BASIC

MATHEMATICS

for the

College Student

Published by Kaplan Educational Centers
888 Seventh Avenue
New York, NY 10106

Copyright © 1999 by Kaplan Educational Centers

All rights reserved. No part of this book may be reproduced or transmitted in any form or by any means, electronic or mechanical, including photocopying, recording, or by any information storage and retrieval system, without the written permission of the Publisher, except where permitted by law.

Portions of this text were adapted from:

Basic Mathematics, Eighth Edition, by Marvin L. Bittinger
Copyright © 1999 Addison-Wesley Longman, Inc., Reading MA

Prealgebra, Second Edition, by Marvin L. Bittinger and David J. Ellenbogen
Copyright © 1996 Addison-Wesley Longman, Inc., Reading MA

Adaptation copyright © 1999 by Kaplan
Adaptation published by arrangement with Addison Wesley Longman, Inc., Reading MA

Cover photo: © Corbis 1999

Kaplan® is a registered trademark of Kaplan Educational Centers.

Lead Faculty: Becky Blackwell, Coordinator; Debbie Moran, Maxine Smith, Leigh Ann Wheeler
Managing Editor: Philip Vlahakis
Development Editors: Ruth Baygell, Abby Tanenbaum
Layout Design/Manager: Pamela Beaulieu
Cover Design: Deborah Wolfe
Executive Editor: Ed Stanford
Executive Director Higher Education: Marty Vespo

Manufactured in the United States of America
July 1999
First Printing

ISBN: 1-58059-921-4

Contents

Acknowledgements

This book is drawn from Basic Mathematics by Marvin L. Bittinger and Prealgebra by Marvin L. Bittinger and David J. Ellenbogen. A team of dedicated math faculty at Greenville Technical College have carefully and energetically adapted these books. Addison Wesley Longman, publisher of the Bittinger texts, has graciously granted permission for this adaptation.

Lead faculty for this project were: Becky Blackwell, coordinator; Debbie Moran, Maxine Smith, and Leigh Ann Wheeler. This book has benefited greatly from their teaching insights, their long experience using the Bittinger texts, and their willingness to share ideas and to analyze new approaches in order to improve student success.

A special thanks to Dr. Kay Grastie, Vice President for Education, for her amazing energy and leadership throughout this project, and to Dr. Thomas Barton, President, for his continuing support and dedication to the partnership between Kaplan and Greenville Technical College.

Editorial development and production was a Kaplan team effort, coordinated by Phil Vlahakis and Ed Stanford, with help from Lora Shapiro and Abby Tanenbaum. Pamela Beaulieu both designed the book and managed the electronic formatting. Additional formatting was performed by Martha Arango, Alisa Caratozzolo, Sarah Carnevale, Laurel Douglas, and Monica McCready. Copy editing and proof reading were done by Ruth Baygell, Colette Conboy, Rebecca Emery, and David Rodman.

To the Student

Many students ask, "Why do we have to study mathematics?" Mathematics is an important tool used in solving problems in the "real world." A recent survey of business and industry showed that employers desire to hire people with strong mathematical and problem-solving skills. If you think back over the past week, there are likely many times when you have used mathematics. You are constantly exposed to mathematics, even if itís only something like hearing sports commentators give statistical information.

Many of you have possessed some of these math skills but may have forgotten them. This course is designed to refresh your memory and refine these skills.

There may be some mathematical concepts taught in this course that you believe will never be used in your career or daily life. Even if this turns out to be true, the study of these concepts will aid in improving your critical thinking skills and will make you a stronger problem solver.

Throughout this book, you will find many tips on how to make learning and remembering math easier. One goal of this course is to help make studying math more fun and more meaningful. We know that if you apply these skills and your mind is open to learning, you CAN be successful in mathematics.

Chapter R is a "review" chapter. It will not be covered in class. However, this chapter contains skills that you will be expected to know how to perform without the use of a calculator. The rest of the book builds on these skills.

Where to Begin: the Review Chapter

Chapter R, the review chapter, serves two purposes:

It can be used to strengthen your mathematical skills.

It can be used as a reference.

The material in Chapter R covers the skills you need in order to succeed in the rest of this course, and you need to be able to perform those skills without using a calculator.

How do you decide if you need to study Chapter R?

You make already know all or most of these skills and not need to review. The quick and easy way to decide if you need to work through Chapter R is to take the pretest that begins on the following page. The test is designed to help you assess your current skills. The test will probably only take about 30-45 minutes, but you can take as much time as you want.

Remember: to get an accurate picture of your own current skills, take the test without using a calculator.

As soon as you have finished, score yourself to determine if you need to study any parts of Chapter R before you go on to Chapter 1. The answers are shown on the page immediately following the test. The test is divided into 7 sections that match each section of Chapter R. If you should miss more than one problem from a section, then you need to read and review that section.

Chapter R Pretest

Remember: If you use a calculator on this test, you will not get an accurate picture of your math skills.

Section R.1

1. Write a word name for 76,021,009.

2. Write standard notation for three million, seventeen thousand five.

3. What does the digit 7 mean in the number 123,476,801?

4. In the number 48,613,245, what digit tells the number of hundred thousands?

Section R.2

Add.

5.
```
  24,852
+  7549
```

6.
```
   1948
  67,000
     25
+   116
```

7.
```
  49,006
+  3,724
```

8.
```
  89,900,422
   5,673,060
  22,652,303
+   575,215
```

Section R.3

Subtract.

9.
```
  18,008
-  7,549
```

10.
```
  1,325,649
-   89,604
```

11.
```
  7106
-  526
```

12.
```
  600,000
- 523,814
```

Section R.4

13. Round 87,499 to the nearest thousand.

14. Round 7,854,952 to the nearest hundred.

In questions 15 and 16, use < or > for □ to write a true sentence.

15. 999 □ 99

16. 687 □ 786

Section R. 5

Multiply

17. 97 × 59

18. 46 × 10,000,000

19. 9883 · 4276

20. 450,821 · 7,007

Section R.6

Divide.

21. $8{,}762{,}000 \div 1000$ **22.** $8\overline{)12{,}127}$ **23.** $64\overline{)8009}$ **24.** $88{,}993 \div 89$

Section R. 7

25. Identify the numerator of $\dfrac{13}{55}$.

26. A math class has 23 students. 19 of the students are male. What fraction of the students are male?

27. Using the information in question 26, what fraction of the students are female?

28. What fraction of the rectangle is shaded?

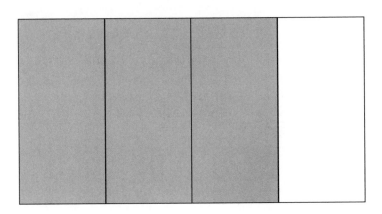

Answers for Pretest

The Pretest is divided into the seven sections of Chapter R. Now that you've completed the Pretest, score your own answers, using the answers given below.

The purpose of the Pretest is to decide whether or not you need to read parts of the Review Chapter before you go on to Chapter 1. If you missed more than one problem in any one section, you need to read that section in Chapter R.

Section R.1

1. Seventy-six million, twenty-one thousand nine.
2. 3,017,005
3. seven ten thousands
4. 6

Section R.2

5. 32,401
6. 69,089
7. 52,730
8. 118,801,000
9. 10,459
10. 1,236,045
11. 6,580
12. 76,186

Section R.4

13. 87,000
14. 7,855,000
15. 999 > 99
16. 687 < 786

Section R.5

17. 5723
18. 460,000,000
19. 42,259,708
20. 3,158,902,747

Section R.6

21. 8762
22. 1515 R7
23. 125 R 9
24. 999 R82

Section R.7

25. 13
26. $\dfrac{19}{23}$
27. $\dfrac{4}{23}$
28. $\dfrac{3}{4}$

R

Review of Arithmetic

An Application

Total sales, in millions of dollars, of bicycles and related sporting supplies were $2973 in 1992, $3534 in 1993, $3470 in 1994, and $3435 in 1995 (*Source:* National Sporting Goods Association). Find the total sales for the entire four-year period.

The Mathematics

Since we are combining sales, addition can be used.

2973 + 3534 + 3470 + 3435

This is how addition can occur in applications and problem solving.

Write a word name.

1. 57

2. 29

3. 88

R.1 Standard Notation

We study mathematics in order to be able to solve problems. In this chapter, we learn how to use operations on the whole numbers. We begin by studying how numbers are named.

a Word Names

"Three," "two hundred one," and "forty-two" are **word names** for numbers. When we write word names for two-digit numbers like 42, 76, and 91, we use hyphens. For example, U.S. Olympic team pitcher Michelle Granger can pitch a softball at a speed of 72 mph. A word name for 72 is "seventy-two."

Examples Write a word name.

1. 43   Forty-three   **2.** 91   Ninety-one

Do Margin Exercises 1–3.

For large numbers, digits are separated into groups of three, called **periods**. Each period has a name: *ones, thousands, millions, billions,* and so on. When we write or read a large number, we start at the left with the largest period. The number named in the period is followed by the name of the period; then a comma is written and the next period is named. Recently, the U.S. national debt was $5,103,040,000,000. We can use a **place-value** chart to illustrate how to use periods to read the number 5,103,040,000,000.

PLACE-VALUE CHART														
Trillions			Billions			Millions			Thousands			Ones		
		5	1	0	3	0	4	0	0	0	0	0	0	0
Hundreds	Tens	Ones	Hundreds	Tens	Ones	Hundreds	Tens	Ones	Hundreds	Tens	Ones	Hundreds	Tens	Ones

Periods → (leftmost)

5 trillion,   103 billion,   40 million,   0 thousand,   0 ones

This number should be read as five trillion, one hundred three billion, forty million.

Example 3 Write a word name for 46,605,314,732.

Forty-six billion,

     six hundred five million,

         three hundred fourteen thousand,

            seven hundred thirty-two

The word "and" *should not* appear in word names for whole numbers. Although we commonly hear such expressions as "two hundred *and* one," the use of "and" is not, strictly speaking, correct in word names for whole numbers. For decimal notation, it is appropriate to use "and" for the decimal point. For example, 317.4 is read as "three hundred seventeen *and* four tenths."

Do Margin Exercises 4–7.

b From Word Names to Standard Notation

Standard notation is the numerical form of a number.

Example 4   Write standard notation.

Five hundred six million,
   three hundred forty-five thousand,
      two hundred twelve

Standard notation is 506,345,212.

Do Margin Exercise 8.

c Digits

A **digit** is a number 0, 1, 2, 3, 4, 5, 6, 7, 8, or 9 that names a place-value location.

Examples   What does the digit 8 mean in each case?

5. 278,342   8 thousands
6. 872,342   8 hundred thousands
7. 28,343,399,223   8 billions

Do Margin Exercises 9–12.

Example 8   *Dunkin Donuts.* On an average day about 2,739,526 Dunkin Donuts are served in the United States. In 2,739,526, what digit tells the number of:

a) Hundred thousands   7
b) Thousands   9

Do Margin Exercises 13–16.

Write a word name.

4. 204

5. 79,204

6. 1,879,204

7. 22,301,879,204

8. Write standard notation.

Two hundred thirteen million, one hundred five thousand, three hundred twenty-nine

What does the digit 2 mean in each case?

9. 526,555

10. 265,789

11. 42,789,654

12. 24,789,654

Golf Balls. On an average day, Americans buy 486,575 golf balls. In 486,575, what digit tells the number of:

13. Thousands?

14. Ten thousands?

15. Ones?

16. Hundreds?

Exercise Set R.1

a Write a word name.

1. 85

2. 48

3. 88,000

4. 45,987

5. 123,765

6. 111,013

7. 7,754,211,577

8. 43,550,651,808

Write a word name for the number in the sentence.

9. *NBA Salaries.* In a recent year, the average salary of a player in the NBA was $1,867,000.

10. The area of the Pacific Ocean is about 64,186,000 square miles.

11. *Population.* The population of South Asia is about 1,583,141,000.

12. *Monopoly.* In a recent Monopoly game sponsored by McDonald's restaurants, the odds of winning the grand prize was estimated to be 467,322,388 to 1.

b Write standard notation.

13. Two million, two hundred thirty-three thousand, eight hundred twelve

14. Three hundred fifty-four thousand, seven hundred two

15. Eight billion

16. Seven hundred million

Write standard notation for the number in the sentence.

17. *Light Distance.* Light travels nine trillion, four hundred sixty billion kilometers in one year.

18. *Pluto.* The distance from the sun to Pluto is three billion, six hundred sixty-four million miles.

19. *Area of Greenland.* The area of Greenland is two million, nine hundred seventy-four thousand, six hundred square kilometers.

20. *Memory Space.* On computer hard drives, one gigabyte is actually one billion, seventy-three million, seven hundred forty-one thousand, eight hundred twenty-four bytes of memory.

| **c** | What does the digit 5 mean in each case?

21. 235,888   **22.** 253,888   **23.** 488,526   **24.** 500,346

In 89,302, what digit tells the number of:

25. Hundreds?   **26.** Thousands?   **27.** Tens?   **28.** Ones?

Synthesis

Exercises designated as *Synthesis exercises* differ from those found in the main body of the exercise set. The icon ❖ denotes synthesis exercises that are writing exercises. Writing exercises are meant to be answered in one or more complete sentences. Because answers to writing exercises often vary, they are not listed at the back of the book.

29. ❖ Write an English sentence in which the number 260,000,000 is used.

30. ❖ Explain why we use commas when writing large numbers.

31. How many whole numbers between 100 and 400 contain the digit 2 in their standard notation?

Write an addition sentence that corresponds to the situation.

1. John has 8 music CDs in his backpack. Then he buys 2 educational CDs at the bookstore. How many CDs does John have in all?

2. Sue earns $45 in overtime pay on Thursday and $33 on Friday. How much overtime pay does she earn altogether on the two days?

Write an addition sentence that corresponds to the situation.

3. A car is driven 100 mi from Austin to Waco. It is then driven 93 mi from Waco to Dallas. How far is it from Austin to Dallas along the same route?

4. A coaxial cable 5 ft (feet) long is connected to a cable 7 ft long. How long is the resulting cable?

5. Two trucks haul sand to a construction site to use in a driveway. One hauls 6 cu yd and the other hauls 8 cu yd. Altogether, how many cubic yards of sand have they hauled to the site?

6. A football fan drives to all college football games using a motor home. On one trip the fan buys 80 gallons (gal) of gasoline and on another, 56 gal. How many gallons were bought in all?

R.2 Addition

a Addition and the Real World

Addition of whole numbers corresponds to combining or putting things together. Let's look at various situations in which addition applies.

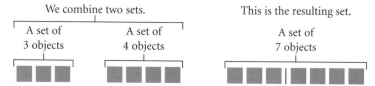

The addition that corresponds to the figure above is

$$3 + 4 = 7.$$

The number of objects in a set can be found by counting. We count and find that the two sets have 3 members and 4 members, respectively. After combining, we count and find that there are 7 objects. We say that the **sum** of 3 and 4 is 7. The numbers added are called **addends**.

$$\underset{\text{Addend}}{3} \quad + \quad \underset{\text{Addend}}{4} \quad = \quad \underset{\text{Sum}}{7}$$

Example 1 Write an addition sentence that corresponds to this situation.

A student has $3 and earns $10 more. How much money does the student have?

An addition that corresponds is $3 + $10 = $13.

Do Margin Exercises 1 and 2.

Addition also corresponds to combining distances or lengths.

Example 2 Write an addition sentence that corresponds to this situation

A car is driven 44 mi from San Francisco to San Jose. It is then driven 42 mi from San Jose to Oakland. How far is it from San Francisco to Oakland along the same route?

44 mi + 42 mi = 86 mi

Do Margin Exercises 3–6.

b | Addition of Whole Numbers

To add numbers, we add the ones digits first, then the tens, then the hundreds, and so on.

Example 3 Add: 7312 + 2504.

Place values are lined up in columns.

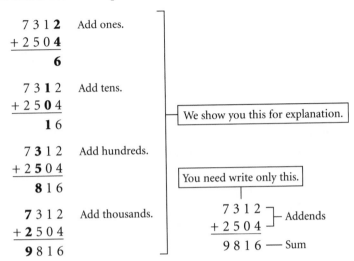

```
  7 3 1 2    Add ones.
+ 2 5 0 4
        6
```

```
  7 3 1 2    Add tens.
+ 2 5 0 4
      1 6
```

```
  7 3 1 2    Add hundreds.
+ 2 5 0 4
    8 1 6
```

```
  7 3 1 2    Add thousands.
+ 2 5 0 4
  9 8 1 6
```

We show you this for explanation.

You need write only this.

```
  7 3 1 2  ⎤─ Addends
+ 2 5 0 4  ⎦
  9 8 1 6  ─ Sum
```

Do Margin Exercise 7.

Example 4 Add: 6878 + 4995.

```
    1
  6 8 7 8    Add ones. We get 13 ones, or 1 ten + 3 ones.
+ 4 9 9 5    Write 3 in the ones column and 1 above the tens.
        3    This is called carrying, or regrouping.
```

```
  1 1
  6 8 7 8    Add tens. We get 17 tens, or 1 hundred + 7 tens.
+ 4 9 9 5    Write 7 in the tens column and 1 above the hundreds.
      7 3
```

```
  1 1 1
  6 8 7 8    Add hundreds. We get 18 hundreds, or 1 thousand + 8 hundreds.
+ 4 9 9 5    Write 8 in the hundreds column and 1 above the thousands.
    8 7 3
```

```
  1 1 1
  6 8 7 8    Add thousands. We get 11 thousands.
+ 4 9 9 5
1 1 8 7 3
```

Do Margin Exercises 8 and 9.

7. Add.

```
  6 2 0 3
+ 3 5 4 2
```

8.
```
  7 9 6 8
+ 5 4 9 7
```

9.
```
  9 8 0 4
+ 6 3 7 8
```

Add from the top.

10.
```
   9
   9
   4
 + 5
```

11.
```
   8
   6
   9
   7
 + 4
```

12. Add from the bottom.
```
   9
   9
   4
 + 5
```

When we add three numbers, like $2 + 3 + 6$, we can add 3 and 6, and then 2. We can show this with parentheses:

$$2 + (3 + 6) = 2 + 9 = 11.$$ Parentheses tell what to do first.

We could also add 2 and 3, and then 6:

$$(2 + 3) + 6 = 5 + 6 = 11.$$

Either way we get 11. It does not matter how we group the numbers. This illustrates the **associative law of addition**, $a + (b + c) = (a + b) + c$. We can also add whole numbers in any order. That is, $2 + 3 = 3 + 2$. This illustrates the **commutative law of addition**, $a + b = b + a$. Together the commutative and associative laws tell us that to add more than two numbers, we can use any order and grouping we wish.

Here are three different approaches to addition using the associative and commutative laws. Decide which way works best for you.

Example 5 Add from the top.

```
   8
   9
   7
 + 6
```

We first add 8 and 9, getting 17; then 17 and 7, getting 24; then 24 and 6, getting 30.

```
  8
  9  →  17
  7        7  →  24
+ 6               6  →  30
 30  ←────────────────────  You write only this.
```

Do Margin Exercises 10 and 11.

Example 6 Add from the bottom.

```
  8               8  →  30
  9        9  →  22
  7  →  13
+ 6
 30  ←──  You still write the answer here.
```

Do Margin Exercise 12.

Sometimes it is easier to look for pairs of numbers whose sums are 10 or 20 or 30, and so on.

Examples Add.

7.

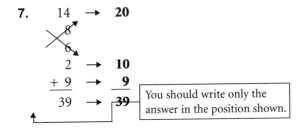

| You should write only the answer in the position shown. |

8. $23 + 19 + 7 + 21 + 4 = 74$

$$30 + 40 + 4$$
$$74$$

Do Margin Exercises 13–15.

Example 9 Add: $2391 + 3276 + 8789 + 1498$.

```
    2
  2 3 9 1     Add ones: We get 24, so we have 2 tens + 4 ones.
  3 2 7 6     Write 4 in the ones column and 2 above the tens.
  8 7 8 9
+ 1 4 9 8
        4
```

```
  3 2
  2 3 9 1     Add tens: We get 35 tens, so we have 30 tens + 5 tens.
  3 2 7 6     This is also 3 hundreds + 5 tens. Write 5 in the tens column
  8 7 8 9     and 3 above the hundreds.
+ 1 4 9 8
      5 4
```

```
  1 3 2
  2 3 9 1     Add hundreds: We get 19 hundreds, or 1 thousand +
  3 2 7 6     9 hundreds. Write 9 in the hundreds column and
  8 7 8 9     1 above the thousands.
+ 1 4 9 8
    9 5 4
```

```
  1 3 2
  2 3 9 1     Add thousands: We get 15 thousands.
  3 2 7 6
  8 7 8 9
+ 1 4 9 8
1 5 9 5 4
```

Do Margin Exercise 16.

Add. Look for pairs of numbers whose sums are 10, 20, 30, and so on.

13.
```
  1 5
    7
    5
    3
+   8
```

14. $6 + 12 + 14 + 8 + 7$

15. $27 + 8 + 13 + 2 + 11$

16. Add.
```
  1 9 3 2
  6 7 2 3
  9 8 7 8
+ 8 9 4 1
```

Exercise Set R.2

a Write an addition sentence that corresponds to the situation.

1. Isabel receives 7 e-mail messages on Tuesday and 8 on Wednesday. How many e-mail messages did she receive altogether on the two days?

2. At a construction site, there are two gasoline containers to be used by earth-moving vehicles. One contains 400 gal and the other 200 gal. How many gallons do both contain altogether?

3. A builder buys two parcels of land to build a housing development. One contains 500 acres and the other 300 acres. What is the total number of acres purchased?

4. During March and April, Will earns extra money doing income taxes part time. In March he earned $220, and in April he earned $340. How much extra did he earn altogether in March and April?

b Add.

5.
$$\begin{array}{r} 364 \\ + 23 \\ \hline \end{array}$$

6.
$$\begin{array}{r} 1521 \\ + 348 \\ \hline \end{array}$$

7.
$$\begin{array}{r} 1716 \\ +3482 \\ \hline \end{array}$$

8.
$$\begin{array}{r} 7503 \\ +2683 \\ \hline \end{array}$$

9.
$$\begin{array}{r} 86 \\ +78 \\ \hline \end{array}$$

10.
$$\begin{array}{r} 73 \\ +69 \\ \hline \end{array}$$

11.
$$\begin{array}{r} 99 \\ + 1 \\ \hline \end{array}$$

12.
$$\begin{array}{r} 999 \\ + 11 \\ \hline \end{array}$$

13. 789 + 111

14. 839 + 386

15. 909 + 101

16. 707 + 909

17. 8113 + 390

18. 271 + 3338

19. 356 + 4910

20. 280 + 34,702

21. 3870 + 92 + 7 + 497

22. 10,120 + 12,989 + 5738

23.
$$\begin{array}{r} 5093 \\ +3217 \\ \hline \end{array}$$

24.
$$\begin{array}{r} 3654 \\ +2700 \\ \hline \end{array}$$

25.
$$\begin{array}{r} 4825 \\ +1783 \\ \hline \end{array}$$

26.
$$\begin{array}{r} 6775 \\ +1432 \\ \hline \end{array}$$

27.	9999 + 6 7 8 5	28.	4 5,8 7 9 + 2 1,7 8 6	29.	2 3,4 4 3 + 1 0,9 8 9	30.	6 7,6 5 4 + 9 8,7 8 6
31.	7 7,5 4 3 + 2 3,7 6 7	32.	4 4,6 5 4 + 4,7 6 5	33.	9 9,9 9 9 + 1 1 2	34.	1 2 7,5 5 6 + 6 8,7 6 6

Add from the top. Then check by adding from the bottom.

35.	7 9 4 + 8	36.	4 3 9 1 + 8	37.	8 6 2 3 + 7	38.	9 4 7 8 + 7

Add. Look for pairs of numbers whose sums are 10, 20, 30, and so on.

39.	7 1 8 3 3 7 + 2	40.	2 3 1 6 1 1 1 8 + 1 9	41.	4 5 2 5 3 6 4 4 + 8 0	42.	3 8 2 7 3 2 1 4 + 7 6

Add.

43.	2 3 6 2 + 4 5	44.	4 3 1 1 + 3 7	45.	4 5 1 3 6 + 8 6 2	46.	3 1 7 5 3 + 9 2 4
47.	2,6 0 3 2 8,2 1 4 + 6,1 0 9	48.	9 3,2 4 9 1,2 6 8 + 7 4,8 2 3	49.	1 2,0 7 0 2,9 5 4 + 3,4 0 0	50.	4 2,4 8 7 8 3,1 4 1 + 3 6,7 1 2

51.
$$\begin{array}{r} 327 \\ 428 \\ 569 \\ 787 \\ +209 \\ \hline \end{array}$$

52.
$$\begin{array}{r} 989 \\ 566 \\ 834 \\ 920 \\ +703 \\ \hline \end{array}$$

53.
$$\begin{array}{r} 4835 \\ 729 \\ 9204 \\ 8986 \\ +7931 \\ \hline \end{array}$$

54.
$$\begin{array}{r} 5,946 \\ 834 \\ 12,956 \\ 928,342 \\ 34,901 \\ +56,000 \\ \hline \end{array}$$

55.
$$\begin{array}{r} 2037 \\ 4923 \\ 3471 \\ +1248 \\ \hline \end{array}$$

56.
$$\begin{array}{r} 4567 \\ 1023 \\ 4821 \\ +3683 \\ \hline \end{array}$$

57.
$$\begin{array}{r} 3420 \\ 8719 \\ 4312 \\ +6203 \\ \hline \end{array}$$

58.
$$\begin{array}{r} 2003 \\ 149 \\ 58 \\ +3426 \\ \hline \end{array}$$

59.
$$\begin{array}{r} 5,678,987 \\ 1,409,312 \\ 898,888 \\ +4,777,910 \\ \hline \end{array}$$

60.
$$\begin{array}{r} 78,899,311 \\ 6,784,170 \\ 11,541,913 \\ +100,817 \\ \hline \end{array}$$

Skill Maintenance

The exercises that follow begin an important feature called skill maintenance exercises. These exercises provide an ongoing review of any preceding objective in the book. You will see them in virtually every exercise set. It has been found that this kind of extensive review can significantly improve your performance on a final examination.

61. Write a word name for the number in the following sentence:
In a recent year, the gross revenue of the NBA was $924,600,000 (***Source:*** *Wall Street Journal*).

62. What does the digit 8 mean in 486,205?

Synthesis

63. ❖ Describe a situation that corresponds to the addition 80 sq ft + 140 sq ft.

64. ❖ Explain in your own words what the associative law of addition means.

65. A fast way to add all the numbers from 1 to 10 inclusive is to pair 1 with 9, 2 with 8, and so on. Use a similar approach to add all the numbers from 1 to 100 inclusive.

R.3 Subtraction

a Subtraction and the Real World

Subtraction of whole numbers corresponds to taking away objects from a set.

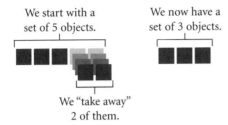

We start with a set of 5 objects.

We now have a set of 3 objects.

We "take away" 2 of them.

The subtraction that corresponds to the figure above is as follows.

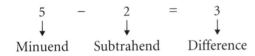

$$5 \quad - \quad 2 \quad = \quad 3$$

Minuend   Subtrahend   Difference

A **difference** is the result of subtracting one number from another.

Examples   Write a subtraction sentence that corresponds to the situation.

1. Juan goes to a music store and chooses 10 CDs to take to the listening station. He rejects 7 of them, but buys the rest. How many CDs did Juan buy?

There are 10 CDs to begin with.

He rejects 7 of them.

He buys the remaining 3.

$$10 \quad - \quad 7 \quad = \quad 3$$

2. A student has $300 and spends $85 for office supplies. How much money is left?

Amount to begin with

Amount spent for office supplies

Amount left

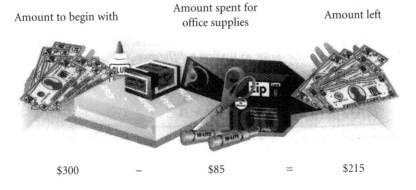

$$\$300 \quad - \quad \$85 \quad = \quad \$215$$

Do Margin Exercises 1 and 2.

Write a subtraction sentence that corresponds to the situation.

1. A contractor removes 5 cu yd of sand from a pile containing 67 cu yd. How many cubic yards of sand are left in the pile?

2. Sparks Electronics owns a field next door that has an area of 20,000 sq ft. Deciding they need more room for parking, the owners have 12,000 sq ft paved. How many square feet of field are left unpaved?

Write an addition sentence to check.

3. $7 - 5 = 2$

4. $17 - 8 = 9$

5. Subtract.

$$
\begin{array}{r}
7\,8\,9\,3 \\
-\,4\,0\,9\,2 \\
\hline
\end{array}
$$

---

b │ Checking the Answer

Addition is used to check subtraction. For example, $5 - 2$ is actually asking us what number which when added to 2 gives 5. Thus for the subtraction sentence

$$5 - 2 = 3, \qquad \text{Taking away 2 from 5 gives 3.}$$

We can check our answer by writing the addition sentence.

$$5 = 3 + 2. \qquad \text{Putting back the 2 gives 5 again.}$$

Example 3   Write the addition check: $8 - 5 = 3$.

$$8 - 5 = 3$$

This number gets added (after 3).

By the commutative law of addition, there is also another addition sentence:

$$8 = 5 + 3.$$

$$8 = 3 + 5$$

The addition sentence is $8 = 3 + 5$.

Do Margin Exercises 3 and 4.

c │ Subtraction of Whole Numbers

To subtract numbers, we subtract the ones digits first, then the tens, then the hundreds, and so on.

Example 4   Subtract: $9768 - 4320$.

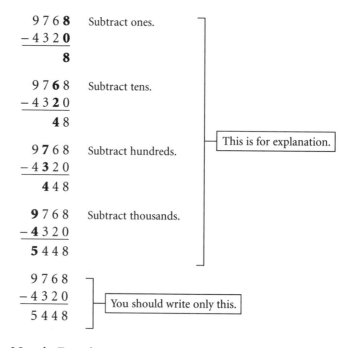

Do Margin Exercise 5.

Sometimes we need to borrow.

Example 5   Subtract: 6246 − 1879.

$$\begin{array}{r} {\scriptstyle 3\ 16} \\ 6\,2\,\cancel{4}\,\cancel{6} \\ -\,1\,8\,7\,9 \\ \hline \end{array}$$ We cannot subtract 9 ones from 6 ones, but we can subtract 9 ones from 16 ones. We borrow 1 ten to get 16 ones.

$$\begin{array}{r} {\scriptstyle \ \ 13} \\ {\scriptstyle 1\ \ 3\ 16} \\ 6\,\cancel{2}\,\cancel{4}\,\cancel{6} \\ -\,1\,8\,7\,9 \\ \hline \end{array}$$ We cannot subtract 7 tens from 3 tens, but we can subtract 7 tens from 13 tens. We borrow 1 hundred to get 13 tens.

$$\begin{array}{r} {\scriptstyle 11\ 13} \\ {\scriptstyle 5\ 1\ \ 3\ 16} \\ \cancel{6}\,\cancel{2}\,\cancel{4}\,\cancel{6} \\ -\,1\,8\,7\,9 \\ \hline \end{array}$$ We cannot subtract 8 hundreds from 1 hundred, but we can subtract 8 hundreds from 11 hundreds. We borrow 1 thousand to get 11 hundreds.

We can always check the answer by adding it to the number being subtracted.

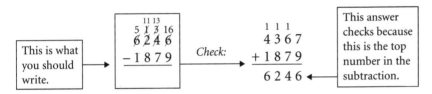

This is what you should write. → $$\begin{array}{r} {\scriptstyle 11\ 13} \\ {\scriptstyle 5\ 1\ \ 3\ 16} \\ \cancel{6}\,\cancel{2}\,\cancel{4}\,\cancel{6} \\ -\,1\,8\,7\,9 \\ \hline \end{array}$$ *Check:* $$\begin{array}{r} {\scriptstyle 1\ 1\ 1} \\ 4\,3\,6\,7 \\ +\,1\,8\,7\,9 \\ \hline 6\,2\,4\,6 \end{array}$$ ← This answer checks because this is the top number in the subtraction.

Do Margin Exercises 6 and 7.

Example 6   Subtract: 902 − 477.

$$\begin{array}{r} {\scriptstyle 12} \\ \cancel{9}\,\cancel{0}\,\cancel{2} \\ -\,4\,7\,7 \\ \hline 4\,2\,5 \end{array}$$ We cannot subtract 7 ones from 2 ones. We have 9 hundreds, or 90 tens. We borrow 1 ten to get 12 ones. We then have 89 tens.

Do Margin Exercises 8 and 9.

Example 7   Subtract: 8003 − 3667.

$$\begin{array}{r} {\scriptstyle 7\ 9\ 9\ 13} \\ \cancel{8}\,\cancel{0}\,\cancel{0}\,\cancel{3} \\ -\,3\,6\,6\,7 \\ \hline 4\,3\,3\,6 \end{array}$$ We have 8 thousands, or 800 tens. We borrow 1 ten to get 13 ones. We then have 799 tens.

Examples

8. Subtract: 6000 − 3762.

$$\begin{array}{r} {\scriptstyle 5\ 9\ 9\ \mathbf{10}} \\ \cancel{6}\,\cancel{0}\,\cancel{0}\,\cancel{0} \\ -\,3\,7\,6\,2 \\ \hline 2\,2\,3\,8 \end{array}$$

9. Subtract: 6024 − 2968.

$$\begin{array}{r} {\scriptstyle \ \ \ \ 11} \\ {\scriptstyle 5\ 9\ 1\ 14} \\ \cancel{6}\,\cancel{0}\,\cancel{2}\,\cancel{4} \\ -\,2\,9\,6\,8 \\ \hline \end{array}$$

Do Margin Exercises 10–12.

Subtract. Check by adding.

6. $$\begin{array}{r} 8\,6\,8\,6 \\ -\,2\,3\,5\,8 \\ \hline \end{array}$$ **7.** $$\begin{array}{r} 7\,1\,4\,5 \\ -\,2\,3\,9\,8 \\ \hline \end{array}$$

Subtract.

8. $$\begin{array}{r} 7\,0 \\ -\,1\,4 \\ \hline \end{array}$$ **9.** $$\begin{array}{r} 5\,0\,3 \\ -\,2\,9\,8 \\ \hline \end{array}$$

Subtract.

10. $$\begin{array}{r} 7\,0\,0\,7 \\ -\,6\,3\,4\,9 \\ \hline \end{array}$$ **11.** $$\begin{array}{r} 6\,0\,0\,0 \\ -\,3\,1\,4\,9 \\ \hline \end{array}$$

12. $$\begin{array}{r} 9\,0\,3\,5 \\ -\,7\,4\,8\,9 \\ \hline \end{array}$$

Exercise Set R.3

a Write a subtraction sentence that corresponds to the situation. You need not carry out the subtraction.

1. Jeanne has $1260 in her college checking account. She spends $450 for her food bill at the dining hall. How much is left in her account?

2. *Frozen Yogurt.* A dispenser at a frozen yogurt store contains 126 ounces (oz) of strawberry yogurt. A 13-oz cup is sold to a customer. How much is left in the dispenser?

3. A chef pours 5 oz of salsa from a jar containing 16 oz. How many ounces are left?

4. *Chocolate Cake.* One slice of chocolate cake with fudge frosting contains 564 calories. One cup of hot cocoa made with skim milk contains 188 calories. How many more calories are in the cake than in the cocoa?

b Write an addition sentence to check.

5. $7 - 4 = 3$

6. $12 - 5 = 7$

7. $13 - 8 = 5$

8. $9 - 9 = 0$

9. $23 - 9 = 14$

10. $20 - 8 = 12$

11. $43 - 16 = 27$

12. $51 - 18 = 33$

c Subtract.

13.
$$\begin{array}{r} 16 \\ -\ 4 \\ \hline \end{array}$$

14.
$$\begin{array}{r} 86 \\ -13 \\ \hline \end{array}$$

15.
$$\begin{array}{r} 65 \\ -21 \\ \hline \end{array}$$

16.
$$\begin{array}{r} 87 \\ -34 \\ \hline \end{array}$$

17.
$$\begin{array}{r} 866 \\ -333 \\ \hline \end{array}$$

18.
$$\begin{array}{r} 526 \\ -323 \\ \hline \end{array}$$

19.
$$\begin{array}{r} 4547 \\ -3421 \\ \hline \end{array}$$

20.
$$\begin{array}{r} 6875 \\ -2111 \\ \hline \end{array}$$

21. $86 - 47$

22. $73 - 28$

23. $625 - 327$

24. $726 - 509$

25. 835 − 609

26. 953 − 246

27. 981 − 747

28. 887 − 698

29. $\begin{array}{r} 7769 \\ -2387 \\ \hline \end{array}$

30. $\begin{array}{r} 6431 \\ -2896 \\ \hline \end{array}$

31. $\begin{array}{r} 3982 \\ -2489 \\ \hline \end{array}$

32. $\begin{array}{r} 7650 \\ -1765 \\ \hline \end{array}$

33. $\begin{array}{r} 5046 \\ -2859 \\ \hline \end{array}$

34. $\begin{array}{r} 6308 \\ -2679 \\ \hline \end{array}$

35. $\begin{array}{r} 7640 \\ -3809 \\ \hline \end{array}$

36. $\begin{array}{r} 8003 \\ -599 \\ \hline \end{array}$

37. $\begin{array}{r} 12,647 \\ -4,899 \\ \hline \end{array}$

38. $\begin{array}{r} 16,222 \\ -5,888 \\ \hline \end{array}$

39. $\begin{array}{r} 46,771 \\ -12,977 \\ \hline \end{array}$

40. $\begin{array}{r} 95,654 \\ -48,985 \\ \hline \end{array}$

41. 10,002 − 7834

42. 23,048 − 17,592

43. 90,237 − 47,209

44. 84,703 − 298

45. $\begin{array}{r} 80 \\ -24 \\ \hline \end{array}$

46. $\begin{array}{r} 40 \\ -37 \\ \hline \end{array}$

47. $\begin{array}{r} 90 \\ -54 \\ \hline \end{array}$

48. $\begin{array}{r} 90 \\ -78 \\ \hline \end{array}$

49. $\begin{array}{r} 140 \\ -56 \\ \hline \end{array}$

50. $\begin{array}{r} 470 \\ -188 \\ \hline \end{array}$

51. $\begin{array}{r} 690 \\ -236 \\ \hline \end{array}$

52. $\begin{array}{r} 803 \\ -418 \\ \hline \end{array}$

53. $\begin{array}{r} 903 \\ -132 \\ \hline \end{array}$

54. $\begin{array}{r} 6408 \\ -258 \\ \hline \end{array}$

55. $\begin{array}{r} 2300 \\ -109 \\ \hline \end{array}$

56. $\begin{array}{r} 3506 \\ -1293 \\ \hline \end{array}$

57. $\begin{array}{r} 6808 \\ -3059 \\ \hline \end{array}$

58. $\begin{array}{r} 7840 \\ -3027 \\ \hline \end{array}$

59. $\begin{array}{r} 8092 \\ -1073 \\ \hline \end{array}$

60. $\begin{array}{r} 6007 \\ -1589 \\ \hline \end{array}$

61. 5843 − 98

62. 10,002 − 398

63. 101,734 − 5760

64. 15,017 − 7809

65. 10,008 − 19

66. 21,043 − 8909

67. 83,907 − 89

68. 311,568 − 19,394

69. $\begin{array}{r} 7000 \\ -2794 \\ \hline \end{array}$

70. $\begin{array}{r} 8001 \\ -6543 \\ \hline \end{array}$

71. $\begin{array}{r} 48,000 \\ -37,695 \\ \hline \end{array}$

72. $\begin{array}{r} 17,043 \\ -11,598 \\ \hline \end{array}$

Skill Maintenance

73. What does the digit 7 mean in 6,375,602?

74. Write a word name for 6,375,602.

75. Write the number that means 2 ten thousands + 9 thousands + 7 hundreds + 8 ones.

76. Add: 9807 + 12,885.

Synthesis

77. ❖ Is subtraction commutative (is there a commutative law of subtraction)? Why or why not?

78. ❖ Describe a situation that corresponds to the subtraction $20 − $17.

Subtract.

79. 3,928,124 − 1,098,947

80. 21,431,206 − 9,724,837

81. Fill in the missing digits to make the equation true:
9,☐48,621 − 2,097☐81 = 7,251,140.

R.4 Rounding and Order

a Rounding

We round numbers in various situations if we do not need an exact answer. For example, we might round to check if an answer to a problem is reasonable or to check a calculation done by hand or on a calculator. We might also round to see if we are being charged the correct amount in a store.

To understand how to round, we first look at some examples using number lines, even though this is not the way we normally do rounding.

Example 1 Round 47 to the nearest ten.

Here is a part of a number line; 47 is between 40 and 50.

Since 47 is closer to 50, we round up to 50.

Example 2 Round 42 to the nearest ten.

42 is between 40 and 50.

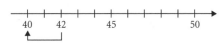

Since 42 is closer to 40, we round down to 40.

Do Margin Exercises 1–4.

Example 3 Round 45 to the nearest ten.

45 is halfway between 40 and 50.

We could round 45 down to 40 or up to 50. We agree to round up to 50.

▶ When a number is halfway between rounding numbers, round up.

Do Margin Exercises 5–7.

Here is a rule for rounding.

To round to a certain place:
a) Locate the digit in that place.
b) Consider the next digit to the right.
c) If the digit to the right is 5 or higher, round up.
d) Change all digits to the right of the rounding location to zeros.

Round to the nearest ten.

1. 37

2. 52

3. 73

4. 98

Round to the nearest ten,

5. 35

6. 75

7. 85

Round to the nearest ten.

8. 137

9. 473

10. 235

11. 285

Round to the nearest hundred.

12. 641

13. 759

14. 750

15. 9325

Round to the nearest thousand.

16. 7896

17. 8459

18. 19,343

19. 68,500

Example 4 Round 6485 to the nearest ten.

a) Locate the digit in the tens place.

6 4 **8** 5
   ↑

b) Consider the next digit to the right.

6 4 8 **5**
     ↑

c) Since that digit is 5 or higher, round 8 tens up to 9 tens.

d) Change all digits to the right of the tens digit to zeros.

6 4 9 0 ← This is the answer.

Example 5 Round 6485 to the nearest hundred.

a) Locate the digit in the hundreds place.

6 **4** 8 5
  ↑

b) Consider the next digit to the right.

6 4 **8** 5
   ↑

c) Since that digit is 5 or higher, round 4 hundreds up to 5 hundreds.

d) Change all digits to the right of hundreds to zeros.

6 5 0 0 ← This is the answer.

Example 6 Round 6485 to the nearest thousand.

a) Locate the digit in the thousands place.

6 4 8 5
↑

b) Consider the next digit to the right.

6 **4** 8 5
  ↑

c) Since that digit is 4 or lower, then 6 thousands stays as 6 thousands.

d) Change all digits to the right of thousands to zeros.

6 0 0 0 ← This is the answer.

CAUTION! 7000 is not a correct answer to Example 6. It is incorrect to round from the ones digit over, as follows: 6485, 6490, 6500, 7000.

Do Margin Exercises 8–19.

b | Order

We know that 2 is not the same as 5. We express this by the sentence $2 \neq 5$. We also know that 2 is less than 5. We can see this order on a number line: 2 is to the left of 5. The number 0 is the smallest whole number.

▶ For any whole numbers a and b:

1. $a < b$ (read "a is less than b" when read from left to right) is true when a is to the left of b on a number line.

2. $a > b$ (read "a is greater than b" when read from left to right) is true when a is to the right of b on a number line.

We call $<$ and $>$ **inequality symbols**.

Note: The symbol $<$ or $>$ always points to the smaller number.

Example 7   Use $<$ or $>$ for $\square$ to write a true sentence: $7 \square 11$.

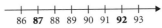

Since 7 is to the left of 11, $7 < 11$.

Example 8   Use $<$ or $>$ for $\square$ to write a true sentence: $92 \square 87$.

Since 92 is to the right of 87, $92 > 87$.

Do Margin Exercises 20–25.

Use $<$ or $>$ for $\square$ to write a true sentence. Draw a number line if necessary.

20. $8 \square 12$

21. $12 \square 8$

22. $76 \square 64$

23. $64 \square 76$

24. $217 \square 345$

25. $345 \square 217$

Exercise Set R.4

a Round to the nearest ten.

1. 48   **2.** 17   **3.** 67   **4.** 99

5. 731   **6.** 532   **7.** 895   **8.** 798

Round to the nearest hundred.

9. 146   **10.** 874   **11.** 957   **12.** 650

13. 9079   **14.** 4645   **15.** 32,850   **16.** 198,402

Round to the nearest thousand.

17. 5876   **18.** 4500   **19.** 7500   **20.** 2001

21. 45,340   **22.** 735,562   **23.** 373,405   **24.** 6,713,855

b Use < or > for □ to write a true sentence. Draw a number line if necessary.

25. 0 □ 17   **26.** 32 □ 0   **27.** 34 □ 12   **28.** 28 □ 18

29. 1000 □ 1001   **30.** 77 □ 117   **31.** 133 □ 132   **32.** 999 □ 997

33. 460 □ 17   **34.** 345 □ 456   **35.** 37 □ 11   **36.** 12 □ 32

Skill Maintenance

Add.

37. 67,789
 $+18,965$

38. 9002
 $+4587$

Subtract.

39. 67,789
 $-18,965$

40. 9002
 -4587

Synthesis

41. ❖ When rounding 748 to the nearest hundred, a student rounds to 750 and then to 800. What mistake is the student making?

42. ❖ Explain how rounding can be useful when shopping for groceries.

R.5 Multiplication

a | Multiplication and the Real World

Multiplication of whole numbers corresponds to two kinds of situations.

Repeated Addition

The multiplication 3×5 corresponds to this repeated addition:

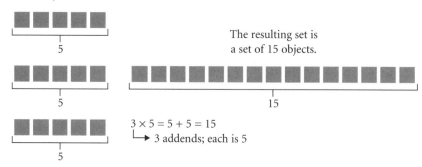

We combine 3 sets
of 5 objects each.

The resulting set is
a set of 15 objects.

$3 \times 5 = 5 + 5 = 15$
3 addends; each is 5

We say that the *product* of 3 and 5 is 15. The numbers 3 and 5 are called *factors*.

$$3 \quad \times \quad 5 \quad = \quad 15$$

Factors   Product

Product
A product is the result of multiplying two or more numbers.

Factors
The numbers we multiply together are called factors.

Rectangular Arrays

The multiplication 3×5 corresponds to this rectangular array:
3 rows with 5 objects in each row

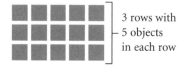

3 rows with
5 objects
in each row

When you write a multiplication sentence corresponding to a real-world situation, you should think of either a rectangular array or repeated addition. In some cases, it may help to think both ways.

Symbols Used for Multiplication

$\times$ the letter x

$\cdot$ a dot placed mid-height between the factors

2(3)   parentheses around one or more of the factors
(2)3
or (2)(3)

Examples   Write a multiplication sentence that corresponds to the situation.

1. It is known that Americans drink 24 million gal of soft drinks per day (*per day* means *each day*). What quantity of soft drinks is consumed every 5 days?

    We draw a picture or at least visualize the situation. Repeated addition fits best in this case.

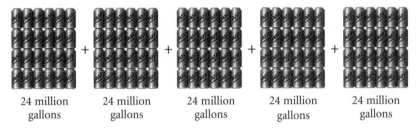

24 million gallons   24 million gallons   24 million gallons   24 million gallons   24 million gallons

5 · 24 million gallons = 120 million gallons

= 1 million gallons

2. One side of a building has 6 floors with 7 windows on each floor. How many windows are there on that side of the building?

    We have a rectangular array and can easily draw a sketch.

$6 \cdot 7 = 42$

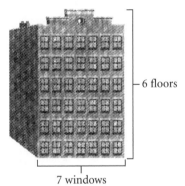

— 6 floors

7 windows

Do Margin Exercises 1–3.

Write a multiplication sentence that corresponds to the situation.

1. Marv practices for the U.S. Open bowling tournament. He bowls 8 games a day for 7 days. How many games does he play altogether for practice?

2. A lab technician pours 75 milliliters (mL) of acid into each of 10 beakers. How much acid is poured in all?

3. *Checkerboard.* A checkerboard consists of 8 rows with 8 squares in each row. How many squares in all are there on a checkerboard?

Multiply.

4. $\begin{array}{r} 4\,5 \\ \times\,2\,3 \\ \hline \end{array}$

5. 48×63

b | Multiplication of Whole Numbers

To find 54×32, we can use repeated addition:

$$54 + 54 + 54 + \ldots + 54.$$
$$\underbrace{\qquad\qquad\qquad\qquad}_{\text{32 of these}}$$

The associative law allows us to rewrite this as

$$(54 + 54 + 54 + \ldots + 54) + 54 + 54.$$
$$\underbrace{\qquad\qquad\qquad}_{\text{30 of these}}\quad\underbrace{\qquad}_{\text{2 of these}}$$

Thus we can determine the product $54 \cdot 32$ by adding the products $54 \cdot 30$ and $54 \cdot 2$.

$$\begin{array}{r} \overset{1}{5}\,4 \\ \times\,3\,0 \\ \hline 1\,6\,2\,0 \end{array} \quad + \quad \begin{array}{r} 5\,4 \\ \times\,\,\,2 \\ \hline 1\,0\,8. \end{array}$$

Because the results are added, we usually present the work this way.

$$\begin{array}{r} 5\,4 \\ \times\,3\,2 \\ \hline 1\,0\,8 \\ 1\,6\,2\,0 \\ \hline 1\,7\,2\,8 \end{array}$$

$\quad$ 108 $\quad$ Multiplying by 2
$\quad$ 1620 $\quad$ Multiplying by 30
$\quad$ 1728 $\quad$ Adding

Example 3 Multiply 43×57.

$$\begin{array}{r} \overset{2}{5}\,7 \\ \times\,4\,3 \\ \hline \mathbf{1\,7\,1} \end{array}$$

$\quad$ Multiplying by 3.

$$\begin{array}{r} \overset{2}{} \\ \overset{2}{5}\,7 \\ \times\,4\,3 \\ \hline 1\,7\,1 \\ \mathbf{2\,2\,8\,0} \end{array}$$

$\quad$ Multiplying by 40. (We write a 0 and then multiply 57 by 4.)

You may have learned that such a 0 does not have to be written. You may omit it if you wish. If you do omit it, remember, when multipluying by tens, to put the answer in the tens place.

$$\begin{array}{r} \overset{2}{} \\ \overset{2}{5}\,7 \\ \times\,4\,3 \\ \hline 1\,7\,1 \\ 2\,2\,8\,0 \\ \hline \mathbf{2\,4\,5\,1} \end{array}$$

$\quad$ Adding.

Do Margin Exercises 4 and 5.

Example 4   Multiply: 457×683.

```
      5 2
      6 8 3
    × 4 5 7
    4 7 8 1      Multiplying 683 by 7


      4 1
      5 2
      6 8 3
    × 4 5 7
    4 7 8 1
  3 4 1 5 0      Multiplying 683 by 50


      3 1
      4 1
      5 2
      6 8 3
    × 4 5 7
    4 7 8 1
  3 4 1 5 0
  2 7 3 2 0 0    Multiplying 683 by 400
  3 1 2,1 3 1    Adding
```

Do Margin Exercises 6 and 7.

Zeros in Multiplication

Example 5   Multiply: 306×274.

```
    2 7 4
  × 3 0 6
    1 6 4 4      Multiplying by 6
  8 2 2 0 0      Multiplying by 3 hundreds.
               (We write 00 and then multiply 274 by 3.)
  8 3,8 4 4      Adding
```

Do Margin Exercises 8–10.

Example 6   Multiply: 360×274.

```
    2 7 4
  × 3 6 0
  1 6 4 4 0      Multiplying by 6 tens.
               (We write 0 and then multiply 274 by 6.)
  8 2 2 0 0      Multiplying by 3 hundreds.
               (We write 00 and then multiply 274 by 3.)
  9 8,6 4 0      Adding
```

Do Margin Exercises 11–14.

Multiply.

6. $\begin{array}{r} 7\,4\,6 \\ \times\ \ 6\,2 \\ \hline \end{array}$

7. 245×837

Multiply.

8. $\begin{array}{r} 4\,7\,2 \\ \times\,3\,0\,6 \\ \hline \end{array}$

9. 408×704

10. $\begin{array}{r} 2\,3\,4\,4 \\ \times\,6\,0\,0\,5 \\ \hline \end{array}$

Multiply.

11. $\begin{array}{r} 4\,7\,2 \\ \times\,8\,3\,0 \\ \hline \end{array}$

12. $\begin{array}{r} 2\,3\,4\,4 \\ \times\,7\,4\,0\,0 \\ \hline \end{array}$

13. 100×562

14. 1000×562

15. a) Find $23 \cdot 47$.

b) Find $47 \cdot 23$.

c) Compare your answers to parts (a) and (b).

Multiply.

16. $5 \cdot 2 \cdot 4$

17. $5 \cdot 1 \cdot 3$

Note the following.

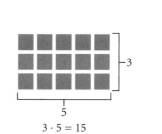 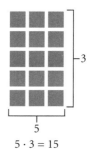

$$3 \cdot 5 = 15 \qquad 5 \cdot 3 = 15$$

If we rotate the array on the left, we get the array on the right. The answers are the same. We call this the **commutative law of multiplication**. It says that we can multiply two numbers in any order, $a \cdot b = b \cdot a$, and still get the same answer.

Do Margin Exercise 15.

To multiply three or more numbers, we usually group them so that we multiply two at a time. Consider $2 \cdot (3 \cdot 4)$ and $(2 \cdot 3) \cdot 4$. The parentheses tell what to do first:

$$2 \cdot (3 \cdot 4) = 2 \cdot (12) = 24. \quad \text{We multiply 3 and 4, then 2.}$$

We can also multiply 2 and 3, then 4:

$$(2 \cdot 3) \cdot 4 = (6) \cdot 4 = 24.$$

Either way we get 24. It does not matter how we group the numbers. This illustrates that **multiplication is associative**: $a \cdot (b \cdot c) = (a \cdot b) \cdot c$. Together the commutative and associative laws tell us that to multiply more than two numbers, we can use any order and grouping we wish.

Do Margin Exercises 16 and 17.

c Multiplying by Multiples of 10, 100, and 1000

Multiplying by a Multiple of 10

We begin by considering multiplication by multiples of 10, 100, and 1000. These are numbers such as 10, 20, 30, 100, 400, 1000, and 7000.

We know that

$$50 = 5 \text{ tens} \quad 340 = 34 \text{ tens} \quad \text{and} \quad 2340 = 234 \text{ tens}$$
$$= 5 \cdot 10, \quad = 34 \cdot 10, \quad = 234 \cdot 10.$$

Turning this around, we see that to multiply any number by 10, all we need do is write a 0 on the end of the number.

> ▶ To multiply a number by 10, write 0 on the end of the number.

Examples Multiply.

7. $10 \cdot 6 = 60$

8. $10 \cdot 47 = 470$

9. $10 \cdot 583 = 5830$

Do Margin Exercises 18–22.

Let's find $4 \cdot 90$. This is $4 \cdot (9 \text{ tens})$, or 36 tens. The procedure is the same as multiplying 4 and 9 and writing a 0 on the end. Thus, $4 \cdot 90 = 360$.

Examples Multiply.

10. $5 \cdot 70 = 350$
    └── $5 \cdot 7$, then write a 0

11. $8 \cdot 80 = 640$

12. $5 \cdot 60 = 300$

Do Margin Exercises 23 and 24.

Multiplying by a Multiple of 100

Note the following:

$$300 = 3 \text{ hundreds} \quad 4700 = 47 \text{ hundreds} \quad \text{and} \quad 56{,}800 = 568 \text{ hundreds}$$
$$= 3 \cdot 100, \quad = 47 \cdot 100, \quad = 568 \cdot 100.$$

Turning this around, we see that to multiply any number by 100, all we need do is write two 0's on the end of the number.

> ▶ To multiply a number by 100, write two 0's on the end of the number.

Multiply.

18. $10 \cdot 7$

19. $10 \cdot 45$

20. $10 \cdot 273$

21. $10 \cdot 10$

22. $10 \cdot 100$

Multiply.

23.   7 0
   $\times\ 8$
  ‾‾‾‾‾

24.   6 0
   $\times\ 6$
  ‾‾‾‾‾

Multiply.

25. $100 \cdot 7$ **26.** $100 \cdot 23$

27. $100 \cdot 723$ **28.** $100 \cdot 100$

29. $100 \cdot 1000$

Multiply.

30. $\begin{array}{r} 700 \\ \times \quad 8 \\ \hline \end{array}$

31. $\begin{array}{r} 400 \\ \times \quad 4 \\ \hline \end{array}$

Multiply.

32. $1000 \cdot 9$

33. $1000 \cdot 852$

Multiply.

34. $1000 \cdot 10$

35. $3 \cdot 4000$

36. $9 \cdot 8000$

37. $9000 \cdot 6$

Examples   Multiply.

13. $100 \cdot 6 = 600$

14. $100 \cdot 39 = 3900$

15. $100 \cdot 448 = 44{,}800$

Do Margin Exercises 25–29

Let's find $4 \cdot 900$. This is $4 \cdot (9$ hundreds$)$.

$$4 \cdot (9 \cdot 100)$$
$$(4 \cdot 9) \cdot 100 \qquad \text{Associative property of multiplication}$$
$$36 \cdot 100$$
$$3600$$

This is the same as multiplying 4 and 9 and writing two 0's on the end. Thus, $4 \cdot 900 = 3600$.

Examples   Multiply.

16. $6 \cdot 800 = 4800$
   $6 \cdot 8$, then write 00

17. $9 \cdot 700 = 6300$

18. $5 \cdot 500 = 2500$

Do Margin Exercises 30 and 31.

Multiplying by a Multiple of 1000

Note the following:

$$6000 = 6 \text{ thousands} \quad \text{and} \quad 19{,}000 = 19 \text{ thousands}$$
$$= 6 \cdot 1000 \qquad\qquad\qquad = 19 \cdot 1000.$$

Turning this around, we see that to multiply any number by 1000, all we need do is write three 0's on the end of the number.

> ▶ To multiply a number by 1000, write three 0's on the end of the number.

Examples   Multiply.

19. $1000 \cdot 8 = 8000$

20. $2000 \cdot 13 = 26{,}000$

21. $1000 \cdot 567 = 567{,}000$

Do Margin Exercises 32–37.

Multiplying Multiples by Multiples

Let's multiply 50 and 30. This is $50 \cdot (3 \text{ tens})$, or 150 tens, or 1500. The procedure is the same as multiplying 5 and 3 and writing two 0's on the end.

> To multiply multiples of tens, hundreds, thousands, and so on:
> **a)** Multiply the one·digit numbers.
> **b)** Count the number of zeros.
> **c)** Write that many 0's on the end.

Examples   Multiply.

22.
$$\begin{array}{r} 80 \\ \times\,60 \\ \hline 4800 \end{array}$$
1 zero at end
1 zero at end
$6 \cdot 8$, then write 00

23.
$$\begin{array}{r} 800 \\ \times\,60 \\ \hline 48{,}000 \end{array}$$
2 zeros at end
1 zero at end
$6 \cdot 8$, then write 000

24.
$$\begin{array}{r} 800 \\ \times\,600 \\ \hline 480{,}000 \end{array}$$
2 zeros at end
2 zeros at end
$6 \cdot 8$, then write 0,000

24.
$$\begin{array}{r} 800 \\ \times\,50 \\ \hline 40{,}000 \end{array}$$
2 zeros at end
1 zero at end
$5 \cdot 8$, then write 000

Do Margin Exercises 38–40.

Multiply.

38.
$$\begin{array}{r} 80 \\ \times 70 \\ \hline \end{array}$$

39.
$$\begin{array}{r} 800 \\ \times\ 70 \\ \hline \end{array}$$

40.
$$\begin{array}{r} 600 \\ \times\ 30 \\ \hline \end{array}$$

Exercise Set R.5

a Write a multiplication sentence that corresponds to the situation.

1. The *Los Angeles Sunday Times* crossword puzzle is arranged rectangularly with squares in 21 rows and 21 columns. How many squares does the puzzle have altogether?

2. A computer screen consists of small rectangular dots called pixels. How many pixels are there on a screen that has 600 rows with 800 pixels in each row?

3. A typical beverage carton contains 8 cans, each of which holds 12 oz. How many ounces are there in the carton?

4. There are 7 days in a week. How many days are there in 18 weeks?

b Multiply.

5.
$$\begin{array}{r} 8\,7 \\ \times 1\,0 \\ \hline \end{array}$$

6.
$$\begin{array}{r} 1\,0\,0 \\ \times\ \ 9\,6 \\ \hline \end{array}$$

7.
$$\begin{array}{r} 2\,3\,4\,0 \\ \times 1\,0\,0\,0 \\ \hline \end{array}$$

8.
$$\begin{array}{r} 8\,0\,0 \\ \times\ \ 7\,0 \\ \hline \end{array}$$

9.
$$\begin{array}{r} 6\,5 \\ \times\ \ 8 \\ \hline \end{array}$$

10.
$$\begin{array}{r} 8\,7 \\ \times\ \ 4 \\ \hline \end{array}$$

11.
$$\begin{array}{r} 9\,4 \\ \times\ \ 6 \\ \hline \end{array}$$

12.
$$\begin{array}{r} 7\,6 \\ \times\ \ 9 \\ \hline \end{array}$$

13.
$$\begin{array}{r} 6\,5\,2 \\ \times 1\,0\,0 \\ \hline \end{array}$$

14.
$$\begin{array}{r} 6\,5\,2 \\ \times\ \ 1\,0 \\ \hline \end{array}$$

15.
$$\begin{array}{r} 4\,3\,7\,1 \\ \times 1\,0\,0\,0 \\ \hline \end{array}$$

16.
$$\begin{array}{r} 4\,3\,7\,1 \\ \times\ \ 1\,0\,0 \\ \hline \end{array}$$

17.
$$\begin{array}{r} 4\,0\,0 \\ \times 3\,0\,0 \\ \hline \end{array}$$

18.
$$\begin{array}{r} 4\,0\,0\,0 \\ \times\ \ 2\,0\,0 \\ \hline \end{array}$$

19.
$$\begin{array}{r} 6\,0\,0\,0 \\ \times\ \ 2\,0 \\ \hline \end{array}$$

20.
$$\begin{array}{r} 4\,0\,0\,0 \\ \times 4\,0\,0\,0 \\ \hline \end{array}$$

21.
$$\begin{array}{r} 8\,0\,0\,0 \\ \times\ \ 1\,0 \\ \hline \end{array}$$

22. $3 \cdot 509$

23. $7 \cdot 806$

24. $7(9229)$

25. $4(7867)$

26. $90(53)$

27. $60(78)$

28. $(47)(85)$

29. $(34)(87)$

30.
$$\begin{array}{r} 640 \\ \times\ 72 \\ \hline \end{array}$$

31.
$$\begin{array}{r} 666 \\ \times\ 66 \\ \hline \end{array}$$

32.
$$\begin{array}{r} 444 \\ \times\ 33 \\ \hline \end{array}$$

33.
$$\begin{array}{r} 509 \\ \times\ 88 \\ \hline \end{array}$$

34.
$$\begin{array}{r} 509 \\ \times 408 \\ \hline \end{array}$$

35.
$$\begin{array}{r} 432 \\ \times 375 \\ \hline \end{array}$$

36.
$$\begin{array}{r} 853 \\ \times 936 \\ \hline \end{array}$$

37.
$$\begin{array}{r} 346 \\ \times 650 \\ \hline \end{array}$$

38.
$$\begin{array}{r} 489 \\ \times 340 \\ \hline \end{array}$$

39.
$$\begin{array}{r} 7080 \\ \times\ 160 \\ \hline \end{array}$$

40.
$$\begin{array}{r} 4378 \\ \times 2694 \\ \hline \end{array}$$

41.
$$\begin{array}{r} 8007 \\ \times\ 480 \\ \hline \end{array}$$

42.
$$\begin{array}{r} 6428 \\ \times 3224 \\ \hline \end{array}$$

43.
$$\begin{array}{r} 8928 \\ \times 3172 \\ \hline \end{array}$$

44.
$$\begin{array}{r} 3482 \\ \times\ 104 \\ \hline \end{array}$$

45.
$$\begin{array}{r} 6408 \\ \times 6064 \\ \hline \end{array}$$

46.
$$\begin{array}{r} 5006 \\ \times 4008 \\ \hline \end{array}$$

47.
$$\begin{array}{r} 6789 \\ \times 2330 \\ \hline \end{array}$$

48.
$$\begin{array}{r} 5608 \\ \times 4500 \\ \hline \end{array}$$

49.
$$\begin{array}{r} 4560 \\ \times 7890 \\ \hline \end{array}$$

50.
$$\begin{array}{r} 876 \\ \times 345 \\ \hline \end{array}$$

51.
$$\begin{array}{r} 355 \\ \times 299 \\ \hline \end{array}$$

52.
$$\begin{array}{r} 7889 \\ \times 6224 \\ \hline \end{array}$$

53.
$$\begin{array}{r} 6501 \\ \times 3449 \\ \hline \end{array}$$

54.   5 5 5
    $\times$ 5 5

55.   8 8 8
     $\times$ 8 8

56.   7 3 4
    $\times 4\,0\,7$

57.   5 0 8 0
     $\times$ 3 0 2

Skill Maintenance

58. Add.

    2 0
    8 5 0
    +3 5 0 0

59. Subtract.

    6 0 0 3
    −2 8 9 4

60. Round 2345 to the nearest ten, then to the nearest hundred, and then to the nearest thousand.

Synthesis

61. ❖ Explain in your own words what it means to say that multiplication is commutative.

62. ❖ Describe a situation that corresponds to the multiplication 4 · $150.

R.6 Division

a Division and the Real World

Division of whole numbers corresponds to two kinds of situations. In the first, consider the division $20 \div 5$, read "20 divided by 5." We can think of 20 objects arranged in a rectangular array. We ask "How many rows, each with 5 objects, are there?"

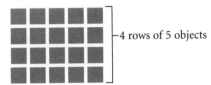

Since there are 4 rows of 5 objects each, we have

$$20 \div 5 = 4.$$

In the second situation, we can ask, "If we make 5 rows, how many objects will there be in each row?"

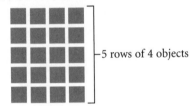

Since there are 4 objects in each of the 5 rows, we have

$$20 \div 5 = 4.$$

The *dividend* is what we are dividing into. The result of the division is the *quotient*.

We say that the **dividend** is 20, the **divisor** is 5, and the **quotient** is 4.

$$
\begin{array}{ccccc}
20 & \div & 5 & = & 4 \\
\downarrow & & \downarrow & & \downarrow \\
\text{Dividend} & & \text{Divisor} & & \text{Quotient}
\end{array}
$$

▸ We also write a division such as $20 \div 5$ as
$$\frac{20}{5} \text{ or } 5\overline{)20}.$$

Write a division sentence that corresponds to the situation. You need not carry out the division.

1. There are 112 students in a college band, and they are marching with 14 in each row. How many rows are there?

2. A college band is in a rectangular array. There are 112 students in the band, and they are marching in 8 rows. How many students are there in each row?

Example 1   Write a division sentence that corresponds to this situation.

A parent gives $24 to 3 children, with each child getting the same amount. How much does each child get?

We think of an array with 3 rows. Each row will go to a child. How many dollars will be in each row?

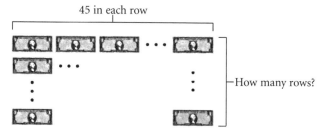
} 3 rows with 8 in each row

$$24 \div 3 = 8$$

Example 2   Write a division sentence that corresponds to this situation. You need not carry out the division.

How many mailboxes that cost $45 each can be purchased for $495?

We think of an array with 45 one-dollar bills in each row. The money in each row will buy a mailbox. How many rows will there be?

45 in each row

—How many rows?

▶ Whenever we have a rectangular array, we know the following:
(The total number) ÷ (The number of rows) =
(The number in each row).

Also:
(The total number) ÷ (The number in each row) =
(The number of rows).

Do Margin Exercises 1 and 2.

By looking at rectangular arrays, we can see how multiplication and division are related. The following array shows that $4 \cdot 5 = 20$.

$$4 \cdot 5 = 20$$

The array also shows the following:

$$20 \div 5 = 4 \quad \text{and} \quad 20 \div 4 = 5.$$

Division is actually defined in terms of multiplication. For example, $20 \div 5$ is defined to be the number that when multiplied by 5 gives 20. Thus, every division sentence can be written as a multiplication sentence.

$20 \div 5 = 4$ Division sentence

$20 = 4 \cdot 5$ Division written as multiplication

Every division sentence can be written as a multiplication sentence.

Example 3   Write the division sentence as a multiplication sentence: $12 \div 6 = 2$.

We have

$12 \div 6 = 2$ Division sentence

$12 = 2 \cdot 6.$ Division written as multiplication

The multiplication sentence is $12 = 2 \cdot 6$.

By the commutative law of multiplication, there is also another multiplication sentence: $12 = 6 \cdot 2$.

Do Margin Exercises 3 and 4.

For every multiplication sentence, we can write a division sentence, as we can see from the preceding array.

Example 4   Using the multiplication sentence: $7 \cdot 8 = 56$.

We have

$7 \cdot 8 = 56$ $7 \cdot 8 = 56$

This factor becomes a divisor.   This factor becomes a divisor.

$7 = 56 \div 8$ $8 = 56 \div 7$

The division sentences are $7 = 56 \div 8$ and $8 = 56 \div 7$.

Do Margin Exercises 5 and 6.

Write the division as a multiplication sentence.

3. $15 \div 3 = 5$

4. $72 \div 8 = 9$

Using the multiplication sentences, write two division sentences.

5. $6 \cdot 2 = 12$

6. $7 \cdot 6 = 42$

b | Division of Whole Numbers

Multiplication can be thought of as repeated addition. Division can be thought of as repeated subtraction. Compare.

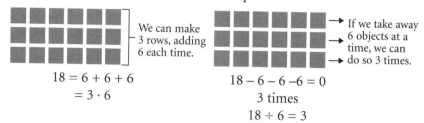

$$18 = 6 + 6 + 6$$
$$= 3 \cdot 6$$

We can make 3 rows, adding 6 each time.

If we take away 6 objects at a time, we can do so 3 times.

$$18 - 6 - 6 - 6 = 0$$
3 times
$$18 \div 6 = 3$$

To divide by repeated subtraction, we keep track of the number of times we subtract.

Example 5 Divide by repeated subtraction: $20 \div 4$.

```
  2 0
-   4  →
  1 6
-   4  →
  1 2
-   4  →       We subtracted 5 times, so 20 ÷ 4 = 5.
    8
-   4  →
    4
-   4  →
    0
```

Example 6 Divide by repeated subtraction: $23 \div 5$.

```
  2 3
-   5  →
  1 8
-   5  →
  1 3
-   5  →       We subtracted 4 times.
    8
-   5  →
    3  →       We have 3 left. This number is
               called the remainder.
```

We write

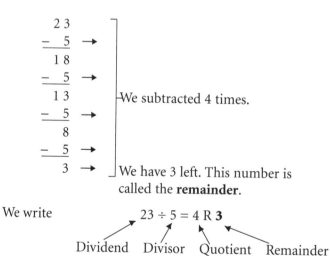

$$23 \div 5 = 4 \text{ R } 3$$

Dividend   Divisor   Quotient   Remainder

CHECKING DIVISIONS. To check a division, we multiply. Suppose we divide 98 by 2 and get 49:

$$98 \div 2 = 49.$$

To check, we multiply the quotient and the divisor and add the remainder. This answer should result in the dividend. In this case, 49 (quotient) · 2 (divisor) + 0 (remainder) = 98. This is true, so our answer checks.

Example 7 Check the division in Example 6.

We found that $23 \div 5 = 4$ R 3. To check, we multiply 5 by 4. This gives us 20. Then we add 3 to get 23. The dividend is 23, so the answer checks.

Do Margin Exercises 7–10.

Long division is a process you have to go through when dividing larger numbers. The process, as shown in the example below, is simple: Estimate, multiply, subtract, and bring down. Repeat this process until you have used all the digits in the dividend.

Example 8 $5\overline{)3\,6\,4\,2}$

$\begin{array}{r} ? \\ 5\overline{)3\,6\,4\,2} \end{array}$ First, try dividing 5 (the divisor) into 3 (the first digit of the dividend). We know that doesn't work.

$\begin{array}{r} ? \\ 5\overline{)3\,6\,4\,2} \end{array}$ So, we then try dividing 5 into 36. The question is "What times 5 will give an answer close to 36 but not greater than 36?"

$\begin{array}{r} 7 \\ 5\overline{)3\,6\,4\,2} \end{array}$ ESTIMATE 7. Put a 7 above the 6 in 36 (7 is now the first digit in the quotient). Next MULTIPLY 7 x 5 and put the result (35) underneath 36.

$\begin{array}{r} 7 \\ 5\overline{)3\,6\,4\,2} \\ 3\,5 \\ \hline 1 \end{array}$ SUBTRACT 35 from 36, leaving 1. How do you know your estimate was good? What's left over (1) is less than the divisor (5).

$\begin{array}{r} 7 \\ 5\overline{)3\,6\,4\,2} \\ 3\,5 \\ \hline 1\,4 \end{array}$ BRING DOWN the 4 (the next digit in the dividend) to make the new number 14.

$\begin{array}{r} 7\,2 \\ 5\overline{)3\,6\,4\,2} \\ 3\,5 \\ \hline 1\,4 \\ 1\,0 \\ \hline 4\,2 \end{array}$ Now, divide 5 into 14 using the same process as above. *Estimate* 2, which becomes the next digit in the quotient, and after *multiplying, subtracting,* and *bringing down* the 2 (the last digit in the dividend), we are left with 42.

$\begin{array}{r} 7\,2\,8 \\ 5\overline{)3\,6\,4\,2} \\ 3\,5 \\ \hline 1\,4 \\ 1\,0 \\ \hline 4\,2 \\ 4\,0 \\ \hline 2 \end{array}$ We now need to divide 5 into 42 using the same process. *Estimate* 8, which becomes the last digit in the quotient, and after *multiplying* and *subtracting,* we now have a 2 remaining at the bottom.

Since there are no digits left in the dividend to bring down, and 2 is smaller than 5, we are finished. Thus 2 is "left over" and it is called the "remainder." The answer (quotient) to this division problem is 728 with a remainder of 2. We write this as 728 R 2.

To check, we multiply the quotient 728 by the divisor 5. This gives us 3640. Then we add 2 (the remainder) to get 3642. The dividend is 3642, so the answer checks.

Divide by repeated subtraction. Then check.

7. $54 \div 9$

8. $61 \div 9$

9. $53 \div 12$

10. $157 \div 24$

Divide and check.

11. 4$\overline{)235}$

12. 6$\overline{)8855}$

13. 5$\overline{)5075}$

14. 9$\overline{)6031}$

Do Margin Exercises 11 and 12.

Example 9 7$\overline{)2901}$

7$\overline{)2901}$ First, try dividing 7 (the divisor) into 2 (the first digit of the dividend). We know that doesn't work.

7$\overline{)2901}$ So, we then try dividing 7 into 29 and the question is "What times 7 will get us an answer close to 29 but not greater than 29?"

← **Estimate not good**

$\begin{array}{r} 3 \\ 7\overline{)2901} \\ 21 \\ \hline 8 \end{array}$

↑
Not good

ESTIMATE 3. Put a 3 above the 9 in 29 (3 is now the first digit in the quotient). Next MULTIPLY 3 x 7 and put the result (21) underneath 29.

SUBTRACT 21 from 29, leaving 8. But, 8 is NOT less than 7 and thus, our estimate was not right. We know we have to get a number greater than 21 so instead of estimating 3, try estimating 4.

← **Estimate is good**

$\begin{array}{r} 4 \\ 7\overline{)2901} \\ 28 \\ \hline 1 \end{array}$

↑
Good

ESTIMATE 4. Put a 4 above the 9 in 29 (4 is now the first digit in the quotient). Next MULTIPLY 4 x 7 and put the result (28) underneath 29.

SUBTRACT 28 FROM 29, LEAVING 1. Since 1 is less than the divisor (7), so our estimate is good.

$\begin{array}{r} 4 \\ 7\overline{)2901} \\ 28 \\ \hline 10 \end{array}$

BRING DOWN the 0 (note, 0 is treated just like any other digit in the dividend) to make the new number 10.

$\begin{array}{r} 4 \\ 7\overline{)2901} \\ 28 \\ \hline 10 \\ 7 \\ \hline 31 \\ 28 \\ \hline 3 \end{array}$

Continue the process (estimate, multiply, subtract, bring down) until you have used all of the digits in the dividend.

The answer (quotient) to this division problem is 414 with a remainder of 3 or 414 R 3.

To check, we multiply the quotient 414 by the divisor 7. This gives us 2898. Then we add 3 (the remainder) to get 2901. The dividend is 2901, so the answer checks.

Do Margin Exercises 13–14.

Example 10 $15\overline{)4527}$

$$\begin{array}{r} ? \\ 15\overline{)4527} \end{array}$$

First, try dividing 15 (the divisor) into 4 (the first digit of the dividend). We know that doesn't work.

$$\begin{array}{r} 3 \\ 15\overline{)4527} \\ 45 \end{array}$$

So, we then try dividing 15 into 45 and the question is "What times 15 will get us an answer close to 45 but not greater than 45?"

ESTIMATE 3. Put a 3 above the 5 in 45 (3 is now the first digit in the quotient). Next MULTIPLY 3 x 15 and put the result (45) underneath the 45 in the dividend.

$$\begin{array}{r} 3 \\ 15\overline{)4527} \\ 45 \\ \hline 0 \end{array}$$

SUBTRACT 45 from 45, leaving 0. Was our estimate good? Yes, because 0 is less than 15 (the divisor).

$$\begin{array}{r} 30 \\ 15\overline{)4527} \\ 45 \\ \hline 02 \end{array}$$

BRING DOWN the 2 to make the new number 02. A zero at the beginning of a number can be ignored, which means we are left with 2. Now we need to find the number that when multiplied by 15 gives us a number that is close to, but not greater than 2. Only 0 can accomplish this. Put a 0, now the second digit in the quotient, above the 2 in the dividend.

$$\begin{array}{r} 301 \\ 15\overline{)4527} \\ 45 \\ \hline 02 \\ 0 \\ \hline 27 \\ 15 \\ \hline 12 \end{array}$$

Multiply 0 x 15 to get 0, and put that 0 underneath the 2. Subtract 0 from 2 to get 2. Now bring down the 7 to make 27.

Continue the process until you have used all of the digits in the dividend. The answer (quotient) to this division problem is 301 with a remainder of 12 or 301 R12.

To check, we multiply the quotient 301 by the divisor 15. This gives us 4515. Then we add 12 (the remainder) to get 4527. The dividend is 4527, so the answer checks.

Do Margin Exercises 15 and 16.

Divide.

15. $27\overline{)9724}$

16. $15\overline{)44,847}$

Exercise Set R.6

a Write a division sentence that corresponds to the situation. You need not carry out the division.

1. *Canyonlands.* The trail boss for a trip into Canyonlands National Park divides 760 pounds (lb) of equipment among 4 mules. How many pounds does each mule carry?

2. *Surf Expo.* In a swimwear showing at Surf Expo, a trade show for retailers of beach supplies, each swimsuit test takes 8 minutes (min). If the show runs for 240 min, how many tests can be scheduled?

3. A lab technician pours 455 mL of sulfuric acid into 5 beakers, putting the same amount in each. How much acid is in each beaker?

4. A computer screen is made up of a rectangular array of pixels. There are 480,000 pixels in all, with 800 pixels in each row. How many rows are there on the screen?

Write the division as a multiplication sentence.

5. $18 \div 3 = 6$

6. $72 \div 9 = 8$

7. $22 \div 22 = 1$

8. $32 \div 1 = 32$

9. $54 \div 6 = 9$

10. $72 \div 8 = 9$

11. $37 \div 1 = 37$

12. $28 \div 28 = 1$

Using the multiplication sentence write two division sentences.

13. $9 \times 5 = 45$

14. $2 \cdot 7 = 14$

15. $37 \cdot 1 = 37$

16. $4 \cdot 12 = 48$

17. $8 \times 8 = 64$

18. $9 \cdot 7 = 63$

19. $11 \cdot 6 = 66$

20. $1 \cdot 43 = 43$

b Divide.

21. $277 \div 5$

22. $699 \div 3$

23. $864 \div 8$

24. $869 \div 8$

25. $4\overline{)1228}$

26. $3\overline{)2124}$

27. $6\overline{)4521}$

28. $9\overline{)9110}$

29. $297 \div 4$

30. $389 \div 2$

31. $738 \div 8$

32. $881 \div 6$

33. $5\overline{)8515}$

34. $3\overline{)6027}$

35. $9\overline{)8888}$

36. $8\overline{)4139}$

37. $127{,}000 \div 10$

38. $127{,}000 \div 100$

39. $127{,}000 \div 1000$

40. $4260 \div 10$

41. $70\overline{)3692}$

42. $20\overline{)5798}$

43. $30\overline{)875}$

44. $40\overline{)987}$

45. $852 \div 21$

46. $942 \div 23$

47. $85\overline{)7672}$

48. $54\overline{)2729}$

49. $111\overline{)3219}$

50. $102\overline{)5612}$

51. $8\overline{)843}$

52. $7\overline{)749}$

53. $5\overline{)8047}$

54. $9\overline{)7273}$

55. $5\overline{)5036}$

56. $7\overline{)7074}$

57. $1058 \div 46$

58. $7242 \div 24$

59. $3425 \div 32$

60. $48\overline{)4899}$

61. $24\overline{)8880}$

62. $36\overline{)7563}$

63. $28\overline{)17,067}$

64. $36\overline{)28,929}$

65. $80\overline{)24,320}$

66. $90\overline{)88,560}$

67. $285\overline{)999,999}$

68. $306\overline{)888,888}$

69. $456\overline{)3,679,920}$

70. $803\overline{)5,622,606}$

Skill Maintenance

71. Round 6825 to the nearest hundred.

72. Use < or > for □ to write a true sentence.
888 □ 788

73. Add $17 + 11,036$.

74.
$$\begin{array}{r} 8000 \\ -\ 6251 \\ \hline \end{array}$$

75. $630(27) = \underline{\hspace{2cm}}$

76. Subtract $54 - 14$ and write an addition sentence as a check.

R.7 Fractions

The study of arithmetic begins with the set of whole numbers

  0, 1, 2, 3, 4, 5, 6, 7, 8, 9, 10, 11, and so on.

The need soon arises for fractional parts of numbers such as halves, thirds, fourths, and so on. Here are some examples:

$\frac{1}{25}$ of the parking spaces in a commercial area in the state of Indiana are to be marked for the handicapped.

$\frac{1}{11}$ of all women develop breast cancer.

$\frac{1}{4}$ of the minium daily requirement of calcium is provided by a cup of frozen yogurt.

$\frac{43}{100}$ of all corporate travel money is spent on airfares.

a | Identifying Numerators and Denominators

The following are some additional examples of fractions:

$$\frac{1}{2}, \quad \frac{3}{8}, \quad \frac{8}{5}, \quad \frac{11}{23}$$

This way of writing number names is called **fractional notation**. The top number is called the **numerator** and the bottom number is called the **denominator**.

Example 1   Identify the numerator and the denominator.

$\dfrac{7}{8}$ ← Numerator
     ← Denominator

Do Margin Exercises 1–3.

b | Writing Fractional Notation

Example 2   What part is shaded?

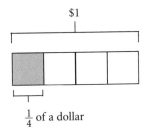

$\frac{1}{4}$ of a dollar

When an object is divided into 4 parts of the same size, each of these parts is $\frac{1}{4}$ of the object. Thus, *one-fourth* is shaded.

Do Margin Exercises 4–7.

Identify the numerator and the denominator.

1. $\dfrac{1}{6}$ **2.** $\dfrac{5}{7}$ **3.** $\dfrac{22}{3}$

What part is shaded?

4. $1

5.   1 mile

6.
1 gallon

7.

What part is shaded?

8.

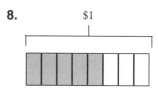

9.

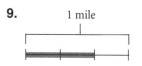

10.

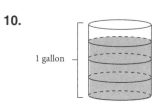

11.

What part is shaded?

12.

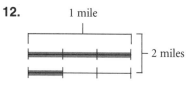

13.

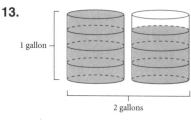

14. What part of the set of tools in Example 5 are hammers?

15. What part of this set is shaded?

16. What part of this set are or were United States presidents? are recording stars?

Abraham Lincoln
Whitney Houston
Garth Brooks
Bill Clinton
Sheryl Crow
Gloria Estefan

Example 3 What part is shaded?

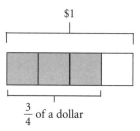

$\frac{3}{4}$ of a dollar

The object is divided into 4 parts of the same size, and 3 of them are shaded. This is $3 \cdot \frac{1}{4}$, or $\frac{3}{4}$. Thus , $\frac{3}{4}$ (three-fourths) of the object is shaded.

Do Margin Exercises 8–11.

Fractions greater than I correspond to situations like the following.

Example 4 What part is shaded?

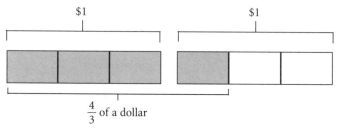

$\frac{4}{3}$ of a dollar

We divide the two objects into 3 parts each and take 4 of those parts. We have more than one whole object. In this case, it is $4 \cdot \frac{1}{3}$, or $\frac{4}{3}$

Do Margin Exercises 12 and 13.

Fractional notation also corresponds to situations involving part of a set.

Example 5 What part of this set, or collection, of tools are wrenches?

There are 5 tools, and 3 are wrenches. We say that three-fifths of the tools are wrenches; that is, $\frac{3}{5}$ of the set consists of wrenches.

Do Margin Exercises 14–16.

Circle graphs, or pie charts, areoften used to illustrate the relationships of fractional parts of a whole. The following graph shows color preferences of bicycles.

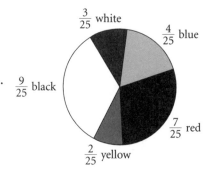

$\frac{3}{25}$ white

$\frac{4}{25}$ blue

$\frac{9}{25}$ black

$\frac{7}{25}$ red

$\frac{2}{25}$ yellow

Fractional Notation for 1

The number 1 corresponds to situations like those shown here.

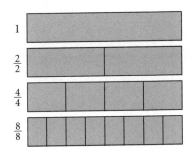

If we divide an object into parts and take all of them, we get the shole object. For example,

$$\frac{2}{2} = 1, \qquad \frac{14}{14} = 1, \qquad \frac{8}{8} = 1$$

Do Margin Exercises 17–20.

c   What is a Mixed Number?

A symbol like $2\frac{3}{4}$ is called a mixed number.

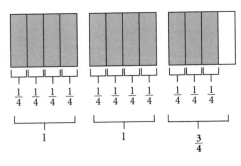

$$2\frac{3}{4} \quad \text{means} \quad 2 \ + \ \frac{3}{4}$$

This is a whole number.   This is a fraction less than 1.

Examples   Convert to a mixed number.

1. $7 + \frac{2}{5} = 7\frac{2}{5}$

2. $4 + \frac{3}{10} = 4\frac{3}{10}$

Do Margin Exercises 21–23.

Simplify.

17. $\frac{1}{1}$ **18.** $\frac{4}{4}$

19. $\frac{34}{34}$ **20.** $\frac{100}{100}$

Convert to a mixed number.

21. $1 + \frac{2}{3}$

22. $8 + \frac{3}{4}$

23. $12 + \frac{2}{3}$

Exercise Set R.7

a Identify the numerator and the denominator.

1. $\dfrac{3}{4}$ **2.** $\dfrac{9}{10}$ **3.** $\dfrac{11}{20}$ **4.** $\dfrac{18}{5}$

b What part of the object or set of objects is shaded?

5.

6.
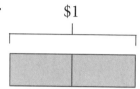

7.
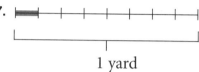
1 yard

8.

9.

1 year

10.
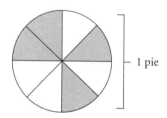
1 pie

11.
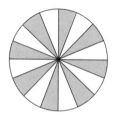

12.
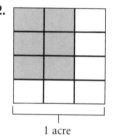
1 acre

13.
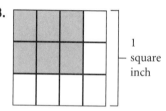
1 square inch

14.
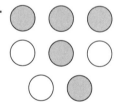

15.

16.

17.

c What part of the object or set of objects is shaded?

18. 1 gold bar

19.
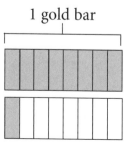
1 quart

20. 1 foot
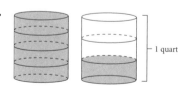

1

Basic Arithmetic Properties

An Application

Years divisible by 4 are leap years, except those indicating the beginning of a century (last two digits 00) in which case they must be divisible by 400 in order to be leap years.

Determine whether or not 1492 was a leap year.

The Mathematics

To see if a large number is divisible by 4, we need only check if its last two digits are divisible by 4. So, to find out if 1492 was a leap year, we need to determine if 92 is divisible by 4.

This application appears in section 1.3.

Introduction

In this chapter, we will look at fundamental properties of numbers that will be critical for current and future studies of mathematics. We will also look at exponential notation and see how to carry out operations in the correct order. Finally, we will examine the important connection between multiples, factors and divisibility and learn about prime factorization and least common multiples.

1.1 Properties of Numbers

In your previous experiences with numbers, you have used properties of addition, subtraction, multiplication and division. These properties will now be stated formally using letters to represent numbers. As we work through this book, you will find that these properties are also true for integers, fractions and decimals.

a Addition Facts

The addition of numbers corresponds to combining or putting things together. The result of combining two or more numbers is called the **sum**, and the numbers that are added together are called the **addends**.

$$\underset{\text{addend}}{10} \quad \underset{+}{+} \quad \underset{\text{addend}}{7} \quad \underset{=}{=} \quad \underset{\text{sum}}{17}$$

Properties of Addition

You have probably noticed that we can add numbers in any order. For example, $4 + 10 = 10 + 4$. We call this special property the **Commutative Property of Addition**.

▶ **Commutative Property of Addition**

For all numbers a and b,

$a + b = b + a$

When adding three numbers, such as $2 + 3 + 6$, we can add 3 and 6, and then add 2. We can show this with parentheses:

$$2 + (3 + 6) = 2 + 9 = 11. \qquad \text{Parentheses tell what to do first.}$$

We could also add 2 and 3, and then 6:

$$(2 + 3) + 6 = 5 + 6 = 11.$$

Either way, 11 is the sum. Thus, $2 + (3 + 6) = (2 + 3) + 6$. It does not matter how we group the numbers when adding. This illustrates the **Associative Property of Addition**.

▶ **Associative Property of Addition**

For all numbers a, b and c,

$a + (b + c) = (a + b) + c$

Together the commutative and associative properties tell us that to add numbers, we can use any order or grouping we wish.

As you know, the sum of 0 and any number is that number. For example, if we have a set of 4 objects and add 0 objects to it, we still have 4 objects. Similarly, if we have a set with 0 objects and add 4 objects to it, we have a set with 4 objects. Thus, $4 + 0 = 4$ and $0 + 4 = 4$. This property is know as the **Identity Property of Zero**.

> **Identity Property of Zero**
>
> For any number a,
>
> $a + 0 = a$
>
> or
>
> $0 + a = a$

The number 0 is called the **additive identity** because when 0 is added to a number, the sum is *identical* to the original number.

Real-life problems often occur that can be solved by writing an addition statement. These problems may include any of the following key words or phrases.

Key Words or Phrases	Example	Symbols
plus	3 plus 6	3 + 6
added to	4 added to 1	1 + 4
more than	2 more than 16	16 + 2
increased by	7 increased by 3	7 + 3
sum	the sum of 8 and 0	8 + 0
total	the total of 9 and 4	9 + 4

Sometimes it is helpful to first write the statement in words, and then translate the words to symbols.

b Subtraction Facts

The subtraction of numbers corresponds to two types of situations. One is when you are "taking away" a portion or part of a group of objects, and the other is when you determine "how much more?"

$$9 \quad - \quad 3 \quad = \quad 6$$
$$\text{minuend} \quad - \quad \text{subtrahend} \quad = \quad \text{difference}$$

Example 1 (Taking Away):
At one time CVS carried 759 different types of prescription drugs. Because most insurance companies now require that generic brands be dispensed, CVS is decreasing the number of prescription drugs in their inventory by 48 types. How many drugs are now in CVS's inventory?

$759 - 48 = $ number of drugs now in inventory

Example 2 (How Much More?):
There are 327 students enrolled in Chemistry 100 at Greenville Tech this term, while 270 students are enrolled in Biology 100. How many more students are enrolled in chemistry than in biology?

$327 - 270 = $ how many more students enrolled in chemistry

Properties of Subtraction

The difference of any number and itself is 0. For example, $13 - 13 = 0$. Also, the difference of any number and 0 is the number itself. For example, $32 - 0 = 32$. These properties are called the **Subtraction Properties of Zero**.

> ▶ **Subtraction Properties of Zero**
>
> For any number a,
>
> $a - a = 0$
>
>   and
>
> $a - 0 = a$.

Note that subtraction is neither associative nor commutative. If the order or grouping is changed in subtraction, the answer will also change. This will be further explained in Chapter 3.

With subtraction, there are also key words and phrases that can be helpful in solving problems.

Key Words or Phrases	Example	Symbols
subtract	subtract 3 from 9	$9 - 3$
less than	4 less than 12	$12 - 4$
difference	the difference of 6 and 2	$6 - 2$
take away	8 take away 7	$8 - 7$
decreased by	15 decreased by 5	$15 - 5$
subtracted from	6 subtracted from 10	$10 - 6$
minus	11 minus 2	$11 - 2$
less	4 less 3	$4 - 3$

c | Multiplication Facts

Multiplication of numbers represents repeated addition. For example, $2 + 2 + 2 + 2 + 2 = 2 \cdot 5 = 10$. The numbers that are multiplied are called **factors**, and the result of the multiplication is called the **product**.

$$\underset{\text{factor}}{8} \quad \cdot \quad \underset{\text{factor}}{3} \quad \underset{=}{=} \quad \underset{\text{product}}{24}$$

Properties of Multiplication

Similar to the Commutative Property of Addition, the **Commutative Property of Multiplication** allows the factors to be multiplied in any order. For example, $3 \cdot 5 = 5 \cdot 3$.

> ▶ **Commutative Property of Multiplication**
>
> For any numbers a and b,
>
> $a \cdot b = b \cdot a$.

Like the Associative Property of Addition, the **Associative Property of Multiplication** tells us that it does not matter how we group numbers when multiplying. When multiplying three numbers, such as $2 \cdot 3 \cdot 4$, we can multiply 3 and 4, and then multiply by 2. We can show this with parentheses:

$2 \cdot (3 \cdot 4) = 2 \cdot 12 = 24.$ Parentheses tell what to do first.

We could also multiply 2 and 3, and then multiply by 4:

$(2 \cdot 3) \cdot 4 = 6 \cdot 4 = 24.$

Either way, 24 is the product. Thus, $2 \cdot (3 \cdot 4) = (2 \cdot 3) \cdot 4$. It does not matter how we group the numbers when multiplying. This illustrates the **Associative Property of Multiplication**.

▶ **Associative Property of Multiplication**

For any numbers a, b and c,

$a \cdot (b \cdot c) = (a \cdot b) \cdot c.$

When we multiply a number by 0, the product is always 0. For example, consider $3 \cdot 0$. Since multiplication is defined as repeated addition, we can see that $3 \cdot 0 = 0 + 0 + 0 = 0$.

Consider $0 \cdot 3$. Using repeated addition, we say that this is 0 addends of 3, which is 0. This property is referred to as the **Multiplication Property of Zero**.

▶ **Multiplication Property of Zero**

For any number a,

$a \cdot 0 = 0$
 and
$0 \cdot a = 0.$

As you know, when we multiply a number by 1, the result is the original number. For example, $1 \cdot 5 = 5$. Since multiplication is commutative, we can also show that $5 \cdot 1 = 5$. Thus, we have the following **Identity Property of One**.

▶ **Identity Property of One**

For any number a,

$a \cdot 1 = a$
 or
$1 \cdot a = a.$

The number 1 is called the **multiplicative identity** because when a number is multiplied by 1, the product is *identical* to the original number.

Similar to addition and subtraction, there are key words and phrases useful in problem solving involving multiplication.

Key Words or Phrases	Example	Symbols
times	6 times 7	$6 \cdot 7$
the product of	the product of 8 and 2	$8 \cdot 2$
twice	twice 5	$2 \cdot 5$
double	double 6	$2 \cdot 6$
multiplied by	9 multiplied by 3	$3 \cdot 9$
multiply	multiply 4 by 8	$8 \cdot 4$

Unlike the operations of addition and subtraction, there are a variety of symbols that are used to represent multiplication. These symbols are not dependent on the key words and phrases, and, in general, you may choose which symbol you prefer.

▶ **Multiplication Symbols**

$a \times b$

$a \cdot b$

$a(b)$

$(a)b$

$(a)(b)$

We could have written the previous examples using any of these symbols. For example, 6 times 7, could also have been written as any of the following.

6×7

$6(7)$

$(6)7$

$(6)(7)$

Often, key words and phrases in problems suggest using addition but could be solved using multiplication. For example, to find the total cost of 6 books selling for $15 each, we can either add

$15 + $15 + $15 + $15 + $15 + $15,

or we can multiply $6 \cdot 15.

d Division Facts

As we previously saw, multiplication can be thought of as repeated addition. Division can be thought of as repeated subtraction. For example, $10 - 2 - 2 - 2 - 2 - 2 = 0$. Because we are able to subtract 2 from 10 no more than five times, we can say that 10 divided by 2 equals 5, or

$$\underset{\text{dividend}}{10} \quad \underset{\div}{\div} \quad \underset{\text{divisor}}{2} \quad \underset{=}{=} \quad \underset{\text{quotient}}{5.}$$

$$\text{divisor}\,\overline{)\,\text{dividend}}^{\,\text{quotient}}$$

The quotient of zero divided by any number, except 0, is 0. The quotient of any number divided by 0 is undefined. These properties are known as the **Division Properties of 0**.

▶ **Division Properties of 0**

   a. For any number a, except $a = 0$
      $0 \div a = 0$.

   b. For any number a,
      $a \div 0$ is undefined.

You have probably noted that when a number is divided by itself, the quotient is 1. Also, the quotient of any number divided by 1 is that same number. These properties are referred to as the **Division Properties of 1**.

▶ **Division Properties of 1**

   a. For any number a, except $a = 0$,
      $a \div a = 1$.

   b. For any number a,
      $a \div 1 = a$.

Note that unlike multiplication, division is neither commutative nor associative. This will be further explained later in this book.

As with addition, subtraction and multiplication, there are key words and phrases useful in problem solving dealing with division.

Key Words or Phrases	Example	Symbols
divide	divide 8 by 2	$8 \div 2$
divided by	6 divided by 3	$6 \div 3$
tthe quotient of	the quotient of 12 and 4	$12 \div 4$
divided into	2 divided into 10	$10 \div 2$

There are different symbols that you may use when writing a division problem. As with multiplication, in general, you may choose which symbol to use.

▶ **Division Symbols**

$a \div b$

$b\overline{)a}$

$\frac{a}{b}$

a/b

The previous examples could have been shown using any of the above symbols. For example, 8 divided by 2, could also have been written as any of the following.

$$8 \div 2$$

$$2\overline{)8}$$

$$\frac{8}{2}$$

$$8/2$$

Sometimes, key words and phrases in problems suggest using subtraction but could be solved using division. For example, if you were going to put 70 cans into boxes that hold 10 cans each, the number of boxes needed could be found either by subtracting,

$$70 - 10 - 10 - 10 - 10 - 10 - 10 - 10,$$

or by dividing, $70 \div 10$.

The properties you have studied in this section help form the foundation of all mathematics. In fact, each chapter builds on these properties.

Exercise Set 1.1

Answer the following questions in complete sentences. Writing questions are incorporated throughout this text-book. If you need help getting started, check the answers to questions 1, 3, and 5 to use them as guides for answering other writing questions.

1. In your own words, explain the Commutative Property of Addition. Give a numerical example.

2. In your own words, explain the Commutative Property of Multiplication. Give a numerical example.

3. In your own words, explain the Associative Property of Multiplication. Give a numerical example.

4. In your own words, explain the Associative Property of Addition. Give a numerical example.

5. Why is subtraction not commutative? Give a numerical example.

6. Why is division not commutative? Give a numerical example.

7. Explain the difference between the Identity Property of Zero and the Identity Property of One.

8. In your own words, explain the relationship between a factor and product. Give an example.

9. In your own words explain the relationship between an addend and sum. Give an example.

10. Explain the Division Properties of Zero. Give an example of each.

Write exponential notation.

1. $5 \cdot 5 \cdot 5 \cdot 5$

2. $5 \cdot 5 \cdot 5 \cdot 5 \cdot 5$

3. $10 \cdot 10$

4. $10 \cdot 10 \cdot 10 \cdot 10$

Evaluate.

5. 10^4

6. 10^2

7. 8^3

8. 2^5

1.2 Exponential Notation

a Exponential Notation

Consider the product $3 \cdot 3 \cdot 3 \cdot 3$. Such products occur often enough that mathematicians have found it convenient to create a shorter notation, called **exponential notation**, explained as follows.

$3 \cdot 3 \cdot 3 \cdot 3$ is shortened to 3^4 ← exponent

└─ base

4 factors

We read 3^4 as "three to the fourth power," 5^3 as "five to the third power," or "five cubed," and 5^2 as "five squared."

$$a \cdot a = a^2$$
$$a \cdot a \cdot a = a^3$$
$$a \cdot a \cdot a \cdot a = a^4$$

Example 1 Write exponential notation for $10 \cdot 10 \cdot 10 \cdot 10 \cdot 10$.

Exponential notation is 10^5 ← 5 is the exponent.

└────10 is the base.

Example 2 Write exponential notation for $4 \cdot 4 \cdot 4$.

Exponential notation is 4^3.

Do Margin Exercises 1–4.

b Evaluating Exponential Notation

We evaluate exponential notation by rewriting it as a product and computing the product.

$$a^2 = a \cdot a$$
$$a^3 = a \cdot a \cdot a$$
$$a^4 = a \cdot a \cdot a \cdot a$$

Example 3 Evaluate: 10^3.

$10^3 = 10 \cdot 10 \cdot 10 = 1000$

Example 4 Evaluate: 5^4.

$5^4 = 5 \cdot 5 \cdot 5 \cdot 5 = 625$

CAUTION! 5^4 does not mean $5 \cdot 4$.

Do Margin Exercises 5–8.

Improving Your Math Study Skills

Homework

Before Doing Your Homework

- **Setting.** Consider doing your homework as soon as possible after class, before you forget what you learned in the lecture. Research has shown that after 24 hours, most people forget about half of what is in their short-term memory. To avoid this "automatic" forgetting, you need to transfer the knowledge into long-term memory. The best way to do this with math concepts is to perform practice exercises repeatedly. This is the "drill-and-practice" part of learning math that comes when you do your homework. It cannot be overlooked if you want to succeed in your study of math.

  Try to set a specific time for your homework. Then choose a location that is quiet and uninterrupted. Some students find it helpful to listen to music when doing homework. Research has shown that classical music creates the best atmosphere for studying: Give it a try!

- **Reading.** Before you begin doing the homework exercises, you should reread the assigned material in the textbook. You may also want to look over your class notes again and rework some of the examples given in class.

  You should not read a math textbook as you would a novel or history textbook. Math texts are not meant to be read passively. Be sure to stop and do the margin exercises when directed. Also be sure to reread any paragraphs as you see the need.

While Doing Your Homework

- **Study groups.** For some students, forming a study group can be helpful. Many times, two heads are better than one. Also, it is true that "to teach is to learn again." Thus, when you explain a concept to your classmate, you often gain a deeper understanding of the concept yourself. If you do study in a group, resist the temptation to waste time by socializing.

If you work regularly with someone, be careful not to become dependent on that person. Work on your own some of the time so that you do not rely heavily on others and are able to learn even when they are not available.

- **Notebook.** When doing your homework, consider using notebook paper in a spiral or three-ring binder. You want to be able to go over your homework when studying for a test. Therefore, you need to be able to easily access any problem in your homework notebook. Write legibly in your notebook so you can check over your work. Label each section and each exercise clearly, and show all steps. Your clear writing will also be appreciated by your instructor should your homework be collected. Also, tutors and instructors can be more helpful if they can see and understand all the steps in your work.

  When you are finished with your homework, check the answers to the odd-numbered exercises at the back of the book and make corrections. If you do not understand why an answer is wrong, put a star by it so you can ask questions in class or during the instructor's office hours.

After Doing Your Homework

- **Review.** If you complete your homework several days before the next class, review your work every day. This will keep the material fresh in your mind. You should also review the work immediately before the next class so that you can ask questions as needed.

Exercise Set 1.2

a Write exponential notation.

1. $3 \cdot 3 \cdot 3 \cdot 3$ **2.** $2 \cdot 2 \cdot 2 \cdot 2 \cdot 2$ **3.** $5 \cdot 5$ **4.** $13 \cdot 13 \cdot 13$

5. $7 \cdot 7 \cdot 7 \cdot 7 \cdot 7$ **6.** $10 \cdot 10$ **7.** $10 \cdot 10 \cdot 10$ **8.** $1 \cdot 1 \cdot 1 \cdot 1$

b Evaluate.

9. 7^2 **10.** 5^3 **11.** 9^3 **12.** 10^2

13. 12^4 **14.** 10^5 **15.** 11^2 **16.** 6^3

Skill Maintenance

Add.

17. $234 + 68$ **18.** $75 + 139$

Subtract.

19. $88 - 29$ **20.** $114 - 53$

Multiply.

21. $45(3)$ **22.** $17(12)$

Divide.

23. $103 \div 6$ **24.** $247 \div 8$

Synthesis

Write in exponential notation.

25. $7 \cdot 7 \cdot 7 \cdot 8 \cdot 8 \cdot 8 \cdot 9 \cdot 9 \cdot 9 \cdot 9$ **26.** $5 \cdot 5 \cdot 5 \cdot 11 \cdot 11 \cdot 11 \cdot 11 \cdot 13$

27. $x \cdot x \cdot x \cdot x$ **28.** $y \cdot y \cdot y \cdot y \cdot y \cdot y$

1.3 Multiples, Factors, and Divisibility

The numbers that we multiply are called **factors**. The result of the multiplication is called a **product**. A product is a multiple of any one of its factors.

a | Multiples and Factors

Multiples

A **multiple** of a natural number is a product of it and some natural number. For example, some multiples of 2 are:

> Note that all but the first multiple of a number are *larger* than the number itself.

$$
\begin{bmatrix}
2 \text{ (because } 2 = 1 \cdot \mathbf{2}); \\
4 \text{ (because } 4 = 2 \cdot \mathbf{2}); \\
6 \text{ (because } 6 = 3 \cdot \mathbf{2}); \\
8 \text{ (because } 8 = 4 \cdot \mathbf{2}); \\
10 \text{ (because } 10 = 5 \cdot \mathbf{2}).
\end{bmatrix}
$$

We find multiples of 2 by counting by twos: 2, 4, 6, 8, and so on. We can find multiples of 3 by counting by threes: 3, 6, 9, 12, and so on.

Example 1 Show that each of the numbers 3, 6, 9, and 15 is a multiple of 3.

$$3 = 1 \cdot 3 \qquad 9 = 3 \cdot 3$$
$$6 = 2 \cdot 3 \qquad 15 = 5 \cdot 3$$

Do Margin Exercises 1 and 2.

Example 2 Multiply by 1, 2, 3, and so on, to find ten multiples of 7.

$$
\begin{array}{ll}
1 \cdot 7 = 7 & 6 \cdot 7 = 42 \\
2 \cdot 7 = 14 & 7 \cdot 7 = 49 \\
3 \cdot 7 = 21 & 8 \cdot 7 = 56 \\
4 \cdot 7 = 28 & 9 \cdot 7 = 63 \\
5 \cdot 7 = 35 & 10 \cdot 7 = 70
\end{array}
$$

Do Margin Exercise 3.

Factors

The numbers 15 and 40 are both multiples of 5. Another way of saying this is to state that 5 is a *factor* of both 15 and 40. When a number is expressed as a product of two or more factors, we say that we have *factored* the original number. Thus the word "factor" can be used as either a noun or a verb. Being able to factor is an important skill for our study of fractions.

Looking at the equation $3 \cdot 4 = 12$, we see that 3 and 4 are **factors** of 12. Since $12 = 12 \cdot 1$, we know that 12 and 1 are also factors of 12.

> ▶ A natural number c is a *factor* of the number a if a is the product of c and some natural number. A *factorization* of a number expresses that number as a product of natural numbers.

1. Show that each of the numbers 5, 45, and 100 is a multiple of 5.

2. Show that each of the numbers 10, 60, and 110 is a multiple of 10.

3. Multiply by 1, 2, 3. and so on, to find ten multiples of 5.

Find all the factors of the number. (*Hint:* Find some factorizations of the number.)

4. 6

5. 8

6. 10

7. 32

For example, each of the following represents a factorization of 12.

$12 = 4 \cdot 3$ ← This factorization shows that 4 and 3 are factors of 12.
$12 = 12 \cdot 1$ ← This factorization shows that 12 and 1 are factors of 12.
$12 = 6 \cdot 2$ ← This factorization shows that 6 and 2 are factors of 12.
$12 = 2 \cdot 3 \cdot 2$ ← This factorization shows that 2 and 3 are factors of 12.

Since $n = n \cdot 1$, every number has a factorization and every number has factors even if its only factors may be itself and 1.

Example 3 Find all the factors of 24.

We can write some factorizations and then make a complete list of factors.

$24 = 1 \cdot 24$ $24 = 3 \cdot 8$
$24 = 2 \cdot 12$ $24 = 4 \cdot 6$

← Note that all but one of the factors of a natural number are *less* than the number itself.

Factors: 1, 2, 3, 4, 6, 8, 12, 24.

In part "b" of this section, we will study divisibility rules that will help us find all factors of some numbers more easily.

Do Margin Exercises 4–7.

▶ A number b is said to be *divisible* by another number a if b is a multiple of a.

Thus,

6 is divisible by 2 because 6 is a multiple of 2 ($6 = 3 \cdot \mathbf{2}$);

27 is divisible by 3 because 27 is a multiple of 3 ($27 = 9 \cdot \mathbf{3}$);

100 is divisible by 25 because 100 is a multiple of 25 ($100 = 4 \cdot \mathbf{25}$).

▶ A number b is divisible by another number a if division of b by a results in a remainder of zero. We sometimes say that a divides b "evenly."

Example 4   Determine whether 24 is divisible by 3.

We divide 24 by 3:

$$
\begin{array}{r}
8 \\
3{\overline{\smash{\big)}\,24}} \\
\underline{24} \\
0 \quad \leftarrow \text{zero}
\end{array}
$$

The remainder of 0 indicates that 24 is divisible by 3.

Example 5   Determine whether 98 is divisible by 4.

We divide 98 by 4:

$$
\begin{array}{r}
24 \\
4{\overline{\smash{\big)}\,98}} \\
\underline{8} \\
18 \\
\underline{16} \\
2 \quad \leftarrow \text{Not 0!}
\end{array}
$$

Since the remainder is not 0, we know that 98 is not divisible by 4.

Do Margin Exercises 8–10.

8. Determine whether 16 is divisible by 2.

9. Determine whether 125 is divisible by 5.

10. Determine whether 125 is divisible by 6.

Determine whether the number is divisible by 2.

11. 84

12. 59

13. 998

14. 2225

Determine whether the number is divisible by 3.

15. 111

16. 1111

17. 309

18. 17,216

b | Tests For Divisibility

We now learn quick ways of determining whether numbers are divisible by 2, 3, 5, 6, 9, or 10 without actually performing long division.

Divisibility by 2

You may already know the test for divisibility by 2.

> ▶ A number is divisible by 2 (is *even*) if it has a ones digit of 0, 2, 4, 6, or 8 (that is, it has an even ones digit).

Examples Determine whether the number is divisible by 2. (*Hint:* Add the digits of the number.)

6. 355   *is not* a multiple of 2; **5** is not even.
7. 4786   *is* a multiple of 2; **6** is even.
8. 8990   *is* a multiple of 2; **0** is even.
9. 4261   *is not* a multiple of 2; **1** is not even.

Do Margin Exercises 11–14.

Divisibility by 3

> ▶ A number is divisible by 3 if the sum of its digits is divisible by 3.

Examples Determine whether the number is divisible by 3. (*Hint:* Add the digits of the number.)

10.   18 $1 + 8 = 9$ ⎤   All are divisible by 3 because the
11.   93 $9 + 3 = 12$ ⎟   sums of their digits are divisible by 3.
12.   201 $2 + 0 + 1 = 3$ ⎦

13.   256 $2 + 5 + 6 = 13$ The sum is not divisible by 3, so 256 is not divisible by 3.

Do Margin Exercises 15–18.

Divisibility By 6

A number divisible by 6 is a multiple of 6. But $6 = 2 \cdot 3$, so the number is also a multiple of 2 and 3. Thus a number is divisible by 6 if it is divisible by both 2 and 3.

> ▶ A number is divisible by 6 if its ones digit is even (0, 2, 4, 6, or 8) and the sum of its digits is divisible by 3.

Examples Determine whether the number is divisible by 6.

14. 720

Because 720 is even, it is divisible by 2. Also, $7 + 2 + 0 = 9$, and since 9 is divisible by 3, 720 is divisible by 3.

720            $7 + 2 + 0 = \mathbf{9}$
↑   ↑
Even   Divisible by 3

Thus, 720 is divisible by 6.

15. 471

471 *is not* divisible by 2 because it *is not* even.

47**1**
↑
Not even

Thus, 471 *is not* divisible by 2.

16. 256

256 *is not* divisible by 3 because the sum of its digits *is not* divisible by 3.

$2 + 5 + 6 = \mathbf{13}$
                    ↑
        Not divisible by 3.

Thus, 256 *is not* divisible by 3.

Do Margin Exercises 19–22.

Divisibility By 9

The test for divisibility by 9 is similar to the test for divisibility by 3.

> ▶ A number is divisible by 9 if the sum of its digits is divisible by 9.

Example 17 The number 6984 is divisible by 9 because

$6 + 9 + 8 + 4 = \mathbf{27}$

and 27 is divisible by 9.

Example 18 The number 322 *is not* divisible by 9 because

$3 + 2 + 2 = \mathbf{7}$

and 7 *is not* divisible by 9.

Do Margin Exercises 23–26.

Determine whether the number is divisible by 6.

19. 420

20. 106

21. 321

22. 444

Determine whether the number is divisible by 9.

23. 16

24. 117

25. 930

26. 29,223

Determine whether the number is divisible by 10.

27. 305

28. 300

29. 847

30. 8760

Determine whether the number is divisible by 5.

31. 5780

32. 3427

33. 34,678

34. 7775

Divisibility By 10

▶ A number is divisible by 10 if its ones digit is 0.

We know that this test works because the product of 10 and any number has a ones digit of 0.

Examples   Determine whether the number is divisible by 10.

19. 3440   *is* divisible by 10 because its ones digit is 0.
20. 3447   *is not* divisible by 10 because its ones digit is not 0.

Do Margin Exercises 27–30.

Divisibility By 5

▶ A number is divisible by 5 if its ones digit is 0 or 5.

Examples   Determine whether the number is divisible by 5.

21. 220   *is* divisible by 5 because its ones digit is 0.
22. 475   *is* divisible by 5 because its ones digit is 5.
23. 6514   *is not* divisible by 5 because its ones digit is neither a 0 nor a 5.

Do Margin Exercises 31–34.

To see why the test for 5 works, consider 7830:

$$7830 = \mathbf{10} \cdot 783 = \mathbf{5} \cdot \mathbf{2} \cdot 783.$$

Since 7830 is divisible by 10 and 5 is a factor of 10, it follows that 7830 is divisible by 5.

An Application: Leap Years

Years divisible by 4 are leap years, except those indicating the beginning of a century (last two digits 00), in which case they must be divisible by 400 in order to be leap years. To see if a large number is divisible by 4, we need only check if its last two digits are divisible by 4. For example, the following are all leap years:

1980	(80 is divisible by 4);
1984	(84 is divisible by 4);
1988	(88 is divisible by 4);
2000	(2000 is divisible by 400).

But the following are not leap years:

1981	(81 is *not* divisible by 4);
2100	(2100 is *not* divisible by 400).

Exercises

Determine whether each year is a leap year.

1. 1992
2. 1990
3. 1492
4. 1941
5. 1950
6. 2200
7. 2001
8. 1600

Exercise Set 1.3

a Multiply by 1, 2, 3, and so on, to find ten multiples of the number.

1. 4   **2.** 14   **3.** 20   **4.** 50

5. 3   **6.** 7   **7.** 12   **8.** 17

9. 10   **10.** 6   **11.** 9   **12.** 11

Find all the factors of the number.

13. 16   **14.** 18   **15.** 54   **16.** 48

17. 4   **18.** 9   **19.** 7   **20.** 11

21. 1   **22.** 3   **23.** 98   **24.** 100

25. 42   **26.** 105   **27.** 385   **28.** 110

29. 36   **30.** 196   **31.** 225   **32.** 441

33. Determine if 26 is divisible by 7.   **34.** Determine if 29 is divisible by 9.

35. Determine if 1880 is divisible by 8.   **36.** Determine if 4227 is divisible by 3.

37. Determine if 256 is divisible by 16.   **38.** Determine if 102 is divisible by 4.

39. Determine if 4227 is divisible by 9.   **40.** Determine if 200 is divisible by 25.

41. Determine if 8650 is divisible by 16.   **42.** Determine if 4143 is divisible by 7.

b To answer Exercises 43–48, consider the following numbers. Use the tests for divisibility.

46	300	85
224	36	711
19	45,270	13,251
555	4,444	254,765

43. Which are divisible by 2?

44. Which are divisible by 3?

45. Which are divisible by 10?

46. Which are divisible by 5?

47. Which are divisible by 6?

48. Which are divisible by 9?

To answer Exercises 49–54, consider the following numbers. Do not perform long division.

56	200	75
324	42	812
784	501	2345
55,555	3009	2001

49. Which are divisible by 3?

50. Which are divisible by 2?

51. Which are divisible by 5?

52. Which are divisible by 10?

53. Which are divisible by 9?

54. Which are divisible by 6?

Divide.

55. $9\,4\,)\overline{2\,1\,5\,3}$ **56.** $8\,2\,)\overline{4\,0\,6\,4}$ **57.** $1\,1\,7\,)\overline{4\,4,9\,0\,2}$ **58.** $7\,4\,0\,)\overline{5\,5,2\,0\,0}$

Synthesis

59. ❖ Is every counting number a multiple of 1? Why or why not?

60. ❖ Describe a manner in which Exercises 43, 44, and 46 can be used to answer Exercises 45 and 47.

Find the smallest number that is a multiple of all the given numbers.

61. 2, 3, and 5

62. 3, 5, and 7

63. 4, 6, and 10

64. 6, 10, and 14

65. Describe a test for determining whether a number is divisible by 15.

66. Describe a test for determining whether a number is divisible by 30.

1.4 Prime Factorization

a Prime and Composite Numbers

> A natural number that has only two different natural numbers as factors, itself and 1, is called a *prime number*.
>
> The number 1 is not prime. It does not have two *different* natural numbers as factors.

> The only even prime number is 2. Every other even number is a multiple of two, so no other even numbers are prime.
>
> All other prime numbers are odd, but not every odd number is prime.

Example 1 Tell whether the numbers 2, 3, 5, 7, and 11 are prime.

The number 2 is prime. It has only the factors 1 and 2.
The number 5 is prime. It has only the factors 1 and 5.
The numbers 3, 7, and 11 are also prime.

Example 2 Tell whether the numbers 4, 6, 8, 10, 63, and 1 are prime.

The number 4 is not prime. It has the factors 1, 2, and 4.
The numbers 6, 8, 10, and 63 are not prime. Each has factors other than itself and 1. For instance, 2 is a factor of 6, 8, and 10, while 7 is a factor of 63.
The number 1 is not prime. It does not have 2 natural numbers as factors.

> A natural number, other than 1, that is not prime is called *composite*.

In other words, if a number has at least one factor other than itself and 1, it is composite. Thus,

2, 3, 5, 7, and 11 are prime;
4, 6, 8, 10, and 63 are composite;
1 is neither prime nor composite.

Do Margin Exercise 1.

The following is a table of the prime numbers from 2 to 157. Being able to recognize primes will help save you time as you progress through this text.

A Table of Primes

2, 3, 5, 7, 11, 13, 17, 19, 23, 29, 31, 37, 41, 43, 47, 53, 59, 61, 67, 71, 73, 79, 83, 89, 97, 101, 103, 107, 109, 113, 127, 131, 137, 139, 149, 151, 157

---

1. Tell whether each number is prime, composite, or neither.

1, 4, 6, 8, 13, 19, 41

b Finding Prime Factorizations

To factor a composite number into a product of primes is to find a **prime factorization** of the number. To do this, we consider the primes

2, 3, 5, 7, 11, 13, 17, 19, 23, and so on,

and determine whether a given number is divisible by a prime.

Example 3 Find the prime factorization of 39.

a. We check for divisibility by the first prime, 2. Since 39 is not even, 2 is not a factor of 39.

b. We check for divisibility by the next prime, 3. Since the sum of the digits in 39 is 12, and 12 is divisible by 3, we know that 39 is divisible by 3. We then perform the division.

$$\begin{array}{r} 13 \\ 3\overline{)39} \end{array} \quad R = 0 \quad \text{A remainder of 0 confirms that 3 is a factor of 39.}$$

Because 13 is prime, we are finished. The prime factorization is

$$39 = \mathbf{3 \cdot 13}.$$

Example 4

Find the prime factorization of 76.

a. Since 76 is even, it must have the first prime, 2, as a factor.

$$\begin{array}{r} 38 \\ 2\overline{)76} \end{array} \qquad \text{We can write } 76 = 2 \cdot 38.$$

b. Since 38 is also even, we see that 76 contains a second factor of 2.

$$\begin{array}{r} 19 \\ 2\overline{)38} \end{array} \qquad \text{Note that } 38 = 2 \cdot 19, \text{ so } 76 = 2 \cdot 2 \cdot 19.$$

Because 19 is prime, the complete factorization is

$$76 = \mathbf{2 \cdot 2 \cdot 19}. \quad \text{All factors are prime.}$$

We abbreviate our procedure as follows.

$$\begin{array}{r} 19 \\ 2\overline{)38} \\ 2\overline{)76} \end{array} \qquad \leftarrow\text{We begin here.}$$

$$76 = \mathbf{2 \cdot 2 \cdot 19} \text{ or } 2^2 \cdot 19$$

Multiplication is commutative so a factorization such as $2 \cdot 2 \cdot 19$ could also be expressed as $2 \cdot 19 \cdot 2$ or $19 \cdot 2 \cdot 2$, but the prime factors are still the same. For this reason. we agree that any of these is "the" prime factorization of 76.

> ▶ Each composite number has just one (unique) prime factorization.

Example 5   Find the prime factorization of 72.

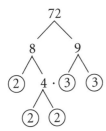

$$72 = 2 \cdot 2 \cdot 2 \cdot 3 \cdot 3 \text{ or } 2^3 \cdot 3^2$$

Another way to find a prime factorization is by using a **factor tree** as follows:

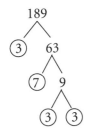

Had we begun with $2 \cdot 36$, $3 \cdot 24$, $4 \cdot 18$, or $6 \cdot 12$, the same prime factorization would result. Try it!

$$72 = 2 \cdot 2 \cdot 2 \cdot 3 \cdot 3 \text{ or } 2^3 \cdot 3$$

Example 6   Find the prime factorization of 189. We can use a string of successive divisions:

$$\begin{array}{r} 7 \\ 3\overline{)21} \\ 3\overline{)63} \\ 3\overline{)189} \end{array}$$

Since 189 is odd, 2 will not be a factor. We begin with 3. Because the sum of the digits $(1 + 8 + 9)$ is 18, which is divisible by 3.

$$189 = 3 \cdot 3 \cdot 3 \cdot 7 \text{ or } 3^3 \cdot 7$$

We can also use a factor tree.

189
3   63
7   9
3   3

$$189 = 3 \cdot 3 \cdot 3 \cdot 7 \text{ or } 3^3 \cdot 7$$

Example 7   Find the prime factorization of 65.

We can use a string of successive divisions:

$$\begin{array}{r} 13 \\ 5\overline{)65} \end{array}$$

65 is not divisible by 2 or 3 but *is* divisible by 5.

$$65 = 5 \cdot 13$$

We can also use a factor tree.

65
5   13

$$65 = 5 \cdot 13$$

Do Margin Exercises 2–7.

Find the prime factorization of the number.

2. 6

3. 12

4. 45

5. 98

6. 126

7. 144

Exercise Set 1.4

a State whether the number is prime, composite, or neither.

1. 17

2. 24

3. 22

4. 31

5. 32

6. 43

7. 31

8. 54

9. 1

10. 2

11. 9

12. 19

13. 47

14. 27

15. 29

16. 49

b Find the prime factorization of the number.

17. 8

18. 16

19. 14

20. 15

21. 22

22. 32

23. 25

24. 40

25. 50

26. 62

27. 169

28. 140

29. 100

30. 110

31. 35

32. 70

33. 78

34. 86

35. 77

36. 99

37. 112

38. 142

39. 300

40. 175

Divide.

41. $0 \div 22$

42. $22 \div 22$

Multiply.

43. $8 \cdot 0$

44. $0 \cdot 13$

Synthesis

45. ❖ Are the divisibility tests useful for finding prime factorizations? Why or why not?

46. ❖ Explain a method for constructing a composite number that contains exactly two factors other than itself and 1.

Find the prime factorization of the number.

47. 7800

48. 2520

49. 2772

50. 1998

51. Describe an arrangement of 54 objects that corresponds to the factorization $54 = 6 \times 9$.

52. Describe an arrangement of 24 objects that corresponds to the factorization $24 = 2 \cdot 3 \cdot 4$.

1.5 Least Common Multiples

a | Finding Least Common Multiples

▶ The **least common multiple**, or LCM, of two natural numbers is the smallest number that is a multiple of both.

Example 1 Find the LCM of 20 and 30.

a. First list some multiples of 20 by multiplying 20 by 1, 2, 3, and so on:

20, 40, 60, 80, 100, 120, 140, 160, 180, 200, 220, 240, ...

b. Then list some multiples of 30 by multiplying 30 by 1, 2, 3, and so on:

30, 60, 90, 120, 150, 180, 210, 240, ...

c. Now list the numbers common to both lists, the *common multiples*:

60, 120, 180, 240, ...

d. These are the common multiples of 20 and 30. Which is the smallest? The LCM of 20 and 30 is **60**.

Do Margin Exercise 1.

Next we develop three methods that are more efficient for finding LCMs. You may choose to learn one method (consult with your instructor), or all three, but if you are going on to a study of algebra, you should definitely learn method 2 or 3.

Method 1: Finding LCMs Using One List of Multiples

▶ *Method 1.* To find the LCM of a set of numbers (9, 12):

a. Determine whether the largest number is a multiple of the others. If it is, it is the LCM. That is, if the largest number has the others as factors, the LCM is that number.

(12 is not a multiple of 9)

b. If not, check multiples of the largest number until you get one that is a multiple of the others.

($2 \cdot 12 = 24$, not a multiple of 9)

($3 \cdot 12 = \mathbf{36}$, a multiple of 9)

c. That number is the LCM.

LCM = **36**

Example 2 Find the LCM of 12 and 15.

a. 15 is not a multiple of 12.

b. Check multiples:

$2 \cdot 15 = 30,$ Not a multiple of 12

$3 \cdot 15 = 45,$ Not a multiple of 12

$4 \cdot 15 = \mathbf{60}.$ A multiple of 12

c. The LCM = **60**.

Do Margin Exercise 2.

Example 3 Find the LCM of 4 and 14.

a. 14 is not a multiple of 4.

b. Check multiples:

$2 \cdot 14 = \mathbf{28}.$ A multiple of 4

c. The LCM = **28**.

Do Margin Exercises 3 and 4.

Example 4 Find the LCM of 8 and 32.

a. 32 is a multiple of 8, so it is the LCM.

b. The LCM = **32**.

Example 5 Find the LCM of 10, 100, and 1000.

a. 1000 is a multiple of 10 and 100, so it is the LCM.

b. The LCM = **1000**.

Do Margin Exercises 5 and 6.

Method 2: Finding LCMs Using Factorizations

A second method for finding LCMs uses prime factorizations. Consider again 20 and 30. Their prime factorizations are

$$20 = 2 \cdot 2 \cdot 5 \text{ and } 30 = 2 \cdot 3 \cdot 5.$$

Let's look at these prime factorizations in order to find the LCM. Any multiple of 20 will have to have *two* 2's as factors and *one* 5 as a factor. Any multiple of 30 will have to have *one* 2, *one* 3, and *one* 5 as factors. The smallest number satisfying all of these conditions is

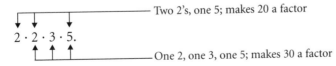

Two 2's, one 5; makes 20 a factor

$2 \cdot 2 \cdot 3 \cdot 5.$

One 2, one 3, one 5; makes 30 a factor

The LCM must have all the factors of 20 and all the factors of 30, but the factors should not be repeated when they are common to both numbers.

2. By examining lists of multiples, find the LCM of 8 and 10.

Find the LCM.

3. 10, 15

4. 6, 8

Find the LCM.

5. 5, 10

6. 20, 40, 80

Use prime factorizations to find the LCM.

7. 8, 10

8. 18, 40

9. 32, 54

The greatest number of times a 2 occurs as a factor of either 20 or 30 is two, and the LCM has 2 as a factor twice. The greatest number of times a 3 occurs as a factor of either 20 or 30 is one, and the LCM has 3 as a factor once. The greatest number of times that 5 occurs as a factor of either 20 or 30 is one, and the LCM has 5 as a factor once. The LCM is the product $2 \cdot 2 \cdot 3 \cdot 5$, or 60.

▶ *Method 2.* To find the LCM of a set of numbers using prime factorizations:

a. Find the prime factorization of each number.

b. Create a product of factors, using each factor the greatest number of times that it occurs in any one factorization.

Example 6 Find the LCM of 6 and 8.

a. Find the prime factorization of each number.

$$6 = 2 \cdot 3, \qquad 8 = 2 \cdot 2 \cdot 2$$

b. Create a product by writing factors, using each the greatest number of times that it occurs in any one factorization.

Consider the factor 2. The greatest number of times that 2 occurs in any one factorization is three. We write **2** as a factor **three** times.

$$2 \cdot 2 \cdot 2 \cdot ?$$

Consider the factor 3. The greatest number of times that 3 occurs in any one factorization is one. We write **3** as a factor **one** time.

$$2 \cdot 2 \cdot 2 \cdot 3 \cdot ?$$

Since there are no other prime factors in either factorization, the

LCM is $2 \cdot 2 \cdot 2 \cdot 3$, or 24.

Example 7 Find the LCM of 24 and 36.

a. Find the prime factorization of each number.

$$24 = 2 \cdot 2 \cdot 2 \cdot 3, \qquad 36 = 2 \cdot 2 \cdot 3 \cdot 3$$

b. Create a product by writing factors, using each the greatest number of times that it occurs in any one factorization.

Consider the factor 2. The greatest number of times that 2 occurs in any one factorization is three. We write **2** as a factor **three** times:

$$2 \cdot 2 \cdot 2 \cdot ?$$

Consider the factor 3. The greatest number of times that 3 occurs in any one factorization is two. We write **3** as a factor **two** times:

$$2 \cdot 2 \cdot 2 \cdot 3 \cdot 3 \cdot ?$$

Since there are no other prime factors in either factorization, the

LCM is $2 \cdot 2 \cdot 2 \cdot 3 \cdot 3$, or 72.

Do Margin Exercises 7–9.

Example 8 Find the LCM of 27, 90, and 84.

a. Find the prime factorization of each number.

$$27 = 3 \cdot 3 \cdot 3, \quad 90 = 2 \cdot 3 \cdot 3 \cdot 5, \quad\quad 84 = 2 \cdot 2 \cdot 3 \cdot 7$$

b. Create a product by writing factors, using each the greatest number of times that it occurs in any one factorization.

Consider the factor 2. The greatest number of times that 2 occurs in any one factorization is two. We write **2** as a factor **two** times:

2 · 2 · ?

Consider the factor 3. The greatest number of times that 3 occurs in any one factorization is three. We write **3** as a factor **three** times:

$$2 \cdot 2 \cdot \mathbf{3} \cdot \mathbf{3} \cdot \mathbf{3} \cdot ?$$

Consider the factor 5. The greatest number of times that 5 occurs in any one factorization is one. We write **5** as a factor **one** time:

$$2 \cdot 2 \cdot 3 \cdot 3 \cdot 3 \cdot \mathbf{5} \cdot ?$$

Consider the factor 7. The greatest number of times that 7 occurs in any one factorization is one. We write **7** as a factor **one** time:

$$2 \cdot 2 \cdot 3 \cdot 3 \cdot 3 \cdot 5 \cdot \mathbf{7} \cdot ?$$

Since no other prime factors are possible in any of the factorizations, the LCM is **2 · 2 · 3 · 3 · 3 · 5 · 7**, or 3780.

The use of exponents might be helpful to you as an extension of the factorization method. Let's reconsider Example 8. We want to find the LCM of 27, 90, and 84. We factor and then convert to exponential notation:

$$27 = 3 \cdot 3 \cdot 3 = 3^3,$$
$$90 = 2 \cdot 3 \cdot 3 \cdot 5 = 2^1 \cdot 3^2 \cdot 5^1, \text{ and}$$
$$84 = 2 \cdot 2 \cdot 3 \cdot 7 = 2^2 \cdot 3^1 \cdot 7^1.$$

Thus the

LCM is $2^2 \cdot 3^3 \cdot 5^1 \cdot 7^1$, or $2^2 \cdot 3^3 \cdot 5 \cdot 7$, or 3780.

Note that in 84, the **2** in 2^2 is the largest exponent of 2 in any of the factorizations. It is also the exponent of 2 in the LCM. It indicates the greatest number of times that 2 occurs as a factor of any of the numbers. Similarly in 27, the **3** in 3^3 is the largest exponent of 3 in any of the factorizations. It is also the exponent of 3 in the LCM. Likewise, the 1's in 5^1 and 7^1 tell us the exponents of 5 and 7 in the LCM. They indicate the greatest number of times that 5 and 7 occur as factors.

Do Margin Exercise 10.

10. Find the LCM of 24, 35, and 45.

> When an exponent is 1, we normally omit writing the exponent.

Find the LCM.

11. 3, 18

12. 12, 24

Find the LCM.

13. 4, 9

14. 5, 6, 7

Example 9 Find the LCM of 7 and 21.

a. Find the prime factorization of each number. Because 7 is prime, it has no prime factorization. We think of $7 = 7$ as a "factorization" in order to carry out our procedure.

$$7 = 7, \qquad 21 = 3 \cdot 7$$

b. Create a product by writing factors, using each the greatest number of times that it occurs in any one factorization.

Consider the factor 7. The greatest number of times that 7 occurs in any one factorization is one. We write **7** as a factor **one** time:

$$7 \cdot ?$$

Consider the factor 3. The greatest number of times that 3 occurs in any one factorization is one. We write **3** as a factor **one** time:

$$7 \cdot 3 \cdot ?$$

Since no other prime factors are possible in any of the factorizations, the

LCM is **7 · 3**, or 21.

Note in Example 9 that 7 is a factor of 21. We stated earlier that if one number is a factor of another, the LCM is the larger of the numbers. Thus, if you note this at the outset, you can find the LCM quickly without using factorizations.

Do Margin Exercises 11 and 12.

Example 10 Find the LCM of 8 and 9.

a. Find the prime factorization of each number.

$$8 = 2 \cdot 2 \cdot 2, \qquad 9 = 3 \cdot 3$$

b. Create a product by writing factors, using each the greatest number of times that it occurs in any one factorization.

Consider the factor 2. The greatest number of times that 2 occurs in any one factorization is three. We write **2** as a factor **three** times.

$$2 \cdot 2 \cdot 2 \cdot ?$$

Consider the factor 3. The greatest number of times that 3 occurs in any one factorization is two. We write **3** as a factor **two** times.

$$2 \cdot 2 \cdot 2 \cdot 3 \cdot 3 \cdot ?$$

Since no other prime factors are possible in any of the factorizations, the

LCM is **2 · 2 · 2 · 3 · 3**, or 72.

Note in Example 10 that the two numbers, 8 and 9, have no common prime factor. When this happens, the LCM is just the product of the two numbers. Thus, when you note this at the outset, you can find the LCM quickly by multiplying the two numbers.

Do Margin Exercises 13 and 14.

Let's compare the two methods considered for finding LCMs: the multiples method and the factorization method.

Method 1, the **multiples method**, can be longer than the factorization method when the LCM is large or when there are more than two numbers.

Method 2, the **factorization method**, works well for several numbers. It is just like a method used in algebra. If you are going to study algebra, you should definitely learn the factorization method.

Method 3: A Third Method for Finding LCMs

Here is another method for finding LCMs that may work well for you. Suppose you want to find the LCM of 48, 72, and 80. Find a prime number that divides any of these numbers with no remainder. Do the division and bring the third number down, unless the third number is divisible by the prime also. Repeat the process until you can divide no more. Multiply, as shown at the right, all the numbers at the side. The LCM is

$$2 \cdot 3 \cdot 2 \cdot 2 \cdot 2 \cdot 3 \cdot 5, \text{ or } 720.$$

Do Margin Exercises 15 and 16.

Find the LCM using method 3.

15. 24, 35, 45

16. 27, 90, 84

Study Tips: Studying for Tests and Making the Most of Tutoring Sessions

We will often present some tips and guidelines to enhance your learning abilities. Sometimes these tips will be focused on mathematics, but sometimes they will be more general, as is the case here where we consider test preparation and tutoring.

Test-Taking Tips

• *Make up your own test questions as you study.* After you have done your homework for a particular objective, write one or two questions on your own that you think might be on a test. You will be amazed at the insight this will provide. You are actually carrying out a task similar to what an instructor does in preparing an exam.

• *When taking a test, read each question carefully and try to do all the questions the first time through, but pace yourself.* Answer all the questions, and mark those to recheck if you have time at the end. Very often, your first hunch will be correct.

• *Try to write your test in a neat and orderly manner.* Very often, your instructor tries to award partial credit when grading an exam. If your test paper is sloppy and disorderly, it is difficult to verify the partial credit. Doing your work neatly can ease such a task on an exam. By using a soft-lead pencil, you can make your writing darker and therefore more readable. Pencil also enables you to erase and correct errors very easily. Sloppy work can also lead to errors.

Making the Most of Tutoring and Help Sessions

Often you may determine that a tutoring session would be helpful. The following comments may help you make the most of such sessions.

• *Work on the topics before you go to the help or tutoring session. Do not go to such sessions viewing yourself as an empty cup and the tutor as a magician who will pour in the learning.* The primary source of your ability to learn is within you. We have seen so many students over the years go to tutoring sessions with no advance preparation. You are often wasting your time and perhaps your money if you are paying for such sessions. Go to class, study the textbook, and mark trouble spots. Then use the tutoring sessions to deal with these difficulties most efficiently.

• *Do not be afraid to ask questions in these sessions.* The more you talk to your tutor, the more the tutor can help you with your difficulties.

• *Try being a "tutor" yourself.* Explaining a topic to someone else—a classmate, your instructor—is often the best way to learn it.

• *What about the student who says, "I could do the work at home, but on the test I made silly mistakes"?* Yes, all of us, including instructors, make silly computational mistakes in class, on homework, and on tests. But your instructor, if he or she has taught for some time, is probably aware that 90% of students who make such comments in truth do not have enough depth of knowledge of the subject matter, and such silly mistakes often are a sign that the student has not mastered the material. There is no way we can make that analysis for you. It will have to be unraveled by some careful soul searching on your part or by a conference with your instructor.

Exercise Set 1.5

a Find the LCM of the set of numbers.

1. 2, 4   **2.** 3, 15   **3.** 10, 25   **4.** 10, 15   **5.** 20, 40

6. 8, 12   **7.** 18, 27   **8.** 9, 11   **9.** 30, 50   **10.** 24, 36

11. 30, 40   **12.** 21, 27   **13.** 18, 24   **14.** 12, 18   **15.** 60, 70

16. 35, 45   **17.** 16, 36   **18.** 18, 20   **19.** 32, 36   **20.** 36, 48

21. 2, 3, 5   **22.** 5, 18, 3   **23.** 3, 5, 7   **24.** 6, 12, 18   **25.** 24, 36, 12

26. 8, 16, 22   **27.** 5, 12, 15   **28.** 12, 18, 40   **29.** 9, 12, 6   **30.** 8, 16, 12

31. 180, 100, 450 **32.** 18, 30, 50, 48 **33.** 8, 48   **34.** 16, 32   **35.** 5, 50

36. 12, 72   **37.** 11, 13   **38.** 13, 14   **39.** 12, 35   **40.** 23, 25

41. 54, 63   **42.** 56, 72   **43.** 81, 90   **44.** 75, 100

Applications of LCMs: Planet Orbits. The earth, Jupiter, Saturn, and Uranus all revolve around the sun. The earth takes 1 yr, Jupiter 12 yr, Saturn 30 yr, and Uranus 84 yr to make a complete revolution. On a certain night, you look at those three distant planets and wonder how many years it will take before they have the same position again. (*Hint:* to find out, you find the LCM of 12, 30, and 84. It will be that number of years.)

45. How often will Jupiter and Saturn appear in the same direction in the night sky as seen from the earth?

46. How often will Jupiter, Saturn, and Uranus appear in the same direction in the night sky as seen from the earth?

Skill Maintenance

47. Joy uses 12 in. of dental floss each day. How long will a 2400 in. container of dental floss last for Joy?

48. A performing arts center was sold out for a musical. Its seats sell for $13 each. Total receipts were $3250. How many seats does this auditorium contain?

49. Multiply: $23 \cdot 345$.

50. List all factors of 36.

51. Find the prime factorization of 98.

52. Subtract: $10,007 - 3068$.

Synthesis

53. ❖ Is the LCM of two prime numbers always their product? Why or why not?

54. ❖ Is the LCM of two numbers always at least twice as large as the larger of the two numbers? Why or why not?

55. Find the LCM of 27, 90, and 84.

56. Find the LCM of 18, 21, and 24.

57. A pencil company uses two sizes of boxes, 5 in. by 6 in. and 5 in. by 8 in. These boxes are packed in bigger cartons for shipping. Find the width and the length of the smallest carton that will accommodate boxes of either size without any room left over. (Each carton can contain only one type of box and all boxes must point in the same direction.)

58. Consider 8 and 12. Determine whether each of the following is the LCM of 8 and 12. Tell why or why not.

    a. $2 \cdot 2 \cdot 3 \cdot 3$
    b. $2 \cdot 2 \cdot 3$
    c. $2 \cdot 3 \cdot 3$
    d. $2 \cdot 2 \cdot 2 \cdot 3$

Review Exercises: Chapter 1

Name the property used in the following:

1. $2 + 3 = 3 + 2$ **2.** $2 + (3 + 4) = (2 + 3) + 4$ **3.** $8 \cdot 2 = 2 \cdot 8$ **4.** $9 \cdot (2 \cdot 3) = (9 \cdot 2) \cdot 3$

5. $7 + 0 = 7$ **6.** $5 - 5 = 0$ **7.** $12 - 0 = 12$ **8.** $23 \cdot 0 = 0$

9. $75 \cdot 1 = 75$ **10.** $67 \div 67 = 1$ **11.** $83 \div 1 = 83$ **12.** $0 \div 99 = 0$

13. $99 \div 0$ is undefined

Write exponential notation.

14. $4 \cdot 4 \cdot 4 \cdot 4 \cdot 4$ **15.** $6 \cdot 6 \cdot 6$

Evaluate.

16. 13^2 **17.** 2^3

Find the first ten multiples of the number.

18. 12   **19.** 8   **20.** Determine if 112 is divisible by 7.

21. Determine if 201 is divisible by 18.

To answer questions 22-27, consider the following numbers. Use the tests for divisibility. Do not perform long division.

555,555   6372   300

90,000   620,844   1432

22. Which numbers are divisible by 2?   **23.** Which numbers are divisible by 3?

24. Which numbers are divisible by 10?   **25.** Which numbers are divisible by 5?

26. Which numbers are divisible by 6?   **27.** Which numbers are divisible by 9?

State whether the number is prime, composite or neither.

28. 57   **29.** 37

Find the factors of the number.

30. 36   **31.** 96   **32.** 75

Find the prime factorization of the number.

33. 70   **34.** 150   **35.** 136   **36.** 429

Find the LCM of the set of numbers.

37. 18, 45   **38.** 6, 16, and 24

Practice Test: Chapter 1

Name the property used in the following:

1. $12 + (2 + 3) = (12 + 2) + 3$

2. $47 \cdot 53 = 53 \cdot 47$

3. Write exponential notation for $7 \cdot 7 \cdot 7 \cdot 7 \cdot 7 \cdot 7 \cdot 7 \cdot 7$.

4. Evaluate 7^3.

5. Find the first ten multiples of 9.

6. Determine if 1784 is divisible by 8.

Use the test for divisiblity to answer questions 7-9. Do not perform long division.

7. Is 4563 divisible by 9? Why or why not?

8. Is 14,636 divisible by 4? Why or why not?

9. Is 942 divisible by 3? Why, or why not?

To answer questions 10-12, consider the following numbers.

13	1	41
21	48	2

10. Which numbers are prime?

11. Which numbers are composite?

12. Which numbers are neither prime nor composite?

Find all the factors of the number.

13. 32

14. 125

15. Find the prime factorization of 60.

16. Find the prime factorization of 108.

17. Find the LCM of 5, 12 and 18.

18. Is subtraction associative? Why or why not?

19. A student claims that $9^2 = 18$. Explain the error in the student's reasoning.

2

Operations on Whole Numbers

Introduction

In this chapter, we study expressions and equations. We learn the difference between the two and how to solve equations. We then apply our skills to estimating and problem solving, and to perimeter and area problems in particular.

2.1 Expression and Equations

2.2 Introduction to Expressions

2.3 Solving Equations

2.4 Perimeter and Area

2.5 Estimating and Problem Solving

An Application

Th costs to a student of attending a community technical college for two years are: first year, $1025; second year $1115. Find the total cost of the education.

The Mathematics

We let n = the total cost of the college education. Since we are combining costs, addition can be used. We translate the problem to this equation:

$$1025 + 1115 = n$$

↑

Here is how addition can occur in problem solving.

1. $93 - 14 \cdot 3$

2. $104 \div 4 + 4$

3. $25 \cdot 26 - (56 + 10)$

4. $75 \div 5 + (83 - 14)$

2.1 Expressions and Equations

a | Simplifying Numerical Expressions

A **numerical expression** consists of numbers and operation signs.

Suppose we have an expression like the following:

$$3 + 4 \cdot 8.$$

How do we find the answer? Do we add 3 to 4 and then multiply by 8, or do we multiply 4 by 8 and then add 3? In the first case, the answer is 56. In the second, the answer is 35. We agree to compute as in the second case.

Consider the expression

$$7 \cdot 14 - (12 + 18).$$

What do the parentheses mean? To deal with these questions, we must make some agreement regarding the order in which we perform operations. The rules are as follows.

▶ **Rules for Order of Operations**

1. Do all calculations within parentheses ( ), brackets [ ], or braces { } before operations outside.

2. Evaluate all exponential expressions.

3. In order from left to right, do all multiplications and divisions.

4. In order from left to right, do all additions and subtractions.

It is worth noting that these are the rules that a computer uses to do computations. In order to program a computer, you must know these rules.

A nice way of remembering the order of operations is

Please	**Excuse**	**My**		**Dear**	**Aunt**		**Sally**
a	x	u		i	d		u
r	p	l		v	d		b
e	o	t		i	i		t
n	n	i		s	t		r
t	e	p	or	i	i	or	a
h	n	l		o	o		c
e	t	i		n	n		t
s	s	c					i
e		a					o
s		t					n
		i					
		o					
		n					

Example 1 Simplify: $16 \div 8 \cdot 2$.

There are no parentheses or exponents, so we start with the third step.

$$16 \div 8 \cdot 2 = \mathbf{2} \cdot 2 \qquad \text{Doing all multiplications and divisions in order from left to right}$$
$$= 4$$

Example 2 Simplify: $7 \cdot 14 - (12 + 18)$.

$$7 \cdot 14 - (12 + 18) = 7 \cdot 14 - \mathbf{30} \qquad \text{Carrying out operations inside parentheses}$$
$$= \mathbf{98} - 30 \qquad \text{Doing all multiplications and divisions}$$
$$= 68 \qquad \text{Doing all additions and subtractions}$$

Do Margin Exercises 1–4 on the previous page.

Example 3 Simplify and compare: $23 - (10 - 9)$ and $(23 - 10) - 9$.

We have

$$23 - (10 - 9) = 23 - \mathbf{1} = 22;$$
$$(23 - 10) - 9 = \mathbf{13} - 9 = 4.$$

We can see that $23 - (10 - 9)$ and $(23 - 10) - 9$ represent different numbers. Thus subtraction is not associative.

Do Margin Exercises 5 and 6.

Example 4 Simplify: $7 \cdot 2 - (12 + 0) \div 3 - (5 - 2)$.

$$7 \cdot 2 - (12 + 0) \div 3 - (5 - 2) = 7 \cdot 2 - \mathbf{12} \div 3 - \mathbf{3} \qquad \text{Carrying out operations inside parentheses}$$
$$= \mathbf{14} - \mathbf{4} - 3 \qquad \text{Doing all multiplications and divisions in order from left to right}$$
$$= 7 \qquad \text{Doing all additions and subtractions in order from left to right}$$

Do Margin Exercise 7.

Example 5 Simplify: $15 \div 3 \cdot 2 \div (10 - 8)$.

$$15 \div 3 \cdot 2 \div (10 - 8) = 15 \div 3 \cdot 2 \div \mathbf{2} \qquad \text{Carrying out operations inside parentheses}$$
$$= \mathbf{5} \cdot 2 \div 2 \qquad \text{Doing all multiplications and divisions in order from left to right}$$
$$= \mathbf{10} \div 2$$
$$= 5$$

Do Margin Exercises 8–10.

Simplify and compare,

5. $64 \div (32 \div 2)$ and $(64 \div 32) \div 2$

6. $(28 + 13) + 11$ and $28 + (13 + 11)$

7. Simplify:
$9 \cdot 4 - (20 + 4) \div 8 - (6 - 2)$

Simplify.

8. $5 \cdot 5 \cdot 5 + 26 \cdot 71 - (16 + 25 \cdot 3)$

9. $30 \div 5 \cdot 2 + 10 \cdot 20 + 8 \cdot 8 - 23$

10. $95 - 2 \cdot 2 \cdot 2 \cdot 5 \div (24 - 4)$

Simplify.

11. $5^3 + 26 \cdot 71 - (16 + 25 \cdot 3)$

12. $(1 + 3)^3 + 10 \cdot 20 + 8^2 - 23$

13. $95 - 2^3 \cdot 5 \div (24 - 4)$

14. *NBA Tall Men.* The heights, in inches, of several of the tallest players in the NBA are given in the bar graph below. Find the average height of these players.

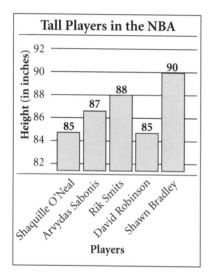

Tall Players in the NBA

Example 6 Simplify: $4^2 \div (10 - 9 + 1)^3 \cdot 3 - 5$.

$$4^2 \div (10 - 9 + 1)^3 \cdot 3 - 5.$$

$= 4^2 \div (\mathbf{1} + 1)^3 \cdot 3 - 5$ Carrying out operations inside parentheses

$= 4^2 \div \mathbf{2^3} \cdot 3 - 5$ Adding inside parentheses

$= \mathbf{16} \div \mathbf{8} \cdot 3 - 5$ Evaluating exponential expressions

$= \mathbf{2} \cdot 3 - 5$
$= \mathbf{6} - 5$ Doing all multiplications and divisions in order from left to right

$= 1$

Do Margin Exercises 11–13.

Example 7 *Average Height of Waterfalls.* The heights of the four highest waterfalls in the world are given in the bar graph at right. Find the average height of all four. To find the **average** of a set of numbers, we first add the numbers and then divide by the number of addends.

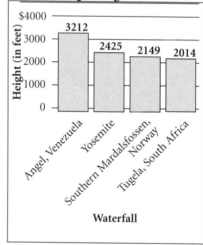

Principal High Waterfalls

Source: World Almanac

The average is given by

$$(3212 + 2425 + 2149 + 2014) \div 4.$$

To find the average, we carry out the computation using the rules for order of operations:

$$(3212 + 2425 + 2149 + 2014) \div 4 = 9800 \div 4$$
$$= 2450.$$

Thus the average height of the four highest waterfalls is 2450 ft.

Do Margin Exercise 14.

b Order of Operations Within Parentheses

When parentheses occur within parentheses, we can make them different shapes, such as [ ] (also called "brackets") and { } (also called "braces"). All of these have the same meaning. When parentheses occur within parentheses, computations in the innermost ones are to be done first.

Example 8 Simplify: $2^3 + 6(2) - (4 + 6 \cdot 2)$.

$2^3 + 6(2) - (4 + 6 \cdot 2)$

$= 2^3 + 6(2) - (4 + \mathbf{12})$ Doing the calculations in parentheses first

$= 2^3 + 6(2) - \mathbf{16}$ Continuing the calculations in parentheses

$= \mathbf{8} + 6(2) - 16$ Evaluating exponential expressions

$= 8 + \mathbf{12} - 16$ Doing all multiplications and divisions in order from left to right

$= \mathbf{20} - 16$ Doing all additions and subtractions in order from left to right

$= 4$

Example 9 Simplify: $16 \div 2 + \{40 - [13 - (4 + 2)]\}$.

$16 \div 2 + \{40 - [13 - (4 + 2)]\}$

$= 16 \div 2 + \{40 - [13 - \mathbf{6}]\}$ Doing the calculations in the innermost parentheses first

$= 16 \div 2 + \{40 - \mathbf{7}\}$ Again, doing the calculations in the innermost parentheses

$= 16 \div 2 + \mathbf{33}$

$= \mathbf{8} + 33$ Doing all multiplications and divisions in order from left to right

$= 41$ Doing all additions and subtractions in order from left to right

Example 10 Simplify: $[25 - (4 + 3) \cdot 3] \div (11 - 7)$.

$[25 - (4 + 3) \cdot 3] \div (11 - 7) = [25 - \mathbf{7} \cdot 3] \div (11 - 7)$

$= [25 - \mathbf{21}] \div (11 - 7)$

$= \mathbf{4} \div \mathbf{4}$

$= 1$

Do Margin Exercises 15–17.

Example 11 Simplify: $3[(120 - 40 \div 4) - (32 \div 8) - 6 \cdot 2]$.

$3[(120 - 40 \div 4) - (32 \div 8) - 6 \cdot 2]$

$= 3[(120 - \mathbf{10}) - \mathbf{4} - 6 \cdot 2]$ Doing the calculations in innermost parentheses first doing multiplication/division in order from left to right

$= 3[\mathbf{110} - 4 - 6 \cdot 2]$ Continuing calculations in innermost parentheses now doing addition/subtraction in order from left to right

$= 3[110 - 4 - \mathbf{12}]$ Performing multiplication within the brackets

$= 3[\mathbf{94}]$ Performing subtraction within the brackets

$= 282$ Multiplying

Do Margin Exercise 18.

Simplify.

15. $9 \cdot 5 + \{6 \div [14 - (5 + 3)]\}$

16. $[18 - (2 + 7) \div 3] - (31 - 10 \cdot 2)$

17. $3 \div 3 + (5 + 2 \cdot 3) + 1^3$

18. $2 + \{(220 - 100 \div 50) - [40 \div 5 - 3 \cdot 2] + 6\}$

Exercise Set 2.1

a Simplify.

1. $12 + (6 + 4)$

2. $(12 + 6) + 18$

3. $52 - (40 - 8)$

4. $(52 - 40) - 8$

5. $1000 \div (100 \div 10)$

6. $(1000 \div 100) \div 10$

7. $(256 \div 64) \div 4$

8. $256 \div (64 \div 4)$

9. $(2 + 5)^2$

10. $2^2 + 5^2$

11. $(11 - 8)^2 - (18 - 16)^2$

12. $(32 - 27)^3 + (19 + 1)^3$

13. $16 \cdot 24 + 50$

14. $23 + 18 \cdot 20$

15. $83 - 7 \cdot 6$

16. $10 \cdot 7 - 4$

17. $10 \cdot 10 - 3 \cdot 4$

18. $90 - 5 \cdot 5 \cdot 2$

19. $4^3 \div 8 - 4$

20. $8^2 - 8 \cdot 2$

21. $17 \cdot 20 - (17 + 20)$

22. $1000 \div 25 - (15 + 5)$

23. $6 \cdot 10 - 4 \cdot 10$

24. $3 \cdot 8 + 5 \cdot 8$

25. $300 \div 5 + 10$

26. $144 \div 4 - 2$

27. $3 \cdot (2 + 8)^2 - 5 \cdot (4 - 3)^2$

28. $7 \cdot (10 - 3)^2 - 2 \cdot (3 + 1)^2$

29. $4^2 + 8^2 \div 2^2$

30. $6^2 - 3^4 \div 3^3$

31. $6 \cdot 11 - (7 + 3) \div 5 - (6 - 4)$

32. $8 \cdot 9 - (12 - 8) \div 4 - (10 - 7)$

33. Find the average of $64, $97, and $121.

34. Find the average of four test grades of 86, 92, 80, and 78.

35. $10^3 - 10 \cdot 6 - (4 + 5 \cdot 6)$

36. $7^2 + 20 \cdot 4 - (28 + 9 \cdot 2)$

37. $120 - 3^3 \cdot 4 \div (5 \cdot 6 - 6 \cdot 4)$

38. $80 - 2^4 \cdot 15 \div (7 \cdot 5 - 45 \div 3)$

b Simplify.

39. $8 \cdot 13 + \{42 \div [18 - (6 + 5)]\}$

40. $72 \div 6 - \{2 \cdot [9 - (4 \cdot 2)]\}$

41. $[14 - (3 + 5) \div 2] - [18 \div (8 - 2)]$

42. $[92 \cdot (6 - 4) \div 8] + [7 \cdot (8 - 3)]$

43. $(82 - 14) \cdot [(10 + 45 \div 5) - (6 \cdot 6 - 5 \cdot 5)]$

44. $(18 \div 2) \cdot \{[(9 \cdot 9 - 1) \div 2] - [5 \cdot 20 - (7 \cdot 9 - 2)]\}$

45. $4 \cdot \{(200 - 50 \div 5) - [(35 \div 7) \cdot (35 \div 7) - 4 \cdot 3]\}$

46. $\{[18 - 2 \cdot 6] - [40 \div (17 - 9)]\} + \{48 - 13 \cdot 3 + [(50 - 7 \cdot 5) + 2]\}$

Skill Maintenance

47. Find the LCM of 14, 21, and 6.

48. Find the LCM of 15, 25, and 40.

49. Write $6 \cdot 6 \cdot 6 \cdot 6 \cdot 6$ in exponential notation.

50. Evaluate 4^3.

Synthesis

51. ❖ The expression $9 - (4 \cdot 2)$ contains parentheses. Are they necessary? Why or why not?

52. ❖ The expression $(3 \cdot 4)^2$ contains parentheses. Are they necessary? Why or why not?

Each of the expressions in Exercises 53–55 is incorrect. First find the correct answer. Then place as many parentheses as needed in the expression in order to make the incorrect answer correct.

53. $1 + 5 \cdot 4 + 3 = 36$

54. $12 \div 4 + 2 \cdot 3 - 2 = 2$

55. $12 \div 4 + 2 \cdot 3 - 2 = 4$

56. Write an expression using $\times$, $+$ and $\div$ and one occurrence each of 1, 2, 3, 4, 5, 6, 7, 8, and 9 to represent 100.

1. Evaluate $a + b$ for $a = 38$ and $b = 26$

2.2 Introduction to Expressions

a Algebraic Expressions

Previously we worked with expressions such as

$$37 + 86, \quad 7 \cdot 8, \quad 19 - 7, \quad \text{and} \quad \frac{24}{3}.$$

We can use letters for numbers and work with *algebraic expressions* such as

$$x + 86, \quad 7 \cdot t, \quad 19 - y, \quad \text{and} \quad \frac{a}{3}.$$

In the expressions above, the letters x, t, y and a are called *variables* because they can represent any number.

2. Evaluate $x - y$ for $x = 57$ and $y = 29$

> ▶ A **variable** is a letter that represents various numbers.

An **algebraic expression** consists of variables, numbers, and operation signs. When we replace a variable by a number, we say that we are substituting for the variable. This process is called **evaluating the expression.**

Example 1 Evaluate $x + y$ for $x = 37$ and $y = 29$.

$x + y$

$37 + 29$ We substitute 37 for x and 29 for y

66 We carry out the addition

The number 66 is the **value** of the expression when $x = 37$ and $y = 29$.

3. Evaluate $4t$ for $t = 15$

Algebraic expressions involving multiplication can be written in several ways. For example, "8 times a" can be written as $8 \times a$, $8 \cdot a$, $8(a)$, or simply $8a$. Two letters written together without a symbol, such as ab, also, indicates a multiplication.

Example 2 Evaluate $3y$ for $y = 14$.

$3y$

$3(14)$ We substitute 14 for y

42 We carry out the multiplication.

The number 42 is the value of the expression when $y = 14$.

Do Margin Exercises 1-3.

Algebraic expressions involving division can also be written in several ways. For example, "8 divided by t" can be written as $8 \div t$, or $8/t$, or $\frac{8}{t}$ where the fraction bar is a division symbol.

Example 3 Evaluate $2x + 3x$ for $x = 7$.

$2x + 3x$

$2(7) + 3(7)$ Substituting 7 for x

$14 + 21$ Multiplying

35 Adding

The number 35 is the value of the expression when $x = 7$.

Do Margin Exercise 4.

Example 4 Evaluate $\dfrac{9C}{5} + 32$ for $C = 20$.

   This expression can be used to find the Fahrenheit temperature that corresponds to 20 degrees Celsius:

$\dfrac{9C}{5} + 32$

$\dfrac{9(20)}{5} + 32$ Substituting 20 for C

$\dfrac{180}{5} + 32$ Multiplying

$36 + 32$ Dividing

68 Adding

Do Margin Exercise 5.

Example 5 Evaluate $5x^2$ for $x = 3$.

   The rules for order of operations specify that the replacement for x be squared first. That result is then multiplied by 5:

$5x^2$

$5(3)^2$ Substituting 3 for x.

$5(9)$ Squaring 3

45 Multiplying

Do Margin Exercises 6 and 7.

b Terms and Factors

As we learned in the previous section, within a given algebraic expression we may find a collection of variables, numbers, and operation signs. In the language of Math there are two other definitions which are important when considering algebraic espressions: *Terms* and *Factors*.

---

4. Evaluate $5x - 3x$ for $x = 4$.

5. Find the Fahrenheit temperature that corresponds to 10 degrees Celsius (see Example 4).

6. Evaluate $3x^2$ for $x = 4$.

7. Evaluate a^4 for $a = 3$.

Terms are those quantities that are separated by addition signs. For example, in the expression $x + 3$, x and 3 are terms. In the expression $7 + x$, 7 is a term and x is a term.

Factors are those quantities that are multiplied. In the expression, $3 \cdot x$, 3 is a factor and x is a factor. In the expression, $7 \cdot x$, 7 is a factor and x is a factor.

Here are some additional examples to illustrate the difference between terms and factors:

$y + 10$	y is a term and 10 is a term
$10 \cdot y$	10 is a factor and y is a factor
$10 \cdot y + 5$	5 is a term and $10y$ (taken as a whole) is a term. 10 and y are each factors of the term $10y$.
$5\,y + 10$	$5y$ is a term and 10 is a term. 5 and y are each factors of the term $5y$.

Example 6 Identify the terms and factors in the following algebraic expression.

$$7x + 5y + 6$$

First, let's look at what parts of the equation are separated by addition signs in each piece of the expression:

$$\underbrace{7 \cdot x}_{\text{Term}} \quad + \quad \underbrace{5 \cdot y}_{\text{Term}} \quad + \quad \underbrace{6}_{\text{Term}}$$

We see that there are three terms in this expression: $7x$, $5y$, and 6.

There are also four factors:

$7x = 7 \cdot x$, so 7 and x are factors of the term $7x$.

$5y = 5 \cdot y$, so 5 and y are factors of the term $5y$.

Example 7

$$4x + 32$$

To identify the terms, we need to look at the parts of the expression separated by addition signs.

$$\underbrace{4x}_{\text{Term}} \quad + \quad \underbrace{32}_{\text{Term}}$$

To identify the factors, we have to look for the multiplication.

$4x = 4 \cdot x$, so 4 and x are factors of the term $4x$.

Exercise Set 2.2

a Evaluate.

1. $6x$, for $x = 7$

2. $7y$, for $y = 7$

3. $\dfrac{x}{y}$, for $x = 9$ and $y = 3$

4. $\dfrac{m}{n}$, for $m = 14$ and $n = 2$

5. $\dfrac{3p}{q}$, for $p = 2$ and $q = 6$

6. $\dfrac{5y}{z}$, for $y = 15$ and $z = 25$

7. $\dfrac{x + y}{5}$, for $x = 10$ and $y = 20$

8. $\dfrac{p - q}{2}$, for $p = 16$ and $q = 2$

9. $3 + 5x$, for $x = 2$

10. $9 - 2x$, for $x = 3$

11. *For perimeter of a rectangle* $2l + 2w$, for $l = 3$ and $w = 4$

12. $3(a + b)$, for $a = 2$ and $b = 4$

13. *For perimeter of a rectangle* $2(l + w)$, for $l = 3$ and $w = 4$

14. $3a + 3b$, for $a = 2$ and $b = 4$

15. $7a - 7b$, for $a = 5$ and $b = 2$

16. $4x - 4y$, for $x = 6$ and $y = 1$

17. $7(a - b)$, for $a = 5$ and $b = 2$

18. $4(x - y)$, for $x = 6$ and $y = 1$

19. *For distance of a timed fall* $16t^2$, for $t = 3$

20. $7n - n^2$, for $n = 5$

21. $9m - m^2$, for $m = 4$

22. $7n - n^2$, for $n = 3$

23. $a + (a - b)^2$, for $a = 6$ and $b = 4$

24. $(x + y)^2 - y$, for $x = 2$ and $y = 3$

25. *For converting Fahrenheit to Celsius* $\dfrac{5(F - 32)}{9}$, for $F = 68$

26. $a \div b - 2$, for $a = 15$ and $b = 5$

Identify the terms in each of the following expressions.

27. $x + 20$

28. $10 + B$

29. $5 + x$

30. $2x + 5$

31. $a + b$

32. $10a + 5b$

33. $2 + 5$

34. $20 + x$

35. $15 + 15$

36. $5x + 9x + y$

37. $a + b + c$

38. $2a + 3b + 5$

Identify the factors in each of the following expressions.

39. $7x$

40. $8 \cdot y \cdot x$

41. $3x + 4y$

42. $9a + 9b$

43. $5 \cdot x \cdot 7$

44. $x + 2y$

45. $y + 4a$

46. $(4 \cdot 14) + 3x$

47. $9xy$

48. $6a + 5 + 3b$

49. $abcd$

50. $2a + 3b + 5$

Skill Maintenance

51. Write a word name for 23,043,921.

52. Multiply: $17 \cdot 53$.

53. Estimate by rounding to the nearest ten. Show your work.
$$5\ 2\ 8\ 3$$
$$-2\ 4\ 7\ 5$$

54. Divide: $2982 \div 3$.

55. On January 6, it snowed 5 in., and on January 7, it snowed 8 in. How much did it snow altogether?

56. On March 9, it snowed 15 in., but on March 10, the sun melted 7 in. How much snow remained?

Synthesis

57. ❖ A student evaluates $a + a^2$ for $a = 5$ and gets 100 as the result. What mistake did the student probably make?

58. Evaluate $a^{1996} - a^{1997}$, for $a = 1$

59. Evaluate $5a^{3a-4}$, for $a = 2$

60. Using the number 13 and the variable x, write an expression using them as terms and write a second expression using them as factors.

2.3 Solving Equations

a Solving by Trial

Let's find a number that we can put in the blank to make this sentence true:

$9 = 3 + \square$

We are asking "9 is 3 plus what number?" The answer is 6.

$9 = 3 + \boxed{6}$

Do Margin Exercises 1 and 2.

A sentence with = is called an **equation**. A **solution** of an equation is a number that makes the sentence true. Thus, 6 is a solution of

$9 = 3 + \square$ because $9 = 3 + \boxed{6}$ is true.

However, 7 is not a solution of

$9 = 3 + \square$ because $9 = 3 + \boxed{7}$ is false.

Do Margin Exercises 3 and 4.

We can use a *variable* instead of a blank. For example,

$9 = 3 + x.$

We call x a **variable** because it can represent any number.

A **solution** is a replacement for the variable that makes the equation true. When we find all the solutions, we say that we have solved the equation.

> ▶ A number sentence with an equal sign (=) is called an **equation**.
>
> ▶ A **solution** is a number that when substituted for the variable makes the equation true. When we find all the solutions, we say that we have **solved** the equation.
>
> ▶ When we have an unknown value that we represent with a letter, we call it a **variable**.

Examples Solve by guess and check.

1. $7 + n = 22$
   (7 plus what number is 22?)
   The solution is 15.

2. $x - 15 = 47$
   (What minus 15 will be 47?)
   The solution is 62.

3. $8 \cdot 23 = y$
   (8 times 23 is what?)
   The solution is 184.

4. $3 \cdot t = 150$
   (3 times what is 150?)
   The solution is 50.

Do Margin Exercises 5-8.

Find a number that makes the sentence true.

1. $8 = 1 + \square$

2. $\square + 2 = 7$

3. Determine whether 7 is a solution of $\square + 5 = 9$.

4. Determine whether 4 is a solution of $\square + 5 = 9$.

Solve by trial.

5. $n + 3 = 8$

6. $x - 2 = 8$

7. $45 \div 9 = y$

8. $10 \div t = 2$

Solve.

9. $346 \cdot 65 = y$

10. $x = 2347 + 6675$

11. $4560 \div 8 = t$

12. $x = 6007 - 2346$

---

b | Solving Equations

We now begin to develop more precise ways to solve certain equations. When an equation has a variable alone on one side, it is easy to see the solution or to compute it. For example, the solution of

$$x = 12$$

is 12. When a calculation is on one side and the variable is alone on the other, we can find the solution by carrying out the calculation.

Example 5   Solve: $x = 245 \cdot 34$.

To solve the equation, we carry out the calculation.

$$
\begin{array}{r}
2\,4\,5 \\
\times \quad 3\,4 \\
\hline
9\,8\,0 \\
7\,3\,5\,0 \\
\hline
8\,3\,3\,0
\end{array}
$$

The solution is 8330.

Do Margin Exercises 9–12.

Look at the equation

$$x + 12 = 27.$$

The equal sign separates an equation into its left and right sides.

To solve the equation, we need to get x alone on one side of the equation. We want $x =$ to a number. To do this, we must first think about the fact that $=$ means both sides are the same. To make sure we keep this balance, whatever we take away from one side will have to be taken away from the other side, and whatever we add to one side will have to be added to the other side.

So, in this example to get x alone, we must remove or "zero out" the 12 on the left hand side. To do this, we have to subtract 12 from the left hand side which means we also have to subtract 12 from the right hand side. Thus,

$$x + 12 = 27$$
$$x + 12 - 12 = 27 - 12 \qquad \text{Subtracting 12 on both sides}$$
$$x + 0 = 15 \qquad \text{Carrying out the subtraction}$$
$$x = 15 \qquad \text{Additive identity}$$

To visualize the addition principle, think of a jeweler's balance. When both sides of the balance hold equal amounts of weight, the balance is level. If weight is added or removed, equally, on both sides, the balance remains level.

> ▶ To solve $x + a = b$, subtract a on both sides.

If we can get an equation in a form with the variable alone on one side, we can "see" the solution.

Example 6   Solve: $t + 28 = 54$.

We have

$$t + 28 = 54$$
$$t + 28 - 28 = 54 - 28 \qquad \text{Subtracting 28 on both sides}$$
$$t + 0 = 26 \qquad \text{Carrying out the subtraction}$$
$$t = 26. \qquad \text{Additive identity}$$

The solution is 26.

Do Margin Exercises 13 and 14.

Example 7   Solve: $182 = 65 + n$.

We have

$$182 = 65 + n$$
$$182 - 65 = 65 + n - 65 \qquad \text{Subtracting 65 on both sides}$$
$$117 = 0 + n \qquad \text{Carrying out the subtraction}$$
$$117 = n. \qquad \text{Additive identity}$$

The solution is 117.

Do Margin Exercise 15.

Example 8   Solve: $7381 + x = 8067$.

We have

$$7381 + x = 8067$$
$$7381 + x - 7381 = 8067 - 7381 \qquad \text{Subtracting 7381 on both sides}$$
$$x = 686.$$

The solution is 686.

Do Margin Exercises 16 and 17.

We now learn to solve equations like $8 \cdot n = 96$. Look at

$$8 \cdot n = 96.$$

We can get n alone by dividing the left hand side by 8. As before, if we do something to one side of the equation, we must do it to the other side, so we must also divide the right hand side by 8

$$\frac{8 \cdot n}{8} = \frac{96}{8} \qquad \text{Dividing by 8 on both sides}$$
$$n = 12. \qquad \text{8 times } n \text{ divided by 8 is } n.$$

Solve.

13. $x + 9 = 17$

14. $77 = m + 32$

15. Solve: $155 = t + 78$

Solve.

16. $4566 + x = 7877$

17. $8172 = h + 2058$

18. Solve: $8 \cdot x = 64$

> To solve $a \cdot x = b$, divide by a on both sides.

Example 9 Solve: $10 \cdot x = 240$.

We have

$$10 \cdot x = 240$$
$$\frac{10 \cdot x}{10} = \frac{240}{10} \qquad \text{Dividing by 10 on both sides}$$
$$x = 24.$$

The solution is 24.

Do Margin Exercises 18 and 19.

19. $144 = 9 \cdot n$

Example 10 Solve: $5202 = 9 \cdot t$.

We have

$$5202 = 9 \cdot t$$
$$\frac{5202}{9} = \frac{9 \cdot t}{9} \qquad \text{Dividing by 9 on both sides}$$
$$578 = t.$$

The solution is 578.

Do Margin Exercise 20.

20. Solve: $5152 = 8 \cdot t$

Example 11 Solve: $14 \cdot y = 1092$.

We have

$$14\,y = 1092$$
$$\frac{14\,y}{14} = \frac{1092}{14} \qquad \text{Dividing by 14 on both sides}$$
$$y = 78.$$

The solution is 78.

Do Margin Exercise 21.

21. Solve: $18y = 1728$

Example 12 Solve: $n \cdot 56 = 4648$.

We have

$$n \cdot 56 = 4648$$
$$\frac{n \cdot 56}{56} = \frac{4648}{56} \qquad \text{Dividing by 56 on both sides}$$
$$n = 83.$$

The solution is 83.

Do Margin Exercise 22.

22. Solve: $n \cdot 48 = 4512$

Exercise Set 2.3

a Solve by guess and check.

1. $x + 0 = 14$

2. $x - 7 = 18$

3. $y \cdot 17 = 0$

4. $56 \div m = 7$

b Solve.

5. $13 + x = 42$

6. $15 + t = 22$

7. $12 = 12 + m$

8. $16 = t + 16$

9. $3 \cdot x = 24$

10. $6 \cdot x = 42$

11. $112 = n \cdot 8$

12. $162 = 9 \cdot m$

13. $4 \cdot 23 = x$

14. $23 \cdot 78 = y$

15. $t = 125 \div 5$

16. $w = 256 \div 16$

17. $p = 908 - 458$

18. $9007 - 5667 = m$

19. $x = 12{,}345 + 78{,}555$

20. $5678 + 9034 = t$

21. $3 \cdot m = 96$

22. $4 \cdot y = 96$

23. $715 = 5 \cdot z$

24. $741 = 3 \cdot t$

25. $10 + x = 89$

26. $20 + x = 57$

27. $61 = 16 + y$

28. $53 = 17 + w$

29. $6 \cdot p = 1944$

30. $4 \cdot w = 3404$

31. $5 \cdot x = 3715$

32. $9 \cdot x = 1269$

33. $47 + n = 84$

34. $56 + p = 92$

35. $x + 78 = 144$

36. $z + 67 = 133$

37. $165 = 11 \cdot n$

38. $660 = 12 \cdot n$

39. $624 = t \cdot 13$

40. $784 = y \cdot 16$

41. $x + 214 = 389$

42. $x + 221 = 333$

43. $567 + x = 902$

44. $438 + x = 807$

45. $18 \cdot x = 1872$

46. $19 \cdot x = 6080$

47. $40 \cdot x = 1800$

48. $20 \cdot x = 1500$

49. $2344 + y = 6400$ **50.** $9281 = 8322 + t$ **51.** $8322 + 9281 = x$ **52.** $9281 - 8322 = y$

53. $234 \cdot 78 = y$ **54.** $10{,}534 \div 458 = q$ **55.** $58 \cdot m = 11{,}890$ **56.** $233 \cdot x = 22{,}135$

Skill Maintenance

Use or $>$ or $<$ to write a true sentence.

57. $123 \;\square\; 789$ **58.** $342 \;\square\; 339$

Divide.

59. $1283 \div 9$ **60.** $17\overline{)5689}$

Synthesis

63. ❖ Describe a procedure that can be used to convert any equation of the form $a + b = c$ to a subtraction equation.

64. ❖ Describe a procedure that can be used to convert any equation of the form $a \cdot b = c$ to a division equation.

Solve.

65. $42x = 556$ **66.** $63x = 3276$

2.4 Perimeter and Area

a | Finding Perimeter

> A **polygon** is a closed geometric figure with three or more sides. The **perimeter of a polygon** is the distance around it, or the sum of the lengths of its sides.

Example 1 Find the perimeter of this polygon.

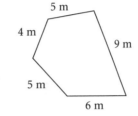

We add the lengths of the sides. Since all the units are the same, we add the numbers, keeping meters (m) as the unit.

Perimeter = 6 m + 5 m + 4 m + 5 m + 9 m
Perimeter = (6 + 5 + 4 + 5 + 9) m
Perimeter = 29 m

Do Margin Exercises 1 and 2.

A **rectangle** is a polygon with four sides and four 90°-angles, like the one shown in Example 2.

> The **perimeter of a rectangle** is 2 times the length plus two times the width, or twice the sum of the length and the width:
>
> $$P = 2 \cdot l + 2 \cdot w$$
>
> **OR**
>
> $$P = 2 \cdot (l + w).$$

Example 2 Using the formula $P = 2 \cdot l + 2 \cdot w$, find the perimeter of a rectangle that is 3 cm by 4 cm.

$$P = 2 \cdot l + 2 \cdot w$$
$$P = 2(3 \text{ cm}) + 2(4 \text{ cm})$$
$$P = 6 \text{ cm} + 8 \text{ cm}$$
$$P = 14 \text{ cm}$$

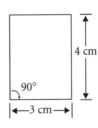

Do Margin Exercises 3–5.

---

1. Find the perimeter of the polygon.

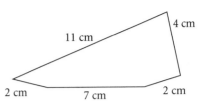

2. Find the perimeter of the polygon.

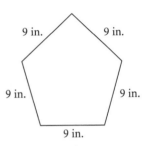

3. Find the perimeter of the rectangle.

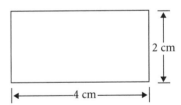

4. Find the perimeter of a rectangle that is 5 yd by 3 yd.

5. Find the perimeter of a rectangle that is 8 km by 8 km.

6. Find the perimeter of a square with sides of length 10 km.

7. Find the perimeter of a square with sides of length 5 yd.

8. Find the perimeter of a square with sides of length 4 km.

9. What is the area of this region? Count the number of square centimeters.

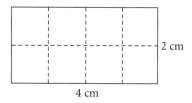

A **square** is a rectangle with all sides the same length.

▶ The **perimeter of a square** is four times the length of a side.

$$P = 4 \cdot s$$

Example 3 Find the perimeter of a square whose sides are 9 mm long

$$P = 4s$$

$$P = 4(9 \text{ mm})$$

$$P = 36 \text{ mm}$$

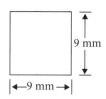

Do Margin Exercises 6–8.

b | Finding Area

We can find the area of a *rectangular region* by filling it with square units. Two such units, a *square inch* and a *square centimeter*, are shown below.

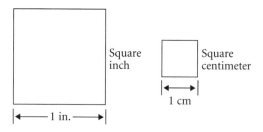

Example 4 What is the area of this region?

We have a rectangular array. Since the region is filled with 12 square centimeters, its area is 12 square centimeters (sq cm), or 12 cm². The number of units is 3 × 4, or 12.

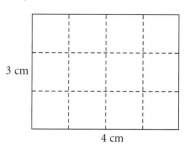

Do Margin Exercise 9.

▶ The **area of a rectangular region** is the product of the length *l* and the width *w*:

$$A = l \cdot w.$$

Example 5   Find the area of a rectangle that is 7 yd by 4 yd.

$$A = l \cdot w$$

$$A = 7 \text{ yd} \cdot 4 \text{ yd}$$

$$A = 7 \cdot 4 \cdot \text{yd} \cdot \text{yd}$$

$$A = 28 \text{ yd}^2$$

We think of yd · yd as (yd)^2 and denote it yd^2. Thus we read "28 yd^2" as "28 square yards."

Do Margin Exercises 10 and 11.

▶ The **area of a square region** is the square of the length of a side:

$A = s \cdot s$ or $A = s^2$.

Example 6   Find the area of a square with sides of length 9 mm.

$$A = s^2$$

$$A = (9 \text{ mm}) \cdot (9 \text{ mm})$$

$$A = 9 \cdot 9 \cdot \text{mm} \cdot \text{mm}$$

$$A = 81 \text{ mm}^2$$

Do Margin Exercise 12–14.

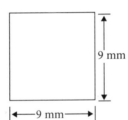

10. Find the area of a rectangle that is 7 km by 8 km.

11. Find the area of a rectangle that is 5 yd by 3 yd.

12. Find the area of a square with sides of length 12 km.

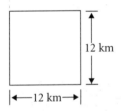

13. Find the area of a square with sides of length 11 m.

14. Find the area of a square with sides of length 14 yd.

Exercise Set 2.4

a Find the perimeter of the polygon.

1.
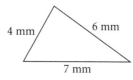
4 mm, 6 mm, 7 mm

2.
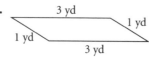
3 yd, 1 yd, 1 yd, 3 yd

3.
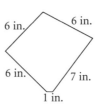
6 in., 6 in., 6 in., 7 in., 1 in.

4.
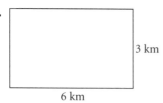
3 km, 6 km

5.
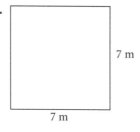
7 m, 7 m

6.
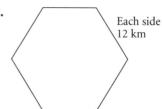
Each side 12 km

Find the perimeter of the rectangle.

7. 5 ft by 10 ft

8. 5 m by 100 m

9. 35 cm by 5 cm

10. 17 yd by 13 yd

Find the perimeter of the square.

11. 22 ft on a side

12. 57 km on a side

13. 46 mm on a side

14. 18 yd on a side

b Find the area.

15.
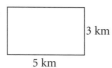
3 km, 5 km

16.
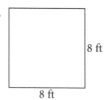
8 ft, 8 ft

17.

4 in., 1 in.

18.
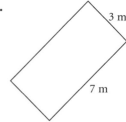
3 m, 7 m

19.

2 yd, 2 yd

20.

3 mi, 3 mi

21.
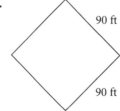
90 ft, 90 ft

22.
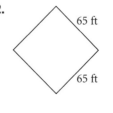
65 ft, 65 ft

Find the area of the rectangle.

23. 5 ft by 10 ft

24. 14 yd by 8 yd

25. 35 cm by 5 cm

26. 3 km by 100 km

27. 4 in. by 8 in.

28. 30 mi by 20 mi

Find the area of the square.

29. 22 ft on a side

30. 18 yd on a side

31. 57 km on a side

32. 46 m on a side

33. 5 yd on a side

34. 7 ft on a side

Skill Maintenance

Evaluate.

35. 5^2

36. 10^2

37. 31^2

Synthesis

38. ❖ Create for a fellow student a development of the formula
$P = 2 \cdot (l + w) = 2 \cdot l + 2 \cdot w$
for the perimeter of a rectangle.

39. ❖ Create for a fellow student a development of the formula
$P = 4 \cdot s$
for the perimeter of a square.

Find the perimeter of the figure in feet.

40. 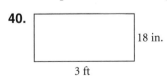 18 in.

3 ft

41. 78 in.

6 yd

42. ❖ The length and the width of one rectangle are each three times the length and the width of another rectangle. Is the area of the first rectangle three times the area of the other rectangle? Why or why not?

43. ❖ Create for a fellow student a development of the formula
$A = l \cdot w$
for the area of a rectangle.

1. Estimate the sum by first rounding to the nearest ten. Show your work.

$$
\begin{array}{r}
74 \\
23 \\
35 \\
+\ 66 \\
\end{array}
$$

2. Estimate the sum by first rounding to the nearest hundred. Show your work.

$$
\begin{array}{r}
650 \\
685 \\
238 \\
+\ 168 \\
\end{array}
$$

2.5 Estimating and Problem-Solving

a Estimating

Estimating is used to simplify a problem so that it can then be solved easily or mentally. Rounding is used when estimating. There are many ways to estimate.

Example 1 Michelle earned $21,791 as a consultant and $17,239 as an instructor in a recent year. Estimate Michelle's yearly earnings.

There are many ways to get an answer, but there is no one perfect answer based on how the problem is worded. Let's consider a couple of methods.

Method 1. Round each number to the nearest thousand and then add.

$$
\begin{array}{r}
21,791 \\
+\ 17,239 \\
\end{array}
\qquad
\begin{array}{r}
22,000 \\
+\ 17,000 \\
\hline
39,000 \\
\end{array}
$$
$\leftarrow$ Estimated answer

Method 2. We might use a less formal approach, depending on how specific we want the answer to be. We note that both numbers are close to 20,000, and so the total is close to **40,000**. In some contexts, such as retirement planning, this might be sufficient.

The point to be made is that estimating can be done in many ways and can have many answers, even though in the problems that follow we ask you to round in a specific way.

Example 2 Estimate this sum by first rounding to the nearest ten:

$$78 + 49 + 31 + 85.$$

We round each number to the nearest ten. Then we add.

$$
\begin{array}{r}
78 \\
49 \\
31 \\
+\ 85 \\
\end{array}
\qquad
\begin{array}{r}
80 \\
50 \\
30 \\
+\ 90 \\
\hline
250 \\
\end{array}
$$
$\leftarrow$ Estimated answer

Do Margin Exercise 1.

Example 3 Estimate this sum by first rounding to the nearest hundred:

$$850 + 674 + 986 + 839.$$

We have

$$
\begin{array}{r}
850 \\
674 \\
986 \\
+\ 839 \\
\end{array}
\qquad
\begin{array}{r}
900 \\
700 \\
1000 \\
+\ 800 \\
\hline
3400 \\
\end{array}
$$

Do Margin Exercise 2.

Example 4 Estimate the difference by first rounding to the nearest thousand: 9324 − 2849.

We have

```
  9 3 2 4      9 0 0 0
− 2 8 4 9    − 3 0 0 0
              6 0 0 0
```

Do Margin Exercises 3 and 4.

Example 5 Estimate the following product by first rounding to the nearest ten and to the nearest hundred: 683 × 457.

Nearest ten	Nearest hundred	Exact
6 8 0	7 0 0	6 8 3
× 4 6 0	× 5 0 0	× 4 5 7
4 0 8 0 0	3 5 0 0 0 0	4 7 8 1
2 7 2 0 0 0		3 4 1 5 0
3 1 2 8 0 0		2 7 3 2 0 0
		3 1 2 1 3 1

Note in Example 5 that the estimate, having been rounded to the nearest ten, is

312,800.

The estimate, having been rounded to the nearest hundred, is

350,000.

Note how the estimates compare to the exact answer,

312,131.

Why does rounding give a larger answer than the exact one?

Do Margin Exercise 5.

b Problem Solving

Estimating and problem solving are the main uses of mathematics. To solve a problem using the operations on the whole numbers, we first look at the situation and estimate a reasonable answer. We try to translate the problem to an equation. Then we solve the equation. We check to see if the solution of the equation is a solution of the original problem. Thus we are using the following five-step strategy.

---

3. Estimate the difference by first rounding to the nearest hundred. Show your work.

```
  9 2 8 5
− 6 7 3 9
```

4. Estimate the difference by first rounding to the nearest thousand. Show your work.

```
  2 3, 2 7 8
− 1 1, 6 9 8
```

5. Estimate the product by first rounding to the nearest ten and then the nearest hundred. Show your work.

```
    8 3 7
  × 2 4 5
```

1. *Familiarize* yourself with the situation.
   a. Read to visualize the situation.
   b. Draw a picture or chart to organize the ingformation.
   c. Identify the unknown and choose a variable to represent it.
   d. Estimate your answer when appropriate.

2. *Translate* the problem into an equation using key words.

3. *Solve* the equation.

4. *Check* the answer for reasonableness by comparing it to your estimate from step one. Then, check the answer in the original wording of the problem.

5. *State* the answer to the problem clearly with appropriate units.

Before looking at the examples and starting the exercises, here are some words and phrases that can help you with Step 2 when translating the problem into an equation

Addition: sum, total, plus, increased by, added to, more than

Subtraction: subtract, less than, difference, take away, decreased by, subtracted from, minus, less, how much more

Multiplication: times, the product of, twice, double, multiplied by, multiply

Division: divide, divided by, the quotient of, divided into

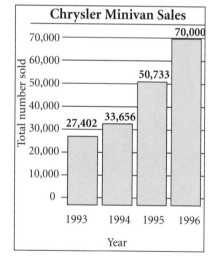

Chrysler Minivan Sales

Example 6 *Minivan Sales.* Recently, sales of minivans have soared. The bar graph at left shows the number of Chrysler Town & Country LXi minivans sold in recent years. Find the total number of minivans sold during those years.

1. **Familiarize.** We can make a drawing or at least visualize the situation.

$$\boxed{27,402} + \boxed{33,656} + \boxed{50,733} + \boxed{70,000} = n$$

| in 1993 | in 1994 | in 1995 | in 1996 | Total sold |

Since we are combining objects, addition can be used. First we define the unknown. We let n = the total number of minivans sold.

As an estimate, we would expect the answer to be larger than the sales in any of the individual years. We can also estimate our answer by rounding. Here, we round to the nearest thousand:

$$27,402 + 33,656 + 50,733 + 70,000$$
$$\approx 27,000 + 34,000 + 51,000 + 70,000$$
$$\approx 182,000.$$

2. **Translate.** We translate to an equation:

$$27,402 + 33,656 + 50,733 + 70,000 = n.$$

3. Solve. We solve the equation by carrying out the addition.

```
  1 1   1
  2 7,4 0 2
  3 3,6 5 6
  5 0,7 3 3
+ 7 0,0 0 0
──────────
1 8 1,7 9 1
```

Thus, $181,791 = n$, or $n = 181,791$.

4. Check. There are many ways in which this can be done. For example, we can repeat the calculation. (We leave this to the student.) Another way is to check the reasonableness of the answer. Since $181,791 \approx 182,000$, our estimate, we have a partial check. If we had an estimate like 236,000 or 580,000, we might be suspicious that our calculated answer is incorrect. Since our estimated answer is close to our calculation, we know that our answer is reasonable.

5. State. The total number of minivans sold during these years is 181,791.

Do Margin Exercise 6.

Example 7 *Hard-Drive Space.* The hard drive on your computer has 572 megabytes (MB) of storage space available. You install a software package called Microsoft® Office, which uses 84 MB of space. How much storage space do you have left after the installation?

1. Familiarize. We first make a drawing or at least visualize the situation. We let M = the amount of space left.

572 MB   84 MB

We note that our answer should be less than the original memory 572 MB. We can also estimate our answer:

$$572 - 84 \approx 600 - 100$$
$$\approx 500.$$

We can expect our answer to be close to 500.

2. Translate. We see that this is a "take-away" situation. We translate to an equation.

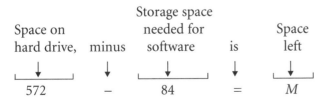

Space on hard drive,	minus	Storage space needed for software	is	Space left
↓	↓	↓	↓	↓
572	−	84	=	M

---

6. *Teacher needs in 2005.* The data in the table show the estimated number of new jobs for teachers in the year 2005. The reason is an expected boom in the number of youngsters under the age of 18. Find the total number of jobs available for teachers in 2005.

Type of Teacher	Number of New Jobs
Secondary	386,000
Aides	364,000
Childcare workers	248,000
Elementary	220,000
Special education	206,000

Source: Bureau of Labor Statistics

7. *Checking Account.* You have $756 in your checking account. You write a check for $387 to pay for a VCR for your campus apartment. How much is left for your checking account?

8. Find the perimeter of (distance around) the figure.

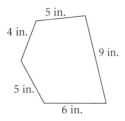

9. A play area is 25 ft by 10 ft. A fence is to be built around the play area. How many feet of fencing will be needed? If fencing costs $5.00 per foot, what will the fencing cost?

3. Solve. This sentence tells us what to do. We subtract.

$$\begin{array}{r} \overset{16}{\underset{4\ \ 6\ 12}{5\ 7\ 2}} \\ -\ 8\ 4 \\ \hline 4\ 8\ 8 \end{array}$$

Thus, $488 = M$, or $M = 488$.

4. Check. Our answer, 488, is reasonable since it is close to our estimate of 500. We can also add the difference, 488, to the subtrahend, 84: $84 + 488 = 572$.

5. State. There are 488 MB of memory left.

Example 8 A computer sales rep travels the following route to visit various electronics stores. How long is the route?

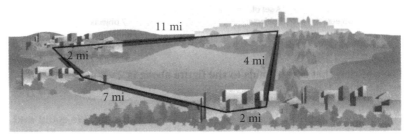

$$P = 2\text{mi} + 7\text{mi} + 2\text{mi} + 4\text{mi} + 11\text{ mi} = 26\text{mi}$$

Do Margin Exercise 7 and 8.

Example 9 A vegetable garden is 20 ft by 15 ft. a fence is to be built around the garden. How many feet of fence will be needed? If fencing sells for $3.00 per foot, what will the fencing cost?

1. Familiarize. We make a drawing and let P = the perimeter.

Since $15 \approx 20$, we can estimate the perimeter as $4(20) = 80$. Then our estimate of the cost would be $80(\$3) = \$240$. Since 15 ft is less than 20 ft, we would expect our answer to be less than $240.

2. Translate. The perimeter of the garden is given by

$$P = 2l + 2w$$
$$P = 2(20 \text{ ft}) + 2(15 \text{ ft})$$

3. Solve. We calculate the perimeter as follows:

$$P = 40 \text{ ft} + 30 \text{ ft}$$
$$P = 70 \text{ ft}$$

Then we multiply by $3.00 to find the cost of the fencing:

$$\text{Cost} = \$3.00 \cdot \text{Perimeter}$$
$$\text{Cost} = \$3.00(70 \text{ ft})$$
$$\text{Cost} = \$210.$$

4. Check. Our answers match our figures from Step One.

5. State. The fencing will cost $210.

Do Margin Exercise 9.

Example 10 *Bed Sheets.* The dimensions of a sheet for a king-size bed are 108 in. by 102 in. What is the area of the sheet? (The dimension labels on sheets list width × length.)

1. Familiarize. We first make a drawing. We let A the area.

Since both sides are about 100 in. we can estimate the area $(l \cdot w)$ by calculating 100 in. $\cdot$ 100 in. = 10,000 in^2.

2. Translate. Using a formula for area, we have

$$A = \text{length} \cdot \text{width} = l \cdot w = 102 \text{ in.} \cdot 108 \text{ in.}$$

3. Solve. We carry out the multiplication.

$$\begin{array}{r} 108 \\ \times 102 \\ \hline 216 \\ 10800 \\ \hline 11016 \end{array}$$

Thus, $A = 11,016$ in^2.

4. Check. 11,016 is close to our estimate of 10,000 so our answer is reasonable.

5. State. The area of a king-size bed sheet is 11,016 in.^{2}

Do Margin Exercise 10.

10. *Bed Sheets.* The dimensions of a sheet for a queen-size bed are 90 in. by 102 in. What is the area of the sheet?

11. *Diet Cola Packaging.* The bootling company also uses 6-can packages. How many 6-can packages can be filled with 2269 cans of cola? How many cans will be left over?

Example 11 *Diet Cola Packaging.* Diet Cola has become very popular in the quest to control our weight. A bottling company produces 2203 cans of cola. How many 8-can packages can be filled? How many cans will be left over?

1. Familiarize. We first draw a picture. We let n the number of 8-can packages to be filled.

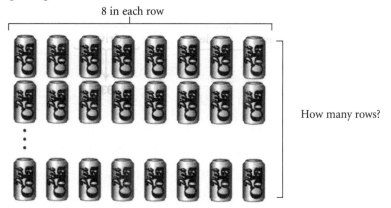

8 in each row

How many rows?

For our estimate, we know that $2400 \div 8 = 300$. Since we have 2203 cans which is less than 2400 cans, we would expect our answer to be less than 300 packages.

2. Translate. We can translate to an equation as follows.

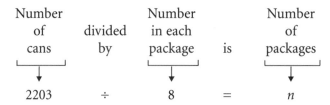

Number of cans	divided by	Number in each package	is	Number of packages
2203	÷	8	=	n

3. Solve. We solve the equation by carrying out the division.

$$
\begin{array}{r}
2\,7\,5 \\
8\overline{)2\,2\,0\,3} \\
-1\,6 \\
\hline
6\,0 \\
-5\,6 \\
\hline
4\,3 \\
4\,0 \\
\hline
3
\end{array}
$$

4. Check. We can check by multiplying the number of packages by 8 and adding the remainder, 3:

$$8 \cdot 275 = 2200 \qquad 2200 + 3 = 2203.$$

5. State. Thus, 275 8-can packages can be filled. There will be 3 cans left over.

Do Margin Exercise 11.

Example 12 *Automobile Mileage.* The Chrysler Town & Country LXi minivan featured in Example 6 gets 18 miles to the gallon (mpg) in city driving. How many gallons will it use in 4932 mi of city driving?

1. **Familiarize.** We first make a drawing. It is often helpful to be descriptive about how you define a variable. In this example, we let g = the number of gallons (g comes from "gallons").

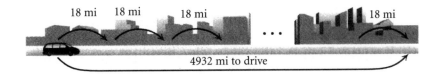

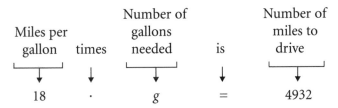

As an estimate, we can see that if 5000 miles were driven and the van average 20 mpg, then the van would use $5000 \div 20 = 250$ gal of gas.

2. **Translate.** Repeated addition applies here. Thus the following multiplication corresponds to the situation.

Miles per gallon	times	Number of gallons needed	is	Number of miles to drive
18	·	g	=	4932

3. **Solve.** To solve the equation, we divide by 18 on both sides.

$$18g = 4932$$
$$\frac{18g}{18} = \frac{4932}{18}$$
$$g = 274$$

$$\begin{array}{r} 274 \\ 18{\overline{\smash{\big)}\,4932}} \\ \underline{3\,6} \\ 1\,3\,3 \\ \underline{-1\,2\,6} \\ 7\,2 \\ \underline{7\,2} \\ 0 \end{array}$$

4. **Check.** To check, we see that 274 is close to our estimate of 250. We could also multiply 274 by 18 ($18 \cdot 274 = 4932$) to check our answer.

5. **State.** The minivan will use 274 gal.

Do Margin Exercise 12.

In the real world, problems may not be stated in written words. You must still become familiar with the situation before you can solve the problem.

12. *Automobile Mileage.* The Chrysler Town & Country LXi minivan gets 24 miles to the gallon (mpg) in country driving. How many gallons will it use in 888 mi of country driving?

13. *Calculator Purchase.*
Bernardo has $76. He wants to purchase a graphing calculator for $94. How much more does he need?

Example 13 *Travel Distance.* Vicki is driving from Indianapolis to Salt Lake City to work during summer vacation. The distance from Indianapolis to Salt Lake City is 1634 mi. She travels 1154 mi to Denver. How much farther must she travel?

1. Familiarize. We first make a drawing or at least visualize the situation. We let x = the remaining distance to Salt Lake City.

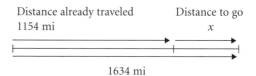

We see that this is a "how-much-more" situation.

If Vicki was going a total of 1600 miles and had already traveled 1100 miles, we see that she would need to travel 500 more miles. If she had already traveled 1200 miles, then she would need to travel 400 more miles. Therefore, we will estimate our answer to be between 400 and 500 miles.

2. Translate. We translate to an equation.

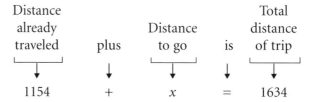

$$1154 + x = 1634$$

3. Solve. We solve the equation.

$$1154 + x = 1634$$

$$1154 + x - 1154 = 1634 - 1154 \qquad \text{Subtracting 1154 on both sides}$$

$$x = 480$$

$$\begin{array}{r} \overset{5\ 13}{1\,\overset{}{6}\,\overset{}{3}\,4} \\ -\ 1\ 1\ 5\ 4 \\ \hline 4\ 8\ 0 \end{array}$$

4. Check. We compare our answer of 480 mi to our estimate and see that it is reasonable. We can also add the difference, 480, to the subtrahend, 1154: 1154 + 480 = 1634.

The answer, 480 mi, checks.

5. State. Vicki must travel 480 mi farther to Salt Lake City.

Do Margin Exercise 13.

Example 14 *Total Cost of VCRs.* What is the total cost of 5 four-head VCRs if each one costs $289?

1. Familiarize. We let $n =$ the cost of 5 VCRs. Repeated addition works well here.

We can also estimate our answer as follows:

$$5 \times 289 \approx 5 \times 300 = 1500.$$

Our estimate is $15,000.

2. Translate. We translate to an equation.

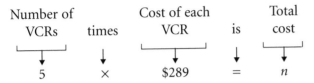

Number of VCRs	times	Cost of each VCR	is	Total cost
5	×	$289	=	n

3. Solve. This sentence tells us what to do. We multiply.

$$\begin{array}{r} {\scriptstyle 4\ 4} \\ 2\ 8\ 9 \\ \times\quad 5 \\ \hline 1\ 4\ 4\ 5 \end{array}$$

Thus, $n = 1445$.

4. Check. We have an answer that is much larger than the cost of any individual VCR, which is reasonable, and we can compare the answer to our estimate from step 1 and see that it is reasonable.

5. State. The total cost of 5 VCRs is $1445.

Do Margin Exercise 14.

14. *Total Cost of Laptop Computers.* What is the total cost of 12 laptop computers with CD-ROM drives and matrix color if each one costs $3249?

Exercise Set 2.5

a Estimate the sum or difference by first rounding to the nearest ten. Show your work.

1.	78 + 97	2.	62 97 46 + 88	3.	8074 − 2347	4.	673 − 28

Estimate the sum by first rounding to the nearest ten. Do any of the given sums seem to be incorrect when compared to the estimate? Which ones?

5.	45 77 25 + 56 343	6.	41 21 55 + 60 177	7.	622 78 81 + 111 932	8.	836 374 794 + 938 3947

Estimate the sum or difference by first rounding to the nearest hundred. Show your work.

9.	7348 + 9247	10.	568 472 938 + 402	11.	6852 − 1748	12.	9438 − 2787

Estimate the sum by first rounding to the nearest hundred. Do any of the given sums seem to be incorrect when compared to the estimate? Which ones?

13.	216 84 745 + 595 1640	14.	481 702 623 + 1043 1849	15.	750 428 63 + 205 1446	16.	326 275 758 + 943 2302

Estimate the sum or difference by first rounding to the nearest thousand. Show your work.

17.	9643 4821 8943 + 7004	18.	7648 9348 7842 + 2222	19.	92,149 − 22,555	20.	84,890 − 11,110

Estimate the product by first rounding to the nearest ten. Show your work.

21.	45 × 67	22.	51 × 78	23.	34 × 29	24.	63 × 54

Estimate the product by first rounding to the nearest hundred. Show your work.

25.	876 × 345	26.	355 × 299	27.	432 × 199	28.	789 × 434

Estimate the product by first rounding to the nearest thousand. Show your work.

29.	5608 × 4576	30.	2344 × 6123	31.	7888 × 6224	32.	6501 × 3449

b Solve.

33. During the first four months of a recent year, Campus Depot Business Machine Company reported the following sales:

January $3572
February 2718
March 2809
April 3177

What were the total sales over this time period?

34. A family travels the following miles during a five-day trip:

Monday 568
Tuesday 376
Wednesday 424
Thursday 150
Friday 224

How many miles did they travel altogether?

Bicycle Sales. The bar graph below shows the total sales, in millions of dollars, for bicycles and related supplies in recent years. Use this graph for Exercises 35–38.

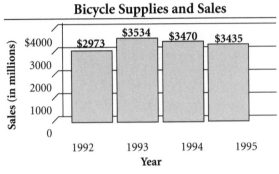

Bicycle Supplies and Sales

Source: National Sporting Goods Association

35. What were the total sales for 1993 and 1994?

36. What were the total sales for 1992 through 1995?

37. How much more were the sales in 1993 than in 1994?

38. How much more were the sales in 1994 than in 1992?

39. *Longest Rivers.* The longest river in the world is the Nile, which has a length of 4145 mi. It is 138 mi longer than the next longest river, which is the Amazon in South America. How long is the Amazon?

40. *Largest Lakes.* The largest lake in the world is the Caspian Sea, which has an area of 317,000 square kilometers (sq km). The Caspian is 288,900 sq km larger than the second largest lake, which is Lake Superior. What is the area of Lake Superior?

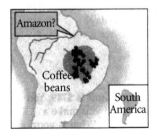

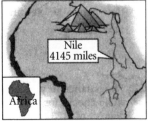

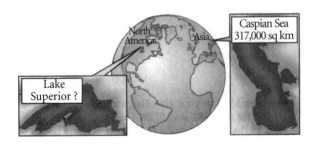

41. *Sheet Perimeter.* The dimensions of a sheet for a queen-size bed are 90 in. by 102 in. What is the perimeter of the sheet?

42. *Sheet Perimeter.* The dimensions of a sheet for a king-size bed are 108 in. by 102 in. What is the perimeter of the sheet?

43. *Paper Quantity.* A ream of paper contains 500 sheets. How many sheets are in 9 reams?

44. *Reading Rate.* Cindy's reading rate is 205 words per minute. How many words can she read in 30 min?

45. *Elvis Impersonators.* When Elvis Presley died in 1977, there were already 48 professional Elvis impersonators (**Source:** *Chance Magazine* 9, no. 1, Winter 1996). In 1995, there were 7328. How many more were there in 1995?

46. *LAV Vehicle.* A combat-loaded U.S. Light Armed Vehicle 25 (LAV-25) weighs 3930 lb more than its empty curb weight. The loaded LAV-25 weighs 28,400 lb. (**Source:** *Car & Driver* 42, no. 1, July 1996: 153-155) What is its curb weight?

47. Dana borrows $5928 for a used car. The loan is to be paid off in 24 equal monthly payments. How much is each payment (excluding interest)?

48. A family borrows $4824 to build a sunroom on the back of their house. The loan is to be paid off in equal monthly payments of $134 (excluding interest). How many months will it take to pay off the loan?

49. *Cheers Episodes.* Cheers is the longest-running comedy in the history of television, with 271 episodes created. A local station picks up the syndicated reruns. If the station runs 5 episodes per week, how many full weeks will pass before it must start over with past episodes? How many episodes will be left for the last week?

50. A lab technician separates a vial containing 70 cubic centimeters (cc) of blood into test tubes, each of which contain 3 cc of blood. How many test tubes can be filled? How much blood is left over?

51. There are 24 hours (hr) in a day and 7 days in a week. How many hours are there in a week?

52. There are 60 min in an hour and 24 hr in a day. How many minutes are there in a day?

53. You have $568 in your checking account. You write checks for $46, $87, and $129. Then you deposit $94 back in the account upon the return of some books. How much is left in your account?

54. The balance in your checking account is $749. You write checks for $34 and $65. Then you make a deposit of $123 from your paycheck. What is your new balance?

55. *NBA Court.* The standard basketball court used by college and NBA players has dimensions of 50 ft by 94 ft (**Source**: National Basketball Association).
   a. What is its area?
   b. What is its perimeter?

56. *High School Court.* The standard basketball court used by high school players has dimensions of 50 ft by 84 ft.
   a. What is its area? What is its perimeter?
   b. How much larger is the area of an NBA court than a high school court? (See Exercise 55)

57. Copies of this book are generally shipped from the warehouse in cartons containing 24 books each. How many cartons are needed to ship 840 books?

58. Sixteen-ounce bottles of catsup are generally shipped in cartons containing 12 bottles each. How many cartons are needed to ship 528 bottles of catsup?

59. Copies of this book are generally shipped from the warehouse in cartons containing 24 books each.How many cartons are needed to ship 1355 books? How many books are left over?

60. Sixteen-ounce bottles of catsup are generally shipped in cartons containing 12 bottles each. How many cartons are needed to ship 1033 bottles of catsup? How many bottles are left over?

61. *Map Drawing.* A map has a scale of 64 mi to the inch. How far apart *in reality* are two cities that are 25 in. apart on the map? How far apart *on the map* are two cities that, in reality, are 1728 mi apart?

62. *Map Drawing.* A map has a scale of 25 mi to the inch. How far apart *on the map* are two cities that, in reality, are 2200 mi apart? How far apart *in reality* are two cities that are 13 in. apart on the map?

63. A carpenter drills 216 holes in a rectangular array in a pegboard. There are 12 holes in each row. How many rows are there?

64. Lou works as a CPA. He arranges 504 entries on a spreadsheet in a rectangular array that has 36 rows. How many entries are in each row?

65. Elaine buys 5 video games at $44 each and pays for them with $10 bills. How many $10 bills did it take?

66. Lowell buys 5 video games at $44 each and pays for them with $20 bills. How many $20 bills did it take?

67. Before going back to college, David buys 4 shirts at $59 each and 6 pairs of pants at $78 each. What was the total cost of this clothing?

68. Ann buys office supplies at Office Depot. One day she buys 8 reams of paper at $24 each and 16 pens at $3 each. How much did she spend?

69. *Index Cards.* Index cards of dimension 3 in. by 5 in. are normally shipped in packages containing 100 cards each. How much writing area is available if one uses the front and back sides of a package of these cards?

70. An office for adjunct instructors at a community college has 6 bookshelves, each of which is 3 ft long. The office is moved to a new location that has dimensions of 16 ft by 21 ft. Is it possible for the bookshelves to be put side by side on the 16-ft wall?

Skill Maintenance

Round 234,562 to the nearest:

71. Hundred.

72. Thousand.

Perform the following operations

73. 2783 + 4602 + 5797 + 8111

74. 28,430 - 11,977

75. 787 · 363

76. 887 · 799

Synthesis

77. ❖ Of the five problem-solving steps listed at the beginning of this section, which is the most difficult for you? Why?

78. ❖ Write a problem for a classmate to solve. Design the problem so that the solution is "The driver still has 329 mi to travel."

79. *Speed of Light.* Light travels about 186,000 miles per second (mi/sec) in a vacuum as in outer space. In ice it travels about 142,000 mi/sec, and in glass it travels about 109,000 mi/sec. In 18 sec, how many more miles will light travel in a vacuum than in ice? in glass?

80. Carney Community College has 1200 students. Each professor teaches 4 classes and each student takes 5 classes. There are 30 students and 1 teacher in each classroom. How many professors are there at Carney Community College?

Review Exercises: Chapter 2

Simplify.

1. $8 \cdot 6 + 17$

2. $10 \cdot 24 - (18 + 2) \div 4 - (9 - 7)$

3. $7 + (4 + 3)^2$

4. $7 + 4^2 + 3^2$

5. $(80 \div 16) \times [(20 - 56 \div 8) + (8 \cdot 8 - 5 \cdot 5)]$

Evaluate.

6. $9x$, for $x = 11$

7. $3a + b$, for $a = 5$ and $b = 7$

8. $\dfrac{x}{y}$ for $x = 63$ and $y = 9$

9. $\dfrac{a - b}{5}$ for $a = 37$ and $b = 2$

10. $8x - 5y$ for $x = 4$ and $y = 6$

Solve.

11. $46 \cdot n = 368$

12. $47 + x = 92$

13. $x = 782 - 236$

14. $y = 247 \div 13$

15. $957 = 33x$

16. $y + 18 = 57$

17. Find the perimeter and area.

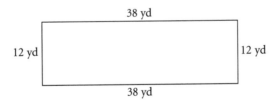

18. Find the perimeter and area.

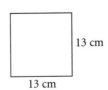

Estimate the sum or difference by rounding to the nearest hundred.

19. 724
     98
   1351
+ 883

20. 14,758
−   604

Estimate the product by rounding to the nearest ten.

21. $649 \cdot 32$

22. $43 \cdot 96$

Solve.

23. An apartment builder bought 3 electric ranges at $299 each and 4 dishwashers at $379 each. What was the total cost?

24. *Lincoln-Head Pennies.* In 1909, the first Lincoln-head pennies were minted. Seventy-three years later, these pennies were first minted with a decreased copper content. In what year was the copper content reduced?

25. A family budgets $4950 for food and clothing and $3585 for entertainment. The yearly income of the family was $28,283. How much of this income remained after these two allotments?

26. A chemist has 2753 mL of alcohol. How many 20-mL beakers can be filled? How much will be left over?

Practice Test: Chapter 2

Simplify.

1. $(10 - 2)^2$

2. $10^2 - 2^2$

3. $(25 - 15) \div 5$

4. $8 \times \{(20 - 11) \cdot [(12 + 48) \div 6 - (9 - 2)]\}$

5. $2^4 + 24 \div 12$

6. Find the average of 97, 98, 87, and 86.

Evaluate.

7. $\dfrac{a - b}{6}$ for $a = 27$ and $b = 3$

8. $8y^2$ for $y = 12$

9. $7x - 2y$ for $x = 5$ and $y = 4$

10. $\dfrac{x^3}{y}$ for $x = 2$ and $y = 8$

Solve.

11. $28 + x = 74$

12. $169 \div 13 = n$

13. $38 \cdot y = 532$

14. $x = 749 - 213$

15. Find the perimeter and area.

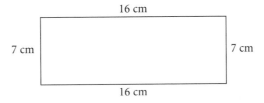

16 cm

7 cm   7 cm

16 cm

16. Find the perimeter and area.

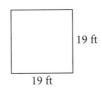

19 ft

19 ft

17. *James Dean.* James Dean was 24 yr old when he died. He was born in 1931. In what year did he die?

18. A beverage company produces 739 cans of soda. How many 8-can packages can be filled? How many cans will be left over?

19. *Area of New England.* Listed below are the areas, in square miles, of the New England states (*Source:* U.S. Bureau of the Census). What is the total area of New England?

Maine	30,865
Massachusetts	7,838
New Hampshire	8,969
Vermont	9,249
Connecticut	4,845
Rhode Island	1,045

20. A rectangular lot measures 200 m by 600 m. What is the area of the lot? What is the perimeter of the lot?

21. A sack of oranges weighs 27 lb. A sack of apples weighs 32 lb. Find the total weight of 16 bags of oranges and 43 bags of apples.

22. A box contains 5000 staples. How many staplers can be filled from the box if each stapler holds 250 staples?

Estimate the sum or difference by rounding to the nearest hundred.

23.
$$\begin{array}{r} 843 \\ 720 \\ 89 \\ + 1199 \\ \hline \end{array}$$

24.
$$\begin{array}{r} 29{,}805 \\ - \quad 3649 \\ \hline \end{array}$$

Estimate the product by rounding to the nearest ten.

25. $961 \cdot 42$ **26.** $87 \cdot 399$

27. Explain how estimating is helpful in solving applied problems.

28. Explain the difference between terms and factors. Give examples of each.

Cumulative Review: Chapters 1-2

1. Write exponential notation for: $14 \cdot 14 \cdot 14 \cdot 14 \cdot 14 \cdot 14 \cdot 14 \cdot 18$.

2. Evaluate 9^4.

Consider the following numbers. Use the tests for divisibility to answer the questions. Do not perform long division.

72,324	416,235
1200	9876
25,432	555

3. Which are divisible by 3?

4. Which are divisible by 4?

5. Which are divisible by 5?

6. Which are divisible by 6?

7. Which are divisible by 9?

Find the prime factorization. Write your answer with exponents.

8. 28

9. 198

10. 2450

11. Find the LCM of 18, 24 and 36.

Simplify.

12. $35 - 25 \div 5 + 2 \cdot 3$

13. $\{17 - [8 - (5 - 2 \cdot 2)]\} \div (3 + 12 \div 6)$

14. $6^2 + 40 \div (8 - 3)$

15. $18 \div 2 \cdot 3$

Evaluate.

16. $\dfrac{x + y}{2}$, for $x = 11$ and $y = 4$

17. $12x - x^2$, for $x = 3$

18. $3x - 4y + 16$, for $x = 8$ and $y = 6$

Solve.

19. $x + 13 = 50$ **20.** $y = 3927 \div 17$ **21.** $y = 99 \cdot 100$

22. $x + 123 = 576$ **23.** $19x = 2698$ **24.** $736 = 23y$

25. Find the perimeter.

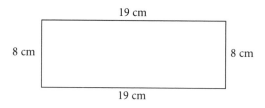

26. Find the area

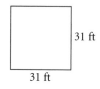

27. *Baseball Salaries.* The average salary of a major-league baseball player was $1,176,967 in 1996 and $512,804 in 1989 (*Source:* Major League Baseball). How much more was the average salary in 1996 than in 1989?

28. *Hotel Room in Las Vegas.* Four of the largest hotels in the United States are in Las Vegas. One has 3174 rooms, the second has 2920 rooms, the third 2832 rooms, and the fourth 2793 rooms. What is the total number of rooms in these four hotels?

29. A student is offered a part-time job paying $3900 a year. How much is each weekly paycheck?

30. Eastside Appliance sells a refrigerator for $600 and $30 tax with no delivery charge. Westside Appliance sells the same model for $560 and $28 tax plus a $25 delivery charge. Which is the better buy?

3

Introduction to Integers and Algebraic Expressions

An Application

The coldest temperature ever recorded in the state of Vermont is fifty degrees below zero Fahrenheit. What integer corresponds to this number?

The Mathematics

Fifty degrees below zero corresponds to

$$-50.$$

This is a negative number.

3.1   Integers and the Number Line

To answer questions such as "How many?", "How much?", and "How far?" we use whole numbers. The set, or collection, of **whole numbers** is 0, 1, 2, 3, 4, 5, 6, 7 ,8, 9, 10, 11, 12, ...

In this section, we extend the set of whole numbers to form the set of integers.

The Set of Integers

To create the set of integers, we begin with the set of whole numbers, 0, 1, 2, 3, and so on. For each natural number 1, 2, 3, and so on, we obtain a new number to the left of zero on the number line:

> For the number 1, there will be an *opposite* number –1 (negative 1).
> For the number 2, there will be an *opposite* number –2 (negative 2).
> For the number 3, there will be an *opposite* number –3 (negative 3), and so on.

The **integers** consist of the whole numbers and these new numbers. We picture them on a number line as follows.

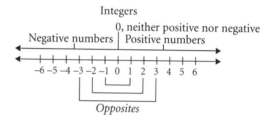

The integers to the left of zero are called **negative integers** and those to the right of zero are called **positive integers**. Zero is neither positive nor negative, but is still considered an integer.

> The integers: ...,–5, –4, –3, –2, –1, 0, 1, 2, 3, 4, 5....

a   Integers and the Real World

Integers are associated with many real-world problems and situations. The following examples will help you get ready to translate problems and situations to mathematical language with integers.

Example 1   Tell which integer corresponds to this situation: The coldest temperature ever recorded in Vermont is 50° below zero Fahrenheit.

50° below zero is –50°

▶ **Integers**

When looking at the number line, the integers consist of the whole numbers, which are 0, the numbers to the right of 0 (the positive numbers), and the numbers to the left of 0 (the negative numbers).

Example 2 Tell which integer corresponds to this situation: Death Valley is 280 feet below sea level.

The integer –280 corresponds to the situation. The elevation is –280 ft.

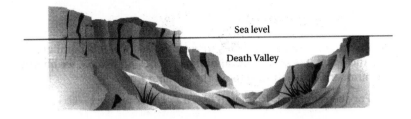

Example 3 Tell which integers correspond to this situation: A bank customer made a $234 deposit on Monday and a $350 withdrawal on Tuesday.

The integers 234 and –350 correspond to the situation. The integer 234 corresponds to the deposit on Monday and –350 corresponds to the withdrawal on Tuesday.

Some common uses for negative integers are as follows:

Time:	Before an event;
Temperature:	Degrees below zero;
Money:	Amount lost, spent, owed, or withdrawn;
Elevation:	Depth below sea level;
Travel:	Motion in the backward (reverse) direction.

Do Margin Exercises 1-4.

Tell which integers correspond to the situation.

1. The halfback gained 8 yd on first down. The quarterback was sacked for a 5-yd loss on second down.

2. The highest Fahrenheit temperature ever recorded in the United States was 134° in Death Valley on July 10, 1913. The coldest Fahrenheit temperature ever recorded in the United States was 80° below zero in Prospect Creek, Alaska, in January of 1971.

3. At 10 sec before liftoff, ignition occurs. At 148 sec after liftoff, the first stage is detached from the rocket.

4. Jeremy owes $137 to the campus bookstore. He has $289 in a savings account.

Use either < or > for □ to write a true sentence.

5. 15 □ 7

6. 12 □ −3

7. −13 □ −3

8. − 4 □ − 2 0

---

b **Order on the Number Line**

Numbers are named in order on the number line, with larger numbers named farther to the right. For any two numbers on the line, the one to the left is less than the one to the right.

Since the symbol < means "is less than" when read from left to right, the sentence −5 < 9 means "−5 is less than 9." The symbol > means "is greater than" when read from left to right so the sentence −4 > −8 means "−4 is greater than −8."

> For any real numbers a and b:
>
> **1.** $a < b$ (read "a is less than b") is true when a is to the left of b on a number line.
>
> **2.** $a > b$ (read "a is greater than b") is true when a is to the right of b on a number line.
>
> We call < and > *inequality symbols*.

Examples Use either < or > for □ to write a true sentence.

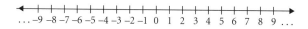
. . . −9 −8 −7 −6 −5 −4 −3 −2 −1 0 1 2 3 4 5 6 7 8 9 . . .

4. −9 □ 2   Since −9 is to the left of 2, we have −9 < 2.

5. 7 □ −13   Since 7 is to the right of −13, we have 7 > −13.

6. −19 □ −6   Since −19 is to the left of −6, we have −19 < −6.

Do Margin Exercises 5-8.

---

c **Absolute Value**

From the number line, we see that numbers like 5 and −5 are the same number of units from zero.

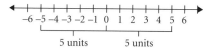

How many units is 5 from 0? How many units is −5 from 0? The number of units we count in either direction from zero is considered to be the distance. Since distance is always considered to be a non-negative number (it is either positive or zero), it follows that 5 is 5 units from 0 and −5 is 5 units from 0.

> The *absolute value* of a number is the number of units from 0 on a number line. We use the symbol $|x|$ to represent the absolute value of a number x.

Examples Find the absolute value.

7. $|-3|$ The distance from –3 to 0 is 3 units, so $|-3| = 3$.

8. $|25|$ The distance from 25 to 0 is 25 units, so $|25| = 25$

9. $|0|$ The distance from 0 to 0 is 0 units, so $|0| = 0$

10. $|-17|$ The distance from –17 to 0 is 17 units, so $|-17| = 17$

11. $|9|$ The distance from 9 to 0 is 9 units, so $|9| = 9$.

Do Margin Exercises 9-12.

d | Opposites

The set of integers is shown below on a number line.

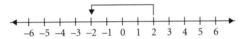

Notice that the left side of zero, which contains the negative numbers, is a reflection of the right side of zero, which contains the positive numbers. Given a number on one side of 0, we can find its opposite on the other side of 0 by *reflecting.* The *reflection* of 2 is –2.

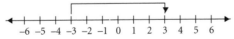

We can read –2 as "negative 2" or "the opposite of 2." We read –x as "the opposite of x."

> ▶ The *opposite* of a number x is named –x.

A number has a numerical part and a sign part. The numerical part tells how many units from zero, and the sign part tells the direction from zero.

Example 12 If x is –3, find –x.

To find the opposite of x when x is –3, we reflect –3 to the other side of 0.

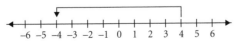

We have $-(-3) = 3$. The opposite of –3 is 3.

Example 13 Find –x when x is 4.

To find the opposite of x when x is 4, we reflect 4 to the other side of 0.

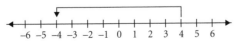

We have $-(4) = -4$. The opposite of 4 is –4.

Find the absolute value.

9. $|18|$

10. $|-9|$

11. $|-29|$

12. $|52|$

In each of the following, use a number line, if necessary.

13. Find −x when x is 1.

14. Find −x when x is −2.

15. Find −x when x is 0.

Find the opposite. (Change the sign.)

16. −4

17. −13

18. 28

19. 0

20. Find −(−x) when x is 4.

21. Find −(−x) when x is 1.

22. Find −(−x) when x is −2.

23. Find −(−x) when x is −5.

Example 14 Find −x when x is 0.

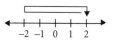

When we try to reflect 0 "to the other side of 0" we go nowhere: −x = 0 when x is 0.

Do Margin Exercises 13-15.

A negative number is sometimes said to have a "negative sign." A positive number is said to have a "positive sign." Replacing a number by its opposite is sometimes called *changing the sign*.

> *Note:* A number written without a sign is understood to be positive.

Examples Find the opposite. (Change the sign.)

15.	−3	−(−3) = 3
16.	−10	−(−10) = 10
17.	0	−(0) = 0
18.	14	−(14) = −14

Do Margin Exercises 16-19.

When a number's sign is changed twice, we return to the original number. This can also be described as taking the opposite of the opposite of a number.

Example 19 Find −(−x) when x is 2.

We replace x by 2. We wish to find −(−(2)).

> When substituting a number for a variable, it is often less confusing if you first enclose the variable within parentheses:
> −(−x) = −(−(x))

Reflecting 2 to the other side of 0 gives us −2. Reflecting again will give us −(−(2)).

We see from the figure that −(−(2)) = 2.

Example 20 Find −(−x) when x is −3.

We replace x by −3. We wish to find −(−(−3)).

Reflecting −3 to the other side of 0 and then back again gives us −3. Thus, −(−(−3)) = −(3) = −3.

Do Margin Exercises 20-23.

Exercise Set 3.1

a Tell which integers correspond to the situation.

1. Redbank, Montana, once recorded temperature of 70° below zero.

2. The Dead Sea, between Jordan and Israel, is 1286 ft below sea level, whereas Mt. Everest is 29,028 ft above sea level.

3. The space shuttle stood ready 3 sec before liftoff. Solid fuel rockets were released 128 sec after liftoff.

4. A student deposited $850 in a savings account. Two weeks later, the student withdrew $432.

b Use either < or > for □ to write a true sentence.

5. 6 □ 0

6. 9 □ 0

7. −9 □ 5

8. 8 □ −8

9. −6 □ 6

10. 0 □ −7

11. −8 □ −5

12. −5 □ −3

13. −5 □ −11

14. −3 □ −4

15. −6 □ −5

16. −10 □ −14

c Find the absolute value.

17. |−3|

18. |−7|

19. |10|

20. |11|

21. |0|

22. |−4|

23. |−24|

24. |−36|

25. |53|

26. |54|

27. |−8|

28. |−79|

d Find −x when x is each of the following.

29. −6

30. −7

31. 6

32. 0

33. −12

34. −19

35. 70

36. 80

Find the opposite. (Change the sign.)

37. −1   **38.** −7   **39.** 7   **40.** 10

41. −14   **42.** −22   **43.** 0   **44.** 1

Find $-(-x)$ when x is each of the following.

45. −7   **46.** −8   **47.** 1   **48.** 2

49. 0   **50.** −2   **51.** −34   **52.** −23

Skill Maintainance

53. Add: 327 + 498.   **54.** Evaluate: 5^3.

55. Multiply: 209 · 34.   **56.** Solve: $300 \cdot x = 1200$.

57. Evaluate: 9^2.   **58.** Multiply: 31 · 50.

Synthesis

59. ❖ Does $-x$ always represent a negative number? Why or why not?

60. ❖ Does $|x|$ always represent a positive number? Why or why not

Solve. Consider only integer replacements.

61. $|x| = 7$

62. $|x| < 2$

63. Simplify $-(-x)$, and $-(-(-x))$.

64. List these integers in order from least to greatest.
2^3, −5, $|-6|$, 4, $|3|$, −100, 0, 3^2, 7^2, 10^2

Improving Your Math Study Skills

Forming Math Study Groups, by James R. Norton

Dr. James Norton has taught at the University of Phoenix and Scottsdale Community College. He has extensive experience with the use of study groups to learn mathematics.

The use of math study groups for learning has become increasingly more common in recent years. Some instructors regard them as a primary source of learning, while others let students form groups on their own.

A study group generally consists of study partners who help each other learn the material and do the homework. You will probably meet outside of class at least once or twice a week. Here are some do's and don'ts to make your study group more valuable.

- DO make the group up of no more than four or five people. Research has shown clearly that this size works best.

- DO trade phone numbers so that you can get in touch with each other for help between team meetings.

- DO make sure that everyone in the group has a chance to contribute.

- DON'T let a group member copy from others without contributing. If this should happen, one member should speak with that student privately; if the situation continues, that student should be asked to leave the group.

- DON'T let the "A" students drop the ball. The group needs them! The benefits to even the best-students are twofold: (1) Other students will benefit from their expertise and (2) the bright students will learn the material better by teaching it to someone else.

DON'T let the slower students drop the ball either. Everyone can contribute something, and being in a group will actually improve their self-esteem as well as their performance.

How do you form study groups if the instructor has not already done so? A good place to begin is to get together with three or four friends and arrange a study time. If you don't know anyone, start getting acquainted with other people in the class during the first week of the semester.

What should you look for in a study partner?

- Do you live near each other to make it easy to get together?

- What are your class schedules like? Are you both on campus? Do you have free time?

- What about work schedules, athletic practice, and other out-of-school commitments that you might have to work around?

Making use of a study group is not a form of cheating." You are merely helping each other learn. So long as everyone in the group is both contributing and doing the work, this method will bring you great success!

Add, using a number line.

1. $3 + (-4)$

2. $-3 + (-5)$

3. $-3 + 7$

4. $-5 + 5$

Write an addition sentence.

5.

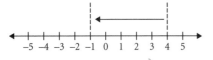

6.

7.

Add. Do not use a number line except as a check.

8. $-5 + (-6)$

9. $-9 + (-3)$

10. $-20 + (-14)$

11. $-11 + (-11)$

3.2 Addition of Integers

a Addition

To explain addition of integers, we can use the number line.

> To do the addition $a + b$, we start at a, and then move according to b.
>
> **a.** If b is positive, we move to the right.
> **b.** If b is negative, we move to the left.
> **c.** If b is 0, we stay at a.

Example 1 Add: $3 + (-5)$.

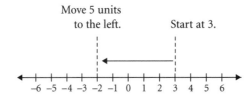

$3 + (-5) = -2$

Example 2 Add: $-4 + (-3)$.

$-4 + (-3) = -7$

Example 3 Add: $-4 + 9$.

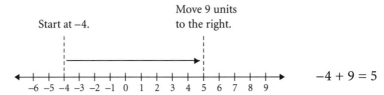

$-4 + 9 = 5$

Do Margin Exercises 1-7.

You may have noticed in Example 2 and Margin Exercises 2 and 6 that any time two negative integers are added, the result is negative.

> To add two negative integers, add their absolute values. The answer is negative.

Examples Add.

4. $-5 + (-7) = -12$ *Think:* Add the absolute values: $5 + 7 = 12$. Make the answer negative, -12.

5. $-8 + (-2) = -10$

Do Margin Exercises 8-11.

When we add a positive integer and a negative integer, as in Examples 1 and 3, the answer is either negative or positive, depending on which number has the greater absolute value.

Additive Inverse

The additive inverse of a is called $-a$ because the sum of any number and its additive inverse always gives 0.

▶ To add a positive integer and a negative integer, find the difference of their absolute values.

a) If the negative integer has the greater absolute value, the answer is negative.

b) If the positive integer has the greater absolute value, the answer is positive.

Add. Do not use a number line except as a check.

12. $-4 + 6$

Examples Add.

6. $3 + (-5) = -2$ *Think:* The absolute values are 3 and 5. The difference is 2. Since the negative number has the larger absolute value, the answer is *negative*, -2.

7. $11 + (-8) = 3$ *Think:* The absolute values are 11 and 8. The difference is 3. The positive number has the larger absolute value, so the answer is *positive*, 3.

13. $-7 + 3$

8. $1 + (-5) = -4$ **9.** $-7 + 4 = -3$

10. $7 + (-3) = 4$ **11.** $-6 + 10 = 4$

14. $5 + (-7)$

We sometimes call $-a$ the **additive inverse** of a, because adding any number to its additive inverse always gives 0, the additive identity:

$$-8 + 8 = 0, \qquad 14 + (-14) = 0, \qquad \text{and } 0 + 0 = 0.$$

15. $10 + (-7)$

▶ When the sum of two numbers is zero, the numbers are called additive inverses or opposites.

For any integer a,
$a + (-a) = -a + a = 0$.

16. $5 + (-5)$

17. $-6 + 6$

Do Margin Exercises 12-19.

18. $-10 + 10$

19. $89 + (-89)$

Add.

20. $(-15) + (-37) + 25 + 42 + (-59) + (-14)$

21. $42 + (-81) + (-28) + 24 + 18 + (-31)$

22.
$$
\begin{array}{r}
-35 \\
17 \\
14 \\
-27 \\
31 \\
+ \quad -12 \\
\hline
\end{array}
$$

▶ **Rules for Addition of Real Numbers**

1. *Positive numbers:* Add the same as arithmetic numbers. The answer is positive.

2. *Negative numbers:* Add absolute values. The answer is negative.

3. *A positive and a negative number*: Subtract the smaller absolute value from the larger. Then:
   a) If the positive number has the greater absolute value, the answer is positive.
   b) If the negative number has the greater absolute value, the answer is negative.
   c) If the numbers have the same absolute value, the answer is 0.

4. *One number is zero:* The sum is the other number.

5. *Additive inverses:* The sum is 0.

Suppose we wish to add several numbers, positive and negative:

$$15 + (-2) + 7 + 14 + (-5) + (-12).$$

Because of the commutative and associative laws for addition, we can group the positive numbers together and the negative numbers together and add them separately. Then we add the two results.

Example 12   Add: $15 + (-2) + 7 + 14 + (-5) + (-12)$.

First add the positive numbers: $15 + 7 + 14 = 36.$

Then add the negative numbers: $-2 + (-5) + (-12) = -19$

Finally, add the results: $36 + (-19) = 17.$

We can also add in any other order we wish, say, from left to right:

$$
\begin{aligned}
15 + (-2) + 7 + 14 + (-5) + (-12) &= 13 + 7 + 14 + (-5) + (-12) \\
&= 20 + 14 + (-5) + (-12) \\
&= 34 + (-5) + (-12) \\
&= 29 + (-12) \\
&= 17.
\end{aligned}
$$

Do Margin Exercises 20-22.

Exercise Set 3.2

a Add, using a number line.

1. $-8 + 3$ **2.** $2 + (-5)$ **3.** $-9 + 5$ **4.** $8 + (-3)$

5. $5 + (-5)$ **6.** $-7 + 7$ **7.** $-8 + (-5)$ **8.** $-3 + (-1)$

Add. Use a number line only as a check.

9. $-5 + (-11)$ **10.** $-3 + (-4)$ **11.** $-6 + (-5)$ **12.** $-10 + (-14)$

13. $9 + (-9)$ **14.** $10 + (-10)$ **15.** $-2 + 2$ **16.** $-3 + 3$

17. $0 + 8$ **18.** $7 + 0$ **19.** $0 + (-8)$ **20.** $-7 + 0$

21. $-25 + 0$ **22.** $-43 + 0$ **23.** $0 + (-27)$ **24.** $0 + (-19)$

25. $17 + (-17)$ **26.** $-13 + 13$ **27.** $-25 + 25$ **28.** $11 + (-11)$

29. $8 + (-5)$ **30.** $-7 + 8$ **31.** $-4 + (-5)$ **32.** $0 + (-3)$

33. $0 + (-5)$ **34.** $10 + (-12)$ **35.** $14 + (-5)$ **36.** $-3 + 14$

37. $-11 + 8$ **38.** $0 + (-34)$ **39.** $-19 + 19$ **40.** $-10 + 3$

41. $-17 + 7$ **42.** $-15 + 5$ **43.** $-17 + (-7)$ **44.** $-15 + (-5)$

45. $11 + (-16)$ **46.** $-7 + 15$ **47.** $-15 + (-6)$ **48.** $-16 + 16$

49. $11 + (-9)$ **50.** $-14 + (-19)$ **51.** $-20 + (-6)$ **52.** $19 + (-19)$

53. $-15 + (-7) + 1$

54. $23 + (-5) + 4$

55. $30 + (-10) + 5$

56. $40 + (-8) + 5$

57. $-23 + (-9) + 15$

58. $-25 + 25 + (-9)$

59. $40 + (-40) + 6$

60. $63 + (-18) + 12$

61. $85 + (-65) + (-12)$

62. $-35 + (-63) + (-27) + (-14) + (-59)$

63. $-24 + (-37) + (-19) + (-45) + (-35)$

64. $75 + (-14) + (-17) + (-5)$

65. $28 + (-44) + 17 + 31 + (-94)$

66. $27 + (-54) + (-32) + 65 + 46$

67. $42 + 21 + (-60) + (-13) + 29$

Skill Maintainance

68. Round to the nearest hundred: 746.

69. Round to the nearest thousand: 32,831.

70. Multiply: $42 \cdot 56$.

71. Divide: $288 \div 9$.

72. Round to the nearest ten: 3496.

Synthesis

73. ❖ Explain in your own words why the sum of two negative numbers is always negative.

74. ❖ A student states that −93 *is* "bigger than" −47. What mistake is the student making?

Add.

75. $-3496 + (-2987)$

76. $497 + (-3028)$

77. For what numbers x is $[x + (-7)]$ positive?

78. For what numbers x is $(-7 + x)$ negative?

Tell whether the sum is positive, negative, or zero.

79. If n is positive and m is negative, then

$-n + m$ is _____.

80. If $n = m$ and n *is* negative,

$-n + (-m)$ is _____.

Improving Your Math Study Skills

Better Test Taking

How often do you make the following statement after taking a test: "I was able to do the homework, but I froze during the test"? Instructors have heard this comment for years, and in most cases, it is merely a coverup for a lack of proper study habits. Here are two related tips, however, to help you with this difficulty. Both are intended to make test taking less stressful by getting you to practice good test-taking habits on a daily basis.

• Treat every homework exercise as if it were a test question. If you had to work a problem at your job with no backup answer provided, what would you do? You would probably work it very deliberately, checking and rechecking every step. You might work it more than one time, or you might try to work it another way to check the result. Try to use this approach when doing your homework. Treat every exercise as though it were a test question and no answer were provided at the back of the book.

• Be sure that you do questions without answers as part of every homework assignment whether or not the instructor has assigned them! One reason a test may seem such a different task is

that questions on a test lack answers. That is the reason for taking a test: to see if you can do the questions without assistance. As part of your test preparation, be sure you do some exercises for which you do not have the answers. Thus when you take a test, you are doing a more familiar task.

The purpose of doing your homework using these approaches is to give you more test-taking practice beforehand. Let's make a sports analogy here. At a basketball game, the players take lots of practice shots before the game. They play the first half, go to the locker room, and come out for the second half. What do they do before the second half, even though they have just played 20 minutes of basketball? They shoot baskets again! We suggest the same approach here. Create more and more situations in which you practice taking test questions by treating each homework exercise like a test question and by doing exercises for which you have no answers. Good luck!

Subtract.

1. $2 - 8$

2. $-6 - 10$

3. $14 - 9$

4. $-8 - (-11)$

5. $-8 - (-2)$

6. $5 - (-8)$

3.3   Subtraction of Integers

a   Subtraction

We now consider subtraction of integers. Subtraction is performed as follows:

▶ For any real numbers a and b,
$$a - b = a + (-b)$$

To subtract, add the opposite, or additive inverse, of the number being subtracted.

▶ To subtract integers:

1. Change the subtraction to addition.

2. Change the number after the subtraction sign to its opposite.

3. Follow the addition rules.

Examples   Subtract.

1. $2 - 6 = 2 + (-6)$ The opposite of 6 is –6. We change the
　　　　$= -4$ subtraction to addition and add the opposite. Instead of subtracting 6, we add –6.

2. $4 - (-9) = 4 + 9$ The opposite of –9 is 9. We change the
　　　　$= 13$ subtraction to addition and add the opposite. Instead of subtracting –9, we add 9.

3. $-3 - 8 = -3 + (-8)$ We change the subtraction to addition and
　　　　$= -11$ add the opposite. Instead of subtracting 8, we add –8.

4. $10 - 7 = 10 + (-7)$ We change the subtraction to addition and
　　　　$= 3$ add the opposite. Instead of subtracting 7, we add –7.

5. $-4 - (-9) = -4 + 9$ Instead of subtracting –9, we add 9.
　　　　$= 5$

6. $-5 - (-3) = -5 + 3$ Instead of subtracting –3, we add 3.
　　　　$= -2$

Do Margin Exercises 1-6.

When several additions and subtractions occur together, we can make them all additions. The commutative law for addition can then be used.

Example 7 Simplify: $-3 - (-5) - 9 + 4 - (-6)$

$$-3 - (-5) - 9 + 4 - (-6) = -3 + 5 + (-9) + 4 + 6 \quad \text{Adding opposites}$$

$$= -3 + (-9) + 5 + 4 + 6 \quad \text{Using the commutative law}$$

$$= -12 + 15 \quad \text{Adding negative and positive numbers separately}$$

$$= 3$$

Do Margin Exercises 7 and 8.

b Problem Solving

Let us see how we can use subtraction of integers to solve problems.

Example 8 The lowest point in Asia is the Dead Sea, which is 400 m below sea level. The lowest point in the United States is Death Valley, which is 86 m below sea level. How much higher is Death Valley than the Dead Sea?

It is helpful to draw a picture of the situation.

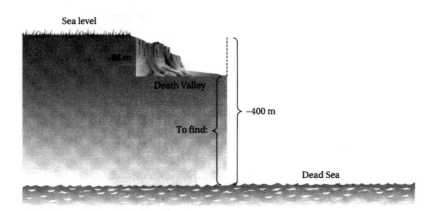

We see that -86 is the higher altitude at Death Valley and -400 is the lower altitude at the Dead Sea. To find how much higher Death Valley is, we subtract:

$$-86 - (-400) = -86 + 400 = 314.$$

Death Valley is 314 m higher than the Dead Sea.

Do Margin Exercises 9 and 10.

Simplify.

7. $-6 - (-2) - (-4) - 12 + 3$

8. $9 - (-6) + 7 - 11 - 14 - (-20)$

Solve.

9. Bo went from being 3 lb overweight to being 12 lb underweight. How many pounds did he lose?

10. In Churchill, Manitoba, Canada, the average daily low temperature in January is $-31°C$ (Celsius). The average daily low temperature in Key West, Florida, is $19°C$. How much higher is the average daily low temperature in Key West, Florida?

Exercise Set 3.3

a Subtract.

1. $2 - 9$ **2.** $3 - 8$ **3.** $0 - 4$ **4.** $0 - 9$

5. $-8 - (-2)$ **6.** $-6 - (-8)$ **7.** $-11 - (-11)$ **8.** $-6 - (-6)$

9. $12 - 16$ **10.** $14 - 19$ **11.** $20 - 27$ **12.** $30 - 4$

13. $-9 - (-3)$ **14.** $-7 - (-9)$ **15.** $-40 - (-40)$ **16.** $-9 - (-9)$

17. $7 - 7$ **18.** $9 - 9$ **19.** $5 - (-5)$ **20.** $4 - (-4)$

21. $8 - (-3)$ **22.** $-7 - 4$ **23.** $-6 - 8$ **24.** $6 - (-10)$

25. $-4 - (-9)$ **26.** $-14 - 2$ **27.** $1 - 8$ **28.** $2 - 8$

29. $-6 - (-5)$ **30.** $-4 - (-3)$ **31.** $8 - (-10)$ **32.** $5 - (-6)$

33. $0 - 10$ **34.** $0 - 18$ **35.** $-5 - (-2)$ **36.** $-3 - (-1)$

37. $-7 - 14$ **38.** $-9 - 16$ **39.** $0 - (-5)$ **40.** $0 - (-1)$

41. $-8 - 0$ **42.** $-9 - 0$ **43.** $7 - (-5)$ **44.** $7 - (-4)$

45. $2 - 25$ **46.** $18 - 63$ **47.** $-42 - 26$ **48.** $-18 - 63$

49. $-71 - 2$ **50.** $-49 - 3$ **51.** $24 - (-92)$ **52.** $48 - (-73)$

53. $-50 - (-50)$ **54.** $-70 - (-70)$

Simplify.

55. $9 - (-4) + 7 - (-2)$

56. $-8 - (-9) + 4 - 7$

57. $-31 + (-28) - (-14) - 17$

58. $-43 - (-19) - (-21) + 25$

59. $-34 - 28 + (-33) - 44$

60. $39 + (-88) - 29 - (-83)$

61. $-93 - (-84) - 41 - (-56)$

62. $84 + (-99) + 44 - (-18) - 43$

63. $-5 - (-30) + 30 + 40 - (-12)$

64. $14 - (-50) + 20 - (-32)$

65. $132 - (-21) + 45 - (-21)$

66. $81 - (-20) - 14 - (-50) + 53$

b Solve.

67. Through exercise, Rosa went from 8 lb above her "ideal" body weight to 9 lb below it. How many pounds did Rosa lose?

68. Chris has $720 in a checking account. If Chris writes a check for $970 to pay for a sound system, by how much is the checking account overdrawn?

69. In 1993, the elevation of the world's deepest offshore oil well was −2860 ft. By 1998, the deepest well was 360 ft deeper. What was the elevation of the deepest well in 1998?

70. You are in debt $95. How much money will you need to make your total assets $213?

71. The deepest point in the Pacific Ocean is the Marianas Trench, with a depth of 34,370 ft. The deepest point in the Atlantic Ocean is the Puerto Rico Trench, with a depth of 28,538 ft. How much higher is the Puerto Rico Trench than the Marianas Trench?

72. The lowest point in Africa is Lake Assal, which is 515 ft below sea level. The lowest point in South America is the Valdes Peninsula, which is 132 ft below sea level. How much lower is Lake Assal than the Valdes Peninsula?

73. A submarine cruising 30 m below the surface dives 50 m lower and then rises 18 m. What is the submarine's new depth?

74. A football team advanced 9 yd on its first play but was penalized 15 yd on its second play. How far did the team advance after the two plays?

Skill Maintainance

Evaluate.

75. 4^3

76. 5^3

77. How many 12-oz cans of soda can be filled with 96 oz of soda?

78. A case of soda contains 24 bottles. If each bottle contains 12 oz, how many ounces of soda are in the case?

Synthesis

79. ❖ If a negative number is subtracted from a positive number, will the result always be positive? Why or why not?

80. ❖ Write a problem for a classmate to solve. Design the problem so that the solution is "The temperature dropped to –9°."

Subtract.

81. $123,907 - 433,789$

82. $23,011 - (-60,432)$

Tell whether the statement is true or false for all integers m and n. If false, show why.

83. $-n = 0 - n$

84. $n - 0 = 0 - n$

85. If $m \neq n$, then $m - n \neq 0$.

86. If $m = -n$, then $m + n = 0$.

87. If $m + n \neq 0$, then m and n are opposites.

88. If $m - n = 0$, then $m = -n$.

89. $m = -n$ if m and n are opposites.

90. If $m = -m$, then $m = 0$.

91. Velma Quarles is a stockbroker. She kept track of the changes in the stock market over a period of 5 weeks. By how many points had the market risen or fallen over this time?

WEEK I	WEEK 2	WEEK 3	WEEK 4	WEEK 5
Down 13 pts	Down 16 pts	Up 36 pts	Down 11 pts	Up 19 pts

3.4 Multiplication of Integers

a Multiplication

Multiplication of integers is very much like multiplication of whole numbers. The only difference is that we must determine whether the answer is positive or negative.

Multiplication of a Positive Integer and a Negative Integer

To see how to multiply a positive integer and a negative integer, consider the pattern of the following.

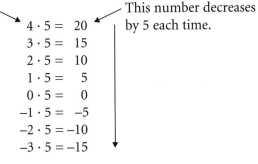

This number decreases by 1 each time.   This number decreases by 5 each time.

$$4 \cdot 5 = 20$$
$$3 \cdot 5 = 15$$
$$2 \cdot 5 = 10$$
$$1 \cdot 5 = 5$$
$$0 \cdot 5 = 0$$
$$-1 \cdot 5 = -5$$
$$-2 \cdot 5 = -10$$
$$-3 \cdot 5 = -15$$

Do Margin Exercise 1.

According to this pattern, the product of a negative integer and a positive integer is negative. This leads to the first part of the rule for multiplying integers.

> ▶ To multiply a positive integer and a negative integer, multiply their absolute values. Then make the answer negative.

Examples Multiply.

1. $8(-5) = -40$ **2.** $20(-1) = -20$ **3.** $-7(-5) = -35$

Do Margin Exercises 2-4.

Multiplication of Two Negative Integers

How do we multiply two negative integers? Again we look for a pattern.

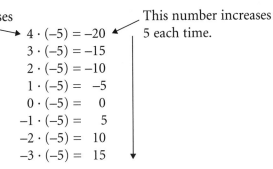

This number decreases by 1 each time.   This number increases 5 each time.

$$4 \cdot (-5) = -20$$
$$3 \cdot (-5) = -15$$
$$2 \cdot (-5) = -10$$
$$1 \cdot (-5) = -5$$
$$0 \cdot (-5) = 0$$
$$-1 \cdot (-5) = 5$$
$$-2 \cdot (-5) = 10$$
$$-3 \cdot (-5) = 15$$

Do Margin Exercise 5.

---

1. Complete, as in the example.

$$4 \cdot 10 = 40$$
$$3 \cdot 10 = 30$$
$$2 \cdot 10 =$$
$$1 \cdot 10 =$$
$$0 \cdot 10 =$$
$$-1 \cdot 10 =$$
$$-2 \cdot 10 =$$
$$-3 \cdot 10 =$$

Multiply.

2. $-3 \cdot 6$

3. $20 \cdot (-5)$

4. $7(-1)$

5. Complete, as in the example.

$$3(-10) = -30$$
$$2(-10) = -20$$
$$1(-10) =$$
$$0(-10) =$$
$$-2(-10) =$$
$$-3(-10) =$$

Multiply.

6. $(-3)(-4)$

7. $-16(-2)$

8. $(-1)(-7)$

Multiply.

9. $0 \cdot (-5)$

10. $-23 \cdot 0$

According to the pattern, the product of two negative integers is positive. This leads to the second part of the rule for multiplying integers.

> ▶ To multiply two negative integers, multiply their absolute values. The answer is positive.

Examples Multiply.

4. $(-2)(-4) = 8$ **5.** $(-10)(-7) = 70$ **6.** $(-9)(-1) = 9$

Do Margin Exercises 6-8.

The following is another way to state the rules we have for multiplication.

> ▶ To multiply two integers:
>
> **a)** Multiply the absolute values.
>
> **b)** If the signs are the same, the answer is positive.
>
> **c)** If the signs are different, the answer is negative.

Note also that Examples 2 and 6 show us that when a number is multiplied by −1, the result is the opposite of that number.

> ▶ For any non-zero integer a,
>
> $a(-1) = (-1)a = -a.$

Multiplication by Zero

The only case that we have not discussed is multiplying by zero. As with other numbers, the product of any integer and 0 is 0.

> ▶ For any integer a,
>
> $a \cdot 0 = 0.$
>
> (The product of 0 and any integer is 0.)

Examples Multiply.

7. $-19 \cdot 0 = 0$ **8.** $0(-7) = 0$

Do Margin Exercises 9 and 10.

b | Multiplication of More than Two Integers

Because of the commutative and the associative laws, to multiply three or more integers, we may group as we please.

Examples Multiply.

9. a) $-8 \cdot 2\,(-3) = -16\,(-3)$ Multiplying the first two numbers.
             $= 48$ Multiplying the results.

  b) $-8(-3) \cdot 2 \;= 24 \cdot 2$ Multiplying the negatives.
              $= 48$ The result is the same as above.

10. $7(-1)(-4)(-2) = (-7)8$ Multiplying the first two numbers
                 $= -56$ and the last two numbers.

11. a) $-5 \cdot (-2) \cdot (-3) \cdot (-6) \;= 10 \cdot 18$ Each pair of negatives gives a
                       $= 180$ positive product.

  b) $-5 \cdot (-2) \cdot (-3) \cdot (-6) \cdot (-1) = 10 \cdot 18\,(-1)$ Making use of example 11a.
                      $= -180$

We can see the following pattern in the results of Examples 9–11.

> ▶ The product of an *even* number of integers is positive. The product of an *odd* number of integers is negative.

Do Margin Exercises 11-13.

Powers of Integers

The result of raising a negative number to a power is positive or negative, depending on the exponent.

Examples Simplify.

12. $(-7)^2 = (-7)(-7) = 49$ The result is positive.

13. $(-4)^3 = (-4)(-4)(-4)$
          $= 16(-4)$
          $= -64$ The result is negative.

14. $(-3)^4 = (-3)(-3)(-3)(-3)$
          $= 9 \cdot 9$
          $= 81$ The result is positive.

15. $(-2)^5 = (-2)(-2)(-2)(-2)(-2)$
          $= 4 \cdot 4 \cdot (-2)$
          $= 16(-2)$
          $= -32$ The result is negative.

Perhaps you noticed the following.

> ▶ When a negative number is raised to an *even* exponent, the result is positive.
>
> When a negative number is raised to an *odd* exponent, the result is negative.

Do Margin Exercises 14-16.

Multiply.

11. $-2 \cdot (-5) \cdot (-4) \cdot (-3)$

12. $(-4)(-5)(-2)(-3)(-1)$

13. $(-1)(-1)(-2)(-3)(-1)(-1)$

Simplify.

14. $(-2)^3$

15. $(-9)^2$

16. $(-1)^7$

Exercise Set 3.4

a Multiply.

1. $-2 \cdot 5$

2. $-8 \cdot 2$

3. $-9 \cdot 2$

4. $-7 \cdot 6$

5. $9 \cdot (-5)$

6. $8 \cdot (-3)$

7. $-10 \cdot 3$

8. $-9 \cdot 8$

9. $-2 \cdot (-5)$

10. $-8 \cdot (-2)$

11. $-9 \cdot (-2)$

12. $-7 \cdot (-6)$

13. $-9 \cdot (-5)$

14. $-8 \cdot (-3)$

15. $-10(-3)$

16. $-9(-8)$

17. $12(-10)$

18. $15(-8)$

19. $-6(-50)$

20. $-25(-8)$

21. $(-35)(-1)$

22. $41(-3)$

23. $(-20)17$

24. $(-1)43$

25. $-23 \cdot 0$

26. $-17 \cdot 0$

27. $0(-14)$

28. $0(-38)$

b Multiply.

29. $2 \cdot (-7) - 5$

30. $(-3) \cdot (-4) \cdot (-5)$

31. $7(-4)(-3)5$

32. $9(-2)(-6)7$

33. $-2(-5)(-7)$

34. $(-2)(-5)(-3)(-5)$

35. $(-3)(-5)(-2)(-1)$

36. $-7(-21)13$

37. $-14(34)12(-1)$

38. $4(-4)(-5)(-12)2$

39. $(-17)(-29)0 \cdot 3$

40. $17(-2)(-8)0 \cdot 5$

Simplify.

41. $(-5)^2$
42. $(-8)^2$
43. $(-10)^3$
44. $(-2)^4$

45. $(-5)^4$
46. $(-1)^5$
47. $(-2)^7$
48. $(-2)^6$

49. $(-3)^5$
50. $(-10)^4$
51. $(-1)^{12}$
52. $(-1)^{13}$

Skill Maintainance

53. Round 532,451 to the nearest hundred.

54. Write standard notation for sixty million.

55. Divide: $2880 \div 436$.

56. Multiply: 75×34.

57. A rectangular rug measures 5 ft by 8 ft. What is the area of the rug?

58. How many 12-egg cartons can be filled with 2880 eggs?

Synthesis

59. ❖ Explain in your own words why $-7(-1)^3$ is the opposite of -7.

60. ❖ Without calculating, which number is larger, $(-3)^7$ or $(-5)^7$? Why?

61. Jo wrote seven checks for $13 each. If she had a balance of $68 in her account, what was her balance after writing the checks?

62. After diving 95 m below the surface, a diver rises at a rate of 7 meters per minute for 9 min. What is the diver's new elevation?

63. $(-5)^3(-1)^{421}$

64. $(-2)5 \cdot [(-1)^{43}]$

65. $[(-2)^3 + 4^2] - (2-7)^2$

66. $-11(-3)^2 - 5^3 - 6^2 - (-4)^2$

67. What must be true of m and n if $-mn$ is to be (a) positive? (b) zero? (c) negative?

Divide.

1. $6 \div (-3)$

2. $\dfrac{-15}{-3}$

3. $-24 \div 8$

4. $\dfrac{-32}{-4}$

5. $\dfrac{30}{-5}$

6. $\dfrac{-45}{9}$

Divide.

7. $\dfrac{-5}{0}$

8. $\dfrac{0}{-3}$

3.5 Division of Integers

a Division of Integers

We now consider division of integers.

▶ The quotient $a \div b$ or $\dfrac{a}{b}$ is the number that when multiplied by b gives a (when $b \neq 0$).

The rules for division are the same as those for multiplication.

▶ To multiply or divide two real numbers:

a) Multiply or divide the absolute values.

b) If the signs are the same, the answer is positive.

c) If the signs are different, the answer is negative.

Examples Divide, if possible. Check your answer.

1. $14 \div (-7) = -2$

2. $\dfrac{-32}{-4} = 8$

3. $\dfrac{-21}{7} = -3$

4. $\dfrac{-17}{0}$ is **undefined.**   *Remember:* When asked to divide a number by 0, we state that the answer is "undefined" because there is no number that when multiplied by 0 gives -17.

5. $0 \div (-5) = 0$ *Think:* What number multiplied by -5 gives 0? The number is 0. *Check:* $0(-5) = 0$.

Example 4 shows why we cannot divide -17 by 0. We can use the same argument to show why we cannot divide other numbers by 0. For example, $25 \div 0$ is undefined because there is no number that when multiplied by 0 gives 25. On the other extreme, $0 \div 0$ is undefined because there are too many numbers q for which $q \cdot 0 = 0$.

Example 5 shows that division *into* 0 is possible. For example $\dfrac{0}{29} = 0$ because $0 \cdot 29 = 0$.

▶ 0 divided by a nonzero number a is 0: $0 \div a = \dfrac{0}{a} = 0$, $a \neq 0$.

Do Margin Exercises 1-8.

b | Order of Operations

When several operations are to be done in a calculation or a problem, we apply the same rules that we did in Section 2.1. We repeat them here for review, now including integers.

> ### Rules for Order of Operations
>
> 1. Do all calculations within parentheses before operations outside.
> 2. Evaluate all exponential expressions.
> 3. In order from left to right, do all multiplications and divisions.
> 4. In order from left to right, do all additions and subtractions.

Examples Simplify.

6. $17 - 10 \div 2 \cdot 4$

There are no parentheses or powers so we start with the third step.

$$
\begin{aligned}
17 - 10 \div 2 \cdot 4 &= 17 - 5 \cdot 4 \\
&= 17 - 20 \\
&= -3
\end{aligned}
$$

Carrying out all multiplications and divisions in order from left to right

7. $|(-2)^3 \div 4| - 5(-2)$

We first simplify within the absolute value signs.

$$
\begin{aligned}
|(-2)^3 \div 4| - 5(-2) &= |-8 \div 4| - 5(-2) && (-2)^3 = (-2)(-2)(-2) = -8 \\
&= |-2| - 5(-2) && \text{Dividing} \\
&= 2 - 5(-2) && \text{Taking the absolute value} \\
&= 2 - (-10) && \text{Multiplying} \\
&= 12 && \text{Subtracting by adding the opposite of } -10
\end{aligned}
$$

A fraction bar is a grouping symbol. It tells us to simplify the numerator and the denominator seperately before dividing.

Example 8 Simplify: $\dfrac{5 - (-3)^2}{-2}$.

$$
\begin{aligned}
\frac{5 - (-3)^2}{-2} &= \frac{5 - 9}{-2} && \text{Simplifying: } (-3)^2 = (-3)(-3) = 9 \\
&= \frac{-4}{-2} && \text{Subtracting} \\
&= 2 && \text{Dividing}
\end{aligned}
$$

Do Margin Exercises 9-11.

Simplify.

9. $5 - (-7)(-3)^2$

10. $(-2) \cdot |3 - 2^2| + 5$

11. $\dfrac{(-5)(-9)}{1 - 2 \cdot 2}$

Exercise Set 3.5

a Divide, if possible. Check each answer.

1. $42 \div (-6)$

2. $\dfrac{35}{-7}$

3. $\dfrac{28}{-2}$

4. $26 \div (-13)$

5. $\dfrac{-16}{8}$

6. $-22 \div (-2)$

7. $\dfrac{-48}{-12}$

8. $-63 \div (-9)$

9. $\dfrac{-72}{8}$

10. $\dfrac{-50}{25}$

11. $-100 \div (-50)$

12. $\dfrac{-400}{8}$

13. $-344 \div 8$

14. $\dfrac{-128}{8}$

15. $\dfrac{200}{-25}$

16. $-651 \div (-31)$

17. $\dfrac{-75}{0}$

18. $\dfrac{0}{-5}$

19. $\dfrac{88}{-11}$

20. $\dfrac{-145}{-5}$

21. $\dfrac{-276}{12}$

22. $\dfrac{-217}{7}$

23. $\dfrac{0}{-9}$

24. $\dfrac{-13}{0}$

25. $\dfrac{19}{-1}$

26. $\dfrac{-17}{1}$

27. $-41 \div 1$

28. $23 \div (-1)$

b Simplify.

29. $8 - 2 \cdot 3 - 9$

30. $8 - (2 \cdot 3 - 9)$

31. $8 - 2 (3 - 9)$

32. $(8 - 2)(3 - 9)$

33. $16 \cdot (-24) + 50$

34. $10 \cdot 20 - 15 \cdot 24$

35. $40 - 3^2 - 2^3$

36. $2^4 + 2^2 - 10$

37. $4 \cdot (6 + 8) \div (4 + 3)$

38. $4^3 + 10 \cdot 20 + 8^2 - 23$

39. $4 \cdot 5 - 2 \cdot 6 + 4$

40. $5^3 + 4 \cdot 9 - (8 + 9 \cdot 3)$

41. $\dfrac{9^2 - 1}{1 - 3^2}$

42. $\dfrac{100 - 6^2}{(-5)^2 - 3^2}$

43. $8(-7) + 6(-5)$

44. $10(-5) \div 1(-1)$

45. $20 \div 5(-3) + 3$

46. $14 \div 2(-6) + 7$

47. $9 \div (-3) \cdot 16 \div 8$

48. $-32 \div 8 \cdot 4 - (-2)$

49. $2 \cdot 3^2 \div 6$

50. $(2 - 5)^2 \div (-9)$

51. $(3 - 8)^2 \div (-1)$

52. $3 - 3^2$

53. $12 - 20^3$

54. $20 + 4^3 \div (-8)$

55. $2 \cdot 10^3 - 5000$

56. $-7(3^4) + 18$

57. $6[9 - (3 - 4)]$

58. $8[(6 - 13) - 11]$

59. $-1000 \div (-100) \div 10$

60. $256 + (-32) \div (-4)$

61. $8 - |7 - 9| \cdot 3$

62. $|8 - 7 - 9| \cdot 2 + 1$

63. $9 - |7 - 3^2|$

64. $9 - |5 - 7|^3$

65. $\dfrac{(-5)^3 + 17}{10(2 - 6) - 2(5 + 2)}$

66. $\dfrac{(3 - 5)^2 - (7 - 13)}{(2 - 5)3 + 2 \cdot 4}$

Skill Maintenance

67. A classroom contains 7 rows of chairs with 6 chairs in each row. How many chairs are there in the classroom?

68. A motorcycle gets 53 miles to the gallon. How many gallons will it take to travel 371 mi?

69. A 7-oz bag of tortilla chips contains 1050 calories. How many calories are in a 1-oz serving?

70. A 7-oz bag of tortilla chips contains 8 g of fat. How many grams of fat are in a carton containing 12 bags of chips?

Synthesis

71. ❖ Explain how multiplication can be used to justify why the quotient of two negative integers is a positive integer.

72. ❖ Explain how multiplication can be used to justify why a negative integer divided by a positive integer is a negative integer.

Simplify.

73. $\dfrac{-2}{1}$

74. $\dfrac{-(2)}{-(-1)}$

75. $-\left(\dfrac{-(2)}{-1}\right)$

76. $-\left(\dfrac{2}{-(1)}\right)$

77. $-\left(\dfrac{-(2)}{-(1)}\right)$

3.6 Solving Equations Using Addition and Subtraction

a In order to solve an equation, we sometimes say that we "add the same number to both sides of the equation." This is also true for subtraction since we can express every subtraction as an addition. Thus, to solve an equation we can also choose to "subtract the same number from both sides of an equation."

> ### ▶ The Addition and Subtraction Principle
>
> To solve $x - a = b$, add a to both sides.
>
> To solve $x + a = b$, subtract a from both sides.

Example 1 Solve: $x + 5 = -7$

$x + 5 = -7$		$x + 5 = -7$
$x + 5 - 5 = -7 - 5$	Subtract 5 from both sides	$\underline{\quad -5 \quad -5 \quad}$
$x + 0 = -12$	Simplifying	$x + 0 = -12$
$x = -12$	Identify property of zero.	$x = -12$

To check the answer substitute –12 in the original equation.

Check:
$$\frac{x + 5 = -7}{-12 + 5 \;\; ? \;\; -7}$$
$$-7 \;\mid\; -7 \quad \text{True}$$

The solution of the original equation is –12.

Do Margin Exercises 1 and 2.

Now we solve an equation with a subtraction by adding the same number to both sides.

Example 2 Solve: $-6 = y - 8$

$$-6 = y - 8$$
$$-6 + 8 = y - 8 + 8 \quad \text{Adding 8 to eliminate } -8 \text{ on the right}$$
$$2 = y$$

Check:
$$\frac{-6 = y - 8}{-6 \;\; ? \;\; 2 - 8}$$
$$-6 \;\mid\; -6 \quad \text{True}$$

The solution is 2

Do Margin Exercises 3 and 4.

Solve:

1. $x + 2 = 11$

2. $x + 7 = 2$

3. $8 = n - 4$

4. $y - 17 = 10$

Exercise Set 3.6

a Solve. Don't forget to check!

1. $x + 5 = 12$

2. $x + 3 = 7$

3. $x + 15 = -5$

4. $y + 8 = 37$

5. $x + 6 = -8$

6. $t + 8 = -14$

7. $x + 16 = -2$

8. $y + 34 = -8$

9. $x - 9 = 6$

10. $x - 9 = 2$

11. $x - 7 = -21$

12. $x - 5 = -16$

13. $5 + t = 7$

14. $6 + y = 22$

15. $-7 + y = 13$

16. $-8 + z = 16$

17. $-3 + t = -9$

18. $-8 + y = -23$

19. $-12 + z = -12$

20. $5 + y = 15$

21. $x + 44 = -10$

22. $x - 3 = -7$

23. $1 + t = -11$

24. $x - 5 = 7$

25. $y + 52 = 6$

26. $35 = 27 + x$

27. $74 = x + 23$

28. $93 = 46 + x$

29. $76 = x - 48$

30. $95 = y - 83$

31. $-97 = 47 + y$

32. $-78 = 28 + x$

Skill Maintenance

Add.

33. $-3 + (-8)$

34. $-143 + (-198)$

35. $32 + (-49)$

Subtract.

36. $-3 - (-8)$

37. $-143 - (-198)$

38. $32 - (-49)$

Multiply.

39. $-3(-8)$

40. $143(-198)$

41. $32(-45)$

Divide.

42. $\dfrac{-24}{-3}$

43. $\dfrac{28314}{198}$

44. $\dfrac{-1568}{32}$

Synthesis

45. ❖ Explain the following mistake made by a fellow student.

$$x + 1 = -5$$
$$x = -4$$

46. ❖ Explain the role of the opposite of a number when using the addition principle.

Solve.

47. $-356 = -699 + t$

Note: ax means $a \cdot x$
For example,
$7x$ means $7 \cdot x$

3.7 Solving Equations Using Multiplication and Division

In Chapter 2 we found when solving equations like $9x = 36$, we divided both sides of the equation by 9 to get $x = 4$. This leads us to another strategy to use with an equation like $\frac{x}{9} = 36$.

To isolate the x term, the left side of the equation needs to be multiplied by 9. To keep the equation "balanced," the right side must also be multiplied by 9. Let us look at these two equations side by side:

$$9x = 36 \qquad\qquad \frac{x}{9} = 36$$

$$\frac{9x}{9} = \frac{36}{9} \qquad\qquad 9 \cdot \frac{x}{9} = 36 \cdot 9$$

$$x = 4 \qquad\qquad x = 324$$

Because $9x$ means $9 \cdot x$ we divide both sides by 9 to isolate x.

Because $\frac{x}{9}$ means $x \div 9$ multiply both sides by 9 to isolate x.

> ▶ **The Multiplication and Division Principle**
>
> For any real numbers a and b, $a \neq 0$
>
> To solve $ax = b$, divide both sides by a
>
> To solve $\frac{x}{a} = b$, multiply both sides by a

1. $-4x = 24$

The Multiplication and Division Principle allows us to multiply or divide by the same non-zero number on both sides of an equation.

Example 1 *Solve:* $-3x = 18$

We have:

$$-3x = 18$$

$$\frac{-3x}{-3} = \frac{18}{-3} \qquad \text{Using the Multiplication and Division Principle and dividing both sides by } -3.$$

$$1 \cdot x = -6 \qquad \text{Simplifying}$$

$$x = -6 \qquad \text{Identify property of 1}$$

Check:
$$\frac{-3x = 18}{\;}$$
$$-3(-6) \overset{?}{\;} 18$$
$$18 \mid 18 \quad \text{True}$$

The solution is -6.

Do Margin Exercise 1.

Example 2 Solve: $3x = -9$

We have:

$$3x = -9$$

$$\frac{3x}{3} = \frac{-9}{3} \qquad \text{Using the Multiplication and Division Principle and dividing both sides by 3.}$$

$$1 \cdot x = -3 \qquad \text{Simplifying}$$

$$x = -3 \qquad \text{Identify property of 1}$$

Check:

$$\frac{3x = -9}{3(-3) \ ? \ -9}$$
$$-9 \ | \ -9 \qquad \text{True}$$

The solution is -3

Do Margin Exercise 2.

Example 3 Solve: $-92 = -4x$

We have:

$$-92 = -4x$$

$$\frac{-92}{-4} = \frac{-4x}{-4} \qquad \text{Using the Multiplication and Division Principle and dividing both sides by } -4.$$

$$23 = 1 \cdot x \qquad \text{Simplifying}$$

$$23 = x \qquad \text{Identity property of 1}$$

Check:

$$\frac{-92 = -4x}{-92 \ ? \ -4(23)}$$
$$-92 \ | \ -92 \qquad \text{True}$$

The solution is 23.

Note: Equations are reversible. Therefore, $-92 = -4x$ is the same as $-4x = -92$.

Both equations have the same solution, $x = 23$.

Do Margin Exercises 3 and 4.

2. $7x = -35$

3. $-5x = -40$

4. $-108 = -6x$

5. $\frac{x}{-8} = -16$

6. $-14 = \frac{t}{2}$

Example 4 Solve: $-20 = \frac{m}{4}$

We have:

$$-20 = \frac{m}{4}$$

$$-20 \cdot 4 = \frac{m}{4} \cdot 4 \qquad \text{Using the Multiplication and Division Principle to multiply both sides by 4.}$$

$$-80 = m \cdot 1 \qquad \text{Simplifying}$$

$$-80 = m \qquad \text{Identify property of 1}$$

Check: $\quad -20 = \frac{m}{4}$

$$-20 \; ? \; \frac{-80}{4}$$

$$-20 \; \Big| \; -20 \qquad \text{True}$$

The solution is -80.

Example 5 Solve: $\frac{x}{-3} = 12$

We have:

$$\frac{x}{-3} = 12$$

$$\frac{x}{-3}(-3) = 12(-3) \qquad \text{Using the Multiplication and Division Principle to multiply both sides by } -3.$$

$$x \cdot 1 = -36 \qquad \text{Simplifying}$$

$$x = -36 \qquad \text{Identify property of 1}$$

Check:

$$\frac{x}{-3} = 12$$

$$\frac{-36}{-3} \; ? \; 12$$

$$12 \; \Big| \; 12 \qquad \text{True}$$

The solution is -36.

Do Margin Exercises 5 and 6.

Exercise Set 3.7

a Solve. Don't forget to check

1. $6x = 36$

2. $4x = 52$

3. $5x = 45$

4. $8x = 56$

5. $84 = 7x$

6. $63 = 7x$

7. $-x = 40$

8. $50 = -x$

9. $-2x = -10$

10. $-78 = -39p$

11. $7x = -49$

12. $9x = -54$

13. $-12x = 72$

14. $-15x = 105$

15. $-21x = -126$

16. $-13x = -104$

17. $\dfrac{t}{7} = -9$

18. $\dfrac{y}{-8} = 11$

19. $\dfrac{x}{3} = 27$

20. $\dfrac{x}{4} = 16$

21. $\dfrac{t}{-3} = 7$

22. $\dfrac{x}{-6} = 9$

23. $\dfrac{m}{-1} = 5$

24. $-8 = \dfrac{z}{-1}$

25. $-9 = \dfrac{t}{-3}$

26. $-4 = \dfrac{y}{2}$

27. $\dfrac{t}{-2} = -27$

28. $\dfrac{x}{-7} = -14$

29. $63x = 441$

30. $27y = 54$

31. $-31y = 217$

32. $-33y = 66$

33. $387m = 3096$

34. $294m = 2352$

Skill Maintenance

35. Evaluate $(-2)^5$

36. Evaluate $(-3)^2 - (-4^2)$

37. Simplify $-12 \div 3 + (-33) - (-4) + 5$

38. Simplify $4(-2) - 6(3 - 5) + (-4)$

39. Simplify $14 - 36 \div 3^2 - 5 - (-2)$

40. A car gets 32 miles to the gallon on the highway. How many gallons (rounded to the neaarest whole number) will be needed to make a 670 mile trip?

Synthesis

41. ❖ Explain the mistake made by a student in solving this problem

$$2x = -5$$
$$x = -10$$

42. ❖ State, in your own words, the Multiplication and Division Principle.

43. ❖ Solve: $0 \cdot x = 7$. Why is there no solution?

44. ❖ Explain how you would solve for x in the following problem

$$\frac{x}{7} = -2$$

Review Exercises: Chapter 3

1. Tell which integers correspond to this situation: Louise has $213 in her savings account and Roger is $53 in debt.

Use either < or > for ☐ to write a true statement.

2. 0 ☐ −5

3. − 7 ☐ 6

4. − 4 ☐ −19

Find the absolute value.

5. $|-39|$

6. $|12|$

7. $|0|$

8. Find $-x$ when $x = -29$.

9. Find $-(-x)$ when $x = 32$.

Simplify.

10. $-14 + 5$

11. $-5 + (-6)$

12. $14 + (-8)$

13. $0 + (-24)$

14. $15 - 24$

15. $9 - (-14)$

16. $-8 - (-7)$

17. $-3 - (-10)$

18. $-3 + 7 + (-8)$

19. $8 - (-9) - 7 + 2$

20. $- 23 \cdot (-4)$

21. $7(-12)$

22. $2(-4)(-5)(-1)$

23. $15 \div (-5)$

24. $\dfrac{-55}{11}$

25. $\dfrac{0}{7}$

26. $(-1)^4$

27. $(-1)^{12}$

28. $(-7)^2$

29. $(-7)^3$

30. $8(6 - 12) - 4 \cdot 3$

31. $\dfrac{12(-4) + 16 \div (-2)}{22 + (-15)}$

32. $[(-8) - (-4)] \div (-2) \div 2$

Solve.

33. $y - 19 = -78$

34. $x + 53 = 16$

35. $17x = -68$

36. $\dfrac{x}{-12} = 32$

Practice Test: Chapter 3

1. Tell which integers correspond to this situation: A company sold 542 fewer units than expected in January and 307 more than expected in February.

2. Use either < or > for □ to write a true statement. $-14 \square -21$

3. Find the absolute value: $|-429|$.

4. Find $-(-x)$ when $x = -19$.

Simplify.

5. $6 + (-17)$

6. $-9 + (-12)$

7. $-8 + 17$

8. $0 - 12$

9. $7 - 22$

10. $-5 - 19$

11. $-8 - (-27)$

12. $17 - (-3) - 5 + 9$

13. $(-4)^3$

14. $13(-10)$

15. $-9 \cdot 0$

16. $-72 \div (-9)$

17. $\dfrac{-56}{7}$

18. $8 \div 2 \cdot 2 - 3^2$

19. $29 - (3 - 5)^2$

20. $(-5)^3$

21. $(-3)^4$

22. $\dfrac{-45(3) + 6(8 - 2)}{(-9)(-11)}$

23. $x - 52 = 17$

24. $y + 29 = 75$

25. $-14x = 42$

26. $\dfrac{y}{18} = 56$

26. Explain how to add 2 numbers with different signs. Give an example.

27. Explain the difference between terms and expressions. Give an example of each.

4

Fractions: Multiplication and Division

Introduction

In this chapter, we consider addition and subtraction using fractional notation. Also discussed are addition, subtraction, multiplication, and division using mixed numbers. We then apply all these operations to solving equations and some applied problems.

An Application

The tape in an audio cassette is played at a rate of $1\frac{7}{8}$ in. per second. A defective tape player has destroyed 30 in. of tape. How many seconds of music have been lost?

This problem appears as Example 8 in Section 4.6.

The Mathematics

We let t = the number of seconds of music lost. The problem then translates to the equation

$$t = 30 \div 1\frac{7}{8}.$$

Division using mixed numbers occurs often in applications and problem solving.

Write as a mixed number.

1. $8 + \dfrac{3}{4}$

2. $12 + \dfrac{2}{3}$

4.1 Introduction to Fractions

a | Proper Fractions, Improper Fractions and Mixed Numbers

Whole numbers are used to count whole units. However, it is often necessary to refer to parts of a whole which are called fractions of a part. For example, a measuring cup can be divided into 4 equal parts. If 3 of these parts are used the fraction $\frac{3}{4}$ can be used to show the part of 1 cup. The 4 in the fraction refers to the total number of equal parts and is called the **denominator**. The 3 tells how many of those parts are used and is called the **numerator**.

$$\frac{3}{4} \begin{array}{l} \leftarrow \text{ the number of parts used} \\ \leftarrow \text{ the number of equal parts of the whole} \end{array}$$

A **proper fraction** is a fraction whose numerator is less than the denominator. Proper fractions are always less than 1. Examples of proper fractions are $\frac{3}{4}, \frac{1}{3}, \frac{7}{8}$ and $\frac{99}{100}$.

An **improper fraction** is a fraction whose numerator is greater than or equal to the denominator. Improper fractions are greater than or equal to 1. Examples of improper fractions are $\frac{4}{3}, \frac{8}{8}, \frac{11}{5}$ and $\frac{100}{99}$.

A symbol like $2\frac{3}{4}$ is called a **mixed number**. A mixed number contains a whole number and a fraction. Mixed numbers are greater than 1.

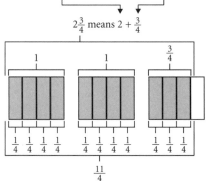

Examples Write as a mixed number.

1. $7 + \dfrac{2}{5} = 7\dfrac{2}{5}$ **2.** $4 + \dfrac{3}{10} = 4\dfrac{3}{10}$

Do Margin Exercises 1 and 2.

The notation $2\frac{3}{4}$ has a plus sign left out. To aid in understanding, we sometimes write the missing plus sign. Similarly, the notation $-5\frac{2}{3}$ has a minus sign left out since $-5\frac{2}{3} = -(5 + \frac{2}{3}) = -5 - \frac{2}{3}$.

Mixed numbers can be displayed easily on a number line, as shown here.

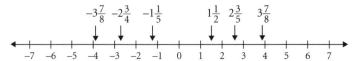

b Changing Mixed Numbers to Improper Fractions

Mixed numbers and improper fractions can both be used to represent the same quantity. Therefore, mixed numbers can be changed to improper fractions, and improper fractions can be changed to mixed numbers.

Examples Convert to an improper fraction.

3. $2\frac{3}{4} = 2 + \frac{3}{4}$ Inserting the missing plus sign

$= \frac{8}{4} + \frac{3}{4}$

$= \frac{11}{4}$

Do Margin Exercises 3 and 4.

From Example 3, we can see a faster way to convert.

> ▶ To convert a mixed number like $2\frac{3}{4}$ to an improper fraction:
>
>   **a.** Multiply: $4 \cdot 2 = 8$.
>
>   **b.** Add: $8 + 3 = 11$.
>
>   **c.** Keep the denominator.
>
> **b.** ↱ $2\frac{3}{4} = \frac{11}{4}$ ↙
> **a.** ↰

Examples Convert to improper fractions.

4. $6\frac{2}{3} = \frac{20}{3}$ $3 \cdot 6 = 18; 18 + 2 = 20$

5. $8\frac{2}{9} = \frac{74}{9}$ $9 \cdot 8 = 72; 72 + 2 = 74$

6. $10\frac{7}{8} = \frac{87}{8}$ $8 \cdot 10 = 80; 80 + 7 = 87$

Do Margin Exercises 5–7.

To find the opposite of the number in Example 4, we can write either $-6\frac{2}{3}$ or $-\frac{20}{3}$. Thus, to convert a negative mixed number to an improper fraction, we remove the negative sign for purposes of computation and then include it in the answer.

Examples Convert to improper fractions.

7. $-2\frac{3}{4} = -\frac{11}{4}$ $4 \cdot 2 = 8; 8 + 3 = 11;$ include the negative sign.

8. $-5\frac{1}{3} = -\frac{16}{3}$ $3 \cdot 5 = 15; 15 + 1 = 16;$ include the negative sign.

9. $-7\frac{5}{6} = -\frac{47}{6}$ $6 \cdot 7 = 42; 42 + 5 = 47;$ include the negative sign.

Do Margin Exercises 8 and 9.

Convert to an improper fraction.

3. $4\frac{2}{5}$

4. $6\frac{1}{10}$

Convert to improper fractions.

5. $4\frac{5}{6}$

6. $9\frac{1}{4}$

7. $20\frac{2}{3}$

Convert to improper fractions.

8. $-6\frac{2}{5}$

9. $-8\frac{3}{7}$

Convert to a mixed number.

10. $\dfrac{11}{10}$

11. $\dfrac{109}{6}$

c | Writing Mixed Numbers

Fractional symbols like $\dfrac{13}{5}$ also indicate division.

> ▶ To convert from fractional notation to a mixed number, divide.
>
> $$\dfrac{13}{5}; \quad 5\overline{)\begin{array}{r} 2 \\ 13 \\ \underline{10} \\ 3 \end{array}} \longrightarrow \text{The quotient}$$
>
> Now divide 3, the remainder, by 5.
>
> $2\dfrac{3}{5};$
>
> $\dfrac{13}{5} = 2\dfrac{3}{5}$

Examples   Convert to a mixed number.

10. $\dfrac{8}{5}$
$\quad 5\overline{)\begin{array}{r} 1 \\ 8 \\ \underline{5} \\ 3 \end{array}}$
So $\dfrac{8}{5} = 1\dfrac{3}{5}$

11. $\dfrac{69}{10}$
$\quad 10\overline{)\begin{array}{r} 6 \\ 69 \\ \underline{60} \\ 9 \end{array}}$
So $\dfrac{69}{10} = 6\dfrac{9}{10}$

12. $\dfrac{123}{8}$
$\quad 8\overline{)\begin{array}{r} 15 \\ 123 \\ \underline{80} \\ 43 \\ \underline{40} \\ 3 \end{array}}$
So $\dfrac{123}{8} = 15\dfrac{3}{8}$

Do Margin Exercises 10 and 11.

The same procedure also works with negative numbers. Of course, the result will be a negative mixed number.

Example 13   Convert $\dfrac{-9}{4}$ to a mixed number.

Since $\quad 4\overline{)\begin{array}{r} 2 \\ 9 \\ \underline{8} \\ 1 \end{array}}$, we have $\dfrac{9}{4} = 2\dfrac{1}{4}$.

Thus, $\dfrac{-9}{4} = -2\dfrac{1}{4}$.

Do Margin Exercises 12 and 13.

Convert to a mixed number.

12. $\dfrac{-12}{5}$

13. $-\dfrac{137}{12}$

d | Finding Mixed Numbers for Quotients

It is quite common when performing long division to express the quotient as a mixed number. As in Examples 10–13, the remainder becomes the numerator of the fractional part of the mixed number.

Example 14   Divide. Write a mixed number for the quotient.

$$7\overline{)6\,3\,4\,1}$$

We first divide as usual.

$$
\begin{array}{r}
9\,0\,5 \\
7\overline{)6\,3\,4\,1} \\
\underline{6\,3} \\
4\,1 \\
\underline{3\,5} \\
6
\end{array}
$$

The answer is 905 R 6. We write a mixed number for the answer as follows:

$$905\frac{6}{7}.$$

The division $6341 \div 7$ can be expressed as an improper fraction or as a mixed number:

$$\frac{6341}{7} = 905\frac{6}{7}.$$

Example 15   Divide. Write a mixed number for the answer.

$$-8915 \div 42$$

We first divide as usual.

$$
\begin{array}{r}
2\,1\,2 \\
42\overline{)8\,9\,1\,5} \\
\underline{8\,4} \\
5\,1 \\
\underline{4\,2} \\
9\,5 \\
\underline{8\,4} \\
1\,1
\end{array}
$$

We see that

$$\frac{8915}{42} = 212\frac{11}{42}.$$

Since 42 is really divided into *negative* 8915, the answer is $-212\frac{11}{42}$.

Do Margin Exercises 14 and 15.

Divide. Write a mixed number for the answer.

14. $6\overline{)4\,8\,4\,7}$

15. $-6053 \div 45$

Simplify. Assume $a \neq 0$.

16. $\dfrac{1}{1}$ **17.** $\dfrac{a}{a}$

18. $\dfrac{-34}{-34}$ **19.** $\dfrac{100}{100}$

20. $\dfrac{-2347}{-2347}$ **21.** $\dfrac{54a}{54a}$

Simplify, if possible. Assume $x \neq 0$.

22. $\dfrac{0}{2}$ **23.** $\dfrac{0}{-8}$

24. $\dfrac{0}{7x}$ **25.** $\dfrac{4-4}{236}$

26. $\dfrac{7}{0}$ **27.** $\dfrac{-4}{0}$

e Some Fractional Notation for Integers

Fractional Notation for 1

The number 1 corresponds to situations like the following.

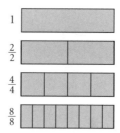

If we divide an object into n parts and take n of them, we get all of the object (1 whole object). Since a negative divided by a negative is a positive, the following is stated for *all* nonzero integers.

> $\dfrac{n}{n} = 1$, for any integer n that is not 0.

Examples   Simplify. Assume $x \neq 0$.

16. $\dfrac{5}{5} = 1$ **17.** $\dfrac{-9}{-9} = 1$ **18.** $\dfrac{17x}{17x} = 1$

Do Margin Exercises 16–21.

Fractional Notation for 0

Consider $\dfrac{0}{4}$. This corresponds to dividing an object into 4 parts and taking none of them. We get 0. This result also extends to all nonzero integers.

> $\dfrac{0}{n} = 0$, for any integer n that is not 0.

Examples   Simplify. Assume $a \neq 0$.

19. $\dfrac{0}{9} = 0$ **20.** $\dfrac{0}{1} = 0$

21. $\dfrac{0}{5a} = 0$ **22.** $\dfrac{0}{-23} = 0$

Fractional notation with a denominator of 0, such as $\dfrac{n}{0}$, is meaningless because we cannot speak of an object divided into *zero* parts. (If it is not divided at all, then we say that it is undivided and remains in one part.)

> $\dfrac{n}{0}$ is not defined.

Do Margin Exercises 22–27.

Other Integers

Consider $\frac{4}{1}$. This corresponds to taking 4 objects and dividing each into 1 part. (We do not divide them.) We have 4 objects.

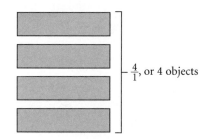

$\frac{4}{1}$, or 4 objects

▶ Any integer divided by 1 is the original integer. That is,

$$\frac{n}{1} = n, \text{ for any integer } n.$$

Examples Simplify.

23. $\dfrac{2}{1} = 2$ **24.** $\dfrac{-9}{1} = -9$ **25.** $\dfrac{3x}{1} = 3x$

Do Margin Exercises 28–31.

Simplify.

28. $\dfrac{8}{1}$

29. $\dfrac{-10}{1}$

30. $\dfrac{-346}{1}$

31. $\dfrac{-5x}{1}$

Exercise Set 4.1

a Identify as a proper fraction, improper fraction or mixed number.

1. $\dfrac{3}{8}$

2. $\dfrac{-2}{5}$

3. $1\dfrac{1}{5}$

4. $\dfrac{6}{5}$

5. $\dfrac{-7}{4}$

6. $8\dfrac{1}{3}$

7. $\dfrac{45}{53}$

8. $\dfrac{-19}{14}$

9. $12\dfrac{2}{7}$

10. $\dfrac{23}{12}$

11. $\dfrac{101}{122}$

12. $\dfrac{215}{116}$

13. $-118\dfrac{3}{8}$

14. $\dfrac{-123}{135}$

15. $-10\dfrac{7}{100}$

b Write as improper fractions.

16. $3\dfrac{2}{5}$

17. $5\dfrac{2}{3}$

18. $6\dfrac{1}{4}$

19. $8\dfrac{1}{2}$

20. $-20\dfrac{1}{8}$

21. $-10\dfrac{1}{3}$

22. $5\dfrac{1}{10}$

23. $8\dfrac{1}{10}$

24. $20\dfrac{3}{5}$

25. $30\dfrac{4}{5}$

26. $-9\dfrac{5}{6}$

27. $-8\dfrac{7}{8}$

28. $8\dfrac{3}{10}$

29. $6\dfrac{9}{10}$

30. $1\dfrac{3}{5}$

31. $1\dfrac{5}{8}$

32. $-12\dfrac{3}{4}$

33. $-15\dfrac{2}{3}$

34. $4\dfrac{3}{10}$

35. $5\dfrac{7}{10}$

36. $7\dfrac{3}{100}$

37. $-5\dfrac{7}{100}$

38. $-6\dfrac{4}{15}$

39. $4\dfrac{23}{50}$

c Convert to mixed numbers.

40. $\dfrac{17}{4}$

41. $\dfrac{18}{5}$

42. $\dfrac{14}{3}$

43. $\dfrac{19}{8}$

44. $\dfrac{-25}{6}$

45. $\dfrac{31}{9}$

46. $\dfrac{57}{10}$

47. $\dfrac{-89}{10}$

48. $\dfrac{53}{7}$

49. $\dfrac{65}{8}$

50. $\dfrac{47}{6}$

51. $\dfrac{-49}{8}$

52. $\dfrac{43}{4}$

53. $\dfrac{38}{9}$

54. $\dfrac{-11}{8}$

55. $\dfrac{29}{6}$

56. $\dfrac{757}{100}$

57. $\dfrac{467}{100}$

58. $-\dfrac{345}{8}$

59. $-\dfrac{223}{4}$

d Divide. Write a mixed number for the answer.

60. $8\overline{)869}$

61. $3\overline{)2126}$

62. $7\overline{)6345}$

63. $9\overline{)9110}$

64. $21\overline{)852}$

65. $85\overline{)7672}$

66. $102\overline{)5612}$

67. $46\overline{)1087}$

68. $-302 \div 15$

69. $-475 \div 13$

70. $472 \div (-21)$

71. $542 \div (-25)$

e Simplify, if possible. Assume all variables are nonzero.

72. $\dfrac{0}{5}$

73. $\dfrac{7}{7}$

74. $\dfrac{15}{1}$

75. $\dfrac{10}{1}$

76. $\dfrac{20}{20}$

77. $\dfrac{-20}{1}$

78. $\dfrac{-14}{-14}$

79. $\dfrac{4a}{1}$

80. $\dfrac{0}{-234}$

81. $\dfrac{37a}{37a}$

82. $\dfrac{3n}{3n}$

83. $\dfrac{0}{-1}$

84. $\dfrac{9x}{9x}$

85. $\dfrac{56}{56}$

86. $\dfrac{-63}{1}$

87. $\dfrac{-3x}{-3x}$

88. $\dfrac{0}{2a}$

89. $\dfrac{0}{8}$

90. $\dfrac{52}{0}$

91. $\dfrac{8-8}{1247}$

92. $\dfrac{7n}{1}$

93. $\dfrac{247}{0}$

94. $\dfrac{6}{7-7}$

95. $\dfrac{15}{9-9}$

Skill Maintenance

Multiply.

96. $-7(30)$

97. $23 \cdot (-14)$

98. $(-71)(-12)0$

99. $32(-29)0$

100. The average annual income of people living in Alaska is $21,932 per person. In Colorado, the average annual income is $19,440. How much more do people in Alaska make, on average, than those living in Colorado?

101. Sandy can type 62 words per minute. How long will it take Sandy to type 12,462 words?

Synthesis

102. ❖ Describe in your own words a method for rewriting an improper fraction as a mixed number.

103. ❖ Describe in your own words a method for rewriting a mixed number as a fraction.

Write a mixed number.

104. There are $\frac{366}{7}$ weeks in a leap year.

105. There are $\frac{365}{7}$ weeks in a year.

106. ❖ Explain in your own words why $\frac{0}{n} = 0$, for any natural number n.

107. ❖ Explain in your own words why $\frac{n}{n} = 1$, for any natural number n.

108. The surface of the earth is 3 parts water and 1 part land. What fractional part of the earth is water? land?

109. A couple had 3 boys, each of whom had three daughters. If each daughter gave birth to 3 sons, what fractional part of the couple's descendants is female?

1. Find $2 \cdot \dfrac{1}{3}$.

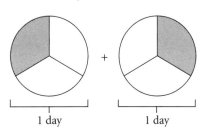

2. Find $5 \cdot \dfrac{1}{8}$.

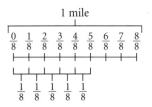

Multiply.

3. $5 \cdot \dfrac{2}{3}$

4. $(-11) \cdot \dfrac{3}{8}$

5. $23 \cdot \dfrac{2}{5}$

6. $x \cdot \dfrac{4}{9}$

4.2 Multiplication

a Multiplication by an Integer

We can find $3 \cdot \dfrac{1}{4}$ by thinking of repeated addition. We add three $\dfrac{1}{4}$'s.

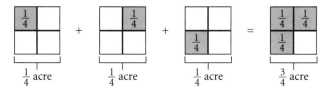

We see that $3 \cdot \dfrac{1}{4} = \dfrac{1}{4} + \dfrac{1}{4} + \dfrac{1}{4} = \dfrac{3}{4}$.

Do Margin Exercises 1 and 2.

▶ To multiply a fraction by a whole number,

   a. write the whole number as a fraction,

   b. multiply the numerators, and

$$6 \cdot \dfrac{4}{5} = \dfrac{6}{1} \cdot \dfrac{4}{5} = \dfrac{6 \cdot 4}{1 \cdot 5} = \dfrac{24}{5}$$

   c. multiply the denominators.

Examples Multiply.

1. $5 \cdot \dfrac{3}{8} = \dfrac{5}{1} \cdot \dfrac{3}{8} = \dfrac{5 \cdot 3}{1 \cdot 8} = \dfrac{15}{8}$

     | Skip this step when you feel comfortable doing so. |

2. $\dfrac{2}{5} \cdot 13 = \dfrac{2}{5} \cdot \dfrac{13}{1} = \dfrac{2 \cdot 13}{5 \cdot 1} = \dfrac{26}{5}$

3. $-10 \cdot \dfrac{1}{3} = \dfrac{-10}{1} \cdot \dfrac{1}{3} = \dfrac{-10}{3}$, or $-\dfrac{10}{3}$ Recall that $\dfrac{-a}{b} = -\dfrac{a}{b}$.

4. $a \cdot \dfrac{4}{7} = \dfrac{a}{1} \cdot \dfrac{4}{7} = \dfrac{4a}{7}$ Recall that $a \cdot 4 = 4 \cdot a$.

Do Margin Exercises 3–6.

b | Multiplication Using Fractional Notation

We find a product such as $\frac{9}{7} \cdot \frac{3}{4}$ as follows.

> To multiply a fraction by a fraction,
>
> **a.** multiply the numerators, and
>
> **b.** multiply the denominators.
>
> $$\frac{9}{7} \cdot \frac{3}{4} = \frac{9 \cdot 3}{7 \cdot 4} = \frac{27}{28}$$

Examples Multiply.

5. $\frac{5}{6} \cdot \frac{7}{4} = \frac{5 \cdot 7}{6 \cdot 4} = \frac{35}{24}$

> Skip this step when you feel comfortable doing so.

6. $\frac{3}{5} \cdot \frac{7}{8} = \frac{3 \cdot 7}{5 \cdot 8} = \frac{21}{40}$

7. $\frac{4}{3} \cdot \frac{y}{9} = \frac{4y}{27}$

8. $(-6)\left(-\frac{4}{5}\right) = \frac{-6}{1} \cdot \frac{-4}{5} = \frac{24}{5}$

Do Margin Exercises 7–10.

Unless one of the factors is a whole number, multiplication of fractions is hard to imagine as repeated addition. Let us see how multiplication of fractions corresponds to situations in the real world. We consider the multiplication

$$\frac{1}{2} \text{ of } \frac{3}{4}$$

We first consider some object and take $\frac{3}{4}$ of it. We divide it into 4 parts and take 3 of them. That is shown in the shading below.

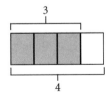

Multiply.

7. $\frac{3}{8} \cdot \frac{5}{7}$

8. $\frac{4}{3} \cdot \frac{8}{5}$

9. $\left(-\frac{3}{10}\right)\left(-\frac{1}{10}\right)$

10. $(-7)\left(\frac{a}{3}\right)$

Next, we take $\frac{1}{2}$ of the result. We divide the same shaded part into 2 parts and take 1 of them. That is shown below as the heavily shaded region.

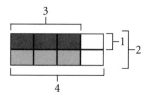

The entire object has been divided into 8 parts, of which 3 have been shaded heavily and 3 have been shaded lightly.

$$\frac{1}{2} \cdot \frac{3}{4} = \frac{1 \cdot 3}{2 \cdot 4} = \frac{3}{8}.$$

The figure above shows a rectangular array inside a rectangular array. The number of pieces in the entire array is $4 \cdot 2$ (the product of the denominators). The number of pieces shaded heavily is $1 \cdot 3$ (the product of the numerators). For the answer, we take 3 pieces out of a set of 8 to get $\frac{3}{8}$. We have shown that $\frac{1}{2}$ of $\frac{3}{4}$ corresponds to the multiplication $\frac{1}{2} \cdot \frac{3}{4}$.

c Solving Problems

Most problems that can be solved by multiplying fractions can be thought of in terms of rectangular arrays.

Example 9   A couple owns a square mile of land. They give $\frac{3}{5}$ of it to their daughter and she gives $\frac{1}{2}$ of her share to her son. How much land goes to the son?

1. *Familiarize.* We draw a picture to help solve the problem. The land may not be square. It could be in a shape like A or B below, or it could even be in more than one piece. But to visualize the problem, we can think of it as a square, as shown by shape C.

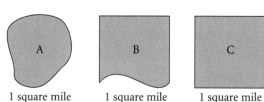

1 square mile   1 square mile   1 square mile

The daughter gets $\frac{3}{5}$ of the land. We shade her part $\frac{3}{5}$.

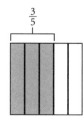

Her son gets $\frac{1}{2}$ of her part. We shade his part darker.

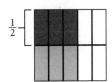

2. Translate. We let n = the amount of land that goes to the son. When we are taking "one-half of three-fifths," the word "of" corresponds to multiplication. Thus the following multiplication sentence corresponds to the situation:

$$n = \frac{1}{2} \cdot \frac{3}{5}$$

3. Solve. The number sentence tells us to multiply:

$$n = \frac{1}{2} \cdot \frac{3}{5}$$

$$n = \frac{3}{10}$$

4. Check. To check, note that 3 of the 10 parts in the above figure have been heavily shaded. The son's portion $(\frac{3}{10})$ is less than his mother's original portion $(\frac{3}{5})$.

5. State. The son gets $\frac{3}{10}$ of a square mile of land.

Do Margin Exercise 11.

We have seen that the area of a rectangular region is found by multiplying length by width. This is true whether length and width are whole numbers or not. Remember, the area of a rectangular region is given by the formula

$$A = l \cdot w \quad (Area = length \cdot width).$$

Example 10 The length of a rectangular button on a calculator is $\frac{7}{10}$ cm (centimeter). The width is $\frac{3}{10}$ cm. What is the area?

1. Familiarize. Recall that area is length times width. We draw a picture, letting A = the area of the calculator key.

2. Translate. Next we translate.

Area	is	Length	times	Width
↓	↓	↓	↓	↓
A	=	$\frac{7}{10}$	$\cdot$	$\frac{3}{10}$

$\frac{3}{10}$ cm

$\frac{7}{10}$ cm

3. Solve. The sentence tells us what to multiply:

$$A = \frac{7}{10} \cdot \frac{3}{10}$$

$$A = \frac{21}{100}$$

11. A resort uses $\frac{3}{8}$ of its land for recreational purposes. Of that, $\frac{1}{2}$ is used for a ski slope. What part of the land is used for the ski slope?

12. The length of a button on a fax machine is $\frac{9}{10}$ cm. The width is $\frac{7}{10}$ cm. What is the area?

13. Of the students at Overton Community College, $\frac{1}{8}$ participate in sports and $\frac{3}{5}$ of these play soccer. What fractional part of the student body plays soccer?

4. Check. *To* check, we can repeat the calculation or draw a grid, as in Example 9. This is left to the student.

5. State. The area of the key is $\frac{21}{100}$ cm².

Do Margin Exercise 12.

Example 11 A cornbread recipe calls for $\frac{3}{4}$ cup of cornmeal. A chef is making $\frac{1}{2}$ of the recipe. How much cornmeal will the chef need?

1. Familiarize. We draw a picture or at least visualize the situation. We let n = *the* amount of cornmeal the chef will need.

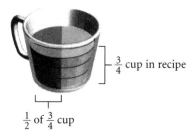

$\frac{3}{4}$ cup in recipe

$\frac{1}{2}$ of $\frac{3}{4}$ cup

2. Translate. The multiplication sentence $\frac{1}{2} \cdot \frac{3}{4} = n$ corresponds to the situation.

3. Solve. We carry out the multiplication:

$$n = \frac{1}{2} \cdot \frac{3}{4}$$

$$n = \frac{3}{8}$$

4. Check. To check, we can determine what fractional part of the drawing has been heavily shaded. This is left to the student.

5. State. The chef will need $\frac{3}{8}$ cup of cornmeal.

Do Margin Exercise 13.

Exercise Set 4.2

a Multiply.

1. $3 \cdot \frac{1}{5}$

2. $2 \cdot \frac{1}{3}$

3. $(-5) \cdot \frac{1}{6}$

4. $(-4) \cdot \frac{1}{7}$

5. $\frac{2}{3} \cdot 7$

6. $\frac{2}{5} \cdot 6$

7. $(-1)\frac{7}{9}$

8. $(-1)\frac{4}{11}$

9. $\frac{2}{5} \cdot x$

10. $\frac{3}{8} \cdot y$

11. $\frac{2}{5}(-3)$

12. $\frac{3}{5}(-4)$

13. $a \cdot \frac{3}{4}$

14. $b \cdot \frac{2}{5}$

15. $17 \cdot \frac{m}{6}$

16. $\frac{n}{7} \cdot 40$

b Multiply.

17. $\frac{1}{2} \cdot \frac{1}{3}$

18. $\frac{1}{4} \cdot \frac{1}{5}$

19. $\left(-\frac{1}{4}\right) \cdot \frac{1}{10}$

20. $\left(-\frac{1}{3}\right) \cdot \frac{1}{10}$

21. $\frac{2}{3} \cdot \frac{1}{5}$

22. $\frac{3}{5} \cdot \frac{1}{5}$

23. $\frac{2}{y} \cdot \frac{x}{5}$

24. $\left(-\frac{3}{4}\right)\left(-\frac{3}{5}\right)$

25. $\left(-\frac{3}{4}\right)\left(-\frac{3}{4}\right)$

26. $\frac{3}{b} \cdot \frac{a}{7}$

27. $\frac{2}{3} \cdot \frac{7}{13}$

28. $\frac{3}{11} \cdot \frac{4}{5}$

29. $\frac{1}{10}\left(-\frac{7}{10}\right)$

30. $\frac{3}{10}\left(-\frac{3}{10}\right)$

31. $\frac{7}{8} \cdot \frac{a}{8}$

32. $\frac{4}{5} \cdot \frac{4}{b}$

33. $\frac{1}{y} \cdot \frac{1}{100}$

34. $\frac{x}{10} \cdot \frac{7}{100}$

35. $\frac{-14}{15} \cdot \frac{13}{19}$

36. $\frac{-12}{13} \cdot \frac{12}{13}$

37. A rectangular cutting board is $\frac{4}{5}$ m long and $\frac{3}{5}$ in wide. What is its area?

38. If each piece of pie is $\frac{1}{6}$ of a pie, how much of the pie is $\frac{1}{2}$ of a piece?

39. A kerosene lamp holds $\frac{5}{8}$ liter of fuel. How much will it hold when it is $\frac{1}{2}$ full?

40. One out of every 15 high school students who go on to college aspires to be a professional actor or musician. One out of 200 college students becomes a professional actor or musician. What fraction of high school students who go on to college become professional actors or musicians?

41. A recipe for a batch of granola calls for $\frac{2}{3}$ cup of molasses. How much molasses is needed to make $\frac{3}{4}$ of a batch?

42. It takes $\frac{2}{3}$ yard of silk to make a bow. How much silk is needed for 5 bows?

43. Out of every 3 tons of municipal waste, 2 tons are dumped in landfills. Of the waste that goes into landfills, $\frac{1}{10}$ is yard trimmings. What fractional part of municipal waste is yard trimmings?

44. Out of every 3 tons of waste that is dumped in landfills, 1 ton is paper and paperboard. If $\frac{2}{3}$ of all municipal waste is landfilled, what fractional part of municipal waste is paper and paperboard that is landfilled?

Skill Maintenance

Simplify.

45. $5 - 3^2$

46. $(5 - 3)^2$

47. $8 \cdot 12 - (7 + 13)$

48. $8 \cdot 12 - 7 + 13$

49. What does the digit 6 mean in 4,678,952?

50. What does the digit 4 mean in 4,678,952?

Synthesis

Multiply. Write the answer using fractional notation.

51. ❖ When calculating the number of buses required to take a group of children to a local amusement park, the organizers calculated $2\frac{1}{2}$ buses. Does this answer make sense? Explain why or why not.

52. ❖ You are helping a student learn how to estimate what the result of $(24)(15)$ should be. Explain how you would go about estimating this.

53. $\left(\frac{1}{3}\right)^2\left(\frac{3}{5}\right)$

54. $\left(\frac{-2}{3}\right)^2\left(\frac{1}{4}\right)$

55. $\left(\frac{2}{5}\right)^3\left(-\frac{7}{9}\right)$

56. $\left(-\frac{1}{2}\right)^5\left(\frac{3}{5}\right)$

57. Evaluate $-\frac{2}{3}xy$ for $x = \frac{2}{5}$ and $y = -\frac{1}{7}$.

Multiply.

1. $\dfrac{1}{2} \cdot \dfrac{8}{8}$ **2.** $\dfrac{3}{5} \cdot \dfrac{x}{x}$

3. $-\dfrac{13}{25} \cdot \dfrac{4}{4}$ **4.** $\dfrac{8}{3}\left(\dfrac{-2}{-2}\right)$

Find another name for the number, but with the denominator indicated. Use multiplying by 1.

5. $\dfrac{4}{3} = \dfrac{?}{9}$ **6.** $\dfrac{3}{4} = \dfrac{?}{-24}$

7. $\dfrac{9}{10} = \dfrac{?}{10x}$ **8.** $\dfrac{3}{15} = \dfrac{?}{45}$

9. $\dfrac{-8}{7} = \dfrac{?}{49}$

4.3 Simplifying

a Multiplying by 1

Recall the following:

$$1 = \frac{1}{1} = \frac{2}{2} = \frac{3}{3} = \frac{4}{4} = \frac{-13}{-13} = \frac{45}{45} = \frac{100}{100} = \frac{n}{n}$$

Any nonzero number divided by itself is 1.

> ▶ When we multiply a number by 1, we get the same number.
>
> $$\frac{3}{5} = \frac{3}{5} \cdot 1 = \frac{3}{5} \cdot \frac{4}{4} = \frac{12}{20}$$

Since $\frac{3}{5} \cdot 1 = \frac{12}{20}$, we know that $\frac{3}{5}$ and $\frac{12}{20}$ are two names for the same number. We also say that $\frac{3}{5}$ and $\frac{12}{20}$ are **equivalent.**

Do Margin Exercises 1–4.

Suppose we want to rename $\frac{2}{3}$, using a denominator of 15. We can multiply by 1 to find equivalent fractions:

$$\frac{2}{3} = \frac{2}{3} \cdot \frac{5}{5} = \frac{2 \cdot 5}{3 \cdot 5} = \frac{10}{15}.$$

We chose $\frac{5}{5}$ for 1 because $15 \div 3$ is 5.

Example 1 Find a name for $\frac{1}{4}$, with a denominator of 24.

Since $24 \div 4 = 6$, we multiply by 1, using $\frac{6}{6}$:

$$\frac{1}{4} = \frac{1}{4} \cdot \frac{6}{6} = \frac{1 \cdot 6}{4 \cdot 6} = \frac{6}{24}.$$

Example 2 Find a name for $\frac{2}{5}$ with a denominator of –35.

Since $-35 \div 5 = -7$, we multiply by 1, using $\frac{-7}{-7}$:

$$\frac{2}{5} = \frac{2}{5}\left(\frac{-7}{-7}\right) = \frac{2(-7)}{5(-7)} = \frac{-14}{-35}.$$

Example 3 Find a name for $\frac{9}{8}$ with a denominator of $8a$.

Since $8a \div 8 = a$, we multiply by 1, using $\frac{a}{a}$, as long as a is not equal to 0 $(a \neq 0)$.

$$\frac{9}{8} \cdot \frac{a}{a} = \frac{9a}{8a}.$$

Do Margin Exercises 5–9.

b Simplifying

All of the following are names for three-fourths:

$$\frac{3}{4}, \frac{-6}{-8}, \frac{9}{12}, \frac{12}{16}, \frac{-15}{-20}.$$

We say that $\frac{3}{4}$ is *simplest* because it has the smallest positive denominator.

To simplify, we reverse the process of multiplying by 1. This is accomplished by removing any factors that the numerator and the denominator have in common.

$$\frac{12}{18} = \frac{2 \cdot 6}{3 \cdot 6} \qquad \text{Factoring the numerator}$$
$$\text{Factoring the denominator}$$

$$= \frac{2}{3} \cdot \frac{6}{6} \qquad \text{Factoring the fraction}$$

> Note that 6 is the *greatest common factor* of 12 and 18.

$$= \frac{2}{3} \cdot 1 \qquad \frac{6}{6} = 1$$

$$= \frac{2}{3} \qquad \text{Removing a factor of 1: } \frac{2}{3} \cdot 1 = \frac{2}{3}$$

Examples Simplify.

4. $\dfrac{-8}{20} = \dfrac{-2 \cdot 4}{5 \cdot 4} = \dfrac{-2}{5} \cdot \dfrac{4}{4} = \dfrac{-2}{5}$

5. $\dfrac{2}{6} = \dfrac{1 \cdot 2}{3 \cdot 2} = \dfrac{1}{3} \cdot \dfrac{2}{2} = \dfrac{1}{3}$

> The number 1 allows for pairing of factors in the numerator and the denominator.

6. $\dfrac{30}{6} = \dfrac{5 \cdot 6}{1 \cdot 6} = \dfrac{5}{1} \cdot \dfrac{6}{6} = \dfrac{5}{1} = 5$

> We could also simplify $\frac{30}{6}$ by doing the division $30 \div 6$. That is, $\frac{30}{6} = 30 \div 6 = 5$.

7. $-\dfrac{15}{10} = -\dfrac{3 \cdot 5}{2 \cdot 5} = -\dfrac{3}{2} \cdot \dfrac{5}{5} = -\dfrac{3}{2}$

8. $\dfrac{3x}{7x} = \dfrac{3 \cdot x}{7 \cdot x} = \dfrac{3}{7} \cdot \dfrac{x}{x} = \dfrac{3}{7}$ $(x \neq 0)$

Do Margin Exercises 10–14.

Simplify.

10. $\dfrac{2}{8}$

11. $\dfrac{-10}{12}$

12. $\dfrac{40}{8}$

13. $\dfrac{4a}{3a}$

14. $-\dfrac{50}{30}$

Simplify.

15. $\dfrac{35}{40}$

16. $\dfrac{801}{702}$

17. $\dfrac{-24}{21}$

18. $-\dfrac{75}{300}$

Prime factorizations can be especially helpful if a fraction contains large numbers.

Example 9 Simplify: $\dfrac{90}{84}$

$$\dfrac{90}{84} = \dfrac{2 \cdot 3 \cdot 3 \cdot 5}{2 \cdot 2 \cdot 3 \cdot 7}$$ Factoring the numerator and the denominator into primes

$$= \dfrac{2 \cdot 3 \cdot 3 \cdot 5}{2 \cdot 3 \cdot 2 \cdot 7}$$ Rearranging so that like primes are above and below each other.

$$= \dfrac{2}{2} \cdot \dfrac{3}{3} \cdot \dfrac{3 \cdot 5}{2 \cdot 7}$$ Factoring the fraction

$$= 1 \cdot 1 \cdot \dfrac{3 \cdot 5}{2 \cdot 7}$$ Recall that $\frac{n}{n} = 1$, for $n \neq 0$.

$$= \dfrac{3 \cdot 5}{2 \cdot 7}$$ Removing the factors $1 \cdot 1$

$$= \dfrac{15}{14}$$

The tests for divisibility are also helpful when simplifying.

$$\dfrac{90}{84} = \dfrac{90 \div 6}{84 \div 6}$$ Since 90 and 84 are both divisible by 2 and 3, they are also divisible by 6.

$$= \dfrac{15}{14}$$

Example 10 Simplify: $\dfrac{105}{135}$

Since both 105 and 135 end in 5, we know that 5 is a factor of both the numerator and the denominator:

$$\dfrac{105}{135} = \dfrac{21 \cdot 5}{27 \cdot 5} = \dfrac{21}{27} \cdot \dfrac{5}{5} = \dfrac{21}{27}$$

A fraction is not "simplified" if common factors of the numerator and the denominator remain. Because 21 and 27 are both divisible by 3, we simplify further:

$$\dfrac{105}{135} = \dfrac{21}{27} = \dfrac{7 \cdot 3}{9 \cdot 3} = \dfrac{7}{9} \cdot \dfrac{3}{3} = \dfrac{7}{9}$$

or using divisibility rules

$$\dfrac{105}{135} = \dfrac{105 \div 5}{135 \div 5}$$

$$= \dfrac{21}{27}$$

$$= \dfrac{21 \div 3}{27 \div 3}$$

$$= \dfrac{7}{9}$$

Do Margin Exercises 15–18.

Canceling

Canceling is a shortcut that you may have used for removing a factor of 1 when working with fractional notation. With *great* concern, we mention it as a way of speeding up your work. Canceling may be done only when removing common factors in numerators and denominators. Each common factor allows us to remove a factor of 1 in a product. In effect, slashes are used to indicate factors of 1 that have been removed. Canceling cannot be done in sums. Our concern is that canceling be done with care and understanding. With canceling, Example 9 might have been written as follows:

$$\frac{90}{84} = \frac{2 \cdot 3 \cdot 3 \cdot 5}{2 \cdot 2 \cdot 3 \cdot 7}$$
Factoring the numerator and the denominator

$$= \frac{\cancel{2} \cdot \cancel{3} \cdot 3 \cdot 5}{\cancel{2} \cdot 2 \cdot \cancel{3} \cdot 7}$$
When a factor equal to 1 is noted, it is "canceled" as shown: $\frac{2 \cdot 3}{2 \cdot 3} = 1$.

$$= \frac{3 \cdot 5}{2 \cdot 7} = \frac{15}{14}$$

CAUTION! The difficulty with canceling is that it is often applied incorrectly in situations like the following:

$$\frac{5}{2} = \frac{\cancel{2} + 3}{\cancel{2}} = 3; \quad \frac{5}{6} = \frac{\cancel{4} + 1}{\cancel{4} + 2} = \frac{1}{2}; \quad \frac{15}{54} = \frac{1\cancel{5}}{\cancel{5}4} = \frac{1}{4}.$$

wrong   wrong   wrong

Clearly, $\frac{5}{2} \neq 3$. Similarly, $\frac{5}{6} \neq \frac{1}{2}$, and $\frac{15}{54} \neq \frac{1}{4}$. In each situation, the numbers canceled did not form a factor equal to 1. Factors are parts of products. For example, in $2 \cdot 3$, the numbers 2 and 3 are factors, but in $2 + 3$, the numbers 2 and 3 are terms, not factors.

▶ **If you cannot factor, do not cancel! If in doubt, do not cancel!**

Exercise Set 4.3

a Find another name for the given number, with the denominator indicated. Use multiplying by 1.

1. $\dfrac{1}{2} = \dfrac{?}{10}$

2. $\dfrac{1}{6} = \dfrac{?}{12}$

3. $\dfrac{3}{4} = \dfrac{?}{-48}$

4. $\dfrac{2}{9} = \dfrac{?}{-18}$

5. $\dfrac{9}{10} = \dfrac{?}{30}$

6. $\dfrac{3}{8} = \dfrac{?}{48}$

7. $\dfrac{11}{5} = \dfrac{?}{30}$

8. $\dfrac{5}{3} = \dfrac{?}{45}$

9. $\dfrac{5}{12} = \dfrac{?}{48}$

10. $\dfrac{7}{8} = \dfrac{?}{56}$

11. $-\dfrac{17}{18} = -\dfrac{?}{54}$

12. $-\dfrac{11}{16} = -\dfrac{?}{256}$

13. $\dfrac{2}{-5} = \dfrac{?}{-25}$

14. $\dfrac{7}{-8} = \dfrac{?}{-32}$

15. $\dfrac{-7}{22} = \dfrac{?}{132}$

16. $\dfrac{-10}{21} = \dfrac{?}{126}$

17. $\dfrac{5}{8} = \dfrac{?}{8x}$

18. $\dfrac{2}{7} = \dfrac{?}{7a}$

19. $\dfrac{7}{11} = \dfrac{?}{11m}$

20. $\dfrac{4}{3} = \dfrac{?}{3n}$

21. $\dfrac{4}{9} = \dfrac{?}{27b}$

22. $\dfrac{8}{11} = \dfrac{?}{55y}$

Simplify.

23. $\dfrac{2}{4}$

24. $\dfrac{3}{6}$

25. $\dfrac{-6}{8}$

26. $\dfrac{-9}{12}$

27. $\dfrac{3}{15}$

28. $\dfrac{8}{10}$

29. $\dfrac{24}{-8}$

30. $\dfrac{36}{-4}$

31. $\dfrac{27}{36}$

32. $\dfrac{30}{40}$

33. $-\dfrac{12}{10}$

34. $-\dfrac{16}{14}$

35. $\dfrac{16}{48}$

36. $\dfrac{150}{25}$

37. $\dfrac{-17}{51}$

38. $\dfrac{-425}{525}$

39. $\dfrac{420}{480}$

40. $\dfrac{180}{240}$

41. $\dfrac{5m}{7m}$

42. $\dfrac{3n}{10n}$

Skill Maintenance

43. A soccer field is 90 yd long and 40 yd wide. What is its area?

44. Yardbird Landscaping buys 13 maple saplings and 17 oak saplings for a project. A maple costs $23 and an oak costs $37. How much is spent altogether for the saplings?

Solve.

45. $30x = 150$

46. $5280 = 1780 + t$

Synthesis

47. ❖ Explain in your own words when it is possible to cancel and when it is not possible to cancel.

48. ❖ Can a fraction be simplified if its numerator and its denominator are two different prime numbers? Why or why not?

49. Sociologists have found that 4 out of 10 people are shy. Write fractional notation for the part of the population that is shy; the part that is not shy. Simplify.

50. Sociologists estimate that 3 out of 20 people are left-handed. In a crowd of 460 people, how many would you expect to be left-handed?

51. The circle graph below shows how high school students rate their schools' ability to teach study habits. What portion of students gave a rating of "fair"? Simplify.

52. The circle graph below shows how long shoppers stay when visiting a mail. What portion of shoppers stay for 2 hr or less?

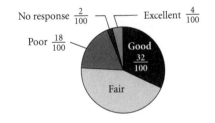

53. Andrea earned $2700 one summer. During the following semester, she spent $1200 for tuition, $540 for rent, and $360 for food. The rest went for miscellaneous expenses. What part of the income went for tuition? rent? food? miscellaneous expenses?

4.4 Multiplying, Simplifying, and More with Area

a Simplifying When Multiplying

We usually want a simplified answer when we multiply. To make such simplifying easier, it is generally best not to calculate the products in the numerator and the denominator until we have first factored and simplified. Consider

$$\frac{3}{8} \cdot \frac{4}{15}$$

We proceed as follows:

$$\frac{3}{8} \cdot \frac{4}{15} = \frac{3 \cdot 4}{8 \cdot 15} \quad \text{We write the products in the numerator and the denominator, but do not carry out the multiplication.}$$

$$= \frac{3 \cdot 2 \cdot 2}{2 \cdot 2 \cdot 2 \cdot 3 \cdot 5} \quad \text{Factoring the numerator and the denominator}$$

$$= \frac{\overset{1}{\cancel{3}} \cdot \overset{1}{\cancel{2}} \cdot \overset{1}{\cancel{2}}}{2 \cdot \underset{1}{\cancel{2}} \cdot \underset{1}{\cancel{2}} \cdot \underset{1}{\cancel{3}} \cdot 5} \quad \text{Cancelling like factors.}$$

$$= \frac{1}{10}$$

The procedure could have been shortened had we noticed that 4 is a factor of the 8 and 3 is a factor of 15:

$$\frac{3}{8} \cdot \frac{4}{15} = \frac{\overset{1}{\cancel{3}}}{\underset{2}{\cancel{8}}} \cdot \frac{\overset{1}{\cancel{4}}}{\underset{5}{\cancel{15}}} = \frac{1 \cdot 1}{2 \cdot 5} = \frac{1}{10}$$

> To multiply and simplify:
>
> **a)** Write the products in the numerator and the denominator, but do not calculate the products.
>
> **b)** Factor the numerator and the denominator.
>
> **c)** Cancel common factors in the numerator and the denominator.
>
> **d)** Calculate the remaining products.

Examples Canceling can be used as follows for these examples.

1. $\dfrac{2}{3} \cdot \dfrac{5}{4} = \dfrac{\overset{1}{\cancel{2}}}{3} \cdot \dfrac{5}{\underset{2}{\cancel{4}}} = \dfrac{5}{6}$

2. $\dfrac{6}{7} \cdot \dfrac{-5}{3} = \dfrac{\overset{2}{\cancel{6}}}{7} \cdot \dfrac{-5}{\underset{1}{\cancel{3}}} = \dfrac{-10}{7}$

3. $\dfrac{2}{3} \cdot \dfrac{3a}{10} = \dfrac{\overset{1}{\cancel{2}}}{\underset{1}{\cancel{3}}} \cdot \dfrac{\overset{1}{\cancel{3}}a}{\underset{5}{\cancel{10}}} = \dfrac{a}{5}$

4. $40 \cdot \dfrac{7}{8} = \dfrac{\overset{5}{\cancel{40}}}{1} \cdot \dfrac{7}{\underset{1}{\cancel{8}}} = \dfrac{35}{1} = 35$

5. $\dfrac{2}{3} \cdot \dfrac{6}{7} \cdot \dfrac{5}{8} = \dfrac{\overset{1}{\cancel{2}}}{\underset{1}{\cancel{3}}} \cdot \dfrac{\overset{2}{\cancel{6}}}{7} \cdot \dfrac{5}{\underset{4}{\cancel{8}}}$

$\qquad\qquad = \dfrac{\overset{1}{\cancel{2}} \cdot 5}{7 \cdot \underset{2}{\cancel{4}}}$ Sometimes additional cancellation is necessary.

$\qquad\qquad = \dfrac{5}{14}$

REMEMBER! If you can't factor, you can't cancel!

Do Margin Exercises 1–5.

b | Solving Problems

Example 6 Subway sells subs by the foot. If one serving is $\frac{2}{3}$ ft long, how many feet will be needed to serve 30 people?

1. *Familiarize.* We first draw a picture or at least visualize the situation. Repeated addition will work here.

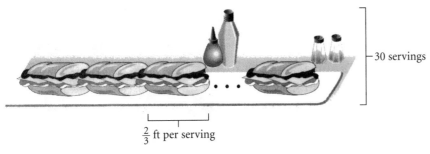

30 servings

$\frac{2}{3}$ ft per serving

We let n = the number of feet of sub needed. To estimate, we note that since it takes less than 1 foot to serve 1 person, it should take less than 30 feet of sub to feed 30 people.

2. *Translate.* The problem translates to the following equation:

$$n = 30 \cdot \dfrac{2}{3}$$

3. *Solve.* To solve the equation, we carry out the multiplication:

$$n = \dfrac{30}{1} \cdot \dfrac{2}{3}$$

$$n = \dfrac{\overset{10}{\cancel{30}}}{1} \cdot \dfrac{2}{\underset{1}{\cancel{3}}}$$

$$n = \dfrac{20}{1}$$

$$n = 20$$

Multiply and simplify.

1. $\dfrac{2}{3} \cdot \dfrac{7}{8}$

2. $\dfrac{4}{5} \cdot \dfrac{-5}{12}$

3. $16 \cdot \dfrac{3}{8}$

4. $\dfrac{5}{2x} \cdot 6$

5. $\dfrac{4}{5} \cdot \dfrac{5}{9} \cdot \dfrac{3}{8}$

6. Yardbird Landscaping uses $\frac{2}{5}$ lb of peat moss for a rosebush. How much will be needed for 25 rosebushes?

4. *Check.* Our answer (20) is less than 30, which meets our expectation from Step 1.

$$20 = 30 \cdot \frac{2}{3}$$

The number 20 checks

5. *State.* Thus, a 20-ft long sub will be needed.

Do Margin Exercise 6.

Area

Multiplication of fractions also occurs when we are solving problems involving the area of a triangle. Consider a triangle with a base of length b and a height of h, as shown.

A rectangle can be formed by splitting and inverting a copy of this triangle:

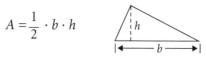

The rectangle's area, $b \cdot h$, is exactly twice the area of the triangle. We have the following result.

> ▶ The area A of a triangle is half the length of the base b times the height h:
>
> $$A = \frac{1}{2} \cdot b \cdot h$$

Example 7 Find the area of this triangle.

$A = \dfrac{1}{2} \cdot b \cdot h$

$A = \dfrac{1}{2} \cdot 9\text{m} \cdot 6\text{m}$

$A = \dfrac{1}{2} \cdot \dfrac{9}{1} \cdot \dfrac{6}{1} \cdot \text{m} \cdot \text{m}$

$A = \dfrac{1}{\underset{1}{2}} \cdot \dfrac{9}{1} \cdot \dfrac{\overset{3}{6}}{1} \cdot \text{m}^2$

$A = \dfrac{27}{1} \text{ m}^2$

$A = 27\text{m}^2$

> *Note:* When multiplying measurements,
> unit · unit = unit².
> Therefore, m · m = m².

Example 8 Find the area of this triangle.

$A = \dfrac{1}{2} \cdot b \cdot h$

$A = \dfrac{1}{2} \cdot \dfrac{10}{3} \text{ cm} \cdot 4 \text{ cm}$

$A = \dfrac{1}{2} \cdot \dfrac{10}{3} \cdot \dfrac{4}{1} \cdot \text{cm} \cdot \text{cm}$

$A = \dfrac{1}{\underset{1}{2}} \cdot \dfrac{\overset{5}{10}}{3} \cdot \dfrac{4}{1} \cdot \text{cm}^2$

$A = \dfrac{20}{3} \text{ cm}^2 \text{ or } 6\dfrac{2}{3} \text{ cm}^2$

Do Margin Exercises 7 and 8.

Find the area.

7.

8.

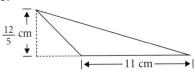

9. Find the area.

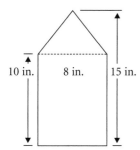

10 in.   8 in.   15 in.

Example 9 Find the area of this kite.

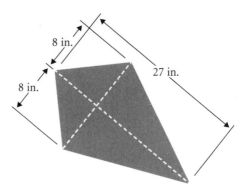

8 in.

8 in.

27 in.

1. *Familiarize.* We look for the kinds of figures whose areas we can calculate using area formulas that we already know.

2. *Translate.* The kite consists of two long triangles, each with a base of 27 in. and a height of 8 in. We can apply the formula $a = \frac{1}{2} \cdot b \cdot h$ for the area of a triangle and then multiply by 2.

3. *Solve.* We have

$$A = \frac{1}{2} \cdot 27 \text{ in.} \cdot 8 \text{ in.}$$

$$A = \frac{1}{2} \cdot \frac{27}{1} \cdot \frac{8}{1} \text{ in.} \cdot \text{in.}$$

$$A = \frac{1}{\cancel{2}_1} \cdot \frac{27}{1} \cdot \frac{\cancel{8}^4}{1} \text{ in}^2$$

$$A = \frac{108}{1} \text{ in}^2$$

$$A = 108 \text{ in}^2$$

Since the kite consists of 2 of these triangles, we double the area by multiplying by 2.

$$2 \cdot 108 \text{ in}^2 = 216 \text{ in}^2$$

4. *Check.* To check, we note that our answer showed that the area of each triangle is 108 in². We know that the area of the rectangle surrounding each triangle will be twice that of the triangle: Area of rectangle = $2 \cdot 108$ in² = 216 in². We compare this figure to the standard calculation of area for a rectangle.

A (rectangle) $= b \cdot h$

A (rectangle) $= 27$ in. $\cdot 8$ in.

A (rectangle) $= 216$ in.²

8 in.

27 in.

Our answer checks.

5. *State.* The area of the kite is 216 in².

Do Margin Exercise 9.

Exercise Set 4.4

a Multiply. Don't forget to simplify.

1. $\dfrac{3}{8} \cdot \dfrac{1}{3}$

2. $\dfrac{4}{5} \cdot \dfrac{1}{4}$

3. $\dfrac{7}{8} \cdot \dfrac{-1}{7}$

4. $\dfrac{5}{6} \cdot \dfrac{-1}{5}$

5. $\dfrac{1}{8} \cdot \dfrac{4}{5}$

6. $\dfrac{2}{5} \cdot \dfrac{1}{6}$

7. $\dfrac{1}{6} \cdot \dfrac{2}{3}$

8. $\dfrac{3}{6} \cdot \dfrac{1}{6}$

9. $\dfrac{12}{-5} \cdot \dfrac{9}{8}$

10. $\dfrac{16}{-15} \cdot \dfrac{5}{4}$

11. $\dfrac{5x}{9} \cdot \dfrac{7}{5}$

12. $\dfrac{25}{4a} \cdot \dfrac{4}{3}$

13. $\dfrac{1}{4} \cdot 8$

14. $\dfrac{1}{6} \cdot 12$

15. $15 \cdot \dfrac{1}{3}$

16. $14 \cdot \dfrac{1}{2}$

17. $-12 \cdot \dfrac{3}{4}$

18. $-18 \cdot \dfrac{5}{6}$

19. $\dfrac{3}{8} \cdot 8a$

20. $\dfrac{2}{9} \cdot 9x$

21. $13\left(\dfrac{-2}{5}\right)$

22. $15\left(\dfrac{-1}{6}\right)$

23. $\dfrac{m}{10} \cdot 28$

24. $\dfrac{n}{8} \cdot 34$

25. $\dfrac{1}{6} \cdot 360x$

26. $\dfrac{1}{3} \cdot 120y$

27. $240\left(\dfrac{1}{-8}\right)$

28. $150\left(\dfrac{1}{-5}\right)$

29. $9 \cdot \dfrac{1}{9}$

30. $4 \cdot \dfrac{1}{4}$

31. $-\dfrac{1}{3} \cdot 3$

32. $-\dfrac{1}{6} \cdot 6$

33. $\dfrac{7}{10} \cdot \dfrac{10}{7}$

34. $\dfrac{8}{9} \cdot \dfrac{9}{8}$

35. $\dfrac{m}{n} \cdot \dfrac{n}{m}$

36. $\dfrac{x}{y} \cdot \dfrac{y}{x}$

37. $\dfrac{4}{10} \cdot \dfrac{5}{10}$

38. $\dfrac{7}{10} \cdot \dfrac{34}{150}$

39. $\dfrac{8}{10} \cdot \dfrac{45}{100}$

40. $\dfrac{3}{10} \cdot \dfrac{8}{10}$

41. $\left(-\dfrac{11}{24}\right)\dfrac{3}{5}$

42. $\left(-\dfrac{15}{22}\right)\dfrac{4}{7}$

43. $\dfrac{10a}{21} \cdot \dfrac{3}{4a}$

44. $\dfrac{17}{18x} \cdot \dfrac{3x}{5}$

45. $\dfrac{3}{4} \cdot \dfrac{8}{7} \cdot \dfrac{5}{6}$

46. $\dfrac{3}{9} \cdot \dfrac{5}{9} \cdot \dfrac{9}{2}$

47. $\dfrac{x}{7} \cdot \dfrac{14}{15} \cdot \dfrac{5}{x}$

48. $\dfrac{7}{18} \cdot \dfrac{9}{13} \cdot \dfrac{26}{11} \cdot \dfrac{33}{14}$

b Solve.

49. Business people have determined that $\frac{1}{4}$ of the addresses on a mailing list will change in one year. A business has a mailing list of 2500 people. After one year, how many addresses on that list will be incorrect?

50. Sociologists have determined that $\frac{2}{5}$ of the people in the world are shy. A sales manager is interviewing 650 people for an aggressive sales position. How many of these people might be shy?

51. A recipe for piecrust calls for $\frac{2}{3}$ cup of flour. A chef is making $\frac{1}{2}$ of the recipe. How much flour should the chef use?

52. Of the students in the entering class, $\frac{2}{5}$ have cameras; $\frac{1}{4}$ of these students also join the college photography club. What fraction of the students in the entering class join the photography club?

53. Jennifer's tuition was $2400. A loan was obtained for $\frac{2}{3}$ of the tuition. How much was the loan?

55. Shawn's tuition was $2800. A loan was obtained for $\frac{3}{4}$ of the tuition. How much was the loan?

55. On a map, 1 in. represents 240 mi. How much does $\frac{2}{3}$ in. represent?

56. On a map, 1 in. represents 120 km. How much does $\frac{3}{4}$ in. represent?

57. The Kelsner family has an annual income of $27,000. Of this, $\frac{1}{4}$ is spent for food, $\frac{1}{5}$ for housing, $\frac{1}{10}$ for clothing, $\frac{1}{9}$ for savings, $\frac{1}{4}$ for taxes, and the rest for other expenses. How much is spent for each?

58. The Jensen family has an annual income of $25,200. Of this, $\frac{1}{4}$ is spent for food, $\frac{1}{5}$ for housing, $\frac{1}{10}$ for clothing, $\frac{1}{9}$ for savings, $\frac{1}{4}$ for taxes, and the rest for other expenses. How much is spent for each?

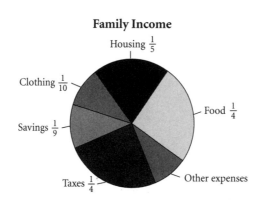

Family Income

Housing $\frac{1}{5}$

Clothing $\frac{1}{10}$

Savings $\frac{1}{9}$

Food $\frac{1}{4}$

Taxes $\frac{1}{4}$

Other expenses

Find the area.

59.
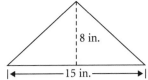
8 in.
|← 15 in. →|

60.
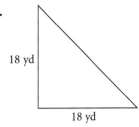
18 yd
18 yd

61.
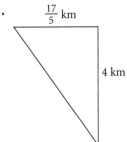
$\frac{17}{5}$ km
4 km

62.
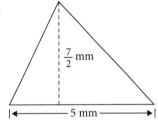
$\frac{7}{2}$ mm
|← 5 mm →|

63.
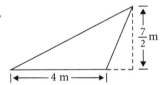
$\frac{7}{2}$ m
|← 4 m →|

64.
|← $\frac{8}{3}$ yd →|
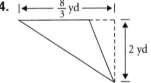
2 yd

65.
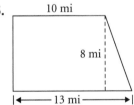
10 mi
8 mi
|← 13 mi →|

66.
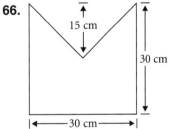
15 cm
30 cm
|← 30 cm →|

67. Find the total area of the sides and ends of the building.

25 ft
11 ft
75 ft
50 ft

68. A rectangular piece of sailcloth is 36 ft by 24 ft. A triangular area with a height of 28 ft and a base of 16 ft is cut from the sailcloth. How much area is left over?

Skill Maintenance

Solve.

69. $48 \cdot t = 1680$

70. $456 + x = 9002$

71. $747 = x + 270$

72. $280 = 4 \cdot t$

Add.

73. $(-39) + (-72)$

74. $-59 + 37$

Synthesis

75. ❖ When multiplying using fractional notation, we form products in the numerator and the denominator, but do not immediately calculate the products. Why?

76. ❖ If a fraction's numerator and denominator have no factors (other than 1) in common, can the fraction be simplified? Why or why not?

77. Of the students entering a college, $\frac{7}{8}$ have completed high school and $\frac{2}{3}$ are older than 20. If $\frac{1}{7}$ of all students are left-handed, what fraction of students entering the college are left-handed high school graduates over the age of 20?

78. Refer to the information in Exercise 77. If 480 students are entering the college, how many of them are left-handed high school graduates 20 years old or younger?

79. Refer to Exercise 77. What fraction of students entering the college did not graduate high school, are 20 years old or younger, and are left-handed?

4.5 Reciprocals and Division

a | Reciprocals

Look at these products:

$$8 \cdot \frac{1}{8} = \frac{8}{8} = 1; \quad \frac{-2}{3} \cdot \frac{3}{-2} = \frac{-6}{-6} = 1.$$

> If the product of two numbers is 1, we say that they are *reciprocals* of each other. To find a reciprocal, interchange the numerator and the denominator.
>
> The numbers $\frac{3}{4}$ and $\frac{4}{3}$ are reciprocals of each other.

Examples Find the reciprocal.

1. The reciprocal of $\frac{4}{5}$ is $\frac{5}{4}$.   Note that $\frac{4}{5} \cdot \frac{5}{4} = \frac{20}{20} = 1$.

2. The reciprocal of $\frac{a}{b}$ is $\frac{b}{a}$.   Note that $\frac{a}{b} \cdot \frac{b}{a} = \frac{ab}{ba} = 1$.

3. The reciprocal of $-\frac{5}{9}$ is $-\frac{9}{5}$.   Negative numbers have negative reciprocals: $\left(-\frac{5}{9}\right)\left(-\frac{9}{5}\right) = \frac{45}{45} = 1$.

4. The reciprocal of $\frac{1}{3}$ is 3.   Note that $\frac{1}{3} \cdot 3 = \frac{1}{3} \cdot \frac{3}{1} = \frac{3}{3} = 1$.

5. The reciprocal of -8 is $-\frac{1}{8}$.   Think of -8 as $-\frac{8}{1} \cdot (-\frac{8}{1})(-\frac{1}{8}) = 1$

6. The reciprocal of 0 is what?   0 has *no* reciprocal because the product of any number and 0 cannot be 1.

> Remember:
>
> | When multiplying or dividing two numbers | **Result** |
> |---|---|
> | with the same signs (either both positive or both negative) | positive |
>
> $$+ \cdot + = +$$
> $$- \cdot - = +$$
>
> | two numbers with different signs | negative |
>
> $$+ \cdot - = -$$
> $$- \cdot + = -$$

Do Margin Exercises 1–5.

> Remember:
>
> A number and its reciprocal have the same sign.

Find the reciprocal.

1. $\dfrac{2}{5}$

2. $\dfrac{7}{a}$

3. -9

4. $\dfrac{1}{5}$

5. $\dfrac{-3}{10}$

Divide and simplify.

6. $\dfrac{6}{7} \div \dfrac{3}{4}$

7. $\left(-\dfrac{2}{3}\right) \div \dfrac{1}{4}$

8. $\dfrac{4}{5} \div 8$

9. $60 \div \dfrac{3a}{5}$

10. $\dfrac{3}{5} \div \dfrac{-3}{5}$

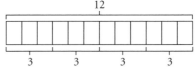

b Division

Recall that $12 \div 3$ means "how many 3's are there in 12?"

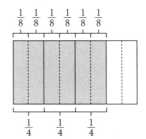

There are four 3's in 12, so let $12 \div 3 = 4$.

Consider the division $\dfrac{3}{4} \div \dfrac{1}{8}$. This asks how many $\dfrac{1}{8}$'s are in $\dfrac{3}{4}$. We can answer this by looking at the figure below.

We see that there are six $\dfrac{1}{8}$'s in $\dfrac{3}{4}$. Thus,

$$\dfrac{3}{4} \div \dfrac{1}{8} = 6.$$

We can check this by multiplying:

$$6 \cdot \dfrac{1}{8} = \dfrac{6}{8} = \dfrac{3}{4}.$$

Here is a faster way to divide.

To divide by a fraction, multiply by its reciprocal:

$$\dfrac{3}{4} \div \dfrac{1}{8} = \dfrac{3}{4} \cdot \dfrac{8}{1} = \dfrac{3}{\overset{}{\underset{1}{4}}} \cdot \dfrac{\overset{2}{8}}{1} = \dfrac{6}{1} = 6$$

Multiply by the reciprocal of the divisor.

▶ Recall that when two numbers with unlike signs are multiplied or divided, the result is negative. When both numbers have the same sign, the result is positive.

Examples   Divide and simplify.

7. $\dfrac{5}{6} \div \dfrac{2}{3} = \dfrac{5}{6} \cdot \dfrac{3}{2} = \dfrac{5}{\underset{2}{6}} \cdot \dfrac{\overset{1}{3}}{2} = \dfrac{5}{4}$

8. $\dfrac{4}{9} \div \left(-\dfrac{2}{3}\right) = \dfrac{4}{9} \cdot \left(-\dfrac{3}{2}\right) = -\left(\dfrac{\overset{2}{4}}{\underset{3}{9}} \cdot \dfrac{\overset{1}{3}}{\underset{1}{2}}\right) = -\dfrac{2}{3}$

9. $\dfrac{3}{4} \div \dfrac{1}{8} = \dfrac{3}{4} \cdot \dfrac{8}{1} = \dfrac{3}{\underset{1}{4}} \cdot \dfrac{\overset{2}{8}}{1} = \dfrac{6}{1} = 6$

10. $\dfrac{2a}{5} \div 7 = \dfrac{2a}{5} \cdot \dfrac{1}{7} = \dfrac{2a}{35}$ **11.** $\dfrac{-3}{5} \div \dfrac{1}{2} = \dfrac{-3}{5} \cdot \dfrac{2}{1} = \dfrac{-6}{5}$

Do Margin Exercises 6–10.

What do we do when a fraction has either a numerator or denominator or both that are fractions? We rewrite the fraction as a division problem.

Example 12

$$\frac{\frac{2}{3}}{\frac{7}{5}} = \frac{2}{3} \div \frac{7}{5} = \frac{2}{3} \cdot \frac{5}{7} = \frac{10}{21}$$

Do Margin Exercise 11.

c Solving Problems

Example 13 Tameka has 51 g (grams) of sulfur. How many test tubes can she fill if each test tube is to contain $\frac{3}{5}$ g?

1. Familiarize. We first make a drawing or at least visualize the situation. Repeated subtraction, or division, will work here.

$\frac{3}{5}$ g per test tube

51 g fills how many test tubes?

We let n = the number of test tubes that can be filled.

If each test tube contained 1 gram, the answer would be 51 test tubes. If each test tube held $\frac{1}{2}$ g, the answer would be 102 test tubes. Since $\frac{3}{5}$ is in between $\frac{1}{2}$ and 1, we expect our answer to be between 51 and 102.

2. Translate. The problem can be translated to the following equation:

$$n = 51 \div \frac{3}{5}.$$

3. Solve. *To* solve the equation, we carry out the division:

$$n = 51 \div \frac{3}{5}$$

$$n = 51 \cdot \frac{5}{3} \qquad \text{Multiplying by the reciprocal}$$

$$n = \frac{51 \cdot 5}{1 \cdot 3}$$

$$n = \frac{\overset{17}{\cancel{51}} \cdot 5}{1 \cdot \underset{1}{\cancel{3}}}$$

$$n = \frac{85}{1}$$

$$n = 85$$

4. Check. 85 is between 51 and 102, and thus is reasonable. We can also do a formal check by multiplying. If each of *85* test tubes contains $\frac{3}{5}$ g of sulfur, a total of

$$\frac{85}{1} \cdot \frac{3}{5} = \frac{\overset{17}{\cancel{85}}}{1} \cdot \frac{3}{\underset{1}{\cancel{5}}} = \frac{51}{1} = 51$$

or 51 g of sulfur is used. Since the problem states that Tameka begins with 51 g, our answer checks.

5. State. Tameka can fill *85* test tubes with sulfur.

Do Margin Exercises 12 and 13.

11. $\dfrac{\frac{4}{5}}{\frac{6}{7}}$

12. Each loop in a spring uses $\frac{3}{8}$ in. of wire. How many loops can be made from 120 in. of wire?

13. For a party, Jana made an 8-foot submarine sandwich. If one serving is $\frac{2}{3}$ ft, how many servings does Jana's sub contain?

Exercise Set 4.5

a Find the reciprocal.

1. $\dfrac{6}{5}$

2. $\dfrac{8}{3}$

3. 4

4. 7

5. $\dfrac{1}{6}$

6. $\dfrac{1}{4}$

7. $-\dfrac{10}{3}$

8. $-\dfrac{12}{5}$

9. $\dfrac{2}{21}$

10. $\dfrac{3}{28}$

11. $\dfrac{2x}{y}$

12. $\dfrac{a}{2b}$

13. $\dfrac{7}{-15}$

14. $\dfrac{-6}{27}$

15. $7m$

16. $5n$

b Divide. Don't forget\ to simplify.

17. $\dfrac{3}{5} \div \dfrac{3}{4}$

18. $\dfrac{2}{3} \div \dfrac{3}{4}$

19. $\dfrac{3}{5} \div \dfrac{-9}{4}$

20. $\dfrac{6}{7} \div \dfrac{-3}{5}$

21. $\dfrac{4}{3} \div \dfrac{1}{3}$

22. $\dfrac{10}{9} \div \dfrac{1}{2}$

23. $\left(-\dfrac{1}{3}\right) \div \dfrac{1}{6}$

24. $\left(-\dfrac{1}{4}\right) \div \dfrac{1}{5}$

25. $\dfrac{3}{8} \div 3$

26. $\dfrac{5}{6} \div 5$

27. $\dfrac{12}{7} \div 4x$

28. $\dfrac{18}{5} \div 2y$

29. $(-12) \div \dfrac{3}{2}$

30. $(-24) \div \dfrac{3}{8}$

31. $28 \div \dfrac{4}{5a}$

32. $40 \div \dfrac{2}{3m}$

33. $\left(-\dfrac{5}{8}\right) \div \left(-\dfrac{5}{8}\right)$

34. $\left(-\dfrac{2}{5}\right) \div \left(-\dfrac{2}{5}\right)$

35. $\dfrac{-8}{15} \div \dfrac{4}{5}$

36. $\dfrac{6}{-13} \div \dfrac{3}{26}$

37. $\dfrac{9}{5} \div \dfrac{4}{5}$

38. $\dfrac{5}{12} \div \dfrac{25}{36}$

39. $120a \div \dfrac{5}{6}$

40. $360n \div \dfrac{8}{7}$

41. Megan uses $\frac{1}{2}$ yd of dental floss each day. How long will a 45-yd container of dental floss last for Megan?

42. Greg use $\frac{2}{5}$ g of toothpaste each time he brushes his teeth. If Greg buys a 30-g tube, how many times will he be able to brush his teeth?

43. A road crew repaves $\frac{1}{12}$ mi of road each day. How long will it take the crew to repave a $\frac{3}{4}$-mi stretch of road?

44. Tiffany has $9 to spend on ride tickets at the fair. If the tickets cost 75¢, or $\$\frac{3}{4}$, each, how many tickets can she purchase?

45. Ryan purchased 6 lb of cold cuts for a luncheon. If Ryan is to allow $\frac{3}{8}$ lb per person, how many people can he invite to the luncheon?

46. Michael's Market prepackages Swiss cheese in $\frac{3}{4}$-lb packages. How many packages can be made from a 12-lb slab of cheese?

47. The Lauren's School District purchased $\frac{3}{4}$ T (ton) of clay. If the clay is to be shared equally among the district's 6 art departments, how much will each art department receive?

48. The Grove community garden is to be split into 16 equally sized plots. If the garden occupies $\frac{3}{4}$ acre of land, how large will each plot be?

49. A piece of wire $\frac{3}{5}$ m long is to be cut into 6 pieces of the same length. What is the length of each piece?

50. A piece of wire $\frac{4}{5}$ m long is to be cut into eight pieces of the same length. What is the length of each piece?

51. A pair of basketball shorts requires $\frac{3}{4}$ yd of nylon. How many pairs of shorts can be made from 24 yd of the fabric?

52. A child's shirt requires $\frac{5}{6}$ yd of cotton fabric. How many shirts can be made from 25 yd of the fabric?

53. How many $\frac{2}{3}$-cup sugar bowls can be filled from 16 cups of sugar?

54. How many $\frac{2}{3}$-cup breakfast bowls can be filled from 10 cups of cornflakes?

Skill Maintenance

Multiply.

55. $(-17)(-30)$

56. $(73)(-4)$

Evaluate each of the following.

57. x^3 for $x = 3$ and $x = -3$

58. $5x^2$ for $x = 4$ and $x = -4$

59. $3x^2$ for $x = 7$ and $x = -7$

60. x^3 for $x = 7$ and $x = -7$

Synthesis

61. ❖ Without performing the division, explain why $5 \div \frac{1}{7}$ is a bigger number than $5 \div \frac{2}{3}$.

62. What number is its own reciprocal? What number has no reciprocal? Explain your answer.

63. A student claims that taking half of a number is the same as dividing that number by $\frac{1}{2}$. Explain the error in his reasoning.

64. $\left(\frac{9}{10} \div \frac{2}{5} \div \frac{3}{8} \right)^2$

65. $\dfrac{\left(-\frac{3}{7} \right)^2 \div \frac{12}{5}}{\left(\frac{-2}{9} \right)\left(\frac{9}{2} \right)}$

4.6 Multiplication and Division Using Mixed Numbers

a Multiplication

> To multiply mixed numbers:
> 1. First convert to improper fractions.
> 2. Multiply.
> 3. When the product is an improper fraction, it can be left as either an improper fraction or converted back to a mixed number.

CAUTION! $2\frac{1}{4} \cdot 3\frac{2}{5} \neq 6\frac{2}{20}$. A common error is to multiply the whole numbers and then the fractions. The correct answer, $\frac{153}{20}$ or $7\frac{13}{20}$, is found after converting to improper fractions before multiplying.

Example 1 Multiply: $6 \cdot 2\frac{1}{2}$.

$$6 \cdot 2\frac{1}{2} = \frac{6}{1} \cdot \frac{5}{2} = \frac{\overset{3}{\cancel{6}}}{1} \cdot \frac{5}{\underset{1}{\cancel{2}}} = \frac{15}{1} = 15$$

Here we write fractional notation.

Do Margin Exercise 1.

Example 2 Multiply: $3\frac{1}{2} \cdot \frac{3}{4}$.

$$3\frac{1}{2} \cdot \frac{3}{4} = \frac{7}{2} \cdot \frac{3}{4} = \frac{21}{8} \text{ or } 2\frac{5}{8}$$

Do Margin Exercise 2.

Example 3 Multiply: $-8 \cdot 4\frac{2}{3}$.

$$-8 \cdot 4\frac{2}{3} = -\frac{8}{1} \cdot \frac{14}{3} = -\frac{112}{3} \text{ or } -37\frac{1}{3}$$

Do Margin Exercise 3.

Example 4 Multiply: $2\frac{1}{4} \cdot 3\frac{2}{5}$.

$$2\frac{1}{4} \cdot 3\frac{2}{5} = \frac{9}{4} \cdot \frac{17}{5} = \frac{153}{20} \text{ or } 7\frac{13}{20}$$

Do Margin Exercise 4.

1. Multiply: $6 \cdot 3\frac{1}{3}$

2. Multiply: $2\frac{1}{2} \cdot \frac{3}{4}$

3. Multiply: $-2 \cdot 6\frac{2}{5}$

4. Multiply: $3\frac{1}{3} \cdot 2\frac{1}{2}$

5. Divide: $84 \div 5\frac{1}{4}$

b Division

The division problem $1\frac{1}{2} \div \frac{1}{6}$ asks "how many $\frac{1}{6}$'s are there in $1\frac{1}{2}$?"

    We see that there are nine $\frac{1}{6}$'s.

This is how we divide $1\frac{1}{2}$ by $\frac{1}{6}$:

$$1\frac{1}{2} \div \frac{1}{6} = \frac{3}{2} \div \frac{1}{6}$$

$$= \frac{3}{2} \cdot \frac{6}{1} = \frac{3}{\overset{}{\underset{1}{2}}} \cdot \frac{\overset{3}{6}}{1} = \frac{9}{1} = 9$$

> To divide mixed numbers,
> 1. Convert to improper fractions.
> 2. Multiply by the reciprocal of the second fraction.
> 3. When the quotient is an improper fraction, it can be left as an improper fraction or converted back to a mixed number.

CAUTION! The reciprocal of $3\frac{1}{5}$ is neither $5\frac{1}{3}$ nor $3\frac{5}{1}$!

Example 5   Divide: $32 \div 3\frac{1}{5}$.

$$32 \div 3\frac{1}{5} = \frac{32}{1} \div \frac{16}{5} \qquad \text{Converting to fractional notation}$$

$$= \frac{32}{\underset{2}{1}} \cdot \frac{5}{16} \qquad \longleftarrow \text{Remember to multiply by the reciprocal.}$$

$$= \frac{\overset{2}{32}}{1} \cdot \frac{5}{\underset{1}{16}}$$

$$= \frac{10}{1}$$

$$= 10$$

Do Margin Exercise 5.

Example 6   Divide: $2\frac{1}{3} \div 1\frac{3}{4}$

$$2\frac{1}{3} \div 1\frac{3}{4} = \frac{7}{3} \div \frac{7}{4}$$

$$= \frac{7}{3} \cdot \frac{4}{7}$$

$$= \frac{\overset{1}{7}}{3} \cdot \frac{4}{\underset{1}{7}}$$

$$= \frac{4}{3} \text{ or } 1\frac{1}{3}$$

Example 7 Divide: $-1\frac{3}{5} \div \left(-3\frac{1}{3}\right)$.

$$-1\frac{3}{5} \div \left(-3\frac{1}{3}\right) = -\frac{8}{5} \div \left(-\frac{10}{3}\right)$$

$$= \frac{8}{5} \cdot \frac{3}{10} \qquad \text{The product or quotient of two negatives is positive.}$$

$$= \frac{\overset{4}{8}}{5} \cdot \frac{3}{\underset{5}{10}}$$

$$= \frac{12}{25}$$

Do Margin Exercises 6 and 7.

---

c Solving Problems

Example 8

The tape in an audio cassette is played at a rate of $1\frac{7}{8}$ in. per second. A defective tape player has destroyed 30 in. of tape. How many seconds of music have been lost?

1. *Familiarize.* We can draw a picture.

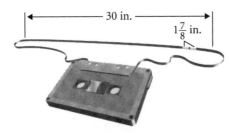

Since each $1\frac{7}{8}$ in. of tape represents 1 sec of lost music, the question can be regarded as asking how many times 30 can be divided by $1\frac{7}{8}$. We let $t =$ the number of seconds of music lost.

To estimate, we note that $1\frac{7}{8}$ in. is a little less than 2 in., and that $30 \div 2 = 15$. Since we're dividing by a number a little less than 2, we would expect the answer to be slightly greater than 15.

2. *Translate.* The situation corresponds to a division sentence:

$$t = 30 \div 1\frac{7}{8}.$$

Divide.

6. $2\frac{1}{4} \div 1\frac{1}{5}$

7. $1\frac{3}{4} \div \left(-2\frac{1}{2}\right)$

8. Kyle's pickup truck travels on an interstate highway at 65 mph for $3\frac{1}{2}$ hr. How far does it travel?

3. Solve. *To* solve the equation, we perform the division:

$$t = 30 \div 1\frac{7}{8}$$

$$t = \frac{30}{1} \div \frac{15}{8}$$

$$t = \frac{30}{1} \cdot \frac{8}{15}$$

$$t = \frac{\overset{2}{\cancel{30}}}{1} \cdot \frac{8}{\underset{1}{\cancel{15}}}$$

$$t = \frac{16}{1}$$

$$t = 16$$

4. Check. We check by comparing to our estimate from Step 1. Since 16 is a little larger than 15, as we predicted, our answer is reasonable.

We also check by multiplying.

If 16 sec of music were lost, then

$$16 \cdot 1\frac{7}{8} = \frac{16}{1} \cdot \frac{15}{8}$$

$$= \frac{\overset{2}{\cancel{16}}}{1} \cdot \frac{15}{\underset{1}{\cancel{8}}}$$

$$= \frac{30}{1} \text{ in.}$$

$$= 30 \text{ in.}$$

9. Holly's minivan travels 302 mi on $15\frac{1}{10}$ gal of gas. How many miles per gallon did it get?

of tape were destroyed. Our answer checks.

5. State. The cassette has lost 16 sec of music.

Do Margin Exercises 8 and 9.

Exercise Set 4.6

a Multiply. Write a mixed number for the answer.

1. $8 \cdot 2\frac{5}{6}$

2. $5 \cdot 3\frac{3}{4}$

3. $3\frac{5}{8} \cdot \frac{2}{3}$

4. $6\frac{2}{3} \cdot \frac{1}{4}$

5. $-9 \cdot 4\frac{2}{5}$

6. $-10 \cdot 7\frac{1}{3}$

7. $4\frac{1}{3} \cdot 6\frac{2}{5}$

8. $7\frac{3}{8} \cdot 4\frac{1}{3}$

9. $3\frac{1}{2} \cdot 2\frac{1}{3}$

10. $4\frac{1}{5} \cdot 5\frac{1}{4}$

11. $-3\frac{2}{5} \cdot 2\frac{7}{8}$

12. $-2\frac{3}{10} \cdot 4\frac{2}{5}$

13. $4\frac{7}{10} \cdot 5\frac{3}{10}$

14. $6\frac{3}{10} \cdot 5\frac{7}{10}$

15. $-20\frac{1}{2} \cdot \left(-10\frac{1}{5}\right)$

16. $-21\frac{1}{3} \cdot \left(-11\frac{1}{3}\right)$

b Divide. Write a mixed number for the answer whenever possible.

17. $20 \div 3\frac{1}{5}$

18. $18 \div 2\frac{1}{4}$

19. $8\frac{2}{5} \div 7$

20. $3\frac{3}{8} \div 3$

21. $4\frac{3}{4} \div 1\frac{1}{3}$

22. $5\frac{4}{5} \div 2\frac{1}{2}$

23. $-1\frac{7}{8} \div 1\frac{2}{3}$

24. $-4\frac{3}{8} \div 2\frac{5}{6}$

25. $5\frac{1}{10} \div 4\frac{3}{10}$

26. $4\frac{1}{10} \div 2\frac{1}{10}$

27. $20\frac{1}{4} \div (-90)$

28. $12\frac{1}{2} \div (-50)$

29. A serving of spaghetti is $1\frac{1}{2}$ cups. How much spaghetti is needed to serve 7 people?

30. The average American woman consumes $1\frac{1}{3}$ tsp of sodium each day. How much sodium would 10 average American women consume in one day?

31. A serving of filleted fish is generally considered to be about $\frac{1}{3}$ lb. How many servings can be prepared from $5\frac{1}{2}$ lb of flounder fillet?

32. A serving of fish steak (cross section) is generally $\frac{1}{2}$ lb. How many servings can be prepared from a cleaned $18\frac{3}{4}$-lb tuna?

33. The weight of water is $62\frac{1}{2}$ lb per cubic foot. What is the weight of $5\frac{1}{2}$ cubic feet of water?

34. The weight of water is $62\frac{1}{2}$ lb per cubic foot. What is the weight of $2\frac{1}{4}$ cubic feet of water?

35. The tape in a VCR operating in the short-play mode travels at a rate of $1\frac{3}{8}$ in. per second. How many inches of tape are used to record for 60 sec in the short-play mode?

36. The tape in an audio cassette is played at the rate of $1\frac{7}{8}$ in. per second. How many inches of tape are used when a cassette is played for $5\frac{1}{2}$ sec?

37. Fahrenheit temperature can be obtained from Celsius (centigrade) temperature by multiplying by $1\frac{4}{5}$ and adding 32°. What Fahrenheit temperature corresponds to a Celsius temperature of 20°?

38. Fahrenheit temperature can be obtained from Celsius (centigrade) temperature by multiplying by $1\frac{4}{5}$ and adding 32°. What Fahrenheit temperature corresponds to the Celsius temperature of boiling water, which is 100°?

39. Listed below are the ingredients for a low-fat, heart-healthy dish called *Chicken à la King*. What are the ingredients for $\frac{1}{2}$ recipe? for 3 recipes?

```
CHICKEN À LA KING

 2  chicken bouillon cubes
1½  cups hot water
 3  tablespoons margarine
 3  tablespoons flour
2½  cups diced cooked chicken
 1  cup cooked peas
 1  4-oz can sliced mushrooms, drained
⅓  cup sliced cooked carrots
¼  cup chopped onions
 2  tablespoons chopped pimiento
 1  teaspoon salt
```

40. Listed below are the ingredients for a low-fat, heart-healthy dish called *Italian Stuffed Peppers*. What are the ingredients for $\frac{1}{2}$ recipe? for 3 recipes?

```
ITALIAN STUFFED PEPPERS

⅓  cup Italian dressing
 4  medium green peppers
 1  quart water
1½  cups cooked brown rice
 1  16-oz can tomato sauce
    (no salt or sugar added)
 1  teaspoon Tamari soy sauce
½  teaspoon basil
 1  clove garlic, minced
⅓  cup onion, chopped
 2  15-oz cans dark red kidney beans
    rinsed and drained
 1  tablespoon parsley, chopped
 4  tablespoons Parmesan cheese
```

41. Most space shuttles orbit the earth once every $1\frac{1}{2}$ hr. How many orbits are made every 24 hr?

42. Turkey contains $1\frac{1}{3}$ servings per pound. How many pounds are needed for 32 servings?

43. Chipper's taxi traveled 213 mi on $14\frac{2}{10}$ gal of gas. How many miles per gallon did it get?

44. Javy's van traveled 385 mi on $15\frac{4}{10}$ gal of gas. How many miles per gallon did it get?

Skill Maintenance

45. Solve: $-7x = 63$

46. On a winter night, the temperature dropped from 7°F to −12°F. How many degrees did it drop?

47. Multiply: $\left(-\dfrac{1}{29}\right)(-29)$.

48. Divide and simplify: $\dfrac{4}{5} \div \dfrac{6}{5}$.

49. Divide: $-198 \div (-6)$

50. Multiply: $(-7)(185)(0)$.

Synthesis

51. ❖ Write a problem for a classmate to solve. Design the problem so that its solution is found by performing the multiplication $4\frac{1}{2} \cdot 33\frac{1}{3}$.

52. ❖ Explain in your own words how to multiply two mixed numbers.

53. ❖ Explain in your own words how to divide two mixed numbers.

54. ❖ A student claims that $4\frac{2}{3} \cdot 2\frac{3}{4} = 8\frac{6}{12} = 8\frac{1}{2}$. Explain the error in her reasoning.

4.7 Solving Equations: The Multiplication Principle

a In Chapters 1 and 2, we learned to solve equations using the multiplication and division principle. Now we know that dividing is the same as multiplying by the reciprocal, so we will refer to this principle only as the multiplication principle.

When both sides of an equation are multiplied by the same number, we say that we are using the **multiplication principle**.

> **▶ The Multiplication Principle**
>
> For any numbers a, b, and c,
>
> if $a = b$, then $c \cdot a = c \cdot b$.

We can multiply by any nonzero number on both sides to produce an equivalent equation. Remember that we can do anything to one side of an equation as long as we do the exact same thing to the other side of the equation.

Example 1 Solve: $\frac{3}{4}x = 15$

Since we are looking for an equation of the form $1 \cdot x = \square$, we multiply by the reciprocal of $\frac{3}{4}$ on both sides.

$$\frac{4}{3} \cdot \frac{3}{4}x = \frac{4}{3} \cdot 15 \qquad \text{Multiplying by the reciprocal}$$

$$1x = \frac{4}{\underset{1}{\cancel{3}}} \cdot \frac{\overset{5}{\cancel{15}}}{1} \qquad \begin{array}{l}\text{The product of a number}\\ \text{and its reciprocal equals 1}\end{array}$$

$$x = 20 \qquad \text{Remember that } 1x \text{ is } x.$$

To confirm that 20 is the solution, we perform a check.

Check:

$$\frac{3}{4}x = 15$$

$$\frac{3}{4} \cdot 20 \; ? \; 15$$

$$\frac{3}{\underset{1}{\cancel{4}}} \cdot \frac{\overset{5}{\cancel{20}}}{1}$$

$$15 = 15 \quad \text{True}$$

Do Margin Exercises 1 and 2.

Solve.

1. $\frac{2}{3}x = 10$

2. $\frac{2}{7}a = -8$

Solve.

3. $\dfrac{3}{4}x = \dfrac{7}{5}$

4. $\dfrac{4}{9}a = 2$

In an expression like $\frac{3}{4}x$, the numerical factor—in this case, $\frac{3}{4}$—is called the **coefficient**. In Example 1, we multiplied on both sides by $\frac{4}{3}$, the reciprocal of the coefficient of x.

Example 2 Solve: $\dfrac{4}{5}x = \dfrac{3}{2}$.

We can multiply both sides by any nonzero number and produce an equivalent equation. Since we are looking for an equation of the form $1x = \square$, we multiply by the reciprocal of $\frac{4}{5}$ on both sides.

$$\frac{4}{5}x = \frac{3}{2}$$

$$\frac{5}{4} \cdot \frac{4}{5}x = \frac{5}{4} \cdot \frac{3}{2} \qquad \text{Using the multiplication principle; note that } \frac{5}{4} \text{ is the reciprocal of the coefficient } \frac{4}{5}.$$

$$1x = \frac{15}{8} \qquad \text{Multiplying}$$

$$x = \frac{15}{8} \qquad \text{Remember that } 1x \text{ is } x.$$

We check to confirm that $\dfrac{15}{8}$ is the solution.

Check:

$$\frac{4}{5}x = \frac{3}{2}$$

$$\frac{4}{5} \cdot \frac{15}{8} \;\overset{?}{\vert}\; \frac{3}{2}$$

$$\frac{\overset{1}{4}}{\underset{1}{5}} \cdot \frac{\overset{3}{15}}{\underset{2}{8}}$$

$$\frac{3}{2} \;\bigg\vert\; \frac{3}{2} \qquad \text{True}$$

> *Note:* Even though the answer could be written as $1\frac{7}{8}$, checking will often be easier if the answer is left as an improper fraction.

Do Margin Exercises 3 and 4.

With practice, two or more steps can sometimes be combined.

Example 3 Solve: $5a = -\dfrac{7}{3}$.

$$5a = -\frac{7}{3}$$

$$\frac{1}{5} \cdot 5a = \frac{1}{5} \cdot \left(-\frac{7}{3}\right) \qquad \text{Multiplying by } \tfrac{1}{5}, \text{ the reciprocal of } 5, \text{ on both sides}$$

$$a = -\frac{7}{15}$$

We check to see that $-\dfrac{7}{15}$ is the solution.

Check:

$$5a = -\frac{7}{3}$$

$$5\left(-\frac{7}{15}\right) \overset{?}{} -\frac{7}{3}$$

$$\frac{\overset{1}{5}}{1}\left(-\frac{7}{\underset{3}{\cancel{15}}}\right) \,\Big|\, -\frac{7}{3}$$

$$-\frac{7}{3} \,\Big|\, -\frac{7}{3} \quad \text{True}$$

The solution is $-\dfrac{7}{15}$

Example 4 Solve: $\dfrac{10}{3} = -\dfrac{4}{9}x$.

$$\frac{10}{3} = -\frac{4}{9}x$$

$$-\frac{9}{4} \cdot \frac{10}{3} = -\frac{9}{4} \cdot \left(-\frac{4}{9}\right)x \qquad \text{The reciprocal of } -\tfrac{4}{9} \text{ is } -\tfrac{9}{4}.$$

$$-\frac{\overset{3}{\cancel{9}}}{\underset{2}{\cancel{4}}} \cdot \frac{\overset{5}{\cancel{10}}}{\underset{1}{\cancel{3}}} = x$$

$$-\frac{15}{2} = x$$

We check to see that $-\dfrac{15}{2}$ is the solution.

Check:

$$\frac{10}{3} = -\frac{4}{9}x$$

$$\frac{10}{3} \overset{?}{} -\frac{4}{9}\left(-\frac{15}{2}\right)$$

$$\frac{10}{3} \,\Big|\, -\frac{\overset{2}{\cancel{4}}}{\underset{3}{\cancel{9}}}\left(-\frac{\overset{5}{\cancel{15}}}{\underset{1}{\cancel{2}}}\right)$$

$$\frac{10}{3} \,\Big|\, \frac{10}{3} \qquad \text{True}$$

The solution is $-\dfrac{15}{2}$.

Do Margin Exercises 5 and 6.

Solve.

5. $-\dfrac{9}{8} = 4x$

6. $-\dfrac{6}{7}a = \dfrac{9}{14}$

Example 5 Solve: $\frac{2}{3}x = 3\frac{1}{4}$.

$$\frac{2}{3}x = 3\frac{1}{4}$$

$$\frac{2}{3}x = \frac{13}{4}$$

$$\frac{3}{2} \cdot \frac{2}{3}x = \frac{13}{4} \cdot \frac{3}{2}$$

$$x = \frac{39}{8} \text{ or } 4\frac{7}{8}$$

We check to see that $\frac{39}{8}$ or $4\frac{7}{8}$ is the solution.

Check:

$$\frac{2}{3}x = 3\frac{1}{4}$$

$$\frac{2}{3}\left(\frac{39}{8}\right) \stackrel{?}{=} \frac{13}{4}$$

$$\frac{\overset{1}{2}}{\underset{1}{3}}\left(\frac{\overset{13}{39}}{\underset{4}{8}}\right)$$

$$\frac{13}{4} \;\bigg|\; \frac{13}{4} \quad \text{True}$$

The solution is $\frac{39}{8}$.

7. $-\frac{4}{5}x = 3\frac{2}{3}$

8. $7\frac{1}{6}y = 9\frac{1}{2}$

Example 6 Solve: $-2\frac{1}{5}x = \frac{4}{7}$.

$$-2\frac{1}{5}x = \frac{4}{7}$$

$$-\frac{11}{5}x = \frac{4}{7}$$

$$-\frac{5}{11}\left(-\frac{11}{5}x\right) = -\frac{5}{11} \cdot \frac{4}{7}$$

$$x = -\frac{20}{77}$$

We check to see that $-\frac{20}{77}$ is the solution.

Do Margin Exercises 7 and 8.

Check:

$$-2\frac{1}{5}x = \frac{4}{7}$$

$$-2\frac{1}{5}\left(-\frac{20}{77}\right) \stackrel{?}{=} \frac{4}{7}$$

$$-\frac{11}{5}\left(-\frac{20}{77}\right)$$

$$-\frac{\overset{1}{11}}{\underset{1}{5}}\left(-\frac{\overset{4}{20}}{\underset{7}{77}}\right)$$

$$\frac{4}{7} \;\bigg|\; \frac{4}{7} \quad \text{True}$$

The solution is $-\frac{20}{77}$.

Exercise Set 4.7

a Use the multiplication principle to solve the equations. Don't forget to check!

1. $\frac{4}{5}x = 16$

2. $\frac{4}{3}x = 20$

3. $2\frac{1}{3}a = 21$

4. $1\frac{3}{5}a = 24$

5. $\frac{2}{7}x = -16$

6. $\frac{3}{8}x = -21$

7. $-10 = \frac{2}{9}a$

8. $-14 = \frac{2}{11}a$

9. $\frac{3}{5}x = \frac{2}{7}$

10. $\frac{3}{7}x = \frac{1}{4}$

11. $1\frac{1}{2}t = \frac{5}{7}$

12. $1\frac{1}{3}t = \frac{2}{11}$

13. $10 = \frac{4}{5}a$

14. $12 = \frac{6}{5}a$

15. $\frac{9}{5}x = \frac{3}{10}$

16. $\frac{10}{3}x = \frac{8}{15}$

17. $-\frac{3}{10}x = 8$

18. $-\frac{2}{11}x = 5$

19. $a \cdot \frac{9}{7} = -\frac{3}{14}$

20. $a \cdot \frac{9}{4} = -\frac{3}{10}$

21. $-2\frac{1}{7} = 1\frac{1}{2}t$

22. $-1\frac{5}{9} = 3\frac{1}{3}t$

23. $x \cdot \frac{5}{16} = \frac{15}{14}$

24. $x \cdot \frac{4}{15} = \frac{12}{25}$

25. $-\frac{3}{20}x = -\frac{21}{10}$

26. $-\frac{7}{25}x = -\frac{21}{10}$

27. $-1\frac{8}{17} = -1\frac{1}{34}a$

28. $-1\frac{4}{15} = -1\frac{1}{27}a$

Skill Maintenance

Simplify.

29. $36 \div (-3)^2 (7 - 2)$

30. $(-37 - 12 + 1) \div (-2)^3$

31. $-13 + 3^2$

32. $-15 + (-2)(-11)$

Synthesis

33. ❖ Example 1 was solved by multiplying by $\frac{4}{3}$ on both sides of the equation. Could we have divided by $\frac{3}{4}$ on both sides instead? Why or why not?

34. ❖ Can $7x = 63$ be solved by multiplying both sides by a number? Why or why not?

Solve using the five-step problem-solving approach.

35.   After driving 180 km, $\frac{5}{8}$ of a trip is completed. How long is the total trip? How many kilometers are left to drive?

36. After driving 240 km, $\frac{3}{5}$ of a trip is completed. How long is the total trip? How many kilometers are left to drive?

37. A package of coffee beans weighed $\frac{21}{32}$ lb when it was $\frac{3}{4}$ full. How much could the package hold when completely filled?

38. After swimming $\frac{2}{7}$ mi, Katie had swum $\frac{3}{4}$ of the race. How long a race was Katie competing in?

4.8 Applications

a Solving applied problems with fractions is similar to solving applied problems with whole numbers. As with all applied problems, we want to consider the 5 Steps for Problem Solving.

▶ **5 Steps for Problem Solving**

1. Familiarize yourself with the situation.

   a. Read to visualize the situation

   b. Draw a picture or chart to organize the information.

   c. Identify the unknown and choose a variable to represent it.

   d. Estimate your answer.

2. Translate the problem into an equation using key words.

3. Solve the equation.

4. Check the answer for reasonableness by comparing it to your estimation from step 1 and then check the answer in the original wording of the problem.

5. State the answer to the problem clearly with appropriate units.

Example 1 You want to have a group of friends over for a chili dinner. You figure about 30 people will come. You plan on buying paper bowls which hold $1\frac{1}{2}$ cups each. What is the minimum amount of chili you should make?

1. **Familiarize.** We first make a drawing to visualize the situation. We let c = cups of chili.

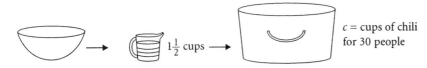

$1\frac{1}{2}$ cups ⟶

c = cups of chili for 30 people

To estimate, we note that if we were making 1 cup of chili per person, we would need to make 30 cups $(1 \cdot 30)$. If we were making 2 cups per person we would need 60 cups $(2 \cdot 30)$. Thus, we know our answer must be between 30 and 60.

2. **Translate.** We know 30 people are attending and will eat at least $1\frac{1}{2}$ cups of chili. Thus,

$$c = 30 \cdot 1\frac{1}{2} \text{ cups}$$

3. **Solve.** To solve we write $1\frac{1}{2}$ cups as an improper fraction, so

$$c = 30 \cdot \frac{3}{2} \text{ cups}$$

$$c = \frac{\overset{15}{\cancel{30}}}{1} \cdot \frac{3}{\underset{1}{\cancel{2}}} \text{ cups}$$

$$c = 45 \text{ cups}$$

1. You wanted to save $1200 over the course of the year. At the end of the year, you saved $\frac{3}{5}$ of the desired amount. How much did you save?

2. For an art project, you have to cut a piece of fabric that is $40\frac{2}{5}$ in. length. Six pieces are needed. What must be the length of each piece?

4. **Check.** First, is our answer reasonable? Yes, because 45 is between 30 and 60 as we expected. Now we can verify it.

$$x = 30 \cdot 1\frac{1}{2}\text{cups}$$

$$45 \ ? \ 30 \cdot 1\frac{1}{2}\text{cups}$$

$$45 \ \bigg| \ \frac{\overset{15}{\cancel{30}}}{1} \cdot \frac{3}{\underset{1}{\cancel{2}}}\text{cups}$$

$$45 \ \bigg| \ 45 \qquad \text{True}$$

5. **State:** 45 cups of chili is the minimum amount to be made.

Do Margin Exercises 1 and 2.

Example 2 Last summer your cousin took a car trip across country. After driving 1810 miles she had completed $\frac{2}{3}$ of the trip. How many miles was the trip?

1. **Familiarize:** Let us first visualize the situation.

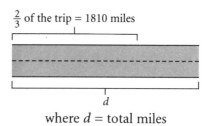

where d = total miles

To estimate, we can divide the trip up into 3 parts. We know the first two parts of the trip $\left(\frac{2}{3}\right)$ was about 1800 miles. That means each part of the trip is about 900 miles ($1800 \div 2$). Thus, we have about 900 miles left to go. Adding 900 to the roughly 1800 miles we've already gone, we expect our answer to be about 2700 miles.

2. **Translate.** Now we translate the information into an equation.

$$\frac{2}{3}d = 1810 \text{ mi}$$

3. **Solve.** To solve we multiply both sides by $\frac{3}{2}$, thus,

$$\frac{3}{2} \cdot \frac{2}{3}d = 1810 \text{ mi} \cdot \frac{3}{2}$$

$$d = \frac{1810}{1} \text{ mi} \cdot \frac{3}{2}$$

$$d = \frac{\overset{905}{\cancel{1810}}}{1} \text{ mi} \cdot \frac{3}{\underset{1}{\cancel{2}}}$$

$$d = 2715 \text{ mi}$$

4. Check. Our answer (2715 miles) makes sense since it is close to our estimate of 2700. We can verify that the distance we calculated is correct.

$$\frac{2}{3}d = 1810 \text{ mi}$$

$$\frac{2}{3}\left(\frac{2715}{1}\right) \; ? \; 1810 \text{ mi}$$

$$\frac{2}{\underset{1}{\cancel{3}}}\left(\frac{\overset{905}{\cancel{2715}}}{1}\right) \; \bigg| \; 1810 \text{ mi}$$

$$1810 \; \bigg| \; 1810 \text{ mi} \quad \text{True}$$

5. State. The total distance of the cross country trip was 2715 miles.

Do Margin Exercise 3.

3. Diane has begun a new exercise program. The first five days she walked $\frac{3}{8}$ mi. each day. Over the three days, how many miles did she cover?

Exercise Set 4.8

a Solve using the 5 Steps for Problem Solving.

1. Anna receives $36 for working a full day doing inventory at a hardware store. How much will she receive for working $\frac{3}{4}$ of the day?

2. After Jack completes 60 hr of teacher training in college, he can earn $45 for working a full day as a substitute teacher. How much will he receive for working $\frac{1}{5}$ of a day?

3. A recipe calls for $\frac{2}{3}$ cup of flour. A chef is making $\frac{1}{2}$ of the recipe. How much flour should the chef use?

4. Liz and her road crew paint the lines in the middle and on the sides of a highway. They average about $\frac{5}{16}$ of a mile each day. How long will it take to paint the lines on 70 mi of highway?

5. After driving 60 km, $\frac{3}{8}$ of a vacation is complete. How long is the total trip?

6. Bernardo usually earns $42 for working a full day. How much does he receive for working $\frac{1}{7}$ of a day?

7. A bucket had 12 L of water in it when it was $\frac{3}{4}$ full. How much could it hold altogether?

8. A tank had 20 L, of gasoline in it when it was $\frac{4}{5}$ full. How much could it hold altogether?

9. After driving 180 kilometers (km), $\frac{5}{8}$ of a trip is completed. How long is the total trip? How many kilometers are left to drive?

10. Irene wants to build a bookcase to hold her collection of favorite videocassette movies. Each shelf in the bookcase will be 27 in. long and each videocassette is $1\frac{1}{8}$ in. thick. How many cassettes can she place on each shelf?

11. One serving of meat is about $3\frac{1}{2}$ oz. Art eats 2 servings a day. How many ounces of meat is this?

12. A bicycle wheel makes $66\frac{2}{3}$ revolutions per minute. If it rotates for 21 min, how many revolutions does it make?

13. *Weight of Water.* The weight of water is $62\frac{1}{2}$ lb per cubic foot. How many cubic feet would be occupied by 250 lb of water?

14. *Weight of Water.* The weight of water is $62\frac{1}{2}$ lb per cubic foot. How many cubic feet would be occupied by 375 lb of water?

Skill Maintenance

Solve.

15. $48 \cdot t = 1680$

16. $74 \cdot x = 6290$

17. $t + 28 = 5017$

18. $456 + x = 9002$

Subtract.

19.
$$9060$$
$$-4387$$

20.
$$7800$$
$$-2462$$

21. Multiply

$$6709$$
$$\times 213$$

22. Round to the nearest hundred: 45,765.

23. Solve: $\frac{5}{7} \cdot t = 420$.

24. Divide and simplify: $\frac{4}{5} \div \frac{6}{5}$.

25. Multiply and simplify: $\frac{3}{8} \cdot \frac{4}{9}$.

Synthesis

26. ❖ Without performing the division, explain why $5 \div \frac{1}{7}$ is a greater number than $5 \div \frac{2}{3}$.

27. $\left(\frac{9}{10} \div \frac{2}{5} \div \frac{3}{8} \right)^2$

28. $\dfrac{\left(\frac{3}{7}\right)^2 \div \frac{12}{5}}{\left(\frac{2}{9}\right)\left(\frac{9}{2}\right)}$

29. ❖ Write a problem for a classmate to solve. Design the problem so that its solution is found by performing the multiplication $4\frac{1}{2} \cdot 33\frac{1}{3}$.

Review Exercises: Chapter 4

Identify as a proper fraction, improper fraction or mixed number.

1. $\dfrac{4}{3}$

2. $-14\dfrac{41}{76}$

3. $\dfrac{19}{19}$

4. $\dfrac{2}{11}$

Write as improper fractions.

5. $-12\dfrac{5}{8}$

6. $23\dfrac{3}{4}$

Convert to mixed numbers.   Divide.

7. $\dfrac{77}{5}$

8. $\dfrac{-85}{7}$

9. $53\overline{)1259}$

10. $6\overline{)2831}$

Simplify if possible. Assume all variables are nonzero.

11. $\dfrac{0}{4}$

12. $\dfrac{23}{23}$

13. $\dfrac{7x}{7x}$

14. $\dfrac{48}{1}$

15. $\dfrac{-10}{15}$

16. $\dfrac{-7}{28}$

17. $\dfrac{9m}{12m}$

18. $\dfrac{-27}{0}$

19. $\dfrac{-9}{-27}$

20. $\dfrac{9n}{1}$

Find another name for the given number, but with the denominator indicated. Use mulitplying by 1.

21. $\dfrac{5}{7} = \dfrac{?}{21}$

22. $\dfrac{-6}{11} = \dfrac{?}{55}$

Find the reciprocal.

23. $\dfrac{5}{9}$

24. -7

25. $\dfrac{1}{8}$

26. $\dfrac{3x}{5y}$

Perform the indicated operation and, if possible, simplify.

27. $\dfrac{2}{7} \cdot \dfrac{3}{5}$

28. $\dfrac{4}{x} \cdot \dfrac{y}{9}$

29. $\dfrac{3}{4} \cdot \dfrac{8}{9}$

30. $\dfrac{-5}{7} \cdot \dfrac{1}{10}$

31. $\dfrac{3a}{10} \cdot \dfrac{2}{15a}$

32. $\dfrac{4a}{7} \cdot \dfrac{7}{4a}$

33. $6 \div \dfrac{5}{3}$

34. $\dfrac{3}{14} \div \dfrac{6}{7}$

35. $180 \div \dfrac{3}{5}$

36. $\dfrac{-5}{36} \div \left(\dfrac{-25}{12}\right)$

37. $14 \div \dfrac{7}{2}a$

38. $\dfrac{-23}{25} \div \dfrac{23}{25}$

Perform the indicated operation. Write a mixed numeral or integer for the answer.

39. $6 \cdot 2\dfrac{2}{3}$

40. $-5\dfrac{1}{4} \cdot \dfrac{2}{3}$

41. $2\dfrac{1}{5} \cdot 1\dfrac{1}{10}$

42. $2\dfrac{2}{5} \cdot 2\dfrac{1}{2}$

43. $27 \div 2\dfrac{1}{4}$

44. $2\dfrac{2}{5} \div \left(-1\dfrac{7}{10}\right)$

45. $3\dfrac{1}{4} \div 26$

46. $4\dfrac{1}{5} \div 4\dfrac{2}{3}$

Use the multiplication principle to solve the equations.

47. $\dfrac{16}{3}a = \dfrac{-40}{9}$

48. $\dfrac{5}{2}x = 20$

49. $\dfrac{-2}{3}x = \dfrac{9}{4}$

50. $-\dfrac{3}{8} = -\dfrac{5}{4}t$

51. $2\dfrac{1}{3} = 1\dfrac{5}{8}x$

52. $-2\dfrac{5}{7}x = \dfrac{10}{21}$

Find the area.

53.

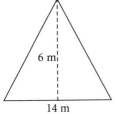

6 m

14 m

54.

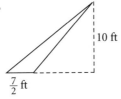

10 ft

$\dfrac{7}{2}$ ft

Solve.

55. The Holtzmnans have drive $\frac{4}{5}$ of a 275-mi trip. How far have they driven?

56. A recipe calls for $\frac{2}{3}$ cup of sugar. In making $\frac{1}{2}$ of this recipe, how much sugar should be used?

57. The Winchester swim team has 4 swimmers in a $\frac{2}{3}$-mi relay race. How far will each person swim?

58. How many $\frac{2}{3}$-cup sugar bowls can be filled from 12 cups of sugar?

Test: Chapter 4

Write as improper fractions.

Convert to a mixed number:

1. $3\frac{1}{2}$

2. $-9\frac{7}{8}$

3. $-\frac{74}{9}$

Simplify if possible. Assume all variables are nonzero.

4. $\frac{26}{1}$

5. $\frac{-12}{-12}$

6. $\frac{0}{-16}$

7. $\frac{12}{24}$

8. $\frac{5x}{45x}$

9. $-\frac{2}{28}$

Perform the indicated operation. Simplify if possible.

10. $\frac{5}{9}\left(-\frac{7}{2}\right)$

11. $\frac{7}{11} \div \frac{3}{4}$

12. $3 \cdot \frac{x}{8}$

13. $28 \div \left(-\frac{6}{7}\right)$

14. $\frac{4a}{13} \cdot \frac{9}{30a}$

Perform the indicated operation. Write a mixed or whole number for the answer.

15. $9 \cdot 4\frac{1}{3}$

16. $6\frac{3}{4} \cdot \left(-2\frac{2}{3}\right)$

17. $-33 \div 5\frac{1}{2}$

18. $2\frac{1}{3} \div 1\frac{1}{6}$

Use the multiplication principle to solve the equations.

19. $\frac{-13}{4a} = 9$

20. $\frac{2}{9x} = \frac{-10}{3}$

21. $\frac{-4}{15} = \frac{2}{5}y$

22. $\frac{-1}{8}x = -\frac{1}{5}$

23. Find the area.

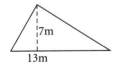

Solve.

24. A $\frac{3}{4}$-lb slab of cheese is shared equally by 5 people. How much does each person receive?

25. Monroe weighs $\frac{3}{7}$ of his dad's weight. If his dad weighs 175 lb, how much does Monroe weigh?

26. Solve: $47 \cdot t = 4747$.

27. Add: $(-93) + (-74)$

28. A student incorrectly insists that $\frac{2}{3} \div \frac{7}{5}$ is $\frac{14}{15}$. What mistake is the student probably making?

29. A student claims that "taking $\frac{1}{2}$ of a number is the same as dividing by $\frac{1}{2}$." Explain the error in this reasoning.

Cumulative Review: Chapters 1-4

1. Find the prime factorization of 250. Write your answer with exponents.

2. Find the LCM of 14, 16 and 56.

Add.

3. $\begin{array}{r} 2{,}7\,3\,9 \\ +\,8{,}2\,4\,3 \\ \hline \end{array}$

4. $-29 + (-14)$

5. $-45 + 12$

Subtract.

6. $\begin{array}{r} 4{,}3\,2\,4 \\ -2{,}1\,9\,5 \\ \hline \end{array}$

7. $17 - 40$

8. $-12 - (-4)$

Multiply and simplify.

9. $\begin{array}{r} 7\,3\,5 \\ \times\ \ 2\,3 \\ \hline \end{array}$

10. $-52 \cdot 6$

11. $\dfrac{6}{7} \cdot (-35x)$

12. $\dfrac{2}{9} \cdot \dfrac{21}{10}$

Divide and simplify.

13. $13\overline{)3058}$

14. $-85 \div 5$

15. $-16 \div \dfrac{4}{7}$

16. $\dfrac{3}{7} \div \dfrac{9}{14}$

17. Round 4514 to the nearest ten.

18. Estimate the product by rounding to the nearest hundred. Show your work.
$$\begin{array}{r} 921 \\ \times\ \ 453 \\ \hline \end{array}$$

19. Find the absolute value: $|879|$.

20. Simplify: $10^2 \div 5(-2) - 8(2 - 8)$.

21. Determine whether 98 is prime, composite, or neither.

22. Evaluate $a - b^2$ for $a = -5$ and $b = 4$.

Solve.

23. $a + 24 = 49$

24. $7x = 63$

25. $\dfrac{2}{9} \cdot a = -10$

26. A 1992 car that gets 31 miles per gallon is traded in toward a 1996 van that gets 26 miles per gallon. How many more miles per gallon did the older vehicle get?

27. A 32-oz soda is poured into 8 glasses. How much will each glass hold if the soda is poured out evenly?

Simplify, if possible.

28. $\dfrac{97}{97}$

29. $\dfrac{59}{1}$

30. $\dfrac{0}{72}$

31. $\dfrac{-10}{54}$

Find the reciprocal.

32. $\dfrac{2}{5}$

33. 17

34. Find another name for $\dfrac{3}{10}$, but with 70 as the denominator. Use multiplying by 1.

35. A babysitter earns $50 for working a full day. How much is earned for working $\dfrac{3}{5}$ of a day?

36. How many $\dfrac{3}{4}$-lb servings can be made from a 9-lb roast?

37. Tony has jogged $\dfrac{2}{3}$ of a course that is $\dfrac{9}{10}$ of a mile long. How far has Tony gone?

38. Evaluate $\dfrac{ab}{c}$ for $a = \dfrac{-2}{5}$, $b = \dfrac{10}{13}$, and $c = \dfrac{26}{27}$.

39. Multiply: $-7\dfrac{3}{4}\left(5\dfrac{1}{3}\right)$

40. Divide: $9\dfrac{4}{5} \div (-7)$

5

Fractions: Addition and Subtraction

An Application

Gail has run $\frac{2}{3}$ mi and will stop running when she has run $\frac{7}{8}$ mi. How much farther does Gail have to go?

The Mathematics

We let d = the distance to go. The problem then translates to this equation:

$$\frac{2}{3} + d = \frac{7}{8}$$

This is an example of how addition using fractional notation occurs in applied problems. This problem appears as Example 9 in 5.2 of this chapter.

1. Find $\frac{1}{5} + \frac{3}{5}$.

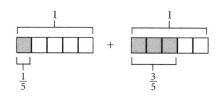

Add and simplify.

2. $\frac{1}{3} + \frac{2}{3}$

3. $\frac{5}{12} + \frac{1}{12}$

4. $\frac{-9}{16} + \frac{3}{16}$

5. $\frac{3}{x} + \frac{-7}{x}$

Remember:

$$\frac{-m}{n} = -\frac{m}{n} = \frac{m}{-n}$$

5.1 Addition and Order

a Like Denominators

Addition using fractional notation corresponds to combining or putting like things together. For example,

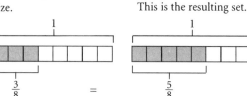

We combine two sets, each of which consists of fractional parts that are the same size.

This is the resulting set.

$$\frac{2}{8} \quad + \quad \frac{3}{8} \quad = \quad \frac{5}{8}$$

2 eighths + 3 eighths = 5 eighths,

or $\frac{2}{8} + \frac{3}{8} = \frac{5}{8}$.

Do Margin Exercise 1.

▶ To add when denominators are the same,

a) add the numerators,

b) keep the denominator, and

$$\frac{2}{6} + \frac{5}{6} = \frac{2+5}{6} = \frac{7}{6}$$

c) simplify, if possible.

Examples Add and simplify, if possible.

1. $\frac{2}{4} + \frac{1}{4} = \frac{2+1}{4} = \frac{3}{4}$ No simplifying is possible.

2. $\frac{3}{12} + \frac{5}{12} = \frac{3+5}{12} = \frac{8}{12} = \frac{4 \cdot 2}{4 \cdot 3} = \frac{2}{3}$ Here we simplified.

3. $\frac{-11}{6} + \frac{3}{6} = \frac{-11+3}{6} = \frac{-8}{6} = \frac{2 \cdot (-4)}{2 \cdot 3}$

$= \frac{-4}{3}$, or $-\frac{4}{3}$. Recall that $\frac{-m}{m} = -\frac{m}{m}$.

4. $-\frac{2}{a} + \left(-\frac{3}{a}\right) = \frac{-2}{a} + \frac{-3}{a} = \frac{-2+(-3)}{a} = \frac{-5}{a}$, or $-\frac{5}{a}$

Do Margin Exercises 2–5.

b Addition Using the Least Common Denominator

At the beginning of this section, we visualized the addition $\frac{2}{8} + \frac{3}{8}$. Consider now the addition $\frac{1}{2} + \frac{1}{3}$.

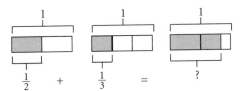

By rewriting $\frac{1}{2}$ as $\frac{1}{2} \cdot \frac{3}{3} = \frac{3}{6}$ and $\frac{1}{3}$ as $\frac{1}{3} \cdot \frac{2}{2} = \frac{2}{6}$, we can determine the sum.

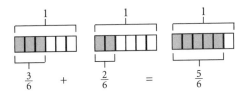

Thus, when denominators differ, before adding we must multiply by 1 to get a common denominator. There is always more than one common denominator that can be used. Consider the addition $\frac{3}{4} + \frac{1}{6}$:

A. $\dfrac{3}{4} + \dfrac{1}{6} = \dfrac{3}{4} \cdot 1 + \dfrac{1}{6} \cdot 1$

$\qquad = \dfrac{3}{4} \cdot \dfrac{6}{6} + \dfrac{1}{6} \cdot \dfrac{4}{4}$ Here 24 is the common denominator.

$\qquad = \dfrac{18}{24} + \dfrac{4}{24}$

$\qquad = \dfrac{22}{24} = \dfrac{11}{12};$

B. $\dfrac{3}{4} + \dfrac{1}{6} = \dfrac{3}{4} \cdot 1 + \dfrac{1}{6} \cdot 1$

$\qquad = \dfrac{3}{4} \cdot \dfrac{3}{3} + \dfrac{1}{6} \cdot \dfrac{2}{2}$ Here 12 is the common denominator.

$\qquad = \dfrac{9}{12} + \dfrac{2}{12}$

$\qquad = \dfrac{11}{12}.$

We had to simplify the sum in (A), but not in (B). In (B), we used the *least* common multiple of the denominators, 12. That number is called the **least common denominator,** or **LCD**.

6. Add. Find the least common denominator.

$$\frac{2}{3} + \frac{1}{6}$$

7. Add: $\frac{3}{8} + \frac{5}{6}$.

▶ To add when denominators are different:

a) Find the least common multiple of the denominators. That number is the least common denominator, LCD.

b) Multiply by 1, using appropriate forms of $\frac{n}{n}$, to find equivalent numbers in which the LCD appears.

c) Add and, if possible, simplify.

Example 5 Add: $\frac{1}{8} + \frac{3}{4}$.

The LCD is 8.   4 is a factor of 8 so the LCM of 4 and 8 is 8.

$$\frac{1}{8} + \frac{3}{4} = \frac{1}{8} + \frac{3}{4} \cdot 1 \qquad \frac{1}{8} \text{ already has the LCD.}$$

$$= \frac{1}{8} + \frac{3}{4} \cdot \frac{2}{2} \qquad \textit{Think: } 4 \times \square = 8. \text{ The answer is 2,}$$
$$\text{so we multiply by 1, using } \frac{2}{2}.$$

$$= \frac{1}{8} + \frac{6}{8}$$

$$= \frac{7}{8}$$

Do Margin Exercise 6.

Example 6 Add: $\frac{5}{6} + \frac{1}{9}$

The LCD is 18. $6 = 2 \cdot 3$ and $9 = 3 \cdot 3$, so the LCM of 6 and 9 is $2 \cdot 3 \cdot 3$, or 18.

$$\frac{5}{6} + \frac{1}{9} = \frac{5}{6} \cdot 1 + \frac{1}{9} \cdot 1$$

$$= \frac{5}{6} \cdot \frac{3}{3} + \frac{1}{9} \cdot \frac{2}{2} \qquad \begin{array}{l} \textit{Think: } 9 \times \square = 18. \\ \text{The answer is 2, so} \\ \text{we multiply by 1, using } \frac{2}{2}. \end{array}$$

$$\qquad\qquad\qquad\qquad \begin{array}{l} \textit{Think: } 6 \times \square = 18. \\ \text{The answer is 3, so} \\ \text{we multiply by 1, using } \frac{3}{3}. \end{array}$$

$$= \frac{15}{18} + \frac{2}{18}$$

$$= \frac{17}{18}$$

Do Margin Exercise 7

Example 7 Add: $\dfrac{3}{-5} + \dfrac{11}{10}$.

$$\dfrac{3}{-5} + \dfrac{11}{10} = \dfrac{-3}{5} + \dfrac{11}{10} \qquad \text{Recall that } \dfrac{m}{-n} = \dfrac{-m}{n}. \text{ The LCD is 10.}$$

$$= \dfrac{-3}{5} \cdot \dfrac{2}{2} + \dfrac{11}{10}$$

$$= \dfrac{-6}{10} + \dfrac{11}{10}$$

$$= \dfrac{5}{10}$$

$$= \dfrac{1}{2}$$

> We may still have to simplify, but simplifying is usually easier if we have used the LCD.

Example 8 Add: $\dfrac{5}{8} + 2$.

$$\dfrac{5}{8} + 2 = \dfrac{5}{8} + \dfrac{2}{1} \qquad \text{Rewriting 2 in fractional notation}$$

$$= \dfrac{5}{8} + \dfrac{2}{1} \cdot \dfrac{8}{8} \qquad \text{The LCD is 8.}$$

$$= \dfrac{5}{8} + \dfrac{16}{8}$$

$$= \dfrac{21}{8}$$

Do Margin Exercises 8 and 9.

Example 9 Add: $\dfrac{9}{70} + \dfrac{11}{21} + \dfrac{-6}{15}$.

We have

$$\dfrac{9}{70} + \dfrac{11}{21} + \dfrac{-6}{15} = \dfrac{9}{2 \cdot 5 \cdot 7} + \dfrac{11}{3 \cdot 7} + \dfrac{-6}{3 \cdot 5}. \qquad \text{Factoring denominators}$$

The LCD is $2 \cdot 5 \cdot 7 \cdot 3$. Then

$$\dfrac{9}{70} + \dfrac{11}{21} + \dfrac{-6}{15} = \dfrac{9}{2 \cdot 5 \cdot 7} \cdot \dfrac{3}{3} + \dfrac{11}{3 \cdot 7} \cdot \dfrac{2 \cdot 5}{2 \cdot 5} + \dfrac{-6}{3 \cdot 5} \cdot \dfrac{7 \cdot 2}{7 \cdot 2}$$

$$= \dfrac{9 \cdot 3}{2 \cdot 5 \cdot 7 \cdot 3} + \dfrac{11 \cdot 2 \cdot 5}{3 \cdot 7 \cdot 2 \cdot 5} + \dfrac{-6 \cdot 7 \cdot 2}{3 \cdot 5 \cdot 7 \cdot 2}$$

$$= \dfrac{27}{3 \cdot 5 \cdot 7 \cdot 2} + \dfrac{110}{3 \cdot 5 \cdot 7 \cdot 2} + \dfrac{-84}{3 \cdot 5 \cdot 7 \cdot 2}$$

$$= \dfrac{53}{3 \cdot 5 \cdot 7 \cdot 2}$$

$$= \dfrac{53}{210}. \qquad \text{We multiplied } 3 \cdot 5 \cdot 7 \cdot 2 \text{ only when we knew we could not simplify.}$$

> In each case, we multiply by 1 to obtain the LCD. To form 1, look at the prime factorization of the LCD and use the factor(s) missing from each denominator.

Do Margin Exercises 10 and 11.

Add.

8. $\dfrac{1}{-6} + \dfrac{7}{18}$

9. $7 + \dfrac{3}{5}$

10. $\dfrac{4}{10} + \dfrac{1}{100} + \dfrac{3}{1000}$

11. $\dfrac{7}{10} + \dfrac{-2}{21} + \dfrac{1}{7}$

Use < or > for □ to write a true sentence.

12. $\dfrac{3}{8} \,\square\, \dfrac{5}{8}$

13. $\dfrac{7}{10} \,\square\, \dfrac{6}{10}$

14. $\dfrac{-2}{9} \,\square\, \dfrac{-5}{9}$

15. $\dfrac{2}{3} \,\square\, \dfrac{3}{4}$

16. $\dfrac{-3}{4} \,\square\, \dfrac{-8}{12}$

17. $\dfrac{5}{6} \,\square\, \dfrac{7}{8}$

---

c | Order

Common denominators are also important for determining the larger of two fractions. When two fractions share a common denominator, the larger number can be found by comparing numerators. For example, 4 is greater than 3, so $\frac{4}{5}$ is greater than $\frac{3}{5}$.

$$\frac{4}{5} > \frac{3}{5}$$

Similarly, because –6 is less than –2, we have

$$\frac{-6}{7} < \frac{-2}{7}.$$

Do Margin Exercises 12–14.

Example 10 Use < or > for □ to write a true sentence:

$$\frac{5}{8} \,\square\, \frac{2}{3}.$$

The student can confirm that the LCD is 24. We multiply by 1 to make the denominators the same:

$$\frac{5}{8} \cdot \frac{3}{3} = \frac{15}{24}; \quad \frac{2}{3} \cdot \frac{8}{8} = \frac{16}{24}.$$

Since 15 < 16, it follows that $\frac{15}{24} < \frac{16}{24}$. Thus,

$$\frac{5}{8} < \frac{2}{3}.$$

Example 11 Use < or > for □ to write a true sentence:

$$-\frac{89}{100} \,\square\, -\frac{9}{10}.$$

The LCD is 100

$$\frac{-9}{10} \cdot \frac{10}{10} = \frac{-90}{100} \qquad \text{We multiply by } \tfrac{10}{10} \text{ to get the LCD.}$$

Since –89 > –90, it follows that $-\frac{89}{100} > -\frac{90}{100}$, so

$$-\frac{89}{100} > -\frac{9}{10}.$$

Do Margin Exercises 15–17

d | Solving Problems

Example 12 A cake recipe calls for $\frac{1}{4}$ cup of oil and $\frac{2}{3}$ cup of milk. How many cups of liquid ingredients are in the recipe?

1. Familiarize. We draw a picture and let n = the total number of cups of liquid ingredients.

$\frac{1}{4}$ cup $\frac{2}{3}$ cup n cups

To estimate the answer to this problem, let us use the fact that $\frac{1}{4}$ is less than $\frac{1}{3}$. Now, if we add $\frac{2}{3}$ cup and an amount slightly smaller than $\frac{1}{3}$, we should have a sum just under 1.

2. Translate. The problem can be translated to an equation as follows.

Amount of oil	plus	Amount of milk	is	Amount of liquid
↓	↓	↓	↓	↓
$\frac{1}{4}$	$+$	$\frac{2}{3}$	$=$	n

3. Solve. To solve the equation, we carry out the addition:

$$\frac{1}{4} + \frac{2}{3} = n \qquad \text{The LCD is 12.}$$

$$\frac{1}{4} \cdot \frac{3}{3} + \frac{2}{3} \cdot \frac{4}{4} = n \qquad \text{Multiplying by 1}$$

$$\frac{3}{12} + \frac{8}{12} = n$$

$$\frac{11}{12} = n.$$

4. Check. $\frac{11}{12}$ cup is just under 1 cup as we estimated in step 1.

5. State. The recipe calls for $\frac{11}{12}$ cup of liquid ingredients.

Do Margin Exercise 18.

18. Maureen bought $\frac{1}{2}$ lb of peanuts and $\frac{3}{5}$ lb of cashews. How many pounds of nuts were bought altogether?

Exercise Set 5.1

a b Add and, if possible, simplify.

1. $\dfrac{2}{9} + \dfrac{4}{9}$

2. $\dfrac{1}{4} + \dfrac{1}{4}$

3. $\dfrac{1}{8} + \dfrac{5}{8}$

4. $\dfrac{7}{8} + \dfrac{1}{8}$

5. $\dfrac{-7}{11} + \dfrac{5}{11}$

6. $\dfrac{7}{12} + \dfrac{-5}{12}$

7. $\dfrac{9}{a} + \dfrac{2}{a}$

8. $\dfrac{5}{m} + \dfrac{3}{m}$

9. $-\dfrac{3}{x} + \left(-\dfrac{7}{x}\right)$

10. $-\dfrac{9}{a} + \dfrac{5}{a}$

11. $\dfrac{1}{8} + \dfrac{1}{6}$

12. $\dfrac{1}{9} + \dfrac{1}{6}$

13. $\dfrac{-4}{5} + \dfrac{7}{10}$

14. $\dfrac{-3}{4} + \dfrac{1}{12}$

15. $\dfrac{5}{12} + \dfrac{3}{8}$

16. $\dfrac{7}{8} + \dfrac{1}{16}$

17. $\dfrac{3}{20} + 4$

18. $\dfrac{2}{15} + 3$

19. $\dfrac{5}{-8} + \dfrac{5}{6}$

20. $\dfrac{5}{-6} + \dfrac{7}{9}$

21. $\dfrac{3}{10} + \dfrac{1}{100}$

22. $\dfrac{9}{10} + \dfrac{3}{100}$

23. $\dfrac{5}{12} + \dfrac{4}{15}$

24. $\dfrac{3}{16} + \dfrac{1}{12}$

25. $\dfrac{9}{10} + \dfrac{-99}{100}$

26. $\dfrac{3}{10} + \dfrac{-27}{100}$

27. $5 + \dfrac{7}{12}$

28. $7 + \dfrac{3}{8}$

29. $-4 + \dfrac{2}{9}$

30. $-3 + \dfrac{7}{8}$

31. $-\dfrac{5}{12} + \dfrac{7}{24}$

32. $-\dfrac{1}{18} + \dfrac{7}{12}$

33. $\dfrac{4}{10} + \dfrac{3}{100} + \dfrac{7}{1000}$

34. $\dfrac{7}{10} + \dfrac{2}{100} + \dfrac{9}{1000}$

35. $\dfrac{3}{10} + \dfrac{5}{12} + \dfrac{8}{15}$

36. $\dfrac{1}{2} + \dfrac{3}{8} + \dfrac{1}{4}$

37. $\dfrac{5}{6} + \dfrac{25}{52} + \dfrac{7}{4}$

38. $\dfrac{15}{24} + \dfrac{7}{36} + \dfrac{91}{48}$

39. $\dfrac{2}{9} + \dfrac{7}{10} + \dfrac{-4}{15}$

40. $\dfrac{5}{12} + \dfrac{-3}{8} + \dfrac{1}{10}$

41. $\frac{5}{8}$ □ $\frac{6}{8}$

42. $\frac{7}{9}$ □ $\frac{5}{9}$

43. $\frac{1}{3}$ □ $\frac{1}{4}$

44. $\frac{1}{8}$ □ $\frac{1}{6}$

45. $\frac{-2}{3}$ □ $\frac{-5}{7}$

46. $\frac{-3}{5}$ □ $\frac{-4}{7}$

47. $\frac{4}{5}$ □ $\frac{5}{6}$

48. $\frac{3}{2}$ □ $\frac{7}{5}$

49. $\frac{19}{20}$ □ $\frac{4}{5}$

50. $-\frac{5}{6}$ □ $-\frac{13}{16}$

51. $\frac{-19}{20}$ □ $\frac{-9}{10}$

52. $\frac{3}{4}$ □ $\frac{11}{15}$

53. $\frac{31}{21}$ □ $\frac{41}{13}$

54. $\frac{-8}{15}$ □ $\frac{-7}{10}$

55. $\frac{12}{7}$ □ $\frac{132}{49}$

56. $\frac{-7}{12}$ □ $\frac{-5}{8}$

d Solve.

57. Rose bought $\frac{1}{3}$ lb of orange pekoe tea and $\frac{1}{2}$ lb of English cinnamon tea. How many pounds of tea were bought?

58. Mitch bought $\frac{1}{4}$ lb of gumdrops and $\frac{1}{2}$ lb of caramels. How many pounds of candy were bought?

59. Chris walked $\frac{7}{8}$ mi to a friend's dormitory, and then $\frac{3}{4}$ mi to class. How far did Chris walk?

60. Kimberly walked $\frac{7}{8}$ mi to the student union, and then $\frac{2}{5}$ mi to class. How far did Kimberly walk?

61. A recipe for bread calls for $\frac{2}{3}$ cup of water, $\frac{1}{4}$ cup of milk, and $\frac{1}{8}$ cup of oil. How many cups of liquid ingredients does the recipe call for?

62. A recipe for muffins calls for $\frac{1}{2}$ qt (quart) of buttermilk, $\frac{1}{3}$ qt of skim milk, and $\frac{1}{16}$ qt of oil. How many quarts of liquid ingredients does the recipe call for?

63. A cubic meter of concrete mix contains 420 kg of cement, 150 kg of stone, and 120 kg of sand. What is the total weight of the cubic meter of concrete mix? What fractional part is cement? stone? sand? Add these amounts. What is the result?

64. A recipe for cherry punch calls for $\frac{1}{5}$ L of ginger ale and $\frac{3}{5}$ L of black cherry soda. How much liquid is needed? If the recipe is doubled, how much liquid is needed? If the recipe is halved, how much liquid is needed?

65. A triathlete runs $\frac{7}{8}$ mi, canoes $\frac{1}{3}$ mi, and swims $\frac{1}{6}$ mi. How many miles does the triathlete cover?

66. A naturalist hikes $\frac{4}{5}$ mi to a lookout, another $\frac{3}{10}$ mi to an osprey's nest, and finally, $\frac{3}{4}$ mi to a campsite. How far did the naturalist hike?

67. A tile $\frac{5}{8}$ in. thick is glued to a board $\frac{7}{8}$ in. thick. The glue is $\frac{3}{32}$ in. thick. How thick is the result?

68. A baker used $\frac{1}{2}$ lb of flour for rolls, $\frac{1}{4}$ lb for donuts, and $\frac{1}{3}$ lb for cookies. How much flour was used?

Skill Maintenance

Subtract.

69. $-7 - 6$

70. $-5 - (-9)$

71. $9 - 17$

72. $-8 - 23$

Evaluate.

73. $\frac{x - y}{3}$, for $x = 7$ and $y = -3$

74. $3(x + y)$ and $3x + 3y$, for $x = 5$ and $y = 9$

Synthesis

75. ❖ Explain in your own words how to add two fractions with different denominators.

76. ❖ To add numbers with different denominators, a student consistently uses the product of the denominators as a common denominator. Is this correct? Why or why not?

77. A guitarist's band is booked for Friday and Saturday night at a local club. The guitarist is part of a trio on Friday and part of a quintet on Saturday. Thus the guitarist is paid one-third of one-half the weekend's pay for Friday and one-fifth of one-half the weekend's pay for Saturday. What fractional part of the band's pay did the guitarist receive for the weekend's work? If the band was paid $1200, how much did the guitarist receive?

Add and, if possible, simplify.

78. $\frac{9}{7x} + \frac{5}{7x}$

79. $\frac{8}{15a} + \frac{2}{15a}$

5.2 Subtraction and Solving Equations

a Subtraction

Like Denominators

Recall that subtraction can be regarded as "take away" or "adding the opposite." Let's use "take away" to find $\frac{4}{8} - \frac{3}{8}$:

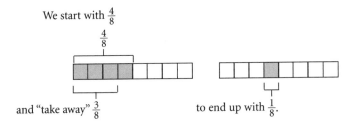

We start with $\frac{4}{8}$

and "take away" $\frac{3}{8}$

to end up with $\frac{1}{8}$.

We start with 4 eighths and take away 3 eighths:

4 eighths − 3 eighths = 1 eighth,

or $\frac{4}{8} - \frac{3}{8} = \frac{1}{8}$.

▶ To subtract when denominators are the same,

a) subtract the numerators,

b) keep the denominator, and

$$\frac{7}{10} - \frac{4}{10} = \frac{7-4}{10} = \frac{3}{10}$$

c) simplify, if possible.

Remember to simplify the answer, if possible.

Examples Subtract and simplify.

1. $\frac{7}{10} - \frac{3}{10} = \frac{7-3}{10} = \frac{4}{10} = \frac{2 \cdot 2}{2 \cdot 5} = \frac{2}{5}$

2. $\frac{8}{9} - \frac{2}{9} = \frac{8-2}{9} = \frac{6}{9} = \frac{3 \cdot 2}{3 \cdot 3} = \frac{2}{3}$

3. $\frac{32}{12} - \frac{35}{12} = \frac{32-35}{12} = \frac{-3}{12} = \frac{3 \cdot (-1)}{3(4)} = -\frac{1}{4}$

Do Margin Exercises 1–3.

Subtract and simplify.

1. $\frac{7}{8} - \frac{3}{8}$

2. $\frac{10}{16} - \frac{4}{16}$

3. $\frac{8}{10} - \frac{13}{10}$

4. Subtract: $\frac{3}{4} - \frac{2}{3}$.

Subtract

5. $\frac{5}{6} - \frac{1}{9}$

6. $\frac{4}{5} - \frac{3}{10}$

7. $\frac{2}{3} - \frac{5}{6}$

Different Denominators

> To subtract when denominators are different:
>
> **a)** Find the least common multiple of the denominators. That number is the least common denominator, LCD.
>
> **b)** Multiply by 1, using appropriate forms of $\frac{n}{n}$, to find equivalent numbers in which the LCD appears.
>
> **c)** Subtract and, if possible, simplify.

Example 4 Subtract: $\frac{2}{5} - \frac{3}{8}$.

The LCM of 5 and 8 is 40. The LCD is 40.

$$\frac{2}{5} - \frac{3}{8} = \frac{2}{5} \cdot \frac{8}{8} - \frac{3}{8} \cdot \frac{5}{5}$$

Think: $8 \times \square = 40$. The answer is 5, so we multiply by 1, using $\frac{5}{5}$.

Think: $5 \times \square = 40$. The answer is 8, so we multiply by 1, using $\frac{8}{8}$.

$$= \frac{16}{40} - \frac{15}{40}$$

$$= \frac{16 - 15}{40} = \frac{1}{40}$$

Do Margin Exercise 4.

Example 5 Subtract: $\frac{7}{12} - \frac{5}{6}$.

Since 6 is a factor of 12, the LCM of 6 and 12 is 12. The LCD is 12.

$$\frac{7}{12} - \frac{5}{6} = \frac{7}{12} - \frac{5}{6} \cdot \frac{2}{2}$$

$$= \frac{7}{12} - \frac{10}{12}$$

$$= \frac{7 - 10}{12}$$ If we prefer, we can add the opposite: $7 + (-10)$.

$$= \frac{-3}{12}$$

$$= \frac{\cancel{3}(-1)}{\cancel{3} \cdot 4}$$ Always simplify, if possible.

$$= \frac{-1}{4}, \text{ or } -\frac{1}{4}$$

Do Margin Exercises 5–7.

Example 6 Subtract: $\dfrac{17}{24} - \dfrac{4}{15}$.

We have

$$\frac{17}{24} - \frac{4}{15} = \frac{17}{3 \cdot 2 \cdot 2 \cdot 2} - \frac{4}{5 \cdot 3}.$$

The LCD is $3 \cdot 2 \cdot 2 \cdot 2 \cdot 5$, or 120. Then

$$\frac{17}{24} - \frac{4}{15} = \frac{17}{3 \cdot 2 \cdot 2 \cdot 2} \cdot \frac{5}{5} - \frac{4}{5 \cdot 3} \cdot \frac{2 \cdot 2 \cdot 2}{2 \cdot 2 \cdot 2}$$

$$= \frac{17 \cdot 5}{3 \cdot 2 \cdot 2 \cdot 2 \cdot 5} - \frac{4 \cdot 2 \cdot 2 \cdot 2}{5 \cdot 3 \cdot 2 \cdot 2 \cdot 2}$$

$$= \frac{85}{120} - \frac{32}{120}$$

$$= \frac{53}{120}.$$

> In each case, we multiply by 1 to obtain the LCD. To form 1, look at the prime factorization of the LCD and use the factor(s) each denominator lacks.

Do Margin Exercise 8.

b Solving Equations

To solve an equation like $x - \frac{1}{9} = \frac{7}{9}$, use the addition principle.

> **The Addition Principle**
>
> For any numbers a, b, and c,
> $$\text{if } a = b, \text{ then } a + c = b + c.$$

To solve $x - \frac{1}{9} = \frac{7}{9}$ using the addition principle, we proceed as follows:

$$x - \frac{1}{9} = \frac{7}{9}$$

$$x - \frac{1}{9} + \frac{1}{9} = \frac{7}{9} + \frac{1}{9} \qquad \text{Using the addition principle: adding } \tfrac{1}{9} \text{ on both sides}$$

$$x + 0 = \frac{7}{9} + \frac{1}{9} \qquad \text{Adding } \tfrac{1}{9} \text{ "undoes" the subtraction of } \tfrac{1}{9} \text{ on the left side.}$$

$$x = \frac{8}{9}.$$

The addition principle gives us a way to form equivalent equations. In our work above, we showed that

$$x - \frac{1}{9} = \frac{7}{9}$$

is equivalent to

$$x = \frac{8}{9}.$$

8. Subtract: $\dfrac{11}{28} - \dfrac{5}{16}$.

9. Solve using the addition principle:

$$x - \frac{3}{5} = \frac{7}{5}.$$

10. Solve: $x - \frac{3}{8} = \frac{1}{6}$. $\frac{4}{24}$

$\frac{3}{8} + \frac{3}{8}$ (handwritten)

$\frac{16}{24} = \frac{2}{3}$ (handwritten)

$\frac{3}{8} \begin{array}{c} 9 \\ \cdot 24 \end{array}$ (handwritten)

$\frac{16}{24}$ (handwritten)

Of course the solution, $\frac{8}{9}$, is more obvious when the variable is isolated on one side of the equation.

To visualize the addition principle, think of a jeweler's balance. When both sides of the balance hold equal amounts of weight, the balance is level. If weight is added or removed, equally, on both sides, the balance remains level.

Do Margin Exercise 9.

Example 7 Solve: $x - \frac{1}{3} = \frac{6}{7}$.

$$x - \frac{1}{3} = \frac{6}{7}$$

$$x - \frac{1}{3} + \frac{1}{3} = \frac{6}{7} + \frac{1}{3} \qquad \text{Using the addition principle:}$$
$$\text{adding } \tfrac{1}{3} \text{ on both sides}$$

$$x + 0 = \frac{6}{7} + \frac{1}{3} \qquad \text{Adding } \tfrac{1}{3} \text{ "undoes" the subtraction of } \tfrac{1}{3}.$$

$$x = \frac{6}{7} \cdot \frac{3}{3} + \frac{1}{3} \cdot \frac{7}{7} \qquad \text{Multiplying by 1 to obtain the LCD, 21}$$

$$x = \frac{18}{21} + \frac{7}{21}$$

$$x = \frac{25}{21}$$

Check:

$$x - \frac{1}{3} = \frac{6}{7}$$

$$\frac{25}{21} - \frac{1}{3} \; ? \; \frac{6}{7}$$

$$\frac{25}{21} - \frac{1}{3} \cdot \frac{7}{7}$$

$$\frac{25}{21} - \frac{7}{21}$$

$$\frac{18}{21}$$

$$\frac{6 \cdot 3}{7 \cdot 3} \bigg| \frac{6}{7}$$

$$\frac{6}{7} \bigg| \frac{6}{7} \quad \text{True}$$

Do Margin Exercise 10.

Recall that subtraction can be regarded as adding the opposite of the number being subtracted. Because of this, the addition principle allows us to subtract the same number on both sides of an equation.

Example 8 Solve: $x + \dfrac{1}{4} = \dfrac{3}{5}$.

$$x + \frac{1}{4} - \frac{1}{4} = \frac{3}{5} - \frac{1}{4}$$

Using the addition principle to add $-\frac{1}{4}$ or to subtract $\frac{1}{4}$ on both sides

$$x + 0 = \frac{3}{5} \cdot \frac{4}{4} - \frac{1}{4} \cdot \frac{5}{5}$$

The LCD is 20. We multiply by 1 to get the LCD.

$$x = \frac{12}{20} - \frac{5}{20}$$

$$x = \frac{7}{20}$$

Check.

$$\begin{array}{c|c} x + \dfrac{1}{4} = \dfrac{3}{5} \\[2mm] \hline \dfrac{7}{20} + \dfrac{1}{4} \ ? \ \dfrac{3}{5} \\[2mm] \dfrac{7}{20} + \dfrac{1}{4} \cdot \dfrac{5}{5} \\[2mm] \dfrac{7}{20} + \dfrac{5}{20} \\[2mm] \dfrac{12}{20} \\[2mm] \dfrac{3 \cdot \cancel{4}}{5 \cdot \cancel{4}} \ \Big| \ \dfrac{3}{5} \\[2mm] \dfrac{3}{5} \ \Big| \ \dfrac{3}{5} \quad \text{True} \end{array}$$

The solution is $\frac{7}{20}$.

Do Margin Exercises 11 and 12.

c Solving Problems

Example 9 Gail has run $\frac{2}{3}$ mi and will stop running when she has run $\frac{7}{8}$ mi. How much farther does Gail have to go?

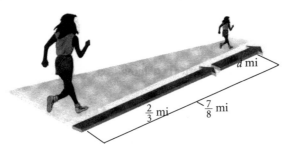

d mi

$\frac{2}{3}$ mi $\frac{7}{8}$ mi

1. *Familiarize.* We first draw a picture or at least visualize the situation. We let d = the distance to go. Given that the total distance ($\frac{7}{8}$ mile) is a little less than one mile, and that Gail has already gone $\frac{2}{3}$ mi, we see that she has a little less than $\frac{1}{3}$ mile to go.

Solve.

11. $x + \dfrac{2}{3} = \dfrac{5}{6}$

12. $\dfrac{3}{5} + t = -\dfrac{7}{8}$

13. There is $\frac{1}{4}$ lb of margarine in a mixing bowl. How much more is needed so that there is $\frac{4}{5}$ lb of margarine in the bowl?

2. Translate. This is a "how much more" situation that can be translated as follows:

Distance already traveled	+	Distance to go	is	Total distance run
↓	↓	↓	↓	↓
$\frac{2}{3}$	+	d	=	$\frac{7}{8}$

3. Solve. To solve the equation, we subtract $\frac{2}{3}$ on both sides:

$$\frac{2}{3} + d - \frac{2}{3} = \frac{7}{8} - \frac{2}{3}$$ Subtracting $\frac{2}{3}$ on both sides

$$d + 0 = \frac{7}{8} \cdot \frac{3}{3} - \frac{2}{3} \cdot \frac{8}{8}$$ The LCD is 24, We multipy by 1 to obtain the LCD.

$$d = \frac{21}{24} - \frac{16}{24}$$

$$d = \frac{5}{24}$$

4. Check. Since $\frac{5}{24}$ is a little less than $\frac{1}{3}$ (note $\frac{1}{3} = \frac{8}{24}$), our answer is reasonable.

We can check our answer by writing:

$$\frac{2}{3} + d = \frac{7}{8}$$

$$\frac{2}{3} + \frac{5}{24} \overset{?}{\mid} \frac{7}{8}$$

$$\frac{2}{3} \cdot \frac{8}{8} + \frac{5}{24}$$

$$\frac{16}{24} + \frac{5}{24}$$

$$\frac{21}{24}$$

$$\frac{7 \cdot 3}{8 \cdot 3}$$

$$\frac{7}{8} \mid \frac{7}{8} \quad \text{True}$$

5. State. Gail has $\frac{5}{24}$ mi to go.

Do Margin Exercise 13.

Example 10 Norma and Steven own $\frac{7}{8}$ acre of land. They give $\frac{1}{3}$ acre to their son and daughter-in-law as a wedding gift. How much land do Norma and Steven still own?

1. *Familiarize.* We first draw a picture or at least visualize the situation. We let r = the number of acres remaining after the gift.

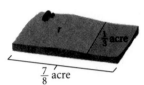

To estimate our answer, we may use the same approach as in Example 9. We know that $\frac{7}{8}$ acre is a little less than 1 acre. One-third was given away, so slightly less than $\frac{2}{3}$ acre still belong to Norma and Steven.

2. *Translate.* The problem translates to a "take-away" situation.

Amount owned originally	minus	Size of gift	is	Amount remaining
↓	↓	↓	↓	↓
$\frac{7}{8}$	$-$	$\frac{1}{3}$	$=$	r

3. *Solve.* To solve the equation, we carry out the subtraction:

$$\frac{7}{8} - \frac{1}{3} = r \qquad \text{The LCD is 24.}$$

$$\frac{7}{8} \cdot \frac{3}{3} - \frac{1}{3} \cdot \frac{8}{8} = r \qquad \text{Multiplying by 1}$$

$$\frac{21}{24} - \frac{8}{24} = r$$

$$\frac{13}{24} = r.$$

4. *Check.* Since $\frac{13}{24}$ acre is a little less than $\frac{2}{3}$ acre (note $\frac{2}{3} = \frac{16}{24}$), $\frac{13}{24}$ acre is a reasonable answer.

5. *State.* Norma and Steven still own $\frac{13}{24}$ acre.

Do Margin Exercise 14.

Example 11 Three sisters work in shifts to keep a local family business running. Mary takes the morning shift working $\frac{2}{5}$ of the work day. Susan works the second shift, working $\frac{1}{3}$ of the work day. Determine how much of the work day the third sister, Diane, works.

1. *Familiarize.* First we will attempt to visualize the situation. Let d = the fraction of the day that Diane will work

Mary 1st Shift $\frac{2}{5}$ day	Susan 2nd Shift $\frac{1}{3}$ day	Diane 3rd Shift d

1 work day

We can see that since our total is represented by 1 work day, the total of the worker's shifts will have to be 1 work day.

14. A $\frac{4}{5}$-cup bottle of salad dressing consists of olive oil and vinegar. The bottle contains $\frac{2}{3}$ cup of oil. How much vinegar is in the bottle?

Mary and Susan each work a little less than $\frac{1}{2}$ workday. However, the sum of their parts of a work day is greater than $\frac{1}{2}$. Therefore, the estimated fraction of the work day remaining that Diane will work is less than $\frac{1}{2}$.

2. Translate. The problem translates to a "combining" situation.

Mary's fraction of the workday	+	Susan's fraction of the workday	+	Diane's fraction of the workday	= 1 work day
↓	↓	↓	↓	↓	↓
$\frac{2}{5}$	+	$\frac{1}{3}$	+	d	= 1 work day

3. Solve. To solve the equation, we first add the fractions on the left side.

$$\frac{2}{5} + \frac{1}{3} + d = 1$$

$$\frac{2}{3} \cdot \frac{3}{3} + \frac{1}{3} \cdot \frac{5}{5} + d = 1 \qquad \text{The LCD is 15.}$$

$$\frac{6}{15} + \frac{5}{15} + d = 1$$

$$\frac{11}{15} + d = 1 \qquad \text{Combining fractions}$$

$$\frac{11}{15} - \frac{11}{15} + d = 1 - \frac{11}{15} \qquad \text{Subtracting } \frac{11}{15} \text{ from both sides.}$$

$$d = \frac{15}{15} - \frac{11}{15} \qquad \text{Writing 1 as an equivalent expression with the LCD of 15.}$$

$$d = \frac{4}{15} \text{ of the work day}$$

4. Check. Since $\frac{4}{15}$ is less than $\frac{1}{2}$ ($\frac{4}{15} = \frac{8}{30}$ and $\frac{1}{2} = \frac{15}{30}$) our answer is reasonable. The work day is defined as 1 unit, so the total of the three shifts could not be larger than 1. To check we go back to the original equation

$$\frac{2}{5} + \frac{1}{3} + d = 1$$

and substitute in $\frac{4}{15}$ to see if the total is 1.

$$\frac{2}{5} + \frac{1}{3} + d = 1$$

$$\frac{2}{5} + \frac{1}{3} + \frac{4}{15}$$

$$\frac{2}{5} \cdot \frac{3}{3} + \frac{1}{3} \cdot \frac{5}{5} + \frac{4}{15} \quad ? \quad \text{The LCD is 15.}$$

$$\frac{6}{15} + \frac{5}{15} + \frac{4}{15}$$

$$\frac{15}{15}$$

$$1 \mid 1 \quad \text{True}$$

So, the answer is correct.

5. State. Diane, who works the third shift, works $\frac{4}{15}$ of the work day.

Exercise Set 5.2

a Subtract, and if possible, simplify.

1. $\dfrac{5}{6} - \dfrac{1}{6}$

2. $\dfrac{7}{5} - \dfrac{2}{5}$

3. $\dfrac{11}{16} - \dfrac{15}{16}$

4. $\dfrac{2}{12} - \dfrac{11}{12}$

5. $\dfrac{2}{3} - \dfrac{1}{9}$

6. $\dfrac{3}{4} - \dfrac{1}{8}$

7. $\dfrac{1}{8} - \dfrac{1}{12}$

8. $\dfrac{1}{6} - \dfrac{1}{8}$

9. $\dfrac{4}{3} - \dfrac{5}{6}$

10. $\dfrac{7}{8} - \dfrac{1}{16}$

11. $\dfrac{5}{6} - \dfrac{1}{2}$

12. $\dfrac{3}{20} - \dfrac{3}{4}$

13. $\dfrac{2}{15} - \dfrac{2}{5}$

14. $\dfrac{3}{4} - \dfrac{3}{28}$

15. $\dfrac{3}{4} - \dfrac{1}{20}$

16. $\dfrac{3}{4} - \dfrac{4}{16}$

17. $\dfrac{2}{15} - \dfrac{5}{12}$

18. $\dfrac{11}{16} - \dfrac{9}{10}$

19. $\dfrac{6}{10} - \dfrac{7}{100}$

20. $\dfrac{9}{10} - \dfrac{3}{100}$

21. $\dfrac{7}{15} - \dfrac{3}{25}$

22. $\dfrac{18}{25} - \dfrac{4}{35}$

23. $\dfrac{69}{100} - \dfrac{9}{10}$

24. $\dfrac{42}{100} - \dfrac{11}{20}$

25. $\dfrac{2}{3} - \dfrac{1}{8}$

26. $\dfrac{3}{4} - \dfrac{1}{2}$

27. $\dfrac{3}{5} - \dfrac{1}{2}$

28. $\dfrac{5}{6} - \dfrac{2}{3}$

29. $\dfrac{-5}{12} - \dfrac{3}{8}$

30. $\dfrac{-7}{12} - \dfrac{2}{9}$

31. $\dfrac{7}{8} - \dfrac{1}{16}$

32. $\dfrac{5}{12} - \dfrac{5}{16}$

33. $\dfrac{17}{25} - \dfrac{4}{15}$

34. $\dfrac{11}{18} - \dfrac{7}{24}$

35. $-\dfrac{23}{25} - \dfrac{112}{150}$

36. $-\dfrac{89}{90} - \dfrac{53}{120}$

b Solve.

37. $x - \dfrac{2}{9} = \dfrac{4}{9}$

38. $x - \dfrac{3}{11} = \dfrac{7}{11}$

39. $a + \dfrac{2}{11} = \dfrac{8}{11}$

40. $a + \dfrac{4}{15} = \dfrac{13}{15}$

41. $n + \dfrac{3}{10} = \dfrac{7}{10}$

42. $n + \dfrac{7}{9} = \dfrac{8}{9}$

43. $x - \dfrac{2}{5} = \dfrac{4}{5}$

44. $x - \dfrac{5}{8} = \dfrac{1}{8}$

45. $a + \dfrac{1}{2} = \dfrac{7}{8}$

46. $a + \dfrac{2}{3} = \dfrac{7}{9}$

47. $x - \dfrac{3}{10} = \dfrac{2}{5}$

48. $x - \dfrac{3}{8} = \dfrac{3}{4}$

49. $\dfrac{2}{3} + x = \dfrac{4}{5}$

50. $\dfrac{4}{5} + x = \dfrac{6}{7}$

51. $\dfrac{3}{8} + a = \dfrac{1}{12}$

52. $\dfrac{5}{6} + a = \dfrac{2}{9}$

53. $n - \dfrac{1}{10} = -\dfrac{1}{30}$

54. $n - \dfrac{3}{4} = -\dfrac{5}{12}$

55. $x + \dfrac{3}{4} = -\dfrac{1}{2}$

56. $x + \dfrac{5}{6} = -\dfrac{11}{12}$

c Solve.

57. Monica spent $\frac{3}{4}$ hr listening to tapes of Beethoven and Brahms. She spent $\frac{1}{3}$ hr listening to only Beethoven. How many hours were spent listening to Brahms?

58. From a $\frac{4}{5}$-lb wheel of cheese, a $\frac{1}{4}$-lb piece was served. How much cheese remained on the wheel?

59. As part of an exercise program, Phil is to walk $\frac{7}{8}$ mi each day. He has already walked $\frac{1}{3}$ mi. How much further should Phil walk?

60. As part of a fitness program, Deb swims $\frac{1}{2}$ mi every day. She has already swum $\frac{1}{5}$ mi. How much further should Deb swim?

61. An ice cream stand was owned by three people. One owned $\frac{7}{12}$ of the business and the second owned $\frac{1}{6}$. How much did the third person own?

62. An estate was left to four children. One received $\frac{1}{4}$ of the estate, the second $\frac{1}{16}$, and the third $\frac{3}{8}$. How much did the fourth receive?

Skill Maintenance

Divide and simplify.

63. $\dfrac{9}{10} \div \dfrac{3}{5}$

64. $\dfrac{3}{7} \div \dfrac{9}{4}$

65. $(-7) \div \dfrac{1}{3}$

66. $8 \div \left(-\dfrac{1}{4}\right)$

67. A small box of cornflakes weighs $\frac{3}{4}$ lb. How much do 8 small boxes of cornflakes weigh?

68. A batch of fudge requires $\frac{3}{4}$ cup of sugar. How much sugar is needed to make 12 batches?

Synthesis

69. ❖ Before subtraction (or addition) of fractions with unlike denominators can be taught, students must first understand multiplication with fractional notation. Why?

70. ❖ Explain in your own words how the addition principle is used to solve equations.

71. A mountain climber, beginning at sea level, climbs $\frac{3}{5}$ km, descends $\frac{1}{4}$ km, climbs $\frac{1}{3}$ km, and then descends $\frac{1}{7}$ km. At what elevation does the climber finish?

Simplify.

72. $\dfrac{10}{7m} - \dfrac{3}{7m}$

73. $\dfrac{12}{5x} - \dfrac{7}{5x}$

74. $-5 \cdot \dfrac{3}{7} - \dfrac{1}{7} \cdot \dfrac{4}{5}$

75. $\left(\dfrac{2}{3}\right)^2 + \left(\dfrac{3}{4}\right)^2$

76. A VCR can record up to 6 hr on one tape. It can also fill that same tape in either 4 hr or 2 hr when running at faster speeds. A tape is placed in the machine, which records for $\frac{1}{2}$ hr at the 4-hr speed and $\frac{3}{4}$ hr at the 2-hr speed. How much time is left on the tape to record at the 6-hr speed?

77. As part of a rehabilitation program, an athlete must swim and then walk a total of $\frac{9}{10}$ km each day. If one lap in the swimming pool is $\frac{3}{80}$ km, how far must the athlete walk after swimming 10 laps?

1. Add.

$$2 \frac{3}{10}$$

$$+ 5 \frac{1}{10}$$

2.

$$8 \frac{2}{5}$$

$$+ 3 \frac{7}{10}$$

5.3 Addition and Subtraction Using Mixed Numbers

a Addition

To find the sum $1 \frac{5}{8} + 3 \frac{1}{8}$, we first add the fractions. Then we add the whole numbers.

$$
\begin{array}{r}
1 \frac{5}{8} \\
+\, 3 \frac{1}{8} \\
\hline
\frac{6}{8}
\end{array}
\qquad
\begin{array}{r}
1 \frac{5}{8} \\
+\, 3 \frac{1}{8} \\
\hline
4 \frac{6}{8} = 4 \frac{3}{4}
\end{array}
$$

Simplify the fractional part of the result when possible.

↑ Add the fractions.   ↑ Add the whole numbers.

Do Margin Exercise 1.

Remember that to add or subtract fractions, a common denominator is always needed.

Example 1   Add: $5 \frac{2}{3} + 3 \frac{5}{6}$. Write a mixed number for the answer. We first rewrite $\frac{2}{3}$, using the LCD, 6. Then we add.

$$
\begin{array}{r}
5 \frac{2}{3} \cdot \frac{2}{2} = \; 5 \frac{4}{6} \\
+\, 3 \frac{5}{6} \quad = +\, 3 \frac{5}{6} \\
\hline
8 \frac{9}{6} = 8 + \frac{9}{6} \\
= 8 + 1 \frac{1}{2} \\
= 9 \frac{1}{2}
\end{array}
$$

To find a mixed number for $\frac{9}{6}$, we divide:

$$
\begin{array}{r}
1 \\
6 \overline{)9} \\
\underline{6} \\
3
\end{array}
\qquad
\frac{9}{6} = 1 \frac{3}{6} = 1 \frac{1}{2}
$$

$\frac{19}{2}$ is also a correct answer, but it is not a mixed number.

Do Margin Exercise 2.

Example 2 Add: $10\frac{5}{6} + 7\frac{3}{8}$.

The LCD is 24.

$$
\begin{aligned}
10\frac{5}{6} \cdot \frac{4}{4} &= 10\frac{20}{24} \\
+ \quad 7\frac{3}{8} \cdot \frac{3}{3} &= + 7\frac{9}{24} \\
\hline
&\quad 17\frac{29}{24} = 18\frac{5}{24}
\end{aligned}
$$

> The fractional part of a mixed number should always be less than 1.

Do Margin Exercise 3.

Examples. In Examples 1 and 2 we could have found the answer by writing the mixed numbers as improper fractions. This method is illustrated below.

3. $5\frac{2}{3} + 3\frac{5}{6} = \frac{17}{3} + \frac{23}{6}$ Converting to improper fractions

$\qquad = \frac{17}{3} \cdot \frac{2}{2} + \frac{23}{6}$ Writing new expression with the LCD of 6

$\qquad = \frac{34}{6} + \frac{23}{6}$

$\qquad = \frac{57}{6}$

$\qquad = 9\frac{3}{6}$ Mixed number form of answer

$\qquad = 9\frac{1}{2}$ Reduced fraction

4. $10\frac{5}{6} + 7\frac{3}{8} = \frac{65}{6} + \frac{59}{8}$ Converting to improper fractions

$\qquad = \frac{65}{6} \cdot \frac{4}{4} + \frac{59}{8} \cdot \frac{3}{3}$ The LCD is 24.

$\qquad = \frac{260}{24} + \frac{177}{24}$

$\qquad = \frac{437}{24}$

$\qquad = 18\frac{5}{24}$ Mixed number form of answer

Do Margin Exercises 4 and 5.

3. Add.

$$
\begin{aligned}
&9\frac{3}{4} \\
+\ &3\frac{5}{6} \\
\hline
\end{aligned}
$$

Change to an improper fraction and then add. Write the answer as a mixed number.

4. $7\frac{1}{6} + 5\frac{2}{3}$

5. $4\frac{3}{10} + 9\frac{11}{15}$

Subtract.

6. $10\frac{7}{8}$

$\underline{-9\frac{3}{8}}$

7. $8\frac{2}{3}$

$\underline{-5\frac{1}{2}}$

---

b **Subtraction**

Example 5   Subtract: $7\frac{3}{4} - 2\frac{1}{4}$.

$$
\begin{array}{cc}
7\dfrac{3}{4} = & 7\dfrac{3}{4} \\[2mm]
-2\dfrac{1}{4} = & -2\dfrac{1}{4} \\ \hline
\dfrac{2}{4} & 5\dfrac{2}{4} = 5\dfrac{1}{2}
\end{array}
$$

$\uparrow$ $\uparrow$

Subtract the   Subtract the
fractions.   whole numbers.

Example 6   Subtract $9\frac{4}{5} - 3\frac{1}{2}$.

The LCD is 10.

$$
\begin{array}{cc}
9\dfrac{4}{5} \cdot \dfrac{2}{2} = & 9\dfrac{8}{10} \\[2mm]
-3\dfrac{1}{2} \cdot \dfrac{5}{5} = & -3\dfrac{5}{10} \\ \hline
& 6\dfrac{3}{10}
\end{array}
$$

Do Margin Exercises 6 and 7.

When subtracting mixed numbers, it may be necessary to borrow, as shown in the next examples.

Example 7.   Subtract: $7\frac{1}{6} - 5\frac{1}{4}$

The LCD is 12.

$$
\begin{array}{cc}
7\dfrac{1}{6} = & 7\dfrac{2}{12} \\[2mm]
-5\dfrac{1}{4} = & -5\dfrac{3}{12}
\end{array}
$$

Notice that we cannot subtract $\frac{3}{12}$ from $\frac{2}{12}$, so we borrow from the whole number 7.

borrow 1 from 7

$$7\frac{1}{6} = 7\frac{2}{12} = 6 + 1\frac{2}{12} = 6 + \frac{14}{12} = 6\frac{14}{12}$$

Now subtract

$$
\begin{array}{ccc}
7\dfrac{1}{6} = & 7\dfrac{2}{12} = & 6\dfrac{14}{12} \\[2mm]
-5\dfrac{1}{4} = & -5\dfrac{3}{12} = & -5\dfrac{3}{12} \\ \hline
& & 1\dfrac{11}{12}
\end{array}
$$

$\leftarrow$ Subtract the fractions

$\uparrow$
Subtract the whole numbers

Example 8. In Example 7 above, we could have found the answer by writing the mixed numbers as improper fractions. The method is illustrated below

$$7\frac{1}{6} - 5\frac{1}{4} = \frac{43}{6} - \frac{21}{4}$$ Converting to improper fractions

$$= \frac{43}{6} \cdot \frac{2}{2} - \frac{21}{4} \cdot \frac{3}{3}$$ The LCD is 12

$$= \frac{86}{12} - \frac{63}{12}$$ Writing new expressions with the LCD

$$= \frac{23}{12}$$ To write a mixed number for $\frac{23}{12}$ we divide $12\overline{)23}$

$$= 1\frac{11}{12}$$ Mixed number form of answer

Do Margin Exercises 8–10.

Example 9 Subtract: $13 - 9\frac{3}{8}$

$$13 = \qquad 12\frac{8}{8} \qquad \longleftarrow \text{Borrow 1 from 13 and write it as } \frac{8}{8}.$$

$$-9\frac{3}{8} = \qquad -9\frac{3}{8}$$
$$\overline{\qquad \qquad 3\frac{5}{8}}$$

Do Margin Exercise 11.

c | Solving Problems

Example 10 On a recent day, the stock of Len & Terry's Homemade, Inc. opened at $\$17\frac{1}{4}$ and climbed $\$1\frac{5}{8}$. What was the stock worth at the close of the business day?

1. *Familiarize.* Note that $1\frac{5}{8}$ is between 1 and 2. Thus we expect the answer to be between $17\frac{1}{4} + 1$, or $18\frac{1}{4}$, and $17\frac{1}{4} + 2$, or $19\frac{1}{4}$. We let $v =$ the value of the stock at the end of the business day.

2. *Translate.* We translate as follows.

Value at opening	+	Amount of increase	=	Value at close
↓	↓	↓	↓	↓
$17\frac{1}{4}$	+	$1\frac{5}{8}$	=	v

Using both methods:

8. Subtract .

$$7\frac{11}{12} - 5\frac{2}{3}$$

9. Subtract by first converting to improper fractions.

$$7\frac{3}{10}$$
$$-2\frac{9}{10}$$
$$\overline{\qquad}$$

10.

$$5\frac{1}{12}$$
$$-1\frac{3}{4}$$
$$\overline{\qquad}$$

11. Subtract

$$5$$
$$-1\frac{1}{3}$$
$$\overline{\qquad}$$

12. A fabric store sold two pieces of linen $3\frac{1}{4}$ yd and $4\frac{5}{6}$ yd long. What was the total length of the linen?

3. Solve. The sentence tells us what to do. We add using the LCD, 8.

$$
\begin{array}{r}
17\frac{1}{4} = \quad 17\frac{1}{4}\cdot\frac{2}{2} = \quad 17\frac{2}{8} \\[2mm]
+\ 1\frac{5}{8} = \ +\ 1\frac{5}{8} \quad = \ +\ 1\frac{5}{8} \\[2mm]
\hline
18\frac{7}{8}
\end{array}
$$

Thus, $v = 18\frac{7}{8}$.

4. Check. To check, we see that the answer is between $18\frac{1}{4}$ and $19\frac{1}{4}$, as predicted in the *Familiarize* step. Since $1\frac{5}{8}$ is between 1 and 2, this serves as a partial check.

5. State. The stock closed at $\$18\frac{7}{8}$.

Do Margin Exercise 12.

Example 11 Recently, in college football, the distance between goalposts was reduced from $23\frac{1}{3}$ to $18\frac{1}{2}$ ft. How much was it reduced?

1. Familiarize. Given that $23\frac{1}{3}$ is between 23 and 24 and $18\frac{1}{2}$ is between 18 and 19 we expect our answer to be close to 5 ($23 - 18 = 5$ or $24 - 19 = 5$).

2. Translate. We translate as follows.

Former distance	−	New distance	=	Amount of reduction
↓	↓	↓	↓	↓
$23\frac{1}{3}$	−	$18\frac{1}{2}$	=	d

3. Solve. To solve the equation, we carry out the subtraction. The LCD is 6.

$$23\frac{1}{3} = \qquad 23\frac{1}{3}\cdot\frac{2}{2} = \qquad 23\frac{2}{6} = \qquad 22\frac{8}{6}$$

$$-18\frac{1}{2} = \qquad -18\frac{1}{2}\cdot\frac{3}{3} = \qquad -18\frac{3}{6} = \qquad -18\frac{3}{6}$$

$$4\frac{5}{6}$$

4. Check. To check, we first note that the answer $4\frac{5}{6}$ is close to the estimation made in Step 1. We can check for accuracy by adding back the distance by which the goal posts were reduced.

$$18\frac{1}{2} + 4\frac{5}{6} = 18\frac{3}{6} + 4\frac{5}{6}$$

$$= 22\frac{8}{6} = 23\frac{2}{6} = 23\frac{1}{3}$$

5. **State.** The reduction in the goalpost distance was $4\frac{5}{6}$ ft.

Do Margin Exercise 13.

▶ **A Number Pattern**

Show that each of the following is true by simplying each side of the equation. Look for a pattern.

$$1 = \frac{1\cdot 2}{2}$$

$$1 + 2 = \frac{2\cdot 3}{2}$$

$$1 + 2 + 3 = \frac{3\cdot 4}{2}$$

$$1 + 2 + 3 + 4 = \frac{4\cdot 5}{2}$$

$$1 + 2 + 3 + 4 + 5 = \frac{5\cdot 6}{2}$$

Exercises   Use the pattern of the above to find the sum without adding.

1. $1 + 2 + 3 + 4 + 5 + 6$
2. $1 + 2 + 3 + 4 + 5 + 6 + 7 + 8$
3. $1 + 2 + 3 + 4 + 5 + 6 + 7 + 8 + 9 + 10 + 11 + 12$
4. $1 + 2 + 3 \ldots + 100$ (the dots stand for the symbols we did not write)

13. A $6\frac{1}{2}$-m pole was set $2\frac{3}{4}$ m in the ground. How much was left above the ground?

Exercise Set 5.3

[a] [b] Perform the indicated operation. Write a mixed number for the answer.

1. $2\dfrac{7}{8}$

   $+ 3\dfrac{5}{8}$

2. $4\dfrac{5}{6}$

   $+ 3\dfrac{5}{6}$

3. $1\dfrac{1}{4}$

   $+ 1\dfrac{2}{3}$

4. $4\dfrac{1}{3}$

   $+ 5\dfrac{2}{9}$

5. $8\dfrac{3}{4}$

   $+ 5\dfrac{5}{6}$

6. $4\dfrac{3}{8}$

   $+ 6\dfrac{5}{12}$

7. $3\dfrac{2}{5}$

   $+ 8\dfrac{7}{10}$

8. $5\dfrac{1}{2}$

   $+ 3\dfrac{7}{10}$

9. $5\dfrac{3}{8}$

   $+ 10\dfrac{5}{6}$

10. $\dfrac{5}{8}$

    $+ 1\dfrac{5}{6}$

11. $12\dfrac{4}{5}$

    $+ 8\dfrac{7}{10}$

12. $15\dfrac{5}{8}$

    $+ 11\dfrac{3}{4}$

13. $14\dfrac{5}{8}$

    $+ 13\dfrac{1}{4}$

14. $16\dfrac{1}{4}$

    $+ 15\dfrac{7}{8}$

15. $4\dfrac{1}{5}$

    $- 2\dfrac{3}{5}$

16. $5\dfrac{1}{8}$

    $- 2\dfrac{3}{8}$

17. $6\dfrac{3}{5}$

    $- 2\dfrac{1}{2}$

18. $7\dfrac{2}{3}$

    $- 6\dfrac{1}{2}$

19. $34\dfrac{1}{3}$

    $- 12\dfrac{5}{8}$

20. $23\dfrac{5}{16}$

    $- 16\dfrac{3}{4}$

21. 21

    $- 8\dfrac{3}{4}$

22. 42

    $- 3\dfrac{7}{8}$

23. 34

    $- 18\dfrac{5}{8}$

24. 23

    $- 19\dfrac{3}{4}$

25. $21\dfrac{1}{6}$

$-13\dfrac{3}{4}$

26. $42\dfrac{1}{10}$

$-23\dfrac{7}{12}$

27. $25\dfrac{1}{9}$

$-13\dfrac{5}{6}$

28. $23\dfrac{5}{16}$

$-14\dfrac{7}{12}$

[a] [b] Change to improper fractions, then add or subtract. Write the answer as a mixed number.

29. $5\dfrac{3}{14} + 3\dfrac{2}{21}$

30. $9\dfrac{1}{2} + 5\dfrac{3}{4}$

31. $9\dfrac{1}{2} - 7\dfrac{3}{8}$

32. $7\dfrac{3}{4} - 2\dfrac{3}{8}$

33. $3\dfrac{7}{8} + 4\dfrac{9}{10}$

34. $5\dfrac{3}{8} + 6\dfrac{2}{7}$

35. $37\dfrac{5}{9} - 25\dfrac{4}{5}$

36. $23\dfrac{1}{6} - 19\dfrac{2}{5}$

37. $2\dfrac{5}{6} + 3\dfrac{1}{3}$

38. $7\dfrac{3}{20} + 1\dfrac{2}{15}$

39. $4\dfrac{3}{11} + 5\dfrac{2}{3}$

40. $4\dfrac{11}{12} + 5\dfrac{7}{10}$

[c] Solve.

41. Alexa purchased two packages of ground turkey weighing $1\dfrac{2}{3}$ lb and $5\dfrac{3}{4}$ lb. What was the total weight of the meat?

42. Hubert purchased two packages of cheese weighing $1\dfrac{1}{3}$ lb and $4\dfrac{3}{5}$ lb. What was the total weight of the cheese?

43. Rocky is $187\dfrac{1}{10}$ cm tall and his daughter is $180\dfrac{3}{4}$ cm tall. How much taller is Rocky?

44. Aunt Louise is $168\dfrac{1}{4}$ cm tall and her son is $150\dfrac{7}{10}$ cm tall. How much taller is Aunt Louise?

45. Janet uses pipes of length $10\dfrac{5}{16}$ ft and $8\dfrac{3}{4}$ ft in the installation of a sink. How much pipe was used?

46. A standard pencil is $16\dfrac{9}{10}$ cm wood and $1\dfrac{9}{10}$ cm eraser. What is the total length of a standard pencil?

47. On a recent day, the stock of Marriott Corporation opened at $\$28\dfrac{7}{8}$ and closed at $\$27\dfrac{1}{4}$. How much did the price of the stock drop that day?

48. A photocopier technician drove $125\dfrac{7}{10}$ mi away from Los Angeles for a repair call. The next day the technician drove $65\dfrac{1}{2}$ mi back toward Los Angeles for another service call. How far was the technician from Los Angeles?

49. Renée is $4\frac{1}{2}$ cm taller than her daughter. The daughter is $169\frac{3}{10}$ cm tall. How tall is Renée?

50. A standard sheet of paper is $8\frac{1}{2}$ in. by 11 in. What is the total distance around (perimeter of) the paper?

51. One standard book size is $8\frac{1}{2}$ in. by $9\frac{3}{4}$ in. What is the total distance around (perimeter of) the front cover of such a book?

52. On a recent day, the stock of Cummins Engine Corporation opened at $\$104\frac{5}{8}$ and dropped $\$1\frac{1}{4}$ during the course of the day. What was the closing price?

53. A plane flew 640 km on a nonstop flight. On the return flight, it landed after having flown $320\frac{3}{10}$ km. How far was it from its original point of departure?

54. Brian is $5\frac{1}{4}$ cm taller than his son. The son is $182\frac{9}{10}$ cm tall. How tall is Brian?

55. Tamika worked $10\frac{1}{2}$ hr over a three-day period. If she worked $2\frac{1}{2}$ hr the first day and $4\frac{1}{5}$ hr the second, how many hours did she work the third day?

56. A painter had $3\frac{1}{2}$ gal of paint. It took $2\frac{3}{4}$ gal to paint a bedroom. It was estimated that it would take $2\frac{1}{4}$ gal to paint the living room. How much more paint was needed?

Find the length d in the figure

57.

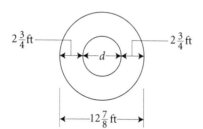

58.

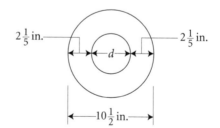

Find the distance around (perimeter of) the figure.

59.

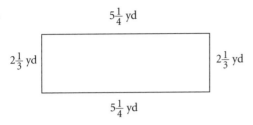

$5\frac{1}{4}$ yd

$2\frac{1}{3}$ yd $2\frac{1}{3}$ yd

$5\frac{1}{4}$ yd

60.

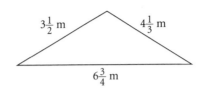

$3\frac{1}{2}$ m $4\frac{1}{3}$ m

$6\frac{3}{4}$ m

Skill Maintenance

61. Divide and simplify: $\frac{12}{25} \div \frac{24}{5}$.

62. Multiply and simplify: $\left(-\frac{15}{9}\right)\left(\frac{18}{39}\right)$.

Synthesis

63. ❖ Is the sum of two mixed numbers always a mixed number? Why or why not?

64. ❖ Write a word problem for a classmate to solve. Design the problem so it uses the equation $x + 4\frac{1}{2} = 10\frac{2}{3}$

65. A post for a pier is 29 ft long. Half of the post extends above the water's surface and $8\frac{3}{4}$ ft of the post is buried in mud. How deep is the water at that location?

66. Solve: $47\frac{2}{3} + n = 56\frac{1}{4}$

1. Simplify:

$$\left(\frac{2}{3}+\frac{3}{4}\right) \div 2\frac{1}{3}-\left(\frac{1}{2}\right)^3.$$

5.4 Order of Operations, Evaluating Expressions, and Problem Solving

a Order of Operations

Suppose we have a calculation like the following:

$$\frac{2}{3}+\frac{1}{5}\cdot\frac{2}{3}$$

The rules we learned for the order of operations for integers also apply to fractions or mixed numbers.

▶ **Rules for Order of Operations**

1. Do all calculations within parentheses (), brackets [], or braces {} before operations outside.

2. Evaluate all exponential expressions.

3. In order from left to right, do all multiplications and divisions.

4. In order from left to right, do all additions and subtractions.

Example 1   Simplify: $\left(\frac{7}{8}-\frac{1}{3}\right)\cdot 48+\left(13+\frac{4}{5}\right)^2$

$$\left(\frac{7}{8}-\frac{1}{3}\right)\cdot 48+\left(13+\frac{4}{5}\right)^2$$

$$=\left(\frac{7}{8}\cdot\frac{3}{3}-\frac{1}{3}\cdot\frac{8}{8}\right)\cdot 48+\left(\frac{13}{1}\cdot\frac{5}{5}+\frac{4}{5}\right)^2 \quad \begin{array}{l}\text{Carrying out operations}\\ \text{inside parantheses first. To}\\ \text{do so, we first multiply by}\\ \text{1 to obtain the LCD.}\end{array}$$

$$=\left(\frac{21}{24}-\frac{8}{24}\right)\cdot 48+\left(\frac{65}{5}+\frac{4}{5}\right)^2$$

$$=\frac{13}{24}\cdot 48+\left(\frac{69}{5}\right)^2 \qquad \text{Completing the operations within parantheses}$$

$$=\frac{13}{24}\cdot 48+\frac{4761}{25} \qquad \text{Evaluating the exponential expressions next}$$

$$=26+\frac{4761}{25} \qquad \text{Multiplying } \frac{13}{\underset{1}{24}}\cdot\frac{\overset{2}{48}}{1}=26$$

$$=26+190\frac{11}{25} \qquad \text{Converting to a mixed number}$$

$$=216\frac{11}{25}\text{, or }\frac{5411}{25} \qquad \text{Adding}$$

Answers can be given using either fractional notation or mixed numbers as desired. Consult with your instructor.

Do Margin Exercise 1.

b | Evaluating Expressions and Problem Solving

Fractions and mixed numbers can appear in algebraic expressions and equations.

Example 2 A train traveling r miles per hour for t hours travels a total of rt miles. (Remember: Distance = Rate · Time.)

a) Find the distance traveled by a 60-mph train in $2\frac{3}{4}$ hr.

We evaluate rt for $r = 60$ and $t = 2\frac{3}{4}$.

$$d = rt$$

$$d = 60 \cdot 2\frac{3}{4}$$

$$d = \frac{60}{1} \cdot \frac{11}{4}$$

$$d = \frac{15 \cdot 4 \cdot 11}{1 \cdot 4}$$

$$d = 165$$

In $2\frac{3}{4}$ hr, a 60-mph train travels 165 mi.

b) Find the distance traveled if the speed of the train is $26\frac{1}{2}$ mph and the time is $2\frac{2}{3}$ hr.

We evaluate rt for $r = 26\frac{1}{2}$ and $t = 2\frac{2}{3}$.

$$d = rt$$

$$d = 26\frac{1}{2} \cdot 2\frac{2}{3}$$

$$d = \frac{53}{2} \cdot \frac{8}{3}$$

$$d = \frac{53 \cdot 2 \cdot 4}{2 \cdot 3}$$

$$d = \frac{212}{3}$$

$$d = 70\frac{2}{3}$$

In $2\frac{2}{3}$ hr, a $26\frac{1}{2}$-mph train travels $70\frac{2}{3}$ mi.

Evaluate.

2. rt for $r = 78$ and $t = 2\frac{1}{4}$

3. $7xy$ for $x = 9\frac{2}{5}$ and $y = 2\frac{3}{7}$

4. $x - y \div z$ for $x = 5\frac{7}{8}, y = \frac{1}{4},$ and $z = 2$

Example 3. Evaluate $x + yz$ for $x = 7\frac{1}{3}, y = \frac{1}{3},$ and $z = 5$.

We substitute and follow the rules for order of operations:

$x + yz$

$7\frac{1}{3} + \frac{1}{3} \cdot 5$ Substitute values for x, y and z.

$7\frac{1}{3} + \frac{1}{3} \cdot \frac{5}{1}$

$7\frac{1}{3} + \frac{5}{3}$ Use order of operations

$7\frac{1}{3} + 1\frac{2}{3}$ ⎤   Adding mixed numbers

$8\frac{3}{3}$

9

Do Margin Exercises 2–4.

c Problem Solving

Example 4 An L -shaped room consists of a rectangle that is $8\frac{1}{2}$ by 11 ft and one that is $6\frac{1}{2}$ by $7\frac{1}{2}$ ft. What is the total area of a carpet that covers the floor?

1. *Familiarize.* In drawing this picture, we see that the room is formed by adding together two rectangles. If we estimate the area of the smaller rectangle it will be between 42ft² (6ft x 7ft) and 56ft (7ft x 8ft). The area of the large rectangle will be between 88ft² (11ft x 8ft) and 99ft² (11ft x 9ft). So the total area will be between 130 ft² (42ft² + 88ft²) and 155ft² (56ft² + 99ft²).

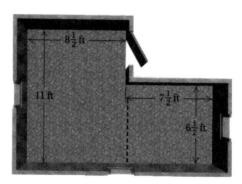

2. *Translate.* The total area is the sum of the areas of the two rectangles. This gives us the following equation:

total area = (area of larger rectangle) + (area of smaller rectangle)

$$a = 8\frac{1}{2} \cdot 11 + 7\frac{1}{2} \cdot 6\frac{1}{2}$$

3. **Solve.** This is a multistep problem. We perform each multiplication and then add. This follows the rules for order of operations:

$$a = 8\frac{1}{2} \cdot 11 + 7\frac{1}{2} \cdot 6\frac{1}{2}$$

$$a = \frac{17}{2} \cdot \frac{11}{1} + \frac{15}{2} \cdot \frac{13}{2}$$

$$a = \frac{17 \cdot 11}{2} + \frac{15 \cdot 13}{2 \cdot 2}$$

$$a = \frac{187}{2} + \frac{195}{4}$$

$$a = \frac{187}{2} \cdot \frac{2}{2} + \frac{195}{4}$$

$$a = \frac{324}{4} + \frac{195}{4}$$

$$a = \frac{569}{4}$$

$$a = 142\frac{1}{4}$$

4. **Check.** The answer $(142\frac{1}{4}\text{ft}^2)$ is within our original estimate.

5. **State.** The total area of the carpet is $142\frac{1}{4}$ ft².

Do Margin Exercise 5.

5. A room is $22\frac{1}{2}$ ft by $15\frac{1}{2}$ ft. A 9-ft by 12-ft Oriental rug is placed in the center of the room. How much area is not covered by the rug?

Exercise Set 5.4

a Simplify.

1. $\dfrac{2}{3} \div \dfrac{4}{3} \div \dfrac{7}{8}$

2. $\dfrac{5}{6} \div \dfrac{3}{4} \div \dfrac{2}{5}$

3. $\dfrac{5}{8} \div \dfrac{1}{4} - \dfrac{2}{3} \cdot \dfrac{4}{5}$

4. $\dfrac{4}{7} \cdot \dfrac{7}{15} + \dfrac{2}{3} \div 8$

5. $\dfrac{3}{4} - \dfrac{2}{3} \cdot \left(\dfrac{1}{2} + \dfrac{2}{5}\right)$

6. $\dfrac{3}{4} \div \dfrac{1}{2} \cdot \left(\dfrac{8}{9} - \dfrac{2}{3}\right)$

7. $28\dfrac{1}{8} - 5\dfrac{1}{4} + 3\dfrac{1}{2}$

8. $10\dfrac{3}{5} - 4\dfrac{1}{10} - 1\dfrac{1}{2}$

9. $\dfrac{7}{8} \div \dfrac{1}{2} \cdot \dfrac{1}{4}$

10. $\dfrac{7}{10} \cdot \dfrac{4}{5} \div \dfrac{2}{3}$

11. $\left(\dfrac{2}{3}\right)^2 - \dfrac{1}{3} \cdot 1\dfrac{1}{4}$

12. $\left(\dfrac{3}{4}\right)^2 + 3\dfrac{1}{2} \div 1\dfrac{1}{4}$

13. $\dfrac{1}{2} - \left(\dfrac{1}{2}\right)^2 + \left(\dfrac{1}{2}\right)^3$

14. $1 + \dfrac{1}{4} + \left(\dfrac{1}{4}\right)^2 - \left(\dfrac{1}{4}\right)^3$

b Evaluate 15–20 for $x = 6\dfrac{1}{4}$, $y = 2\dfrac{1}{2}$, and $z = \dfrac{2}{3}$.

15. $x + y \cdot z$

16. $x \cdot y + z$

17. $z(x + y)$

18. $x \div (y - z)$

19. $x \div y - z$

20. $xz + y$

Evaluate.

21. mv, for $m = 7$ and $v = 3\dfrac{2}{5}$

22. rs, for $r = 5$ and $s = 3\dfrac{1}{7}$

23. rt, for $r = 5\dfrac{2}{3}$ and $t = -2\dfrac{3}{8}$

24. mt, for $m = 6\dfrac{2}{9}$ and $t = -4\dfrac{3}{5}$

16. $3\frac{2}{5}$ 17. $5\frac{2}{3}$ 18. $6\frac{1}{4}$ 19. $8\frac{1}{2}$ 20. $-20\frac{1}{8}$

25. $M \div NP$, for $M = 2\frac{1}{4}$, $N = -5$, and $P = 2\frac{1}{3}$

26. $R \cdot S \div T$, for $R = 4\frac{2}{3}$, $S = 1\frac{3}{7}$, and $T = -5$

27. $a - bc$, for $a = 18$, $b = 2\frac{1}{5}$, and $c = 3\frac{3}{4}$

28. $r + ps$, for $r = 5\frac{1}{2}$, $p = 3$, and $s = 2\frac{1}{4}$

29. $m + n \div p$, for $m = 7\frac{2}{5}$, $n = 4\frac{1}{2}$, and $p = 6$

30. $x - y \div z$, for $x = 9$, $y = 2\frac{1}{2}$, and $z = 3\frac{3}{4}$

31. Find the distance traveled by a car driving at 70mph for $3\frac{1}{3}$hr.

32. Find the distance traveled by a car driving at 55mph for $1\frac{2}{3}$ hr.

33. Over $4\frac{4}{5}$ hours, a bicyclist averaged 19 mph. How far did she travel?

34. A train left the station at noon and had an average running speed of 70 mph. How far had it traveled by 2:40pm? (40 min $= \frac{2}{3}$ hr)

$\boxed{c}$ Solve

35. Jake has a $3\frac{1}{5} \times 4\frac{1}{5}$ ft. piece of fencing which he wants to attach to a $2\frac{1}{5}$ by $4\frac{1}{5}$ ft piece. What will the total area of the fencing be?

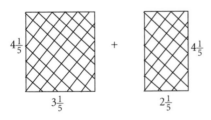

36. You want to practice using your new electric saw, so you take a piece of plywood which measures $3\frac{2}{3}$ ft by $5\frac{2}{3}$ ft and cut from it a square measuring $2\frac{1}{3}$ ft. What is the total area of the plywood after you cut out the square?

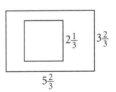

37. A picture has dimensions of $8\frac{1}{2}$ by 11 in. You put a border around it so that it now measures $12\frac{3}{4}$ by $15\frac{1}{4}$ in. How much has the area of the picture increased with the border?

38. Roommates are buying fabric for curtains in their new flat. It comes pre-cut in pieces that measure $5\frac{1}{2}$ ft by $3\frac{1}{2}$ ft. They buy 4 of these pre-cut pieces. What is the total area of the fabric purchased?

39. On a winter night, the temperature dropped from 7°F to −12°F. How many degrees did it drop?

40. Multiply: $(-\frac{1}{29})(-29)$.

41. Divide and simplify: $\frac{4}{5} \div \frac{6}{5}$.

42. Divide: $-198 \div (-6)$.

43. Multiply: $(-7)(185)(0)$.

Synthesis

44. ❖ Write a problem for a classmate to solve. Design the problem so that its solution is found by performing the addition $4\frac{1}{2} + 33\frac{1}{3}$.

45. ❖ Under what circumstances is a pair of mixed numbers more easily added than multiplied?

Simplify.

46. $-8 \div \frac{1}{2} + \frac{3}{4} + \left(-5 - \frac{5}{8}\right)^2$

47. $\left(\frac{5}{9} - \frac{1}{4}\right)(-12) + \left(-4 - \frac{3}{4}\right)^2$

48. $\frac{1}{3} \div \left(\frac{1}{2} - \frac{1}{5}\right) \cdot \frac{1}{4} + \frac{1}{6}$

49. $\frac{7}{8} - 1\frac{1}{8} \cdot \frac{2}{3} + \frac{9}{10} \div \frac{3}{5}$

Evaluate.

50. $ab + ac$ and $a(b + c)$, for $a = 3\frac{1}{4}$, $b = 5\frac{1}{3}$, $c = 4\frac{5}{8}$

51. $ab - ac$ and $a(b - c)$, for $a = 4\frac{1}{6}$, $b = 3\frac{2}{5}$, $c = 5\frac{1}{3}$

Review Exercises: Chapter 5

Add and simplify.

1. $\dfrac{6}{5} + \dfrac{3}{8}$
    2. $\dfrac{5}{16} + \dfrac{1}{12}$
    3. $-\dfrac{6}{5} + \dfrac{11}{15}$
    4. $\dfrac{5}{16} + \dfrac{3}{24}$

Subtract and simplify.

5. $\dfrac{5}{9} - \dfrac{2}{9}$
    6. $\dfrac{3}{4} - \dfrac{7}{8}$
    7. $\dfrac{11}{27} - \dfrac{2}{9}$
    8. $\dfrac{5}{6} - \dfrac{2}{9}$

Use < or > for □ to write a true sentence.

9. $\dfrac{4}{7} \;\boxed{>}\; \dfrac{5}{9}$
    10. $\dfrac{8}{9} \;\square\; \dfrac{11}{13}$

Use < or > for □ to write a true sentence.

11. $\dfrac{4}{7} \;\square\; \dfrac{5}{9}$
    12. $\dfrac{-8}{9} \;\square\; \dfrac{-11}{13}$

Add.

13. $\dfrac{-4}{y} + \left(\dfrac{-8}{y}\right)$
    14. $\dfrac{11}{10} + \dfrac{9}{100} + \dfrac{5}{1000}$

Add. Write a mixed numeral for the answer.

15. $\begin{array}{r} 5\frac{3}{5} \\ + \, 4\frac{4}{5} \\ \hline \end{array}$
    16. $\begin{array}{r} 8\frac{1}{3} \\ + \, 3\frac{2}{5} \\ \hline \end{array}$
    17. $\begin{array}{r} 5\frac{5}{6} \\ + \, 4\frac{5}{6} \\ \hline \end{array}$
    18. $\begin{array}{r} 2\frac{3}{4} \\ + \, 5\frac{1}{2} \\ \hline \end{array}$

Subtract. Write a mixed numeral for the answer.

19. $\begin{array}{r} 12 \\ - \, 4\frac{2}{9} \\ \hline \end{array}$
    20. $\begin{array}{r} 9\frac{3}{5} \\ - \, 4\frac{13}{15} \\ \hline \end{array}$
    21. $4\dfrac{5}{8} - 9\dfrac{3}{4}$
    22. $-7\dfrac{1}{2} - 6\dfrac{3}{4}$

Solve.

23. $x + \dfrac{2}{5} = \dfrac{7}{8}$ **24.** $\dfrac{22}{5} = x + \dfrac{16}{5}$ **25.** $x - \dfrac{2}{3} = -\dfrac{11}{12}$ **26.** $-\dfrac{1}{2} + y = \dfrac{9}{10}$

Simplify.

27. $\dfrac{7}{8} \div \dfrac{1}{2} \cdot \left(\dfrac{6}{7} - \dfrac{2}{7} \right)$ **28.** $\left(\dfrac{5}{8} \right)^2 - \dfrac{7}{16} \div \dfrac{7}{2}$

Evaluate.

29. $5x - y$, for $x = 3\dfrac{1}{5}$ and $y = 2\dfrac{2}{7}$ **30.** $2a \div b$, for $a = 5\dfrac{2}{11}$ and $b = 3\dfrac{4}{5}$

Solve.

31. Alcoa Stock Price. On the first day of trading on the stock market, stock in Alcoa opened at $67\dfrac{3}{4}$ and rose by $2\dfrac{5}{8}$ at the close of trading. What was the stock's closing price?

32. A board $\dfrac{9}{10}$ in. thick is glued to a board $\dfrac{8}{10}$ in. thick. The glue is $\dfrac{3}{100}$ in. thick. How thick is the result?

33. What is the sum of the areas in the figure below?

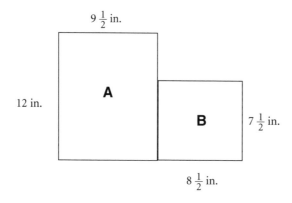

34. In the figure above, how much larger is the area of rectangle A than the area of rectangle B?

35. A wedding-cake recipe requires 12 cups of shortening. Being calorie-conscious, the wedding couple decides to reduce the shortening by 3 5\8 cups and replace it with prune purée. How many cups of shortening are used in their new recipe?

Practice Test: Chapter 5

Perform the indicated operation and, if possible, simplify.

1. $\dfrac{1}{2} + \dfrac{5}{2}$

2. $-\dfrac{7}{8} + \dfrac{2}{3}$

3. $\dfrac{5}{6} - \dfrac{3}{6}$

4. $\dfrac{7}{6} - \dfrac{3}{4}$

5. $\dfrac{5}{8} - \dfrac{17}{24}$

6. $3\dfrac{4}{5} - 9\dfrac{1}{2}$

7. $9\dfrac{1}{4} + 5\dfrac{1}{6}$

8. $\begin{array}{r} 14 \\ -7\dfrac{5}{6} \\ \hline \end{array}$

9. $\begin{array}{r} 10\dfrac{1}{6} \\ -5\dfrac{7}{8} \\ \hline \end{array}$

10. $-\dfrac{15}{x} - \left(\dfrac{-9}{x}\right)$

11. $\dfrac{3}{4} + \dfrac{7}{8} + \dfrac{5}{16}$

Use < or > to write a true statement.

12. $-\dfrac{13}{14} \ \square \ -\dfrac{2}{3}$

13. $\dfrac{5}{8} \ \square \ \dfrac{9}{16}$

Solve.

14. $x + \dfrac{7}{9} = -\dfrac{4}{3}$

15. $y - \dfrac{3}{10} = \dfrac{5}{6}$

16. $\dfrac{6}{25} = \dfrac{7}{15} + t$

Simplify.

17. $\dfrac{2}{3} + 1\dfrac{1}{3} \cdot 2\dfrac{1}{8}$

18. $\left(\dfrac{2}{5} + \dfrac{3}{4} + \dfrac{1}{2}\right) \cdot \dfrac{1}{3}$

Evaluate.

19. $\dfrac{2}{3} ab$, for $a = 7$ and $b = 4\dfrac{1}{5}$

20. $4 + mn$, for $m = 7\dfrac{2}{5}$ and $n = 3\dfrac{1}{4}$

Solve.

21. The weights of two students are $83\frac{2}{3}$ kg and $76\frac{3}{4}$ kg. What is their total weight?

22. A standard piece of paper is $\frac{43}{200}$ m by $\frac{7}{25}$ m. By how much does the length exceed the width?

23. Find the area of the shaded region.

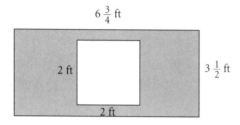

24. Explain how to add fractions with different denominators. Give an example.

25. A student claims that $13\frac{7}{9} - 8\frac{5}{9} = 5\frac{2}{9}$. What mistake is the student making, and how should he have proceeded?

6

Decimals

An Application

As life becomes busier, Americans are eating many more meals outside the home. In 1995, the average check for a casual meal eaten out was $28.90 and in 1996, it was $39.51 (**Source:** Sandelman and Associates. Brea Ca). How much more is the average check for 1996 than that for 1995?

This problem appears as Example 1 in Section 6.9.

The Mathematics

We let c = the additional amount spent in 1996. The problem then translates to the equation

$$\$28.90 + c = 39.51.$$

This equation involves decimal notation, which arises often in applied problems.

Introduction

In this chapter, we consider the operations of addition, subtraction, multiplication, and division with decimals. This will allow us to solve applied probems like the one below. We will also study estimating sums, differences, products, and quotients. Conversion between fractional and decimal notation in which the decimal notation may be repeating will be discussed. We will also work with decimals in equations.

6.1 Decimal Notation

The set of **rational numbers** consists of the integers

$$\ldots, -3, -2, -1, 0, 1, 2, 3, \ldots,$$

and fractions like

$$\frac{1}{2}, \frac{2}{3}, \frac{-7}{8}, \frac{17}{-10}, \text{ and so on.}$$

We used fractional notation for rational numbers in Chapters 4 and 5. In Chapter 6, we will use *decimal notation*. We will still consider the same set of numbers, but now with a different notation. For example, instead of using fractional notation for $\frac{7}{8}$, we use decimal notation, 0.875.

a Decimal Notation and Word Names

Decimal notation for the women's shotput record is 74.249 ft. To understand what 74.249 means, we use a **place-value chart**. The value of each place is $\frac{1}{10}$ as large as the one to its left.

PLACE-VALUE CHART							
Hundreds	Tens	Ones	Tenths	Hundredths	Thousandths	Ten-Thousandths	Hundred-Thousandths
100	10	1	$\frac{1}{10}$	$\frac{1}{100}$	$\frac{1}{1000}$	$\frac{1}{10,000}$	$\frac{1}{100,000}$

$$7 \quad 4 \quad . \quad 2 \quad 4 \quad 9$$

The decimal notation 74.249 means

$$70 + 4 + \frac{2}{10} + \frac{4}{100} + \frac{9}{1000}.$$

A mixed number for 74.249 is $74\frac{249}{1000}$. We read 74.249 as "seventy-four and two hundred forty-nine thousandths." When we come to the decimal point, we read "and."

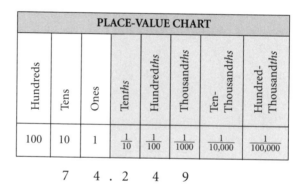

▶ To write a word name from decimal notation,

a. write a word name for the integer (the number named to the left of the decimal point),

397.685
↳ **Three hundred ninety-seven**

b. write the word "and" for the decimal point, and

397.685
Three hundred ninety-seven **and**

c. write a word name for the number named to the right of the decimal point, followed by the place value of the last digit.

397.**685**
Three hundred ninety-seven and **six hundred eighty-five thousandths**

Note: If there are no non-zero digits to the left of the decimal, skip parts *a* and *b*.

Example 1 Write a word name for the number in this sentence: Each person consumes an average of 41.2 gallons of water per year.

Forty-one and two-tenths

Example 2 Write a word name for −410.87.

Negative four hundred ten and eighty-seven hundredths

Example 3 Write a word name for the number in this sentence: The world record in the men's marathon is 2.1833 hours.

Two and one thousand eight hundred thirty-three ten-thousandths

Example 4 Write a word name for 1788.405.

One thousand, seven hundred eighty-eight and four hundred five thousandths

Example 5 Write a word name for 0.0075.

Seventy-five ten-thousandths

Do Margin Exercises 1–5.

Decimal notation is also used with money. It is common on a check to write "and ninety-five cents" as "and $\frac{95}{100}$ dollars."

Example 6 Write a word name for a check amount of $5876.95.

Five thousand, eight hundred seventy-six and $\frac{95}{100}$ dollars

Do Margin Exercises 6.

Write a word name for the number.

1. Each person in this country consumes an average of 21.1 gallons of coffee per year. (**Source:** Department of Agriculture).

2. The racehorse *Swale* won the Belmont Stakes in a time of 2.4533 minutes.

3. −245.89

4. 31,079.764

5. 0.038

Write a word name as on a check.

6. $4217.56

b Converting from Decimal Notation to Fractional Notation

We can find fractional notation as follows:

$$9.875 = 9\frac{875}{1000}$$

Note the following:

$$9.875 \qquad\qquad 9\frac{875}{1000}$$

$$\uparrow \qquad\qquad\qquad \uparrow$$

3 decimal places   3 zeros

Reduce: $\quad 9\dfrac{875}{1000}$

$$9\frac{7}{8} \text{ or } \frac{79}{8}$$

To convert 4.98 to fractional notation:

a. Write the integer

$\qquad\qquad\qquad\qquad\qquad\qquad\qquad$ 4

b. Count the number of digits to the right of the decimal and move the decimal point that number of places to the right.

$\qquad\qquad .98.\quad$ 2 places

c. Write the result over a denominator of 1 followed by that many zeroes.

$\qquad\qquad \dfrac{98}{100}\quad$ 2 zeroes

d. Now write the integer and fractions as a mixed number.

$\qquad\qquad 4\dfrac{98}{100}$

e. Reduce the fraction whenever possible. (*Note:* If the integer portion is 0, omit step a.)

$\qquad\qquad 4\dfrac{49}{50} \text{ or } \dfrac{249}{50}$

Example 7 Write fractional notation for 0.876.

$$0.876 \qquad 0.876. \qquad 0.876 = \frac{876}{1000} = \frac{219}{250}$$

$$\text{3 places} \qquad \text{3 zeros}$$

For a number like 0.876, we generally write a 0 before the decimal to avoid forgetting or overlooking the decimal point.

Example 8 Write fractional notation for 56.23.

$$56.23 \qquad 56.23. \qquad 56.23 = 56\frac{23}{100} \text{ or } \frac{5623}{100}$$

$$\text{2 places} \qquad \text{2 zeros}$$

Negative numbers written in decimal notation can also be converted.

Example 9 Write fractional notation for −1.5018. Do not simplify.

$$-1.5018 \quad -1.5018. \quad -1.5018 = -1\frac{5018}{10,000} = -1\frac{2509}{5000} \text{ or } -\frac{7509}{5000}$$

4 places

Do Margin Exercises 7–10.

c Order

To compare numbers in decimal notation, consider 0.85 and 0.9. First note that $0.9 = 0.90$ because $\frac{9}{10} = \frac{90}{100}$. Also, $0.85 = \frac{85}{100}$. Since $\frac{85}{100} < \frac{90}{100}$, it follows that $0.85 < 0.9$. This leads us to a quick way to compare two numbers named in decimal notation.

> ► To compare two *positive numbers* in decimal notation, start at the left and compare digits with the same place value. When two digits differ, the number with the larger digit is the larger of the two numbers. To ease the comparison, extra zeros can be written to the right of the last decimal place.

Example 10 Which is larger: 2.109 or 2.1?

2.109	2.109	2.109	2.109
↑ The same ↓	↑ The same ↓	↑ The same ↓	↑ Different; 9 is **larger** than 0. ↓
2.1	2.1	2.10	2.100

Thus, 2.109 is **larger**. In symbols, $2.109 > 2.1$.

Example 11 Which is larger: 0.09 or 0.108?

0.09	0.09
↑ The same ↓	↑ Different; 1 is **larger** than 0. ↓
0.108	0.108

Thus, 0.108 is **larger**. In symbols, $0.108 > 0.09$.

As before, a number line can be used to visualize order. We illustrate Examples 10 and 11. Larger numbers are always to the right.

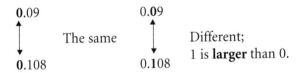

Write fractional notation.

7. 0.896

8. −23.78

9. 5.6789

10. 1.9

Which number is larger?

11. 2.04, 2.039

12. 0.06, 0.008

13. 0.5, 0.58

14. 1, 0.9999

15. 0.8989, 0.09898

16. 21.006, 21.05

17. −34.01, −34.008

18. −9.12, −8.98

Observe from the number line that −2 < −1. Similarly, −1.57 < −1.52.

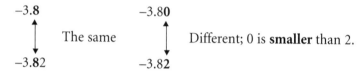

> *Reminder:* For any two numbers on the number line, the number to the left is less than the number on the right.

> To compare two *negative numbers* in decimal notation, start at the left and compare digits with the same place value. When two digits differ, the number with the smaller digit is the larger of the two numbers.

Example 12 Which is **larger**: −3.8 or −3.82?

−3.8 ↕ −3.82   The same

−3.80 ↕ −3.82   Different; 0 is **smaller** than 2.

Thus, −3.8 is **larger**. In symbols, −3.8 > −3.82.

Do Margin Exercises 11–18.

d Rounding

Rounding is done as for whole numbers. To see how, we again make use of a number line.

Example 13 Round 0.37 to the nearest tenth.

Here is part of a number line, magnified.

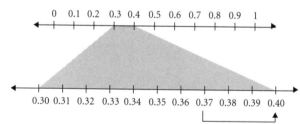

We see that 0.37 is closer to 0.40 than to 0.30. Thus, 0.37 rounded to the nearest tenth is 0.4.

> When rounding the fractional portion a decimal:
>
> **a.** Locate the digit in the rounding place.
> **b.** Consider the next digit to the right.
> **c.** If the digit to the right is 5 or more, round up.
> **d.** Drop all digits to the right of the rounding place.

Example 14   Round 3876.2459 to the nearest tenth.

a. Locate the digit in the tenths place.

3 8 7 6 . **2** 4 5 9
↑

b. Consider the next digit to the right.

3 8 7 6 . 2 **4** 5 9
↰↑

c. Since that digit, **4**, is less than 5, the digits to the right of the tenths place are dropped.

3 8 7 6 . 2   This is the answer.

Example 15   Round 64.7953 to the nearest hundredth.

a. Locate the digit in the hundredths place.

6 4 . 7 **9** 5 3
↑

b. Consider the next digit to the right.

6 4 . 7 9 **5** 3
↰↑

c. Since that digit is 5 or more, round up. Since the hundredths digit becomes 10, we carry 1 to the tenths place. The answer is 64.80. Note that the 0 in 64.80 indicates that the answer is correct to the nearest hundredth.

Example 16   Round 7536.8274 to the nearest thousandth, hundredth, tenth, one, ten, hundred, and thousand.

Thousandth:	7536.827	Ten:	7540
Hundredth:	7536.83	Hundred:	7500
Tenth:	7536.8	Thousand:	8000
One:	7537		

▶ Notice when rounding a decimal to a place value in the integer portion, follow the rules for rounding whole numbers (see R.4) and drop all digits to the right of the decimal.

Example 17   Round –0.06 to the nearest tenth.

a. Locate the digit in the tenths place.

–0 . **0** 6
↑

b. Consider the next digit to the right.

–0 . 0 **6**
↰↑

c. Since that digit, **6**, is greater than 5, round from –0.06 to –0.1.

The answer is –0.1.

Do Margin Exercises 19–37.

Round to the nearest tenth.

19. 2.76   **20.** 13.85

21. –234.448   **22.** 7.009

Round to the nearest hundredth.

23. 0.636   **24.** –7.834

25. 34.695   **26.** –0.025

Round to the nearest thousandth.

27. 0.9434   **28.** –8.0038

29. –43.1119   **30.** 37.4005

Round 7459.3598 to the nearest:

31. Thousandth.

32. Hundredth.

33. Tenth.

34. One.

35. Ten. (*Caution:* "Tens" are not "tenths.")

36. Hundred.

37. Thousand.

STUDY TIPS FOR TROUBLE SPOTS

By now you have probably encountered certain topics that gave you more difficulty than others. It is important to know that this happens to every person who studies mathematics. Unfortunately, frustration is often part of the learning process and it is important not to give up when difficulty arises.

One source of frustration for many students is not being able to set aside sufficient time for studying. Family commitments, work schedules, and recreational activities are just a few of the time demands that many students face. Couple these demands with a math lesson that seems to require a greater than usual amount of study time, and it is no wonder that many students often feel frustrated. Below are some study tips that might be useful if and when troubles arise.

- Realize that everyone—even your instructor—has been stymied at times when studying math. You are not the first person, nor will you be the last, to encounter a "roadblock."

- Whether working alone or with a classmate, try to allow enough study time so that you won't need to constantly glance at a clock. Difficult material is best mastered when your mind is completely focused on the subject matter. Thus, if you are tired, it is usually best to study early the next morning or to take a ten-minute "power-nap" in order to make the most productive use of your time.

- Talk about your trouble spot with a classmate. It is possible that she or he is also having difficulty with the same material. If that is the case, per-

haps the majority of your class is confused and your instructor's coverage of the topic is not yet finished. If your classmate *does* understand the topic that is troubling you, patiently allow him or her to explain it to you. By verbalizing the math in question, your classmate may help clarify the material for both of you. Perhaps you will be able to return the favor for your classmate when he or she is struggling with a topic that you understand.

- Try to study in a "controlled" environment. What we mean by this is that you can often put yourself in a setting that will enable you to maximize your powers of concentration. For example, whereas some students may succeed in studying at home, for many this setting is filled with distractions. Consider a trip to the math center, a library, or an empty classroom if such a setting is more conducive to studying. If you plan on working with a classmate, try to find a location in which conversation will not be bothersome to others.

- When working on difficult material, it is often helpful to first "back up" and review the most recent material that *did* make sense. This can build your confidence and create a momentum that can often carry you through the roadblock. Sometimes a small piece of information that appeared in a previous section is all that is needed for your problem spot to disappear. When the difficult material is finally mastered, try to make use of what is fresh in your mind by taking a "sneak preview" of what your next topic for study will be.

Exercise Set 6.1

a   Write a word name for the number in the sentence.

1. The average age of a bride is 23.2 years.

2. The fastest time in the men's marathon was 2.1083 hours.

3. Each day, the average person spends $7.89 on health care.

4. Recently, one dollar was worth 88.106 Japanese yen.

Write a word name.

5. 42.359

6. 12.345

7. −528.37

8. −6314.201

Write a word name as on a check.

9. $216.99

10. $346.68

11. $47.02

12. $9.85

b   Write fractional notation.

13. 9.2

14. 8.3

15. 0.17

16. 0.89

17. 1.46

18. 2.78

19. −304.7

20. −215.8

21. 3.142

22. 1.732

23. 46.03

24. 53.81

25. −0.00013

26. −0.0109

27. 20.003

28. 1000.3

29. 2.0114

30. 1.0008

31. −4567.2

32. −0.1104

Which number is larger?

33. 0.42, 0.418

34. 0.738, 0.71

35. 0.1, 0.111

36. 31.08, 31.2

37. 0.0009, 0.001

38. −4.056, −4.043

39. −234.07, −235.07

40. 0.99999, 1.0

41. 0.4545, 0.05454

42. −0.6, −0.05

43. −0.54, −0.78

44. 0.432, 0.4325

45. −0.8437, −0.84384

46. −0.872, −0.873

d

Round to the nearest tenth and to the nearest ten.

47. 0.11

48. 0.76

49. −0.16

50. −0.29

51. 0.5794

52. 0.75

53. −2.7449

54. 5.98

55. 13.41

56. −41.23

57. 153.96

58. 36.049

Round to the nearest hundredth and to the nearest one.

59. 0.893

60. 0.675

61. 0.666

62. 4.798

63. −0.4246

64. −6.529

65. 2.396

66. 0.406

67. −0.007

68. −4.889

69. 1.4251

70. 0.66661

Round to the nearest thousandth.

71. 0.3246

72. 0.4278

73. −0.6666

74. −7.4294

75. 17.00153

76. 2.67769

77. 0.0009

78. 123.4562

Skill Maintenance

79. Simplify: $\dfrac{0}{-19}$.

80. Add: $\dfrac{2}{15} + \dfrac{5}{9}$.

81. Subtract: $\dfrac{4}{9} - \dfrac{2}{3}$.

82. Solve: $x + 5 = 3$.

83. Solve: $3x = 21$.

84. Subtract: $\dfrac{3}{14} - \dfrac{2}{7}$.

Synthesis

85. ❖ Explain why −73.69 is smaller than −73.67.

86. ❖ Describe in your own words a procedure for converting from decimal notation to fractional notation.

There are other methods of rounding decimal notation. A computer often uses a method called **truncating.** To round using truncating, simply drop all decimal places past the rounding place, which is the same as changing all digits to the right to zeros. For example, truncating 6.78163 to the third decimal place gives 6.781. Use truncating to round each of the following to the fifth decimal place.

87. 6.78346123

88. −6.783461902

89. 99.999999999

90. 0.07070707

1.   0.8 4 7
       + 1 0.0 7

2.   2.1
       0.7 3 9
     + 3 1.3 6 8 9

Add.

3. 0.02 + 4.3 + 0.649

4. 0.12 + 3.006 + 0.4357

5. 0.4591 + 0.2374 + 8.70894

6.2 Addition and Subtraction with Decimals

a | Addition

Adding with decimal notation is similar to adding whole numbers. First though, we must line up the decimal points. Then we add digits from the right. For example, we add the thousandths, then the hundredths, and so on, carrying when necessary. If desired, we can write extra zeros to the right of the last decimal place so that the number of places is the same.

Example 1   Add: 56.314 + 17.78.

5 6 . 3 1 4 + 1 7 . 7 8 **0**	Lining up the decimal points in order to add Writing an extra zero as a placeholder
5 6 . 3 1 4 + 1 7 . 7 8 0 **4**	Adding thousandths
5 6 . 3 1 4 + 1 7 . 7 8 0 **9** 4	Adding hundredths
1 5 6 . 3 1 4 + 1 7 . 7 8 0 . **0** 9 4	Adding tenths Write a decimal point in the answer. We get 10 tenths = 1 one + 0 tenths, so we carry the 1 to the ones column.
1 1 5 6 . 3 1 4 + 1 7 . 7 8 0 **4** . 0 9 4	Adding ones We get 14 ones = 1 ten + 4 ones, so we carry the 1 to the tens column.
1 1 5 6 . 3 1 4 + 1 7 . 7 8 0 **7** 4 . 0 9 4	Adding tens

Do Margin Exercises 1 and 2.

Remember, we can write extra zeros to the right of the decimal point to get the same number of decimal places without changing the value of the number.

Example 2   Add: 3.42 + 0.237 + 14.1.

3.4 2 **0** 0.2 3 7 + 1 4.1 **0 0**	Lining up the decimal points and writing extra zeros
1 7.7 5 7	Adding

Do Margin Exercises 3–5.

Consider the addition 3456 + 19.347. Keep in mind that an integer, such as 3456, has an "unwritten" decimal point to its right, with 0 fractional parts. When adding, we can always write in that decimal point and extra zeros if desired.

Example 3   Add: 3456 + 19.347.

$$
\begin{array}{r}
3\,4\,5\,6.\mathbf{0\,0\,0} \\
+\quad 1\,9.3\,4\,7 \\
\hline
3\,4\,7\,5.3\,4\,7
\end{array}
$$

Writing in the decimal point and extra zeros

Lining up the decimal points in order to add

Adding

Do Margin Exercises 6 and 7.

b   Subtraction

Subtracting with decimal notation is similar to subtracting whole numbers. First we line up the decimal points. Then we subtract digits, beginning with the rightmost decimal place. For example, we subtract the thousandths, then the hundredths, the tenths, and so on, borrowing when necessary.

Example 4   Subtract: 56.314 − 17.78.

$$
\begin{array}{r}
5\,6.3\,1\,4 \\
-1\,7.7\,8\,\mathbf{0} \\
\end{array}
$$

Lining up the decimal points in order to subtract

Writing an extra 0

$$
\begin{array}{r}
5\,6.3\,1\,4 \\
-1\,7.7\,8\,0 \\
\hline
4
\end{array}
$$

Subtracting thousandths

$$
\begin{array}{r}
^{2\ 11} \\
5\,6.\cancel{3}\,\cancel{1}\,4 \\
-1\,7.7\,8\,0 \\
\hline
3\,4
\end{array}
$$

Borrowing a tenth to subtract hundredths

$$
\begin{array}{r}
^{12} \\
^{5\ 2\ 11} \\
5\,\cancel{6}.\cancel{3}\,\cancel{1}\,4 \\
-1\,7.7\,8\,0 \\
\hline
.5\,3\,4
\end{array}
$$

Borrowing a one to subtract tenths

Writing a decimal point

$$
\begin{array}{r}
^{15\ 12} \\
^{4\ 5\ 2\ 11} \\
\cancel{5}\,\cancel{6}.\cancel{3}\,\cancel{1}\,4 \\
-1\,7.7\,8\,0 \\
\hline
8.5\,3\,4
\end{array}
$$

Borrowing a ten to subtract ones

$$
\begin{array}{r}
^{15\ 12} \\
^{4\ 5\ 2\ 11} \\
\cancel{5}\,\cancel{6}.\cancel{3}\,\cancel{1}\,4 \\
-1\,7.7\,8\,0 \\
\hline
3\,8.5\,3\,4
\end{array}
$$

Subtracting tens

Check:
$$
\begin{array}{r}
^{1\ 1\ 1} \\
3\,8.5\,3\,4 \\
+1\,7.7\,8\,0 \\
\hline
5\,6.3\,1\,4
\end{array}
$$

Do Margin Exercises 8 and 9.

Add.

6. 789 + 123.67

7. 45.78 + 2467 + 1.993

Subtract.

8.
$$
\begin{array}{r}
3\,7.4\,2\,8 \\
-2\,6.6\,7\,4
\end{array}
$$

9.
$$
\begin{array}{r}
0.3\,4\,7 \\
-0.0\,0\,8
\end{array}
$$

Subtract.

10. $1.7 - 0.23$

11. $0.43 - 0.18762$

12. $7.37 - 0.00008$

Subtract.

13. $1277 - 82.78$

14. $5 - 0.0089$

Add.

15. $7.42 + (-9.38)$

16. $-4.201 + 7.36$

17. Add: $-4.95 + (-3.6)$.

Example 5 Subtract: $23.08 - 5.0053$.

$$
\begin{array}{r}
\overset{\scriptstyle 1\ 13}{}\ \overset{\scriptstyle 7\ 9\ 10}{} \\
2\,\cancel{3}.0\,\cancel{8}\cancel{0}\,\cancel{0} \\
-\ 5.0\,0\,5\,3 \\
\hline
1\,8.0\,7\,4\,7
\end{array}
$$

Writing two extra zeros is essential.

Subtracting

Do Margin Exercises 10–12.

As with addition, when subtraction involves a whole number, there is an "unwritten" decimal point that can be written in. Extra zeros can then be written in to the right of the decimal point.

Example 6 Subtract: $456 - 2.467$.

$$
\begin{array}{r}
\overset{\scriptstyle 5\ 9\ 9\ 10}{} \\
4\,5\,\cancel{6}\,\cancel{0}\,\cancel{0}\,\cancel{0} \\
-\ 2.4\,6\,7 \\
\hline
4\,5\,3.5\,5\,3
\end{array}
$$

Writing in the decimal point and extra zeroes.

Subtracting

Do Exercises 13 and 14.

$\boxed{\text{c}}$ Adding and Subtracting with Negatives

Recall that to find the sum of a negative number and a positive number, we find the difference of their absolute values and then use the sign of the number with the greater absolute value.

Example 7 Add: $-13.82 + 4.69$.

a. $|-13.82| = 13.82$, $|4.69| = 4.69$, so $|-13.82| > |4.69|$, and the answer is **negative**.

b.
$$
\begin{array}{r}
\overset{\scriptstyle 7\ 12}{} \\
1\,3.\cancel{8}\,\cancel{2} \\
4.6\,9 \\
\hline
9.1\,3
\end{array}
$$

Finding the difference of the absolute values

Next, use the result of part (a).

c. $-13.82 + 4.69 = -9.13$

Do Margin Exercises 15 and 16.

We can find the sum of two negative numbers by adding the absolute values and making the answer negative.

Example 8 Add: $-2.306 + (-3.125)$.

a.
$$
\begin{array}{r}
2.3\,0\,6 \\
+\ 3.1\,2\,5 \\
\hline
5.4\,3\,1
\end{array}
$$

Adding the absolute values

b. $-2.306 + (-3.125) = -5.431$

The sum of two negatives is negative.

Do Margin Exercise 17

To subtract, we add the opposite of the number being subtracted.

Example 9   Subtract: $-3.1 - 4.8$.

$$-3.1 - 4.8 = -3.1 + (\mathbf{-4.8}) \qquad \text{Adding the opposite of 4.8}$$
$$= -7.9 \qquad \text{The sum of two negatives is negative.}$$

Example 10   Subtract: $-7.9 - (-8.5)$.

$$-7.9 - (-8.5) = -7.9 + \mathbf{8.5} \qquad \text{Adding the opposite of } -8.5$$
$$= 0.6 \qquad \text{Subtracting absolute values. The answer is positive since 8.5 has the larger absolute value.}$$

Do Margin Exercises 18–21.

Subtract.

18. $9.25 - 13.41$

19. $-4.26 - 3.18$

20. $9.8 - (-2.6)$

21. $-5.9 - (-3.2)$

Exercise Set 6.2

a Add.

1.
$$\begin{array}{r} 3\,1 6.2\,5 \\ +\ \ 1\,8.1\,2 \\ \hline \end{array}$$

2.
$$\begin{array}{r} 4\,1.8\,2\,3 \\ +6\,1\,4.9\,1\,5 \\ \hline \end{array}$$

3.
$$\begin{array}{r} 6\,5\,9.4\,0\,3 \\ +9\,1\,6.8\,1\,2 \\ \hline \end{array}$$

4.
$$\begin{array}{r} 3.2\,5 \\ +1\,1\,2\,3.3\,9 \\ \hline \end{array}$$

5.
$$\begin{array}{r} 9.1\,0\,4 \\ +1\,2\,3.4\,5\,6 \\ \hline \end{array}$$

6.
$$\begin{array}{r} 4.1\,5\,2\,3 \\ +3.2\,7\,7\,8 \\ \hline \end{array}$$

7.
$$\begin{array}{r} 6\,1.0\,0\,6 \\ +\ \ 3.4\,0\,7 \\ \hline \end{array}$$

8. $0.8096 + 0.7856$

9. $20.0124 + 30.0124$

10. $0.263 + 0.8$

11. $0.83 + 0.005$

12. $0.347 + 10.04$

13. $0.34 + 3.5 + 0.127 + 768$

14. $2.3 + 0.729 + 23$

15. $17 + 3.24 + 0.256 + 0.3689$

16.
$$\begin{array}{r} 4\,7.8 \\ 2\,1\,9.8\,5\,2 \\ 4\,3.5\,9 \\ +6\,6\,6.7\,1\,3 \\ \hline \end{array}$$

17.
$$\begin{array}{r} 2.7\,0\,3 \\ 7\,8.3\,3 \\ 2\,8.0\,0\,0\,9 \\ +1\,1\,8.4\,3\,4\,1 \\ \hline \end{array}$$

18.
$$\begin{array}{r} 1\,3.7\,2 \\ 9.1\,1\,2 \\ 6\,5\,4\,2.7\,9\,0\,8 \\ +\ \ \ 2\,3.9\,0\,1 \\ \hline \end{array}$$

19. $99.6001 + 7285.18 + 500.042 + 870$

20. $65.987 + 9.4703 + 6744.02 + 1.0003 + 200.895$

b Subtract.

21.
$$\begin{array}{r} 5.2 \\ -3.9 \\ \hline \end{array}$$

22.
$$\begin{array}{r} 1\,1.3\,4\,5 \\ -\ \ 2.1\,0\,5 \\ \hline \end{array}$$

23.
$$\begin{array}{r} 5\,1.3\,1 \\ -\ \ 2.2\,9 \\ \hline \end{array}$$

24.
$$\begin{array}{r} 3\,7.4\,5 \\ -\ \ 6.3\,2 \\ \hline \end{array}$$

25.
```
   2.5
- 0.0 0 2 5
```

26.
```
   2 8.0
-   0.2 8
```

27.
```
   9 2.3 4 1
-     6.4 2
```

28.
```
   0.3 4 6
- 0.0 3 4 6
```

29.
```
   3.0 0 7 4
- 1.3 4 0 8
```

30.
```
   3 2.7 9 7 8
-     0.0 5 9 2
```

31.
```
   6.0 7
- 2.0 0 7 8
```

32.
```
   1.0
- 0.9 9 9 9
```

33. $28.2 - 19.35$

34. $100.12 - 0.112$

35. $34.07 - 30.7$

36. $36.2 - 16.28$

37. $8.45 - 7.405$

38. $3.801 - 2.81$

39. $6.003 - 2.3$

40. $9.087 - 8.807$

41. $1 - 0.0098$

42. $23\ 2 - 1.0908$

43. $100 - 0.34$

44. $624 - 18.79$

45. $7.48 - 2.6$

46. $3 - 2.006$

47. $25.008 - 12.4$

48. $263.7 - 102.08$

49. $2548.98 - 2.007$

50. $19 - 1.198$

51. $45 - 0.999$

52. $10.056 - 0.392$

c Add or subtract, as indicated.

53. $-8.02 + 9.73$

54. $-4.31 + 7.66$

55. $12.9 - 15.4$

56. $27.2 - 31.9$

57. $-2.9 + (-4.3)$

58. $-5.7 + (-1.9)$

59. $-4.301 + 7.68$

60. $-5.952 + 7.98$

61. $-13.4 - 9.2$

62. $-8.7 - 12.4$

63. $-2.1 - (-4.6)$

64. $-4.3 - (-2.5)$

65. $14.301 + (-17.82)$

66. $13.45 + (-18.701)$

67. $7.201 - (-2.4)$

68. $2.901 - (-5.7)$

69. $23.9 + (-9.4)$

70. $43.2 + (-10.9)$

71. $-8.9 - (-12.7)$

72. $-4.5 - (-7.3)$

73. $-4.9 - 5.392$

74. $89.3 - 92.1$

75. $14.7 - 23.5$

76. $-7.201 - 1.9$

Skill Maintenance

77. Simplify: $\dfrac{0}{-92}$.

78. Add: $\dfrac{-2}{7} + \dfrac{5}{21}$.

79. Subtract: $\dfrac{3}{5} - \dfrac{7}{10}$.

80. Solve: $x - 16 = 5$.

81. Solve: $7x = 40$.

82. Subtract: $\dfrac{2}{9} - \dfrac{2}{3}$

Synthesis

83. ❖ A student claims to be able to add negative numbers but not subtract them. What advice would you give this student?

84. ❖ Explain the error in the following: Add.

$$\begin{array}{r} 1\,3.0\,7 \\ +\quad 9.2\,0\,5 \\ \hline 1\,0.5\,1\,2 \end{array}$$

85. ❖ Explain the error in the following: Subtract.

$$\begin{array}{r} 7\,3.0\,8\,9 \\ -\quad 5.0\,0\,6\,1 \\ \hline 2.3\,0\,2\,8 \end{array}$$

6.3 Multiplication with Decimals

a Multiplication

We now consider products like

$$2.3 \times 1.12 \quad \text{or} \quad 0.02 \times 3.412.$$

Note the number of decimal places.

<table>
<tr><td>1.1 2</td><td>(2 decimal places)</td><td>3.4 1 2</td><td>(3 decimal places)</td></tr>
<tr><td>× 2.3</td><td>(1 decimal place)</td><td>× 0.0 2</td><td>(2 decimal places)</td></tr>
<tr><td>2.5 7 6</td><td>(3 decimal places)</td><td>0.0 6 8 2 4</td><td>(5 decimal places)</td></tr>
</table>

It is important to write in this zero.

We have the following rule for multiplying decimals.

▶ To multiply using decimals: 0.8×0.43

a. Ignore the decimal points and multiply as though both factors were whole numbers.

$$\begin{array}{r} {\scriptstyle 2} \\ 0.4\,3 \\ \times\ \ 0.8 \\ \hline \mathbf{3\,4\,4} \end{array}$$ Ignore the decimal points for now.

b. Then place the decimal point in the result. The number of decimal places in the product is the sum of the numbers of places in the factors (count places from the right).

$$\begin{array}{r} 0.4\,3 \quad \text{(2 decimal places)} \\ \times\ \ 0.8 \quad \text{(1 decimal place)} \\ \hline 0.3\,4\,4 \quad \text{(3 decimal places)} \end{array}$$

Example 1 Multiply: 8.3×74.6.

a. Ignore the decimal points and multiply as though factors were whole numbers:

$$\begin{array}{r} {\scriptstyle 3\ \ 4} \\ {\scriptstyle 1\ \ 1} \\ 7.4\,6 \\ \times\ \ 8.3 \\ \hline 2\,2\,3\,8 \\ 5\,9\,6\,8\,0 \\ \hline \mathbf{6\,1\,9\,1\,8} \end{array}$$ We are not yet finished.

b. Place the decimal point in the result. The number of decimal places in the product is the sum, $1 + 1$, of the number of decimal places in the factors.

$$\begin{array}{r} 7.4\,6 \quad \text{(1 decimal place)} \\ \times\ \ 8.3 \quad \text{(1 decimal place)} \\ \hline 2\,2\,3\,8 \\ 5\,9\,6\,8\,0 \\ \hline 6\,1\,9.1\,8 \quad \text{(2 decimal places)} \end{array}$$

Do Margin Exercise 1.

1. Multiply.

$$\begin{array}{r} 7\,6.3 \\ \times\ \ 8.2 \\ \hline \end{array}$$

Multiply.

2.   4 2 1 3
     × 0.0 0 5 1

3. 2.3 × 0.0041

4. 5.2014 × (−2.41)

As we catch on to the skill, we can combine the two steps.

Example 2   Multiply: 0.0032 × 2148.

```
      2 1 4 8    (0 decimal places)
    × 0.0 0 3 2  (4 decimal places)
      4 2 9 6
    6 4 4 4 0
    6.8 7 3 6    (4 decimal places)
```

Example 3   Multiply: −0.14 × 0.867.

Multiplying the absolute values, we have

```
      0.8 6 7    (3 decimal places)
    ×   0.1 4    (2 decimal places)
      3 4 6 8
      8 6 7 0
    0.1 2 1 3 8  (5 decimal places)
```

Since the product of a negative and a positive is negative, the answer is −0.12138.

Do Margin Exercises 2–4.

Suppose that a product involves multiplication by a tenth, hundredth, thousandth, and so on. From the following products, a pattern emerges.

```
    4 5.6        4 5.6         4 5.6          4 5.6
  ×   0.1      × 0.0 1       × 0.0 0 1      × 0.0 0 0 1
    4.5 6        0.4 5 6       0.0 4 5 6      0.0 0 4 5 6
```

Observe the location of the decimal point in each product. Note that in each case the product is *smaller* than 45.6 and contains the digits 456.

> To multiply any number by a tenth, hundredth, thousandth, and so on:
>
> **a.** count the number of decimal places in the tenth, hundredth, or thousandth, and
>
> **b.** move the decimal point that many places to the left. Use zeros as placeholders if necessary.

0.001 × 34.45678

→ **3** places

0.001 × 34.45678 = 0.034.45678

Move **3** places to the left.

0.001 × 34.45678 = 0.03445678

Examples Multiply.

4. $0.1 \times 45 = 4.5$ Moving the decimal point one place to the left

5. $0.01 \times 243.7 = 2.437$ Moving the decimal point two places to the left

6. $0.001 \times (-8.2) = -0.0082$ Moving the decimal point three places to the left

7. $0.0001 \times 536.9 = 0.05369$ Moving the decimal point four places to the left

Do Margin Exercises 5–8.

Next we consider multiplication of a decimal by a power of ten such as 10, 100, 1000, and so on. From the following products, a pattern emerges.

$$
\begin{array}{r}
5.2\,3\,7 \\
\times\;\;\;\;\; 1\,0 \\
\hline
0\,0\,0\,0 \\
5\,2\,3\,7 \\
\hline
5\,2.3\,7\,0
\end{array}
\qquad
\begin{array}{r}
5.2\,3\,7 \\
\times\;\;\;\;\; 1\,0\,0 \\
\hline
0\,0\,0\,0 \\
0\,0\,0\,0 \\
5\,2\,3\,7 \\
\hline
5\,2\,3.7\,0\,0
\end{array}
\qquad
\begin{array}{r}
5.2\,3\,7 \\
\times\;\;\;\;\; 1\,0\,0\,0 \\
\hline
0\,0\,0\,0 \\
0\,0\,0\,0 \\
0\,0\,0\,0 \\
5\,2\,3\,7 \\
\hline
5\,2\,3\,7.0\,0\,0
\end{array}
$$

Observe the location of the decimal point in each product. Note that in each case the product is *larger* than 5.237 and contains the digits 5237.

> ▶ To multiply any number by a power of ten, such as 10, 100, 1000, and so on,
>
> **a.** count the number of zeros, and
>
> $\underset{\text{3 zeros}}{1000} \times 34.45678$
>
> **b.** move the decimal point that many places to the right. Use zeros as placeholders if necessary.
>
> $1000 \times 34.45678 = 34.456.78$
>
>   Move **3** places to the right.
>
> $1000 \times 34.45678 = 34{,}456.78$

Examples Multiply.

8. $10 \times 32.98 = 329.8$ Moving the decimal point one place to the right

9. $100 \times 4.7 = 470$ Moving the decimal point two places to the right; zero is a placeholder here

10. $1000 \times (-2.4167) = -2416.7$ Moving the decimal point three places to the right

11. $10{,}000 \times 7.52 = 75{,}200$ Moving the decimal point four places to the right and using two zeros as placeholders

Do Margin Exercises 9–12.

Multiply.

5. 0.1×359

6. 0.001×732.4

7. $(-0.01) \times 5.8$

8. 0.0001×723.6

Multiply.

9. 10×53.917

10. $100 \times (-62.417)$

11. 1000×64.7

12. $10{,}000 \times 43.01$

Convert the number in the sentence to standard notation.

13. Americans drink 17 million gallons of coffee each day.

14. The population of the world is 5.6 billion.

b | Using Multiplication with Decimal Notation

Naming Large Numbers

We often see notation like the following in newspapers and magazines and on television.

> O'Hare International Airport handles **59.9 million** passengers per year.
> Americans drink **17 million** gallons of coffee each day.
> The population of the world is **5.6 billion**.

To understand such notation, it helps to consider the following table.

> ▶ 1 hundred = 100 → 2 zeros
>
> 1 thousand = 1000 → 3 zeros
>
> 1 million = 1,000,000 → 6 zeros
>
> 1 billion = 1,000,000,000 → 9 zeros
>
> 1 trillion = 1,000,000,000,000 → 12 zeros

To convert to standard notation, we proceed as follows.

Example 12 Convert the number in this sentence to standard notation: O'Hare handles 59.9 million passengers per year.

$$59.9 \text{ million} = 59.9 \times \textbf{1 million}$$
$$= 59.9 \times \textbf{1,000,000} = 59,900,000$$

Do Margin Exercises 13 and 14.

Money Conversion

Converting from dollars to cents is like multiplying by 100. To see why, consider $19.43.

$19.43 = 19.43 × **$1**	We think of $19.43 as 19.43 × 1 dollar or 19.43 × $1.
= 19.43 × **100¢**	Substituting 100¢ for $1: $1 = 100¢
= 1943¢	Multiplying

> ▶ To convert from dollars to cents, move the decimal point two places to the right and change from the $ sign in front to the ¢ sign at the end.

Examples Convert from dollars to cents.

13. $189.64 = 18,964¢
14. $0.75 = 75¢

Do Margin Exercises 15 and 16.

Converting from cents to dollars is like multiplying by 0.01. To see why, consider 65¢.

$$65¢ = 65 \times 1¢$$ We think of 65¢ as 65 × 1 cent, or 65 × 1¢.
$$= 65 \times \$0.01$$ Substituting $0.01 for 1¢: 1¢ = $0.01
$$= \$0.65$$ Multiplying

> ▶ To convert from cents to dollars, move the decimal point two places to the left and change from the ¢ sign at the end to the $ sign in front.

Examples Convert from cents to dollars.

15. 395¢ = $3.95
16. 8503¢ = $85.03

Do Margin Exercises 17 and 18.

c | Evaluating

Frequently algebraic expressions are evaluated using numbers written in decimal notation.

Example 17 Evaluate *Prt* for *P = 80, r = 0.12,* and *t = 0.5.*

We will see later that this product could be used to determine the interest earned on $80, invested at 12 percent simple interest, for half a year. We substitute as follows:

$$Prt = 80(0.12)(0.5)$$

$$Prt = 9.6(0.5)$$

$$Prt = 4.8.$$

Prt is $4.80.

Do Margin Exercise 19.

Convert from dollars to cents.

15. $15.69

16. $0.17

Convert from cents to dollars.

17. 35¢

18. 577¢

19. Evaluate *lwh* for *l* = 3.2, *w* = 2.6, and *h* = 0.8. (This is the formula for the volume of a rectangular box.)

20. Find the area of the stamp in Example 18.

21. Evaluate $6.28rh + 3.14r^2$ for $r = 1.5$ and $h = 5.1$. (This is the formula for the area of an open can.)

Example 18 Find the perimeter of a stamp that is *3.25* cm long and *2.5* cm wide.

Recall that the perimeter, P, of a rectangle of length l and width w is given by the formula

$$P = 2l + 2w.$$

Thus we evaluate $2l + 2w$ for $l = 3.25$ and $w = 2.5$:

$$P = 2l + 2w$$
$$P = 2(\textbf{3.25}) + 2(\textbf{2.5})$$
$$P = 6.5 + 5.0 \qquad \text{Remember the rules for order of operations.}$$
$$P = 11.5.$$

The perimeter is 11.5 cm.

Example 19 Evaluate $9.8t^2$ for $t = 5.1$.

This formula is used in physics to find the distance, in meters, traveled by a falling body. We substitute as follows:

$$9.8\ t^2 = 9.8(5.1)^2$$
$$= 9.8 \cdot 26.01 \qquad \text{Squaring}$$
$$= 254.898. \qquad \text{Multiplying}$$

The distance is 254.898 m.

Do Margin Exercises 20 and 21.

Exercise Set 6.3

a Multiply.

1. 6.8
 $\times$ 7

2. 5.7
 $\times 0.9$

3. 0.8 4
 $\times$ 8

4. 7.3
 $\times 0.6$

5. 6.3
 $\times 0.0\,4$

6. 7.8
 $\times 0.0\,9$

7. 1 7.2
 $\times 0.0\,0\,6$

8. 8.7
 $\times 0.0\,6$

9. 10×23.76

10. 100×2.8793

11. -1000×783.686852

12. -0.34×1000

13. -7.8×100

14. $0.00238 \times (-10)$

15. 0.1×89.23

16. 0.01×789.235

17. 0.001×97.68

18. 8976.23×0.001

19. $28.7 \times (-0.01)$

20. $0.0325 \times (-0.1)$

21. 2.7 3
 $\times$ 1 6

22. 8.2 7
 $\times$ 5.4

23. 0.9 8 4
 $\times$ 3.3

24. 7.4 8 9
 $\times$ 8.2

25. $(-37.4)(-2.4)$

26. $569(-1.05)$

27. $749(-0.43)$

28. $(-876)(-20.4)$

29. 0.8 7
 $\times$ 6 4

30. 7.2 5
 $\times$ 6 0

31. 4 6.5 0
 $\times$ 7 5

32. 8.2 4
 $\times 7\,0\,3$

33. $(-0.231)(-0.5)$

34. $(-12.3)(-1.08)$

35. $9.42 \times (-1000)$

36. $-7.6 \times (-1000)$

37. $-95.3 \times (-0.0001)$

38. $-4.23 \times (-0.001)$

b Convert from dollars to cents.

39. $28.88   **40.** $67.43   **41.** $0.66   **42.** $1.78

Convert from cents to dollars.

43. 34¢   **44.** 95¢   **45.** 3445¢   **46.** 933¢

Convert the number in the sentence to standard notation.

47. In a recent year, the net sales of Morton International, Inc., were $3.6 billion.

48. Annual production of sugarcane is 1.075 billion tons.

49. The total surface area of the earth is 196.8 million square miles.

50. Annual sales of *Sports Illustrated* magazine is 3.2 million copies per year.

c Evaluate.

51. $P + Prt$, for $P = 10,000$, $r = 0.04$, and $t = 2.5$ (*formula for adding interest*)

52. $6.28r(h + r)$, for $r = 10$ and $h = 17.2$ (*surface area of a cylinder*)

53. $vt + 0.5at^2$, for $v = 10$, $t = 1.5$, and $a = 4.9$ (*physics formula*)

54. $4lh + 2h^2$, for $l = 3.5$ and $h = 1.2$ (*surface area of a rectangular prism*)

Find (a) the perimeter and (b) the area of a rectangular room with the given dimensions.

55. 12.5 ft long, 9.5 ft wide

56. 10.25 ft long, 8 ft wide

Skill Maintenance

57. Simplify: $\dfrac{-109}{-109}$.

58. Add: $\dfrac{-2}{10} + \dfrac{4}{15}$.

59. Subtract: $\dfrac{2}{9} - \dfrac{5}{18}$.

60. Solve: $x - 4 = -2$.

61. Add: $-\dfrac{3}{20} + \dfrac{3}{4}$.

62. Simplify: $\dfrac{0}{-19}$.

Synthesis

63. ❖ If two rectangles have the same perimeter, will they also have the same area? Why?

64. ❖ A student insists that 346.708×0.1 is 3467.08. How could you convince the student that a mistake has been made?

Express as a power of 10.

65. (1 trillion) · (1 billion)

66. (1 million) · (1 billion)

6.4 Division with Decimals

a Division

Whole Number Divisors

Now that we have studied multiplication of decimals, we can develop a procedure for division. The following divisions are justified by the multiplication in each *check:*

This is the **dividend.** ⟶ $\dfrac{651}{7} = 93$ *Check:* $7 \cdot 93 = 651$.

This is the **divisor.** ⟶

This is the **quotient.**

$$\frac{65.1}{7} = 9.3 \qquad \textit{Check: } 7 \cdot 9.3 = 65.1.$$

$$\frac{6.51}{7} = 0.93 \qquad \textit{Check: } 7 \cdot 0.93 = 6.51.$$

$$\frac{0.651}{7} = 0.093 \qquad \textit{Check: } 7 \cdot 0.093 = 0.651.$$

Note that the number of decimal places in each quotient is the same as the number of decimal places in the dividend.

> To divide by a whole number,
>
> **a.** place the decimal point directly above the decimal point in the dividend, and
>
> **b.** divide as though dividing whole numbers.

$$
\begin{array}{r}
0.8\,4 \\
7\overline{)5.8\,8} \\
5\,6 \\
\hline
2\,8 \\
2\,8 \\
\hline
0
\end{array}
$$

Example 1   Divide: $82.08 \div 24$.

Place the decimal point.

$$
\begin{array}{r}
3.4\,2 \\
2\,4\overline{)8\,2.0\,8} \\
7\,2 \\
\hline
1\,0\,0 \\
9\,6 \\
\hline
4\,8 \\
4\,8 \\
\hline
0
\end{array}
$$

Divide as though dividing whole numbers.

Estimation can be used as a partial check: $24 \approx 25$ and $82.08 \approx 80$; since $75 \div 25 = 3$. then $80 \div 25$ would be a little more than 3. So 3.42 is a reasonable answer and we have at least a partial check.

Do Margin Exercises 1–3.

Divide.

1. $9\overline{)5.4}$

2. $39.1 \div 23$

3. $8\,2\overline{)3\,8.5\,4}$

Divide.

4. $2\,5\,\overline{)\,8}$

5. $-23 \div 4$

6. $8\,6\,\overline{)\,2\,1.5}$

Extra zeros

Sometimes the division process ends, or terminates, only after we have written some extra zeros to the right of the decimal point. This does not change the value of the number.

Example 2 Divide: $36 \div 8$.

$$
\begin{array}{r}
4. \\
8\,)\overline{3\,6.} \\
\underline{3\,2} \\
4
\end{array}
$$
Place the decimal point and divide to find how many ones.

$$
\begin{array}{r}
4. \\
8\,)\overline{3\,6.0} \\
\underline{3\,2}\downarrow \\
4\,\mathbf{0}
\end{array}
$$
Write an extra zero; this does not change the number.

$$
\begin{array}{r}
4.5 \\
8\,)\overline{3\,6.0} \\
\underline{3\,2}\downarrow \\
4\,0 \\
\underline{4\,0} \\
0
\end{array}
$$
Divide to find how many tenths.

Since the remainder is 0, we are finished.

Example 3 Divide: $-4 \div 25$.

We first consider $4 \div 25$:

$$
\begin{array}{r}
0.1\,6 \\
2\,5\,)\overline{4.0\,0} \\
\underline{2\,5} \\
1\,5\,0 \\
\underline{1\,5\,0} \\
0
\end{array}
$$
← We can write as many extra zeros as needed.

Since a negative number divided by a positive number is negative, the answer is -0.16.

Do Margin Exercises 4–6.

Divisors That Are Not Whole Numbers

Consider the division

$$0.24 \overline{)8.208}$$

We write the division as $\dfrac{8.208}{0.24}$. If we multiply by 1, it is possible to find an equivalent division with a whole-number divisor, as in Examples 1–3:

$$\frac{8.208}{0.24} = \frac{8.208}{0.24} \times \frac{\mathbf{100}}{\mathbf{100}} = \frac{820.8}{24}.$$

Since the divisor is now a whole number, we have effectively traded a "new" problem for an equivalent problem that is more familiar:

$$0.24 \overline{)8.208}$$

is the same as

$$24 \overline{)820.8}$$

▶ To divide when the divisor is not a whole number,

a. move the decimal point (multiply by 10, 100, and so on) to make the divisor a whole number;

$$0.24 \overline{)8.208}$$

Move **2** places to the right.

b. move the decimal point the same number of places (multiply the same way) in the dividend; and

$$0.24 \overline{)8.208}$$

Move **2** places to the right.

c. place the decimal point for the answer directly above the new decimal point in the dividend and divide as though dividing whole numbers.

$$
\begin{array}{r}
3\,4.2 \\
0.24 \overline{)8.2\,0_{\wedge}8} \\
7\,2 \\
\hline
1\,0\,0 \\
9\,6 \\
\hline
4\,8 \\
4\,8 \\
\hline
0
\end{array}
$$

(The new decimal point in the dividend is indicated by a caret.)

7. a. Complete.

$$\frac{3.75}{0.25} = \frac{3.75}{0.25} \times \frac{\mathbf{100}}{\mathbf{100}}$$

$$= \frac{(\quad)}{25}$$

b. Divide.

$$0.2\,5\,\overline{)3.7\,5}$$

Divide.

8. $0.8\,3\,\overline{)4.0\,6\,7}$

9. $-44.8 \div (-3.5)$

10. Divide.

$$1.6\,\overline{)2\,5}$$

Example 4   Divide: $5.848 \div 8.6$.

$$8.6\,\overline{)5.8\,4\,8}$$

Multiply the divisor by 10 (move the decimal point 1 place). Multiply the same way in the dividend (move 1 place).

$$\begin{array}{r} 0.6\,8 \\ 8.6\,\overline{)5.8{\scriptstyle\wedge}4\,8} \\ \underline{5\,1\,6} \\ 6\,8\,8 \\ \underline{6\,8\,8} \\ 0 \end{array}$$

Then divide.

Note: $\dfrac{5.848}{8.6} = \dfrac{5.848}{8.6} \cdot \dfrac{10}{10} = \dfrac{58.48}{86}$.

Do Margin Margin Exercises 7–9.

Example 5   Divide: $12 \div 0.64$.

$$0.6\,4\,\overline{)1\,2.}$$

Put a decimal point at the end of the whole number.

$$0.6\,4\,\overline{)1\,2.0\,0}$$

Multiply the divisor by 100 (move the decimal point 2 places). Multiply the same way in the dividend (move 2 places).

$$\begin{array}{r} 1\,8.7\,5 \\ 0.6\,4\,\overline{)1\,2.0\,0{\scriptstyle\wedge}0\,0} \\ \underline{6\,4} \\ 5\,6\,0 \\ \underline{5\,1\,2} \\ 4\,8\,0 \\ \underline{4\,4\,8} \\ 3\,2\,0 \\ \underline{3\,2\,0} \\ 0 \end{array}$$

Then divide.

Do Margin Exercise 10.

To divide quickly by a thousandth, hundredth, tenth, ten, hundred, and so on, consider the following:

$$\frac{43.9}{100} = \frac{43.9}{100} \cdot \frac{\mathbf{10}}{\mathbf{10}} = \frac{439}{1000} = 0.439;$$

$$\frac{43.9}{0.01} = \frac{43.9}{0.01} \cdot \frac{\mathbf{100}}{\mathbf{100}} = \frac{4390}{1} = 4390.$$

Division of 43.9 by a number greater than 1 results in a quotient *smaller* than 43.9, whereas division by a positive number less than 1 results in a quotient that is *larger* than 43.9.

▶ To divide by a power of ten, such as 10, 100, or 1000, and so on,

a. count the number of zeros in the divisor, and

$$\frac{713.495}{100}$$

└┘→ **2** zeros

b. move the decimal point that number of places to the left.

$$\frac{713.495}{\mathbf{100}}, \qquad 7.13.495 \qquad \frac{713.495}{100} = \frac{7.13495}{1.00} = 7.13495$$

2 places to the left

To divide by a tenth, hundredth, or thousandth, and so on,

a. count the number of decimal places in the divisor, and

$$\frac{89.12}{0.001}$$

└┘→ **3** places

b. move the decimal point that number of places to the right.

$$\frac{89.12}{\mathbf{0.001}}, \qquad 89.120. \qquad \frac{89.12}{0.001} = \frac{89120.}{1.0} = 89{,}120$$

3 places to the right

Example 6 Divide: $\dfrac{0.0732}{10}$

$$\frac{0.0732}{10}, \qquad 0.0.0732, \qquad \frac{0.0732}{10} = 0.00732$$

1 zero   **1** place to the left to change 10 to 1.

Example 7 Divide: $\dfrac{23.738}{0.001}$.

$$\frac{23.738}{\mathbf{0.001}}, \qquad 23.738. \qquad \frac{23.738}{0.001} = 23{,}738$$

3 places to the right to change 0.001 to 1.

Do Margin Exercises 11–14.

Divide.

11. $\dfrac{0.1278}{0.01}$

12. $\dfrac{0.1278}{100}$

13. $\dfrac{98.47}{1000}$

14. $\dfrac{6.7832}{-0.1}$

▶ Summary of Multiplication and Division Shortcuts

To multiply any number by 10, 100, 1000, and so on.

a. count the number of zeros,

b. move the decimal point that many places to the right.

example $32.584 \times 10 = 328.54$
$32.584 \times 100 = 3285.4$
$32.584 \times 1000 = 32,854$

To divide by a power of ten, such as 10, 100, or 1000, and so on,

a. count the number of zeros in the divisor, and

b. move the decimal point that number of places to the left.

example $32.584 \div 10 = 3.2854$
$32.584 \div 100 = 0.32854$
$32.584 \div 100 = 0.032854$

To multiply any number by 0.1, 0.01, 0.001, and so on,

a. count the number of decimal places in the tenth, hundredth, or thousandth, and

b. move the decimal point that many places to the left.

example $32.584 \times 0.1 = 3.2854$
$32.584 \times 0.01 = 0.32854$
$32.584 \times 0.001 = 0.032854$

To divide by 0.1, 0.01, 0.001, and so on.

a. count the number of decimal places in the divisor, and

b. move the decimal point that number of places to the right.

example $32.584 \div 0.1 = 328.54$
$32.584 \div 0.01 = 3285.4$
$32.584 \div 0.001 = 32,854$

b Order of Operations: Decimal Notation

The same rules for order of operations used with integers apply when we are simplifying expressions involving decimal notation.

▶ Rules for Order of Operations

1. Do all calculations within parentheses ( ), brackets [ ], or braces { } before operations outside.

2. Evaluate all exponential expressions.

3. In order from left to right, do all multiplications and divisions.

4. In order from left to right, do all additions and subtractions.

Example 8 Simplify: $(5 - 0.06) \div 2 + 3.42(0.1)$.

$(5 - 0.06) \div 2 + 3.42(0.1) = \mathbf{4.94} \div 2 + 3.42(0.1)$ Carrying out operations inside parentheses

$= \mathbf{2.47} + \mathbf{0.342}$ Doing all multiplications and divisions in order from left to right

$= 2.812$

Example 9 Simplify: $25 - [5.4(1.3^2 + 0.21) \div 0.6]$.

$25 - [5.4(1.3^2 + 0.21) \div 0.6]$

$= 25 - [5.4(\mathbf{1.69} + 0.21) \div 0.6]$ ⎤
$= 25 - [5.4(\mathbf{1.9}) \div 0.6]$ ⎦   Working in the innermost parentheses first

$= 25 - [\mathbf{10.26} \div 0.6]$ Multiplying

$= 25 - 17.1$ Dividing

$= 7.9$

Do Margin Exercises 15 and 16.

Example 10 *Average Movie Revenue.* The bar graph shows movie box-office revenue (money taken in), in billions, in each of the four years from 1993 to 1996. Find the average revenue.

Movie Box Office Revenue
Source: Motion Picture Association of America

To find the average of a set of numbers, we add them. Then we divide by the number of addends. In this case, we are finding the average of 5.2, 5.4, 5.5, and 5.9 (in billions of dollars). The average is given by

$$(5.2 + 5.4 + 5.5 + 5.9) \div 4.$$

Thus

$$(5.2 + 5.4 + 5.5 + 5.9) \div 4 = 22 \div 4 = 5.5.$$

The average box-office revenue was $5.5 billion.

Do Margin Exercise 17.

Simplify.

15. $0.25 \cdot (1 + 0.08) - 0.0274$

16. $[(19.7 - 17.2)^2 + 3] \div 1.25$

17. *Tickets Sold at the Movies.* The number of tickets sold at the movies in each of the four years from 1993 to 1996 is shown in the bar graph below. Find the average number of tickets sold.

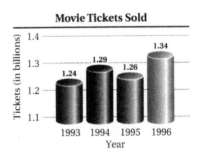
Movie Tickets Sold

Exercise Set 6.4

a Divide.

1. $5 \overline{)7\,3}$

2. $5 \overline{)1\,8}$

3. $4 \overline{)9\,5.1\,2}$

4. $8 \overline{)2\,5.9\,2}$

5. $1\,2 \overline{)8\,9.7\,6}$

6. $2\,3 \overline{)2\,5.0\,7}$

7. $3\,3 \overline{)2\,3\,7.6}$

8. $12.4 \div (-4)$

9. $9.144 \div (-8)$

10. $3.6 \div 4$

11. $12.123 \div 3$

12. $-5.4 \div 6$

13. $-0.35 \div 5$

14. $0.0\,4 \overline{)1.6\,8}$

15. $0.1\,2 \overline{)8.4}$

16. $0.3\,6 \overline{)2.8\,8}$

17. $3.2 \overline{)1\,2\,8}$

18. $2.6 \overline{)1\,0\,4}$

19. $6 \div (-15)$

20. $1.8 \div (-12)$

21. $3\,6 \overline{)1\,4.7\,6}$

22. $2.7\overline{)129.6}$

23. $6.2\overline{)46.5}$

24. $8.5\overline{)27.2}$

25. $39.06 \div (-4.2)$

26. $0.0828 \div (-3.6)$

27. $-5 \div (-8)$

28. $-7 \div (-8)$

29. $0.47\overline{)0.1222}$

30. $0.54\overline{)0.27}$

31. $4.8\overline{)75}$

32. $0.28\overline{)63}$

33. $0.032\overline{)0.07488}$

34. $0.017\overline{)1.581}$

35. $-24.969 \div 82$

36. $-25.221 \div 42$

37. $\dfrac{213.4567}{1000}$

38. $\dfrac{-213.4567}{100}$

39. $\dfrac{-213.4567}{10}$

40. $\dfrac{-213.4567}{0.1}$

41. $\dfrac{1.0237}{0.001}$

42. $\dfrac{1.0237}{-0.01}$

43. $\dfrac{56.78}{-0.001}$

44. $\dfrac{0.5678}{1000}$

45. $\dfrac{743.92}{-100}$

46. $\dfrac{743.92}{-10}$

47. $\dfrac{0.97}{0.1}$

48. $\dfrac{0.97}{0.001}$

49. $\dfrac{75.3}{-0.001}$

50. $\dfrac{-75.3}{1000}$

51. $\dfrac{23{,}001}{100}$

52. $\dfrac{23{,}001}{0.01}$

53. $\dfrac{-57.281}{-10}$

54. $\dfrac{-57.281}{-100}$

b Simplify.

55. $14(82.6 + 67.9)$

56. $(26.2 - 14.8)12$

57. $0.003 + 3.03 \div (-0.01)$

58. $-9.94 + 4.26 \div (6.02 - 4.6) - 0.9$

59. $42(10.6 + 0.024)$

60. $(4.9 - 18.6)13$

61. $4.2(5.7) + 0.7 \div 3.5$

62. $123.3 - 4.24(1.01)$

63. $-9.0072 + 0.04 \div 0.1^2$

64. $12 \div (-0.03) - 12(0.03)^2$

65. $(5 - 0.04)^2 \div 4 + 8.7(0.4)$

66. $(4 - 2.5)^2 \div 100 + 0.1(6.5)$

67. $4 \div 0.4 - 0.1(5) + 0.1^2$

68. $6(0.9) - 0.1 \div 4 + 0.2^3$

69. $5.5^2[(6 - 7.8) \div 0.06 + 0.12]$

70. $12^2 \div (12 + 2.4) - [(2 - 2.4) \div 0.81]$

71. $0.01\{[(4 - 0.25) \div 2.5] - (4.5 - 4.025)\}$

72. $0.03\{2(50.2) - [(8 - 7.5) \div 0.05]\}$

73. Find the average of $1276.59, $1350.49, $1123.78, and $1402.56.

74. Find the average weight of two wrestlers who weigh 308 lb and 296.4 lb.

Global Warming. The following table lists the global average temperature for the years 1984 through 1994. Use the table for Exercises 75 and 76.

YEAR	1986	1987	1988	1989	1990	1991	1992	1993	1994	1995	1996
Global Temperature (in degrees Fahrenheit)	59.29°	59.58°	59.63°	59.45°	59.85°	59.74°	59.23°	59.36°	59.56°	59.72°	59.58°

Source: Lester R. Brown et al., Vital Signs 1997.

75. Find the average temperature for the years 1992 through 1996.

76. Find the average temperature for the years 1987 through 1991.

Skill Maintenance

77. Add: $10\frac{1}{2} + 4\frac{5}{8}$.

78. Subtract: $10\frac{1}{2} - 4\frac{5}{8}$.

79. Simplify: $\frac{36}{42}$.

80. Simplify: $\frac{0}{73}$.

81. Subtract: $7 - 8\frac{2}{3}$.

82. Add: $-5\frac{1}{3} + 7\frac{5}{6}$.

Synthesis

83. ❖ A student insists that $0.247 \div 0.1$ is 0.0247. How could you convince this student that a mistake has been made?

84. ❖ A student insists that $0.247 \div 10$ is 2.47. How could you convince this student that a mistake has been made?

In Exercises 85–88, find the missing value.

85. $439.57 \times 0.01 \div 1000 \times \square = 4.3957$

86. $5.2738 \div 0.01 \times 1000 \div \square = 52.738$

87. $0.0329 \div 0.001 \times 10^4 \div \square = 3290$

88. $0.0047 \times 0.01 \div 10^4 \times \square = 4.7$

1. Estimate to the nearest ten the total cost of one TV and one vacuum cleaner. Which of the following is an appropriate estimate?

   a. $5700   **b.** $570
   c. $790   **d.** $57

2. About how much more does the TV cost than the vacuum cleaner? Estimate to the nearest ten. Which of the following is an appropriate estimate?

   a. $130   **b.** $1300
   c. $580   **d.** $13

6.5 Estimating

a | Estimating Sums, Differences, Products and Quotients

Estimating has many uses. It can be done before a problem is even attempted in order to get an idea of the answer. It can be done afterward as a check, even when we are using a calculator. In many situations, an estimate is all we need. We usually estimate by rounding the numbers so that there are one or two nonzero digits. Consider the following advertisements for Examples 1–4.

Example 1 Estimate to the nearest ten the total cost of one fax machine and one TV.

We are estimating the sum

$$\$466.95 + \$349.95 = \textbf{Total cost.}$$

To estimate to the nearest ten, we round $466.95 to $470 and $349.95 to $350.

$$\$470 + \$350 = \textbf{\$820.}\quad (\textit{Estimated}\text{ total cost})$$

The estimated sum is **$820**.

Do Margin Exercise 1.

Example 2 About how much more does the fax machine cost than the TV? Estimate to the nearest ten.

We are estimating the difference

$$\$466.95 - \$349.95 = \textbf{Price difference.}$$

The estimate to the nearest ten is

$$\$470 - \$350 = \textbf{\$120.}\quad (\textit{Estimated}\text{ price difference})$$

Do Margin Exercise 2.

Example 3 Estimate the total cost of 4 vacuum cleaners.

We are estimating the product

$$4 \times \$219.95 = \textbf{Total cost}.$$

The estimate is found by rounding $219.95 to the nearest ten:

$$4 \times \$220 = \textbf{\$880}.$$

The estimated cost of 4 vacuum cleaners is $880.

Do Margin Exercise 3.

Example 4 About how many fax machines can be bought for $1580?

We estimate the quotient

$$\$1580 \div \$466.95.$$

Since we want a whole-number estimate, we choose our rounding appropriately. Rounding $466.95 to the nearest hundred, we get $500. Since $1580 is close to $1500, which is a multiple of 500, we estimate

$$\$1500 \div \$500 = 3$$

The estimated number of fax machines is 3.

Do Margin Exercise 4.

Example 5 Estimate: 4.8×52. Do not find the actual product. Which of the following is an appropriate estimate?

a. 25   **b.** 250   **c.** 2500   **d.** 360

We have

$$5 \times 50 = \textbf{250}. \qquad (\textit{Estimated} \text{ product})$$

We rounded 4.8 to the nearest one and 52 to the nearest ten. Thus an appropriate estimate is (b).

Do Margin Exercises 5–10.

3. Estimate the total cost of 6 fax machines. Which of the following is an appropriate estimate?
   a. $4400   **b.** $300
   c. $30,000   **d.** $3000

4. About how many vacuum cleaners can be bought for $1100? Which of the following is an appropriate estimate?
   a. 8   **b.** 5
   c. 11   **d.** 124

Estimate the product. Do not find the actual product. Which of the following is an appropriate estimate?

5. 2.4×8
   a. 16   **b.** 34
   c. 125   **d.** 5

6. 24×0.6
   a. 200   **b.** 5
   c. 110   **d.** 20

7. 0.86×0.432
   a. 0.04   **b.** 0.4
   c. 1. 1   **d.** 4

8. 0.82×0.1
   a. 800   **b.** 8
   c. 0.08   **d.** 80

9. 0.12×18.248
   a. 180   **b.** 1.8
   c. 0.018   **d.** 18

10. 24.234×5.2
    a. 200   **b.** 125
    c. 12.5   **d.** 234

Estimate the quotient. Which of the following is an appropriate estimate?

11. $59.78 \div 29.1$
    a. 200   **b.** 20
    c. 2   **d.** 0.2

12. $82.08 \div 2.4$
    a. 40   **b.** 4.0
    c. 400   **d.** 0.4

13. $0.1768 \div 0.08$
    a. 8   **b.** 10
    c. 2   **d.** 20

Example 6 Estimate: $82.08 \div 21$. Which of the following is an appropriate estimate?

    a. 400   **b.** 16   **c.** 40   **d.** 4

This is about $80 \div 20$, so the answer is about **4**. Thus an appropriate estimate is (d).

Example 7 Estimate: $94.18 \div 3.2$. Which of the following is an appropriate estimate?

    a. 30   **b.** 300   **c.** 3   **d.** 60

This is about $90 \div 3$, so the answer is about **30**. Thus an appropriate estimate is (a).

Example 8 Estimate: $0.0156 \div 1.3$. Which of the following is an appropriate estimate?

    a. 0.2   **b.** 0.002   **c.** 0.02   **d.** 20

This is about $0.02 \div 1$, so the answer is about **0.02**. Thus an appropriate estimate is (c).

Do Margin Exercises 11–13.

Exercise Set 6.5

[a] Consider the following advertisements for Exercises 1–8. Estimate the sums, differences, products, or quotients involved in these problems. Indicate which of the choices is an appropriate estimate.

1. Estimate the total cost of one entertainment center and one sound system.
   a. $36   b. $72   c. $3.60   d. $360

2. Estimate the total cost of one entertainment center and one TV.
   a. $410   b. $820   c. $41   d. $4.10

3. About how much more does the TV cost than the sound system?
   a. $500   b. $80   c. $50   d. $5

4. About how much more does the TV cost than the entertainment center?
   a. $100   b. $190   c. $250   d. $150

5. Estimate the total cost of 9 TVs.
   a. $2700   b. $27   c. $270   d. $540

6. Estimate the total cost of 16 sound systems.
   a. $5010   b. $4000   c. $40   d. $410

7. About how many TVs can be bought for $1700?
   a. 600   b. 72   c. 6   d. 60

8. About how many sound systems can be bought for $1300?
   a. 10   b. 5   c. 50   d. 500

Estimate by rounding as directed.

9. $0.02 + 1.31 + 0.34$; nearest tenth

10. $0.88 + 2.07 + 1.54$; nearest one

11. $6.03 + 0.007 + 0.214$; nearest one

12. $1.11 + 8.888 + 99.94$; nearest one

13. $52.367 + 1.307 + 7.324$; nearest one

14. $12.9882 + 1.0115$; nearest tenth

15. $2.678 - 0.445$; nearest tenth

16. $12.9882 - 1.0115$; nearest one

17. $198.67432 - 24.5007$; nearest ten

Estimate. Choose a rounding digit that gives one or two nonzero digits. Indicate which of the choices is an appropriate estimate.

18. $234.12321 - 200.3223$
  a. 600   **b.** 60
  c. 300   **d.** 30

19. 49×7.89
  a. 400   **b.** 40
  c. 4   **d.** 0. 4

20. 7.4×8.9
  a. 95   **b.** 63
  c. 124   **d.** 6

21. 98.4×0.083
  a. 80   **b.** 12
  c. 8   **d.** 0.8

22. 78×5.3
  a. 400   **b.** 800
  c. 40   **d.** 8

23. $3.6 \div 4$
  a. 10   **b.** 1
  c. 0. 1   **d.** 0.01

24. $0.0713 \div 1.94$
  a. 4   **b.** 0.4
  c. 0.04   **d.** 40

25. $74.68 \div 24.7$
  a. 9   **b.** 3
  c. 12   **d.** 120

26. $914 \div 0.921$
  a. 9   **b.** 90
  c. 900   **d.** 0.9

27. *Movie Revenue.* Total summer box-office revenue (money taken in) for the movie *Eraser* was $53.6 million (**Source:** *Hollywood Reporter Magazine*). Each theater showing the movie averaged $6716 in revenue. Estimate how many screens were showing this movie.

28. *Nintendo and the Sears Tower.* The Nintendo Game Boy portable video game is 4.5 in. (0.375 ft) tall (**Source:** Nintendo of America). Estimate how many game units it would take to reach the top of the Sears Tower, which is 1454 ft tall. Round to the nearest one.

Skill Maintenance

Find the prime factorization.

29. 108

30. 400

31. 325

32. 666

Simplify.

33. $\dfrac{125}{400}$

34. $\dfrac{3225}{6275}$

35. $\dfrac{72}{81}$

36. $\dfrac{325}{625}$

Synthesis

37. ❖ A roll of fiberglass insulation costs $21.95. Describe two situations involving estimating and the cost of fiberglass insulation. Devise one situation so that $21.95 is rounded to $22. Devise the other situation so that $21.95 is rounded to $20.

38. ❖ Describe a situation in which an estimation is made by rounding to the nearest 10,000 and then multiplying.

The following were done on a calculator. Estimate to see if the decimal point was placed correctly.

39. $178.9462 \times 61.78 = 11,055.29624$

40. $14,973.35 \div 298.75 = 501.2$

41. $19.7236 - 1.4738 \times 4.1097 = 1.366672414$

42. $28.46901 \div 4.9187 - 2.5081 = 3.279813473$

6.6 More with Fractional Notation and Decimal Notation

a Converting from Fractional Notation to Decimal Notation

If fractional notation has a denominator that is a power of ten, such as 10, 100, 1000, and so on, we can use the following procedure.

> To convert from fractional notation to decimal notation when the denominator is 10, 100, 1000, and so on,
>
> a. count the number of zeros, and
>
> $$\frac{8679}{\mathbf{1000}}$$
>
> → **3** zeros
>
> b. move the decimal point that number of places to the left. Leave off the denominator.
>
> 8.679.
>
> → Move **3** places.

Example 1 Write decimal notation for $\frac{47}{10}$.

$$\frac{47}{10} \qquad 4.7. \qquad \frac{47}{10} = \mathbf{4.7}$$

— **1** zero

Example 2 Write decimal notation for $\frac{123,067}{10,000}$.

$$\frac{123,067}{\mathbf{10,000}} \qquad 12.3067. \qquad \frac{123,067}{10,000} = \mathbf{12.3067}$$

— **4** zeros

Example 3 Write decimal notation for $-\frac{59}{100}$.

$$-\frac{59}{\mathbf{100}} \qquad -0.59. \qquad -\frac{59}{100} = \mathbf{-0.59}$$

— **2** zeros

Do Margin Exercises 1–4.

If a mixed number has a fractional part with a denominator that is a power of ten, such as 10, 100, or 1000, and so on, we first write the mixed number as a sum of a whole number and a fraction. Then we convert to decimal notation.

Example 4 Write decimal notation for $23\frac{59}{100}$.

$$23\frac{59}{100} = 23 + \frac{59}{100} = 23 \text{ and } \frac{59}{100} = 23 + 0.59 = \mathbf{23.59}$$

Write decimal notation.

1. $\frac{743}{100}$

2. $\frac{406}{1000}$

3. $\frac{67,089}{10,000}$

4. $-\frac{9}{10}$

Write decimal notation.

5. $4\frac{3}{10}$

6. $283\frac{71}{100}$

7. $456\frac{13}{100}$

Find decimal notation.

8. $\frac{2}{5}$

9. $\frac{3}{8}$

Example 5 Write decimal notation for $772\frac{129}{10,000}$.

$$772\frac{129}{10,000} = 772 + \frac{129}{10,000} = 772 \text{ and } \frac{129}{10,000} = 772 + 0.0129 = \mathbf{772.0129}$$

Do Margin Exercises 5–7.

b Using Division to Find Decimal Notation

Now that we know how to divide using decimal notation, we can express *any* fraction as a decimal.

Recall that the expression $\frac{a}{b}$ means $a \div b$. This gives us one way of converting fractional notation to decimal notation.

Example 6 Find decimal notation for $\frac{3}{20}$.

We have

$$\frac{3}{20} = 3 \div 20 \qquad \begin{array}{r} 0.1\ 5 \\ 20\overline{)3.0\ 0} \\ \underline{2\ 0} \\ 1\ 0\ 0 \\ \underline{1\ 0\ 0} \\ 0 \end{array} \qquad \frac{3}{20} = \mathbf{0.15}$$

We are finished when the remainder is 0. → 0

Example 7 Find decimal notation for $\frac{7}{8}$.

We have

$$\frac{7}{8} = 7 \div 8 \qquad \begin{array}{r} 0.8\ 7\ 5 \\ 8\overline{)7.0\ 0\ 0} \\ \underline{6\ 4} \\ 6\ 0 \\ \underline{5\ 6} \\ 4\ 0 \\ \underline{4\ 0} \\ 0 \end{array} \qquad \frac{7}{8} = \mathbf{0.875}$$

Do Margin Exercises 8 and 9.

Note that the fractional notation in Examples 6 and 7 had already been simplified as much as possible. Furthermore, note that because each denominator contained only 2's and/or 5's as prime factors, each division eventually led to a remainder of 0.

Often the denominator of a number written in simplified fractional form contains a prime factor other than 2 or 5. In such cases we can still divide to get decimal notation, but answers will be *repeating* decimals. For example, $\frac{5}{6}$ can be converted to decimal notation, but since 6 contains 3 as a prime factor, the answer will be a repeating decimal, as follows.

Example 8 Find decimal notation for $\frac{5}{6}$.

We have

$$\frac{5}{6} = 5 \div 6$$

$$\begin{array}{r} 0.8\,3\,3 \\ 6\overline{)5.0\,0\,0} \\ \underline{4\,8} \\ 2\,0 \\ \underline{1\,8} \\ 2\,0 \\ \underline{1\,8} \\ 2 \end{array}$$

Since 2 keeps reappearing as the remainder, the digit 3 in the quotient will repeat; therefore,

$$\frac{5}{6} = 0.83333 \ldots.$$

The dots indicate an endless sequence of digits in the quotient. When there is a repeating pattern, the dots are often replaced by a bar to indicate the repeating part—in this case, only the 3:

$$\frac{5}{6} = 0.8\overline{3}.$$

Do Margin Exercises 10 and 11.

Example 9 Find decimal notation for $-\frac{4}{11}$.

First consider $\frac{4}{11}$. Because 11 is not a product of 2's and/or 5's, we expect a repeating decimal:

$$\frac{4}{11} = 4 \div 11$$

$$\begin{array}{r} 0.3\,6\,3\,6 \\ 11\overline{)4.0\,0\,0\,0} \\ \underline{3\,3} \\ 7\,0 \\ \underline{6\,6} \\ 4\,0 \\ \underline{3\,3} \\ 7\,0 \\ \underline{6\,6} \\ 4 \end{array}$$

Since 7 and 4 keep reappearing as remainders, the sequence of digits "36" repeats in the quotient, and

$$\frac{4}{11} = 0.363636\ldots, \quad \text{or} \quad 0.\overline{36}$$

Thus, $-\frac{4}{11} = -0.\overline{36}$.

Do Margin Exercises 12 and 13.

Find decimal notation.

10. $\frac{1}{6}$

11. $\frac{2}{3}$

Find decimal notation.

12. $\frac{5}{11}$

13. $-\frac{12}{11}$

14. Find decimal notation for $\frac{5}{7}$.

Example 10 Find decimal notation for $\frac{3}{7}$.

Because 7 is not a product of 2's and/or 5's, we again expect a repeating decimal:

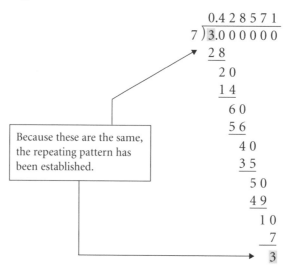

Because these are the same, the repeating pattern has been established.

Since we have already divided 7 into 3, the sequence of digits "428571" repeats in the quotient, and

$$\frac{3}{7} = 0.428571428571..., \quad \text{or} \quad 0.\overline{428571}.$$

It is possible for the repeating part of a repeating decimal to be so long that it will not fit on a calculator. For example, when $\frac{5}{97}$ is written in decimal form, its repeating part is 96 digits long! Most calculators round off repeating decimals to 9 or 10 decimal places.

Do Margin Exercise 14.

c Rounding Repeating Decimals

In applied problems, repeating decimals are generally rounded to a predetermined degree of accuracy.

Example 11 Round $4.\overline{27}$ to the nearest thousandth.

We first rewrite the decimal without the bar. The repeating part is rewritten until we have passed the thousandths place:

$$4.\overline{27} = 4.2727....$$

Now we round as in Section 6. 1.

a. Locate the digit in the thousandths place.   4.2 7 **2** 7 ...
                                                                    ↑

b. Consider the next digit to the right.   4.2 7 **2** 7 ...
                                                                    └↱

c. Since that digit, 7, is greater than or equal to 5, round up.

   4.273   This is the answer.

Examples Round each to the nearest tenth, hundredth, and thousandth.

	Nearest tenth	Nearest hundredth	Nearest thousandth
12. $0.8\overline{3} = 0.83333\ldots$	0.8	0.83	0.833
13. $3.\overline{09} = 3.090909\ldots$	3.1	3.09	3.091
14. $0.\overline{714285} = 0.714285714285\ldots$	0.7	0.71	0.714
15. $5.\overline{89} = 5.8989\ldots$	5.9	5.90	5.899

Do Margin Exercises 15–18.

d | More with Conversions

Recall that fractional notation like $\frac{3}{10}$ or $-\frac{71}{1000}$ can be converted quickly to decimal notation, without performing long division. When a denominator is a factor of 10, 100, and so on, it is often easy to obtain decimal notation by finding (perhaps mentally) an equivalent fraction with a denominator of 10, 100, or some other power of 10.

Example 16 Find decimal notation for $\frac{3}{20}$.

Note that 20 is a factor of 100 ($20 \cdot 5 = 100$). Thus, by using $\frac{5}{5}$ as an expression for 1, we can easily find an equivalent fraction with a denominator that is a power of 10:

$$\frac{3}{20} = \frac{3}{20} \cdot \frac{5}{5} = \frac{15}{100} = 0.15.$$

Example 17 Find decimal notation for $-\frac{7}{500}$.

Since $500 \cdot 2 = 1000$, a power of 10, we use $\frac{2}{2}$ as an expression for 1:

$$-\frac{7}{500} = -\frac{7}{500} \cdot \frac{2}{2} = -\frac{14}{1000} = -0.014.$$

Example 18 Find decimal notation for $\frac{9}{25}$.

$$\frac{9}{25} = \frac{9}{25} \cdot \frac{4}{4} = \frac{36}{100} = 0.36 \qquad \text{Using } \tfrac{4}{4} \text{ for 1 to get a denominator of 100}$$

Example 19 Find decimal notation for $\frac{7}{4}$.

$$\frac{7}{4} = \frac{7}{4} \cdot \frac{25}{25} = \frac{175}{100} = 1.75 \qquad \text{Using } \tfrac{25}{25} \text{ for 1 to get a denominator of 100; you might also note that 7 quarters is \$1.75.}$$

Do Margin Exercises 19–22.

Round each to the nearest tenth, hundredth, and thousandth.

15. $0.\overline{6}$

16. $0.6\overline{08}$

17. $6.2\overline{45}$

18. $3.\overline{69}$

Find decimal notation. Use multiplying by 1.

19. $\dfrac{4}{5}$

20. $-\dfrac{9}{20}$

21. $\dfrac{7}{200}$

22. $\dfrac{33}{25}$

Exercise Set 6.6

a Find decimal notation.

1. $\dfrac{8}{10}$

2. $\dfrac{1}{10}$

3. $-\dfrac{29}{100}$

4. $-\dfrac{17}{100}$

5. $\dfrac{97}{10}$

6. $\dfrac{73}{10}$

7. $\dfrac{889}{100}$

8. $\dfrac{694}{100}$

9. $\dfrac{-2508}{10}$

10. $\dfrac{-6701}{10}$

11. $-\dfrac{3798}{1000}$

12. $-\dfrac{78}{1000}$

13. $\dfrac{78}{10,000}$

14. $\dfrac{904}{10,000}$

15. $\dfrac{56,788}{100,000}$

16. $\dfrac{19}{100,000}$

17. $\dfrac{2713}{100}$

18. $\dfrac{6743}{100}$

19. $-\dfrac{66}{100}$

20. $-\dfrac{178}{100}$

21. $99\dfrac{44}{100}$

22. $4\dfrac{909}{1000}$

23. $3\dfrac{798}{1000}$

24. $67\dfrac{83}{100}$

25. $2\dfrac{1739}{10,000}$

26. $9243\dfrac{1}{10}$

27. $8\dfrac{953,073}{1,000,000}$

28. $2256\dfrac{3059}{10,000}$

b, **d** Find decimal notation.

29. $\dfrac{7}{16}$

30. $\dfrac{13}{20}$

31. $\dfrac{13}{40}$

32. $\dfrac{1}{16}$

33. $\dfrac{1}{5}$

34. $\dfrac{3}{20}$

35. $\dfrac{17}{20}$

36. $\dfrac{3}{40}$

37. $\dfrac{21}{40}$

38. $-\dfrac{39}{40}$

39. $-\dfrac{51}{40}$

40. $\dfrac{19}{40}$

41. $\dfrac{13}{25}$

42. $\dfrac{21}{125}$

43. $\dfrac{2502}{125}$

44. $\dfrac{121}{200}$

45. $\dfrac{-1}{4}$

46. $\dfrac{-1}{2}$

47. $\dfrac{23}{40}$

48. $\dfrac{11}{20}$

49. $-\dfrac{5}{8}$

50. $-\dfrac{19}{16}$

51. $\dfrac{37}{25}$

52. $\dfrac{18}{25}$

53. $\dfrac{4}{15}$

54. $\dfrac{7}{9}$

55. $\dfrac{1}{3}$

56. $\dfrac{1}{9}$

57. $\dfrac{-4}{3}$

58. $\dfrac{-8}{9}$

59. $\dfrac{7}{6}$

60. $\dfrac{7}{11}$

61. $\dfrac{4}{7}$

62. $\dfrac{14}{11}$

63. $-\dfrac{11}{12}$

64. $-\dfrac{5}{12}$

c

65–70. (odd) Round each answer of the odd-numbered Exercises 53–63 to the nearest tenth, hundredth, and thousandth.

71–76. (even) Round each answer of the even-numbered Exercises 54–64 to the nearest tenth, hundredth, and thousandth.

Skill Maintenance

77. Subtract: $20 - 16\frac{3}{5}$.

78. Add: $14\frac{3}{5} + 16\frac{1}{10}$.

79. Simplify: $\frac{95}{-1}$.

80. Solve: $5x = -20$.

81. Simplify: $9 - 4 + 2 \div (-1) \cdot 6$.

82. Simplify: $\frac{-9}{-9}$.

Synthesis

83. ❖ When is long division *not* the fastest way of converting a fraction to decimal notation?

84. Explain the error in the following and give the correct answer.

$$4.60\overline{24} = 4.60246024\ldots$$

85. ❖ Describe two different real-life situations when you would want to have information given to you in decimal form as opposed to fractional form. When in real life would you prefer to have information in fractional form?

86. ❖ Without doing the division, how would you know whether $\frac{4}{27}$ would result in a repeating decimal when converted to decimal notation? Write a step-by-step process for determining that.

Solve.

1. $23x = 96.6$

2. $1.25t = 7.125$

Solve.

3. $x + 9.8 = 12.4$

4. $6.5 + t = -4.3$

6.7 Solving Equations

Earlier, we saw how the addition and multiplication principles can be used to solve equations. We now use those same properties to solve equations involving decimals.

a | Equations with One Variable Term

Recall that to solve equations like $3x = 12$, we can use the multiplication principle to multiply by $\frac{1}{3}$ on both sides. This is the same as dividing by 3 on both sides. The same procedure works with decimals.

Example 1   Solve: $3.4x = 6.97$.

We have

$$3.4x = 6.97$$
$$\frac{3.4x}{3.4} = \frac{6.97}{3.4} \qquad \text{Dividing by 3.4}$$
$$x = 2.05.$$

$$
\begin{array}{r}
2.0\,5 \\
3.4.\,\overline{)6.9\,7\,0} \\
\underline{6\ 8} \\
1\ 7\ 0 \\
\underline{1\ 7\ 0} \\
0
\end{array}
$$

To check, we can approximate: Note that $3.4 \approx 3.5$ and $2.05 \approx 2$. Since $3.5 \cdot 2 = 7.0 \approx 6.97$, we have a partial check. The solution is 2.05.

Do Margin Exercises 1 and 2.

To solve equations like $x + 7 = -3$, we used the addition principle to add -7 on both sides or, equivalently, to subtract 7 on both sides. The same approach is used with decimals.

Example 2   Solve: $x + 7.4 = -3.1$.

We have

$$x + 7.4 = -3.1$$
$$x + 7.4 + (-7.4) = -3.1 + (-7.4) \qquad \text{Adding } -7.4 \text{ on both sides}$$
$$x = -10.5.$$

To check, note that $-10.5 + 7.4 = -3.1$. The solution is -10.5.

Do Margin Exercises 3 and 4.

Exercise Set 6.7

a Solve. Remember to check.

1. $4.2x = 39.06$

2. $36y = 14.76$

3. $x + 17.5 = 29.15$

4. $t + 50.7 = -54.07$

5. $1000y = 9.0678$

6. $789.23 = 0.25q$

7. $3.205 + m = -22.456$

8. $4.26 + q = 58.32$

9. $-23.4 = 5.2a$

10. $-40.74 = 4.2x$

11. $-9.2x = -94.76$

12. $-7.6a = -29.64$

13. $t - 19.27 = 24.51$

14. $t - 3.012 = 10.478$

15. $1048.8 = -23t$

16. $28.2x = 423$

17. $-5.9 + m = 8.42$

18. $-7.31 + m = 2.9$

19. $x + 13.9 = 4.2$

20. $x + 15.7 = 3.1$

21. $23.1 + y = 12.06$

22. $31.4 + y = 15.09$

Skill Maintenance

23. Simplify: $\dfrac{-43}{-43}$.

24. Add: $\dfrac{4}{9} + \dfrac{5}{6}$.

25. Subtract: $\dfrac{7}{10} - \dfrac{3}{25}$.

26. Simplify: $\dfrac{0}{-18}$.

27. Add: $-17 + 24 + (-9)$.

28. Solve: $x - 10 = 14$.

Synthesis

29. ❖ Is it possible for an equation like $x + 3 = x + 5$ to have a solution? Why or why not?

Solve.

30. $0 \cdot x = 0$

31. $0 \cdot x = 9$

32. $4|x| = 48$

33. $2|x| = -12$

34. A student makes a calculation and gets an answer of 22.5. On the last step, the student multiplies by 0.3 when division by 0.3 should have been done. What should the correct answer be?

6.8 Statistics

Statistics is the name of the branch of mathematics which studies and analyzes data. Data are often available regarding some kind of application involving mathematics. We can use tables and graphs of various kinds to show information about the data and to extract information from the data that can lead us to make analyses and predictions. Graphs allow us to communicate a message from the data.

For example, the following show data regarding credit-card spending between Thanksgiving and Christmas in recent years. Examine each method of presentation. Which method, if any, do you like the best and why? Which do you like the least and why?

PARAGRAPH FORM

The National Credit Counseling Services has recently released data regarding credit-card spending between Thanksgiving and Christmas for various years. In 1991, spending was $59.8 billion; in 1992, it was $66.8 billion; in 1993, it was $79.1 billion; in 1994, it was $96.9 billion; in 1995, it was $116.3 billion; and finally, in 1996, it was $131.4 billion.

TABLE

Year	Credit-Card Spending from Thanksgiving to Christmas (in billions)
1991	$ 59.8
1992	66.8
1993	79.1
1994	96.9
1995	116.3
1996	131.4

Source: RAM Research Group,
National Credit Counseling Services

PICTOGRAPH

Credit-Card Spending from Thanksgiving to Christmas

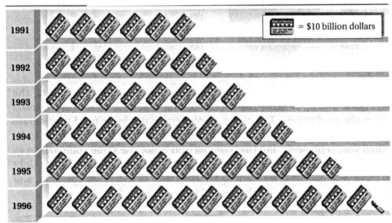

BAR GRAPH

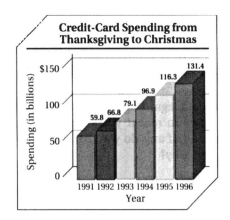

LINE GRAPH

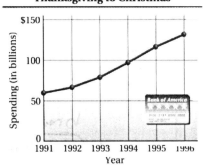

CIRCLE, OR PIE, GRAPH

Most people would not find the paragraph method for displaying the data most useful. It takes time to read, and it is hard to look for a trend and make predictions. The circle, or pie, graph might be used to compare what part of the entire amount of spending over the six years each individual year represents, but that comparison is not the same comparison as those presented by the bar and line graphs. The bar and line graphs might be more worthwhile if we want to see the trend of increased spending and to make predictions about the years 1997 and beyond.

In this section, we will learn how to extract information from various kinds of tables and graphs.

a | Mean, Median, Mode and Range

A **statistic** is a number describing a set of data. One statistic is a *center point* that characterizes the data. *Mean*, *median*, and *mode* are different types of center points.

Mean

The most common kind of center point is the *mean*, or *average*, of a set of numbers.

Let's consider the data on credit-card spending (given in billions):

$59.8, $66.8, $79.1, $96.9, $116.3, $131.4.

What is the *average* of the numbers? First, we add the numbers:

59.8 + 66.8 + 79.1 + 96.9 + 116.3 + 131.4 = 550.3.

Next, we divide by the number of data items, 6:

$$\frac{550.3}{6} \approx \$91.7 \text{ (in billions)} \qquad \text{Rounding to the nearest tenth}$$

Note that

91.7 + 91.7 + 91.7 + 91.7 + 91.7 + 91.7 = 550.2 ≈ 550.3.

Had credit card spending been $91.7 billion per year for 6 years, we would have approximately the same total ($550.3 billion.)

Therefore, the number 91.7 is called the **average** of the set of numbers. It is also called the **arithmetic** (pronounced ăr′ ith-mĕt′-ik) **mean** or simply the **mean**.

> ▶ To find the **mean (average)** of a set of numbers, add the numbers and then divide by the number of items of data.

Example 1 On a 4-day trip, a car was driven the following number of miles each day: 240, 302, 280, 320. What was the average number of miles per day?

$$\frac{240 + 302 + 280 + 320}{4} = \frac{1142}{4}, \quad \text{or} \quad 285.5$$

The car was driven an average of 285.5 mi per day. Had the car been driven exactly 285.5 mi each day, the same total distance (1142 mi) would have been traveled.

Do Margin Exercises 1–4.

Example 2 *Food Waste.* Courtney is a typical American consumer. In the course of 1 yr, she discards 100 lb of food waste. What is the average number of pounds of food waste discarded each week? Round to the nearest tenth.

We already know the total amount of food waste for the year. Since there are 52 weeks in a year, we divide by 52 and round:

$$\frac{100}{52} \approx 1.9.$$

On average, Courtney discards 1.9 lb of food waste per week.

Do Margin Exercise 5.

Find the mean (average).

1. 14, 175, 36

2. 75, 36.8, 95.7, 12.1

3. A student scored the following on five tests: 68, 85, 82, 74, 96. What was the average score?

4. In the first five games, a basketball player scored points as follows: 26, 21, 13, 14, 23. Find the average number of points scored per game.

5. *Food Waste.* Courtney also composts (converts to dirt) 5 lb of food waste each year. How much, on average, does Courtney compost per month? Round to the nearest tenth.

6. Gas Mileage. According to recent EPA estimates, a Toyota Camry LE can be expected to travel 209 mi (city) on 11 gal of gasoline (*Source: Popular Science Magazine*). What is the average number of miles expected per gallon?

7. GPA. Jennifer earned the following grades one semester.

Grade	Number of Credit Hours in Course
B	3
C	4
C	4
A	2

What was Jennifer's grade point average? Assume that the grade point values are 4.0 for an A, 3.0 for a B, and so on. Round to the nearest tenth.

Example 3 Gas Mileage. According to recent EPA estimates, an Oldsmobile Aurora can be expected to travel 204 mi (city) on 12 gal of gasoline. What is the average number of miles expected per gallon?

We divide the total number of miles, 204, by the number of gallons, 12:

$$\frac{204}{12} = 17 \text{ mpg.}$$

The Aurora's expected average is 17 miles per gallon.

Do Margin Exercise 6.

Example 4 GPA. In most colleges, students are assigned grade point values for grades obtained. The *grade point average*, or *GPA*, is the average of the grade point values for each credit hour taken. At many colleges, grade point values are assigned as follows:

A: 4.0
B: 3.0
C: 2.0
D: 1.0
F: 0.0

Tom earned the following grades for one semester. What was his grade point average?

Course	Grade	Number of Credit Hours in Course
History	B	4
Basic mathematics	A	5
English	A	5
French	C	3
Physical education	F	1

To find the GPA, we first multiply the grade point value by the number of credit hours in the course and then add, as follows:

History	**3.0**(4) = 12
Basic mathematics	**4.0**(5) = 20
English	**4.0**(5) = 20
French	**2.0**(3) = 6
Physical education	**0.0**(1) = 0
	58 (Total)

The total number of credit hours taken is 4 + 5 + 5 + 3 + 1, or 18. We divide 58 by 18 and round to the nearest tenth:

$$\text{GPA} = \frac{58}{18} \approx 3.2.$$

Tom's grade point average was 3.2.

Do Margin Exercise 7.

Median

Another type of center-point statistic is the *median*. Medians are useful when we wish to de-emphasize unusually extreme scores. For example, suppose a small class scored as follows on an exam.

Phil: 78   Pat: 56
Jill: 81   Olga: 84
Matt: 82

Let's first list the scores in order from smallest to largest:

56, 78, **81**, 82, 84.
        ↑
   Middle score

The middle score—in this case, 81—is called the **median**. Note that because of the extremely low score of 56, the average of the scores is 76.2. In this example, the median may be a more appropriate center-point statistic.

Example 5   What is the median of this set of numbers?

99, 870, 91, 98, 106, 90, 98

We first rearrange the numbers in order from smallest to largest. Then we locate the middle number, 98.

90, 91, 98, **98**, 99, 106, 870
              ↑
      Middle number

The median is 98.

Do Margin Exercises 8–10.

> ▶ Once a set of data is listed in order, from smallest to largest, the **median** is the middle number if there is an odd number of data items. If there is an even number of items, the median is the number that is the average of the two middle numbers.

Example 6   What is the median of this set of numbers?

69, 80, 61, 63, 62, 65

We first rearrange the numbers in order from smallest to largest. There is an even number of numbers. We look for the middle two, which are 63 and 65. The median is halfway between 63 and 65, the number 64.

61, 62, 63, 65, 69, 80   The average of the middle numbers
        ↑   is $\frac{63+65}{2}$, or 64.
The median is 64.

Find the median.
8. 17, 13, 18, 14, 19

9. 20, 14, 13, 19, 16, 18, 17

10. 78, 81, 83, 91, 103, 102, 122, 119, 88

Find the median and the range.

11. $1300, $2000, $1900, $1600, $1800, $1400

12. 68, 34, 67, 69, 34, 70

Find the modes of these data.

13. 23, 45, 45, 45, 78

14. 34, 34, 67, 67, 68, 70

15. 13, 24, 27, 28, 67, 89

16. In a lab, Gina determined the mass, in grams, of each of five eggs:

15 g, 19 g, 19 g, 14 g, 18 g.

  a. What is the mean?
  b. What is the median?
  c. What is the mode?
  d. What is the range?

Range

Another term used to interpret data is the *range*. The **range** of a set of data is the difference between the greatest and least numbers in the set. In example 6, the range would be $80 - 61 = 19$.

Example 7 What is the median and the range of this set of yearly salaries?

$$\$35,000, \quad \$500,000, \quad \$28,000, \quad \$34,000$$

We rearrange the numbers in order from smallest to largest. The two middle numbers are $34,000 and $35,000. Thus the median is halfway between $34,000 and $35,000 (the average of $34,000 and $35,000):

$$\$28,000, \quad \$34,000, \quad \$35,000, \quad \$500,000$$

$$\text{Median} = \frac{\$34,000 + \$35,000}{2} = \frac{\$69,000}{2} = \$34,500.$$

$$\text{Range} = \text{highest value} - \text{lowest value}$$
$$= \$500,000 - \$28,000 = \$471,000$$

Do Margin Exercises 11 and 12.

Mode

The final type of centerpoint statistic is the **mode**.

> ▶ The **mode** of a set of data is the number or numbers that occur most often. If each number occurs the same number of times, there is *no* mode.

Example 8 Find the mode of these data.

13,   14,   **17**,   **17**,   18,   19

The number that occurs most often is 17. Thus the mode is 17.

A set of data has just one average (mean) and just one median, but it can have more than one mode. It is also possible for a set of data to have no mode—when all numbers are equally represented. For example, the set of data 5, 7, 11, 13, 19 has no mode.

Example 9 Find the modes of these data.

33,   **34**,   **34**,   **34**,   35,   36,   **37**,   **37**,   **37**,   38,   39,   40

There are two numbers that occur most often, 34 and 37. Thus the modes are 34 and 37.

Do Margin Exercises 13–16.

b Reading and Interpreting Tables and Graphs

Tables

A **table** is often used to present data in rows and columns.

Example 10 *Cereal Data.* Let's assume that you generally have a 2-cup bowl of cereal each morning. The following table lists nutritional information for five name-brand cereals. (It does not consider the use of milk, sugar, or sweetener.) The data have been determined by doubling the information given for a 1-cup serving that is found in the Nutrition Facts panel on a box of cereal.

Cereal	Calories	Fat	Total Carbohydrate	Sodium
Ralston Rice Chex	240	0 g	54 g	460 mg
Kellogg's Complete Bran Flakes	240	1.3 g	64 g	613.3 mg
Kellogg's Special K	220	0 g	44 g	500 mg
Honey Nut Cheerios	240	3 g	48 g	540 mg
Wheaties	220	2 g	48 g	440 mg

a. Which cereal has the least amount of sodium per serving?

b. Which cereal has the greatest amount of fat?

c. Which cereal has the least amount of fat?

d. Find the average total carbohydrate in the cereals.

Careful examination of the table will give the answers.

a. To determine which cereal has the least amount of sodium, look down the column headed "Sodium" until you find the smallest number. That number is 440 mg. Then look across that row to find the brand of cereal, Wheaties.

b. To determine which cereal has the greatest amount of fat, look down the column headed "Fat" until you find the largest number. That number is 3 g. Then look across that row to find the cereal, Honey Nut Cheerios.

c. To determine which cereal has the least amount of fat, look down the column headed "Fat" until you find the smallest number. There are two listings of 0 g. Then look across those rows to find the cereals, Ralston Rice Chex and Kellogg's Special K.

d. Find the average of all the numbers in the column headed "Total Carbohydrate":

$$\frac{54 + 64 + 44 + 48 + 48}{5} = 51.6 \text{ g.}$$

The average total carbohydrate content is 51.6 g.

Do Margin Exercises 17–23.

Use the table in Example 10 to answer each of the following.

17. Which cereal has the most total carbohydrate?

18. Which cereal has the least total carbohydrate?

19. Which cereal has the least number of calories?

20. Which cereal has the greatest number of calories?

21. Find the average amount of sodium in the cereals.

22. Find the median of the amount of sodium in the cereals.

23. Find the mean, the median, and the mode of the number of calories in the cereals.

Use the Nutrition Facts data from the Wheaties box and the bowl of cereal described in Example 11 to answer each of the following.

24. How many calories from fat are in your bowl of cereal?

Example 11 *Wheaties Nutrition Facts.* Most foods are required by law to provide factual information regarding nutrition, as shown in the following table of Nutrition Facts from a box of Wheaties cereal. Although this can be very helpful to the consumer, one must be careful in interpreting the data. The % Daily Value figures shown here are based on a 2000-calorie diet. Your daily values may be higher or lower, depending on your calorie needs or intake.

Nutrition Facts

Serving Size 1 cup (30g)
Servings Per Container 17

Amount Per Serving	Wheaties	with ½ cup skim milk
Calories	110	150
Calories from Fat	10	10

	% Daily value**	
Total Fat 1g*	2%	2%
Saturated Fat 0g	0%	0%
Cholesterol 0mg	0%	1%
Sodium 220mg	9%	12%
Potassium 110mg	3%	9%
Total Carbohydrate 24g	8%	10%
Dietary Fiber 3g	12%	12%
Sugars 4g		
Other Carbohydrate 17g		
Protein 3g		

Vitamin A	25%	30%
Vitamin C	25%	25%
Calcium	0%	15%
Iron	45%	45%
Vitamin D	10%	25%
Thiamin	25%	30%
Riboflavin	25%	35%
Niacin	25%	25%
Vitamin B$_6$	25%	25%
Folic Acid	25%	25%
Phosphorus	10%	20%
Magnesium	8%	10%
Zinc	4%	8%
Copper	4%	4%

*Amount in Cereal. A serving of cereal plus skim milk provides 1g fat, less than 5mg cholesterol, 280mg sodium, 310mg potassium, 30g carbohydrate (10g sugars), and 7g protein.

**Percent Daily Values are based on a 2,000 calorie diet. Your daily values may be higher or lower depending on your calorie needs.

25. A nutritionist recommends that you look for foods that provide 10% or more of the daily value for iron. Do you get that with your bowl of Wheaties?

26. How much sodium have you consumed?

27. What daily value of sodium have you consumed?

28. How much protein have you consumed?

Suppose your morning bowl of cereal consists of 2 cups of Wheaties together with 1 cup of skim milk, with artificial sweetener containing 0 calories.

a. How many calories have you consumed?

b. What percent of the daily value of total fat have you consumed?

c. A nutritionist recommends that you look for foods that provide 10% or more of the daily value for vitamin C. Do you get that with your bowl of Wheaties?

d. Suppose you are trying to limit your daily caloric intake to 2500 calories. How many bowls of cereal would it take to exceed the 2500 calories, even though you probably would not eat just cereal?

Careful examination of the table of nutrition facts will give the answers.

a. Look at the column marked "with ½ cup skim milk" and note that 1 cup of cereal with ½ cup skim milk contains 150 calories. Since you are having twice that amount, you are consuming

$$2 \times 150, \text{ or } 300 \text{ calories.}$$

b. Read across from "Total Fat" and note that in 1 cup of cereal with ½ cup skim milk, you get 2% of the daily value of fat. Since you are doubling that, you get 4% of the daily value of fat.

c. Find the row labeled "Vitamin C" on the left and look under the column labeled "with ½ cup skim milk." Note that you get 25% of the daily value for "1 cup with ½ cup of skim milk," and since you are doubling that, you are more than satisfying the 10% requirement.

d. From part (a), we know that you are consuming 300 calories per bowl. Dividing 2500 by 300 gives $\frac{2500}{300} \approx 8.33$. Thus if you eat 9 bowls of cereal in this manner, you will exceed the 2500 calories.

Do Exercises 24–28.

Pictographs

Pictographs (or *picture graphs*) are another way to show information. Instead of actually listing the amounts to be considered, a **pictograph** uses symbols to represent the amounts. In addition, a *key* is given telling what each symbol 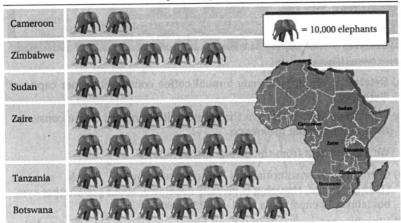 represents.

Example 12 *Elephant Population.* The following pictograph shows the elephant population of various countries in Africa. Located on the graph is a key that tells you that each symbol represents 10,000 elephants.

Elephant Population

Source: National Geographic

a. Which country has the greatest number of elephants?

b. Which country has the least number of elephants?

c. How many more elephants are there in Zaire than in Botswana?

We can compute the answers by first reading the pictograph.

a. The country with the most symbols has the greatest number of elephants: Zaire, with $11 \times 10{,}000$, or 110,000 elephants.

b. The countries with the fewest symbols have the least number of elephants: Cameroon and Sudan, each with $2 \times 10{,}000$, or 20,000 elephants.

c. From part (a), we know that there are 110,000 elephants in Zaire. In Botswana there are $7 \times 10{,}000$, or 70,000 elephants. Thus there are $110{,}000 - 70{,}000$, or 40,000 more elephants in Zaire than in Botswana.

Do Exercises 29–31.

You have probably noticed that, although they seem to be very easy to read, pictographs are difficult to draw accurately because whole symbols reflect loose approximations due to significant rounding. In pictographs, you also need to use some mathematics to find the actual amounts.

Use the pictograph in Example 12 to answer each of the following.

29. How many elephants are there in Tanzania?

30. How does the elephant population of Zimbabwe compare to that of Cameroon?

31. What is the average number of elephants in these six countries?

Use the bar graph in Example 13 to answer each of the following.

32. About how much fat is in the plain single sandwich?

33. Find the average number of fat grams for these 6 Wendy's sandwiches.

34. Which sandwiches contain 20 g or more of fat?

Bar Graphs

A **bar graph** is convenient for showing comparisons because you can tell at a glance which amount represents the largest or smallest quantity. Of course, since a bar graph is a more abstract form of pictograph, this is true of pictographs as well. However, with bar graphs, a *second scale* is usually included so that a more accurate determination of the amount can be made.

Example 13 *Fat Content in Fast Foods.* Wendy's Hamburgers is a national food franchise. The following bar graph shows the fat content of various sandwiches sold by Wendy's.

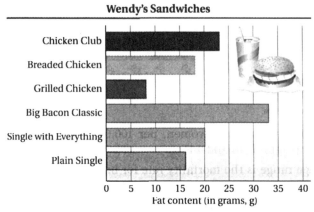

Wendy's Sandwiches

Source: Wendy's International

a. About how much fat is in a chicken club sandwich?

b. Which sandwich contains the least amount of fat?

c. Which sandwich contains about 20 g of fat?

d. What is the range of fat grams in Wendy's sandwiches?

We look at the graph to answer the questions.

a. We move to the right along the bar representing chicken club sandwiches. We can read, fairly accurately, that there is approximately 23 g of fat in the chicken club sandwich.

b. The shortest bar is for the grilled chicken sandwich. Thus that sandwich contains the least amount of fat.

c. We locate the line representing 20 g and then go up until we reach a bar that ends at approximately 20 g. We then go across to the left and read the name of the sandwich, which is the "Single with Everything."

d. We can easily see from this graph that the range would be the difference between the fat grams of the Big Bacon Classic and the Grilled Chicken, 33–8, which equals 25.

Do Exercises 32–34.

Bar graphs are often drawn vertically and sometimes a double bar graph is used to make comparisons.

Example 14 *Breast Cancer.* The following graph indicates the incidence and mortality rates of breast cancer for women of various age groups.

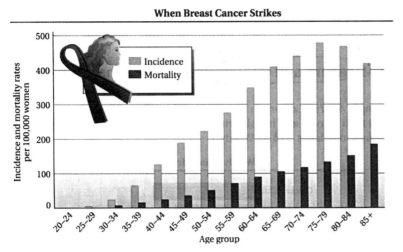

When Breast Cancer Strikes

Source: National Cancer Institute

a. Approximately how many women, per 100,000, develop breast cancer between the ages of 40 and 44?

b. In what age range is the mortality rate for breast cancer approximately 100 for every 100,000 women?

c. In what age range is the incidence of breast cancer the highest?

d. Does the incidence of breast cancer seem to increase from the youngest to the oldest age group?

We look at the graph to answer the questions.

a. We go to the right, across the bottom, to the gray bar above the age group 40–44. Next, we go up to the top of that bar and, from there, back to the left to read approximately 130 on the vertical scale. About 130 out of every 100,000 women develop breast cancer between the ages of 40 and 44.

b. We read up the vertical scale to the number 100. From there we move to the right until we come to the top of a black bar. Moving down that bar, we find that in the 65–69 age group, about 100 out of every 100,000 women die of breast cancer.

c. We look for the tallest gray bar and read the age range below it. The incidence of breast cancer is highest for women in the 75–79 age group.

d. Looking at the heights of the bars, we see that the incidence of breast cancer increases to a high point in the 75–79 age group and then decreases.

Do Exercises 35–38.

Use the bar graph in Example 14 to answer each of the following.

35. Approximately how many women, per 100,000, develop breast cancer between the ages of 35 and 39?

36. In what age group is the mortality rate the highest?

37. In what age group do about 350 out of every 100,000 women develop breast cancer?

38. Does the breast-cancer mortality rate seem to increase from the youngest to the oldest age group?

Use the line graph in Example 15 to answer each of the following.

39. For which month were new home sales lowest?

40. Between which months did new home sales decrease?

41. Find the range in the number of new home sales for the twelve-month period. Answer may vary with your estimation of each point on the graph.

Line Graphs

Line graphs are often used to show a change over time as well as to indicate patterns or trends.

Example 15 *New Home Sales.* The following line graph shows the number of new home sales, in thousands, over a twelve-month period. The jagged line at the base of the vertical scale indicates an unnecessary portion of the scale. Note that the vertical scale differs from the horizontal scale so that the data can be shown reasonably.

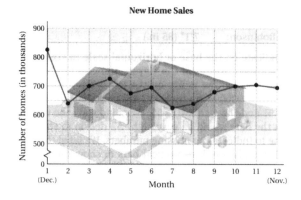

a. For which month were new home sales the greatest?

b. Between which months did new home sales increase?

c. For which months were new home sales about 700 thousand?

We look at the graph to answer the questions.

a. The greatest number of new home sales was about 825 thousand in month 1.

b. Reading the graph from left to right, we see that new home sales increased from month 2 to month 3, from month 3 to month 4, from month 5 to month 6, from month 7 to month 8, from month 8 to month 9, from month 9 to month 10, and from month 10 to month 11.

c. We look from left to right along the line at 700.

We see that points are closest to 700 thousand at months 3, 6, 10, 11, and 12. The mode appears to be 700 thousand since 5 of the 12 months are approximately 700,000.

Do Exercises 39–41.

Example 16 *Monthly Loan Payment.* Suppose that you borrow $110,000 at an interest rate of 9% to buy a home. The following graph shows the monthly payment required to pay off the loan, depending on the length of the loan. (*Caution:* A low monthly payment means that you will pay more interest over the duration of the loan.)

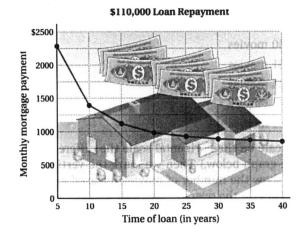

$110,000 Loan Repayment

a. Estimate the monthly payment for a loan of 15 yr.

b. What time period corresponds to a monthly payment of about $1400?

c. By how much does the monthly payment decrease when the loan period is increased from 10 yr to 20 yr?

We look at the graph to answer the questions.

a. We find the time period labeled "15" on the bottom scale and move up from that point to the line. We then go straight across to the left and find that the monthly payment is about $1100.

b. We locate $1400 on the vertical axis. Then we move to the right until we hit the line. The point $1400 crosses the line at the 10-yr time period.

c. The graph shows that the monthly payment for 10 yr is about $1400; for 20 yr, it is about $990. Thus the monthly payment is decreased by $1400 − $990, or $410. (It should be noted that you will pay back $990 · 20 · 12 − $1400 · 10 · 12, or $69,600, more in interest for a 20-yr loan.)

Do Exercises 42–44.

Use the line graph in Example 16 to answer each of the following.

42. Estimate the monthly payment for a loan of 25 yr.

43. What time period corresponds, to a monthly payment of about $850?

44. By how much does the monthly payment decrease when the loan period is increased from 5 yr to 20 yr?

45. *Planetary Moons.* Make a horizontal bar graph to show, the number of moons orbiting, the various planets.

Planet	Number of Moons
Earth	1
Mars	2
Jupiter	16
Saturn	18
Uranus	15
Neptune	8
Pluto	1

c Drawing Bar and Line Graphs

Example 17 *Heights of NBA Centers.* Listed below are the heights of some of the tallest centers in the NBA (*Source:* National Basketball Association). Make a vertical bar graph of the data.

Shaquille O'Neal:	7'1" (85 in.)
Shawn Bradley:	7'6" (90 in.)
Rik Smits:	7'4" (88 in.)
Gheorghe Muresan:	7'7" (91 in.)
Arvydas Sabonis:	7'3" (87 in.)
David Robinson:	7'1" (85 in.)

First, we indicate on the base or horizontal scale in six equally spaced intervals the different names of the players and give the horizontal scale the title "Players." (See the figure on the left below.) Then we label the vertical scale with "Height (in inches)." We note that the range of the numbers (in inches) is from 85 to 91. We could start the vertical scaling at 0, but then the bars would be very high. We decide to start at 83, using the jagged line to indicate the missing numbers. We label the marks by 1's from 83 to 91. Finally, we draw vertical bars to show the various heights (in inches), as shown in the figure on the right below. We give the graph the overall title "NBA Centers."

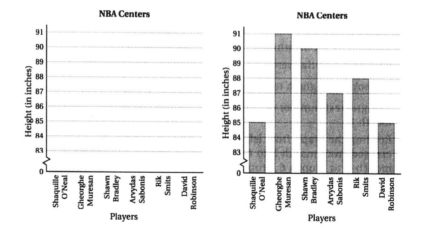

Do Exercise 45.

Example 18 *Movie Releases.* Draw a line graph to show how the number of movies released each year has changed over a period of 6 yr. Use the following data (*Source:* Motion Picture Association of America).

1991:	164 movies
1992:	150 movies
1993:	161 movies
1994:	184 movies
1995:	234 movies
1996:	260 movies

First, we indicate on the horizontal scale the different years and title it "Year." (See the graph below.) Then we mark the vertical scale appropriately by 50's to show the number of movies released and title it "Number per Year." We also give the overall title "Movies Released" to the graph.

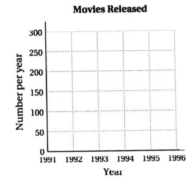

Next, we mark at the appropriate level above each year the points that indicate the number of movies released. Then we draw line segments connecting the points. The change over time can now be observed easily from the graph.

Do Exercise 46.

46. *SAT Scores.* Draw a line graph to show how the average combined verbal-math SAT score has changed over a period of 6 yr. Use the following data (*Source:* The College Board).

1991:	999
1992:	1001
1993:	1003
1994:	1003
1995:	1010
1996:	1013

Exercise Set 6.8

a For each set of numbers, find the mean, the median, any modes that exist and the range.

1. 16, 18, 29, 14, 29, 19, 15

2. 72, 83, 85, 88, 92

3. 5, 30, 20, 20, 35, 5, 25

4. 13, 32, 25, 27, 13

5. 1.2, 4.3, 5.7, 7.4, 7.4

6. 13.4, 13.4, 12.6, 42.9

7. 234, 228, 234, 229, 234, 278

8. $29.95, $28.79, $30.95, $29.95

9. The following temperatures were recorded for seven days in Hartford:

43°, 40°, 23°, 38°, 54°, 35°, 47°.

What was the average temperature? the median? the mode?

10. Lauri Merten, a professional golfer, scored 71, 71, 70, and 68 to win the U.S. Women's Open in a recent year. What was the average score? the median? the mode?

11. *Gas Mileage.* According to recent EPA estimates, an Achieva can be expected to travel 297 mi (highway) on 9 gal of gasoline (*Source: Motor Trend Magazine*). What is the average number of miles expected per gallon?

12. *Gas Mileage.* According to EPA estimates an Aurora can be expected to travel 192 mi (highway) on 8 gal of gasoline (*Source: Motor Trend Magazine*). What is the average number of miles expected per gallon?

GPA. In Exercises 13 and 14 are the grades of a student for one semester. In each case, find the grade point average. Assume that the grade point values are 4.0 for an A, 3.0 for a B, 2.0 for a C, 1.0 for a D, and 0.0 for an F. Round to the nearest tenth.

13.

Grades	Number of Credit Hours in Course
B	4
B	5
B	3
C	4

14.

Grades	Number of Credit Hours in Course
A	5
B	4
B	3
C	5

15. The following prices per pound of Atlantic salmon were found at five fish markets:

$7.99, $9.49, $9.99, $7.99, $10.49.

What was the average price per pound? the median price? the mode?

16. The following prices per pound of Vermont cheddar cheese were found at five supermarkets:

$4.99, $5.79, $4.99, $5.99, $5.79.

What was the average price per pound? the median price? the mode?

b

Planets. Use the following table, which lists information about the planets, for Exercises 17–26.

Planet	Average Distance from Sun (in miles)	Diameter (in miles)	Length of Planet's Day in Earth Time (in days)	Time of Revolution in Earth Time (in years)
Mercury	35,983,000	3,031	58.82	0.24
Venus	67,237,700	7,520	224.69	0.62
Earth	92,955,900	7,926	1.00	1.00
Mars	141,634,800	4,221	1.03	1.88
Jupiter	483,612,200	88,846	0.41	11.86
Saturn	888,184,000	74,898	0.43	29.46
Uranus	1,782,000,000	31,763	0.45	84.01
Neptune	2,794,000,000	31,329	0.66	164.78
Pluto	3,666,000,000	1,423	6.41	248.53

Source: Handy Science Answer Book, Gale Research, Inc.

17. Find the average distance from the sun to Jupiter.

18. How long is a day on Venus?

19. Which planet has a time of revolution of 164.78 yr?

20. Which planet has a diameter of 4221 mi?

21. Which planets have an average distance from the sun that is greater than 1,000,000 mi?

22. Which planets have a diameter that is less than 100,000 mi?

23. About how many earth diameters would it take to equal one Jupiter diameter?

24. How much longer is the longest time of revolution than the shortest?

25. What are the mean, the median, the mode, and the range of the diameters of the planets?

26. What are the mean, the median, the mode, and the range of the average distances from the sun of the planets?

Heat Index. In warm weather, a person can feel hotter due to reduced heat loss from the skin caused by higher humidity. The **temperature-humidity index**, or **apparent temperature**, is what the temperature would have to be with no humidity in order to give the same heat effect. The following table lists the apparent temperatures for various actual temperatures and relative humidities. Use this table for Exercises 27–38.

Actual Temperature (°F)	Relative Humidity									
	10%	20%	30%	40%	50%	60%	70%	80%	90%	100%
	Apparent Temperature (°F)									
75°	75	77	79	80	82	84	86	88	90	92
80°	80	82	85	87	90	92	94	97	99	102
85°	85	88	91	94	97	100	103	106	108	111
90°	90	93	97	100	104	107	111	114	118	121
95°	95	99	103	107	111	115	119	123	127	131
100°	100	105	109	114	118	123	127	132	137	141
105°	105	110	115	120	125	131	136	141	146	151

In Exercises 27–30, find the apparent temperature for the given actual temperature and humidity combinations.

27. 80°, 60%   **28.** 90°, 70%   **29.** 85°, 90%   **30.** 95°, 80%

31. How many temperature-humidity combinations give an apparent temperature of 100°?

32. How many temperature-humidity combinations give an apparent temperature of 111°?

33. At a relative humidity of 50%, what actual temperatures give an apparent temperature above 100°?

34. At a relative humidity of 90%, what actual temperatures give an apparent temperature above 100°?

35. At an actual temperature of 95°, what relative humidities give an apparent temperature above 100°?

36. At an actual temperature of 85°, what relative humidities give an apparent temperature above 100°?

37. At an actual temperature of 85°, by how much would the humidity have to increase in order to raise the apparent temperature from 97° to 111°?

38. At an actual temperature of 80°, by how much would the humidity have to increase in order to raise the apparent temperature from 87° to 102°?

Global Warming. Ecologists are increasingly concerned about global warming, that is, the trend of average global temperatures to rise over recent years. One possible effect is the melting of the polar icecaps. Use the following table for Exercises 39–42

Year	Average Global Temperature (°F)
1986	59.29°
1987	59.58°
1988	59.63°
1989	59.45°
1990	59.85°
1991	59.74°
1992	59.23°
1993	59.36°
1994	59.56°
1995	59.72°
1996	59.58°

Source: Vital Signs, 1997

39. Find the average global temperatures in 1986 and 1987. What was the percent of increase in the temperature from 1986 to 1987?

40. Find the average global temperatures in 1992 and 1993. What was the percent of increase in the temperature from 1992 to 1993?

41. Find the average of the average global temperatures for the years 1986 to 1988. Find the average of the average global temperatures for the years 1994 to 1996. By how many degrees does the latter average exceed the former?

42. Find the average of the average global temperatures for the years 1994 to 1996. Find the ten-year average of the average global temperatures for the years 1987 to 1996. By how many degrees does the former average exceed the latter?

Mountain Bikes. The following pictograph shows sales of mountain bikes for a bicycle company for six consecutive years. Use the pictograph for Exercises 43–50.

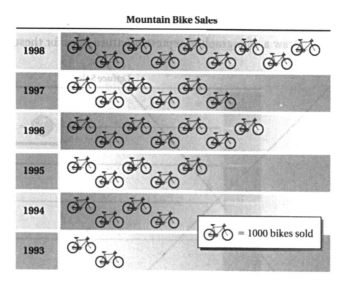

Mountain Bike Sales

= 1000 bikes sold

43. In which year was the greatest number of bikes sold?

44. Between which two consecutive years was there the greatest growth?

45. Between which two years did the least amount of positive growth occur?

46. How many sales does one bike symbol represent?

47. Approximately how many bikes were sold in 1996?

48. Approximately how many more bikes were sold in 1998 than in 1993?

49. In which year was there actually a decline in the number of bikes sold?

50. The sales for 1998 were how many times the sales for 1993?

Chocolate Desserts. The following horizontal bar graph shows the average caloric content of various kinds of chocolate desserts. Use the bar graph for Exercises 51–62.

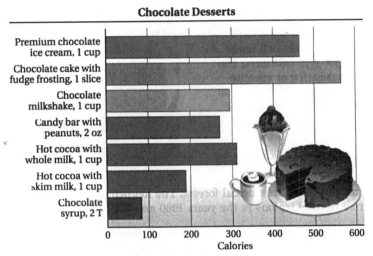

Chocolate Desserts

Source: Better Homes and Gardens, December 1996

Source: Better Homes and Gardens, December 1996

51. Estimate how many calories there are in 1 cup of hot cocoa with skim milk.

52. Estimate how many calories there are in 1 cup of premium chocolate ice cream.

53. Which dessert has the highest caloric content?

54. Which dessert has the lowest caloric content?

55. Which dessert contains about 460 calories?

56. Which desserts contain about 300 calories?

57. How many more calories are there in 1 cup of hot cocoa made with whole milk than in 1 cup of hot cocoa made with skim milk?

58. Fred generally drinks a 4-cup chocolate milkshake. How many calories does he consume?

59. Kristin likes to eat 2 cups of premium chocolate ice cream at bedtime. How many calories does she consume?

60. Barney likes to eat a 6-oz chocolate bar with peanuts for lunch. How many calories does he consume?

61. Paul adds a 2-oz chocolate bar with peanuts to his diet each day for 1 yr (365 days) and makes no other changes in his eating or exercise habits. Consumption of 3500 extra calories will add about 1 lb to his body weight. How many pounds will he gain?

62. Tricia adds one slice of chocolate cake with fudge frosting to her diet each day for 1 yr (365 days) and makes no other changes in her eating or exercise habits. Consumption of 3500 extra calories will add about 1 lb to her body weight. How many pounds will she gain?

Deforestation. The world is gradually losing its tropical forests. The following vertical triple bar graph shows the amount of forested land of three tropical regions in the years 1980 and 1990. Use the bar graph for Exercises 63–70.

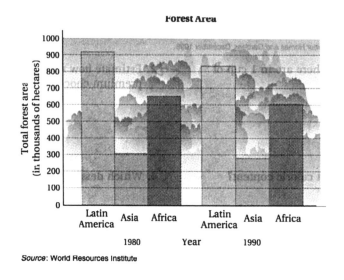

Forest Area

Source: World Resources Institute

63. What was the forest area of Latin America in 1980?

64. What was the forest area of Africa in 1990?

65. Which region experienced the greatest loss of forest area from 1980 to 1990?

66. Which region experienced the smallest loss of forest area from 1980 to 1990?

67. Which region had a forest area of about 600 thousand hectares in 1990?

68. Which region had a forest area of about 300 thousand hectares in 1980?

69. What was the average forest area in Latin America for the two years?

70. What was the average forest area in Asia for the two years?

71. *Commuting Time.* The following table lists the average commuting time in metropolitan areas with more than 1 million people. Make a vertical bar graph to illustrate the data.

City	Commuting Time (in minutes)
New York	30.6
Los Angeles	26.4
Phoenix	23.0
Dallas	24.1
Indianapolis	21.9
Orlando	22.9

Source: Census Bureau

Use the data and the bar graph in Exercise 71 to do Exercises 72–75.

72. Which city has the greatest commuting time?

73. Which city has the least commuting time?

74. What was the average commuting time for all six cities?

75. What was the median commuting time for the six cities?

76. *Deaths from Driving Incidents.* The following table lists for various years the number of driving incidents that resulted in death. Make a horizontal bar graph illustrating the data.

Year	Number of Incidents Causing Death
1990	1129
1991	1297
1992	1478
1993	1555
1994	1669
1995	1708

Source: AAA Foundation

Use the data and the bar graph in Exercise 76 to do Exercises 77–80.

77. Between which two years was the greatest increase in the number of incidents causing death?

78. Between which two years was the smallest increase in the number of incidents causing death?

79. What was the average number of incidents causing death over the 6-yr period?

80. What was the median number of incidents causing death over the 6-yr period?

Average Salary of Major League Baseball Players. The following graph shows the average salary of major-league baseball players over a recent 7-yr period. Use the graph for Exercises 81–86.

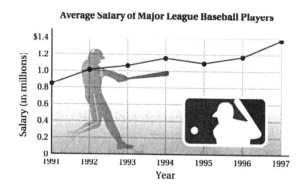

81. In which year was the average salary the highest?

82. In which year was the average salary the lowest?

83. What was the difference in salary between the highest and lowest salaries?

84. Between which two years was the increase in salary the greatest?

85. Between which two years did the salary decrease?

86. What was the percent of increase in salary between 1991 and 1996?

Make a line graph of the data in the following tables (Exercises 87 and 92), using time on the horizontal scale.

87. *Ozone Layer.*

Year	Ozone Level (in parts per billion)
1991	2981
1992	3133
1993	3148
1994	3138
1995	3124

Source: National Oceanic and Atmospheric Administration

Use the data and the line graph in Exercise 87 to do Exercises 88–91.

88. Between which two years was the increase in the ozone level the greatest?

89. Between which two years was the decrease in the ozone level the greatest?

90. What was the average ozone level over the 5-yr period?

91. What was the median ozone level over the 5-yr period?

92. *Motion Picture Expense.*

Year	Average Expense per Picture (in millions)
1991	$38.2
1992	42.4
1993	44.0
1994	50.4
1995	54.1
1996	61.0

Source: Motion Picture Association of America

Use the data and the line graph in Exercise 92 to do Exercises 93–98

93. Between which two years was the increase in motion-picture expense the greatest?

94. Between which two years was the increase in motion-picture expense the least?

95. What was the average motion-picture expense over the 6-yr period?

96. What was the median motion-picture expense over the 6-yr period?

97. What was the average motion-picture expense from 1991 through 1993?

98. What was the average motion-picture expense from 1994 through 1996?

Skill Maintenance

Multiply.

99. $14 \cdot 14$

100. $\dfrac{2}{3} \cdot \dfrac{2}{3}$

101. $3\dfrac{1}{2} \cdot 5\dfrac{2}{3} - 2\dfrac{1}{8} \div 1\dfrac{3}{4}$

102. A car is driven 700 mi in 5 days. At this rate, how far will it have been driven in 24 days?

Synthesis

103. ❖ Compare bar graphs and line graphs. Discuss why you might use one over the other to graph a particular set of data.

104. ❖ Can bar graphs always, sometimes, or never be converted to line graphs? Why?

105. Referring to Exercise 92, what do you think was the average expense per picture in 1997? Justify your answer. How could you tell for sure?

106. ❖ You are applying for an entry-level job at a large firm. You can be informed of the mean, median, or mode salary. Which of the three figures would you request? Why?

107. ❖ Is it possible for a driver to average 20 mph on a 30-mi trip and still receive a ticket for driving 75 mph? Why or why not?

Bowling Averages. Bowling averages are always computed by rounding down to the nearest integer. For example, suppose a bowler gets a total of 599 for 3 games. To find the average, we divide 599 by 3 and drop the amount to the right of the decimal point:

$$\frac{599}{3} \approx 199.67. \quad \text{The bowler's average is 199.}$$

In each case, find the bowling average.

108. 547 in 3 games

109. 4621 in 27 games

110. ***Hank Aaron.*** Hank Aaron averaged $34\frac{7}{22}$ home runs per year over a 22-yr career. After 21 yr, Aaron had averaged $35\frac{10}{21}$ home runs per year. How many home runs did Aaron hit in his final year?

111. ❖ What advantage(s) does a table have over a pictograph?

6.9 Applications and Problem Solving

a Solving applied problems with decimals is like solving applied problems with whole numbers. We translate first to an equation that corresponds to the situation. Then we solve the equation.

Example 1 *Eating Out.* More and more Americans are eating meals outside the home. The following graph compares the average check for meals of various types for the years 1995 and 1996. How much more is the average check for casual dining in 1996 than in 1995?

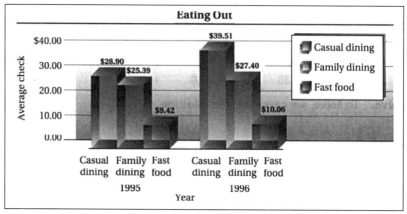

Eating Out

Source: Sandelman and Associates, Brea, California

1. **Familiarize.** We use the bar graph to visualize the situation and to obtain the appropriate data. We let c = the additional amount spent in 1996.

   Estimate: To estimate, we note from the graph that for 1995, the average check for casual dining was almost $30.00. For 1996, it was almost $40.00. Since $40 is $10 more than $30, we expect our answer to be about $10.

2. **Translate.** This is a "how-much-more" situation. We translate as follows, using the data from the bar graph.

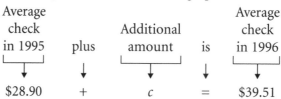

3. **Solve.** We solve the equation, first subtracting 28.90 from both sides:

$$28.90 + c - \mathbf{28.90} = 39.51 - \mathbf{28.90}$$
$$c = 10.61.$$

$$\begin{array}{r} \overset{8\ 15}{3\,9.\!\cancel{5}\,1} \\ -\ 2\,8.9\,0 \\ \hline 1\,0.6\,1 \end{array}$$

4. **Check.** $10.61 is close to our estimate so our answer is reasonable. We can check more precisely by adding 10.61 to 28.90 to get 39.51.

5. **State.** The average check for casual dining in 1996 was $10.61 more than in 1995.

Do Margin Exercise 1.

---

1. *Body Temperature.* Normal body temperature is 98.6°F. When fevered, most people will die if their bodies reach 107°F. This is a rise of how many degrees?

Example 2 *Injections of Medication.* A patient was given injections of 2.8 mL, 1.35 mL, 2.0 mL, and 1.88 mL over a 24-hr period. What was the total amount of the injections?

1. **Familiarize.** We make a drawing or at least visualize the situation. We let t = the total amount of the injections.

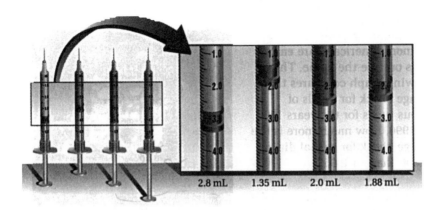

Estimate: To estimate, we can round each of the numbers given and add:

$$2.8 + 1.35 + 2.0 + 1.88 \approx 3 + 1 + 2 + 2$$
$$\approx 8$$

We would expect our answer to be close to 8 mL.

2. **Translate.** Amounts are being combined. We translate to an equation:

First plus second plus third plus fourth is total.

$$2.8 + 1.35 + 2.0 + 1.88 = t$$

3. **Solve.** To solve, we carry out the addition.

```
  2 1
  2.8 0
  1.3 5
  2.0 0
+ 1.8 8
  8.0 3
```

Thus, $t = 8.03$.

4. **Check.** Our answer, 8.03, is reasonable since it is close to our estimate, 8.

   If we had gotten an answer like 80.3 or 0.803, then our estimate, 8, would have told us that we did something wrong, like not lining up the decimal points. We can also check by repeating our addition.

5. **State.** The total amount of the injections was 8.03 mL.

Do Margin Exercise 2.

2. Each year, the average American drinks about 49.0 gal of soft drinks, 41.2 gal of water, 25.3 gal of milk, 24.8 gal of coffee, and 7.8 gal of fruit juice. What is the total amount that the average American drinks? (*Source:* U.S. Department of Agriculture)

Liquids Consumed per Year

3. *Printing Costs.* At a printing company, the cost of copying is 12 cents per page. How much, in dollars, would it cost to make 466 copies?

Example 3 *IRS Driving Allowance.* In a recent year, the Internal Revenue Service allowed a tax deduction of 31¢ per mile for mileage driven for business purposes. What deduction, in dollars, would be allowed for driving 127 mi?

1. Familiarize. We first make a drawing or at least visualize the situation. Repeated addition fits this situation. We let d = the deduction, in dollars, allowed for driving 127 mi.

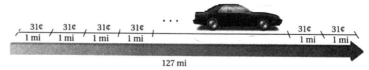

Estimate. To get a rough estimate, we note that if the distance was 100 miles, our deduction would be 31¢, one hundred times, which equals $31.00. Thus we expect our answer to be somewhat more than $31.00.

2. Translate. We translate as follows.

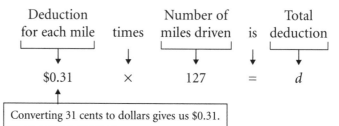

Converting 31 cents to dollars gives us $0.31.

3. Solve. To solve the equation, we carry out the multiplication.

$$
\begin{array}{r}
1\,2\,7 \\
\times\ \ 0.3\,1 \\
\hline
1\,2\,7 \\
3\,8\,1\,0 \\
\hline
3\,9.3\,7
\end{array}
$$

Thus, $d = 39.37$.

4. Check. 39.37 is somewhat more than our estimate so it is reasonable. For a more precise check we could divide 39.37 by 0.31 to see if we get 127.

5. State. The total allowable deduction would be $39.37.

Do Margin Exercise 3.

Example 4 *Loan Payments.* A car loan of $7382.52 is to be paid off in 36 monthly payments. How much is each payment?

1. Familiarize. We first make a drawing. We let n = the amount of each payment.

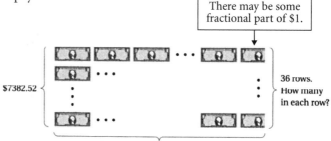

Estimate: As an estimate, we could look at $8000 ÷ $40 = $200. We would expect our answer to be around $200.

2. **Translate.** The problem can be translated to the following equation, thinking that

(Total loan) ÷ (Number of payments) = Amount of each payment
$$\$7382.52 \div 36 = n.$$

3. **Solve.** To solve the equation, we carry out the division.

```
        2 0 5.0 7
 3 6 ) 7 3 8 2.5 2
       7 2
         1 8 2
         1 8 0
             2 5 2
             2 5 2
                 0
```

Thus, n = 205.07.

4. **Check.** Our answer is reasonable when we compare it to our estimate in step 1.

5. **State.** Each payment is $205.07.

Do Margin Exercise 4.

The area of a rectangular region is given by the formula *Area = Length · Width*, or $A = l \cdot w$. We can use this formula with decimal notation.

Example 5 *Poster Area.* A rectangular poster measures 73.2 cm by 61.8 cm. Find the area.

1. **Familiarize.** We first make a drawing, letting A = the area.

Estimate. To estimate, we can use easier numbers, 70 and 60 instead of 73.2 and 61.8 and 60 · 70 = 4200. Since we rounded both numbers down, we should expect our answer to be somewhat more than 4200.

2. **Translate.** Then we use the formula $A = l \cdot w$ and translate:

$$A = 73.2 \times 61.8.$$

4. *Loan Payments.* A loan of $4425 is to be paid off in 12 monthly payments. How much is each payment?

5. A standard-size index card measures 12.7 cm by 7.6 cm. Find its area.

3. Solve. We solve by carrying out the multiplication.

$$
\begin{array}{r}
7\,3.2 \\
\times \quad 6\,1.8 \\
\hline
5\,8\,5\,6 \\
7\,3\,2\,0 \\
4\,3\,9\,2\,0\,0 \\
\hline
4\,5\,2\,3.7\,6
\end{array}
$$

Thus, $A = 4523.76$.

4. Check. Our answer was somewhat more than our estimate so it is reasonable. We could also repeat our calculation as a further check.

5. State. The area is 4523.76 cm^2.

Do Margin Exercise 5.

Example 6 *Cost of Crabmeat.* One pound of crabmeat makes 3 servings at the Key West Seafood Restaurant. It costs $14.98 per pound. What is the cost per serving? Round to the nearest cent.

1. Familiarize. We let c = the cost per serving.

Estimate: To estimate, we note that each pound of crab meat costs about $15.00. Since each pound makes 3 servings, it's easy to see that 3 servings costs about $15.00. Thus, one serving will cost approximately $15 ÷ 3 = $5.00.

6. One pound of lean boneless ham contains 4.5 servings. It costs $3.99 per pound. What is the cost per serving? Round to the nearest cent.

2. Translate. We translate as follows.

Cost per serving	is	Cost per pound	divided by	Number of servings per pound
↓	↓	↓	↓	↓
c	=	14.98	÷	3

3. Solve. To solve, we carry out the division.

$$
\begin{array}{r}
4.9\,9\,3\,3 \\
3\overline{)1\,4.9\,8\,0\,0} \\
\underline{1\,2} \\
2\,9 \\
\underline{2\,7} \\
2\,8 \\
\underline{2\,7} \\
1\,0 \\
\underline{9} \\
1\,0
\end{array}
\qquad c = 4.99\overline{3}
$$

4. Check. Our answer is very close to our estimate so it is very reasonable.

5. State. We round $4.99\overline{3}$ and find the cost per serving to be $4.99.

Do Margin Exercise 6.

Multistep Problems

Example 7 *Gas Mileage.* A driver filled the gasoline tank and noted that the odometer read 67,507.8. After the next filling, the odometer read 68,006.1. It took 16.5 gal to fill the tank. How many miles per gallon (mpg) did the driver get?

1. Familiarize. We first make a drawing.

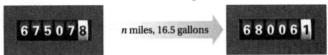

This is a two-step problem. First, we find the number of miles that have been driven between fillups. We let n = the number of miles driven.

Estimate. Sometimes when estimating, your real life experiences enable you to predict a reasonable answer. In this case, a reasonable gas mileage would be 15–35 mpg.

2., 3. Translate and **Solve.** This is a "how-much-more" situation. We translate and solve as follows.

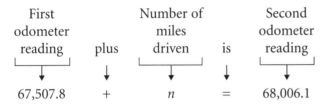

To solve the equation, we subtract 67,507.8 on both sides:

$$n - 67{,}507.8 = 68{,}006.1 - 67{,}507.8$$
$$n = 498.3.$$

$$\begin{array}{r} 6\,8{,}0\,0\,6.1 \\ -\,6\,7{,}5\,0\,7.8 \\ \hline 4\,9\,8.3 \end{array}$$

Second, we divide the total number of miles driven by the number of gallons. This gives us m = the number of miles per gallon—that is, the mileage. The division that corresponds to the situation is

$$498.3 \div 16.5 = m.$$

To find the number m, we divide.

$$\begin{array}{r} 3\,0.2 \\ 1\,6.5\,\overline{)\,4\,9\,8.3\,0} \\ \underline{4\,9\,5\,0} \\ 3\,3\,0 \\ \underline{3\,3\,0} \\ 0 \end{array}$$

Thus, $m = 30.2$.

4. Check. To check, we first multiply the number of miles per gallon times the number of gallons:

$$16.5 \times 30.2 = 498.3.$$

Then we add 498.3 to 67,507.8:

$$67{,}507.8 + 498.3 = 68{,}006.1.$$

The mileage 30.2 checks.

5. State. The driver got 30.2 miles per gallon.

Do Margin Exercise 7.

7. *Gas Mileage.* A driver filled the gasoline tank and noted that the odometer read 38,320.8. After the next filling, the odometer read 38,735.5. It took 14.5 gal to fill the tank. How many miles per gallon did the driver get?

Example 8 *Home-Cost Comparison.* Suppose you own a home, and it is valued at $250,000 in Indianapolis, Indiana. What would it cost to buy a similar (replacement) home in Beverly Hills, California? To find out, we can use an index table prepared by Coldwell Banker Real Estate Corporation (***Source:*** Coldwell Banker Real Estate Corporation. For a complete index table, contact your local representative.). We use the following formula:

$$\begin{bmatrix} \text{Cost of your} \\ \text{home in new city} \end{bmatrix} = \begin{bmatrix} \text{Value of} \\ \text{your home} \end{bmatrix} \div \begin{bmatrix} \text{Index of} \\ \text{your city} \end{bmatrix} \times \begin{bmatrix} \text{Index of} \\ \text{new city} \end{bmatrix}$$

Find the cost of your Indianapolis home in Beverly Hills.

State	City	Index
California	San Francisco	286
	Beverly Hills	376
	Fresno	82
Indiana	Indianapolis	79
	Fort Wayne	69
Arizona	Phoenix	90
	Tucson	79
Illinois	Chicago	214
	Naperville	101
Texas	Austin	89
	Dallas	70
	Houston	61
Florida	Miami	85
	Orlando	76
	Tampa	72
Massachusetts	Wellesley	231
	Cape Cod	84
Georgia	Atlanta	81
New York	Queens	179
	Albany	89

1. **Familiarize.** We let C = the cost of the home in Beverly Hills. We use the table and look up the indexes of the city in which you now live and the city to which you are moving.

   Estimate. For our estimate, we could round as follows:

   $$C = \$250{,}000 \div 79 \times 376$$

   $$C \approx \$250{,}000 \div 100 \times 400$$

   $$C \approx \$1{,}000{,}000.$$

2. **Translate.** Using the formula, we translate to the following equation:

   $$C = \$250{,}000 \div 79 \times 376.$$

3. **Solve.** To solve, we carry out the computations using the rules for order of operations (see Section 6.4):

   $$C = \$250{,}000 \div 79 \times 376$$

   $C = \$3164.557 \times 376$ Carrying out the division first

   $C \approx \$1{,}189{,}873.$ Carrying out the multiplication and rounding to the nearest one

4. **Check.** Since $\$1{,}189{,}873 \approx \$1{,}000{,}000$, our answer is reasonable.

5. **State.** A home selling for $250,000 in Indianapolis would cost about $1,189,873 in Beverly Hills.

Do Margin Exercises 8 and 9.

8. *Home-cost Comparison.* Find the replacement cost of a $250,000 home in Indianapolis if you were to try to replace it when moving to Dallas.

9. Find the replacement cost of a $250,000 home in Phoenix if you were to try to replace it when moving to Chicago.

Exercise Set 6.9

a Solve.

1. What is the cost of 8 pairs of socks at $4.95 per pair?

2. What is the cost of 7 shirts at $32.98 each?

3. *Gasoline Cost.* What is the cost, in dollars, of 17.7 gal of gasoline at 119.9 cents per gallon? (119.9 cents = $1.199) Round the answer to the nearest cent.

4. *Gasoline Cost.* What is the cost, in dollars, of 20.4 gal of gasoline at 149.9 cents per gallon? Round the answer to the nearest cent.

5. Roberto bought a CD for $16.99 and paid with a $20 bill. How much change did he receive?

6. Madeleine buys a book for $44.68 and pays with a $50 bill. How much change does she receive?

7. *Body Temperature.* Normal body temperature is 98.6°F. During an illness, a patient's temperature rose 4.2°. What was the new temperature?

8. *Blood Test.* A medical assistant draws 9.85 mL of blood and uses 4.68 mL, in a blood test. How much is left?

9. *Lottery Winnings.* In Texas, one of the state lotteries is called "Cash 5." In a recent weekly game, the lottery prize of $127,315 was shared equally by 6 winners. How much was each winner's share? Round to the nearest cent.

10. A group of 4 students pays $40.76 for lunch. What is each person's share?

11. A rectangular parking lot measures 800.4 ft by 312.6 ft. What is its area?

12. A rectangular fenced yard measures 40.3 yd by 65.7 yd. What is its area?

13. **Odometer Reading.** A family checked the odometer before starting a trip. It read 22,456.8 and they know that they will be driving 234.7 mi. What will the odometer read at the end of the trip?

14. **Miles Driven.** Petra bought gasoline when the odometer read 14,296.3. At the next gasoline purchase, the odometer read 14,515.8. How many miles had been driven?

15. **Eating Habits.** Each year, Americans eat 24.8 billion hamburgers and 15.9 billion hot dogs. How many more hamburgers than hot dogs do Americans eat?

16. **Gas Mileage.** A driver wants to estimate gas mileage per gallon. At 36,057.1 mi, the tank is filled with 10.7 gal. At 36,217.6 mi, the tank is filled with 11.1 gal. Find the mileage per gallon. Round to the nearest tenth.

17. **Jet-Powered Car.** A jet-powered car was measured on a computer to go from a speed of mach 0.85 to mach 1.15 (mach 1.0 is the speed of sound). What was the difference in these speeds?

18. **Fat Content.** There is 0.8 g of fat in one serving $(3\frac{1}{2}$ oz) of raw scallops. In one serving of oysters, there is 2.5 g of fat. How much more fat is in one serving of oysters than in one serving of scallops?

19. **Gas Mileage.** Peggy filled her van's gas tank and noted that the odometer read 26,342.8. After the next filling, the odometer read 26,736.7. It took 19.5 gal to fill the tank. How many miles per gallon did the van get?

20. **Gas Mileage.** Peter filled his Honda's gas tank and noted that the odometer read 18,943.2. After the next filling, the odometer read 19,306.2. It took 13.2 gal to fill the tank. How many miles per gallon did the car get?

21. The water in a filled tank weighs 748.45 lb. One cubic foot of water weighs 62.5 lb. How many cubic feet of water does the tank hold?

22. **Highway Routes.** You can drive from home to work using either of two routes:

    Route A: Via interstate highway, 7.6 mi, with a speed limit of 65 mph.
    Route B: Via a country road, 5.6 mi, with a speed limit of 50 mph.

    Assuming you drive at the posted speed limit, which route takes less time? (Use the formula *Distance = Speed × Time.*)

23. Cost of Video Game. The average video game costs 25 cents and runs for 1.5 min. Assuming a player does not win any free games and plays continuously, how much money, in dollars, does it cost to play a video game for 1 hr?

24. Property Taxes. The Colavitos own a house with an assessed value of $124,500. For every $1000 of assessed value, they pay $7.68 in taxes. How much do they pay in taxes?

Find the distance around (perimeter of) the figure.

25.

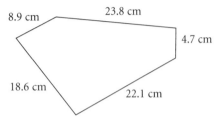

26.

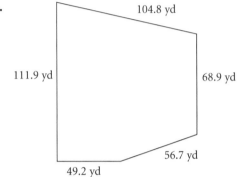

Find the length *d* in the figure.

27.

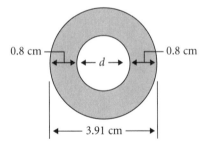

28.

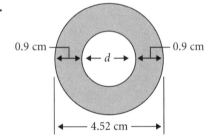

29. Calories Burned Mowing. A person weighing 150 lb burns 7.3 calories per minute while mowing a lawn with a power lawnmower (*Source:* Hanely Science Answer Book). How many calories would be burned in 2 hr of mowing?

30. Lot A measures 250.1 ft by 302.7 ft. Lot B measures 389.4 ft by 566.2 ft. What is the total area of the two lots?

31. Holly had $1123.56 in her checking account. She wrote checks of $23.82, $507.88, and $98.32 to pay some bills. She then deposited a bonus check of $678.20. How much is in her account after these changes?

32. Natalie Clad had $185.00 to spend for fall clothes: $44.95 was spent for shoes, $71.95 for a jacket, and $55.35 for pants. How much was left?

33. A rectangular yard is 20 ft by 15 ft. The yard is covered with grass except for an 8.5-ft square flower garden. How much grass is in the yard?

34. Rita earns a gross paycheck (before deductions) of $495.72. Her dedctions are $59.60 for federal income tax, $29.00 for FICA, and $29.00 for medical insurance. What is her take-home paycheck?

35. *Batting Average.* In a recent year, Bernie Williams of the New York Yankees got 168 hits in 551 times at bat. What part of his at-bats were hits? Give decimal notation to the nearest thousandth. (This is a player's *batting average.*)

36. *Batting Average.* In a recent year, Chipper Jones of the Atlanta Braves got 185 hits in 598 times at bat. What was his batting average? Give decimal notation to the nearest thousandth. (See Exercise 35.)

37. It costs $24.95 a day plus 27 cents per mile to rent a compact car at Shuttles Rent-a-Car. How much, in dollars, would it cost to drive the car 120 mi in 1 day?

38. Zachary worked 53 hr during a week one summer. He earned $6.50 per hour for the first 40 hr and $9.75 per hour for overtime (hours exceeding 40). How much did Zachary earn during the week?

39. A family of five can save $6.72 per week by eating cooked cereal instead of ready-to-eat cereal. How much will they save in 1 year? Use 52 weeks for 1 year.

40. A medical assistant prepares 200 injections, each with 2.5 mL of penicillin. How much penicillin is used in all?

41. A restaurant owner bought 20 dozen eggs for $13.80. Find the cost of each egg to the nearest tenth of a cent (thousandth of a dollar).

42. *Weight Loss.* A person weighing 170 lb burns 8.6 calories per minute while mowing a lawn. One must burn about 3500 calories in order to lose 1 lb. How many pounds would be lost by mowing for 2 hr? Round to the nearest tenth.

43. *Soccer Field.* The dimensions of a World Cup soccer field are 114.9 yd by 74.4 yd. The dimensions of a standard football field are 120 yd by 53.3 yd. How much greater is the area of a soccer field?

44. *Construction Pay.* A construction worker is paid $13.50 per hour for the first 40 hr of work, and time and a half, or $20.25 per hour, for any overtime exceeding 40 hr per week. One week she works 46 hr. How much is her pay?

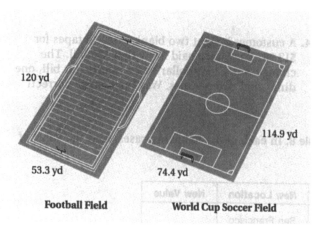

120 yd

53.3 yd

Football Field

114.9 yd

74.4 yd

World Cup Soccer Field

45. *Loan Payment.* In order to make money on loans, financial institutions are paid back more money than they loan. You borrow $120,000 to buy a house and agree to make monthly payments of $880.52 for 30 yr. How much do you pay back altogether? How much more do you pay back than the amount of the loan?

46. *Car-Rental Cost.* Enterprise Rent-A-Car charges $59.99 per day plus $0.25 per mile for a luxury sedan (*Source:* Enterprise Rent-A-Car). How much is the rental charge for a 4-day trip of 876 mi?

Airport Passengers. The following graph shows the number of passengers in a recent year who traveled through the country's busiest airports. (Use the graph for Exercises 47–50.)

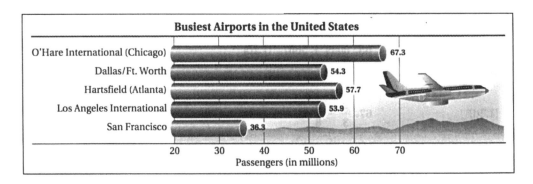

Busiest Airports in the United States

O'Hare International (Chicago) 67.3
Dallas/Ft. Worth 54.3
Hartsfield (Atlanta) 57.7
Los Angeles International 53.9
San Francisco 36.3

Passengers (in millions)

47. How many more passengers does O'Hare handle than San Francisco?

48. How many more passengers does Hartsfield handle than Los Angeles?

49. How many passengers do Dallas/Ft. Worth and San Francisco handle altogether?

50. How many passengers do all these airports handle altogether?

51. *Body Temperature.* Normal body temperature is 98.6°F. A baby's bath water should be 100°F. How many degrees above normal body temperature is this?

52. *Body Temperature.* Normal body temperature is 98.6°F. The lowest temperature at which a patient has survived is 69°F. How many degrees below normal is this?

53. A student used a $20 bill to buy a poster for $10.75. The change was a five-dollar bill, three one-dollar bills, a dime, and two nickels. Was the change correct?

54. A customer bought two blank cassette tapes for $13.88. They were paid for with a $20 bill. The change was a five-dollar bill, a one-dollar bill, one dime, and two pennies. Was the change correct?

Home-Cost Comparison. Use the table and formula from Example 8. In each of the following cases, find the value of the house in the new location.

	Value	Present Location	New Location	New Value
55.	$125,000	Fresno	San Francisco	
56.	$180,000	Chicago	Beverly Hills	
57.	$96,000	Indianapolis	Tampa	
58.	$300,000	Miami	Queens	
59.	$240,000	San Francisco	Atlanta	
60.	$160,000	Cape Cod	Phoenix	

Skill Maintenance

Add.

61. $4569 + 1766$

62. $\frac{2}{3} + \frac{5}{8}$

63. $4\frac{1}{3} + 2\frac{1}{2}$

64. $\frac{5}{6} + \frac{7}{10}$

65. $8099 + 5667$

Subtract.

66. $4569 - 1766$

67. $\frac{2}{3} - \frac{5}{8}$

68. $4\frac{1}{3} - 2\frac{1}{2}$

69. $\frac{5}{6} - \frac{7}{10}$

70. $8099 - 5667$

Solve.

71. If a water wheel made 469 revolutions at a rate of $16\frac{3}{4}$ revolutions per minute, how long did it rotate?

72. If a bicycle wheel made 480 revolutions at a rate of $66\frac{2}{3}$ revolutions per minute, how long did it rotate?

Synthesis

73. ❖ Write a problem for a classmate to solve. Design the problem so that the solution is "Mona's Buick got 23.5 mpg."

74. ❖ Write a problem for a classmate to solve. Design the problem so that the solution is "The larger field is 200 m² bigger."

75. You buy a half-dozen packs of basketball cards with a dozen cards in each pack. The cost is a dozen cents for each half-dozen cards. How much do you pay for the cards?

Review Exercises: Chapter 6

Write a word name:

1. 3.47 **2.** − 597.253 **3.** − 0.031 **4.** 0.0056

Write fractional notation.

5. 0.09 **6.** − 3.0227 **7.** − 4.561 **8.** 0.089

Which number is larger?

9. 0.034, 0.0185 **10.** − 0.67, − 0.19

Round 17,4287 to the nearest:

11. Tenth **12.** Hundredth

Perform the indicated operation.

13.
$$236.231$$
$$263.4$$
$$+ \quad 0.198$$

14.
$$37.645$$
$$-8.497$$

15. 219.3 + 2.8 + 7

16. 745.0109 − 59.959 **17.** −37.8 + (−19.5) **18.** (−3.7)(0.29) **19.**
$$24.68$$
$$\times \ 1000$$

20. $\dfrac{25}{80}$ **21.** $\dfrac{82.9}{-0.01}$ **22.** 11.52 ÷ (−7.2) **23.** $\dfrac{276.3}{1000}$

24. Convert 1549 cents to dollars.

25. Convert $8.29 to cents.

Evaluate

26. $P - Prt$, for $P = 1000$, $r = 0.05$, and $t = 1.5$.

27. $vt + 0.5\ at^2$, for $v = 8$, $t = 2.5$, and $a = 5.1$.

Simplify.

28. $9 - 3.2(-1.5) + 5.2^2$

29. $(8 - 1.23) \div 4 + 5.6(0.02)$

30. $(1 + 0.07)^2 + 10^3 \div 10^2 + [4(10.1 - 5.6) + 8(11.3 - 7.8)]$

31. Estimate the sum $7.298 + 3.961$ to the nearest tenth.

32. Which of the following is an appropriate estimate of $7.9 \cdot 4.8$?

a) 240   b) 24   c) 40   d) 4

Find decimal notation.

33. $-\dfrac{13}{5}$ **34.** $\dfrac{32}{25}$ **35.** $\dfrac{13}{4}$ **36.** $-\dfrac{7}{6}$

37. $-\dfrac{913}{100,000}$ **38.** $-\dfrac{13}{9}$ **39.** $4\dfrac{45}{100}$

40. Round $248.\overline{27}$ to the nearest hundreth.

Solve. Remember to check.

41. $4.1x = -12.3$ **42.** $-4.5x = 3.9$ **43.** $x - 4.7 = 19.13$ **44.** $9.4 + y = 6.1$

FedEx Mailing Costs. Federal Express has three types of delivery service for packages of various weights, as shown in the following table. Use this table for Exercises 45–49.

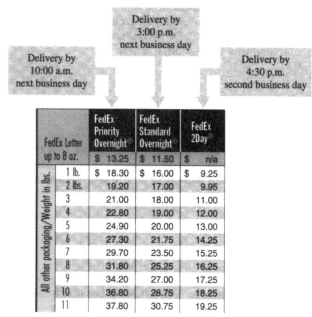

FedEx Letter up to 8 oz.	FedEx Priority Overnight	FedEx Standard Overnight	FedEx 2Day
	$ 13.25	$ 11.50	$ n/a
1 lb.	$ 18.30	$ 16.00	$ 9.25
2 lbs.	19.20	17.00	9.95
3	21.00	18.00	11.00
4	22.80	19.00	12.00
5	24.90	20.00	13.00
6	27.30	21.75	14.25
7	29.70	23.50	15.25
8	31.80	25.25	16.25
9	34.20	27.00	17.25
10	36.80	28.75	18.25
11	37.80	30.75	19.25

All other packaging/Weight in lbs.

Source: Federal Express Corporation

45. Find the cost of a 3-lb FedEx Priority Overnight delivery.

46. Find the cost of a 10-lb FedEx Standard Overnight delivery.

47. How much would you save by sending the package listed in Exercise 45 by FedEx 2Day delivery?

48. How much would you save by sending the package in Exercise 46 by FedEx 2Day delivery?

49. Is there any difference in price between sending a 5-oz package FedEx Priority Overnight and sending an 8-oz package in the same way?

Find the average.

50. 26, 34, 43, 51

51. 0.2, 1.7, 1.9, 2.4

52. $2, $14, $17, $17, $21, $29

Find the median.

53. 26, 34, 43, 51

54. 0.2, 1.7, 1.9, 2.4

55. $2, $14, $17, $17, $21, $29

Find the mode.

56. 26, 34, 43, 26, 51

57. 0.2, 0.2, 0.2, 1.7, 1.9, 2.4

58. $2, $14, $17, $17, $21, $29

Find the range.

59. 0.2, 0.2, 0.2, 1.7, 1.9, 2.4

60. $2, $14, $17, $17, $21, $29

61. A student obtained the following grades one semester. What was the student's GPA? Assume that the grade values are 4.0 for an A, 3.0 for a B, 2.0 for a C, and 1.0 for a D.

Calorie Content in Fast Foods. Wendy's Hamburgers is a national food franchise. The following bar graph shows the calorie content of various sandwiches sold by Wendy's. Use the bar graph for Exercises 62-69.

Wendy's Sandwiches

Source: Wendy's International

62. How many calories are in a Single with Everything?

63. How many calories are in a breaded chicken sandwich?

64. Which sandwich has the highest caloric content?

65. Which sandwich has the lowest caloric content?

66. Which sandwich contains about 360 calories?

67. Which sandwich contains about 500 calories?

68. How many more calories are in a chicken club than in a Single with Everything?

69. How many more calories are in a Big Bacon Classic than in a plain single?

Accidents of Drivers by Age. The following line graph shows the number of accidents per 100 drivers, by age. Use the graph for Exercises 70–75.

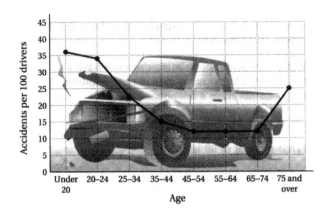

70. Which age group has the most accidents per 100 drivers?

71. What is the fewest number of accidents per 100 in any age group?

72. How many more accidents do people over 75 yr of age have than those in the age range of *65-74*?

73. Between what ages does the number of accidents stay basically the same?

74. How many fewer accidents do people 25-34 yr of age have than those *20-24* yr of age?

75. Which age group has accidents more than three times as often as people 55-64 yr of age?

Hotel Preferences. This circle graph shows hotel preferences for travelers. Use the graph for Exercises 76–79.

Types of Hotels

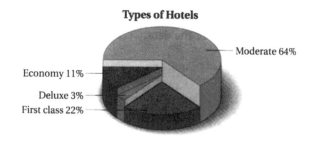

Moderate 64%

Economy 11%

Deluxe 3%

First class 22%

76. What percent of travelers prefer a first-class hotel?

77. What percent of travelers prefer an economy hotel?

78. Suppose 2500 travelers arrive in a city one day. How many of them might seek a moderate room?

79. What percent of travelers prefer either a first-class or a deluxe hotel?

Solve.

80. In the United States, there are 51.81 telephone poles for every 100 people. In Canada, there are 40.65. How many more telephone poles for every hundred people are there in the United States?

81. A farmer has 4 corn fields. One year the harvest in each field was 1419.3 bushels, 1761.8 bushels, 1095.2 bushels, and 2088.8 bushels. What was the year's total harvest?

82. The average person drinks 3.48 cups of tea per day. How many cups of tea are drunk in a week? in a month (30 days)?

83. In 1970, the average age of a first-time groom was 23.2. In 1990, the average age was 26.1. How much older was the average groom in 1990 than in 1970?

84. A florist sold 13 potted palms for a total of $423.65. What was the cost for each palm? Round to the nearest cent.

85. A taxi driver charges $7.25 plus 95 cents a mile for out-of-town fares. How far can an out-of-towner travel on $15.23?

Practice Test: Chapter 6

1. Write a word name for 7.023

Write fractional notation.

2. -0.2 **3.** 7.308   **4.** Which number is larger?
0.0189, 0.19

Round 9.4523 to the nearest

5. tenth.   **6.** thousandth.

Perform the indicated operation.

7.
$$\begin{array}{r} 402.3 \\ 2.81 \\ + 0.109 \end{array}$$

8.
$$\begin{array}{r} 0.125 \\ \times\ 0.24 \end{array}$$

9.
$$\begin{array}{r} 213.45 \\ \times\ 0.001 \end{array}$$

10.
$$\begin{array}{r} 52.091 \\ -\ 7.345 \end{array}$$

11. $-9.5 + 7.3$ **12.** $342.9 + 8.1 + 5.37$ **13.** $2 - 0.0054$ **14.** $25\overline{)11}$

15. $3.3\overline{)100.32}$ **16.** $\dfrac{-346.82}{100}$ **17.** Convert \$179.82 to cents.

18. Evaluate $2l + 2w + 2h$, for $l = 2.4$, $w = 1.3$ and $h = 0.8$.

Simplify.

19. $20 \div (5 - 2)^2 - 8.4$ **20.** $10^3 \{[(22.402 - 0.35) \div 7.4] - (0.332 - 0.022)\}$

Find decimal notation.

21. $-\dfrac{11}{9}$ **22.** $\dfrac{4}{5}$

Solve.

23. $-8.2y = 521.356$ **24.** $17.7 + x = 2.53$

Retirement Savings. The following table lists estimates of the type of retirement savings a person should have, based on his or her yearly income, age, gender, and marital status. Use the table for Exercises 1–6.

Household Yearly Income	Age			
	35	45	55	65
Couple				
$ 50,000	$ 2,756	$ 34,443	$117,739	$187,593
$100,000	$ 28,850	$101,462	$261,139	$474,590
$150,000	$ 60,538	$200,825	$468,837	$820,215
Single Male				
$ 50,000	$ 2,558	$ 38,939	$125,420	$180,953
$100,000	$ 26,345	$115,816	$275,744	$472,326
$150,000	$ 53,519	$209,960	$468,259	$779,456
Single Female				
$ 50,000	$ 35,158	$ 69,391	$121,242	$181,577
$100,000	$ 90,601	$193,985	$341,413	$504,500
$150,000	$152,725	$326,846	$565,817	$831,025

25. What is the recommended retirement savings for a 55-year-old single female with an annual income of $100,000?

26. What type of person(s) needs a retirement savings of $474,590?

27. How much more retirement savings does a 45-year-old single female with an income of $100,000 need than a comparable single male?

28. Find the mean.
[26, 32, 46, 35, 29, 73, 49, 35, 46, 38]

29. Find the median.
[38, 34, 31, 33, 35, 23, 23, 24]

30. Find the mode.
[45, 44, 55, 45, 55, 45, 49]

31. Find the range.
[100, 98, 88, 86, 94, 103, 77, 90]

32. Find the student's GPA from the following. Assume that A = 4.0, B = 3.0, C = 2.0, etc.

Course	Grade	Credit Hours
Algebra	A	5
History	B	3
Biology	C	4
English	A	3

The graph below shows the sales (in millions of dollars) for ABC Corporatio

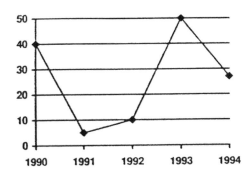

33. How much greater were sales in 1990 than 1991?

34. Between which two years was the most significant increase in sales?

35. Compare and contrast bar graphs and line graphs. Discuss why you might use one over the other to graph a particular set of data.

36. Explain the process of changing a decimal to a fractiuon. Give an example.

Cumulative Review: Chapters 1-6

Convert to fractional notation.

1. $2\dfrac{2}{9}$

2. 3.052

Find decimal notation.

3. $\dfrac{7}{5}$

4. $-\dfrac{6}{11}$

5. Determine whether 43 is prime, composite, or neither.

6. Determine whether 2,053,752 is divisible by 4.

Calculate.

7. $48 + 12 \div 4 - 10 \cdot (2) + 6892 \div 4$

8. $4.7 - \{0.1[1.2(3.95 - 1.65) + 1.5 \div 2.5]\}$

Round to the nearest hundredth.

9. 584.903

10. $218.\overline{5}$

11. Estimate the product $16.392 \cdot 9.715$ by rounding to the nearest one.

12. Estimate by rounding to the nearest tenth: $2.714 + 4.562 - 3.31 - 0.0023$.

13. Estimate the product $6418 \cdot 1984$ by rounding to the nearest hundred.

14. Estimate the quotient $717.832 + 124.998$ by rounding to the nearest ten.

Add and simplify.

15.
$$2\dfrac{1}{4}$$
$$+\ 3\dfrac{4}{5}$$

16.
$$\begin{array}{r} 3\,4,9\,2\,1 \\ 9\,3,0\,9\,2 \\ +\,1\,1,1\,0\,3 \\ \hline \end{array}$$

17. $\dfrac{1}{6} + \dfrac{2}{3} + \dfrac{8}{9}$

18. $-143.9 + 2.053$

Subtract and simplify.

19. $723{,}041 - 12{,}904$

20. $19 - 5.903$

21. $5\frac{1}{7} - 4\frac{3}{7}$

22. $\frac{10}{11} - \frac{9}{10}$

Multiply and simplify.

23. $\frac{3}{8} \cdot \frac{4}{9}$

24. $\begin{array}{r} 2\,5\,3\,2 \\ \times\, 2\,1\,0\,0 \\ \hline \end{array}$

25. $\begin{array}{r} 2\,3.9 \\ \times\, 0.2 \\ \hline \end{array}$

26. $\begin{array}{r} 2\,7.9\,4\,3\,1 \\ \times\,\, 0.0\,0\,1 \\ \hline \end{array}$

Divide and simplify.

27. $1\,6.5\,\overline{)3\,5.0\,1\,3}$

28. $2\,6\,\overline{)4\,7{,}9\,1\,8}$

29. $13.8621 \div 0.001$

30. $\frac{4}{9} \div -\frac{8}{15}$

Solve.

31. $8.32 + x = 9.1$

32. $-75 \cdot x = 2100$

33. $y \cdot 9.47 = 81.6314$

34. $1062 + y = 368{,}313$

35. $t + \frac{5}{6} = \frac{8}{9}$

36. $\frac{7}{8} \cdot t = \frac{7}{16}$

Solve.

37. In a recent year, there were 1952 heart transplants, 9004 kidney transplants, 3229 liver transplants, and 89 pancreas transplants (Source: U.S. Department of Health). How many transplants of these four organs were performed that year?

38. After making a $150 down payment on a sofa, of the total cost was paid. How much did the sofa cost?

39. There are 60 seconds in a minute and 60 minutes in an hour. How many seconds are in a day?

40. A student's tuition was $3600. A loan was obtained for $\frac{2}{3}$ of the tuition. How much was the loan?

41. The balance in a checking account is $314.79. After a check is written for $56.02, what is the balance in the account?

42. A clerk in a delicatessen sold $1\frac{1}{2}$ lb of ham, $2\frac{3}{4}$ lb of turkey, and $2\frac{1}{4}$ lb of roast beef. How many pounds of meat were sold?

43. A baker used $\frac{1}{2}$ lb of sugar for cookies, $\frac{2}{3}$ lb of sugar for pie, and $\frac{5}{6}$ lb of sugar for cake. How much sugar was used in all?

44. A rectangular family room measures 19.8 ft by 23.6 ft. Find its area.

45. Simplify:

$$\left(\frac{3}{4}\right)^2 - \frac{1}{8} \cdot \left(3 - 1\frac{1}{2}\right)^2.$$

46. Find the mean: 80, 75, 90, 82, 85, 95.

47. Find the median: 20, 40, 32, 23, 18, 20, 30.

48. Find the mode: 140, 137, 142, 156, 137, 156, 137.

49. Find the range: 82, 78, 89, 80, 95, 76, 93.

50. Evaluate.

$$\frac{3x - 7y}{2z}, \text{ for } x = -7$$

$$y = -3 \text{ and } z = 2.$$

Scientific Calculators

Using a Scientific Calculator

Calculator usage has become commonplace in business and daily living. For this reason, we have included a brief section on the basic operation of a scientific calculator.

Features and required procedures vary widely among scientific calculators. If you are unfamiliar with the use of your particular calculator, consult its manual or your instructor.

The calculator is a remarkable tool for both students and teachers, but remember, it is not a substitute for learning the concepts.

a | Operations With Real Numbers

To enter a negative number, we use the $+/-$ key. To enter −5, we press 5 and then $+/-$. The display then reads

$$-5.$$

Example 1 Evaluate: $-8 - (-2.3)$.

We press the following keys:

8 $+/-$ $-$ 2 $\cdot$ 3 $+/-$ $=$.

The answer is −5.7.

Do Margin Exercises 1 and 2.

b | Exponential Expressions

To evaluate exponential expressions, we use the x^y key to raise any base to a power. On some calculators, this key is denoted y^x, a^x, or $\wedge$. The keystrokes will make more sense if we say "raised to the" as we press the x^y key.

Evaluate.

1. $-5 - (-13)$

2. $-13 + 72 + (-20) + (-23)$

Evaluate.

3. 3^8

4. 15^3

5. 23^2

6. 2^{10}

7. 7^4

Evaluate.

8. $(1.8)^4$

9. $(0.3)^5$

Example 2   Evaluate: 3^5.

We find 3^5 using the following keystrokes:

[3] [x^y] [5] [=] .

The answer, 243, is displayed in the window:

243 .

Since raising a number to the second power is frequently encountered in mathematics, most calculators have a key for this, [x^2].

Example 3   Evaluate: 15^2.

We find 15^2 using the following keystrokes:

[1] [5] [x^2] .

The display shows 225 without our having pressed the [=] key.

In Example 2, the [x^y] key can be used to evaluate 15^2 but the [x^2] key requires fewer keystrokes.

Do Margin Exercises 3-7

We can easily raise decimal notation to a power using a calculator.

Example 4   Find: $(1.2)^3$.

To find $(1.2)^3$, we press the following keys:

[1] [·] [2] [x^y] [3] [=] .

The answer, 1.728, appears in the window.

Do Margin Exercises 8 and 9.

Example 5   When using a calculator to calculate numbers like $(-39)^4$, it is important to use the correct sequence of keystrokes. On most calculators, the appropriate keystrokes are

[3] [9] [+/−] [x^y] [4] [=] .

Note that in this instance, pressing the key to change a number's sign is more convenient than multiplying by −1. Had we expressed −39 as −1 · 39, the following keystrokes would be needed:

[1] [+/−] [×] [3] [9] [=] [x^y] [4] [=] .

c | Order of Operations

The order of operations is built into most scientific calculators.

Example 6 Calculate: $36 \div 2 \cdot 3 - 4 \cdot 4$.

To calculate $36 \div 2 \cdot 3 - 4 \cdot 4$, we press the following keys:

$\boxed{3}\ \boxed{6}\ \boxed{\div}\ \boxed{2}\ \boxed{\times}\ \boxed{3}\ \boxed{-}\ \boxed{4}\ \boxed{\times}\ \boxed{4}\ \boxed{=}$.

The answer, 38, is displayed in the window.

$\boxed{38}$.

When parentheses appear in the problem, we must enter the operation preceding the parentheses.

Do Margin Exercises 10-13.

Example 7 Calculate: $36 \div (2 \cdot 3 - 4) \cdot 4$.

We press the following keys:

$\boxed{3}\ \boxed{6}\ \boxed{\div}\ \boxed{(}\ \boxed{2}\ \boxed{\times}\ \boxed{3}\ \boxed{-}\ \boxed{4}\ \boxed{)}\ \boxed{\times}\ \boxed{4}\ \boxed{=}$.

The answer, 72, is displayed in the window.

Example 8 Calculate: $(15 + 3)^3 + 4(12 - 7)^2$.

We calculate using the following keystrokes:

$\boxed{(}\ \boxed{1}\ \boxed{5}\ \boxed{+}\ \boxed{3}\ \boxed{)}\ \boxed{x^y}\ \boxed{3}\ \boxed{+}\ \boxed{4}\ \boxed{\times}\ \boxed{(}\ \boxed{1}\ \boxed{2}\ \boxed{-}$
$\boxed{7}\ \boxed{)}\ \boxed{x^2}\ \boxed{=}$

The answer is 5932.

Do Margin Exercises 14-18.

Even when the order of operations is built in, parentheses must be inserted at times.

Example 9 Calculate: $\dfrac{80}{8 - 6}$.

We press

$\boxed{8}\ \boxed{0}\ \boxed{\div}\ \boxed{(}\ \boxed{8}\ \boxed{-}\ \boxed{6}\ \boxed{)}\ \boxed{=}$.

The display reads 40, the correct answer:

$\boxed{40}$.

Use a calculator to determine each of the following.

10. $(-23)^6$

11. $(-104)^3$

12. $(-17)^5$

13. $(-4)^{10}$

Calculate.

14. $68 - 8 \div 4 + 3 \cdot 5$

15. $50 - 8 \cdot 3 + 4(5^2 - 2)$

16. $35 - (-16) - (-21) + 9^2$

17. $[3 + 2(10 - 4)^2] - 20 \div 5$

18. $\{(150 \cdot 5) \div [(3 \cdot 16) \div (8 \cdot 3)]\} + 25 \cdot (12 \div 4)$

Calculate.

19. $\dfrac{1200}{30 - 18}$

20. $\dfrac{50 - 5}{5 + 10}$

Calculate.

21. $\dfrac{7}{8} - \dfrac{1}{3}$

22. $\dfrac{2}{3} + \dfrac{1}{4} - \dfrac{2}{5}$

23. $3\dfrac{1}{4} + 9\dfrac{5}{6}$

24. $\dfrac{2}{5} \cdot \dfrac{14}{11} - \dfrac{1}{2}$

25. $2\dfrac{1}{2} \div 1\dfrac{1}{4}$

Evaluate and express the answer in decimal notation

26. $\dfrac{3}{5}\left(\dfrac{19}{4} - \dfrac{1}{8}\right)$

27. $\dfrac{3}{8} + \dfrac{3}{4} + \dfrac{1}{2}$

28. $\dfrac{1}{8}\left(\dfrac{1}{2} \div \dfrac{2}{3}\right) + \dfrac{7}{32}$

In Example 9, if we had not inserted the parentheses, 80 would have been divided by 8 *before* the 6 had been subtracted, given an incorrect answer of 4.

Wrong!

Do Margin Exercises 19 and 20.

d Fractional Notation

The $\boxed{a^{b/c}}$ key allows us to compute with fractional notation and mixed numerals.

Example 10 Calculate: $\dfrac{1}{2} + 3\dfrac{1}{5} - \dfrac{4}{9}$.

To enter the problem, we use the following keystrokes:

The display in the window is in the form

$$3 \llcorner 23 \llcorner 90 .$$

This means that the answer is $3\dfrac{23}{90}$.

If we press the SHFT key and the $\boxed{d/c}$ key, the answer is converted from a mixed numeral to fractional notation:

$$293 \llcorner 90 ,$$

which means $\dfrac{293}{90}$.

Do Margin Exercises 21-25

The $\boxed{a^{b/c}}$ key can also convert an answer in fractional notation to decimal notation.

Example 11 Calculate $\dfrac{1}{2}\left(\dfrac{3}{5} - \dfrac{1}{8}\right)$ and express the answer in decimal notation.

We press the following keys:

$$\boxed{1}\ \boxed{a^{b/c}}\ \boxed{2}\ \boxed{\times}\ \boxed{(}\ \boxed{3}\ \boxed{a^{b/c}}\ \boxed{5}\ \boxed{-}\ \boxed{1}\ \boxed{a^{b/c}}\ \boxed{8}\ \boxed{)}\ \boxed{=} .$$

The display reads

$$19 \llcorner 80 ,$$

which means $\dfrac{19}{80}$. We now press $\boxed{a^{b/c}}$ to convert $\dfrac{19}{80}$ to decimal notation:

$$0.2375 .$$

The answer is 0.2375.

Do Margin Exercises 26-28

Calculator Exercises

Evaluate using your calculator.

1 . $42 \div (-6)$ **2.** $-63 \div (-9)$ **3.** $\dfrac{-48}{-12}$ **4.** $\dfrac{28}{-2}$ **5.** $\dfrac{0}{-9}$

6. $\dfrac{-13}{0}$ **7.** $40 - 3^2 - 2^3$ **8.** $2^4 + 2^2 - 10$ **9.** $8 - 2(3 - 9)$ **10.** $(8 - 2)(3 - 9)$

11. $\dfrac{4(6 + 8)}{4 + 3}$ **12.** $\dfrac{10(-5)}{5(-1)}$ **13.** $-8 + 4(7 - 9) + 5$ **14.** $-3[2 + (-5)]$

15. $7[4 - (-3)] + 5[32 - (-4)]$ **16.** $(8 - 7 - 9)2 + 1$ **17.** $9 - (7 - 32)$ **18.** $9 - (5 - 7)^2$

19. $\dfrac{(-5)3 + 17}{10(2 - 6) - 2(5 + 2)}$ **20.** $\dfrac{(3 - 5)2 - (7 - 13)}{(2 - 5)3 + 2(4)}$

21. $[14 - (3 + 5) \div 2] - [18 \div (8 - 2)]$ **22.** $[92(6 - 4) \div 8] + [7(8 - 3)]$

23. $8(13) + \{42\,[18 - (6 + 5)]\}$ **24.** $72 \div 6 - \{2[9 - (4 \cdot 2)]\}$

25. $8 \div 2\{[(9 \cdot 9 - 1) \div 2] - [5 \cdot 20 - (7 \cdot 9 - 2)]\}$ **26.** $\dfrac{2}{3} \div \dfrac{4}{3} \div \dfrac{7}{8}$ **27.** $\dfrac{5}{8} \div \dfrac{1}{4} - \dfrac{2}{3} \cdot \dfrac{4}{5}$

28. $\dfrac{3}{4} - \dfrac{2}{3}\left(\dfrac{1}{2} + \dfrac{2}{5}\right)$ **29.** $10\dfrac{3}{5} - 4\dfrac{1}{10} - 1\dfrac{1}{2}$ **30.** $\left(\dfrac{3}{4}\right)^2 + 3\dfrac{1}{2} \div 1\dfrac{1}{4}$ **31.** $\dfrac{1}{2} - \left(\dfrac{1}{2}\right)^2 + \left(\dfrac{1}{2}\right)^3$

32. $1 + \dfrac{1}{4} + \left(\dfrac{1}{4}\right)2 - \left(\dfrac{1}{4}\right)3$

Ratio and Proportion

7

An Application

To determine the number of fish in a lake, a conservationist catches 225 fish, tags them, and throws them back into the lake. Later, 108 fish are caught, and it is found that 15 of them are tagged. Estimate how many fish are in the lake.

The Mathematics

We let F = the number of fish in the lake. Then we translate to a proportion.

Each of these is a ratio.

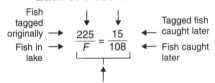

This is a proportion.

Introduction

The mathematics of the application below shows what is called a *proportion*. The expressions on either side of the equals sign are called *ratios*. In this chapter, we use ratios and proportions to solve problems such as this one. We will also study such topics as rates, unit pricing, and similar triangles.

1. Find the ratio of 5 to 11.

2. Find the ratio of 57.3 to 86.1.

3. Find the ratio of $6\frac{3}{4}$ to $7\frac{2}{5}$.

4. The average American drinks 182.5 gal of liquid each year. Of this, 21.1 gal is milk. Find the ratio of milk drunk to total amount drunk.

5. *Fat Content.* In one serving ($3\frac{1}{2}$ oz) of raw scallops, there is 0.8 g of fat. In one serving of oysters, there is 2.5 g of fat. Find the ratio of fat in one serving of oysters to that in one serving of scallops.

6. A pitcher gives up 4 earned runs in $7\frac{2}{3}$ innings of pitching. Find the ratio of earned runs to number of innings pitched.

7.1 Introduction to Ratios

a Ratios

▶ A **ratio** is the quotient of two quantities.

For example, each day in this country about 5200 people die. Of these, 1070 die of cancer. The *ratio* of those who die of cancer to those who die is shown by the fractional notation

$$\frac{1070}{5200} \text{ or by the notation } 1070{:}5200.$$

We read such notation as "the ratio of 1070 to 5200," listing the numerator first and the denominator second.

▶ The **ratio** of a to b is given by $\frac{a}{b}$, where a is the numerator and b is the denominator, or by a: b.

Example 1 Find the ratio of 7 to 8.

The ratio is $\frac{7}{8}$, or 7:8.

Example 2 Find the ratio of 31.4 to 100.

The ratio is $\frac{31.4}{100}$, or 31.4:100.

Example 3 Find the ratio of $4\frac{2}{3}$ to $5\frac{7}{8}$. You need not simplify.

The ratio is $\frac{4\frac{2}{3}}{5\frac{7}{8}}$, or $4\frac{2}{3}{:}5\frac{7}{8}$

Do Margin Exercises 1-3.

In most of our work, we will use fractional notation for ratios.

Example 4 Hank Aaron hit 755 home runs in 12,364 at-bats. Find the ratio of at-bats to home runs.

The ratio is $\frac{12{,}264}{755}$.

Example 5 A family earning $21,400 per year allots about $3210 for car expenses. Find the ratio of car expenses to yearly income.

The ratio is $\frac{3210}{21{,}400}$.

Do Margin Exercises 4-6.

Example 6 In the triangle at right:

a) What is the ratio of the length of the longest side to the length of the shortest side?

$$\frac{5}{3}$$

b) What is the ratio of the length of the shortest side to the length of the longest side?

$$\frac{3}{5}$$

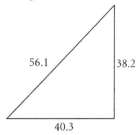

Do Margin Exercise 7.

b Simplifying Notation for Ratios

Sometimes a ratio can be simplified. This provides a means of finding other numbers with the same ratio.

Example 7 Find the ratio of 6 to 8. Then simplify and find two other numbers in the same ratio.

We write the ratio in fractional notation and then simplify:

$$\frac{6}{8} = \frac{2 \cdot 3}{2 \cdot 4} = \frac{\overset{1}{\cancel{2}} \cdot 3}{\underset{1}{\cancel{2}} \cdot 4} = \frac{3}{4}$$

Thus, 3 and 4 have the same ratio as 6 and 8. We can express this by saying "6 is to 8" as "3 is to 4."

Do Margin Exercise 8.

Example 8 Find the ratio of 2.4 to 10. Then simplify and find two other numbers in the same ratio.

We first write the ratio. Next, we multiply by 1 to clear the decimal from the numerator. Then we simplify:

$$\frac{2.4}{10} = \frac{2.4}{10} \cdot \frac{10}{10} = \frac{24}{100} = \frac{\overset{1}{\cancel{4}} \cdot 6}{\underset{1}{\cancel{4}} \cdot 25} = \frac{6}{25}$$

Thus, 2.4 is to 10 as 6 is to 25.

Do Margin Exercises 9 and 10.

Example 9 A standard television screen with a length of 16 in. has a width or height of 12 in. What is the ratio of length to width?

The ratio is $\dfrac{16}{12} = \dfrac{\overset{1}{\cancel{4}} \cdot 4}{\underset{1}{\cancel{4}} \cdot 3} = \dfrac{4}{3}$.

Thus we can say that the ratio of length to width is 4 to 3.

Do Margin Exercise 11.

7. In the triangle below, what is the ratio of the length of the shortest side to the length of the longest side?

8. Find the ratio of 18 to 27. Then simplify and find two other numbers in the same ratio.

9. Find the ratio of 3.6 to 12. Then simplify and find two other numbers in the same ratio.

10. Find the ratio of 1.2 to 1.5. Then simplify and find two other numbers in the same ratio.

11. In Example 9, what is the ratio of the length of the shortest side of the television screen to the length of the longest side?

Exercise Set 7.1

a Find fractional notation for the ratio. You need not simplify.

1. 4 to 5

2. 3 to 2

3. 178 to 572

4. 329 to 967

5. 0.4 to 12

6. 2.3 to 22

7. 3.8 to 7.4

8. 0.6 to 0.7

9. 56.78 to 98.35

10. 456.2 to 333.1

11. $8\frac{3}{4}$ to $9\frac{5}{6}$

12. $10\frac{1}{2}$ to $43\frac{1}{4}$

13. One person in four plays a musical instrument. In a typical group of people, what is the ratio of those who play an instrument to total number of people? What is the ratio of those who do not play an instrument to those who do?

14. Of the 365 days in each year, it takes 107 days of work for the average person to pay his or her taxes. What is the ratio of days worked for taxes to total number of days in a year?

15. *Corvette Accidents.* Of every 5 fatal accidents involving a Corvette, 4 do not involve another vehicle (*Source: Harper's Magazine*). Find the ratio of fatal accidents involving just a Corvette to those involving a Corvette and at least one other vehicle.

16. *New York Commuters.* Of every 5 people who commute to work in New York City, 2 spend more than 90 min a day commuting (*Source: The Amicus Journal*). Find the ratio of people whose daily commute to New York exceeds 90 min a day to those whose commute is 90 min or less.

17. In this rectangle, find the ratios of length to width and of width to length.

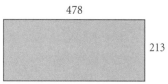

18. In this right triangle, find the ratios of shortest length to longest length and of longest length to shortest length.

b Simplify the ratio.

19. 4 to 6

20. 6 to 10

21. 18 to 24

22. 28 to 36

23. 4.8 to 10

24. 5.6 to 10

25. 2.8 to 3.6

26. 4.8 to 6.4

27. 20 to 30

28. 40 to 60

29. 56 to 100

30. 42 to 100

31. 128 to 256   **32.** 232 to 116   **33.** 0.48 to 0.64   **34.** 0.32 to 0.96

35. The ratio of Americans aged 18-24 living with their parents is 54 to 100. Find the ratio and simplify.

36. Of every 100 hr, the average person spends 8 hr cooking. Find the ratio of hours spent cooking to total number of hours and simplify.

37. In this right triangle, find the ratio of shortest length to longest length and simplify.

38. In this rectangle, find the ratio of width to length and simplify.

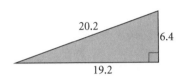

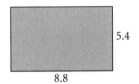

Skill Maintenance

Use = or ≠ for □ to write a true sentence.

39. $\frac{12}{8}$ □ $\frac{6}{4}$

40. $\frac{4}{7}$ □ $\frac{5}{9}$

Divide. Write decimal notation for the answer.

41. 200 ÷ 4   **42.** 95 ÷ 10   **43.** −232 ÷ 16   **44.** 342 ÷ −2.25

Solve.

45. Rocky is $187\frac{1}{10}$ cm tall and his daughter is $180\frac{3}{4}$ cm tall. How much taller is Rocky?

46. Aunt Louise is $168\frac{1}{4}$ cm tall and her son is $150\frac{7}{10}$ cm tall. How much taller is Aunt Louise?

Synthesis

47. ❖ Can every ratio be written as the ratio of some number to 1? Why or why not?

48. ❖ What can be concluded about a rectangle's width if the ratio of length to perimeter is 1 to 3? Make some sketches and explain your reasoning.

49. ▦ In 1996, the total payroll of major league baseball teams was $937,905,284. The New York Yankees won the World Series that year. Their payroll was the highest at $61,511,870. Find the ratio in decimal notation of the Yankees payroll to the overall payroll.

50. ▦ See Exercise 49. In 1995, the total payroll of major league baseball teams was $927,334,416. Find the ratio of the payroll in 1996 to the payroll in 1995.

51. Find the ratio of $3\frac{3}{4}$ to $5\frac{7}{8}$ and simplify.

Exercises 52 and 53 refer to a common fertilizer known as "5, 10, 15." This mixture contains 5 parts of potassium for every 10 parts of phosphorus and 15 parts of nitrogen (this is often denoted 5:10:15).

52. Find the ratio of potassium to nitrogen and of nitrogen to phosphorus.

53. Simplify the ratio 5:10:15.

What is the rate, or speed, in miles per hour?

1. 45 mi, 9 hr

2. 120 mi, 10 hr

3. 3 mi, 10 hr

What is the rate, or speed, In feet per second?

4. 2200 ft, 2 sec

5. 52 ft, 13 sec

6. 232 ft, 16 sec

7. A well-hit golf ball can travel 500 ft in 2 sec. What is the rate, or speed, of the golf ball in feet per second?

8. A leaky faucet can lose 14 gal of water in a week. What is the rate in gallons per day?

7.2 Rates and Unit Prices

a A **rate** is a special ratio where the denominator is equal to 1. Therefore, the numerator could be a decimal. Suppose that a car is driven 200 km in 4 hr. The ratio

$$\frac{200 \text{ km}}{4 \text{ hr}}, \text{ or } 50 \frac{\text{km}}{\text{hr}}, \text{ or } 50 \frac{\text{km}}{\text{hr}}, \text{ or } 50 \text{ kilometers per hour, or } 50 \text{ km/hr}$$

> Recall that "per" means "division," or "for each."

is the rate traveled in kilometers per hour, which is the division of the number of kilometers by the number of hours. A rate of distance traveled to time is also called **speed**.

Example 1 A European driver travels 145 km on 2.5 L of gas. What is the rate in kilometers per liter?

$$\frac{145 \text{ km}}{2.5 \text{ L}}, \text{ or } 58 \frac{\text{km}}{\text{L}}$$

Example 2 It takes 60 oz of grass seed to seed 3000 sq ft of lawn. What is the rate in ounces per square foot?

$$\frac{60 \text{ oz}}{3000 \text{ sq ft}} = \frac{1}{50} \frac{\text{oz}}{\text{sq ft}}, \text{ or } 0.02 \frac{\text{oz}}{\text{sq ft}}$$

Example 3 A cook buys 10 lb of potatoes for $3.69. What is the rate in cents per pound?

$$\frac{\$3.69}{10 \text{ lb}} = \frac{369 \text{ cents}}{10 \text{ lb}}, \text{ or } 36.9 \frac{\text{cents}}{\text{lb}}$$

Example 4 A student nurse working in a health center earned $3690 for working 3 months one summer. What was the rate of pay per month?

The rate of pay is the ratio of money earned per length of time worked, or

$$\frac{\$3690}{3 \text{ mo}} = 1230 \frac{\text{dollars}}{\text{month}}, \text{ or } \$1230 \text{ per month.}$$

Example 5 *Strikeout-to-Home-Run Ratio* One year Gary Sheffield of the Florida Marlins had the lowest strikeout-to-home-run ratio in the major leagues. He had 66 strikeouts and 42 home runs. What was his strikeout-to-home -run ratio?

$$\frac{66 \text{ strikeouts}}{42 \text{ home runs}} \approx 1.57 \frac{\text{strikeouts}}{\text{home runs}}$$

Do Margin Exercises 1-8

b Unit Pricing

> A **unit price** or **unit rate** is the ratio of price to the number of units.

By carrying out the division indicated by the ratio, we can find the price per unit.

Example 6 A customer bought a 20-lb box of powdered detergent for $19.47. What is the unit price in dollars per pound?

The unit price is the price in dollars for each pound.

$$\text{Unit price} = \frac{\text{Price}}{\text{Number of units}}$$

$$= \frac{\$19.47}{20 \text{ lb}} = \frac{19.47}{20} \cdot \frac{\$}{\text{lb}}$$

$$= 0.9735 \text{ dollars per pound}$$

$$= \$0.9735/\text{lb}$$

For comparison shopping, it helps to find unit prices.

Example 7 Which has the lower unit price?

A   B

To find out, we compare the unit prices—in this case, the price per ounce.

For can A: $\dfrac{48 \text{ cents}}{14 \text{ oz}} \approx 3.429\dfrac{\text{cents}}{\text{oz}} \approx 3.429\text{¢/oz}$

For can B: We need to find the total number of ounces:

1 lb, 15 oz = 16 oz + 15 oz = 31 oz.

Then $\dfrac{99 \text{ cents}}{31 \text{ oz}} \approx 3.194\dfrac{\text{cents}}{\text{oz}} \approx 3.194\text{¢/oz}$

Thus can B has the lower unit price.

In many stores, unit prices are now listed on the items or the shelves.

Do Margin Exercise 9 and 10.

9. A customer bought a 14-oz package of oat bran for $2.89. What is the unit price in cents per ounce? Round to the nearest hundredth of a cent.

10. Which has the lower unit price? [*Note:* 1 qt = 32 fl oz (fluid ounces).]

A   B

11. A 64 oz carton of orange juice costs $2.56 and a 16 oz can costs $0.88. How many cents per ounce does each carton cost?

Example 8 A 5-lb bag of dog food costs $4.50. A 20-lb bag is priced at $14.95. How many cents per pound does each size cost?

Since the question asks for cents per pound and the price is given in dollars per pound, the first step will be to convert the dollars to cents.

For the smaller bag: $4.50 = 450 cents

$$\frac{450 \text{ cents}}{5 \text{ lb}} = 90 \frac{\text{cents}}{\text{lb}} = 90¢/\text{lb}$$

For the larger bag: $14.95 = 1495 cents

$$\frac{1495 \text{ cents}}{20 \text{ lb}} = 74.75 \frac{\text{cents}}{\text{lb}} = 74.75¢/\text{lb}$$

Do Margin Exercise 11.

Exercise Set 7.2

a In Exercises 1-6, find the rate as a ratio of distance to time.

1. 120 km, 3 hr

2. 18 mi, 9 hr

3. 440 m, 40 sec

4. 200 mi, 25 sec

5. 342 yd, 2.25 days

6. 492 m, 60 sec

7. A car is driven 500 mi in 20 hr. What is the rate in miles per hour? in hours per mile?

8. A student eats 3 hamburgers in 15 min. What is the rate in hamburgers per minute? in minutes per hamburger?

9. A long-distance telephone call between two cities costs $5.75 for 10 min. What is the rate in cents per minute?

10. An 8-lb boneless ham contains 36 servings of meat. What is the ratio in servings per pound?

11. To water a lawn adequately requires 623 gal of water for every 1000 ft². What is the rate in gallons per square foot?

12. A car is driven 200 km on 40 L of gasoline. What is the rate in kilometers per liter?

13. Light travels 186,000 mi in 1 sec. What is its rate, or speed, in miles per second?

14. Sound travels 1100 ft in 1 sec. What is its rate, or speed, in feet per second?

15. Impulses in nerve fibers travel 310 km in 2.5 hr. What is the rate, or speed, in kilometers per hour?

16. A black racer snake can travel 4.6 km in 2 hr. What is its rate, or speed, in kilometers per hour?

17. A jet flew 2660 mi in 4.75 hr. What was its speed?

18. A turtle traveled 0.42 mi in 2.5 hr. What was its speed?

b

19. The fabric for a wedding gown costs $80.75 for 8.5 yd. Find the unit price.

20. An 8-oz bottle of shampoo costs $2.59. Find the unit price.

21. A 2-lb can of decaffeinated coffee costs $6.59. What is the unit price in cents per ounce? Round to the nearest hundredth of a cent.

22. A 24-can package of 12-oz cans of orange soda costs $6.99. What is the unit price in cents per ounce? Round to the nearest hundredth of a cent.

23. A $\frac{2}{3}$-lb package of Monterey Jack cheese costs $2.89. Find the unit price in dollars per pound. Round to the nearest hundredth of a dollar.

24. A $1\frac{1}{4}$-lb container of cottage cheese costs $1.62. Find the unit price in dollars per pound.

Which has the lower unit price?

25.

CHILI SAUCE
Brand A: 18 oz for $1.79
Brand B: 16 oz for $1.65

26.

NAPKINS
Brand A: 140 napkins for $2.69
Brand B: 125 napkins for $2.39

27.

GRAPEFRUIT JUICE
Brand A: $3.89 for 2 qt
Brand B: $5.79 for 48 oz

28.

EVAPORATED MILK
Brand A: 79 cents for 12 oz
Brand B: $2.69 for 1 qt, 8 oz

29.

SOAP
Brand A: $2.09 for 3 bars
Brand B: $1.58 for 2 bars

30.

BROCCOLI SOUP
Brand A: 8.25 oz for 96 cents
Brand B: 10.75 oz for $1.11

31.

FANCY TUNA
Brand A- $1.19 for $6\frac{1}{8}$ oz
Brand B: $1.11 for 6 oz

32.

FLOUR
Brand A: $1.25 for 3 lb, 2 oz
Brand B: $0.99 for 28 oz

33.

SPARKLING WATER
The same kind of water is sold in two types of bottle. Which type has the lower unit price?
Six 10-oz bottles for $3.09, or Four 12-oz bottles for $2.39

34.

COLA
The same kind of cola is sold in two types of container. Which type has the lower unit price?
Six 12-oz cans for $2.19, or One 30-oz bottle for 79¢

35.

INSTANT PUDDING (SAME BRAND)
Package A: 5.9 oz for 99¢
Package B: 3.9 oz for 63¢

36.

TACO SHELLS (SAME BRAND)
Package A: 18 in a box for $2.49
Package B: 12 in a box for $1.99

37.

BROCCOLI SOUP
Big Chunk: 10.5 oz, 2 for $1.59
Bert's: 11 oz for $ 0.82

38.

GRAPE JELLY
The same kind of jelly is sold in two sizes. Which size has the lower unit price?
18 oz for $1.59, or 32 oz for $3.59

Skill Maintenance

Solve.

39. There are 20.6 million people in this country who play the piano and 18.9 million who play the guitar. How many more play the piano than the guitar?

40. A serving of fish steak (cross section) is generally $\frac{1}{2}$ lb. How many servings can be prepared from a cleaned $18\frac{3}{4}$-lb tuna?

Multiply.

41.
$$\begin{array}{r} 45.67 \\ \times\ \ 2.4 \\ \hline \end{array}$$

42.
$$\begin{array}{r} 678.19 \\ \times\ \ 100 \\ \hline \end{array}$$

43. 84.3×-69.2

44. -1002.56×-465

Synthesis

45. ❖ The unit price of an item generally drops when larger packages of that item are purchased. Why?

46. ❖ Suppose that the same type of juice is available in two sizes and that the larger bottle has the lower unit price. if the larger bottle costs $3.79 and contains twice as much juice, what can you conclude about the price of the smaller bottle? Why?

47. Recently, certain manufacturers have been changing the size of their containers in such a way that the consumer thinks the price of a product has been lowered when in reality, a higher unit price is being charged.

a) Some aluminum juice cans are now concave (curved in) on the bottom. Suppose the volume of the can in the figure has been reduced from a fluid capacity of 6 oz to 5.5 oz, and the price of each can has been reduced from 65¢ to 60¢. Find the unit price of each container in cents per ounce.

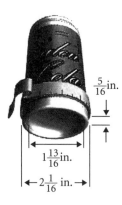

$\frac{5}{16}$ in.

$1\frac{13}{16}$ in.

$2\frac{1}{16}$ in.

b) Suppose that at one time the cost of a certain kind of paper towel was $0.89 for a roll containing 78 ft² of absorbent surface. Later the surface area was changed to 65 ft² and the price was decreased to $0.79. Find the unit price of each product in cents per square foot. Which is the best buy?

48. In 1994, Coca-Cola introduced a 20-oz soda bottle. At first it was sold for 64¢ a bottle, the same price as their 16-oz bottle. After about a month, the price of a 20-oz bottle rose to 80¢. How did the unit price change for a consumer who made the switch from the 16-oz to the 20-oz bottle?

49. Suppose that a pasta manufacturer shrinks the size of a box from 1 lb to 14 oz, but keeps the price at 85 cents a box. How does the unit price change?

7.3 Proportions

a Proportion

When two pairs of numbers (such as 3, 2 and 6, 4) have the same ratio, we say that they are **proportional.** The equation

$$\frac{3}{2} = \frac{6}{4}$$

states that the pairs 3, 2 and 6, 4 are proportional. Such an equation is called a **proportion.** We sometimes read $\frac{3}{2} = \frac{6}{4}$ as "3 is to 2 as 6 is to 4."

Since ratios are represented by fractional notation, we can test whether two ratios are the same by using the test for equality of fractions.

Example 1 Determine whether 1, 2 and 3, 6 are proportional.

We can use cross products:

$$1 \cdot 6 = 6 \quad \frac{1}{2} \quad \frac{3}{6} \quad 2 \cdot 3 = 6.$$

Since the cross products are the same, $6 = 6$, we know that $\frac{1}{2} = \frac{3}{6}$, so the numbers are proportional.

Example 2 Determine whether 2, 5 and 4, 7 are proportional.

We can use cross products:

$$2 \cdot 7 = 14 \quad \frac{2}{5} \quad \frac{4}{7} \quad 5 \cdot 4 = 20.$$

Since the cross products are not the same, $14 \neq 20$, we know that $\frac{2}{5} \neq \frac{4}{7}$, the numbers are not proportional.

Do Margin Exercises 1–3.

Example 3 Determine whether 3.2, 4.8 and 0.16, 0.24 are proportional.

We can use cross products:

$$3.2(0.24) = 0.768 \quad \frac{3.2}{4.8} \quad \frac{0.16}{0.24} \quad 4.8(0.16) = 0.768.$$

Since the cross products are the same, $0.768 = 0.768$, we know that $\frac{3.2}{4.8} = \frac{0.16}{0.24}$, so the numbers are proportional.

Do Margin Exercises 4 and 5.

Determine whether the two pairs of numbers are proportional.

1. 3, 4 and 6, 8

2. 1, 4 and 10, 39

3. 1, 2 and 20, 39

Determine whether the two pairs of numbers are proportional.

4. 6.4, 12.8 and 5.3, 10.6

5. 6.8, 7.4 and 3.4, 4.2

6. Determine whether $4\frac{2}{3}$, $5\frac{1}{2}$ and 14, $16\frac{1}{2}$ are proportional.

7. Solve: $\dfrac{x}{63} = \dfrac{2}{9}$.

Example 4 Determine whether $4\frac{2}{3}$, $5\frac{1}{2}$ and $8\frac{7}{8}$, $16\frac{1}{3}$ are proportional.

We can use cross products:

$$4\frac{2}{3} \cdot 16\frac{1}{3} = \frac{14}{3} \cdot \frac{49}{3} \qquad \begin{array}{cc} 4\frac{2}{3} & 8\frac{7}{8} \\ \hline 5\frac{1}{2} & 16\frac{1}{3} \end{array} \qquad 5\frac{1}{2} \cdot 8\frac{7}{8} = \frac{11}{2} \cdot \frac{71}{8}$$

$$= \frac{686}{9} \qquad\qquad\qquad = \frac{781}{16}$$

$$= 76\frac{2}{9} \qquad\qquad\qquad = 48\frac{13}{16}.$$

Since the cross products are not the same, $76\frac{2}{9} \neq 48\frac{13}{16}$, we know that the numbers are not proportional.

Do Margin Exercise 6.

b Solving Proportions

Let's now look at solving proportions. Consider the proportion

$$\frac{x}{3} = \frac{4}{6}.$$

One way to solve a proportion is to use cross products. Then we can divide on both sides to get the variable alone:

$x \cdot 6 = 3 \cdot 4$	Setting cross products equal
$x \cdot 6 = 12$	Multiplying
$\dfrac{x \cdot 6}{6} = \dfrac{12}{6}$	Dividing both sides by 6
$x = 2$	Dividing

We can check that 2 is the solution by replacing x with 2 and using cross products:

$$2 \cdot 6 = 12 \qquad \begin{array}{cc} 2 & 4 \\ \hline 3 & 6 \end{array} \qquad 3 \cdot 4 = 12.$$

Since the cross products are the same, it follows that $\frac{2}{3} = \frac{4}{6}$ so the numbers 2, 3 and 4, 6 are proportional, and 2 is the solution of the equation.

> ▶ To solve $\dfrac{x}{a} = \dfrac{c}{d}$, set cross products equal and solve for x.

Do Margin Exercise 7.

Example 5 Solve: $\dfrac{x}{7} = \dfrac{5}{3}$. Write a mixed number for the answer.

We have

$$\frac{x}{7} = \frac{5}{3}$$

$3 \cdot x = 7 \cdot 5$ Setting cross products equal

$3x = 35$ Multiplying

$\dfrac{3x}{3} = \dfrac{35}{3}$ Dividing both sides by 3

$x = \dfrac{35}{3}$, or $11\dfrac{2}{3}$.

The solution is $11\frac{2}{3}$.

Do Margin Exercise 8.

Example 6 Solve: $\dfrac{7.7}{15.4} = \dfrac{y}{2.2}$.

We have

$$\frac{7.7}{15.4} = \frac{y}{2.2}$$

$7.7 \cdot 2.2 = 15.4 \cdot y$ Setting cross products equal

$16.94 = 15.4y$ Multiplying

$\dfrac{16.94}{15.4} = \dfrac{15.4y}{15.4}$ Dividing both sides by 15.4

$1.1 = y.$ Dividing

The solution is 1.1.

Do Margin Exercise 9.

Example 7 Solve: $\dfrac{8}{x} = \dfrac{5}{3}$. Write decimal notation for the answer.

We have

$$\frac{8}{x} = \frac{5}{3}$$

$8 \cdot 3 = x \cdot 5$ Setting cross products equal

$24 = 5x$ Multiplying

$\dfrac{24}{5} = \dfrac{5x}{5}$ Dividing both sides by 5

$\dfrac{24}{5} = x$ Dividing

$4.8 = x.$ Simplifying

The solution is 4.8.

Do Margin Exercise 10.

8. Solve: $\dfrac{x}{9} = \dfrac{5}{4}$.

9. Solve: $\dfrac{21}{5} = \dfrac{n}{2.5}$.

10. Solve: $\dfrac{6}{x} = \dfrac{25}{11}$.

11. Solve: $\dfrac{0.4}{0.9} = \dfrac{4.8}{t}$.

12. Solve:

$$\dfrac{8\frac{1}{3}}{x} = \dfrac{10\frac{1}{2}}{3\frac{3}{4}}.$$

Example 8 Solve: $\dfrac{3.4}{4.93} = \dfrac{10}{n}$.

We have

$$\dfrac{3.4}{4.93} = \dfrac{10}{n}$$

$3.4 \cdot n = 4.93 \cdot 10$ Setting cross products equal

$3.4n = 49.3$ Multiplying

$\dfrac{3.4n}{3.4} = \dfrac{49.3}{3.4}$ Dividing both sides by 3.4

$n = 14.5$ Simplifying

The solution is 14.5.

Do Margin Exercise 11.

Example 9 Solve: $\dfrac{4\frac{2}{3}}{5\frac{1}{2}} = \dfrac{14}{x}$. Write a mixed number for the answer.

We have

$$\dfrac{4\frac{2}{3}}{5\frac{1}{2}} = \dfrac{14}{x}$$

$4\dfrac{2}{3} \cdot x = 14 \cdot 5\dfrac{1}{2}$ Setting cross products equal

$\dfrac{14}{3}x = 14 \cdot \dfrac{11}{2}$ Converting to fractional notation and multiplying

$\dfrac{3}{14} \cdot \dfrac{14}{3}x = 14 \cdot \dfrac{11}{2} \cdot \dfrac{3}{14}$ Multiplying both sides by the reciprocal of $\frac{14}{3}$

$x = \cancel{14} \cdot \dfrac{11}{2} \cdot \dfrac{3}{\cancel{14}}$ Multiplying by the reciprocal of the divisor

$x = \dfrac{33}{2}$, or $16\dfrac{1}{2}$.

The solution is $16\dfrac{1}{2}$.

Do Margin Exercise 12.

Exercise Set 7.3

a Determine whether the two pairs of numbers are proportional.

1. 5, 6 and 7, 9

2. 7, 5 and 6, 4

3. 1, 2 and 10, 20

4. 7, 3 and 21, 9

5. 2.4, 3.6 and 1.8, 2.7

6. 4.5, 3.8 and 6.7, 5.2

7. $5\frac{1}{3}$, $8\frac{1}{4}$ and $2\frac{1}{5}$, $9\frac{1}{2}$

8. $2\frac{1}{3}$, $3\frac{1}{2}$ and 14, 21

b Solve.

9. $\dfrac{18}{4} = \dfrac{x}{10}$

10. $\dfrac{x}{45} = \dfrac{20}{25}$

11. $\dfrac{x}{8} = \dfrac{9}{6}$

12. $\dfrac{8}{10} = \dfrac{n}{5}$

13. $\dfrac{t}{12} = \dfrac{5}{6}$

14. $\dfrac{12}{4} = \dfrac{x}{3}$

15. $\dfrac{2}{5} = \dfrac{8}{n}$

16. $\dfrac{10}{6} = \dfrac{5}{x}$

17. $\dfrac{n}{15} = \dfrac{10}{30}$

18. $\dfrac{2}{24} = \dfrac{x}{36}$

19. $\dfrac{16}{12} = \dfrac{24}{x}$

20. $\dfrac{7}{11} = \dfrac{2}{x}$

21. $\dfrac{6}{11} = \dfrac{12}{x}$

22. $\dfrac{8}{9} = \dfrac{32}{n}$

23. $\dfrac{20}{7} = \dfrac{80}{x}$

24. $\dfrac{5}{x} = \dfrac{4}{10}$

25. $\dfrac{12}{9} = \dfrac{x}{7}$

26. $\dfrac{x}{20} = \dfrac{16}{15}$

27. $\dfrac{x}{13} = \dfrac{2}{9}$

28. $\dfrac{1.2}{4} = \dfrac{x}{9}$

29. $\dfrac{t}{0.16} = \dfrac{0.15}{0.40}$

30. $\dfrac{x}{11} = \dfrac{7.1}{2}$

31. $\dfrac{100}{25} = \dfrac{20}{n}$

32. $\dfrac{35}{125} = \dfrac{7}{m}$

33. $\dfrac{7}{\frac{1}{4}} = \dfrac{28}{x}$

34. $\dfrac{x}{6} = \dfrac{1}{6}$

35. $\dfrac{\frac{1}{4}}{\frac{1}{2}} = \dfrac{\frac{1}{2}}{x}$

36. $\dfrac{1}{7} = \dfrac{x}{4\frac{1}{2}}$

37. $\dfrac{1}{2} = \dfrac{7}{x}$

38. $\dfrac{x}{3} = \dfrac{0}{9}$

39. $\dfrac{\frac{2}{7}}{\frac{3}{4}} = \dfrac{\frac{5}{6}}{y}$

40. $\dfrac{\frac{5}{4}}{\frac{5}{8}} = \dfrac{\frac{3}{2}}{Q}$

41. $\dfrac{2\frac{1}{2}}{3\frac{1}{3}} = \dfrac{x}{4\frac{1}{4}}$

42. $\dfrac{5\frac{1}{5}}{6\frac{1}{6}} = \dfrac{y}{3\frac{1}{2}}$

43. $\dfrac{1.28}{3.76} = \dfrac{4.28}{y}$

44. $\dfrac{10.4}{12.4} = \dfrac{6.76}{t}$

45. $\dfrac{10\frac{3}{8}}{12\frac{2}{3}} = \dfrac{5\frac{3}{4}}{y}$

46. $\dfrac{12\frac{7}{8}}{20\frac{3}{4}} = \dfrac{5\frac{2}{3}}{y}$

Skill Maintenance

Use = or ≠ for □ to write a true sentence.

47. $\dfrac{3}{4} \; \square \; \dfrac{5}{6}$

48. $\dfrac{18}{24} \; \square \; \dfrac{36}{48}$

49. $\dfrac{7}{8} \; \square \; \dfrac{7}{9}$

50. $\dfrac{19}{37} \; \square \; \dfrac{15}{29}$

Divide. Write decimal notation for the answer.

51. $-260 \div -4$

52. $395 \div -10$

53. $4648 \div 16$

54. $3427 \div 2.25$

Synthesis

55. ❖ Instead of setting cross products equal, a student solves $\frac{x}{7} = \frac{5}{3}$ (see Example 5) by multiplying on both sides by the least common denominator, 21. Is the student's approach a good one? Why or why not?

56. ❖ An instructor predicts that a student's test grade will be proportional to the amount of time the student spends studying. What is meant by this? Write an example of a proportion that involves the grades of two students and their study times.

▦ Solve.

57. $\dfrac{1728}{5643} = \dfrac{836.4}{x}$

58. $\dfrac{328.56}{627.48} = \dfrac{y}{127.66}$

7.4 Applications of Proportions

a | Proportions have applications in such diverse fields as business, chemistry, health sciences, and home economics, as well as to many areas of daily life. Proportions are most useful in making predictions.

Example 1 *Predicting Total Distance.* Donna drives her delivery van 800 mi in 3 days. At this rate, how far will she drive in 15 days?

1. Familiarize. We let d = the distance traveled in 15 days.

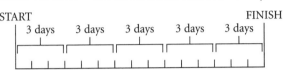

To estimate, we can break up the distance into five 3-day segments (15 days in total). Since each 3-day segment corresponds to 800 miles, we should anticipate that Donna will travel $5 \cdot 800$ or 4000 miles in 15 days.

2. Translate. We translate to a proportion. We make each side the ratio of distance to time, with distance in the numerator and time in the denominator.

$$\text{Distance in 15 days} \rightarrow \frac{d}{15} = \frac{800}{3} \leftarrow \text{Distance in 3 days}$$
$$\text{Time} \rightarrow \qquad\qquad\qquad \leftarrow \text{Time}$$

It may help to verbalize the proportion above as "the unknown distance d is to 15 days, as the known distance 800 miles is to 3 days."

3. Solve. Next, we solve the proportion:

$\quad 3 \cdot d = 15 \cdot 800 \qquad$ Setting cross products equal

$\quad 3d = 12,000 \qquad\quad$ Multiplying

$\quad \dfrac{3d}{3} = \dfrac{12,000}{3} \qquad$ Dividing both sides by 3

$\quad d = 4000. \qquad\qquad$ Simplifying

4. Check. Our answer matches our estimate so it is very reasonable. We can also substitute into the proportion and check cross products:

$\quad \dfrac{4000}{15} = \dfrac{800}{3};$

$\quad 4000 \cdot 3 = 12,000; \quad 15 \cdot 800 = 12,000$

The cross products are the same.

5. State. Donna drives 4000 mi in 15 days.

Do Margin Exercise 1.

Proportion problems can be solved in more than one way. In Example 1, any one of the following is an appropriate translation:

$$\frac{800}{3} = \frac{d}{15}, \qquad \frac{15}{d} = \frac{3}{800}, \qquad \frac{15}{3} = \frac{d}{800}, \qquad \frac{800}{d} = \frac{3}{15}$$

1. *Calories Burned.* The author of this book generally exercises three times per week. The readout on a stairmaster machine tells him that if he exercises for 24 min, he will burn 356 calories. How many calories will he burn if he exercises for 30 min?

2. *Predicting Paint Needs.* Lowell and Chris run a summer painting company to support their college expenses. They can paint 1700 ft² of clapboard with 4 gal of paint. How much paint would be needed for a building with 6000 ft² of clapboard?

3. *Purchasing Shirts.* If 2 shirts can be bought for $47, how many shirts can be bought with $200?

Example 2 *Predicting Medication.* To control a fever, a doctor suggests that a child who weighs 28 kg be given 420 mg of Tylenol. If the dosage is proportional to the child's weight, how much Tylenol is recommended for a child who weighs 35 kg?

1. Familiarize. We let t = the number of milligrams of Tylenol. Since we want to find the amount of Tylenol for a child who weighs somewhat more than 28 kg, we expect the answer to be somewhat more than 420 mg of Tylenol (since 35 kg is somewhat more than 28 kg).

2. Translate. We translate to a proportion, keeping the amount of Tylenol in the numerators.

$$\text{Tylenol suggested} \rightarrow \frac{420}{28} = \frac{t}{35} \leftarrow \text{Tylenol suggested}$$
$$\text{Child's weight} \rightarrow \qquad\qquad \leftarrow \text{Child's weight}$$

3. Solve. Next, we solve the proportion:

$$420 \cdot 35 = 28 \cdot t \qquad \text{Setting cross products equal}$$

$$14{,}700 = 28t \qquad \text{Multiplying}$$

$$\frac{14{,}700}{28} = \frac{28t}{28} \qquad \text{Dividing by 28 on both sides}$$

$$525 = t. \qquad \text{Simplifying}$$

4. Check. 525 mg is somewhat more than 420 mg, as predicted in step 1, so our answer is reasonable. As a more precise check, we substitute into the proportion and check cross products:

$$\frac{420}{28} = \frac{525}{35};$$
$$420 \cdot 35 = 14{,}700; \qquad 28 \cdot 525 = 14{,}700.$$

The cross products are the same.

5. State. The dosage for a child who weighs 35 kg is 525 mg

Do Margin Exercise 2.

Example 3 *Purchasing Tickets.* Carey bought 8 tickets to an international food festival for $52. How many tickets could she purchase with $90?

1. Familiarize. We let n = the number of tickets that can be purchased with $90. If we doubled our money ($52 · 2) we would have $104 and be able to purchase twice the number of tickets: 16. Since $90 is somewhat less than $104, $90 should buy us somewhat less than 16 tickets.

2. Translate. We translate to a proportion, keeping the number of tickets in the numerators.

$$\text{Tickets} \rightarrow \frac{8}{52} = \frac{n}{90} \leftarrow \text{Tickets}$$
$$\text{Cost} \rightarrow \qquad\qquad \leftarrow \text{Cost}$$

3. Solve. Next, we solve the proportion:

$$52 \cdot n = 8 \cdot 90 \qquad \text{Setting cross products equal}$$

$$52n = 720 \qquad \text{Multiplying}$$

$$\frac{52n}{52} = \frac{720}{52} \qquad \text{Dividing by 52 on both sides}$$

$$n \approx 13.8. \qquad \text{Simplifying and rounding}$$

Because it is impossible to buy a fractional part of a ticket, we must round our answer *down* to 13.

4. Check. 13 is somewhat less than our estimate of 16, so our answer is reasonable. As a more precise check, we can use a different approach. We find the cost per ticket and then divide $90 by that price. Since

$$52 \div 8 = 6.50 \quad \text{and} \quad 90 \div 6.50 \approx 13.8,$$

we have a check.

5. State. Carey could purchase 13 tickets with $90.

Do Margin Exercise 3.

Example 4 *Women's Hip Measurements.* For improved health, it is recommended that a woman's waist-to-hip ratio be 0.85 (or lower) (***Source:*** David Schmidt, "Lifting Weight Myths," *Nutrition Action Newsletter* 20, no 4, October 1993). Marta's hip measurement is 40 in. To meet the recommendation, what should Marta's waist measurement be?

Hip measurement is the largest measurement around the widest part of the buttocks.

Waist measurement is the smallest measurement below the ribs but above the navel.

1. Familiarize. Note that $0.85 = \frac{85}{100}$. We let w = Marta's waist measurement. To estimate, we should recognize that the recommended ratio requires that the waist be somewhat smaller than the hips.

2. Translate. We translate to a proportion as follows:

$$\begin{array}{c} \text{Waist measurement} \rightarrow \\ \text{Hip measurement} \rightarrow \end{array} \frac{w}{40} = \frac{85}{100} \begin{array}{c} \searrow \text{Recommended} \\ \nearrow \text{waist-to-hip ratio} \end{array}$$

3. Solve. Next, we solve the proportion:

$$100 \cdot w = 40 \cdot 85 \qquad \text{Setting cross products equal}$$

$$100w = 3{,}400 \qquad \text{Multiplying}$$

$$\frac{100w}{100} = \frac{3{,}400}{100} \qquad \text{Dividing by 100 on both sides}$$

$$w = 34. \qquad \text{Simplifying}$$

4. Check. 34 (the waist measurement) is somewhat smaller than 40 (the hip measurement) so our answer is reasonable. As a more precise check, we divide 34 by 40:

$$34 \div 40 = 0.85.$$

This is the desired ratio.

5. State. Marta's recommended waist measurement is 34 in. (or less).

Do Margin Exercise 4.

4. *Men's Hip Measurements.* It is recommended that a man's waist-to-hip ratio be 0.95 (or lower). Malcolm's hip measurement is 40 in. To meet the recommendation, what should Malcolm's waist measurement be?

5. *Construction Plans.* in Example 5, the length of the actual deck is 28.5 ft. What is the length of the deck on the blueprints?

Example 5 *Construction Plans.* Architects make blueprints of projects being constructed. These are scale drawings in which lengths are in proportion to actual sizes. The Hennesseys are constructing a rectangular deck just outside their house. The architectural blueprints are rendered such that $\frac{3}{4}$ in. on the drawing is actually 2.25 ft on the deck. The width of the deck on the drawing is 4.3 in. How wide is the deck in reality?

1. **Familiarize.** We let w = the width of the deck. Since 3\4 in. translates to 2.25 ft., 1 in. would translate to a bit more than that—say 3 ft. If every inch of drawing is 3 ft in reality, we can see that 4 inches of drawing would be 12 ft in reality ($3 \cdot 4 = 12$). Since 4 in. is close to 4.3 in., 12 ft is a good estimate.

2. **Translate.** Then we translate to a proportion, using 0.75 for $\frac{3}{4}$ in.

$$\text{Measure on drawing} \rightarrow \frac{0.75}{2.25} = \frac{4.3}{w} \leftarrow \text{Width on drawing} \atop \leftarrow \text{Width on deck}$$

3. **Solve.** Next, we solve the proportion:

$0.75 \cdot w = 2.25 \cdot 4.3$ Setting cross products equal

$0.75w = 9.675$ Multiplying

$\dfrac{0.75w}{0.75} = \dfrac{9.675}{0.75}$ Dividing by 0.75 on both sides

$w = 12.9.$ Simplifying

4. **Check.** 12. 9 is close to our estimate of 12 from step 1, so it is reasonable. As a more precise check, we substitute into the proportion and check cross products:

$$\frac{0.75}{2.25} = \frac{4.3}{12.9};$$

$0.75(12.9) = 9.675; \quad 2.25(4.3) = 9.675.$

The cross products are the same.

5. **State.** The width of the deck is 12.9 ft.

Do Margin Exercise 5.

Example 6 *Estimating a Wildlife Population.* To determine the number of fish in a lake, a conservationist catches 225 fish, tags them, and throws them back into the lake. Later, 108 fish are caught, and it is found that 15 of them are tagged. Estimate how many fish are in the lake.

1. **Familiarize.** We let F = the number of fish in the lake. Since 225 is just a sample of the fish in the lake, we expect the answer to be much larger than 225.

2. **Translate.** We translate to a proportion as follows:

   Fish tagged originally → $\dfrac{225}{F} = \dfrac{15}{108}$ ← Tagged fish caught later
   Fish in lake →   ← Fish caught later

3. **Solve.** Next, we solve the proportion:

   $225 \cdot 108 = F \cdot 15$ Setting cross products equal

   $24{,}300 = 15 \cdot F$ Multiplying

   $\dfrac{24{,}300}{15} = \dfrac{15F}{15}$ Dividing by 15 on both sides

   $1620 = F.$ Simplifying

4. **Check.** Our answer is much larger than 225, as we predicted in step 1. For a precise check, we substitute into the proportion and check cross products:

   $\dfrac{225}{1620} = \dfrac{15}{108};$

   $225 \cdot 108 = 24{,}300; \quad 1620 \cdot 15 = 24{,}300.$

   The cross products are the same.

5. **State.** We estimate that there are 1620 fish in the lake.

Do Margin Exercise 6.

6. *Estimating a Deer Population.* To determine the number of deer in a forest, a conservationist catches 612 deer, tags them, and releases them. Later, 244 deer are caught, and it is found that 72 of them are tagged. Estimate how many deer are in the forest.

Exercise Set 7.4

a Solve.

1. *Travel Distance.* Monica bicycled 234 mi in 14 days. At this rate, how far would Monica travel in 42 days?

2. *Gasoline Mileage.* Chuck's van traveled 84 mi on 6.5 gal of gasoline. At this rate, how many gallons would be needed to travel 126 mi?

3. If 2 tee shirts cost $18.80, how much would 9 tee shirts cost?

4. If 2 bars of soap cost $0.89, how many bars of soap can be purchased with $6.50?

5. In the rectangular paintings below, the ratio of length to height is the same. Find the height of the larger painting.

6. In the rectangles below, the ratio of length to width is the same. Find the width of the larger rectangle.

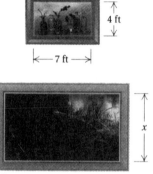

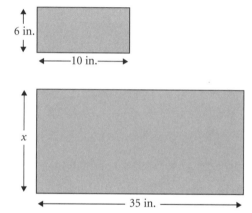

7. A bookstore manager knows that 24 books weigh 37 lb. How much do 40 books weigh?

8. *Turkey Servings.* An 8-lb turkey breast contains 36 servings of meat. How many pounds of turkey breast would be needed for 54 servings?

9. *Maple Syrup.* When 38 gal of maple sap are boiled down, the result is 2 gal of maple syrup. How much sap is needed to produce 9 gal of syrup?

10. In a class of 40 students, on average, 6 will be left-handed. If a class includes 9 "lefties," how many students would you estimate are in the class?

11. *Coffee.* Coffee beans from 14 trees are required to produce the 17 lb of coffee that the average person in the United States drinks each year. How many trees are required to produce 375 lb of coffee?

12. Jean bought a new car. In the first 8 months, it was driven 10,000 km. At this rate, how many kilometers will the car be driven in 1 yr?

13. A college advertises that its student-to-faculty ratio is 14 to 1. If 56 students register for Introductory Spanish, how many sections of the course would you expect to see offered?

14. In a metal alloy, the ratio of zinc to copper is 3 to 13. If there are 520 lb of copper, how many pounds of zinc are there?

15. *Deck Sealant.* Bonnie can waterproof 450 ft^2 of decking with 2 gal of sealant. How many gallons should Bonnie buy for a 1200-ft^2 deck?

16. *Paint Coverage.* Fred uses 3 gal of paint to cover 1275 ft^2 of siding. How much siding can Fred paint with 7 gal of paint?

17. *Estimating a Deer Population.* To determine the number of deer in a game preserve, a forest ranger catches 318 deer, tags them, and releases them. Later, 168 deer are caught, and it is found that 56 of them are tagged. Estimate how many deer are in the game preserve.

18. *Estimating a Trout Population.* To determine the number of trout in a lake, a conservationist catches 112 trout, tags them, and throws them back into the lake. Later, 82 trout are caught, and it is found that 32 of them are tagged. Estimate how many trout there are in the lake.

19. *Grass-Seed Coverage.* It takes 60 oz of grass seed to seed 3000 ft^2 of lawn. At this rate, how much would be needed for 5000 ft^2 of lawn?

20. *Grass-Seed Coverage.* In Exercise 19, how much seed would be needed for 7000 ft^2 of lawn?

21. *Quality Control.* A quality-control inspector examined 200 lightbulbs and found 18 of them to be defective. At this rate, how many defective bulbs will there be in a lot of 22,000?

22. A professor must grade 32 essays in a literature class. She can grade 5 essays in 40 min. At this rate, how long will it take her to grade all 32 essays?

23. *Map Scaling.* On a road atlas map, 1 in. represents 16.6 mi. If two cities are 3.5 in. apart on the map, how far apart are they in reality?

24. *Map Scaling.* On a map, $\frac{1}{4}$ in. represents 50 mi. If two cities are $3\frac{1}{4}$ in. apart on the map, how far apart are they in reality?

25. *Snow to Water.* Under typical conditions, $1\frac{1}{2}$ ft of snow will melt to 2 in. of water. To how many inches of water will $5\frac{1}{2}$ ft of snow melt?

26. *Tire Wear.* Tires are often priced according to the number of miles that they are expected to be driven. Suppose a tire priced at $59.76 is expected to be driven 35,000 mi. How much would you pay for a tire that is expected to be driven 40,000 mi?

27. *College Expenses.* A student attends a university whose academic year consists of two 16-week semesters. She budgets $800 for incidental expenses for the academic year. After 3 weeks, she has spent $80 for incidental expenses. Assuming the student continues to spend at the same rate, will the budget for incidental expenses be adequate? If not, when will the money be exhausted and how much more will be needed to complete the year?

28. *Sound-System Expense.* A basic sound system consists of a CD player, a receiver-amplifier, and two speakers. A rule of thumb used to estimate the relative investment in these components is 1:3:2. That is, the receiver-amplifier should cost three times the amount spent on the CD player and the speakers should cost twice as much as the amount spent on the CD player.

a) You have $1800 to spend. How should you allocate the funds if you use this rule of thumb?

b) How should you allocate a budget of $3000?

Earned Run Average. In baseball, the average number of earned runs given up by a pitcher in 9 innings is the pitcher's *earned run average,* or *ERA.* For example, John Smoltz of the Atlanta Braves gave up 83 earned runs in $253\frac{2}{3}$ innings during the year in which he earned the Cy Young award as the finest pitcher in the National League. His earned average is found by solving the following proportion:

$$\frac{\text{ERA}}{9} = \frac{83}{253\frac{2}{3}}$$

$$\text{ERA} = \frac{9 \cdot 83}{253\frac{2}{3}} \approx 2.94.$$

Complete the following table to find the ERA of each National League pitcher in the same year.

	Player	Team	Earned Runs	Innings Pitched	ERA
	John Smoltz	Atlanta Braves	83	$253\frac{2}{3}$	2.94
29.	Greg Maddux	Atlanta Braves	74	245	
30.	Jaime Navarro	Chicago Cubs	103	$236\frac{2}{3}$	
31.	Kevin Ritz	Colorado Rockies	125	213	
32.	Hideo Nomo	Los Angeles Dodgers	81	$228\frac{1}{3}$	

Skill Maintenance

Solve.

33. Dallas, Texas, receives an average of 31.1 in. (78.994 cm) of rain and 2.6 in. (6.604 cm) of snow each year (Source: National Oceanic and Atmospheric Administration).

a) What is the total amount of precipitation in inches?

b) What is the total amount of precipitation in centimeters?

34. The distance, by air, from New York to St. Louis is 876 mi (1401.6 km) and from St. Louis to Los Angeles is 1562 mi (2499.2 kin).

a) How far, in miles, is it from New York to Los Angeles?

b) How far, in kilometers, is it from New York to Los Angeles?

Synthesis

35. ❖ Polly solved Example 1 by forming the proportion $\frac{15}{3} = \frac{x}{800}$ whereas Rudy wrote $\frac{800}{15} = \frac{3}{x}$. Are both approaches valid? Why or why not.

36. ❖ Rob's waist and hips measure 35 in. and 33 in., respectively (see Margin Exercise 4). Suppose that Rob can either gain or lose 1 in. from one of his measurements. Where should the inch come from or go to? Why?

37. ▦ Carney College is expanding from 850 to 1050 students. To avoid any rise in the student-to-faculty ratio, the faculty of 69 professors must also increase. How many new faculty positions should be created?

38. ▦ In recognition of her outstanding work, Sheri's salary has been increased from $26,000 to $29,380. Tim is earning $23,000 and is requesting a proportional raise. How much more should he ask for?

39. Sue can paint 950 ft² with 2 gal of paint. How many gallons should Sue buy in order to paint a 30-ft by 100-ft wall?

40. Cy Young, one of the greatest baseball pitchers of all time, had an earned run average of 2.63. He pitched more innings, 7356, than anyone in the history of baseball. How many earned runs did he give up?

1. This pair of triangles is similar. Find the missing length x.

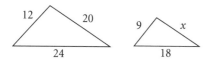

Note: As you look at the examples of similar triangles (at left), be aware that when uppercase letters (such as A) are used along with lowercase letters (such as *a*), they do not necessarily represent the same value.

7.5 Similar Triangles

a | Proportions and Similar Triangles

Look at the pair of triangles below. Note that they appear to have the same shape, but their sizes are different. These are examples of **similar triangles.** By using a magnifying glass, you could imagine enlarging the smaller triangle to get the larger. This process works because the corresponding sides of each triangle have the same ratio. That is, the following proportion is true.

  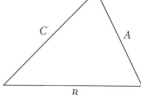

$$\frac{a}{A} = \frac{b}{B} = \frac{c}{C}$$

▶ **Similar triangles** have the same shape. Their corresponding sides have the same ratio—that is, they are proportional.

Example 1 The triangles at right are similar triangles. Find the missing length x.

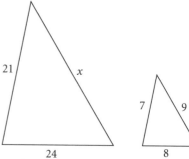

The ratio of x to 9 is the same as the ratio of 24 to 8. We get the proportion

$$\frac{x}{9} = \frac{24}{8}.$$

We solve the proportion:

$8 \cdot x = 9 \cdot 24$	Setting cross products equal
$8x = 216$	Multiplying
$\dfrac{8x}{8} = \dfrac{216}{8}$	Dividing by 8 on both sides
$x = 27.$	Simplifying

The missing length x is 27. We could have also used: $\frac{x}{9} = \frac{21}{7}$ to find x.

Do Margin Exercise 1.

Similar triangles and proportions can often be used to find lengths that would ordinarily be difficult to measure. For example, we could find the height of a flagpole without climbing it or the distance across a river without crossing it.

Example 2   How high is a flagpole that casts a 56-ft shadow at the same time that a 6-ft man casts a 5-ft shadow?

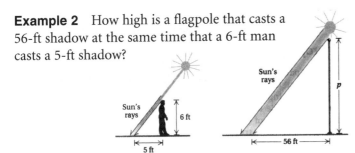

If we use the sun's rays to represent the third side of the triangle in our drawing of the situation, we see that we have similar triangles. Let p = the height of the flagpole. The ratio of 6 to p is the same as the ratio of 5 to 56. Thus we have the proportion

$$\text{Height of man} \rightarrow \frac{6}{p} = \frac{5}{56}. \leftarrow \text{Length of shadow of man}$$
$$\text{Height of pole} \rightarrow \qquad\qquad \leftarrow \text{Length of shadow of pole}$$

Solve: $6 \cdot 56 = 5 \cdot p$ Setting cross products equal

$\qquad\quad 336 = 5p$ Multiplying

$\qquad\quad \dfrac{336}{5} = \dfrac{5p}{5}$ Dividing by 5 on both sides

$\qquad\quad 67.2 = p$ Simplifying

The height of the flagpole is 67.2 ft.

Do Margin Exercise 2.

Example 3   *F-106 Blueprint.* A blueprint for an F-106 Delta Dart fighter plane is a scale drawing. Each wing of the plane has a triangular shape. The blueprint shows similar triangles. Find the length of side a of the wing.

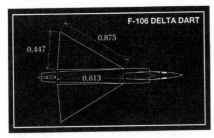

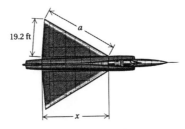

We let a = the length of the wing. Thus we have the proportion

$$\text{Length on the blueprint} \rightarrow \frac{0.447}{19.2} = \frac{0.875}{a}. \leftarrow \text{Length on the blueprint}$$
$$\text{Length of the wing} \rightarrow \qquad\qquad\qquad \leftarrow \text{Length of the wing}$$

Solve: $0.447 \cdot a = 19.2 \cdot 0.875$ Setting cross products equal

$\qquad\quad 0.447a = 16.8$ Multiplying

$\qquad\quad \dfrac{0.447a}{0.447} = \dfrac{16.8}{0.447}$ Dividing by 0.447 on both sides

$\qquad\quad a = \dfrac{16.8}{0.447}$ Simplifying

$\qquad\quad a \approx 37.6 \text{ ft}$

The length of side a of the wing is about 37.6 ft.

Do Margin Exercise 3.

2. How high is a flagpole that casts a 45-ft shadow at the same time that a 5.5-ft woman casts a 10-ft shadow?

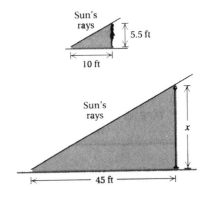

3. *F-106 Blueprint.* Referring to Example 3, find the length x of the wing.

4. The sides in the rectangles below are proportional. Find the width of the larger rectangle.

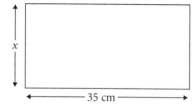

b Proportions and Other Geometric Shapes

When one geometric figure is a magnification of another, the corresponding ratios of the lengths within each figure are proportional. Thus in Example 1 we could have also used the proportions

$$\frac{x}{21} = \frac{9}{7} \text{ or } \frac{x}{24} = \frac{9}{8}.$$

Example 4   The sides in the rectangles below are proportional. Find the width of the larger rectangle.

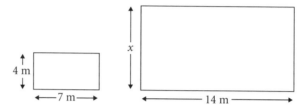

We let x = the width of the larger rectangle. Then we translate into a proportion.

$$\text{Width} \to \frac{4}{7} = \frac{x}{14} \leftarrow \text{Width}$$
$$\text{Length} \to \qquad\qquad \leftarrow \text{Length}$$

Solve: $4 \cdot 14 = 7 \cdot x$ Setting cross products equal

$56 = 7x$ Multiplying

$\dfrac{56}{7} = \dfrac{7x}{7}$ Dividing both sides by 7

$8 = x$ Simplifying

Thus the width of the larger rectangle is 8 m.

Do Margin Exercise 4.

Proportions involving measurements found in geometric figures have important uses in engineering, surveying, architecture, and art design.

Example 5   A scale model of an addition to an athletic facility is 12 cm wide at the base and rises to a height of 15 cm. If the actual base is to be 116 ft, what will be the height of the addition?

5. Refer to the figures in Example 5. If a model skylight is 3 cm wide, how wide will the actual skylight be?

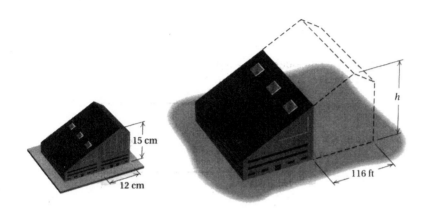

We let h = the height of the addition. Then we translate into a proportion.

$$\text{Width} \rightarrow \frac{12}{15} = \frac{116}{h} \leftarrow \text{Width}$$
$$\text{Height} \rightarrow \qquad\qquad \leftarrow \text{Height}$$

Other proportions could have been used. To solve for h, we simplify $\frac{12}{15}$ and find cross-products:

$\dfrac{4}{5} = \dfrac{116}{h}$ Rewriting $\frac{12}{15}$ as $\frac{4}{5}$

$4h = 5 \cdot 116$ Setting cross products equal

$4h = 580$ Multiplying

$\dfrac{4h}{4} = \dfrac{580}{4}$ Dividing both sides by 4

$h = 145$ Simplifying

Thus the height of the addition will be 145 ft.

Do Margin Exercise 5.

Exercise Set 7.5

a The triangles in each exercise are similar. Find the missing lengths.

1.

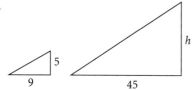

2.

3.

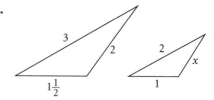

4.

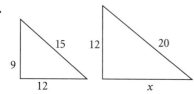

5.

6.

7.

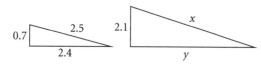

8.

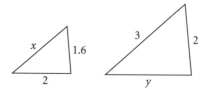

9. When a tree 8 m high casts a shadow 5 m long, how long a shadow is cast by a person 2 m tall?

10. How high is a flagpole that casts a 42-ft shadow at the same time that a $5\frac{1}{2}$-ft woman casts a 7-ft shadow?

11. How high is a tree that casts a 27-ft shadow at the same time that a 4-ft fence post casts a 3-ft shadow?

12. How high is a tree that casts a 32-ft shadow at the same time that an 8-ft light pole casts a 9-ft shadow?

13. Find the height *h* of the wall.

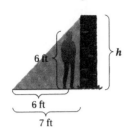

14. Find the length *L* of the lake.

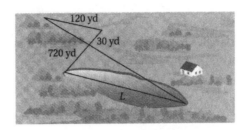

15. Find the distance across the river. Assume that the ratio of *d* to 25 ft is the same as the ratio of 40 ft to 10 ft.

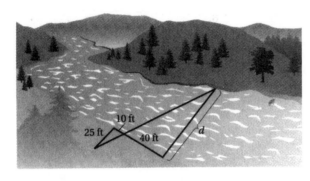

16. To measure the height of a hill, a string is drawn tight from level ground to the top of the hill. A 3-ft yardstick is placed under the string, touching it at point *P*, a distance of 5 ft from point *G*, where the string touches the ground. The string is then detached and found to be 120 ft long. How high is the hill?

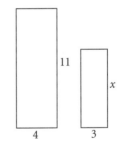

b The sides in each pair of figures are proportional. Find the missing lengths.

17.

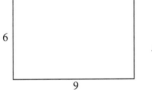

18.

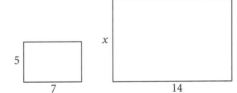

19.

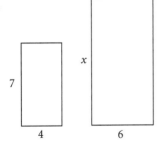

20.

21.

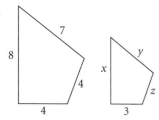

22.

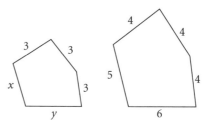

23.

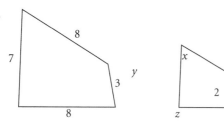

24.

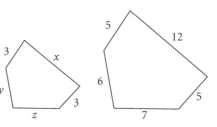

25.

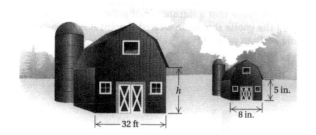

26.

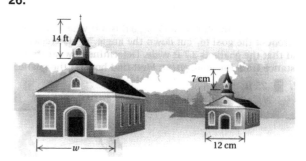

27. A scale model of an addition to an athletic facility is 12 cm wide at the base and rises to a height of 15 cm. If the actual base is to be 116 ft, what will be the height of the addition?

28. Refer to the figures in Exercise 27. If a model skylight is 3 cm wide, how wide will the actual skylight be?

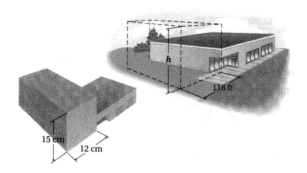

Skill Maintenance

29. A student has $34.97 to spend for a book at $49.95, a CD at $14.88, and a sweatshirt at $29.95. How much more money does the student need to make these purchases?

30. Divide: $-80.892 \div -8.4$.

Multiply.

31. -8.4×80.892

32. 0.01×-274.568

33. 100×274.568

34. 0.002×274.568

Synthesis

35. ❖ Is it possible for two triangles to have two pairs of sides that are proportional without the triangles being similar? Why or why not?

36. ❖ Design for a classmate a problem involving similar triangles for which

$$\frac{18}{128.95} = \frac{x}{789.89}.$$

Hockey Goals. An official hockey goal is 6 ft wide. To make scoring more difficult, goalies often locate themselves far in front of the goal to "cut down the angle." In Exercises 37 and 38, suppose that a slapshot from point A is attempted and that the goalie is 2.7 ft wide. Determine how far from the goal the goalie should be located if point A is the given distance from the goal. (*Hint:* First find how far the goalie should be from point A.)

37. ▦ 25 ft

38. ▦ 35 ft

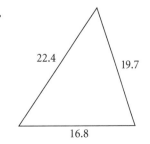

39. ▦ A miniature basketball hoop is built for the model referred to in Exercise 27. An actual hoop is 10 ft high. How high should the model hoop be? Round to the nearest thousandth of a centimeter.

▦ Solve. Round the answer to the nearest thousandth.

40. $\dfrac{8664.3}{10{,}344.8} = \dfrac{x}{9776.2}$

41. $\dfrac{12.0078}{56.0115} = \dfrac{789.23}{y}$

▦ The triangles in each exercise are similar triangles. Find the lengths not given.

42.

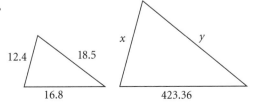

43.

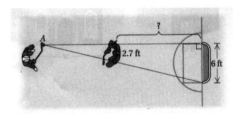

Review Exercises: Chapter 7

Write fractional notation for the ratio. Do not simplify.

1. 47 to 84   **2.** 46 to 1.27   **3.** 83 to 100   **4.** 0.72 to 197

5. In a recent year in the United States, 2,312,203 people died. Of these, 537,969 died of cancer. (Source: U.S. National Center for Health Statistics) Write fractional notation for the ratio of the number of people who die of cancer to the number of people who die.

Simplify the ratio.

6. 9 to 12

7. 3.6 to 6.4

8. What is the rate in miles per hour? 117.7 miles, 5 hours

9. A lawn requires 319 gal of water for every 500 ft². What is the rate in gallons per square foot?

10. What is the rate in dollars per kilogram? $355.04, 14 kilograms

11. Turkey Servings. A 25-lb turkey serves 18 people. What is the rate in servings per pound?

12. A 1-lb, 7-oz package of flour costs $1.30. Find the unit price in cents per ounce. Round to the nearest tenth of a cent.

13. Unit Pricing. It costs 79 cents for a $14\frac{1}{2}$ oz can of tomatoes. Find the unit price in cents per ounce. Round to the nearest hundredth of a cent.

Which has the lower unit price?

14.

WHITE BREAD
Brand A: 16 oz for 89 cents
Brand B: 12 oz for 65 cents

15.

CANNED PINEAPPLE JUICE
Brand A: 16 oz for 89 cents
Brand B: 18 oz for $1.26

Determine whether the two pairs of numbers are proportional.

16. 9, 15 and 36, 59

17. 24, 37 and 40, 46.25

Solve.

18. $\dfrac{8}{9} = \dfrac{x}{36}$

19. $\dfrac{6}{x} = \dfrac{48}{56}$

20. $\dfrac{120}{\frac{3}{7}} = \dfrac{7}{x}$

21. $\dfrac{4.5}{120} = \dfrac{0.9}{x}$

Solve.

22. If 3 dozen eggs cost $2.67, how much will 5 dozen eggs cost?

23. Quality Control. A factory manufacturing computer circuits found 39 defective circuits in a lot of 65 circuits. At this rate, how many defective circuits can be expected in a lot of 585 circuits?

24. A train travels 448 mi in 7 hr. At this rate, how far will it travel in 13 hr?

25. Fifteen acres are required to produce 54 bushels of tomatoes. At this rate, how many acres are required to produce 97.2 bushels of tomatoes?

26. It is known that 5 people produce 13 kg of garbage in one day. San Diego, California, has 1,150,000 people. How many kilograms of garbage are produced in San Diego in one day?

27. Under typical conditions, $1\frac{1}{2}$ ft of snow will melt to 2 in. of water. To how many inches of water will $4\frac{1}{2}$ ft of snow melt?

28. In Michigan, there are 2.3 lawyers for every 1000 people. The population of Detroit is 4,307,000. (Source: U.S. Bureau of the Census) How many lawyers would you expect there to be in Detroit?

29. The following triangles are similar. Find x and y.

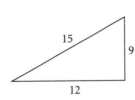 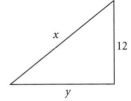

30. How high is a billboard that casts a 25-ft shadow at the same time that an 8-ft sapling casts a 5-ft shadow

31. The lengths in the figure below are proportional. Find the missing lengths.

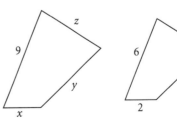

Test: Chapter 7

Write fractional notation for the ratio. Do not simplify.

1. 85 to 97

2. 0.34 to 124

Simplify the ratio.

3. 18 to 20

4. 0.75 to 0.96

5. What is the rate in feet per second?
   10 feet, 16 seconds

6. Ham Servings. A 12-lb shankless ham contains 16 servings. What is the rate in servings per pound?

7. A 1-lb, 2-oz package of Mahi Mahi fish costs $3.49. Find the unit price in cents per ounce. Round to the nearest hundredth of a cent.

8. Which orange juice has the lower unit price?

   Brand A: $1.19 for 12 oz.
   Brand B: $1.33 for 16 oz.

Determine whether the two pairs of numbers are proportional.

9. 7, 8 and 63, 72

10. 1.3, 3.4 and 5.6, 15.2

Solve.

11. $\dfrac{9}{4} = \dfrac{27}{x}$

12. $\dfrac{150}{2.5} = \dfrac{x}{6}$

Solve.

13. A woman traveled 432 km in 12 hr. At this rate, how far would she travel in 42 hr?

14. If 2 cans of apricots cost $3.39, how many cans of apricots can you buy for $74.58?

15. Time Loss. A watch loses 2. min in 10 hr. At this rate, how much will it lose in 24 hr?.

16. Map Scaling. On a map, 3 in. represents 225 mi. If two cities are 7 in. apart on the map, how far apart are they in reality?

17. Tower Height. A birdhouse built on a pole that is 3 m high casts a shadow 5 m long. At the same time, the shadow of a tower is 110 m long. How high is the tower?

The lengths in each pair of figures are proportional. Find the missing lengths.

18.

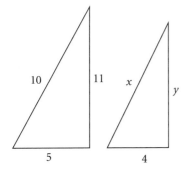

19.

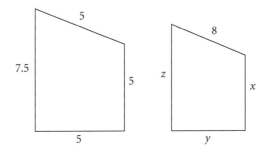

20. In your own words, explain how to solve a proportion.

21. Give an example NOT used on this test of how a ratio can be used in the real world.

8

Percent Notation

An Application

In a treadmill test, a doctor's goal is to get the patient to reach his or her *maximum heart rate,* in beats per minute. The maximum heart rate is found by subtracting the patient's age from 220 and taking 85% of the result. What is the maximum heart rate for a man of age 55?

This problem appears as Exercise 11 in exercise set 8.5a.

The Mathematics

We let x = the maximum heart rate and the problem is rephrased and translated as follows:

$$\begin{array}{ccccc} \text{What} & \text{is} & 85\% & \text{of} & 220 - 55? \\ \downarrow & \downarrow & \downarrow & \downarrow & \downarrow \\ x & = & 85\% & \cdot & (220 - 55) \end{array}$$

Introduction

This chapter introduces a new kind of notation for numbers. We will see that $\frac{3}{8}$, 0.375, and 37.5% are all names for the same number. Then we will use percent notation and equations to solve applied problems.

8.1 Percent Notation

a | Understanding Percent Notation

Of all wood harvested, 35% of it is used for paper production. What does this mean? It means that, on average, of every 100 tons of wood harvested, 35 tons is used to produce paper. Thus, 35% is a ratio of 35 to 100, or $\frac{35}{100}$.

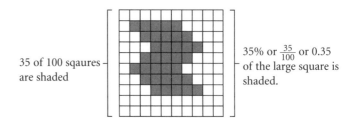

35 of 100 sqaures are shaded

35% or $\frac{35}{100}$ or 0.35 of the large square is shaded.

Percent notation is used extensively in our lives. Here are some examples:

> Astronauts lose 1% of their bone mass for each month of weightlessness.
> 95% of hair spray is alcohol.
> 55% of all baseball merchandise sold is purchased by women.
> 62.4% of all aluminum cans were recycled in a recent year.
> 56% of all fruit juice purchased is orange juice.
> 45.8% of us sleep between 7 and 8 hours per night.
> 74% of the times a major-league baseball player strikes out swinging, the pitch was out of the strike zone.

Percent notation is often represented by pie charts to show how the parts of a quantity are related. For example, the chart below relates the amounts of different kinds of juices that are sold.

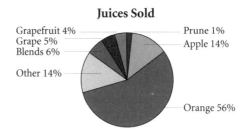

Juices Sold

Grapefruit 4%
Grape 5%
Blends 6%
Other 14%
Prune 1%
Apple 14%
Orange 56%

Source: Beverage Marketing Corporation

> ▶ The notation **n%** means "*n* per hundred."

This definition leads us to the following equivalent ways of defining percent notation.

> **Percent notation, $n\%$,** is defined using:
>
> ratio → $n\% =$ the ratio of n to $100 = \frac{n}{100}$;
>
> fractional notation → $n\% = n \cdot \frac{1}{100}$;
>
> decimal notation → $n\% = n(0.01)$.

Example 1   Write three kinds of notation for 35%.

Using ratio: $35\% = \dfrac{35}{100}$ A ratio of 35 to 100

Using fractional notation: $35\% = 35 \cdot \dfrac{1}{100}$ Replacing % with $\cdot \frac{1}{100}$

Using decimal notation: $35\% = 35 \cdot 0.01$ Replacing % with $\cdot \, 0.01$

Example 2   Write three kinds of notation for 67.8%.

Using ratio: $67.8\% = \dfrac{67.8}{100}$ A ratio of 67.8 to 100

Using fractional notation: $67.8\% = 67.8 \cdot \dfrac{1}{100}$ Replacing % with $\cdot \frac{1}{100}$

Using decimal notation: $67.8\% = 67.8 \cdot 0.01$ Replacing % with $\cdot \, 0.01$

Do Margin Exercises 1–3.

b Converting from Percent Notation to Decimal Notation

Consider 78%. To convert to decimal notation, we can think of percent notation as a ratio and write

$78\% = \dfrac{78}{100}$ Using the definition of percent as a ratio

$ = 0.78.$ Converting to decimal notation

Similarly,

$4.9\% = \dfrac{4.9}{100}$ Using the definition of percent as a ratio

$ = 0.049.$ Converting to decimal notation

We could also convert 78% to decimal notation by replacing "%" with "× 0.01" and write

$78\% = 78 \cdot 0.01$ Replacing % with × 0.01

$ = 0.78.$ Multiplying

Similarly,

$4.9\% = 4.9 \cdot 0.01$ Replacing % with × 0.01

$ = 0.049.$ Multiplying

Write three kinds of notation as in Examples 1 and 2.

1. 70%

2. 23.4%

3. 100%

It is thought that the Roman Emperor Augustus began percent notation by taxing goods sold at a rate of $\frac{1}{100}$. In time, the symbol "%" evolved by interchanging the parts of the symbol "100" to "$\frac{0}{0}$" and then to "%."

Find decimal notation.

4. 34%

5. 78.9%

Find decimal notation for the percent notation in the sentence.

6. People forget 83% of all names they learn.

7. Soft drink sales in the United States have grown 4.2% annually over the past decade.

Dividing by 100 amounts to moving the decimal point two places to the left, which is the same as multiplying by 0.01. This leads us to a quick way to convert from percent notation to decimal notation: We drop the percent symbol and move the decimal point two places to the left.

> To convert from percent notation to decimal notation, 36.5%
>
> **a.** replace the percent symbol % with × 0.01, and 36.5(0.01)
>
> **b.** multiply by 0.01, which means move the decimal point two places to the left. 0.36.5 Move 2 places to the left.
>
> 36.5% = 0.365

Example 3 Find decimal notation for 99.44%.

a. Replace the percent symbol with × 0.01. 99.44(0.01)
b. Move the decimal point two places to the left. 0.99.44

Thus, 99.44% = 0.9944.

Example 4 The interest rate on a $2\frac{1}{2}$ year certificate of deposit is 5.1%. Find decimal notation for 5.1%.

a. Replace the percent symbol with × 0.01. 5.1(0.01)
b. Move the decimal point two places to the left. 0.05.1

Thus, 5.1% = 0.051.

Do Margin Exercises 4–7.

c | Converting from Decimal Notation to Percent Notation

To convert 0.38 to percent notation, we can first write fractional notation, as follows:

$0.38 = \frac{38}{100}$ Converting to fractional notation

$= 38\%.$ Using the definition of percent as a ratio

Note that 100% = 100 × 0.01 = 1. Thus to convert 0.38 to percent notation, we can multiply by 1, using 100% as a symbol for 1. Then

$0.38 = 0.38 \cdot 1$

$= 0.38 \cdot 100\%$

$= 0.38 \cdot 100 \cdot 0.01$

$= 38 \cdot 0.01$

$= 38\%.$ Replacing "× 0.01" with the % symbol

Even more quickly, since 0.38 = 0.38 × 100%, we can simply multiply 0.38 by 100 and write the % symbol.

To convert from decimal notation to percent notation, multiply by 100%—that is, move the decimal point two places to the right and write a percent symbol.

▶ To convert from decimal notation to percent notation, multiply by 100%. That is,

$0.675 = 0.675 \times 100\%$

a. move the decimal point two places to the right, and

0.67.5   Move 2 places to the right.

b. write a % symbol.

67.5%

$0.675 = 67.5\%$

Example 5 Find percent notation for 1.27.

a. Move the decimal point two places to the right.

1.27.

b. Write a % symbol.

127%

Thus, 1.27 = 127%.

Example 6 Television sets are on 0.25 of the time. Find percent notation for 0.25.

a. Move the decimal point two places to the right.

0.25.

b. Write a % symbol.

25%

Thus, 0.25 = 25%.

Example 7 Find percent notation for 5.6.

a. Move the decimal point two places to the right, adding an extra zero.

5.60.

b. Write a % symbol.

560%

Thus, 5.6 = 560%.

Do Margin Exercises 8–12.

Find percent notation.

8. 0.24

9. 3.47

10. 1

Find percent notation for the decimal notation in the sentence.

11. Blood is 0.9 water.

12. Of those accidents requiring medical attention, 0.108 of them occur on roads.

Exercise Set 8.1

a Write three kinds of notation as in Examples 1 and 2 in Section 8.1a.

1. 90%   **2.** 58.7%   **3.** 12.5%   **4.** 130%

b Find decimal notation.

5. 67%   **6.** 17%   **7.** 45.6%   **8.** 76.3%   **9.** 59.01%

10. 30.02%   **11.** 10%   **12.** 40%   **13.** 1%   **14.** 100%

15. 200%   **16.** 300%   **17.** 0.1%   **18.** 0.4%   **19.** 0.09%

20. 0.12%   **21.** 0.18%   **22.** 5.5%   **23.** 23.19%   **24.** 87.99%

Find decimal notation for the percent notation in the sentence.

25. On average, about 40% of the body weight of an adult male is muscle.

26. On average, about 23% of the body weight of an adult female is muscle.

27. A person's brain is 2.5% of his or her body weight.

28. It is known that 16% of all dessert orders in restaurants is for pie.

29. It is known that 62.2% of us think Monday is the worst day of the week.

30. Of all 18-year-olds, 68.4% have a driver's license.

c Find percent notation.

31. 0.47   **32.** 0.87   **33.** 0.03   **34.** 0.01   **35.** 8.7

36. 4   **37.** 0.334   **38.** 0.889   **39.** 0.75   **40.** 0.99

41. 0.4　　　　　**42.** 0.5　　　　　**43.** 0.006　　　　　**44.** 0.008　　　　　**45.** 0.017

46. 0.024　　　　　**47.** 0.2718　　　　　**48.** 0.8911　　　　　**49.** 0.0239　　　　　**50.** 0.00073

Find percent notation for the decimal notation in the sentence.

51. Around the fourth of July, about 0.000104 of all children aged 15 to 19 suffer injuries from fireworks.

52. About 0.144 of all children are cared for by relatives.

53. It is known that 0.24 of us go to the movies once a month.

54. It is known that 0.458 of us sleep between 7 and 8 hours.

55. Of all CDs purchased, 0.581 of them are pop/rock.

56. About 0.026 of all college football players go on to play professional football.

Skill Maintenance

Convert to a mixed numeral.

57. $\dfrac{100}{3}$　　　　　**58.** $\dfrac{75}{2}$　　　　　**59.** $\dfrac{-75}{8}$　　　　　**60.** $\dfrac{-297}{16}$

Convert to decimal notation.

61. $-\dfrac{2}{3}$　　　　　**62.** $-\dfrac{1}{3}$　　　　　**63.** $\dfrac{5}{6}$　　　　　**64.** $\dfrac{17}{12}$

Synthesis

65. ❖ What would you do to an entry on a calculator in order to get percent notation? Explain.

66. ❖ What would you do to percent notation on a calculator in order to get decimal notation? Explain.

8.2 Percent Notation and Fractional Notation

a | Converting from Fractional Notation to Percent Notation

Consider the fractional notation $\frac{7}{8}$. To convert to percent notation, we use two skills we already have. We first find decimal notation by dividing:

$$\frac{7}{8} = 0.875$$

Then we convert the decimal notation to percent notation. We move the decimal point two places to the right

$$0.8\ 7.5$$

and write a % symbol:

$$\frac{7}{8} = 87.5\%, \text{ or } 87\tfrac{1}{2}\%$$

▶ To convert from fractional notation to percent notation,

$\frac{3}{5}$ Fractional notation

a. find decimal notation by division, and

$$\begin{array}{r} 0.6 \\ 5 \overline{)\ 3.0} \\ \underline{3.0} \\ 0 \end{array}$$ or $\boxed{3}\ \boxed{\div}\ \boxed{5}\ \boxed{=}$

b. convert the decimal notation to percent notation.

$0.6 = 0.60 = 60\%$ Percent

$\frac{3}{5} = 60\%$ notation

Example 1 Find percent notation for $\frac{3}{8}$.

a. Find decimal notation by division.

$$\frac{3}{8} = 0.375$$

Calculator Spotlight

Conversion. Calculators are often used when we are converting fractional notation to percent notation. We simply perform the division on the calculator and then convert the decimal notation to percent notation. For example, percent notation for $\frac{17}{40}$ can be found by pressing

$\boxed{1}\ \boxed{7}\ \boxed{\div}$
$\boxed{4}\ \boxed{0}\ \boxed{=}$

and then converting the result, 0.425, to percent notation, 42.5%.

Exercises

Find percent notation. Round to the nearest hundredth of a percent.

1. $\frac{13}{25}$ 2. $\frac{5}{13}$

3. $\frac{42}{39}$ 4. $\frac{12}{7}$

5. $\frac{217}{364}$ 6. $\frac{2378}{8401}$

Answers

1. 52%
2. 38.46%
3. 107.69%
4. 171.43%
5. 59.62%
6. 28.31%

b. Convert the decimal notation to percent notation. Move the decimal point two places to the right, and write a % symbol.

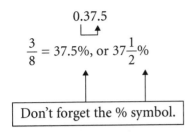

$$\frac{3}{8} = 37.5\%, \text{ or } 37\frac{1}{2}\%$$

Don't forget the % symbol.

Do Margin Exercises 1 and 2.

Example 2 Of all meals, $\frac{1}{3}$ are eaten outside the home. Find percent notation for $\frac{1}{3}$.

a. Find decimal notation by division.

$$\frac{1}{3} = 0.333...$$

We get a repeating decimal: $0.\overline{3}$

b. Convert the answer to percent notation.
Because conversion from a decimal to a percent requires the decimal point to be moved two places to the right and the bar only appears to the right of the decimal, $0.\overline{3}$ should be written as $0.33\overline{3}$.

$$0.33.\overline{3}$$

$$\frac{1}{3} = 33.3\%, \text{ or } 33\frac{1}{3}\%$$

Do Margin Exercises 3 and 4.

In some cases, division is not the fastest way to convert. The following are some optional ways in which conversion might be done.

Example 3 Find percent notation for $\frac{69}{100}$.

We use the definition of percent as a ratio.

$$\frac{69}{100} = 69\%$$

Example 4 Find percent notation for $\frac{17}{20}$.

We multiply by 1 to get 100 in the denominator. We think of what we have to multiply 20 by in order to get 100. That number is 5, so we multiply by 1 using $\frac{5}{5}$.

$$\frac{17}{20} \cdot \frac{5}{5} = \frac{85}{100} = 85\%$$

Note that this shortcut works only when the denominator is a factor of 100.

Do Margin Exercises 5 and 6.

Find percent notation.

1. $\frac{1}{4}$ **2.** $\frac{5}{8}$

3. The human body is $\frac{2}{3}$ water. Find percent notation for $\frac{2}{3}$.

4. Find percent notation: $\frac{5}{6}$

Find percent notation.

5. $\frac{57}{100}$ **6.** $\frac{19}{25}$

Find fractional notation.

7. 60%

8. 3.25%

9. $66\frac{2}{3}\%$

10. Complete this table.

Fractional Notation	$\frac{1}{5}$		
Decimal Notation		$0.83\overline{3}$	
Percent Notation			$37\frac{1}{2}\%$

b **Converting from Percent Notation to Fractional Notation**

To convert from percent notation to fractional notation,	30% Percent notation
a. use the definition of percent as a ratio, and	$\frac{30}{100}$
b. simplify, if possible.	$\frac{3}{10}$ Fractional notation

Example 5 Find fractional notation for 75%.

$$75\% = \frac{75}{100} \qquad \text{Using the definition of percent}$$

$$= \frac{3 \cdot \overset{1}{\cancel{25}}}{4 \cdot \underset{1}{\cancel{25}}} \qquad \text{Simplifying}$$

$$= \frac{3}{4}$$

Example 6 Find fractional notation for 62.5%.

$$62.5\% = \frac{62.5}{100} \qquad \text{Using the definition of percent}$$

$$= \left(\frac{62.5}{100}\right)\left(\frac{10}{10}\right) \qquad \text{Multiplying by 1 to eliminate the decimal point in the numerator}$$

$$= \frac{625}{1000}$$

$$= \frac{5 \cdot \overset{1}{\cancel{125}}}{8 \cdot \underset{1}{\cancel{125}}} \qquad \text{Simplifying}$$

$$= \frac{5}{8}$$

Example 7 Find fractional notation for $16\frac{2}{3}\%$.

$$16\frac{2}{3}\% = \frac{50}{3}\% \qquad \text{Converting from the mixed number to fractional notation}$$

$$= \left(\frac{50}{3}\right)\left(\frac{1}{100}\right) \qquad \text{Using the definition of percent}$$

$$= \frac{\overset{1}{\cancel{50}} \cdot 1}{3 \cdot \underset{2}{\cancel{100}}} \qquad \text{Simplifying}$$

$$= \frac{1}{6}$$

Do Margin Exercises 7-10.

The table on the inside front cover lists decimal, fractional, and percent equivalents used so often that it would speed up your work if you learned them. For example, $\frac{1}{3} = 0.\overline{3}$, so we say that the **decimal equivalent** of $\frac{1}{3}$ is $0.\overline{3}$, or that $0.\overline{3}$ has the **fractional equivalent** $\frac{1}{3}$.

Exercise Set 8.2

a Find percent notation.

1. $\dfrac{41}{100}$ **2.** $\dfrac{36}{100}$ **3.** $\dfrac{5}{100}$ **4.** $\dfrac{1}{100}$ **5.** $\dfrac{2}{10}$ **6.** $\dfrac{7}{10}$

7. $\dfrac{3}{10}$ **8.** $\dfrac{9}{10}$ **9.** $\dfrac{1}{2}$ **10.** $\dfrac{3}{4}$ **11.** $\dfrac{5}{8}$ **12.** $\dfrac{1}{8}$

13. $\dfrac{4}{5}$ **14.** $\dfrac{2}{5}$ **15.** $\dfrac{2}{3}$ **16.** $\dfrac{1}{3}$ **17.** $\dfrac{1}{6}$ **18.** $\dfrac{5}{6}$

19. $\dfrac{4}{25}$ **20.** $\dfrac{17}{25}$ **21.** $\dfrac{1}{20}$ **22.** $\dfrac{31}{50}$ **23.** $\dfrac{17}{50}$ **24.** $\dfrac{3}{20}$

Find percent notation for the fractional notation in the sentence.

25. Bread is $\dfrac{9}{25}$ water.

26. Milk is $\dfrac{7}{8}$ water.

Write percent notation for the fractions in this pie chart.

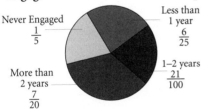

Engagement Times of Married Couples

Never Engaged $\dfrac{1}{5}$

Less than 1 year $\dfrac{6}{25}$

1–2 years $\dfrac{21}{100}$

More than 2 years $\dfrac{7}{20}$

27. $\dfrac{21}{100}$

28. $\dfrac{1}{5}$

29. $\dfrac{6}{25}$

30. $\dfrac{7}{20}$

b Find fractional notation. Simplify.

31. 85%

32. 55%

33. 62.5%

34. 12.5%

35. $33\frac{1}{3}\%$

36. $83\frac{1}{3}\%$

37. $16.\overline{6}\%$

38. $66.\overline{6}\%$

39. 7.25%

40. 4.85%

41. 0.8%

42. 0.2%

43. $25\frac{3}{8}\%$

44. $48\frac{7}{8}\%$

45. $78\frac{2}{9}\%$

46. $16\frac{5}{9}\%$

47. $64\frac{7}{11}\%$

48. $73\frac{3}{11}\%$

49. 150%

50. 110%

51. 0.0325%

52. 0.419%

53. $33.\overline{3}\%$

54. $83.\overline{3}\%$

Find fractional notation for the percents in this bar graph.

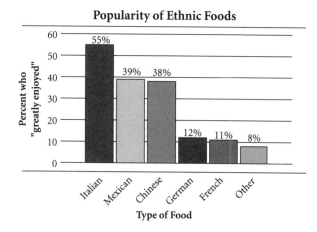

Popularity of Ethnic Foods

55. 55%

56. 39%

57. 38%

58. 12%

59. 11%

60. 8%

Note that there were multiple responses.

Find fractional notation for the percent notation in the sentence.

61. A 30-gram cup of Wheaties supplies 25% of the minimum daily requirement of vitamin A.

62. A 30-gram cup of Wheaties supplies 45% of the minimum daily requirement of iron.

63. The interest rate on a 5-yr certificate of deposit was 5.69%.

64. One year the sales of *USA Today* increased 7.2%.

Complete the table.

65.

Fractional Notation	Decimal Notation	Percent Notation
$\frac{1}{8}$		$12\frac{1}{2}\%$ or 12.5%
$\frac{1}{6}$		
		20%
	0.25	
		$33\frac{1}{3}\%$ or $33.\overline{3}\%$
		$37\frac{1}{2}\%$ or 37.5%
		40%
$\frac{1}{2}$	0.5	50%

66.

Fractional Notation	Decimal Notation	Percent Notation
$\frac{3}{5}$		
	0.625	
$\frac{2}{3}$		
	0.75	75%
$\frac{4}{5}$		
$\frac{5}{6}$		$83\frac{1}{3}\%$ or $83.\overline{3}\%$
$\frac{7}{8}$		$87\frac{1}{2}\%$ or 87.5%
		100%

67.

Fractional Notation	Decimal Notation	Percent Notation
	0.5	
$\frac{1}{3}$		
		25%
		$16\frac{2}{3}\%$ or $16.\overline{6}\%$
	0.125	
$\frac{3}{4}$		
	$0.8\overline{3}$	
$\frac{3}{8}$		

68.

Fractional Notation	Decimal Notation	Percent Notation
		40%
		$62\frac{1}{2}\%$ or 62.5%
	0.875	
$\frac{1}{1}$		
	0.6	
	$0.\overline{6}$	
$\frac{1}{5}$		

Skill Maintenance

Solve.

69. $13x = -910$

70. $15y = 75$

71. $-0.05b = 20$

72. $3 = 0.16b$

73. $\dfrac{24}{37} = \dfrac{15}{x}$

74. $\dfrac{17}{18} = \dfrac{x}{27}$

Convert to a mixed number.

75. $\dfrac{100}{3}$

76. $\dfrac{75}{2}$

77. $\dfrac{-250}{3}$

78. $-\dfrac{123}{6}$

79. $\dfrac{345}{8}$

80. $\dfrac{373}{6}$

81. $\dfrac{75}{4}$

82. $\dfrac{67}{9}$

Synthesis

83. ❖ Is it always best to convert from fractional notation to percent notation by first finding decimal notation? Why or why not?

84. ❖ Athletes sometimes speak of "giving 110%" effort. Does this make sense? Why or why not?

Find percent notation.

85. $\dfrac{41}{369}$

86. $\dfrac{54}{999}$

Find decimal notation.

87. $\dfrac{14}{9}\%$

88. $\dfrac{19}{12}\%$

8.3 Solving Percent Problems Using Equations

a Translating to Equations

To solve a problem involving percents, it is helpful to translate first to an equation.

Example 1 Translate:

$$23\% \quad of \quad 5 \quad is \quad what?$$
$$23\% \quad \cdot \quad 5 \quad = \quad a$$

▶ **"Of"** translates to " · " or " × ". **"Is"** translates to "=".

"What" translates to any letter. % translates to "$\times \frac{1}{100}$" or "$\times 0.01$".

Example 2 Translate:

$$What \quad is \quad 11\% \quad of \quad 49$$
$$a \quad = \quad 11\% \quad \cdot \quad 49 \qquad \text{Any letter can be used.}$$
$$a \quad = \quad 11(0.01)(49)$$

Do Margin Exercises 1 and 2.

Example 3 Translate:

$$3 \quad is \quad 10\% \quad of \quad what?$$
$$3 \quad = \quad 10\% \quad \cdot \quad b$$
$$3 \quad = \quad 10(0.01)b$$

Example 4 Translate:

$$45\% \quad of \quad what \quad is \quad 23?$$
$$45\% \quad \cdot \quad b \quad = \quad 23$$
$$45(0.01)b \qquad = \quad 23$$

Do Margin Exercises 3 and 4.

Example 5 Translate:

$$10 \quad is \quad what \quad percent \quad of \quad 20?$$
$$10 \quad = \quad n \quad \% \quad of \quad 20$$
$$10 \quad = \quad n(0.01)(20)$$

Example 6 Translate:

$$What \quad percent \quad of \quad 50 \quad is \quad 7?$$
$$n \quad \% \quad \cdot \quad 50 \quad = \quad 7$$
$$n(0.01)(50) \qquad = \quad 7$$

Do Margin Exercises 5 and 6.

Translate to an equation. Do not solve.

1. 12% of 50 is what?

2. What is 40% of 60?

Translate to an equation. Do not solve.

3. 45 is 20% of what?

4. 120% of what is 60?

Translate to an equation. Do not solve.

5. 16 is what percent of 40?

6. What percent of 84 is 10.5?

b | Solving Percent Problems

In solving percent problems, we use the *Translate* and *Solve* steps in the problem-solving strategy used throughout this text.

Percent problems are actually of three different types. Although the method we present does *not* require that you be able to identify which type we are studying, it is helpful to know them.

We know that

15 is 25% of 60, or

$15 = 25\% \times 60$.

We can think of this as:

> ▶ Amount = Percent number × Base.

Each of the three types of percent problems depends on which of the three pieces of information is missing.

Example 7

a. Finding the *amount* (the result of taking the percent)

Example: <u>What</u>   is   25%   of   60?

Translate: a =   25%   ·   60

Solve: a = $25(0.01)(60)$

a =   15

Thus, 15 is 25% of 60. The answer is 15.

b. Finding the *base* (the number you are taking the percent of)

Example: 15   is   25%   of   <u>what number?</u>

Translate: 15   =   25%   · b

Solve: 15   = $25(0.01)b$

15   = $0.25b$

$$\frac{15}{0.25} = \frac{0.25b}{0.25}$$

60   = b

Thus, 15 is 25% of 60. The answer is 60.

c. Finding the *percent number* (the percent itself)

Example: 15   is   <u>what percent</u>   of   60?

Translate: 15   =   p%   ·   60

Solve:

$$15 = p(0.01)(60)$$
$$15 = 0.6p$$
$$\frac{15}{0.6} = \frac{0.6p}{0.6}$$
$$25 = p$$

Thus, 15 is 25% of 60. The answer is 25%.

CAUTION! When a question asks "what percent?," be sure to give the answer in percent notation.

Example 8 120% of $42 is what?

Translate: $120\% \times 42 = a.$

Solve:

$$120(0.01)(42) = a$$
$$50.4 = a$$
$$\$50.40 = a$$

Thus, 120% of $42 is $50.40. The answer is $50.40.

Example 9 $16\frac{2}{3}\%$ of what is 15?

Translate: $16\frac{2}{3}\% \cdot b = 15$

$$16\frac{2}{3}\left(\frac{1}{100}\right)b = 15$$

Solve:

$$\frac{\overset{1}{50}}{3}\left(\frac{1}{\underset{2}{100}}\right)b = 15$$

$$\frac{1}{6}b = 15$$

$$6 \cdot \frac{1}{6}b = 6 \cdot 15$$

$$b = 90$$

Thus, $16\frac{2}{3}\%$ of 90 is 15. The answer is 90.

Do Margin Exercises 7–12.

Solve.

7. What is 12% of 50?

8. 64% of $55 is what?

9. $33\frac{1}{3}\%$ of what is 7?

10. $60 is 120% of what?

11. 16 is what percent of 40?

12. What percent of $84 is $10.50?

Exercise Set 8.3

a Translate to an equation. Do not solve.

1. What is 32% of 78?

2. 98% of 57 is what?

3. 89 is what percent of 99?

4. What percent of 25 is 8?

5. 13 is 25% of what?

6. 21.4% of what is 20?

b Solve.

7. What is 85% of 276?

8. What is 74% of 53?

9. 150% of 30 is what?

10. 100% of 13 is what?

11. What is 6% of $300?

12. What is 4% of $45?

13. 3.8% of 50 is what?

14. $33\frac{1}{3}$% of 480 is what? (Hint: $33\frac{1}{3}\% = \frac{1}{3}$.)

15. $39 is what percent of $50?

16. $16 is what percent of $90?

17. 20 is what percent of 10?

18. 60 is what percent of 20?

19. What percent of $300 is $150?

20. What percent of $50 is $40?

21. What percent of 80 is 100?

22. What percent of 60 is 15?

23. 20 is 50% of what?

24. 57 is 20% of what?

25. 40% of what is $16?

26. 100% of what is $74?

27. 56.32 is 64% of what?

28. 71.04 is 96% of what?

29. 70% of what is 14?

30. 70% of what is 35?

31. What is $62\frac{1}{2}$% of 10?

32. What is $35\frac{1}{4}$% of 1200?

33. What is 8.3% of $10,200?

34. What is 9.2% of $5600?

Skill Maintenance

Write fractional notation.

35. 0.09

36. 1.79

37. 0.875

38. 0.9375

Write decimal notation.

39. $\frac{89}{100}$

40. $\frac{7}{100}$

41. $\frac{3}{10}$

42. $\frac{17}{1000}$

Synthesis

43. ❖ Write a question that could be translated to the equation
$$25 = 4\%b.$$

44. ❖ To calculate a 15% tip on a $24 bill, a customer adds $2.40 and half of $2.40, or $1.20, to get $3.60. Is this procedure valid? Why or why not?

Solve.

45. ▦ What is 7.75% of $10,880?
Estimate _____
Calculate _____

46. ▦ 50,951.775 is what percent of 78,995?
Estimate _____
Calculate _____

47. *Recyclables.* It is estimated that 40% to 50% of all trash is recyclable. If a community produces 270 tons of trash, how much of their trash is recyclable?

48. 40% of $18\frac{3}{4}$% of $25,000 is what?

8.4 Solving Percent Problems Using Proportions

a Translating to Proportions

A percent is a ratio of some number to 100. For example, 75% is the ratio $\frac{75}{100}$. The numbers 3 and 4 have the same ratio as 75 and 100. Thus,

$$75\% = \frac{75}{100} = \frac{3}{4}$$

To solve a percent problem using a proportion, we translate as follows:

$$\text{Percent Number} \longrightarrow \frac{P}{100} \longleftarrow 100 \qquad = \qquad \frac{a}{b} \begin{array}{l} \longleftarrow \text{Amount} \\ \longleftarrow \text{Base} \end{array}$$

> You might find it helpful to read this as "part is to whole as part is to whole."

For example,
60% of 25 is 15

translates to

$$\frac{60}{100} = \frac{15}{25} \qquad \begin{array}{l} \longleftarrow \text{Amount} \\ \longleftarrow \text{Base} \end{array}$$

When a percent problem is written in the general form:

percent of base is amount

it can be separated into the following parts:

| $P\%$ | | of B | | is A |

and will translate into the following proportion:

$$\frac{P}{100} = \frac{A}{B}.$$

You may already be familiar with this as

$$\frac{P}{100} = \frac{IS}{OF}$$

A clue in translating is that the base, b, corresponds to 100 and usually follows the wording "percent of." Also, $P\%$ always translates to $\frac{P}{100}$. Whatever follows the verb "*is*," is the amount.

Another aid in translating is to make a comparison drawing. To do this, we start with the percent side and list 0% at the top and 100% near the bottom. Then we estimate where the specified percent—in this case, 60%—is located. The corresponding quantities are then filled in. The base—in this case, 25—always corresponds to 100% and the amount—in this case, 15—corresponds to the specified percent.

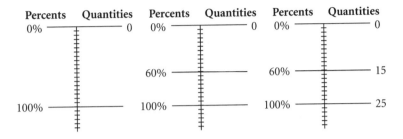

The proportion can then be read easily from the drawing.

Example 1 Translate to a proportion.

$$23\% \text{ of } 5 \text{ is } \underline{what}?$$

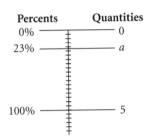

number of   base   amount
hundredths

$$\frac{23}{100} = \frac{a}{5}$$

Example 2 Translate to a proportion.

$$\underline{What} \text{ is } 124\% \text{ of } 49?$$

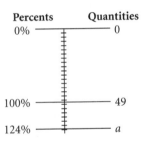

amount   number of   base
          hundredths

$$\frac{124}{100} = \frac{a}{49}$$

Do Margin Exercises 1–3.

Example 3 Translate to a proportion.

$$3 \text{ is } 10\% \text{ of } \underline{what}?$$

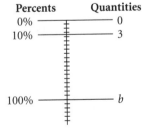

amount   number of   base
          hundredths

$$\frac{10}{100} = \frac{3}{b}$$

Translate to a proportion. Do not solve.

1. 12% of 50 is what?

2. What is 40% of 60?

3. 130% of 72 is what?

Translate to a proportion.
Do not solve.

4. 45 is 20% of what?

5. 120% of what is 60?

Translate to a proportion.
Do not solve.

6. 16 is what percent of 40?

7. What percent of 84 is 10.5?

8. Solve:

20% of what is $45?

Example 4   Translate to a proportion.

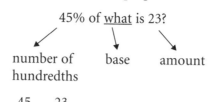

$$\frac{45}{100} = \frac{23}{b}$$

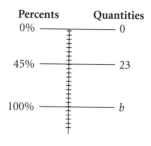

Do Margin Exercises 4 and 5.

Example 5   Translate to a proportion.

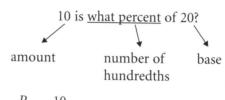

$$\frac{P}{100} = \frac{10}{20}$$

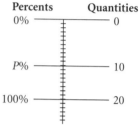

Example 6   Translate to a proportion.

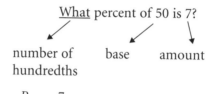

$$\frac{P}{100} = \frac{7}{50}$$

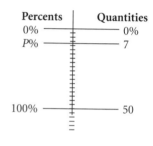

Do Margin Exercises 6 and 7.

b Solving Percent Problems

After a percent problem has been translated to a proportion, we solve as in Section 7.3.

Example 7   5% of what is $20?

number of   base   amount
hundredths

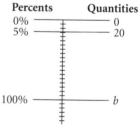

Translate: $\dfrac{5}{100} = \dfrac{20}{b}$

Solve: $5 \cdot b = 100 \cdot 20$ Setting cross products equal

$$\frac{5 \cdot b}{5} = \frac{100 \cdot \overset{4}{\cancel{20}}}{5}$$ Dividing by 5

$b = 400$ Simplifying

Thus, 5% of $400 is $20. The answer is $400.

Do Margin Exercise 8.

Example 8   120% of 42 is <u>what</u>?

number of hundredths   base   amount

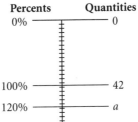

Translate: $\dfrac{120}{100} = \dfrac{a}{42}$

Solve: $120 \cdot 42 = 100 \cdot a$ Setting cross products equal

$\dfrac{120 \cdot 42}{100} = \dfrac{100 \cdot a}{100}$ Dividing by 100

$\dfrac{5040}{100} = a$

$50.4 = a$ Simplifying

Thus, 120% of 42 is 50.4. The answer is 50.4.

Do Margin Exercises 9 and 10.

Example 9   3 is 16% of <u>what</u>?

amount   number of hundredths   base

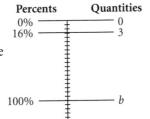

Translate: $\dfrac{3}{b} = \dfrac{16}{100}$

Solve: $3 \cdot 100 = b \cdot 16$ Setting cross products equal

$\dfrac{3 \cdot 100}{16} = \dfrac{b \cdot 16}{16}$ Dividing by 16

$\dfrac{3 \cdot 100}{16} = b$

$18.75 = b$ Multiplying and dividing

Thus, 3 is 16% of 18.75. The answer is 18.75.

Do Margin Exercise 11.

Solve.

9. 64% of 55 is what?

10. What is 12% of 50?

11. Solve:

60 is 120% of what?

12. Solve:

$12 is what percent of $40?

13. Solve:

What percent of 84 is 10.5?

Example 10 $10 is <u>what percent</u> of $20?

amount   number of   base
hundredths

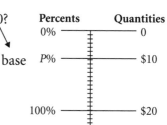

Translate: $\dfrac{10}{20} = \dfrac{P}{100}$

Solve: $10 \cdot 100 = 20 \cdot P$ Setting cross products equal

$\dfrac{10 \cdot 100}{20} = \dfrac{20 \cdot P}{20}$ Dividing by 20

$\dfrac{1000}{20} = P$

$50 = P$

Thus, $10 is 50% of $20. The answer is 50%.

Do Margin Exercise 12.

Example 11 <u>What percent</u> of 50 is 16?

number of   base   amount
hundredths

Translate: $\dfrac{P}{100} = \dfrac{16}{50}$

Solve: $50 \cdot P = 100 \cdot 16$ Setting cross products equal

$\dfrac{50 \cdot P}{50} = \dfrac{100 \cdot 16}{50}$ Dividing by 50

$P = \dfrac{1600}{50}$

$P = 32$

Thus, 32% of 50 is 16. The answer is 32%.

Do Margin Exercise 13.

Exercise Set 8.4

a Translate to a proportion. Do not solve.

1. What is 37% of 74?

2. 66% of 74 is what?

3. 4.3 is what percent of 5.9?

4. What percent of 6.8 is 5.3?

5. 14 is 25% of what?

6. 133% of what is 40?

b Solve.

7. What is 76% of 90?

8. What is 32% of 70?

9. 70% of 660 is what?

10. 80% of 920 is what?

11. What is 4% of 1000?

12. What is 6% of 2000?

13. 4.8% of 60 is what?

14. 63.1% of 80 is what?

15. $24 is what percent of $96?

16. $14 is what percent of $70?

17. 102 is what percent of 100?

18. 103 is what percent of 100?

19. What percent of $480 is $120?

20. What percent of $80 is $60?

21. What percent of 160 is 150?

22. What percent of 33 is 11?

23. $18 is 25% of what?

24. $75 is 20% of what?

25. 60% of what is 54?

26. 80% of what is 96?

27. 65.12 is 74% of what?

28. 63.7 is 65% of what?

29. 80% of what is 16?

30. 80% of what is 10?

31. What is $62\frac{1}{2}$% of 40?

32. What is $43\frac{1}{4}$% of 2600?

33. What is 9.4% of $8300?

34. What is 8.7% of $76,000?

Skill Maintenance

Solve.

35. $\dfrac{x}{188} = \dfrac{2}{47}$

36. $\dfrac{15}{x} = \dfrac{3}{800}$

37. $\dfrac{4}{7} = \dfrac{x}{14}$

38. $\dfrac{612}{t} = \dfrac{72}{244}$

39. $\dfrac{5000}{t} = \dfrac{3000}{60}$

40. $\dfrac{75}{100} = \dfrac{n}{20}$

41. $\dfrac{x}{1.2} = \dfrac{36.2}{5.4}$

42. $\dfrac{y}{1\frac{1}{2}} = \dfrac{2\frac{3}{4}}{22}$

Solve.

43. A recipe for muffins calls for $\frac{1}{2}$ qt of buttermilk, $\frac{1}{3}$ qt of skim milk, and $\frac{1}{16}$ qt of oil. How many quarts of liquid ingredients does the recipe call for?

44. The Ferristown School District purchased $\frac{3}{4}$ ton (T) of clay. If the clay is to be shared equally among the district's 6 art departments, how much will each art department receive?

Synthesis

45. ❖ In your own words, list steps that a classmate could use to solve any percent problem in this section.

46. ❖ In solving Example 10, a student simplifies $\frac{10}{20}$ before solving. Is this a good idea? Why or why not?

Solve.

47. ▦ What is 8.85% of $12,640?
Estimate _____
Calculate _____

48. ▦ 78.8% of what is 9809.024?
Estimate _____
Calculate _____

8.5 Applications of Percent

a | Applied Problems Involving Percent

Applied problems involving percent occur in a variety of everyday situations. These may be solved using either the percent equation or the percent proportion. Use whichever method you prefer.

The following two examples demonstrate that either method can be used.

When applying percent to real situations it is important to remember that the actual data of the situation is being compared to a control group of 100. For instance: if in a group of 900 people there are 225 people wearing red hats, then in a control group of 100 people 25 of them would be wearing red hats. Both ratios $\frac{225}{900}$ and $\frac{25}{100}$ compare the number of people wearing red hats to the total of number of people in the group. The numerators of the two ratios both represent the number of people wearing red hats. One numerator is the number of red hats in the real situation and the other numerator is the number of red hats in the control group. Both ratios simplify to $\frac{1}{4}$. So 25% of the actual group of 900 people are wearing red hats.

Example 1 *Paper Recycling.* In a recent year, the United States generated 73.3 million tons of paper waste, of which 20.5 million tons were recycled. What percent of paper waste was recycled?

1. *Familiarize.* The question asks for a percent. We let n = the percent of paper waste that was recycled.

   Estimate. We know that 10% of 73.3 is 7.33. Since 10% ≈ 7 tons of waste, then 30% ≈ 21 tons of waste. This is close to 20.5 so we should expect an answer close to 30%.

2. *Translate.* We can rephrase the question and translate to either an equation or proportion as follows:

   20.5 million is what percent of 73.3 million

Equation	*Proportion*
$20,500,000 = n\% \cdot 73,300,000$	$\dfrac{\text{amount (is)}}{\text{base(of)}} = \dfrac{\text{percent}}{100}$
	$\dfrac{20,500,000}{73,300,000} = \dfrac{P}{100}$

3. *Solve the Equation*   *Solve the Proportion*

$20,500,000 = n(0.01) \cdot 73,300,000$

$20,500,000 = n(0.01 \cdot 73,300,000)$ $(20,500,000)(100) = P(73,300,000)$

$20,500,000 = n(730,000)$ $\dfrac{(20,500,000)(100)}{73,300,000} = P$

$\dfrac{20,500,000}{730,000} = \dfrac{n(730,000)}{730,000}$

$28 = n$ $28 = P$

1. *Desserts.* If a restaurant sells 250 desserts in an evening, it is typical that 40 of them will be pie. What percent of the desserts sold will be pie?

2. *Desserts.* Of all desserts sold in restaurants, 20% of them are chocolate cake. One evening a restaurant sells 250 desserts. How many were chocolate cake?

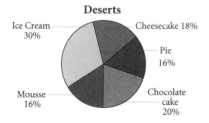

Deserts

Ice Cream 30%
Cheesecake 18%
Pie 16%
Mousse 16%
Chocolate cake 20%

4. *Check.* The initial estimate was 30%, which is close to the answer, 28%.

5. *State.* About 28% of the paper waste was recycled.

Do Margin Exercise 1.

Example 2 *Junk Mail.* The U.S. Postal Service estimates that we read 78% of the junk mail we receive. Suppose that a business sends out 9500 advertising brochures. How many brochures can the business expect to be opened and read?

1. *Familiarize.* We can draw a pie chart to help familiarize ourselves with the problem. We let a = the number of brochures that are opened and read.

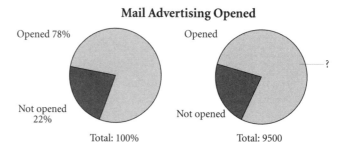

Mail Advertising Opened

Opened 78%

Not opened 22%

Total: 100%

Opened

Not opened

?

Total: 9500

Estimate. Since 78% ≈ 80% and 9500 ≈ 10,000, an estimation would be 80% of the 10,000 brochures will be read. Performing this calculation, we expect that about 8000 brochures will be read.

2. *Translate.* We can rephrase the question and translate to either an equation or proportion as follows. What number is 78% of 9500?

Equation	*Proportion*
$a = 78\% \cdot 9500$	$\dfrac{\text{amount (is)}}{\text{base (of)}} = \dfrac{\text{percent}}{100}$
	$\dfrac{a}{9500} = \dfrac{78}{100}$

3. *Solve the Equation.*

$a = 78(0.01) \cdot 9500$

$a = 0.78 \cdot 9500$

$a = 7410$

Solve the Proportion

$a(100) = (78)(9500)$

$\dfrac{a(100)}{100} = \dfrac{(78)(9500)}{100}$

$a = 7410$

4. *Check.* Since the estimate was 8000, the answer 7410 is reasonable.

5. *State.* The business can expect 7410 of its brochures to be opened and read.

Do Margin Exercise 2.

▶ ▦ **Calculator Spotlight**

[%] *Key* Many calculators have a percent key This key can be useful in calculations like 78% × 9500, as in Example 2, but you may need to change the order to 9500 × 78%. To do the calculation, press

[9] [5] [0] [0] [×] [7] [8] [SHFT] [%]

The displayed result is 7410.

Check your manual for other procedures for determining percents.

Exercises

Calculate.

1. 250 × 20%   **2.** 37% × 18,924

3. 67.2% × 124,898   **4.** 56,788.22 × 64.2%

Answers

1. 50
2. 7001.88
3. 83,931.456
4. 36,458.03724

Use the circle graph in Example 3 to answer each of the following.

3. Which item costs the least?

4. What percent of the total cost is spent on toys?

5. How much of the $6600 lifetime cost of owning a dog is for grooming?

6. What part of the expense is for supplies and for buying the dog?

b **Circle Graphs**

Reading and Interpreting

Example 3 *Costs of Owning a Dog.* The following circle graph shows the relative costs of raising a dog from birth to death.

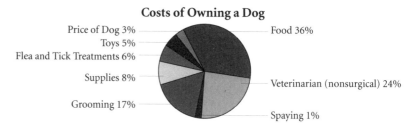

Costs of Owning a Dog

Price of Dog 3%
Toys 5%
Flea and Tick Treatments 6%
Supplies 8%
Grooming 17%
Food 36%
Veterinarian (nonsurgical) 24%
Spaying 1%

Source: The American Pet Products Manufacturers Association

a. Which item costs the most?

b. What percent of the total cost is spent on grooming?

c. Which item involves 24% of the cost?

d. The American Pet Products Manufacturers Association estimates that the total cost of owning a dog for its lifetime is $6600. How much of that amount is spent for food?

e. What percent of the expense is for grooming and flea and tick treatments?

We look at the sections of the graph to find the answers.

a. The largest section (or sector) of the graph, 36%, is for food.

b. We see that grooming is 17% of the cost.

c. Nonsurgical veterinarian bills account for 24% of the cost.

d. The section of the graph representing food costs is 36%; 36% of $6600 is $2376.

e. In a circle graph, we can add percents for questions like this. Therefore,

17% (grooming) + 6% (flea and tick treatments) = 23%.

Do Margin Exercises 3–6.

Drawing Circle Graphs

To draw a circle graph, or pie chart, like the one in Example 3, think of a pie cut into 100 equally sized pieces. We would then shade in a wedge equal in size to 36 of these pieces to represent 36% for food. We shade a wedge equal in size to 5 of these pieces to represent 5% for toys, and so on.

Example 4 *Fruit Juice Sales.* The percents of various kinds of fruit juice sold are given in the list at right (Source: Beverage Marketing Corporation).Use this information to draw a circle graph.

Apple:	14%
Orange:	56%
Blends:	6%
Grape:	5%
Grapefruit:	4%
Prune:	1%
Other:	14%

Using a circle marked with 100 equally spaced ticks, we start with the 14% given for apple juice. We draw a line from the center to any one tick. Then we count off 14 ticks and draw another line. We shade the wedge and label the wedge as shown in the figure on the left below.

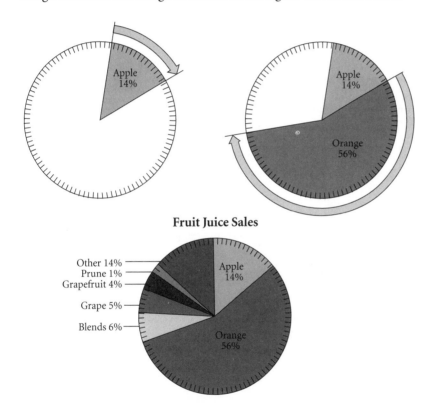

Fruit Juice Sales

To shade a wedge for orange juice, at 56%, we count off 56 ticks and draw another line. We shade the wedge with a different shading and label the wedge as shown in the figure on the right above. Continuing in this manner, we obtain the graph shown above. Finally, we give the graph the overall title "Fruit Juice Sales."

Do Margin Exercise 7.

7. *Lengths of Engagement of Married Couples.* The data below relate the percent of married couples who were engaged for a certain time period before marriage (*Source:* Bruskin Goldring Research). Use this information to draw a circle graph.

Less than 1 yr:	24%
1–2 yr:	21%
More than 2 yr:	35%
Never engaged:	20%

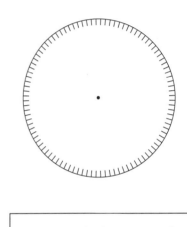

These circles have 100 tick marks so that they can easily represent percent. However, circles are sometimes divided into 360 tick marks to represent degrees.

c Percent of Increase or Decrease

Percent is often used to state increases or decreases. For example, the average salary of an NBA basketball player increased from $1.558 million in 1994 to $1.867 million in 1995. To find the *percent of increase* in salary, we first subtract to find out how much more the salary was in 1995:

New salary	less	Original salary	is	Amount of increase
$1.867 million	–	$1.558 million	=	$0.309 million

Let's first look at this with a drawing.

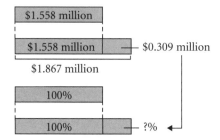

Then we determine what percent of the original amount the increase was. Since $0.309 million = $309,000, we are asking

$309,000 is what percent of $1,558,000?

This translates to the following:

$$309,000 = x(0.01)(1,558,000)?$$

This is an equation of the type studied in Sections 8.3 and 8.4. Solving the equation, we can confirm that $0.309 million, or $309,000, is about 19.8% of $1.558 million. Thus the percent of increase in salary was 19.8%.

▶ To find a percent of increase or decrease:

  a. Find the amount of increase or decrease.

  b. Then determine what percent this is of the **original amount**.

  $P\% \cdot$ original amount = increase or decrease

  OR

  $$\frac{\text{increase or decrease}}{\text{original amount}} = \frac{P}{100}$$

Example 5 *Digital-Camera Screen Size.* The diagonal of the display screen of a digital camera was recently increased from 1.8 in. to 2.5 in. What was the percent of increase in the diagonal?

1. *Familiarize.* We note that the increase in the diagonal was 2.5 − 1.8, or 0.7 in. A drawing can help us to visualize the situation. We let n = the percent of increase.

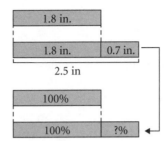

Estimate: Estimate by calculating various percents of 1.8. First, 50% of 1.8 is 0.9. This is bigger than 0.7 so decrease the calculation to 40% of 1.8. This gives 0.72, which is very close to 0.7, but still a little too big. We can estimate the answer would be slightly smaller than 40%.

2. *Translate*: We rephrase the question and then translate to solve:

$$0.7 \quad \text{is} \quad \text{what percent} \quad \text{of} \quad 1.8 \text{ inches?}$$

Equation:

$$0.7 = p(0.01) \cdot 1.8$$

Proportion:

$$\frac{p}{100} = \frac{0.7}{1.8}$$

3. *Solve*:

$$0.7 = 0.018p$$

$$\frac{0.7}{0.018} = \frac{0.018p}{0.018}$$

$$38.9 \approx p$$

Solve:

$$1.8 \cdot p = 100(0.7)$$

$$\frac{1.8p}{1.8} = \frac{70}{1.8}$$

$$p \approx 38.9$$

4. *Check*: Since our answer, 38.9%, agrees with our estimate, this is a reasonable answer.

5. *State*: The percent of increase of the screen diagonal is 38.9%

Do Margin Exercise 8.

What do we mean when we say that the price of Swiss cheese has decreased 8%? If the price was $5.00 per pound and it went down to $4.60 per pound, then the decrease is $0.40, which is 8% of the original price. We can see this in the following figure.

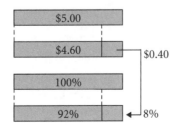

8. *Automobile Price.* The price of an automobile increased from $15,800 to $17,222. What was the percent of increase?

9. *Fuel Bill.* By using only cold water in the washing machine, a household with a monthly fuel bill of $78.00 can reduce their bill to $74.88. What is the percent of decrease?

Example 6 *Fuel Bill.* With proper furnace maintenance, a family that pays a monthly fuel bill of $78.00 can reduce their bill to $70.20. What is the percent of decrease?

1. *Familiarize.* We find the amount of decrease and then make a drawing.

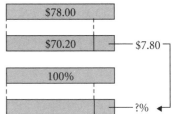

$$
\begin{array}{ll}
7\,8.0\,0 & \text{Original bill} \\
-7\,0.2\,0 & \text{New bill} \\
\hline
7.8\,0 & \text{Decrease}
\end{array}
$$

We let n = the percent of decrease.

Estimate. The question is $7.80 is what percent of $78? Since $7.80 ≈ $8 and $78 ≈ $80, we can get an estimate by using these numbers which are easier to work with. Since 8 is 10% of 80, then 10% is our estimate.

2. *Translate.*

Equation:

7.8	is	what	percent	of	78?
↓	↓	↓	↓	↓	↓
7.8	=	n	(0.01)	·	78

Proportion:

$$\frac{n}{100} = \frac{7.8}{78}$$

3. *Solve.*

Equation:

$$7.8 = 0.78n$$

$$\frac{7.8}{0.78} = \frac{0.78n}{0.78}$$

$$10 = n$$

Proportion:

$$78n = 100(7.8)$$

$$\frac{78n}{78} = \frac{780}{78}$$

$$n = 10$$

4. *Check.* Our answer matches our estimate so it is very reasonable.

5. *State.* The percent of decrease of the fuel bill is 10%.

Do Margin Exercise 9.

Example 7 A part-time teacher's aide earns $9700 one year and receives a 6% raise the next. What is the new salary?

1. *Familiarize.* We make a drawing.

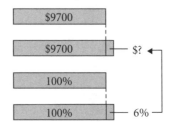

Estimate. This is a two-step problem. First we find the increase and then we will add it to the original salary. We let a = the salary raise. The increase will be 6% of $9700. Since $9700 is close to $10,000, we can estimate the increase to be $600 (6% of $10,000 = $600). Adding $600 to $9700, we get $10,300 as an estimate.

2. *Translate.* We rephrase the question and translate as follows.

Equation:

What is 6% of 9700

$\downarrow$ $\downarrow$ $\downarrow$ $\downarrow$ $\downarrow$

a = 6(0.01) · 9700

Proportion:

$$\frac{6}{100} = \frac{a}{9700}$$

3. *Solve.*

Equation:

$a = .06(9700)$

$a = 582$

Proportion:

$100a = 58{,}200$

$$\frac{100a}{100} = \frac{58{,}200}{100}$$

$a = 582$

Next, we add $582 to the old salary:

$9700 + $582 = $10{,}282.

4. *Check.* $10,282 is close to our estimate of $10,300 so it is reasonable.

5. *State.* The new salary is $10,282.

Do Margin Exercise 10.

▶ ## Calculator Spotlight

The ⬚%⬚ Key and Percent of Increase or Decrease. On a calculator with a percent key, there may be a fast way to find the result of adding or subtracting a percent from a number. In Example 7, the result of taking 6% of $9700 and adding it to $9700 might be found by pressing

9 7 0 0 × 6 SHFT % +

The displayed result would be

10,282 .

If the salary had been reduced by 6%, the computation would be

9 7 0 0 × 6 SHFT % −

The displayed result would be

9118 .

Check your manual for other procedures for determining percents.

Exercises

Use a calculator with a ⬚%⬚ key.

1. Find the result of Margin Exercise 10.

2. Find the result of Margin Exercise 10 if the salary were decreased by 9%.

---

10. A part-time salesperson earns $9800 one year and gets a 9% raise the next. What is the new salary?

Exercise Set 8.5

[a] Solve.

1. *Left-handed Professional Bowlers.* It has been determined by sociologists that 17% of the population is left-handed. Each tournament conducted by the Professional Bowlers Association has 120 entrants. How many would you expect to be left-handed? not left-handed? Round to the nearest one.

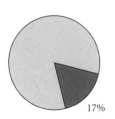

17%

Total: 120

2. *Advertising Budget.* A common guideline for businesses is to use 5% of their operating budget for advertising. Ariel Electronics has an operating budget of $8000 per week. How much should it spend each week for advertising? for other expenses?

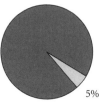

5%

Total: $8000

3. Of all moviegoers, 67% are in the 12-29 age group. A theater held 800 people for a showing of *Star Trek-18*. How many were in the 12-29 age group? not in this age group?

4. Deming, New Mexico, claims to have the purest drinking water in the world. It is 99.9% pure. If you had 240 L of water from Deming, how much of it, in liters, would be pure? impure?

5. A baseball player gets 13 hits in 40 at-bats. What percent are hits? not hits?

6. On a test of 80 items, Erika had 76 correct. What percent were correct? incorrect?

7. A lab technician has 680 mL of a solution of water and acid; 3% is acid. How many milliliters are acid? water?

8. A lab technician has 540 mL of a solution of alcohol and water; 8% is alcohol. How many milliliters are alcohol? water?

9. *TV Usage.* Of the 8760 hr in a year, most television sets are on for 2190 hr. What percent is this?

10. *Colds from Kissing.* In a medical study, it was determined that if 800 people kiss someone who has a cold, only 56 will actually catch a cold. What percent is this?

11. *Maximum Heart Rate.* Treadmill tests are often administered to diagnose heart ailments. A guideline in such a test is to try to get you to reach your maximum heart rate, in beats per minute. The maximum heart rate is found by subtracting your age from 220 and then multiplying by 85%. What is the maximum heart rate of someone whose age is 25? 36? 48? 55? 76? Round to the nearest one.

12. It costs an oil company $40,000 a day to operate two refineries. Refinery A accounts for 37.5% of the cost, and refinery B for the rest of the cost.
  a. What percent of the cost does it take to run refinery B?
  b. What is the cost of operating refinery A? refinery B?

Musical Recordings. This circle graph, in the shape of a CD, shows music preferences of customers on the basis of music store sales. Use the graph for Exercises 13–18.

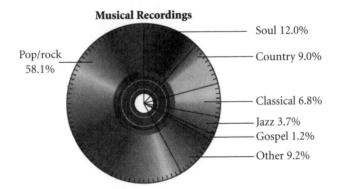

Musical Recordings

Soul 12.0%
Country 9.0%
Pop/rock 58.1%
Classical 6.8%
Jazz 3.7%
Gospel 1.2%
Other 9.2%

13. What percent of all recordings sold are jazz?

14. Together, what percent of all recordings sold are either soul or pop/rock?

15. Lou's Music Store sells 3000 recordings a month. How many are country?

16. Al's Music Store sells 2500 recordings a month. How many are gospel?

17. What percent of all recordings sold are classical?

18. Together, what percent of all recordings sold are either classical or jazz?

Family Expenses. This circle graph shows expenses as a percent of income in a family of four. (Note: Due to rounding, the sum of the percents is 101% instead of 100%.) Use the graph for Exercises 19–22.

Family Expenses

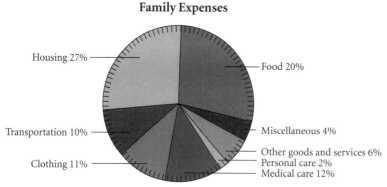

Source: Bureau of Labor Statistics

19. Which item accounts for the greatest expense?

20. In a family with a $2000 monthly income, how much is spent for transportation?

21. Some surveys combine medical care with personal care. What percent would be spent on those two items combined?

22. In a family with a $2000 monthly income, what is the ratio of the amount spent on medical care to the amount spent on personal care?

Use the given information to complete a circle graph. Note that each circle is divided into 100 sections. (Circle graphs for Exercises 27 and 28 should be drawn on a separate sheet of paper.)

23. *Where Homebuyers Prefer to Live.*

City:	4%
Rural:	30%
Outlying suburbs:	34%
Nearby suburbs:	30%
Other:	2%

24. *How Vacation Money is Spent.*

Transportation:	15%
Meals:	20%
Lodging:	32%
Recreation:	18%
Other:	15%

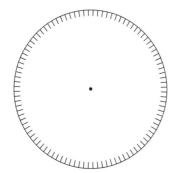

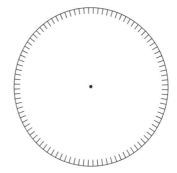

25. *Pilots' Ages.*

20-29:	6%
30-39:	32%
40-49:	36%
50-59:	26%

Source: Federal Aviation Administration

26. *Sources of Water.*

Drinking water:	29%
Tea and coffee:	24%
Vegetables:	9%
Milk/dairy products:	9%
Soft drinks:	8%
Other:	21%

Source: U.S. Department of Agriculture

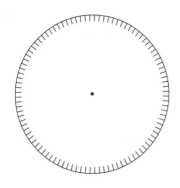

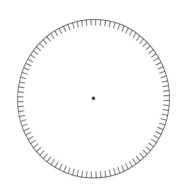

27. *Holiday Gift Giving by Men.*

More than 30 gifts:	14%
21-30 gifts:	13%
11-20 gifts:	32%
6-10 gifts:	24%
1-5 gifts:	13%
0 gifts:	4%

Source: Maritz AmeriPoll

28. *Reasons for Drinking Coffee.*

To get going in the morning:	32%
Like the taste:	33%
Not sure:	2%
To relax:	4%
As a pick-me-up:	10%
A habit:	19%

Source: LMK Associates survey for Au Bon Pain Co., Inc.

c Solve.

29. The amount in a savings account increased from $200 to $216. What was the percent of increase?

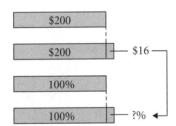

30. The population of a small mountain town increased from 840 to 882. What was the percent of increase?

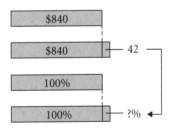

31. During a sale, a dress decreased in price from $90 to $72. What was the percent of decrease?

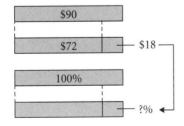

32. A person on a diet goes from a weight of 125 lb to a weight of 110 lb. What is the percent of decrease

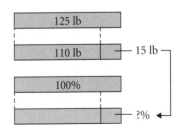

33. A person earns $28,600 one year and receives a 5% raise in salary. What is the new salary?

34. A person earns $20,400 one year and receives an 8% raise in salary. What is the new salary?

35. The value of a car typically decreases by 30% in the first year. A car is bought for $18,000. What is its value one year later?

36. One year the pilots of an airline shocked the business world by taking an 11% pay cut. The former salary was $55,000. What was the reduced salary?

37. *World Population.* World population is increasing by 1.6% each year. In 1999, it was 6.0 billion. How much will it be in 2000? 2001? 2002?

38. *Cooling Costs.* By increasing the thermostat from 72° to 78°, a family can reduce its cooling bill by 50%. If the cooling bill was $106.00, what would the new bill be? By what percent has the temperature been increased?

39. *Car Depreciation.* A car generally depreciates 30% of its original value in the first year. A car is worth $25,480 after the first year. What was its original cost? (*Hint:* The second year value of the car is 70% of the original value.)

40. *Car Depreciation.* Given normal use, an American-made car will depreciate 30% of its original cost the first year and 14% of its remaining value in the second year. What is the value of a car at the end of the second year if its original cost was $36,400? $28,400? $26,800?

41. *Tipping.* Diners frequently add a 15% tip when charging a meal to a credit card. What is the total amount charged if the cost of the meal, without tip, is $15? $34? $49?

42. *Two-by-Four.* A cross-section of a standard or nominal "two-by-four" board actually measures $1\frac{1}{2}$ in. by $3\frac{1}{2}$ in. The rough board is 2 in. by 4 in. but is planed and dried to the finished size. What percent of the cross-sectional area of the wood is removed in planing and drying?

43. *MADD.* Despite efforts by groups such as MADD (Mothers Against Drunk Driving), the number of alcohol-related deaths is rising after many years of decline. The data in the table shows the number of deaths from 1986 to 1995.

a. What is the percent of increase in the number of alcohol-related deaths from 1994 to 1995?

b. What is the percent of decrease in the number of alcohol-related deaths from 1986 to 1994?

Alcohol-Related Traffic Deaths	
Back on the Increase!!	
Year	**Deaths**
1986	24,045
1987	23,641
1988	23,626
1989	22,436
1990	22,084
1991	19,887
1992	17,859
1993	17,473
1994	16,589
1995	17,274

Source: National Highway Traffic Safety Administration

44. *Fetal Acoustic Stimulation.* Each year there are about 4 million births in the United States. Of these, about 120,000 births occur in breech position (delivery of a fetus with the buttocks or feet appearing first). A new technique, called fetal acoustic stimulation (FAS), uses sound directed through a mother's abdomen in order to stimulate movement of the fetus to a safer position. In a recent study of this low-risk and low-cost procedure, FAS enabled doctors to turn the baby in 34 of 38 cases (**Source:** Johnson and Elliott, "Fetal Acoustic Stimulation, an Adjunct to External Cephalic Versions: A Blinded, Randomized Crossover Study," *American Journal of Obstetrics & Gynecology* **173**, no. 5 (1995): 1369-1372).

a. What percent of U.S. births are breech?

b. What percent (rounded to the nearest tenth) of cases showed success with FAS?

c. About how many breech babies yearly might be turned if FAS could be implemented in all births in the United States?

d. Breech position is one reason for performing Caesarean section (or C-section) birth surgery. Researchers expect that FAS alone can eliminate the need for about 2000 C-sections yearly in the United States. Given this information, how many yearly C-sections are due to breech position alone?

45. *Strike Zone.* In baseball, the *strike zone* is normally a 17-in. by 40-in. rectangle. Some batters give the pitcher an advantage by swinging at pitches thrown out of the strike zone. By what percent is the area of the strike zone increased if a 2-in. border is added to the outside?

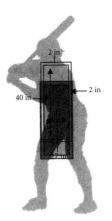

46. Tony is planting grass on a 24-ft by 36-ft area in his back yard. He installs a 6-ft by 8-ft garden. By what percent has he reduced the area he has to mow?

Skill Maintenance

Convert to decimal notation.

47. $\dfrac{25}{11}$ **48.** $\dfrac{11}{25}$ **49.** $\dfrac{27}{8}$ **50.** $\dfrac{43}{9}$ **51.** $\dfrac{23}{25}$

52. $\dfrac{20}{24}$ **53.** $\dfrac{14}{32}$ **54.** $\dfrac{2317}{1000}$ **55.** $\dfrac{34{,}809}{10{,}000}$ **56.** $\dfrac{27}{40}$

Synthesis

57. Which is better for a wage earner, and why: a 10% raise followed by a 5% raise a year later, or a 5% raise followed by a 10% raise a year later?

58. Write a problem for a classmate to solve. Design the problem so that the solution is "Jackie's raise was $7\frac{1}{2}$%."

59. A worker receives raises of 3%, 6%, and then 9%. By what percent has the original salary increased?

60. A workers' union is offered either a 5% ""across-the-board" raise in which all salaries would increase 5%, or a flat $1650 raise for each worker. If the total payroll for the 123 workers is $4,213,365, which offer should the union select? Why?

61. *Adult Height.* It has been determined that at the age of 10, a girl has reached 84.4% of her final adult growth. Cynthia is 4 ft, 8 in. at the age of 10. What will be her final adult height?

62. *Adult Height.* It has been determined that at the age of 15, a boy has reached 96.1% of his final adult height. Claude is 6 ft, 4 in. at the age of 15. What will be his final adult height?

63. If p is 120% of q, then q is what percent of p?

64. A coupon allows a couple to have dinner and then have $10 subtracted from the bill. Before subtracting $10, however, the restaurant adds a tip of 15%. If the couple is presented with a bill for $44.05, how much would the dinner (without tip) have cost without the coupon?

8.6 Consumer Applications: Sales Tax, Commission, and Discount

As in previous sections, the applied problems in this section can be solved by using either the percent equation or the percent proportion. When setting up a proportion for any of these applications, the numerators of each fraction are referring to the same thing using different notation.

Example: For the tax proportion, $\dfrac{\text{tax rate}}{100} = \dfrac{\text{amount of tax}}{\text{total sales}}$, the numerators both show *how much tax*. The percent side(left side) of the proportion always shows how much tax on $100 and the right side shows the amount of tax for a specific situation.

In general, the left side numerator is the rate (%), and the right side numerator is the numerical amount whether it be dollars, cents, number of people, etc.

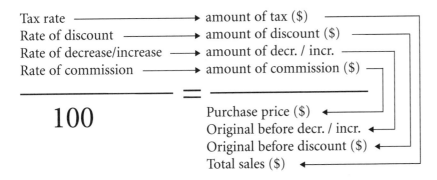

Likewise, a general percent equation would be written like this:

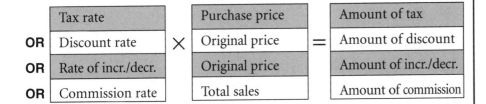

1. *Connecticut.* The sales tax rate in Connecticut is 8%. How much tax is charged on the purchase of a refrigerator that sells for $668.95? What is the total price?

2. *New Jersey.* Morris buys 5 blank audiocassettes in New Jersey, where the sales tax rate is 7%. If each tape costs $2.95, how much tax will be charged? What is the total price?

Sales tax refers to an amount of money.

Sales tax rate refers to a percent.

---

a | Sales Tax

Sales tax computations represent a special type of percent of increase problem. The sales tax rate in Arkansas is 3%. This means that the tax is 3% of the purchase price. Suppose the purchase price on a coat is $124.95. The sales tax is then

3% of $124.95, or 0.03(124.95),

or

3.7485, or $3.75.

The total that you pay is the price plus the sales tax:

$124.95 + $3.75, or $128.70.

Bill:	
Purchase price =	$124.95
Sales tax (3% of $124.95) =	+ 3.75
Final price	$128.70

▶ **Sales tax** = Sales tax rate × Purchase price

OR $\dfrac{\text{Sales tax rate}}{100} = \dfrac{\text{Sales tax}}{\text{Purchase price}}$

Total price = Purchase price + Sales tax

Example 1 *Florida.* The sales tax rate in Florida is 6%. How much tax is charged on the purchase of 3 CDs at $13.95 each? What is the total price?

a. We first find the cost of the CDs. It is

3($13.95) = $41.85.

b. The sales tax on items costing $41.85 is

$$
\begin{aligned}
\text{Sales tax} &= \text{Sales tax rate} \times \text{Purchase price} \\
t &= (6\%) \cdot (\$41.85) \\
t &= 0.06(\$41.85) \\
t &= \$2.511
\end{aligned}
$$

Thus the tax is $2.51 (rounding to the nearest cent).

c. The total price is given by the purchase price plus the sales tax:
total price = purchase price + sales tax.
$$
\begin{aligned}
p &= \$41.85 + \$2.51 \\
p &= \$44.36.
\end{aligned}
$$

Do Margin Exercises 1 and 2.

Example 2 The sales tax is $32 on the purchase of an $800 sofa. What is the sales tax rate?

Rephrase: Sales tax is what percent of purchase price?

Translate: 32   = r%   ×   800

Solve: $$32 = r(0.01)(800)$$
$$32 = 8r$$
$$\frac{32}{8} = \frac{8r}{8}$$
$$4 = r$$

The sales tax rate is 4%.

Do Margin Exercise 3.

Example 3 The sales tax on a laser printer is $31.74 and the sales tax rate is 5%. Find the purchase price (the price before taxes are added).

Rephrase: Sales tax is 5% of what?

Translate: 31.74   =   5% × b

Solve: $$31.74 = 0.05b$$
$$\frac{31.74}{0.05} = \frac{0.05b}{0.05}$$
$$634.8 = b.$$

The purchase price is $634.80.

Do Margin Exercise 4.

3. The sales tax is $33 on the purchase of a $550 washing machine. What is the sales tax rate?

4. The sales tax on a television is $25.20 and the sales tax rate is 6%. Find the purchase price (the price before taxes are added).

5. Raul's commission rate is 30%. What is the commission from the sale of $18,760 worth of air conditioners?

b Commission

When you work for a **salary**, you receive the same amount of money each week or month. When you work for a **commission**, you are paid a percentage of the total sales for which you are responsible.

> **Commission** = Commission rate × Sales
>
> or $\dfrac{\text{Commission rate}}{100} = \dfrac{\text{commission}}{\text{sales}}$

Example 4 A salesperson's commission rate is 20%. What is the commission from the sale of $25,560 worth of stereophonic equipment?

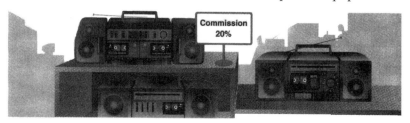

Rephrase:	Commission	=	Commission rate	×	Sales
Translate:	C	=	20%	×	$25,560
Solve:	C	=	0.20($25,560)		
	C	=	$5112		

The commission is $5112.

Do Margin Exercise 5.

Commission refers to an amount of money.

Commission rate refers to a percent.

6. Liz earns a commission of $6000 selling $24,000 worth of refrigerators. What is the commission rate?

Example 5 Dawn earns a commission of $3000 selling $60,000 worth of farm machinery. What is the commission rate?

Rephrase:	Commission	=	Commission rate	×	Sales
Translate:	3,000	=	r%	×	$60,000
Solve:	3,000	=	r%(60,000)		
	3,000	=	r(0.01)(60,000)		
	3,000	=	600r		
	$\dfrac{3,000}{600}$	=	$\dfrac{600r}{600}$		
	5	=	r		

The commission rate is 5%.

Do Margin Exercise 6.

Example 6 Joyce's commission rate is 25%. She receives a commission of $425 on the sale of a motorbike. How much did the motorbike cost?

Rephrase: Commission = Commission rate × Sales

Translate: 425 = 25% × S

Solve:

$$425 = 0.25S$$

$$\frac{425}{0.25} = \frac{0.25S}{0.25}$$

$$1700 = S$$

The motorbike costs $1700.

Do Margin Exercise 7.

c | Discount

Suppose that the regular price of a rug is $60, and the rug is on sale at 25% off. Since 25% of $60 is $15, the sale price is $60 − $15, or $45. We call $60 the **original**, or **marked price**, 25% the **rate of discount**, $15 the **discount**, and $45 the **sale price**. Note that discount problems are a type of percent of decrease problem.

> **Discount** = Rate of discount × Original price
>
> or $\dfrac{\text{rate of discount}}{100} = \dfrac{\text{Discount}}{\text{Original Price}}$
>
> **Sale price** = Original price − Discount

7. Ben's commission rate is 16%. He receives a commission of $268 from sales of clothing. How many dollars worth of clothing were sold?

> **Discount** refers to an amount of money.
>
> **Discount rate** refers to a percent.

8. A suit marked $140 is on sale at 24% off. What is the discount? the sale price?

9. A pair of hiking boots is reduced from $75 to $60. Find the rate of discount.

Example 7 A rug marked $240 is on sale at 25% off. What is the discount? the sale price?

a. *Rephrase:* *Discount* = *Rate of discount* × *Original price*

Translate: D = 25% × 240

Solve: D = 25(0.01)(240)
D = 0.25(240)
D = 60

The discount is $60.

b.   *Saleprice* = *Marked price* − *Discount*

S = 240 − 60
S = 180

The sale price is $180.

Do Margin Exercise 8

Example 8 An antique table is marked down from $620 to $527. What is the rate of discount?

We first find the discount by subtracting the sale price from the original price:

Discount = 620 − 527
D = 93

The discount is $93.

Next, we use the equation for discount:

Discount = *Rate of discount* × *Original price*
93 = r% × 620.

93 = r(0.01)(620)
93 = 6.2r
$\dfrac{93}{6.2}$ = $\dfrac{6.2r}{6.2}$

15 = r

The discount rate is 15%.

Do Margin Exercise 9.

Exercise Set 8.6

a Solve.

1. *Indiana.* The sales tax rate in Indiana is 5%. How much tax is charged on a generator costing $586? What is the total price?

2. *New York City.* The sales tax rate in New York City is 8.25%. How much tax is charged on photo equipment costing $248? What is the total price?

3. *Illinois.* The sales tax rate in Illinois is 6.25%. How much tax is charged on a purchase of 5 telephones at $53 apiece? What is the total price?

4. *Kentucky.* The sales tax rate in Kentucky is 6%. How much tax is charged on a purchase of 5 teapots at $37.99 apiece? What is the total price?

5. The sales tax is $48 on the purchase of a dining room set that sells for $960. What is the sales tax rate?

6. The sales tax is $15 on the purchase of a diamond ring that sells for $500. What is the sales tax rate?

7. The sales tax is $35.80 on the purchase of a refrigerator-freezer that sells for $895. What is the sales tax rate?

8. The sales tax is $9.12 on the purchase of a patio set that sells for $456. What is the sales tax rate?

9. The sales tax on a used car is $100 and the sales tax rate is 5%. Find the purchase price (the price before taxes are added).

10. The sales tax on the purchase of a new boat is $112 and the sales tax rate is 2%. Find the purchase price.

11. The sales tax on a dining room set is $28 and the sales tax rate is 3.5%. Find the purchase price.

12. The sales tax on a stereo is $66 and the sales tax rate is 5.5%. Find the purchase price.

13. The sales tax rate in Dallas is 1% for the city and 6% for the state. Find the total amount paid for 2 shower units at $332.50 apiece.

14. The sales tax rate in Omaha is 1.5% for the city and 5% for the state. Find the total amount paid for 3 air conditioners at $260 apiece.

15. The sales tax is $1030.40 on an automobile purchase of $18,400. What is the sales tax rate?

16. The sales tax is $979.60 on an automobile purchase of $15,800. What is the sales tax rate?

b Solve.

17. Sondra's commission rate is 6%. What is the commission from the sale of $45,000 worth of furnaces?

18. Jose's commission rate is 32%. What is the commission from the sale of $12,500 worth of sailboards?

19. Vince earns $120 selling $2400 worth of television sets. What is the commission rate?

20. Donna earns $408 selling $3400 worth of shoes. What is the commission rate?

21. An art gallery's commission rate is 40%. They receive a commission of $392. How many dollars worth of artwork were sold?

22. A real estate agent's commission rate is 7%. She receives a commission of $5600 on the sale of a home. How much did the home sell for?

23. A real estate commission is 6%. What is the commission on the sale of a $98,000 home?

24. A real estate commission is 8%. What is the commission on the sale of a piece of land for $68,000?

25. Bonnie earns $280.80 selling $2340 worth of tee shirts. What is the commission rate?

26. Chuck earns $1147.50 selling $7650 worth of ski passes. What is the commission rate?

27. Miguel's commission is increased according to how much he sells. He receives a commission of 5% for the first $2000 and 8% on the amount over $2000. What is the total commission on sales of $6000?

28. Lucinda earns a salary of $500 a month, plus a 2% commission on sales. One month, she sold $990 worth of encyclopedias. What were her wages that month?

c Find what is missing.

29.

Marked Price	Rate of Discount	Discount	Sale Price
$300	10%		

30.

Marked Price	Rate of Discount	Discount	Sale Price
$2000	40%		

31.

$17.00	15%		

32.

$20.00	25%		

33.

	10%	$12.50	

34.

	15%	$65.70	

35.

$600		$240	

36.

$12,800		$1920	

37. Find the discount and the rate of discount for the ring in this ad.

38. Find the discount and the rate of discount for the calculator in this ad.

39. Find the marked price and the rate of discount for the camcorder in this ad.

40. Find the marked price and the rate of discount for the cedar chest in this ad.

Skill Maintenance

Solve.

41. $\dfrac{x}{12} = \dfrac{24}{16}$

42. $\dfrac{7}{2} = \dfrac{11}{x}$

43. $0.64 \cdot x = 170$

44. $28.5 = 25.6y$

Find decimal notation.

45. $\dfrac{5}{9}$

46. $\dfrac{23}{11}$

47. $\dfrac{11}{12}$

48. $\dfrac{13}{7}$

49. $\dfrac{15}{7}$

50. $\dfrac{19}{12}$

Convert to standard notation.

51. $4.03 trillion

52. 5.8 million

53. 42.7 million

54. 6.09 trillion

Synthesis

55. ❖ Is the following ad mathematically correct? Why or why not?

30% OFF

$6.95
Regularly $9.95

Famous Maker Watches
Choose from men's and ladies' casual or dress designs.

Limited time offer.

56. ❖ If a discount of 25% is followed by an increase of 25%, is the item back to the original price? Why or why not?

57. ❖ Which is better, a discount of 40% or a discount of 20% followed by another of 20%? Explain.

58. A real estate commission rate is 7.5%. A house sells for $98,500. How much does the seller get for the house after paying the commission?

59. *People Magazine.* In a recent subscription drive, *People* offered a subscription of 52 weekly issues for a price of $1.89 per issue. They advertised that this was a savings of 29.7% off the newsstand price. What was the newsstand price?

60. Gordon receives a 10% commission on the first $5000 in sales and 15% on all sales beyond $5000. If Gordon receives a commission of $2405, how much did he sell? Use a calculator and trial and error if you wish.

61. Herb collects baseball memorabilia. He bought two autographed plaques, but became short of funds and had to sell them quickly for $200 each. On one, he made a 20% profit and on the other, he lost 20%. Did he make or lose money on the sale?

62. Tee shirts are being sold at the mall for $5 each, or 3 for $10. If you buy three tee shirts, what is the rate of discount?

8.7 Consumer Applications: Interest

a Simple Interest

Suppose you put $100 into an investment for 1 year. The $100 is called the **principal**. If the **interest rate** is 8%, in addition to the principal, you get back 8% of the principal, which is

> 8% of $100,   or 0.08×100,   or $8.00.

The $8.00 is called the **simple interest**. It is, in effect, the price that a financial institution pays for the use of the money over time.

> The **simple interest** I on principal P, invested for t years at interest rate r, is given by
>
> $I = P \cdot r \cdot t$.
>
> Since t is in years, the interest rate must be an annual rate.

Example 1 What is the interest on $2500 invested at an annual interest rate of 6% for 1 year?

We use the formula $I = P \cdot r \cdot t$:

$$I = (\$2500)(6\%)(1)$$
$$I = (\$2500)(0.06)$$
$$I = \$150.$$

The interest for 1 year is $150.

Do Margin Exercise 1.

Example 2 What is the interest on a principal of $2500 invested at an annual interest rate of 6% for $\frac{1}{4}$ year?

We use the formula $I = P \cdot r \cdot t$:

$$I = (\$2500)(6\%)\left(\frac{1}{4}\right)$$
$$I = (\$2500)(0.06)\left(\frac{1}{4}\right)$$
$$I = \$37.50.$$

The interest for $\frac{1}{4}$ year is $37.50.

Do Margin Exercise 2.

1. What is the interest on $4300 invested at an interest rate of 14% for 1 year?

2. What is the interest on a principal of $4300 invested at an interest rate of 14% for $\frac{3}{4}$ year?

3. The Glass Nook borrows $4800 at 7% for 30 days. Find **a.** the amount of simple interest due and **b.** the total amount that must be paid after 30 days.

When investing or borrowing money the amount paid back equals the principal plus the interest. For example, in example 1, the payback to the investor would equal $2500 + $150 = $2650.

> **Payback** = Principal + Interest

When time is given in days, we usually divide it by 365 to express the time as a fractional part of a year. This is because we are using annual interest, so time needs to be expressed in years or part of a year.

Example 3 To pay for a shipment of tee shirts, New Wave Designs borrows $8000 at 9% annual interest for 60 days. Find **a.** the amount of simple interest that is due and **b.** the total amount that must be paid after 60 days.

a. We express 60 days as a fractional part of a year:

$$I = P \cdot r \cdot t$$

$$I = (\$8000)(9\%)\left(\frac{60}{365}\right)$$

$$I = (\$8000)(0.09)\left(\frac{60}{365}\right)$$

$$I = \$118.36.$$

The interest due for 60 days is $118.36.

b. The total amount to be paid after 60 days is the principal plus the interest:

Payback = Principal + Interest

Payback = $8,000 + $118.36.

Payback = $8,118.36.

The total amount due is $8118.36.

Do Margin Exercise 3.

Exercise Set 8.7

a Find the simple interest.

Principal	Annual Rate of interest	Time
1. $200	13%	1 year
2. $450	18%	1 year
3. $2000	12.4%	$\frac{1}{2}$ year
4. $200	7.7%	$\frac{1}{2}$ year
5. $4300	14%	$\frac{1}{4}$ year
6. $2000	15%	$\frac{1}{4}$ year

Solve. Assume that all interest rates are annual.

7. CopiPix, Inc., borrows $10,000 at 9% for 60 days. Find (a) the amount of interest due and (b) the total amount that must be paid after 60 days.

8. Sal's Laundry borrows $8000 at 10% for 90 days. Find (a) the amount of interest due and (b) the total amount that must be paid after 90 days.

9. Animal Instinct, a pet supply shop, borrows $6500 at 8% for 90 days. Find (a) the amount of interest due and (b) the total amount that must be paid after 90 days.

10. Andante's Cafe borrows $4500 at 9% for 60 days. Find (a) the amount of interest due and (b) the total. amount that must be paid after 60 days.

11. Jean's Garage borrows $5600 at 10% for 30 days. Find (a) the amount of interest due and (b) the total amount that must be paid after 30 days.

12. Shear Delights, a hair salon, borrows $3600 at 8% for 30 days. Find (a) the amount of interest due and (b) the total amount that must be paid after 30 days.

Skill Maintenance

Solve.

13. $\dfrac{9}{10} = \dfrac{x}{5}$

14. $\dfrac{7}{x} = \dfrac{4}{5}$

15. $\dfrac{3}{4} = \dfrac{6}{x}$

16. $\dfrac{7}{8} = \dfrac{x}{100}$

Convert to a mixed number.

17. $\dfrac{100}{3}$

18. $\dfrac{-64}{17}$

19. $\dfrac{-38}{3}$

20. $\dfrac{38}{11}$

Convert from a mixed number to fractional notation.

21. $1\dfrac{1}{17}$

22. $20\dfrac{9}{10}$

23. $-101\dfrac{1}{2}$

24. $-32\dfrac{3}{8}$

Synthesis

Assume all interest rates are annual.

25. ❖ A college student borrows $1800 for six months at 10% annual interest. What would be the amount of each monthly payment?

26. ❖ A firm must choose between borrowing $5000 at 10% for 30 days and borrowing $10,000 at 8% for 60 days. Give arguments in favor of and against each option.

27. ▦ What is the simple interest on $24,680 at 7.75% for $\frac{3}{4}$ year?

28. ▦ Sometimes 360 days is used instead of 365 days when calculating interest for less than a year. Which gives the most interest, $1000 \cdot 8\% \cdot \frac{30}{360}$, or $1000 \cdot 8\% \cdot \frac{30}{365}$?

Review Exercises: Chapter 8

Important Properties and Formulas

Commission = Commission rate = rate × sales × Original price

Sale price = Original price – Discount

Compounded interest: $A = P \cdot \left(1 + \frac{r}{n}\right)^{n \cdot t}$

Discount = Rate of discount

Simple interest: $I = P \cdot r \cdot t$

Find percent notation.

1. 0.483

2. 0.36

3. $\frac{3}{8}$

4. $\frac{1}{3}$

Find decimal notation.

5. 73.5%

6. $6\frac{1}{2}$%

Find fractional notation.

7. 24%

8. 6.3%

Translate to an equation. Then solve.

9. 30.6 is what percent of 90?

10. 63 is 84 percent of what?

11. What is $38\frac{1}{2}$% of 168?

Translate to a proportion. Then solve.

12. 24 percent of what is 16.8?

13. 42 is what percent of 30?

14. What is 10.5% of 84?

Solve.

15. Food expenses account for 26% of the average family's budget. A family makes $2300 one month. How much do they spend for food?

16. The price of a television set was reduced from $350 to $308. Find the percent of decrease in price.

17. Jerome County has a population that is increasing 3% each year. This year the population is 80,000. What will it be next year?

18. The price of a box of cookies increased from $1.70 to $2.04. What was the percent of increase in the price?

19. Carney College has a student body of 960 students. Of these, 17.5% are seniors. How many students are seniors?

Solve.

20. A state charges a meals tax of $4\frac{1}{2}$%. What is the meals tax charged on a dinner party costing $320?

21. In a certain state, a sales tax of $378 is collected on the purchase of a used car for $7560. What is the sales tax rate?

---

22. Kim earns $753.50 selling $6850 worth of televisions. What is the commission rate?

23. An air conditioner has a marked price of $350. It is placed on sale at 12% off. What are the discount and the sale price?

24. A fax machine priced at $305 is discounted at the rate of 14%. What are the discount and the sale price?

25. An insurance salesperson receives a 7% commission. If $42,000 worth of life insurance is sold, what is the commission?

Solve.

26. What is the simple interest on $1800 at 6% for $\frac{1}{3}$ year?

27. The Dress Shack borrows $24,000 at 10% simple interest for 60 days. Find (a) the amount of interest due and (b) the total amount that must be paid after 60 days.

28. What is the simple interest on $2200 principal at the annual interest rate of 5.5% for 1 year?

Hotel Preferences. This circle graph shows hotel preferences for travelers. Use the graph for Exercises 29–32.

Types of Hotels

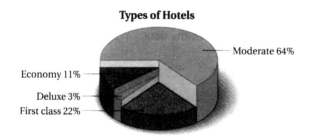

Economy 11%
Deluxe 3%
First class 22%
Moderate 64%

29. What percent of travelers prefer a first-class hotel?

30. What percent of travelers prefer an economy hotel?

31. Suppose 2500 travelers arrive in a city one day. How many of them might seek a moderate room?

32. What percent of travelers prefer either a first-class or a deluxe hotel?

Practice Test: Chapter 8

1. Find decimal notation for 89%.

2. Find percent notation for 0. 674.

3. Find percent notation for $\frac{11}{8}$.

4. Find fractional notation for 65%.

5. Translate to an equation, then solve.

   What is 40% of 55?

6. Translate to a proportion, then solve.

   What percent of 80 is 65?

Solve.

7. *Weight of Muscles.* The weight of muscles in a human body is 40% of total body weight. A person weighs 125 lb. What do the muscles weight?

8. The population of Rippington increased from 500 to 3600. Find the xpercent of increase in population.

9. *Arizona Tax Rate.* The sales tax rate in Arizona is 5%. How much tax is charged on a purchase of $324? What is the total price?

10. Gwen's commission rate is 15%. What is the commission from the sale of $4200 worth of merchandise?

11. The marked price of a CD player is $200 and the item is on sale at 20% off. What are the discount and the sale price?

12. What is the simple interest on a principal of $120 at the annual interest rate of 7.1% for 1 year.

13. The Burnham Parents–Teachers Association invests $5200 at an annual rate of 6% simple interest. How much is in the account after $\frac{1}{2}$ year?

14. A white iron day-bed with brass account is normally priced at $249. It is being advertised on sale for $118 (springs included). Find the discount and the discount rate of the bed as advertised.

A family with an annual income of $45,000 kept track of their expenses. The next circle graph shows the percentages of how their income was spent. Use the circle graph to answer the following questions.

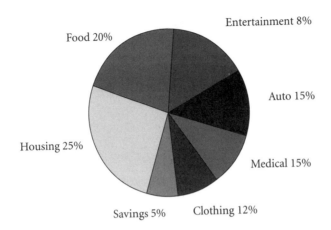

Entertainment 8%

Food 20%

Auto 15%

Housing 25%

Medical 15%

Savings 5%   Clothing 12%

15. On what category did the family spend the most?

16. How much money was spent on food? (Amount, not percent.)

17. How much was spent on Entertainment?

18. What percent more did the family spend on food than medical?

19. What kind of graph would best show a pattern or trend over a certain time period?

20. Explain how to change a decimal to a percent. Give an example.

Cumulative Review: Chapters 1-8

1. Find fractional notation for 0.091.

2. Find decimal notation for $\frac{13}{6}$.

3. Find decimal notation for 3%.

4. Find percent notation for $\frac{9}{8}$.

5. Write fractional notation for the ratio 5 to 0.5.

6. Find the rate in kilometers per hour.

350 km, 15 hr

Use <, >, or = for □ to write a true sentence.

7. $\frac{5}{7}$ □ $\frac{6}{8}$

8. -3.78 □ -37.8

Estimate the sum or difference by rounding to the nearest hundred.

9. 263,961 + 32,090 + 127.89

10. 73,510 − 23,450

11. Calculate: $46 - [4(6 + 4 \div 2) + 2 \cdot 3 - 51$.

12. List the terms: $5x + 9 + 7x + 5$.

Perform the indicated operation and simplify.

13 $\frac{6}{5} + 1\frac{5}{6}$

14. −46.9 + 32.7

15.
$$\begin{array}{r} 4\,8\,7,0\,9\,4 \\ 6,9\,3\,6 \\ +\ \ 2\,1,1\,2\,0 \\ \hline \end{array}$$

16. 35 − 34.98

17. $3\frac{1}{3} - 2\frac{2}{3}$

18. $-\frac{8}{9} - \frac{6}{7}$

19. $\frac{7}{9} \cdot \frac{3}{14}$

20. $(-32)(-4)(-3)$

21.
$$\begin{array}{r} 4\,6.0\,1\,2 \\ \times\ \ \ 0.0\,3 \\ \hline \end{array}$$

22. $6\frac{3}{5} \div 4\frac{2}{5}$

23. 431.2 ÷ 35.2

23. $1\,5\overline{)1\,8\,5\,0}$

Solve.

25. $36 \cdot x = 3420$

26. $y + 142.87 = 151$

27. $\dfrac{2}{15} \cdot t = -\dfrac{6}{5}$

28. $\dfrac{3}{4} + x = \dfrac{5}{6}$

29. $-9x = 16$

30. $\dfrac{16}{n} = \dfrac{21}{11}$

31. Out of 60 questions, a student correctly answered 45 questions. What percent were correct?

32. Find the simple interest on a loan of $750 at 8% annual interest for 3 years.

33. Find the mean: 19, 29, 34, 39, 45.

34. Find the median: 7, 7, 12, 15, 19.

35. Find the perimeter of a 15-in. by 15-in. chessboard.

36. Find the area of a 40-yd by 80-yd yd soccer field.

Solve.

37. A 12-oz box of cereal costs $1.80. Find the unit price in cents per ounce.

38. A bus travels 456 km in 6 hr. At this rate, how far would the bus travel in 8 hr?

39. In a recent year, Americans threw away 50 million lb of paper. It is projected that this will increase to 65 million lb in the year 2000. Find the percent of increase.

40. The state of Utah has an area of 1,722,850 mi². Of this area, 60% is owned by the government. How many square miles are owned by the government?

41. How many pieces of ribbon $1\frac{4}{5}$ yd long can be cut from a length of ribbon 9 yd long?

42. A student walked $\frac{7}{10}$ km to school and then $\frac{8}{10}$ km to the library. How far did the student walk?

9

Geometry and Measures

An Application

A standard-sized slow-pitch softball diamond is a square with sides of length 65 ft. What is the perimeter of this softball diamond? (This is the distance you would have to run if you hit a home run.)

This problem appears as Exercise 47 in Exercise Set 9.7.

The Mathematics

We find the perimeter by finding the distance around the square:

$P = 65 \text{ ft} + 65 \text{ ft} + 65 \text{ ft} + 65 \text{ ft}$

$P = 4 \cdot (65 \text{ ft}) = 260 \text{ ft}$

↑

This is the perimeter.

9.1 Linear Measures

Length, or distance, is one kind of measure. To find lengths, we start with some **unit segment** and assign to it a measure of 1 unit. Suppose $\overline{AB}$ below is a unit segment.

Let's measure segment $\overline{CD}$ below, using $\overline{AB}$ as our unit segment.

Since we can place 4 unit segments end to end along $\overline{CD}$, the measure of $\overline{CD}$ is 4 units.

Sometimes we have to use parts of units, called **subunits**. For example, the measure of the segment $\overline{MN}$ below is $1\frac{1}{2}$ units. We pace one unit segment and one half-unit segment end to end.

Do Margin Exercises 1–4

a American Measures

American units of length are related as follows

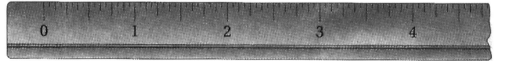

(Actual size, in inches.)

> **American Units of Length**
>
> 12 inches (in.) = 1 foot (ft)   3 feet = 1 yard (yd)
>
> 36 inches = 1 yard   5280 feet = 1 mile (mi)

The symbolism 13 in. = 13" and 27 ft = 27' is also used for inches and feet. American units have also been called "English," or "British-American," because at one time they were used by both countries. Today both Canada and England have officially converted to the metric system. However, if you travel in England, you will still see units such as "miles" on road signs.

 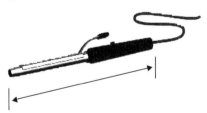

To change from certain American units to others, we make substitutions. Such a substitution is usually helpful when we are converting from a larger unit to a smaller one.

Example 1 Complete: 1 yd = _____ in.

$$1 \text{ yd} = 3 \text{ ft}$$

$= 3 \cdot 1$ ft	We think of 3 ft as $3 \cdot$ ft, or $3 \cdot 1$ ft.
$= 3 \cdot 12$ in.	Substituting 12 in. for 1 ft
$= 36$ in.	Multiplying

Example 2 Complete: 7 yd = _____ in.

$$7 \text{ yd} = 7 \cdot 1 \text{ yd}$$

$= 7 \cdot 3$ ft	Substituting 3 ft for 1 yd
$= 7 \cdot 3 \cdot 1$ ft	
$= 7 \cdot 3 \cdot 12$ in.	Substituting 12 in. for 1 ft; $7 \cdot 3 = 21; 21 \cdot 12 = 252$
$= 252$ in.	

Do Margin Exercises 5–7

Sometimes it helps to use multiplying by 1 in. making conversions. For example, 12 in. = 1 ft, so

$$\frac{12 \text{ in.}}{1 \text{ ft}} = 1 \text{ and } \frac{1 \text{ ft}}{12 \text{ in.}} = 1.$$

If we divide 12 in. by 1 ft or 1 ft by 12 in., we get 1 because the lengths are the same. Let's first convert from smaller to larger units.

Example 3 Complete: 48 in. = _____ ft.

We want to convert from "in." to "ft." We multiply by 1 using an equivalent ratio for 1 with "in." on the bottom and "ft" on the top to eliminate inches and to convert to feet:

$$48 \text{ in.} = \frac{48 \text{ in.}}{1} \cdot \frac{1 \text{ ft}}{12 \text{ in.}}$$

Multiplying by 1 using $\frac{1 \text{ ft}}{12 \text{ in.}}$ to eliminate in.

$$= \frac{\overset{4}{\cancel{48 \text{ in.}}}}{1} \cdot \frac{1 \text{ ft}}{\underset{1}{\cancel{12 \text{ in.}}}}$$

Simplifying

$$= \frac{4 \cdot 1 \text{ ft}}{1 \cdot 1}$$

$$= 4 \text{ ft.}$$

Converting units using this process is called "canceling" units.

Do Margin Exercises 8 and 9.

Complete.

5. 8 yd = _____ in.

6. 14.5 yd = _____ ft

7. 3.8 mi = _____ in.

Complete.

8. 72 in. = _____ ft

9. 17 in. = _____ ft

Complete.

10. 24 ft = _____ yd

11. 35 ft = _____ yd

Complete.

12. 26,400 ft = _____ mi

13. 2650 ft = _____ mi

14. Complete. Use multiplying by 1.

8 yd = _____ in.

Example 4 Complete: 25 ft = _____ yd.

Since we are converting from "ft" to "yd," we choose a ratio for 1 with "yd" on the top and "ft" on the bottom:

$$25 \text{ ft} = \frac{25 \text{ ft}}{1} \cdot \frac{1 \text{ yd}}{3 \text{ ft}}$$

3 ft = 1 yd, so $\frac{3 \text{ ft}}{1 \text{ yd}} = 1$, and $\frac{1 \text{ yd}}{3 \text{ ft}} = 1$. We use $\frac{1 \text{ yd}}{3 \text{ ft}}$ to eliminate ft.

$$= \frac{25 \text{ ft}}{1} \cdot \frac{1 \text{ yd}}{3 \text{ ft}}$$

$$= \frac{25}{3} \text{ yd}$$

$$= 8\frac{1}{3} \text{ yd, or } 8.\overline{3} \text{ yd.}$$

Do Margin Exercises 10 and 11.

Example 5 Complete: 23,760 ft = _____ mi.

We choose a ratio for 1 with "mi" on the top and "ft" on the bottom:

$$23,760 \text{ ft} = \frac{23,760 \text{ ft}}{1} \cdot \frac{1 \text{ mi}}{5280 \text{ ft}}$$

5280 ft = 1 mi, so $\frac{1 \text{ mi}}{5280 \text{ ft}} = 1$.

$$= \frac{23,760 \text{ ft}}{1} \cdot \frac{1 \text{ mi}}{5280 \text{ ft}}$$

$$= \frac{23,760}{5280} \text{ mi}$$

Simplify using a calculator.

$$= 4.5 \text{ mi, or } 4\frac{1}{2} \text{ mi.}$$

Do Margin Exercises 12 and 13.

We can also use multiplying by 1 to convert from larger to smaller units. Let's redo Example 2.

Example 6 Complete: 7 yd = _____ in.

$$7 \text{ yd} = \frac{7 \text{ yd}}{1} \cdot \frac{3 \text{ ft}}{1 \text{ yd}} \cdot \frac{12 \text{ in.}}{1 \text{ ft}}$$

$$= (7 \cdot 3 \cdot 12) \text{ in.}$$

$$= 252 \text{ in.}$$

Do Margin Exercise 14.

b The Metric System

The **metric system** is used in most countries of the world, and the United States is now making greater use of it as well. The metric system does not use inches, feet, pounds, and so on, although units for time and electricity are the same as those you use now.

An advantage of the metric system is that it is easier to convert from one unit to another. That is because the metric system is based on the number 10. Multipying and dividing by powers of 10 is easier than using numbers such as 12, 36, and 5280.

The basic unit of length is the **meter**. It is just over a yard. In fact, 1 meter ≈ 1.1 yd.

(Comparative sizes are shown.)

1 Meter

1 Yard

The other units of length are multiples of the length of a meter:

10 times a meter, 100 times a meter, 1000 times a meter, and so on,

or fractions of a meter:

$\frac{1}{10}$ of a meter, $\frac{1}{100}$ of a meter, $\frac{1}{1000}$ of a meter, and so on.

▶ **Metric Units of Length**

1 *kilo*meter (km) = 1000 meters (m)

1 *hecto*meter (hm) = 100 meters (m)

1 *deka*meter (dam) = 10 meters (m)

1 meter (m) | *dam* and *dm* are not used often. |

1 *deci*meter (dm) = $\frac{1}{10}$ meter (m)

1 *centi*meter (cm) = $\frac{1}{100}$ meter (m)

1 *milli*meter (mm) = $\frac{1}{1000}$ meter (m)

You should memorize these names and abbreviations. Think of *kilo-* for 1000, *hecto-* for 100, *deka-* for 10, *deci-* for $\frac{1}{10}$, *centi-* for $\frac{1}{100}$ and *milli-* for $\frac{1}{1000}$. We will also use these prefixes when considering units of area, capacity, and mass.

Thinking Metric

To familiarize yourself with metric units, consider the following.

1 kilometer (1000 meters)   is slightly more than $\frac{1}{2}$ mile (0.6 mi).

1 meter   is just over a yard (1.1 yd).

1 centimeter (0.01 meter)   is a little more than the width of a paperclip (about 0.3937 inch).

1 cm

1 inch is about 2.54 centimeters.

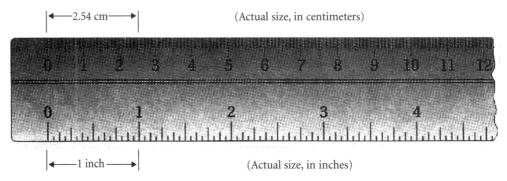

1 millimeter is about the diameter of a paperclip wire.

1 mm

The millimeter (mm) is used to measure small distances, especially in industry.

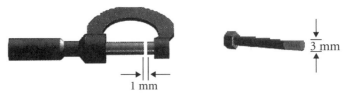

In many countries, the centimeter (cm) is used for body dimensions and clothing sizes.

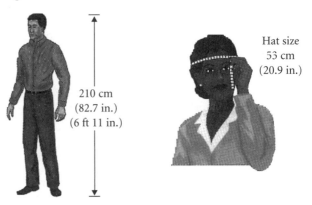

Hat size
53 cm
(20.9 in.)

210 cm
(82.7 in.)
(6 ft 11 in.)

The meter (m) is used for expressing dimensions of larger objects—say, the length of a building—and for shorter distances, such as the length of a rug.

 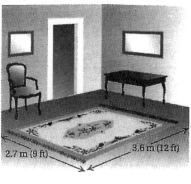

25 m (82.5 ft)   2.7 m (9 ft)   3.6 m (12 ft)

The kilometer(km) is used for longer distances, mostly in cases where miles are now being used.

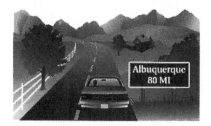 

Do Margin Exercises 15–20.

Changing Metric Units

Example 7   Complete: 4 km _____ m.

$$4 \text{ km} = 4 \cdot 1 \text{ km}$$

$$= 4 \cdot 1000 \text{ m} \qquad \text{Substituting 1000 m for 1 km}$$

$$= 4000 \text{ m}$$

Do Margin Exercises 21 and 22.

Since

$$\frac{1}{10}\text{m} = 1 \text{ dm}, \qquad \frac{1}{100}\text{m} = 1 \text{ cm}, \quad \text{and} \qquad \frac{1}{1000}\text{m} = 1 \text{ mm},$$

it follows that

▶ 1 m = 10 dm   1 m = 100 cm,   and   1 m = 1000 mm.

Memorizing these will help you to write forms of 1 when making conversions.

Complete with mm, cm, m, or km.

15. A stick of gum is 7 _____ long.

16. Minneapolis is 3213 _____ from San Fransisco.

17. A penny is 1 _____ thick.

18. The halfback ran 7 _____ .

19. The book is 3 _____ thick.

20. The desk is 2 _____ long.

Complete.

21. 23 km = _____ m

22. 4 hm = _____ m

Complete.

23. 1.78 m = _____ cm

24. 9.04 m = _____ mm

Complete.

25. 7814 m = _____ km

26. 7814 m = _____ dam

Example 8   Complete: 93.4 m = _____ cm.

We want to convert from "m" to "cm." We multiply by 1 using a ratio for 1 with "m" on the bottom and "cm" on the top to eliminate meters and convert to centimeters:

$$93.4 \text{ m} = \frac{93.4 \text{ m}}{1} \cdot \frac{100 \text{ cm}}{1 \text{ m}}$$ Multiplying by 1 using $\frac{100 \text{cm}}{1 \text{ m}}$

$$= \frac{93.4 \text{ m̸}}{1} \cdot \frac{100 \text{ cm}}{1 \text{ m̸}}$$

$$= 93.4 \cdot 100 \text{ cm}$$

$$= 9340 \text{ cm.}$$ Multiplying by 100 moves the decimal point two places to the right.

Example 9   Complete: 0.248 m = _____ mm.

We are converting from "m" to "mm," so we choose a ratio for 1 with "mm" on the top and "m" on the bottom:

$$0.248 \text{ m} = \frac{0.248 \text{ m}}{1} \cdot \frac{1000 \text{ mm}}{1 \text{ m}}$$ Multiplying by 1 using $\frac{1000 \text{mm}}{1 \text{ m}}$

$$= \frac{0.248 \text{ m̸}}{1} \cdot \frac{1000 \text{ mm}}{1 \text{ m̸}}$$

$$= 0.248 \cdot 1000 \text{ mm}$$

$$= 248 \text{ mm.}$$ Multiplying by 1000 moves the decimal point three places to the right.

Do Margin Exercises 23 and 24.

Example 10   Complete: 2347 m = _____ km.

$$2347 \text{ m} = \frac{2347 \text{ m}}{1} \cdot \frac{1 \text{ km}}{1000 \text{ m}}$$ Multiplying by 1 using $\frac{1 \text{ km}}{1000 \text{ m}}$

$$= \frac{2347 \text{ m̸}}{1} \cdot \frac{1 \text{ km}}{1000 \text{ m̸}}$$

$$= \frac{2347}{1000} \text{ km}$$

$$= 2.347 \text{ km}$$ Dividing by 1000 moves the decimal point three places to the left.

Do Margin Exercises 25 and 26.

Sometimes we multiply by 1 more than once.

Example 11 Complete: 8.42 mm = _____ cm.

$$8.42 \text{ mm} = \frac{8.42 \text{ mm}}{1} \cdot \frac{1 \text{ m}}{1000 \text{ mm}} \cdot \frac{100 \text{ cm}}{1 \text{ m}}$$

Multiplying by 1 using $\frac{1 \text{ m}}{1000 \text{ mm}}$ and $\frac{100 \text{ cm}}{1 \text{ m}}$

$$= \frac{8.42 \text{ mm}}{1} \cdot \frac{1 \text{ m}}{1000 \text{ mm}} \cdot \frac{100 \text{ cm}}{1 \text{ m}}$$

$$= \frac{8.42 \,(100) \text{ cm}}{1000}$$

$$= \frac{842 \text{ cm}}{1000}$$

$$= 0.842 \text{ cm}$$

Do Margin Exercises 27 and 28.

Mental Conversion

Look back over the examples and exercises done so far and you will see that changing from one unit to another in the metric system amounts to only the movement of a decimal point. That is because the metric system is based on 10. Let's find a faster way to convert. Look at the following table.

1000 m	100 m	10 m	1 m	0.1 m	0.01 m	0.001m
1 km	1 hm	1 dam	1 m	1 dm	1 cm	1 mm

Each place in the table has a value $\frac{1}{10}$ of the unit to the left or 10 times the unit to the right. Thus moving one place in the table corresponds to one decimal place. Let's convert mentally.

Example 12 Complete: 8.42 mm = _____ cm.

Think: To go from mm to cm in the table is a move of one place to the left. Thus we move the decimal point one place to the left.

1000 m	100 m	10 m	1 m	0.1 m	0.01 m	0.001m
1 km	1 hm	1 dam	1 m	1 dm	**1 cm**	**1 mm**

1 place to the left

8.42   0.8.42   8.42 mm = 0.842 cm

Example 13 Complete: 1.886 km = _____ cm.

Think: To go from km to cm is a move of five places to the right. Thus we move the decimal point five places to the right.

1000 m	100 m	10 m	1 m	0.1 m	0.01 m	0.001m
1 **km**	1 hm	1 dam	1 m	1 dm	**1 cm**	1 mm

5 places to the right

1.886   1.88600.   1.886 km = 188,600 cm

Complete.

27. 9.67 mm = _____ cm

28. 89 km = _____ cm

Complete. Try to do this mentally using the table.

29. 6780 m = _____ km

30. 9.74 m = _____ mm

31. 1 mm = _____ cm

32. 845.1 mm = _____ dm

Complete.

33. 100 yd = _____ m
(length of a football field)

34. 500 mi = _____ km
(Indianapolis 500-mile race)

35. 2383 km = _____ mi
(distance from St. Louis to Phoenix)

Example 14 Complete: 3 m = _____ cm.

Think: To go from m to cm in the table is a move of two places to the right. Thus we move the decimal point two places to the right.

1000 m	100 m	10 m	1 m	0.1 m	0.01 m	0.001m
1 km	1 hm	1 dam	1 **m**	1 dm	1 cm	1 **mm**

2 places to the right

3   3.00.   3 m = 300 cm

You should try to make metric conversions mentally as much as possible.

The fact that conversions can be done so easily is an important advantage of the metric system. The most commonly used metric units of length are km, m, cm, and mm. We have purposely used these more often than the others in the exercises.

Do Margin Exercises 29–32.

Converting Between American and Metric Units

We can make conversions between American and metric units by using the following table. Again, we either make a substitution or multiply by 1 appropriately.

Metric	American
1 m	39.37 in.
1 m	3.3 ft
1 m	1.1 yd
0.303 m	1 ft
2.54 cm	1 in.
1 km	0.621 mi
1.609 km	1 mi

Example 15 Complete: 26.2 mi = _____ km. (This is the length of the Olympic marathon.)

26.2 mi = 26.2 · 1 mi
≈ 26.2 · 1.609 km
≈ 42.1558 km

Example 16 Complete: 100 m = _____ yd. (This is the length of a dash in track.)

$$100 \text{ m} \approx \frac{100 \text{ m}}{1} \cdot \frac{1.1 \text{ yd}}{1 \text{ m}}$$

$$\approx \frac{100 \text{ m\!\!\!/}}{1} \cdot \frac{1.1 \text{ yd}}{1 \text{ m\!\!\!/}}$$

$$\approx 110 \text{ yd}$$

Do Margin Exercises 33–35.

c | Perimeter

Perimeter has been studied in previous sections of this book as an application for adding numbers. The perimeter is the total distance around a figure. When calculating the perimeter of squares and rectangles, there are formulas that can be used.

Perimeter of a rectangle: $P = 2L + 2W$

Perimeter of a square: $P = 4s$

It is important to realize that all the units that are given for the measurements of the sides must be the same. For example, we cannot add inches to feet or millimeters to centimeters. If the dimensions of a figure are not given in the same unit, then conversions must be made *before* calculating the perimeter.

Example 17 Find the perimeter of the rectangle that has a length of 4 feet and a width of 28 inches.

Drawing a picture may be helpful.

4 ft

28 in.

Next, you should notice that the units are different. Unless the question specifies which unit to use, either would be fine. Since 28 inches is between 2 ft and 3 ft and therefore cannot be expressed as a whole number of feet, it would be easier to convert all dimensions to inches.

Begin by changing 4 ft to inches.

$$4 \text{ ft} = \frac{4 \text{ ft}}{1} \cdot \frac{12 \text{ in.}}{1 \text{ ft}} \qquad \text{Multiplying by 1 using 12 in.} = 1 \text{ ft}$$

$$= \frac{4 \cancel{\text{ft}}}{1} \cdot \frac{12 \text{ in.}}{1 \cancel{\text{ft}}}$$

$$= (4 \cdot 12)\text{in.}$$

$$= 48 \text{ in.}$$

Now we have the dimension in inches ($L = 48$ in. and $W = 28$ in.), and the calculation for the perimeter can be done:

$P = 2L + 2W$

$P = 2(48 \text{ in.}) + 2(28 \text{ in.})$ Substitute values for L and W

$P = 96 \text{ in.} + 56 \text{ in.}$

$P = 152 \text{ in.}$

The perimeter of a rectangle 4 ft by 28 in. is 152 in.

Do Margin Exercises 36–39.

Find the perimeter.

36.

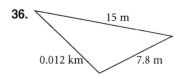

15 m

0.012 km

7.8 m

37.

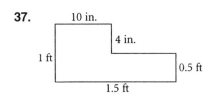

10 in.

4 in.

1 ft

0.5 ft

1.5 ft

38. A rectangle 4.7 yd by 2.4 yd.

Exercise Set 9.1

a Complete.

1. 1 ft = _____ in.

2. 1 yd = _____ ft

3. 1 in. = _____ ft

4. 1 mi = _____ yd

5. 1 mi = _____ ft

6. 1 ft= _____ yd

7. 3 yd = _____ in.

8. 10 yd = _____ ft

9. 84 in. = _____ ft

10. 48 ft = _____ yd

11. 18 in. = _____ ft

12. 29 ft = _____ yd

13. 5 mi = _____ ft

14. 5 mi = _____ yd

15. 36 in. = _____ ft

16. 11,616 ft = _____ mi

17. 10 ft = _____ yd

18. 9.6 yd = _____ ft

19. 10 mi = _____ ft

20. 31,680 ft = _____ mi

21. $4\frac{1}{2}$ ft = _____ yd

22. 48 in. = _____ ft

23. 36 in. = _____ yd

24. 20 yd = _____ in.

25. 330 ft = _____ yd

26. 5280 yd = _____ mi

27. 3520 yd = _____ mi

28. 25 mi = _____ ft

29. 100 yd = _____ ft

30. 480 in. = _____ ft

31. 360 in. = _____ ft

32. 720 in. = _____ yd

33. 1 in. = _____ yd

34. 25 in. = _____ ft

35. 2 mi = _____ in.

36. 63,360 in. = _____ mi

b Complete. Do as much as possible mentally.

37. a) 1 km = _____ m

38. a) 1 hm = _____ m

39. a) 1 dam = _____ m

b) 1 m = _____ km

b) 1 m = _____ hm

b) 1 m = _____ dam

40. a) l dm= _____ m

41. a) 1 cm = _____ m

42. a) 1 mm = _____ m

b) 1 m= _____ dm

b) 1 m = _____ cm

b) 1m = _____ mm

43. 6.7 km = _____ m

44. 27 km = _____ m

45. 98 cm = _____ m

46. 0.789 cm = _____ m

47. 8921 m = _____ km

48. 8664 m = _____ km

49. 56.66 m = _____ km

50. 4.733 m = _____ km

51. 5666 m = _____ cm

52. 869 m = _____ cm

53. 477 cm = _____ m

54. 6.27 mm = _____ m

55. 6.88 m = _____ cm

56. 6.88 m = _____ dm

57. 1 mm = _____ cm

58. 1 cm = _____ km

59. 1 km = _____ cm

60. 2 km = _____ cm

61. 14.2 cm = _____ mm

62. 25.3 cm = _____ mm

63. 8.2 mm = _____ cm

64. 9.7 mm = _____ cm

65. 4500 mm = _____ cm

66. 8,000,000 m = _____ km

67. 0.024 mm = _____ m

68. 60,000 mm = _____ dam

69. 6.88 m = _____ dam

70. 7.44 m = _____ hm

71. 2.3 dam = _____ dm

72. 9 km = _____ hm

73. 392 dam = _____ km

74. 0.056 mm = _____ dm

Complete.

75. 330 ft = _____ m
(length of most baseball foul lines)

76. 12 in. = _____ cm

77. 1171.352 km = _____ mi
(distance from Cleveland to Atlanta)

78. 2 m = _____ ft
(length of a desk)

79. 65 mph = _____ km/h
(common speed limit in the United States)

80. 100 km/h = _____ mph
(common speed limit in Canada)

81. 180 mi = _____ km
(distance from Indianapolis to Chicago)

82. 141,600,000 mi = _____ km
(farthest distance of Mars from the sun)

83. 70 mph = _____ km/h
(interstate speed limit in the United States)

84. 60 km/h = _____ mph
(city speed limit in Canada)

85. 10 yd = _____ m
(length needed for a first down in football)

86. 450 ft = _____ m
(length of a long home run in baseball)

c Find the perimeter of the polygon.

87.
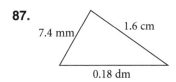
7.4 mm   1.6 cm
0.18 dm

88.
140 in.
1.2 yd   1.2 yd
140 in.

89.
3.5 in.   3.5 in.
3.5 in.   0.125 yd
0.5 in.

90.
40 hm
5.6 km

91.
3250 mm
3.25 m

92.
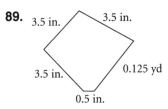
Each side $\frac{1}{6}$ km

Find the perimeter of the rectangle.

93. 5 ft by 2 yd

94. 250 cm by 100 m

95. 340 mm by 4.9 cm

96. $8\frac{1}{2}$ ft by $4\frac{1}{3}$ yd

Find the perimeter of the square.

97. $3\frac{3}{4}$ ft on a side

98. 1.8 km on a side

99. 7.2 mm on a side

100. $2\frac{1}{4}$ yd on a side

Skill Maintenance

101. Multiply (3.14)(4.41). Round to the nearest hundredth.

102. Multiply: $4 \cdot 20\frac{1}{8}$.

103. Multiply: $48 \cdot \frac{1}{12}$

Find decimal notation for the percent notation in the sentence.

104. Blood is 90% water.

105. Of those accidents requiring medical attention, 10.8% of them occur on roads.

Find fractional notation for the percent notation in the sentence.

106. Of all 18-year-olds, 27.5% are registered to vote.

107. Of all those who buy CDs, 57% are in the 20–39 age group.

Convert to percent notation.

108. $\dfrac{11}{8}$

109. $\dfrac{2}{3}$

110. $\dfrac{1}{4}$

Find the simplified fractional notation for the ratio.

111. In Washington, D.C., there are 36.1 lawyers for every 1000 people. What is the ratio of lawyers to people? What is the ratio of people to lawyers?

112. In a bread recipe, there are 2 cups of milk to 12 cups of flour. What is the ratio of cups of milk to cups of flour?

Synthesis

113. ❖ Explain the error in the following:
    23 in. = 23(12 ft) = 276 ft.

114. ❖ Describe two methods of making unit conversions discussed in this section.

115. ▦ *National Debt.* Recently the national debt was $5.103 trillion. To get an idea of this amount, picture that if that many $1 bills were stacked on top of each other, they would reach 1.382 times the distance to the moon. The distance to the moon is 238,866 mi. How thick, in inches, is a $1 bill?

116. ❖ Explain in your own words why metric units are easier to work with than American units.

117. ❖ Would you expect the world record for the 100-m dash to be longer or shorter than the record for the 100-yd dash? Why?

Complete.

118. ▦ 2 mi = _____ cm

119. ▦ 10 km = _____ in.

120. ▦ Audio cassettes are generally played at a rate of $1\frac{7}{8}$ inches per second. How many meters of tape are used for a 60-min cassette? (*Note:* A 60-min cassette has 30 min of playing time on each side.)

121. ▦ In a recent year, the world record for the 100-m dash was 9.86 see. How fast is this in miles per hour? Round to the nearest tenth of a mile per hour.

9.2   Area

a Rectangles and Squares

Area of rectangles and squares was studied earlier in the text as an application for multiplying numbers. Area is defined as the number of square units that cover the interior of a polygon. Specifically, the formulas used were:

Area of a rectangle: $A = L \cdot W$

Area of a square: $A = s^2$

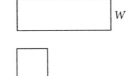

Just as when calculating perimeter, the dimensions of the figure must all be the same unit before calculating area. ***The resulting answer is always in square units.*** For example, 12 square feet can be expressed as 12 sq. ft or 12 ft².

Example 1

Find the area of a rectangle that is 250 cm by 1.2 meters.

Make a drawing of the rectangle

Notice that the units are different. Choose whether you would like to change the units to meters or centimeters. For this example, the conversion will be made to centimeters.

$$1.2\ m = \frac{1.2\ m}{1} \cdot \frac{100cm}{1\ m}$$

$$= \frac{1.2\ \cancel{m}}{1} \cdot \frac{100cm}{1\ \cancel{m}}$$

$$= (1.2)(100)cm$$

$$= 120\ cm$$

> *Note:* You can also convert by moving the decimal point two places to the right.

Now calculate the area using $L = 250$ cm and $W = 120$ cm:

$A = L \cdot W$

$A = (120\ cm) \cdot (250\ cm)$

$A = (120 \cdot 250)(cm \cdot cm)$

$A = 30{,}000\ cm^2$ *Note:* cm · cm = cm²

The area of the rectangle is 30,000 cm².

Do Margin Exercises 1–3.

Find the area

1. A rectangle that is 40 ft by 10 yd

2.

21 in.

4.5 yd

3. A square that is 32 cm on each side

b | Converting Units of Area

It is often necessary to convert units of area. Suppose the area of a room is 360 ft^2, and the carpet you want for the room is sold in yd^2. The 360 ft^2 can be changed to yd^2 without going back and measuring the room in yards. **The conversion numbers used when converting square units are not the same as those used when converting linear units.**

American Units

Let's do some conversions from one American unit of area to another.

This diagram shows that 1 square yard can be divided into 9 smaller square units that are each 1 square foot. Example 2 shows how this conversion is done using unit cancellation.

Example 2 Complete: 1 yd^2 = _____ ft^2

$1 \text{ yd}^2 = 1 \text{ yd} \cdot 1 \text{ yd}.$

$$= \frac{1 \text{ yd} \cdot 1 \text{ yd}}{1} \cdot \frac{3 \text{ ft}}{1 \text{ yd}} \cdot \frac{3 \text{ ft}}{1 \text{yd}} \qquad \text{yd}^2 = \text{yd} \cdot \text{yd}$$

$$= \frac{1 \; \cancel{\text{yd}} \cdot \cancel{\text{yd}}}{1} \cdot \frac{3 \text{ ft}}{1 \; \cancel{\text{yd}}} \cdot \frac{3 \text{ ft}}{1 \; \cancel{\text{yd}}} \qquad \text{Multiply by 1 using } \frac{3 \text{ ft}}{1 \text{ yd}}$$

$$= (1 \cdot 3 \cdot 3) \cdot \text{ft} \cdot \text{ft}$$

$$= 9 \text{ ft}^2$$

Example 3 Complete: 1 ft^2 = _____ in.^{2}

$$1 \text{ ft}^2 = \text{ft} \cdot \text{ft} \qquad\qquad \text{ft}^2 = \text{ft} \cdot \text{ft}$$

$$= \frac{1 \text{ ft} \cdot \text{ft}}{1} \cdot \frac{12 \text{ in.}}{1 \text{ ft}} \cdot \frac{12 \text{ in.}}{1 \text{ ft}}$$

$$= \frac{1 \; \cancel{\text{ft}} \cdot \cancel{\text{ft}}}{1} \cdot \frac{12 \text{ in.}}{1 \; \cancel{\text{ft}}} \cdot \frac{12 \text{ in.}}{1 \; \cancel{\text{ft}}} \qquad \text{Multiply by 1 using } \frac{12 \text{ in.}}{1 \text{ ft}}$$

$$= (1 \cdot 12 \cdot 12) \cdot \text{in.} \cdot \text{in.}$$

$$= 144 \text{ in.}^2 \qquad\qquad \text{in.} \cdot \text{in.} = \text{in.}^2$$

American units are related as follows.

> ▶ 1 yd^2 = 9 ft^2
>
> 1 ft^2 = 144 in.^{2}
>
> 1 mi^2 = 640 acres
>
> 1 acre = 43,560 ft^2

Example 4 Complete: $360 \text{ ft}^2 = \underline{\hspace{1cm}} \text{ yd}^2$.

We are converting from "ft²" to "yd²." Thus we choose a ratio for 1 with yd² on top and ft² on the bottom.

$$360 \text{ ft}^2 = \frac{360 \text{ ft}^2}{1} \cdot \frac{1 \text{ yd}^2}{9 \text{ ft}^2} \qquad \text{Multiplying by 1 using } \frac{1 \text{ yd}^2}{9 \text{ ft}^2}$$

$$= \frac{360 \cancel{\text{ft}^2}}{1} \cdot \frac{1 \text{ yd}^2}{9 \cancel{\text{ft}^2}}$$

$$= \frac{360}{9} \text{ yd}^2$$

$$= 40 \text{ yd}^2$$

So the amount of carpet needed for the room described above is 40 yd.

Example 5 Complete: $7 \text{ mi}^2 = \underline{\hspace{1cm}} \text{ acres}$.

$$7 \text{ mi}^2 = \frac{7 \text{ mi}^2}{1} \cdot \frac{640 \text{ acres}}{1 \text{ mi}^2} \qquad \text{Multiplying by 1 using } \frac{640 \text{ acres}}{1 \text{ mi}^2}$$

$$= \frac{7 \cancel{\text{mi}^2}}{1} \cdot \frac{640 \text{ acres}}{1 \cancel{\text{mi}^2}}$$

$$= 4480 \text{ acres}$$

Do Margin Exercises 4–8.

Metric Units

Let's now convert from one metric unit of area to another.

Example 6 Complete: $1 \text{ km}^2 = \underline{\hspace{1cm}} \text{ m}^2$.

$$1 \text{ km}^2 = 1 \text{ km} \cdot 1 \text{ km}$$

$$= \frac{1 \text{ km} \cdot \text{km}}{1} \cdot \frac{1000 \text{ m}}{1 \text{ km}} \cdot \frac{1000 \text{ m}}{1 \text{ km}}$$

$$= \frac{1 \cancel{\text{km}} \cdot \cancel{\text{km}}}{1} \cdot \frac{1000 \text{ m}}{1 \cancel{\text{km}}} \cdot \frac{1000 \text{ m}}{1 \cancel{\text{km}}}$$

$$= (1{,}000 \cdot 1{,}000) \text{m} \cdot \text{m}$$

$$= 1{,}000{,}000 \text{ m}^2$$

Example 7 Complete: $1 \text{ m}^2 = \underline{\hspace{1cm}} \text{ cm}^2$.

$$1 \text{m}^2 = 1 \text{ m} \cdot \text{m}$$

$$= \frac{1 \text{ m} \cdot \text{m}}{1} \cdot \frac{100 \text{ cm}}{1 \text{ m}} \cdot \frac{100 \text{ cm}}{1 \text{ m}}$$

$$= \frac{1 \cancel{\text{m}} \cdot \cancel{\text{m}}}{1} \cdot \frac{100 \text{ cm}}{1 \cancel{\text{m}}} \cdot \frac{100 \text{ cm}}{1 \cancel{\text{m}}}$$

$$= (100 \cdot 100) \text{ cm} \cdot \text{cm}$$

$$= 10{,}000 \text{ cm}^2$$

Do Margin Exercises 9 and 10.

Complete.

4. $8 \text{ yd}^2 = \underline{\hspace{1cm}} \text{ ft}^2$

5. $5 \text{ yd}^2 = \underline{\hspace{1cm}} \text{ ft}^2$

6. $20 \text{ ft}^2 = \underline{\hspace{1cm}} \text{ in.}^2$

7. $360 \text{ in.}^2 = \underline{\hspace{1cm}} \text{ ft}^2$

8. $5 \text{ mi}^2 = \underline{\hspace{1cm}} \text{ acres}$

Complete.

9. $1 \text{ m}^2 = \underline{\hspace{1cm}} \text{ mm}^2$

10. $1 \text{ cm}^2 = \underline{\hspace{1cm}} \text{ mm}^2$

Complete.

11. $2.88 \text{ m}^2 = $ _____ cm^2

12. $4.3 \text{ mm}^2 = $ _____ cm^2

13. $678,000 \text{ m}^2 = $ _____ km^2

Mental Conversion

To convert mentally, we first note that $10^2 = 100$, $100^2 = 10,000$, and $0.1^2 = 0.01$. We use the diagram as before and **multiply the number of moves by 2** to determine the number of moves of the decimal point.

1000 m	100 m	10 m	1 m	0.1 m	0.01 m	0.001m
1 km	1 hm	1 dam	1 m	1 dm	1 cm	1 mm

Example 8 Complete: $3.48 \text{ km}^2 = $ _____ m^2.

Think: To go from km to m in the table is a move of 3 places to the right.

1000 m	100 m	10 m	1 m	0.1 m	0.01 m	0.001m
1 **km**	1 hm	1 dam	1 **m**	1 dm	1 cm	1 mm

3 moves to the right

So we move the decimal point $2 \cdot 3$, or 6 places to the right.

$3.48 \qquad 3.480000. \qquad 3.48 \text{ km}^2 = 3,480,000 \text{ m}^2$

6 places to the right

Example 9 Complete: $586.78 \text{ cm}^2 = $ _____ m^2.

Think: To go from cm to m in the table is a move of 2 places to the left.

1000 m	100 m	10 m	1 m	0.1 m	0.01 m	0.001m
1 km	1 hm	1 dam	1 **m**	1 dm	1 **cm**	1 mm

2 moves to the left

So we move the decimal point $2 \cdot 2$, or 4 places to the left.

$586.78 \qquad 0.0586.78 \qquad 586.78 \text{ cm}^2 = 0.058678 \text{ m}^2$

4 places to the left

Do Margin Exercises 11–13.

c | Areas of Parallelograms, Triangles, and Trapezoids

Parallelograms

A **parallelogram** is a closed four-sided figure with two pairs of parallel sides, as shown below.

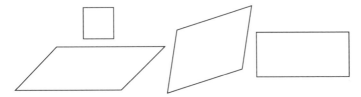

To find the area of a parallelogram, consider the one below.

If we cut off a piece and move it to the other end, we get a rectangle.

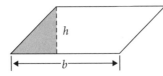 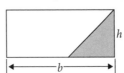

We can find the area by multiplying the length b, called a **base**, by h, called the **height**.

▶ The **area of a parallelogram** is the product of the length of a base b and the height h:

$$A = b \cdot h.$$

Example 10   Find the area of this parallelogram.

$A = b \cdot h$

$A = (7 \text{ km})(5 \text{ km})$

$A = 35 \text{ km}^2$

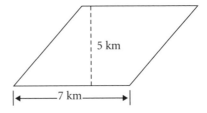

Find the area.

14.

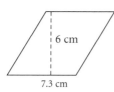

6 cm

7.3 cm

15.

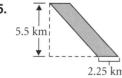

5.5 km

2.25 km

Example 11 Find the area of this parallelogram.

$A = b \cdot h$

$A = (1.2 \text{ m})(6 \text{ m})$

$A = 7.2 \text{ m}^2$

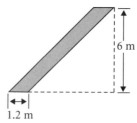

6 m

1.2 m

Do Margin Exercises 14 and 15.

Triangles

To find the area of a triangle, think of cutting out another just like it.

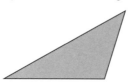

Then place the second one like this.

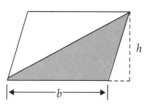

h

b

The resulting figure is a parallelogram whose area is

$b \cdot h$.

The triangle we started with has half the area of the parallelogram, or

$\frac{1}{2} \cdot b \cdot h$.

> The **area of a triangle** is half the length of the base times the height:
> $A = \frac{1}{2} \cdot b \cdot h$.
>
> h
> b

Example 12 Find the area of this triangle.

$A = \frac{1}{2} \cdot b \cdot h$

$A = \frac{1}{2} (9 \text{ m})(6 \text{ m})$

$A = 27 \text{ m}^2$

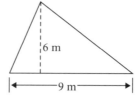

6 m

9 m

Example 13 Find the area of this triangle.

$$A = \frac{1}{2} \cdot b \cdot h$$

$$A = \frac{1}{2} (6.25 \text{ m})(5.5 \text{ m})$$

$$A = (0.5)(6.25)(5.5)\text{cm}^2$$

$$A = 17.1875 \text{ cm}^2$$

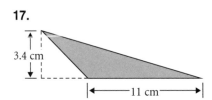

5.5 cm

6.25 cm

Do Margin Exercises 16 and 17

Trapezoids

A **trapezoid** is a polygon with four sides, two of which, the **bases**, are parallel to each other.

To find the area of a trapezoid, think of cutting out another just like it.

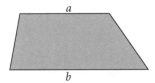

a

b

Then place the second one like this.

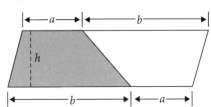

a   *b*

h

b   *a*

The resulting figure is a parallelogram whose area is $h = (a + b)$.

The base is $a + b$.

The trapezoid we started with has half the area of the parallelogram or $\frac{1}{2} \cdot h \cdot (a + b)$.

> The **area of a trapezoid** is half the product of the height and the sum of the lengths of the parallel sides, or the product of the height and the average length of the bases:
>
> $$A = \frac{1}{2} \cdot h \cdot (a + b) = h\left(\frac{a + b}{2}\right).$$

a

h

b

Find the area.

16.

12 m

16 m

17.

3.4 cm

11 cm

Find the area.

18.

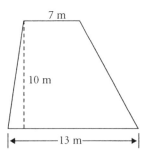

19.

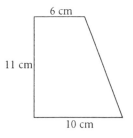

Find the area.

20.

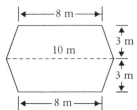

Example 14 Find the area of this trapezoid.

$$A = \frac{1}{2} \cdot h \cdot (a + b)$$

$$= \frac{1}{2} \cdot 7 \text{ cm} \cdot (12 + 18) \text{ cm}$$

$$= \frac{7 \cdot 30}{2} \cdot \text{cm}^2$$

$$= \frac{7 \cdot \overset{15}{\cancel{30}}}{\underset{1}{\cancel{2}}} \text{ cm}^2$$

$$= 105 \text{ cm}^2$$

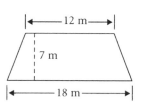

Do Margin Exercises 18 and 19.

Solving Applied Problems

Example 15 Find the area of this kite.

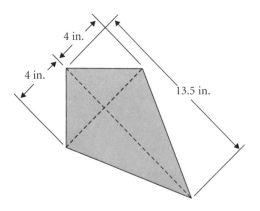

1. *Familiarize.* We look for the kinds of figures whose areas we can calculate using area formulas that we already know.

2. *Translate.* The kite consists of two triangles, each with a base of 13.5 in. and a height of 4 in. We can apply the formula $A = \frac{1}{2} \cdot b \cdot h$ for the area of a triangle and then multiply by 2.

3. *Solve.* We have the area of one triangle:

$$A = \frac{1}{2} \cdot (13.5 \text{ in.}) \cdot (4 \text{ in.}) = 27 \text{ in.}^2$$

Since there are 2 triangles that make up the kite, we multiply by 2:

$$2 \cdot 27 \text{ in.}^2 = 54 \text{ in.}^2$$

4. *Check.* We can check by repeating the calculations.

5. *State.* The area of the kite is 54 in.²

Do Margin Exercise 20.

Exercise Set 9.2

a Find the area.

1.

3000 m
5 km

2.

1.5 ft
18 in.

3.

$\frac{1}{6}$ ft
0.7 in.

4.

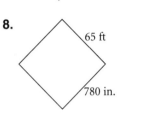

220 cm
3.8 m

5.

$2\frac{1}{2}$ yd
$7\frac{1}{2}$ ft

6.

$3\frac{1}{2}$ mi
18,480 ft

7.

90 ft
30 yd

8.

65 ft
780 in.

b Complete.

9. 1 ft² = _____ in.²

10. 1 yd² = _____ ft²

11. 1 mi² = _____ acres

12. 1 acre = _____ ft²

13. 1 in.² = _____ ft²

14. 1 ft² = _____ yd²

15. 22 yd² = _____ ft²

16. 40 ft² = _____ in.²

17. 44 yd² = _____ ft²

18. 144 ft² = _____ yd²

19. 20 mi² = _____ acres

20. 576 in.² = _____ ft²

21. 1 mi² = _____ ft²

22. 1 mi² = _____ yd²

23. 720 in.² = _____ ft²

24. 27 ft² = _____ yd²

25. 144 in.² = _____ ft²

26. 72 in.² = _____ ft²

27. 1 acre = _____ mi²

28. 4 acres = _____ ft²

29. 5.21 km² = _____ m²

30. 65 km² = _____ m²

31. 0.014 m² = _____ cm²

32. 0.028 m² = _____ mm²

33. 2345.6 mm² = _____ cm²

34. 8.38 cm² = _____ mm²

35. 852.14 cm² = _____ m²

36. 125 mm² = _____ m²

37. 250,000 mm² = _____ cm²

38. 2400 mm² = _____ cm²

39. 472,800 m² = _____ km²

40. 1.37 cm² = _____ mm²

c Find the area.

41.

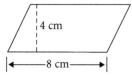

42.

43.

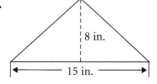

44.

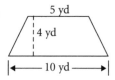

45.

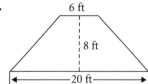

46.

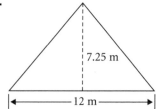

47.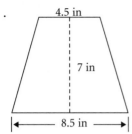
4.5 in
7 in
8.5 in

48.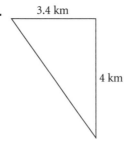
3.4 km
4 km

49.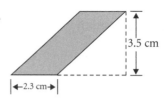
3.5 cm
2.3 cm

50.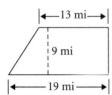
13 mi
9 mi
19 mi

51.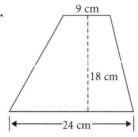
9 cm
18 cm
24 cm

52.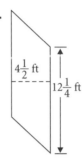
$4\frac{1}{2}$ ft
$12\frac{1}{4}$ ft

53.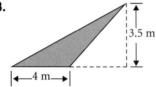
3.5 m
4 m

54.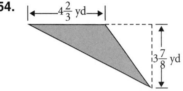
$4\frac{2}{3}$ yd
$3\frac{7}{8}$ yd

b Find the area of the shaded region.

55.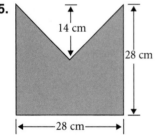
14 cm
28 cm
28 cm

56.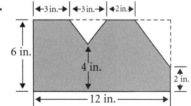
3 in. 3 in. 2 in.
6 in.
4 in.
2 in.
12 in.

57.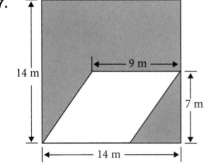
14 m
9 m
7 m
14 m

58. A rectangular piece of sailcloth is 36 ft by 24 ft. A triangular area with a height of 4.6 ft and a base of 5.2 ft is cut from the sailcloth. What is the area of the left over sailcloth?

Skill Maintenance

Convert to fractional notation.

59. 35%

60. 85.5%

61. $37\frac{1}{2}\%$

62. $66.\overline{6}\%$

63. $83.\overline{3}\%$

64. $16\frac{2}{3}\%$

Solve.

65. A ream of paper contains 500 sheets. How many sheets are there in 15 reams?

66. A lab technician separates a vial containing 140 cubic centimeters of blood into test tubes, each of which contains 3 cubic centimeters of blood. How many test tubes can be filled? How much blood is left over?

Synthesis

67. ❖ Explain how the area of a parallelogram can be found by considering the area of a rectangle.

68. ❖ Explain how the area of a triangle can be found by considering the area of a parallelogram.

9.3 Circles

a Radius and Diameter

At the right is a circle with center O. Segment $\overline{AC}$ is a *diameter*. A **diameter** is a segment that passes through the center of the circle and has endpoints on the circle. Segment $\overline{OB}$ is called a *radius*. A **radius** is a segment with one endpoint on the center and the other endpoint on the circle.

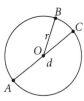

> Suppose that d is the diameter of a circle and r is the radius. Then
> $$d = 2 \cdot r \text{ and } r = \frac{d}{2}$$

Example 1 Find the length of a radius of this circle.

$$r = \frac{d}{2}$$
$$r = \frac{12 \text{ m}}{2}$$
$$r = 6 \text{ m}$$

The radius is 6 m.

Example 2 Find the length of a diameter of this circle.

$$d = 2r$$
$$d = 2 \cdot \frac{1}{4} \text{ ft}$$
$$d = \frac{1}{2} \text{ ft}$$

The diameter is $\frac{1}{2}$ ft.

Do Margin Exercises 1 and 2.

b Circumference

The **circumference** of a circle is the distance around it. Calculating circumference is similar to finding the perimeter of a polygon.

To find a formula for the circumference of any circle given its diameter, we first need to consider the ratio $\frac{C}{d}$. Take a 12-oz soda can and measure the circumference C with a tape measure. Also measure the diameter d. The results are shown in the figure. Then

$$\frac{C}{d} = \frac{7.8 \text{ in.}}{2.5 \text{ in.}} \approx 3.1.$$

$C = 7.8$ in.

$d = 2.5$ in.

Find the area.

1. Find the length of a radius.

18 "

2. Find the length of a diameter.

$2\frac{1}{2}$ ft

Calculator Spotlight

On certain, calculators, there is a pi key, $\boxed{\pi}$.

You can use a $\boxed{\pi}$ key for most computations instead of stopping to round the value of π. Rounding, if necessary, is done at the end.

Exercises

1. If you have a $\boxed{\pi}$ key on your calculator, to how many places does the key give the value of π ?

2. Find the circumference and the area of a circle with a radius of 225.68 in.

3. Find the area of a circle with a diameter of $46\frac{12}{13}$ in.

4. Find the area of a large irrigated farming circle with a diameter of 400 ft.

Answers

1. Varies
2. 1417.99 in.; 160,005.91 in²
3. 1729.27 in²

3. Find the circumference of this circle.

4. Find the circumference of this circle.

Suppose we did this with cans and circles of several sizes. We would get a number close to 3.1. For any circle, if we divide the circumference C by the diameter d, we get the same number. We call this number π (pi). Pi (π) is an irrational number. Irrational numbers are non-ending, non-repeating decimal numbers and therefore cannot be written in fractional form ($\frac{a}{b}$). Pi is not the only irrational number. We will use other irrational numbers later in the chapter.

> $\frac{C}{d} = \pi$ or $C = \pi \cdot d$. The number π is about 3.14, or about $\frac{22}{7}$.
>
> Since the π key on the calculator provides a closer approximation to π than 3.14 or $\frac{22}{7}$, we will use the calculator and round to the nearest thousandth.

Example 3 Find the circumference of this circle.

$C = \pi \cdot d$
$C = \pi (6 \text{ cm})$
$C \approx 18.850 \text{ cm}$

The circumference is about 18.850 cm.

Do Margin Exercise 3.

Since $d = 2 \cdot r$, where r is the length of a radius, it follows that

$C = \pi \cdot d = \pi \cdot (2 \cdot r)$.

> $C = 2 \pi r$

Example 4 Find the circumference of this circle.

$C = 2 \cdot \pi \cdot r$
$C = 2 \cdot \pi \cdot 70 \text{ in.}$
$C \approx 439.823 \text{ in.}$

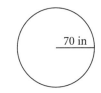

The circumference is about 439.823 in.

Do Margin Exercises 4.

Example 5 Find the perimeter of this figure.

We let P = the perimeter. We see that we have half a circle attached to a square. Thus we add half the circumference to the lengths of the three line segments.

$P = 3 \cdot s + \frac{1}{2}(2\pi r)$

$P = 3(9.4 \text{ km}) + \frac{1}{2}(2 \cdot \pi \cdot 4.7 \text{ km})$

$P \approx 42.965 \text{ km}$

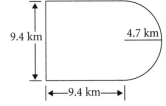

The perimeter is about 42.965 km.

Do Margin Exercise 5.

c Area

Below is a circle of radius *r*.

Think of cutting half the circular region into small pieces and arranging them as shown below.

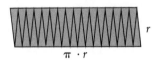

$\pi \cdot r$

Then imagine cutting the other half of the circular region and arranging the pieces in with the others as shown below.

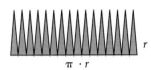

$\pi \cdot r$

This is almost a parallelogram. The base has length $\frac{1}{2} \cdot 2 \cdot \pi \cdot r$, or $\pi \cdot r$ (half the circumference) and the height is *r*. Thus the area is

$(\pi \cdot r) \cdot r$, or πr^2

This is the area of a circle.

> The **area of a circle** with radius of length *r* is given by
>
> $A = \pi \cdot r^2.$

Example 6 Find the area of this circle.

$A = \pi r^2$

$A = \pi (14 \text{ cm})^2$

$A \approx 615.752 \text{ cm}^2$

14 cm

The area is about 615.752 cm².

Do Margin Exercise 6.

---

5. Find the perimeter of this figure.

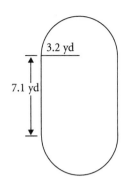

3.2 yd

7.1 yd

6. Find the area of this circle.

5 km

7. Find the area of this circle.

10.4 cm

8. Which is larger and by how much: a 10-ft square flower bed or a 12-ft diameter flower bed?

Example 7 Find the area of this circle. Round to the nearest thousandth.

$A = \pi\,r^2$

$A = \pi\,(2.1\ \text{m})^2$

$A \approx 13.854\ \text{m}^2$

The area is about 13.854 m².

2.1 m

Do Margin Exercise 7.

d Solving Applied Problems

Example 8 *Area of Pizza Pan.* Which makes a larger pizza and by how much: a 16-in. square pizza pan or a 16-in. diameter circular pizza pan?

First, we make a drawing of each.

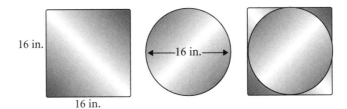

16 in.

16 in.

16 in.

From the drawings we would expect the square pan to have the larger area.

Then we compute areas.

The area of the square is

$A = s^2$

$A = (16\ \text{in.})^2$

$A = 256\ \text{in}^2$

The diameter of the circle is 16 in., so the radius is $\dfrac{16\ \text{in.}}{2}$, or 8 in. The area of the circle is

$A = \pi\,r^2$

$A = \pi\,(8\ \text{in.})^2$

$A \approx 201.062\ \text{in}^2$

We see that the square pizza pan is larger by about

256 in.² − 201.062 in.², or 54.938 in.²

Thus the square pan makes the larger pizza, by about 54.938 in.²

Do Margin Exercise 8.

Exercise Set 9.3

a, **b**, **c** For each circle, find the length of a diameter, the circumference, and the area. Calculate answers to 3 decimal places using the π key.

1.

7 cm

2.

8 m

3.

$\frac{3}{4}$ in.

4.

$8\frac{2}{3}$ mi

For each circle, find the length of a radius, the circumference, and the area.

5.

32 ft

6.

24 in.

7.

1.4 cm

8.

60.9 km

d Solve.

9. The top of a soda can has a 6-cm diameter. What is its radius? its circumference? its area?

10. A penny has a 1-cm radius. What is its diameter? its circumference? its area?

11. A radio station is allowed by the FCC to broadcast over an area with a radius of 220 mi. How much area is this?

12. *Pizza Areas.* Which is larger and by how much: a 12-in. circular pizza or a 12-in. square pizza?

13. *Dimensions of a Quarter.* The circumference of a quarter is 7.85 cm. What is the diameter? the radius? the area?

14. *Dimensions of a Dime.* The circumference of a dime is 2.23 in. What is the diameter? the radius? the area?

15. *Gypsy-Moth Tape.* To protect an elm tree in your backyard, you need to attach gypsy moth caterpillar tape around the trunk. The tree has a 1.1-ft diameter. What length of tape is needed?

16. *Silo.* A silo has a 10-m diameter. What is its circumference?

17. *Swimming-Pool Walk.* You want to install a 1-yd-wide walk around a circular swimming pool. The diameter of the pool is 20 yd. What is the area of the walk?

18. *Roller-Rink Floor.* A roller rink floor is shown below. What is its area? If hardwood flooring costs $10.50 per square meter, how much will the flooring cost?

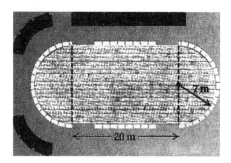

Find the perimeter.

19.

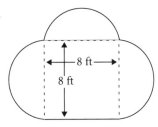

8 ft

8 ft

20.

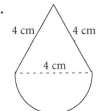

4 cm   4 cm

4 cm

21.

4 yd

4 yd

22.

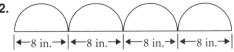

|←—8 in.—→|←—8 in.—→|←—8 in.—→|←—8 in.—→|

23.

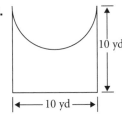

10 yd

|←——— 10 yd ———→|

24.

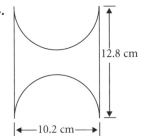

12.8 cm

|←——10.2 cm——→|

Find the area of the shaded region.

25.

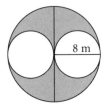

8 m

26.

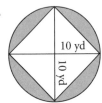

10 yd

10 yd

27. |←——— 2.8 cm ———→|

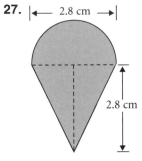

2.8 cm

28.

8 km

8 km

29.

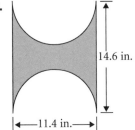

14.6 in.

|←——11.4 in.——→|

30.

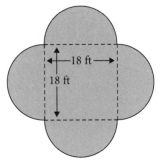

18 ft

18 ft

Skill Maintenance

Convert to percent notation.

31. 0.875   **32.** 0.58   **33.** $0.\overline{6}$ **34.** 0.4361

Convert to percent notation.

35. $\frac{3}{8}$ **36.** $\frac{5}{8}$ **37.** $\frac{2}{3}$ **38.** $\frac{1}{5}$

Change to improper fractions.

39. $3\frac{7}{8}$ **40.** $8\frac{1}{3}$ **41.** $13\frac{1}{6}$ **42.** $39\frac{7}{13}$

Simplify.

43. $\frac{4}{5} + 3\frac{7}{8}$ **44.** $\frac{1}{11} \cdot \frac{7}{15}$ **45.** $\frac{2}{3} + \frac{7}{15} + \frac{8}{9}$ **46.** $\frac{8}{9} + \frac{4}{5} + \frac{13}{14}$

47. $\frac{57}{100} - \frac{1}{10} + \frac{9}{1000}$ **48.** $\frac{23}{24} + \frac{38}{39} + \frac{61}{60}$ **49.** $11\frac{29}{80} + 10\frac{14}{15} \cdot 24\frac{2}{17}$ **50.** $\frac{13}{14} + 9\frac{5}{8} - 1\frac{23}{28} \cdot 1\frac{36}{73}$

Synthesis

51. ❖ Explain why a 16-in.-diameter pizza that costs $16.25 is a better buy than a 10-in.-diameter pizza that costs $7.85.

52. ❖ The radius of one circle is twice the size of another circle's radius. Is the area of the first circle twice the area of the other circle? Why or why not?

53. ▦ The distance from Kansas City to Indianapolis is 500 mi. A car was driven this distance using tires with a radius of 14 in. How many revolutions of each tire occurred on the trip?

54. ▦ $\pi \approx \frac{3927}{1250}$ is another approximation for π. Find decimal notation using a calculator. Round to the nearest thousandth.

55. *Tennis Balls.* Tennis balls are usually packed vertically three in a can, one on top of another. Suppose the diameter of a tennis ball is d. Find the height of the stack of balls. Find the circumference of one ball. Which is greater? Explain.

1. Complete:

5 gal = _____ pt.

2. Complete:

80 qt = _____ gal.

9.4 Capacity, Weight, Mass, and Time

a Capacity

To answer a question like "How much soda is in the can?" we need measures of **capacity**. American units of capacity are ounces, or fluid ounces, cups, pints, quarts, and gallons. These units are related as follows.

> **AMERICAN UNITS OF CAPACITY**
>
> 1 gallon (gal) = 4 quarts (qt)   1 pt = 16 ounces (oz)
> 1 qt = 2 pints (pt)   1 pt = 2 cups
>   1 cup = 8 oz

Example 1 Complete: 9 gal = _____ oz.

We convert as follows:

$$9 \text{ gal} = \frac{9 \text{ gal}}{1} \cdot \frac{4 \text{ qt}}{1 \text{ gal}} \cdot \frac{2 \text{ pt}}{1 \text{ qt}} \cdot \frac{16 \text{ oz}}{1 \text{ pt}}$$

$$= \frac{9 \text{ gal}}{1} \cdot \frac{4 \text{ qt}}{1 \text{ gal}} \cdot \frac{2 \text{ pt}}{1 \text{ qt}} \cdot \frac{16 \text{ oz}}{1 \text{ pt}}$$

$$= (9 \cdot 4 \cdot 2 \cdot 16) \text{ oz}$$

$$= 1152 \text{ oz}$$

Do Margin Exercise 1.

Example 2 Complete: 24 qt = _____ gal.

In this case, we multiply by 1 using 1 gal in the numerator, since we are converting to gallons, and 4 qt in the denominator, since we are converting from quarts.

$$24 \text{ qt} = \frac{24 \text{ qt}}{1} \cdot \frac{1 \text{ gal}}{4 \text{ qt}}$$

$$= \frac{\overset{6}{24 \text{ qt}}}{1} \cdot \frac{1 \text{ gal}}{\underset{1}{4 \text{ qt}}}$$

$$= 6 \text{ gal}$$

After completing Example 2, we can check whether the answer is reasonable. We are converting from smaller to larger units, so our answer has fewer larger units.

Do Margin Exercise 2.

Thinking Metric

The base unit of capacity in the metric system is the **liter.** A liter is just a bit more than a quart. It is defined as follows.

> ### ▶ METRIC UNITS OF CAPACITY
>
> 1 liter (L) = 1000 cubic centimeters (1000 cm³)
>
> The script letter ℓ is also used for "liter."

The metric prefixes are also used with liters. The most common is **milli-**. The milliliter (mL) is, then, $\frac{1}{1000}$ liter. Thus,

> ▶   1 L = 1000 mL = 1000 cm³;
>
> 0.001 L = 1 mL = 1 cm³.

Although the other metric prefixes are rarely used for capacity, we display them in the following table as we did for linear measure.

1000 L	100 L	10 L	1 L	0.1 L	0.01 L	0.001 L
1 kL	1 hL	1 daL	1 L	1 dL	1cL	1 mL (cc)

A preferred unit for drug dosage is the milliliter (mL) or the cubic centimeter (cm³). The notation "cc" is also used for cubic centimeter, especially in medicine. The milliliter and the cubic centimeter represent the same measure of capacity. A milliliter is about $\frac{1}{5}$ of a teaspoon.

> ▶ 1 mL = 1 cm³ = 1 cc

Volumes for which quarts and gallons are used are expressed in liters. Large volumes in business and industry are expressed using measures of cubic meters (m³).

Do Margin Exercises 3–6.

Example 3 Complete: 4.5 L _____ mL.

    4.5 L = 4.5 × 1 L = 4.5 × 1000 mL   Substituting 1000 mL for 1 L
          = 4500 mL

OR

1000 L	100 L	10 L	1 L	0.1 L	0.01 L	0.001 L
1 kL	1 hL	1 daL	1 **L**	1 dL	1cL	1 **mL** (cc)

                              3 places to the right

    4.5 L = 4.500. mL

          = 4500 mL

Complete with mL or L.

3. The patient received an injection of 2 _____ of penicillin.

4. There are 250 _____ in a coffee cup.

5. The gas tank holds 80 _____.

6. Bring home 8 _____ of milk.

Complete.

7. 0.97 L = _____ mL

8. 8990 mL = _____ L

9. A physician ordered 4800 mL, of 0.9% saline solution. How many liters were ordered?

10. A prescription calls for 4 oz of ephedrine.

   a) For how many milliliters is the prescription?

   b) For how many liters is the prescription?

Example 4 Complete: 280 mL = _____ L.

$$280 \text{ mL} = 280 \times 1 \text{ mL}$$
$$= 280 \times 0.001 \text{ L} \qquad \text{Substituting } 0.001 \text{ L for } 1 \text{ mL}$$
$$= 0.28 \text{ L}$$

OR

1000 L	100 L	10 L	1 L	0.1 L	0.01 L	0.001 L
1 kL	1 hL	1 daL	**1 L**	1 dL	1cL	**1 mL** (cc)

3 places to the left

$$280 \text{ mL} = .280. \text{ L}$$
$$= 0.28 \text{ L}$$

Do Margin Exercises 7 and 8.

b **Solving Applied Problems**

The metric system has extensive usage in medicine.

Example 5 *Medical Dosage.* A physician ordered 3.5 L of 5% dextrose in water. How many milliliters were ordered?

We convert 3.5 L to milliliters:

$$3.5 \text{ L} = 3.5 \times 1 \text{ L} = 3.5 \times 1000 \text{ mL} = 3500 \text{ mL}.$$

The physician ordered 3500 mL.

Do Margin Exercise 9.

Example 6 *Medical Dosage.* In pharmaceutical work, liquids at the drugstore are given in liters or milliliters, but a physician's prescription is given in ounces. For conversion, a druggist knows that 1 oz = 29.57 mL. A prescription calls for 3 oz of ephedrine. For how many milliliters is the prescription?

We convert as follows:

$$3 \text{ oz} = \frac{3 \text{ oz}}{1} \cdot \frac{29.57 \text{ mL}}{1 \text{ oz}}$$
$$= \frac{3 \text{ o\!\!\!/z}}{1} \cdot \frac{29.57 \text{ mL}}{1 \text{ o\!\!\!/z}}$$
$$= 3 \, (29.57) \text{mL}$$
$$= 88.71 \text{ mL}.$$

The prescription calls for 88.71 mL of ephedrine.

Do Margin Exercise 10.

c | Weight: The American System

The American units of weight are as follows.

> ▶ **AMERICAN UNITS OF WEIGHT**
>
> $$1 \text{ ton (T)} = 2000 \text{ pounds (lb)}$$
> $$1 \text{ lb} = 16 \text{ ounces (oz)}$$

The term "ounce" used here for weight is different from the "ounce" we use for capacity.

Example 7 A well-known hamburger is called a "quarter-pounder." Find its name in ounces: a "_____ ouncer."

$$\frac{1}{4} \text{ lb} = \frac{1 \text{ lb}}{4} \cdot \frac{16 \text{ oz}}{1 \text{ lb}}$$

$$= \frac{1 \cancel{\text{lb}}}{\cancel{4}_{1}} \cdot \frac{\overset{4}{\cancel{16}} \text{ oz}}{1 \cancel{\text{lb}}}$$

$$= 4 \text{ oz}$$

A "quarter-pounder" can also be called a "four-ouncer."

Example 8 Complete: 15,360 lb = _____ T.

$$15{,}360 \text{ lb} = \frac{15{,}360 \cancel{\text{lb}}}{1} \cdot \frac{1 \text{ T}}{2000 \cancel{\text{lb}}}$$

$$= \frac{15{,}360}{2000} \text{ T}$$

$$= 7.68 \text{ T}$$

Do Margin Exercises 11–13.

d | Mass: The Metric System

There is a difference between **mass** and **weight**, but the terms are often used interchangeably. People sometimes use the word "weight" instead of "mass." Weight is related to the force of gravity. The farther you are from the center of the earth, the less you weigh. Your mass stays the same no matter where you are.

The basic unit of mass is the **gram** (g), which is the mass of 1 cubic centimeter (1 cm³ or 1 mL) of water. Since a cubic centimeter is small, a gram is a small unit of mass.

$$1 \text{ g} = 1 \text{ gram} = \text{the mass of } 1 \text{ cm}^3 \text{ (1 mL) of water}$$

---

11. 5 lb = _____ oz

12. 8640 lb = _____ T

13. 1 T = _____ oz

Complete with mg, g, kg, or t.

14. A laptop computer has a mass of 6 _____.

15. That person has a body mass of 85.4 _____.

16. This is a 3-_____ vitamin.

17. A pen has a mass of 12 _____.

18. A minivan has a mass of 3 _____.

The following table shows the metric units of mass. The prefixes are the same as those for length and capacity.

▶ **METRIC UNITS OF MASS**

1 metric ton (t) = 1000 kilograms (kg)

1 *kilo*gram (kg) = 1000 grams (g)

1 *hecto*gram (hg) = 100 grams (g)

1 *deka*gram (dag) = 10 grams (g)

1 gram (g)

1 *deci*gram (dg) = $\frac{1}{10}$ gram (g)

1 *centi*gram (cg) = $\frac{1}{100}$ gram (g)

1 *milli*gram (mg) = $\frac{1}{1000}$ gram (g)

Thinking Metric

One gram is about the mass of 1 raisin or 1 paperclip. Since 1 kg is about 2.2 lb, 1000 kg is about 2200 lb, or 1 metric ton (t), which is just a little more than 1 American ton (T).

1 gram   1 kilogram   1 pound

Small masses, such as dosages of medicine and vitamins, may be measured in milligrams (mg). The gram (g) is used for objects ordinarily measured in ounces, such as the mass of a letter, a piece of candy, a coin, or a small package of food.

15 g

Each 2.5 mg

2 g

Ground beef
2 lb (0.9 kg)

90 kg

The kilogram (kg) is used for larger food packages, such as meat, or for human body mass. The metric ton (t) is used for very large masses, such as the mass of an automobile, a truckload of gravel, or an airplane.

Do Margin Exercises 14–18.

Changing Units Mentally

As before, changing from one metric unit to another amounts to only the movement of a decimal point. We use this table.

1000 g	100 g	10 g	1 g	0.1 g	0.01 g	0.001 g
1 kg	1 hg	1 dag	1 g	1 dg	1 cg	1 mg

Example 9 Complete: 8 kg = _____ g.

Think: To go from kg to g in the table is a move of three places to the right. Thus we move the decimal point three places to the right.

1000 g	100 g	10 g	1 g	0.1 g	0.01 g	0.001 g
1 **kg**	1 hg	1 dag	1 **g**	1 dg	1 cg	1 mg

3 places to the right

8.0   8.000.   8 kg = 8000 g

Example 10 Complete: 4235 g = _____ kg.

Think: To go from g to kg in the table is a move of three places to the left. Thus we move the decimal point three places to the left.

1000 g	100 g	10 g	1 g	0.1 g	0.01 g	0.001 g
1 **kg**	1 hg	1 dag	1 **g**	1 dg	1 cg	1 mg

3 places to the left

4235.0   4.235.0   4235 g = 4.235 kg

Do Margin Exercises 19 and 20.

Complete.

19. 6.2 kg = _____ g

20. 304.8 cg = _____ g

Complete.

21. 7.7 cg = _____ mg

22. 2344 mg = _____ cg

23. 67 dg = _____ mg

Example 11 Complete: 6.98 cg = _____ mg.

Think: To go from cg to mg is a move of one place to the right. Thus we move the decimal point one place to the right.

1000 g	100 g	10 g	1 g	0.1 g	0.01 g	0.001 g
1 kg	1 hg	1 dag	l g	1 dg	1 **cg**	1 **mg**

1 place to the right

6.98   6.9.8   6.98 cg = 69.8 mg

The most commonly used metric units of mass are kg, g, cg, and mg. We have purposely used those more often than the others in the exercises.

Example 12 Complete: 89.21 mg = _____ g.

Think: To go from mg to g is a move of three places to the left. Thus we move the decimal point three places to the left.

1000 g	100 g	10 g	1 g	0.1 g	0.01 g	0.001 g
1 kg	1 hg	1 dag	l **g**	1 dg	1 cg	1 **mg**

3 places to the left

89.21   0.089.21   89.21 mg = 0.08921 g

Do Margin Exercises 21–23.

e | Time

A table of units of time is shown below. The metric system sometimes uses "h" for hour and "s" for second, but we will use the more familiar "hr" and "sec."

> **UNITS OF TIME**
>
> 1 day = 24 hours (hr)   1 year (yr) = $365\frac{1}{4}$ days
>
>   1 hr = 60 minutes (min)
>   1 week (wk) = 7 days
>   1 min = 60 seconds (sec)

Since we cannot have $\frac{1}{4}$ day on the calendar, we give each year 365 days and every fourth year 366 days (a leap year), unless it is a year at the beginning of a century not divisible by 400.

Example 13 Complete: 1 hr = _____ sec.

$$1 \text{ hr} = \frac{1 \cancel{hr}}{1} \cdot \frac{60 \cancel{min}}{1 \cancel{hr}} \cdot \frac{60 \text{ sec}}{1 \cancel{min}}$$

$$= (60 \cdot 60) \text{ sec}$$

$$= 3600 \text{ sec}$$

Example 14 Complete: 5 yr = _____ days.

$$5 \text{ yr} = \frac{5 \cancel{yr}}{1} \cdot \frac{365\frac{1}{4} \text{ days}}{1 \cancel{yr}}$$

$$= (5 \cdot 365\frac{1}{4}) \text{ days}$$

$$= 1826\frac{1}{4} \text{ days}$$

Example 15 Complete: 4320 min = _____ days.

$$4320 \text{ min} = 4320 \cancel{min} \cdot \frac{1 \cancel{hr}}{60 \cancel{min}} \cdot \frac{1 \text{ day}}{24 \cancel{hr}}$$

$$= \frac{4320}{60 \cdot 24} \text{ days}$$

$$= 3 \text{ days}$$

Do Margin Exercises 24–27.

Complete.

24. 2hr = _____ min

25. 4 yr = _____ days

26. 1 day = _____ min

27. 168 hr = _____ wk

9.4 Exercise Set

a Complete.

1. I L = _____ mL = _____ cm^3

2. _____ L = 1 mL = _____ cm^3

3. 87 L = _____ mL

4. 806 L = _____ mL

5. 49 mL = _____ L

6. 19 mL = _____ L

7. 0.401 mL = _____ L

8. 0.816 mL = _____ L

9. 78.1 L = _____ cm^3

10. 99.6 L = _____ cm^3

11. 10 qt = _____ oz

12. 9.6 oz = _____ pt

13. 20 cups = _____ pt

14. 1 gal = _____ oz

15. 8 gal = _____ qt

16. 1 gal = _____ cups

b Solve.

17. *Medical Dosage.* A physician ordered 0.5 L of normal saline solution. How many millilliters were ordered?

18. *Medical Dosage.* A patient received 84 mL per hour of normal saline solution. How many liters did the patient receive in a 24-hr period?

19. *Medical Dosage.* A doctor wants a patient to receive 3 L of a normal saline solution in a 24-hr period. How many milliliters per hour must the nurse administer?

20. *Medical Dosage.* A doctor tells a patient to purchase 0.5 L of hydrogen peroxide. Commerically, hydrogen peroxide is found on the shelf in bottles that hold 4 oz, 8oz, and 16oz. Which bottle comes closest to filling the prescription? (1 qt = 32 oz)

21. *Wasting Water.* Many people leave the water running while they are brushing their teeth. Suppose that 32 oz of water is wasted in such a way each day by one person. How much water, in gallons, is wasted in a week? in a month (30 days)? in a year? Assuming each of the 261 million people in this country wastes water in this way, estimate how much water is wasted in a day; in a year.

22. Each can in a six-pack of cola contains 12 oz. How many pints are in a six-pack of cola?

c Complete.

23. 1 T = _____ lb

24. 1 lb= _____ oz

25. 6000 lb = _____ T

26. 8 T = _____ lb

27. 4 lb = _____ oz

28. 10 lb = _____ oz

29. 6.32 T = _____ lb

30. 8.07 T = _____ lb

31. 3200 oz = _____ T

32. 6400 oz = _____ T

33. 80 oz = _____ lb

34. 960 oz = _____ lb

d Complete.

35. 1 kg = _____ g

36. 1 hg = _____ g

37. 1 dag = _____ g

38. 1 dg = _____ g

39. 1 cg = _____ g

40. 1 mg = _____ g

41. 1 g = _____ mg

42. 1 g = _____ cg

43. 1 g = _____ dg

44. 25 kg = _____ g

45. 234 kg = _____ g

46. 9403 g = _____ kg

47. 5200 g = _____ kg

48. 1.506 kg = _____ g

49. 67 hg = _____ kg

50. 45 cg = _____ g

51. 0.502 dg = _____ g

52. 0.0025 cg = _____ mg

53. 8492 g = _____ kg

54. 9466 g = _____ kg

55. 585 mg = _____ cg

56. 96.1 mg = _____ cg

57. 8 kg = _____ cg

58. 0.06 kg = _____ mg

59. 1 t = _____ kg

60. 2 t = _____ kg

61. 3.4 cg = _____ dag

62. 115 mg = _____ g

e Complete.

63. 1 day = _____ hr

64. 1 hr = _____ min

65. 1 min = _____ sec

66. 1 wk = _____ days

67. 1 yr = _____ days

68. 2 yr = _____ days

69. 180 sec = _____ hr

70. 60 sec = _____ hr

71. 492 sec = _____ min
(the amount of time it takes for
the rays of the sun to reach the
earth)

72. 18,000 sec = _____ hr

73. 156 hr = _____ days

74. 444 hr = _____ days

75. 645 min = _____ hr

76. 375 min = _____ hr

77. 2 wk = _____ hr

78. 4 hr = _____ sec

79. 756 hr = _____ wk

80. 166,320 min = _____ wk

81. 2922 wk = _____ yr

82. 623 days = _____ wk

Skills Maintenance

83. Find the simple interest on $600 at 6.4% for $\frac{1}{2}$ yr. **84.** Find the simple interest on $600 at 8% for 2 yr.

Evaluate.

85. 10^3 **86.** 15^2 **87.** 7^2 **88.** 4^3

Solve.

89. *Sales Tax.* In a certain state, a sales tax of $878 is collected on the purchase of a car for $17,560. What is the sales tax rate?

90. *Commission Rate.* Rich earns $1854.60 selling $16,860 worth of cellular phones. What is the commission rate?

Synthesis

91. ❖ What advantages does the use of metric units of capacity have over that of American units?

92. ❖ Give at least two reasons why someone might prefer the use of grams to the use of ounces.

93. ❖ Describe a situation in which one object weighs 70 kg, another object weighs 3 g, and a third object weighs 125 mg.

Complete. Use 1 kg = 2.205 lb and 453.5 g = 1 lb. Round to four decimal places.

94. ▦ 1 lb = _____ kg

95. ▦ 1 g = _____ lb

96. Estimate the number of years in one million seconds.

97. Estimate the number of years in one billion seconds.

98. Estimate the number of years in one trillion seconds.

Medical Applications. Another metric unit used in medicine is the microgram (μg). It is defined as follows.

> ▶ 1 microgram = 1 μg = $\frac{1}{1,000,000}$ g;   1,000,000 μg = 1g

Thus a microgram is one millionth of a gram, and one million micrograms is one gram.

Complete.

99. 1 mg =_____ μg

100. 1 μg = _____ mg

101. A physician orders 125 μg of digoxin. For how many milligrams is the prescription?

102. A physician orders 0.25 mg of reserpine. For how many micrograms is the prescription?

103. A medicine called sulfisoxazole usually comes in tablets that are 500 mg each. A standard dosage is 2 g. How many tablets would have to be taken in order to achieve this dosage?

104. Quinidine is a liquid mixture, part medicine and part water. There is 80 mg of Quinidine for every milliliter of liquid. A standard dosage is 200 mg. How much of the liquid mixture would be required in order to achieve the dosage?

105. A medicine called cephalexin is obtainable in a liquid mixture, part medicine and part water. There is 250 mg of cephalexin in 5 mL of liquid. A standard dosage is 400 mg. How much of the liquid would be required in order to achieve the dosage?

106. A medicine called Albuterol is used for the treatment of asthma. It typically comes in an inhaler that contains 18 g. One actuation, or inhalation, is 90 mg.
a) How many actuations are in one inhaler?
b) A student is going away for 4 months of college and wants to take enough Albuterol to last for that time. Assuming that she will need 4 actuations per day, estimate about how many inhalers the student will need for the 4-month period.

9.5 Volume

a Rectangular Solids

The **volume** of a **rectangular solid** is the number of unit cubes needed to fill it.

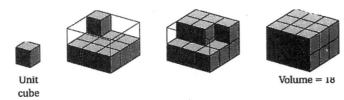

Unit cube

Volume = 18

Two other units are shown below.

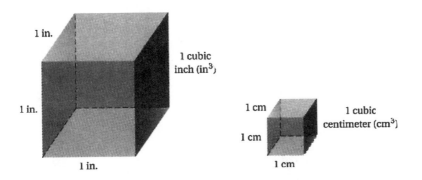

1 in.

1 in.

1 in.

1 cubic inch (in³)

1 cm

1 cm

1 cm

1 cubic centimeter (cm³)

Example 1 Find the volume.

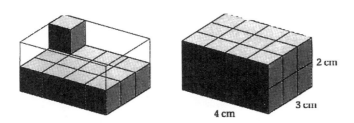

2 cm

3 cm

4 cm

The figure is made up of 2 layers of 12 cubes each, so its volume is 24 cubic centimeters (cm³).

Do Margin Exercise 1.

▶ The **volume of a rectangular solid** is found by multiplying length by width by height:

$$V = l \cdot w \cdot h.$$

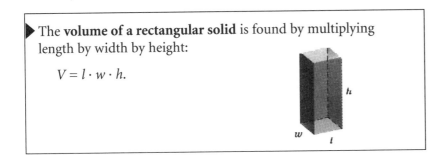

h

w

l

1. Find the volume.

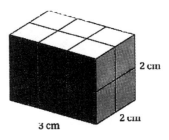

2 cm

3 cm

2 cm

2. In a recent year, people in the United States bought enough unpopped popcorn to provide every person in the country with a bag of popped corn measuring 2 ft by 2 ft by 5 ft. Find the volume of such a bag.

3. *Cord of Wood.* A cord of wood is 4 ft by 4 ft by 8 ft. What is the volume of a cord of wood?

4. Find the volume of the cylinder.

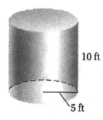

10 ft

5 ft

5. Find the volume of the cylinder.

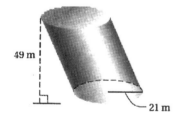

49 m

21 m

Example 2 The largest piece of luggage that you can carry on an airplane meaures 23 in. by 10 in. by 13 in. Find the volume of this solid.

$$V = l \cdot w \cdot h$$
$$V = (23 \text{ in.})(10 \text{ in.})(13 \text{ in.})$$
$$V = 2990 \text{ in}^3$$

Do Margin Exercise 2 and 3.

b | Cylinders

A rectangular solid is shown below. Note that we can think of the volume as the product of the area of the base times the height:

$$V = l \cdot w \cdot h$$
$$V = (l \cdot w) \cdot h$$
$$V = (\text{Area of the base}) \cdot h$$
$$V = B \cdot h,$$

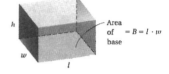

where B represents the area of the base.

Like rectangular solids, **circular cylinders** have bases of equal area that lie in parallel planes. The bases of circular cylinders are circular regions.

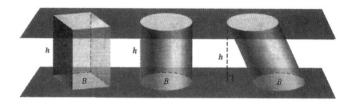

The volume of a circular cylinder is found in a manner similar to finding the volume of a rectangular solid. The volume is the product of the area of the base times the height. The height is always measured perpendicular to the base.

> ▶ The **volume of a circular cylinder** is the product of the area of the base B and the height h:
>
> $$V = B \cdot h, \quad \text{or} \quad V = \pi \cdot r^2 \cdot h$$

Example 3 Find the volume of this circular cylinder.

$$V = Bh = \pi \cdot r^2 \cdot h$$
$$V = \pi (4 \text{ cm})^2 (12 \text{ cm})$$
$$V \approx 603.186 \text{ cm}^3$$

12 cm

4 cm

Do Margin Exercises 4 and 5.

c | Spheres

A **sphere** is the three-dimensional counterpart of a circle. It is the set of all points in space that are a given distance (the radius) from a given point (the center).

We find the volume of a sphere as follows.

> ▶ The **volume of a sphere** of radius r is given by
> $$V = \frac{4}{3} \cdot \pi \cdot r^3.$$

Example 4 *Bowling Ball.* The radius of a standard-sized bowling ball is 4.2915 in. Find the volume of a standard-sized bowling ball. Round to the nearest thousandth of a cubic inch.

$$V = \frac{4}{3} \cdot \pi \cdot r^3$$
$$V = \frac{4}{3}\pi(4.2915 \text{ in.})^3$$
$$V \approx 331.067 \text{ in.}^3$$

Do Margin Exercises 6 and 7.

d | Cones

Consider a circle in a plane and choose any point P not in the plane. The circular region, together with the set of all segments connecting P to a point on the circle, is called a **circular cone**.

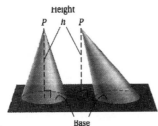

We find the volume of a cone as follows.

> ▶ The **volume of a circular cone** with base radius r is one-third the product of the base area and the height:
> $$V = \frac{1}{3} \cdot B \cdot h = \frac{1}{3}\pi \cdot r^2 \cdot h$$

Example 5 Find the volume of this circular cone.

$$V = \frac{1}{3}\pi \cdot r^2 \cdot h$$
$$V = \frac{1}{3}\pi(3 \text{ cm})^2(7 \text{ cm})$$
$$V \approx 65.973 \text{ cm}^3$$

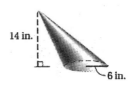

Do Margin Exercises 8 and 9.

6. Find the volume of the sphere.

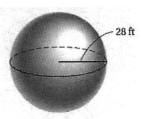

7. The radius of a standard-sized golf ball is 2.1 cm. Find its volume.

8. Find the volume of this cone.

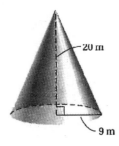

9. Find the volume of this cone.

10. *Medicine Capsule.* A cold capsule is 8 mm long and 4 mm in diameter. Find the volume of the capsule. (*Hint:* First find the length of the cylindrical section.)

Calculator Spotlight

Exercises

1. *Measuring the volume of a cloud.* Using a calculator with a $\boxed{\pi}$ key, find the volume of a spherical cloud with a 1000-m diameter.

2. The box shown is just big enough to hold 3 golf balls. If the radius of a golf ball is 2.1 cm, how much air surrounds the three balls?

Answers

1. 523,598,775.6 m³
2. 105.887 cm³

e | Solving Applied Problems

Example 6 *Propane Gas Tank.* A propane gas tank is shaped like a circular cylinder with half of a sphere at each end. Find the volume of the tank if the cylindrical section is 5 ft long with a 4-ft diameter.

1. Familiarize. We first make a drawing.

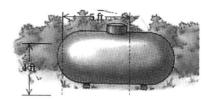

2. Translate. This is a two-step problem. We first find the volume of the cylindrical portion. Then we find the volume of the two ends and add. Note that the radius is 2 ft and that together the two ends make a sphere.

When V is total volume, we have

Total volume	is	Volume of the cylinder	plus	Volume of the sphere
$\downarrow$	$\downarrow$	$\downarrow$	$\downarrow$	$\downarrow$
V	$=$	$\pi \cdot r^2 \cdot h$	$+$	$\frac{4}{3} \cdot \pi \cdot r^3$
V	$=$	$\pi \cdot (2 \text{ ft})^2 \cdot 5 \text{ ft}$	$+$	$\frac{4}{3} \cdot \pi \cdot (2 \text{ ft})^3.$

3. Solve. The volume of the cylinder is approximately

$$V \approx \pi \, (2 \text{ ft})^2 \, (5 \text{ ft})$$
$$V \approx 62.832 \text{ ft}^3$$

The volume of the two ends is approximately

$$V = \frac{4}{3}\pi \, (2 \text{ ft})^3$$
$$V \approx 33.510 \text{ ft}^3$$

The total volume is approximately

$$V \approx 62.832 \text{ ft}^3 + 33.510 \text{ ft}^3$$
$$V \approx 96.342 \text{ ft}^3.$$

4. Check. The check is left to the student.

5. State. The volume of the tank is about 96.342 ft³.

Do Margin Exercise 10.

Exercise Set 9.5

a Find the volume.

1.

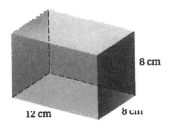

8 cm

12 cm   8 cm

2.

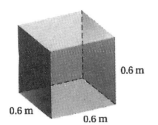

0.6 m

0.6 m   0.6 m

3.

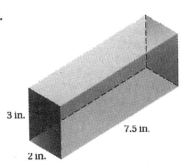

3 in.   7.5 in.

2 in.

4.

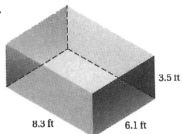

3.5 ft

8.3 ft   6.1 ft

5.

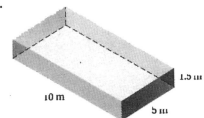

1.5 m

10 m   5 m

6.

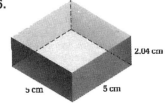

2.04 cm

5 cm   5 cm

7.

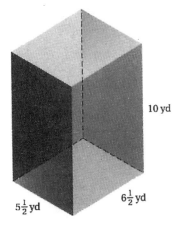

10 yd

$5\frac{1}{2}$ yd $6\frac{1}{2}$ yd

8.

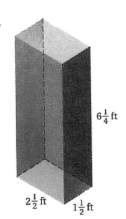

$6\frac{1}{4}$ ft

$2\frac{1}{2}$ ft $1\frac{1}{2}$ ft

b Find the volume of the circular cylinder.

9.

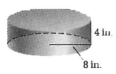

4 in.

8 in.

10.

13 ft

10 ft

11.

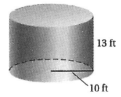

4.5 cm

5 cm

12.

40 cm

4 cm

13.

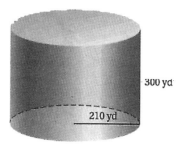

300 yd

210 yd

14.

28 km

4 km

c Find the volume of the sphere.

15.

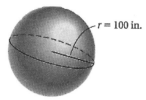

r = 100 in.

16.

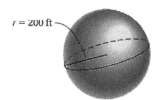

r = 200 ft

17.

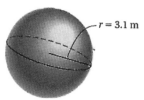

r = 3.1 m

18.

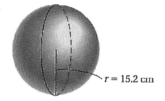

r = 15.2 cm

19.

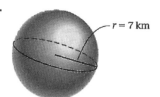

r = 7 km

20.

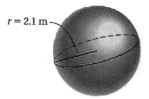

r = 2.1 m

d Find the volume of the circular cone.

21.

100 ft

33 ft

22.

10 m

3 m

23.

12 cm

1.4 cm

24.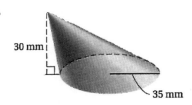

30 mm

35 mm

e Solve.

25. The diameter of the base of a circular cylinder is 14 yd. The height is 220 yd. Find the volume.

26. A rung of a ladder is 2 in. in diameter and 16 in. long. Find the volume.

27. *Barn Silo.* A barn silo, excluding the top, is a circular cylinder. The silo is 6 m in diameter and the height is 13 m. Find the volume.

28. A log of wood has a diameter of 12 cm and a height of 42 cm. Find the volume.

29. *Tennis Ball.* The diameter of a tennis ball is 6.5 cm. Find the volume.

30. *Spherical Gas Tank.* The diameter of a spherical gas tank is 6 m. Find the volume.

31. *Volume of Earth.* The diameter of the earth is about 3980 mi. Find the volume of the earth. Round to the nearest ten thousand cubic miles.

32. The volume of a ball is 36π cm³. Find the dimensions of a rectangular box that is just large enough to hold the ball.

Skill Maintenance

Convert.

33. 11 yd = _____ in.

34. 15,840 ft = _____ mi

35. 42 ft = _____ yd

36. 48 mi = _____ ft

37. 144 in. = _____ ft

38. 5.3 mi = _____ in.

Synthesis

39. ❖ The design of a modern home includes a cylindrical tower that will be capped with either a 10-ft-high dome or a 10-ft-high cone. Which type of cap will be more energy-efficient and why?

40. ▦ A 2-cm-wide stream of water passes through a 30-m garden hose. At the instant that the water is turned off, how many liters of water are in the hose?

41. ▦ A hot water tank is a right circular cylinder with a base of diameter 16 in and height 5 ft. Find the volume of the tank in cubic feet. One cubic foot of water is about 7.5 gal. About how many gallons will the tank hold?

42. ▦ An ice cream cone with a $1\frac{1}{4}$-in. radius and a $4\frac{1}{2}$-in. depth is filled. How much ice cream is in the cone?

Name the angle in four different ways.

1.

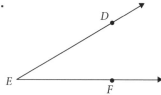

2.

9.6 Angles and Triangles

a Measuring Angles

An **angle** is a set of points consisting of two **rays**, or half-lines, with a common endpoint. The endpoint is called the **vertex**.

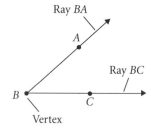

The rays are called the *sides*. The angle above can be named

angle *ABC*,   ∠*ABC*,   ∠*CBA*,   or   ∠*B*.

Note that the name of the vertex is either in the middle or, if no confusion results, listed by itself.

Do Margin Exercises 1 and 2.

Measuring angles is similar to measuring segments. To measure angles, we start with some arbitrary angle and assign to it a measure of 1 unit. We call it a *unit angle*. Suppose that ∠*U*, below, is a unit angle. Let's measure ∠*DEF*. If we made 3 copies of ∠*U*, they would "fill up" ∠DEF. Thus the measure of ∠*DEF* would be 3 units.

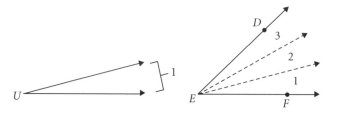

The unit most commonly used for angle measure is the degree. Below is such a unit. Its measure is 1 degree, or 1°.

Here are some other angles with their degree measures.

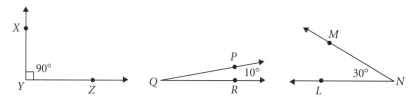

To indicate the *measure* of ∠*XYZ*, we write *m* ∠*XYZ* = 90°. The symbol □ is sometimes drawn on a figure to indicate a 90° angle.

A device called a **protractor** is used to measure angles. Protractors have two scales. To measure an angle like ∠Q below, we place the protractor's ▲ at the vertex and line up one of the angle's sides at 0°. Then we check where the angle's other side crosses the scale. In the figure below, 0° is on the inside scale, so we check where the angle's other side crosses the inside scale. We see that m ∠Q = 145°. The notation m ∠Q is read "the measure of angle Q."

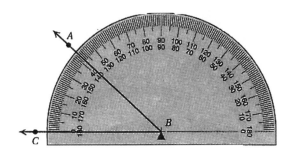

Do Margin Exercise 3.

Let's find the measure of ∠ABC. This time we will use the 0° on the outside scale. We see that m ∠ABC = 42°.

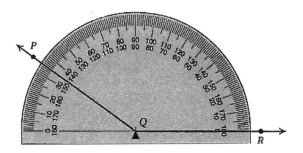

Do Margin Exercise 4.

3. Use a protractor to measure this angle.

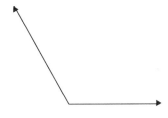

4. Use a protractor to measure this angle.

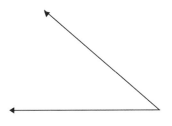

Classify the angle as right, straight, acute, or obtuse. Use a protractor if necessary,

5.

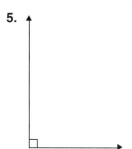

6.

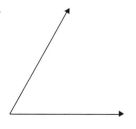

7.

8.

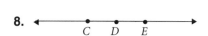

The following are ways in which we classify angles.

> ▶ **Right angle:** An angle whose measure is 90°.
>
> **Straight angle:** An angle whose measure is 180°.
>
> **Acute angle:** An angle whose measure is greater than 0° and less than 90°.
>
> **Obtuse angle:** An angle whose measure is greater than 90° and less than 180°.

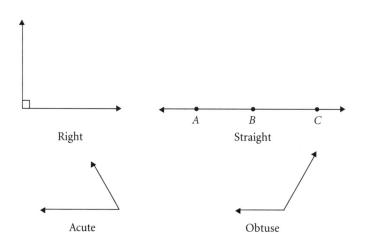

Do Margin Exercises 5–8.

c **Triangles**

A **triangle** is a polygon made up of three segments, or sides. Consider these triangles. The triangle with vertices *A*, *B*, and *C* can be named △*ABC*.

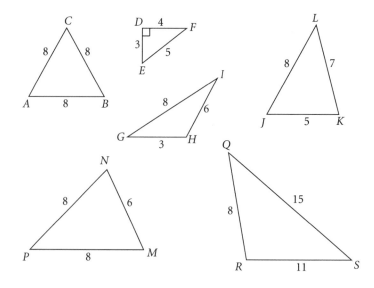

We can classify triangles according to sides and according to angles.

> **Equilateral triangle:** All sides are the same length.

Isosceles triangle: Two or more sides are the same length.

Scalene triangle: All sides are of different lengths.

Right triangle: One angle is a right angle.

Obtuse triangle: One angle is an obtuse angle.

Acute triangle: All three angles are acute.

Do Margin Exercises 9–12.

d | Sum of the Angle Measures of a Triangle

The sum of the angle measures of a triangle is 180°. To see this, note that we can think of cutting apart a triangle as shown on the left below. If we reassemble the pieces, we see that a straight angle is formed.

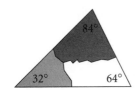 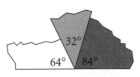

$$64° + 32° + 84° = 180°$$

> In any triangle *ABC*, the sum of the measures of the angles is 180°:
>
> $$m(\angle A) + m(\angle B) + m(\angle C) = 180°.$$

Do Margin Exercise 13.

If we know the measures of two angles of a triangle, we can calculate the third.

Example 1 Find the missing angle measure.

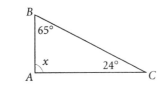

$$m(\angle A) + m(\angle B) + m(\angle C) = 180°$$
$$x + 65° + 24° = 180°$$
$$x + 89° = 180°$$
$$x + 89° - 89° = 180° - 89°$$
$$x = 91°$$

Do Margin Exercise 14.

9. Which triangles on the previous page are:
   a) equilateral?
   b) isosceles?
   c) scalene?

10. Are all equilateral triangles isosceles?

11. Are all isosceles triangles equilateral?

12. Which triangles on the previous page are:
    a) right triangles?
    b) obtuse triangles?
    c) acute triangles?

13. Find $m(\angle P) + m(\angle Q) + m(\angle R)$.

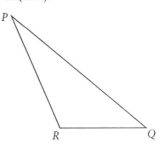

14. Find the missing angle measure.

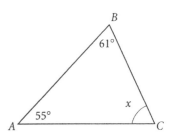

Exercise Set 9.6

[a] Name the angle in four different ways.

1.

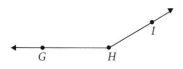

2.

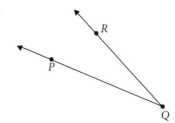

Use a protractor to measure the angle.

3.

4.

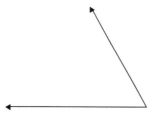

5.

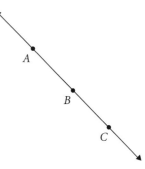

6.

7.

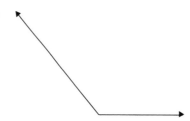

8.

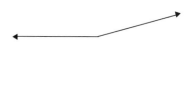

[b]

9.–16. Classify each of the angles in Exercises 1–8 as right, straight, acute, or obtuse.

17.–20. Classify each of the angles in Margin Exercises 1–4 as right, straight, acute, or obtuse.

[c] Classify the triangle as equilateral, isosceles, or scalene. Then classify it as right, obtuse, or acute.

21.

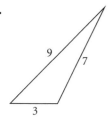

22.

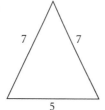

23.

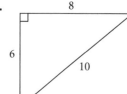

24.

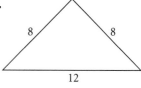

25.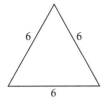

26.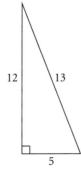

27.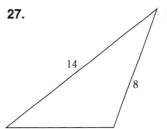

28.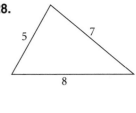

d Find the missing angle measure.

29.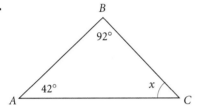

30.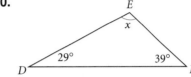

31.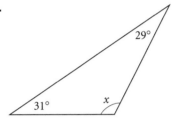

32.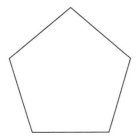

Skill Maintenance

In each of Exercises 33–36, find the simple interest.

33. On $24,000 at an interest rate of 6.4% for 3 yr

34. On $8500 at an interest rate of 10% for 2.5 yr

35. On $6400 at an interest rate of 9.6% for 150 days

36. On $4200 at an interest rate of 10.5% for 60 days

Synthesis

37. ❖ Explain how you might use triangles to find the sum of the angle measures of this figure.

38. Find $m \angle ACB$, $m \angle CAB$, $m \angle EBC$, $m \angle EBA$, $m \angle AEB$, and $m \angle ADB$ in the rectangle shown below.

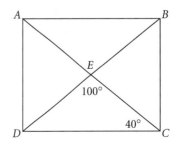

Find the square.

1. 9^2 **2.** 10^2

3. 11^2 **4.** 12^2

> It would be helpful to memorize the squares of numbers from 1 to 25.

5. 13^2 **6.** 14^2

7. 15^2 **8.** 16^2

9. 17^2 **10.** 18^2

11. 20^2 **12.** 25^2

Simplify. The results of Exercises 1–12 above may be helpful here.

13. $\sqrt{9}$ **14.** $\sqrt{16}$

15. $\sqrt{121}$ **16.** $\sqrt{100}$

17. $\sqrt{81}$ **18.** $\sqrt{64}$

19. $\sqrt{324}$ **20.** $\sqrt{400}$

21. $\sqrt{225}$ **22.** $\sqrt{169}$

23. $\sqrt{1}$ **24.** $\sqrt{0}$

9.7 Square Roots and the Pythagorean Theorem

a   Square Roots

> ▶ If a number is a product of two identical factors, then either factor is called a **square root** of the number. (If $a = c^2$, then c is a square root of a.) The symbol $\sqrt{}$ (called a **radical sign**) is used in naming square roots.

For example, $\sqrt{36}$ is read as "the square root of 36."

$$\sqrt{36} = \sqrt{6 \cdot 6} = 6 \qquad \text{The square root of 36 is 6 because } 6^2 = 36.$$

Example 1   Simplify: $\sqrt{25}$.

$$\sqrt{25} = \sqrt{5 \cdot 5} = 5 \qquad \text{The square root of 25 is 5 because } 5^2 = 25.$$

Example 2   Simplify: $\sqrt{144}$.

$$\sqrt{144} = \sqrt{12 \cdot 12} = 12 \qquad \text{The square root of 144 is 12 because } 12^2 = 144.$$

CAUTION! It is common to confuse squares and square roots. A number squared is that number multiplied by itself. For example, $16^2 = 16 \cdot 16 = 256$. A square root of a number is a number that when multiplied by itself gives the original number. For example, $\sqrt{16} = 4$, because $4 \cdot 4 = 16$.

Examples   Simplify.

3. $\sqrt{4} = 2$ **4.** $\sqrt{256} = 16$ **5.** $\sqrt{361} = 19$

Do Margin Exercises 1–24.

b   Approximating Square Roots

Square roots of some numbers are irrational numbers. For example,

$$\sqrt{2}, \quad \sqrt{3}, \quad \sqrt{39}, \quad \text{and} \quad \sqrt{70}$$

are irrational numbers. We can approximate these square roots. For example, consider the following decimal approximations for $\sqrt{2}$. Each gives a closer approximation.

$$\sqrt{2} \approx 1.4 \qquad \text{because } (1.4)^2 = 1.96,$$
$$\sqrt{2} \approx 1.41 \qquad \text{because } (1.41)^2 = 1.9881,$$
$$\sqrt{2} \approx 1.414 \qquad \text{because } (1.414)^2 = 1.999396,$$
$$\sqrt{2} \approx 1.4142 \qquad \text{because } (1.4142)^2 = 1.99996164.$$

How do we find such approximations? We use a calculator.

Example 6 Approximate $\sqrt{3}$, $\sqrt{27}$, and $\sqrt{180}$ to three decimal places. Use a calculator.

We use a calculator to find each square root. Since more than three decimal places are given, we round back to three places.

$$\sqrt{3} \approx 1.732,$$
$$\sqrt{27} \approx 5.196,$$
$$\sqrt{180} \approx 13.416.$$

As a check, note that $1 \cdot 1 = 1$ and $2 \cdot 2 = 4$, so we expect $\sqrt{3}$ to be between 1 and 2. Similarly, we expect $\sqrt{27}$ to be between 5 and 6 and $\sqrt{180}$ to be between 13 and 14.

Do Margin Exercises 25–27.

c The Pythagorean Theorem

A **right triangle** is a triangle with a 90° angle, as shown here.

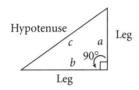

In a right triangle, the longest side is called the **hypotenuse**. It is also the side opposite the right angle. The other two sides are called **legs**. We generally use the letters *a* and *b* for the lengths of the legs and *c* for the length of the hypotenuse. They are related as follows.

▶ **The Pythagorean Theorem**

In any right triangle, if *a* and *b* are the lengths of the legs and *c* is the length of the hypotenuse, then

$$a^2 + b^2 = c^2, \text{ or}$$
$$(\text{Leg})^2 + (\text{Other leg})^2 = (\text{Hypotenuse})^2.$$

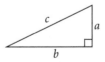

The equation $a^2 + b^2 = c^2$ is called the **Pythagorean equation**.

Approximate to three decimal places.

25. $\sqrt{5}$

26. $\sqrt{78}$

27. $\sqrt{168}$

Calculator Spotlight

Most calculators have a square root key, $\boxed{\sqrt{\ }}$. On some calculators, square roots are found by pressing the $\boxed{x^2}$ key after first pressing a key labeled $\boxed{\text{2nd}}$ or $\boxed{\text{SHFT}}$. (On these calculators, finding square roots is a secondary function.)

To find an approximation for $\sqrt{30}$, we simply press

$\boxed{\text{2nd}}$ $\boxed{\sqrt{\ }}$ $\boxed{3}$ $\boxed{0}$ $\boxed{\text{ENTER}}$.

The value 5.477225575 appears.

It is always best to wait until calculations are complete before rounding off. For example, to round $9 \cdot \sqrt{5}$ to the nearest tenth, we do *not* first determine that $\sqrt{5} \approx 2.2$. Rather, we press

$\boxed{9}$ $\boxed{\times}$ $\boxed{\text{2nd}}$ $\boxed{\sqrt{\ }}$ $\boxed{5}$ $\boxed{\text{ENTER}}$.

The result, 20.1246118, is then rounded to 20.1.

Exercises

Round to the nearest tenth.

1. $\sqrt{43}$ 2. $\sqrt{94}$
3. $7 \cdot \sqrt{8}$ 4. $5 \cdot \sqrt{12}$
5. $\sqrt{35} + 19$ 6. $17 + \sqrt{57}$
7. $13 \cdot \sqrt{68} + 14$
8. $24 \cdot \sqrt{31} - 18$
9. $5 \cdot \sqrt{30} - 3 \cdot \sqrt{14}$
10. $7 \cdot \sqrt{90} + 3 \cdot \sqrt{40}$

28. Find the length of the hypotenuse of this right triangle. Give an exact answer and an approximation to three decimal places.

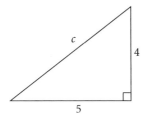

The **Pythagorean theorem** is named for the Greek mathematician Pythagoras (569?-500? B.C.). We can think of this relationship as adding areas.

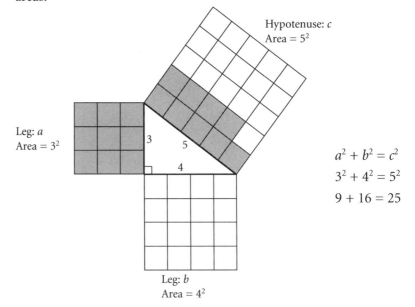

$$a^2 + b^2 = c^2$$
$$3^2 + 4^2 = 5^2$$
$$9 + 16 = 25$$

If we know the lengths of any two sides of a right triangle, we can use the Pythagorean equation to determine the length of the third side.

Example 7 Find the length of the hypotenuse of this right triangle. Give an exact answer and an approximation to three decimal places.

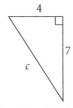

We substitute 4 for a and 7 for b in the Pythagorean equation:

$$a^2 + b^2 = c^2$$
$$4^2 + 7^2 = c^2 \qquad \text{Substituting}$$
$$16 + 49 = c^2$$
$$65 = c^2.$$

The solution of this equation is the square root of 65. We approximate the square root using a calculator.

Exact answer: $\qquad\qquad c = \sqrt{65}$
Approximate answer: $\qquad c \approx 8.062 \qquad$ Using a calculator

Do Margin Exercise 28.

Example 8 Find the length b for the right triangle shown. Give an exact answer and an approximation to three decimal places.

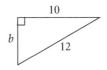

We substitute in the Pythagorean equation. Next we solve for b^2 and then b, as follows:

$$a^2 + b^2 = c^2$$
$$10^2 + b^2 = 12^2 \qquad \text{Substituting}$$
$$100 + b^2 = 144$$
$$100 + b^2 - 100 = 144 - 100 \qquad \text{Subtracting 100 on both sides}$$
$$b^2 = 144 - 100$$
$$b^2 = 44$$

Exact answer: $\qquad b = \sqrt{44}$

Approximation: $\qquad b \approx 6.633.$ $\qquad$ Using a calculator

Do Margin Exercises 29–31.

Example 9 *Height of Ladder.* A 12-ft ladder leans against a building. The bottom of the ladder is 7 ft from the building. How high is the top of the ladder? Give an exact answer and an approximation to the nearest tenth of a foot.

1. **Familiarize.** We first make a drawing. In it we see a right triangle. We let h = the unknown height.

Since the ladder represents the hypotenuse (the longest side of the triangle) we know that our answer must be less than 12 ft.

2. **Translate.** We substitute 7 for a, h for b, and 12 for c in the Pythagorean equation:

$$a^2 + b^2 = c^2 \qquad \text{Pythagorean equation}$$
$$7^2 + h^2 = 12^2.$$

3. **Solve.** We solve for h^2 and then h:

$$49 + h^2 = 144$$
$$49 + h^2 - 49 = 144 - 49$$
$$h^2 = 144 - 49$$
$$h^2 = 95$$

Exact answer: $\qquad h = \sqrt{95}$

Approximation: $\qquad h \approx 9.7$ ft.

4. **Check.** $7^2 + (\sqrt{95})^2 = 49 + 95 = 144 = 12^2$. This also agrees with the estimate.

5. **State.** The top of the ladder is $\sqrt{95}$ or about 9.7 ft from the ground.

Do Margin Exercise 32.

Find the length of the leg of the right triangle. Give an exact answer and an approximation to three decimal places.

29.

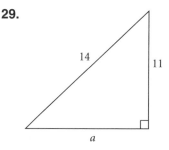

30.

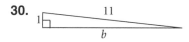

31.

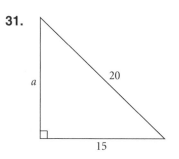

32. How long is a guy wire reaching from the top of an 18-ft pole to a point on the ground 10 ft from the pole? Give an exact answer and an approximation to the nearest tenth of a foot.

Excercise Set 9.7

a Simplify.

1. $\sqrt{100}$ **2.** $\sqrt{25}$ **3.** $\sqrt{441}$ **4.** $\sqrt{225}$

5. $\sqrt{625}$ **6.** $\sqrt{576}$ **7.** $\sqrt{361}$ **8.** $\sqrt{484}$

9. $\sqrt{529}$ **10.** $\sqrt{169}$ **11.** $\sqrt{10,000}$ **12.** $\sqrt{4,000,000}$

b Approximate to three decimal places.

13. $\sqrt{48}$ **14.** $\sqrt{17}$ **15.** $\sqrt{8}$ **16.** $\sqrt{3}$

17. $\sqrt{18}$ **18.** $\sqrt{7}$ **19.** $\sqrt{6}$ **20.** $\sqrt{61}$

21. $\sqrt{10}$ **22.** $\sqrt{21}$ **23.** $\sqrt{75}$ **24.** $\sqrt{220}$

25. $\sqrt{196}$ **26.** $\sqrt{123}$ **27.** $\sqrt{183}$ **28.** $\sqrt{300}$

c Find the length of the third side of the right triangle. Give an exact answer and an approximation to three decimal places.

29.

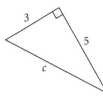

30.

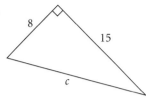

31.

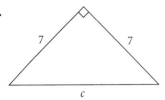

32.

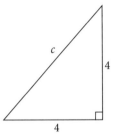

33.

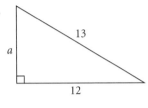

34.

35.

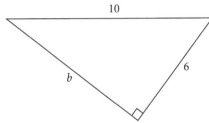

36.

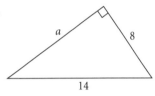

In a right triangle, find the length of the side not given. Give an exact answer and an approximation to three deicimal places.

37. $a = 5$, $b = 12$

38. $a = 10$, $b = 24$

39. $a = 18$, $c = 30$

40. $a = 9$, $c = 15$

41. $b = 1$, $c = 20$

42. $a = 1$, $c = 32$

43. $a = 1$, $c = 15$

44. $a = 3$, $b = 4$

In Exercises 45–52, give an exact answer and an approximation to the nearest tenth.

45. How long must a wire be in order to reach from the top of a 13-m telephone pole to a point on the ground 9 m from the base of the pole?

46. How long is a light cord reaching from the top of a 12-ft pole to a point on the ground 8 ft from the base of the pole?

47. *Softball Diamond.* A slow-pitch softball diamond is actually a square 65 ft on a side. How far is it from home plate to second base?

48. *Baseball Diamond.* A baseball diamond is actually a square 90 ft on a side. How far is it from home plate to second base?

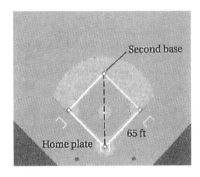

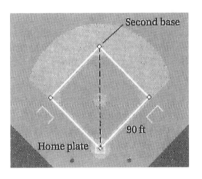

49. How tall is this tree?

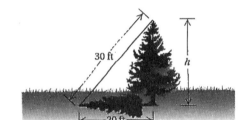

50. How far is the base of the fence post from point *A*?

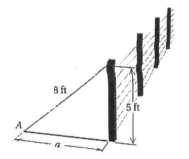

51. An airplane is flying at an altitude of 4100 ft. The slanted distance directly to the airport is 15,100 ft. How far is the airplane horizontally from the airport?

52. A surveyor had poles located at points *P*, *Q*, and *R* around a lake. The distances that the surveyor was able to measure are marked on the drawing. What is the approximate distance from *P* to *R* across the lake?

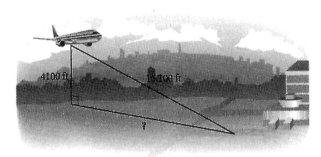

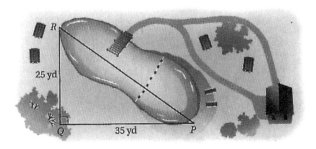

Convert to decimal notation.

53. 45.6%

54. 16.34%

55. 123%

56. 99%

57. 0.41%

58. 3%

Solve.

59. Food expenses account for 26% of the average family's budget. A family makes $1800 one month. How much do they spend for food?

60. The price of a cellular phone was reduced from $350 to $308. Find the percent of decrease in price.

61. A county has a population that is increasing by 4% each year. This year the population is 180,000. What will it be next year?

62. The price of a box of cookies increased from $2.85 to $3.99. What was the percent of increase in the price?

63. A college has a student body of 1850 students. Of these, 17.5% are seniors. How many students are seniors?

64. A state charges a meals tax of $4\frac{1}{2}$%. What is the meals tax charged on a dinner party costing $540?

Synthesis

65. ❖ Write a problem similar to Exercises 49–52 for a classmate to solve. Design the problem so that its solution involves the length $\sqrt{58}$ m.

66. ❖ Give an argument that could be used to convince a classmate that $\sqrt{2501}$ is not a whole number. Do not use a calculator.

67. ▦ Find the area of the trapezoid shown.

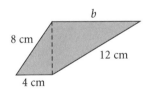

68. A 19-in television set has a rectangular screen whose diagonal is 19 in. The ratio of length to width in a conventional television set is 4 to 3. Find the length and the width of the screen. Round to the nearest hundredth.

Review Exercises: Chapter 9

Important Properties and Formulas

American Units of Length:	12 in. = 1 ft; 3 ft = 1 yd; 36 in. = 1 yd; 5280 ft = 1 mi
Metric Units of Length:	1 km = 1000 m; 1 hm = 100 m; 1 dam = 10 m;
	1 dm = 0.1 m; 1 cm = 0.01 m; 1 mm = 0.001 m
American-Metric Converson:	1 m = 39.37 in.; 1 m = 3.3 ft; 0.303 m = 1ft;
	2.54 cm = 1 in.; 1 km = 0.621 mi; 1.609 km = 1 mi
Perimeter of a Rectangle:	$P = 2 \cdot (l + w)$, or $P = 2 \cdot l + 2 \cdot w$
Perimeter of a Square:	$P = 4 \cdot s$
Area of a Rectange:	$A = l \cdot w$
Area of a Square:	$A = s \cdot s$, or $A = s^2$
Area of a Parallelogram:	$A = b \cdot h$
Area of a Triangle:	$A = \frac{1}{2} b \cdot h$
Area of a Trapezoid:	$A = \frac{1}{2} \cdot h \cdot (a + b)$
Radius and Diameter of a Circle:	$d = 2 \cdot r$, or $r = \frac{d}{2}$
Circumference of a Circle:	$C = \pi \cdot d$, or $C = 2 \cdot \pi \cdot r$
Area of a Circle:	$A = \pi \cdot r \cdot r$, or $A = \pi \cdot r^2$
Pythagorean Equation:	$a^2 + b^2 = c^2$

Complete.

1. 8 ft = _____ yd

2. $\frac{5}{6}$ yd = _____ in.

3. 0.3 mm = _____ cm

4. 4 m = _____ km

5. 2 yd = _____ in.

6. 4 km = _____ cm

7. 14 in. = _____ ft

8. 15 cm = _____ m

9. 200 m = _____ yd

10. 20 mi = _____ km

11.
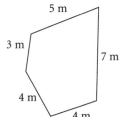

12.
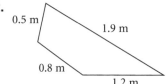

13. The dimensions of a standard-sized tennis court are 78 ft by 36 ft. Find the perimeter and the area of the tennis court.

14. Find the length of a diagonal from one corner to another of the tennis court in Exercise 13.

Find the perimeter and the area.

15.

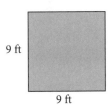

9 ft

9 ft

16.

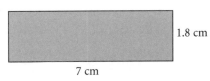

1.8 cm

7 cm

Find the area.

17.

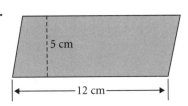

5 cm

12 cm

18.

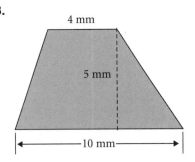

4 mm

5 mm

10 mm

19.

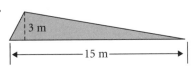

3 m

15 m

20.

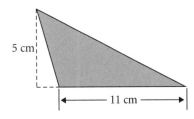

5 cm

11 cm

21.

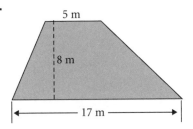

5 m

8 m

17 m

22.

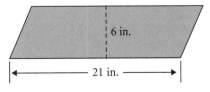

6 in.

21 in.

23. A grassy area is to be seeded around three sides of a building and has equal width on the three sides, as shown below. What is the seeded area?

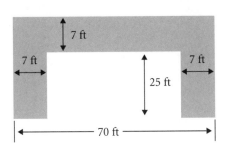

7 ft

7 ft

7 ft

25 ft

70 ft

Complete.

24. 4 yd 2 = _____ ft²

25. 0.3 km² = _____ m²

26. 2070 in² = _____ ft²

27. 600 cm² = _____ m²

Find the length and radius of the circle.

28.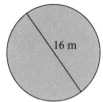

16 m

29.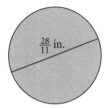

$\frac{28}{11}$ in.

30.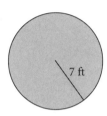

7 ft

31.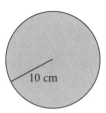

10 cm

32. Find the circumference of the circle in Exercise 28.

33. Find the circumference of the circle in Exercise 29.

34. Find the area of the circle in Exercise 28.

35. Find the area of the circle in Exercise 29.

36. Find the area of the shaded region.

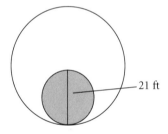

21 ft

Important Properties and Formulas

Volume of a Rectangular Solid:	$V = l \cdot w \cdot h$
American Units of Capacity:	1 gal = 4 qt; 1 qt = 2 pt; 1 pt = 16 oz;
	1 pt = 2 cups; 1 cup = 8 oz
Metric Units of Capacity:	1 L = 1000 mL = 1000 cm^3
Volume of a Circular Cylinder:	$V = \pi \cdot r^2 \cdot h$
Volume of a Sphere:	$V = \frac{4}{3} \cdot \pi \cdot r^3$
Volume of a Cone:	$V = \frac{1}{3} \cdot \pi \cdot r^2 \cdot h$
American System of Weights:	1 T = 2000 lb; 1 lb = 16 oz
Metric System of Mass:	1 t = 1000 kg; 1 kg = 1000 g; 1 hg = 100 g; 1 dag = 10 g;
	1 dg = 0.1 g; 1 cg = 0.01 g; 1 mg = 0.001 g
Units of Time:	1 min = 60 sec; 1 hr = 60 min; 1 day = 24 hr;
	1 wk = 7 days; 1 yr = 365.25 days
Temperature Conversion:	$F = \frac{9}{5}(C + 32); C = \frac{5}{9}(F - 32)$
Sum of Angle Measures of a Triangle:	$m(\angle A) + m(\angle B) + m(\angle C) = 180°$

Complete.

37. 7 lb = _____ oz

38. 4 g = _____ kg

39. 16 min = _____ hr

40. 464 mL = _____ L

41. 3 min = _____ sec

42. 4.7 kg = _____ g

43. 8.07 T = _____ lb

44. 0.83 L = = _____ mL

45. 6 hr = _____ days

46. 4 cg = _____ g

47. 0.2 g = _____ mg

48. 0.0003 kg = _____ cg

49. 60 mL = _____ L

50. 0.8 T = _____ lb

51. 0.4 L = _____ mL

52. 20 oz = _____ lb

53. 5 min = _____ sec

54. 20 gal = _____ pt

55. 960 oz = _____ gal

56. 54 qt = _____ gal

57. A physician prescribed 780 mL per hour of a certain intravenous fluid for a patient. How many liters of fluid did this patient receive in one day?

Find the volume.

58.

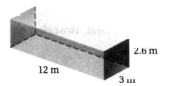

59.

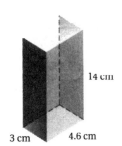

Find the volume.

60.

100 ft

10 ft

61.

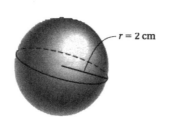

r = 2 cm

62.

4.5 in.

1 in.

Use a protractor to measure each angle.

63.

64.

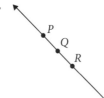

P

Q

R

65.

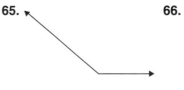

66.

67.–70. Classify each of the angles in Exercises 63–66 as right, straight, acute, or obtuse. [9.6b]

Use the following triangle for Exercises 71–73.

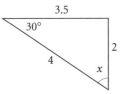

3.5

30°

2

4

x

71. Find the missing angle measure.

72. Classify the triangle as equilateral, isosceles, or scalene.

73. Classify the triangle as right, obtuse, or acute.

In a right triangle, find the length of the side not given. Give an exact answer and an approximation to three decimal places.

74. $a = 15, b = 25$

75. $a = 7, c = 10$

Find the length of the side not given. Give an exact answer and an approximation to three decimal places. [8.7c]

76.

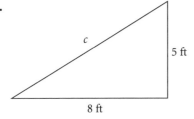

c

5 ft

8 ft

77.

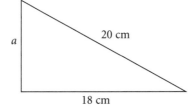

20 cm

a

18 cm

78. How long is a wire reaching from the top of a 24-ft pole to a point on the ground 16 ft from the base of the pole?

79. How tall is this tree?

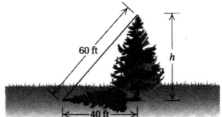

60 ft

h

40 ft

Practice Test: Chapter 9

Complete.

1. 4 ft = _____ in.

2. 4, in. = _____ ft

3. 6 km = _____ m

4. 8.7 mm. = _____ cm

5. 200 yd = _____ m

6. 2400, km = _____ mi

Find the perimeter and the area.

7.
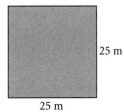
7.01 cm

9.4 cm

8.
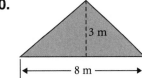
25 m

25 m

Find the area.

9.
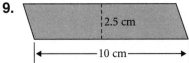
2.5 cm

10 cm

10.

3 m

8 m

11.
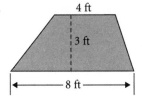
4 ft

3 ft

8 ft

12. Find the length of a diameter of this circle.

13. Find the length of a radius of this circle.

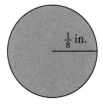
$\frac{1}{8}$ in.

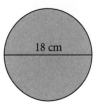
18 cm

14. Find the circumference of the circle in Question 12.

15. Find the area of the circle in Question 13.

16. Find the area of the shaded region.

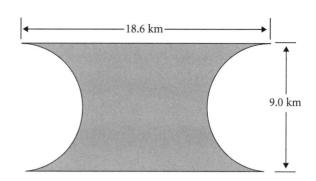

17. Simplify: $\sqrt{225}$.

18. Approximate to three decimal places: $\sqrt{87}$.

In a right triangle, find the length of the side not given. Give an exact answer and an approximation to three decimal places.

19. $a = 24, b = 32$

20. $a = 2, c = 8$

21.

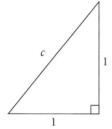

22.

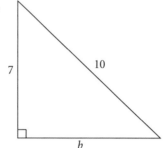

23. How long must a wire be in order to reach from the top of a 13-m antenna to a point on the ground 9 m from the base of the antenna?

24. Find the volume.

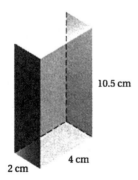

Complete.

25. 3080 mL = _____ L

26. 0.24 L   = _____ mL

27. 4 lb = _____ oz

28. 4.11 T = _____ lb

29. 3.8 kg = _____ g

30. 4.325 mg = _____ cg

31. 2200 mg = _____ g

32. 5 hr = _____ min

33. 15 days = _____ hr

34. 64 pt = _____ qt

35. 10 gal = _____ oz

36. 5 cups = _____ oz

---

38. A twelve-box carton of 12-oz juice boxes comes in a rectangular box 101 in. by 8 in. by 5 in. What is the volume of the carton?

Find the volume.

39.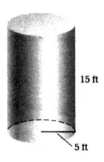

15 ft

5 ft

40.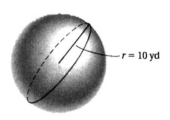

$r = 10$ yd

41.

12 cm

3 cm

Use a protractor to measure each angle.

42.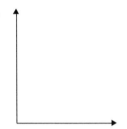

43.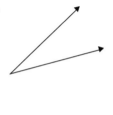

44.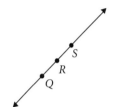

S

R

Q

45.

46.–49. Classify each of the angles in Questions 42–45 as right, straight, acute, or obtuse.

Use the following triangle for Questions 50–52.

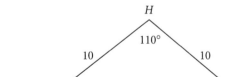

H

110°

10   10

35°   x

A   F

50. Find the missing angle measure.

51. Classify the triangle as equilateral, isosceles, or scalene.

52. Classify the triangle as right, obtuse, or acute.

53. List as many reasons as you can for continuing our use of the American system of measurement instead of changing to the metric system.

10

Algebra

An Application

The Iditarod sled-dog race extends for 1049 mi from Anchorage to Nome. If a Musher is twice as far from Anchorage as from Nome, how many miles has the musher traveled?

The Mathematics

We let x = the distance that the musher is from Nome. We can then translate the problem to this equation:

$$x + 2x = 1049.$$

Add.

1. $-13.2 + -9.1$

2. $-78 + (-93)$

3. $-\dfrac{2}{11} + \left(-\dfrac{7}{11}\right)$

4. $-\dfrac{3}{8} + \left(-\dfrac{7}{15}\right)$

5. $-8.9 + 17.5$

6. $8.9 + (-17.5)$

7. $-\dfrac{7}{15} + \dfrac{13}{15}$

8. $\dfrac{7}{15} + \left(-\dfrac{13}{15}\right)$

10.1   Expressions and Equations

In this section, we will review operations with signed numbers, algebraic expressions and solving one-step equations.

a   Operations with Signed Numbers

> ▶ To add real numbers with the same sign, add their absolute values.
>
>   a.) If the numbers are negative, the answer is negative.
>
>   b.) If the numbers are positive, the answer is positive.

Examples   Add.

1. $6.2 + 3.5 = 9.7$

2. $-6.2 + (-3.5) = -9.7$

3. $\dfrac{2}{9} + \dfrac{5}{9} = \dfrac{7}{9}$

4. $-\dfrac{2}{9} + \left(-\dfrac{5}{9}\right) = -\dfrac{7}{9}$

Do Margin Exercises 1–4.

> ▶ To add a positive and a negative real number, find the difference of their absolute values.
>
>   a.) If the negative number has the greater absolute value, the answer is negative.
>
>   b.) If the positive number has the greater absolute value, the answer is positive.

Examples   Add.

5. $-13.5 + 6.3 = -7.2$

6. $13.5 + (-6.3) = 7.2$

7. $-\dfrac{11}{13} + \dfrac{5}{13} = -\dfrac{6}{13}$

8. $\dfrac{11}{13} + \left(-\dfrac{5}{13}\right) = \dfrac{6}{13}$

Do Margin Exercises 5–8

▶ To subtract two real numbers, add the opposite, or additive inverse, of the number being subtracted.

Examples Subtract.

9. $9.2 - 11.5 = 9.2 + (-11.5) = -2.3$

10. $-9.2 - 11.5 = -9.2 + (11.5) = -20.7$

11. $9.2 - (-11.5) = 9.2 + 11.5 = 20.7$

12. $-9.2 - (-11.5) = -9.2 + 11.5 = 2.3$

Do Margin Exercises 9–12.

▶ To multiply or divide two real numbers:

  a) Multiply or divide the absolute values.

  b) If the signs are the same, the answer is positive.

  c) If the signs are different, the answer is negative.

Examples Multiply or divide as indicated.

13. $(-7)(-3) = 21$

14. $(-7)(3) = -21$

15. $(7)(-3) = -21$

16. $\frac{-72}{8} = -9$

17. $\frac{-72}{-8} = 9$

18. $\frac{72}{-8} = -9$

Do Margin Exercises 13–18.

▶ The product of an even number of negative real numbers is positive.

The product of an odd number of negative numbers is negative.

Examples Multiply.

19. $(-2)(-1)(3)(-1)(-4) = 24$

20. $(-2)(-1)(3)(-1)(4) = -24$

Subtract.

9. $23.8 - 56.2$

10. $-23.8 - 56.2$

11. $23.8 - (-56.2)$

12. $-23.8 - (-56.2)$

Multiply or divide as indicated.

13. $(-15)(-3)$

14. $(-15)(3)$

15. $(15)(-3)$

16. $\frac{-56}{7}$

17. $\frac{-56}{-7}$

18. $\frac{56}{-7}$

Multiply.

19. $(-5)(-1)(-1)(3)(2)(-1)$

20. $(-5)(-1)(-1)(-3)(2)(-1)$

21. Evaluate $7x - 2y$ for $x = 6$ and $y = -8$.

22. Evaluate $\frac{x+y}{-6}$ for $x = -47$ and $y = 35$.

b | Evaluating Expressions

Recall. that an algebraic expression consists of variables, numbers and operations signs. We *cannot solve expressions,* however, we **can evaluate expressions** for given values. We do this by replacing the variables with the given values.

Examples

21. Evaluate $2x + 3y$ for $x = -5$ and $y = 7$
We substitute -5 for x and 7 for y
and follow the order of operations.

$2x + 3y$

$2(-5)+3(7)$

$-10 + 21$

11

22. Evaluate $\frac{x-y}{5}$ for for $x = 27$ and $y = 32$

$\frac{x-y}{5}$

$\frac{27-32}{5}$

$\frac{-5}{5}$

-1

Do Margin Exercises 21 and 22

c | Solving One-Step Equations

Recall that to solve the equation $x + a = b$ for x, we can add or subtract the same number to both sides of the equation. The goal is to isolate the variable x on one side of the equation.

> ▶ **The Addition Principle**
>
> For any real numbers a, b and c.
>
> $a = b$ is equivalent to $a + b = c$.

Examples Solve the following.

23. $x + 1.8 = 2.7$

$$\underline{-1.8 \quad -1.8}$$

$$x = 0.9$$

24. $y - 2.8 = -7.6$

$$\underline{+2.8 \quad +2.8}$$

$$y = -4.8$$

Do Margin Exercises 23 and 24.

Remember, that to solve the equation $ax = b$ for x, we can multiply or divide both sides of the equation by the same nonzero number. The goal is for the coefficient of x to be positive 1.

▶ **The Multiplication and Division Principle**

For any real numbers a, b and c, $c \neq 0$,

$a = b$ is equivalent to $ac = bc$ or $\frac{a}{c} = \frac{b}{c}$

Examples Solve the following.

25. $-8x = 72$

$$\frac{-8x}{-8} = \frac{72}{-8}$$

$$x = -9$$

26. $\frac{y}{6} = -42$

$$6\left(\frac{y}{6}\right) = 6(-42)$$

$$y = -252$$

27. $-\frac{2}{3}x = 8$

$$-\frac{3}{2}\left(-\frac{2}{3}x\right) = \overset{4}{\cancel{8}}(-\frac{3}{\underset{1}{\cancel{2}}})$$

$$1 \cdot x = -12$$

$$x = -12$$

Do Margin Exercises 25–27.

Solve the following.

23. $x + 9.5 = 3.2$

24. $y - 4.7 = 6.1$

25. $5x = -105$

26. $\frac{y}{-3} = -13$

27. $-\frac{4}{5}y = -16$

Calculator Spotlight

Let's do some calculations with real numbers on a calculator. To enter a negative number on some calculators, we use the $\boxed{+/-}$ key. To enter −5, we press $\boxed{5}$ and then $\boxed{+/-}$. The display then reads

$$-5$$

Some graphing calculators use an opposite key $\boxed{(-)}$. To enter −5 on such a grapher, we press $\boxed{(-)}$ $\boxed{5}$. To do a calculation like −8 − (−2.3), we press the following keys.

$\boxed{8}$ $\boxed{+/-}$ $\boxed{-}$ $\boxed{2}$ $\boxed{.}$ $\boxed{3}$ $\boxed{+/-}$ $\boxed{=}$

or

$\boxed{(-)}$ $\boxed{8}$ $\boxed{-}$ $\boxed{(-)}$ $\boxed{2}$ $\boxed{.}$ $\boxed{3}$ $\boxed{ENTER}$.

The answer is −5.7.

Note that we did not need grouping symbols, or parentheses, in the preceding keystrokes. Many calculators do provide grouping symbols. Such keys may appear as $\boxed{(}$ and $\boxed{)}$ or $\boxed{[(...]}$ and $\boxed{...)]}$. To do a calculation like −7(2 − 9) − 20 on such a calculator, we press the following keys:

$\boxed{7}$ $\boxed{+/-}$ $\boxed{\times}$ $\boxed{(}$ $\boxed{2}$ $\boxed{-}$ $\boxed{9}$ $\boxed{)}$
$\boxed{-}$ $\boxed{2}$ $\boxed{0}$ $\boxed{=}$

or

$\boxed{(-)}$ $\boxed{7}$ $\boxed{(}$ $\boxed{2}$ $\boxed{-}$ $\boxed{9}$ $\boxed{)}$
$\boxed{-}$ $\boxed{2}$ $\boxed{0}$ $\boxed{ENTER}$

The multiplication key $\boxed{\times}$ could also be used but often that is not necessary on a graphing calculator. The answer is 29.

If we want to enter a power like $(-39)^4$, the keystrokes are

$\boxed{3}$ $\boxed{9}$ $\boxed{+/-}$ $\boxed{y^x}$ $\boxed{4}$ $\boxed{=}$

or

$\boxed{(}$ $\boxed{(-)}$ $\boxed{3}$ $\boxed{9}$ $\boxed{)}$ $\boxed{\wedge}$ $\boxed{4}$ $\boxed{ENTER}$.

The answer is 2,313,441.
To find -39^4, think of the calculation as -1×39^4. The keystrokes are

$\boxed{1}$ $\boxed{+/-}$ $\boxed{\times}$ $\boxed{3}$ $\boxed{9}$ $\boxed{y^x}$ $\boxed{4}$ $\boxed{=}$

or

$\boxed{(-)}$ $\boxed{3}$ $\boxed{9}$ $\boxed{\wedge}$ $\boxed{4}$ $\boxed{ENTER}$.

The answer is −2,313,441.

To simplify an expression like

$$\frac{38 + 143}{2 - 47},$$

we use groupong symbols to write it as

$$(38 + 142) \div (2- 47)$$

We then press

$\boxed{(}$ $\boxed{3}$ $\boxed{8}$ $\boxed{+}$ $\boxed{1}$ $\boxed{4}$ $\boxed{2}$ $\boxed{)}$ $\boxed{\div}$
$\boxed{(}$ $\boxed{2}$ $\boxed{-}$ $\boxed{4}$ $\boxed{7}$ $\boxed{)}$ $\boxed{=}$.

The answer is −4.

Exercises

Press the appropriate keys so that your calculator displays each of the following numbers.

1. −9   **2.** −57

3. −1996   **4.** −24.7

Evaluate.

5. $-8 + 4(7 - 9) + 5$ **6.** $-3[2 + (-5)]$

7. $7[4 - (-3)] + 5[3^2 - (-4)]$

Evaluate.

8. $(-7)^6$ **9.** $(-17)^5$

10. $(-104)^3$ **11.** -7^6

12. -17^5 **13.** -104^3

Calculate

14. $\dfrac{36 - 178}{5 + 30}$ **15.** $\dfrac{311 - 17^2}{2 - 13}$

16. $785 - \dfrac{285 - 5^4}{17 + 3 \cdot 51}$

17. Consider only the numbers 2, 4, 6, and 8. Assume that each can be placed in a blank as follows:
$$\square \div \square \cdot \square - \square^2$$
What placement of the numbers in the blanks yields the largest number?

18. Consider only the numbers 2, 4, 6, and 8. Assume that each can be placed in a blank as follows:
$$\square - \square + \square^2 \div \square$$
What placement of the numbers in the blanks yields the largest number?

In Exercises 19 and 20, place one of + , − , x, and ÷ in each blank to make a true sentence

19. $-32 \,\square\, (88 \,\square\, 29) = -1888$

20. $3^5 \,\square\, 10^2 \,\square\, 5^2 = -22.57$

Improving Your Math Study Skills

Tips from a Former Student

A former student of Professor Bittinger, Mike Rosenborg earned a master's degree in mathematics and now teaches mathematics. Here are some of his study tips.

- Because working problems is the best way to learn math, instructors generally assign lots of problems. Never let yourself get behind in your math homework.

- If you are struggling with a math concept, do not give up. Ask for help from your friends and your instructor. Since each concept is built on previous concepts, any gaps in your understanding will follow you through the entire course, so make sure you understand each concept as you go along.

- Math contains many rules that cannot be "bent." Don't try inventing your own rules and still expect to get correct answers. Although there is usually more than one way to solve a problem, each method must follow the established rules.

- Read your textbook! It will often contain the tips and help you need to solve any problem with which you're struggling. It may also bring out points that you missed in class or that your instructor may not have covered.

- Learn to use scratch paper to jot down your thoughts and to draw pictures. Don't try to figure everything out "in your head." You will think more clearly and accurately this way.

- When preparing for a test, it is often helpful to work at least two problems per section as practice: one easy and one difficult. Write out all the new rules and procedures your test will cover, and then read through them twice. Doing so will enable you to both learn and retain them better.

- Some people like to work in study groups, while others prefer solitary study. Although it's important to be flexible, it's more important that you be comfortable with your study method, so consider trying both. You may find one or the other or a combination of both effective.

- Most schools have classrooms set up where you can get free help from math tutors. Take advantage of this, but be sure you do the work first. Don't let your tutor do all the work for you–otherwise you'll never learn the material.

- In math, as in many other areas of life, patience and persistence are virtues–cultivate them. "Cramming" for an exam will not help you learn and retain the material.

- Do your work neatly and in pencil. Then if you make a mistake, it will be relatively easy to find and correct. Write out each step in the problem's solution; don't skip steps or take shortcuts. Each step should follow clearly from the preceding step, and the entire solution should be easy to follow. If you understand the concepts and get a wrong answer, the first thing you should look for is a small" mistake, like writing a + " instead of a "–".

Exercise Set 10.1

a Perform the indicated operations.

1. $-\dfrac{5}{8} - \dfrac{3}{4}$

2. $85 + (-65)$

3. $-3.2 - 5.8$

4. $-7(-3.1)$

5. $-\dfrac{3}{5} + \dfrac{2}{5}$

6. $-6.6 \div 3.3$

7. $8 - (-9.3)$

8. $\dfrac{2}{3}\left(-\dfrac{3}{5}\right)$

9. $-6.3\,(2.7)$

10. $-\dfrac{3}{8} \div \left(-\dfrac{8}{3}\right)$

11. $-71 - 2$

12. $0.99 - 1$

13. $-7.9 + (-6.5)$

14. $-\dfrac{5}{6} + \dfrac{2}{3}$

15. $-5.7 + (-7.2) + 6.6$

16. $48 - (-73)$

17. $-\dfrac{5}{9}\left(\dfrac{3}{4}\right)$

18. $\dfrac{-9}{17 - 17}$

19. $\dfrac{200}{-25}$

20. $0.87 - 1$

21. $-\dfrac{5}{9} + \left(-\dfrac{5}{18}\right)$

22. $-4(-3.2)$

23. $-\dfrac{5}{8} + \left(-\dfrac{1}{3}\right)$

24. $1.5 - (-3.5)$

25. $-\dfrac{3}{4} - \dfrac{2}{3}$

26. $-5(-6)$

27. $3 - 5.7$

28. $\left(-\dfrac{5}{6}\right)\left(\dfrac{1}{8}\right)\left(-\dfrac{3}{7}\right)\left(-\dfrac{1}{7}\right)$

29. $-6.2(8.5)$

30. $-2.7 - 5.9$

31. $24 - (-92)$

32. $-\dfrac{3}{7} + \left(-\dfrac{2}{5}\right)$

33. $63 + (-18)$

34. $-\dfrac{3}{5} + \left(-\dfrac{2}{15}\right)$

35. $75 + (-14) + (-17) + (-5)$

36. $-\dfrac{3}{8}\left(-\dfrac{2}{9}\right)$

37. $-44.1 \div (-6.3)$

38. $\dfrac{-8}{-5 + 5}$

39. $-10.3 + (-7.5) + 3.1$

40. $\dfrac{-1.7}{20}$

41. $\dfrac{-17.8}{3.2}$

42. $\left(\dfrac{4}{5}\right)\left(-\dfrac{2}{3}\right)\left(-\dfrac{15}{7}\right)\left(\dfrac{1}{2}\right)$

43. $\dfrac{48.6}{-3}$

44. $-\dfrac{8}{3}\left(\dfrac{9}{4}\right)$

45. $-44 + \left(-\dfrac{3}{8}\right) + 95 + \left(-\dfrac{5}{8}\right)$

46. $-6(-4)$

47. $\dfrac{5}{7}\left(-\dfrac{2}{3}\right)$

48. $-\dfrac{3}{8} - (-\dfrac{1}{2})$

49. $-49 - 3$

50. $-\dfrac{5}{8} + \dfrac{1}{4}$

51. $-\dfrac{5}{8}\left(-\dfrac{2}{5}\right)$

52. $\dfrac{12}{5} - \dfrac{12}{5}$

53. $\dfrac{-64}{-7}$

54. $(-6)(-7)(-8)(-9)(-10)$

55. $7 - 10.53$

56. $6.1 - (-13.8)$

57. $-\dfrac{3}{4} - \left(-\dfrac{2}{3}\right)$

58. $\dfrac{-145}{-5}$

59. $\dfrac{-11}{-13}$

60. $-\dfrac{5}{8} - \left(-\dfrac{3}{4}\right)$

61. $-\dfrac{4}{7} - \left(-\dfrac{10}{7}\right)$

62. $-\dfrac{2}{7} \div \left(-\dfrac{4}{9}\right)$

63. $-\dfrac{3}{5} \div \left(-\dfrac{5}{8}\right)$

64. $\dfrac{81}{-9}$

65. $(-5)(-6)(-7)(-8)(-9)(10)$

66. $-\dfrac{5}{8} \div \left(-\dfrac{6}{5}\right)$

b Evaluate.

67. $6x$, for $x = 7$

68. $9t$, for $t = 8$

69. $\dfrac{x}{y}$ for $x = 9$ and $y = 3$

70. $\dfrac{m}{n}$, for $m = 18$ and $n = 3$

71. $3p$, for $p = -2$ and $q = 6$

72. $\dfrac{5y}{z}$, for $y = -15$ and $z = -25$

76. $\dfrac{x + y}{5}$, for $x = 10$ and $y = 20$

77. $\dfrac{p - q}{2}$, for $p = 17$ and $q = 3$

78. $3 + 5x$, for $x = -2.8$

79. $9 - 2x$, for $x = 3$

80. $7x - 2y$, for $x = -2$ and $y = 5$

81. $-4x + 11y$, for $x = 6.2$ and $y = -1.3$

82. $x + 24 = 117$

83. $x + \dfrac{7}{9} = \dfrac{4}{3}$

84. $\dfrac{7}{9}t = -\dfrac{4}{3}$

85. $\dfrac{14}{25} = \dfrac{x}{54}$

86. $-423 = 16t$

87. $\dfrac{2}{3}y = \dfrac{16}{27}$

88. $34.56 + n = 67.9$

89. $t + \dfrac{7}{25} = \dfrac{5}{7}$

90. $8.32 + x = 9.1$

91. $-75x = 2100$

92. $9.47y = 81.6314$

93. $1062 - y = -368{,}313$

94. $t + \dfrac{5}{6} = \dfrac{8}{9}$

95. $\dfrac{7}{8}t = \dfrac{7}{16}$

Skill Maintenance

96. Find the area of a rectangle that is 8.4 cm by 11.5 cm.

97. Find the prime factorization of 750.

98. Find the LCM of 36 and 54.

99. Find the area of a square whose sides are of length 11.km.

Evaluate.

100. 4^3

101. 5^3

Solve.

102. How many 12-oz cans of soda can be filled with 96 oz of soda?

103. A case of soda contains 24 bottles. If each bottle contains 12 oz, how many ounces of soda are in the case?

Synthesis

104. ❖ If a negative number is subtracted from a positive number, will the result always be positive? Why or why not?

105. ❖ Write a problem for a classmate to solve. Design the problem so that the solution is "The temperature dropped to −9°."

Subtract.

106. ▦ $123{,}907 - 433{,}789$

107. ▦ $23{,}011 - (-60{,}432)$

Tell whether the statement is true or false for all integers m and n. If false, find a number that shows why.

108. $-n = 0 - n$

109. $n - 0 = 0 - n$

110. If $m \neq n$, then $m - n \neq 0$.

111. If $m = -n$, then $m + n = 0$.

112. If $m + n = 0$, then m and n are opposites.

113. If $m - n = 0$, then $m = -n$.

114. $m = -n$ if m and n are opposites.

115. If $m = -m$, then $m = 0$.

116. Velma Quarles is a stockbroker. She kept track of the changes in the stock market over a period of 5 weeks. By how many points had the market risen or fallen over this time?

Week 1	Week 2	Week 3	Week 4	Week 5
Down 13 pts	Down 16 pts	Up 36 pts	Down 11 pts	Up 19 pts

1. Evaluate $3(x + y)$ and $3x + 3y$ for $x = 5$ and $y = 7$.

2. Evaluate $6x + 6y$ and $6(x + y)$ for $x = 10$ and $y = 5$.

3. Evaluate $4(x + y)$ and $4x + 4y$ for $x = 11$ and $y = 5$.

10.2 Distributive Properties, Factoring and Collecting Like Terms

a | Distributive Properties

Let's consider the **distributive** properties of real numbers. They are the basis of many procedures in both arithmetic and algebra and are probably the most important properties that we use to manipulate algebraic expressions. The first distributive property involves two operations: addition and multiplication.

Let's begin by considering a multiplication problem from arithmetic:

$$
\begin{array}{r}
4\,5 \\
\times\ \ 7 \\
\hline
3\,5 \\
2\,8\,0 \\
\hline
3\,1\,5
\end{array}
$$

← This is $7 \cdot 5$.
← This is $7 \cdot 40$.
← This is the sum $7 \cdot 40 + 7 \cdot 5$.

To carry out the multiplication, we actually added two products. That is,

$$7 \cdot 45 = 7(40 + 5) = 7 \cdot 40 + 7 \ 5.$$

Let's examine this further. If we wish to multiply a sum of several numbers by a factor, we can either add and then multiply or multiply and then add.

Example 6 Evaluate $5(x + y)$ and $5x + 5y$ for $x = 2$ and $y = 8$ and compare the results.

We substitute 2 for x and 8 for y in each expression. Then we use the rules for order of operations to calculate.

a) $5(x + y) = 5(2 + 8)$
$\quad\quad\quad\quad = 5(10)$ Adding within parentheses first, and then multiplying
$\quad\quad\quad\quad = 50$

b) $5x + 5y = 5 \cdot 2 + 5 \cdot 8$
$\quad\quad\quad\quad = 10 + 40$ Multiplying first and then adding
$\quad\quad\quad\quad = 50$

We see that the expressions $5(x + y)$ and $5x + 5y$ are equivalent.

Do Margin Exercises 1–3.

> **The Distributive Property of Multiplication Over Addition**
>
> For any numbers a, b, and c,
>
> $$a(b + c) = ab + ac.$$

In the statement of the distributive property, we know that in an expression such as $ab + ac$, the multiplications are to be done first according to the rules for order of operations. So, instead of writing $(4 \cdot 5) + (4\ 7)$, we can write $4 \cdot 5 + 4 \cdot 7$. However, in $a(b + c)$, we cannot omit the parentheses. If we did we would have $ab + c$, which means $(ab) + c$. For example, $3(4 + 2) = 18$, but $3 \cdot 4 + 2 = 14$.

The second distributive property relates multiplication and subtraction. This property says that to multiply by a difference, we can either subtract and then multiply or multiply and then subtract.

> **▶ The Distributive Property of Multiplication Over Subtraction**
>
> For any numbers a, b, and c,
>
> $a(b - c) = ab - ac.$

We often refer to "the distributive property" when we mean *either* or both of these properties.

Do Margin Exercises 4–6.

What do we mean by the terms of an expression? **Terms** are separated by addition signs. If there are subtraction signs, we can find an equivalent expression that uses addition signs.

Example 2 What are the terms of $3x - 4y + 2z$?

$3x - 4y + 2z = 3x + (-4y) + 2z$ Separating parts with + signs

The terms are $3x$, $-4y$, and $2z$.

Do Margin Exercises 7 and 8.

The distributive properties are the basis for a procedure in algebra called **multiplying**. In an expression such as $8(a + 2b - 7)$, we multiply each term inside the parentheses by 8:

$8(a + 2b - 7) = 8 \cdot a + 8 \cdot 2b - 8 \cdot 7 = 8a + 16b - 56.$

Because multiplication is commutative, $(b + c)a = a(b + c)$ and $(b - c)a = a(b - c)$

$(a + 2b - 7)8 = 8 \cdot a + 8 \cdot 2b - 8 \cdot 7 = 8a + 16b - 56$

Examples Multiply.

3. $9(x - 5) = 9x - 9(5)$ Using the distributive property
$\qquad = 9x - 45$ of multiplication over subtraction

4. $\frac{2}{3}(w + 1) = \frac{2}{3} \cdot w + \frac{2}{3} \cdot 1$ Using the distributive property of
$\qquad\qquad$ multiplication over addition

$\qquad = -\frac{2}{3}w + \frac{2}{3}$

---

4. Evaluate $7(x - y)$ and $7x - 7y$ for $x = 9$ and $y = 7$.

5. Evaluate $6x - 6y$ and $6(x - y)$ for $x = 10$ and $y = 5$.

6. Evaluate $2(x - y)$ and $2x - 2y$ for $x = 11$ and $y = 5$.

What are the terms of the expression?

7. $5x - 4y + 3$

8. $-4y - 2x + 3z$

Multiply.

9. $3(x-5)$

10. $(x+1)5$

11. $\dfrac{5}{4}(x-y+4)$

12. $(x-3)(-2)$

13. $-5(x-2y+4z)$

Example 5 Multiply: $-4(x-2y+3z)$.

$-4(x-2y+3z) = -4 \cdot x - (-4)(2y) + (-4)(3z)$ Using both distributive properties

$= -4x - (-8y) + (-12z)$ Multipying

$= -4x + 8y - 12z$

We can also do this problem by first finding an equivalent expression with all plus signs and then multiplying:

$-4(x-2y+3z) = -4[x + (-2y) + 3z]$

$= -4 \cdot x + (-4)(-2y) + (-4)(3z) = -4x + 8y - 12z.$

Do Margin Exercises 9–13.

b Factoring

Factoring is the reverse of multiplying. To factor, we can use the distributive properties in reverse:

$$ab + ac = a(b+c) \text{ and } ab - ac = a(b-c).$$

> ▶ To **factor** an expression is to find an equivalent expression that is a product.

Look at Example 3. To *factor* $9x - 45$, we find an equivalent expression that is a product, $9(x-5)$. When all the terms of an expression have a factor in common, we can "factor it out" using the distributive properties. Note the following.

$9x$ has the factors **9**, -9, 3, -3, 1, -1, x, $-x$, $3x$, $-3x$, $9x$, $-9x$;

-45 has the factors 1, -1, 3, -3, 5, -5, **9**, -9, 15, -15, 45, -45.

We remove the largest common factor. In this case, that factor is 9. Thus,

$$9x - 45 = 9 \cdot x - 9 \cdot 5$$
$$= 9(x-5).$$

Remember that an expression is factored when we find an equivalent expression that is a product.

Examples Factor.

6. $5x - 10 = 5 \cdot x - 5 \cdot 2$ Try to do this step mentally.

$= 5(x-2)$ ←   You can check by multiplying.

7. $9x + 27y - 9 = 9 \cdot x + 9 \cdot 3y - 9 \cdot 1$

$= 9(x + 3y - 1)$

CAUTION! Note that although $3(3x + 9y - 3)$ is also equivalent to $9x + 27y - 9$, it is not the desired form. However, we can complete the process by factoring out another factor of 3:

$9x + 27y - 9 = 3(3x + 9y - 3) = 3 \cdot 3 (x + 3y - 1) = 9 (x + 3y - 1).$

Remember to factor out the *largest common factor.*

Examples Factor. Try to write just the answer, if you can.

8. $5x - 5y = 5(x - y)$

9. $-3x + 6y - 9z =$
3$(-x + 2y - 3z)$ or $-3(x - 2y + 3z)$.

We usually factor out a negative when the first term is negative.

10. $18z - 12x - 24 = 6(3z - 2x - 4)$

Remember that you should always check such factoring by multiplying. Keep in mind that an expression is factored when it is written as a product.

Do Margin Exercises 14–17.

d Collecting Like Terms

Terms such as $5x$ and $-4x$, whose variable factors are exactly the same, are called like terms. Similarly, numbers, such as -7 and 13, are like terms. Also, $3y^2$ and $9y^2$ are like terms because the variables are raised to the same power. Terms such as $4y$ and $5y^2$ are not like terms, and $7x$ and $2y$ are not like terms.

The process of **collecting like terms** is based on the distributive properties. We can also apply the distributive property when a factor is on the right.

Examples Collect like terms. Try to write just the answer, if you can.

11. $4x + 2x = (4 + 2)x = 6x$ Factoring out the x using a distributive property

12. $2x + 3y - 5x - 2y = 2x - 5x + 3y - 2y$

$$= (2 - 5)x + (3 - 2)y = -3x + y$$

13. $3x - x = (3 - 1)x = 2x$

14. $x - 0.24x = 1 \cdot x - 0.24x = (1 - 0.24)x = 0.76x$

15. $x - 6x = 1 \cdot x - 6 \cdot x = (1 - 6)x = -5x$

16. $4x - 7y + 9x - 5 + 3y - 8 = 13x - 4y - 13$

17. $\frac{2}{3}a - b + \frac{4}{5}a + \frac{1}{4}b - 10 = \frac{2}{3}a - 1 \cdot b + \frac{4}{5}a + \frac{1}{4}b - 10$

$$= \left(\frac{2}{3} + \frac{4}{5}\right)a + \left(-1 + \frac{1}{4}\right)b - 10$$

$$= \left(\frac{10}{15} + \frac{12}{15}\right)a + \left(-\frac{4}{4} + \frac{1}{4}\right)b - 10$$

$$= \frac{22}{15}a - \frac{3}{4}b - 10$$

Do Margin Exercises 18–24.

Factor.

14. $6z - 12$

15. $3x - 6y + 9$

16. $16a - 36b + 42$

17. $-12x + 32y - 16z$

Collect like terms.

18. $6x - 3x$

19. $7x - x$

20. $x - 9x$

21. $x - 0.41x - 2x - y$

22. $5x + 4y - 2x - y$

23. $3x - 7x - 11 + 8y + 4 - 13y$

24. $-\frac{2}{3}x - \frac{3}{5}x + y + \frac{7}{10}x - \frac{2}{9}y$

Exercise Set 10.2

a Evaluate

1. $10(x + y)$ and $10x + 10y$, for $x = 20$ and $y = 4$

2. $5(a + b)$ and $5a + 5b$, for $a = 16$ and $b = 6$

3. $10(x - y)$ and $10x - 10y$, for $x = 20$ and $y = 4$

4. $5(a - b)$ and $5a - 5b$, for $a = 16$ and $b = 6$

Multiply.

5. $2(b + 5)$

6. $4(x + 3)$

7. $7(1 - t)$

8. $4(1 - y)$

9. $6(5x + 2)$

10. $9(6m + 7)$

11. $7(x + 4 + 6y)$

12. $(5x + 8 + 3p)$

13. $-7(y - 2)$

14. $-9(y - 7)$

15. $-9(-5x - 6y + 8)$

16. $-7(-2x - 5y + 9)$

17. $\frac{3}{4}(x - 3y - 2z)$

18. $\frac{2}{5}(2x - 5y - 8z)$

19. $3.1(-1.2x + 3.2y - 1.1)$

20. $-2.1(-4.2x - 4.3y - 2.2)$

b Factor. Check by multiplying.

21. $2x + 4$

22. $5y + 20$

23. $30 + 5y$

24. $7x + 28$

25. $14x + 21y$

26. $18a + 24b$

27. $5x + 10 + 15y$

28. $9a + 27b + 81$

29. $8x - 24$

30. $10x - 50$

31. $32 - 4y$

32. $24 - 6m$

33. $8x + 10y - 22$

34. $9a + 6b - 15$

35. $-18x - 12y + 6$

36. $14x + 21y + 7$

c Collect like terms.

37. $9a + 10a$

38. $14x + 3x$

39. $10a - a$

40. $-10x + x$

41. $2x + 9z + 6x$

42. $3a - 5b + 4a$

43. $41a + 90 - 60a - 2$

44. $42x - 6 - 4x + 20$

45. $23 + 5t + 7y - t - y - 27$

46. $95 - 90d - 87 - 9d + 3 + 7d$

47. $11x - 3x$

48. $9t - 13t$

49. $6n - n$

50. $10t - t$

51. $y - 17y$

52. $5m - 8m + 4$

53. $-8 + 11a - 5b + 6a - 7b + 7$

54. $8x - 5x + 6 + 3y - 2y - 4$

55. $9x + 2y - 5x$

56. $8y - 3z + 4y$

57. $\frac{11}{4}x + \frac{2}{3}y - \frac{4}{5}x - \frac{1}{6}y + 12$

58. $\frac{13}{2}a + \frac{9}{5}b - \frac{2}{3}a - \frac{3}{10}b - 42$

59. $2.7x + 2.3y - 1.9x - 1.8y$

60. $6.7a + 4.3b - 4.1a - 2.9b$

Skill Maintenance

For a circle with the given radius, find the diameter, the circumference, and the area.

61. $r = 15$ yd

62. $r = 8.2$ m

63. $r = 191$ mi

64. $r = 2400$ cm

For a circle with the given diameter, find the radius, the circumference, and the area.

65. $d = 20$ mm

66. $d = 264$ km

67. $d = 4.6$ ft

68. $d = 10.3$ m

Synthesis

69. ❖ Determine whether $(a + b)^2$ and $a^2 + b^2$ are equivalent for all real numbers. Explain.

70. ❖ The distributive law is introduced before the material on collecting like terms. Why do you think this is?

1. Solve: $9x + 6 = 51$

Solve.

2. $8x - 4 = 28$

3. $-\dfrac{1}{2}x + 3 = 1$

10.3 Solving Equations Using the Addition and Multiplication Principles

a Applying Both Principles

Consider the equation $3x + 4 = 13$. It is more complicated than those in the preceding two sections. In order to solve such an equation, we first isolate the x-term, $3x$, using the addition principle. Then we apply the multiplication principle to get x by itself.

Example 1 Solve: $3x + 4 = 13$.

$$3x + 4 = 13$$

$$3x + 4 - 4 = 13 - 4 \qquad \text{Using the addition principle: adding } -4 \text{ or subtracting 4 on both sides}$$

$$3x = 9 \qquad \text{Simplifying}$$

$$\frac{3x}{3} = \frac{9}{3} \qquad \text{Using the multiplication principle: multiplying by } \tfrac{1}{3} \text{ or dividing by 3 on both sides}$$

$$x = 3 \qquad \text{Simplifying}$$

Check:

$$\begin{array}{c|c} 3x + 4 = 13 \\ \hline 3 \cdot 3 + 4 \; ? \; 13 \\ 9 + 4 \; \Big| \\ 13 \; \Big| & \text{True} \end{array}$$

The solution is 3.

Do Margin Exercise 1.

Example 2 Solve: $-5x - 6 = 16$.

$$-5x - 6 = 16$$

$$-5x - 6 + 6 = 16 + 6 \qquad \text{Adding 6 on both sides}$$

$$-5x = 22$$

$$\frac{-5x}{-5} = \frac{22}{-5} \qquad \text{Dividing by 5 on both sides}$$

$$x = \frac{-22}{5}, \text{ or } -4\frac{2}{5} \qquad \text{Simplifying}$$

Check:

$$\begin{array}{c|c} -5x - 6 = 16 \\ \hline -5\left(-\frac{22}{5}\right) - 6 \; ? \; 16 \\ 22 - 6 \; \Big| \\ 16 \; \Big| & \text{True} \end{array}$$

The solution is $\dfrac{22}{5}$.

Do Margin Exercises 2 and 3.

Example 3 Solve: $45 - x = 13$.

$$45 - x = 13$$
$$-45 + 45 - x = -45 + 13 \qquad \text{Adding } -45 \text{ on both sides}$$
$$x = -32 \qquad\qquad x = -1 \cdot x$$
$$-1 \cdot x = 32$$
$$\frac{-1 \cdot x}{-1} = \frac{-32}{-1} \qquad \text{Dividing by 1 on both sides. (We could have multiplied by 1 on both sides instead. That would also change the sign on both sides.)}$$
$$x = 32$$

Check: $\quad\dfrac{45 - x = 13}{45 - 32 \; \overset{?}{} \; 13}$
$$\qquad\qquad 13 \mid \quad \text{True}$$

The solution is 32.

Do Margin Exercise 4.

Example 4 Solve: $16.3 - 7.2y = -8.18$.

$$16.3 - 7.2y = 8.18$$
$$-16.3 + 16.3 - 7.2y = -16.3 + (-8.18) \quad \text{Adding } -16.3 \text{ on both sides}$$
$$-7.2y = -24.48$$
$$\frac{-7.2y}{-7.2} = \frac{-24.48}{-7.2} \qquad\qquad \text{Dividing by 7.2 on both sides}$$
$$y = 3.4$$

Check: $\quad\dfrac{16.3 - 7.2y = -8.18}{16.3 - 7.2(3.4) \; \overset{?}{} \; -8.18}$
$$\qquad 16.3 - 24.48 \mid$$
$$\qquad\qquad -8.18 \mid \qquad \text{True}$$

The solution is 3.4.

Do Margin Exercises 5 and 6.

b Collecting Like Terms

If there are like terms on one side of the equation, we collect them before using the addition or multiplication principle.

Example 5 Solve: $3x + 4x = -14$.

$$3x + 4x = -14$$
$$7x = -14 \qquad \text{Collecting like terms}$$
$$\frac{7x}{7} = \frac{-14}{7} \qquad \text{Dividing by 7 on both sides}$$
$$x = -2.$$

Using a calculator, the number -2 checks, so the solution is -2.

Do Margin Exercises 7 and 8.

---

4. Solve: $-18 - x = -57$

Solve.

5. $-4 - 8x = 8$

6. $41.68 = 4.7 - 8.6y$

Solve.

7. $4x + 3x = -21$

8. $x - 0.09x = 728$

9. Solve: $7y + 5 = 2y + 10$.

Solve.

10. $5 - 2y = 3y - 5$

11. $7x - 17 + 2x = 2 - 8x + 15$

12. $3x - 15 = 5x + 2 - 4x$

If there are like terms on opposite sides of the equation, we get them on the same side by using the addition principle. Then we collect them. In other words, we get all terms with a variable on one side and all numbers on the other.

Example 6 Solve: $2x - 2 = -3x + 3$.

$$2x - 2 = -3x + 3$$
$$2x - 2 + 2 = -3x + 3 + 2 \qquad \text{Adding 2}$$
$$2x = -3x + 5 \qquad \text{Collecting like terms}$$
$$2x + 3x = -3x + 5 + 3x \qquad \text{Adding } 3x$$
$$5x = 5 \qquad \text{Simplifying}$$
$$\frac{5x}{5} = \frac{5}{5} \qquad \text{Dividing by 5}$$
$$x = 1 \qquad \text{Simplifying}$$

Check:
$$\begin{array}{c|c} 2x - 2 = -3x + 3 \\ \hline 2 \cdot 1 - 2 \ ? \ -3 \cdot 1 + 3 \\ 2 - 2 \ | \ -3 + 3 \\ 0 \ | \ 0 \end{array} \qquad \text{True}$$

The solution is 1.

Do Margin Exercise 9.

In Example 6, we used the addition principle to get all terms with a variable on one side and all numbers on the other side. Then we collected like terms and proceeded as before. If there are like terms on one side at the outset, they should be collected first.

Example 7 Solve: $6x + 5 - 7x = 10 - 4x + 3$.

$$6x + 5 - 7x = 10 - 4x + 3$$
$$-x + 5 = 13 - 4x \qquad \text{Collecting like terms}$$
$$4x - x + 5 = 13 - 4x + 4x \qquad \text{Adding } 4x$$
$$3x + 5 = 13 \qquad \text{Simplifying}$$
$$3x + 5 - 5 = 13 - 5 \qquad \text{Subtracting 5}$$
$$3x = 8 \qquad \text{Simplifying}$$
$$\frac{3x}{3} = \frac{8}{3} \qquad \text{Dividing by 3}$$
$$x = 3 \qquad \text{Simplifying}$$

The number $\frac{8}{3}$ checks, So $\frac{8}{3}$ is the solution.

Do Margin Exercises 10–12.

Clearing Fractions and Decimals

For the equations considered thus far, we generally use the addition principle first. There are, however, some situations in which it is to our advantage to use the multiplication principle first. Consider, for example,

$$\frac{1}{2}x = \frac{3}{4}.$$

The LCM of the denominators is 4. If we multiply by 4 on both sides, we get $2x = 3$, which has no fractions. We have "cleared fractions." Now consider

$$2.3x = 4.78.$$

If we multiply by 100 on both sides, we get $230x = 478$, which has no decimal points. We have "cleared decimals." The equations are then easier to solve. It is your choice whether to clear fractions or decimals, but doing so often eases computations.

In what follows, we use the multiplication principle first to "clear," or "eliminate," fractions or decimals. For fractions, the number by which we multiply is the **least common multiple of all the denominators.**.

Example 8 Solve:

$$\frac{2}{3}x - \frac{1}{6} + \frac{1}{2}x = \frac{7}{6} + 2x.$$

The number 6 is the least common multiple of all the denominators. We multiply by 6 on both sides:

$$6\left(\frac{2}{3}x - \frac{1}{6} + \frac{1}{2}x\right) = 6\left(\frac{7}{6} + 2x\right) \quad \text{Multiplying by 6 on both sides}$$

$$6 \cdot \frac{2}{3}x - 6 \cdot \frac{1}{6} + 6 \cdot \frac{1}{2}x = 6 \cdot \frac{7}{6} + 6 \cdot 2x \quad \text{Using the distributive properties.}$$

↑ ↑ ↑ ↑ ↑   (*Caution!* Be sure to multiply

all the terms by 6.)

$4x - 1 + 3x = 7 + 12x$	Simplifying. Note that the fractions are cleared.
$7x - 1 = 7 + 12x$	Collecting like terms
$7x - 1 - 12x = 7 + 12x - 12x$	Subtracting $12x$
$-5x - 1 = 7$	Simplifying
$-5x - 1 + 1 = 7 + 1$	Adding 1
$-5x = 8$	Collecting like terms
$x = -\frac{8}{5}$	Multiplying by $-\frac{1}{5}$ or dividing by -5.

The number $-\frac{8}{5}$ checks and is the solution.

Do Margin Exercise 13.

13. Solve: $\frac{7}{8}x - \frac{1}{4} + \frac{1}{2}x = \frac{3}{4} + x.$

14. Solve: $41.68 = 4.7 - 8.6y$

Solve.

15. $2(2y + 3) = 14$

16. $5(3x - 2) = 35$

To illustrate clearing decimals, we repeat Example 4, but this time we clear the decimals first.

Example 9   Solve: $16.3 - 7.2y = -8.18$.

The greatest number of decimal places in any one number is *two*. Multiplying by 100, which has *two* 0's, will clear the decimals.

$$100(16.3 - 7.2y) = 100(-8.18)$$ Multiplying by 100 on both sides

$$100(16.3) - 100(7.2y) = 100(-8.18)$$ Using a distributive property

$$1630 - 720y = 818$$ Simplifying

$$1630 - 720y - 1630 = 818 - 1630$$ Subtracting 1630 on both sides

$$720y = 2448$$ Collecting like terms

$$-\frac{720y}{720} = -\frac{2448}{720}$$ Dividing by -720 on both sides

$$y = 3.4$$

The number 3.4 checks and is the solution.

Do Margin Exercise 14.

c Equations Containing Parentheses

To solve certain kinds of equations that contain parentheses, we first use the distributive properties to remove the parentheses. Then we proceed as before.

Example 10   Solve: $4x = 2(12 - 2x)$.

$$4x = 2(12 - 2x)$$

$$4x = 24 - 4x$$ Using a distributive property to multiply and remove parentheses

$$4x + 4x = 24 - 4x + 4x$$ Adding $4x$ to get all x-terms on one side

$$8x = 24$$ Collecting like terms

$$\frac{8x}{8} = \frac{24}{8}$$ Dividing by 8

$$x = 3$$

Check:

$$\frac{4x = 2(12 - 2x)}{4 \cdot 3 \; ? \; 2(12 - 2 \cdot 3)}$$
$$12 \; \Big| \; 2(12 - 6)$$
$$\Big| \; 2 \cdot 6$$
$$\Big| \; 12 \qquad \text{True}$$

We use the rules for order of operations to carry out the calculations on each side of the equation.

The solution is 3

Do Margin Exercises 15 and 16.

Here is a procedure for solving the types of equation discussed in this section.

▶ **An Equation Solving Procedure**

1. Multiply on both sides to clear the equation of fractions or decimals. (This is optional, but it can ease computations.)

2. If parentheses occur, multiply using the distributive properties to remove them.

3. Collect like terms on each side, if necessary.

4. Get all terms with variables on one side and all constant terms on the other side, using the *addition principle*.

5. Collect like terms again, if necessary.

6. Multiply or divide to solve for the variable, using the *multiplication principle*.

7. Check all possible solutions in the original equation.

Example 11 Solve: $2 - 5(x + 5) = 3(x - 2) - 1$.

$2 - 5\,(x + 5) = 3\,(x - 2) - 1$

$2 - 5x - 25 = 3x - 6 - 1$ Using the distributive properties to multiply and remove parentheses

$-5x - 23 = 3x - 7$ Collecting like terms

$-5x - 23 + 5x = 3x - 7 + 5x$ Adding $5x$

$-23 = 8x - 7$ Collecting like terms

$-23 + 7 = 8x - 7 + 7$ Adding 7

$-\dfrac{16}{8} = \dfrac{8x}{8}$ Dividing by 8

$-2 = x$

Check:

$$\begin{array}{c|c}\multicolumn{2}{c}{2 - 5(x + 5) = 3(x - 2) - 1} \\ \hline 2 - 5(-2 + 5) \;?\; & 3(-2 - 2) - 1 \\ 2 - 5(3) & 3(-4) - 1 \\ 2 - 15 & -12 - 1 \\ -13 & -13 \end{array}$$ True

The solution is 2.

Note that the solution of $-2 = x$ is -2, which is also the solution of $x = -2$.

Do Margin Exercises 17 and 18.

Solve.

17. $3(7 + 2x) = 30 + 7(x - 1)$

18. $4(3 + 5x) - 4 = 3 + 2(x - 2)$

Calculator Spotlight

Checking Solutions of Equations

Calculators can be used to check solutions of equations. We can replace the variable with the solution and evaluate each side of the equation separately.

Example 15 Check to see if 5 is a solution of the equation:

$$3(x - 5) + 4(x + 3) = 2(x - 6) + 34.$$

To check using a calculator, we first evaluate the left side:

The display reads 32:

32

We then evaluate the right side:

$$\boxed{2}\ \boxed{\times}\ \boxed{(}\ \boxed{5}\ \boxed{-}\ \boxed{6}\ \boxed{)}\ \boxed{+}\ \boxed{3}\ \boxed{4}\ \boxed{=}.$$

Again, the display reads 32:

32

Since the left side is the same as the right side, the solution checks.

Check to see of the given number is a solution of the equation using a calculator.

1. $3(5x - 9) + 2(x + 3) = -5(3x - 7) + 8$; $x = 2$
Yes

2. $2(3x - 5) + 7x = 3x - (x + 3) + 20$; $x = 3$
No

3. $20(x - 39) = 5x - 432$; $x = 23\frac{1}{5}$
Yes

4. $-\frac{1}{2}x + 8 = \frac{11}{2}x - 6$; $x = -28$
No

5. $-(x - 3) - (x - 4) = 2x + 3$; $x = 1$
Yes

Exercise Set 10.3

a Solve. Don't forget to check!

1. $5x + 6 = 31$

2. $8x + 6 = 30$

3. $8x + 4 = 68$

4. $8z + 7 = 79$

5. $4x - 6 = 34$

6. $4x - 11 = 21$

7. $3x - 9 = 33$

8. $6x - 9 = 57$

9. $7x + 2 = -54$

10. $5x + 4 = -41$

11. $-45 = 3 + 6y$

12. $-91 = 9t + 8$

13. $-4x + 7 = 35$

14. $-5x - 7 = 108$

15. $-7x - 24 = -129$

16. $-6z - 18 = -132$

b Solve.

17. $5x + 7x = 72$

18. $4x + 5x = 45$

19. $8x + 7x = 60$

20. $3x + 9x = 96$

21. $4x + 3x = 42$

22. $6x + 19x = 100$

23. $-6y - 3y = 27$

24. $-4y - 8y = 48$

25. $7y - 8y = -15$

26. $-10y - 3y = -39$

27. $10.2y - 73y = -58$

28. $6.8y - 2.4y = -88$

29. $x + \dfrac{1}{3}x = 8$

30. $x + \dfrac{1}{4}x = 10$

31. $8y - 35 = 3y$

32. $4x - 6 = 6x$

33. $8x - 1 = 23 - 4x$

34. $5y - 2 = 28 - y$

35. $2x - 1 = 4 + x$

36. $5x - 2 = 6 + x$

37. $6x + 3 = 2x + 11$

38. $5y + 3 = 2y + 15$

39. $5 - 2x = 3x - 7x + 25$

40. $10 - 3x = 2x - 8x + 40$

41. $4 + 3x - 6 = 3x + 2 - x$

42. $5 + 4x - 7 = 4x - 2 - x$

43. $4y - 4 + y + 24 = 6y + 20 - 4y$

44. $5y - 7 + y = 7y + 21 - 5y$

Solve. (Hint: Fractions or decimals can be cleared before solving.)

45. $\frac{7}{2}x + \frac{1}{2}x = 3x + \frac{3}{2} + \frac{5}{2}x$

46. $\frac{7}{8}x - \frac{1}{4} + \frac{3}{4}x = \frac{1}{16} + x$

47. $\frac{2}{3} + \frac{1}{4}t = \frac{1}{3}$

48. $-\frac{3}{2} + x = -\frac{5}{6} - \frac{4}{3}$

49. $\frac{2}{3} + 3y = 5y - \frac{2}{15}$

50. $\frac{1}{2} + 4m = 3m - \frac{5}{2}$

51. $\frac{5}{3} + \frac{2}{3}x = \frac{25}{12} + \frac{5}{4}x + \frac{3}{4}$

52. $1 - \frac{2}{3}y = \frac{9}{5} - \frac{y}{5} + \frac{3}{5}$

53. $2.1x + 45.2 = 3.2 - 8.4x$

54. $0.96y - 0.79 = 0.21y + 0.46$

55. $1.03 - 0.62x = 0.71 - 0.22x$

56. $1.7t + 8 - 1.62t = 0.4t - 0.32 + 8$

57. $\frac{2}{7}x - \frac{1}{2}x = \frac{3}{4}x + 1$

58. $\frac{5}{16}y + \frac{3}{8}y = 2 + \frac{1}{4}y$

c Solve.

59. $3(2y - 3) = 27$

60. $4(2y - 3) = 28$

61. $40 = 5(3x + 2)$

62. $9 = 3(5x - 2)$

63. $2(3 + 4m) - 9 = 45$

64. $3(5 + 3m) - 8 = 88$

65. $5r - (2r + 8) = 16$

66. $6b - (3b + 8) = 16$

67. $6 - 2(3x - 1) = 2$

68. $10 - 3(2x - 1) = 1$

69. $5(d + 4) = 7(d - 2)$

70. $3(t - 2) = 9(t + 2)$

71. $8(2t + 1) = 4(7t + 7)$

72. $7(5x - 2) = 6(6x - 1)$

73. $3(r - 6) + 2 = 4(r + 2) - 21$

74. $5(t + 3) + 9 = 3(t - 2) + 6$

75. $19 - (2x + 3) = 2(x + 3) + x$

76. $13 - (2c + 2) = 2(c + 2) + 3c$

77. $0.7(3x + 6) = 1.1 - (x + 2)$

78. $0.9\ (2x + 8) = 20 - (x + 5)$

79. $a + (a - 3) = (a + 2) - (a + 1)$

80. $0.8 - 4(b - 1) = 0.\,2 + 3(4 - b)$

Skill Maintenance

Divide.

81. $22.1 \div 3.4$

82. $-22.1 \div (-3.4)$

83. $22.1 \div (-3.4)$

84 $-22.1 \div 3.4$

Factor.

85. $7x - 21 - 14y$

86. $25a - 625b + 75$

87. $42t + 14m - 56$

88. $16a - 64b + 224 - 32q$

89. Find $-(-x)$ when $x = -8$.

90. Use $<$ or $>$ for $\square$ to write a true sentence:
$-15 \,\square\, -13$.

91. ❖ A student begins solving the equation $\frac{2}{3}x + 1 = \frac{5}{6}$ by multiplying by 6 on both sides. Is this a wise thing to do? Why or why not?

92. ❖ Describe a procedure that a classmate could use to solve the equation $ax + b = c$ for x.

Solve.

93. $\dfrac{y-2}{3} = \dfrac{2-y}{5}$

94. $3x = 4x$

95. $5 + 2y = \dfrac{25}{12} + \dfrac{5y+3}{4}$

96. ▦ $0.05y - 1.82 = 0.708y - 0.504$

97. $\dfrac{2}{3}(2x - 1) = 10$

98. $\dfrac{2}{3}\left(\dfrac{7}{8} - 4x\right) - \dfrac{5}{8} = \dfrac{3}{8}$

99. The perimeter of the figure shown is 15 cm. Solve for x.

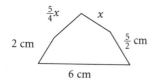

Review Exercises: Chapter 10

Compute and simplify.

1. $4 + (-7)$

2. $-\dfrac{2}{3} + \dfrac{1}{12}$

3. $6 + (-9) + (-8) - 7$

4. $-3.8 + 5.1 + (-12) + (-4.3) + 10$

5. $-3 - (-7)$

6. $\dfrac{9}{10} - \dfrac{1}{2}$

7. $-3.8 - 4.1$

8. $-9 \cdot -6$

9. $-2.7(3.4)$

10. $\dfrac{2}{3} \cdot \left(-\dfrac{3}{7}\right)$

11. $3 \cdot (-7) \cdot (-2) \cdot (-5)$

12. $35 \div (-5)$

13. $-5.1 \div 1.7$

14. $-\dfrac{3}{11} \div \left(-\dfrac{4}{11}\right)$

Evaluate the following for $x = 4$, $y = 3$ and $z = -2$.

15. xyz

16. $2x + 5z$

17. $\dfrac{xy}{2z}$

18. $-7x + 11y$

Multiply.

19. $7(2x + 3y - 1)$

20. $(7x - 4)(-5)$

21. $-11(8x - 17)$

22. $13(6x - 3y + 7)$

Factor.

23. $15x - 45$

24. $7x - 14y + 35$

25. $-24x + 8y - 12$

Collect like terms.

26. $9x - 14 - 5x - 3$

27. $6.5a - 8.2b - 3.1a + 6.2$

28. $\frac{3}{4}x - \frac{1}{8}y - \frac{2}{3}x + \frac{3}{5} - \frac{3}{4}y$

Solve.

29. $x + 5 = -17$

30. $-8x = -56$

31. $-\frac{x}{4} = 48$

32. $n - 7 = -6$

33. $15x = -35$

34. $x - 11 = 14$

35. $-\frac{2}{3} + x = -\frac{1}{6}$

36. $\frac{4}{5}y = -\frac{3}{16}$

37. $y - 0.9 = 9.09$

38. $5 - x = 13$

Solve.

39. $5t + 9 = 3t - 1$

40. $7x - 6 = 25x$

41. $\frac{1}{4}x - \frac{5}{8} = 3$

42. $14y = 23y - 17 - 10$

43. $0.22y - 0.6 = 0.12y + 3 - 0.8y$

44. $\frac{1}{4}x - \frac{1}{8}x = 3 - \frac{1}{16}x$

45. $4(x + 3) = 36$

46. $3(5x - 7) = -66$

47. $8(x - 2) = 5(x + 4)$

48. $-5x + 3(x + 8) = 16$

Practice Test: Chapter 10

Compute and simplify.

1. $3.1 - (-4.7)$

2. $-8 + 4 + (-7) + 3$

3. $-\dfrac{1}{3} + \dfrac{3}{8}$

4. $2 - (-8)$

5. $3.2 - 5.7$

6. $\dfrac{1}{8} - \left(-\dfrac{3}{4}\right)$

7. $4 \cdot (-12)$

8. $-\dfrac{1}{2} \cdot \left(-\dfrac{3}{8}\right)$

9. $-45 \div 5$

10. $-\dfrac{3}{5} \div \left(-\dfrac{4}{5}\right)$

11. Evaluate $\dfrac{a-b}{6}$ for $a = -8$ and $b = 10$.

Multiply.

12. $-6(5x - 4y + 2)$

13. $(9x - 11y - 6)(-7)$

Factor.

14. $-22x + 33y + 44$

15. $75x - 150$

Collect like terms.

16. $-12x + 17 + 13x - 10y - 17$

17. $3x = -18$

18. $-\dfrac{4}{7}x = -28$

19. $3t + 7 = 2t - 5$

20. $\dfrac{1}{2}x - \dfrac{3}{5} = \dfrac{2}{5}$

21. $-\dfrac{2}{5} + x - \dfrac{3}{4}$

22. $0.4p + 0.2 = 4.2p - 7.8 - 0.6p$

23. $3(x + 2) = 27$

24. $-3x - 6(x - 4) = 9$

25. Explain the distributive law in your own words. Give an example.

Cumulative Review: Chapters 1-10

Perform the indicated operations and simplify.

1. $4\frac{2}{3} + 5\frac{1}{2}$

2. $\left(\frac{1}{4}\right)^2 \div \left(\frac{1}{2}\right)^3 \cdot (10.3)(4)$

3. $120.5 - 32.98$

4. $-27{,}148 \div 22$

5. $14 \div [33 \div 11 + 0 \cdot 2 - (15 - 3)]$

6. $8^3 + 45 \cdot 24 - 9^2 \div 3$

Find fractional notation.

7. -6.23

8. 210%

Use $<$, $>$, or for $\square$ to write a true sentence.

9. $\frac{5}{6} \square \frac{7}{8}$

10. $\frac{5}{12} \square \frac{3}{10}$

Complete.

11. $6 \text{ oz} = \underline{\hspace{2cm}} \text{ lb}$

12. $23.5 \text{m}^2 = \underline{\hspace{2cm}} \text{ cm}^2$

13. $0.087 \text{ L} = \underline{\hspace{1cm}} \text{ mL}$

14. $2.5 \text{ yd} = \underline{\hspace{2cm}} \text{ in.}$

15. $3 \text{ yd}^2 = \underline{\hspace{2cm}} \text{ ft}^2$

16. $17 \text{ cm} = \underline{\hspace{2cm}} \text{ m}$

17. Find the perimeter and the area.

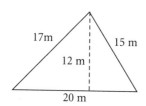

18. Collect like terms: $12a - 7 - 3a - 9$.

19. Evaluate: $9x - 7y$, for $x = 3.2$ and $y = -8.5$

This line graph shows the average number of pounds of apples eaten per person in the United States for the years 1984–1988.

20. What was the average number of pounds of apples that each person ate in 1987?

21. In what year did apple consumption decrease?

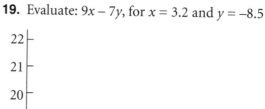

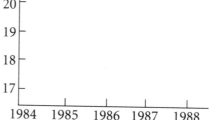

Solve.

22. $\dfrac{12}{15} = \dfrac{x}{18}$ **23.** $1 - 7x = 4 - (x + 9)$ **24.** $-15x = 265$ **25.** $x + \dfrac{3}{4} = \dfrac{7}{8}$

26. A case of returnable bottles contains 24 bottles. Several students find that together they have 168 bottles. How many cases can they fill?

27. Americans own 52 million dogs, 56 million cats, 45 million birds, 250 million fish, and 125 million other creatures as house pets. How many pets do Americans own?

28. Find the mean: 49, 53, 60, 62, 69.

29. What is the simple interest on $800 at 12% annual interest for $\frac{1}{4}$ year?

30. How long must a rope be in order to reach from the top of an 8-m tree to a point on the ground 15 m from the bottom of the tree?

31. The sales tax on a purchase of $5.50 is $0.33. What is the sales tax rate?

32. A bolt of fabric in a fabric store has $10\frac{3}{4}$ yd on it. A customer purchases $8\frac{5}{8}$ yd. How many yards remain on the bolt?

33. What is the cost, in dollars, of 15.6 gal of gasoline at 139.9¢ per gallon? Round to the nearest cent.

34. A box of powdered milk that makes 20 qt costs $4.99. A box that makes 8 qt costs $1.99. Which size has the lower unit price?

35. It is $\frac{7}{10}$ km from Ida's dormitory to the library. She starts to walk there, changes her mind after going $\frac{1}{4}$ of the distance, and returns home. How far did Ida walk?

Final Practice Test

This exam reviews the entire textook. A question may arise as to what notation to use for a particular problem or exercise. While there is no hard-and-fast rule, especially as you use mathematics outside the classroom, here is the guideline that we follow: Use the notation given in the problem. That is, if the problem is given using mixed numbers, give the answer in mixed numbers. If the problem is given in decimal notation, give the answer in decimal notation. You may NOT use a calculator in questions.

1. Find the prime factorization of 2100.

2. Find the LCM of 6, 15 and 25.

Simplify.

3. $4(-6) \div [3(7-5)^2]$

4. $10 \div 2(20) - 5^2$

5. Evaluate $\dfrac{a^2 - b}{3}$ for $a = -9$ and $b = -6$.

Solve.

6. $6c = -72$

7. $7.32 + y = 2.4$

8. $12y = -288$

9. $-833 \div 17 = x$

10. Find the perimeter and the area.

2.5 m

10.3 m

11. Find $-(-x)$ when $x = -17$.

Simplify.

12. $-45 + 9$

13. $-9 - (-13)$

14. $(-15)(-2)$

15. $(-3)(-1)(2)(1)(-1)$

16. $3\frac{1}{5} - 2\frac{3}{4}$

17. $-\frac{5}{12} + \frac{7}{18}$

18. $-\frac{99a}{50} \div \left(-\frac{33a}{10}\right)$

19. $-7\frac{1}{4} \cdot 3\frac{3}{5}$

20. $0.15(2.35)$

21. $-3.78 \div 2.8$

22. $2.35 + (-1.68) + 3.6$

23. $-\frac{290c}{15c}$

Solve.

24. $-3.9y = 249.6$

25. $-\frac{2}{3}t = -\frac{5}{6}$

26. $\frac{5}{8} + y = \frac{7}{3}$

27. Evaluate:

$16x + 5y$, for $x = \frac{3}{8}$ and $y = -\frac{4}{5}$

28. Find the area:

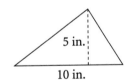

5 in.

10 in.

29. Round $21.\overline{83}$ to the nearest hundredth.

30. Find decimal notation for $\frac{5}{8}$.

31. Find fractional notation for -14.125

Simplify.

32. $(-7)^2 - 5[2(8 - 12) \div (-4)]^2$

Use the following set of numbers to answer questions 33-36.
3, 6, 10, 12, 5, 7, 2, 9, 5, 11.

33. Find the mean.

34. Find the median.

35. Find the mode.

36. Find the range.

37. This line graph shows the prime rate (the interest rate charged by banks to their best customers) in June for several years.

　a) What was the highest prime rate?

　b) Between what two consecutive years did the prime rate decrease the most?

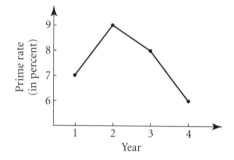

38. How much more profit did Company C make than Company D did?

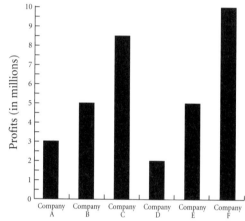

You may use your calculator for the rest of the exam.

39. Simplify the ratio 6.3 to 4.2.

40. Is the following a true proportion?

$$\frac{3}{5} = \frac{45}{75}$$

41. Eight gallons of paint covers 200 square feet. How much paint is needed to cover 325 square feet?

42. Eighteen ounces of a fruit drink costs $3.06. Find the unit price in cents per ounce.

43. Determine which item of sugar is the best buy.

Brand A	5 lb	for	$1.59
Brand B	7.5 lb	for	$1.99

44. Solve for x.

$$\frac{25}{12} = \frac{8}{x}$$

45. A map scale is $\frac{1}{8}$ in. = 5 mi. If two cities are 2 in. apart on the map, what is the actual distance between the cities?

46. These triangles are similar. Find the missing lengths.

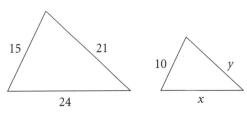

47. Convert 48% to a decimal.

48. What is 4.5% of 82?

49. 63 is 35% of what number?

50. What is the percent increase if the number of children born at a hospital grows from 750 to 900?

51. What amount more has Judy budgeted for rent than for food? (Amount, not percent!)

Judy's 1999 Budget
(Salary = $30,000)

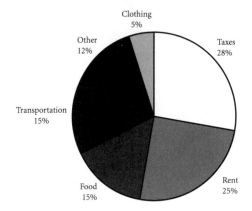

Clothing 5%
Other 12%
Taxes 28%
Transportation 15%
Food 15%
Rent 25%

52. 15 ft = _____ yd

53. 2371 m = _____ km

54. 5 L = _____ mL

55. 7 T = _____ lb

56. 24 hr = _____ min

57. 5.34 kg = _____ g

58. 75.4 mg = _____ cg

59. 80 oz = _____ pt

Find the area.

60.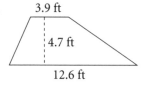
3.9 ft

4.7 ft

12.6 ft

61.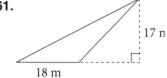
17 n

18 m

62.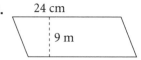
24 cm

9 m

63. Find the radius, the circumference, and the area of this circle.

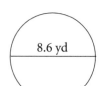
8.6 yd

64. Find the volume.

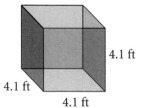
4.1 ft

4.1 ft

4.1 ft

Find the volume.

65.
1000 mi

10 mi

66.
10 m

67.
1000 in.

10 in.

68. Multiply.

$-7(3x - 2y + 8)$

69. Factor.

$18x - 24y + 114$

70. Collect like terms.

$-2.5x + 17 + 9.6y - 19.5 + 13x$

Solve.

71. $0.5m - 13 = 17 + 2.5m$

72. $8z + 3 = 7z - 4$

73. $-2(2x - 3) = 4(2x + 2)$

74. $\dfrac{7}{4}x - \dfrac{1}{2} = \dfrac{1}{8} + x$

75. A machine wraps 134 candy bars per minute. How long does it take this machine to wrap 8710 bars?

76. A share of stock bought for $29\frac{5}{8}$ dropped $3\frac{7}{8}$ before it was resold. What was the price when it was resold?

77. At the start of a trip, a car's odometer read 27,428.6 mi and at the end of the trip the reading was 27,914.5 mi. How long was the trip?

78. From an income of $32,000, amounts of $6400 and $1600 are paid for federal and state taxes. How much remains after these taxes have been paid?

79. A lifeguard is paid $47 a day for 9 days. How much was received?

80. What is the simple interest on $4000 principal at 8% annual interest for $\frac{3}{4}$ year?

81. A real estate agent received $5880 commission on the sale of an $84,000 home. What was the rate of commission?

82. Ace Car Rentals charges $35 a day plus 15 cents a mile for a van rental. If a couple's one-day van rental cost $68, how many miles did they drive?

83. Find the length of the third side of this right triangle. Give an exact answer and an approximation to three decimal places.

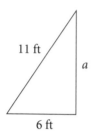

11 ft

a

6 ft

84. Explain the order of operations and its importance in mathematics.

85. Explain the commutative property of multiplication and give an example.

86. Explain the difference between an expression and an equation. Give an example of each.

Answer Key

Chapter R

Margin Exercises R.1

1. fifty-seven   **2.** twenty-nine   **3.** eighty-eight
4. two hundred four   **5.** seventy-nine thousand, two hundred four   **6.** one million, eight hundred seventy-nine thousand, two hundred four   **7.** twenty-two billion, three hundred one million, eight hundred seventy-nine thousand, two hundred four
8. 213,105,329   **9.** 2 ten thousands
10. 2 hundred thousands   **11.** 2 millions
12. 2 ten millions   **13.** 6   **14.** 8   **15.** 5   **16.** 5

Exercise Set R.1

1. eighty-five   **3.** eighty-eight thousand
5. one hundred twenty-three thousand, seven hundred sixty-five   **7.** seven billion, seven hundred fifty-four million, two hundred eleven thousand, five hundred seventy-seven   **9.** one million, eight hundred sixty-seven thousand dollars   **11.** one billion, five hundred eighty-three million, one hundred forty-one thousand
13. 2,233,812   **15.** 8,000,000,000
17. 9,460,000,000,000   **19.** 2,974,600   **21.** 5 thousands   **23.** 5 hundreds   **25.** 3   **27.** 0
31. 131

Margin Exercises R.2

1. 10   **2.** $78   **3.** 193 mi   **4.** 12 ft   **5.** 14 cu yd
6. 136 gal   **7.** 9,745   **8.** 13,465   **9.** 16,182
10. 27   **11.** 34   **12.** 27   **13.** 38   **14.** 47
15. 61   **16.** 27,474

Exercise Set R.2

1. 15   **3.** 800   **5.** 387   **7.** 5,198   **9.** 164
11. 100   **13.** 900   **15.** 1,010   **17.** 8,503
19. 5,266   **21.** 4,466   **23.** 8,310   **25.** 6,608
27. 16,784   **29.** 34,432   **31.** 101,310   **33.** 100,111
35. 28   **37.** 26   **39.** 67   **41.** 230   **43.** 130
45. 1,349   **47.** 36,926   **49.** 18,424   **51.** 2,320
53. 31,685   **55.** 11,679   **57.** 22,654
59. 12,765,097   **61.** nine hundred twenty-four million, six hundred thousand dollars   **65.** 5050

Margin Exercises R.3

1. 62 cu yd   **2.** 8000 sq ft   **3.** $7 = 2 + 5$ **4.** $17 = 9 + 8$ **5.** 3,801   **6.** 6,328   **7.** 4,747   **8.** 56
9. 205   **10.** 658   **11.** 2,851   **12.** 1,546

Exercise Set R.3

1. $\$1260 - \$450 = \$810$ **3.** $16 - 5 = 11$
5. $7 = 3 + 4$ **7.** $13 = 5 + 8$ **9.** $23 = 14 + 9$
11. $43 = 27 + 16$ **13.** 12   **15.** 44   **17.** 533
19. 1,126   **21.** 39   **23.** 298   **25.** 226   **27.** 234
29. 5,382   **31.** 1,493   **33.** 2,187   **35.** 3,831
37. 7,748   **39.** 33,794   **41.** 2,168   **43.** 43,028
45. 56   **47.** 36   **49.** 84   **51.** 454   **53.** 771
55. 2,191   **57.** 3,749   **59.** 7,019   **61.** 5,745
63. 95,974   **65.** 9,989   **67.** 83,818   **69.** 4,206
73. 10,305   **73.** 7 ten thousands   **75.** 29,708
79. 2,829,177   **81.** 3, 4

Margin Exercises R.4

1. 40   **2.** 50   **3.** 70   **4.** 100   **5.** 40   **6.** 80
7. 90   **8.** 140   **9.** 470   **10.** 240   **11.** 290
12. 600   **13.** 800   **14.** 800   **15.** 9,300
16. 8,000   **17.** 8,000   **18.** 19,000   **19.** 69,000
20. <   **21.** >   **22.** >   **23.** <   **24.** <   **25.** >

Exercise Set R.4

1. 50   **3.** 70   **5.** 730   **7.** 900   **9.** 100
11. 1,000   **13.** 9,100   **15.** 32,900   **17.** 6,000
19. 8,000   **21.** 45,000   **23.** 373,000   **25.** <
27. >   **29.** <   **31.** >   **33.** >   **35.** >
37. 86,754   **39.** 48,824

Margin Exercises R.5

1. $8 \cdot 7 = 56$ **2.** $75 \text{ mL} \cdot 10 = 750 \text{ mL}$ **3.** $8 \cdot 8 = 64$
4. 1,035   **5.** 3,024   **6.** 46,252   **7.** 205,065
8. 144,432   **9.** 287,232   **10.** 14,075,720
11. 391,760   **12.** 17,345,600   **13.** 56,200
14. 562,000   **15.** a) 1081   b) 1081   **16.** 40
17. 15   **18.** 70   **19.** 450   **20.** 2,730   **21.** 100
22. 1,000   **23.** 560   **24.** 360   **25.** 700
26. 2,300   **27.** 72,300   **28.** 10,000   **29.** 100,000
30. 5,600   **31.** 1,600   **32.** 9,000   **33.** 852,000
34. 10,000   **35.** 12,000   **36.** 72,000   **37.** 54,000
38. 5,600   **39.** 56,000   **40.** 18,000

Exercise Set R.5

1. $21 \cdot 21 = 441$ **3.** $8 \cdot 12 = 96$ **5.** 870
7. 2,340,000   **9.** 520   **11.** 564   **13.** 65,200
15. 4,371,000   **17.** 120,000   **19.** 120,000
21. 80,000   **23.** 5,642   **25.** 31,468   **27.** 4,680
29. 2,958   **31.** 43,956   **33.** 44,792   **35.** 162,000
37. 224,900   **39.** 1,132,800   **41.** 3,843,360

43. 28,319,616   **45.** 38,858,112   **47.** 15,818,370
49. 35,978,400   **51.** 106,145   **53.** 22,421,949
55. 78,144   **57.** 1,534,160   **59.** 3,109

Margin Exercises R.6

1. 8   **2.** 14   **3.** $15 = 5 \cdot 3$ **4.** $72 = 9 \cdot 8$
5. $12 \div 6 = 2$, $12 \div 2 = 6$ **6.** $42 \div 7 = 6$, $42 \div 6 = 7$
7. 6   **8.** 6 R 7   **9.** 4 R 5   **10.** 6 R 13   **11.** 58 R 3
12. 1,475 R 5   **13.** 1015   **14.** 670 R 1   **15.** 360 R 4
16. 2,989 R 12

Exercise Set R.6

1. 190   **3.** 91   **5.** $6 \cdot 3 = 18$ **7.** $22 \cdot 1 = 22$
9. $9 \cdot 6 = 54$ **11.** $37 \cdot 1 = 37$ **13.** $45 \div 9 = 5$, $45 \div 5 = 9$
15. $37 \div 1 = 37$, $37 \div 37 = 1$ **17.** $64 \div 8 = 8$, $64 \div 8 = 8$
19. $66 \div 11 = 6$, $66 \div 6 = 11$ **21.** 55 R 2
23. 108   **25.** 307   **27.** 753 R 3
29. 74 R 1   **31.** 92 R 2   **33.** 1703   **35.** 987 R 5
37. 12,700   **39.** 127   **41.** 52 R 52   **43.** 29 R 5
45. 40 R 12   **47.** 90 R 22   **49.** 29   **51.** 105 R 3
53. 1,609 R 2   **55.** 1,007 R 1   **57.** 23   **59.** 107 R 1
61. 370   **63.** 609 R 15   **65.** 304   **67.** 3,508 R 219
69. 8070   **71.** 6,800   **73.** 11,053   **75.** 17,010

Margin Exercises R.7

1. 1 = numerator, 6 = denominator
2. 5 = numerator, 7 = denominator
3. 22 = numerator, 3 = denominator   **4.** $\frac{1}{2}$ **5.** $\frac{1}{3}$
6. $\frac{1}{3}$ **7.** $\frac{1}{6}$ **8.** $\frac{5}{8}$ **9.** $\frac{2}{3}$ **10.** $\frac{3}{4}$ **11.** $\frac{4}{6}$
12. $1\frac{1}{3}$ or $\frac{4}{3}$ **13.** $1\frac{3}{4}$ or $\frac{7}{4}$ **14.** $\frac{2}{5}$ **15.** $\frac{2}{3}$
16. $\frac{2}{6}, \frac{4}{6}$ **17.** 1   **18.** 1   **19.** 1   **20.** 1   **21.** $1\frac{2}{3}$
22. $8\frac{3}{4}$ **23.** $12\frac{2}{3}$

Exercise Set R.7

1. 3 = numerator, 4 = denominator
3. 11 = numerator, 20 = denominator   **5.** $\frac{2}{4}$
7. $\frac{1}{8}$ **9.** $\frac{1}{4}$ **11.** $\frac{8}{16}$ **13.** $\frac{6}{12}$ **15.** $\frac{5}{10}$ **17.** $\frac{3}{6}$
19. $1\frac{1}{3}$ or $\frac{4}{3}$

Chapter 1

Exercise Set 1.1

1. The Commutative Property of Addition allows us to add numbers in any order. For example $8 + 2 = 10$ and $2 + 8 = 10$ **3.** The Associate Property of Multiplication allows groupings to change when multiplying. For example, $2 \cdot (5 \cdot 6) = (2 \cdot 5) \cdot 6 = 10 \cdot 6 = 60$. In these examples, parentheses tell us what operation to perform first.   **5.** The Commutative Property of Addition says that the order of the numbers being added can be changed without affecting the sum. However, when subtracting, if the order is changed, the answer is also changed. For example, $7 - 2$ does not equal $2 - 7$

Margin Exercises 1.2

1. 54   **2.** 55   **3.** 102   **4.** 104   **5.** 10000
6. 100   **7.** 512   **8.** 32

Exercise Set 1.2

1. 3^4 **3.** 5^2 **5.** 7^5 **7.** 10^3 **9.** 49   **11.** 729
13. 20736   **15.** 121   **17.** 302   **19.** 59   **21.** 135
23. 17 R1   **25.** $7^3 \cdot 8^3 \cdot 9^4$ **27** x^4

Margin Exercises 1.3

1. $5 = 1 \cdot 5$; $45 = 9 \cdot 5$; $100 = 20 \cdot 5$ **2.** $10 = 1 \cdot 10$; $60 = 6 \cdot 10$; $110 = 11 \cdot 10$ **3.** 5, 10, 15, 20, 25, 30, 35, 40, 45, 50   **4.** 1, 2, 3, 6   **5.** 1, 2, 4, 8   **6.** 1, 2, 5, 10
7. 1, 2, 4, 8, 16, 32   **8.** yes   **9.** yes   **10.** no
11. yes   **12.** no   **13.** yes   **14.** no   **15.** yes
16. no   **17.** yes   **18.** no   **19.** yes   **20.** no
21. no   **22.** yes   **23.** no   **24.** yes   **25.** no
26. yes   **27.** no   **28.** yes   **29.** no   **30.** yes
31. yes   **32.** no   **33.** no   **34.** yes

Margin Exercises 1.4

1. 1:neither; 4:composite; 6:composite; 8:composite; 13:prime; 19:prime; 41:prime   **2.** $2 \cdot 3$ **3.** $2 \cdot 2 \cdot 3$
4. $3 \cdot 5 \cdot 5$ **5.** $2 \cdot 7 \cdot 7$ **6.** $2 \cdot 7 \cdot 7$ **7.** $2 \cdot 3 \cdot 3 \cdot 7$

Exercise Set 1.4

1. prime   **3.** composite   **5.** composite   **7.** prime
9. neither   **11.** composite   **13.** prime   **15.** prime
17. 2^3 **19.** $2 \cdot 7$ **21.** $2 \cdot 11$ **23.** 5^2 **25.** $2 \cdot 5^2$
27. 13^2 **29.** $2^2 \cdot 5^2$ **31.** $5 \cdot 7$ **33.** $2 \cdot 3 \cdot 13$
35. $7 \cdot 11$ **37.** $2^4 \cdot 7$ **39.** $2^2 \cdot 5^2 \cdot 3$ **41.** 0
43. 0   **47.** $2^3 \cdot 3 \cdot 5^2 \cdot 13$ **49.** $2^2 \cdot 3^2 \cdot 7 \cdot 11$

Margin Exercises 1.5

1. 45   **2.** 40   **3.** 30   **4.** 24   **5.** 10   **6.** 80
7. 40   **8.** 360   **9.** 864   **10.** 756   **11.** 18
12. 24   **13.** 36   **14.** 210   **15.** 2520   **16.** 3780

Exercise Set 1.5

1. 4   **3.** 50   **5.** 40   **7.** 54   **9.** 150   **11.** 120
13. 72   **15.** 420   **17.** 144   **19.** 288   **21.** 30
23. 105   **25.** 72   **27.** 60   **29.** 36   **31.** 900
33. 48   **35.** 50   **37.** 143   **39.** 420   **41.** 378
43. 810   **45.** Every 420 years.   **47.** 200 days.
49. 7935   **51.** $2 \cdot 7$ squared   **53.** Yes.   **55.** 1260
57. 5 in. by 24 in.

Chapter 1 Review Exercises

1. Commutative property of addition   **2.** Associative property of addition   **3.** Commutative property of multiplication   **4.** Associative law of multiplication
5. Identity property of zero   **6.** Subtraction property of zero   **7.** Subtraction property of zero
8. Multiplication property of zero   **9.** Identity property of one   **10.** Division property of one
11. Division property of one   **12.** Division property of zero   **13.** Division property of zero   **14.** 4^5
15. 5^3 **16.** 169   **17.** 8   **18.** 12, 24, 36, 48, 60, 72, 84, 96, 108, 120   **19.** 8, 16, 24, 32, 40, 48, 56, 64, 72, 80
20. yes   **21.** no   **22.** 6372, 300, 1432, 90,000, 620,844   **23.** 555,555, 6372, 300, 90,000, 620,844
24. 300, 90,000   **25.** 555,555, 300, 90,000
26. 6372, 300, 90,000, 620,844   **27.** 6372, 90,000
28. composite   **29.** prime   **30.** 2, 3, 4, 6, 9, 12, 18
31. 2, 48, 3, 32, 4, 24, 6, 16, 8, 12   **32.** 3, 25, 5, 15
33. $5 \cdot 2 \cdot 7$ **34.** $5 \cdot 5 \cdot 2 \cdot 3$ **35.** $17 \cdot 2 \cdot 2 \cdot 2$
36. $3 \cdot 143$ **37.** 90   **38.** 96

Chapter 1 Practice Test

1. Associate property of addition   **2.** Commutative property of multiplication   **3.** 7^8 **4.** 343
5. 9, 18, 27, 36, 45, 54, 63, 72, 81, 90   **6.** yes
7. yes, the sum of the digits is divisible by 9
8. yes, the last two digits are divisible by 4
9. yes, the sum of the digits is divisible by 3
10. 2, 13, 41   **11.** 21, 48   **12.** 1   **13.** 2, 4, 8, 16
14. 5, 25   **15.** $5 \cdot 3 \cdot 2 \cdot 2$ **16.** $3 \cdot 3 \cdot 3 \cdot 2 \cdot 2$
17. 180   **18.** no, the grouping is changed, the answer will also change.   **19.** The student has multiplied 9×2 but should have raised 9 to the second power $(9 \cdot 9)$

Chapter 2

Margin Exercises 2.1

1. 51   **2.** 30   **3.** 584   **4.** 84   **5.** 4, 1
6. 52, 52   **7.** 29   **8.** 1,880   **9.** 253   **10.** 93
11. 1,880   **12.** 305   **13.** 93   **14.** 87 in
15. 46   **16.** 4   **17.** 13   **18.** 224

Exercise Set 2.1

1. 22   **3.** 20   **5.** 100   **7.** 1   **9.** 49   **11.** 5
13. 434   **15.** 41   **17.** 88   **19.** 4   **21.** 303
23. 20   **25.** 70   **27.** 295   **29.** 32   **31.** 62
33. 94   **35.** 906   **37.** 102   **39.** 110   **41.** 7
43. 544   **45.** 708   **47.** 42   **49.** 6^5
53. 24, $1 + 5 \cdot (4 + 3)$ **55.** 7, $12 \div (4 + 2) \cdot 3 - 2$

Margin Exercises 2.2

1. 64   **2.** 28   **3.** 60   **4.** 8   **5.** 50°
6. 48   **7.** 81

Exercise Set 2.2

1. 42   **3.** 3   **5.** 1   **7.** 6   **9.** 13   **11.** 14
13. 14   **15.** 21   **17.** 21   **19.** 144   **21.** 20
23. 10   **25.** 20°   **27.** x, 20   **29.** 5, x **31.** a, b
33. 2, 5   **35.** 15, 15   **37.** a, b, c **39.** 7, x
41. 3, x, 4, y **43.** 5, x, 7
45. 4, a   **47.** 9, x, y **49.** a, b, c, d **51.** twenty-three million, forty-three thousand, nine hundred twenty-one   **53.** 2,800   **55.** 13 in   **59.** 20

Margin Exercises 2.3

1. 7   **2.** 5   **3.** FALSE   **4.** TRUE   **5.** 5
6. 10   **7.** 5   **8.** 5   **9.** 22490   **10.** 9022
11. 570   **12.** 3661   **13.** 8   **13.** 45   **15.** 77
16. 3311   **17.** 6114   **18.** 8   **19.** 16   **20.** 644
21. 96   **22.** 94

Exercise Set 2.3

1. 14   **3.** 0   **5.** 29   **7.** 0   **9.** 8   **11.** 14
13. 92   **15.** 25   **17.** 450   **19.** 90900   **21.** 32
23. 143   **25.** 79   **27.** 45   **29.** 324   **31.** 743
33. 37   **35.** 66   **37.** 15   **39.** 48   **41.** 175
43. 335   **45.** 104   **47.** 45   **49.** 4056   **51.** 17603
53. 18252   **55.** 205   **57.** <   **59.** 142 R 5
63. 13 R 10

Margin Exercises 2.4

1. 26 cm   **2.** 45 in   **3.** 12 cm   **4.** 16 yd
5. 32 km   **6.** 40 km   **7.** 20 yd   **8.** 16 km
9. 8 cm²   **10.** 56 km²   **11.** 15 yd²
12. 144 km²   **13.** 121 m²   **14.** 196 yd²

Exercise Set 2.4

1. 17 mm   **3.** 26 in   **5.** 28 m   **7.** 30 ft
9. 80 cm   **11.** 88 ft   **13.** 184 mm   **15.** 15 km²
17. 4 in²   **19.** 4 yd²   **21.** 8,100 ft²   **23.** 50 ft²
25. 175 cm²   **27.** 32 in²   **29.** 484 ft²
31. 3,249 km²   **33.** 25 yd²   **35.** 25   **37.** 961
41. 49 ft

Margin Exercises 2.5

1. 200   **2.** 1800   **3.** 2,600   **4.** 11,000
5. 210,000; 160,000   **6.** 1,424,000   **7.** $369
8. 29 in   **9.** 70 ft; $350   **10.** 9180 in²
11. 378 R 1   **12.** 37 gal   **13.** $18   **14.** $38,988

Exercise Set 2.5

1. 180   **3.** 5,720   **5.** 220   **7.** 890   **9.** 16,500
11. 5,200   **13.** 1,600   **15.** 1,500   **17.** 31,000
19. 69,000   **21.** 3,500   **23.** 900   **25.** 270,000
27. 80,000   **29.** 30,000,000   **31.** 48,000,000
33. $12,276   **35.** $7,004   **37.** $64
39. 4007 mi   **41.** 384 in   **43.** 4,500   **45.** 7,280
47. $247   **49.** 54 R 1   **51.** 168 hr   **53.** $400
55. 4700 ft², 288 ft   **57.** 35   **59.** 56 R 11
61. 1600 mi, 27 in   **63.** 18   **65.** $22
67. $704   **69.** 3000 sq in   **71.** 234,600
73. 21,293   **75.** 285,681   **79.** 792,000 mi,
1,386,000 mi

Chapter 2 Review Exercises

1. 65   **2.** 233   **3.** 56   **4.** 32   **5.** 260
6. 99   **7.** 22   **8.** 7   **9.** 7   **10.** 2
11. 8   **12.** 45   **13.** 546   **14.** 19
15. 29   **16.** 39   **17.** A = 456 yd², P = 100 yd
18. A = 169 cm², P = 52 cm   **19.** 3056
20. 14,154   **21.** 19,500   **22.** 4000
23. $2413   **24.** 1982   **25.** $19,748
26. 1371 beakers, 13 mL left over

Chapter 2 Practice Test

1. 64   **2.** 96   **3.** 2   **4.** 216   **5.** 18
6. 92   **7.** 4   **8.** 1152   **9.** 27   **10.** 1

11. 46   **12.** 13   **13.** 14   **14.** 536
15. P = 46 cm, A = 112 cm²
16. P = 76 cm, A = 361 cm²   **17.** 1955
18. 92 packages, 8 left over   **19.** 62,811 mi²
20. A = 120,000 m², P = 1600 m   **21.** 1808 lb.
22. 20   **23.** 2800   **24.** 26,156   **25.** 38,400
26. 36,000

Chapter 2 Cumulative Review

1. $14^7 \cdot 18$ **2.** 6561   **3.** 72,324, 416,235, 1200,
9876, 555   **4.** 72,234; 1200; 9876; 25,432
5. 416,235, 1200, 555   **6.** 72,324, 1200, 9876
7. 72,324   **8.** $2 \cdot 2 \cdot 7$ **9.** $2 \cdot 3 \cdot 3 \cdot 11$
10. $2 \cdot 5 \cdot 5 \cdot 7 \cdot 7$ **11.** 72   **12.** 36   **13.** 2
14. 44   **15.** 27   **16.** $\frac{15}{2}$ **17.** 27   **18.** 16
19. 37   **20.** 231   **21.** 9900   **22.** 453   **23.** 142
24. 32   **25.** 54 cm   **26.** 961 ft²   **27.** $664,163
28. 11,719   **29.** $75   **30.** Westside Appliance

Chapter 3

Margin Exercises 3.1

1. 8 - gain; 5 - loss   **3.** −10 - time before liftoff ; 148
sec after liftoff   **5.** >   **7.** <   **9.** 18   **11.** 29
13. −1   **15.** 0   **17.** 13   **19.** 0   **21.** 1   **23.** −5

Exercise Set 3.1

1. −70° - Montana temperature   **3.** −3 sec - before
liftoff; 128 sec after liftoff   **5.** >   **7.** <   **9.** <
11. <   **13.** >   **15.** <   **17.** 3   **19.** 10   **21.** 0
23. 24   **25.** 53   **27.** 8   **29.** 6   **31.** −6   **33.** 12
35. −70   **37.** 1   **39.** −7   **41.** 14   **43.** 0   **45.**
−7   **47.** 1   **49.** 0   **51.** −34   **53.** 825   **55.**
7,106   **57.** 81   **61.** $x = \pm 7$ **63.** $x; -x$

Margin Exercises 3.2

1. −1   **3.** 4   **5.** 4 + (−5)   **7.** −3 + 8   **9.** −12
11. −22   **13.** −4   **15.** 3   **17.** 0   **19.** 0   **21.** −56

Exercise Set 3.2

1. −5   **3.** −4   **5.** 0   **7.** −13   **9.** −16   **11.** −11
13. 0   **15.** 0   **17.** 8   **19.** −8   **21.** −25   **23.** −27
25. 0   **27.** 0   **29.** 3   **31.** −9   **33.** −5   **35.** 9
37. −3   **39.** 0   **41.** −10   **43.** −24   **45.** −5
47. −21   **49.** 2   **51.** −26   **53.** −21   **55.** 25
57. −17   **59.** 6   **61.** 8   **63.** 160   **65.** −62
67. 19   **69.** 33,000   **71.** 32   **75.** −6,483

77. $x > 7$

Margin Exercises 3.3

1. –6   **3.** 5   **5.** –6   **7.** –9   **9.** 15 lb.

Exercise Set 3.3

1. –7   **3.** –4   **5.** –6   **7.** 0   **9.** –4   **11.** –7
13. –6   **15.** 0   **17.** 0   **19.** 10   **21.** 11   **23.** –14
25. 5   **27.** –7   **29.** –1   **31.** 18   **33.** –10
35. –3   **37.** –21   **39.** 5   **41.** –8   **43.** 12
45. –23   **47.** –68   **49.** –73   **51.** 116   **53.** 0
55. 22   **57.** –62   **59.** –139   **61.** 6   **63.** 107
65. 219   **67.** 17 lbs.   **69.** –3,220 ft.   **71.** 5,832 ft.
73. 62 m   **75.** 64   **77.** 8   **81.** –309,882   **83.** T
85. T   **87.** F   **89.** T   **91.** Up 15 pts.

Margin Exercises 3.4

1. 20; 10; 0; –10; –20; –30   **3.** –100   **5.** –10, 0, 20, 30
7. 32   **9.** 0   **11.** 120   **13.** 6   **15.** 81

Exercise Set 3.4

1. –10   **3.** –18   **5.** –45   **7.** –30   **9.** 10   **11.** 18
13. 45   **15.** 30   **17.** –120   **19.** 300   **21.** 35
23. –340   **25.** 0   **27.** 0   **29.** 70   **31.** 420
33. –70   **35.** 30   **37.** 5,712   **39.** 0   **41.** 25
43. –1,000   **45.** 625   **47.** –128   **49.** –243   **51.** 1
53. 532,500   **55.** 6 R 264   **57.** 40 sq. ft.   **61.** –$23
63. 125   **65.** –17   **67. a)** m or n must be negative
but not both   **b)** m or n must be zero   **c)** m and n
must both be positive or both be negative

Margin Exercises 3.5

1. –2   **3.** –3   **5.** –6   **7.** undefined   **9.** 68
11. –15

Exercise Set 3.5

1. –7   **3.** –14   **5.** –2   **7.** 4   **9.** –9   **11.** 2
13. –43   **15.** –8   **17.** undefined   **19.** –8
21. –23   **23.** 0   **25.** –19   **27.** –41
29. –7   **31.** 20   **33.** –334   **35.** 23   **37.** 8
39. 12   **41.** –10   **43.** –86   **45.** –9   **47.** –6
49. 3   **51.** –25   **53.** –7,988   **55.** –3,000   **57.** 60
59. 1   **61.** 2   **63.** 7   **65.** 2   **67.** 42   **69.** 150
oz.   **71.** *   **73.** –2   **75.** –2   **77.** –2

Margin Exercises 3.6

1. $x = 9$ **3.** $n = 12$

Exercise Set 3.6

1. $x = 7$ **3.** $x = -20$ **5.** $x = -14$ **7.** $x = -18$
9. $x = 15$ **11.** $x = -14$ **13.** $t = 2$ **15.** $y = 20$
17. $t = -6$ **19.** $z = 0$ **21.** $x = -54$ **23.** $t = -12$
25. $y = -46$ **27.** $x = 51$ **29.** $x = 124$
31. $y = -144$ **33.** –11   **35.** –17   **37.** 55
39. 24   **41.** –1440   **43.** 143   **47.** 343

Margin Exercises 3.7

1. $x = -6$ **3.** $x = 8$ **5.** $x = 128$

Exercise Set 3.7

1. $x = 6$ **3.** $x = 9$ **5.** $x = 12$ **7.** $x = -40$
9. $x = 5$ **11.** $x = -7$ **13.** $x = -6$ **15.** $x = 6$
17. $t = -63$ **19.** $x = 81$ **21.** $t = -21$ **23.** $m = -5$
25. $t = 27$ **27.** $t = 54$ **29.** $x = 7$ **31.** $y = -7$
33. $m = 8$ **35.** –32   **37.** –28   **39.** 7

Chapter 3 Review Exercises

1. 213 and –53   **2.** >   **3.** <   **4.** >   **5.** 39
6. 12   **7.** 0   **8.** 29   **9.** 32   **10.** –9   **11.** –11
12. 6   **13.** –24   **14.** –9   **15.** 23   **16.** –1   **17.** 7
18. –4   **19.** 12   **20.** 92   **21.** –84   **22.** –40
23. –3   **24.** –5   **25.** 0   **26.** 1   **27.** 1   **28.** 49
29. –343   **30.** 36   **31.** –8   **32.** 1   **33.** $y = -59$
34. $x = -37$ **35.** $x = -4$ **36.** $x = -384$

Chapter 3 Practice Test

1. –542 and 307   **2.** >   **3.** 429   **4.** –19   **5.** –11
6. –21   **7.** 9   **8.** –12   **9.** –15   **10.** –24   **11.** 19
12. 24   **13.** –64   **14.** –130   **15.** 0   **16.** 8
17. –8   **18.** –7   **19.** 25   **20.** –125   **21.** 81
22. –1   **23.** $x = 69$ **24.** $y = 46$ **25.** $x = -3$
26. $y = 1008$

Chapter 4

Margin Exercises 4.1

1. $8\frac{3}{4}$ **2.** $12\frac{2}{3}$ **3.** $\frac{22}{5}$ **4.** $\frac{61}{10}$ **5.** $\frac{29}{6}$ **6.** $\frac{37}{4}$
7. $\frac{62}{3}$ **8.** $\frac{-32}{5}$ **9.** $-\frac{59}{7}$ **10.** $1\frac{1}{10}$ **11.** $18\frac{1}{6}$
12. $-2\frac{2}{5}$ **13.** $-11\frac{5}{12}$ **14.** $807\frac{5}{6}$ **15.** $-134\frac{23}{45}$
16. 1   **17.** 1   **18.** 1   **19.** 1   **20.** 1   **21.** 1
22. 0   **23.** 0   **24.** 0   **25.** 0   **26.** not defined
27. not defined   **28.** 8   **29.** –10   **30.** –346
31. $-5x$

Exercise Set 4.1

1. P **3.** M **5.** I **7.** P **9.** M **11.** P **13.** M **15.** M **17.** $\frac{17}{3}$ **19.** $\frac{17}{2}$ **21.** $-\frac{31}{3}$ **23.** $\frac{81}{10}$ **25.** $\frac{154}{5}$ **27.** $-\frac{71}{8}$ **29.** $\frac{69}{10}$ **31.** $\frac{13}{8}$ **33.** $-\frac{47}{3}$ **35.** $\frac{57}{10}$ **37.** $-\frac{507}{100}$ **39.** $\frac{223}{50}$ **41.** $3\frac{3}{5}$ **43.** $2\frac{3}{8}$ **45.** $3\frac{4}{9}$ **47.** $-8\frac{9}{10}$ **49.** $8\frac{1}{8}$ **51.** $-6\frac{1}{8}$ **53.** $4\frac{2}{9}$ **55.** $4\frac{5}{6}$ **57.** $4\frac{67}{100}$ **59.** $-55\frac{3}{4}$ **61.** $708\frac{2}{3}$ **63.** $1{,}012\frac{2}{9}$ **65.** $90\frac{22}{85}$ **67.** $23\frac{29}{46}$ **69.** $-36\frac{7}{13}$ **71.** $-21\frac{17}{25}$ **73.** 1 **75.** 10 **77.** -20 **79.** $4a$ **81.** 1 **83.** 0 **85.** 1 **87.** 1 **89.** 0 **91.** 0 **93.** not defined **95.** not defined **97.** -322 **99.** 0 **101.** 201 min **105.** $52\frac{1}{7}$ **109.** $\frac{3}{10}$

Margin Exercises 4.2

1. $\frac{2}{3}$ **2.** $\frac{5}{8}$ **3.** $\frac{10}{3}$ **4.** $-\frac{33}{8}$ **5.** $\frac{46}{5}$ **6.** $\frac{4x}{9}$ **7.** $\frac{15}{56}$ **8.** $\frac{32}{15}$ **9.** $-\frac{3}{100}$ **10.** $-\frac{7a}{3}$ **11.** $\frac{3}{16}$ **12.** $\frac{63}{100}$ sq. cm **13.** $\frac{3}{40}$

Exercise Set 4.2

1. $\frac{3}{5}$ **3.** $-\frac{5}{6}$ **5.** $\frac{14}{3}$ **7.** $-\frac{7}{9}$ **9.** $\frac{2x}{5}$ **11.** $-\frac{6}{5}$ **13.** $\frac{3a}{4}$ **15.** $\frac{17m}{6}$ **17.** $\frac{1}{6}$ **19.** $-\frac{1}{40}$ **21.** $\frac{2}{15}$ **23.** $\frac{2x}{5y}$ **25.** $\frac{9}{16}$ **27.** $\frac{14}{39}$ **29.** $-\frac{7}{100}$ **31.** $\frac{7a}{64}$ **33.** $\frac{1}{100y}$ **35.** $-\frac{182}{285}$ **37.** $\frac{12}{25}$ sq. m **39.** $\frac{5}{16}$ **41.** $\frac{1}{2}$ **43.** $\frac{2}{30}$ **45.** -4 **47.** 76 **49.** 6 one hundred thousands **53.** $\frac{3}{45}$ **55.** $-\frac{56}{1125}$ **57.** $\frac{4}{105}$

Margin Exercises 4.3

1. $\frac{8}{16}$ **2.** $\frac{3x}{5x}$ **3.** $-\frac{52}{100}$ **4.** $\frac{-16}{-6}$ **5.** 12 **6.** -18 **7.** $9x$ **8.** 9 **9.** -56 **10.** $\frac{1}{4}$ **11.** $-\frac{5}{6}$ **12.** 5 **13.** $\frac{4}{3}$ **14.** $-\frac{5}{3}$ **15.** $\frac{7}{8}$ **16.** $\frac{89}{78}$ **17.** $-\frac{8}{7}$ **18.** $-\frac{1}{4}$

Exercise Set 4.3

1. 5 **3.** -36 **5.** 27 **7.** 66 **9.** 20 **11.** 51 **13.** 10 **15.** -42 **17.** $5x$ **19.** $7m$ **21.** $12b$ **23.** $\frac{1}{2}$ **25.** $-\frac{3}{4}$ **27.** $\frac{1}{5}$ **29.** -3 **31.** $\frac{3}{4}$ **33.** $-\frac{6}{5}$ **35.** $\frac{1}{3}$ **37.** $-\frac{1}{3}$ **39.** $\frac{7}{8}$ **41.** $\frac{5}{7}$ **43.** 3,600 sq. yds **45.** $x = 5$ **49.** $\frac{2}{5}$ shy; $\frac{3}{5}$ not shy **51.** $\frac{11}{25}$ **53.** Tuition $= \frac{4}{9}$; Rent $= \frac{1}{5}$; Food $= \frac{2}{15}$; Misc. $= \frac{7}{9}$

Margin Exercises 4.4

1. $\frac{7}{12}$ **2.** $-\frac{1}{3}$ **3.** 6 **4.** $\frac{15}{x}$ **5.** $\frac{1}{6}$ **6.** 10 lb. **7.** 96 sq. m **8.** $13\frac{1}{5}$ cm **9.** 100 sq. in

Exercise Set 4.4

1. $\frac{1}{8}$ **3.** $-\frac{1}{8}$ **5.** $\frac{1}{10}$ **7.** $\frac{1}{9}$ **9.** $-2\frac{7}{10}$ **11.** $\frac{7x}{9}$ **13.** 2 **15.** 5 **17.** -9 **19.** $3a$ **21.** $-5\frac{1}{5}$ **23.** $\frac{14m}{5}$ **25.** $60x$ **27.** -30 **29.** 1 **31.** -1 **33.** 1 **35.** 1 **37.** $\frac{1}{5}$ **39.** $\frac{9}{25}$ **41.** $-\frac{11}{40}$ **43.** $\frac{5}{14}$ **45.** $\frac{5}{7}$ **47.** $\frac{2}{3}$ **49.** 625 **51.** $\frac{1}{3}$ cup **53.** $1,600 **55.** 160 mi. **57.** $6,750 = food $5,400 = housing $2,700 = clothing $3,000 = savings $6,750 = taxes $2,400 = other expenses **59.** 60 sq. in **61.** $6\frac{4}{5}$ sq. km **63.** 7 sq. m **65.** 92 sq. m **67.** 6800 sq. ft **69.** $t = 35$ **70.** $x = 8{,}546$ **71.** $x = 477$ **72.** $t = 70$ **73.** -111 **77.** $\frac{1}{12}$ **79.** $\frac{1}{168}$

Margin Exercises 4.5

1. $\frac{5}{2}$ **2.** $\frac{a}{7}$ **3.** $-\frac{1}{9}$ **4.** 5 **5.** $-\frac{10}{3}$ **6.** $1\frac{1}{7}$ **7.** $-2\frac{2}{3}$ **8.** $\frac{1}{10}$ **9.** $\frac{100}{a}$ **10.** -1 **11.** $\frac{14}{15}$ **12.** 320 **13.** 12

Exercise Set 4.5

1. $\frac{5}{6}$ **3.** $\frac{1}{4}$ **5.** 6 **7.** $-\frac{3}{10}$ **9.** $\frac{21}{2}$ **11.** $\frac{y}{2x}$ **13.** $-\frac{15}{7}$ **15.** $\frac{1}{7m}$ **17.** $\frac{4}{5}$ **19.** $-\frac{4}{15}$ **21.** 4 **23.** -2 **25.** $\frac{1}{8}$ **27.** $\left(\frac{3}{7}\right)x$ **29.** -8 **31.** $35a$ **33.** 1 **35.** $-\frac{2}{3}$ **37.** $2\frac{1}{4}$ **39.** $144a$ **41.** 90 days **43.** 9 days **45.** 16 people **47.** $\frac{1}{8}T$ **49.** $\frac{1}{10}m$ **51.** 32 **53.** 24 **55.** 510 **57.** 27; -27 **59.** 147; 147 **65.** $-\frac{15}{196}$

Margin Exercises 4.6

1. 20 **2.** $1\frac{7}{8}$ **3.** $-12\frac{4}{5}$ **4.** $8\frac{1}{3}$ **5.** 16 **6.** $1\frac{7}{8}$ **7.** $-\frac{7}{10}$ **8.** $227\frac{1}{2}$ mi. **9.** 20 $\frac{\text{mi}}{\text{gal}}$

Exercise Set 4.6

1. $22\frac{2}{3}$ **3.** $2\frac{5}{12}$ **5.** $-39\frac{3}{5}$ **7.** $27\frac{11}{15}$ **9.** $8\frac{1}{6}$

11. $-9\frac{31}{40}$ **13.** $24\frac{91}{100}$ **15.** $209\frac{1}{10}$ **17.** $6\frac{1}{4}$

19. $1\frac{1}{5}$ **21.** $3\frac{9}{16}$ **23.** $-1\frac{1}{8}$ **25.** $1\frac{8}{43}$ **27.** $-\frac{9}{40}$

29. $10\frac{1}{2}$ cups **31.** $16\frac{1}{2}$ **33.** $343\frac{3}{4}$ lbs.

35. $82\frac{1}{2}$ in. **37.** $68°$ **39.** 1; 6 chicken bouillon $\frac{3}{4}$; $4\frac{1}{2}$ cup hot water $1\frac{1}{2}$; 9 tbsp. margarine $1\frac{1}{2}$; 9 tbsp. flour $1\frac{1}{4}$; $7\frac{1}{2}$ cups diced chicken $\frac{1}{2}$; 3 cups peas $\frac{1}{2}$; 3 mushrooms $\frac{1}{6}$; 1 cups carrots $\frac{1}{8}$; $\frac{3}{4}$ cups onions 1; 6 tbsp. pimento $\frac{1}{2}$; 3 tsp. salt **41.** 16 orbits **43.** 15 $\frac{\text{mi.}}{\text{gal}}$ **45.** $x = -9$

47. 1 **49.** 33

Margin Exercises 4.7

1. $x = 15$ **2.** $a = -28$ **3.** $x = 1\frac{13}{15}$ **4.** $a = 4\frac{1}{2}$

5. $x = -\frac{9}{32}$ **6.** $a = -\frac{3}{4}$ **7.** $x = -4\frac{7}{12}$ **8.** $y = 1\frac{14}{43}$

Exercise Set 4.7

1. $x = 20$ **3.** $a = 9$ **5.** $x = -56$ **7.** $a = -45$

9. $x = \frac{10}{21}$ **11.** $t = \frac{10}{21}$ **13.** $a = 12\frac{1}{2}$ **15.** $x = \frac{1}{6}$

17. $x = -26\frac{2}{3}$ **19.** $a = -\frac{1}{6}$ **21.** $t = -1\frac{3}{7}$

23. $x = 3\frac{3}{7}$ **25.** $x = 14$ **27.** $a = 1\frac{3}{7}$ **29.** 20

31. -4 **35.** 288 km; 108 km **37.** $\frac{7}{8}$ lb.

Margin Exercises 4.8

1. \$720 **2.** $6\frac{11}{15}$

Exercise Set 4.8

1. \$27 **3.** $\frac{1}{3}$ cup **5.** $x = 160$ km **7.** 16L

9. 288 km; 108 km **11.** 7oz. **13.** 4 cu. ft

15. $t = 35$ **17.** $x = 85$ **19.** $x = 8,546$ **21.** 5,338

23. 45,800 **25.** $\frac{2}{3}$ **27.** 36

Chapter 4 Review Exercises

1. improper **2.** mixed number **3.** improper
4. proper **5.** $-\frac{101}{5}$ **6.** $\frac{95}{4}$ **7.** $15\frac{2}{5}$ **8.** $-12\frac{1}{7}$

9. $23\frac{40}{53}$ **10.** $471\frac{5}{6}$ **11.** 0 **12.** 1 **13.** 1

14. 48 **15.** $-\frac{11}{15}$ **16.** $-\frac{1}{4}$ **17.** $\frac{3}{4}$ **18.** undefined

19. $\frac{1}{3}$ **20.** $9n$ **21.** $\frac{15}{21}$ **22.** $-\frac{30}{55}$ **23.** $\frac{9}{5}$

24. $-\frac{1}{7}$ **25.** 8 **26.** $\frac{5y}{3x}$ **27.** $\frac{6}{35}$ **28.** $\frac{4y}{9x}$ **29.** $\frac{2}{3}$

30. $-\frac{1}{14}$ **31.** $\frac{1}{25}$ **32.** 1 **33.** $\frac{18}{5}$ **34.** $\frac{1}{4}$

35. 300 **36.** $\frac{1}{15}$ **37.** $4a$ **38.** -1 **39.** 16

40. $-3\frac{1}{2}$ **41.** $2\frac{21}{50}$ **42.** 6 **43.** 12 **44.** $-1\frac{7}{17}$

45. $\frac{1}{8}$ **46.** $\frac{9}{10}$ **47.** $-\frac{5}{6}$ **48.** 8 **49.** $-3\frac{3}{8}$

50. $\frac{3}{10}$ **51.** $\frac{56}{39}$ **52.** $-\frac{2}{15}$ **53.** 42 m **54.** $17\frac{1}{2}$ ft^2

55. 22 mi **56.** $\frac{1}{3}$ cup **57.** $\frac{1}{6}$ mi **58.** 18

Chapter 4 Practice Test

1. $\frac{7}{2}$ **2.** $-\frac{79}{8}$ **3.** $-8\frac{2}{9}$ **4.** 26 **5.** 1 **6.** 0

7. $\frac{1}{2}$ **8.** $\frac{1}{9}$ **9.** $-\frac{1}{14}$ **10.** $-\frac{35}{18}$ **11.** $\frac{28}{33}$ **12.** $\frac{3x}{8}$

13. $-\frac{98}{3}$ **14.** $\frac{6}{65}$ **15.** 39 **16.** -18 **17.** -6

18. 2 **19.** $-\frac{13}{36}$ **20.** $-\frac{1}{15}$ **21.** $-\frac{2}{3}$ **22.** $\frac{8}{5}$

23. $45\frac{1}{2}$ m^2 **24.** $\frac{3}{20}$ lb **25.** 75 lb

26. 101 **27.** -167

Chapter 4 Cumulative Review

1. $5^3 \cdot 2$ **2.** 112 **3.** 10,982 **4.** -43 **5.** -33
6. 2129 **7.** -23 **8.** -8 **9.** 16,905 **10.** -312
11. $-30x$ **12.** $\frac{7}{15}$ **13.** 235 R 3 **14.** -17

15. -28 **16.** $\frac{2}{3}$ **17.** 4510 **18.** 450,000 **19.** 879

20. 8 **21.** composite **22.** -21 **23.** 25 **24.** 9

25. -45 **26.** 5 mpg **27.** 4 oz **28.** 1 **29.** 59

30. 0 **31.** $-\frac{5}{27}$ **32.** $\frac{5}{2}$ **33.** $\frac{1}{17}$ **34.** $\frac{21}{70}$

35. \$30 **36.** 12 **37.** $\frac{3}{5}$ mi **38.** $\frac{54}{169}$ **39.** $-\frac{124}{3}$

40. $-\frac{7}{5}$

Chapter 5

Margin Exercises 5.1

1. $\frac{4}{5}$ **2.** 1 **3.** $\frac{1}{2}$ **4.** $-\frac{3}{8}$ **5.** $-\frac{4}{x}$ **6.** $\frac{5}{6}$; LCD = 6

7. $1\frac{5}{24}$; LCD = 24 **8.** $\frac{2}{9}$; LCD = 18 **9.** $\frac{38}{5}$; LCD = 5

10. $\frac{413}{1000}$; LCD = 1000 **11.** $\frac{157}{210}$; LCD = 210 **12.** $<$

13. $>$ **14.** $>$ **15.** $<$ **16.** $<$ **17.** $<$
18. $1\frac{1}{10}$ lb.

5.1 Exercise Set

1. $\frac{2}{3}$ **3.** $\frac{3}{4}$ **5.** $\frac{-2}{11}$ **7.** $\frac{11}{a}$ **9.** $\frac{-10}{x}$ **11.** $\frac{7}{24}$

13. $\frac{-1}{10}$ **15.** $\frac{19}{24}$ **17.** $\frac{83}{20}$ **19.** $\frac{5}{24}$ **21.** $\frac{31}{100}$

23. $\frac{41}{60}$ **25.** $\frac{-9}{100}$ **27.** $\frac{67}{12}$ **29.** $\frac{-34}{9}$ **31.** $\frac{-1}{8}$

33. $\frac{437}{1000}$ **35.** $\frac{5}{4}$ **37.** $\frac{239}{78}$ **39.** $\frac{59}{90}$ **41.** $<$

43. $>$ **45.** $>$ **47.** $<$ **49.** $<$ **51.** $<$ **53.** $<$

55. > **57.** $\frac{5}{6}$ lb. **59.** $1\frac{5}{8}$ mi. **61.** $1\frac{1}{24}$ cup

63. 690 kg.; $\frac{14}{23}$; $\frac{5}{23}$; $\frac{4}{23}$ **65.** $1\frac{3}{8}$ mi. **67.** $1\frac{19}{32}$ in.

69. −13 **71.** −8 **73.** $3\frac{1}{3}$ **77.** $\frac{4}{15}$; $320 **79.** $\frac{2}{3a}$

5.2 Margin Exercises

1. $\frac{1}{2}$ **2.** $\frac{3}{8}$ **3.** $\frac{-1}{2}$ **4.** $\frac{1}{12}$ **5.** $\frac{13}{18}$ **6.** $\frac{1}{2}$ **7.** $\frac{-1}{6}$

8. $\frac{9}{112}$ **9.** $x = 2$ **10.** $x = \frac{13}{24}$ **11.** $x = \frac{1}{6}$

12. $t = \frac{-59}{40}$ **13.** $\frac{11}{20}$ lb. **14.** $\frac{2}{15}$ cup

5.2 Exercise Set

1. $\frac{2}{3}$ **3.** $\frac{-1}{4}$ **5.** $\frac{5}{9}$ **7.** $\frac{1}{24}$ **9.** $\frac{1}{2}$ **11.** $\frac{1}{3}$

13. $\frac{-4}{15}$ **15.** $\frac{7}{10}$ **17.** $\frac{-17}{60}$ **19.** $\frac{53}{100}$ **21.** $\frac{26}{75}$

23. $\frac{-21}{100}$ **25.** $\frac{13}{24}$ **27.** $\frac{1}{10}$ **29.** $\frac{-19}{24}$ **31.** $\frac{13}{16}$

33. $\frac{31}{75}$ **35.** $\frac{-5}{3}$ **37.** $x = \frac{2}{3}$ **39.** $a = \frac{6}{11}$

41. $n = \frac{2}{5}$ **43.** $x = 1\frac{1}{5}$ **45.** $a = \frac{3}{8}$ **47.** $x = \frac{7}{10}$

49. $x = \frac{2}{15}$ **51.** $a = \frac{-7}{24}$ **53.** $n = \frac{1}{15}$ **55.** $x = -1\frac{1}{4}$

57. $\frac{5}{12}$ hr **59.** $\frac{13}{24}$ mi. **61.** $\frac{1}{4}$ **63.** $1\frac{1}{2}$ **65.** −21

67. 6 lb. **71.** $\frac{227}{420}$ km. **73.** $\frac{1}{x}$ **75.** $1\frac{1}{144}$

77. $\frac{21}{40}$ km

5.3 Margin Exercises

1. $7\frac{2}{5}$ **2.** $12\frac{1}{10}$ **3.** $13\frac{7}{12}$ **4.** $12\frac{5}{6}$ **5.** $14\frac{1}{30}$

6. $1\frac{1}{2}$ **7.** $3\frac{1}{6}$ **8.** $2\frac{1}{4}$ **9.** $4\frac{2}{5}$ **10.** $3\frac{1}{3}$ **11.** $3\frac{2}{3}$

12. $8\frac{1}{12}$ yd. **13.** $3\frac{3}{4}$ m

5.3 Exercise Set

1. $6\frac{1}{2}$ **3.** $2\frac{11}{12}$ **5.** $14\frac{7}{12}$ **7.** $12\frac{1}{10}$ **9.** $16\frac{5}{24}$

11. $21\frac{1}{2}$ **13.** $27\frac{7}{8}$ **15.** $1\frac{3}{5}$ **17.** $4\frac{1}{10}$ **19.** $21\frac{17}{24}$

21. $12\frac{1}{4}$ **23.** $15\frac{3}{8}$ **25.** $7\frac{5}{12}$ **27.** $11\frac{5}{18}$ **29.** $8\frac{13}{42}$

31. $2\frac{1}{8}$ **33.** $8\frac{31}{40}$ **35.** $11\frac{34}{45}$ **37.** $6\frac{1}{6}$ **39.** $9\frac{31}{33}$

41. $7\frac{5}{12}$ lb. **43.** $6\frac{7}{20}$ cm **45.** $19\frac{1}{6}$ ft. **47.** $1\frac{5}{8}$

49. $173\frac{4}{5}$ cm **51.** $36\frac{1}{2}$ in **53.** $319\frac{7}{10}$ km

55. $3\frac{4}{5}$ hr. **57.** $7\frac{3}{8}$ ft. **59.** $15\frac{1}{6}$ yd. **61.** $\frac{1}{10}$

65. $5\frac{3}{4}$ ft.

5.4 Margin Exercises

1. $\frac{27}{56}$ **2.** $175\frac{1}{2}$ **3.** $159\frac{4}{5}$ **4.** $5\frac{3}{4}$ **5.** $240\frac{3}{4}$ ft.

5.4 Exercise Set

1. $\frac{4}{7}$ **3.** $1\frac{29}{30}$ **5.** $\frac{3}{20}$ **7.** $26\frac{3}{8}$ **9.** $\frac{7}{16}$ **11.** $\frac{1}{36}$

13. $\frac{3}{8}$ **15.** $7\frac{11}{12}$ **17.** $5\frac{5}{6}$ **19.** $1\frac{5}{6}$ **21.** $23\frac{4}{5}$ mi.

23. $13\frac{11}{24}$ **25.** $-\frac{27}{140}$ **27.** $12\frac{3}{4}$ **29.** $18\frac{1}{4}$

31. $233\frac{1}{3}$ mi **33.** $91\frac{1}{5}$ mi **35.** $22\frac{17}{25}$ sq ft

37. $100\frac{15}{16}$ sq in **39.** 19°F **41.** $\frac{2}{3}$ **43.** 0

47. $18\frac{41}{48}$ **49.** $\frac{13}{8}$ **51.** $-8\frac{1}{18}$; $-8\frac{1}{18}$

Chapter 5 Review Exercises

1. $\frac{63}{40}$ **2.** $\frac{19}{48}$ **3.** $\frac{-7}{15}$ **4.** $\frac{7}{16}$ **5.** $\frac{1}{3}$ **6.** $\frac{-1}{8}$

7. $\frac{5}{27}$ **8.** $\frac{11}{18}$ **9.** > **10.** > **11.** < **12.** <

13. $\frac{-12}{y}$ **14.** $\frac{1195}{1000}$ **15.** $10\frac{2}{5}$ **16.** $11\frac{11}{15}$ **17.** $10\frac{2}{3}$

18. $8\frac{1}{4}$ **19.** $11\frac{7}{9}$ **20.** $4\frac{11}{15}$ **21.** $-5\frac{1}{8}$ **22.** $-14\frac{1}{4}$

23. $\frac{19}{40}$ **24.** $\frac{6}{5}$ **25.** $\frac{-1}{4}$ **26.** $1\frac{4}{10}$ **27.** 1

28. $\frac{17}{64}$ **29.** $13\frac{5}{7}$ **30.** $\frac{30}{11}$ **31.** $70\frac{3}{8}$ **32.** $1\frac{73}{100}$

in. **33.** $177\frac{3}{4}$ in² **34.** $50\frac{1}{4}$ in² **35.** $8\frac{3}{8}$ cups

Chapter 5 Practice Test

1. 3 **2.** $\frac{-5}{24}$ **3.** $\frac{1}{3}$ **4.** $\frac{5}{12}$ **5.** $\frac{-1}{3}$ **6.** $5\frac{7}{10}$

7. $14\frac{5}{12}$ **8.** $6\frac{1}{6}$ **9.** $4\frac{7}{24}$ **10.** $\frac{-6}{x}$ **11.** $1\frac{15}{16}$

12. < **13.** > **14.** $\frac{-5}{9}$ **15.** $1\frac{4}{30}$ **16.** $\frac{-17}{75}$

17. $\frac{1}{2}$ **18.** $\frac{11}{20}$ **19.** $19\frac{3}{5}$ **20.** $28\frac{1}{20}$

21. $160\frac{5}{12}$ kg **22.** $\frac{13}{200}$ m **23.** $19\frac{5}{8}$

Chapter 6

Margin Exercises 6.1

1. Twenty-one and one tenth **2.** Two and four thousand five hundred thirty-three ten-thousandths **3.** Negative two hundred forty-five and eighty-nine hundredths **4.** Thirty-one thousand, seventy-nine and seven hundred sixty-four thousandths **5.** Thirty-eight thousandths **6.** Four thousand, two hundred seventeen and $\frac{56}{100}$ dollars **7.** $\frac{112}{125}$ **8.** $-23\frac{39}{50}$ or $-\frac{1189}{50}$

9. $5\frac{6789}{10000}$ or $\frac{56789}{10000}$ **10.** $1\frac{9}{10}$ or $\frac{19}{10}$

11. 2.04 **12.** 0.06 **13.** 0.58 **14.** 1 **15.** 0.8989

16. 21.05 **17.** −34.008 **18.** −8.98 **19.** 2.8

20. 13.9 **21.** −234.4 **22.** 7.0 **23.** 0.64

24. −7.83 **25.** 34.70 **26.** −0.03 **27.** 0.943

28. −8.004 **29.** −43.112 **30.** 37.401

31. 7459.360 **32.** 7459.36 **33.** 7459.4 **34.** 7459

35. 7460 **36.** 7500 **37.** 7000

Exercise Set 6.1

1. Twenty-three and two tenths   **3.** Seven and eighty-nine hundredths   **5.** Forty-two and three hundred fifty-nine thousandths   **7.** Negative five hundred twenty-eight and thirty-seven hundredths   **9.** Two hundred sixteen and $\frac{99}{100}$ dollars   **11.** Forty-seven and $\frac{2}{100}$ dollars   **13.** $\frac{9}{15}$ or $\frac{46}{5}$ **15.** $\frac{17}{100}$ **17.** $1\frac{23}{100}$ or $\frac{73}{50}$ **19.** $-304\frac{7}{10}$ or $-\frac{3047}{10}$ **21.** $3\frac{71}{500}$ or $\frac{1571}{500}$ **23.** $46\frac{3}{100}$ or $\frac{4603}{100}$ **25.** $-\frac{13}{100000}$ **27.** $20\frac{3}{1000}$ or $\frac{20003}{1000}$ **29.** $2\frac{57}{5000}$ or $\frac{10057}{5000}$ **31.** $-4567\frac{1}{5}$ or $\frac{22836}{5}$ **33.** 0.42   **35.** 0.111   **37.** 0.001   **39.** −234.07   **41.** 0.4545   **43.** −0.54   **45.** −0.8437   **47.** 0.1   **49.** −0.2   **51.** 0.6   **53.** −2.7   **55.** 13.4   **57.** 154.0   **59.** 0.9   **61.** 0.67   **63.** −0.42   **65.** 2.40   **67.** −0.01   **69.** 1.43   **71.** 0.325   **73.** −0.667   **75.** 17.002   **77.** 0.001   **79.** 0   **81.** $-\frac{2}{9}$ **83.** $x = 7$ **87.** 6.78346   **89.** 99.99999

Margin Exercises 6.2

1. 10.917   **2.** 34.2079   **3.** 4.969   **4.** 3.5617   **5.** 9.40544   **6.** 912.67   **7.** 2514.773   **8.** 10.754   **9.** 0.339   **10.** 1.47   **11.** 0.24238   **12.** 7.36992   **13.** 1194.22   **14.** 4.9911   **15.** −1.96   **16.** 3.159   **17.** −8.55   **18.** −4.16   **19.** −7.44   **20.** 12.4   **21.** −2.7

Exercise Set 6.2

1. 334.37   **3.** 1576.215   **5.** 132.56   **7.** 64.413   **9.** 50.0248   **11.** 0.835   **13.** 771.967   **15.** 20.8649   **17.** 227.468   **19.** 8754.8221   **21.** 1.3   **23.** 49.02   **25.** 2.4975   **27.** 85.921   **29.** 1.6666   **31.** 4.0622   **33.** 8.85   **35.** 3.37   **37.** 1.045   **39.** 3.703   **41.** 0.9902   **43.** 99.66   **45.** 4.88   **47.** 12.608   **49.** 2546.973   **51.** 44.001   **53.** 1.71   **55.** −2.5   **57.** −7.2   **59.** 3.379   **61.** −22.6   **63.** 2.5   **65.** −3.519   **67.** 9.601   **69.** 14.5   **71.** 3.8   **73.** −10.292   **75.** −8.8   **77.** 0   **79.** $-\frac{1}{10}$ **81.** $x = 5\frac{5}{7}$

Margin Exercises 6.3

1. 625.66   **2.** 21.4863   **3.** 0.00943   **4.** −12.535374   **5.** 35.9   **6.** 0.7324   **7.** −0.058   **8.** 0.07236   **9.** 539.17   **10.** −6,241.7   **11.** 64,700   **12.** 430,100   **13.** 17,000,000   **14.** 5,600,000,000   **15.** 1569¢   **16.** 17¢   **17.** $0.35   **18.** $5.77   **19.** 6.656   **20.** 8.125 cm²   **21.** 6.656

Exercise Set 6.3

1. 47.6   **3.** 6.72   **5.** 0.252   **7.** 0.1032   **9.** 237.6   **11.** −783686.852   **13.** −780   **15.** 8.923   **17.** 0.09768   **19.** −0.287   **21.** 43.68   **23.** 3.2472   **25.** 89.76   **27.** −322.07   **29.** 55.68   **31.** 3487.5   **33.** 0.1155   **35.** −9420   **37.** 0.00953   **39.** 2888¢   **41.** 66¢   **43.** $0.34   **45.** $34.45   **47.** $3,600,000,000.00   **49.** 196,800,000   **51.** 11,000   **53.** 20.5125   **55. a.** 44 ft;   **b.** 118.75 ft²   **57.** 1   **59.** $-\frac{1}{18}$ **61.** $\frac{3}{5}$ **63.** No.   **65.** 1×10^{21}

Margin Exercises 6.4

1. 0.6   **2.** 1.7   **3.** 0.47   **4.** 0.32   **5.** −5.75   **6.** 0.25   **7. a.** 375;   **b.** 15   **8.** 4.9   **9.** 12.8   **10.** 15.625   **11.** 12.78   **12.** 0.001278   **13.** 0.09847   **14.** −67.832   **15.** 0.2426   **16.** 7.4   **17.** 1.2825

Exercise Set 6.4

1. 14.6   **3.** 23.78   **5.** 7.48   **7.** 7.2   **9.** −1.143   **11.** 4.041   **13.** −0.07   **15.** 70   **17.** 40   **19.** −0.4   **21.** 0.41   **23.** 7.5   **25.** −9.3   **27.** 0.625   **29.** 0.26   **31.** 15.625   **33.** 2.34   **35.** −0.3045   **37.** 0.2134567   **39.** −21.34567   **41.** 1023.7   **43.** −56780   **45.** −7.4392   **47.** 9.7   **49.** −75300   **51.** 230.01   **53.** 5.7281   **55.** 2107   **57.** −0.0273   **59.** 446.208   **61.** 24.14   **63.** −5.0072   **65.** 9.6304   **67.** 9.51   **69.** −903.87   **71.** −0.00325   **73.** $1,288.36   **75.** 59.49°   **77.** $15\frac{1}{8}$ **79.** $\frac{6}{7}$ **81.** $-1\frac{2}{3}$ **85.** 1000   **87.** 100

Margin Exercises 6.5

1. b   **2.** a   **3.** d   **4.** b   **5.** a   **6.** d   **7.** b   **8.** c   **9.** b   **10.** b   **11.** c   **12.** a   **13.** c

Exercise Set 6.5

1. d   **3.** c   **5.** a   **7.** c   **9.** 1.6   **11.** 6   **13.** 60   **15.** 2.3   **17.** 180   **19.** a   **21.** c   **23.** a   **25.** b   **27.** 7981 screens   **29.** $2^2 \cdot 3^3$ **31.** $5^2 \cdot 13$ **33.** $\frac{5}{16}$ **35.** $\frac{8}{9}$ **39.** yes   **41.** no

Margin Exercises 6.6

1. 7.43   **2.** 0.406   **3.** 6.7089   **4.** −0.9   **5.** 4.3   **6.** 283.71   **7.** 456.13   **8.** 0.4   **9.** 0.375   **10.** $0.1\overline{6}$ **11.** $0.\overline{6}$ **12.** $0.\overline{45}$ **13.** $-1.\overline{09}$ **14.** $0.\overline{714285}$ **15.** 0.7; 0.67; 0.667   **16.** 0.6; 0.61; 0.608   **17.** 6.2; 6.25; 6.245   **18.** 3.7; 3.70; 3.697   **19.** 0.8   **20.** −0.45   **21.** 0.035   **22.** 1.32

Exercise Set 6.6

1. 0.8 **3.** −0.29 **5.** 9.7 **7.** 8.89 **9.** −250.8
11. −3.798 **13.** 0.0078 **15.** 0.56788 **17.** 27.13
19. −0.66 **21.** 99.44 **23.** 3.798 **25.** 2.1739
27. 8.953073 **29.** 0.4375 **31.** 0.325 **33.** 0.2
35. 0.85 **37.** 0.525 **39.** −1.275 **41.** 0.52
43. 20.016 **45.** −0.25 **47.** 0.575 **49.** −0.625
51. 1.48 **53.** $0.2\overline{6}$ **55.** $0.\overline{3}$ **57.** $-1.\overline{3}$ **59.** $1.1\overline{6}$
61. $0.\overline{571428}$ **63.** $-0.91\overline{6}$ **65.** 0.3; 0.27; 0.267
67. −1.3; −1.33; −1.333 **69.** 0.6; 0.57; 0.571
71. 0.8; 0.78; 0.778 **73.** −0.9; −0.89; −0.889
75. 1.3; 1.27; 1.273 **77.** $3\frac{2}{5}$ **79.** −95 **81.** −7

Margin Exercises 6.7

1. $x = 4.2$ **2.** $t = 5.7$ **3.** $x = 2.6$ **4.** $t = -10.8$

Exercise Set 6.7

1. $x = 9.3$ **3.** $x = 11.65$ **5.** $y = 0.0090678$
7. $m = -25.661$ **9.** $a = -4.5$ **11.** $x = 10.3$
13. $t = 43.78$ **15.** $t = -45.6$ **17.** $m = 14.32$
19. $x = -9.7$ **21.** $y = -11.04$ **23.** 1 **25.** $\frac{29}{50}$
27. −2 **29.** no **31.** $x =$ undefined
33. $x =$ undefined

Margin Exercises 6.8

1. 75 **2.** 54.9 **3.** 81 **4.** 19.4 **5.** 0.4 lb
6. 19 miles per gallon **7.** 2.5 GPA **8.** 17 **9.** 17
10. 91 **11.** Median = $1700; range = $700
12. Median = 67.5; range = 36 **13.** 45 **14.** 34, 67
15. no mode **16. a.** 17 g; **b.** 18 g; **c.** 19 g;
d. 4 g **17.** Kellogg's Complete Bran Flakes
19. Kellogg's Special K and Wheaties **21.** 510.7 mg
23. Mean = 232, median = 230, mode = 240 **25.** yes
27. 24% **29.** 60,000 elephants **31.** 55,000
elephants **33.** 20 g **35.** 75 women **37.** 60 − 64
39. Month 7 **41.** 160 homes **43.** 35 years

Exercise Set 6.8

1. Mean = 20; median = 18; mode = 29; range = 15
3. Mean = 20; median = 22.5; modes = 5 and 20;
range = 30 **5.** Mean = 5.2; median = 5.7; mode = 7.4;
range = 6.2 **7.** Mean = 239.5; median = 234; mode =
234; range = 50 **9.** Average = 40°; median = 40°;
no mode **11.** 33 miles per gallon **13.** GPA = 2.8
15. Average = $9.19; median = $9.49; mode = $7.99
17. 483,612,200 miles **19.** Neptune **21.** All of
them **23.** 11.2 Earth diameters **25.** Mean = 27,884
miles; median = 7926 miles; no mode; range = 87,423
miles **27.** 92° **29.** 108° **31.** 3
33. 90° and above **35.** 30% and above **37.** 50%

39. 0.49% **41.** 0.12° **43.** 1998 **45.** 1994 to 1995
47. 7000 bikes **49.** 1997 **51.** 190 calories
53. Chocolate cake with fudge frosting **55.** Premium
chocolate ice cream **57.** 125 calories
59. 920 calories **61.** 28 lb **63.** 300,000 hectares
65. Latin America **67.** Africa **69.** 915,000 hectares
73. Indianapolis **75.** 23.55 minutes **77.** 1991 and
1992 **79.** 1473 **81.** 1997 **83.** $0.55 million
85. 1994 and 1995 **89.** 1994 and 1995
91. 3133 ppb **93.** 1995 and 1996 **95.** $48.6 million
97. $41.5 million **99.** 196 **101.** $18\frac{13}{21}$ **109.** 171

Margin Exercises 6.9

1. 8.4° **2.** 148.1 gallons **3.** $55.92 **4.** $368.75
5. 96.52 cm² **6.** $0.89 **7.** 28.6 miles per gallon
8. $221,519 **9.** $594,444

Exercise Set 6.9

1. $39.60 **3.** $21.22 **5.** $3.01 **7.** 102.8°
9. $21,219.17 **11.** 250,205.04 ft² **13.** 22,691.5
15. 8.9 billion hamburgers **17.** mach 0.3
19. 20.2 miles per gallon **21.** 11.9752 cubic feet
23. $10.00 **25.** 78.1 cm **27.** 2.31 cm
29. 876 calories **31.** $1,171.74 **33.** 291.5 yd²
35. 0.305 **37.** $57.35 **39.** $349.44 **41.** 5.8 cents
43. 2152.56 yd² **45.** $316,987.20, −$196,987.20
47. 31 million **49.** 90.6 million **51.** 1.4° **53.** no
55. $435,975.61 **57.** $87,493.67 **59.** $67,972.03
61. 6335 **63.** $6\frac{5}{6}$ **65.** 13766 **67.** $\frac{1}{24}$ **69.** $\frac{2}{15}$
71. 28 minutes **75.** $144.00

Chapter 6 Review Exercises

1. three and forty-seven hundredths **2.** negative five
hundred and ninety-seven and two hundred and fifty-
three thousandths **3.** negative thirty one thousandths
4. fifty six ten thousandths **5.** $\frac{9}{100}$ **6.** $-3\frac{227}{10000}$
7. $-4\frac{561}{1000}$ **8.** $\frac{89}{1000}$ **9.** 0.034 **10.** −0.19
11. 17.4 **12.** 17.43 **13.** 499.829 **14.** 29.148
15. 229.1 **16.** 685.0519 **17.** − 57.3 **18.** − 1.073
19. 24,680 **20.** 3.2 **21.** − 8290 **22.** − 1.6
23. .2763 **24.** $15.49 **25.** 829 cents **26.** 925
27. 35.9375 **28.** 40.84 **29.** 1.8045 **30.** 57.1449
31. 11.3 **32.** c **33.** −2.6 **34.** 1.28 **35.** 3.25
36. $-1.1\overline{6}$ **37.** −.00913 **38.** $-1.\overline{4}$ **39.** 4.45
40. 248.27 **41.** −3 **42.** $.86\overline{6}$ **43.** 23.83
44. −3.3 **45.** $21.00 **46.** $28.75 **47.** $10.00
48. $10.50 **49.** no **50.** 38.5 **51.** 1.55
52. $16.\overline{6}$ **53.** 38.5 **54.** 1.8 **55.** $17 **56.** 26
57. 0.2 **58.** $17 **59.** .2 to 2.4 **60.** $2 to $29
61. 2.93 **62.** 420 **63.** 440 **64.** Big Bacon Classic
65. Grilled Chicken **66.** Plain single **67.** Chicken

club **68.** 80 **69.** 250 **70.** Under 20 **71.** 12
72. 13 **73.** 45–74 **74.** 11 **75.** Under 20
76. 22% **77.** 11% **78.** 1600 **79.** 25%
80. 11.16 **81.** 6365.1 bushels **82.** 24.36; 104.4
83. 2.9 **84.** $32.59 **85.** 8.4 mi

Chapter 6 Practice Test

1. seven and $\frac{23}{100}$ **2.** $-\frac{1}{5}$ **3.** $7\frac{308}{1000}$ **4.** .19
5. 9.5 **6.** 9.452 **7.** 405.219 **8.** .03 **9.** .21345
10. 44.746 **11.** -2.2 **12.** 356.37 **13.** 1.9946
14. .44 **15.** 30.4 **16.** 3.4682 **17.** 17,982 cents
18. 9 **19.** 7.6 **20.** 2670 **21.** $1.\overline{2}$ **22.** .$\overline{8}$
23. -63.58 **24.** -15.17 **25.** $341,413
26. Couple, age 65; yearly income $150,000
27. $78,169 **28.** $45.\overline{4}$ **29.** 32 **30.** 45
31. 77 to 103 **32.** 2.867 **33.** $35 million
34. 1992 to 1993

Chapters 1-6 Cumulative Review

1. $\frac{20}{9}$ **2.** $\frac{3052}{1000}$ **3.** 1.4 **4.** $0.\overline{54}$ **5.** Prime
6. Yes **7.** 1754 **8.** 4.364 **9.** 584.90
10. 218.56 **11.** 160 **12.** 4 **13.** 12,800,000
14. 6 **15.** $6\frac{1}{20}$ **16.** 139,116 **17.** $\frac{31}{18}$
18. 145.953 **19.** 710,137 **20.** 13.097 **21.** $\frac{5}{7}$
22. $\frac{1}{110}$ **23.** $\frac{1}{6}$ **24.** 5,317,200 **25.** 4.78
26. 0.0279431 **27.** 2.122 **28.** 1843 **29.** 13,862.1
30. $\frac{5}{6}$ **31.** .78 **32.** 28 **33.** 8.62 **34.** 367,251
35. $\frac{1}{18}$ **36.** $\frac{1}{2}$ **37.** 14,274 **38.** $500
39. 86,400 **40.** $2400 **41.** $258.77 **42.** $6\frac{1}{2}$ lb
43. 2 lb **44.** 467.28 ft² **45.** $\frac{9}{32}$ **46.** 84.5
47. 23 **48.** 137 **49.** 76 to 95 **50.** 0

Scientific Calculators

Margin Exercises

1. 8 **2.** 16 **3.** 6561 **4.** 3375 **5.** 529
6. 1024 **7.** 2401 **8.** 10.4976 **9.** 0.00243
10. 148,035,889 **11.** -1124864 **12.** $-1,419,857$
13. 1,048,576 **14.** 81 **15.** 118 **16.** 153
17. 71 **18.** 375 **19.** 100 **20.** 3 **21.** $.541\overline{6}$
22. $51.1\overline{6}$ **23.** $13.08\overline{3}$ **24.** $.00\overline{90}$ **25.** 2
26. 5.55 **27.** 1.625 **28.** .3125

Chapter 7

Margin Exercises 7.1

1. 5 : 11 or $\frac{5}{11}$ **2.** $\frac{57.3}{86.1}$ or $\frac{57.3}{86.1}$ **3.** $6\frac{3}{4} : 7\frac{2}{5}$ or $\frac{135}{148}$
4. 21.1 : 182.5 or $\frac{21.1}{182.5}$ **5.** 2.5 : .8 or $\frac{2.5}{0.8}$
6. $4 : 7\frac{2}{3}$ or $\frac{12}{23}$ **7.** $\frac{38.2}{56.1}$ **8.** $\frac{18.2}{27}; \frac{2}{3}$ **9.** $\frac{3.6}{12}; \frac{3}{10}$
10. $\frac{1.2}{1.5}; \frac{4}{5}$ **11.** $\frac{12}{16}; \frac{3}{4}$

Exercise Set 7.1

1. $\frac{4}{5}$ **3.** $\frac{178}{572}$ **5.** $\frac{0.4}{12}$ **7.** $\frac{3.8}{7.4}$ **9.** $\frac{56.78}{98.35}$
11. $\frac{8\frac{3}{4}}{9\frac{5}{6}}$ **13.** $\frac{1}{4}; \frac{3}{4}$ **15.** $\frac{\frac{4}{5}}{\frac{1}{5}}$ **17.** $\frac{478}{213}; \frac{213}{478}$ **19.** $\frac{2}{3}$
21. $\frac{3}{4}$ **23.** $\frac{12}{25}$ **25.** $\frac{7}{9}$ **27.** $\frac{2}{3}$ **29.** $\frac{23}{50}$ **31.** $\frac{1}{2}$
33. $\frac{3}{4}$ **35.** $\frac{27}{50}$ **37.** $\frac{32}{101}$ **39.** $=$ **41.** 50
43. -14.5 **45.** $6\frac{7}{20}$ cm **49.** .066 **51.** $\frac{30}{47}$
53. 1 : 2 : 3

Margin Exercises 7.2

1. $\frac{45}{9}$ or 5 mi./hr. **2.** 12 mi./hr **3.** $\frac{3}{10}$ mi./hr
4. 1110 ft\sec **5.** 4 ft/sec **6.** $14\frac{1}{2}$ ft/sec
7. 250 ft./sec **8.** 2 gal/day **9.** 21 ¢/oz.
10. A **11.** 4 ¢/oz.; $5\frac{1}{2}$ ¢/oz.

Exercise Set 7.2

1. 40 km/hr **3.** 11 m/sec **5.** 152 yd/day **7.** 25
mi/hr **9.** $57\frac{1}{5}$ ¢/min **11.** .623 gal/sq. ft **13.**
186,000 mi/sec **15.** 124 km/hr **17.** 560 mi/hr
19. $9.5/yd **21.** 20.59 ¢/oz. **23.** $4.34/lb. **25.** A
27. A **29.** A **31.** B **33.** A **35.** B **37.** B
39. 1.7 million **41.** 109.608 **43.** $-5,833.56$
47. a) 10.8¢; 10.9¢ **49.** -0.8¢

Margin Exercises 7.3

1. Proportional **2.** Not Proportional **3.** Not
Proportional **4.** Proportional **5.** Not Proportional
6. Not Proportional **7.** $x = 14$ **8.** $x = 11\frac{1}{4}$
9. $n = 17.5$ **10.** $x = 2.64$ **11.** $t = 10.8$
12. $x = 2\frac{41}{42}$

Exercise Set 7.3

1. Not Proportional **3.** Proportional
5. Proportional **7.** Not Proportional **9.** $x = 45$
11. $x = 12$ **13.** $t = 10$ **15.** $n = 20$ **17.** $n = 5$
19. $x = 18$ **21.** $x = 22$ **23.** $x = 28$ **25.** $x = 9\frac{1}{3}$
27. $x = 2\frac{8}{9}$ **29.** $t = 0.06$ **31.** $n = 5$ **33.** $x = 1$
35. $x = 1$ **37.** $x = 14$ **39.** $y = 2\frac{3}{16}$ **41.** $x = 3\frac{3}{16}$
43. $y = 12.573$ **45.** $y = 7\frac{5}{249}$ **47.** not equal
48. = **49.** not equal **51.** 65 **53.** 290.5
57. 2,731.369

Margin Exercises 7.4

1. 445 cal. **2.** 14.118 gal. **3.** 8 shirts **4.** 38 in.
5. 9.5 in. **6.** 2,074 deer

Exercise Set 7.4

1. 702 mi. **3.** $84.60 **5.** $x = 8$ **7.** $61\frac{2}{3}$ lb.
9. 171 gal. **11.** 308 trees **13.** 4 sections
15. $5\frac{1}{3}$ gal. **17.** 954 deer **19.** 100 oz **21.** 1980
23. 58.1 **25.** $7\frac{1}{3}$ in. **27.** No; Week 30; $53.33
29. $2.72 **31.** 5.28 **33. a)** 33.7 in. **b)** 85.598 cm.
37. 16 **39.** 7 gal.

Margin Exercises 7.5

1. $x = 15$ **2.** 24.75 ft. **3.** 34.92 ft. **4.** $x = 21$ cm.
5. 29 ft.

Exercise Set 7.5

1. h = 25 **3.** $x = 1\frac{1}{3}$ **5.** $x = 6\frac{3}{4}$; $y = 9$ **7.** $x = 7.5$;
$y = 7.2$ **9.** $1\frac{1}{4}$ m **11.** 36 ft **13.** 7 ft **15.** 100 ft
17. $x = 4$ **19.** $x = 10\frac{1}{2}$ **21.** $x = 6$; $y = 5\frac{1}{4}$; $z = 3$
23. $x = 5\frac{1}{3}$; $y = 4\frac{2}{3}$; $z = 5\frac{1}{3}$ **25.** h = 20 in
27. h = 145 ft **29.** $59.81 **31.** −679.493
33. 27,456.8 **37.** $13\frac{3}{4}$ ft. **39.** 1,034 cm
41. $y = 3681.437$ **43.** $x = .352$; $y = .4$

Chapter 7 Review Exercises

1. $\frac{47}{84}$ **2.** $\frac{46}{1.27}$ **3.** $\frac{83}{100}$ **4.** $\frac{0.72}{197}$ **5.** $\frac{537,969}{2,312,203}$
6. $\frac{3}{4}$ **7.** $\frac{9}{16}$ **8.** 23.54 mi/hr **9.** 0.638 gal/ft²
10. $25.36/kg **11.** 0.72 serving/lb **12.** 5.7 cents/oz
13. 5.45 cents/oz **14.** B **15.** B **16.** No
17. No **18.** 32 **19.** 7 **20.** $\frac{1}{40}$ **21.** 24
22. $4.45 **23.** 351 **24.** 832 mi **25.** 27 acres
26. 2,900,000 kg **27.** 6 in. **28.** Approximately
9906 **29.** $x = 20$, $y = 16$ **30.** 40 ft
31. $x = 3$, $y = 9$, $z = 7\frac{1}{2}$

Chapter 7 Practice Test

1. $\frac{85}{97}$ **2.** $\frac{0.3}{124}$ **3.** $\frac{9}{10}$ **4.** $\frac{25}{32}$ **5.** 0.625 ft/sec
6. $1\frac{1}{3}$ servings/lb **7.** 19.39 cents/oz **8.** B **9.** Yes
10. No **11.** 12 **12.** 360 **13.** 1512 km **14.** 44
15. 4.8 min **16.** 525 mi **17.** 66 m **18.** 173.736
19. −0.9944

Chapter 8

Margin Exercises 8.1

1. $\frac{70}{100}$; $70 \cdot \frac{1}{100}$; $70 \cdot 0.01$ **2.** $\frac{23.4}{100}$; $23.4 \cdot \frac{1}{100}$; $23.4 \cdot 0.01$
3. $\frac{100}{100}$; $100 \cdot \frac{1}{100}$; $100 \cdot 0.01$ **4.** 0.34 **5.** 0.789
6. 0.83 **7.** 0.042 **8.** 24% **9.** 347% **10.** 100%
11. 90% **12.** 10.80%

Exercise Set 8.1

1. $\frac{90}{100}$; $90 \cdot \frac{1}{100}$; $90 \cdot 0.01$ **3.** $\frac{12.5}{100}$; $12.5 \cdot \frac{1}{100}$; $12.5 \cdot 0.01$
5. 0.67 **7.** 0.456 **9.** 0.5901 **11.** 0.1 **13.** 0.01
15. 2 **17.** 0.001 **19.** 0.0009 **21.** 0.0018
23. 0.2319 **25.** 0.4 **27.** 0.025 **29.** 0.622
31. 47% **33.** 3% **35.** 870% **37.** 33.4%
39. 75% **41.** 40% **43.** 0.6% **45.** 1.7%
47. 27.18% **49.** 2.39% **51.** 0.0104% **53.** 24%
55. 58.1% **57.** $33\frac{1}{3}$ **59.** $-9\frac{3}{8}$ **61.** $-0.66\overline{6}$
63. $-0.83\overline{3}$

Margin Exercises 8.2

1. 25% **2.** 62.50% **3.** 66.67% **4.** 83.33%
5. 57% **6.** 76% **7.** $\frac{3}{5}$ **8.** $\frac{31}{4}$ **9.** $\frac{2}{3}$
10.

$\frac{1}{5}$	$\frac{5}{6}$	$\frac{3}{8}$
0.200	0.833	0.375
20.00%	$83\frac{1}{3}$%	$37\frac{1}{2}$

Exercise Set 8.2

1. 41% **3.** 5% **5.** 20% **7.** 30% **9.** 50%
11. 62.50% **13.** 80% **15.** $66\frac{2}{3}$% **17.** $16\frac{2}{3}$%
19. 16% **21.** 5% **23.** 34% **25.** 36% **27.** 21%
29. 24% **31.** $\frac{17}{20}$ **33.** $\frac{5}{8}$ **35.** $\frac{1}{3}$ **37.** $\frac{1}{6}$
39. $\frac{29}{40}$ **41.** $\frac{4}{5}$ **43.** $\frac{203}{800}$ **45.** $\frac{176}{225}$ **47.** $\frac{711}{1100}$
49. $\frac{11}{2}$ **51.** $\frac{31}{4}$ **53.** $\frac{1}{3}$ **55.** $\frac{11}{20}$ **57.** $\frac{19}{50}$
59. $\frac{11}{100}$ **61.** $\frac{1}{4}$ **63.** $\frac{569}{10000}$

65.

Fractional	Decimal	Percent
$\frac{1}{8}$	0.125	12.50%
$\frac{1}{6}$	0.16666	16.67%
$\frac{1}{5}$	0.2	20%
$\frac{1}{4}$	0.25	25%
$\frac{1}{3}$	0.33333	33.30%
$\frac{3}{8}$	0.375	37.50%
$\frac{2}{5}$	0.4	40%
$\frac{1}{2}$	0.5	50%

67.

Fractional	Decimal	Percent
$\frac{1}{2}$	0.5	50.00%
$\frac{1}{3}$	0.333333	33.33%
$\frac{1}{4}$	0.25	25%
$\frac{1}{6}$	0.16666666	16.66%
$\frac{1}{8}$	0.125	12.50%
$\frac{3}{4}$	0.75	75.00%
$\frac{5}{6}$	0.833333	83.33%
$\frac{3}{8}$	0.375	37.5%

69. $x = -70$ **71.** $b = -400$ **73.** $x = 23.125$
75. $33\frac{1}{3}$ **77.** $-83\frac{1}{3}$ **79.** $43\frac{1}{4}$ **81.** $18\frac{3}{4}$
85. 11.11% **87.** 155.55%

Margin Exercises 8.3

1. $12(0.01)(50) = x$ **3.** $45 = 20(0.01)x$
5. $16 = (0.01)n \cdot 40$ **7.** 6 **9.** 21 **11.** 40%

Exercise Set 8.3

1. $n = 32(0.01)(78)$ **3.** $89 = x(0.01)(99)$
5. $13 = 25(0.01)x$ **7.** 234.6 **9.** 45 **11.** 18
13. 1.9 **15.** 68% **17.** 200% **19.** 50%
21. 1.25% **23.** 40 **25.** $40 **27.** 88 **29.** 20
31. 6.25 **33.** $846.60 **35.** $\frac{9}{10}$ **37.** $\frac{7}{8}$ **39.** 0.89
41. 0.03 **45.** Est: 852.5; Calc: 843.2
47. 108 to 135 tons

Margin Exercises 8.4

1. $\frac{12}{100} = \frac{x}{50}$ **3.** $\frac{130}{100} = \frac{x}{72}$ **5.** $\frac{120}{100} = \frac{60}{x}$
7. $\frac{x}{100} = \frac{10.5}{84}$ **9.** 35.2 **11.** 50 **13.** 12.50%

Exercise Set 8.4

1. $\frac{37}{100} = \frac{x}{74}$ **3.** $\frac{x}{100} = \frac{4.3}{5.9}$ **5.** $\frac{25}{100} = \frac{14}{x}$ **7.** 68.4
9. 462 **11.** 40 **13.** 2.88 **15.** 25% **17.** 102%
19. 25% **21.** 93.75% **23.** $72 **25.** 90
27. 88 **29.** 20 **31.** 25 **33.** $780.20 **35.** $x = 8$
37. $x = 8$ **39.** $t = 100$ **41.** $x = 8.0\overline{4}$ **43.** $\frac{43}{48}$ qt.

Margin Exercises 8.5

1. 16% **3.** Spaying **5.** $1,122 **9.** 4%

Exercise Set 8.5

1. 20 left; 100 right **3.** 536; 264 **5.** 32.5%; 67.5%
7. 20.4mL acid; 659.6mL water **9.** 25% **11.** 166, 156, 146, 140, 75 **13.** 3.70% **15.** 270 **17.** 6.8
19. Housing **21.** 14% **29.** 8% **31.** 20%
33. $30,030 **35.** $12,600 **37.** 6.096; 6.194; 6.293
39. $36,400 **41.** $17.25; $39.10; $56.35
43. a. 3.965% **b.** 28.16% **45.** 17.50%
47. 2.272727 **49.** 3.375 **51.** 0.92 **53.** 0.4375
55. 0.0034809 **59.** 18% **61.** 5 ft. 8 in.
63. 83.33%

Margin Exercises 8.6

1. $53.52; $722.47 **3.** 6% **5.** $5,628 **7.** $1,675
9. 20%

Exercise Set 8.6

1. $29.30; $615.30 **3.** $16.56; $281.56 **5.** 5%
7. 4% **9.** $2,000 **11.** $800 **13.** $711.55
15. 5.60% **17.** $2,700 **19.** 5% **21.** $980
23. $5,880 **25.** 12% **27.** $420

29.

Marked	Disc. Rate	Discount	Sales Price
$300	10%	$30	$270

31.

Marked	Disc. Rate	Discount	Sales Price
$17	15%	$2.55	$14.45

33.

Marked	Disc. Rate	Discount	Sales Price
$125	10%	$12.50	$112.50

35.

Marked	Disc. Rate	Discount	Sales Price
$600	40%	$240	$360

37. $387; 30.4% **39.** $460; 18.043% **41.** 18
43. 265.625 **45.** 0.5555 **47.** 0.9166
49. 2.142857 **51.** 4,030,000,000,000
53. 42,700,000 **59.** $2.69 **61.** He bought the plaques for $416.67 and sold them for $400 so he lost money **62.** $33\frac{1}{3}$%

Margin Exercises 8.7

1. $602 **3.** $27.62; $4827.62

Exercise Set 8.7

1. $26 **3.** $124 **5.** $150.50 **7.** $147.95; $10,147.95 **9.** $128.22; $6628.22 **11.** $46.03; $5646.03 **13.** 4.5 **15.** 8 **17.** $33\frac{1}{3}$ **19.** $-12\frac{2}{3}$
21. $\frac{18}{17}$ **23.** $-\frac{203}{2}$ **27.** $1,434.53

Review Exercises: Chapter 8

1. 48.3% **2.** 36% **3.** 37.5%, or $37\frac{1}{2}$%
4. $33.\overline{3}$% or $33\frac{1}{3}$% **5.** 0.735 **6.** 0.065 **7.** $\frac{6}{25}$
8. $\frac{63}{1000}$ **9.** $30.6 = x\% \cdot 90$; 34 **10.** $63 = 84\% \cdot n$; 75
11. $y = 38\frac{1}{2}\% \cdot 168$; 64.68 **12.** $\frac{24}{100} = \frac{16.8}{b}$; 70
13. $\frac{42}{30} = \frac{N}{100}$; 140% **14.** $\frac{10.5}{100} = \frac{a}{84}$; 8.82 **15.** $598
16. 12% **17.** 82,400 **18.** 20% **19.** 168
20. $14.40 **21.** 5% **22.** 11% **23.** $42;$308
24. $42.70; $262.30 **25.** $2940 **26.** $36
27. a) $394.52 **b)** $24,394.52 **28.** $121
29. 22% **30.** 11% **31.** 1600 **32.** 25%

Practice Test: Chapter 8

1. .89 **2.** 67.4% **3.** 137.5% **4.** $\frac{13}{20}$
5. $a = 40\% \cdot 55$; 22 **6.** $\frac{N}{100} = \frac{65}{80}$; 81.25% **7.** 50 lb
8. 140% **9.** $16.20 **10.** $630 **11.** $40; $160
12. $8.52 **13.** $5356 **14.** $131.95; 52.8%
15. Housing **16.** $9000 **17.** $3600 **18.** 5%

Cumulative Review: Chapter 8

1. $\frac{91}{1000}$ **2.** $2.\overline{16}$ **3.** 0.03 **4.** 112.5% **5.** $\frac{5}{0.5}$
6. $23\frac{1}{3}$ km **7.** < **8.** > **9.** 296,200 **10.** 50,000
11. 13 **12.** $-2x - 14$ **13.** $3\frac{1}{30}$ **14.** -14.2
15. 515,150 **16.** $35 - 34.98$ **17.** $\frac{2}{3}$ **18.** $-\frac{110}{63}$
19. $\frac{1}{6}$ **20.** -384 **21.** 1.38036 **22.** $1\frac{1}{2}$
23. 12.25 **24.** 123 R 5 **25.** 95 **26.** 8.13
27. -9 **28.** $\frac{1}{12}$ **29.** $-\frac{16}{9}$ **30.** $8\frac{8}{21}$ **31.** 75%
0.75 **32.** $180 **33.** 33.2 **34.** 12 **35.** 60 in.
36. 3200 yd² **37.** 15 $\frac{cents}{oz}$ **38.** 608 km **39.** 30%
40. 1,033,710 mi² **41.** 5 **42.** $\frac{3}{2}$ km

Chapter 9

Margin Exercises 9.1

1. 2 **2.** 3 **3.** $1\frac{1}{2}$ **4.** $2\frac{1}{2}$ **5.** 288 **6.** 43.5
7. 240,768 **8.** 6 **9.** $1\frac{5}{12}$ **10.** 8 **11.** $11\frac{2}{3}$
12. 5 **13.** 0.502 **14.** 288 **15.** cm **16.** km
17. mm **18.** m **19.** cm **20.** m **21.** 23,000
22. 400 **23.** 178 **24.** 9,040 **25.** 7,814
26. 781.4 **27.** 0.967 **28.** 8,900,000 **29.** 6.78
30. 9,740 **31.** 0.1 **32.** 8.451 **33.** 90.909
34. 804.5 **35.** 1,479.843 **36.** 34.8 m **37.** 50 in.
38. 11.28 sq. yd.

Exercise Set 9.1

1. 12 **3.** 0.083 **5.** 5,280 **7.** 108 **9.** 7
11. $1\frac{1}{2}$ **13.** 26,400 **15.** 3 **17.** $3\frac{1}{3}$ **19.** 52,800
21. 1.5 **23.** 1 **25.** 110 **27.** 2 **29.** 300
31. 30 **33.** $\frac{1}{36}$ **35.** 126,720 **37. a)** 1000
b) .001 **39. a)** 10 **b)** 0.1 **41. a)** 0.01 **b)** 100
43. 6,700 **45.** 0.98 **47.** 8.921 **49.** 0.056666
51. 566,600 **53.** 4.77 **55.** 688 **57.** 0.1
59. 100,000 **61.** 142 **63.** 0.82 **65.** 450
67. .000024 **69.** .688 **71.** 230 **73.** 3.92
75. 100 **77.** 727.41 **79.** 104.585 **81.** 289.62
83. 112.63 **85.** 9.09 **87.** 41.4 mm **89.** 15.5 in.
91. 13 m **93.** 22 ft. **95.** 778 mm **97.** 15 ft.
99. 28.8 mm **101.** 13.85 **102.** 80.5 **103.** 4
104. 0.9 **105.** 0.108 **106.** $\frac{11}{40}$ **107.** $\frac{57}{100}$
108. 137.5% **109.** $66\frac{2}{3}$% **110.** 25%
111. $\frac{361}{10,000}$; $27\frac{253}{361}$ **112.** $\frac{1}{6}$ **115.** 0.0041
119. 327,272.73 in. **121.** 22.7 $\frac{mi}{hr}$

Margin Exercises 9.2

1. 1,200 sq. ft. **2.** 3,402 sq. in. **3.** 1,024 sq cm
4. 72 sq. ft. **5.** 45 sq. ft. **6.** 2,880 sq in
7. 2.5 sq. ft **8.** 3,330 acres **9.** 1,000,000
10. 100 **11.** 28,800 **12.** 0.043 **13.** 0.678
14. 43.8 sq. cm **15.** 12.375 sq km **16.** 96 sq. m
17. 18.7 sq. cm **18.** 100 sq. m **19.** 88 sq cm
20. 54 sq m

Exercise Set 9.2

1. 15 sq. km **3.** 1.4 sq. in **5.** 56.25 sq. ft
7. 900 sq. yd. **9.** 144 sq. in **11.** 640 **13.** 0.007
15. 198 **17.** 396 **19.** 12,800 **21.** 27,878,400
23. 5 **25.** 1 **27.** 0.00156 **29.** 5,210,000
31. 140 **33.** 23.456 **35.** 0.085 **37.** 2,500
39. 0.473 **41.** 32 sq. cm **43.** 60 sq. in.
45. 104 sq. ft **47.** 45.5 sq. in **49.** 8.05 sq. cm
51. 297 sq. cm **53.** 7 sq. m **55.** 588 sq. cm
57. 133 sq. m **59.** $\frac{35}{100}$ **61.** $\frac{3}{8}$ **63.** $\frac{833}{1000}$
65. 7,500

Margin Exercises 9.3

1. 9 in. **2.** 5 ft. **3.** 62.832 m **4.** 87.965
5. 34.306 yd. **6.** 78.54 sq. km. **7.** 339.794 sq. cm.
8. 12 ft is larger by 13.097 sq ft.

Exercise Set 9.3

1. 14 cm; 43.982 cm; 153.938 sq. cm   **3.** $1\frac{1}{2}$ in;
4.712 in; 1.767 sq. in   **5.** 16 ft.; 100.531 ft.;
804.247 sq ft.   **7.** 0.7 cm; 4.398 cm; 1.539 sq. cm
9. 3 cm; 18.857 cm; 28.274 sq. cm   **11.** 152,052.956 sq.
mi   **13.** 2.5 cm; 1.25cm; 4.909 sq. cm   **15.** 3.456 ft.
17. 65.973 sq. yd.   **19.** 45.699   **21.** 26.85 yd
23. 45.708 yd   **25.** 97.389 sq. m   **27.** 12.716 sq. m
29. 64.37 sq. in.   **31.** 87.5%   **33.** $66\frac{2}{3}$%
35. 37.5%   **37.** $66\frac{2}{3}$%   **39.** $\frac{31}{8}$ **41.** $\frac{78}{6}$
43. $4\frac{27}{40}$ **45.** $2\frac{1}{45}$ **47.** $\frac{479}{1000}$ **49.** $275\frac{199}{4080}$
53. 360,143.24 revs.   **55.** 3d; pi times d;
Circumference is greater since pi > 3

Margin Exercises 9.4

1. 40   **2.** 20   **3.** mL   **4.** mL   **5.** L   **6.** L
7. 970   **8.** 8.99   **9.** 4.8   **10. a)** 118.28 mL
b) .11828L   **11.** 80   **12.** 4.32   **13.** 32,000
14. kg.   **15.** kg.   **16.** mg.   **17.** g.   **18.** t
19. 6200   **20.** 3.048   **21.** 77   **22.** 234.4
23. 6700   **24.** 120   **25.** 1461   **26.** 1440   **27.** 1

Exercise Set 9.4

1. 1000; 1000;   **3.** 87,000   **5.** 0.049   **7.** 0.000401
9. 78,100   **11.** 320   **13.** 10   **15.** 32   **17.** 500mL
19. 125mL   **21.** 1.75 $\frac{gal.}{wk.}$; 7.5 $\frac{gal.}{wk.}$ **23.** 2000   **25.** 3
27. 64   **29.** 12,640   **31.** 0.1   **33.** 5   **35.** 1,000
37. 10   **39.** $\frac{1}{100}$ **41.** 1,000   **43.** 10   **45.** 234,000
47. 5.2   **49.** 6.7   **51.** 0.0502   **53.** 8.492
55. 58.5   **57.** 800,000   **59.** 1,000   **61.** 0.0034
63. 24   **65.** 60   **67.** $365\frac{1}{4}$ **69.** 0.05   **71.** 8.2
73. 6.5   **75.** 10.75   **77.** 336   **79.** 4.5   **81.** 56
83. $19.2   **85.** 1,000   **87.** 49   **89.** 5%
95. 0.0022   **97.** 32   **99.** 1,000   **101.** 0.125
103. 4   **105.** 8 mL

Margin Exercises 9.5

1. 12 cu cm   **2.** 20 cu ft   **3.** 128 cu ft
4. 785.398 cu ft   **5.** 67,886.618 cu m
6. 91,952.244 cu ft   **7.** 38.792 cu cm
8. 1,696.459 cu m   **9.** 527.787 cu in
10. 50.265 cu mm

Exercise Set 9.5

1. 768 cu cm   **3.** 45 cu in   **5.** 75 cu m
7. $357\frac{1}{2}$ cu yd   **9.** 804.247 cu in   **11.** 353.429 cu cm
13. 41,563,235.7 cu yd   **15.** 4,188,786.66 cu in
17. 124.788 cu m   **19.** 1,436.754 cu km
21. 114,039.717 cu ft   **23.** 24.63 cu cm

25. 33,866.34 cu yd   **27.** 367.566 cu m
29. 143.793 cu cm   **31.** 33,010,140,000 cu mi
33. 396   **35.** 14   **37.** 12   **41.** 6.97 cu ft; 52.3 gal

Margin Exercises 9.5

1. Angle DEF; angle FED; ∠DEF; ∠FED; ∠E
2. Angle PQR; angle RQP; ∠PQR; ∠RQP; ∠Q
3. 127°   **4.** 33°   **5.** Right   **6.** Acute   **7.** Obtuse
8. Straight   **9. a)** ΔABC;   **b)** ΔABC, ΔMPN;
c) ΔDEF   **10.** Yes   **11.** No   **12. a)** ΔEDF;
b) ΔGHI , ΔQRS;   **c)** ΔABC, ΔPMN, ΔJKL
13. 180°   **14.** 64°

Exercise Set 9.6

1. Angle GHI, angle IHG, ∠GHI, ∠IHG, ∠H   **3.** 10°
5. 180°   **7.** 130°   **9.** Obtuse   **11.** Acute
13. Straight   **15.** Obtuse   **17.** Acute   **19.** Obtuse
21. Scalene; Obtuse   **23.** Scalene; Right
25. Equilateral; Acute   **27.** Scalene; Obtuse
29. 46°   **31.** 120°   **33.** $4,608   **35.** $252.49

Margin Exercises 9.7

1. 81   **2.** 100   **3.** 121   **4.** 144   **5.** 169   **6.** 196
7. 225   **8.** 256   **9.** 289   **10.** 324   **11.** 400
12. 625   **13.** 3   **14.** 4   **15.** 11   **16.** 10   **17.** 9
18. 8   **19.** 18   **20.** 20   **21.** 15   **22.** 13   **23.** 1
24. 0   **25.** 2.236   **26.** 8.832   **27.** 12.961
28. $c = \sqrt{41}$; $c \approx 6.403$ **29.** $a = \sqrt{75}$; $a \approx 8.66$
30. $b = \sqrt{120}$; $b \approx 10.954$ **31.** $a = \sqrt{175}$; $a \approx 13.220$
32. $\sqrt{424}$ ft. ≈ 20.6 ft.

Exercise Set 9.7

1. 10   **3.** 21   **5.** 25   **7.** 19   **9.** 23   **11.** 100
13. 6.928   **15.** 2.828   **17.** 4.243   **19.** 2.449
21. 3.162   **23.** 8.66   **25.** 14   **27.** 13.528
29. $c = \sqrt{34} \approx 5.831$ **31.** $c = \sqrt{98} \approx 9.889$
33. $a = 5$ **35.** $b = 8$ **37.** $c = 13$ **39.** $b = 24$
41. $a = \sqrt{399} \approx 19.975$ **43.** $b = \sqrt{224} \approx 14.967$
45. $\sqrt{250}$ m ≈ 15.8 m   **47.** $\sqrt{8450}$ ft ≈ 91.9 ft.
49. $h = \sqrt{500}$ ft ≈ 22.4 ft   **51.** $\sqrt{211,200,000}$ ft $\approx$
14,532.7 ft   **53.** 0.456   **55.** 1.23   **57.** 0.0041
59. $468   **61.** 187,200   **63.** About 324
67. 47.8 sq. cm

Chapter 9 Review Exercises

1. $2\frac{2}{3}$ **2.** 30 **3.** 0.03 **4.** 0.004 **5.** 72

6. 400,000 **7.** $1\frac{1}{6}$ **8.** 0.15 **9.** 220 **10.** 32.18

11. 23 m **12.** 4.4 m **13.** 228 ft; 2808 ft²

14. 85.9 ft **15.** 36 ft; 81 ft² **16.** 17.6 cm; 12.6 cm²

17. 60 cm² **18.** 35 mm² **19.** 22.5 m²

20. 27.5 cm² **21.** 88 m² **22.** 126 in² **23.** 840 ft²

24. 36 **25.** 300,000 **26.** 14.375 **27.** 0.06

28. 8 m **29.** $\frac{14}{11}$ in., or $1\frac{3}{11}$ in. **30.** 14 ft

31. 20 cm **32.** 50.24 m **33.** 8 in.

34. 200.96 m² **35.** $5\frac{1}{11}$ in² **36.** 1038.555 ft²

37. 112 **38.** 0.004 **39.** $\frac{4}{15}$ **40.** 0.464 **41.** 180

42. 4700 **43.** 16,140 **44.** 830 **45.** $\frac{1}{4}$ **46.** 0.04

47. 200 **48.** 30 **49.** 0.06 **50.** 1600 **51.** 400

52. $1\frac{1}{4}$ **53.** 50 **54.** 160 **55.** 7.5 **56.** 13.5

57. 18.72 L **58.** 93.6 m³ **59.** 193.2 cm³

60. 31,400 ft³ **61.** 33.493 cm³ **62.** 4.71 in³

63. 54° **64.** 180° **65.** 140° **66.** 90° **67.** Acute

68. Straight **69.** Obtuse **70.** Right **71.** 60°

72. Scalene **73.** Right **74.** $c = \sqrt{850}$

75. $b = \sqrt{51}$ **76.** $c = \sqrt{89}$ **77.** $a = \sqrt{76}$

78. 28.8 ft **79.** 44.7 ft.

Chapter 9 Practice Test

1. 48 **2.** $\frac{1}{3}$ **3.** 6000 **4.** 0.87 **5.** 181.8

6. 1490.4 **7.** 32.82 cm; 65.894 cm²

8. 100 m; 625 m² **9.** 25 cm² **10.** 12 m²

11. 18 ft² **12.** $\frac{1}{4}$ in. **13.** 9 cm **14.** $\frac{11}{14}$ in.

15. 254.34 cm² **16.** 103.815 km² **17.** 15

18. 9.327 **19.** $c = 40$ **20.** $b = \sqrt{60}$ **21.** $c = \sqrt{2}$

22. $b = \sqrt{51}$ **23.** 15.8 m **24.** 84 cm³ **25.** 3.08

26. 240 **27.** 64 **28.** 8220 **29.** 3800

30. 0.4325 **31.** 2.2 **32.** 300 **33.** 360 **34.** 32

35. 1280 **36.** 40 **37.** 420 in³ **38.** 1177.5 ft³

39. 4186.6 yd³ **40.** 113.04 cm³ **41.** 90 degrees

42. 35 degrees **43.** 180 degrees **44.** 113 degrees

45. Right **46.** Acute **47.** Straight **48.** Obtuse

49. 35 degrees **50.** Isosceles **51.** Obtuse

Chapter 10

Margin Exercises 10.1

1. −22.3 **2.** −171 **3.** $-\frac{9}{11}$ **4.** $-\frac{101}{120}$ **5.** 8.6

6. −8.6 **7.** $\frac{2}{5}$ **8.** $-\frac{2}{5}$ **9.** −32.4 **10.** −80

11. 80 **12.** 32.4 **13.** 45 **14.** −45 **15.** −45

16. −8 **17.** 8 **18.** −8 **19.** 30 **20.** −30

21. 58 **22.** 2 **23.** $x = -6.3$ **24.** 10.8

25. $x = -21$ **26.** $y = 39$ **27.** $y = 20$

Exercise Set 10.1

1. $-1\frac{3}{8}$ **3.** −9 **5.** $-\frac{1}{5}$ **7.** 17.3 **9.** −17.01

11. −73 **13.** −0.01 **15.** −6.3 **17.** $-\frac{5}{12}$ **19.** −8

21. $-\frac{5}{6}$ **23.** $-\frac{23}{24}$ **25.** $-1\frac{5}{12}$ **27.** −2.7 **29.** −52.7

31. 116 **33.** 45 **35.** 39 **37.** 7 **39.** −14.7

41. −5.563 **43.** −16.2 **45.** 50 **47.** $-\frac{10}{21}$

49. −52 **51.** $\frac{1}{4}$ **53.** $9\frac{1}{7}$ **55.** −3.53 **57.** $-\frac{1}{12}$

59. $\frac{11}{13}$ **61.** $\frac{6}{7}$ **63.** $\frac{24}{25}$ **65.** −151,200 **67.** 42

69. 3 **71.** −1 **73.** 6 **75.** −11 **77.** −24

79. $x = 93$ **81.** $t = -1\frac{5}{7}$ **83.** $t = -26.438$

85. $n = 33.34$ **87.** $x = .78$ **89.** $y = 8.62$

91. $t = \frac{1}{18}$ **93.** 96.6 sq. cm **94.** $2 \cdot 3 \cdot 53$

95. 18 **97.** 64 **99.** 8 **103.** −309,882 **105.** T

107. T **109.** T **111.** T

Margin Exercise 10.2

1. 36; 36 **2.** 90; 90 **3.** 60; 60 **4.** 14; 14

5. 30; 30 **6.** 12; 12 **7.** $5x, 4y, 3$ **8.** $-4y, -2x, 3z$

9. $3x - 15$ **10.** $5x + 5$ **11.** $\frac{5}{4}x - \frac{5}{4}y + 5$

12. $-2x + 6$ **13.** $-5x + 10y - 20z$ **14.** $6(z - 2)$

15. $3(x - 2y + 3)$ **16.** $2(8a - 18b + 21)$

17. $-4(3x + 8y - 4z)$ **18.** $3x$ **19.** $6x$ **20.** $-8x$

21. $0.59x$ **22.** $3x + 3y$ **23.** $-4x - 5y - 7$

24. $\frac{1}{10}x + \frac{7}{9}y - \frac{2}{3}$

Exercise Set 10.2

1. 240; 240 **3.** 160; 160 **5.** $2b + 10$ **7.** $7 - 7t$

9. $30x + 12$ **11.** $7x + 42y + 28$ **13.** $-7y + 14$

15. $45x + 54y - 72$ **17.** $3\backslash 4\, x - \frac{9}{4}y - \frac{3}{2}z$

19. $-3.72x + 9.92y - 3.41$ **21.** $2(x + 2)$

23. $5(6 + y)$ **25.** $7(2x + 3y)$ **27.** $5(x + 3y + 2)$

29. $8(x - 3)$ **31.** $4(8 - y)$ **33.** $2(4x + 5y - 11)$

35. $-6(3x - 2y - 1)$ **37.** $19a$ **39.** $9a$ **41.** $8x + 9z$

43. $-19a + 88$ **45.** $4t + 6y - 4$ **47.** $8x$ **49.** $5n$

51. $-16y$ **53.** $17a - 12b - 1$ **55.** $4x + 2y$

57. $\frac{39}{20}x + \frac{1}{2}y + 12$ **59.** $0.8x + .5y$ **61.** 30 yd.;

94.248 yd.; 706.858 sq. yd. **63.** 19 mi.; 59.69 mi.;

283.528 sq. mi. **65.** 10 mm; 62.832 mm;

314 .159 sq. mm **67.** 2.3 ft.; 14.451 ft.; 16.619 sq. ft.

Margin Exercises 10.3

1. 5 **2.** 4 **3.** 4 **4.** 39 **5.** $-\frac{3}{2}$ **6.** −4.3

7. −3 **8.** 800 **9.** 1 **10.** 2 **11.** 2 **12.** $\frac{17}{2}$

13. $\frac{8}{3}$ **14.** −4.3 **15.** 2 **16.** 3 **17.** −2

18. $-\frac{1}{2}$

Exercise Set 10.3

1. 5   **3.** 8   **5.** 10   **7.** 14   **9.** −8   **11.** −8
13. −7   **15.** 15   **17.** 6   **19.** 4   **21.** 6   **23.** −3
25. 15   **27.** −20   **29.** 6   **31.** 7   **33.** 2   **35.** 5
37. 2   **39.** 10   **41.** 4   **43.** 0   **45.** −1   **47.** $-\frac{4}{3}$
49. $\frac{2}{5}$ **51.** −2   **53.** −4   **55.** $\frac{4}{5}$ **57.** $-\frac{28}{27}$ **59.** 6
61. 2   **63.** 6   **65.** 8   **67.** 1   **69.** 17   **71.** $-\frac{5}{3}$
73. −3   **75.** 2   **77.** $-\frac{51}{31}$ **79.** 2   **81.** 6.5
83. −6.5   **85.** $7(x-3-2y)$ **87.** $14(3t+m-4)$
89. −8   **93.** 2   **95.** −2   **97.** 8   **99.** 2cm

Chapter 10 Review Exercises

1. − 3   **2.** $-\frac{7}{12}$ **3.** −18   **4.** −5   **5.** 4   **6.** $-\frac{14}{10}$
7. − 7.9   **8.** 54   **9.** −9.18   **10.** $-\frac{2}{7}$ **11.** −210
12. − 7   **13.** 3   **14.** $\frac{3}{4}$ **15.** −24   **16.** −2
17. −3   **18.** 5   **19.** $14x+21y-7$ **20.** $-35x+20$
21. $-88x+187$ **22.** $78x-39y+91$ **23.** $15(x-3)$
24. $7(x-2y+5)$ **25.** $4(-6x+2y-3)$ **26.** $4x-17$
27. $3.4a-8.2b+6.2$ **28.** $\frac{x}{12}-\frac{7}{8}y+\frac{3}{5}$ **29.** −22
30. 7   **31.** −192   **32.** 1   **33.** $-\frac{7}{3}$ **34.** 25
35. $\frac{1}{2}$ **36.** $-\frac{15}{64}$ **37.** 9.99   **38.** −8   **39.** −5
40. $-\frac{1}{3}$ **41.** 4   **42.** 3   **43.** 4   **44.** 16   **45.** 6
46. −3   **47.** 12   **48.** 4

Chapter 10 Practice Test

1. 7.8   **2.** − 8   **3.** $\frac{7}{40}$ **4.** 10   **5.** −2.5   **6.** $\frac{7}{8}$
7. −48   **8.** $\frac{3}{16}$ **9.** −9   **10.** $\frac{3}{4}$ **11.** −3
12. $-30x-4y+2$ **13.** $-63x+77y+42$
14. $11(2x+3y+4)$ **15.** $75(x-2)$ **16.** $x-10y$
17. −6   **18.** 49   **19.** −12   **20.** 2   **21.** $-\frac{7}{20}$
22. 2.5   **23.** 7   **24.** $\frac{5}{3}$

Chapter 10 Cumulative Review

1. $10\frac{1}{6}$ **2.** 49.2   **3.** 87.52   **4.** −1234   **5.** 2
6. 1565   **7.** $-\frac{623}{1000}$ **8.** 21\10   **9.** <   **10.** >
11. $\frac{3}{8}$ **12.** 235000   **13.** 87   **14.** 90   **15.** 27
16. 0.17   **17.** $52m; 120m^2$ **18.** $9a-16$ **19.** −30.7
20. 20 lb   **21.** 1985   **22.** 14.4   **23.** 1   **24.** $-\frac{53}{3}$
25. $\frac{1}{8}$ **26.** 7   **27.** 528 million   **28.** 58.6
29. $24   **30.** 17 m   **31.** 6%   **32.** $2\frac{1}{8}$ yd
33. $21.82   **34.** The 8-qt box   **35.** $\frac{7}{20}$ km

Index

D

Data, 119, 339-341, 343-346, 350, 352-353, 361-364, 366, 389, 465, 469, 479

Decigram, 540

Decimals, 54, 599-601, 604, 285, 296-297, 299, 301, 303, 305, 307, 309, 311, 313, 315, 317, 319, 321, 328, 330, 336, 366

Decimeter, 505

Decrease, 610, 350-351, 362-363, 470-473, 477, 479, 481, 485, 495, 569

Denominator, 163, 178-179, 182, 196-202, 210-211, 213, 236, 242, 244-248, 252-255, 264, 288, 327-328, 331, 400, 404, 416-417, 447, 536, 49, 52

Diameter, 355, 506, 529-530, 532-533, 535, 552, 555, 570, 575, 595

Difference, 17, 55-56, 61, 580, 591, 93, 102, 117-118, 120, 124, 126, 132, 134, 147, 157, 176, 298, 322, 344, 348, 362, 375, 382, 499, 539,

Digits, 7

Digoxin, 548

Dime, 379, 533

Dimension, 121, 129, 511

Dimensions, 121, 128-129, 279, 310, 378, 506-507, 511, 517, 533, 555, 570

Discount, 439, 481, 483, 485-90, 495-497

Discuss, 364, 389

Discussed, 601, 158, 177, 285, 516

Dish, 223

Dishwashers, 132

Disorderly, 86

Dispensed, 55

Dispenser, 20

Display, 393-396, 584, 602, 471, 537

Displayed, 394-395, 178, 467, 473

Displaying, 340

Displays, 584

Distance, 8, 579, 611, 103, 111, 120, 124, 140-141, 233, 243, 257-258, 268-269, 272-273, 275, 279, 308, 341, 355, 368, 375-376, 404, 407, 417, 422, 425-426, 431, 433, 501-502, 510-511, 514, 516, 529, 535, 550, 568,

Distributive properties, 579, 590-593, 595, 599-601, 609

Dividend, 59, 311, 313-314, 39, 42-45

Divisibility rules, 65-71,

Division, 39-47, 59-61, 66, 162-163, 170-174, 211-213, 215-221, 223, 225, 235, 285, 311-317,

Divisor, 59, 212, 311, 313-316, 414, 39, 41-45

Dollars, converting from, 127, 287, 306-307, 310, 317, 368, 374, 376-377, 380, 389, 404-406, 611

E

Earned interest, 585, 116, 201, 242, 307, 342, 377, 400, 404, 424-425, 14

Effective yield, 585

Eight, 215, 287, 8

Elbow (see Smoltz)

English system of measures, 251, 342, 388, 502,

Equations, 579-583, 585, 587, 589, 596-597, 599-603, 605, 93-95, 97, 99, 105-107, 109, 137, 167, 169-171, 173, 177, 225, 227, 229, 237, 239, 243, 253, 255, 257, 259, 261, 263, 275, 285, 336-337, 439, 453, 455, 457

Equilateral triangle, 559-560, 574, 577

Equivalent expressions and equations, 582-583, 590-592, 595, 196, 225-226, 246, 254-255, 260, 313, 331, 441, 448, 503

Estimating and problem-solving, 93, 116-117, 195, 285, 322-323, 325-326, 371, 421, 423, 44

Evaluating expressions, 62, 582, 96-97, 100, 243, 274-275, 277, 279, 307

Exponential notation, 393, 53, 62-64, 83, 89, 91, 94, 96-97, 99, 135, 163, 274, 316

Exponents, 83, 95, 135, 241

Expressions, 393, 579-583, 585, 587, 589-590, 93-97, 99-101, 103-104, 137-138, 140, 142, 144, 146, 148, 150, 152, 154, 156, 158, 160, 162-164, 166, 168, 170, 172, 174-176, 243, 267, 274-275, 277, 279, 307, 316, 399, 7

F

Factor, 56, 61, 65, 70, 75-77, 81-84, 590, 592-594, 605, 607, 609, 102, 197-199, 202-203, 226, 246-247, 254-255, 328, 331, 447, 562, 41

Factoring, 579, 590-593, 595, 197-199, 202, 247

Factorization, 53, 65-66, 75-79, 82-85, 88, 90-91, 588, 135, 241, 247, 255, 326

Factors, 53, 56, 62, 65-67, 69, 71-73, 75-76, 79-84, 88, 90-91, 592-593, 101-102, 104, 134, 189, 197-199, 202, 210, 303, 328, 562, 28-29

Fahrenheit, 101, 103, 137-139, 222, 321 445, 543

Fractions, 54, 65, 599, 601, 604, 177-190, 192, 194, 196, 198, 200, 202, 204, 206, 208, 210, 212-214, 216-218, 220, 222, 224, 226, 228, 230-232, 234, 236-240, 242-244, 246, 248, 250, 252, 254, 256, 258, 260, 262-268, 270-272, 274-276, 278, 280-284, 286, 288, 411, 449, 505, 535, 5, 49-51

S0-ADA-175

Organizational Behavior and Management

Sixth Edition

JOHN M. IVANCEVICH

Cullen Professor of Organizational Behavior and Management

MICHAEL T. MATTESON

Professor Emeritus of Organizational Behavior and Management

Both of University of Houston

Boston   Burr Ridge, IL   Dubuque, IA   Madison, WI   New York   San Francisco   St. Louis
Bangkok   Bogotá   Caracas   Kuala Lumpur   Lisbon   London   Madrid   Mexico City
Milan   Montreal   New Delhi   Santiago   Seoul   Singapore   Sydney   Taipei   Toronto

McGraw-Hill Higher Education 🌀

A Division of The **McGraw-Hill** *Companies*

ORGANIZATIONAL BEHAVIOR AND MANAGEMENT
Published by McGraw-Hill, an imprint of The McGraw-Hill Companies, Inc. 1221 Avenue of the Americas, New York, NY, 10020. Copyright © 2002, 1999, 1996, 1993, 1990, 1987 by The McGraw-Hill Companies, Inc. All rights reserved. No part of this publication may be reproduced or distributed in any form or by any means, or stored in a data base or retrieval system, without the prior written consent of The McGraw-Hill Companies, Inc., including, but not limited to, in any network or other electronic storage or transmission, or broadcast for distance learning. Some ancillaries, including electronic and print components, may not be available to customers outside the United States.

The book is printed on acid-free paper.

domestic   1 2 3 4 5 6 7 8 9 0 DOW/DOW 0 9 8 7 6 5 4 3 2 1
international   1 2 3 4 5 6 7 8 9 0 DOW/DOW 0 9 8 7 6 5 4 3 2 1

ISBN 0-07-243638-7

Publisher: *John E. Biernat*
Senior editor: *John Weimeister*
Editorial assistant: *Trina Hauger*
Marketing manager: *Lisa Nicks*
Project manager: *Scott Scheidt*
Production associate: *Gina Hangos*
Producer, Media technology: *Jenny R. Williams*
Cover design: *Matthew Baldwin*
Cover image: *© SIS Rob Colvin*
Senior supplement coordinator: *Rose M. Range*
Printer: *R. R. Donnelley & Sons Company*
Typeface: *10.5/12 Berkeley Medium*
Compositor: *Carlisle Communications, Ltd.*

Library of Congress Cataloging-in-Publication Data

Ivancevich, John M.
     Organizational behavior and management / John M. Ivancevich, Michael R. Mattteson.—
6th ed.
        p. cm.
     Includes index.
     ISBN 0-07-243638-7 (alk. paper)
     1. Organizational behavior. I. Matteson, Michael T. II. Title.

HD58.7 .I89 2002
658.4—dc21   2001030498

INTERNATIONAL EDITION ISBN 0-07-112219-2
Copyright © 2002. Exclusive rights by The McGraw-Hill Companies, Inc. for manufacture and export.
This book cannot be re-exported from the country to which it is sold by McGraw-Hill.
The International Edition is not available in North America.

www.mhhe.com

This book is dedicated to each member
of our immediate families.

Brief Contents

Contents

PART V

ORGANIZATIONAL DESIGN, CHANGE, AND INNOVATION   *567*

CHAPTER 15

Organizational Structure and Design   *569*

CHAPTER 16

Managing Organizational Change and Innovation   *625*

Organizational Behavior and Management continues to be well received by colleagues. The book's sixth edition is based on reviewers' comments, suggestions, and requests as well as our teaching from the book, observing the dramatic changes occurring around the world, and striving to provide a comprehensive, accurate, and up-to-date picture of organizational behavior and management knowledge, applications, controversy, and concerns. As the first decade of the 21st century unfolds with all of the swift environmental changes impacting managers, it is still the people (clerks, technicians, project leaders, programmers, engineers) who provide an organization's services or products. This book is about people who work in or telework with organizations—their needs, thoughts, behaviors, and emotions.

We have reviewed and considered many suggestions from colleagues, students, and previous users of the book. The basic structure has been kept much as it was originally, but we have significantly updated, streamlined, and/or expanded the content of each chapter. We have, in each new edition, added more comprehensive treatment of the content base. Content has been streamlined, as well as related to events, activities, and decisions made in organizational life. And, of course, we have updated all the information. Our intention in making these substantive changes has been to offer an intensive treatment of organizational behavior and management that helps instructors teach easily and effectively. As dedicated teachers, we revise with our fellow teachers and the student population in mind. This book was not written as a research message or as a new theoretical model. Like its predecessors, the sixth edition of *Organizational Behavior and Management* contains knowledge that applies both inside and outside the classroom.

Can the serious theory and research basis of organizational behavior and management be presented to students in an exciting and challenging way? We believe it can. Thus, we expanded the theory, research, and applications of the subject matter in the revision of the book. The sixth edition differs from the previous editions in these ways:

1. Additional content makes it more comprehensive.
2. The application of theory and research in actual organizations is further emphasized with more examples, new elements, and Internet exercises.
3. More international and multicultural examples showing applications of principles and models are provided. International and multicultural issues, debates, concepts, and examples are interspersed throughout the book and its elements.
4. Fundamental themes covering managing diversity and demographic changes, technological changes, total quality, ethics, and globalization are woven throughout the book. These themes are consistent with the recommendations for balanced subject matter coverage made by the American Assembly of Collegiate Schools of Business/International Association for Management Education. This internationally acclaimed accrediting body establishes the boundaries for appropriate topic coverage.

5. The end-of-chapter elements—readings, exercises, and cases—have been re-done. After listening to users and potential users, we have added, retained, or deleted, a number of elements for students and instructors. The elements included in the final array are considered by the authors, reviewers, and text users as relevant, teachable, and complete.

6. The materials—text, readings, exercises, and cases—stimulate students to think about how they would respond if they were in the situation being discussed or displayed.

With *Organizational Behavior and Management* (OBM), students become involved participants in learning about behavior and management within work settings. We have designed the book with instructional flexibility in mind. OBM combines text, readings, self-learning exercises, group participation exercises, and cases. These elements are aimed at students interested in understanding, interpreting, and attempting to predict the behavior of people working in organizations.

Organizational functioning is complex. No single theory or model of organizational behavior has emerged as the best or most practical. Thus, managers must be able to probe and diagnose organizational situations when they attempt to understand, interpret, and predict behavior. OBM devotes considerable attention to encouraging the development of these probing and diagnostic skills. The first step in this development is for each reader to increase his or her own self-awareness. Before a person can diagnose why another person (a friend, subordinate, or competitor) is behaving in a particular way, he or she must conduct a self-analysis. This introspective first step is built into each chapter's content and into the learning elements found at the end of OBM's chapters. The content and these elements encourage the students to relate their own knowledge and experience to the text, readings, exercises, and cases in the book.

FRAMEWORK OF THE BOOK

The book is organized into five parts containing a total of 16 chapters and two appendices. The framework highlights behavior, structure, and processes that are part of organizational life. The five parts are as follows:

Part One   "The Field of Organizational Behavior." The first chapter of OBM, "Introduction to Organizational Behavior," introduces the field of organizational behavior and explores the how, what, why, and when of organizational behavior as viewed and practiced by managers. Chapter 2, "Organizational Culture," covers such issues as internal culture, cultural diversity, and cross-cultural research.

Part Two   "Understanding and Managing Individual Behavior." These five chapters focus on the individual, including topics such as "Individual Differences and Work Behavior" (Chapter 3), "Motivation" (Chapter 4), "Evaluation, Feedback, and Reward of Individual Behavior" (Chapter 5), "Job Design" (Chapter 6), and "Organizational Stress An Individual View" (Chapter 7).

Part Three   "Group Behavior and Interpersonal Influence." These two topics are explored in a three-chapter sequence: Chapter 8, "Group Behavior and Work Teams"; Chapter 9, "Intergroup Conflict and Negotiations"; and Chapter 10, "Organizational Power and Politics."

Part Four   "Organizational Processes" are covered in four chapters. Two leadership chapters are presented: Chapter 11, "Leadership," and Chapter 12, "Leadership: Developing Applications," Chapter 13 covers "Communication," and Chapter 14 focuses on "Decision Making."

Part Five   "Organizational Design, Change, and Innovation." Two chapters make up the final part: Chapter 15, "Organizational Structure and Design," and Chapter 16, "Managing Organizational Change and Innovation."

FEATURES OF THE SIXTH EDITION

First, this edition includes 16 readings, 24 exercises, and 16 cases. These end-of-chapter elements were selected because of their relevance to the chapter content and because of feedback from adopters. Second, weaving global events, situations, and examples throughout the content, elements, and end-of-chapter material was purposefully directed. Globalization is such a vital area that it must be presented and covered throughout the book. Third, managing diversity in the workplace is presented and discussed throughout the text. Fourth, total quality management (TQM) is a major philosophy and practice that influences a firm's culture and competitiveness. Thus, TQM is introduced and reviewed. Fifth, ethics and ethical behavior are topics of major concern throughout the world. Examples, incidents, and debates that present ethical dilemmas are integrated into the book.

Sixth, the text introduces realism and relevance. Hundreds of real-world examples of decisions, situations, problem solving, successes, and failures are presented. Fortune 1000 companies do not dominate this book. Smaller and medium-size firms that students may not be familiar with are also used to illustrate organizational behavior and management activities. Finally, we have taken the time and space to explain the concepts, frameworks, and studies presented in the text. It was our intention not to be an encyclopedia of terms and references to colleagues. Instead, we use the ideas, work, and concepts of colleagues only when they add learning value to the chapter content. The goal of each presentation is to present something of value. A "cookbook" list of terms, names, historical points of reference, or empirical studies often becomes pedantic and boring. Comments on previous editions of this text suggest that the book is readable and teachable. These are attributes that are important to the success of the book.

A total of 140 learning and knowledge enrichment elements are provided in the form of Encounters, Management Pointers, You Be The Judge, readings, exercises and cases. These can be used by instructors in any combination that fits the course objectives, teaching style, and classroom situation.

Encounters   Forty-four chapter encounters are interspersed throughout the text. They focus on ethical issues, global examples, and general organizational behavior and management activities. The encounters bring the concepts to life by presenting a meaningful example of activity that ties in with the chapter content.

Management Pointers   A total of 24 management pointers are used with at least one in each chapter. This new element explains, in straightforward terms, principles of how to manage and how-to lead. These principles are easy to understand and use and are based on experience, theory, and empirical research.

You Be The Judge   Another new element in this edition, "You Be The Judge," features 16 problems, dilemmas, or issues requiring students to make a decision and solve the dilemma, problem, or situation. These action-oriented elements are intended to increase student involvement.

Readings   The book contains 16 carefully selected classic or contemporary readings from a variety of sources (e.g., *Academy of Management Executive, Harvard Business Review, Issues and Observations, Fast Company, Organizational Dynamics*). Each of the readings is tied to the chapter's content.

Exercises   *OBM* also includes 24 self-learning and group exercises. Some of the exercises allow the individual student to participate in a way that enhances self-knowledge. These self-learning exercises illustrate how to gather and use feedback properly and emphasize the uniqueness of perception, values, personality, and communication abilities. In addition, a number of exercises apply theories and principles from the text in group activities. Working in groups is a part of organizational life, so these exercises introduce a touch of reality. Group interaction can generate debates, lively discussions, testing of personal ideas, and sharing of information.

Furthermore, the exercises are designed to involve the instructor in the learning process. Your participation allows you to try out techniques and patterns of behavior and to integrate exercise materials with the text. None of the exercises require advance preparation for the instructor, although some require returning to a particular section or model in the chapter for information. The main objective is to get the reader involved. We want an involved, thinking, and questioning reader.

Cases   *OBM* contains 16 full-length cases. These cases reflect a blend of old- and new-economy examples, principles, and lessons. Lessons can and are still being learned from what we now refer to as the old-economy organizations (pre-1985). These realistic, dynamic cases link theory, research, and practice. They provide an inside view of various organizational settings and dynamics. The cases, like the real world, do not have one "right" solution. Instead, each case challenges students to experience the complexity of the work environment as if they were managers. The cases also are an invaluable teaching tool. They encourage the individual student to probe, diagnose, and creatively solve real problems. Group participation and learning are encouraged meanwhile through in-class discussion and debate. The questions at the end of each case are used to guide the discussion. A case analysis should follow the following format:

1. Read the case quickly.
2. Reread the case using the following model:
    a. Define the major problem in the case in organizational behavior and management terms.
    b. If information is incomplete, which it is likely to be, make realistic assumptions.

c. Outline the probable causes of the problem.

d. Consider the costs and benefits of each possible solution.

e. Choose a solution and describe how you would implement it.

f. Go over the case again. Make sure the questions at the end of the case are answered, and make sure your solution is efficient, feasible, ethical, legally defensible, and can be defended in classroom debate.

Video Cases   In addition to the 16 chapter-ending cases __ video cases have been added at the ends of the parts for this edition of *OBM*. These cases are designed to be used with the video that accompanies the text.

Marginal Notations   Marginal notations are used to highlight main points and to encourage the reader to think of how the ideas and concepts fit together. These marginal notations connect the text with the end-of-chapter readings, exercises, and cases. Every reading, exercise, and case elaborates some point made in that chapter; the marginal notation draws attention to these discussions by indicating the relevant reading, exercise, or case.

Thus, the instructor can use the marginal notations to determine the best point in the lecture to incorporate each reading, exercise, or case in reviewing the chapter and to understand how each fits into the overall framework of ideas in that chapter.

The marginal notations serve to encourage students to tie together and integrate ideas, concepts, and techniques. It is important that text content be lively, realistic, and stimulating to a reader. Thus, the marginal notations help to put the reader in the position of fitting the parts, pieces, and ideas together to improve learning.

Irwin/McGraw-Hill Internet Support Site → *www.mhhe.com/business/ management/ivancevich*   This edition, like the previous one, has an Internet site, which will provide up-to-date data, information, profiles, and examples that can be used with the chapter content and elements. The Internet resources will enable the student to probe more deeply into an event, company, person, or situation. A *password*-protected portion of the site, consisting of supplemental lecture material and other downloadable supplemental teaching materials, is available to instructors only. The vast array of information available on the Internet will allow students to enrich the content being read and discussed in class with current events occurring within organizations.

Other Learning Devices   Learning objectives open each chapter to start the reader thinking about concepts, practices, and concerns. Each chapter also includes two or three Encounters and an end-of-chapter Summary, which is a brief review of main points brought out in the chapter. In addition, a review and discussion section containing 10 questions is presented at the end of each chapter to test the students' understanding.

An important part of any course is vocabulary building. Thus we provide a thorough Glossary of terms at the end of the book. Before a quiz or test, students should go through the glossary and pick out words that they will be expected to know and use.

Although it is difficult to paint a world-renowned portrait of organizational behavior and management, we were determined to help the reader paint his or her own picture. We hope the text, readings, exercises, cases, and learning and knowledge enrichment help you become an adventurous explorer of how organizational behavior and management occurs within organizations.

Internet Enrichment   The Internet was created over 25 years ago as a project of the U.S. Department of Defense, specifically, the Defense Advanced Research Projects Administration, or DARPA. Its goal was to provide a way for widely separated computers to transfer information and data and to make these data communications as robust and reliable as possible. DARPA wanted to make a network that was smart enough to recover on its own from problems such as power failures and interruptions in communication lines.

Eventually, the government dropped the idea that its network was only useful for defense-related projects, and the network became known as Arpanet. The government then began connecting many of the country's universities to the network. Since then, generations of students have studied, used, and improved what we now call the Internet.

Although the Internet began as a government research project and was funded by tax dollars for years, the government is not involved in it anymore. The government might still be one of the largest single users of the Internet, but it no longer funds new development or supports any of the costs associated with maintaining the network. The Internet is completely self-sufficient.

Only a few years ago, the Internet was still relatively unknown outside of scientific and technical communities. That has changed dramatically in just a short time. After two decades of development and improvements, the Internet has exploded into the mainstream.

People were initially attracted to the Internet because it connected them to the world at large. They could exchange electronic mail, participate in discussions (via Usenet newsgroups), and easily exchange programs and data with others around the world using the Internet's file-transfer facilities.

Technically, the Internet isn't a network of computers—it's a network of networks. Local networks throughout the world are tied together by wires, telephone lines, fiber-optic cables, microwave transmissions, and satellites in orbit. But the details of how data gets from one computer on the Internet to another are invisible to the user.

The Internet is dramatically different from online services such as CompuServe and America Online. These companies sell access to their computers; think of them as gigantic bulletin board systems owned and operated by a company. What you see and what you can do with them are limited to what they allow you to see and do. To avoid losing their entire memberships to the Internet, these services have found it necessary to offer access to the Internet and the World Wide Web. They determine which parts of the Internet you can access, however, and some of them charge extra for Internet access, even for sending e-mail to an Internet address.

Until recently, using the Internet generally meant using programs and tools on Unix computers. Long after the personal computer craze was in full swing, the Internet was still an arcane concept to many PC and Mac users—even to many people who considered themselves experts with personal computers, software, and networking.

All of this began to change, though, with the development of high-speed modems and a software hack called *Serial Line Internet Protocol* (SLIP). When 14.4 Kbps modems entered the market, it suddenly became practical to connect PCs and Macintosh computers to the Internet, and SLIP software made it possible to extend the Internet from centrally located networks to the PC user at home or in the office.

High-speed modems and SLIP have resulted in a wave of new products—both hardware and software—that make it easy to connect a home or office computer to the Internet. As a result, excitement about the Internet has been snowballing for nearly three years and students, along with millions of other users, have become the beneficiaries.

The huge high-speed trunk lines that run between countries and major cities are usually owned and maintained by big telecommunications companies. For example, AT&T and Sprint own and maintain good-sized chunks of the trunk lines that snake around the country and the world. For the most part, it's not terribly important to these companies that their lines are being used for Internet traffic; that's just what a telecommunications company does. When there is demand for data communications, the companies try to meet that demand with service. When the demand is high enough, they lay another fiber trunk or launch another satellite.

The World Wide Web   For all its technological wonder, the Internet has suffered for years from a reputation of being difficult to learn, hard to use, and downright homely compared to the sexy interfaces of bulletin board systems, online services, and most of the software that people use on personal computers.

The World Wide Web has changed all this. The Web has quickly become the graphical user interface to the Internet, and it stands unrivaled by any online service in terms of both aesthetics and flexibility.

To access the Web, you use a program called a *Web browser.* A Web browser is a program on your own computer that knows how to retrieve pages of text and graphics from other computers on the Internet. Embedded in these pages are symbols (called *links* or *hyperlinks*) telling your Web browser where to find other related pages on the Internet. A browser displays links differently from the surrounding text. (For example, it may display links in blue, as underlined text, or as 3-D buttons.) When you click on a link, it loads another page of text and graphics. This is called *following a link,* and a concept of following links to related pages of information is called *hypertext.*

Part of the reason for the Web's huge and rapid success is that it's easy to use: It's as simple as clicking a mouse button. In each chapter you will be provided with addresses that you can enter, and then simply click to find the information you want or need.

Just as you need an e-mail address so people can communicate with you, files on the Internet need an address so people can access them. A file's address is known as its *Uniform Resource Locator* or *URL.* Each chapter has URLs that will link to specific information associated with human resource issues, concerns, challenges, or opportunities.

The first page of any site is called the *home page.* The home page is simply a starting point. You will need a browser, a program that permits you to visit different URLs on the Internet/World Wide Web. Two of the most widely used browsers are Internet Explorer and Netscape Navigator. They are the Coke and Pepsi of browsers. A browser displays a document from the Internet on your computer screen.

Another key to the Web's magic is its simplicity. Web "pages" are simply files residing on the hundreds of thousands of computers connected to the Internet. To "serve" the pages when they're requested by a browser, all a computer needs is another simple program called a *Web server*. The Web server just waits and listens for requests from Web browsers. When a request comes in, it finds the requested file and sends it back to the browser.

Search Engines   Getting information is made easier if you know the URL of the Web site that contains what you want. But what if you don't know the URL? Don't worry—all you need to use is a *search engine*. A search engine is a Web site that enables you to enter a query and provides a list of hyperlinks (text or graphics that when clicked take you to a different page on the same site or to a completely different site). Some of the better known and used search engines are:

www.google.com
www.northernlight.com
www.altavista.com
www.excite.com
www.lycos.com
www.hotbot.com
www.goto.com
www.yahoo.com

Type in the URL of a search engine in the address bar of your Web browser (Explorer or Netscape) and press *enter*. You can take it from there by clicking your mouse and typing in some words in the search bar that describe what you are looking for, and then pressing *enter*. Don't be surprised if your search for human resource management information turns up hundreds or even thousands of Web pages. Since the Internet/World Wide Web is expanding and changing every day, you need to keep your favorite URLs current.

The Internet/World Wide Web will serve you well in this and in other courses. As you use this invaluable resource more, you will become more comfortable and proficient. Think of the Internet/World Wide Web as your own personal tutor that can be used when you need to improve your understanding of an HRM issue, topic, subject, or situation.

Resources to Use with the Textbook   There are numerous resources relevant to this course and its topic areas that can be found on the World Wide Web. Listed below by topic are some of the thousands of sites that can enhance your learning. We provide these addresses and encourage you to take a look at those sites that suit your interest.

Communication

www.genelevine.com/papers/18.html
st1.yahoo.com/forleaders/emcom.html
www.leadsolutions.com
www.acertraining.com.au/peopleskills.html
www.members.tripod.com/~cooperate/impcom.html~
www.ee.ed.ac.uk/~gerard/management/art7.html~

Conflict Resolution

www.geocities.com/Athens/8945/sycho.html

www.cmhc.com/psyhelp/chap13.html

www.commnet.edu/QVCTC/classes.conflict.author.html

web.utk.edu/~susanart~

Goal Setting

www.andersonplan.com.au/wb/goals1.html#Smart

www.mindzone.net/special_report.html

www.mindtools.com/page6.html

www.gapmtn.com/goalsetting.html

www.adv-leadership-grp.com

www.bouldercycling.com

www.gsu.edu/~gsolnmm/

Motivation

www.qmtheory.com

www.engr.uark.edu/~whl/herzberg.html

www.com/criv/motivate.html

www.mcrel.org/products/noteworthy/barbaram.html/

www.epic.com/MOTIV/MOTIVITIP>html

www.motivateus.com/

www.themms.com

//miinc.com

www.consumermotivation.com

Empowerment

www.empowerment-now.com

www.innovint.com

www.peoplepositive.com

//members.aol.com/empower16/steps.html

www.empowermentworks.com/index.html#programs

www.timsystem.com/timesystem/methods/book/empowerm.html

www.city.grande-prairie.ab.ca/self_emp.html

Leadership

www.oise.on.ca/%7Ebwillard/leadaid.html

www.leadershipmanagement.com/

www.onnow.com/events/3769.shtml

www.cmd-glg.com/

www.communityleadership.org/overview.html

www.emergingleader.som
www.balacreates.com
www.newleadership.com
www.lios.org/
www.np.ac.sg
www.leadership.mindgarden

Teams

www.oeg.net/twkmod.html
www.teamresources.com/
www.yrokteam.com/custom.html
www.iain.co.uk/mrt.html
www.hummerextereme.com/
CorporateMainMenu.html

Stress

www.onhealth.com/ch1/in-depth/item/0.1007.2557.00html
www.health-net.com/stress.html
//primusweb.com/finesspartner/library/weight/stresmgt.html
www.mediconsult.com/stress/shareware
www.mindtools.com/smpage.html
www.stressfree.com
www.gday-mate.com
www.lindaland.com/stressbook/bookindex.html
www.arc.sbc.edu/stress.html
//hammock.ifas.ufl.edu/txt/fairs/30922
www.tcfn.org/chestheart/articles/workst~1.html
//fitlife.com/health/stress.shtml

In addition to these OBM topic-related sites, you may want to explore a few broad resource locations.

Academy of Management—*www.aom.pace.edu*
American Assembly of Collegiate Schools of Business (AACSB)—
    www.aacsb.edu
Business Newspapers—*www.amcity.com*
Business Research Resource—*www.ceoexpress.com*
Career Assessment Tools—*www.jobweb.org/cataputt/assess.htm*
Career Development Links—*www.superperformance.com/businesslinks.html*
Codes and Principles of Ethics—*www.goodmoney.com/directry_codes.htm*
Diversity Issues—*www.diversity.dtg.com*
Ethical Topics—*www.scu.edu/ethics/about/*
Fast Company—*www.fastcompany.com*
Federal Government Information—*www.infoctr.edu/fwl/*

Gateway to Business Publications—*www.clickit.com/touch/home/htm*

Global Business Resources—*http.library.nyenrode.nl*

Human Resource Management—
   www.btintenet.com/!alan.price/hrm/chap10/ch10-links.html

Information on Companies—*www.companiesoloine.com*

Knowledge Management—*www.brint.com/km/*

Management Archives—*www.alaska.edu/uas/other.shtml*

Managerial Career Advice—*www.monsterhr.com*

SUPPLEMENTARY MATERIALS

OBM includes a variety of supplementary materials, all designed to provide additional classroom support for instructors. These materials are as follows:

Instructor's Manual and Test Bank   The instructor's manual and the test bank were prepared by Anne Cowden.

The instructor's manual is organized to follow each chapter in the text. It includes chapter objectives, chapter synopses, chapter outlines with tips and ideas, and project and class speaker ideas. Encounter discussion questions and suggested answers are also provided to help you incorporate these dynamic features into your lecture presentations. Suggested transparencies, term-paper topics, and reading, exercise, and case notes are also included.

The test bank has been completely updated to complement the sixth edition of the text. This testing resource contains approximately 75 true/false, multiple choice, and essay questions per chapter. Each question is classified according to level of difficulty and contains a page reference to the text. Additionally, the test bank includes questions that test students on concepts presented in the readings to enhance the integrative nature of the text.

Powerpoint   A Powerpoint slide presentation includes approximately 100 slides corresponding to the lecture notes found in the instructor's manual.

Color Acetates and Transparency Masters   These include reproductions of the Powerpoint slides that can be used to visually enhance the classroom presentations.

Video   The videotape contains several segments, primarily drawn from the NBC News Archives, covering various topics presented within the main text.

Computest   Irwin/McGraw-Hill's test-generation software allows instructors to add and edit questions online and select questions based on type, level of difficulty, or key word. In addition, those without access to a microcomputer, or who prefer not to create tests, can use Irwin/McGraw-Hill's Teletest service. The complete package we provide in the form of *OBM* and supplements is designed to encourage greater efficiency in learning, studying, retention, and applications. Let us know at Irwin/McGraw-Hill whether we are doing a good job and what we can do to improve.

Contributors   The authors wish to acknowledge the many scholars, managers, and researchers who contributed to OBM. We are indebted to all those individuals who granted permission for the use of readings, exercises, and cases. There were also adopters who made many useful suggestions, offered materials to incorporate, and let us know what worked well. These adopters are too numerous to list, but we appreciate your votes of confidence, your willingness to help us improve the book, and the obvious dedication each of you has to teaching.

In addition, the book was shaped significantly by two colleagues, James Donnelly, Jr., and James Gibson at the University of Kentucky. These two colleagues have shared and put into practice a common belief that teaching and learning about organizational behavior and management can be an exhilarating and worthwhile experience. Roger Blakeney, Dick DeFrank, Bob Keller, Tim McMahon, Dale Rude, and Jim Phillips, all at the University of Houston; Dave Schweiger at the University of South Carolina; and Art Jago at the University of Missouri have exchanged materials, ideas, and opinions with the authors over the years, and these are reflected in *OBM*.

We are indebted to our panel of reviewers, who provided detailed and incisive feedback for the preparation of various editions of the book. These reviewers include:

Jane L. Swanson—Southern Illinois University
Sandra Hartman—University of New Orleans
Kenneth E. Newgren—Illinois State University
Janet E. Gross—Taylor University
Mark Somers—New Jersey Institute of Technology

The typing support and efforts of Ginger Roberts is certainly appreciated. Ginger has made significant commitments to work on page after page of detailed comments, instructions, and suggestions. She is able to make sense out of reams of output. Finally, the book is dedicated to our former organizational behavior and management students at the University of Maryland, the University of Kentucky, and the University of Houston. We also dedicate this textbook to the students who are and will be the managers so vital to the improvement of the overall quality of life in society in the 21st century.

John M. Ivancevich
Michael T. Matteson

I
Part

The Field of Organizational Behavior

What really binds men together is their culture, the ideas and the standards they have in common.

Ruth Benedict *Patterns of Culture* (1934)

1

Introduction to Organizational Behavior

After completing Chapter 1, you should be able to:

Learning Objectives

- Discuss the importance of human resources to organizational success.

- Describe the disciplines that have contributed to the field of organizational behavior.

- Discuss the importance of understanding behavior in organizations.

- Explain the goal approach to defining and measuring effectiveness.

- Explain the relationship between quality and organizational effectiveness.

Imagine going to work in an office, plant, or store and finding coworkers who are excited about their jobs, managers who listen carefully to workers' comments about the job, and a general atmosphere that is vibrant. What a pleasant setting where people want to work hard, have pride in the job they are doing, trust each other, and share ideas on how to improve performance—a setting in which groups work together, solve problems, set high-quality standards, and enjoy the diversity of each coworker's family, ethnic, and religious background.

Is this just an illusion or a dream of an ideal work setting? This is a sketch of a work setting that any manager would cherish, enjoy, and strive to maintain. It is a picture of the kind of workplace that managers should use as a target to achieve. This is the kind of workplace that will have to be created if a firm, entrepreneur, or institution is to survive in the coming years.

www.ge.com

Jack Welch, chief executive officer (CEO) of General Electric, once known as a traditional hard-edge authoritarian manager, has become a more human resource–oriented manager. In earlier days Mr. Welch had a reputation for eliminating entire layers of employees. He was referred to as "Neutron Jack." People were eliminated, but the firm remained in tact. Welch's learning that the human being is essential and the key to an organization's success is captured in his view that:

> The talents of our people are greatly underestimated and their skills are underutilized. Our biggest task is to fundamentally redesign our relationship with our employees. The objective is to build a place where people have the freedom to be creative, where they feel a sense of accomplishment—a place that brings out the best in everybody.[1]

Another visionary leader who values human assets is Percy Barnevik, CEO of Asia Brown Boveri (ABB). He captured the importance of people when he stated:

www.abb.com

> There is a tremendous unused potential in our people. Our organizations ensure they only use 5 to 10 percent of their abilities at work. Outside of work they engage the other 90 to 95 percent to run their households, lead a Boy Scout troop, or build a summer home. We have to learn how to recognize and employ that untapped ability that each individual brings to work every day.[2]

Welch and Barnevik's views about people are likely to still be significant far into the 21st century. In addition to being people-sensitive and astute, managers and leaders will need other skills and competencies. The next generation of leaders will need the charm of a debutante, the flexibility of a gymnast, and the quickness and agility of a cheetah. A second-language ability and a working knowledge of technology and the law will also help. Since change is so widespread and frequent, managers will have to be entrepreneurial. Waiting to be instructed on what to do and how to work with people will not be tolerated. The core 21st century qualities needed to create the ideal work atmosphere[3] begin with intelligence, passion, a strong work ethic, a team orientation, and a genuine concern for people.

---

[1]Sumantra Ghoshal and Christopher A. Bartlett, *The Individualized Corporation* (New York: Harper Business, 1997), pp. 7–8.

[2]Ibid., p. 8.

[3]Diane Brady, "Wanted: Eclectic Visionary with a Sense of Humor," *Business Week*, August 28, 2000, pp. 143–44.

Organizational Encounter 1.1

People Are the Key to Success

Top managers at *Fortune's* most admired companies take their mission statements seriously and expect everyone else to do likewise. Mission statements—often viewed by the troops as platitudinous—surprisingly get lots of respect from executives like General Electric's Jack Welch. Welch says, "Making your numbers but not demonstrating our values is grounds for dismissal." Instead of some vague expression of values, GE uses a clear and specific list—succinct enough to fit on a wallet-sized card—that keeps everybody pulling in the same direction. "Most companies have created a sketch of the culture they want to build," says Bruce Pfau, a managing director of the Hay Group. "By contrast, the most admired companies have something closer to a detailed architectural blueprint, and they are constantly referring to it." For instance, lots of companies say they want global thinkers, but Procter & Gamble and Citibank back that up with action: Fully half of senior managers at both U.S. companies are non-Americans.

The most admired firms go well beyond the resume and put candidates through intense psychological testing. Federal Express, for instance, looks for what the company calls "risk taking and courage of conviction." You probably won't land a job at Disney unless you have an "up personality." Procter & Gamble's strategy is to hire the best young people now and develop them over their entire careers, so CEO John Pepper visits college campuses to seek out what he calls "the lifeblood of our future."

Intel spends an impressive 6 percent of its total payroll—$160 million last year—on its in-house university, and all senior managers must do a teaching stint there every quarter. Everyone who aspires to senior management at SmithKline Beecham has to have "2+2+2" experience—hands-on experience in two businesses, in two roles (say, manufacturing and finance), in two countries. And the most admired companies' CEOs, like Bertelsmann's Mark Wossner and Gillette's Alfred Zeien, personally coach the most promising young talent.

The *Fortune* most admired companies hire people not for a single job but for a career. At Citibank, a talent inventory program keeps track of about 10,000 employees worldwide—how they're doing, what skills they need to work on, and where else in the company they might thrive. Citibank human resources chief Larry Phillips calls the program "critical" to the company's global growth.

ww.sb.com

ww.
ertelsmann.
om

ww.
tibank.com

ww.pg.com

ww.fedex.
om

Source: Each year *Fortune* publishes a detailed account of the most admired organizations. See Anne Fisher, "The World's Most Admired Companies," *Fortune*, October 27, 1997, pp. 220–40 and John Curran, "GE Capital: Jack Welch's Secret Weapon," *Fortune*, November 10, 1997, pp. 116–34.

ENVIRONMENTAL FORCES RESHAPING MANAGEMENT PRACTICE

A number of forces are reshaping the nature of managing within organizations. A limited number of companies have recognized these forces and are working to channel their managerial talents to accomplish goals by using their knowledge about each of these six major forces: power of human resources, globalism, cultural diversity, the rapidity of change, a new worker-employer psychological contract, and technology.[4]

The first force at work is the **power** of human resources. The way people (managers, technicians, and staff specialists) work, think, and behave dictates the direction and success of a firm. Unfortunately, there is a shrinking workforce and a shortage of technically skilled workers. Managing human resources as valuable assets to be maintained and improved is now more important than ever.

To compete effectively as we enter the 21st century, **globalism** must be understood and addressed. Global competition characterized by networks that bring together countries, institutions, and people are beginning to dominate the global economy. Of the largest 25 corporations in terms of market value, 14 are

---

[4]"The Global 1,000," *Business Week,* July 10, 2000, pp. 107–38.

American, 3 are Japanese, and 3 are British.[5] As a result of global integration, the growth rate of world trade has increased faster than that of world gross domestic product. That is, the trading of goods and services among nations has been increasing faster than the actual world production of goods. In order to survive the fast-paced changes in the global world, firms must make not only capital investments but also investments in people. How well a firm recruits, selects, retains, and motivates a skilled workforce will have a major impact on its ability to compete in the more globally interdependent world.

The **culturally diverse** workforce is becoming a reality in the United States. As the complexion of America's workforce changes, managers and coworkers need to learn more about each other so that a receptive work culture is created. While Japan and the European Union are basically racially homogeneous societies, the United States is racially diverse and has been rapidly increasing its workforce diversity since the 1970s. Not only are racial and ethnic diversity growing, but more women, older workers, and people with disabilities are entering the workforce in increasing numbers. The workforce in the year 2000 was considered middle aged, about 50 percent were between the ages of 35 and 54, and about 50 percent of the workers were women. The minority share of the workforce in the year 2000 was about 25 percent.[6]

African Americans, Hispanics, and Asians are now the fastest-growing parts of the U.S. employee mix. About 27 percent of the U.S. workforce is likely to be nonwhite by the year 2005.[7] Increased minority and female participation in the workforce raises a number of issues managers must address in order to remain competitive globally. Are minorities and women ready to take over high-paying, higher-status jobs? Unless organizations properly train and prepare minorities and women for significant jobs, institutions are not going to be competitive.

The **rapidity of change** is another crucial force to recognize. The fax machine, Internet, genetic engineering, microchips, crumbling socialist empires, and more demanding consumers who want better-quality products and services at a lower price and on time are some of the changes sweeping the world. Understanding, accommodating, and using change is now a part of a manager's job requirement.

The elements of change include almost instantaneous communication and computation.[8] Technological connectivity is putting everything online, which has resulted in the shrinking of space and distance. Intangible value of all kinds, such as service and information, is growing at a rapid speed. The modern manager is going to have to be adaptable to such rapid change. Those that fail to understand speed and resist how fast adaptation must come about will have problems.

The new worker-employer **psychological contract** is another force. From the employer's view, employees do not have lifetime jobs, guaranteed advancement or raises, and assurance that their work roles will be fixed. Employees believe that

---

[5]Gary Hamel, "Revamping the Corporation from the Inside Out," *Business 2.0,* September 26, 2000, pp. 136–38.

[6]Peter Coy, "The Creative Economy," *Business Week,* August 28, 2000, pp. 76–82.
[7]Ibid.
[8]James Gleick, *Faster* (New York: Pantheon, 1999), p. 18.

employers must be honest, open, and fair and also be willing to give workers a larger say in their jobs. Employees also want organizations to pay more attention to their family situations and their physical and mental health. Employees want employers to appreciate the humanness of workers.

Another major force influencing management is **technology**. In a general sense, technology is the processes that convert raw materials or intellectual capital into products or services. The technology of an organization influences the work flow, structure, systems, and philosophy in a significant manner. Today, computer technology is so pervasive and powerful that it needs to be understood to be used effectively.[9]

The semiconductor pioneer Gordon Moore predicted in 1965 that chip density—and all kinds of computer power—would double every 18 months or so. This had been right on target. Moore's law highlighted the speed-up in technological pace.

In the agricultural era, land was the core factor in achieving competitive advantage. The landowners were dominant in shaping markets, policies, and legislation. In this information age we use computer technology and human assets to operate, maintain, and invent new computer systems that are more powerful than the previous computer generation. Organizations in their quest for competitive advantage must attract, retain, and recognize crucial human assets to continue advancing.

www.microsoft.com

www.disney.com

www.gs.com

Microsoft, Goldman Sachs, and Walt Disney are sought out by talented technology-savvy job candidates. In examining the programs, practices, and approaches used by these and other firms, it is obvious that valuing those who have knowledge about how to use technology is a priority. Technology can yield competitive advantages only when it is utilized effectively.

The six forces—power of human resources, globalism, cultural diversity, the rapidity of change, a new worker-employer psychological contract, and technology—are facts facing managers. Resisting the reality of these forces will likely lead to unnecessary conflict, reduced managerial and nonmanagerial performance, and lost opportunities. In managerial terms, failing to cope and deal with these forces will likely result in job dissatisfaction, poor morale, reduced commitment, lower work quality, burnout, poor judgment, and a host of unhealthy consequences.

The purpose of this book is to help you learn how to manage and lead individuals and groups as resources of organizations. These resources are operating in a world surrounded by change. Organizations are essential to the way our society operates in the world. In industry, education, health care, and defense, organizations have created impressive gains for the standard of living and the worldwide image of entire nations. The size of the organizations with which you deal daily should illustrate the tremendous political, economic, and social powers they separately possess. For example, your college has much economic, political, and social power in its community. If a large firm announced that it was closing its plant in your community, the resulting impact might be devastating economically. On the other hand, if General Motors announced it was opening an automobile assembly plant in your community, the impact probably would be very positive.

---

[9]John A. Byrne, "Management by Web," *Business Week,* August 28, 2000, pp. 84–96.

Ford and Delta Connect Employees to the Net

Ford announced that it will offer a desktop computer, printer, and Internet access to its 350,000 worldwide employees for $5 per month. Tara Parker, a Ford factory worker, was excited since up to this point she couldn't afford a computer. The technology revolution was beyond her financial means. Ford decided that e-business technology and skills could be improved only through use and practice.

Delta Air Lines, Inc., also announced plans to provide its 72,000 employees computers, printers, and Internet access for a $12 monthly fee. Computer access was considered to be more than just another perk. It was essential for the future.

More and more firms are joining the leaders Ford and Delta in offering inexpensive computers as an important benefit. This can help employees develop the abilities and skills needed by their organizations. Today, firms are searching everywhere for people who understand and can use computers and other technology. In a skills-short job market, developing your own provides a competitive edge.

Ford also believes that plugging everyone into the Net will make it easier to communicate throughout the world. Computers at a low price are not only a good deal for Ford, but a wonderful opportunity for employees to improve their confidence about using computer technology.

www.ford com

www.delta com

Source: Kathleen Kerwin, Peter Burrows, and Dean Foust, "Workers of the World, Log On," *Business Week*, February 21, 2000, p. 521.

Organizations are, however, much more than means for providing goods and services.[10] They create the settings in which most of us spend our lives. In this respect, they have profound influence on employee behavior. However, because large-scale organizations have developed only in recent times, we are just now beginning to recognize the necessity for studying them. Researchers have just begun the process of developing ways to study the behavior of people in organizations.

The Origins of Management

The modern study of management started around 1900.[11] It is probable, however, that the management process first began in the family organization, later expanded to the tribe, and finally pervaded the formalized political units such as those found in early Babylonia (5000 B.C.) The Egyptians, Chinese, Greeks, and Romans were all noted in history for major managerial feats such as building of the pyramids, organizing governments, planning military maneuvers, operating trading companies that traversed the world, and controlling a geographically dispersed empire.

A Brief History Lesson A review of the early history of management dating back over 7,000 years ago suggests that management as a process was based on trial and error, with little or no theory and virtually no sharing of ideas and practices. This lack of sharing slowed the influence of management practices throughout the world. Management for thousands of years was based on trying an approach that seemed to be suited for accomplishing a particular goal. There was no common body of knowledge or theoretical basis for managing the Roman empire or building the Great Pyramid of Cheops.

---

[10]Roger Lewin and Birute Regime, *The Same at Work* (New York: Simon & Schuster, 2000).

[11]John M. Ivancevich, Peter Lorenzi, Steven J. Skinner, and Philip B. Crosby, *Management: Quality and Competitiveness* (Burr Ridge, IL: Irwin, 1997), pp. 30–52.

The period between 1700 and 1785 is referred to as the Industrial Revolution in England.[12] As a nation, England changed dramatically from a rural society to the workshop of the world. She was the first nation to successfully make the transition from a rural-agrarian society to an industrial-commercial society.[13] Management of the workshops of England was characterized by an emphasis on efficiency, strict controls, and rigid rules and procedures.

Industrialization   A new industrial era began in the United States around the time of the Civil War. There was a dramatic expansion of mechanical industries such as the railroad. In addition, large industrial manufacturing complexes grew in importance. Attempts to better plan, organize, and control the work of these complexes led managers to discuss their situations and present papers at meetings. The first modern era management publications were published in engineering journals.

www.wharton.upenn.edu

In 1881, a new way to study management started with a $100,000 gift by Joseph Wharton to the University of Pennsylvania to establish a management department in a college. The management curriculum at that time covered such topics as strikes, business law, the nature of stocks and bonds, and principles of work cooperation.

www.ideafinder.com/facts/ inventors/taylor.htm

Scientific Management   In 1886, an engineer named Frederick W. Taylor presented a paper at a national meeting of engineers entitled, "The Engineer As an Economist." This paper and others prepared by Taylor expressed his philosophy of **scientific management**.[14] Taylor's major thesis was that maximum good for society can come only through the cooperation of management and labor in the application of scientific methods. He stated that the principles of management were to:

- Develop a science for each element of an employee's work, which replaces the old rule-of-thumb method.
- Scientifically select and then train, teach, and develop the worker, whereas in the past a worker chose the work to do and was self-trained.
- Heartily cooperate with each other to ensure that all work was done in accordance with the principles of science.
- Assure an almost equal division of the work and the responsibility between management and nonmanagers.

These four principles constituted Taylor's concept of scientific management. Some regard him as the father of present-day management. Even if this is considered an exaggerated viewpoint, Taylor was a key figure in the promotion of the role of management in organizations. He has had a lasting impact on a unified, coherent method to improve the way managers perform their jobs.

www.hrmguide.co.uk/history/ classical-organization-theory- modified.htm

Functions of Management   Henri Fayol, a French industrialist, presented what is considered the first comprehensive statement of a general theory of management.

---

[12]Ibid., pp. 3–14.

[13]Claude S. George, Jr., *The History of Management Thought* (Englewood Cliffs, NJ: Prentice-Hall, 1968), p. 47.

[14]Andrea Gabor, *The Capitalist Philosophers* (New York: Times Books, 2000), pp. 3–44.

First published in France in 1916,[15] Fayol's *Administrative Industrielle et genérále* was largely ignored in the United States until it was translated into English in 1949.

Fayol attributed his success in managing a large mining firm to his system of management which he believed could be taught and learned. He emphasized the importance of carefully practicing efficient planning, organizing, commanding, coordinating, and controlling.

Fayol's approach was a significant contribution in that it presented three important developments that have had a lasting impact on the field.

1. Management is a separate body of knowledge that can be applied in any type of organization.
2. A theory of management can be learned and taught.
3. There is a need for teaching management in colleges.

Two of Fayol's functions—planning, and controlling—are introduced in Appendix 1–A accompanying this chapter. The organizing function is covered in Chapters 6 and 15.

THE IMPORTANCE OF STUDYING ORGANIZATIONAL BEHAVIOR

Why do employees behave as they do in organizations? Why is one individual or group more productive than another? Why do managers continually seek ways to design jobs and delegate authority? These and similar questions are important to the relatively new field of study known as **organizational behavior**. Understanding the behavior of people in organizations has become increasingly important as management concerns—such as employee productivity, the quality of work life, job stress, and career progression—continue to make front-page news.

Clearly understanding that organizational behavior (OB) has evolved from multiple disciplines, we will use the following definition of OB throughout this book:

> The study of human behavior, attitudes, and performance within an organizational setting; drawing on theory, methods, and principles from such disciplines as psychology, sociology, and cultural anthropology to learn about individual, groups, structure, and processes.

This multidisciplinary-anchored view of organizational behavior illustrates a number of points. First, OB is a *way of thinking*. Behavior is viewed as operating at individual, group, and organizational levels. This approach suggests that when studying OB, we must identify clearly the level of analysis being used—individual, group, and/or organizational. Second, OB is *multidisciplinary*. This means that it utilizes principles, models, theories, and methods from other disciplines. The study of OB is not a discipline or a generally accepted science with an established theoretical foundation. It is a field that only now is beginning to grow and develop in stature and impact. Third, there is a distinctly *humanistic orientation* within organizational behavior. People and their attitudes, perceptions, learning

---

[15]Henri Fayol, *General and Industrial Management*, trans. J. A. Conbrough (Geneva: International Management Institute, 1929).

capacities, feelings, and goals are of major importance to the organization. Fourth, the field of OB is *performance-oriented.* Why is performance low or high? How can performance be improved? Can training enhance on-the-job performance? These are important issues facing practicing managers. Fifth, since the field of OB relies heavily on recognized disciplines, the role of the *scientific method* is deemed important in studying variables and relationships. As the scientific method has been used in conducting research on organizational behavior, a set of principles and guidelines on what constitutes good research has emerged.[16] Finally, the field has a distinctive *applications orientation;* it is concerned with providing useful answers to questions which arise in the context of managing organizations.[17]

Leaders and Organizational Behavior   Leaders of workers, managers, and administrators in organizations are challenged by many changes occurring within and outside of institutions. Terms such as *transformation, cultural diversity, global competitiveness*, and *reengineering* are used freely by experts and non-experts. Each of these concepts points out that leaders are being asked to perform effectively in a changing world.

In addition to the changing makeup and diversity of the workforce is the increased emphasis that consumers are placing on *value.*[18] The trend among consumers is to consider the total value of a product or service. Today, more than ever, customers expect organizations to be responsive to their needs, provide prompt service and delivery, and provide top-quality goods or services at the best price possible.

Along with an increasingly diverse workforce and demanding customers, leaders must contend with changes in both domestic and **global** markets and competition. Today in a global market, richer, more educated, and more demanding customers exist in every competitive country. The global market wants a world of easy access to products and services. Leaders must assure customers that their high-quality goods or services will be available when the consumer wants them and at a competitive price. Establishing the work team, department, or organization that can respond, compete, and negotiate globally is what leaders are being asked to accomplish.

For over three decades, the development of the integrated circuit has permitted an increasing amount of information to be processed or stored on a single microchip. The leaders within organizations are asked to efficiently use and manage the available information technology so that the firm can compete globally. The Internet is an example of an electronic information-sharing system. A national web of high-speed networks links business, state, university, and regional computer systems. Information is passed from one network to another. The dramatic growth of the Internet has resulted in managers from around the world sharing data and ideas with like-minded peers. The length of time it takes an idea to circulate or a problem to be considered by peers across the ocean has dropped from

---

[16]Edward E. Lawler III, "Challenging Traditional Research Assumptions," in *Doing Business That Is Useful for Theory and Practice,* ed. Edward E. Lawler III, Alan M. Mohrman, Jr., Susan A. Mohrman, Gerald E. Ledford, Jr., and Thomas G. Cummings (San Francisco: Jossey-Bass, 1985).

[17]Roderick Martin, "The New Behaviorism: A Critique of Economist and Organization," *Human Relations,* September 1993, pp. 1085–1101.

[18]Moore, op. cit.

weeks to hours. The potential for using information technology and other technologies in managing workers, motivating an individual, or altering the structure of an organization is endless.

Everything facing a leader in an organization is in motion or churning. Properly aligning the human resources of the organization with the changes occurring requires an understanding of such phenomena as the organization's environment, individual characteristics, group behavior, organizational structure and design, decision making, and organizational change processes. The modern day impetus of aligning human resources with organizational factors was initiated with the Hawthorne Studies.

The Hawthorne Studies   From 1900 to 1930 Taylor's concept of scientific management dominated thought about management. His approach focused on maximizing worker output. However, Taylor's emphasis on output and efficiency didn't address employees' needs. Trade unions rebelled against Taylor's focus on scientific management principles.

Mary Parker Follet was opposed to Taylor's lack of specific attention to human needs and relationships in the workplace. She was one of the first management theorists to promote participatory decision making and decentralization. Her view emphasized individual and group needs. The human element was the focus of Follet's view about how to manage. However, she failed to produce empirical evidence to support her views. Industry leaders wanted concrete evidence that focusing on human resources would result in higher productivity. Some concrete evidence became available from data collected in the Hawthorne Studies.

A team of Harvard University researchers was asked to study the activities of work groups at Western Electric's Hawthorne plant outside of Chicago (Cicero, Illinois).[19] Before the team arrived, an initial study at the plant examined the effects of illumination on worker output. It was proposed that illumination would affect the work group's output. One group of female workers completed its job tasks in a test room where the illumination level remained constant. The other study group was placed in a test room where the amount of illumination was changed (increased and decreased).

In the test room where illumination was varied, worker output increased when illumination increased. This, of course, was an expected result. However, output also increased when illumination was decreased. In addition, productivity increased in the control group test room, even though illumination remained constant throughout the study.

The Harvard team was called in to solve the mystery. The team concluded that something more than pay incentives was improving worker output within the work groups. The researchers conducted additional studies on the impact of rest pauses, shorter working days, incentives, and type of supervision on output. They also uncovered what is referred to as the "Hawthorne Effect" operating within the study groups.[20] That is, the workers felt important because someone

---

[19]E. Mayo, *The Social Problems of Industrial Civilization* (Boston: Harvard University Press, 1945).

[20]F. J. Roethlisberger and W. J. Dickson, *Management and the Worker* (Cambridge, MA: Harvard University Press, 1939).

was observing and studying them at work. Thus, they produced more because of being observed and studied.

Elton Mayo, Fritz Roethlisberger, and William Dickson were the leaders of the Harvard study team. They continued their work at the Hawthorne plant from 1924 to 1932. Eight years of study included over 20,000 Western Electric employees.

The Harvard researchers found that individual behaviors were modified within and by work groups. In a study referred to as the "bank wiring room," the Harvard researchers were again faced with some perplexing results. The study group only completed two terminals per worker daily. This was considered to be a low level of output.

The bank wiring room workers appeared to be restricting output. The work group members were friendly, got along well on and off the job, and helped each other. There appeared to be a practice of protecting the slower workers. The fast producers did not want to outperform the slowest producers. The slow producers were part of the team and fast workers were instructed to "slow it down." The group formed an informal production norm of only two completed boards per day.

The Harvard researchers learned that economic rewards did not totally explain worker behavior. Workers were observant, complied with norms, and respected the informal social structure of their group. It was also learned that social pressures could restrict output.

Interviews conducted years after the Hawthorne Studies with a small number of actual study participants and a reanalysis of data clearly raised some doubts about a number of the original conclusions.[21] The conclusion that supportive managers helped boost productivity is considered incorrect by critics. Instead, the fear of job loss during the Great Depression and managerial discipline, not the practices of supportive managers, are considered responsible for the higher rate of productivity in the relay assembly test room experiments. The Hawthorne Studies, however, are still considered the major impetus behind the emphasis on understanding and dealing with human resources.

The Hawthorne studies are perhaps the most-cited research in the applied behavioral science area, but they are not referred to as the most rigorous series of studies. Nonetheless, the Hawthorne studies did point out that workers are more complex than economic theories of the time proposed. Workers respond to group norms, social pressures, and observation. In 1924 to 1932, these were important revelations that changed the way management viewed workers.

FRAMING THE STUDY OF ORGANIZATIONAL BEHAVIOR

The text frames in Exhibit 1.1 are a set of reference points to create a way to consider organizations. The study of the environment, individual and interpersonal influence, and group structure and design processes is done with the concept of effectiveness in mind. Managers and leaders think about and dissect mentally the organizational task they face to accomplish effectiveness. Unless effectiveness is achieved over time, the very existence of the enterprise is in jeopardy.

---

[21]H. McIlvaine Parsons, "Hawthorne: A Early OBM Experiment," *Journal of Organizational Behavior Management*, February 1992, pp. 27–44 and R. G. Greenwood, A. A. Bolton, and B. A. Greenwood, "Hawthorne a Half Century Later: Relay Assembly Participants Remember," *Journal of Management*, Fall-Winter 1983, pp. 217–31.

EXHIBIT 1.1
Topics in Studying
and Understanding
Organizational
Behavior

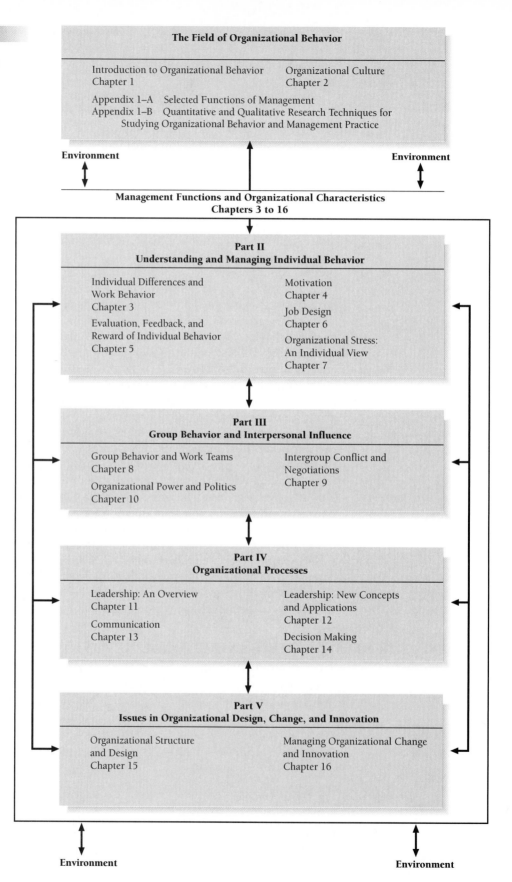

The Field of Organizational Behavior

Introduction to Organizational Behavior   Organizational Culture
Chapter 1   Chapter 2

Appendix 1–A   Selected Functions of Management
Appendix 1–B   Quantitative and Qualitative Research Techniques for
                 Studying Organizational Behavior and Management Practice

Environment   Environment

Management Functions and Organizational Characteristics
Chapters 3 to 16

Part II
Understanding and Managing Individual Behavior

Individual Differences and   Motivation
Work Behavior   Chapter 4
Chapter 3   Job Design
Evaluation, Feedback, and   Chapter 6
Reward of Individual Behavior   Organizational Stress:
Chapter 5   An Individual View
                                    Chapter 7

Part III
Group Behavior and Interpersonal Influence

Group Behavior and Work Teams   Intergroup Conflict and
Chapter 8   Negotiations
Organizational Power and Politics   Chapter 9
Chapter 10

Part IV
Organizational Processes

Leadership: An Overview   Leadership: New Concepts
Chapter 11   and Applications
Communication   Chapter 12
Chapter 13   Decision Making
                                    Chapter 14

Part V
Issues in Organizational Design, Change, and Innovation

Organizational Structure   Managing Organizational Change
and Design   and Innovation
Chapter 15   Chapter 16

Environment   Environment

The Organization's Environment

Organizations exist in societies and are created by societies. Within a society many factors impinge upon the effectiveness of an organization, and management must be responsive to them. Every organization must respond to the needs of its customers or clients, to legal and political constraints, and to economic and technological changes and developments. The model reflects environmental forces interacting within the organization; throughout our discussion of each aspect of the model, the relevant environmental factors will be identified and examined.

Managers constantly are receiving information, examples, data, and gossip about the external environment. When Dell Computer is working on a new computer, Gateway managers are hearing about what is occurring. The environmental "sound bites" provide managers with a picture of what he or she is facing in terms of competition, new products, regulations, and a host of other environmental forces. Eventually, the manager must pause and ask: "How should I respond to the environmental stimuli?" Answering this and similar questions is difficult, but the environment is so pervasive that eventually managers must pay attention.

The Individual in the Organization   Individual performance is the foundation of organization performance. Understanding individual behavior therefore is critical for effective management, as illustrated in this account:

> Ted Johnson has been a field representative for a major drug manufacturer since he graduated from college seven years ago. He makes daily calls on physicians, hospitals, clinics, and pharmacies as a representative of the many drugs his firm manufactures. During his time in the field, prescription rates and sales for all of his firm's major drugs have increased, and he has won three national sales awards given by the firm. Yesterday Ted was promoted to sales manager for a seven-state region. He no longer will be selling but instead will be managing 15 other representatives. Ted accepted the promotion because he believes he knows how to motivate and lead salespeople. He commented: "I know the personality of salespeople. They are special people. I know what it takes to get them to perform. Remember that I am one. I know their values and attitudes and what it takes to motivate them. I know I can motivate a sales force."

In his new job, Ted Johnson will be trying to maximize the individual performance of 15 sales representatives. In doing so he will be dealing with several facets of individual behavior. Our model includes three important influences on individual behavior and motivation in organizations: individual characteristics, individual motivation, and rewards.

Individual Characteristics   Because organizational performance depends on individual performance, managers such as Ted Johnson must have more than a passing knowledge of the determinants of individual performance. Social psychology contributes a great deal of relevant knowledge about the relationships among attitudes, perceptions, personality, values, and individual performance. Managers cannot ignore the necessity for acquiring and acting on their knowledge of the individual characteristics of both their subordinates and themselves.

Individual Motivation   Motivation and ability to work interact to determine performance. Motivation theory attempts to explain and predict how the behavior

Organizational Encounter 1.3

Working Smarter

When a Raleigh, North Carolina, Internet startup down-sized Forsyth's job, she was not too upset. She had developed an aversion to the 50- and 60-hour workweeks, the chaotic working conditions, and the lack of a job description. The mother of two now works in publishing, finds her current employer more "family friendly," and enjoys keeping to a 40-hour workweek.

Jeff, an early member of the Netscape management team, left his position thanks to a nice nest egg generated from the sale of Netscape to America Online. Today, he works part-time as an investor and advisor to small Internet startups. He is able to play with his three children, make them lunch, and even tag along on school field trips. After his 18-hour days at Netscape, Jeff's time with his children "seems like mundane stuff, but when you finally get a chance to do it, you appreciate it."

Despite the fact that Americans have always placed great stock in hard work, there is growing evidence that "working hard" may not mean "working long." According to the Bureau of Labor Statistics, the proportion of Americans working 49 hours or more a week has remained steady in recent years, after rising in the late 1980s and early 1990s. In the late 1980s, 29.5 percent of managers and professionals reported working 49 hours or more a week, as compared to 24 percent in the early 1980s. But in the past several years, the percentage of managers and professionals working 49 hours or more a week has begun to fall to the current rate of 27.9 percent.

It appears that America's work ethic is changing from working hard to working smart. It is more than simply a work/life issue, however, in that a basic American social value of more hard work is being transformed into "work smart but don't forget your other life obligations." How will this change the workplace? Will hourly workers decline overtime opportunities more consistently? Will they move to ensure (through their union) that their workweek remains consistent and does not include continual overtime requests? Will the 40-hour workweek be challenged (as it has in some European countries)? How will this change the pace of productivity? In trying to recruit and retain workers, how will HR professionals cultivate and promote this new social value to attract and retain workers?

These and other similar questions are being asked and debated by managers who must lead in an era of intense competition, globalization, and shortages of skilled workers in a number of industries.

http://stat bls.gov/ blshome. htm

Source: Adapted from Shel Leonard, "Is America's Work Ethic Changing?" *HR Magazine*, April 2000, p. 224.

of individuals is aroused, started, sustained, and stopped. Unlike Ted Johnson, not all managers and behavioral scientists agree on what is the "best" theory of motivation. In fact, motivation is so complex that it may be impossible to have an all-encompassing theory of how it occurs. However, managers must still try to understand it. They must be concerned with motivation because they must be concerned with performance.

Rewards   One of the most powerful influences on individual performance is an organization's reward system. Management can use rewards (or punishment) to increase performance by employees. Management also can use rewards to attract skilled employees to join the organization. Paychecks, raises, and stock options are important aspects of the reward system, but they are not the only aspects. Ted Johnson makes this point very clear in the account when he states; "I know what it takes to get them to perform." Performance of the work itself can provide employees with rewards, particularly if job performance leads to a sense of personal responsibility, autonomy, and meaningfulness.

Stress   Stress is an important result of the interaction between the job and the individual. Stress in this context is a state of imbalance within an individual that often manifests itself in such symptoms as insomnia, excessive perspiration, nervousness, and irritability. Whether stress is positive or negative depends on the individual's tolerance level. People react differently to situations that outwardly would seem to induce the same physical and psychological demands. Some individuals respond positively through increased motivation and commitment to finish the job. Other individuals respond less desirably by turning to such outlets as alcoholism and drug abuse. Hopefully, Ted Johnson will respond positively to the stresses of his new job as sales manager.

Management's responsibility in managing stress has not been clearly defined, but there is growing evidence that organizations are devising programs to deal with work-induced stress.

Group Behavior and Influence Interpersonal   Interpersonal influence and group behavior are also powerful forces affecting organizational performance. The effects of these forces are illustrated in the following account:

> Kelley McCaul spent 2 1/2 years as a teller in the busiest branch of First National Bank. During that time she developed close personal friendships with her coworkers. These friendships extended off the job as well. Kelly and her friends formed a wine-and-cheese club and were the top team in the bankwide-bowling league. In addition, several of the friends took ski trips together each winter.
>
> Two months ago Kelly was promoted to branch manager. She was excited about the new challenge but was a little surprised that she got the promotion since some other likely candidates in the branch have been with the bank longer. She began the job with a great deal of optimism and believed her friends would be genuinely happy for her and supportive of her efforts. However, since she became branch manager, things haven't seemed quite the same. Kelly can't spend nearly as much time with her friends because she is often away from the branch attending management meetings at the main office. A computer training course she must attend two evenings a week has caused her to miss the last two wine-and-cheese club meetings, and she senses that some of her friends have been acting a little differently toward her lately.
>
> Recently, Kelly said, "I didn't know that being part of the management team could make that much difference. Frankly, I never really thought about it. I guess I was naive. I'm seeing a totally different perspective of the business and have to deal with problems I never knew about."

Kelly McCaul's promotion has made her a member of more than one group. In addition to being a member of her old group of friends at the branch, she also is a member of the management team. She is finding out that group behavior and expectations have a strong impact on individual behavior and interpersonal influence. Our model includes four important aspects of group and interpersonal influence on organization behavior: leadership, group behavior, intergroup behavior and conflict, and organizational power and politics.

Group Behavior   Groups form because of managerial action, and also because of individual efforts. Managers create work groups to carry out assigned jobs and tasks. Such groups, created by managerial decisions, are termed *formal groups.* The group that Kelly McCaul manages at her branch is a formal group.

Groups also form as a consequence of employees' actions. Such groups, termed *informal groups,* develop around common interests and friendships. The wine-and-cheese club at Kelly McCaul's branch is an informal group. Though not sanctioned by management, groups of this kind can affect organizational and individual performance. The effect can be positive or negative, depending on the intention of the group's members. If the group at Kelly's branch decided informally to slow the work pace, this norm would exert pressure on individuals who wanted to remain a part of the group. Effective managers recognize the consequences of an individual's need for affiliation.

Work teams are in vogue across industries. However, some managers really don't know how, when, or where to use them properly.

Intergroup Behavior and Conflict   As groups function and interact with other groups, they develop their own unique set of characteristics, including structure, cohesiveness, roles, norms, and processes. As a result, groups may cooperate or compete with other groups, and intergroup competition can lead to conflict. If the management of Kelly's bank instituted an incentive program with cash bonuses to the branch bringing in the most new customers, this might lead to competition and conflict among the branches. While conflict among groups can have beneficial results for an organization, too much or the wrong kinds of intergroup conflict can have very negative results. Thus, managing intergroup conflict is an important aspect of managing organizational behavior.

Power and Politics   Power is the ability to get someone to do something you want done or to make things happen in the way you want them to happen. Many people in our society are very uncomfortable with the concept of power, and some are very offended by it. This is because the essence of power is control over others. To many Americans, control over others is an offensive thought. However, power is a reality in organizations. Managers derive power from both organizational and individual sources. Kelly McCaul has power by virtue of her position in the formal hierarchy of the bank. She controls performance evaluations and salary increases. However, she also may have power because her coworkers respect and admire the abilities and expertise she possesses. Managers therefore must become comfortable with the concept of power as a reality in organizations and managerial roles.

ORGANIZATIONAL PROCESSES, STRUCTURE, AND DESIGN

To work effectively in organizations managers must have a clear understanding of the organizational structure. Viewing an organization chart on a piece of paper or framed on a wall, one sees only a configuration of positions, job duties, and lines of authority among the parts of an organization. However, organizational structures can be far more complex than that, as illustrated in the following account:

> Dr. John Rice recently was appointed dean of the business school at a major university. Prior to arriving on campus, Rice spent several weeks studying the funding, programs, faculty, students, and organizational structure of the business school. He was trying to develop a list of priorities for things he believed would require immediate attention during his first year as dean. The president of the university had requested that he have such a list of priorities available when he arrive on campus.
>
> During his first official meeting with the president, Rice was asked the question he fully expected to be asked: "What will be your number one priority?" Rice replied: "Although money is always a problem, I believe the most urgent need is to reorganize the business school. At present, students can major in only one of two departments—accounting and business administration. The accounting department has 20 faculty members. The business administration department has 43 faculty mem-

bers, including 15 in marketing, 16 in management, and 12 in finance. I foresee a college with four departments—accounting, management, marketing, and finance—each with its own chairperson. First, I believe such a structure will enable us to better meet the needs of our students. Specifically, it will facilitate the development of major programs in each of the four areas. Students must be able to major in one of the four functional areas if they are going to be prepared adequately for the job market. Finally, I believe such an organizational structure will enable us to more easily recruit faculty since they will be joining a group with interests similar to their own."

As this account indicates, an organization's structure is the formal pattern of activities and interrelationships among the various subunits of the organization. Our model includes two important aspects of organizational structure: the actual structure of the organization itself and job design.

Organizational Processes   Certain behavioral processes give life to an organization. When these processes do not function well, unfortunate problems can arise, as illustrated in this account:

> When she began to major in marketing as a junior in college, Debra Washney knew that someday she would work in that field. Once she completed her MBA, she was more positive than ever that marketing would be her life's work. Because of her excellent academic record, she received several outstanding job offers. She decided to accept the job offer she received from one of the nation's largest consulting firms. She believed this job would allow her to gain experience in several areas of marketing and to engage in a variety of exciting work. On her last day on campus, she told her favorite professor: "This has got to be one of the happiest days of my life, getting such a great career opportunity."
>
> Recently, while visiting the college placement office, the professor was surprised to hear that Debra had told the placement director that she was looking for another job. Since she had been with the consulting company less than a year, the professor was somewhat surprised. He decided to call Debra and find out why she wanted to change jobs. This is what she told him: "I guess you can say my first experience with the real world was 'reality shock.' Since being with this company, I have done nothing but gather data on phone surveys. All day long I sit and talk on the phone, asking questions and checking off the answers. In graduate school I was trained to be a manager, but here I am doing what any high school graduate can do. I talked to my boss, and he said that all employees have to pay their dues. Well, why didn't they tell me this while they were recruiting me? To say there was a conflict between the recruiting information and the real world would be a gross understatement. I'm an adult—why didn't they provide me with realistic job information, then let me decide if I want it? A little bit of accurate communication would have gone a long way."

This book includes information on behavioral processes that contribute to effective organizational performance, leadership, communication, decision making, organizational change and development, and stress management.

Leadership   Leaders exist within all organizations. Like the bank's Kelly McCaul, they may be found in formal groups, but they also may be found in informal groups. Leaders may be managers or nonmanagers. The importance of effective leadership in obtaining individual, group, and organizational performance is so critical that it has stimulated a great deal of effort to determine the causes of such leadership. Some people believe that effective leadership depends on traits

Receiving Feedback Regularly

You Be the Judge

At New Hope Communication in Boulder, Colorado, a questionnaire is included in every paycheck asking for feedback in four key areas: the employees' feelings about their financial package; their feelings toward other employees; their feelings about the skills they are developing; and their overall feelings about their job.

and certain behaviors—separately and in combination. Other people believe that one leadership style is effective in all situations. Still others believe that each situation requires a specific leadership style.

Communication Process   Organizational survival is related to the ability of management to receive, transmit, and act on information. The communication process links the people, teams, and external stakeholders. Information integrates the activities of the organization with the demand of the environment. But information also integrates the internal activities of the organization. Debra Washney's problem arose because the information that flowed *from* the organization was different from the information that flowed *within* the organization.

At New Hope Communication a unique method of communication is explained in the box, You Be the Judge.

Decision-Making Process   The quality of decision making in an organization depends on selecting proper goals and identifying means for achieving them. With good integration of behavioral and structural factors, management can increase the probability that high-quality decisions will be made. Debra Washney's experience illustrates inconsistent decision making by different organizational units (personnel and marketing) in the hiring of new employees. Organizations rely on individual decisions as well as group decisions, and effective management requires knowledge of both types of decisions.

Communication and feedback is considered the "breakfast of champions" at New Hope. You be the judge. Do you think this is a good management approach? Why? These days it is common to read about managerial decisions that are considered unethical. It is now accepted that most decisions made in an organization are permeated by ethics.[22] Managers are powerful, and, where power exists, there is potential for good and evil. Recent headlines emphasize the ethical nature of decision making: "Large Brokerage House Pays Large Bonuses to Top Managers for Months before Declaring Bankruptcy"; "Lawyers and Arbitrators Trade Inside Information"; and "How Companies Spy on Employees."

The power of managers is clearly portrayed when they make decisions about employees' well being, distribute organizational resources, and design and implement rules and policies. In Debra Washney's case, she claims that the consulting firm didn't provide a realistic job preview. She is making a statement that suggests unethical behavior on the part of the individuals who interviewed her for the consulting firm job. Was this the right thing for the company to do? Debra suggests that it was not the right thing or the ethical way to

---

[22]John L. Akula, "Business Crime: What to Do When the Law Pursues You," *Sloan Management Review,* Spring 2000, pp. 29–42.

conduct an interview. Ethical dilemmas will be discussed throughout this book because managers and workers must make decisions everyday that have an ethical component.[23]

Structure of the Organization   The structure of the organization refers to the components of the organization and how these components fit together. Dr. Rice plans to alter the basic structure of the business school. The result of his effort will be a new structure of ranks and authority relationships that he believes will channel the behavior of individuals and groups toward higher levels of performance in the business school.

Job Design   This aspect of structure refers to the processes by which managers specify the contents, methods, and relationships of jobs and specific task assignments to satisfy both organizational and individual needs and requirements. Dr. Rice will have to define the content and duties of the newly created chairperson positions and the relationship of those persons to the dean's office and to the individual faculty members in each department.

Organizational Change and Development Processes   Managers sometimes must consider the possibility that effective organizational functioning can be improved by making significant changes in the total organization. Organizational change and development represent planned attempts to improve overall individual, group, and organizational performance. Debra Washney might well have been spared the disappointment she experienced had an organizational development effort uncovered and corrected the inconsistent communication and decision making that brought about Debra's unhappiness. Concerted, planned, and evaluative efforts to improve organizational functioning have great potential for success.

EFFECTIVENESS IN ORGANIZATIONS

For centurys economists, philosophers, engineers, military generals, government leaders, and managers have attempted to define, measure, analyze, and capture the essence of effectiveness. Adam Smith wrote in the *Wealth of Nations* over two centuries ago that efficiency of operations could be achieved most easily through high degrees of specialization.

Whether, and how, managers can influence effectiveness is difficult to determine. There is still confusion about how to manage within organizations so that organizational effectiveness is the final result. Problems of definition, criteria identification, and finding the best model to guide research and practice continue to hinder, block, and discourage practitioners and researchers. Instead of simply ignoring effectiveness because of underlying confusion, we believe important insights can be found by attempting to clarify various perspectives.

The field of organizational behavior focuses on three **levels of analysis:** (1) individual, (2) group, and (3) organizational. Theorists and researchers in organizational behavior have accumulated a vast amount of information about each of these levels. These three levels of analysis also coincide with the three levels of

---

[23]Chris Turner, *All Hat and No Cattle* (New York: Perseus, 1999).

managerial responsibility; that is, managers are responsible for the effectiveness of individuals, groups of individuals, and organizations themselves.

www.levistrauss.com

During California's frenzied Gold Rush in 1853, Levi Strauss, a Bavarian immigrant, arrived in San Francisco aboard a clipper ship.[24] He quickly discovered that the prospectors wanted sturdy pants that could survive the rigors of digging for gold. So he created the world's first jeans. Word of the quality of the pants spread like wildfire and the Levi's legend was born. Today the firm enjoys annual sales of $6 billion.

Levi's has emphasized quality, being socially responsible, and using the most talented people the firm can recruit to work for the firm. The value of each individual, the effective leadership of work groups, and the success of the enterprise has been the emphasis at Levi Strauss since its founding. Long before a stream of firms paid attention to flatter hierarchies, cultural diversity, empowerment, quality, and globalization, Levi's was leading the way. Levi's embraced the view that every organizational decision should be ethically grounded in what is right.[25]

In its values-based philosophy, Levi's management emphasizes what it aspires to be in terms of effectiveness. The firm believes that if specific values are practiced, effectiveness within the firm and in competitive markets will result.[26] A few of Levi's value principles are:

Behaviors. Management must exemplify "directness, openness to influence, commitment to the success of others, and willingness to acknowledge our own contributions to problems.

Diversity. Levi's "values a diverse workforce (age, sex, ethnic group, etc.) at all levels of the organization. . . . Differing points of view will be sought; diversity will be valued and honestly rewarded, not suppressed."

Recognition. Levi's "will provide greater recognition—both financial and public—for individuals and teams that contribute to our success. . . ."

Ethical Practices. Management should epitomize "the stated standards of ethical behavior. We must provide clarity about our expectations and must enforce these standards throughout the corporation."

Empowerment. Management must "increase the authority and responsibility of those closest to our products and customers. By actively pushing the responsibility, trust, and recognition into the organization, we can harness and release the capabilities of our people."

Levi's is not offered as an example of a perfect company. Like every firm, there are problems. Being slow to adopt new fashion trends is a criticism that is well founded. Levi's is struggling with a generation gap problem. It's trying to attract 14 to 17-year-olds without turning off older people with fashions. As Levi's plodded along, fashion shifted to big-pocketed cargo pants, and Levi's seemed to sit and watch.[27] The result was that many young people would not

---

[24]Cindy Waxer, "501 Blues," *Business 2.0,* January 2000, pp. 53–54.

[25]Richard Mitchell and Michael O'Neal, "Managing by Values," *Business Week,* August 1, 1994, pp. 46–52.

[26]Levi Strauss & Co. Annual Report, 1999.

[27]"Can Levi's Be Cool Again," *Business Week,* March 13, 2000, pp. 144–48.

wear Levi's. Despite problems, Levi's appears to have enough leaders and managers pulling together and creating a unique philosophy of dealing with customers and employees. The Levi's corporate culture is recognized by many to be very effective for permitting individuals and groups to perform at their most effective levels.

Perhaps the modern-era starting point of understanding effectiveness within organizations is the scientific management views of Frederick Taylor that were introduced earlier. Taylor's work used motion and time studies to find the "one best way" to do an effective (efficient) job. In Taylor's viewpoint, the principle of specialization was causally linked to effectiveness.

The Goal Approach

The goal approach to defining and measuring effectiveness is the oldest and most widely used evaluation technique.[28] In the view of this approach, an organization exists to accomplish goals. An early but influential practitioner and writer on management and organizational behavior stated: "What we mean by effectiveness . . . is the accomplishment of recognized objectives of cooperative effort. The degree of accomplishment indicates the degree of effectiveness."[29] The idea that organizations, as well as individuals and groups, should be evaluated in terms of goal accomplishment has widespread appeal. The goal approach reflects purposefulness, rationality, and achievement—the fundamental tenets of contemporary Western societies.

Many management practices are based on the goal approach. One widely used practice is management by objectives. Using this practice, managers specify in advance the goals they expect their subordinates to accomplish and periodically evaluate the degree to which the subordinates have accomplished these goals. The actual specifics of management by objectives vary from case to case. In some instances, the manager and subordinate discuss the objectives and attempt to reach mutual agreement. In other instances, the manager simply assigns the goals. The idea of management by objectives is to specify in advance the goals to be sought.

Yet the goal approach, for all of its appeal and apparent simplicity, has problems.[30] These are some of its more widely recognized difficulties:

1. Goal achievement is not readily measurable for organizations that do not produce tangible outputs. For example, the stated goal of a college may be "to provide a liberal education at a fair price." The question is: How would one know whether the college achieves that goal? What is a liberal education? What is a fair price? For that matter, what is education?

2. Organizations attempt to achieve more than one goal, and achievement of one goal often precludes or diminishes their ability to achieve other goals. A business firm may state that its goal is to attain a maximum profit and to

[28]Stephen Strasser, J. D. Eveland, Gaylord Cummins, O. Lynn Deniston, and John H. Romani, "Conceptualizing the Goal and System Models of Organizational Effectiveness," *Journal of Management Studies*, July 1981, p. 323.

[29]Chester I. Barnard, *The Functions of the Executive* (Cambridge, MA: Harvard University Press, 1938), p. 55.

[30]Dick Satran, "Life after Microsoft," *Smart Business*, October 2000, pp. 123–27.

provide absolutely safe working conditions. These two goals are in conflict because each of these goals is achieved at the expense of the other.

3. The very existence of a common set of official goals to which all members are committed is questionable. Various researchers have noted the difficulty of obtaining consensus among managers as to the specific goals of their organization.[31]

4. Sometimes, even if stated goals are achieved, the organization is considered to be ineffective.

Despite the problems of the goal approach, it continues to exert a powerful influence on the development of management and organizational behavior theory and practice. Saying that managers should achieve the goals of the organization is easy. Knowing how to do this is more difficult. The alternative to the goal approach is the systems theory approach. Through systems theory, the concept of effectiveness can be defined in terms that enable managers to take a broader view of the organization and to understand the causes of individual, group, and organizational effectiveness.

The Systems Theory Approach

Systems theory enables you to describe the behavior of organizations both internally and externally. Internally, you can see how and why people within organizations perform their individual and group tasks. Externally, you can relate the transactions of organizations with other organizations and institutions. All organizations acquire resources from the outside environment of which they are a part and, in turn, provide goods and services demanded by the larger environment. Managers must deal simultaneously with the internal and external aspects of organizational behavior. This essentially complex process can be simplified, for analytical purposes, by employing the basic concepts of systems theory.

In systems theory, the organization is seen as one element of a number of elements that act interdependently. The flow of inputs and outputs is the basic starting point in describing the organization. In the simplest terms, the organization takes resources (inputs) from the larger system (environment), processes these resources, and returns them in changed form (output). Exhibit 1.2 displays the fundamental elements of the organization as a system.

An example of a systems explanation of organizational behavior is found in companies doing business in Germany. The German federal government has passed a new packaging law that is extremely tough.[32] Companies must take back and recycle packaging used during transport or arrange for someone else to do so. As of July 1, 1995, 80 percent of the packaging must be collected. Germany's law applies to everyone. The environmental cleanup will influence how business is conducted in every firm doing business in Germany.

Hewlett-Packard, an American computer company, has redesigned its packaging worldwide to make it easier to recycle in Germany. Where possible, it has

www.aicgs.org/irc/rigs/
federal.htm

---

[31]Arnoldo C. Hax and Dean L. Wilde, II, "The Detta Model: Adaptive Management for a Changing World," *Sloan Management Review,* Winter 1999, pp. 11–28.

[32]"Recycling in Germany: A Wall of Waste," *The Economist,* November 30, 1991, p. 73.

EXHIBIT 1.2
The Basic Elements of a System

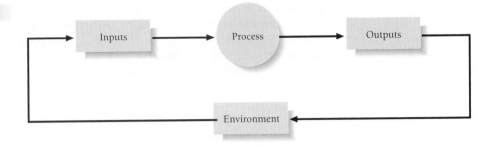

switched to cardboard, hired designers to alter products, and conducted marketing research surveys to determine if German consumers would accept products in reused boxes (they would). The inputs, processes, and outputs of Hewlett-Packard are influenced by the external environmental requirement.

Germany plans to extend recycling to manufacturers of cars and electronic goods, such as computers and televisions. Volkswagen has already practiced to the point of stripping down an automobile in 20 minutes.

Systems theory can also describe the behavior of individuals and groups. The "inputs" of individual behavior are "causes" that arise from the workplace. For example, the cause could be the directives of a manager to perform a certain task. The input (cause) is then acted on by the individual's mental and psychological processes to produce a particular outcome. The outcome that the manager prefers is, of course, compliance with the directive, but depending on the states of the individual's processes, the outcome could be noncompliance. Similarly, you can describe the behavior of a group in systems theory terms. For example, the behavior of a group of employees to unionize (outcome) could be explained in terms of perceived managerial unfairness in the assignment of work (input) and the state of the group's cohesiveness (process). We use the term **systems theory** throughout this text to describe and explain the behavior of individuals and groups in organizations.

Systems Theory and Feedback The concept of the organization as a system related to a larger system introduces the importance of feedback. As mentioned, the organization is dependent on the environment not only for its inputs but also for the acceptance of its outputs. It is critical, therefore, that the organization develop means for adjusting to environmental demands. The means for adjustment are information channels that enable the organization to recognize these demands. In business organizations, for example, market research is an important feedback mechanism. Other forms of feedback are customer complaints, employee comments, and financial reports.

In simplest terms, feedback refers to information that reflects the outcomes of an act or a series of acts by an individual, a group, or an organization. Throughout this text, you will see the importance of responding to the content of the feedback information.

Examples of the Input-Output Cycle The business firm has two major categories of inputs: human and natural resources. Human inputs consist of the people who work in the firm. They contribute their time and energy to the organization in exchange for wages and other rewards, tangible and intangible. Natural resources consist of the nonhuman inputs processed or used in combination with the human element to provide other resources. A steel mill must have people and blast furnaces (along with other tools and machinery) to process iron ore into steel and steel products. An auto manufacturer takes steel, rubber, plastics, and fabrics and—in combination with people, tools, and equipment—uses them to make automobiles. A business firm survives as long as its output is purchased in the market in sufficient quantities and at prices that enable it to replenish its depleted stock of inputs.

Similarly, a university uses resources to teach students, to do research, and to provide technical information to society. The survival of a university depends on its ability to attract students' tuitions and taxpayers' dollars in sufficient amounts to pay the salaries of its faculty and staff as well as the costs of other resources. If a university's output is rejected by the larger environment, so that students enroll elsewhere and taxpayers support other public endeavors, or if a university is guilty of expending too great an amount of resources in relation to its output, it will cease to exist. Like a business firm, a university must provide the right output at the right price if it is to survive.[33]

Systems theory emphasizes two important considerations: (1) the ultimate survival of the organization depends on its ability to adapt to the demands of its environment, and (2) in meeting these demands, the total cycle of input-process-output must be the focus of managerial attention. Therefore, the criteria of effectiveness must reflect each of these two considerations, and you must define effectiveness accordingly. The systems approach accounts for the fact that resources have to be devoted to activities that have little to do with achieving the organization's primary goal.[34] In other words, adapting to the environment and maintaining the input-process-output flow require that resources be allocated to activities that are only indirectly related to that goal.

The "learning organization" has evolved out of the systems view of organizations. The systems view has encouraged the feeling that everyone in the organization is involved in achieving the goals of the firm.[35] Thus, the effectiveness of an organization is, to a large extent, dependent on how well everyone is able to work together to achieve the goals.

An organization learns by acquiring knowledge, distributing information, and interpreting information in a manner that results in learning, adaptation, and change becoming a part of the firm's culture. According to Senge, organizational learning is both generative and facilitative. Generative learning is learning how to learn.[36] Facilitative learning is learning to learn through teaching. When a system fosters both types of learning, the overall level of organizational learning is likely to accelerate.

Senge suggests that people learn faster by using what he calls "microworlds." A "microworld" compresses time and space so that it becomes possible to ex-

---

[33]Kim Cameron, "Measuring Organizational Effectiveness in Institutions of Higher Education," *Administrative Science Quarterly,* December 1978, pp. 604–29.

[34]Robert J. Grossman, "Make Ergonomics Go," *HR Magazine,* April 2000, pp. 36–45.

[35]Brian Dumaine, "Mr. Learning Organization," *Fortune,* October 7, 1994, pp. 147–55.

[36]Peter M. Senge, *The Fifth Discipline* (New York: Doubleday, 1990).

Management Pointer 1.1

IMPROVING EFFECTIVENESS: A FEW HINTS

Highly effective and productive organizations in different industries seem to possess and cultivate some similar characteristics. Managers can lead the way to higher levels of effectiveness by:

1. Providing opportunities for training and continuous learning.
2. Sharing information with employees.
3. Encouraging cross-development partnerships.
4. Linking compensation to performance.
5. Avoiding layoffs.
6. Being a supportive role model.
7. Respecting the differences across employees.
8. Being a good listener.

periment and to learn when the consequences of our decisions are in the future and are distant parts (e.g., another plant or in another laboratory) of the organization.[37] Aeronautical engineering using wind tunnels to test products are engaged in "microworld learning." Managers using white-water rafting as a team-building training exercise are using the microworld. Using role-playing exercises in a college course to help develop interpersonal skills is a form of a microworld laboratory.

Hanover Insurance has created a microworld learning laboratory. Managers are engaged in a number of cost, quality, customer service, and personal interaction problems. The lab emphasizes systems thinking and learning how one part of the business is interconnected with another part of the business. The time pressure introduced into the lab work, the realism, and the forces in the insurance industry environment make the experience exhausting, educational, and developmental.[38]

The following Management Pointer provides a few genuine hints for improving organizational effectiveness.

THE TIME DIMENSION MODEL OF ORGANIZATIONAL EFFECTIVENESS

The concept of organizational effectiveness presented in this book relies on the previous discussion of systems theory, but we must develop one additional point: the dimension of time. Recall that two main conclusions of systems theory are: (1) effectiveness criteria must reflect the entire input-process-output cycle, not simply output, and (2) effectiveness criteria must reflect the interrelationships between the organization and its outside environment. Thus:

1. Organizational effectiveness is an all-encompassing concept that includes a number of component concepts.
2. The managerial task is to maintain the optimal balance among these components.

Much additional research is needed to develop knowledge about the components of effectiveness. There is little consensus about these relevant components, about the interrelationships among them, and about the effects of managerial action on them.[39] In this textbook we attempt to provide the basis for asking questions about what constitutes effectiveness and how the qualities that characterize effectiveness interact.

According to systems theory, an organization is an element of a larger system, the environment. With the passage of time, every organization takes, processes,

---

[37]Tracy E. Benson, "The Learning Organization: Heading toward Places Unimaginable," *Industry Week*, January 4, 1993, p. 18.

[38]Ibid., pp. 322–35.

[39]R. F. Zammuto, "A Comparison of Multiple Constituency Models of Organizational Effectiveness," *Academy of Management Review*, October 1984, pp. 606–16.

EXHIBIT 1.3
Time Dimension Model of Effectiveness

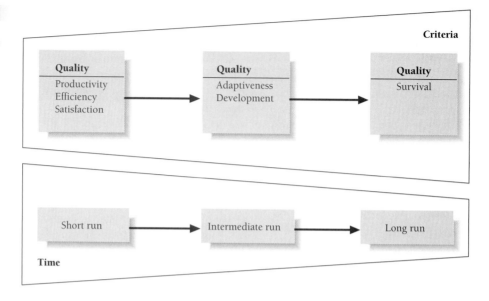

and returns resources to the environment. The ultimate criterion of organizational effectiveness is whether the organization survives in the environment. Survival requires adaptation, and adaptation often involves predictable sequences. As the organization ages, it probably will pass through different phases. It forms, develops, matures, and declines in relation to environmental circumstances. Organizations and entire industries rise and fall. Today, the personal-computer industry is on the rise, and the steel industry is declining. Marketing experts acknowledge the existence of product-market life cycles. Organizations also seem to have life cycles. Consequently, the appropriate criteria of effectiveness must reflect the stage of the organization's life cycle.[40]

Managers and others with interests in the organization must have indicators that assess the probability of the organization's survival. In actual practice, managers use a number of short-run indicators of long-run survival. Among these indicators are measurements of productivity, efficiency, accidents, turnover, absenteeism, quality, rate of return, morale, and employee satisfaction.[41] The overarching criterion that cuts across each time dimension is *quality*. Unless quality is perceived by customers, there will be no survival. Any of these criteria can be relevant for particular purposes. For simplicity, we will use four criteria of short-run effectiveness as representatives of all such criteria. They are quality, productivity, efficiency, and satisfaction.

Three intermediate criteria in the time dimension model are quality, adaptiveness, and development. The final two long-run criteria are quality and survival. The relationships between these criteria and the time dimension are shown in Exhibit 1.3.

---

[40]Kim S. Cameron and David A. Whetten, "Perceptions of Organizational Effectiveness over Organizational Life Cycles," *Administrative Science Quarterly*, December 1981, pp. 525–44, and R. E. Quinn and Kim Cameron, "Organizational Life Cycles and Shifting Criteria of Effectiveness: Some Preliminary Evidence," *Management Science*, January 1983, pp. 33–51.

[41]Chris Angyis, *Flawed Advice and the Management Trap* (New York: Oxford University Press, 2000).

CRITERIA OF EFFECTIVENESS

In the time dimension model, criteria of effectiveness typically are stated in terms of the short run, the intermediate run, and the long run. Short-run criteria are those referring to the results of actions concluded in a year or less. Intermediate-run criteria are applicable when you judge the effectiveness of an individual, group, or organization for a longer time period, perhaps five years. Long-run criteria are those for which the indefinite future is applicable. We will discuss six general categories of effectiveness criteria, beginning with those of a short-run nature.

Quality

J. M. Juran and W. Edwards Deming, in 1950, were prophets without honor in their own country, the United States. These two Americans emphasized the importance of quality. There is now a belief that, in order to survive, organizations must design products, make products, and treat customers in a close-to-perfection way. Close-to-perfection means that quality is now an imperative.[42]

More than any other single event, the 1980 NBC White Paper, "If Japan Can . . . Why Can't We?" illustrates the importance of quality. The television program showed how, in 30 years, the Japanese had risen from the ashes of World War II to economic gianthood with products of superior quality. That is, Japanese organizational effectiveness centered on the notion of quality. The Japanese interpret quality as it relates to the customer's perception. Customers compare the actual performance of the product or evaluate the service being provided to their own set of expectations. The product or service either passes or fails. Thus, quality has nothing to do with how shiny or good looking something is or with how much it costs. Quality is defined as meeting customers' needs and expectations.

In today's competitive global world, the effective company is typically the one that provides customers with quality products or services. Retailers, bankers, manufacturers, lawyers, doctors, airlines, and others are finding out that, to stay in business (survival in effectiveness terms), the customer must be kept happy and satisfied.

Each of the criteria of effectiveness discussed above is significant. However, the one element that executives now recognize as being perhaps the most crucial is quality.

For more than four decades, W. Edwards Deming and J. M. Juran have been the advocates of quality.[43] Deming is the guru of statistical quality control (SQC). He is the namesake of Japan's most prestigious quality award, the Deming prize, created in 1951.

Juran is best known for his concept of total quality control (TQC). This is the application of quality principles to all company programs, including satisfying internal customers. In 1954 Juran first described his method in Japan. He has become an important inspiration to the Japanese because he applied quality to everyone from the top of the firm to the clerical staff.

Today the Japanese, Europeans, Americans, and others who want to compete on the international level have learned a lot about Deming's, Juran's, and other quality improvement methods. Managers have learned that simply paying lip

---

[42]Darryl D. Enos, *Performance Improvement: Making It Happen* (New York: St. Lucie Press, 2000).
[43]Ibid.

service to quality and what it means is not enough. If managers are to be effective over the short and long run, they must translate quality improvement into results: more satisfied customers, a more involved workforce, better designed products, and more creative approaches to solving problems. Competition is sparking a long overdue concern about quality. In many organizations, quality is now the top priority in the short, intermediate, and long run.[44]

In December 1994, IBM stopped shipping personal computers (PCs) based on Intel's Pentium chip because of a quality problem. Quality is a top priority at IBM as it attempts to capture more of the PC market. Pentium PCs, at the time of the IBM stoppage, were the hottest selling computers.[45] However, IBM lab tests indicated that Pentium chips could generate errors in high-intensity mathematical calculations.

A quality flaw in Pentium chips could ruin IBM's attempt to become a competitive force in PCs. IBM claims that it is watching out for its customers. The IBM lab tests found that, if a Pentium PC was turned on and it ran through random calculations, an error would occur once in 9 billion tries. The chip, about the size of a 35mm slide, contains 3.3 million transistors. To fix the flaw, Pentium designers are inserting the missing transistors into a new chip.

The IBM stoppage of shipment created strained relations between the firm and the supplier, Intel. Andrew Grove, chief executive officer at Intel, stated that IBM overreacted in stopping shipment considering a one in 9 billion chance of a quality problem.[46] This debate and concern illustrates how important quality is in terms of competition, public relations, and overall image.[47]

Productivity

As used here, productivity reflects the relationship between inputs (e.g., hours of work, effort, use of equipment) and output (e.g., personal computers produced, customer complaints handled, trucks loaded). The concept excludes any consideration of efficiency, which is defined below. The measures of productivity such as profit, sales, market share, students graduated, patients released, documents processed, clients serviced, and the like, depend upon the type of industry or institution that is being discussed. Every institution has outputs and inputs that need to be in alignment with the organization's mission and goals. These measures relate directly to the output consumed by the organization's customers and clients.

Efficiency

Efficiency is defined as the ratio of outputs to inputs. The short-run criterion focuses attention on the entire input-process-output cycle, yet it emphasizes the input and process elements. Among the measures of efficiency are rate of return on capital or assets, unit cost, scrappage and waste, downtime, occupancy rates, and cost per patient, per student, or per client. Measures of efficiency inevitably must

[44]Shaker A. Zahra, "The Changing Rules of Global Competitiveness in the 21st Century," *Academy of Management Executive,* February 1999, pp. 36–42.

[45]Kevin Maney, "Intel May Get Chip on Its Shoulder," *USA Today,* December 13, 1994, p. 3B.

[46]Bruce Horovitz, "Intel Needs Damage Control," *USA Today,* December 13, 1994, p. 35.

[47]James Overstreet, "Consumers Calm about Pentium Chip Flaw," *USA Today,* December 14, 1994, p. 1B.

be in ratio terms; the ratios of benefit to cost or to time are the general forms of these measures.

Satisfaction

The idea of the organization as a social system requires that some consideration be given to the benefits received by its participants as well as by its customers and clients. Satisfaction and *morale* are similar terms referring to the extent to which the organization meets the needs of employees. We use the term *satisfaction* to refer to this criterion. Measures of satisfaction include employee attitudes, turnover, absenteeism, tardiness, and grievances.

Adaptiveness

Adaptiveness is the extent to which the organization can and does respond to internal and external changes. Adaptiveness in this context refers to management's ability to sense changes in the environment as well as changes within the organization itself. Ineffectiveness in achieving production, efficiency, and satisfaction can signal the need to adapt managerial practices and policies. Or the environment may demand different outputs or provide different inputs, thus necessitating change. To the extent that the organization cannot or does not adapt, its survival is jeopardized.

How can you really know whether the organization is effectively adaptive?

There are short-run measures of effectiveness, but there are no specific and concrete measures of adaptiveness. Management can implement policies that encourage a sense of readiness for change, and certain managerial practices, if implemented, facilitate adaptiveness. For example, managers can invest in employee-training programs and career counseling. They can encourage and reward innovation and risk-taking behavior. Yet, when the time comes for an adaptive response, the organization either adapts or it does not adapt—and that is the ultimate measure.

Development

This criterion measures the ability of the organization to increase its capacity to deal with environmental demands. An organization must invest in itself to increase its chances of survival in the long run. The usual development efforts are training programs for managerial and nonmanagerial personnel. More recently the range of organizational development has expanded to include a number of psychological and sociological approaches.

Time considerations enable you to evaluate effectiveness in the short, intermediate, and long run. For example, you could evaluate a particular organization as effective in terms of production, satisfaction, and efficiency criteria but as ineffective in terms of adaptiveness and development. A manufacturer of buggy whips may be optimally effective because it can produce buggy whips better and faster than any other producer in the short run but still have little chance of survival because no one wants to buy its products. Thus, maintaining optimal balance means, in part, balancing the organization's performance over time.

The time dimensions model of effectiveness enables us to understand the work of managers in organizations. The basic job of managers is to identify and influence the causes of individual, group, and organizational effectiveness in the short, intermediate, and long run. Let us examine the nature of managerial work in that light.

Summary of Key Points

- The key to an organization's success is the institution's human resources. Organizations need human resources that work hard, think creatively, and perform excellently. Rewarding, encouraging, and nurturing the human resources in a timely and meaningful manner is what is required.

- A number of contributing disciplines stand out such as psychology, sociology, and cultural anthropology. Psychology has contributed information and data about motivation, personality, perception, job satisfaction, and work stress. Sociology has offered information about group dynamics, communication problems, organizational change, and formal organization structure. Cultural anthropology has contributed information about culture, comparative attitudes, and cross-cultural studies.

- The behavior of employees is the key to achieving effectiveness. People behave in many predictable and unpredictable ways. Each person has a unique behavioral pattern. Managers must observe, respond to, and cope with the array of behavior patterns displayed by employees.

- The "effect" is the behavior or reaction of a person who is being observed. Individuals who are being observed are likely to react in a nonroutine way because they are being watched or are a part of an experiment.

- Employers and employees enter into a psychological contract. The employer believes that no worker is guaranteed a lifelong job or pay raise. If the worker's performance is good and profit is earned, then employment continues and pay raises are provided. Employees today believe that employers should be honest, concerned about their families, and interested in their overall health. These assumptions are the basis of what is called the *new* psychological agreement.

- Quality definitions are abundant. We opted for a straightforward definition: Quality is meeting customers' needs and expectations. The perception of customers (e.g., patients, clients, or students) is the focal point of our definition. The technological aspects of a product or the elegance of providing a service are not included in our definition. Instead, needs and expectations being met is the key.

  The importance of quality is that it is the core concept that overarches any effectiveness criteria. Production in terms of quantity is important, but the quality of this output is more important.

- The goal approach is based on the idea that organizations are rational, purposive entities that pursue specific missions, goals, and objectives. For example, how well Delta Airlines is performing—that is, how effective they are—is reviewed and analyzed in terms of how the mission, goals, and objectives are being accomplished in the short, intermediate, and long run.

- Managers do not generally walk around handing out behavioral science-type questionnaires or attitude surveys to determine satisfaction. They do, however, engage in observation, listening, and talking with employees. Attempting to acquire insight about attitudes, feelings, and emotions coupled with examining records of absenteeism, tardiness, accident rates, turnover, and grievances provide managers with a general picture of the degree and type of satisfaction among workers.

- The text will attempt to convince you that intuition is practiced by everyone, but, in terms of dealing with the behavior of employees, it is better to learn more on a systematic approach. One systematic approach starts with thinking about the effectiveness criteria of an organization. What are they and how do we accomplish them? We are firm advocates of the fact that managing people is an art. However, knowing what the literature has to say, what other managers have learned, and how people interact in organizations has a scientific basis. The educated man or woman who will manage others in the future needs a lot of intuition, but he or she also needs to use any scientifically derived hints, pointers, or principles that are available.

Review and Discussion Questions

1. Why is management so necessary in an organization of any size—hospital, bank, or school?

2. Frequently, organizations are described in terms used to refer to personality characteristics—dynamic, greedy, creative, conservative, and so on. Is this a valid way to describe organizations? Does this mean that the people in the organization possess the same characteristics?

3. What knowledge about human behavior in the workplace was uncovered by the Hawthorne studies?

4. What are the main differences in taking a goal or a systems approach when interpreting organizational effectiveness?

5. How would you determine whether a large public hospital in your city (community or regional) is effective?

6. Today in the fast-paced, global, and technological environment, it is important for an organization of any size to be adaptive. What does globalization mean to firms like Cisco, Coca-Cola, and Dell Computer?

7. Frederick Taylor's views are considered outmoded by some critics of scientific management. Do you agree? Why?

8. How can the leaders with increasingly diverse workforces manage them more effectively to compete more effectively in world markets?

9. Is it correct to assume that the practice of management is dominated by American practices? Why?

10. What behavioral sciences have contributed to the field of study that is called *organizational behavior*? Explain.

READING 1.1 Managing Oneself

Peter F. Drucker

History's great achievers—Napoleon, da Vinci, Mozart, for instance—have always managed themselves. That, in large measure, is what makes them great achievers. But they are rare exceptions, so unusual both in their talents and their accomplishments as to be considered outside the boundaries of ordinary human existence. Now, most of us, even those of us with modest endowments, will have to learn to manage ourselves. We will have to learn to develop ourselves. We will have to place ourselves where we can make the greatest contribution. And we will have to stay mentally alert and engaged during a 50-year working life, which means knowing how and when to change the work we do.

WHAT ARE MY STRENGTHS?

Most people think they know what they are good at. They are usually wrong. More often, people know what they are not good at—and even then more people are wrong than right. And yet, a person can perform only from strength. One cannot build performance on weaknesses, let alone on something one cannot do at all.

Throughout history, people had little need to know their strengths. A person was born into a position and a line of work: The peasant's son would also be a peasant; the artisan's daughter, an artisan's wife; and so on. But now people have choices. We need to know our strengths in order to know where we belong.

The only way to discover your strengths is through feedback analysis. Whenever you make a key decision or take a key action, write down what you expect will happen. Nine or 12 months later, compare the actual results with your expectations. I have been practicing this method for 15 to 20 years now, and every time I do it, I am surprised. The feedback analysis showed me, for instance—and to my great surprise—that I have an intuitive understanding of technical people, whether they are engineers or accountants or market researchers. It also showed me that I don't really resonate with generalists.

Feedback analysis is by no means new. It was invented sometime in the 14th century by an otherwise totally obscure German theologian and picked up quite independently, some 150 years later, by John Calvin and Ignatius Loyola, each of whom incorporated it into the practice of his followers. In fact, the steadfast focus on performance and results that this habit produces explains why the institutions these two men founded, the Calvinist church and the Jesuit order, came to dominate Europe within 30 years.

Practiced consistently, this simple method will show you within a fairly short period of time, maybe two or three years, where your strengths lie—and this is the most important thing to know. The method will show you what you are doing or failing to do that deprives you of the full benefits of your strengths. It will show you where you are not particularly competent. And finally, it will show you where you have no strengths and cannot perform.

Several implications for action follow from feedback analysis. First and foremost, concentrate on your strengths. Put yourself where your strengths can produce results.

Second, work on improving your strengths. Analysis will rapidly show where you need to improve skills or acquire new ones. It will also show the gaps in your knowledge—and those can usually be filled. Mathematicians are born, but everyone can learn trigonometry.

Third, discover where your intellectual arrogance is causing disabling ignorance and overcome it. Far too many people—especially people with great expertise in one area—are contemptuous of knowledge in other areas or believe that being bright is a substitute for knowledge. First-rate engineers, for instance, tend to take pride in not knowing anything about people. Human beings, they believe, are much too disorderly for the good engineering mind. Human resources professionals, by contrast, often pride themselves on their ignorance of elementary accounting or of quantitative methods altogether. But taking pride in such ignorance is self-defeating. Go to work on acquiring the skills and knowledge you need to fully realize your strengths.

It is equally essential to remedy your bad habits—the things you do or fail to do that inhibit your effectiveness and performance. Such habits will quickly show up in the feedback. For example, a planner may find that his beautiful plans fail because he does not follow through on them. Like so many brilliant people, he believes that ideas move mountains. But bulldozers move mountains; ideas show where the bulldozers should go to work. This planner will have to learn that the work does not stop when the plan is completed. He must find people to carry out the plan and explain it to them. He must adapt and change it as he puts it into action. And finally, he must decide when to stop pushing the plan.

Source: Peter F. Drucker *Harvard Business Review*, March–April 1999, pp. 65–74.

At the same time, feedback will also reveal when the problem is a lack of manners. Manners are the lubricating oil of an organization. It is a law of nature that two moving bodies in contact with each other create friction. This is as true for human beings as it is for inanimate objects. Manners—simple things like saying "please" and "thank you" and knowing a person's name or asking after her family—enable two people to work together whether they like each other or not. Bright people, especially bright young people, often do not understand this. If analysis shows that someone's brilliant work fails again and again as soon as cooperation from others is required, it probably indicates a lack of courtesy—that is, a lack of manners.

Comparing your expectations with your results also indicates what not to do. We all have a vast number of areas in which we have no talent or skill and little chance of becoming even mediocre. In those areas a person—and especially a knowledge worker—should not take on work, jobs, and assignments. One should waste as little effort as possible on improving areas of low competence. It takes far more energy and work to improve from incompetence to mediocrity than it takes to improve from first-rate performance to excellence. And yet most people—especially most teachers and most organizations—concentrate on making incompetent performers into mediocre ones. Energy, resources, and time should go instead toward making a competent person into a star performer.

HOW DO I PERFORM?

Amazingly few people know how they get things done. Indeed, most of us do not even know that different people work and perform differently. Too many people work in ways that are not their ways, and that almost guarantees nonperformance. For knowledge workers, How do I perform? Maybe an even more important question than, What are my strengths?

Like one's strengths, how one performs is unique. It is a matter of personality. Whether personality be a matter of nature or nurture, it surely is formed long before a person goes to work. And *how* a person performs is a given, just as *what* a person is good at or not good at is a given. A person's way of performing can be slightly modified, but it is unlikely to be completely changed—and certainly not easily. Just as people achieve results by doing what they are good at, they also achieve results by working in the ways that they perform best. A few common personality traits usually determine how a person performs.

Am I a Reader or a Listener?   The first thing to know is whether you are a reader or a listener. Rarely are people both, few people know which of the two they are. Some examples will show how damaging such ignorance can be.

When Dwight Eisenhower was commander in chief of the Allied forces in Europe, he was the darling of the press.

His press conferences were famous for their style—General Eisenhower showed total command of whatever question he was asked, and he was able to describe a situation and explain a policy in two or three beautifully polished and elegant sentences. Ten years later, the same journalists who had been his admirers held President Eisenhower in open contempt. He never addressed the questions, they complained, but rambled on endlessly about something else. And they constantly ridiculed him for butchering the King's English in incoherent and ungrammatical answers.

Eisenhower apparently did not know that he was a reader, not a listener. When he was commander in chief in Europe, his aides made sure that every question from the press was presented in writing at least half an hour before a conference was to begin. And then Eisenhower was in total command. When he became president, he succeeded two listeners, Franklin D. Roosevelt and Harry Truman. Both men knew themselves to be listeners and both enjoyed free-for-all press conferences. Eisenhower may have felt that he had to do what his two predecessors had done. As a result, he never even heard the questions journalists asked. And Eisenhower is not even an extreme case of a nonlistener.

A few years later, Lyndon Johnson destroyed his presidency, in large measure, by not knowing that he was a listener. His predecessor, John Kennedy, was a reader who had assembled a brilliant group of writers as his assistants, making sure that they wrote to him before discussing their memos in person. Johnson kept these people on his staff—and they kept on writing. He never, apparently, understood one word of what they wrote. Yet as a senator, Johnson had been superb, for parliamentarians have to be, above all, listeners.

Few listeners can be made, or can make themselves, into competent readers—and vice versa. The listener who tries to be a reader will, therefore, suffer the fate of Lyndon Johnson, whereas the reader who tries to be a listener will suffer the fate of Dwight Eisenhower. They will not perform or achieve.

How Do I Learn?   The second thing to know about how one performs is to know how one learns. Many first-class writers—Winston Churchill is but one example—do poorly in school. They tend to remember their schooling as pure torture. Yet few of their classmates remember it the same way. They may not have enjoyed the school very much, but the worst they suffered was boredom. The explanation is that writers do not, as a rule, learn by listening and reading. They learn by writing. Because schools do not allow them to learn this way, they get poor grades.

Schools everywhere are organized on the assumption that there is only one right way to learn and that it is the same way for everybody. But to be forced to learn in the way a school teaches is sheer hell for students who learn differently. Indeed, there are probably half a dozen different ways to learn.

There are people, like Churchill, who learn by writing. Some people learn by taking copious notes. Beethoven, for example, left behind an enormous number of sketchbooks, yet he said he never actually looked at them when he composed. Asked why he kept them, he is reported to have replied, "If I don't write it down immediately, I forget it right away. If I put it into a sketchbook, I never forget it and I never have to look it up again." Some people learn by doing. Others learn by hearing themselves talk.

A chief executive I know who converted a small and mediocre family business into the leading company in its industry was one of those people who learn by talking. He was in the habit of calling his entire senior staff into his office once a week, then talking at them for two or three hours. He would raise policy issues and argue three different positions on each one. He rarely asked his associates for comments or questions; he simply needed an audience to hear himself talk. That's how he learned. And although he is a fairly extreme case, learning through talking is by no means an unusual method. Successful trial lawyers learn the same way, as do many medical diagnosticians (and so do I).

Of all the important pieces of self-knowledge, understanding how you learn is the easiest to acquire. When I ask people, "How do you learn?" most of them know the answer. But when I ask, "Do you act on this knowledge?" few answer yes. And yet, acting on this knowledge is the key to performance; or rather, *not* acting on this knowledge condemns one to nonperformance.

How do I perform? and How do I learn? are the first questions to ask. But they are by no means the only ones. To manage yourself effectively, you also have to ask, Do I work well with people or am I a loner? And if you do work well with people, you then must ask, In what relationship?

Some people work best as subordinates. General George Patton, the great American military hero of World War II, is a prime example. Patton was America's top troop commander. Yet when he was proposed for an independent command, General George Marshall, the U.S. chief of staff—and probably the most successful at picking leaders in U.S. history—said, "Patton is the best subordinate the American army has ever produced, but he would be the worst commander."

Some people work best as team members. Others work best alone. Some are exceptionally talented as coaches and mentors; others are simply incompetent as mentors.

Another crucial question is, Do I produce results as a decision maker or as an adviser? A great many people perform best as advisers but cannot take the burden and pressure of making the decision. A good many other people, by contrast, need an adviser to force themselves to think;

then they can make decisions and act on them with speed, self-confidence, and courage.

This is a reason, by the way, that the number-two person in an organization often fails when promoted to the number-one position. The top spot requires a decision maker. Strong decision makers often put somebody they trust into the number-two spot as their adviser—and in that position the person is outstanding. But in the number-one spot, the same person fails. He or she knows what the decision should be, but cannot accept the responsibility of actually making it.

Other important questions to ask include, Do I perform well under stress or do I need a highly structured and predictable environment? Do I work best in a big organization or a small one? Few people work well in all kinds of environments. Again and again, I have seen people who were very successful in large organizations flounder miserably when they moved into smaller ones. And the reverse is equally true.

The conclusion bears repeating: Do not try to change yourself—you are unlikely to succeed. But work hard to improve the way you perform. And try not to take on work you cannot perform or perform poorly.

WHAT ARE MY VALUES?

To be able to manage yourself, you finally have to ask, What are my values? This is not a question of ethics. With respect to ethics, the rules are the same for everybody, and the test is a simple one. I call it the "mirror test."

In the early years of this century, the most highly respected diplomat of all the great powers was the German ambassador in London. He was clearly destined for great things—to become the country's foreign minister, at least, if not its federal chancellor. Yet in 1906 he abruptly resigned rather than preside over a dinner given by the diplomatic corps for Edward VII. The king was a notorious womanizer and made it clear what kind of dinner he wanted. The ambassador is reported to have said, "I refuse to see a pimp in the mirror in the morning when I shave."

That is the mirror test. Ethics requires that you ask yourself, What kind of person do I want to see in the mirror in the morning? What is ethical behavior in the present situation? But ethics are only part of a value system—especially of an organization's value system.

To work in an organization whose value system is unacceptable or incompatible with one's own condemns a person both to frustration and to nonperformance.

Consider the experience of a highly successful human resources executive whose company was acquired by a bigger organization. After the acquisition, she was promoted to do the kind of work she did best, which included selecting people for important positions. The executive deeply believed that a company should hire people for such positions from the outside only after exhausting all the inside possibilities. But her new company believed in first looking outside "to bring in fresh blood." There is something to be said for both approaches—in my experience, the proper one is to hire from both inside and outside the company. They are, however, fundamentally incompatible—not as policies but as values. They bespeak different views of the relationship between organizations and people; different views of the responsibility of an organization to its people and their development; and different views of a person's most important contribution to an enterprise. After several years of frustration, the executive quit—at considerable financial loss. Her values and the values of the organization simply were not compatible.

Whether a business should be run for short-term results or with a focus on the long-term is likewise a question of values. Financial analysts believe that businesses can be run for both simultaneously. Successful businesspeople know better. To be sure, every company has to produce short-term results and long-term growth, and each company will determine its own priority. This is not primarily a disagreement about economics. It is fundamentally a value conflict regarding the function of a business and the responsibility of management.

Value conflicts are not limited to business organizations. One of the fastest-growing pastoral churches in the United States measures success by the number of new parishioners. Its leadership believes that what matters is how many newcomers join the congregation. The good Lord will then minister to their spiritual needs or at least to the needs of a sufficient percentage. Another pastoral, evangelical church believes that what matters is people's spiritual growth. The church eases out newcomers who join but do not enter into its spiritual life.

Again, this is not a matter of numbers. At first glance, it appears that the second church grows more slowly. But it retains a far larger proportion of newcomers than the first one does. Its growth, in other words, is more solid. This is also not a theological problem, or only secondarily so. It is a problem about values. In a public debate, one pastor argued, "Unless you first come to church, you will never find the gate to the Kingdom of Heaven."

"No," answered the other. Until you first look for the gate to the Kingdom of Heaven, you don't belong in church."

Organizations, like people, have values. To be effective in an organization, a person's value must be compatible with the organization's values. They do not need to be the same, but they must be close enough to coexist. Otherwise, the person not only will be frustrated but also will not produce results.

A person's strengths and the way that person performs rarely conflict; the two are complementary. But there is sometimes a conflict between a person's values and his or her strengths. What one does well—even very well and successfully—may not fit with one's value system. In that case, the work may not appear to be worth devoting one's life to (or even a substantial portion thereof).

Allow me to interject a personal note. Many years ago, I too had to decide between my values and what I was doing successfully. I was doing very well as a young investment banker in London in the mid-1930s, and the work clearly fit my strengths. Yet I did not see myself making a contribution as an asset manager. People, I realized, were what I valued, and I saw no point in being the richest man in the cemetery. I had no money and no other job prospects. Despite the continuing Depression, I quit—and it was the right thing to do. Values, in other words, are and should be the ultimate test.

WHERE DO I BELONG?

A small number of people know very early where they belong. Mathematicians, musicians, and cooks, for instance, are usually mathematicians, musicians, and cooks by the time they are four or five years old. Physicians usually decide on their careers in their teens, if not earlier. But most people, especially highly gifted people, do not really know where they belong until they are well past their mid-twenties. By that time, however, they should know the answers to the three questions: What are my strengths? How do I perform? And, What are my values? And then they can and should decide where they belong.

Or rather, they should be able to decide where they do *not* belong. The person who has learned that he or she does not perform well in a big organization should have learned to say no working in a large firm. The person who has learned that he or she is not a decision maker should have learned to say no to a decision-making assignment. A General Patton (who probably never learned this himself) should have learned to say no to an independent command.

Equally important, knowing the answer to these questions enables a person to respond to an opportunity, an *offer*, or an assignment, "Yes, I will do that. But this is the way I should be doing it. This is the way it should be structured. This is the way the relationships should be. These are the kind of results you should expect from me, and in this time frame because this is who I am."

Successful careers are not planned. They develop when people are prepared for opportunities because they know their strengths, their method of work, and their values. Knowing where one belongs can transform an ordinary person—hard working and competent but otherwise mediocre—into an outstanding performer.

WHAT SHOULD I CONTRIBUTE?

Throughout history, the great majority of people never had to ask the question, What should I contribute? They were told what to contribute, and their tasks were dictated either by the work itself—as it was for the peasant or artisan—or by a master or a mistress, as it was for domestic servants. And until very recently, it was taken for granted that most people were subordinates who did as they were told. Even in the 1950s and 1960s, the new-knowledge workers (the so-called organization men) looked to their company's personnel department to plan their careers.

Then in the late 1960s, no one wanted to be told what to do any longer. Young men and women began to ask, What do I want to do? And what they heard was that the way to contribute was to "do your own thing." But this solution was as wrong as that of the organization men. Very few of the people who believed that doing one's own thing would lead to contribution, self-fulfillment, and success achieved any of the three.

But still, there is no return to the old answer of doing what you are told or assigned to do. Knowledge workers in particular have to learn to ask a question that has not been asked before: What *should* my contribution be? To answer it, they must address three distinct elements: What does the situation require? Given my strengths, my way of performing, and my values, how can I make the greatest contribution to what needs to be done? And finally, What results have to be achieved to make a difference?

Consider the experience of a newly appointed hospital administrator. The hospital was big and prestigious, but it had been coasting on its reputation for 30 years. The new administrator decided that his contribution should be to establish a standard of excellence in one important area within two years. He chose to focus on the emergency room, which was big, visible, and sloppy. He decided that every patient who came into the ER had to be seen by a qualified nurse within 60 seconds. Within 12 months, the hospital's emergency room had become a model for all hospitals in the United States, and within another two years, the whole hospital had been transformed.

As this example suggests, it is rarely possible—or even particularly fruitful—to look too far ahead. A plan can usually cover no more than 18 months and still be reasonable clear and specific. So the question in most cases should be, Where and how can I achieve results that will make a difference within the next year and a half? The answer must balance several things. First, the results should be hard to achieve—they should require "stretching," to use the current buzzword. But also, they should be within reach. To aim at results that cannot be achieved—or that can be achieved only under the most unlikely circumstances—is not being ambitious; it is being foolish. Second, the results should be meaningful. They should make a difference. Finally, results should be visible and, if at all possible, measurable. From this will come a course of action: what to do, where and how to start, and what goals and deadlines to set.

RESPONSIBILITY FOR RELATIONSHIPS

Very few people work by themselves and achieve results by themselves—a few great artists, a few great scientists, a few great athletes. Most people work with others and are effective with other people. That is true whether they are members of an organization or independently employed. Managing yourself requires taking responsibility for relationships. This has two parts.

The first is to accept the fact that other people are as much individuals as you yourself are. They perversely insist on behaving like human beings. This means that they too have their strengths; they too have their ways of getting things done; they too have their values. To be effective, therefore, you have to know the strengths, the performance modes, and the values of your coworkers.

That sounds obvious, but few people pay attention to it. Typical is the person who was trained to write reports in his or her first assignment because that boss was a reader. Even if the next boss is a listener, the person goes on writing reports that, invariably, produce no results. Invariably the boss will think the employee is stupid, incompetent, and lazy, and he or she will fail. But that could have been avoided if the employee had only looked at the new boss and analyzed how *that* boss performs.

Bosses are neither a title on the organization chart nor a "function." They are individuals and are entitled to do their work in the way they do it best. It is incumbent on the people who work with them to observe them, to find out how they work, and to adapt themselves to what makes their bosses most effective. This, in fact, is the secret of "managing" the boss.

The same holds true for all your coworkers. Each works his or her way, not your way. And each is entitled to work in his or her way. What matters is whether they perform and what their values are. As for how they perform—each is likely to do it differently. The first secret of effectiveness is to understand the people you work with and depend on so that you can make use of their strengths, their ways of working, and their values. Working relationships are as much based on the people as they are on the work.

The second part of relationship responsibility is taking responsibility for communication. Whenever I, or any other consultant, start to work with an organization, the first thing I hear about are all the personality conflicts. Most of these arise from the fact that people do not know what other people are doing and how they do their work, or what contribution the other people are concentrating on and what results they expect. And the reason they do not know is that they have not asked and therefore have not been told.

This failure to ask reflects human stupidity less than it reflects human history. Until recently, it was unnecessary to tell any of these things to anybody. In the medieval city, everyone in a district plied the same trade. In the countryside, everyone in a valley planted the same crop as soon as the frost was out of the ground. Even those few people who did things that were not common worked alone, so they did not have to tell anyone what they were doing.

Today the great majority of people work with others who have different tasks and responsibilities. The marketing vice president may have come out of sales and know everything about sales, but she knows nothing about the things she has never done—pricing, advertising, packaging, and the like. So the people who do these things must make sure that the marketing vice president understands what they are trying to do, why they are trying to do it, how they are going to do it, and what results to expect.

If the marketing vice president does not understand what these high-grade knowledge specialists are doing, it is primarily their fault, not hers. They have not educated her. Conversely, it is the marketing vice president's responsibility to make sure that all of her coworkers understand how she looks at marketing: what her goals are, how she works, and what she expects of herself and of each one of them.

Even people who understand the importance of taking responsibility for relationships often do not communicate sufficiently with their associates. They are afraid of being thought presumptuous or inquisitive or studied. They are wrong. Whenever someone goes to his or her associates and says, "This is what I am good at. This is how I work. These are my values. This is the contribution I plan to concentrate on and the results I should be expected to deliver," the response is always, "This is most helpful. But why didn't you tell me earlier?"

And one gets the same reaction—without exception, in my experience—if one continues by asking, "And what do I need to know about your strengths, how you perform, your values, and your proposed contribution?" In fact, knowledge workers should request this of everyone with whom they work, whether a subordinate, superior, colleague, or team member. And again, whenever this is done, the reaction is always, "Thanks for asking me. But why didn't you ask me earlier?"

Organizations are no longer built on force but on trust. The existence of trust between people does not necessarily mean that they like one another. It means that they understand one another. Taking responsibility for relationships is therefore an absolute necessity. It is a duty. Whether one is a member of the organization, a consultant to it, a supplier, or a distributor, one owes that responsibility to all one's coworkers: those whose work one depends on as well as those who depend on one's own work.

THE SECOND HALF OF YOUR LIFE

When work for most people meant manual labor, there was no need to worry about the second half of life. They simply kept on doing what you had always done. And if they were lucky enough to survive 40 years of hard work in the mill or on the railroad, they were quite happy to spend the rest of your life doing nothing. Today, however, most work is knowledge work, and knowledge workers are not "finished" after 40 years on the job; they are merely bored.

We hear a great deal of talk about the midlife crisis of the executive. It is mostly boredom. At 45, most executives have reached the peak of their business careers, and they know it. After 20 years of doing very much the same kind of work, they are very good at their jobs. But they are not learning or contributing or deriving challenge and satisfaction from the job. And yet they are still likely to face another 20 if not 25 years of work. That is why managing oneself increasingly leads one to begin a second career.

There are three ways to develop a second career. The first is actually to start one. Often this takes nothing more than moving from one kind of reorganization to another: the divisional controller in a large corporation, for instance, becomes the controller of a medium-sized hospital. But there are also growing numbers of people who move into different lines of work altogether: the business executive or government official who enters the ministry at 45, for instance; or the midlevel manager who leaves corporate life after 20 years to attend law school and become a small-town attorney.

We will see many more second careers undertaken by people who have achieved modest success in their first jobs. Such people have substantial skills, and they know how to work. They need a community—the house is empty with the children gone—and they need income as well. But above all, they need challenge.

The second way to prepare for the second half of your life is to develop a parallel career. Many people who are very successful in their first careers stay in the work they have been doing, either on a full-time or a part-time or consulting basis. But in addition, they create a parallel job, usually in a nonprofit organization, that takes another 10 hours of work a week. They might take over the administration of their church, for instance, or the presidency of the local girl scouts council. They might run the battered women's shelter, work as a children's librarian for the local public library, sit on the school board, and so on.

Finally, there are the social entrepreneurs. These are usually people who have been very successful in their first careers. They love their work, but it no longer challenges them. In many cases they keep on doing what they have been doing all along but spend less and less of their time on it. They also start another activity, usually a nonprofit one. My fried Bob Buford, for example, built a very successful television company that he still runs. But he has also founded and built a successful nonprofit organization that works with Protestant churches, and he is building another to teach social entrepreneurs how to manage their own nonprofit ventures while still running their original businesses.

People who manage the second half of their lives may always be a minority. The majority may "retire on the job" and count the years until their actual retirement. But it is this minority, the men and women who see a long working-life expectancy as an opportunity both for themselves and for society, who will become leaders and models.

There is one prerequisite for managing the second half of your life: You must begin long before you enter it. When it first became clear 30 years ago that working-life expectancies were lengthening very fast, many observers (including myself) believed that retired people would increasingly become volunteers for nonprofit institutions. That has not happened. If one does not begin to volunteer before one is 40 or so, one will not volunteer once past 60.

Similarly, all the social entrepreneurs I know began to work in their chosen second enterprise long before they reached their peak in their original business. Consider the example of a successful lawyer, the legal counsel to a large corporation, who has started a venture to establish model schools in his state. He began to do volunteer legal work for the schools when he was around 35. He was elected to the school board at age 40. At age 50, when he amassed a fortune, he started his own enterprise to build and to run model schools. He is, however, still working nearly full-time as the lead counsel in the company he helped found as a young lawyer.

There is another reason to develop a second major interest, and to develop it early. No one can expect to live very long without experiencing a serious setback in his or her life or work. There is the competent engineer who is passed over for promotion at age 45. There is the competent college professor who realizes at age 42 that she will never get a professorship at a big university, even though she may be fully qualified for it. There are tragedies in one's family life: the breakup on one's marriage or the loss of a child. At such times, a second major interest—not just a hobby—may make all the difference. The engineer, for example, now knows that he has not been very successful in his job. But in his outside activity—as church treasurer, for example—he is a success. His family may break up, but in that outside activity there is still a community.

In a society in which success has become so terribly important, having options becomes increasingly vital. Historically, there was no such thing as "success." The overwhelming majority of people did not expect anything but to stay in their "proper station," as an old English prayer goes. The only mobility was downward mobility.

In a knowledge society, however, we expect everyone to be a success. This is clearly an impossibility. For a great many people, there is at best an absence of failure. Whenever there is success, there has to be failure. And then it is vitally important for the individual, and equally so for the individual's family, to have an area in which he or she can contribute, make a difference, and be *somebody*. That means finding a second area—whether in a second career, a parallel career, or a social venture—that offers an opportunity for being a leader, for being respected, for being a success.

The challenges of managing oneself may seem obvious, if not elementary. And the answers may seem self-evident to the point of appearing naive. But, managing oneself requires new and unprecedented things from the individual, and especially from the knowledge worker. In effect, managing oneself demands that each knowledge worker think and behave like a chief executive officer. Further, the shift from manual workers who have to manage themselves profoundly challenges social structure. Every existing society, even the most individualistic one, takes two things for granted, if only subconsciously: that organizations outlive workers and that most people stay put.

But today the opposite is true. Knowledge workers outlive organizations, and they are mobile. The need to manage oneself is therefore creating a revolution in human affairs.

Exercises

EXERCISE 1.1   Initial View of Organizational Behavior

Now that you have completed Chapter 1, which sets the tone for the book *Organizational Behavior and Management,* complete the following exercise. This should be used as your beginning *baseline* assumptions, opinions, and understanding of organizational behavior. Once you have completed the course (book), we will again

Source: Adapted from Robert Weinberg and Walter Nord, "Coping with "It's All Common Sense,' "*Exchange: The Organizational Behavior Teaching Journal,* 7, no. 2 (1982), pp. 29–32. Used with permission.

take another look at your assumptions, opinions, and understanding.

This exercise contains 20 pairs of statements about organizational behavior. For each pair, circle the letter preceding the statement which you think is most accurate. Circle only *one* letter in each pair.

After you have circled the letter, indicate how certain you are of your choice by writing 1, 2, 3, or 4 on the line following each item according to the following procedure.

Place a "1" if you are *very uncertain* that your choice is correct.
Place a "2" if you are *somewhat uncertain* that your choice is correct.

Place a "3" if you are *somewhat certain* that your choice is correct.
Place a "4" if you are *very certain* that your choice is correct.

Do not skip any pairs.

1. *a.* A supervisor is well advised to treat, as much as possible, all members of his/her group exactly the same way.
   b. A supervisor is well advised to adjust his/her behavior according to the unique characteristics of the members of his/her group. _____

2. *a.* Generally speaking, individual motivation is greatest if the person has set goals for himself/herself that are *difficult* to achieve.
   b. Generally speaking, individual motivation is greatest if the person has set goals for himself/herself that are *easy* to achieve. _____

3. *a.* A major reason why organizations are not so productive as they could be these days is that managers are too concerned with managing the work group rather than the individual.
   b. A major reason why organizations are not so productive as they could be these days is that managers are too concerned with managing the individual rather than the work group. _____

4. *a.* Supervisors who, sometime prior to becoming a supervisor, have performed the job of the people they are currently supervising are apt to be more effective supervisors than those who have never performed that particular job.
   b. Supervisors who, sometime prior to becoming a supervisor, have performed the job of the people they are currently supervising are apt to be less-effective supervisors than those who have never performed that particular job. _____

5. *a.* On almost every matter relevant to the work, managers are well advised to be completely honest and open with their subordinates.
   b. There are very few matters in the work place where managers are well advised to be completely honest and open with their subordinates. _____

6. *a.* One's need for power is a better predictor of managerial advancement than one's motivation to do the work well.
   b. One's motivation to do the work well is a better predictor of managerial advancement than one's need for power. _____

7. *a.* When people fail at something, they try harder the next time.
   b. When people fail at something, they quit trying. _____

8. *a.* Performing well as a manager depends most on how much education you have.
   b. Performing well as a manager depends most on how much experience you have. _____

9. *a.* The most effective leaders are those who give more emphasis to getting the work done than they do to relating to people.
   b. The effective leaders are those who give more emphasis to relating to people than they do to getting the work done. _____

10. *a.* It is very important for a leader to "stick to his/her guns."
    b. It is *not* very important for a leader to "stick to his/her guns." _____

11. *a.* Pay is the most important factor in determining how hard people work.
    b. The nature of the task people are doing is the most important factor in determining how hard people work. _____

12. *a.* Pay is the most important factor in determining how satisfied people are at work.
    b. The nature of the task people are doing is the most important factor in determining how satisfied people are at work. _____

13. *a.* Generally speaking, it is correct to say that a person's attitudes cause his/her behavior.
    b. Generally speaking, it is correct to say that a person's attitudes are primarily rationalizations for his/her behavior. _____

14. *a.* Satisfied workers produce more than workers who are not satisfied.
    b. Satisfied workers produce no more than workers who are not satisfied. _____

15. *a.* The notion that most semi-skilled workers desire work that is interesting and meaningful is most likely incorrect.
    b. The notion that most semi-skilled workers desire work that is interesting and meaningful is most likely correct. _____

16. *a.* People welcome change for the better.

b. Even if change is for the better, people will resist it. _____

17. a. Leaders are born, not made.
    b. Leaders are made, not born. _____

18. a. Groups make better decisions than individuals.
    b. Individuals make better decisions than groups. _____

19. a. The statement, "A manager's authority needs to be commensurate with his/her responsibility" is, practically speaking, a very meaningful statement.
    b. The statement, "A manager's authority needs to be commensurate with his/her responsibility" is, practically speaking, a basically meaningless statement. _____

20. a. A major reason for the relative decline in North American productivity is that the division of labor and job specialization have gone too far.
    b. A major reason for the relative decline in North American productivity is that the division of labor and job specialization have not been carried far enough. _____

Cases

CASE 1.1   Drexler's Bar-B-Que

Change seems to be a fact of life, yet in Texas some things remain the same—for instance, people's love for Texas-style barbecue. As you drive from Houston to Waco, for example, you will see many roadside stands asking you to stop by and sample different forms of bbq or bar b q (the tastes vary as much as the spellings and both are often inspired). In the cities, there are many restaurants, several of them large chains, that compete with smaller, neighborhood businesses for the barbecue portion of individuals' dining out budgets.

Survival can sometimes depend on the restaurant's ability to identify and capitalize on "windows of opportunity." Small businesses are presumed to be more flexible, having the ability to react more quickly to changes when they occur; but the risk is also greater for them than for large organizations, which can more easily absorb losses. But although there may be differences in scale, an important question for all organizations is whether they have the willingness and the ability to take advantage of opportunities as they arise.

Drexler's Bar-B-Que is located at 2020 Dowling Street in an area of Houston called the "Third Ward"—an economically disadvantaged neighborhood not far from downtown—and has been "in the family" almost forever. The more recent history, however, begins in the late 1940s, when a great uncle of the present owners operated the establishment as Burney's BBQ. He died in the late 1950s, and an uncle of the present owners took over the restaurant and, because of a leasing arrangement with another popular barbeque restaurant in southwest Houston,

changed the name of the restaurant to Green's Barbecue. In the 1970s, James Drexler, 12 years old, began working with his uncle and learned the secrets of the old family recipes for the barbecue beef, chicken, and sausage. He learned the business from the ground up. In 1982, when his uncle died, James and his mother took over the business, ended the leasing arrangement, and, in 1985, renamed it Drexler's Bar-B-Que. To this day, it continues to be a family affair, but there has been increased specialization in tasks as business has grown. James Drexler continues to do all the meat preparation, his mother, Mrs. Eunice Scott, handles the other food preparation (the standard fare is potato salad, cole slaw, barbeque beans, and slices of white bread), and his sister, Virginia Scott, manages the front operations—customer orders and the cash register. There are only two or three other full-time employees, although sometimes during the summer a couple of nephews work part-time.

Drexler's is a family business with strong underlying values and is recognized for this in the neighborhood. Despite the success of the business and the increased patronage of individuals from other parts of the city (many of whom previously had few occasions to do more than drive through the Third Ward), the Drexlers have never considered moving from their original location. The current head of the family, Mrs. Scott, influences the culture of the organization and the values underpinning it. Her values of honesty, hard work, and treating people fairly and with respect—and her faith in God—permeate the atmosphere and operations of Drexler's. She moves through the restaurant inquiring about individual needs—equally for long-time customers and new ones—and always with a smile and warm greeting for all. She is there every day

Source: Case was written by Forrest F. Aven, Jr., University of Houston-Downtown and V. Jean Ramsey, Texas Southern University.

the restaurant is open and holds the same set of high standards for her as she does for others who work in the restaurant.

Values also get played out in the way in which Drexler's Bar-B-Que "gives back to" the surrounding African American community. Drexler's has, for many years, sponsored a softball team and a local Boy Scout troop. Youths from the neighborhood have opportunities to go camping and visit a local amusement park because the family believes that a business should not just involve itself in the community but has the obligation to aggressively seek out opportunities to help others.

In some ways it would appear that Drexler's is not very flexible or adaptable. The restaurant always closes at 6:00 P.M. and is closed on Sundays and Mondays. The menu has remained the same for many years. Drexler's has always been well known in Houston's African American community, especially in the southwest portion of the city. Regular customers have frequented the restaurant for many years, and a successful side business of catering social functions has also developed. Business has improved every year. During the early 1990s, the business had grown to a point where the small, somewhat ramshackle, restaurant could no longer service the demand—there simply were not enough tables or space. So the decision was made in 1994 to close the business for six months, completely raze the building, and rebuild a new and modern restaurant (with additional space attached for future expansion into related, and unrelated, businesses by other family members). It was a good decision—upon reopening, business doubled. But the biggest test of the restaurant's ability to adapt to changes came on a cold February day.

Mrs. Scott has two sons, James and Clyde Drexler. James is the coowner of the restaurant, and Clyde is an NBA basketball player. In 1994, Clyde Drexler appeared at the restaurant to generate publicity for the reopening. But on February 14, 1995, he was traded from the Portland Trailblazers to the local NBA franchise, the Houston Rockets. Clyde had played his collegiate ball at the local university and was popular in the city of Houston. He and Hakeem Olajuwon, the "star" of the Rockets team, had played together at the University of Houston and were part of the team known as the Phi Slamma Jamma. Clyde had been a very successful member of the Portland team; he had been selected to play on several all-star teams, had played for two NBA championships, and was a member of the original Dream Team that sent NBA players to the 1992 Summer Olympics.

The Houston Rockets, the defending NBA champions, were struggling during that winter of 1995. The acquisition of Clyde Drexler was seen as a "blockbuster" and a key to helping the team repeat as NBA champions. The city was overjoyed with the idea that a local hero was returning home to assist the team in winning once more the championship.

The initial news of the trade brought many new customers to the restaurant. As the Rockets progressed through the playoffs during the spring of 1995, even more customers came. Some days, the restaurant had to close early because it ran out of food. During the semifinals with San Antonio and the finals with Orlando, there appeared to be as many newspaper articles and television reports originating from the restaurant as from the basketball arena. A radio station staged an event outside the restaurant for fans to earn tickets to the game. A major local newspaper gave the restaurant a favorable review in the food section. Many Rockets fans saw frequenting the restaurant as a way to connect to the ball team and came to hug Mrs. Scott or chat with her about her son, Clyde, or both. When the Rockets clinched their second NBA championship, the many now knew about the Rockets, and many now knew of Drexler's Bar-B-Que.

The restaurant has since become the hub of several businesses located side by side. In addition to her two sons, Mrs. Scott has four daughters. Virginia Scott, who is heavily involved in the restaurant, is also coowner of a beauty salon, with another sister, Charlotte Drexler. A bakery is owned and operated by a cousin, Barbara Wiltz. A bookstore with a sports emphasis is leased to a nonfamily member. In January 1996, a new addition was made to the building, and a significantly expanded catering business was begun. Meanwhile, the restaurant has increased its neighborhood involvement by offering free Thanksgiving and Christmas dinners to neighborhood residents in a neighborhood park.

QUESTIONS:

1. What role do values play in how the Drexler's restaurant interfaces with its neighbors and customers?
2. Is Drexler's an effective organization? Why?
3. Apply the systems model to illustrate how Drexler's Bar-B-Que operates with its environment.

1-A

Selected Functions
of Management

This appendix is designed to provide text users with a general background of the practice of management.[1] The skills managers use, the roles managers must perform, and those crucial functions of managing within organizations are also concisely introduced. The appendix is intended to serve as a refresher or as a brief introduction to managerial practice. Managers who are also viewed as leaders are tremendous resources for helping organizations, individuals, and work teams accomplish meaningful objectives. Effectiveness in an organization does not just happen. Dedicated and skillful managers and nonmanagers carrying out specific roles make it happen. Managers influence effectiveness by defining objectives, recognizing and minimizing obstacles to the achievement of these objectives, and effectively planning, organizing, leading, and controlling all available resources to attain high levels of effectiveness. The skillful manager is able to manage and monitor effectiveness in such a way that objectives are achieved because he or she is action oriented and doesn't simply sit back and let things happen.

The term *productivity* has been used to indicate specifically what is being accomplished. Productiv-ity is defined in a general sense as the relationship between real inputs and real outputs, or the *measure* of how well resources (human, technological, financial) are combined and utilized to produce a result desired by management. Productivity is a component of performance, not a synonym for it. As the highest order of resources, human beings are responsible for utilizing all other resources. People design and operate the technology and work flow; they purchase and use raw materials; they produce the product or service; they sell the product or service. People make a company effective or ineffective, and they must be skillfully managed if an organization is to function and survive.

A successful manager possesses certain qualities in applying his or her skills and carrying out various managerial roles. One insightful study conducted by Harbridge House, a Boston consulting firm, identified the qualities of a successful manager.[2] The profile seems to fit managers regardless of age, sex, industry, size of the organization, or the corporate culture. The study identified the following qualities:

1. *Provides clear direction.* An effective manager needs to establish explicit goals and standards for people. He or she must communicate group goals, not just individual goals. The

[1]Comprehensive and up-to-date viewpoints of what constitutes management are presented in James H. Donnelly, Jr., James L. Gibson, and John M. Ivancevich, *Fundamentals of Management* (Burr Ridge, IL: McGraw Hill/Irwin, 1998) and John M. Ivancevich, Peter Lorenzi, Steven J. Skinner, and Philip B. Crosby, *Management: Quality and Competitiveness* (Burr Ridge, IL: Irwin, 1997).

[2]"A Checklist of Qualities That Make a Good Boss," *Nation's Business,* November 1984, p. 100.

manager must involve people in setting these goals and not simply dictate them himself. She or he must be clear and thorough in delegating responsibility.

2. *Encourages open communication.* The manager must be candid in dealing with people. He or she must be honest and direct. "People want straight information from their bosses," the study says, "and managers must establish a climate of openness and trust."

3. *Coaches and supports people.* This means being helpful to others, working constructively to correct performance problems, and going to bat with superiors for subordinates. This last practice "was consistently rated as one of the most important aspects of effective leadership."

4. *Provides objective recognition.* The manager must recognize employees for good performance more often than she criticizes them for problems. Rewards must be related to the quality of job performance, not to seniority or personal relationships. "Most managers don't realize how much criticism they give," the study says. "They do it to be helpful, but positive recognition is what really motivates people."

5. *Establishes ongoing controls.* This means following up on important issues and actions and giving subordinates feedback.

6. *Selects the right people to staff the organization.*

7. *Understands the financial implications of decisions.* This quality is considered important even for functional managers, such as those in personnel/human resources and research and development, who do not have responsibility for the bottom line.

8. *Encourages innovation and new ideas.* Employees rate this quality important in even the most traditional or conservative organizations.

9. *Gives subordinates clear-cut decisions when they are needed.* "Employees want a say in things," the report says, "but they don't want endless debate. There's a time to get on with things, and the best managers know when that time comes."

10. *Consistently demonstrates a high level of integrity.* The study shows that most employees want to work for a manager they can respect.

If any one quality stood out in the study, it was the importance of open and honest communication. Above all other things, a manager must be honest when dealing with employees.

THE MANAGEMENT SYSTEM

As any organization increases in size and complexity, its management must adapt by becoming more specialized. This section addresses some results of specialization of the management process.

Types of Managers

The history of most ongoing firms reveals an evolution through which the management cadre has grown from one manager with many subordinates to a team of many managers with many subordinates. The development of different types of managers has occurred as a result of this evolution. Three broad categories of managers exist in most organizations (e.g., over 100 employees).

First-Line Management   These managers coordinate the work of others who are not themselves managers. Those at the level of *first-line management* are often called *supervisors, office managers,* or *foremen.* These are typically the entry-level line positions of recent college graduates. The subordinates of a first-line manager may be blue-collar workers, salespersons, accounting clerks, or scientists, depending on the particular tasks that the subunit performs: for example, production, marketing, accounting, or research. Whatever the case, first-line managers are responsible for the basic work of the organization according to *plans* provided by their superiors. First-line managers are in daily contact with their subordinates, and they are ordinarily assigned the job because of their ability to work with people. They must work with their own subordinates and with other first-line supervisors whose tasks are related to their own.

Middle Management   The middle manager is known in many organizations as the departmental manager, plant manager, or director of operations. Unlike first-line managers, those in *middle management* plan, organize, lead, and control the activity of other managers; yet, like first-line managers, they are subject to the managerial efforts of a superior.

The middle manager coordinates the activity (for example, marketing) of a subunit.

Top Management   A small cadre of managers, which usually includes a chief executive officer, president, or vice president, constitutes the *top management*. Top management is responsible for the performance of the entire organization through the middle managers. Unlike other managers, the top manager is accountable to none other than the owners of the resources used by the organization. Of course, the top-level manager is dependent on the work of all of her subordinates to accomplish the organization's goals and mission.

Managerial Skills

Regardless of the level of management, managers must possess and seek to further develop many critical skills. A *skill* is an ability or proficiency in performing a particular task. Management skills are learned and developed. Various skills classifications have been suggested as being important in performing managerial roles.

Technical Skills   Technical skill is the ability to use *specific* knowledge, techniques, and resources in performing work. Accounting supervisors, engineering directors, or nursing supervisors must have the technical skills to perform their management jobs. Technical skills are especially important at the first-line management level, since daily work-related problems must be solved.

Analytical Skills   This skill involves using scientific approaches or techniques to solve management problems. In essence, it is the ability to identify key factors and understand how they interrelate and the roles they play in a situation. An analytical skill is actually an ability to diagnose and evaluate. Such skills are needed to understand the problem and to develop a plan of action. Without analytical proficiency, there is little hope for long-term success.

Decision-Making Skills   All managers must make decisions or choose from among alternatives, and the quality of these decisions determines their degree of effectiveness. A manager's decision-making skill in selecting a course of action is greatly influenced by his or her analytical skill. Poor analyti-

cal proficiency will inevitably result in inefficient, spotty, or inadequate decision making.

Computer Skills   One of the most profound and far-reaching trends in the world is the interconnection of individual computers. The information age sweeping the world requires managers who understand and can use the product of computers. Computer abilities are important because using computers substantially increases a manager's productivity. Computers can perform in minutes tasks in financial analysis, human resource planning, and other areas that otherwise take hours, even days to complete. The computer is an especially helpful tool for decision making. The computer instantly places at a manager's fingertips a vast array of information in a flexible and usable form. Software enables managers to manipulate the data and perform "what if?" scenarios, looking at the projected impact of different decision alternatives.

Human Relations Skills   Since managers must accomplish much of their work through other people, their ability to work with, communicate with, and understand others is most important. The human relations skill is essential at every organizational level of management; it is a reflection of a manager's leadership abilities.

Communication Skills   Effective communication—the written and oral transmission of common understanding—is vital for effective managerial performance. The skill is critical to success in every field, but it is crucial to managers who must achieve results through the efforts of others. Communication skills involve the ability to communicate in ways that other people understand, and to seek and use feedback from employees to ensure that one is understood.

Conceptual Skills   These skills consist of the ability to see the big picture, the complexities of the overall organization, and how the various parts fit together. Recall that in our discussions of the systems approach as a way to thinking about organizations, we stressed the importance of knowing how each part of the organization interrelates and contributes to the overall objectives of the organization.

While the above skills are all-important, the relative importance of each will vary according to the level of

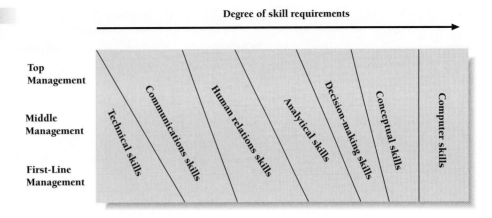

EXHIBIT 1.4
Managerial Skills and Management Level

Degree of skill requirements

Top Management

Middle Management

First-Line Management

Technical skills • Communications skills • Human relations skills • Analytical skills • Decision-making skills • Conceptual skills • Computer skills

the manager in the organization. Exhibit 1.4 illustrates the skills required at each level. For example, note that technical and human relations skills are more important at lower levels of management. These managers have greater contact with the work being done and the people doing the work. Communication and computer skills are equally important at all levels of management. Analytical skills are slightly more important at higher levels of management where the environment is less stable and problems are less predictable. Finally, decision-making and conceptual skills are extremely critical to the performance of top managers. Top management's primary responsibility is to make the key decisions that are executed or implemented at lower levels. This requires that top management see the big picture in order to identify opportunities in the environment and develop strategic plans to capitalize on these opportunities. The many skills required of an effective manager is one of the reasons so many individuals find the field so challenging.

Managerial Roles

We know that managers perform at different hierarchical levels and require an array of skills. At this point, we want to examine what managers actually do and how they spend their time. One of the most frequently cited studies of managerial roles was conducted by Henry Mintzberg. He observed and interviewed five chief executives from different industries for a two-week period. He determined that managers serve in 10 different but closely related roles.[3] These

[3]Henry Mintzberg, *The Nature of Managerial Work* (Englewood Cliffs, NJ: Prentice-Hall, 1980).

are illustrated in Exhibit 1.5. The figure indicates that the 10 roles can be separated into three categories: interpersonal roles, informational roles, and decisional roles. Exhibit 1.6 briefly describes each role and lists the specific activities each comprises.

Interpersonal Roles   The three roles of figurehead, leader, and liaison grow out of the manager's formal authority and focus on interpersonal relationships. By assuming these roles, the manager is also able to perform informational roles, which, in turn, lead directly to the performance of decisional roles.

All managerial jobs require some duties that are symbolic or ceremonial in nature. Some examples of the *figurehead role* include a college dean who hands

EXHIBIT 1.5
Managerial Roles

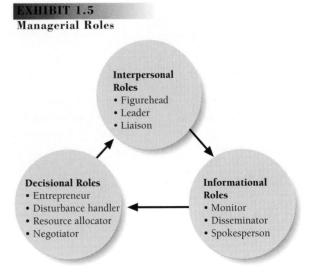

Interpersonal Roles
• Figurehead
• Leader
• Liaison

Decisional Roles
• Entrepreneur
• Disturbance handler
• Resource allocator
• Negotiator

Informational Roles
• Monitor
• Disseminator
• Spokesperson

EXHIBIT 1.6   Mintzberg's 10 Management Roles: Description and Activities

Roles	Description	Identifiable Activities
A. Interpersonal		
1. Figurehead	Symbolic head, obliged to perform a number of routine duties of a legal or social nature	Ceremony, status, requests, solicitations
2. Leader	Responsible for the motivation and activation of subordinates, responsible for staffing, training, and associated duties	Virtually all managerial activities involving subordinates
3. Liaison	Maintains self-developed network of outside contacts and informers who provide favors and information	Acknowledgments of mail, external board work, other activities involving outsiders
B. Informational		
1. Monitor	Seeks and receives wide variety of special information (much of it current) to develop a thorough understanding of the organization and environment, emerges as nerve center of internal and external information of the organization	Handling all main and contacts, which are primarily informational, such as periodical news and observational tours
2. Dissemenitor	Transmits information received from outsiders or from subordinates to members of the organization, some information factual, some involving interpretation and integration	Forwarding mail into the organization for informational purposes, verbal contacts involving information flow to subordinates including review sessions and spontaneous communication
3. Spokesperson	Transmits information to outsiders on the organization's plans, policies, actions, and results, serves as expert on the organization's industry	Board meetings, handling mail and contacts involving transmission of information to outsiders
C. Decisional		
1. Entrepreneur	Searches the organization and its environment for opportunities and initiates "improvement projects" to bring about change, supervises design of certain projects as well	Strategy and review sessions involving initiation or design of improvement projects
2. Disturbance Handler	Responsible for corrective action when the organization faces important, unexpected disturbances	Strategy and review involving disturbances and crises
3. Resource Allocator	Responsible for the allocation of organizational resources of all kinds—in effect the making or approving of all significant organizational decisions	Scheduling, requests for authorization, any activity involving budgeting and the programming of subordinates' work
4. Negotiator	Responsible for representing the organization at major negotiations	Negotiation

Adapted from H. Mintzberg, *The Nature of Managerial Work* (Englewood Cliffs, NJ: Prentice-Hall, 1980), pp. 91–92.

out diplomas at graduation, a shop supervisor who attends the wedding of a subordinate's daughter, and a mayor of New York who gives the key to the city to an astronaut.

The manager's *leadership role* involves directing and coordinating the activities of subordinates. This may involve staffing (hiring, training, promoting, dismissing) and motivating subordinates. The leadership role here also involves controlling, making sure that things are going according to plan.

The *liaison role* involves managers in interpersonal relationships outside of their area of command. This role may involve contacts both inside and outside the organization. Within the organization, managers must interact with numerous other managers and other individuals. They must maintain good relations with the managers who send work to the unit as well as those who receive work from the unit. For example, a college dean must interact with individuals throughout a university campus, a supervisory nurse in an operating room must interact with supervisors of various other groups of nurses, and a production supervisor must interact with engineering supervisors and sales managers. Managers also often have interactions with important people outside the organization. It is easy to see that the liaison role can often consume a significant amount of a manager's time.

Informational Roles
The *informational role* establishes the manager as the central point for receiving and sending nonroutine information. As a result of the three interpersonal roles discussed above, the manager builds a network of interpersonal contacts. The contacts aid him or her in gathering and receiving information as a monitor and transmitting that information as the disseminator and spokesperson.

The *monitor role* involves examining the environment in order to gather information, changes, opportunities, and problems that may affect the unit. The formal and informal contacts developed in the liaison role are often useful here. The information gathered may be competitive moves that could influence the entire organization or the knowledge of whom to call if the usual supplier of an important part cannot fill an order.

The *disseminator role* involves providing important or privileged information to subordinates. The president of a firm may learn during a lunch conversation that a large customer of the firm is on the verge of bankruptcy. Upon returning to the office, the president contacts the vice president of marketing, who in turn instructs the sales force not to sell anything on credit to the troubled company.

In the *spokesperson role,* the manager represents the unit to other people. This representation may be internal when a manager makes the case for salary increases to top management. It may also be external when an executive represents the organization's view on a particular issue of public interest to a local civic organization.

Decisional Roles
Developing interpersonal relationships and gathering information are important, but they are not ends in themselves. They serve as the basic inputs to the process of decision making. Some people believe *decisional roles*—entrepreneur, disturbance handler, resource allocator, and negotiator—are a manager's most important roles.

The purpose of the *entrepreneur role* is to change the unit for the better. The effective first-line supervisor is continually looking for new ideas or new methods to improve the unit's performance. The effective college dean is continually planning changes that will advance the quality of education. The effective marketing manager continually seeks new product ideas.

In the *disturbance handler role,* managers make decisions or take corrective action in response to pressure that is beyond their control. Usually the decisions must be made quickly, which means that this role takes priority over other roles. The immediate goal is to bring about stability. When an emergency room supervisor responds quickly to a local disaster, a plant supervisor reacts to a strike, or a first-line manager responds to a breakdown in a key piece of equipment, they are dealing with disturbances in their environment. They must respond quickly and must return the environment to stability.

The *resource allocator role* places a manager in the position of deciding who will get what resources. These resources include money, people, time, and equipment. Invariably there are not enough resources to go around, and the manager must allocate the scarce goods in many directions. Resource allocation, therefore, is one of the most critical of the manager's decisional roles. A first-line supervisor must decide whether an overtime schedule should be established or whether part-time workers should be hired. A college dean must decide which courses to offer next semester, based on available faculty. The president of the United States must decide whether to allocate more to defense and less to social programs.

In the *negotiator role*, a manager must bargain with other units and individuals to obtain advantages for her unit. The negotiations may concern work, performance, objectives, resources, or anything else influencing the unit. A sales manager may negotiate with the production department over a special order for a large customer. A first-line supervisor may negotiate for new typewriters, while a top-level manager may negotiate with a labor union representative.

Mintzberg suggests that recognizing these 10 roles serves three important functions. First, they help explain the job of managing while emphasizing that all the roles are interrelated. Neglecting one or more of the roles hinders the total progress of the manager. Second, a team of employees cannot function effectively if any of the roles is neglected. Teamwork in an organizational setting requires that each role be performed consistently. Finally, the magnitude of the 10 roles points out the importance of managing time effectively, an essential responsibility of managers if they are to successfully perform each of the 10 roles.

The skilled manager performing the 10 roles engages in carrying out specific management functions. Four of the most important functions are planning, organizing, directing, and controlling. Leadership is the focus of the directing functions and is thoroughly treated in Chapters 10 and 11. Similarly, Chapter 14 addresses multiple aspects of the organizing function. The remaining planning and controlling functions of management will be discussed in this appendix. A more detailed and complete discussion of these functions is available in James H. Donnelly, James L. Gibson, and John M. Ivancevich's text entitled, *Fundamentals of Management* (Burr Ridge, IL: Irwin, 1995). This text focuses on management and the historical evolution of managerial practices in a global world. This and other up-to-date management textbooks provide, in much more detail, a complete picture of managerial issues, successes, and failures. That is, a realistic picture of how management is practiced is available in many excellent textbooks, readers, and professional books.

PLANNING

Planning is a keystone management function. Although some environments are less predictable than others, *all* organizations operate in uncertain environments. For an organization to succeed, management somehow must cope with, and adapt to, change and uncertainty. Planning, if used properly, offers management help in adapting to change. If an organization does no planning, its position and fate in the future will mostly be the result of any momentum built up previously and of luck (hopefully, good). On its own, the organization would follow some kind of course during the next five years. If management wishes to have any control over that course, however, it *must* plan. Otherwise, it will have to rely on defensive reactions rather than on planned actions. Management will be forced to respond to current pressures rather than the organization's long-run needs.

In one way or another, every manager plans. However, the approach to planning, the manner of arriving at plans, and the completeness of plans can differ greatly from organization to organization. Formal planning (as distinguished from the informal planning that we do in thinking through proposed actions prior to their execution) is an activity that distinguishes managers from nonmanagers. Formal planning also distinguishes effective managers from ineffective ones.

If you want to effectively manage the performance of individuals, groups, and organizations, you must understand the concept of, and the necessity for, planning. Planning is that part of the management process that attempts to define the organization's future. More formally, *planning includes all the activities that lead to the definition of objectives and to the determination of appropriate courses of action to achieve those objectives.*

To justify the time and resources expended in planning, distinct benefits must accrue to the planner. The major benefits include the following:

1. Planning forces managers to think ahead.
2. It leads to the development of performance standards that enable more effective management control.
3. Having to formulate plans forces management to articulate clear objectives.
4. Planning enables an organization to be better prepared for sudden developments.

Understanding the Need for Planning

You cannot develop a sound plan at any level of an organization without first understanding and appreciating the *necessity* for planning. If a manager does not believe in the value of planning (and some managers do not), it is unlikely that he or she will develop a useful plan.

To better appreciate the need for planning, consider the following three important factors.

1. *Increasing organization complexity.* As organizations become more complex, the manager's job also becomes bigger and more complicated by the interdependence among the organization's various parts. It is virtually impossible to find an organization (or even a division of an organization) in which the decisions of the various functions, such as research and development, production, finance, and marketing, can be made independently of one another. The more products an organization offers and the more markets it competes in, the greater the volume of its decisions.

   Planning enables each unit in the organization to define the job that needs to be done and the way to go about doing it. With such a blueprint of objectives, there is less likelihood of changing direction, costly improvising, or making mistakes.

2. *Increased external change.* A major role of managers has always been that of change initiator. A manager must be an innovator and doer, someone in constant search of new markets, businesses, and expanded missions. Rapid rates of change in the external environment will force managers at all levels to focus on larger issues rather than solely on solving internal problems. The faster the pace of change becomes, the greater the necessity for organized responses at all levels in the organization. And organized responses spring from well-thought-out plans.

3. *Planning and other management functions.* The need for planning also is illustrated by the relationship between planning and the other management functions. We already know that planning is the beginning of the management process. Before a manager can organize, or control, he or she must have a plan. Otherwise, these activities have no purpose or direction. Clearly defined objectives and well-developed strategies set the other management functions into motion.

The effect of planning on the other management functions can be understood by considering its influence on the function of control. Once a plan has been translated from intentions into actions, its relationship to the control function becomes obvious. As time passes, managers can compare actual results with the planned results. The comparisons can lead to corrective action.

The Elements of Planning

The planning function requires managers to make decisions about four fundamental elements of plans. They are:

1. Objectives
2. Actions
3. Resources
4. Implementation

Objectives are integral to plans because they specify future conditions that the planner deems satisfactory. For example, the statement, "The firm's objective is to achieve a 12 percent rate of return on invested capital by the end of 1996" refers to a future, satisfactory condition.

Actions are the specified, preferred means to achieve the objectives. The preferred course of action to lead to a 12 percent return might be to engage in a product development effort so that five new products are introduced in 1999.

Resources are constraints on the courses of action. For example: "The total cost to be incurred in the development of five new products must not exceed $10 million." A plan should specify the kinds and amounts of resources required, as well as the potential sources and allocations of those resources. Specifying resource constraints also involves *budgeting*—identifying the sources and levels of resources that can be committed to planned courses of action.

Finally, a plan must include ways and means to implement the intended actions. *Implementation* involves the assignment and direction of personnel to carry out the plan.

Establishing objectives and prescribing actions also require *forecasting* the future. A manager cannot plan without explicit consideration of future events and contingencies that could affect what will be possible to accomplish.

Although the four elements of the planning function are discussed separately, they are in fact intertwined. Objectives must be set according to what is possible, given the forecasts of the future and the budgets of resources. Moreover, availability of resources can be affected by the very actions that management plans. In the previous example, if a 12 percent return is not achieved, $10 million may not be available because stockholders, bondholders, or other sources of capital will not invest the funds. Then, other action may not be feasible.

In some organizations, planning is the combined effort of managers and staff personnel. In other organizations, planning is done by the top-management group. In still others, it is done by one individual. Planning activities can range from complex, formal procedures to simple and informal ones. Although the form of planning activities varies from organization, the substance is the same. Plans and planning inherently involve objectives, actions, resources, and implementation directed toward improving an organization's performance in the future.

STRATEGIC PLANNING

Because the internal and external environment of organizations are changing so rapidly, there is increased pressure on top management to respond. In order to respond more accurately, on a more timely schedule, and with a direction or course of action in mind, managers are increasingly turning to the use of strategic planning. Strategic planning is a process that involves the review of market conditions; customer needs; competitive strengths and weaknesses; sociopolitical, legal, and economic conditions; technological developments; and the availability of resources that lead to the specific opportunities or threats facing the organization. In practice, *the development of strategic plans involves taking information from the environment and deciding upon an organizational mission and upon objectives, strategies, and a portfolio plan.*

As indicated, to develop a unity of purpose across the organization, the strategic planning process must be tied to objectives and goals at all levels of management.

The basic questions that must be answered when an organization decides to examine and restate its mission are "What is our business?" and "What should it be?" While the questions may appear simple, they are in fact such difficult and critical ones that the major responsibility for answering them must be with top management.

The Environment of Strategic Planning

Any strategic planning effort requires an analysis of those factors in the organization's environment that may have an influence on the selection of appropriate objectives and strategies. Also some organizations must survive in more uncertain environments than others. In fact, an important goal of a strategic planner is to anticipate change that is beyond the control of the organization so that change within the organization's control can be initiated.

The Strategic Planning Process

The output of the strategic planning process is the development of a strategic plan. There are four components to such plans: mission, objectives, strategies, and the portfolio plan.

The organization's environment supplies the resources that sustain the organization, whether it is a business organization, a college or university, or a governmental agency.

In exchange for these resources, the organization must supply the environment with goods and services at an acceptable price and quality. In other words, every organization exists to accomplish something in the larger environment, and that purpose or mission usually is clear at the start. As time passes, however, the organization expands, the environment changes, and managerial personnel change. And one or more things are likely to occur. First, the original purpose may become irrelevant as the organization expands into new products, new markets, and even new industries. Second, the original mission may remain relevant, but some managers begin to lose interest in it. Finally, changes in the environment may make the original mission inappropriate. The result of any or all of these three conditions is a "drifting" organization, without a clear mission or purpose to guide critical decisions. When this occurs, management must renew the search for purpose or restate the original purpose or mission.

The mission statement should be a long-run vision of what the organization is trying to become—the unique aim that differentiates it from similar organizations. The need is not for a stated purpose (such as "to fulfill all the cosmetic needs of women") that would enable stockholders and managers to feel good or to promote public relations. Rather, the need is for a stated mission that provides direction and significance to all members of the organization, regardless of their level.

A critical phase of planning is the determination of future outcomes that, if achieved, enable the organization to satisfy the expectations of its relevant environment. These desired future outcomes are objectives. Organizational objectives are the end points of an organization's mission and are what it seeks through the ongoing, long-run operations of the organization. The organizational mission is defined into a finer set of specific and achievable organizational objectives.

As with the statement of mission, organizational objectives are more than good intentions. In fact, if formulated properly, they will accomplish the following:

1. They will be capable of being converted into specific actions.
2. They will provide direction. That is, organizational objectives serve as a starting point for more specific and detailed objectives at lower levels in the organization. Each manager will then know how his objectives relate to those at higher levels.
3. They will establish long-run priorities for the organization.
4. They will facilitate management control, because they will serve as standards against which overall organizational performance can be evaluated.

Organizational objectives are necessary in any and all areas that may influence the performance and long-run survival of the organization. When an organization has formulated its mission and developed its objectives, it knows where it wants to go. The next management task is to develop a "grand design" to get there. This grand design constitutes the organizational strategies. The role of strategy in strategic planning is to identify the general approaches that the organization will utilize to achieve its organizational objectives. It involves the choice of major directions the organization will take in pursuing its objectives.

Achieving organizational objectives comes about in two ways. They are accomplished by better man-aging what the organization is presently doing and/or finding new things to do. In choosing either or both of these paths, it then must decide whether to concentrate on present customers, to see new ones, or both.

The final phase of the strategic planning process is the formulation of the organizational portfolio plan. In reality, most organizations at a particular time are a portfolio of businesses. For example, an appliance manufacturer may have several product lines (such as televisions, washers and dryers, refrigerators, stereos) as well as two divisions (consumer appliances and industrial appliances). A college or university will have numerous schools (e.g., education, business, law, engineering) and several programs within each school. The YMCA has hotels, camps, spas, and schools.

Managing such groups of businesses is made a little easier if resources and cash are plentiful and each group is experiencing growth and profits. Unfortunately, providing larger and larger budgets each year to all businesses is not feasible. Many are not experiencing growth, and profits and/or resources (financial and nonfinancial) are becoming more and more scarce. In such a situation, choices must be made, and some method is necessary to help management make the choices. Management must decide which businesses to build, maintain, or eliminate or which new businesses to add.

CONTROLLING

The controlling function consists of actions and decisions managers undertake to ensure that actual results are consistent with desired results. The key to effective controlling is to plan for specific results. Unless managers decide in advance what level of performance they want, they will have no basis for judging actual performance. As described in earlier chapters, when managers plan, they establish the ways and means to achieve objectives. These objectives are the targets, the desired results, that management expects the organization to achieve.

After planning, managers must deploy their organizations' resources to achieve results. And although resources can be allocated and activities can be planned, managers must recognize that unforeseen events such as fuel shortages, strikes, machine breakdowns, competitive actions, and new governmental regulations or tax law changes can sidetrack the organization from its initial plans. Thus, managers must be prepared and able to redirect their organization's activities toward accomplishing the original objectives. To do this, managers must understand the concept of necessary conditions for control.

Effective control requires three basic conditions: (1) *standards* that reflect the ideal outcomes, (2) *information* that indicates deviations between actual and standard results, and (3) *corrective action* for any deviations between actual and standard results. The logic is evident: Without standards, there can be no way of knowing the situation; and without provision for action to correct deviations, the entire control process becomes a pointless exercise.

Standards

Standards are derived from objectives and have many of the same characteristics. Like objectives, standards are targets; to be effective, they must be stated clearly and be related logically to objectives. Standards are the criteria that enable managers to evaluate future, current, or past actions. They are measured in a variety of ways, including physical, monetary, quantitative, and qualitative terms. The various forms standards take depend on *what* is being measured and on *the managerial level responsible* for taking corrective action.

As a manager is promoted in the organization, the standards for which he or she is accountable become more abstract, and the causes for deviations become more difficult to identify. Chief executive officers gauge the success of their organizations against standards such as "service to the public," "quality health care," and "customer satisfaction." These abstract criteria have no obvious method of measurement. But managers at the top of an organization are not the only ones who must deal with difficult-to-measure standards. For example, managers of staff units that provide service to line units also have problems determining standards to guide their units' actions.

Information

Information that reports actual performance and permits appraisal of that performance against standards is necessary. Such information is most easily acquired for activities that produce specific results. For example, production and sales activities have easily identifiable end products for which information is readily obtainable. The performance of legal departments, research and development units, or human resources management departments is more difficult to evaluate, however, because the outputs of these units are difficult to measure.

Corrective Action

Corrective action depends on the discovery of deviations and the ability to take necessary action. The people responsible for taking the corrective action must know (1) that they are indeed responsible and (2) that they have the assigned authority to take those steps. The jobs and position descriptions must include specific statements clearly delineating these two requirements. Otherwise, the control function likely will fall short of its potential contribution to organizational performance. Responsibilities that fall between the jobs of two individuals are undesirable, but sometimes unavoidable. Managers who work in organizations facing uncertain and unpredictable environments often confront unanticipated situations—the kinds not stated in job descriptions.

The control function involves implementing methods that will provide answers to three basic questions: (1) What are the planned and expected results? (2) By what means can the actual results be compared to the planned results? (3) What corrective action is appropriate from which authorized person?

Control methods can be classified according to their foci. Three different types of control methods are precontrol, concurrent, and feedback. (See Exhibit 1.7).

Precontrol Precontrol methods increase the possibility that future actual results will compare favorably with planned results. Policies are important precontrol methods since they define appropriate future action. Other precontrol methods involve human, capital, and financial resources.

Precontrol of *human resources* depends on job requirements. Job requirements predetermine the skills needed by the job holders. How specific the skills must be will depend on the nature of the task. At the shop level, for example, the skills needed may include specific physical attributes and degrees of manual dexterity. On the other hand, the job requirements for management and staff personnel can be more difficult to define with concrete measurements.

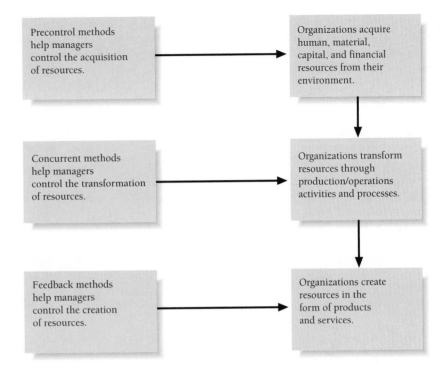

EXHIBIT 1.7
Three Types of Control Methods

Precontrol methods help managers control the acquisition of resources.

→ Organizations acquire human, material, capital, and financial resources from their environment.

Concurrent methods help managers control the transformation of resources.

→ Organizations transform resources through production/operations activities and processes.

Feedback methods help managers control the creation of resources.

→ Organizations create resources in the form of products and services.

Concurrent Control   Concurrent control consists primarily of actions by supervisors who direct the work of their subordinates. Direction refers to the acts managers undertake (1) to instruct subordinates in the proper methods and procedures and (2) to oversee the work of subordinates to ensure that it is done properly. Direction follows the formal chain of command, since the responsibility of each manager is to interpret for subordinates the orders received from higher echelons. The relative importance of direction depends almost entirely on the nature of the tasks performed by subordinates. The manager of an assembly line that produces a component part requiring relatively simple manual operations may seldom engage in direction. On the other hand, the manager of a research and development unit must devote considerable time to direction. Research work is inherently more complex and varied than manual work and requires more interpretation and instruction.

Feedback   Feedback control employs historical outcomes as bases for correcting future actions. For example, a firm's financial statement can be used to evaluate the acceptability of historical results and to determine if changes should be made in future re-

source acquisitions or operational activities. Four feedback methods are widely used in business: financial statement analysis, standard cost analysis, employee performance evaluation, and quality control.

A firm's accounting system is a principal source of information from which managers can evaluate historical results. Periodically, managers receive financial statements, which usually include a balance sheet, an income statement, and a sources-and-uses-of-funds statement. These statements summarize and classify the effects of transactions in terms of assets, liabilities, equity, revenues, and expenses—the principal components of the firm's financial structure.

Standard cost accounting systems are a major contribution of scientific management. A standard cost system provides information that enables management to compare actual costs with predetermined (standard) costs. Management then can take appropriate corrective action or assign others the authority to take action. The first uses of standard cost accounting were concerned with manufacturing costs. In recent years, however, standard cost accounting has been applied to selling expenses and general and administrative expenses.

The most difficult feedback control method is *performance evaluation*. Yet good performance evaluation is important, because people are the most crucial resource in any organization. Effective business firms, hospitals, universities, and governments must have people who are effectively performing their assigned duties. Evaluating individual or group performance can be very difficult, however, because the standards for performance seldom are objective and straightforward. Furthermore, many managerial and nonmanagerial jobs do not produce outputs that can be counted, weighted, and evaluated in objective terms.

Each control method, whether precontrol, concurrent control, or feedback, requires the same three fundamental elements: standards, information, and corrective action. Of the three, information is the element most critical for effective control. Managers act on the basis of information—reports, documents, position papers, and analyses. Without information, standards could not be set, and corrective action could not be taken.

This appendix was intended to provide the basics of management. These basics apply to any organizational setting—domestic or global. The millions of managers practicing around the world each add their own personality, intellect, and style to interactions with peers, superiors, subordinates, and constituents of the enterprise. As this text will illustrate, there is no one best management or leadership approach. There is, however, the need for every manager to plan, organize, and control. How effective he or she is in carrying out these functions is not always accurately assessed or determined. The importance, however, of planning, organizing, directing, and controlling will become clearer as you proceed with the text and classroom discussion.

Quantitative and Qualitative Research Techniques for Studying Organizational Behavior and Management Practice

SOURCES OF KNOWLEDGE ABOUT ORGANIZATIONS

The vast majority of the research reports and writing on organizations are contained in technical papers known as journals. Some of these journals, such as the *Academy of Management Review,* are devoted entirely to topics of management and organization, while journals such as *Organizational Behavior and Human Decision Processes* are devoted largely to the results of laboratory studies. Such journals as the *Harvard Business Review* are general business journals, while the *American Sociological Review* and the *Journal of Applied Psychology* are general behavioral science journals. These business and behavioral science journals often contain articles of interest to studies of management. Exhibit 1.8 presents a selective list of journals.

The sources in Exhibit 1.8 provide information, data, and discussion about what is occurring within and among organizations. This knowledge base provides managers with available research information that could pove useful in their own organizations or situations.

HISTORY AS A WAY OF KNOWING ABOUT ORGANIZATIONS

The oldest approach to the study of organizations is through the history of organizations, societies, and institutions. Throughout human history, people have joined with others to accomplish their goals, first in families, later in tribes and other more sophisticated political units. Ancient peoples constructed pyramids, temples, and ships; they created systems of government, farming, commerce, and warfare. For example, Greek historians tell us that it took 100,000 men to build the Great Pyramid of Khufu in Egypt. The project took more than 20 years to complete. It was almost as high as the Washington Monument and had a base that would cover eight football fields. Remember, these people had no construction equipment or computers. One thing they did have, though, was organization.

EXHIBIT 1.8   Selected Sources of Writing and Research on Organization

1. *Academy of Management Journal*	14. *Human Organization*	27. *Management Review*
2. *Academy of Management Review*	15. *Human Resource Management*	28. *Management Science*
3. *Academy of Management Executive*	16. *HR Magazine*	29. *Organizational Behavior and Human Decision Processes*
4. *Administrative Science Quarterly*	17. *Industrial and Labor Relations Review*	
5. *Advanced Management Journal*	18. *Industrial Engineering*	30. *Organizational Dynamics*
6. *American Sociological Review*	19. *Industrial Management Review*	31. *Online Learning*
7. *Business Horizons*	20. *Journal of Applied Behavioral Science*	32. *Personnel Psychology*
8. *Business Management*	21. *Journal of Applied Psychology*	33. *Public Administration Review*
9. *California Management Review*	22. *Journal of Business*	34. *Sloan Management Review*
10. *Decision Sciences*	23. *Journal of International Business Studies*	35. *Strategic Management Journal*
11. *Fortune*	24. *Journal of Management*	36. *Training and Development Journal*
12. *Hospital and Health Services Administration*	25. *Journal of Management Studies*	37. *Training*
13. *HR Focus*	26. *Management International Review*	

While these "joint efforts" did not have formal names such as "XYZ Corporation," the idea of "getting organized" was quite widespread throughout early civilizations. The literature of the times refers to such managerial concepts as planning, staff assistance, division of labor, control, and leadership.[1]

The administration of the vast Roman Empire required the application of organization and management concepts. In fact, it has been said that "the real secret of the greatness of the Romans was their genius for organization."[2] This is because the Romans used certain principles of organization to coordinate the diverse activities of the empire.

If judged by age alone, the Roman Catholic Church would have to be considered the most effective organization of all time. While its success is the result of many factors, one of these factors is certainly the effectiveness of its organization and management. For example, a hierarchy of authority, a territorial organization, specialization of activities by function, and use of the staff principle were integral parts of early church organization.

Finally, it is not surprising that some important concepts and practices in modern organizations can be traced to military organizations. This is because, like the church, military organizations were faced with problems of managing large, geographically dispersed groups. As did the church, military organizations adopted early the concept of staff as an advisory function for line personnel.

Knowledge of the history of organizations in earlier societies can be useful for the future manager. In fact, many of the early concepts and practices are being utilized successfully today. However, you may ask whether heavy reliance on the past is a good guide to the present and future. We shall see that time and organizational setting have much to do with what works in management.

EXPERIENCE AS A WAY OF KNOWING ABOUT ORGANIZATIONS

Some of the earliest books on management and organizations were written by successful practitioners. Most of these individuals were business executives, and their writings focused on how it was for them during their time with one or more companies. They usually put forward certain general principles or practices that had worked well for them. Although using the writings and experiences of practitioners

---

[1] For an excellent discussion of organizations in ancient societies, see Claude S. George, Jr., *The History of Management Thought* (Englewood Cliffs, NJ: Prentice-Hall, 1968), pp. 3–26.

[2] James D. Mooney, *The Principles of Organization* (New York: Harper & Row, 1939), p. 63.

sounds practical, it has its drawbacks. Successful managers are susceptible to the same perceptual phenomena as each of us. Their accounts, therefore, are based on their own preconceptions and biases. No matter how objective their approaches, the accounts may not be entirely complete or accurate. In addition, the accounts also may be superficial since they often are after-the-fact reflections of situations in which, when the situations were occurring, the managers had little time to think about how or why they were doing something. As a result, the suggestions in such accounts often are oversimplified. Finally, as with history, what worked yesterday may not work today or tomorrow.[3]

SCIENCE AS A WAY OF KNOWING ABOUT ORGANIZATIONS

We have noted that a major interest in this book was the behavioral sciences, which have produced theory, research, and generalizations concerning the behavior, structure, and processes of organizations. The interest of behavioral scientists in the problems of organizations is relatively new, becoming popular in the early 1950s. At that time, an organization known as the Foundation for Research on Human Behavior was established. The objectives of this organization were to promote and support behavioral science research in business, government, and other types of organizations.

Many advocates of the scientific approach believe that practicing managers and teachers have accepted prevalent practices and principles without the benefit of scientific validation. They believe that scientific procedures should be used whenever possible to validate practice. Because of their work, many of the earlier practices and principles have been discounted or modified, and others have been validated.

Research in the Behavioral Sciences

Present research in the behavioral sciences is extremely varied with respect to the scope and methods used. One common thread among the various disciplines is the study of human behavior through the use of scientific procedures. Thus, it is necessary to examine the nature of science as it is applied to human behavior. Some critics believe that a science of human behavior is unattainable and that the scientific procedures used to gain knowledge in the physical sciences cannot be adapted to the study of humans, especially humans in organizations.

The authors do not intend to become involved in these arguments. However, we believe that the scientific approach is applicable to management and organizational studies.[4] Furthermore, as we have already pointed out, there are means other than scientific procedures that have provided important knowledge concerning people in organizations.

The manager of the future will draw from the behavioral sciences just as the physician draws from the biological sciences. The manager must know what to expect from the behavioral sciences, their strengths and weaknesses, just as the physician must know what to expect from bacteriology and how it can serve as a diagnostic tool. However, the manager, like the physician, is a practitioner. He or she must make decisions in the present, whether or not science has all the answers, and certainly cannot wait until it finds them before acting.

The Scientific Approach

Most current philosophers of science define *science* in terms of what they consider to be its one universal and unique feature: *method.* The greatest advantage of the scientific approach is that it has one characteristic not found in any method of attaining knowledge: *self-correction.*[5] The scientific approach is an objective, systematic, and controlled process with built-in checks all along the way to knowledge. These checks control and verify the scientist's activities and conclusions to enable the attainment of knowledge independent of the scientist's own biases and preconceptions.

---

[3]Ian I. Mitroff, "Why Our Old Pictures of the World Do Not Work Anymore," in *Doing Research That Is Useful for Theory and Research,* ed. E. E. Lawler III, et al. (San Francisco: Jossey-Bass, 1985), pp. 18–44.

[4]A similar debate has taken place for years over the issue of whether management is a science. For relevant discussions, the interested reader should consult R. E. Gribbons and S. D. Hunt, "Is Management a Science?" *Academy of Management Review,* January 1978, pp. 139–43; O. Behling, "Some Problems in the Philosophy of Science of Organizations," *Academy of Management Review,* April 1978, pp. 193–201; and O. Behling, "The Case for the Natural Science Model for Research in Organizational Behavior and Organization Theory," *Academy of Management Review,* October 1980, pp. 483–90.

[5]See Fred N. Kerlinger, *Foundations of Behavioral Research* (New York: Holt, Rinehart & Winston, 1973), p. 6.

EXHIBIT 1.9   Characteristics of the Scientific Approach

1. *The procedures are public.* A scientific report contains a complete description of what was done to enable other researchers in the field to follow each step of the investigation as if they were actually present.

2. *The definitions are precise.* The procedures used, the variables measured, and how they were measured must be clearly stated. For example, if examining motivation among employees in a given plant, it would be necessary to define what is meant by motivation and how it was measured (for example, number of units produced, number of absences).

3. *The data collecting is objective.* Objectivity is a key feature of the scientific approach. Bias in collecting and interpreting data has no place in science.

4. *The finding must be replicable.* This enables another interested researcher to test the results of a study by attempting to reproduce them.

5. *The approach is systematic and cumulative.* This relates to one of the underlying purposes of science, to develop a unified body of knowledge.

6. *The purposes are explanation, understanding, and prediction.* All scientists want to know "why" and "how." If they determine "why" and "how" and are able to provide proof, they can then predict the particular conditions under which specific events (human behavior in the case of behavioral sciences) will occur. Prediction is the ultimate objective of behavioral science as it is of all science.

Source: Bernard Berelson and Gary A. Steiner, *Human Behavior: An Inventory of Scientific Findings* (New York: Harcourt Brace Jovanovich, 1964), pp. 16–18.

Most scientists agree that there is no single scientific method. Instead, there are several methods that scientists can and do use. Thus, it probably makes more sense to say that there is a scientific approach. Exhibit 1.9 summarizes the major characteristics of this approach. While only an "ideal" science would exhibit all of them, they are nevertheless the hallmarks of the scientific approach. They exhibit the basic nature—objective, systematic, controlled—of the scientific approach, which enables others to have confidence in research results. What is important is the overall fundamental idea that the scientific approach is a controlled rational process.

Methods of Inquiry Used by Behavioral Scientists

How do behavioral scientists gain knowledge about the functioning organizations?[6] Just as physical scientists have certain tools and methods for obtaining information, so do behavioral scientists. These usually are referred to as research designs. In broad terms, three basic designs are used by behavioral scientists: the case study, the field study, and the experiment.

Case Study   A case study attempts to examine numerous characteristics of one or more people, usually over an extended time period. For years, anthropologists have studied the customs and behavior of various groups by actually living among them. Some organizational researchers have done the same thing. They have worked and socialized with the groups of employees they were studying.[7] The reports on such investigations usually are in the form of a case study. For example, a sociologist might report the key factors and incidents that led to a strike by a group of blue-collar workers.

The chief limitations of the case-study approach for gaining knowledge about the functioning of organizations are:

1. Rarely can you find two cases that can be meaningfully compared in terms of essential characteristics. In other words, in another firm of another size, the same factors might not have resulted in a strike.

2. Rarely can case studies be repeated or their findings verified.

3. The significance of the findings is left to the subjective interpretation of the researcher. Like the

---

[6]A cross-section of papers on gaining knowledge about organizations can be found in Thomas S. Bateman and Gerald R. Ferris, *Methods and Analysis in Organizational Research* (Reston, VA: Reston Publishing, 1984).

[7]See E. Chinoy, *The Automobile Worker and the American Dream* (Garden City, NY: Doubleday, 1955), and D. Roy, "Banana Time—Job Satisfaction and Informal Interaction," *Human Organization,* 1960, pp. 158–69.

practitioner, the researcher attempts to describe reality, but it is reality as perceived by one person (or a very small group). The researcher has training, biases, and preconceptions that inadvertently can distort the report. A psychologist may give an entirely different view of a group of blue-collar workers than would be given by a sociologist.

4. Since the results of a case study are based on a sample of one, the ability to generalize from them may be limited.[8]

Despite these limitations, the case study is widely used as a method of studying organizations. It is extremely valuable in answering exploratory questions.

Field Study   In attempts to add more reality and rigor to the study of organizations, behavioral scientists have developed several systematic field research techniques such as personal interviews, observation, archival data, and questionnaire surveys. These methods are used individually or in combination. They are used to investigate current practices or events, and with these methods, unlike with some other methods, the researcher does not rely entirely on what the subjects say. The researcher may personally interview other people in the organization—fellow workers, subordinates, and superiors—to gain a more balanced view before drawing conclusions.[9] In addition, archival data, records, charts, and statistics on file may be used to analyze a problem or hypothesis.

A very popular field study technique involves the use of expertly prepared questionnaires. Not only are such questionnaires less subject to unintentional distortion than personal interviews, but they also enable the researchers to greatly increase the number of individuals participating. The questionnaire enables the collection of data on particular charac-

teristics that are of interest (for example, equity, accuracy, and clarity).

In most cases, surveys are limited to a description of the current state of the situation. However, if researchers are aware of factors that may account for survey findings, they can make conjectural statements (known as hypotheses) about the relationship between two or more factors and relate the survey data to those factors. Thus, instead of just describing perceptions of performance evaluation, the researchers could make finer distinctions (for example, distinctions regarding job tenure, salary level, or education) among groups of ratees. Comparisons and statistical tests could then be applied to determine differences, similarities, or relationships. Finally, longitudinal studies involving observations made over time are used to describe changes that have taken place. Thus, in the situation described here, we can become aware of changes in overall ratee perceptions of appraisal interviews over time, as well as ratee perceptions relating to individual managers.[10]

Despite their advantages over many of the other methods of gaining knowledge about organizations, field studies are not without problems. Here again, researchers have training, interests, and expectations that they bring with them.[11] Thus, a researcher inadvertently may ignore a vital technological factor when conducting a study of employee morale while concentrating only on behavioral factors. Also, the fact that a researcher is present may influence how the individual responds. This weakness of field studies has long been recognized and is noted in some of the earliest field research in organizations.

Experiment   The experiment is potentially the most rigorous of scientific techniques. For an investigation to be considered an experiment, it must contain two elements—manipulation of some independent variable and observation or measurement of the results (dependent variable) while maintaining all other factors unchanged. Thus, in an organi-

---

[8]Based in part on Robert J. House, "Scientific Investigation in Management," *Management International Review,* 1970, pp. 141–42. The interested reader should see G. Morgan and L. Smircich, "The Case for Qualitative Research," *Academy of Management Review,* October 1980, pp. 491–500, and L. R. Jauch, R. N. Osborn, and T. N. Martin, "Structured Content Analysis of Cases: A Complementary Method for Organizational Research," *Academy of Management Review,* October 1980, pp. 517–26.

[9]See G. R. Salancik, "Field Stimulations for Organizational Behavior Research," *Administrative Science Quarterly,* December 1979, pp. 638–49, for an interesting approach to field studies.

[10]The design of surveys and the development and administration of questionnaires are better left to trained individuals if valid results are to be obtained. The interested reader might consult Seymour Sudman and Norman M. Bradburn, *Asking Questions: A Practical Guide to Questionnaire Design* (San Francisco: Jossey-Bass, 1982).

[11]For an excellent article on the relationship between what researchers want to see and what they do see, consult G. Nettler, "Wanting and Knowing," *American Behavioral Scientist,* July 1973, pp. 5–26.

zation, a behavioral scientist could change one organizational factor and observe the results while attempting to keep everything else unchanged.[12] There are two general types of experiments.

In a **laboratory experiment**, the environment is created by the researcher. For example, a management researcher may work with a small, voluntary group in a classroom. The group may be students or managers. They may be asked to communicate, perform tasks, or make decisions under different sets of conditions designated by the researcher. The laboratory setting permits the researcher to control closely the conditions under which observations are made. The intention is to isolate the relevant variables and to measure the response of dependent variables when the independent variable is manipulated. Laboratory experiments are useful when the conditions required to test a hypothesis are not practically or readily obtainable in natural situations and when the situation to be studied can be replicated under laboratory conditions. For such situations, many schools of business have behavioral science laboratories where such experimentation is done.

In a **field experiment**, the investigator attempts to manipulate and control variables in the natural setting rather than in a laboratory. Early experiments in organizations included manipulating physical working conditions such as rest periods, refreshments, and lighting. Today, behavioral scientists attempt to manipulate a host of additional factors.[13] For example, a training program might be introduced for one group of managers but not for another. Comparisons of performance, attitudes, and so on, could be obtained later at one point or at several different points (a longitudinal study) to determine what effect, if any, the training program had on the managers' performances and attitudes.

The experiment is especially appealing to many researchers because it is the prototype of the scientific approach. It is the ideal toward which every science strives. However, while its potential is still great, the experiment has not produced a great breadth of knowledge about the functioning of organizations. Laboratory experiments suffer the risk of artificiality. The results of such experiments often do not extend to real organizations. Teams of business administration or psychology students working on decision problems may provide a great deal of information for researchers. Unfortunately, it is questionable whether this knowledge can be extended to a group of managers or nonmanagers making decisions under severe time constraints.[14]

Field experiments also have drawbacks. First, researchers cannot control every possible influencing factor (even if they knew them all) as they can in a laboratory. Here again, the fact that a researcher is present may make people behave differently, especially if they are aware that they are participating in an experiment. Experimentation in the behavioral sciences and, more specifically, experimentation in organizations are complex matters.

In a **true experiment**, the researcher has complete control over the experiment: the who, what, when, where, and how. A quasi-experiment, on the other hand, is an experiment in which the researcher lacks the degree of control over conditions that is possible in a true experiment. In the vast majority of organizational studies, it is impossible to completely control everything. Thus, quasi-experiments typically are the rule when organizational behavior is studied via an experiment.

Finally, with each of the methods of inquiry utilized by behavioral scientists, some type of measurement usually is necessary. For knowledge to be meaningful, it often must be compared with or related to something else. As a result, research questions (hypotheses) usually are stated in terms of how differences in the magnitude of some variable are related to differences in the magnitude of some other variable.

The variables studied are measured by research instruments. Those instruments may be psychological tests, such as personality or intelligence tests,

---

[12]For a volume devoted entirely to experiments in organizations, see W. M. Evan, ed., *Organizational Experiments: Laboratory and Field Research* (New York: Harper & Row, 1971). Also see J. A. Walters, P. F. Salipante, Jr., and W. W. Notz, "The Experimenting Organization: Using the Results of Behavioral Science Research," *Academy of Management Review*, July 1978, pp. 483–92.

[13]See an account of the classic Hawthorne studies in Fritz J. Roethlisberger and W. J. Dickson, *Management and the Worker* (Boston: Division of Research, Harvard Business School, 1939). The original purpose of the studies, which were conducted at the Chicago Hawthorne Plant of Western Electric, was to investigate the relationship between productivity and physical working conditions.

[14]For a discussion of this problem, see K. W. Weick, "Laboratory Experimentation with Organizations: A Reappraisal," *Academy of Management Review*, January 1977, pp. 123–27.

questionnaires designed to obtain attitudes or other information, such as a questionnaire, or in some cases, electronic devices to measure eye movement or blood pressure.

It is very important that a research instrument be both reliable and valid. Reliability is the consistency of the measure. In other words, repeated measures with the same instrument should produce the same results or scores. Validity is concerned with whether the research instrument actually measures what it is supposed to be measuring. Thus, it is possible for a research instrument to be reliable but not valid. For example, a test designed to measure intelligence could yield consistent scores over a large number of people but not be measuring intelligence.

Meta-Analysis

A method of statistical analysis called *meta-analysis* that summarizes findings across independent studies is being used with some frequency.[15] The logic of meta-analysis is that researchers can arrive at a clearer, more accurate conclusion regarding a research area such as selection screening, team-building effectiveness, or conflict resolution methods by combining or aggregating the results of many studies of the area. It is assumed that aggregation of results presents a "truer or more accurate picture than would be found in any single study." A typical meta-analysis might combine 30 or 40 individual empirical studies. For example, Ones, Viswesvaran, and Schmidt studied the relationship between scores on a type of employment screening test called an *integrity (honesty) test* and certain aspects of behavior.[16] By using meta-analysis Ones and her coresearchers combined the results of many different studies statistically and there estimated the correlation coefficient (.41) between the test score and supervising ratings of job performance.

There are some potential issues to be concerned about in using meta-analysis. What studies should be included in the aggregate pool? What level of research design rigor should be used to include stud-

ies in the pool? There is also the issue of including only published studies. How about studies with nonsupportive results that are generally not published? These are issues that need to be considered so that the "truest" picture can be provided.[17]

QUALITATIVE RESEARCH

Instead of using experimental designs and concentrating on measurement issues, some researchers use qualitative research procedures. The notion of applying qualitative research methods to studying behavior within organizations recently has been addressed in leading research outlets.[18] The term *qualitative methods* is used to describe an array of interpretative techniques that attempt to describe and clarify the meaning of naturally occurring phenomena. It is by design rather open-ended and interpretative. The researcher's interpretation and description are the significant data collection acts in a qualitative study. In essence, qualitative data are defined as those (1) whose meanings are subjective, (2) that are rarely quantifiable, and (3) that are difficult to use in making quantitative comparisons.

Using both quantitative and qualitative methods in the same study can, in some cases, achieve a comprehensiveness that neither approach, if used alone, could achieve.[19] Another possible advantage of the combined use of the quantitative and qualitative methods is that the use of multiple methods could help check for congruence in findings. This is extremely important, especially when prescribing management interventions on the basis of research.[20]

The quantitative approach to organizational behavior research is exemplified by precise definitions, control groups, objective data collection, use of the scientific method, and replicable findings. The importance of reliability, validity, and accurate measurement is always stressed. On the other hand, qualitative research is more concerned with the meaning of what is observed. Since organizations are

[15]Hunter, J. E. and Schmidt, F. L., *Method of Meta-Analysis: Correcting Error and Bias in Research Findings* (Newburg Park, CA: Sage, 1990).

[16]D. Ones, C. Viswesvaran, and F. L. Schmidt, "Comprehensive Meta-Analysis of Integrity Test Validates: Findings and Implications for Personnel Selection and Theories of Job Performance," *Journal of Applied Psychology,* December 1993, pp. 679–703.

[17]A. Rosenthal, "Writing Articles for Psychological Bulletin," *Psychological Bulletin,* September 1995, pp. 183–92.

[18]John Van Maanen, ed., *Qualitative Methodology* (Beverly Hills, CA: Sage Publications, 1983).

[19]Christopher Stone, "Qualitative Research: A Viable Psychological Alternative," *Psychological Reports,* Winter 1985, pp. 63–75.

[20]Laura D. Goodwin and William L. Goodwin, "Qualitative vs. Quantitative Research, or Qualitative and Quantitative Research," *Nursing Research,* November–December 1984, pp. 378–80.

so complex, a range of quantitative and qualitative techniques can be used side by side to learn about individual, group, and organizational behavior.[21]

Qualitative methodology uses the experience and intuition of the researcher to describe the organizational processes and structures being studied. The data collected by a qualitative researcher requires him or her to become very close to the situation or problem being studied. For example, one qualitative method used is called the *ethnographic method* by anthropologists.[22] Here the researcher typically studies a phenomenon for long periods of time as a participant-observer. The researcher becomes part of the situation being studied to feel what it is like for the people in that situation. The researcher becomes totally immersed in other people's realities.

Participant observation usually is supplemented by a variety of quantitative data collection tools such as structured interviews and self-report questionnaires. A variety of techniques is used so that the researcher can cross-check the results obtained from observation and recorded in field notes.

In training researchers in the ethnographic method, it is a common practice to place them in unfamiliar settings. A researcher may sit with and listen to workers on a production line, drive around in a police car to observe police officers, or do cleanup work in a surgical operating room. The training is designed to improve the researcher's ability to record, categorize, and code what is being observed.

An example of qualitative research involvement is present in Van Maanen's participant-observer study of a big-city police department. He went through police academy training and then accompanied police officers on their daily rounds. He functioned with police officers in daily encounters. Thus, he was able to provide vivid descriptions of what police work was like.[23]

Other qualitative techniques include content analysis (e.g., the researcher's interpretation of field notes), informal interviewing, archival data surveys and historical analysis, and the use of unobtrusive measures (e.g., data whose collection is not influ-

enced by a researcher's presence). An example of the last would be the wear and tear on a couch in a cardiologist's office. As reported in the discussion of Type A Behavior Pattern in Chapter 7 the wear and tear was on the edges of the couch, which suggested anxiety and hyperactive behavior. Qualitative research appears to rely more on multiple sources of data than on any one source. The current research literature suggests a number of characteristics associated with qualitative research.[24]

1. *Analytical induction.* Qualitative research begins with the closeup, first-hand inspection of organizational life.
2. *Proximity.* Researchers' desire to witness first-hand what is being studied. If the application of rewards is what is being studied, the researcher would want to observe episodes of reward distribution.
3. *Ordinary behavior.* The topics of research interest should be ordinary, normal, routine behaviors.
4. *Descriptive emphasis.* Qualitative research seeks descriptions for what is occurring in any given place and time. The aim is to disclose and reveal, not merely to order data and to predict.
5. *Shrinking variance.* Qualitative research is geared toward the explanation of similarity and coherence. Greater emphasis is placed on commonality and on things shared in organizational settings than on things not shared.
6. *Enlightening the consumer.* The consumer of qualitative research could be a manager. A major objective is to enlighten without confusing him or her. This is accomplished by providing commentary that is coherent and logically persuasive.

Researchers and managers do not have to choose either quantitative or qualitative research data and interpretation. There are convincing and relevant arguments that more than one method of research should be used when studying organizational behavior. Quantitative and qualitative research methods and procedures have much to offer practicing managers. Blending and integrating quantitative and qualitative research are what researchers and managers must do in the years ahead to better understand, cope with, and modify organizational behavior.

---

[21]Richard L. Daft, "Learning the Craft of Organizational Research," *Academy of Management Review,* October 1983, pp. 539–46.

[22]Anthony F. C. Wallace, "Paradigmatic Processes in Cultural Change," *American Anthropologist,* 1972, pp. 467–78.

[23]John Van Maanen, J. M. Dobbs, Jr., and R. R. Faulkner, *Varieties of Qualitative Research* (Beverly Hills, CA: Sage Publications, 1982).

[24]Van Maanen, *Qualitative Methodology,* pp. 255–56.

2

Organizational Culture

After completing Chapter 2, you should be able to:

Learning Objectives

- Define the terms *organizational culture, socialization,* and *career.*

- Explain why it is too simplistic to assume that managers can state that they are creating a firm's culture.

- Describe the relationship between a society's culture and organizational culture.

- Explain why valuing diversity has become an important leadership requirement.

- Identify specific practices and programs used by organizations to facilitate socialization.

When a person moves from one firm to another, or even from one department to another in the same firm, he or she senses and experiences differences between the environments. Attempting to adjust to these different environments involves learning new values, processing information in new ways, and working within an established set of norms, customs, and rituals. The adaptation to new environments is becoming a common occurrence and is likely to remain so into the 21st century. Although adaptation is difficult, it can be better understood by learning about organizational culture.[1]

ORGANIZATIONAL CULTURE

www.broadmoor.com

www.bayarea.citysearch.com

www.thebreakers.com

www.mcdonalds.com

If a person walks into the Broadmoor Hotel in Colorado Springs, the Breakers Hotel in West Palm Beach, or the St. Francis Hotel in San Francisco, there is a certain atmosphere, feeling, and style that is unique. These hotels have a personality, a charm, a feel. They have a cultural anchor that influences the way customers respond and the way employees interact with customers. McDonald's also sends off a powerful cultural message.[2] The 13,000 restaurants in the McDonald's network all pay attention to quality, service, and cleanliness. Ray Kroc, the founder, instilled these cultural anchors to McDonald's. He had a significant influence on what McDonald's is throughout the world from Tokyo to Chicago to Moscow. Kroc projected his vision and his openness about what McDonald's would be to customers. He gave McDonald's a purpose, goals, and a cultural base. Whether the discussion focuses on a grand hotel that exudes culture or a McDonald's restaurant that projects its founder's vision of the business, culture is a part of organizational life that influences the behavior, attitudes, and overall effectiveness of employees.

Organizational Culture Defined

Despite being an important concept, organizational culture as a perspective to understand the behavior of individuals and groups within organizations has its limitations. First, it is not the only way to view organizations. We have already discussed the goal and systems view without even mentioning culture. Second, like so many concepts, organizational culture is not defined the same way by any two popular theorists or researchers. Some of the definitions of culture are as follows:

- Symbols, language, ideologies, rituals, and myths[3]
- Organizational scripts derived from the personal scripts of the organization's founder(s) or dominant leader(s)
- Is a product; is historical; is based upon symbols; and is an abstraction from behavior and the products of behavior[4]

---

[1]Harrison M. Trice and Janice M. Beyer, *The Cultures of Work Organizations* (Englewood Cliffs, NJ: Prentice-Hall, 1993).

[2]Gary Hoover, Alta Campbell, and Patricia S. Spain (eds.), *Profiles of over 500 Major Corporations* (Austin, TX: Reference Press, Inc., 2000), p. 364.

[3]A.M. Pettegrew, "On Studying Cultures," *Administrative Science Quarterly*, December 1979, pp. 579–81.

[4]D. Jongeward, *Everybody Wins: Transactional Analysis Applied to Organizations* (Reading, MA: Addison-Wesley Publishing, 1973).

Organizational culture is what employees perceive and how this perception creates a pattern of beliefs, values, and expectations. Edgar Schein defined culture as:

> A pattern of basic assumptions—invented, discovered, or developed by a given group as it learns to cope with the problems of external adaptation and internal integration—that has worked well enough to be considered valid and, therefore, to be taught to new members as the correct way to perceive, think, and feel in relation to those problems.[5]

www.jcpenny.com
www.compaq.com

The Schein definition points out that culture involves assumptions, adaptations, perceptions, and learning. He further contends that an organization's culture such as Walt Disney's or J. C. Penney's or Compaq Computer has three layers. Layer I includes artifacts and creations which are visible but often not interpretable. An annual report, a newsletter, wall dividers between workers, and furnishings are examples of artifacts and creations. At Layer II are values or the things that are important to people. Values are conscious, affective desires or wants. In Layer III are the basic assumptions people make that guide their behavior. Included in this layer are assumptions that tell individuals how to perceive, think about, and feel about work, performance goals, human relationships, and the performance of colleagues. Exhibit 2.1 presents the Schein three-layer model of organizational culture.

www.cisco.com

Asking Cisco Systems or Walt Disney employees about their firm's organizational culture is not likely to reveal much. A person's feelings and perceptions are usually kept at the subconscious level. The feelings one has about a stay at Motel 6 or a stay at the St. Francis Hotel are often difficult to express. The culture of a firm can be inferred by looking at those aspects that are perceptible. For example, four specific manifestations of culture at Walt Disney are shared things (wearing the Walt Disney uniform to fit the attraction), shared sayings (a good "Mickey" is a compliment for doing a good job), shared behavior (smiling at customers and being polite), and shared feelings (taking pride in working at Disney).

www.the-body-shop.com
:www.jnj.com
www.benjerry.com

Companies such as Johnson & Johnson, The Body Shop, and Ben & Jerry's Ice Cream have established credos based on values and ethical principles that serve to project to others what they believe and to guide behavior. Ethics Encounter 2.1 presents a sample of the credos of these three firms.

Organizational Culture and Its Effects

Since organizational culture involves shared expectations, values, and attitudes, it exerts influence on individuals, groups, and organizational processes. For example, members are influenced to be a good citizen and to go along. Thus, if quality customer service is important in the culture, then individuals are expected to adopt this behavior.

Thus, if, on the other hand, adhering to a specific set of procedures in dealing with customers is the norm, then this type of behavior would be expected, recognized, and rewarded.

Researchers who have suggested and studied the impact of culture of employees indicate that it provides and encourages a form of stability.[6] There is a feeling of stability, as well as a sense of organizational identity provided by an organization's culture. Walt Disney is able to attract, develop, and retain top-quality employees

---

[5]Edgar H. Schein, *Organizational Culture and Leadership* (San Francisco: Jossey-Bass, 1985), p. 9.

[6]Michael Zwell, *Creating a Culture of Competence* (New York: John Wiley, 2000).

EXHIBIT 2.1

Schein's Three-Layer
Organizational Model

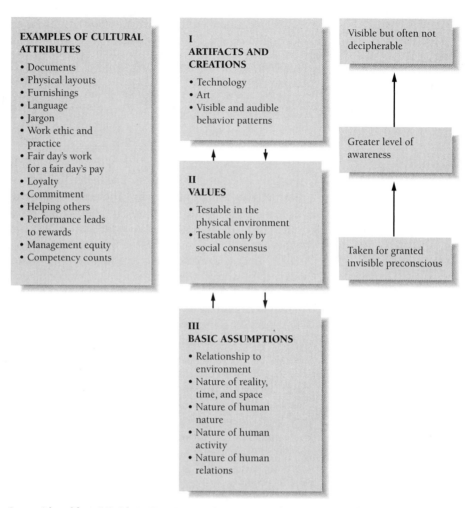

EXAMPLES OF CULTURAL ATTRIBUTES

- Documents
- Physical layouts
- Furnishings
- Language
- Jargon
- Work ethic and practice
- Fair day's work for a fair day's pay
- Loyalty
- Commitment
- Helping others
- Performance leads to rewards
- Management equity
- Competency counts

I ARTIFACTS AND CREATIONS

- Technology
- Art
- Visible and audible behavior patterns

II VALUES

- Testable in the physical environment
- Testable only by social consensus

III BASIC ASSUMPTIONS

- Relationship to environment
- Nature of reality, time, and space
- Nature of human nature
- Nature of human activity
- Nature of human relations

Visible but often not decipherable

Greater level of awareness

Taken for granted invisible preconscious

Source: Adapted form E.H. Schein, "Does Japanese Management Style Have a Message for American Managers?" *Sloan Management Review,* Fall 1981, p. 64

because of the firm's stability and the pride of identity that goes with being a part of the Disney team.

It has become useful to differentiate between strong and weak cultures.[7] A strong culture is characterized by employees sharing core values. The more employees share and accept the core values, the stronger the culture is and the more influential it is on behavior. Religious organizations, cults, and some Japanese firms such as Toyota are examples of organizations that have strong, influential cultures.

An American firm with a notoriously strong and influential culture is Southwest Airlines. Herb Kelleher, one of the founders, is largely responsible for the strong culture. Along with Roland King, Kelleher rather impulsively decided to start another airline.[8] At Southwest, employees are expected to learn more than one job

www.iflyswa.com
www.tke.org/kellerher.html

---

[7]Ibid.

[8]J. Freiburg and K. Freiburg, *NUTS! Southwest Airlines Crazy Recipe for Business and Personal Success* (Austin, TX: Bard Books, 1996).

Ethics Encounter 2.1

Credos of Three Firms

JOHNSON & JOHNSON, OUR CREDO

We believe our first responsibility is to the doctors, nurses, and patients, to mothers and fathers and all others who use our products and services. In meeting their needs, everything we do must be of high quality. We must constantly strive to reduce our costs in other to maintain reasonable prices. Customers' orders must be serviced promptly and accurately. Our suppliers and distributors must have an opportunity to make a fair profit.

We are responsible to our employees, the men and women who work with us throughout the world. Everyone must be considered as an individual. We must respect their dignity and recognize their merit. They must have a sense of security in their jobs. Compensation must be fair and adequate, and working conditions clean, orderly, and safe. We must be mindful of ways to help our employees fulfill their family responsibilities. Employees must feel free to make suggestions and complaints. There must be equal opportunity for employment, development, and advancement for those qualified. We must provide competent management, and their actions must be just and ethical.

THE BODY SHOP INTERNATIONAL, WHAT WE'RE ALL ABOUT

The Body Shop manufactures and sells naturally based cosmetics, skin and hair care products, using high-quality ingredients to make original and exclusive products.

The Body Shop believes in an honest approach to selling cosmetics. We don't promote idealized notions of beauty, nor do we claim our products will perform miracles. Our products are straightforward, designed to meet the real needs of real people. That is why they're sold in five sizes. Through our refill bar and minimal packaging, we conserve resources, reduce waste, and save customers money.

The Body Shop practices basic good housekeeping: energy efficiency, waste minimization, and utilization of renewable resources whenever possible. This is the very least we can do while we continue the search for ways to reduce our impact on the environment.

The Body Shop believes that profits and principles should go hand in hand. We are against animal testing in the cosmetics industry. We campaign for human and civil rights. We are committed to establishing trading partnerships with indigenous peoples and grass roots communities. And we seek alternatives to the conventional ways of doing business.

BEN & JERRY'S STATEMENT OF MISSION

Ben & Jerry's is dedicated to the creation and demonstration of a new corporate concept of linked prosperity. Our mission consists of three interrelated parts:

- **Product Mission:** To make, distribute and sell the finest quality all natural ice cream and related products in a wide variety of innovative flavors made from Vermont dairy products.
- **Social Mission:** To operate the company in a way that actively recognizes the central role that business plays in the structure of society by innovative ways to improve the quality of life of a broad community: local, national, and international.
- **Economic Mission:** To operate the company on a sound financial basis of profitable growth, increasing value for our shareholders and creating career opportunities and financial rewards for our employees.

Underlying the mission of Ben & Jerry's is the determination to seek new and creative ways of addressing all three parts, while holding a deep respect for individuals, inside and outside the company, and for the communities of which they are a part.

Source: See Web sites (October 1, 2000) www.jnj.com, www.the-body-shop.com, and www.benjerry.com. Raymond E. Miles, Charles C. Snow, John A. Mathews, Grant Miles, and Henry J. Coleman, Jr., "Organizing in the Knowledge Age: Anticipating the Cellular Form," *The Academy of Management Executive*, November 1997, pp. 42–45.

and help one another when needed. To show his own commitment, Kelleher often pitches in to help employees as he travels around doing business. Stories about Kelleher's pitching in are legendary at Southwest. One tells of how Kelleher sat next to mailing operators through one night and later into the morning doing the same work they did. He often gets off at a location, goes down to baggage, and pitches in handling bags. The day before Thanksgiving one year, which is the busiest day of the year, Kelleher worked in baggage all day despite a pouring rain.[9]

---

[9]Alan Farnham, "The Trust Gap," *Fortune*, December 4, 1989, pp. 56–74, 78.

The closeness of the employees at Southwest is expressed as having fun and working hard. One researcher who studied the airline concluded:

> The atmosphere at Southwest Airlines shows that having fun is a value that pervades every part of the organization. Joking, cajoling, and prank-pulling at Southwest Airlines are representative of the special relationships that exist among the employees in the company.[10]

At Southwest fun involves flight attendants singing the safety instructions to passengers and pilots telling jokes over the PA system. On some flights attendants don masks of cartoon characters and entertain the children and parents on flights. Making customers feel comfortable and helping them laugh are considered important at Southwest Airlines.[11]

The strong culture that has evolved at Southwest Airlines was created by the founder and the employees. They make it a distinct culture and influence everyone within the firm.

Popular best-seller books provide anecdotal evidence about the powerful influence of culture on individuals, groups, and processes. Heroes and stories about firms are interestingly portrayed.[12] However, theoretically based and empirically valid research on culture and its impact is still quite sketchy. Questions remain about the measures used to assess culture, and definitional problems have not been resolved. There has also been the inability of researchers to show that a specific culture contributes to positive effectiveness in comparison to less-effective firms with another cultural profile. Comparative cultural studies are needed to better understand how culture impacts behavior.

Creating Organizational Culture

Can a culture be created that influences behavior in the direction management desires? This is an intriguing question. An attempt and an experiment to create a positive, productive culture was conducted in a California electronics firm.[13] Top managers regularly meet to establish the core values of the firm. A document was developed to express the core values as: "paying attention to detail," "doing it right the first time," "delivery defect-free products," and "using open communications." The document of core values was circulated to middle-level managers who refined the statements. Then the refined document was circulated to all employees as the set of guiding principles of the firm.

An anthropologist was in the firm at the time working as a software trainer. He insightfully analyzed what actually occurred in the firm. There was a gap between the management-stated culture and the firm's actual working conditions and practices. Quality problems existed throughout the firm. There was also a strictly enforced chain of command and a top-down-only communication system. The cultural creation experiment was too artificial and was not taken seriously by employees.

---

[10]Keom L. Freiberg, The *Heart and Spirit of Transformation Leadership: A Qualitative Case Study of Herb Kelleher's Passion for Southwest Airlines,* Doctoral Dissertation, University of San Diego, 1987, p. 234.

[11]Eryn Brown, "America's Most Admired Companies," *Fortune,* March 1, 1999, pp. 68–73.

[12]William A. Cohen, *The New Art of the Leader* (Englewood Cliffs, NJ: Prentice-Hall, 2000).

[13]Peter C. Reynolds, "Imposing a Corporate Culture," *Psychology Today,* March 1987, pp. 33–38.

The consequences of creating a culture in the California firm included decreased morale, increased turnover, and a poorer financial performance. Ultimately, the firm filed for bankruptcy and closed its doors.

The California electronics firm case points out that artificially imposing a culture is difficult. Imposing a culture is often met with resistance. It is difficult to simply create core values. Also, when a disparity exists between reality and a stated set of values, employees become confused, irritated, and skeptical. They also usually lack enthusiasm and respect when a false image is portrayed. Creating a culture apparently just doesn't happen because a group of intelligent, well-intentioned managers meet and prepare a document.

John Nordstrom, a Swedish immigrant who settled in Seattle, created the Nordstrom department store culture which rests with the principle that "the customer is always right." The company relies on experienced, acculturated "Nordies" to direct new employees on how to provide superb customer service.[14]

Nordstrom's unique approach to customer service is legendary in the retail industry.

- One customer fell in love with a particular pair of pleated burgundy slacks that were on sale at Nordstrom downtown Seattle store. Unfortunately, the store was out of her size. The sales associate got cash from her department manager, went to a competitor's store across the street, bought the slacks at full price, brought them back, and sold them to the customer at Nordstrom's lower sales price.

- A Nordstrom customer inadvertently left her airline ticket on a counter. The sales associate tried to get the lost ticket problem solved by calling the airline. No luck. She then hailed a cab, headed for the airport, and made a personal delivery to the customer.

The founder started Nordstrom's commitment to customers and today's employees carry on this dedication. The Nordstrom Handbook for employees lists rules as follows:

> **Rule #1: Use your good judgement in all situations.**
> **There will be no additional rules.**

www.wetfeet.com/asp/home.asp
www.nordstrom.com

At Nordstrom the culture has evolved over time and is now embedded in the cultural fabric of the firm. Rituals, history, humor, and common sense have resulted in Nordstrom's being recognized as a leader in how to treat customers. The culture reinforces this leadership role every single day.

Cultures seem to evolve over a period of time as did McDonald's, Walt Disney's, and Nordstrom's. Schein describes this evolution as follows:

> The culture that eventually evolves in a particular organization is . . . a complex outcome of external pressures, internal potentials, responses to critical events, and, probably, to some unknown degree, chance factors that could not be predicted from a knowledge of either the environment or the members.[15]

---

[14]R. Spector and D. McCarthy. *The Nordstrom Way: The Inside Story of America's #1 Customer Service Company* (New York: John Wiley, 1995).

[15]Schein, *Organizational Culture and Leadership*, pp. 83–89.

EXHIBIT 2.2 The Evolution of a Positive Culture

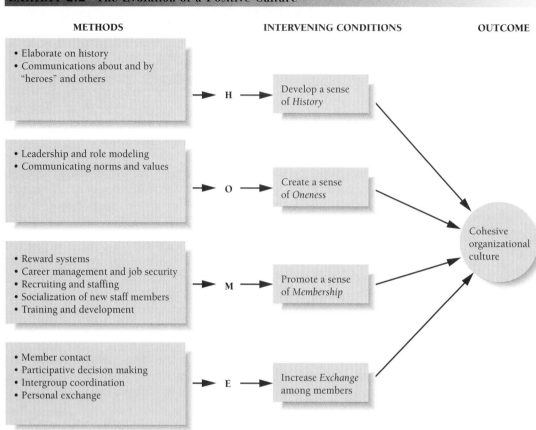

Source: Warren Gross and Shula Shichman, "How to Grow an Organizational Culture," *Personnel,* September 1987, pp. 52–56, © 1987 American Management Association, New York. All rights reserved.

A model that illustrates the evolution of culture and its outcome is presented in Exhibit 2.2. The model emphasizes an array of methods and procedures that managers can use to foster a cohesive culture. In examining this model, recall the California electronics firm and the limited methods it used to generate a quick-fix culture. In Exhibit 2.2 there is an emphasis on the word *home*, which suggests the importance of history, oneness, membership, and exchange among employees.

INFLUENCING CULTURE CHANGE

There is a limited amount of research done on cultural change. The difficulty in creating a culture is made even more complex when attempting to bring about a significant cultural change. The themes that appear in discussing change are these:

- Cultures are so elusive and hidden that they cannot be adequately diagnosed, managed, or changed.
- Because it takes difficult techniques, rare skills, and considerable time to understand a culture and then additional time to change it, deliberate attempts at culture change are not really practical.

EXHIBIT 2.3
Changing Culture
Intervention Points

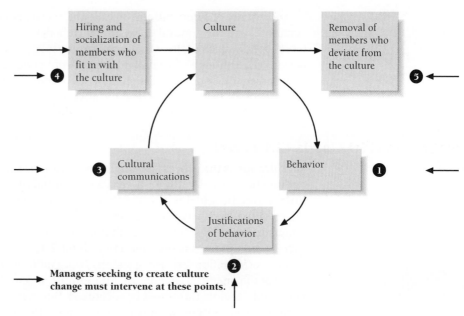

Source: Lisa A. Mainiero and Cheryl L. Tromley, *Developing Managerial Skills in Organizational Behavior* (Englewood Cliffs, NJ: Prentice Hall, 1989), p. 403

- Cultures sustain people throughout periods of difficulty and serve to ward off anxiety. One of the ways they do this is by providing continuity and stability. Thus, people will naturally resist change to a new culture.[16]

These three views suggest that managers who are interested in attempting to produce cultural changes face a difficult task. There are, however, courageous managers who believe that they can intervene and make changes in the culture. Exhibit 2.3 presents a view of five intervention points for managers to consider.[17]

A considerable body of knowledge suggests that one of the most effective ways of changing people's beliefs and values is to first change their behavior (intervention 1).[18] However, behavior change does not necessarily produce culture change because of the process of justification. The California electronics example clearly illustrates this point. Behavioral compliance does not mean cultural commitment. Managers must get employees to see the inherent worth in behaving in a new way (intervention 2). Typically, communications (intervention 3) is the method used by managers to motivate the new behaviors. Cultural communications can include announcements, memos, rituals, stories, dress, and other forms of communications.

---

[16]Joel R. Katzenbach, *The Path to Peak Performance* (Cambridge, MA: Harvard Business School Press 2000).

[17]Vijay Sathe, "Implications of Corporate Culture: A Manager's Guide to Action," *Organizational Dynamics,* Autumn 1983, pp. 4–13.

[18]Charles A. O'Reilly III, Jennifer Chatman, and David F. Caldwell, "People and Organizational Culture: A Profile Comparison to Assessing Person-Organization Fit," *Academy of Management Journal,* September 1991, pp. 487–516.

Another set of interventions include the socialization of new members (intervention 4) and the removal of existing members who deviate from the culture (intervention 5). Each of these interventions must be done after careful diagnoses are performed. Although some individuals may not perfectly fit the firm's culture, they may possess exceptional skills and talents. Weeding out cultural misfits might be necessary, but it should only be done after weighing the costs and benefits of losing talented performers who deviate from the core cultural value system.

SOCIALIZATION AND CULTURE

Socialization is the process by which organizations bring new employees into the culture. In terms of culture, there is a transmittal of values, assumptions, and attitudes from the older to the newer employees. Intervention 4 in Exhibit 2.3 emphasizes the "fit" between the new employee and the culture. Socialization attempts to make this "fit" more comfortable for the employee and the firm. The socialization process is presented in Exhibit 2.4.

The socialization process goes on throughout an individual's career. As the needs of the organization change, for example, its employees must adapt to those new needs; that is, they must be socialized. But even as we recognize that socialization is ever present, we must also recognize that it is more important at some times than at others. For example, socialization is most important when an individual first takes a job or takes a different job in the same organization. The socialization process occurs throughout various career stages, but individuals are more aware of it when they change jobs or change organizations.[19]

Newcomers at Nordstrom encounter the culture norms at the initial employee orientation meeting. They are given a five-inch by eight-inch card which reads:

> **Welcome to Nordstrom: We're glad to have you with our company. Our number-one goal is to provide outstanding customer service. Set both your personal and professional goals high. We have great confidence in your ability to achieve them.[20]**

Socialization Stages

The stages of socialization coincide generally with the stages of a career. Although researchers have proposed various descriptions of the stages of socialization,[21] three stages sufficiently describe it: (1) anticipatory socialization, (2) accommodation, and (3) role management.[22] Each stage involves specific activities that, if undertaken properly, increase the individual's chances of having an effective career. Moreover, these stages occur continuously and often simultaneously.

---

[19]Edgar Schein, *The Corporate Cultural Survival Guide: Sense and Nonsense about Culture Change* (San Francisco: Jossey-Bass, 1999).

[20]Spector and McCarthy, *The Nordstrom Way*, pp. 15–16.

[21]Samuel B. Bacharach, Pete Bamberger, Valerie McKinney, Boundary Management Tactics and Logics of Action: The Case of Peer-Support Providers; *Administrative Science Quarterly*, December 2000, pp. 704–736.

[22]These stages are identified by Daniel C. Feldman, "A Contingency Theory of Socialization," *Administrative Science Quarterly*, September 1967, pp. 434–35. The following discussion is based heavily on this work as well as on Daniel C. Feldman, "A Practical Program for Employee Socialization," *Organizational Dynamics,* Autumn 1976, pp. 64–80; and Daniel C. Feldman, "The Multiple Socialization of Organization Members," *Academy of Management Review,* June 1981, pp. 309–18.

EXHIBIT 2.4
**The Process of
Organizational
Socialization**

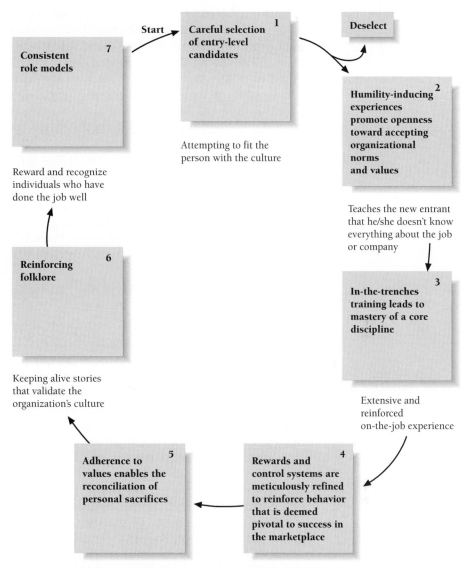

Source: Adapted from R. T. Pascale, "The Paradox of 'Corporate Culture': Reconciling Ourselves to Socialization," *California Management Review,* Winter 1985, p. 38. © by the Regents of the University of California. Reprinted with permission of the Regents.

Anticipatory Socialization

The first stage involves all those activities the individual undertakes prior to entering the organization or to taking a different job in the same organization. The primary purpose of these activities is to acquire information about the new organization and/or new job.

People are vitally interested in two kinds of information prior to entering a new job or organization. First, they want to know as much as they can about what working for the organization is really like. This form of learning about the organization is actually attempting to assess the firm's culture. Second, they want to know whether they are suited to the jobs available in the organization. Individuals seek out this information with considerable effort when they are faced with the decision to take a job, whether it be their first one or one that comes along by way of transfer or promotion. At these times, the information is specific to the job or the organization. We also form impressions about jobs and organizations in less-formal ways. For example, our friends and relatives talk of their experiences. Parents impart both positive and negative information to their offspring regarding the world of work. Although we continually receive information about this or that job or organization, we are more receptive to such information when faced with the necessity to make a decision.

It is desirable, of course, that the information transmitted and received during the anticipatory stage accurately and clearly depicts the organization and the job. However, we know that individuals differ considerably in the way they decode and receive information. Yet if the fit between the individual and the organization is to be optimal, two conditions are necessary: The first condition is *realism*. Both the individual and the organization must portray themselves realistically. The second condition is *congruence*. This condition is present when the individual's skills, talents, and abilities are fully utilized by the job. Either their overutilization or underutilization results in incongruence and, consequently, poor performance.[23]

Accommodation

The second stage of socialization occurs after the individual becomes a member of the organization, after he or she takes the job. During this stage, the individual sees the organization and the job for what they actually are. Through a variety of activities, the individual attempts to become an active participant in the organization and a competent performer on the job. This breaking-in period is ordinarily stressful for the individual because of anxiety created by the uncertainties inherent in any new and different situation. Apparently, individuals who experienced realism and congruence during the anticipatory stage have a less stressful accommodation stage. Nevertheless, the demands on the individual do indeed create situations that induce stress.

Four major activities comprise the accommodation stage: All individuals, to a degree, must engage in (1) establishing new interpersonal relationships with both coworkers and supervisors, (2) learning the task required to perform the job, (3) clarifying their role in the organization and in the formal and informal groups relevant to that role, and (4) evaluating the progress they are making toward satisfying the demands of the job and the role. Readers who have been through the accommodation stage probably recognize these four activities and recall more or less favorable reactions to them.

If all goes well in this stage, the individual feels a sense of acceptance by coworkers and supervisors and experiences competence in performing job tasks. The breaking-in period, if successful, also results in role definition and congruence of evaluation. These four outcomes of the accommodation stage (acceptance, competence, role definition, and congruence of evaluation) are experienced by all new employees to a greater or lesser extent. However, the relative value of each of these outcomes varies from person to person.[24] Acceptance by

---

[23]Feldman, "A Practical Program," pp. 65–66.

[24]Robert T. Carter (ed.), *Addressing Cultural Issues in Organizations: Beyond the Corporate Context* (Thousand Oaks, CA, 2000).

the group may be a less-valued outcome for an individual whose social needs are satisfied off the job, for example. Regardless of these differences due to individual preferences, each of us experiences the accommodation stage of socialization and ordinarily moves on to the third stage.

Role Management

In contrast to the accommodation stage, which requires the individual to adjust to demands and expectations of the immediate work group, the role management stage takes on a broader set of issues and problems. Specifically, during the third stage, conflicts arise. One conflict is between the individual's work and home lives.

For example, the individual must divide time and energy between the job and his or her role in the family. Since the amount of time and energy are fixed and the demands of work and family seemingly insatiable, conflict is inevitable. Employees unable to resolve these conflicts are often forced to leave the organization or to perform at an ineffective level. In either case, the individual and the organization are not well served by unresolved conflict between work and family.

The second source of conflict during the role management stage is between the individual's work group and other work groups in the organization. This source of conflict can be more apparent for some employees than for others. For example, as an individual moves up in the organization's hierarchy, he or she is required to interact with various groups both inside and outside the organization. Each group can and often does place different demands on the individual, and to the extent that these demands are beyond the individual's ability to meet, stress results. Tolerance for the level of stress induced by these conflicting and irreconcilable demands varies among individuals. Generally, the existence of unmanaged stress works to the disadvantage of the individual and the organization.

CHARACTERISTICS OF EFFECTIVE SOCIALIZATION

Organizational socialization processes vary in form and content from organization to organization. Even with the same organization, various individuals experience different socialization processes. For example, the accommodation stage for a college-trained management recruit is quite different from that of a person in the lowest-paid occupation in the organization. As John Van Maanen has pointed out, socialization processes are not only extremely important in shaping the individuals who enter an organization, they are also remarkably different from situation to situation.[25] This variation reflects either lack of attention by management to an important process or the uniqueness of the process as related to organizations and individuals. Either explanation permits the suggestion that, while uniqueness is apparent, some general principles can be implemented in the socialization process.[26]

Effective Anticipatory Socialization

The organization's primary activities during the first stage of socialization are *recruitment* and *selection* and *placement* programs. If these programs are effective,

---

[25]J. Van Maanen, "People Processing: Strategies for Organizational Socialization," *Organizational Dynamics*, Summer 1978, pp. 18–36.

[26]The following discussion reflects the research findings of Feldman, "A Practical Program."

new recruits in an organization should experience the feeling of *realism* and *congruence*. In turn, accurate expectations about the job result from realism and congruence.

Recruitment programs are directed toward new employees, those not now in the organization. It is desirable to give prospective employees information not only about the job but also about those aspects of the organization that affect the individual. It is nearly always easier for the recruiter to stress job-related information to the exclusion of organization-related information. Job-related information is usually specific and objective, whereas organization-related information is usually general and subjective. Nevertheless, the recruiter should, to the extent possible, convey factual information about such matters as pay and promotion policies and practices, objective characteristics of the work group the recruit is likely to join, and other information that reflects the recruit's concerns.

Selection and placement practices, in the context of anticipatory socialization, are important conveyers of information to employees already in the organization. Of prime importance is the manner in which individuals view career paths in organizations. As noted earlier, the stereotypical career path is one that involves advancement up the managerial hierarchy. This concept, however, does not take into account the differences among individuals toward such moves. Greater flexibility in career paths would require the organization to consider lateral or downward transfers.[27]

Effective Accommodation Socialization

Five different activities comprise effective accommodation socialization. They are (1) designing orientation programs, (2) structure training programs, (3) providing performance evaluation information, (4) assigning challenging work, and (5) assigning demanding bosses.

Orientation programs are seldom given the attention they deserve. The first few days on the new job can have very strong negative or positive impacts on the new employee. Taking a new job involves not only new job tasks but also new interpersonal relationships. The new person comes into an ongoing social system which has evolved a unique set of values, ideals, frictions, conflicts, friendships, coalitions, and all the other characteristics of work groups. If left alone, the new employee must cope with the new environment in ignorance, but if given some help and guidance, he or she can cope more effectively.[28]

Thus, organizations should design orientation programs that enable new employees to meet the rest of the employees as soon as possible. Moreover, specific individuals should be assigned the task of orientation. These individuals should be selected for their social skills and be given time off from their own work to spend with the new people. The degree to which the orientation program is formalized can vary, but in any case, the program should not be left to chance.

Training programs are invaluable in the breaking-in stage. Without question, training programs are necessary to instruct new employees in proper techniques and to develop requisite skills. Moreover, effective training programs provide fre-

[27]Gerald R. Ferris (ed.), *Research in Personnel and Human Resources Management* (Stamford, CT: JAI Press, 2000).

[28]Ibid.

quent feedback about progress in acquiring the necessary skills. What is not so obvious is the necessity of integrating formal training with the orientation program.

Performance evaluation, in the context of socialization, provides important feedback about how well the individual is getting along in the organization. Inaccurate or ambiguous information regarding this important circumstance can only lead to performance problems. To avoid these problems, it is imperative that performance evaluation sessions take place in face-to-face meetings between the individual and manager and that in the context of the job the performance criteria must be as objective as possible. Management by objectives and behaviorally anchored rating scales are particularly applicable in these settings.

Assigning challenging work to new employees is a principal feature of effective socialization programs. The first jobs of new employees often demand far less of them than they are able to deliver. Consequently, they are unable to demonstrate their full capabilities, and in a sense they are being stifled. This is especially damaging if the recruiter was overly enthusiastic in "selling" the organization when they were recruited.

Assigning demanding bosses is a practice that seems to have considerable promise for increasing the retention rate of new employees. In this context, *demanding* should not be interpreted as "autocratic." Rather, the boss most likely to get new hires off in the right direction is one who has high but achievable expectations for their performance. Such a boss instills the understanding that high performance is expected and rewarded; equally important, the boss is always ready to assist through coaching and counseling.

Socialization programs and practices intended to retain and develop new employees can be used separately or in combination. A manager is well advised to establish policies most likely to retain those recent hires who have the highest potential to perform effectively. This likelihood is improved if the policies include realistic orientation and training programs, accurate performance evaluation feedback, and challenging initial assignments supervised by supportive, performance-oriented managers.

Effective Role Management Socialization

Organizations that effectively deal with the conflicts associated with the role management stage recognize the impact of such conflicts on job satisfaction and turnover. Even though motivation and high performance may not be associated with socialization activities, satisfaction and turnover are, and organizations can ill-afford to lost capable employees.

Retention of employees beset by off-job conflicts is enhanced in organizations that provide professional counseling and that schedule and adjust work assignments for those with particularly difficult conflicts at work and home. Of course, these practices do not guarantee that employees can resolve or even cope with the conflict. The important point, however, is for the organization to show good faith and make a sincere effort to adapt to the problems of its employees. Exhibit 2.5 summarizes what managers can do to encourage effective socialization.

Mentors and Socialization

In the medical field, young interns learn proper procedures and behavior from established physicians; Ph.D. graduate students learn how to conduct organizational research from professors who have conducted studies. What about the

EXHIBIT 2.5   A Checklist of Effective Socialization PracticesSocialization Stage Practices

Anticipatory socialization	1. Recruitment using realistic job previews
	2. Selection and placement using realistic career paths
Accommodation socialization	1. Tailor-made and individualized orientation programs
	2. Social as well as social skills training
	3. Supportive and accurate feedback
	4. Challenging work assignments
	5. Demanding but fair supervisors
Role management socialization	1. Provision of professional counseling
	2. Adaptive and flexible work assignments
	3. Sincere person-oriented managers

process of learning or working with a senior person called a *mentor* in work settings? In Greek mythology, the mentor was the designation given to a trusted and experienced advisor. Odysseus, absent from home because of the Trojan Wars, charged his servant mentor with the task of educating and guiding his son. In work organizations, a mentor can provide coaching, friendship, sponsorship, and role modeling to a younger, less-experienced protégé. In working with younger or new employees, a mentor can satisfy his or her need to have an influence on another employee's career. Some organizations use mentoring as a means of developing its own leaders. Organizational Encounter 2.1 discusses eight applied principles of mentoring that can work on the job or in the community.

Research has indicated that a majority of managers reported having had at least one mentoring relationship during their careers.[29] Kram has identified two general functions of mentoring which she designated as career functions and psychosocial functions. The career functions include sponsorship, exposure and visibility, coaching, production, and challenging assignments. The psychological functions are role modeling, acceptance and confirmation, counseling, and friendship.[30]

Although mentoring functions can be important in socializing a person, it is not clear that a single individual must play all of these roles. New employees can obtain valuable career and psychosocial influences from a variety of individuals—managers, peers, trainers, and personal friends. At Ford Motor Company, a study was conducted to develop guidelines to socialize new management trainees.

Most mentor-mentee relationships develop over time. There appear to be several distinct phases of mentor-mentee relationships. Exhibit 2.6 presents a four-phase model proposed by Kram. The reasons that cause movement in the relationship are described as turning points. Initiation, cultivation, separation, and redefinition cover general time periods of six months to more than five years.

---

[29]Herminia Ibarra, "Making Partner: A Mentor's Guide for a Psychological Journey," *Harvard Business Review,* March-–April 2000, pp. 146–155.

[30]Kathy E. Kram, "Phases of the Mentor Relationship," *Academy of Management Journal,* December 1983, pp. 608–25.

Eight Ways to Be a Great Mentor

Mentoring is a set of skills for a special relationship, sometimes more honest and more intense than a marriage. To learn more about mentoring principles, Frank Horton is a good place to start. Frank works at a unique nonprofit employment training program called *STRIVE* (Support and Training Results in Valuable Employment), based in Harlem in New York City. Frank has mentored thousands of women and men—many of whom have never held a job. Frank's unique methods have been widely celebrated by the *New York Times*, the *Wall Street Journal*, and two profiles on *60 Minutes*. Here are Frank's tips on how to have one of the greatest relationships in life: a mentor.

1. *The most valuable technique?* It's to understand how much fear the person has. What are they afraid of? Authority figures? Their own inadequacy? That they don't wear the right clothes or have the right background? I determine who they are by what they fear. Then I work on what their fear is.

2. *Don't be afraid to be honest.* People don't really like you unless you challenge them. I look for people's sensitivities, stuff they thought they'd hidden, and I tell people exactly what I see in them. "Oh, you don't do what you're told," I tell them. "Probably because you don't know how to say no, because you grew up thinking that good people don't question authority, they just don't show up and/or they turn passive." It shocks my mentorees to realize I can see through them straight to the heart of their motivations. That's how I gain their confidence. First I get their attention. If you don't gain their respect, they don't see you as important, and they don't learn.

3. *Get a mentor yourself.* The best way to learn how to mentor is to be mentored. My mentor is my boss, Rob Carmona. There are times when I'll call him at two in the morning. It has nothing to do with the job. It has to do with me, how I see me, how I see the world, and what's going around in my head.

4. *Get your mentorees to agree with your style of intervention.* What are the shortfalls in their skills or in their behavior? Then devise a plan, with or without their assistance, to move them forward. And they've

got to buy into the plan. I tell my mentorees, "This is what we're going to do with you." Make it precise. Don't say, "We're going to meet twice a week and talk." Say, "We're gonna meet twice a week, and we're gonna talk about _____."

5. *Don't keep your feelings bottled up.* I don't keep any of it inside. I talk. All the Strive mentors do; we dump it all out. I understand that initially I have to provide the energy. I'm the source. I plug in and get them going. But after awhile my mentorees have to give me something back. If I'm energetic, they have to be just as energetic so that we click and move forward.

6. *Understand that mentoring is a very important relationship, not just for the mentoree but for you.* Sometimes the mentoring relationship is like a marriage. You think with a spouse you share everything? Never. You give people different parts of you. You're different with your wife or your husband than you are with your friends or your family. So there are parts of people you are married to you'll never get to know. A mentor provides a different kind of a relationship. You decided to be with your spouse for your life and with a mentor, maybe a year, maybe two years, and you'll see.

7. *Work at building trust and at feeling it yourself.* I didn't trust people for years because as a child it seemed as if no one was there to help me. I was an angry individual. Coming into Strive has helped me channel that anger into what I do. People see it as passion, which it is, but initially it was just anger at the shortcomings of the world.

8. *Recognize this is a process that's going to change both of you.* A mentor needs to understand that in the process of mentoring, she's going to change as much as the person she's mentoring. You can't come in with this notion of, "Oh, I'm just going to mentor today. It's not going to affect me." It's going to affect you—in a lot of different ways.

Remember, mentoring is not just work. It's a relationship. With any real relationship, you'll want to put all of yourself into it.

Source: *www.village.com/working diva/mentoring/mentor*, October 1, 2000.

EXHIBIT 2.6	Phases of the Mentor Relationship	
Phase	**Definition**	**Turning Points**[*]
Initiation	A period of six months to a year during which time the relationship gets started and begins to have importance for both managers.	Fantasies become concrete expectations.
		Expectations are met; senior manager provides coaching, challenging work, visibility; junior manager provides technical assistance, respect, and desire to be coached.
		There are opportunities for interaction around work tasks.
Cultivation	A period of two to five years during which time the range career and psychosocial functions provided expanded to a maximum.	Both individuals continue to benefit from the relationship.
		Opportunities for meaningful and more frequent interaction increase.
		Emotional bond deepens and intimacy increases.
Separation	A period of six months to two years after a significant change in the structural role relationship and/or in the emotional experience of the relationship.	Junior manager no longer wants guidance but rather the opportunity to work more autonomously.
		Senior manager faces midlife crisis and is less available to provide mentoring functions.
		Job rotation or promotion limits opportunities for continued interaction; career and psychosocial functions can no longer be provided.
		Blocked opportunity creates resentment and hostility that disrupt positive interaction.
Redefinition	An indefinite period after the separation phase, during which time the relationship is ended or takes on significantly different characteristics, making it a more peerlike friendship.	Stresses of separation diminish, and new relationships are formed.
		The mentor relationship is no longer needed on its previous form.
		Resentment and anger diminish; gratitude and appreciation increase.
		Peer status is achieved.

*Examples of the most frequently observed psychological and organizational factors that cause movement into the current relationship phase.

Source: Kathy E. Kram, "Phases of the Mentor Relationship," *Academy of Management Journal,* December 1983, p. 622. Used with permission.

The benefits that result from mentoring can extend beyond the individuals involved. Mentoring can contribute to employee motivation, retention, and the cohesiveness of the organization.[31] The organization's culture can be strengthened by passing the core values from one generation to the next.

The increasing diversity of the workforce adds a new dimension to the mentor-mentee matching process. People are attracted to mentors who talk, look, act, and communicate like them. Gender, race, ethnicity, and religion can all play a role in matching. If mentor-mentee matching is left to occur naturally, women, blacks, Hispanics, and Asians may be left out.[32] The underrepresentation of these groups in management-level positions needs to be evaluated in each firm that considers using mentor-mentee matching. One study showed that cross-gender mentor

---

[31]Ibarra, "Making Partner."

[32]Ibid.

————— **Management Pointer 2.1** —————

MENTORING GUIDELINES

A number of guidelines that can be useful in mentoring programs include:

1. Do not dictate mentoring relationships, but encourage leaders/managers to serve as mentors.

2. Train mentors in how to be effective in mentoring others.

3. Include in the firm's newsletter or in other forms of mass communication (print and electronic) an occasional story of mentoring as reported by a current top-level executive. He or she will explain how a mentor helped them succeed.

4. Inform employees about the benefits and difficulties of mentor relationships with individuals of different gender and race.

5. Make sure there is diversity among the mentors. All mentors should be trained in dealing with diversity.

relationships can be beneficial. The results of 32 mentor-mentee pairings (14 male-female; 18 female-female) found that male-female mentor matchings can be successful.[33]

ORGANIZATIONAL CULTURE AND SOCIETAL VALUE SYSTEMS

Organizations are able to operate efficiently only when shared values exist among the employees. **Values** are the conscious, affective desires or wants of people that guide behavior. An individual's personal values guide behavior on and off the job. If a person's set of values are important, it will guide the person and also enable the person to behavior consistently across situations.

Values are a society's ideas about what is right or wrong—such as the belief that hurting someone physically is immoral. Values are passed from one generation to the next and are communicated through education systems, religion, families, communities, and organizations.[34]

One useful framework for understanding the importance of values in organizational behavior is provided by Hofstede. The result of his research of 116,000 people in 50 countries has been a four-value dimension framework.[35] He proposes four value dimensions: (1) power distance, (2) uncertainty avoidance, (3) individualism, and (4) masculinity.

Power distance is the level of acceptance by a society of the unequal distribution of power in organizations. The extent to which unequal power is accepted by subordinates in organizations differs across countries. In countries in which people display high power distance (e.g., Malaysia), employees acknowledge the boss's authority and typically follow the chain of command. This respectful response results, predictably, in more centralized authority and structure. In countries where people display low power distance (e.g., Denmark), superiors and subordinates are likely to regard one another as equal in power, resulting in a more decentralized and less rigid management structure and style.

The concept of uncertainty avoidance refers to the extent to which people in a society feel threatened by ambiguous situations. Countries with a high level of uncertainty avoidance (e.g., Japan) tend to have specific rules, laws, and procedures. Managers in these countries tend to have a propensity for low-risk decision making, and employees exhibit little aggressiveness. In countries with lower levels of uncertainty avoidance (e.g, Great Britain), organizational activities are less formal, more risk taking occurs, and there is high job mobility.

Individualism refers to the tendency of people to fend for themselves and their family. In countries that value individualism (e.g., United States), individual ini-

[33]Ronald D. Brown, "The Role of Identification in Mentoring Female Protégés," *Group and Organization Studies,* March-June 1986, p. 72.

[34]Geert Hofstede, *Cultures and Organizations,* (New York: McGraw-Hill, 1991), pp. 8–10.

[35]Geert Hofstede, "National Cultures in Four Dimensions," *International Studies of Management and Organization,* Spring-Summer 1983, pp. 31–42.

EXHIBIT 2.7 Cultural Values

	Hofstede's Dimensions				
Region/Country	**Individualism-Collectivism**	**Power Distance**	**Uncertainty Avoidance**	**Masculinity-Femininity**	**Other Dimensions**
North America (USA)	Individualism	Low	Medium	Masculine	
Japan	Collectivism	High and low	High	Masculine and feminine	*Amae* (mutual dependence): authority is respected, but superior must be a warm leader
Europe: Anglo Germanic	Individualism	Low/medium	Low/medium	Masculine	
West Slavic West Urgic Near Eastern	Medium individualism	Low	Medium/high	Medium/high masculine	
Balkanic	Collectivism	High	High	Medium masculine	
Nordic	Medium/high individualism	Low	Low/medium	Feminine	
Latin Europe	Medium/high individualism	High	High	Medium masculine	
East Slavic	Collectivism	Low	Medium	Masculine	
China	Collectivism	Low	Low	Masculine and feminine	Emphasis on tradition, Marxism, Leninism, and Mao Zedong thought
Africa	Collectivism	High	High	Feminine	Colonial traditions; tribal customs
Latin America	Collectivism	High	High	Masculine	Extroverted; prefer orderly customs and procedures

Source: Raghu Nath and Kunal K. Sadhu, "Comparative Analysis, Conclusions, and Future Directions," in *Comparative Management—A Regional View,* Raghu Nath, ed. (Cambridge, M.A.: Ballinger Publishing Company, 1988), p. 273.

tiative and achievement are highly valued and the relationship of the individual with organizations is one of independence.

In countries such as Pakistan, where low individualism exists, one finds tight social frameworks and emotional dependence on belonging to the organization. These countries emphasize collectivism. Japan is a collectivist country in which the will of the group rather than the individual predominates. Collectivist societies value harmony, whereas individualistic cultures value self-respect and autonomy.

Masculinity refers to the degree of traditionally "masculine" values—assertiveness and materialism for others. In comparison, femininity emphasizes "feminine" values—a concern for relationships and the quality of life. In highly masculine societies (e.g., Austria), one finds considerable job stress and conflict between the job and family roles. In countries with low masculinity (e.g., Switzerland), one finds less conflict and stress.

The results of Hofstede's research are shown in what he calls "maps of the world." The maps show at a glance the similarities and differences in work values across nations. A summary of Hofstede's, based on geographical regions, is presented in Exhibit 2.7. The four cultural values dimensions are interdependent and complex.[36] Consequently, the effects of values on workplace productivity, attitudes, and effectiveness are difficult to determine. Managers must be cautious about grossly overgeneralizing. For example, not all Americans value individualism, a low power distance, moderate uncertainty, and masculinity.

A society's values have an impact on organizational values because of the interactive nature of work, leisure, family, and community.[37] American culture has historically given work a central place in the constellation of values. Work remains a source of self-respect and material reward in the United States. Work also serves as a place to achieve personal growth and fulfillment. As the demographics and makeup of the workforce become more culturally diverse, it will become extremely important for managers to learn about the value system and orientations of the changing workforce.[38] Does the value mix change or is it different for African Americans, Mexican Americans, immigrants, physically challenged workers, and others who are increasing in numbers in the society and in the workforce? This is a question that Hofstede's research, new research, and extensive analysis and debate will need to cover more thoroughly in the next few decades.

SOCIALIZING A CULTURALLY DIVERSE WORKFORCE HERE

www.eeoc.gov

The United States society consists of people with many religions, many cultures, and many different roots: African, European, Asian, South American, Middle Eastern, and Indian. Today, African Americans, Asian Americans, and Hispanics constitute about 21 percent of the American population. In 2000, about 51 percent of the total workforce were female.

We hear a lot about diversity, but what it means is sometimes confusing.[39] Diversity is not a synonym for equal employment opportunity (EEO). Nor is it another word for affirmative action. Diversity is the vast array of physical and cultural differences that constitute the spectrum of human differences. Six core dimensions of diversity exist: age, ethnicity, gender, physical attributes, race, and sexual/affectional orientation. These are the core elements of diversity that have a lifelong impact on behavior and attitudes.

---

[36]Simcha Ronen and Oded Shenkar, "Clustering Countries on Attitudinal Dimensions: A Review and Synthesis," *Academy of Management Review,* August 1985, pp. 435–54.

[37]Mary Jo Hatch, "Dynamics of Organizational Culture," *Academy of Management Review,* October 1993, pp. 657–93.

[38]J. Colvin, "The 50 Best Companies for Asians, Blacks, and Hispanics," *Fortune,* September 2000, pp. 53–57.

[39]Robert J. Grossman, "Race in the Workplace," *HR Magazine,* March 2000, pp. 40–45 and David A. Thomas and Suzy Wetlauffer, "A Question of Color: A Debate On Race in the U.S. Workplace," *Harvard Business Review,* September–October 1997, pp. 118–132.

Microsoft of Redmond, Washington, is a firm that places a premium on diversity and has created a culture that reflects the value of differences across people. Microsoft has grown from a small start-up to the largest software firm in the world in a few years. Management at Microsoft believe that its growth is made possible by having a proactive diversity program. A Microsoft philosophy is to make "customers and employees" feel welcome. A diversity staff implements diversity training programs, updates benefits policies, and investigates any cases of discrimination and harassment.[40]

Microsoft's diversity advisory council includes representatives from employee groups of persons with disabilities, women, gay persons, African Americans, Hispanics, American Indians, Jewish Americans, and Asian Indian Americans, and it continually grows as new groups emerge. The council helps Microsoft formulate policy, identify problems, and create a supportive work atmosphere.[41]

Microsoft believes that people from different backgrounds and with a range of talents add to the cultural fabric and the effectiveness of the firm. Microsoft's philosophy is:

> We must make our products assessable to all types of consumers, and therefore we must market them differently to each group. An adverse company is better able to sell to a diverse world.

There are secondary forms of diversity that can be changed. These are differences that people acquire, discard, or modify throughout their lives. Secondary dimensions of diversity include educational background, marital status, religious belief, and work experience.

Valuing diversity from an organizational and leadership perspective means understanding and valuing core and secondary diversity dimension differences between oneself and others. An increasingly important goal in a changing society is to understand that all individuals are different and to appreciate these differences.[42] Diversity Encounter 2.1 offers a few diversity questions that may give you some idea about how much you know or do not know about other races, ethnic groups, and religions.

Management's Ability to Capitalize on Diversity

Due to the changing demographics in the United States, differences in the employee pool are going to continue to increase over the next few decades. Managers will have to study socialization much more closely and intervene so that the maximum benefits result from hiring an increasingly diverse workforce. Studying the ethnic background and national cultures of these workers will have to be taken seriously. The managerial challenge will be to identify ways to integrate the increasing number and mix of people from diverse national cultures into the workplace. Some obvious issues for managers of ethnically diverse workforces to consider are these:

---

[40]Rama D. Jager and Rafael Ortez, *In the Company of Giants* (New York: McGraw-Hill, 1997).

[41]Ibid.

[42]Norma Carr-Ruffino, *Managing Diversity* (Cincinnati, OH: International Thomas Publishing, 1996), pp. 6–8.

Learning About Diversity

Learning about other ethnic groups, races, and religions has become an important organizational issue in terms of showing understanding about the totality of other people. Let's simply list a number of points that students, managers, and people in general should know about.

- **What race are Hispanics?** Black, white, brown? The correct answer is all of the above. *Hispanic* refers not only to a race, but also to an origin or an ethnicity. There are Hispanic segments—Cubans, Puerto Ricans, Mexicans, Salvadorans, and others who are different in their indigenous ancestry, origins, accents, and many other characteristics.
- **What is Confucianism?** Confucianism is the major religious influence on Chinese, Japanese, Korean, and Vietnamese cultures. Confucianism emphasizes response to authority, especially parents and teachers; hard work; discipline and the ability to delay gratification; harmony in relationships; and the importance of the group.
- **Does the term African American apply to all blacks?** No. Black Americans came from different cultures besides those in Africa. Caribbean, Central American, and South American cultures have provided the United States with many talented blacks. Just as there is in the general population, a great variety exists in lifestyle, career choice, educational level attained, and value systems across segments of the over 30 million Black American (includes African and other cultural backgrounds) population.

Should a manager know what the terms *Hispanic, Confucianism,* and *African American* mean? We think so and believe that cultural and religious awareness are going to become more important as the workforce increases in terms of race, ethnic, and religious diversity. Managers and leaders in organizations need to develop a style and pattern of behavior that appeals to and reaches all segments of the diverse workforce. Although the United States has never had a homogeneous culture or population, it is now not possible to ignore the mix of diverse workers, colleagues, customers, suppliers, and owners facing the organization.

Source: Adapted from John Naisbitt, *Global Paradox* (New York: Morrow, 1994), pp. 227–35; Marlene L. Rossman, *Multicultural Marketing* (New York: AMACOM, 1994), pp. 46–52.

- Coping with employees' unfamiliarity with the English language
- Increased training for service jobs that require verbal skills
- Cultural (national) awareness training for the current workforce
- Learning which rewards are valued by different ethnic groups
- Developing career development programs that fit the skills, needs, and values of the ethnic group
- Rewarding managers for effectively recruiting, hiring, and integrating a diverse workforce
- Spending time not only focusing on ethnic diversity, but also learning more about age, gender, and workers with disability diversity

www.merck.com

Socializing involving an ethnically diverse workforce is a two-way proposition. Not only must the manager learn about the employees' cultural background, but the employee must learn about the rituals, customs, and values of the firm or the work unit.[43] Awareness workshops and orientation sessions are becoming more popular every day. Merck has an educational program to raise its employees'

---

[43]G.R. Carroll and M.T. Hannan, *The Demography of Corporations and Industries* (Princeton, NJ: Princton University Press, 2000).

Coping With Stereotypes

You Be the Judge

Asian Americans (Chinese, Filipino, Japanese, Korean, Asian Indian, southeast Asian, and others) must deal with many stereotypes and myths. They have been dealing with overt prejudice since Chinese immigrants first came to the United States over 150 years ago. Today, third- and fourth-generation Asian Americans tend to be very Americanized. As a group, they have higher educational achievement than average. Asian Americans also hold higher-status jobs than average, yet make less income. Why? You be the judge!

awareness and attitudes about women and minorities.[44] The program emphasizes how policies and systems can be tailored to meet changes in the demographics of the workplace. Procter & Gamble has stressed the value of diversity. The firm uses multicultural advisory teams, minority and women's networking conferences, and "onboarding" programs to help new women and minority employees become acclimated and productive as quickly as possible. Ortho Pharmaceutical initiated a program to "manage diversity" that is designed to foster a process of cultural transition within the firm. Northeastern Products Company established an on-site English as a Second Language (ESL) program to meet the needs of Hispanic and Asian employees. A buddy system has been established at Ore-Ida. A buddy (English speaker) is assigned to a new employee (first language is not English) to assist him or her with communication problems.

Global competition, like changing domestic demographics, is placing a new requirement on managers to learn about unfamiliar cultures from which new employees are coming. The emphasis on open expression of diversity in the workforce is paralleled by a social movement toward the retention of ethnic roots. The "new ethnicity," a renewed awareness and pride of cultural heritage, can become an advantage of American firms operating in foreign countries.[45] Using the multicultural workforce to better compete, penetrate and succeed in foreign cultures is one potential benefit of managing diversity effectively.

Certainly, claiming that having employees from different cultural backgrounds only provides benefits is misleading. Ethnic and cultural diversity creates some potential problems like communications, misunderstanding, and responding to authority. The managers involved in this socialization process need to clearly recognize the benefits and the potential problems of working with a more diverse workforce. In the You Be the Judge illustration, there appears to be a problem regarding the status of Asian Americans and the income they earn.

SOCIALIZATION AS AN INTEGRATION STRATEGY

It is possible to view socialization as a form of organizational integration. Specifically, socialization from the integration perspective is a strategy for achieving congruence of organizational and individual goals. Thus, socialization is an important and powerful process for transmitting the organizational culture.[46]

---

[44]David Jamieson and Julie O'Mara, *Managing Workforce 2000* (San Francisco: Jossey-Bass, 1991), pp. 84–89.

[45]Jacqueline A. Gilbert and John M. Ivancevich, "Value Diversity: A Tale of Two Organizations," *Academy of Management Review,* February 2000, pp. 93–105.

[46]Carter, *Addressing Cultural Issues.*

The content of socialization strategies are practices and policies that have appeared in many places throughout this text. Here we can summarize not only our discussion of socialization processes but also cast some important organization behavior concepts and theories in a different framework.

Organizational integration is achieved primarily by aligning and integrating the goals of individuals with the objectives of organizations. The greater the congruity between individual goals and organization objectives, the greater the integration. The socialization process achieves organization integration by, in effect, undoing the individual's previously held goals and creating new ones that come closer to those valued by the organization. In its most extreme form, this undoing process involves debasement techniques such as those experienced by U.S. Marine Corps recruits, military academy plebes, and fraternity and sorority pledges.

Integration of organizational and individual interests can also involve ethical issues. These ethical issues are most evident when the two parties do not share the same information or hold the same legitimate power.

The common thread recommended to organizational leaders in any country is the active role played by the leader and the group members in integrating goals and objectives. Effective socialization, particularly during the accommodation and role management stages, requires joint and supportive efforts of leaders and subordinates alike. The remainder of the book attempts to illustrate that an understanding of organizational and national culture, socialization, and diversity has become an important requirement for achieving effectiveness. Competition, markets, and people are so complex that using the talents and skills of every single worker has become a valued competence of today's leaders within organizations.

Summary of Key Points

- *Culture* is a pattern of assumptions that are invented, discovered, or developed to learn to cope with organizational life. *Socialization* is the process by which organizations bring new employees into the culture. *Career* is the individually perceived sequence of attitudes and behaviors associated with the work-related experiences and activities over the span of the person's life.

- Simply declaring that "this" will be the culture is not realistic. Culture evolves over a period of time. It can be influenced by powerful individuals such as Ray Kroc at McDonald's, Walt Disney, or John Nordstrom, but typically evolves and becomes real when people interact and work together.

- Organizations can achieve effectiveness only when employees share values. The values of an increasingly diverse workforce are shaped long before a person enters an organization. Thus, it is important to recruit, select, and retain employees whose values best fit the values of the firm.

- Socialization is the process by which organizations bring new employees into the culture. There is a passing of values, assumptions, and attitudes from the older to the newer workers.

Review and Discussion Questions

1. Organizational culture is a difficult concept to diagnose. How would you diagnose the culture of an office or a manufacturing plant?

2. A growing number of Americans work for foreign-owned firms in the United States. Do you think that these American employees are being influenced by the approach to management and the culture of the country that owns the firm? Explain.

3. Identify the three socialization stages. Which of these stages is most important for developing high-performing employees? Explain.

4. Since the process of organizational socialization is inevitable, why is it important that it be managed?

5. How can a leader or founder help create a strong culture in an organization? Can any founder create a culture? Explain.

6. Hofstede's research indicates that national cultures exist. Do you believe that in a heterogeneous nation, such as the United States, a national culture that is shared by society does exist?

7. What should managers of diverse workforces know about differences in values among individuals?

8. Point out three assumptions about the culture of the last (or present) firm by which you were employed.

9. What can a leader do to promote cultural change that helps improve the overall effectiveness of an organization?

10. Why is culture so difficult to measure or assess?

READING 2.1 Levels of Culture

11th juror: (rising) "I beg pardon, in discussing. . . ."

10th juror: (interrupting and mimicking) "I beg pardon. What are you so goddam polite about?"

11th juror: (looking straight at the 10th juror) "For the same reason you're not. It's the way I was brought up."

—From Reginald Rose, Twelve Angry Men

Twelve Angry Men is an American theatre piece which became a famous motion picture starring Henry Fonda. The play was written in 1955. The scene consists of the jury room of a New York court of law. Twelve jury members who have never met before have to decide unanimously on the guilt or innocence of a boy from a slum area, accused of murder. The quote above is from the second and final act when emotions have reached a boiling point. It is a confrontation between the tenth juror, a garage owner, and the eleventh juror, a European-born, probably Austrian, watchmaker. The tenth juror is irritated by what he sees as the excessively polite manners of the other man. But the watchmaker cannot behave otherwise. After many years in his new home country, he still behaves the way he was raised. He carries within himself an indelible pattern of behavior.

DIFFERENT MINDS BUT COMMON PROBLEMS

The world is full of confrontations between people, groups, and nations who think, feel, and act differently. At the same time, these people, groups, and nations, just like our twelve angry men, are exposed to common problems which demand cooperation for their solution. Ecological, economical, military, hygienic, and meteorological developments do not stop at national or regional borders. Coping with the threats of nuclear warfare, acid rain, ocean pollution, extinction of animals, AIDS, or a worldwide recession demands cooperation of opinion leaders from many countries. They in their turn need the support of broad groups of followers in order to implement the decisions taken.

Understanding the differences in the ways these leaders and their followers think, feel, and act is a condition for bringing about worldwide solutions that work. Questions of economic, technological, medical, or bio-

Source: Geert Hofstede, *Cultures and Organizations* (New York: McGraw-Hill, 1991), pp. 3–19.

logical cooperation have too often been considered as merely technical. One of the reasons why so many solutions do not work or cannot be implemented is because differences in thinking among the partners have been ignored. Understanding such difference is at least as essential as understanding the technical factors.

The objective of this book is to help in dealing with the differences in thinking, feeling, and acting of people around the globe. It will show that, although the variety in people's minds is enormous, there is a structure in this variety which can serve as a basis for mutual understanding.

CULTURE AS MENTAL PROGRAMMING

Every person carries within him or herself patterns of thinking, feeling, and potential acting which were learned throughout their lifetime. Much of it has been acquired in early childhood, because at that time a person is most susceptible to learning and assimilating. As soon as certain patterns of thinking, feeling, and acting have established themselves within a person's mind, (s)he must unlearn these before being able to learn something different, and unlearning is more difficult than learning for the first time.

Using the analogy of the way in which computers are programmed, this book will call such patterns of thinking, feeling, and acting *mental programs*, or, as the subtitle goes, *"software of the mind."* This does not mean, of course, that people are programmed the way computers are. A person's behavior is only partially predetermined by her or his mental programs: (s)he has a basic ability to deviate from them and to react in ways which are new, creative, destructive, or unexpected. The *"software of the mind"* this book is about only indicates what reactions are likely and understandable, given one's past.

The sources of one's mental programs lie within the social environments in which one grew up and are collected in one's life experiences. The programming starts within the family; *it* continues within the neighborhood, at school, in youth groups, at the workplace, and in the living community. The European watchmaker from the quote at the beginning of this chapter came from a country and a social class in which polite behavior is still at a premium today. Most people from the environment would have reacted as he did. The American garage owner, who worked himself up from the slums, acquired quite different mental programs. Mental programs vary as much as the social environments in which they were acquired.

A customary term for such mental software is *culture*. This word has several meanings, all derived from its Latin source, which refers to the tilling of the soil. In most Western languages, "culture" commonly means "civilization" or "refinement of the mind" and in particular the results of such refinement, like education, art, and literature. This is "culture in the narrow sense": I sometimes call it "culture one." Culture as mental software, however, corresponds to a much broader use of the word which is common among social anthropologists: this is "culture two," and it is the concept which will be used throughout this book.

Social (or cultural) anthropology is the science of human societies, in particular (although not only) traditional or "primitive" ones. In social anthropology, "culture" is a catchword for all those patterns of thinking, feeling, and acting referred to in the previous paragraphs. Not only those activities supposed to refine the mind are included in "culture two," but also the ordinary and menial things in life: greeting, eating, showing or not showing feelings, keeping a certain physical distance form others, making love, or maintaining body hygiene. Politicians and journalists sometimes confuse culture two and culture one without being aware of it: the adaptation problems of immigrants to their new host country are discussed in terms of promoting folk dance groups. But culture two deals with much more fundamental human processes than culture one; it deals with the things that hurt.

Culture (two) is always a collective phenomenon, because it is at least partly shared with people who live or lived within the same social environment, which is where it was learned. It is *the collective programming of the mind which distinguishes the members of one group or category*[1] *of people from another.*[2]

Culture is learned, not inherited. It derives from one's social environment, not from one's genes. Culture should be distinguished from human nature on one side, and from an individual's personality on the other (see Exhibit 2.8), although exactly where the borders lie between human nature and culture, and between culture and personality, is a matter of discussion among social scientist.

Human nature is what all human beings, from the Russian professor to the Australian aborigine, have in common: it represents the universal level in one's mental software. It is inherited with one's genes; within the computer analogy it is the "operating system" which determines one's physical and basic psychological functioning. The human ability to feel fear, anger, love, joy, sadness, the

[1]A *group* means a number of people in contact with each other. A *category* consists of people who, without necessarily having contact, have something in common: e.g., all women managers, or all people born before 1940.

[2]The concept of a "collective programming of the mind" resembles the concept of *habitus* proposed by the French sociologist Pierre Bourdieu: "Certain conditions of existence produce a habitus, a system of permanent and transferable dispositions. A habitus . . . functions as the basis for practices and images . . . which can be collectively orchestrated without an actual conductor." (Bourdieu, 1980, pp. 88–89, translation by GH)

EXHIBIT 2.8

Three Levels of Uniqueness in Human Mental Programming

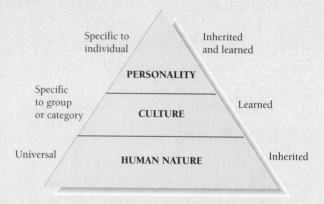

need to associate with others, to play and exercise oneself, the facility to observe the environment and to talk about it with other humans all belong to this level of mental programming. However, what one does with these feelings, how one expresses fear, joy, observations, and so on, is modified by culture. Human nature is not as "human" as the term suggests, because certain aspects of it are shared with parts of the animal world.[3]

The *personality* of an individual, on the other hand, is her/his unique personal set of mental programs which (s)he does not share with any other human being. It is based upon traits which are partly inherited with the individual's unique set of genes and partly learned. "Learned" means: modified by the influence of collective programming (culture) *as well as* unique personal experiences.

Cultural traits have often been attributed to heredity because philosophers and other scholars in the past did not know how to explain otherwise the remarkable stability of differences in culture patterns among human groups. They underestimated the impact of learning from previous generations and of teaching to a future generation what one has learned oneself. The role of heredity is exaggerated in the pseudo-theories of *race*, which have been responsible, among other things, for the Holocaust organized by the Nazis during the Second World War. Racial and ethnic strife is often justified by unfounded arguments of cultural superiority and inferiority.

In the USA, a heated scientific discussion erupted in the late 1960s on whether blacks were genetically less intelligent than whites.[4] The issue became less popular in

[3]"Sociobiology" is an area of study which tries to illustrate how some human social behaviors have analogies in the animal world. From these analogies, sociobiology infers that these social behaviors are biologically (i.e., genetically) determined. See Wilson (1975); for criticisms, see Gregory et al., (eds.) (1978).

[4]The name of Professor A. R. Jensen is linked with the genetic inferiority thesis.

the 1970s, after some researchers had demonstrated that, using the same logic and tests, Asians in the USA on average scored *more* in intelligence than whites. It is extremely difficult, if not impossible, to find tests that are culture free. This means that they reflect only ability, not the differences in, for example, social opportunity. There is little doubt that, on average, blacks in the USA (and other minority and even majority groups in other countries) have fewer *opportunities* than whites.

CULTURAL RELATIVISM

The student of culture finds human groups and categories thinking, feeling, and acting differently, but there are no scientific standards for considering one group as intrinsically superior or inferior to another. Studying differences in culture among groups and societies presupposes a position of cultural relativism.[5] Claude Lévi-Strauss, the grand old man of French anthropology, has expressed it as follows:

> Cultural relativism affirms that one culture has no absolute criteria for judging the activities of another culture as "low" or "noble." However, every culture can and should apply such judgment to its own activities, because is members are actors as well as observers.[6]

Cultural relativism does not imply normlessness for oneself, nor for one's society. It does call for suspending judgment when dealing with groups or societies different from one's own. One should think twice before applying the norms of one person, group, or society to another. Information about the nature of the cultural differences between societies, their roots, and their consequences should precede judgment and action.

Even after having been informed, the foreign observer is still likely to deplore certain ways of the other society. If (s)he is professionally involved in the other society, for example as an expatriate manager or development assistance expert, (s)he may very well want to induce changes. In colonial days, foreigners often wielded absolute power in other societies and they could impose their rules on it. In these postcolonial days, foreigners who want to change something in another society will have to negotiate their interventions. Again, negotiation is more likely to succeed when the parties concerned understand the reasons for the differences in viewpoints.

SYMBOLS, HEROES, RITUALS, AND VALUES

Cultural differences manifest themselves in several ways. From the many terms used to describe manifestations of culture, the following four together cover the total con-

[5]U.S. professor Allan Bloom warns against a cultural relativism in American universities which he calls "nihilism," but he uses the word "culture" in the sense of "culture one." (Bloom, 1988, first published in the U.S. in 1987)

[6]Translation by GH from Lévi-Strauss and Eribon (1988, p. 229).

EXHIBIT 2.9

The "Onion Diagram": Manifestations of Culture at Different Levels of Depth

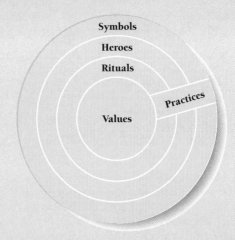

cept rather neatly: symbols, heroes, rituals, and values. In Exhibit 2.9, these are illustrated as the skins of an onion, indicating that symbols represent the most superficial and values the deepest manifestations of culture, with heroes and rituals in between.

Symbols are words, gestures, pictures, or objects that carry a particular meaning which is only recognized by those who share the culture. The words in a language or jargon belong to this category, as do dress, hairstyles, Coca-Cola, flags, and status symbols. New symbols are easily developed and old ones disappear; symbols from one cultural group are regularly copied by others. This is why symbols have been put into the outer, most superficial layer of Exhibit 2.9.

Heroes are persons, alive or dead, real or imaginary, who possess characteristics which are highly prized in a culture, and who thus serve as models for behavior. Even fantasy or cartoon figures, like Batman or, as a contrast, Snoopy in the U.S., Asterix in France, or Ollie B. Bommel (Mr. Bumble) in the Netherlands, can serve as cultural heroes. In this age of television, outward appearances have become more important in the choice of heroes than they were before.

Rituals are collective activities, technically superfluous in reaching desired ends, but which, within a culture, are considered as socially essential; they are therefore carried out for their own sake. Ways of greeting and paying respect to others, and social and religious ceremonies are examples. Business and political meetings organized for seemingly rational reasons often serve mainly ritual purposes, like allowing the leaders to assert themselves.

In Exhibit 2.9, symbols, heroes, and rituals have been subsumed under the term *practices*. As such, they are visible to an outside observer; their cultural meaning, however, is invisible and lies precisely and only in the way these practices are interpreted by the insiders.

The core of culture according to Exhibit 2.9 is formed by *values*. Values are broad tendencies to prefer certain states of affairs over others. Values are feelings with an arrow to it; they have a plus and a minus side. They deal with:

evil vs. good
dirty vs. clean
ugly vs. beautiful
unnatural vs. natural
abnormal vs. normal
paradoxical vs. logical
irrational vs. rational

Values are among the first things children learn—not consciously, but implicitly. Development psychologists believe that by the age of 10, most children have their basic value system firmly in place, and after that age, changes are difficult to make. Because they were acquired so early in our lives, many values remain unconscious to those who hold them. Therefore they cannot be discussed, nor can they be directly observed by outsiders. They can only be inferred from the way people act under various circumstances.

For systematic research on values, inferring them from people's actions is cumbersome and ambiguous. Various paper-and-pencil questionnaires have been developed which ask for people's preferences among alternatives. The answers should not be taken too literally; in practice, people will not always act as they have scored on the questionnaire. Still the questionnaires provide useful information because they show differences in answers between groups or categories of respondents. For example, suppose a question asks for one's preference for time off from work versus more pay. An individual employee who states (s)he prefers time off may in fact choose the money if presented with the actual choice, but if in group A more people claim preferring time off than in group B, this does indicate a cultural difference between these groups in the relative value of free time versus money.

In interpreting people's statements about their values, it is important to distinguish between the *desirable* and the *desired*: how people think the world ought to be versus what people want for themselves. Questions about the desirable refer to people in general and are worded in terms of right/wrong, agree/disagree, or something similar. In the abstract, everybody is in favor of virtue and opposed to sin, and answers about the desirable express people's views about what represents virtue and what corresponds to sin. The desired, on the contrary, is worded in terms of "you" or "me" and what we consider important, what we want for ourselves, including our less-virtuous desires. The desirable bears only a faint resemblance to actual behavior,

but even statements about the desired, although closer to actual behavior, should not necessarily correspond to the way people really behave when they have to choose.

What distinguishes the desirable from the desired is the nature of the *norms* involved. Norms are the standards for values that exist within a group or category of people.[7] In the case of the desirable, the norm is absolute, pertaining to what is ethically right. In the case of the desired, the norm is statistical; it indicates the choices actually made by the majority. The desirable relates more to ideology, the desired to practical matters.

"Interpretations of value studies which neglect the difference between the desirable and the desired may lead to paradoxical results. A case in which the tow produced diametrically opposed answers was found in the IBM studies (see later in this chapter). Employees in different countries were asked for their agreement or disagreement with the statement. "Employees in industry should participate more in the decisions made by management." This is a statement about the desirable. In another question, people were asked whether they personally preferred a manager who "usually consults with subordinates before reaching a decision." This is a statement about the desired. A comparison between the answers to these two questions revealed that employees in countries where the manager who consults was less popular, agreed more with the general statement that employees should participate more, and vice versa; maybe the ideology served as a compensation for the day-to-day relationship with the boss (Hofstede, 1980, p. 109; 1984, p. 82).

LAYERS OF CULTURE

As almost everyone belongs to a number of different groups and categories of people at the same time, people unavoidably carry several layers of mental programming within themselves, corresponding to different levels of culture. For example:

- A national level according to one's country (or countries for people who migrated during their lifetimes);
- A regional and/or ethnic and/or religious and/or linguistic affiliation level, as most nations are composed of culturally different regions and/or ethnic and/or religious and/or language groups;
- A gender level, according to whether a person was born as a girl or as a boy;
- A generation level, which separates grandparents from parents from children;

---

[7]In popular parlance, the words "norm" and "value" are often used indiscriminately, or the twin expression "values and norms" is handled as an inseparable pair, like Laural and Hardy. In this latter case, one of the two words is redundant.

- A social class level, associated with educational opportunities and with a person's occupation or profession; and
- For those who are employed, an organizational or corporate level according to the way employees have been socialized by their work organization.

Additions to this list are easy to make. The mental programs from these various levels are not necessarily in harmony. In modern society they are often partly conflicting: for example, religious values may conflict with generation values, gender values with organizational practices. Conflicting mental programs within people make it difficult to anticipate their behavior in a new situation.

NATIONAL CULTURE DIFFERENCES

Human societies have existed for at least 10,000 years, possibly much longer. Archaeologists believe that the first humans led a nomadic existence as hunter-gatherers. After many thousands of years, some of them settled down as farmers. Gradually, some farming communities grew into larger settlements, which became towns, cities, and finally modern megalopolises like Mexico City with over 25 million inhabitants.

Different human societies have followed this development to different extents, so that hunter-gatherers survive even today (according to some, the modern urban yuppy has reverted to a hunting-gathering state). As the world became more and more populated, an amazing variety of answers was found to the basic question of how people can live together and form some kind of a structured society.

In the fertile areas of the world, large empires had already been built several thousand years ago, usually because the rulers of one part succeeded in conquering other parts. The oldest empire in existence within living memory is China. Although it had not always been unified, the Chinese empire possessed a continuous history of about 4,000 years. Other empires disintegrated: in the eastern Mediterranean and southwestern part of Asia, empires grew, flourished, and fell, only to be succeeded by others: the Sumerian, Babylonian, Assyrian, Egyptian, Persian, Greek, Roman, and Turkish states, to mention only a few. The South Asian subcontinent and the Indonesian archipelago had their empires, such as the Maurya, the Gupta, and later the Moghul in India, and the Majapahit on Java; in Central and South America, the Aztec, Maya, and Inca empires have left their monuments. In Africa, Ethiopia, and Benin are examples of ancient states.

Next to and often within the territory of these larger empires, small units survived in the form of tribes or independent small "kingdoms." Even now, in New Guinea most of the population lives in small and relatively isolated tribes, each with its own language, and hardly integrated into the larger society.

The invention of "nations," political units into which the entire world is divided and to one of which every human being is supposed to belong—as manifested by her or his passport—is a recent phenomenon in human history. Earlier, there were states, but not everybody belonged to one of these or identified with one. The nation system was only introduced worldwide in the mid-twentieth century. It followed the colonial system which had developed during the preceding three centuries. In this colonial period, the technologically advanced countries of Western Europe divided among themselves virtually all the territories of the globe which were not held by another strong political power. The borders between the ex-colonial nations still reflect the colonial legacy. In Africa, particularly, national borders correspond more to the logic of the colonial powers than to the cultural dividing lines of the local populations.

Nations, therefore, should not be equated to *societies.* Historically, societies are organically developed forms of social organization, and the concept of the common culture applies, strictly speaking, more to societies than to nations. Nevertheless, many nations do form historically developed wholes even if they consist of clearly different groups and even if they contain less-integrated minorities.

Within nations that have existed for some time there are strong forces towards further integration: (usually) one dominant national language, common mass media, a national education system, a national army, a national political system, national representation in sports events with a strong symbolic and emotional appeal, a national market for certain skills, products, and services. Today's nations do not attain the degree of internal homogeneity of the isolated, usually nonliterate societies studied by field anthropologists, but they are the source of a considerable amount of common mental programming of their citizens.[8]

On the other hand, there remains a tendency for ethnic, linguistic, and religious groups to fight for recognition of their own identity, if not for national independence; this tendency has been increasing rather than decreasing in the latter part of the twentieth century. Examples are the Ulster Roman Catholics, the Belgian Flemish, the Basques in Spain and France, the Kurds in Iran, Iraq, Syria, and Turkey, and many of the ethnic groups in the Soviet Union.

In research on cultural differences, nationality— the passport one holds—should therefore be used with care.

---

[8]Some nations are less culturally integrated than others. Examples are some of the ex-colonies and multilingual, multiethnic countries such as Yugoslavia, Belgium, or Malaysia. Yet even in these countries, ethnic and/or linguistic groups which consider themselves as very different from each other may have common traits in comparison to the populations of other countries. I have shown this to be the case for the two language groups of Belgium. (1980, pp. 335ff; 1984, pp. 228ff)

Yet it is often the only feasible criterion for classification. Rightly or wrongly, collective properties are ascribed to the citizens of certain countries; people refer to "typically American," "typically German," or "typically Japanese" behavior. Using nationality as a criterion is a matter of expediency, because it is immensely easier to obtain data for nations than for organic homogeneous societies. Nations as political bodies supply all kinds of statistics about their populations. Survey data, i.e., the answers of people on paper-and-pencil questionnaires related to their culture, are also mostly collected through national networks. Where it is possible to separate results by regional, ethnic, or linguistic group, this should be done.

A strong reason for collecting data at the level of nations is that one of the purposes of the research is to promote cooperation among nations. As was argued at the beginning of this chapter, the (over 200) nations that exist today populate one single world and we either survive or perish together. So it makes practical sense to focus on cultural factors separating or uniting nations.

DIMENSIONS OF NATIONAL CULTURES

In the first half of the twentieth century, social anthropology has developed the conviction that all societies, modern or traditional, face the same basic problems; only the answers differ. American anthropologists, in particular Ruth Benedict (1887–1948) and Margaret Mead (1901–1978), played an important role in popularizing this message for a wide audience.

The logical next step was that social scientists attempted to identify *what* problems were common to all societies, through conceptual reasoning and reflection upon field experiences, as well as through statistical studies. In 1954, two Americans, the sociologist Alex Inkeles and the psychologist Daniel Levinson, published a broad survey of the English-language literature on national culture. They suggested that the following issues qualify as common basic problems worldwide, with consequences for the functioning of societies, of groups within those societies, and of individuals within those groups:

1. Relation to authority.
2. Conception of self, in particular:
   a. The relationship between individual and society; and
   b. The individual's concept of masculinity and femininity.
3. Ways of dealing with conflicts, including the control of aggression and the expression of feelings. (Inkeles and Levinson, 1969, pp. 447ff.)

Twenty years later I was given the opportunity of studying a large body of survey data about the values of people in over 50 countries around the world. These people worked in the local subsidiaries of one large multinational corporation—IBM. At first sight, it may seem surprising that employees of a multinational—a very special kind of people—could serve for identifying difference in *national* value systems. However, from one country to another they represent almost perfectly matched samples; they are similar in all respects except nationality, which makes the effect of nationality differences in their answers stand out unusually clearly.

A statistical analysis of the answers on questions about the values of similar IBM employees in different countries revealed common problems, but with solutions differing from country to country, in the following areas:

1. Social inequality, including the relationship with authority;
2. The relationship between the individual and the group;
3. Concepts of masculinity and femininity—the social implications of having been born as a boy or a girl; and
4. Ways of dealing with uncertainty, relating to the control of aggression and the expression of emotions.

These empirical results covered amazingly well the areas predicted by Inkeles and Levinson 20 years before. The discovery of their prediction provided strong support for the theoretical importance of the empirical findings. Problems which are basic to all human societies should turn up in different studies regardless of the approaches followed. The Inkeles and Levinson study is not the only one whose conclusions overlap with mine, but it is the one that most strikingly predicts what I found.[9]

The four basic problem areas defined by Inkeles and Levinson and empirically found in the IBM data represent *dimensions* of cultures. A dimension is an aspect of a culture that can be measured relative to other cultures. The basic problem areas correspond to dimensions which I named *power distance* (from small to large), *collectivism* versus *individualism*, *femininity* versus *masculinity*, and *uncertainty avoidance* (from weak to strong). Each of these terms existed already in some part of the social sciences, and they seemed to apply reasonably well to the basic problem area each dimension stands for. Together they form a four-dimensional (4-D) model of differences among national cultures. Each country in this model is characterized by a score on each of the four dimensions.

A dimension groups together a number of phenomena in a society which were empirically found to occur in combination, even if at first sight there does not always seem to be a logical necessity for their going together. The logic of societies, however, is not the same as the logic of the individuals looking at them. The grouping of the different aspects of a dimension is always based on statistical

---

[9]See Hofstede (1980 or 1984) for the first analysis covering 40 countries, and Hofstede (1983, pp. 335–55) for a later extension.

relationships, that is, on *trends* for these phenomena to occur in combination, not on iron links. Some aspects in some societies may go against a general trend found across most other societies. Because they are found with the help of statistical methods, dimensions can only be detected on the basis of information about a certain number of countries—say, at least 10. In the case of the IBM research, I was fortunate to obtain comparable data about culturally determined values from 50 countries and three multi-country regions, which made the dimensions within their differences stand out quite clearly.

More recently, a fifth dimension of differences among national cultures was identified, opposing a *long-term orientation* in life to a *short-term orientation*. The fact that it had not been encountered earlier can be attributed to a cultural bias in the minds of the various scholars studying culture, including myself. We all shared a "Western" way of thinking. The new dimension was discovered when Michael Harris Bond, a Canadian located in the Far East for many years, studied people's values around the world using a questionnaire composed by "Eastern," in this case Chinese, minds. Besides adding this highly relevant new dimension, Bond's work showed the all-pervading impact of culture; even the minds of the researchers studying it are programmed according to their own particular cultural framework.

The scores for each country on one dimension can be pictured as points along a line. For two dimensions at a time, they become points in a diagram. For three dimensions, they could, with some imagination, be see as points in space. For four or five dimensions, they become difficult to envisage. This is a disadvantage of the dimensional model. Another way of picturing differences among countries (or other social systems) is through *typologies* instead of dimensions. A typology describes a number of ideal types, each of them easy to imagine. Dividing countries into the First, Second, and Third World is such a typology. A more sophisticated example is found in the work of the French political historian Emmanuel Todd, who divides the cultures of the world according to the family structure traditionally prevailing in that culture. He arrives at eight types, four of which occur in Europe. Todd's thesis is that these historically preserved family structures explain the success of a particular type of political ideology in a country (Todd, 1983).

Whereas typologies are easier to grasp than dimensions, they are still problematic in empirical research. Real cases seldom fully correspond to one single ideal type. Most cases are hybrids, and arbitrary rules have to be made for classifying them as belonging to one of the types. With a dimensional model, on the contrary, cases can always be scored unambiguously. On the basis of their dimension scores, cases can *afterwards* empirically be sorted into clusters with similar scores. These clusters then form an empirical typology. More than 50 countries in the IBM study could, on the basis of their 4-D scores, be sorted into 13 such clusters.[10]

In practice, typologies and dimensional models can be considered as complementary. Dimensional models are preferable for research but typologies for teaching purposes. This book will use a kind of typology approach for explaining each of the five dimensions. For every separate dimension, it describes the two opposite extremes, which can be seen as ideal types. Some of the dimensions are subsequently taken two by two, which creates four ideal types. However, the country scores on the dimensions will show that most real cases are somewhere in between the extremes pictured.

CULTURAL DIFFERENCES ACCORDING TO REGION, RELIGION, GENDER, GENERATION, AND CLASS

Regional, ethnic, and *religious* cultures account for differences within countries; ethnic and religious groups often transcend political country borders. Such groups form minorities at the crossroads between the dominant culture of the nation and their own traditional group culture. Some assimilate into the mainstream, although this may take a generation or more; others continue to stick to their own ways. The U.S. as the world's most prominent example of a people composed of immigrants, shows examples of both assimilation (the "melting pot") and retention of group identities over generations (an example are the Pennsylvania Dutch). Discrimination according to ethnic origin delays assimilation and represents a problem in many countries. Regional, ethnic, and religious cultures can be described in the same terms as national cultures, basically, the same dimensions which were found to differentiate among national cultures apply to these differences within countries.

Religious affiliation by itself is less culturally relevant than is often assumed. If we trace the religious history of countries, then the religion a population has embraced along with the version of that religion seem to have been a *result* of previously existing cultural value patterns as much as a *cause* of cultural differences. The great religions of the world, at some time in their history, have all undergone profound schisms: between Roman Catholics, Easter Orthodox, and various Protestant groups in Christianity; between Sunni and Shia in Islam; between liberals and various fundamentalist groups in Jewry; between Hinayana and Mahayana in Buddhism. Cultural differences among groups of believers have always plays a major role in such schisms. For example, the Reformation movement within the Roman Catholic Church in the sixteenth century initially affected all of Europe. However, in

---

[10]Hofstede (1980, p. 334; 1984, p. 229) shows 11 clusters among the first 40 countries studied, and the later article in Hofstede (1983, p. 346) extends this to 13 clusters among 50 countries and three regions.

countries which more than a thousand years earlier had belonged to the Roman Empire, a Counter-Reformation reinstated the authority of the Roman church. In the end, the Reformation only succeeded in countries without a Roman tradition. Although today most of Northern Europe is Protestant and most of Southern Europe Roman Catholic, it is not this religious split which is at the origin of the cultural differences between North and South but the inheritance of the Roman Empire. This does not exclude that once a religion has settled, it does reinforce the value patterns on the basis of which it was adopted by making these into core elements in its teachings.

Gender differences are not usually described in terms of cultures. It can be revealing to do so. If we recognize that within each society there is a men's culture which differs from a women's culture, this helps to explain why it is so difficult to change traditional gender roles. Women are not considered suitable for jobs traditionally filled by men, not because they are technically unable to perform these jobs, but because women do not carry the symbols, do not correspond to the hero images, do not participate in the rituals or foster the values dominant in the men's culture; and vice versa. Feelings and fears about behaviors by the opposite sex are of the same order of intensity as the reactions of people exposed to foreign cultures.

Generation differences in symbols, heroes, rituals, and values are evident to most people. They are often overestimated. Complaints about youth having lost respect for the values of their elders have been found on Egyptian papyrus scrolls dating from 2000 BC and in the writings of Hesiod, a Greek author from the end of the eighth century BC. Many differences in practices and values between generations will be just normal attributes of age which repeat themselves for each successive pair of generations. Historical events, however, do affect some generations in a special way. The Chinese who were of student age during the Cultural Revolution stand witness to this. The development of technology also leads to a difference between generations which is unique.

Not all values and practices in a society, however, are affected by technology or its products. If young Turks drink Coca-Cola, this does not necessarily affect their attitudes toward authority. In some respects, young Turks differ from old Turks, just as young Americans differ from old Americans. Such differences often involve the relatively superficial spheres of symbols and heroes, of fashion and consumption. In the sphere of values, i.e., fundamental attitudes towards life and towards other people, young Turks from young Americans just as much as old Turks differ from old Americans. There is no evidence that the cultures of present-day generations from different countries are converging.

Social classes carry different class cultures. Social class is associated with educational opportunities and with a person's occupation or profession; this even applies in countries which their governments call socialist, preaching a classless society. Education and occupation are in themselves powerful sources of cultural learning. There is no standard definition of social class which applies across all countries, and people in different countries distinguish different types and numbers of class. The criteria for allocating a person to a class are often cultural; symbols play an important role, such as accents in speaking the national language, the use and nonuse of certain words, and manners. The confrontation between the two jurors in *Twelve Angry Men* also contains a class component.

Gender, generation, and class cultures can only partly be classified by the four dimensions found for national cultures. This is because they are not *groups* but *categories* of people. Countries (and ethnic groups too) are integrated social systems. The four dimensions apply to the basic problems of such systems. Categories like gender, generation, or class are only parts of social systems and therefore not all dimensions apply to them. Gender, generation, and class cultures should be described in their own terms, based on special studies of such cultures.

ORGANIZATIONAL CULTURES

Organizational or corporate cultures have been a fashionable topic since the early 1980s. At that time, the management literature began to popularize the claim that the "excellence" of an organization is contained in the common ways by which its members have learned to think, feel and act. "Corporate culture" is a soft, holistic concept with, however, presumed hard consequences. I once called it "the psychological assets of an organization, which can be used to predict what will happen to its financial assets in five years' time."

Organization sociologists have stressed the role of the soft factor in organizations for more than half a century. Using the label "culture" for the shared mental software of the people in an organization is a convenient way of repopularizing these sociological views. Yet organizational "cultures" are a phenomenon *per se*, different in many respects from national cultures. An organization is a social system of a different nature than a nation; if only because the organization's members usually had a certain influence in their decision to join it, are only involved in it during working hours, and may one day leave it again.

Research results about national cultures and their dimensions proved to be only partly useful for the understanding of organizational cultures. The part of this book which deals with organizational culture differences is not based on the IBM studies but on a special research project carried out by IRIC, the Institute for Research on Intercultural Cooperation, within 20 organizational units in Denmark and the Netherlands.

Exercises

EXERCISE 2.1   Assessing and Considering Organizational Culture

Listed below are what two researchers refer to as specific manifestations of organizational culture. Enterprises over a period of time illustrate or use these cultural factors to strengthen and perpetuate the culture. Some of the widely publicized firms such as Harley-Davidson, Merck, Nike, Compaq Computer, Intel, Amazon.com, Oracle, Honda, Nestlé, Hershey, and Coca-Cola have distinct and strongly influential cultures.

Rite | A relatively elaborate, dramatic planned set of activities that combines various forms of cultural expressions and that often has both practical and expressive consequences.

Ritual | A standardized, detailed set of techniques and behaviors that manages anxieties but seldom produces intended, practical consequences of any importance.

Myth | A dramatic narrative of imagined events, usually used to explain origins or transformations of something; also, an unquestioned belief about the practical benefits of certain techniques and behaviors that is not supported by demonstrated facts.

Saga | A historical narrative of some wonderful event that has a historical basis but has been embellished with fictional details.

Folktale | A completely fictional narrative.

Symbol | Any object, act, event, quality, or relation that serves as a vehicle for conveying meaning, usually by representing another thing.

Language | A particular manner in which members of a group use vocal sounds and written signs to convey meanings to each other.

Gesture | Movements of parts of the body used to express meanings.

Physical setting | Those things that physically surround people and provide them with immediate sensory stimuli as they carry out culturally expressive activities.

Artifact | Material objects manufactured by people to facilitate culturally expressive activities.

The instructor will divide the class into groups of five or six to discuss each of manifestations in terms of: (1) a firm the students have worked in and (2) a popular firm such as the widely publicized enterprises listed above. The groups should also discuss the following:

1. How managers can influence the cultural factors listed in the table.
2. Which of the factors listed in the table apply to the school/university they are now attending.
3. Why culture can influence the morale of employees.

The exercise can be completed in one or two classes (45–90 minutes). After the group discusses the questions and issues in the first class, a second class can be used to review each of the group's considerations and findings.

Exercises

EXERCISE 2.2   Determining your Diversity Quotient (DQ)

Lee Gardenswartz and Anita Rowe are well-known and highly regarded diversity management trainers and advocates. They have developed a number of interesting approaches to managing diverse work groups. Listed below is a short nine-item diversity quotient scale. Take the short questionnaire and score your own answers. The DQ could be used by the instructor as a discussion starter in class.

Source: Adapted from Lee Gardenswartz and Anita Rowe, "What's Your Diversity Quotient?" *Managing Diversity Newsletter*, Jamestown, New York (undated).

DIVERSITY QUESTIONNAIRE

Directions

Indicate your views by placing a T (true) next to each of these nine statements.

1. I know about the rules and customs of several different cultures.   _____
2. I know that I hold stereotypes about other groups.   _____
3. I feel comfortable with people of different backgrounds from my own.   _____
4. I associate with people who are different from me.   _____
5. I find working on a multicultural team satisfying.   _____
6. I find change stimulating and exciting.   _____
7. I enjoy learning about other cultures.   _____
8. When dealing with someone whose English is limited, I show patience and understanding.   _____
9. I find that spending time building relationships with others is useful because more gets done.   _____

Interpretation

The more true responses you have, the more adaptable and open you are to diversity.

If you have five or more true responses, you probably are someone who finds value in cross-cultural experiences.

If you have less than five true responses, you may be resistant to interacting with people who are different from you. If that is the case, you may find that your interactions with others are sometimes blocked.

Cases

CASE 2.1   The Consolidated Life Case: Caught between Corporate Cultures

PART I

It all started so positively. Three days after graduating with his degree in business administration, Mike Wilson started his first day at a prestigious insurance company—Consolidated Life. He worked in the Policy Issue Department. The work of the department was mostly clerical and did not require a high degree of technical knowledge. Given the repetitive and mundane nature of the work, the successful worker had to be consistent and willing to grind out paperwork.

Rick Belkner was the division's vice president, "the man in charge" at the time. Rick was an actuary by training, a technical professional whose leadership style was laissez-faire. He was described in the division as "the mirror of whomever was the strongest personality around him." It was also common knowledge that Rick made $60,000 a year while he spent his time doing crossword puzzles.

Mike was hired as a management trainee and promised a supervisory assignment within a year. However, because of a management reorganization, it was only six weeks before he was placed in charge of an eight-person unit.

The reorganization was intended to streamline workflow, upgrade and combine the clerical jobs, and make greater use of the computer system. It was a drastic depar-ture from the old way of doing things and created a great deal of animosity and anxiety among the clerical staff.

Management realized that a flexible supervisory style was necessary to pull off the reorganization without immense turnover, so they gave their supervisors a free hand to run their units as they saw fit. Mike used this latitude to implement group meetings and training classes in his unit. In addition he assured all members raises if they worked hard to attain them. By working long hours, participating in the mundane tasks with his unit, and being flexible in his management style, he was able to increase productivity, reduce errors, and reduce lost time. Things improved so dramatically that he was noticed by upper management and earned a reputation as a "superstar" despite being viewed as free spirited and unorthodox. The feeling was that his loose, people-oriented management style could be tolerated because his results were excellent.

A CHANCE FOR ADVANCEMENT

After a year, Mike received an offer from a different Consolidated Life division located across town. Mike was asked to manage an office in the marketing area. The pay was excellent and it offered an opportunity to turn around an office in disarray. The reorganization in his present division at Consolidated was almost complete and most of his mentors and friends in management had moved on to other jobs. Mike decided to accept the offer.

In his exit interview he was assured that if he ever wanted to return, a position would be made for him. It

Source: Joseph Weiss, Mark Wahlstrom, and Edward Marshall, *Journal of Management Case Studies*, Fall 1986, pp. 238–43.

was clear that he was held in high regard by management and staff alike. A huge party was thrown to send him off.

The new job was satisfying for a short time but it became apparent to Mike that it did not have the long-term potential he was promised. After brining on a new staff, computerizing the office, and auditing the books, he began looking for a position that would both challenge him and give him the autonomy he needed to be successful.

Eventually word got back to his former vice president, Rick Belkner, at Consolidated Life that Mike was looking for another job. Rick offered Mike a position with the same pay he was now receiving and control over a 14-person unit in his old division. After considering other options, Mike decided to return to his old division feeling that he would be able to progress steadily over the next several years.

ENTER JACK GREELY; RETURN MIKE WILSON

Upon his return to Consolidated Life, Mike became aware of several changes that had taken place in the six months since his departure. The most important change was the hiring of a new divisional senior vice president, Jack Greely. Jack had been given total authority to run the division. Rick Belkner now reported to Jack.

Jack's reputation was that he was tough but fair. It was necessary for people in Jack's division to do things his way and "get the work out."

Mike also found himself reporting to one of his former peers, Kathy Miller, who had been promoted to manager during the reorganization. Mike had always "hit it off" with Kathy and foresaw no problems in working with her.

After a week, Mike realized the extent of the changes that had occurred. Gone was the loose, casual atmosphere that had marked his first tour in the division. Now, a stricter, task-oriented management doctrine was practiced. Morale of the supervisory staff had decreased to an alarming level. Jack Greely was the major topic of conversation in and around the division. People joked that MBO now meant "management by oppression."

Mike was greeted back with comments like "Welcome to prison" and "Why would you come back here? You must be desperate!" It seemed like everyone was looking for new jobs or transfers. Their lack of desire was reflected in the poor quality of work being done.

MIKE'S IDEA: SUPERVISORS' FORUM

Mike felt that a change in the management style of his boss was necessary in order to improve a frustrating situation. Realizing that it would be difficult to affect his style directly, Mike requested permission from Rick Belkner to form a Supervisors' Forum for all managers on Mike's level in the division. Mike explained that the purpose would be to enhance the existing management-training program. The Forum would include weekly meetings, guest speakers, and discussions of topics relevant to the division and the industry. Mike thought the forum would show Greely that he was serious about both his job and improving morale in the division. Rick gave the OK for an initial meeting.

The meeting took place and 10 supervisors who were Mike's peers in the company eagerly took the opportunity to "Blue Sky" it. There was a euphoric attitude about the group as they drafted their statement of intent. It read as follows:

TO: Rick Belkner
FROM: New Issue Services Supervisors
SUBJECT: Supervisors' Forum

On Thursday, June 11, the Supervisors' Forum held its first meeting. The objective of the meeting was to identify common areas of concern among us and to determine topics that we might be interested in pursuing.

The first area addressed was the void that we perceived exists in the management-training program. As a result of conditions beyond anyone's control, many of us over the past year have held supervisory duties without the benefit of formal training or proper experience. Therefore, what we propose is that we utilize the Supervisors' Forum as a vehicle with which to enhance the existing management-training program. The areas that we hope to affect with this supplemental training are: a) morale/job satisfaction; b) quality of work and service; c) productivity; and d) management expertise as it relates to the life insurance industry. With these objectives in mind, we have outlined below a list of possible activities that we would like to pursue.

1. Further utilization of the existing "in-house" training programs provided for manager trainees and supervisors, i.e., Introduction to Supervision, E.E.O., and Coaching and Counseling.

2. A series of speakers from various sections in the company. This would help expose us to the technical aspects of their departments and their managerial style.

3. Invitations to outside speakers to address the Forum on management topics such as managerial development, organizational structure and behavior, business policy, and the insurance industry. Suggested speakers could be area college professors, consultants, and state insurance officials.

4. Outside training and visits to the field. This could include attendance at seminars concerning management theory and development relative to the insurance industry. Attached is a representative sample of a program we would like to have considered in the future.

In conclusion, we hope that this memo clearly illustrates what we are attempting to accomplish with this program. It is our hope that the above outline will be able to give the Forum credibility and establish it as an effective tool for all levels of management within New Issue. By supplementing our on-the-job training with a series of speakers and classes, we aim to develop prospective management personnel with a broad perspective of both the life insurance industry and management's role in it. Also, we would like to extend an invitation to the underwriters to attend any programs at which the topic of the speaker might be of interest to them.

cc: J. Greely
                                         Managers

The group felt the memo accurately and diplomatically stated their dissatisfaction with the current situation. However, they pondered what the results of their actions would be and what else they could have done.

PART II

An emergency management meeting was called by Rick Belkner at Jack Greely's request to address the "union" being formed by the supervisors. Four general managers, Rick Belkner, and Jack Greely were at that meeting. During the meeting it was suggested the Forum be disbanded to "put them in their place." However, Rick Belkner felt that, if "guided" in the proper direction, the Forum could die from lack of interest. His stance was adopted but it was common knowledge that Jack Greely was strongly opposed to the group and wanted its founders dealt with. His comment was, "It's not a democracy and they're not a union. If they don't like it here, then they can leave." A campaign was directed by the managers to determine who the main authors of the memo were so they could be dealt with.

About this time, Mike's unit had made a mistake on a case, which Jack Greely was embarrassed to admit to his boss. This embarrassment was more than Jack Greely cared to take from Mike Wilson. At the managers' staff meeting that day, Jack stormed in and declared that the next supervisor to "screw up" was out the door. He would permit no more embarrassments of his division and repeated his earlier statement about "people leaving if they didn't like it here." It was clear to Mike and everyone else present that Mike Wilson was a marked man.

Mike had always been a loose, amiable supervisor. The major reason his units had been successful was the attention he paid to each individual and how they interacted with the group. He had a reputation for fairness, was seen as an excellent judge of personnel for new positions, and was noted for his ability to turn around people who had been in trouble. He motivated people through a dynamic, personable style and was noted for his general lack of re-

gard for rules. He treated rules as obstacles to management and usually used his own discretion as to what was important. His office had a sign saying "Any fool can manage by rules. It takes an uncommon man to manage without any." It was an approach that flew in the face of company policy, but it had been overlooked in the past because of his results. However, because of Mike's actions with the Supervisors' Forum, he was now regarded as a thorn in the side, not a superstar, and his oddball style only made things worse.

Faced with the fact that he was rumored to be out the door, Mike sat down to appraise the situation.

PART III

Mike decided on the following course of action:

1. Keep the Forum alive but moderate its tone so it didn't step on Jack Greely's toes.
2. Don't panic. Simply outwork and outsmart the rest of the division. This plan included a massive retraining and remotivation of his personnel. He implemented weekly meetings, cross training with other divisions, and a lot of interpersonal "stroking" to motivate the group.
3. Evoke praise from vendors and customers through excellent service and direct that praise to Jack Greely.

The results after eight months were impressive. Mike's unit improved the speed of processing 60 percent and lowered errors 75 percent. His staff became the most highly trained in the division. Mike had a file of several letters to Jack Greely that praised the unit's excellent service. In addition, the Supervisors' Forum had grudgingly attained credibility, although the scope of activity was restricted. Mike had even improved to the point of submitting reports on time as a concession to management.

Mike was confident that the results would speak for themselves. However, one month before his scheduled promotion and one month after an excellent merit raise in recognition of his exceptional work record, he was called into his supervisor's, Kathy Miller's, office. She informed him that after long and careful consideration the decision had been made to deny his promotion because of his lack of attention to detail. This did not mean he was not a good supervisor, just that he needed to follow more instead of taking the lead. Mike was stunned and said so. But, before he said anything else, he asked to see Rick Belkner and Jack Greely the next day.

THE SHOWDOWN

Sitting face to face with Rick and Jack, Mike asked if they agreed with the appraisal Kathy had discussed with him. They both said they did. When asked if any other supervisor surpassed his ability and results, each stated

Mike was one of the best, if not *the* best they had. Then why, Mike asked, would they deny him a promotion when others of less ability were approved. The answer came from Jack: "It's nothing personal, but we just don't like you. We don't like your management style. You're an odd-ball. We can't run a division with 10 supervisors all doing different things. What kind of a business do you think we're running here? We need people who conform to our style and methods so we can measure their results objectively. There is no room for subjective interpretation. It's our feeling that if you really put your mind to it, you can be an excellent manager. It's just that you now create trouble and rock the boat. We don't need that. It doesn't matter if you're the best now, sooner or later as you go up the ladder, you will be forced to pay more attention to administrative duties and you won't handle them well. If we correct your bad habits now, we think you can go far."

Mike was shocked. He turned to face Rick and blurted out nervously, "You mean it doesn't mater what my results are? All that matters is how I do things?" Rick leaned back in his chair and said in a casual tone, "In so many words, Yes."

Mike left the office knowing that his career at Consolidated was over and immediately started looking for a new job. What had gone wrong?

EPILOGUE

After leaving Consolidated Life, Mike Wilson started his own insurance, sales, and consulting firm, which specialized in providing corporate risk managers with insurance protection and claims-settlement strategies. He works with a staff assistant and one other associate. After three years, sales averaged over $7 million annually, netting approximately $125,000 to $175,000 before taxes to Mike Wilson.

During a return visit to Consolidated Life, three years after his departure, Mike found Rick Belkner and Jack Greely still in charge of the division in which Mike had worked. The division's size had shrunk by 50 percent. All of the members of the old Supervisor's Forum had left. The reason for the decrease in the division's size was that computerization had removed many of the people's tasks.

QUESTIONS:

1. Can a manager such as Jack have such an impact on the culture of a workplace? Explain.
2. How was the Forum perceived by Jack?
3. What norms of expected behavior did Mike violate, if any?
4. How could Mike have done a better job of diagnosing the culture at Consolidated Life after Jack had joined the firm?

II

Part

Understanding and Managing
Individual Behavior

*Be what you are. This is the first step toward
becoming better than you are.*

Julius Charles Hare and Augustus William Hare,   *Guesses At Truth* (1827)

WHY INDIVIDUAL DIFFERENCES ARE IMPORTANT

Individual differences are important in studying organizational behavior and management for a very important reason: Individual differences have a direct effect on behavior. Every person is unique because of their background, individual haracteristics, needs, and how they perceive the world and other individuals. People who perceive things differently behave differently. People with different attitudes respond differently to directives. People with different personalities interact differently with bosses, coworkers, subordinates, and customers. In a multitude of different ways individual differences shape organizational behavior, and consequently, individual and organizational success. Individual differences, for example, help explain why some people embrace change and others are fearful of it. Or why some employees will be productive only if they are closely supervised, while others will be productive only if they are not. Or why some workers learn new tasks more effectively than others. There is virtually no area of organizational activity that is not affected by individual differences.

A helpful way to think about the importance of individual differences in influencing work behavior is through the use of the **attraction-selection-attrition (ASA) framework**.[1] According to ASA, attraction to an organization, selection by it, and attrition from it results in particular kinds of people being in the organization. These people, in turn, determine organizational behavior.

The ASA cycle works something like this: Different people are *attracted* to different careers and organizations as a function of their own abilities, interests, and personalities. Similarly, organizations *select* employees on the basis of the needs the organization has. *Needs* refers not only to skills and abilities, but also to individual attributes such as values and personality. Not all attraction decisions and selection decisions work out, however. *Attrition* occurs when individuals discover they do not like being part of the organization and elect to resign, or when the organization determines an individual is not succeeding and elects to terminate. Each phase of this ASA cycle is significantly influenced by the characteristics—individual differences—of each person.

In a very real sense, the essence of any organization is defined by the people who work there. The people who work there, and those who do not, are a function of the ASA cycle. Since the ASA cycle is strongly influenced by individual differences, it is not an overstatement to describe individual variables like those discussed in the remainder of this chapter as critical building blocks in the success or failure of any organization.

Any attempt to learn why people behave as they do in organizations requires some understanding of individual differences. Managers spend considerable time making judgments about the fit between individuals, jobs tasks, and effectiveness. Such judgments are influenced typically by both the manager's and the subordinate's individual characteristics. Making decisions about who will perform what tasks in a particular manner—without some understanding of behavior—can lead to irreversible long-run problems.

Each individual is different from every other individual in many respects. A manager needs to ask how such differences influence the behavior and performance of employees. This chapter highlights some of the important individual

---

[1]B. Schneider, H. W. Goldstein, and D. B. Smith, "The ASA Framework: An Update," *Personnel Psychology*, Autumn 1996, pp. 747–74.

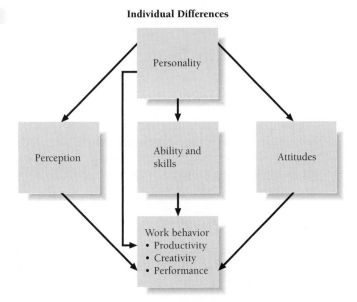

EXHIBIT 3.1
Individual Differences
in the Workplace

Individual Differences

differences that can help explain why one person is a significantly better or poorer performer than another person. Differences among people require forms of adjustment for both the individual and those for whom she or he will work. Managers who ignore such differences often become involved in practices which hinder achieving organizational and personal goals.

THE BASIS FOR UNDERSTANDING WORK BEHAVIOR

Demographic factors such as age, race, and gender influence individual differences. In addition, a person's genetics influence such individual differences as temperament. Another set of factors from a person's environmental background (e.g., urban versus rural, single parent versus dual parent, poor, middle class, or wealthy) impact a person's personality and behavior. For example, a middle-class Caucasian boy from Chicago is likely to respond, behave, and even talk differently than an African American boy born and raised in Athens, Georgia.

In order to understand individual differences, heredity and personal environment need to be weighed and considered. Even when these factors are understood, it is still difficult to accurately predict behavior. A person's behavior at work, in school, or in the home is a complex interaction of the type variable depicted in Exhibit 3.1. This graphical portrayal of individual differences is only a starting point and shows some of the large number of variables that influence behavior.

Exhibit 3.1 suggests that effective managerial practice requires that individual behavior differences be recognized and, when feasible, taken into consideration while carrying out the job of managing organizational behavior. To understand *individual differences,* a manager must (1) observe and recognize the differences, (2) study relationships between variables that influence individual behavior, and (3) discover relationships. For example, a manager is in a better position to make optimal decisions if he or she knows what the attitudes, perceptions, and mental abilities of employees are as well as how these and other variables are related. It also is important to know how each variable influences performance. Being able

Case 3.1

Bob Knowlton

to observe differences, understand relationships, and predict linkages can facilitate managerial attempts to improve performance.

Work behavior is anything a person does in the work environment. *Talking* to a manager, *listening* to a coworker, *creating* a new method of following up on a sale, *filing* a report, *typing* a memo, *placing* a completed unit in inventory, and *learning* how to use the firm's accounting system are all work behaviors. However, so are *daydreaming* about being on the golf course, *socializing with friends* around the water cooler, and *sabotaging* a new piece of equipment. Some of these behaviors contribute to productivity; others are nonproductive or even counterproductive. Nonetheless, they are all examples of behaviors engaged in by individuals in work settings. In this chapter we will attempt to provide a basis for better understanding why these behaviors occur.

INDIVIDUAL VARIABLES

The individual variables presented in Exhibit 3.1 are classified as hereditary and life environment, factors, perception, abilities and skills, attitudes, and personality. These variables all impact what is designated as a person's personality.

Heredity Factors

Heredity provides a genetic explanation of some aspects of human variability. Included in discussions of heredity are debates about gender, race, and ethnic background. Psychological, mental, and moral differences are influenced by genetic inheritance. The genetic basis of individual differences is complicated and controversial. The debate of whether human behavior is determined largely by heredity or by environment has been going on for almost 100 years. It lies at the center of such topics as the reasons for differences between men and women, higher and lower IQs, and the raising of twins in separate environments. For example, studies suggest that identical twins raised apart are more similar to each other (behaviorally) than to other adoptive family members.[2]

Another example of an important heredity difference is that of gender. Possible gender-related differences have received particular attention in regard to professional and managerial careers. It has been argued, for example, that men will make better managers because they are more assertive, that women are less committed to organizational careers because of family considerations, or that men are less sensitive to the feelings of others. While it is true that some examples supporting each of these generalizations can be found, so also can one find multiple examples which refute them. Indeed, research suggests that most of the stereotypical differences frequently used to describe males and females in organizations are simply not valid.[3]

It is important to understand that the perception that these differences exist influences the behavior of both men and women in organizations. A male manager, for example, who assumes a female employee is less committed to the organization because of family responsibilities is likely—perhaps unconsciously—to

Reading 3.1

One More Time: Do Female and Male Managers Differ?

---

[2]Thomas J. Bouchard, Sr., "Genetic and Environmental Influences on Intelligence and Special Mental Abilities", *American Journal of Human Biology,* April 1998, pp. 253–275 and Lawrence Wright, *Twins: And What They Tell Us About What We Are.* News: John Wiley, 1999.

[3]Karen S. Lyness and Donna E. Thompson, "Climbing the Corporate Ladder: Do Female and Male Executives Follow the Same Route?" *Journal of Applied Psychology,* February 2000, pp. 86–101.

Can Jobs Be Gender Stereotyped?

You Be the Judge

One of the more important—and interesting—individual difference variables is gender. While many gender distinctions are more imagined than actual, there are nonetheless some real differences. Men tend to be taller than women and women tend to live longer than men, to mention just a couple. It is also true that there are some real differences in the proportion of males and females in certain jobs. A significant majority of nurses are female, for example. Similarly, most electricians are male. There are, however, no true gender differences that would dictate that nurses had to be women, or that electricians had to be men. Still, many people believe that some jobs are "female" and others are "male."

Such a person was a male manager for a Washington, DC, company. When a receptionist's position became available in his office, he instructed one of his female employees to fill the vacant position with a woman. The notion of having a male receptionist simply did not fit his stereotype of this job category. In a number of different ways he made it clear that "men are not receptionists." Clearly upset by this kind of thinking, the female employee who had been instructed to fill this position with a woman sued her employer for sex discrimination.

How would you have ruled in this case? Is this sex discrimination? Do you think any laws were broken here? If not, should there be a law against such behavior?

behave differently toward her than he otherwise would. In turn, the female employee's behavior will likely be influenced—again, perhaps unconsciously—by the manager's behavior.

Abilities and Skills

Some employees, though highly motivated, simply do not have the abilities or skills to perform well. Abilities and skills play a major role in individual behavior and performance.[4] **Ability** is a person's talent to perform a mental or physical task. Skill is a learned talent that a person has acquired to perform a task. A person's ability is generally stable over time. Skills change as one's training or experience occurs. A person can be trained and consequently new skills are acquired.

The presence or absence of various abilities and skills has an obvious relationship to job performance. Managers must attempt to match a person's abilities and skills to the job requirements. This matching process is important since no amount of leadership, motivation, or organizational resources can make up for deficiencies in abilities or skills (although, clearly some skills can be improved with practice and training). Job analysis is a widely used technique that takes some of the guesswork out of matching. Job analysis is the process of defining and studying a job in terms of tasks or behaviors and specifying the responsibilities, education, and training needed to perform the job successfully. Job analysis will be discussed in more detail in Chapter 6.

An individual ability that has been identified and suggested as being important is referred to as **emotional intelligence**. Daniel Goleman, a psychologist, suggests that emotional intelligence (designated as EQ) is more significant in

---

[4]For a discussion of the nature of ability-performance relationships, see W. M. Coward and P. R. Sackett, "Linearity of Ability-Performance Relationships: A Reconfirmation," *Journal of Applied Psychology,* June 1990, pp. 297–300.

terms of understanding individuals than general intelligence (IQ).[5] EQ has its roots in the concept of "social intelligence" identified originally by E.L. Thorndike in 1920. He defined *social intelligence* as the ability to understand individuals to act wisely in human relations.

According to emotional intelligence theorists and researchers, it involves abilities in five areas:

- *Self-awareness*—observing oneself and recognizing a feeling as it happens
- *Managing emotions*—handling feelings so that they are appropriate
- *Motivating oneself*—channeling emotions to accomplish goals
- *Empathy*—sensitivity to the feelings of others and appreciating the differences in how people feel about things
- *Handling relationships*—Managing emotions in others

www.eiconsortium.org/ goleman.htm

Researchers are investigating dimensions of EQ by increasing related concepts such as social skills, interpersonal competence, psychological maturity, and emotional awareness. There is to date no widely accepted test to gauge a person's emotional intelligence. Much more psychometrically sound research is needed before a widely accepted and easy-to-implement measure is adopted by managers.

General lists of high and low EQ are suggested as only starting points in understanding the concept. For example, individuals with high EQ are intrinsically motivated, interested in the feelings of others, not afraid to express feelings, not dominated by fear, worry, and guilt, realistic, not motivated by power, wealth, and fame, and comfortable talking about feelings. The low EQ person is not able to take responsibility for feelings, unforgiving, rigid and inflexible, acts out feelings rather than talking them out, not open to new ideas and facts, and a poor listener.[6]

Available research on EQ in a multinational consulting firm found that partners with higher EQs scored higher on scales and produced $1.2 more profit from accounts than did lower EQ partners.[7]

In a beverage firm, using standard methods to hire division presidents, 50 percent left within two years, and most because of poor performance. The firm began using emotional competencies such as imitative, self-confidence, and leadership in selecting division presidents. The result was only 6 percent turnover over a two-year period. Also, the high EQ presidents were more likely to perform in the top third based on salary bonuses for division performance. They also outperformed goals by 15 to 20 percent. Presidents with lower EQ scores underperformed goals by almost 20 percent.[8]

Perception

Perception is the cognitive process by which an individual selects, organizes, and gives meaning to environment stimuli. Because each person gives his or her own meaning to stimuli, different individuals will "see" the same thing in different

---

[5]Daniel Goleman, *Working with Emotional Intelligence* (New York: Bantam, 1998).

[6]R. E. Boyotes, Presentation to the Linkage Conference on Emotional Intelligence, Chicago, IL, September 27, 1999.

[7]Hendrie Weisinger, *Emotional Intelligence at Work*. San Francisco: Jossey Base, 2000.

[8]D. C. McClelland, "Identifying Competencies with Behavioral-Event Interviews," *Psychological Science*, Spring 1999, pp. 331–39.

EXHIBIT 3.2
The Perceptual Process: An Individual Interpretation

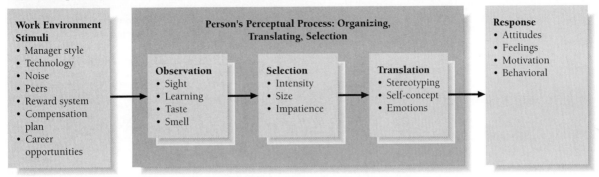

Work Environment Stimuli
- Manager style
- Technology
- Noise
- Peers
- Reward system
- Compensation plan
- Career opportunities

Person's Perceptual Process: Organizing, Translating, Selection

Observation
- Sight
- Learning
- Taste
- Smell

Selection
- Intensity
- Size
- Impatience

Translation
- Stereotyping
- Self-concept
- Emotions

Response
- Attitudes
- Feelings
- Motivation
- Behavioral

ways. When we comment to a classmate, "This course is boring," what we really mean is, "This class bores me." While we think we are describing some objective reality, we are in fact describing our subjective reactions to that reality.[9]

Individuals are constantly bombarded by environmental stimuli which impact their senses of sight, hearing, smell, taste, and touch. The exact stimuli that a person focuses on is based on what he or she chooses to pay attention to at a particular moment. For example, an irate manager screaming out a directive may result in a subordinate ignoring an alarm bell signaling the identification of a defective Pentium III processor unit. The subordinate is shutting out the noisy alarm to focus on the words, body language, and overall behavior of the manager.

Exhibit 3.2 illustrates the basic framework and elements of perception operating as a cognitive process. Each person makes personal/individual choices and responds differently. Understanding perceptual interpretation helps managers explain why individual differences must be considered at work. People see the world around them in their own unique way and behaviorally respond according to their interpretation.

Individuals try to make sense of environmental stimuli by observation, selection, and translation. Each of these three activities is influenced by the type of factors displayed in Exhibit 3.2. Perceptual selection is the process of focusing on the stimuli that are important, large, or intense.

In general, people perceive stimuli that satisfy needs, emotions, attitudes, or their self-concept. This is the translation portion of Exhibit 3.2. If a person has a need to receive positive feedback on performance, then the positive statements made by her boss will be remembered more clearly and accurately than the negative statements she received. Again, the notions of observing, selecting, and translating are linked to form the perceptual process, which precedes any response. There are three internal responses illustrated—attitudes, feelings, and motivation.

There is the possibility that a person's perception is inaccurate. Misinterpreting stimuli can result in perceptual errors. The research literature on interviewing

---

[9]Mary Ann Von Glinow, "On Minority Rights and Majority Accommodations," *Academy of Management Review,* April 1996, pp. 346–51.

> **EXHIBIT 3.3   The Perceptual Gap between Supervisor and Subordinates**
>
> | Types of Recognition | Frequency with Which Supervisors Say They Give Various Types of Recognition for Good Performance | Frequency with Which Subordinates Say Supervisors Give Various Types of Recognition for Good Performance |
> | --- | --- | --- |
> | Gives privileges | 52% | 14% |
> | Gives more responsibility | 48 | 10 |
> | Gives a pat on the back | 82 | 13 |
> | Gives sincere and thorough praise | 80 | 14 |
> | Trains for better jobs | 64 | 9 |
> | Gives more interesting work | 51 | 3 |

Source: Adapted from Rensis Likert, *New Patterns in Management* (New York: McGraw-Hill, 1961), p. 91.

suggests that interviewers rate candidates who are similar in appearance, background, and interests higher than candidates who are dissimilar.[10] This is referred to as the "similar-to-me perception error." There is also a tendency to make quick first impression errors based on the first few minutes of an interview. This first impression error can eliminate too many good job candidates, which is detrimental to a firm.[11]

Since perception refers to the acquisition of specific knowledge about stimuli at any particular moment, it occurs whenever stimuli activate the senses. Perception involves cognition (knowledge). Thus, perception includes the interpretation of objects, symbols, and people in the light of pertinent experiences. In other words, perception involves receiving stimuli, organizing the stimuli, and translating or interpreting the organized stimuli so as to influence behavior and form attitudes.

Each person selects various cues that influence his or her perception of people, objects, and symbols. Because of these factors and their potential for imbalance, people often misperceive another person, group, or object. To a considerable extent, people interpret the behavior of others in the context in which they find themselves. A classic study reported by Rensis Likert clearly illustrates this. He examined the perceptions of superiors and subordinates to determine the amounts and types of recognition that subordinates received for good performance. Both supervisors and subordinates were asked how often superiors provided rewards for good work. The results are presented in Exhibit 3.3.

There were significant differences in what the two groups perceived. Each group viewed the type of recognition being given at a different level. The subordinates in most cases reported that very little recognition was being provided by their supervisors and that rewards were provided infrequently. The superiors, on the other hand, saw themselves as giving a wide variety of rewards for good performance. The two groups were looking at the same objective reality and very

Exercise 3.1

Testing Your Assumptions about People

---

[10]Jim Meade, "The Right System Can Help You Keep Track of Job Applicants," *HR Magazine*, September 2000, pp. 80–85.

[11]Ibid.

honestly reaching quite different conclusions. The situation was the same, but their interpretation of the situation was markedly different.

Stereotyping   *Stereotyping* is a translation step in the perceptual process employed to assist individuals in dealing with massive information-processing demands. In this regard it represents a useful, even essential, way of categorizing individuals (or events, organizations, etc.) on the basis of limited information or observation. The process of forming stereotypes and placing individuals in certain categories on the basis of these stereotypes is a perceptual one. When we speak of the Germans as efficient, the Italians as great lovers, or the French as outstanding cooks, we are engaging in nationality stereotyping. Since many stereotypes relate to ethnic group membership, it is important to distinguish between a stereotype and a prejudice. A prejudice is a stereotype that refuses to change when presented with information indicating the stereotype is inaccurate. Stereotypes can be helpful; prejudice is never helpful.

Although it is often assumed that stereotyping is inherently bad or wrong, this is not the case. Stereotyping is a useful process that greatly increases our efficiency in making sense out of our environment. Nonetheless, stereotyping can and does lead to perceptual inaccuracies and negative consequences.[12] To the extent that stereotypes create social injustice, result in poorer decision making, stifle innovation, or cause underutilization of human resources, they contribute to ineffectiveness and inefficiency. For example, employers' stereotypes regarding disabled workers may be an important source of the employment problems these workers frequently experience. Inaccurate stereotypes include beliefs that disabled workers lack job-related abilities, have lower performance levels, and have higher absenteeism and turnover rates. Objective data, on the other hand, consistently reveal that these stereotypes are false.[13]

The Manager's Characteristics   As the "similar-to-me" illustration shows, people frequently use themselves as benchmarks in perceiving others. Research suggests that (1) knowing oneself makes it easier to see others accurately, (2) one's own characteristics affect the characteristics identified in others, and (3) persons who accept themselves are more likely to see favorable aspects of other people.

Basically, these conclusions suggest that managers perceiving the behavior and individual differences of employees are influenced by their own traits. If they understand that their own traits and values influence perception, they probably can perform a more accurate evaluation of their subordinates. A manager who is a perfectionist tends to look for perfection in subordinates, while a manager who is quick in responding to technical requirements looks for this ability in his subordinates.

——— Management Pointer 3.1 ———

STEREOTYPING

How to Pay Attention to One's Stereotyping

1. Remember that stereotypes are frequently based on little or inaccurate information.

2. Always be willing to change or add information that will improve the accuracy of your stereotypes.

3. Understand that stereotypes rarely accurately apply to a specific individual. Judgments based on personal knowledge of a specific person are almost always more accurate than using a broad category to which that person belongs.

---

[12]See, for example, Jo Ann Lee, Dawn Castella, and Millard McClunery, "Sexual Stereotypes and Perceptions of Competence and Qualifications," *Psychological Reports*, April 1997, pp. 419–28.

[13]Dianna Stone and Adrienne Colella, "A Model of Factors Affecting the Treatment of Disabled Individuals in Organizations," *Academy of Management Review*, April 1966, pp. 352–401.

Situational Factors   The press of time, the attitudes of the people a manager is working with, and other situational factors will all influence perceptual accuracy. If a manager is pressed for time and has to immediately fill an order, then her perceptions will be influenced by the time constraints. The press of time literally will force the manager to overlook some details, to rush certain activities, and to ignore certain stimuli such as requests from other managers or from superiors.

Needs and Perceptions   Perceptions are influrnced significantly by needs and desires. In other words, the employee; the manager, the vice president, and the director see what they want to see. Like the mirrors in the fun house at the amusement park, the work can be distorted; the distortion is related to needs and desires.

The influence of needs in shaping perceptions has been studied in laboratory settings. For instance, subjects at various stages of hunger were asked to report what they saw in ambiguous drawings flashed before them. It was found that as hunger increased up to a certain point, the subjects saw more and more of the ambiguous drawings as articles of food. The hungry subjects saw steaks, salads, and sandwiches, while the subjects who recently had eaten saw nonfood images in the same drawings.[14]

Perception and Behavior

It is often said that perception *is* reality. That is, what an employee perceives to be real is, in fact for that employee, reality. Since behavior is greatly influenced by our personal interpretation of reality, it is easy to understand why our perceptual processes are potent determinants of behavior. One approach that provides a basis for understanding the relationship between perception and behavior is *attribution theory*. Attribution theory is concerned with the process by which individuals interpret events around them as being caused by a relatively stable portion of their environment.[15] In short, attribution theory attempts to explain the *why* of behavior. Exhibit 3.4 displays the attribution process.

According to attribution theory, it is the perceived causes of events, not the actual ones, that influence people's behavior. More specifically, individuals will attempt to analyze why certain events have occurred, and the results of that analysis will influence their behavior in the future. As the example in Exhibit 3.4 will indicate, an employee who receives a raise will attempt to attribute the raise to some underlying cause. If the employee perceives the explanation for the raise to be the fact that she is a hard worker and consequently concludes that working hard leads to rewards in this organization, she would decide to continue working hard in the future. Another employee may attribute his raise to the fact that he participates in the company's bowling team and decide it makes sense to continue bowling for that reason. Thus, in both cases employees have made decisions affecting their future behaviors on the basis of their attributions. Subsequent events will be interpreted by these two employees based on their attributions of why these events happened and will be either reinforced or modified depending on future events.

---

[14]J. A. Deutsch, W. G. Young, and T. J. Kalogeris, "The Stomach Signals Satiety," *Science,* April 1978, pp. 23–33.

[15]H. H. Kelly, "Attribution Theory in Social Psychology," in *Nebraska Symposium on Motivation,* D. Levine, ed. (Lincoln: University of Nebraska Press, 1967).

EXHIBIT 3.4
The Attribution Process

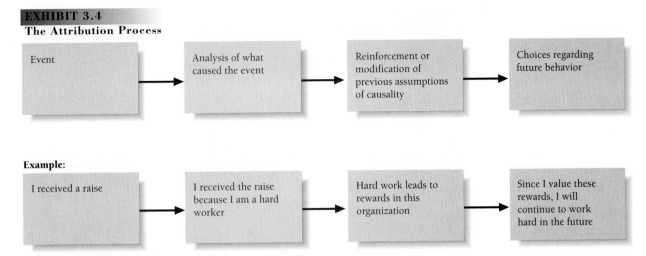

| Event | Analysis of what caused the event | Reinforcement or modification of previous assumptions of causality | Choices regarding future behavior |

Example:

| I received a raise | I received the raise because I am a hard worker | Hard work leads to rewards in this organization | Since I value these rewards, I will continue to work hard in the future |

Source: Adapted from Abraham Korman, *Organizational Behavior* (Engelwood Cliffs, NJ: Prentice Hall, 1977), p. 273.

The attribution process also can be important in understanding the behavior of other people. The behavior of others can be examined on the basis of its **distinctiveness, consistency,** and **consensus.** Distinctiveness is the degree to which a person behaves similarly in different situations. Consistency is the degree to which a person engages in the same behaviors at different times. Consensus is the degree to which other people are engaging in the same behavior. Knowing the extent to which a person's behavior exhibits these qualities can be very useful in helping us better understand that behavior.

Exhibit 3.5 casts these qualities in the form of questions, the answers to which can lead us to some conclusions about the behavior in question. Let's look at an example. Caroline has done poorly on a test in her organizational behavior class and has expressed her concern to her professor. Her professor, in trying to understand the possible reasons for her behavior (doing poorly on the test) tries to determine its degree of distinctiveness, consistency, and consensus. If Caroline tends to do poorly on tests in other courses (low distinctiveness), has performed poorly on earlier tests in her management class (high consistency), and if no other students did poorly on the test (low consensus), the professor might make an internal attribution regarding Caroline's behavior. That is, the explanation for the poor test is to be found within Caroline (lack of motivation, poor study habits, etc.). On the other hand, if Caroline does well on tests in other courses (high consensus), the professor might make an external attribution about the behavior. That is, the explanation for the poor test may be found in factors outside Caroline herself (the professor put together a poor test, used the wrong answer key, etc.). The important point here is that the attributions made regarding why the events took place have important implications for dealing with the problem.

Not all attributions, of course, are correct. Another important contribution made by attribution theory is the identification of systematic errors or biases that distort attributions. One such error is called the **fundamental attribution error.** The fundamental attribution error is a tendency to underestimate the importance of external factors and overestimate the importance of internal factors when making attributions about the behavior of others. An example might be

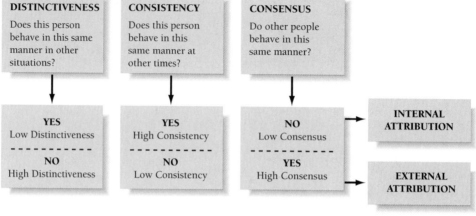

EXHIBIT 3.5
Internal and External Attributions

| **DISTINCTIVENESS** Does this person behave in this same manner in other situations? | **CONSISTENCY** Does this person behave in this same manner at other times? | **CONSENSUS** Do other people behave in this same manner? |

| **YES** Low Distinctiveness | **YES** High Consistency | **NO** Low Consensus | → **INTERNAL ATTRIBUTION** |
| **NO** High Distinctiveness | **NO** Low Consistency | **YES** High Consensus | → **EXTERNAL ATTRIBUTION** |

that of a shop floor supervisor who attributes a high injury rate to employee carelessness (a cause internal to the employee), instead of considering the possibility the equipment is old and in poor repair (a cause external to the employee). Another frequent error is the **self-serving bias**. This is reflected in the tendency people have to take credit for successful work and deny responsibility for poor work. The self-serving bias leads us to conclude that when we succeed it is a result of our outstanding efforts, while when we fail it is because of factors beyond our control. Organizational Encounter 3.1 describes attributions some might feel reflect a bias.

The managerial implications of an attributional approach to understanding work behavior are important. In order to influence employee behavior, the manager must understand the attributions employees make. Further, the manager must be aware that his own attributions may be different from theirs. For example, if a manager perceives employees' poor performance to be the result of lack of effort, she may attempt to increase motivation levels. On the other hand, if employees perceive performance problems to be attributable to lack of supervisory guidance, the efforts made by the manager are not likely to have the desired effect on performance. Managers cannot assume that their attributions will be the same as their employees'. Neither can they assume their own attributions are error-free. Knowing this, coupled with an effort to understand what attributions employees make, can greatly enhance the manager's ability to have a positive effect on employee behavior.

Attitudes

Attitudes are determinants of behavior because they are linked with perception, personality, feelings, and motivation. An attitude is a mental state of readiness learned and organized through experience, exerting a specific influence on a person's response to people, objects, and situations with which it is related. Each of us has attitudes on numerous topics—computers, jogging, restaurants, friends, jobs, religion, the government, elder care, crime, education, income taxes.

Organizational Encounter 3.1

Employee Responsibility for Declining Productivity: Is the Self-Serving Bias at Work?

In the 1970 and 1980s the United States declining productivity was a growing concern among organizational researchers, executives, boards of directors, and various public and private interest groups. Public pronouncements by executives regarding a cause for this phenomenon—particularly when they know their remarks will be attributed to them by name—identify a host of factors contributing to the decline. Yet when these same executives are responding *anonymously* to a survey, the outcome is much different.

When such a survey was conducted by First Pennsylvania Bank, almost 70 percent of the several hundred executives from the eastern and northeastern parts of the country who responded attributed the cause of productivity decline largely to the poor attitudes and resulting bad habits of the workforce—*not* due to the lack of capital investment, and *not* due to technology or bad management. Unfortunately, the attributions the workers made for the decline were not included in the survey.

The executives' attributions of poor worker attitudes being responsible for the productivity decline may be a classic example of an attribution error as discussed in this text. A case may be made for suggesting that management is guilty of the self-serving bias. By "blaming" the workers, management protects itself from having to assume responsibility.

In reality, productivity declines are a function of numerous interacting factors, one of which probably is poor worker attitudes but another of which is probably ineffective management. Also, in fairness, it should be pointed out that had workers been surveyed, they may have made some self-serving attributions of their own: They may have blamed management.

This definition of attitude has certain implications for the manager. First, attitudes are learned. Second, attitudes define one's predispositions toward given aspects of the world. Third, attitudes provide the emotional basis of one's interpersonal relations and identification with others. And fourth, attitudes are organized and are close to the core of personality. Some attitudes are persisten and enduring. Yet, like each of the psychological variables, attitudes are subject to change.[16]

Attitudes are intrinsic parts of a person's personality. However, a number of theories attempt to account for the formation and change of attitudes. One such theory proposes that people "seek a congruence between their beliefs and feelings toward objects" and suggests that the modification of attitudes depends on changing either the feelings or the beliefs.[17] The theory proposes that cognition, affect, and behavior determine attitudes, and that attitudes, in turn, determine cognition, affect, and behavior. The **cognitive** component of an attitude consists of the person's perceptions, opinions, and beliefs. It refers to the thought processes with special emphasis on rationality and logic. An important element of cognition is the evaluative beliefs held by a person. Evaluative beliefs are manifested in the form of favorable or unfavorable impressions that a person holds toward an object or person.

Affect is the emotional component of an attitude and is often learned from parents, teachers, and peer group members. It is the part of an attitude that is associated with "feeling" a certain way about a person, group, or situation. The *behavioral* component of an attitude refers to the tendency of a person to act in a certain way toward someone or something. A person may act in a warm, friendly, aggres-

---

[16]Ann M. Ryan, David Chan, Robert E. Ployhart, and Auen L. Seale, "Employee Attitude Surveys in a Multinational Organization: Considering Language and Culture in Assessing Measurement," *Personnel Psychology,* Spring 1999, pp. 37–58.

[17]Robert Roe and Peter Ester, "Values and Work: Empircal Findings and Theoretical Perspectives," *Applied Psychology: An International Review,* January 1999, pp. 1–21.

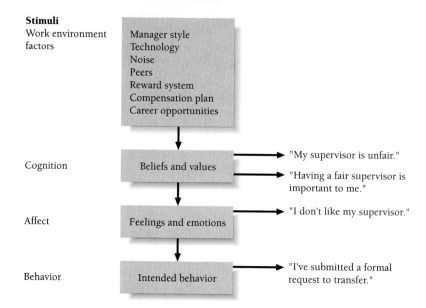

EXHIBIT 3.6
The Three Components
of Attitudes: Cognition,
Affect, Behavior

sive, hostile, teasing, or apathetic way, or in any number of other ways. Such actions could be measured to examine the behavioral component of attitudes.

Sometimes there may be discrepancies between attitudes and behaviors. That is, the behavioral component of an attitude held by someone might suggest behavior different from or even opposed to the actual behavior engaged in by the individual. This kind of discrepancy is called cognitive dissonance. An example of cognitive dissonance could be that of an individual who has the attitude that smoking is bad for one's health but who continues to smoke anyway. Such an inconsistency between beliefs and behavior is thought to create discomfort and a desire on the part of the individual to eliminate or reduce the inconsistency. In the smoking example, this could mean changing beliefs about the negative health consequences ("They really haven't *proven* that smoking is bad for you"), or modifying the behavior (quitting, cutting back, or switching to a "safer" brand). The concept of cognitive dissonance is developed further in Chapter 14.

Exhibit 3.6 presents the three components of attitudes in terms of work environment factors such as job design, company policies, and fringe benefits. These stimuli trigger cognitive (thought), affective (emotional), and behavioral responses. In essence, the stimuli result in the formation of attitudes which then lead to one or more responses.

The theory of cognitive, affective, and behavioral components as determinants of attitudes has a significant implication for managers. The theory implies that the manager must be able to demonstrate that the positive aspects of contributing to the organization outweigh the negative aspects. It is through attempts to develop generally favorable attitudes toward the organization and the job that many managers achieve effectiveness.

Changing Attitudes   Managers are often faced with the task of changing attitudes because previously structured attitudes hinder job performance. Although many variables affect attitude change, they all can be described in terms of three general factors: trust in the sender, the message itself, and the situation.[18] If employees do not trust the manager, they will not accept the manager's message or change an attitude. Similarly, if the message is not convincing, there will be no pressure to change.

The greater the prestiage of the communicator, the greater the attitude change that is produced. A manager who has little prestiage and is not shown respect by peers and superiors will be in a difficult position if the job requires changing the attitudes of subordinates so they will work more effectively.

Liking the communicator can lead to attitude change because people try to identify with a liked communicator and tend to adopt attitudes and behaviors of the liked person. Not all managers, however, are fortunate enough to be liked by each of their subordinates. Therefore, it is important to recognize the importance of trust in the manager as a condition for liking the manager.

Even if a manager is trusted, presents a convincing message, and is liked, the problems of changing people's attitudes are not easily solved. An important factor is the strength of the employee's commitment to an attitude. A worker who has decided not to accept a promotion is committed to the belief that it is better to remain in his or her present position than to accept the promotion. Attitudes that have been expressed publicly are more difficult to change because the person has shown commitment, and to change would be to admit a mistake.

How much you are affected by attempts to change your attitude depends in part on the situation. When people are listening to or reading a persuasive message, they sometimes are distracted by other thoughts, sounds, or activities. Studies indicate that if people are distracted while they are listening to a message, they will show more attitude change because the distraction interferes with silent counterarguing.[19]

Distraction is just one of many situational factors that can increase persuasion. Another factor that makes people more susceptible to attempts to change attitudes is pleasant surroundings. The pleasant surroundings may be associated with the attempt to change the attitude.

Attitudes and Job Satisfaction   *Job satisfaction* is an attitude people have about their jobs. It results from their perception of their jobs and the degree to which there is a good fit between the individual and organization.[20] A number of factors have been associated with job satisfaction. Among the more important ones are these:

> *Pay*—the amount of pay received and the perceived fairness of that pay
>
> *Work itself*—the extent to which job tasks are considered interesting and provide opportunities for learning and accepting responsibility
>
> *Promotion opportunities*—the availability of opportunities for advancement
>
> *Supervision*—the technical competence and the interpersonal skills of one's immediate boss

---

[18]Jonathan L. Freedom, Merrill Carlsmith, and David Sears, *Social Psychology* (Englewood Cliffs, NJ: Prentice Hall, 1974), p. 271.

[19]R. A. Osterhouse and T. C. Brock, "Distraction Increases Yielding to Propaganda by Inhibiting Counterarguing," *Journal of Personality and Social Psychology,* March 1977, pp. 344–58.

[20]Virginia Postrel, *The Future and Its Enemies,* (New York: Free Press, 1999).

Coworkers—the extent to which coworkers are friendly, competent, and supportive

Working conditions—the extent to which the physical work environment is comfortable and supportive of productivity

Job security—the belief that one's position is relatively secure and continued employment with the organization is a reasonable expectation

—**Management Pointer 3.2**—

ATTITUDES

How to Increase Your Effectiveness in Changing Attitudes

1. It's easier to make small changes than large ones. If the change you want is a large one, you will be more effective if you concentrate on gradually changing the attitude over a period of time.

2. The key to changing an attitude is to identify the beliefs or values that are part of it and then provide the attitude holder with information that will alter those beliefs or values.

3. Don't overlook the setting in which the attempted change occurs. Make it as pleasant and enjoyable as possible.

4. People will more likely change their attitudes when it is to their advantage to do so. Help identify reasons that changing the attitude is a good idea.

Many organizations recognize the importance of the potential link between job satisfaction and a number of desirable organizational outcomes. Ben and Jerry's Homemade, Inc., for example, is very proactive in providing a work environment it believes increases satisfaction, and consequently, productivity. This multimillion-dollar ice cream maker has established an employee-run "Joy Committee." The sole purpose of this committee is to suggest and implement activities that make Ben and Jerry's a fun place to work. Among other innovations, the committee has sponsored an official tacky dress-up day in which employees were encouraged to wear their most outlandish and stylistically incorrect outfits. On another occasion the company hired masseuses to reduce stress during their busiest season. Employees could take a break for a half hour and have a massage. Through these and other personnel policies, Ben and Jerry's is committed to increasing employee satisfaction.[21]

Another company committed to building and maintaining high levels of job satisfaction is Patagonia, a manufacturer of high-quality sportswear and equipment. At Patagonia, employees are expected to put in at least five hours a day at the office between the core hours of 9 A.M. and 3 P.M. The remaining three hours can be scheduled when and where the employee desires. Consequently, it is not unusual to find people playing volleyball or spending a couple of hours surfing during the middle of the day (Patagonia offices are located about a mile from the Pacific Ocean). At the same time, neither is it unusual to see employees, or "Patagoniacs" as they like to be called, hard at work in their offices until 9 P.M. or later. Patagonia also realizes that such things as challenging jobs and real participation in decision making contribute to organizational and job satisfaction as well.[22]

Satisfaction and Job Performance   One of the most widely debated and controversial issues in the study of job satisfaction is its relationship to job performance or effectiveness.[23] There general views of this relationship have been advanced: (1) job satisfaction causes job performance; (2) job performance causes job satisfaction; and (3) the job satisfaction–job performance relationship is moderated by other variables such as rewards. Exhibit 3.7 shows each of these viewpoints.

---

[21]Ben and Jerry's, Annual report, 2000.

[22]See, for example, A. Cohen, "Organizational Commitment and Turnover: A Meta-Analysis," *Academy of Management Journal*, October 1993, pp. 1140–57.

[23]For examples of satisfaction and performance research citations, see Ann Marie Ryan, Mark Schmit, and Raymond Johnson, "Attitudes and Effectiveness: Examining Relations at an Organizational Level," *Personnel Psychology*, Winter 1996, pp. 853–82.

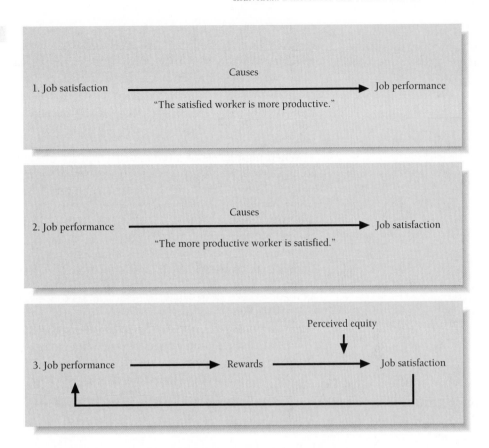

EXHIBIT 3.7
Satisfaction-
Performance
Relationships:
Three Views

The first two views have mixed, but generally weak, research support. Most studies dealing with the performance-satisfaction relationship have found low association between performance and satisfaction. The evidence is rather convincing that a satisfied employee is not necessarily a high performer. Managerial attempts to make everyone satisfied will not necessarily yield high levels of productivity. Likewise, the assumption that a high-performing employee is likely to be satisfied is not well supported.

The third view suggests that satisfaction and performance are related only under certain conditions. A number of other factors, such as employee participation, have been posited as affecting the relationship.[24] Most attention, however, has focused on rewards as moderating the relationship. Generally, this view suggests that the rewards one receives as a consequence of good performance, and the degree to which these rewards are perceived as reasonable or equitable, affect both the extent to which satisfaction results from performance and the extent performance is affected by satisfaction. This means that if an employee is rewarded for good performance and if the reward is deemed fair by the employee, job satisfaction will increase (or remain high). This in turn will have a positive effect on performance, leading to additional rewards and continued higher levels of job satisfaction.

---

[24]J. A. Wagner III, "Participation's Effects on Performance and Satisfaction: A Reconsideration of Research Evidence," *Academy of Management Review,* April 1994, pp. 312–30.

There is a great deal we do not yet understand regarding the role of job satisfaction. It is clear, however, that it can affect a number of important performance variables. Absenteeism and turnover, for example, have been frequently associated with satisfaction, although the relationship is not a strong one.[25] Increasing job performance and employee productivity will continue to be a major management focus in the 21st century. As long as this remains the case, it is unlikely that interest in job satisfaction will diminish among either organizational researchers or managers.

When high levels of job dissatisfaction are present and a manager has an incomplete understanding of the problem with subordinates, he or she needs to take action. The high levels of job dissatisfaction may be a result of perceptual inaccuracies, a misalignment of people with jobs, or poor managerial practices. Would you rather manage a group of job-satisfied or job-dissatisfied people? Most rational managers would want to be around job-satisfied people. For this common-sense reason alone, in spite of the nonconclusive research findings, the job satisfaction factor is still given time, attention, and analysis by most managers.

Personality

The relationship between behavior and personality is perhaps one of the most complex matters that managers have to understand. When we speak about an individual's personality we are referring to *a relatively stable set of feelings and behaviors that have been significantly formed by genetic and environmental factors.* Although many aspects of personality formation, development, and expression are not perfectly understood, certain principles are generally accepted as being true. Some of these are:

1. Personality appears to be organized into patterns which are, to some degree, observable and measurable.
2. Personality has superficial aspects, such as attitudes toward being a team leader, and a deeper core, such as sentiments about authority or the strong work ethic.
3. Personality involves both common and unique characteristics. Every person is different from every other person in some respects and similar to other persons in other respects.

Your own personality did not just suddenly or randomly happen. It is the product of a number of forces that together have helped shape the unique individual that you are. Exhibit 3.8 presents some of these major forces.

Personality is a product of both nature and nurture. Nature refers to the hereditary forces in Exhibit 3.8. The genetic makeup you inherited from your mother and father has partially determined the personality you have today. While scientists have yet to identify specific "personality" genes, it is clear heredity is an important determiner of personality. Research on identical twins who have been

---

[25]See, for example, Chi-sum Wong, Chun Hui, and Kenneth S. Law, "Causal Relationships between Attitudinal Antecedents to Turnover," *Academy of Management Best Paper Proceedings,* August 1995, pp. 342–46. For a somewhat different view, see Thomas W. Lee, Terence R. Mitchell, Lowell Wise, and Steven Fireman, "An Unfolding Model of Voluntary Employee Turnover," *Academy of Management Journal,* February 1966, pp. 5–36.

EXHIBIT 3.8
**Some Major Forces
Influencing
Personality**

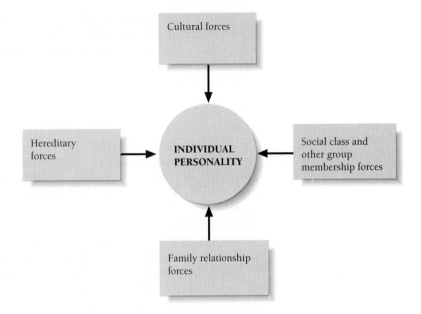

reared apart suggests that hereditary factors may account for as much as half of the variation in different personalities.[26] Heredity is not a constant factor in personality, however. The importance of heredity varies from one personality trait to another. For example, heredity generally is more important in determining a person's temperament than values and ideals.

The remaining forces depicted in Exhibit 3.8 are part of the nurture side of the personality equation. *Nurture* refers to the pattern of life experiences you have. *Family relationship* forces are an important part of nurture. This includes the experiences you had with parents, siblings, and other family members. How your parents expressed their feelings, how strict or permissive they were, how many siblings you had, where you were in the birth order (were you an only child or first, middle or last child, etc.), the role grandparents played in your upbringing, are all examples of family relationship forces that played a role in shaping what your personality is today.

The degree to which every person is molded by *culture* is significant. We frequently do not comprehend the impact of culture in shaping our personalities. It happens gradually, and usually there is no alternative but to accept the culture. The stable functioning of a society requires that there be shared patterns of behavior among its members and that there be some basis for knowing how to behave in certain situations. To ensure this, the society institutionalizes various patterns of behavior. The institutionalization of some patterns of behavior means that most members of a culture will have many common personality characteristics. At the same time, however, there is a great deal of cultural diversity within our society. The effective management of such diversity, and the differences that may exist within an organization's workforce because of it, is a critical and challenging task.

---

[26]Bouchard, *op.cit.*

Increasingly in today's world, business operations are international in scope. This means they are frequently multicultural as well. Thus, while most members of a culture will share similar personality characteristics, there may be significant differences across cultures. One of the challenges of doing business in a global economy is understanding and respecting cultural differences, particularly as they may affect personality and behavior.

Social class also is important in shaping personality. The various neighborhoods of cities and towns tend to be populated by different social classes, each with its own mores. The neighborhood or community where a child grows up is the setting in which he or she learns about life. Social class influences the person's self-perception, perception of others, and perceptions of work, authority, and money. In terms of such pressing organizational problems as adjustment, quality of work life, and dissatisfaction, the manager attempting to understand employees must give attention to social class factors.

A review of each of the major forces that shapes personality indicates that managers have little control over these determinants. However, no manager should conclude that personality is therefore an unimportant factor in workplace behavior. Employee behavior cannot be understood without considering the concept of personality. In fact, personality is so interrelated with perception, attitudes, learning, and motivation that any analysis of behavior is grossly incomplete unless personality is considered.

The Big Five Personality Model   Personality is a term used to describe a great many feelings and behaviors. Literally hundreds of personality dimensions or traits have been identified or suggested by psychologists over the last century. Over the last couple of decades, however, a consensus has begun to emerge that five dimensions largely describe human personality.[27] Out of this consensus has evolved the "Big Five" personality model, suggesting that the following factors are central to describing personality: Extroversion, Emotional stability, Agreeableness, Conscientiousness, and Openness to experience. Each of the five is briefly described below. As you read these descriptions, reflect on the extent to which each of the factors describes your own personality.

Extroversion refers to the tendency to be sociable, friendly, and expressive. People high in extroversion may be talkative, gregarious, impetuous, expressive, and assertive. They will tend to enjoy interacting with coworkers and typically seek positions where there is a good deal of social interaction. People low on this factor will tend to be reserved, quiet, and introverted.

Emotional stability refers to the tendency to experience positive emotional states. Feeling psychologically secure, calm, and relaxed are consistent with having high emotional stability. On the other hand, anxiety, depression, anger, and embarrassment are characteristics of low emotional stability. The low stability individual is more likely to experience job-related stress, a topic discussed in detail in Chapter 7.

Being courteous, forgiving, tolerant, trusting, and soft-hearted are traits associated with **agreeableness**. The person we describe as "someone who gets along well with others" is high on agreeableness. It is a dimension that can help make

---

[27]J. M. Digman, "Personality Structure: Emergence of the Five-Factor Model," *Annual Review of Psychology,* 1990, pp. 195–214.

someone an effective team player and can pay off in jobs where developing and maintaining good interpersonal relationships is important. Individuals low on agreeableness are often described as rude, cold, uncaring, unsympathetic, and antagonistic.

Conscientiousness is exhibited by those who are described as dependable, organized, and responsible. It also includes attributes such as perseverance, hard work, and achievement orientation. It is not hard to understand why it is a dimension that is highly valued by organizations. Employees who are low on conscientiousness tend to be sloppy, inefficient, careless, even lazy.

The final dimension is **openness to experience**. This dimension reflects the extent to which an individual has broad interests and is willing to be a risk-taker. Specific traits include curiosity, broad-mindedness, creativity, imagination, and intelligence. It is an asset in jobs where change is constant and where innovation is important. Those low on this dimension tend to be unimaginative, conventional, and habit-bound.

Personality and Behavior

An issue of interest to behavioral scientists, organizational researchers, and managers is whether personality factors such as those measured by psychological inventories can predict behavior or performance in organizations. Many companies think they can. August Forge Corporation, for example, uses personality tests as a tool in hiring, training, and promoting, as well as in other personnel decisions. The test used by August Forge measures traits such as patience, independence, and exactitude.

Available research indicates that to varying degrees dimensions in the Big Five models are predictive of job performance. The conscientiousness dimension consistently predicts job performance criteria across all occupational groups.[28] Other dimensions are predictive for some groups and not others. Extroversion is a valid predictor of managerial success, for example; emotional stability is related to police job performance; openness to experience predicts success in a variety of training programs.[29] It is interesting that relationships among the Big Five dimensions and job performance also apply across country borders. Very similar relationships have been demonstrated to exist in Great Britain, Germany, France, The Netherlands, Norway, and Spain.[30]

A review of the entire range of personality research suggests that even with the "Big Five" there is no one trait or group of traits that predicts with precision how well someone will perform on a project, in a job, or completing work. It would be more beneficial to attempt to match the person with the job. The person should also be attempting to find the right or best fit. Using only scores on a personality test are subject to misalignments and poor fit. Working hard at the "fit" is likely to result in higher levels of job satisfaction, more positive attitudes, and better relationships among peers.

---

[28]Murray R. Barrick and Michael K. Mount, "The Big Five Personality Dimensions and Job Performance: A Meta-Analysis," *Personnel Psychology*, Spring 1991, pp. 1–26.

[29]Ibid.

[30]R. R. McCraw and P. T. Costa, "A Big Five Factor Theory of Personality," In L. A. Pervin and O. P. John (eds.), *Handbook of Personality*, 2nd ed. (New York: Guilford, 1999), pp. 139–53.

Personality Paradox

Ovick Kar, executive vice president of TCT Technical Training in Fremont, California, couldn't figure out why he was losing members of his sales force left and right. Kar discovered that even new salespeople quickly turned sour on the job at the fast-growing networking and telecommunications training company that specialized in online learning. "We were hiring people we thought matched our needs, but there was high turnover and disillusionment in [the sales] area," he recalls.

In an effort to better match candidates with the company's culture and job roles, TCT decided to look beyond resumes and work histories and into the minds and hearts of potential hires. At a seminar, Kar learned about the Predictive Index, or PI, a personality measuring tool distributed by Praendix/PI Management Resources of Wellesley Hills, Massachusetts.

The tool helps Kar determine whether a person's style is "naturally" suited to a particular job. Once Kar started to screen candidates using PI, he says, the company's retention problems vanished.

It's not unusual for companies to use personality tests to help determine whom they will hire, retain, and promote. A 1999 survey of 1,054 human resources managers conducted by the American Management Association shows that 44 percent used personality testing to select employees. And these numbers don't include companies that use less-orthodox methods of gauging personalities, such as handwriting analysis or astrological charts.

In the high-tech and Internet industries, where turnover is rampant and employee loyalty scarce, such tests promise to help select devoted employees who won't jump ship the moment things get tough. Employers also rely on personality testing to discover all the intangibles that don't get listed on a resume or that don't surface during an interview: whether a candidate thrives on stress and multitasking or whether he gets energy from working alone and doing long-term research. But in some cases these tests can be inaccurate, unethical, and harmful to employees and job candidates, so employers and recruiters must use caution when incorporating them into their hiring and advancement programs.

Personality tests serve one basic purpose: to see how well your personality "fits" the ideal personality for a given job or career path. For example, a salesperson must be outgoing and perform well in social situations; an engineer should be comfortable with periods of isolation and deep thought.

Of course, none of this is terribly scientific. It's up to a company to determine the ideal personality for the position it fills. Then it's up to the candidate to give an accurate portrait of himself.

Personality testing can be traced back to the early 20th century, when "quadrant theory" was developed, and it became popular in the workplace in the late 1970s when David Keirsey published his book *Please Understand Me*, which made Myers-Briggs a household name. Quadrant theory holds that people can be described as a combination of distinct personality types. Myers-Briggs scores test-takers on category pairings: Introvert/extrovert; intuitive/sensing; thinking/feeling; and judging/per-

www.tctte com

www.keirs com

www.mbty guide.com type/type.

A complete personality assessment of the Big Five rarely is employed for staffing decisions or in organizational behavior research. Typically, a few select personality traits are used to more closely examine the relationship between behavior and performance. We will look at three such characteristics as examples: locus of control, self-efficacy, and creativity.

Locus of Control   The *locus of control* of individuals determines the degree to which they believe their behaviors influence what happens to them.[31] Some people believe they are autonomous—that they are masters of their own fate and have personal responsibility for what happens to them. When they perform well, they believe it is because of their effort or skill. They are called **internals**. Others view themselves as helpless pawns of fate, controlled by outside forces over which they have little, if any, influence. When they perform well, they believe it

---

[31]J. R. Rotter, "Generalized Expectancies for Internal versus External Control of Reinforcement," *Psychological Monographs* 1, no. 609 (1966), pp. 1–28.

ceiving. For instance, a person who scores as an "ENFJ" is characterized as an "extrovert, intuitive, feeling, judging" type.

While Myers-Briggs is a general personality inventory, other tests are more directly related to matching people with careers. Susanne Millar, a senior consultant at Praendex/PI Management Resources, says most of her clients work in the high-tech industry. Candidates must sift through a list of 86 adjectives and choose which ones describe how they think other people expect them to behave at work. Then, using the same list of adjectives, they pick the words they think best describe themselves.

Part of the score is based on how different a person's "natural" style is from what is required for the job. The bigger the discrepancy, the less likely it is that the person is suited for a particular position.

Despite the insight learned about job candidates from personality assessments, employers should look at such tests as just one factor in determining whether a candidate is suitable for a hire or promotion.

If used appropriately, personality tools can provide employers that extra bit of assurance that the individual they hire will mesh with the company culture and can handle the job. A thorough evaluation of the available tools is an important first step: Has the test been verified against more complicated personality-assessing techniques such as psychiatric examinations? Does the company grading the test have expertise in psychology, and which companies are its other clients? Check references and talk to past clients about the results the tests achieved.

Finally, don't use just one approach. Linda Berens, director of Temperament Research Institute in Huntington Beach, California, advises her clients to combine personality tests with other interviewing methods, since "no instruments are 100 percent accurate."

Psychological Toolbox

A SAMPLE OF PERSONALITY TESTING RESOURCES.

- **Myers-Biggs Personality Inventory** tests and information can be found at www.keirsey.com, a Web site devoted to the work of David Keirsey, advocate of the Myers-Briggs model, and from the consulting firm Delta Associates at www.deltaassociates.com
- **Management Psychology Group** in Atlanta offers online personality assessments to companies and teams, as well as in-person evaluations of company culture and job candidates. More information at www.managementpsychology.com
- **Praedix/PI Management Resources**, based in Wellesley Hills, Massachusetts, offers corporate training in personality assessment using the Predictive Index. More information at www.piresources.com/pindex.html.
- **Temperament Research Institute** in Huntington Beach, California, offers seminars and uses Myers-Briggs and other tests to train managers at www.tri-network.com

---

Source: Annalee Newitz, "The Personality Paradox, *The Industry Standard*, October 2, 2000, pp. 210–14, and Richard S. Lazarus, "Toward Better Research on Stress and Coping," *American Psychologist*, June 2000, pp. 665–73.

---

is due to luck or because it was an easy task. They are **externals**. Some research suggests that externals score low on the Big Five dimensions of extroversion and emotional stability.[32] If you believe that the grades you typically receive in school are due to the particular classes you took, the characteristics of your professors, or the type of tests given, you are probably an external. On the other hand, if you think your grades typically reflect the amount of time and effort you devoted to a particular class and your knowledge of the subject matter, you are most likely an internal.

In organizational settings internals usually do not require as much supervision as do externals, because they are more likely to believe their own work behavior will influence outcomes such as performance, promotions, and pay. Some research suggest locus of control is related to moral behavior, with internals doing what they think is right and being willing to suffer the consequences

---

[32]Jesus F. Salgado, "The Five Factor Model of Personality and Job Performance in the European Community," *Journal of Applied Psychology*, February 1997, pp. 30–43.

Ethics Encounter 3.1

Can Locus of Control Predict Unethical Behavior?

In recent years we have seen a varied array of media reports of wrongdoing and unethical behavior in business, government, and education. Savings & loan institutions, Wall Street firms, universities with government contracts, and military procurement agencies are but a few of the entities that have made headlines. Are there personality factors that are related to choices individuals make to behave ethically or unethically? Some recent research on ethical decision making sheds some light on this question. A partial description of a portion of this research follows.

In this study individuals with an average of five years' work experience participated in an in-basket exercise in which they played the role of Pat Sneed, a national sales manager for an electronics firm. Among the dozen or so items in the in-basket were two that required decisions involving ethical concerns. In one, a regional sales director informs Sneed that one of his sales representatives is paying kickbacks. Sneed must decide whether or not to put an

end to the kickbacks. In the second situation, Sneed receives a memo from the vice president of production which indicates the vice president has decided to change the material used in a product to save production costs. The memo advises that customers should not be informed of this change despite problems it might create. Sneed must decide what, if anything, to do. Responses by study participants to these two situations were judged on the basis of preestablished criteria to be either ethical or unethical.

Internal locus of control participants demonstrated more ethical behavior, than their *external* counterparts. In fact, locus of control showed nearly twice as much effect on ethical decision making as did the combination of all of the several other variables which were included. The researchers suggest organizations may wish to assess locus of control when selecting managers for positions involving ethical decision making, although they acknowledge potential problems in doing so.

Source: The research described is reported in L. K. Trevino and S. A. Youngblood, "Bad Apples in Bad Barrels: A Casual Analysis of Ethical Decision-Making Behavior," *Journal of Applied Psychology,* August 1990, pp. 378–86.

for doing so.[33] Ethics Encounter 3.1 demonstrates a possible relationship between locus of control and ethical behavior.

Self-Efficacy   *Self-efficacy* relates to personal beliefs regarding competencies and abilities. Specifically, it refers to one's belief in one's ability to successfully complete a task. Individuals with a high degree of self-efficacy firmly believe in their performance capabilities. The concept of self-efficacy includes three dimensions: magnitude, strength, and generality.

Magnitude refers to the level of task difficulty that individuals believe they can attain. For example, Jim may believe he can put an arrow in the archery range target 6 times in 10 attempts. Sara may feel she can hit the target 8 times; thus, Sara has a higher magnitude of self-efficacy regarding this task than Jim. *Strength* refers to whether the belief regarding magnitude is strong or weak. If in the previous example Jim is moderately certain he can hit the target six times, while Sara is positive she can achieve eight hits, Sara is displaying greater strength of belief in her ability than is Jim. Finally, *generality* indicates how generalized across different situations the belief in capability is. If Jim thinks he can hit the target equally well with a pistol and rifle and Sara does not think she can, Jim is displaying greater generality than is Sara.

Beliefs regarding self-efficacy are learned. The most important factor in the development of self-efficacy appears to be past experiences. If over a period of time we attempt a task and are increasingly successful in our performance, we are

---

[33]L. K. Trevino and S. A. Youngblood, "Bad Apples in Bad Barrels: A Causal Analysis of Ethical Decision-Making Behavior and Human Resource Management," *Academy of Management Review,* July 1987, pp. 472–85.

likely to develop self-confidence and an increasing belief in our ability to perform the task successfully; conversely, if we repeatedly fail in our attempts to perform a task well, we are not as likely to develop strong feelings of self-efficacy. It is important to realize, however, that self-efficacy tends to be task specific; that is, a belief that we can perform very well in one job does not necessarily suggest a corresponding belief in our ability to excel in other jobs.

Feelings of self-efficacy have a number of managerial and organizational implications. Gist suggests that the self-efficacy concept has a number of theoretical and practial implications for organizational behavior and human resource management.[34] Included in the implications she suggests are important relationships among feelings of self-efficacy and performance appraisals, goal setting, and the use of incentives. Self-efficacy beliefs may also be important to consider in employee selection and training decisions and in identifying candidates for leadership positions.

Creativity   Creativity is a personality trait that involves the ability to break away from habit-bound thinking and produce novel and useful ideas. Creativity produces innovation, and innovation is the lifeblood of a growing number of corporations. 3M is famous for its creativity and product innovation. Rubbermaid introduces one new product a day. These companies, and others, such as Hewlett-Packard, Walt Disney, Home Depot, and Apple Computer are well known for their efforts to stimulate creativity.

Creativity is a personality trait that can be encouraged and developed within organizations by giving people opportunity and freedom to think in unconventional ways.[35] For example, one of the major impediments to increasing creativity in work settings is the fear of failure. If an organization is intolerant of mistakes and failure, it should not expect employees to take the risks often inherent in creative approaches to problems. At Heinz's highly successful frozen foods subsidiary, Ore-Ida, management is aware that creative behavior will sometimes result in mistakes. They have defined what they call the "perfect failure" and have arranged for a cannon to be shot off in celebration every time one occurs. The cannon symbolizes that a failure has occurred, been learned from, and is forgotton. Because failures are openly discussed and treated positively, the risk-taking behavior that management attempts to nourish is continued.

Each of the individual difference variables discussed here—heredity factors, abilities and skills, perception, attitudes, and personality—impact organizational effectiveness and efficiency. Managers who ignore the importance of these variables do themselves, their employees, and their organizations a disservice. As we proceed through the next four chapters focusing on individual-level behavior, keep in mind how these individual differences help shape the behavior and performance of employees.

Management Pointer 3.3

CREATIVITY

How to Develop Employee Creativity

1. Encourage everyone to view old problems from new perspectives.

2. Make certain people know that it is OK to make mistakes.

3. Provide as many people with as many new work experiences as you can.

4. Set an example in your own approach to dealing with problems and opportunities.

---

[34]M. E. Gist, "Self-Efficacy: Implications for Organizational Behavior and Human Resource Management," *Academy of Management Review,* July 1987, pp. 472–85.

[35]*Annual Report,* Heinz Co., 2000.

Summary of Key Points

- Major individual variables that influence work behavior include demographic factors (e.g., age, sex, race), abilities and skills, perception, attitudes, and personality. These combine with various organizational variables (resources, leadership, rewards, job design, structure) to shape productive, nonproductive, and counterproductive work behaviors.

- Attributions we make about why an event occurs influence our behavior. The process involves analyzing why something has happened (attributing a cause to the event) and fitting that explanation into a general framework that provides a basis for subsequent behavior. Thus our behavior is shaped by our perception of *why* certain things happen.

- Stereotyping is a process employed to assist us in dealing more efficiently with massive information demands. It can be a useful, even necessary, perceptual process. A prejudice is a particular form of stereotyping that resists change even in the face of contrary information. Many stereotypes can be helpful; prejudice is never helpful.

- An attitude is a learned predisposition to respond favorably or unfavorably to people, objects, and situations with which it is related. An attitude consists of a cognitive component (beliefs), an affect component (feelings), and a behavioral component which consists of the individual's behavioral intentions.

- Although the job satisfaction–job performance relationship is a complex one that is not fully understood, it seems clear that these two variables are related under certain conditions. One current view is that the rewards one receives as a consequence of good performance, and the degree to which these rewards are perceived as reasonable, affect both the extent to which satisfaction results from performance and the extent performance is affected by satisfaction.

- Major forces influencing the nature of an individual's personality include (1) heredity factors, (2) parent-child and family relationships, (3) social class and other group membership forces, and (4) cultural factors. The latter is particularly critical as cross-cultural interactions increase in today's global business envionment.

- The Big Five personality model suggests that five dimensions are central to describing personality. These five are extroversion, emotional stability, agreeableness, conscientiousness, and openness to experience. Every individual's personality reflects differing degrees of these five factors.

- There are numerous personality factors that operate to influence behavior. Three that are frequently identified as important in explaining behavior and performance are locus of control, self-efficacy, and creativity.

Review and Discussion Questions

1. So many factors influence an individual's behavior that it is impossible to accurately predict what that behavior will be in all situations. Why then should managers take time to understand individual differences?

2. In what ways can stereotyping be a helpful process? Can a stereotype be useful even if it is not entirely accurate? Are we better off by getting rid of our stereotypes or by making them more accurate?

3. From the standpoint of managing people effectively, which is more important to the manager: subordinates' perceptions of the behavior or the actual behavior itself? Explain.

4. Think of an important attitude you have regarding a career. Identify the three components of that attitude and indicate what each outcome response would be.

5. How can a manager use an understanding of emotional intelligence to explain the poor interpersonal skills of a person?

6. Your text identified job satisfaction as an important attitude. What other attitudes might be important in work settings?

7. Are you an internal or an external? Would you rather have a boss who is an internal or an external? Why?

8. A criticism of some organizations is that all its employees have the same personality. Why might this be desirable from the organization's perspective? How might this be counterproductive?

9. As a manager, how might you increase a subordinate's feelings of self-efficacy regarding a job assignment? How might you attempt to increase the creativity of your subordinates?

10. "If everyone were alike, the task of managing organizations would be much easier." Do you agree or disagree with this statement? Explain.

READING 3.1   One More Time: Do Female and Male Managers Differ?

Gary N. Powell

Do female and male managers differ in the personal qualities they bring to their jobs? Yes, if you believe two recent articles in influential business magazines. Jan Grant, in a 1988 *Organizational Dynamics* article entitled "Women as Managers: What They Can Offer to Organizations,"[1] asserted that women have unique qualities that make them particularly well-suited as managers. Instead of forcing women to fit the male model of managerial success, emphasizing such qualities as independence, competitiveness, forcefulness, and analytical thinking. Grant argued that organizations should place greater emphasis on such female qualities as affiliation and attachment, cooperativeness, nurturance, and emotionality.

Felice Schwartz's 1989 *Harvard Business Review* article, "Management Women and the New Facts of Life,"[2] triggered a national debate over the merits of "mommy tracks" (though she did not use this term herself). She proposed that corporations (1) distinguish between "career-primary women" who put their careers first, and "career-and-family" women who seek a balance between career and family, (2) nurture the careers of the former group as potential top executives, and (3) offer flexible work arrangements and family supports to the latter group in exchange for lower opportunities for career advancement. Women were assumed to be more interested in such arrangements, and thereby less likely to be suitable top executives than men; there has been less discussion over the merits of "daddy tracks."

Male and female managers certainly differ in their success within the managerial ranks. Although women have made great strides in entering management since 1970, with the overall proportion of women managers rising from 16 percent to 40 percent, the proportion of women who hold top management positions is less than 3 percent.[3] This could be due simply to the average male manager being older and more experienced than the average female manager. After all, managerial careers invariably

start at the bottom. If there were no basic differences between male and female managers, it would be just a matter of time until the proportion of women was about the same at all managerial levels.

But are there basic differences between male and female managers? Traditional sex role stereotypes state that males are more masculine (e.g., self-reliant, aggressive, competitive, decisive) and females more feminine (e.g., sympathetic, gentle, shy, sensitive to the needs of others).[4] Grant's views of male-female differences mirrored these stereotypes. However, there is disagreement over the applicability of these stereotypes to managers. Three distinct points of view have emerged:

1. *No differences.* Women who pursue the nontraditional career of manager reject the feminine stereotype and have needs, values, and leadership styles similar to those of men who pursue managerial careers.
2. *Stereotypical differences.* Female and male managers differ in ways predicted by stereotypes, as a result of early socialization experiences that reinforce masculinity in males and femininity in females.
3. *Nonstereotypical differences.* Female and male managers differ in ways opposite to stereotypes because women managers have to be exceptional to compensate for early socialization experiences that are different from those of men.

I recently conducted an extensive review of research on sex differences in management to determine the level of support for each of these viewpoints.[5] I considered four types of possible differences: in behavior, motivation, commitment, and subordinates' responses (see Exhibit 3.9).

The Review

The two most frequently studied types of managerial behavior are task-oriented and people-oriented behavior.[6] *Task-oriented behavior* is directed toward subordinates' performance and includes initiating work, organizing it, and setting deadlines and standards. *People-oriented*

Source: Gary N. Powell, "One More Time: Do Female and Male Managers Differ?" *Academy of Management Executive,* August 1990, pp. 68–75.

[1] J. Grant, "Women as Managers: What They Can Offer to Organizations," *Organizational Dynamics,* Winter 1988, pp. 56–63.

[2] F. N. Schwartz, "Management Women and the New Facts of Life," *Harvard Business Review,* January–February 1989, pp. 65–76.

[3] U.S. Department of Labor, Bureau of Labor Statistics, *Employment and Earnings* (October 1989), Table A–22, p. 29; *Handbook of Labor Statistics,* Bulletin 2175 (December 1983), Table 16, pp. 44–46; J. B. Forbes, J. E. Piercy, and T. L. Hayes. "Women Executives: Breaking Down Barriers?" *Business Horizons,* November–December 1988, pp. 6–9.

[4] For a review of research on sex role stereotypes, see D. N. Ruble and T. N. Ruble, "Sex Stereotypes," in A. G. Miller, ed., *In the Eye of the Beholder* (New York: Praeger, 1982).

[5] For a full report of this review with complete references, see G. N. Powell, Chapter 5, "Managing People," in *Women and Men in Management* (Newbury Park, CA: Sage, 1988).

[6] The technical terms used by researchers for these types of behavior are "initiating structure behavior" and "consideration behavior."

EXHIBIT 3.9   Sex Differences in Management: Selected Results

Dimension	Results
Behavior:	
Task-oriented	No difference.
People-oriented	No difference.
Effectiveness ratings	Stereotypical difference in evaluations of managers in laboratory studies: Males favored. No difference in evaluations of actual managers.
Response to poor performer	Stereotypical difference: Males use norm of equity, whereas females use norm of equality.
Influence strategies	Stereotypical difference: Males use a wider range of strategies, more positive strategies, and less negative strategies. The difference diminishes when women managers have high self-confidence.
Motivation	No difference in some studies.
	Nonstereotypical difference in other studies: Female motivational profile is close to that associated with successful managers.
Commitment	Inconsistent evidence regarding difference.
Subordinates responses	Stereotypical difference in responses to managers in laboratory studies; Managers using style that matches sex role stereotype are favored.
	No difference in responses to actual managers.

behavior is directed toward subordinates' welfare and includes seeking to build their self-confidence, making them feel at ease, and soliciting their input about matters that affect them.

There have been numerous studies of whether female and male leaders differ in these two types of behavior, including (1) laboratory studies in which individuals are asked to react to a standardized description of a female or male leader or are led by a female or male leader on a simulated work task, and (2) field studies comparing female and male leaders in actual organizational settings. Laboratory studies control the variable under investigation better, but they provide less information about the manager. Thus, they are more likely to yield results that support stereotypes of managers than field studies.

Sex role stereotypes suggest that men, being masculine, will be higher in task-oriented behavior, and women, being feminine, will be higher in people-oriented behavior. However, sex role stereotypes are not supported when the results of different studies are considered as a whole. According to a "meta-analysis" of research studies, male and female leaders exhibit similar amounts of task-oriented and people-oriented behavior regardless of the type of study.

Male leaders have been rated as more effective in laboratory studies, but male and female leaders are seen as similarly effective in the "the real world."[7]

There are some possible sex differences in managerial behavior that are under investigation. For example, some evidence supporting the "stereotypical differences" view suggests that female and male managers differ in their responses to poor performers. Males may follow a norm of *equity,* basing their response on whether they believe the poor performance is caused by lack of ability or lack of effort, and females a norm of *equality,* treating all poor performers alike regardless of the assumed cause.[8] Other evidence suggests that female and male managers differ in the strategies they use to influence subordinates (see Exhibit 3.9), but that this difference diminishes as women managers gain self-confidence in their jobs.[9] Overall, though, the pattern of research results on sex differences in managerial behavior favors the "no differences" view.

Female managers are at least as motivated as male managers. Some studies have found that female and male managers score essentially the same on psychological tests of motives that predict managerial success, supporting the "no differences" view. When sex differences have been found, they have supported the "nonstereotypical differences" view. For example, in a study of nearly 2,000 managers, women managers reported lower basic needs and higher

[7]G. H. Dobbins and S. J. Platz, "Sex Differences in Leadership: How Real Are They?" *Academy of Management Review* 11, 1986, pp. 118–27.

[8]G. H. Dobbins, "Effects of Gender on Leaders' Responses to Poor Performers: An Attributional Interpretation," *Academy of Management Journal* 28, 1985, pp. 587–98.

[9]D. Instone, B. Major, and B. B. Bunker, "Gender, Self-Confidence, and Social Influence Strategies: An Organizational Simulation," *Journal of Personality and Social Psychology* 44, 1983, pp. 322–33.

needs for self-actualization. Compared with males, female managers were more concerned with opportunities for growth, autonomy, and challenge and less concerned with work environment and pay. The women managers were judged to exhibit a "more mature and higher-achieving motivational profile" than their male counterparts.[10]

There is disagreement about whether female and male managers possess different levels of commitment.[11] Some studies have found that women are more committed as a group than males; other studies have found that women are less committed; and still other studies have found no sex difference in commitment. Instead, factors other than sex have been linked more conclusively to commitment. For example, age and education are positively associated with commitment. Greater job satisfaction, more meaningful work, and greater utilization of skills also are associated with stronger commitment.[12]

Even if male and female managers did not differ in any respect, their subordinates still could react to them differently. Subordinates' responses to managers have varied according to the type of study. Some laboratory studies have found that managers are judged more favorably when their behavior fits the appropriate sex role stereotype. Female managers using a people-oriented leadership style have been evaluated more positively than male managers using that style; and the male managers using a task-oriented style have been evaluated more positively than female managers using that style. However, subordinates do not respond differently to actual male and female managers, supporting the "no differences" view. Once subordinates have worked for both female and male managers, the effects of stereotypes disappear and managers are treated as individuals rather than representatives of their sex.[13]

In summary, sex differences are absent in task-oriented behavior, people-oriented behavior, effectiveness ratings of actual managers, and subordinates' responses to actual managers. Stereotypical differences in some types of managerial behavior and in some ratings of managers in laboratory studies favor male managers. On the other hand, where differences in motivational profiles appear, they are nonstereotypical and favor female managers. Although results regarding sex differences in commitment are inconclusive, sex differences are not as extensive as other types of differences.

This review supports the "no differences" view of sex differences in management. There is not much difference between the needs, values, and leadership styles of male and female managers. The sex differences that have been found are few, found in laboratory studies more than field studies, and tend to cancel each other out.

Implications for Organizations

The implications of this review are clear: *If there are no differences between male and female managers, companies should not act as if there are.* Instead they should follow two principles in their actions:

1. To be gender-blind in their decisions regarding open managerial positions and present or potential managers, except when consciously trying to offset the effects of past discrimination
2. To try to minimize differences in the job experiences of their male and female managers, so that artificial sex differences in career success do not arise

Grant based her recommendations on a "stereotypical differences" view. She argued that organizations will benefit from placing greater value on women's special qualities.[14]

These "human resources" skills are critical in helping to stop the tide of alienation, apathy, cynicism, and low morale in organizations. . . . If organizations are to become more humane, less alienating, and more responsive to the individuals who work for them, they will probably need to learn to value process as well as product. Women have an extensive involvement in the processes of our society—an involvement that derives from their greater participation in the reproductive process and their early experience of family life. . . . Thus women may indeed be the most radical force available in bringing about organizational change.

Human resources skills are certainly essential to today's organizations. Corporations that are only concerned with getting a product out and pay little attention to their employees' needs are unlikely to have a committed workforce or to be effective in the long run. However, women are at risk when corporations assume that they have a monopoly on human resource skills. The risk is that they will be placed exclusively in managerial jobs that particularly call for social sensitivity and interpersonal skills in dealing with individuals and special-interest groups, e.g., public relations, human resources management, consumer affairs, corporate social responsibility. These jobs are typically staff functions, peripheral to the more powerful line

[10]S. M. Donnell and J. Hall, "Men and Women as Managers: A Significant Case of No Significant Difference," *Organizational Dynamics*, Spring 1980, p. 71.

[11]Commitment to work, job, career, and organizations have all been examined in different streams of research. This article simply refers to commitment in general, since each type of commitment suggests a greater degree of involvement in work in spite of fine difference among them.

[12]L. H. Chusmir, "Job Commitment and the Organizational Woman," *Academy of Management Review* 7, 1982, pp. 595–602.

[13]K. M. Bartol and D. A. Butterfield, "Sex Effects in Evaluating Leaders," *Journal of Applied Psychology* 61, 1976, pp. 446–54; J. Adams, R. W. Rice, and J. Instone, "Follower Attitudes toward Women and Judgments Concerning Performance by Female and Male Leaders," *Academy of Management Journal* 27, 1984, pp. 636–43.

[14]Grant, p. 62.

functions of finance, sales, and production and seldom regarded in exalted terms by line personnel. Women managers are disproportionately found in such jobs, outside the career paths that most frequently lead to top management jobs.[15] Corporations that rely on Grant's assertions about women's special abilities could very well perpetuate this trend. Thus it is very important that the facts about sex differences in management be disseminated to key decision makers. When individuals hold onto stereotypical views about sex differences despite the facts, either of the two approaches may be tried:

1. Send them to programs such as cultural diversity workshops to make them aware of the ways in which biases related to sex (as well as race, age, etc.) can affect their decisions and to learn how to keep these biases from occurring. For example, Levi Strauss put all of its executives, including the president, through an intensive three-day program designed to make them examine their attitudes toward women and minorities on the job.[16]
2. Recognize that beliefs and attitudes are difficult to change and focus on changing behavior instead. If people are motivated to be gender-blind in their decision-making by an effective performance appraisal and reward system backed by the CEO, they often come to believe in what they are doing.[17]

Organizations should do whatever they can to equalize the job experience of equally-qualified female and male managers. This means abandoning the model of a successful career as an uninterrupted sequence of promotions to positions of greater responsibility heading toward the top ranks. All too often, any request to take time out from career for family reasons, either by a woman or a man, is seen as evidence of lack of career commitment.

Schwartz based her recommendations on a real sex difference: More women than men leave work for family reasons due to the demands of maternity and the differing traditions and expectations of the sexes. However, her solution substitutes a different type of sex difference, that such women remain at work with permanently reduced career opportunities. It does not recognize that women's career orientation may change during their careers. Women could temporarily leave the fast track for the mommy track, but then be ready and able to resume the fast track later. Once they were classified as career-and-

family, they would find it difficult to be reclassified as career-primary even if their career commitment returned to its original level.

Corporations would offer daddy tracks as well as mommy tracks and accurately believe that they were treating their female and male employees alike. However, if women tended to opt for such programs more than men and anyone who opted for one was held back in pursuing a future managerial career, the programs would contribute to a sex difference in access to top management positions. Automatic restrictions should not be placed on the later career prospects of individuals who choose alternative work arrangements. Those who wish to return to the fast track should be allowed to do so once they demonstrate the necessary skills and commitment.

There are other ways by which organizations can minimize sex differences in managers' job experiences. For example, the majority of both male and female top executives have had one or more mentors, and mentorship has been critical to their advancement and success.[18] However, as Kathy Kram, an expert on the mentoring process, observed, "It's easier for people to mentor people like themselves."[19] Lower-level female managers have greater difficulty in finding mentors than male managers at equivalent levels, due to the smaller number of female top executives. Unless companies do something, this gives lower-level male managers an advantage in getting ahead.

Some companies try to overcome barriers of sex by assigning highly-placed mentors to promising lower-level managers. For example, at the Bank of America, senior executives are asked to serve as mentors for three or four junior managers for a year at a time. Formal mentoring programs also have been implemented at the Jewel Companies, Aetna, Bell Labs, Merrill Lynch, and Federal Express. Such programs do not guarantee career success for the recipients of mentoring, of course. However, they do contribute to making mentors more equally available for male and female managers.[20]

Companies also influence job experiences through the training and development programs that they encourage or require their managers to take. These programs contribute to a sex difference in job experiences if (1) men and women are systematically diagnosed to have different

[15]G. N. Powell, "Career Development and the Woman Manager: A Social Power Perspective," *Personnel*, May–June 1980, pp. 22–32.

[16]P. Watts, "Bias Busting: Diversity Training in the Workplace," *Management Review*, December 1987, pp. 51–54; B. Zeitz and L. Dusky, "Levi Strauss," in *The Best Companies for Women* (New York: Simon and Schuster, 1988).

[17]L. Festinger. *A Theory of Cognitive Dissonance* (Evanston, IL: Row, Peterson, 1957).

[18]*The Corporate Woman Officer* (New York: Heidrich & Struggles, 1986); G. R. Roche, "Much Ado about Mentors," *Harvard Business Review*, January–February 1979, pp. 14–28; D. M. Hunt and C. Michael, "Mentorship: A Career Training and Development Tool," *Academy of Management Review* 8, 1983, pp. 475–85; R. N. Noe, "Women and Mentoring: A Review and Research Agenda," *Academy of Management Review* 13, 1988, pp. 65–78.

[19]"Women and Minority Workers in Business Find a Mentor Can Be a Rare Commodity," *Wall Street Journal*, November 11, 1987, p. 39.

[20]K. E. Kram, Chapter 7, "Creating Conditions That Encourage Mentoring," in *Mentoring at Work* (Glenview, IL: Scott, Foresman, 1985).

developmental needs and thereby go through different programs, or (2) men and women are deliberately segregated in such programs. Both of these conditions have been advocated and met in the past. For example, in a 1972 article in *Personnel Journal*, Marshall Brenner concluded that[21]

> women will, for the immediate future, generally require different managerial development activities than men. This is based on research showing that, in general, they have different skills and different attitudes toward the managerial role than men do.

This review suggests the opposite, particularly for women and men who are already in management positions. Women managers do not need to be sent off by themselves for "assertiveness training"—they already know how to be assertive. Instead, they need access to advanced training and development activities, such as executive MBAs or executive leadership workshops, just like male managers do.

Some of the available activities, such as the Executive Women Workshop offered by the Center for Creative Leadership (CCL), are open only to women. In addition, some companies, such as Northwestern Bell, have their own executive leadership programs for women only. Such programs, when attended voluntarily, provide women managers a useful opportunity to "share experiences and ideas with other executive women in a unique environment," as the CCL's catalogue puts it, as well as provide valuable executive training.[22] In general, though, women and men should be recommended for training and development programs according to their individual needs rather than their sex. Almost half of the companies regarded as "the best companies for women" in a recent book rely on training and workshops to develop their high-potential managerial talent. However, many of these companies, including Bidermann Industries, General Mills, Hewitt Associates, Neiman-Marcus, and PepsiCo. have no special programs for women: they simply assign the best and brightest people regardless of sex.[23]

In conclusion, organizations should not assume that male and female managers differ in personal qualities. They also should make sure that their policies, practices, and programs minimize the creation of sex differences in managers' experiences on the job. There is little reason to believe that either women or men make superior managers, or that women and men are different types of managers. Instead, there are likely to be excellent, average, and poor managerial performers within each sex. Success in today's highly competitive marketplace calls for organizations to make the best use of the talent available to them. To do this, they need to identify, develop, encourage, and promote the most effective managers, regardless of sex.

[21]M. H. Brenner, "Management Development for Women," *Personnel Journal*, March 1972, p. 166.

[22]*Programs: Center for Creative Leadership.* Greensboro, NC 15. July 1988–June 1989.

[23]Zeitz & Dusky, *The Best Companies.* "Levi Strauss".

Exercises

EXERCISE 3.1   Testing Your Assumptions about People

To enable you to examine your assumptions about people, their work, and how to get them to do the work that is expected, the following test will be helpful. Simply check the appropriate column beside each of the 15 statements that are presented. Read each statement and *immediately* place a check in one of the four columns. Because the test is designed to measure your assumptions, not your carefully reasoned responses, answer at once, not after "qualifying" the statement or looking for the "right" answer.

There are no right or wrong answers, and the "best" answer is the one that describes what you actually believe; any other answer will only cloud the picture this test is trying to obtain—your instinctive pattern of behavior.

Think of "people" in a rather general sense, not as specific individuals. You are trying to analyze your general pattern of behavior—the image that you project to others. It should take you no more than 3 to 4 minutes to complete the quiz.

	Strongly Disagree	Disagree	Agree	Strongly Agree
1. Almost everyone could improve their job performance considerably if they really wanted to.	_____	_____	_____	_____
2. It is unrealistic to expect people to show the same enthusiasm for their work as for their leisure activities.	_____	_____	_____	_____
3. Even when given encouragement by the boss, very few people show the desire to improve themselves on the job.	_____	_____	_____	_____
4. If you give people enough money, they are less likely to worry about such intangibles as status or recognition.	_____	_____	_____	_____
5. When people talk about wanting more-responsible jobs, they usually mean they want more money and status.	_____	_____	_____	_____
6. Because most people don't like to make decisions on their own, it is hard to get them to assume responsibility.	_____	_____	_____	_____
7. Being tough with people usually will get them to do what you want.	_____	_____	_____	_____
8. A good way to get people to do more work is to crack down on them once in a while.	_____	_____	_____	_____
9. It weakens people's prestige whenever they have to admit that a subordinate has been right and they have been wrong.	_____	_____	_____	_____
10. The most effective manager is one who gets the results expected, regardless of the methods used in handling people.	_____	_____	_____	_____
11. It is too much to expect that people will try to do a good job without being prodded by their boss.	_____	_____	_____	_____
12. The boss who expects people to set their own standards for performance probably will find that they don't set them very high.	_____	_____	_____	_____
13. If people don't use much imagination and ingenuity on the job, it's probably because relatively few have much of either.	_____	_____	_____	_____
14. One problem in asking for the ideas of subordinates is that their perspective is too limited for their suggestions to be of much practical value.	_____	_____	_____	_____
15. It is only human nature for people to try to do as little work as they can get away with.	_____	_____	_____	_____
Total for Each Column				
"Weighting" Each Column	× 1_____	× 2_____	× 3_____	× 4_____
Total Score				_____

Source: Adapted from Roger Fritz, *Rate Your Executive Potential* (New York: John Wiley and Sons, 1988), pp. 61–64.

To Score the Test

Total the number of marks in each column. Obviously, unless you have skipped a question, the four totals should add up to 15.

Now "weight" your answer by multiplying each column total by the figure given (that is, the total in the *strongly disagree* column × 1, the *disagree* column total × 2, the *agree* column total × 3, and the *strongly agree* column × 4). Enter the answers at the ends of the appropriate columns.

Add the four weighted column totals together to obtain your total score. The total should fall somewhere between 15 and 60. The theory is that your assumptions about people and their work leads you to develop a certain style of management.

To determine where your score would fall in Exhibit 3.10, place an "X" along the continuum, and circle it.

The range from A to D at the top of the table provides for all possible sets of assumptions regarding people and their work. The segment from A to M represents various degrees of autocratic or authoritarian management styles, while the segment from M to D covers different levels of democratic or developmental styles of management.

EXHIBIT 3.10	Your Leadership Style				
Style	60 A	Autocratic	33–30 M	Developmental	15 D
Often called . . .		Boss		Leader	
Motivates from . . .		Fear		Inspiration	
Supervision is . . .		Close		General	

Exercises

EXERCISE 3.2   Personality Insights

The following 27 statements are designed to provide some insights regarding how you see yourself. In the blank space next to each of these statements, write the number which best describes how strongly you agree or disagree with the statement, or how true or false the statement is as it applies to you. The numbers represent the following:

5 = Strongly Agree, or Definitely True

4 = Generally Agree, or Mostly True

3 = Neither Agree nor Disagree, Neither True nor False

2 = Generally Disagree, or Mostly False

1 = Strongly Disagree, or Definitely False

Example:

___2___   You enjoy playing "bridge."

(The "2" in the space next to the statement indecates that you generally disagree: you are more negative than neutral about enjoying "bridge.")

_____ 1. In some circumstances in the past you have taken the lead.

_____ 2. Everyone should place trust in a supernatural force whose decisions he or she always obeys.

_____ 3. You like to perform activities involving selling or salesmanship.

_____ 4. As a rule you assess your previous actions closely.

_____ 5. You often observe those around you to see how your words and actions affect them.

_____ 6. What you earn depends on what you know and how hard you work.

_____ 7. Generally, those in authority do their share of the unpleasant jobs without passing them on to others.

_____ 8. The remedy for social problems depends on eliminating dishonest, immoral, and mentally inferior people.

_____ 9. Most people today earn their pay by their own work.

_____10. The lowest type of person is the one who does not love and respect his parents.

_____11. There are two kinds of people: the weak and the strong.

_____12. You are the kind of person who tends to look into and analyze himself or herself.

_____13. Your promotions depend more on who you know than on how well you do your work.

_____14. All children should be taught obedience and respect for authority.

_____15. Those who are in public offices usually put their own interest ahead of the public interest.

_____16. Many bosses actually deserve lower pay than their employees.

_____17. Taking on important responsibilities like starting your own company is something you would like to do.

_____18. An insult to your good name should never go unpunished.

_____19. In a meeting you will speak up when you disagree with someone you are convinced is wrong.

_____20. Thinking about complex problems is enjoyable to you.

_____21. Generally, people are well paid for their contributions to society.

_____22. It is better to work for a good boss than for yourself.

_____23. Many times you would like to know the real reasons why some people behave as they do.

_____24. In the long run, we each get what we deserve.

_____25. Most organizations believe in paying a fair day's wages for a fair day's work.

Source: This self-feedback experiential exercise is reprinted with permission from the *Subordinates' Management Styles Survey* by Bernard M. Bass, Enzo R. Valenzi, and Larry D. Eldridge.

_____26. Getting ahead is based more on your performance than your politics.

_____27. You can't expect to be treated fairly by those above you unless you insist on it.

Take your answers to the above questions and enter them below in the appropriate space. In those cases where there is an asterisk before the number, use *reverse scoring* by subtracting your score from six, that is, a 1 becomes a 5, a 4 becomes a 2, and so forth. Asterisks indicate that you must change originally high scores to low ones and vice versa.

Group 1	Group 2	Group 3	Group 4
6. _____	1. _____	*2. _____	4. _____
7. _____	3. _____	*8. _____	5. _____
9. _____	17. _____	*10. _____	12. _____
*13. _____	19. _____	*11. _____	20. _____
*15. _____	*22. _____	*14. _____	23. _____
*16. _____	Total _____	*18. _____	Total _____
21. _____		Total _____	
24. _____			
25. _____			
26. _____			
*27. _____			
Total			

Now take each of your totals and divide by the number of answers so as to obtain your average respones, that is 2.3, 3.2, 4.1, and so forth. On a scale of 1–5, this measures how you see yourself in each of these four areas.

Average Score

The four areas, represented by Groups 1–4, respectively, are:

_____ 1. Fair—this score measures the extent to which you see the world as treating you fairly.

_____ 2. Assertive—this score measures the extent to which you see yourself as aggressive.

_____ 3. Equalitarian—this score measures the extent to which you see yourself as nonauthoritarian.

_____ 4. Introspective—this score measures the extent to which you see yourself as thinking about things that go on around you and trying to determine why they occur.

Cases

CASE 3.1   Bob Knowlton

Bob Knowlton was sitting alone in the conference room of the laboratory. The rest of the group had gone. One of the secretaries had stopped and talked for a while about her husband's coming induction into the army and had finally left. Bob, alone in the laboratory, slid a little further down in his chair, looking with satisfaction at the results of the first test fun of the new photon unit.

He liked to stay after the others had gone. His appointment as project head was still new enough to give him a deep sense of pleasure. His eyes were on the graphs before him, but in his mind he could hear Dr. Jerrold, the project head, saying again, "There's one thing about this place you can bank on. The sky is the limit for a man who can produce!" Knowlton felt again the tingle of happiness and embarrassment. Well, dammit, he said to himself, he had produced. He wasn't kidding anybody. He had come to the Simmons Laboratories two years ago. During a routine testing of some rejected Clanson components, he had stumbled on the idea of the photon correlator, and the rest just happened. Jerrold had been enthusiastic: A separate

project had been set up for further research and development of the device, and he had gotten the job of running it. The whole sequence of events still seemed a little miraculous to Knowlton.

He shrugged out of the reverie and bent determinedly over the sheets when he heard someone come into the room behind him. He looked up expectantly; Jerrold often stayed late himself and now and then dropped in for a chat. This always made the day's end especially pleasant for Bob. It wasn't Jerrold. The man who had come in was a stranger. He was tall, thin, and rather dark. He wore steel-rimmed glasses and had a very wide leather belt with a large brass buckle. Lucy remarked later that it was the kind of belt the Pilgrims must have worn.

The stranger smiled and introduced himself. "I'm Simon Fester. Are you Bob Knowlton?" Bob said yes, and they shook hands. "Doctor Jerrold said I might find you in. We were talking about your work, and I'm very much interested in what you are doing." Bob waved to a chair.

Fester didn't seem to belong in any of the standard categories of visitors: customer, visiting fireman, stockholder. Bob pointed to the sheets on the table. "There are the preliminary results of a test we're running. We've got a new gadget by the tail and we're trying to understand it. It's not finished, but I can show you the section we're testing."

Source: This case was prepared by Professor Alex Bavelas for courses in management of research and development conducted at the School of Industrial Management, Massachusetts Institute of Technology, Cambridge, and is used with his permission.

He stood up, but Fester was deep in the graphs. After a moment, he looked up with an odd grin. "These look like plots of a Jennings surface. I've been playing around with some autocorrelation functions of surfaces—you know that stuff." Bob, who had no idea what he was referring to, grinned back and nodded, and immediately felt uncomfortable. "Let me show you the monster," he said, and led the way to the workroom.

After Fester left, Knowlton slowly put the graphs away, feeling vaguely annoyed. Then, as if he had made a decision, he quickly locked up and took the long way out so that he would pass Jerrold's office. But the office was locked. Knowlton wondered whether Jerrold and Fester had left together.

The next morning, Knowlton dropped into Jerrold's office, mentioned that he had talked with Fester, and asked who he was.

"Sit down for a minute," Jerrold said, "I want to talk to you about him. What do you think of him?" Knowlton replied truthfully that he thought Fester was very bright and probably very competent. Jerrold looked pleased.

"We're taking him on," he said. "He's had a very good background in a number of laboratories, and he seems to have ideas about the problems we're tackling here." Knowlton nodded in agreement, instantly wishing that Fester would not be placed with him.

"I don't know yet where he will finally land," Jerrold continued, "but he seems interested in what you are doing. I thought he might spend a little time with you by way of getting started." Knowlton nodded thoughtfully. "If his interest in your work continues, you can add him to your group."

"Well, he seemed to have some good ideas even without knowing exactly what we are doing," Knowlton answered. "I hope he stays; we'd be glad to have him."

Knowlton walked back to the lab with mixed feelings. He told himself that Fester would be good for the group. He was no dunce; he'd produce. Knowlton thought again of Jerrold's promise when he had promoted him—"the man who produces gets ahead in this outfit." The words seemed to carry the overtones of a threat now.

That day Fester didn't appear until midafternoon. He explained that he had had a long lunch with Jerrold, discussing his place in the lab. "Yes," said Knowlton, "I talked with Jerry this morning about it, and we both thought you might work with us for awhile."

Fester smiled in the same knowing way that he had smiled when he mentioned the Jenning surfaces. "I'd like to," he said.

Knowlton introduced Fester to the other members of the lab. Fester and Link, the mathematician of the group, hit it off well together and spent the rest of the afternoon discussing a method of analysis of patterns that Link had been worrying over the last month.

It was 6:30 when Knowlton finally left the lab that night. He had waited almost eagerly for the end of the day to come—when they would all be gone and he could sit in the quiet rooms, relax, and think it over. "Think what over?" he asked himself. He didn't know. Shortly after 5 P.M. they had almost all gone except Fester, and what followed was almost a duel. Knowlton was annoyed that he was being cheated out of his quiet period and finally resentfully determined that Fester should leave first.

Fester was sitting at the donference table reading, and Knowlton was sitting at his desk in the little glass-enclosed cubby he used during the day when he needed to be undisturbed. Fester had gotten the last year's progress reports out and was sutdying them carefully. The time dragged. Knowlton doodled on a pad, the tension growing inside him. What the hell did Fester think he was going to find in the reports?

Knowlton finally gave up and they left the lab together. Fester took several of the reports with him to study in the evening. Knowlton asked him if he thought the reports gave a clear picture of the lab's activities.

"They're excellent," Fester answered with obvious sincerity. "They're not only good reports; what they report is damn good, too!" Knowlton was surprised at the relief he feld and grew almost jovial as he said good-night.

Driving him, Knowlton felt more optimistic about Fester's presence in the lab. He had never fully understood the analysis that Kink was attempting. If there was anything wrong with Link's approach, Fester would probably spot it. "And if I'm any judge," he murmured, "he won't be especially diplomatic about it."

He described Fester to his wife, who was amused by the broad leather belft and brass buckle.

"It's the kind of belt that Pilgrims must have worn," she laughed.

"I'm not worried about how he holds his pants up," he laughed with her. "I'm afraid that he's the kind that just has to make like a genius twice each day. And that can be pretty rough on the group."

Knowlton had been asleep for several hours when he was jerked awake by the telephone. He realized it had rung several times. He swung off the bed muttering about damn fools and telephones. It was Fester. Without any excuses, apparently oblivious of the time, he plunged into an excited recital of how Link's patterning problem could be solved.

Knowlton covered the mouthpiece to answer his wife's stage-whispered "Who is it?" "It's the genius," replied Knowlton.

Fester, completely ignoring the fact that it was 2:00 in the morning, proceeded in a very excited way to start in the middle of an explanation of a competely new approach to certain of the photon lab problems that he had stumbled on while analyzing past experiments. Knowlton managed to put some enthusiasm in his own voice and stood there, half-dazed and very uncomfortable, listening to Fester talk endlessly about what he had discovered. It was probably not only a new approach but also an analysis which showed the inherent weakness of the previous experiment and how experimentation along that line would certainly have been inconclusive. The following day Knowlton spent the entire morning with Fester and Link, the mathematician, the customary morning meeting of Bob's group having been called off so that Fester's work of the previous night could be gone over intensively. Fester was very anxious that this be done, and Knowlton was not too unhappy to call the meeting off for reasons of his own.

For the next several days Fester sat in the back office that had been turned over to him and did nothing but read the progress reports of the work that had been done in the last six months. Knowlton caught himself feeling apprehensive about the reaction that Fester might have to some of his work. He was a little surprised at his own feelings. He had always been proud—although he had put on a convincingly modest face—of the way in which new ground in the study of photon measuring devices had been broken in this group. Now he wasn't sure, and it seemed to him that Fester might easily show that the line of research they had been following was unsound or even unimaginative.

The next morning (as was the custom), the members of the lab, including the girls, sat around a conference table. Bob always prided himself on the fact that the work of the lab was guided and evaluated by the group as a whole, and he was fond of repeating that it was not a waste of time to include secretaries in such meetings. Often, what started out as a boring recital of fundamental assumptions to a naive listener, uncovered new ways of regarding these assumptions that would not have occurred to the researcher who had long ago accepted them as a necessary basis for his work.

These group meetings also served Bob in another sense. He admitted to himself that he would have felt far less secure if he had had to direct the work out of his own mind, so to speak. With the group meeting as the principle of leadership, it was always possible to justify the exploration of blind alleys because of the general educative effect on the team. Fester was there; Lucy and Martha were there; Link was sitting next to Fester, their conversation concerning Link's mathematical study apparently continuing from yesterday. The other members, Bob Davenport, George Thurlow, and Arthur Oliver, were waiting quietly.

Knowlton, for reasons that he didn't quite understand, proposed for discussion this morning a problem that all of them had spent a great deal of time on previously with the conclusion that a solution was impossible, that there was no feasible way of treating it in an experimental fashion. When Knowlton proposed the problem, Davenport remarked that there was hardly any use of going over it again, that he was satisfied that there was no way of approaching the problem with the equipment and the physical capacities of the lab.

This statement had the effect of a shot of adrenaline on Fester. He said he would like to know what the problem was in detail and, walking to the blackboard, began setting down the "factors" as various members of the group began discussing the problem and simultaneously listing the reasons why it had been abandoned.

Very early in the description of the problem it was evident that Fester was going to disagree about the impossibility of attacking it. The group realized this, and finally the descriptive materials and their recounting of the reasoning that had led to its abandonment dwindled away. Fester began his statement which, as it proceeded, might well have been prepared the previous night although Knowlton knew this was impossible. He couldn't help being impressed with the organized and logical way that Fester was presenting ideas that must have occurred to him only a few minutes before.

Fester had some things to say, however, which left Knowlton with a mixture of annoyance, irritation, and, at the same time, a rather smug feeling of superiority over Fester in at least one area. Fester was of the opinion that the way that the problem had been analyzed was really typical of group thinking, and with an air of sophistication which made it difficult for a listener to dissent, he proceeded to comment on the American emphasis on team ideas, satirically describing the ways in which they led to a "high level of mediocrity."

During this time Knowlton observed that Link stared studiously at the floor, and he was very conscious of George Thurlow's and Bob Davenport's glances toward him at several points of Fester's little speech. Inwardly, Knowlton couldn't help feeling that this was one point at least in which Fester was off on the wrong foot. The whole lab, following Jerry's lead, talked if not practiced the theory of small research teams as the basic organization for effective research. Fester insisted that the problem could be approached and that he would like to study it for a while himself.

Knowlton ended the morning session by remarking that the meetings would continue and that the very fact that a supposedly insoluble experimental problem was now going to get another chance was another indication of the value of such meetings. Fester immediately remarked that he was not at all averse to meetings for the purpose of informing the group of the progress of its members—that the point he wanted to make was that creative advances were seldom accomplished in such meetings, that they were made by the individual "living with" the problem closely and continuously, a sort of personal relationship to it.

Knowlton went on to say to Fester that he was very glad that Fester had raised these points and that he was sure the group would profit by reexamining the basis on which they had been operating. Knowlton agreed that individual effort was probably the basis for making the major advances but that he considered the group meetings useful primarily because of the effect they had on keeping the group together and on helping the weaker members of the group keep up with the ones who were able to advance more easily and quickly in the analysis of problems.

It was clear as days went by and meetings continued that Fester came to enjoy them because of the pattern which the meetings assumed. It became typical for Fester to hold forth, and it was unquestionably clear that he was more brilliant, better prepared on the various subjects which were germane to the problem being studied, and more capable of going ahead than anyone there. Knowlton grew increasingly disturbed as he realized that his leadership of the group had been, in fact, taken over.

Whenever the subject of Fester was mentioned in occasional meetings with Dr. Jerrold, Knowlton would comment only on the ability and obvious capacity for work that Fester had. Somehow he never felt that he could mention his own discomforts, not only because they revealed a weakness on his own part but also because it was quite clear that Jerrold himself was considerably impressed with Fester's work and with the contacts he had with him outside the photon laboratory.

Knowlton now began to feel that perhaps the intellectual advantages that Fester had brought to the group did not quite compensate for what he felt were evidences of a breakdown in the cooperative spirit he had seen in the group before Fester's coming. More and more of the morning meetings were skipped. Fester's opinion concerning the abilities of others of the group, with the exception of Link, was obviously low. At times during morning meetings or in smaller discussions he had been on the point of rudeness, refusing to pursue an argument when he claimed it was based on another person's ignorance of the facts involved. His impatience of others led him to also make similar remarks to Dr. Jerrold. Knowlton inferred this from a conversation with Jerrold in which Jerrold asked whether Davenport and Oliver were going to be continued on; and his failure to mention Link, the mathematician, led Knowlton to feel that this was the result of private conversations between Fester and Jerrold.

It was not difficult for Knowlton to make a quite convincing case on whether the brilliance of Fester was sufficient recompense for the beginning of this breaking up of the group. He took the opportunity to speak privately with Davenport and with Oliver, and it was quite clear that both of them were uncomfortable because of Fester. Knowlton didn't press the discussion beyond the point of hearing them in one way or another say that they did feel awkward and that it was sometimes difficult for them to understand the arguments he advanced, but often embarrassing to ask him to fill in the background on which his arguments were based. Knowlton did not interview Link in this manner.

About six months after Fester's coming into the photon lab, a meeting was scheduled in which the sponsors of the research were coming to get some idea of the work and its progress. It was customary at these meetings for project heads to present the research being conducted in their groups. The members of each group were invited to other meetings which were held later in the day and open to all, but the special meetings were usually made up only of project heads, the head of the laboratory, and the sponsors.

As the time for the special meeting approached, it seemed to Knowlton that he must avoid the presentation at all cost. His reasons for this were that he could not trust himself to present the ideas and work that Fester had advanced because of his apprehension as to whether he could present them in sufficient detail and answer such questions about them as might be asked. On the other hand, he did not feel he could ignore these newer lines of work and present only the material that he had done or that had been started before Fester's arrival. He felt also that it would not be beyond Fester at all, in his blunt and undiplomatic way—if he were present at the meeting, that is—to make comments on his [Knowlton's] presentation and reveal Knowlton's inadequacy. It also seemed quite clear that it would not be easy to keep Fester from attending the meeting, even though he was not on the administrative level of those invited.

Knowlton found an opportunity to speak to Jerrold and raised the question. He remarked to Jerrold that with the meetings coming up and with the interest in the work and with the contributions that Fester had been making, he would probably like to come to these meetings, but there was a question of the feelings of the others in the group if Fester alone were invited. Jerrold passed this over very lightly by saying that he didn't think the group would fail to understand Fester's rather different position and that he thought that Fester by all means should be invited. Knowlton immediately said he had thought so, too; that Fester should present the work because much of it was work he had done; and as Knowlton put it, that this would be a nice way to recognize Fester's contributions and to reward him, as he was eager to be recognized as a productive member of the lab. Jerrold agreed, and so the matter was decided.

Fester's presentation was very successful and in some ways dominated the meeting. He attracted the interest and attention of many of those who had come, and a long discussion followed his presentation. Later in the evening—with the entire laboratory staff present—in the cocktail period before the dinner, a little circle of people formed about Fester. One of them was Jerrold himself, and a lively discussion took place concerning the application of

Fester's theory. All of this disturbed Knowlton, and his reaction and behavior were characteristic. He joined the circle, praised Fester to Jerrold and to others, and remarked on the brilliance of the work.

Knowlton, without consulting anyone, began at this time to take some interest in the possibility of a job elsewhere. After a few weeks he found that a new laboratory of considerable size was being organized in a nearby city and that the kind of training he had would enable him to get a project-head job equivalent to the one he had at the lab with slightly more money.

He immediately accepted it and notified Jerrold by a letter, which he mailed on a Friday night to Jerrold's home. The letter was quite brief, and Jerrold was stunned. The letter merely said that he had found a better position; that there were personal reasons why he didn't want to appear at the lab any more; that he would be glad to come back at a later time from where he would be, some 40 miles away, to assist if there was any mixup at all in the past work; that he felt sure that Fester could, however, supply any leadership that was required for the group; and that his decision to leave so suddenly was based on some personal problems—he hinted at problems of health in his family, his mother and father. All of this was fictitious, of course. Jerrold took it at face value but still felt that this was very strange behavior and quite unaccountable, for he had always felt his relationship with Knowlton had been warm and that Knowlton was satisfied and, as a matter of fact, quite happy and productive.

Jerrold was considerably disturbed, because he had already decided to place Fester in charge of another project that was going to be set up very soon. He had been wondering how to explain this to Knowlton, in view of the obvious help Knowlton was getting from Fester and the high regard in which he held him. Jerrold had, as a matter of fact, considered the possibility that Knowlton could add to his staff another person with the kind of background and training that had been unique in Fester and had proved so valuable.

Jerrold did not make any attempt to meet Knowlton. In a way, he felt aggrieved about the whole thing. Fester, too, was surprised at the suddenness of Knowlton's departure, and when Jerrold, in talking to him, asked him whether he had reasons to prefer to stay with the photon group instead of the project for the Air Force which was being organized, he chose the Air Force project and went on to that job the following week. The photon lab was hard hit. The leadership of the lab was given to Link with the understanding that this would be temporary until someone could come in to take over.

QUESTIONS:

1. What was the major problem that faced Knowlton?
2. What ego-defense mechanisms did Knowlton personally use?
3. Could Rotter's notion of locus of control be used to analyze Bob Knowlton's situation?

4

Chapter

Motivation

After completing Chapter 4, you should be able to:

Learning Objectives

- Describe the three distinct components of motivation.

- Identify the need levels in Maslow's hierarchy.

- Explain Alderfer's ERG Theory.

- Compare motivators with hygiene factors.

- Discuss the factors that reflect a high need for achievement.

- Define the key terms in expectancy theory.

- Distinguish between inputs and outputs in equity theory.

- Identify the key steps in goal setting.

- Describe the concept of the psychological contract.

www.ibm.com

A part of the stories about the culture of IBM involves a situation involving the company's founder Thomas Watson. One of his top senior managers made a very costly mistake costing IBM about $3 million. The manager started to clean out his desk and be ready for the inevitable "pink slip" firing. When Watson came to his office to talk, the manager started, "I know why you're here. I'll offer my resignation and leave." Watson looked at the manager and warmly replied: "You don't think I would let you go after I just spent $3 million to train you." Watson valued the manager, knew the individual wanted to do well, but had failed.[1]

Although, the manager's performance in this case was not achieved, he exerted every effort to do the job. Watson wanted to provide a positive motivation atmosphere at IBM. This IBM story has become a part of the firm's cultural history concerning motivation. The manager was an important part of IBM and despite his failure in this case, the leader of the firm was there to support the manager's willingness to perform.

No one questions the central role motivation plays in shaping behavior and, specifically, in influencing work performance in organizations.[2] Nonetheless, as important as motivation is, it is not the only factor that determines performance. Over the years, a variety of other variables thought to play an important role in performance have been suggested. These include ability, instinct, and aspiration level as well as personal factors such as age, education, and family background.

One way of conceptualizing the various determinants of performance is illustrated in Exhibit 4.1. As can be seen from this exhibit, job performance may be viewed as a function of the **capacity** to perform, the **opportunity** to perform, and the **willingness** to perform. The capacity to perform relates to the degree to which an individual possesses task-relevant skills, abilities, knowledge, and experiences. Unless an employee knows what is supposed to be done and how to do it, high levels of job performance are not possible. Having the opportunity to perform is also a critical ingredient in the performance recipe. An employee assembling a product in a manufacturing plant who constantly experiences equipment failures and a shortage of needed components is clearly going to be unable to perform at the same level as a worker who does not encounter those difficulties. Similarly, an accountant who must make entries in a hand ledger does not have the same opportunity to perform as one who has access to an electronic spreadsheet. Sometimes employees may lack the opportunity to perform not because of poor equipment or outdated technology, but because of poor decisions and outdated attitudes.

The third factor, willingness to perform, relates to the degree to which an individual both desires and is willing to exert effort toward attaining job performance. It is, in other words, motivation, and it is what this chapter is about. No combination of capacity and opportunity will result in high performance in the absence of some level of motivation or willingness to perform.

From a managerial perspective, it is important to realize that the presence of motivation per se, coupled with a capacity and opportunity to perform, does not ensure high performance levels. It is a rare manager who has not at some point concluded that performance would be much higher if "I could just get my peo-

---

[1] Story still related by executive level and operating manager level at IBM, October 2000.

[2] M. L. Ambrose and C. T. Kulek, "Old Friends New Faces: Motivation Research in the 1990s," *Journal of Management*, Summer 1999, pp. 231–37.

EXHIBIT 4.1
Determinants of Job Performance

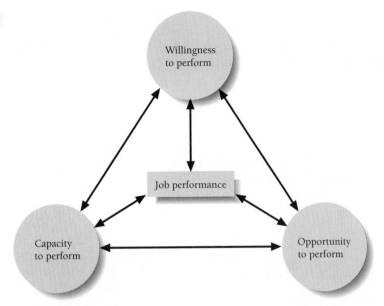

Source: Adapted from M. Blumberg and C. Pringle, "The Missing Opportunity in Organizational Research: Some Implications for a Theory of Work Performance," *Academy of Management Review,* October 1982, p. 565.

ple motivated." In all likelihood, those individuals are already motivated; what that manager really wants is motivation that results in more or different kinds of behaviors. To understand this distinction it is helpful to think of motivation as being made up of at least three distinct components: direction, intensity, and persistence.

Direction relates to what an individual chooses to do when presented with a number of possible alternatives. When faced with the task of completing a report requested by management, for example, an employee may choose to direct effort toward completing the report or toward solving the crossword puzzle in the morning newspaper (or any number of other possible activities). Regardless of which option is selected, the employee is motivated. If the employee selects the first alternative, the direction of his or her motivation is consistent with that desired by management. If the employee chooses the second alternative, the direction is counter to that desired by management, but the employee is nonetheless motivated.

The *intensity* component of motivation refers to the strength of the response once the choice (direction) is made. Using the previous example, the employee may choose the proper direction (working on the report) but respond with very little intensity. Intensity, in this sense, is synonymous with effort. Two people may focus their behavior in the same direction, but one may perform better because he or she exerts more effort than the other. An attribute frequently used to describe an outstanding professional athlete is intensity. When coaches speak of an athlete as playing with a great deal of intensity, they are describing the amount of effort the player invests in the game.

Finally, *persistence* is an important component of motivation. Persistence refers to the staying power of behavior or how long a person will continue to devote effort. Some people will focus their behavior in the appropriate direction and

Organizational Encounter 4.1

What Different Groups Want

A diverse workforce makes the identification of what employees want from their work, identity, and managers more difficult. Since people perceive the environment, stimuli, and organizational programs differently, careful analysis of individual and group differences is a challenging task for managers. Listed below are groups of workers and general statements about what they want. As is true in life not every person wants the same rewards from working. A general classification of various groups and their preferences are presented for consideration.

Able-Bodied People Want
- To develop more ease in dealing with physically disabled people
- To give honest feedback and appropriate support without being patronizing or overprotective

Younger and Older Employees Want
- To have more respect for their life experiences
- To be taken seriously
- To be challenged by their organizations, not patronized

Disabled People Want
- To have greater acknowledgment of and focus on abilities, rather than on disabilities
- To be challenged by colleagues and organizations to be the best
- To be included, not isolated

Heterosexuals Want
- To become more aware of lesbian and gay issues
- To have a better understanding of the legal consequences of being gay in America
- To increase dialogue about personal issues with lesbians and gay men

Gay Men and Lesbians Want
- To be recognized as equal contributors
- To have equal employment protection
- To have increased awareness among people regarding the impact of heterosexism in the workplace

Women Want
- To be recognized as equal contributors
- To have active support of male colleagues
- To have work and family issues actively addressed by organizations

Men Want
- To have the same freedom to grow/feel that women have
- To be perceived as allies, not the enemy
- To bridge the gap with women at home and at work

People of Color Want
- To be valued as unique individuals, as members of ethnically diverse groups, as people of different races and as equal contributors
- To establish more open, honest, working relationships with people of other races and ethnic groups
- To have the active support of white people in fighting racism

White People Want
- To have their ethnicity acknowledged
- To reduce discomfort, confusion, and dishonesty in dealing with people of color
- To build relationships with people of color based on common goals, concerns, and mutual respect for differences

Source: M. A. Bond and J. L. Pyle, "The Ecology of Diversity in Organizational Settings: Lessons from a Case Study," *Human Relations*, 1998, pp. 589–624; and A. Vincola, "Work and Life: In Search of the Missing Links," *HR Focus*, August 1998, pp. 3–5.

do so with a high degree of intensity but only for a short period of time. Individuals who tackle a task enthusiastically but quickly tire of it, or burn out and seldom complete it, lack this critical attribute in their motivated behavior. Thus, the manager's real challenge is not so much one of increasing motivation per se but of creating an environment wherein employee motivation is channeled in the right direction at an appropriate level of intensity and continues over time.

THE STARTING POINT: THE INDIVIDUAL

Most managers must motivate a diverse and, in many respects, unpredictable group of people. The diversity results in different behavioral patterns that are in some manner related to needs and goals. Organizational Encounter 4.1 presents

EXHIBIT 4.2   "What Do You Like about Your Current Job?"

	% of Respondents
People and work environment	66
Good management practices	33
Challenging and exciting jobs	33
Flexibility	24
Salary	19
Autonomy	16
Training and learning opportunities	13
Stock options	9
Technology	8
Team work	8

Source: Adapted from Good Manager Employee Motivation Survey 2000. See www:goalmanager.com/ i101internal30.cap. October 4, 2000.

a wide range of preferences. This type of diversity makes the manager's motivational work very challenging.

Needs refer to deficiencies an individual experiences at a particular time. The deficiencies may be physiological (e.g., a need for food), psychological (e.g., a need for self-esteem), or sociological (e.g., a need for social interaction). Needs are viewed as energizers or triggers of behavioral responses. The implication is that when need deficiencies are present, the individual is more susceptible to a manager's motivational efforts.

The importance of goals in any discussion of motivation is apparent. The motivational process, as interpreted by most theorists, is goal-directed. The goals, or outcomes, that an employee seeks are viewed as forces that attract the person. The accomplishment of desirable goals can result in a significant reduction in need deficiencies.

A survey of a general population conducted by a goal manager asked people, "What do you like about your jobs?" The responses showed a diverse range of answers as presented in Exhibit 4.2.

As illustrated in Exhibit 4.3, people seek to reduce various need deficiencies. Need deficiencies trigger a search process for ways to reduce the tension caused by the deficiencies. A course of action is selected, and goal-directed (outcome-directed) behavior occurs. After a period of time, managers assess that behavior, and the performance evaluation results in some type of reward or punishment. Such outcomes are weighed by the person, and the need deficiencies are reassessed. This, in turn, triggers the process, and the circular pattern is started once again.

Each person is attracted to some set of goals. If a manager is to predict behavior with any accuracy, he or she must know something about an employee's goals and about the actions the employee will take to achieve them. There is no shortage of motivation theories and research findings that attempt to provide explanations of the behavior-outcome relationship. Individual theories can be classified as representing either a **content** or a **process** approach to motivation.

EXHIBIT 4.3
The Motivational Process: A General Model

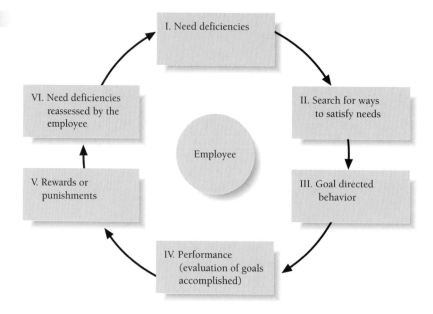

Content approaches focus on identifying specific motivation factors. Process approaches focus on describing how behavior is motivated. Exhibit 4.4 summarizes the basic characteristics of content and process theories of motivation from a managerial perspective.

Both categories of theories have important implications for managers, who are—by the nature of their jobs—involved with the motivational process. We will examine several examples of both types, beginning with the content approaches.

CONTENT APPROACHES

The content theories of motivation focus on the factors within the person that energize, direct, sustain, and stop behavior. They attempt to determine the specific needs that motivate people. Four important content approaches to motivation are: (1) Maslow's need hierarchy, (2) Alderfer's ERG theory, (3) Herzberg's two-factor theory, and (4) McClelland's learned needs theory. Each of these four theories has had an impact on managerial practices and will be considered in the paragraphs that follow.

Maslow's Need Hierarchy

The crux of Maslow's theory is that needs are arranged in a hierarchy.[3] The lowest-level needs are the physiological needs, and the highest-level needs are the self-actualization needs. These needs are defined to mean the following:

1. *Physiological.* The need for food, drink, shelter, and relief from pain.
2. *Safety and security.* The need for freedom from threat, that is, the security from threatening events or surroundings.

---

[3]A. H. Maslow and A. R. Kaplan, *Maslow on Management* (New York: John Wiley, 1998).

EXHIBIT 4.4   Managerial Perspective of Content and Process Theories of Motivation

Theoretical Base	Theoretical Explanation	Founders of the Theories	Managerial Application
Content	Focuses on factors within the person that energize, direct, sustain, and stop behavior. These factors can only be inferred.	Maslow—five-level need hierarchy Alderfer—three-level hierarchy (ERG) Herzberg—two major factors called hygiene-motivators McClelland—three learned needs acquired from the culture: achievement, affiliation, and power	Managers need to be aware of differences in needs, desires, and goals because each individual is unique in many ways.
Process	Describes, explains, and analyzes how behavior is energized, directed, sustained, and stopped.	Vroom—an expectance theory of choices Adams—equity theory based on comparisons that individuals make Locke—goal-setting theory that conscious goals and intentions are the determinants of behavior	Managers need to understand the process of motivation and how individuals make choices based on preferences, rewards, and accomplishments.

3. *Belongingness, social, and love.* The need for friendship, affiliation, interaction, and love.

4. *Esteem.* The need for self-esteem and for esteem from others.

5. *Self-actualization.* The need to fulfill oneself by making maximum use of abilities, skills, and potential.

Exhibit 4.5 shows the hierarchical nature of Maslow's theory. For each of the five need levels, the exhibit provides examples of work-related factors that might be associated with need satisfaction.

Maslow's theory assumes that a person attempts to satisfy the more basic needs (physiological) before directing behavior toward satisfying upper-level needs. Several other crucial points in Maslow's thinking are important to understanding the need-hierarchy approach.

1. A satisfied need ceases to motivate. For example, when a person decides that he or she is earning enough pay for contributing to the organization, money loses its power to motivate.

2. Unsatisfied needs can cause frustration, conflict, and stress. From a managerial perspective, unsatisfied needs are dangerous because they may lead to undesirable performance outcomes.

3. Maslow assumes that people have a need to grow and develop and, consequently, will strive constantly to move up the hierarchy in terms of need satisfaction. This assumption may be true for some employees but not others.

EXHIBIT 4.5
Maslow's Need
Hierarchy Related
to the Job

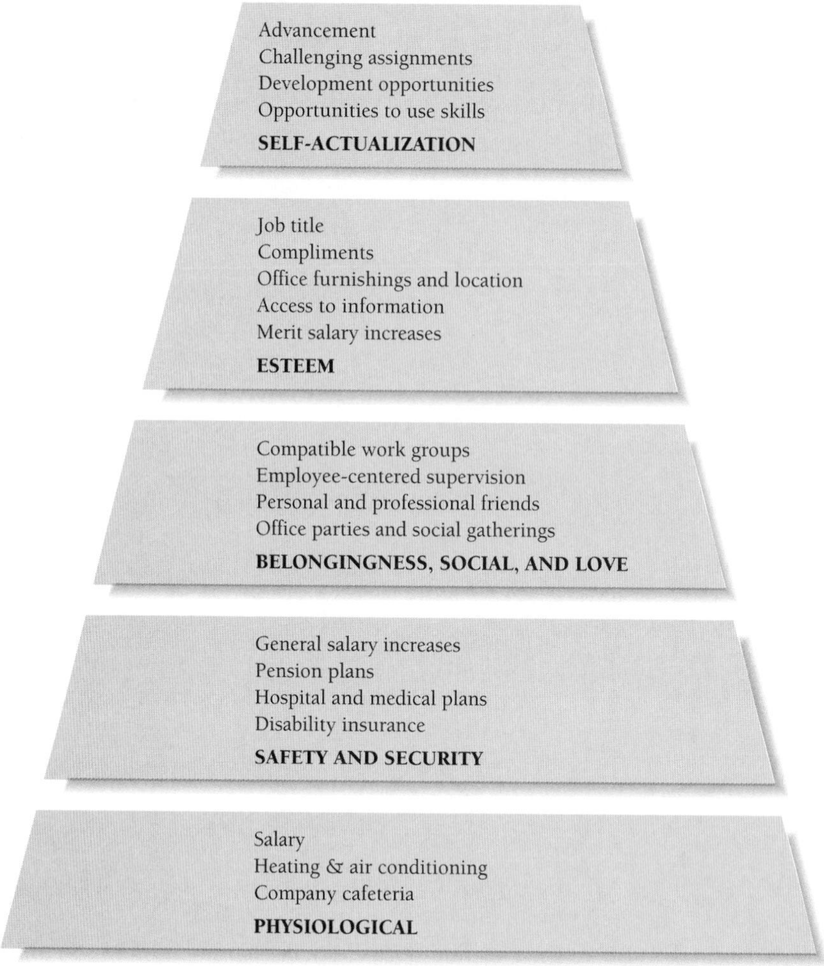

Advancement
Challenging assignments
Development opportunities
Opportunities to use skills
SELF-ACTUALIZATION

Job title
Compliments
Office furnishings and location
Access to information
Merit salary increases
ESTEEM

Compatible work groups
Employee-centered supervision
Personal and professional friends
Office parties and social gatherings
BELONGINGNESS, SOCIAL, AND LOVE

General salary increases
Pension plans
Hospital and medical plans
Disability insurance
SAFETY AND SECURITY

Salary
Heating & air conditioning
Company cafeteria
PHYSIOLOGICAL

Mary Kay, Inc. uses the full range of Maslow's need hierarchy to motivate its 500,000 beauty consultants. The company is still most well known for its reward of the Mary Kay Pink Cadillac for outstanding sales and team building. Consultants report that they are motivated by commissions and incentives (pay), being a part of a team (belongingness and social), recognition (esteem), and the privilege to help others (self-actualization). Mary Kay management appears to understand motivation and needs. Pay, incentives, recognition, autonomy, and helping others succeed are a combination of factors that the consultants seek.[4]

Maslow proposed that the typical adult in society has satisfied about 85 percent of the physiological need; 70 percent of the safety and security needs; 50 percent of the belongingness, social, and love needs; 40 percent of the esteem need; and 10 percent of the self-actualization need. Many critics disagree with these figures, however, particularly the 10 percent figure for self-actualization.

Several research studies have attempted to test the need-hierarchy theory. The first field-reported research that tested a modified version of Maslow's need hier-

---

[4]Mary Kay, Annual Report, 1999.

archy was performed by Porter.[5] At the time of the initial studies, Porter assumed that physiological needs were being adequately satisfied for managers, so he substituted a higher-order need called *autonomy,* defined as the person's satisfaction with opportunities to make independent decisions, set goals, and work without close supervision.

Research studies have reported:

1. Managers higher in the organization chain of command place greater emphasis on self-actualization and autonomy.[6]
2. Managers at lower organizational levels in small firms (less than 500 employees) are more satisfied than their counterpart managers in large firms (more than 5,000 employees); however, managers at upper levels in large companies are more satisfied than their counterparts in small companies.[7]
3. American managers overseas are more satisfied with autonomy opportunities than are their counterparts working in the United States.[8]

Despite these findings, a number of issues remain regarding the need-hierarchy theory. First, data from managers in two different companies provided little support that a hierarchy of needs exists.[9] The data suggested that only two levels of needs exist: one is the physiological level, and the other is a level which includes all other needs. Further evidence also disputes the hierarchy notions.[10] Researchers have found that as managers advance in an organization, their needs for security decrease, with a corresponding increase in their needs for social interaction, achievement, and self-actualization.

Alderfer's ERG Theory

Alderfer agrees with Maslow that individual needs are arranged in a hierarchy. However, his proposed need hierarchy involves only three sets of needs:[11]

1. *Existence.* Needs satisfied by such factors as food, air, water, pay, and working conditions.
2. *Relatedness.* Needs satisfied by meaningful social and interpersonal relationships.
3. *Growth.* Needs satisfied by an individual making creative or productive contributions.

---

[5]Lyman W. Porter, "A Study of Perceived Need Satisfaction in Bottom and Middle-Management Jobs," *Journal of Applied Psychology,* February 1961, pp. 1–10.

[6]Lyman W. Porter, *Organizational Patterns of Managerial Job Attitudes* (New York: American Foundation for Management Research, 1964).

[7]Lyman W. Porter, "Job Attitudes in Management: Perceived Deficiencies in Need Fulfillment as a Function of Size of the Company," *Journal of Applied Psychology,* December 1963, pp. 386–97.

[8]John M. Ivancevich, "Perceived Need Satisfaction of Domestic versus Overseas Managers," *Journal of Applied Psychology,* August 1969, pp. 274–78.

[9]Edward E. Lawler, III and J. L. Suttle, "A Causal Correlation Test of the Need Hierarchy Concept," *Organizational Behavior and Human Performance,* April 1972, pp. 265–87.

[10]Douglas T. Hall and K. E. Nougaim, "An Examination of Maslow's Need Hierarchy in an Organizational Setting," *Organizational Behavior and Human Performance,* February 1968, pp. 12–35.

[11]Clayton P. Alderfer, Existence, Relatedness, and Growth: Human Needs in Organizational Settings (New York: Free Press, 1972).

Alderfer's three needs—existence (E), relatedness (R), and growth (G), or ERG—correspond to Maslow's in that the existence needs are similar to Maslow's physiological and safety categories; the relatedness needs are similar to the belongingness, social, and love category; and the growth needs are similar to the esteem and self-actualization categories.

In addition to a difference in the number of categories, Alderfer's ERG theory and Maslow's need hierarchy differ on how people move through the different sets of needs. Maslow proposed that unfulfilled needs are predominant and that the next-higher level of needs isn't activated or triggered until the predominant need is adequately satisfied. Thus, a person only progresses up the need hierarchy once her lower-level need is adequately satisfied. In contrast, Alderfer's ERG theory suggests that, in addition to the satisfaction-progression process that Maslow proposed, a frustration-regression process is also at work. That is, if a person is continually frustrated in attempts to satisfy growth needs, relatedness needs reemerge as a major motivating force, causing the individual to redirect efforts toward satisfying a lower-order need category.

Alderfer's ERG explanation of motivation provides an interesting suggestion to managers about behavior. If a subordinate's higher-order needs (for example, growth) are being blocked, perhaps because of a company policy or lack of resources, then it's in the manager's best interest to attempt to redirect the subordinate's efforts toward relatedness or existence needs. The ERG theory implies that individuals are motivated to engage in behavior to satisfy one of the three sets of needs.

The ERG theory hasn't stimulated a great deal of research. Thus, empirical verification can't be claimed for the ERG model. Salancik and Pfeffer proposed that need models such as Maslow's and Alderfer's have become popular because they are consistent with other theories of rational choice and because they attribute freedom to individuals. The idea that individuals shape their actions to satisfy unfulfilled needs gives purpose and direction to individual activity. Furthermore, need explanations are also popular, despite little research verification, because they are simple and easily expressed views of human behavior.[12]

Herzberg's Two-Factor Theory

Herzberg developed a content theory known as the two-factor theory of motivation.[13] The two factors are called the dissatisfiers-satisfiers or the hygiene motivators or the extrinsic-intrinsic factors, depending on the discussant of the theory. The original research which led to the theory gave rise to two specific conclusions. First, there is a set of *extrinsic* conditions, the job context, which results in dissatisfaction among employees when the conditions are not present. If these conditions are present, this does not necessarily motivate employees. These conditions are the *dissatisfiers* or *hygiene* factors, since they are needed to maintain at least a level of "no dissatisfaction." They include:

1. Salary
2. Job security

---

[12]Gerald R. Salancik and Jeffrey Pfeffer, "An Examination of Need-Satisfaction Models of Job Attitudes," *Administrative Science Quarterly,* September 1977, pp. 427–56.

[13]Frederick Herzberg, B. Mausner, and B. Snyderman, *The Motivation to Work* (New York: John Wiley & Sons, 1959).

3. Working conditions
4. Status
5. Company procedures
6. Quality of technical supervision
7. Quality of interpersonal relations among peers, with superiors, and with subordinates

Second, a set of *intrinsic* conditions—the job content—when present in the job, builds strong levels of motivation that can result in good job performance. If these conditions are not present, jobs do not prove highly satisfying. The factors in this set are called the *satisfiers* or *motivators* and include:

1. Achievement
2. Recognition
3. Responsibility
4. Advancement
5. The work itself
6. The possibility of growth

These motivators are directly related to the nature of the job or task itself. When present, they contribute to satisfaction. This, in turn, can result in intrinsic task motivation.[14]

www.mapnp.org/library/
prsn-wll/job-stfy.htm

Herzberg suggests that motivators (intrinsic conditions) and hygiene can be applied to understanding factory (extrinsic conditions) workers in most countries and cultures. Exhibit 4.6 which combines the research and reports of a number of researchers supports the application of Herzberg's two-factor explanation across diverse cultures. For example, in Italy 60 percent of the workers indicated that motivators accounted for job satisfaction. On the other hand, 90 percent of workers in Finland reported that motivators accounted for job satisfaction.[15]

Herzberg's model basically assumes that job satisfaction is not a unidimensional concept. His research leads to the conclusion that two continua are needed to correctly interpret job satisfaction. Exhibit 4.7 presents two different views of job satisfaction. Prior to Herzberg's work, those studying motivation viewed job satisfaction as a unidimensional concept; that is, they placed job satisfaction at one end of a continuum and job dissatisfaction at the other end of the same continuum. This meant that if a job condition caused job satisfaction, removing it would cause job dissatisfaction. Similarly, if a job condition caused job dissatisfaction, removing it would cause job satisfaction.

One appealing aspect of Herzberg's explanation of motivation is that the terminology is work-oriented. There is no need to translate psychological terminology into everyday language. Despite this important feature, Herzberg's work has been criticized for a number of reasons. For example, some researchers believe that Herzberg's work oversimplifies the nature of job satisfaction. Other critics focus on Herzberg's methodology, which requires people to look at themselves retrospectively. Still other critics charge that Herzberg has directed little attention toward testing the motivational and performance consequences of the theory. In his

---

[14]Thad Green, *Motivation Management: Fueling Performance by Discovering What People Believe about Themselves and Their Organizations* (Palo Alto, CA: Davies-Black, 2000).

EXHIBIT 4.7
Traditional versus
Herzberg View of Job
Satisfaction

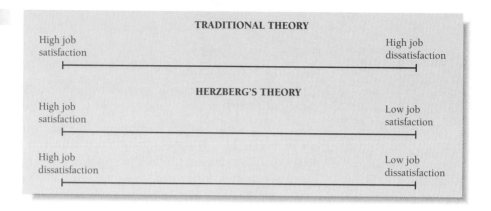

TRADITIONAL THEORY

High job   High job
satisfaction   dissatisfaction

HERZBERG'S THEORY

High job   Low job
satisfaction   satisfaction

High job   Low job
dissatisfaction   dissatisfaction

EXHIBIT 4.6	**Motivators and Hygienes across Cultures**	
Motivators	**Satisfying Job Events**	**Dissatisfying Job Events**
United States	80%	20%
Japan	82%	40%
Finland	90%	18%
Hungary	78%	30%
Italy	60%	35%
Hygienes		
United States	20%	75%
Japan	10%	65%
Finland	10%	80%
Hungary	22%	78%
Italy	30%	70%

Source: Adapted from K. Roberts, E. E. Kossek, and C. Ozeki. "Managing the Global Workforce: Challenges and Strategies." *Academy of Management Executive,* 1998, 12(4), 98–106. S. A. Snell, C. C. Snow, S. Canney Davidson, and D. C. Hambrick. Designing and Supporting Transnational Teams: The Human Rresource Agenda. *Human Resource Management,* 1998, 37, pp. 147–58; and F. Herzberg, Worker's Needs: The Same Around the World. *Industry Week,* September 21, 1987, 29–32.

original study, only self-reports of performance were used, and in most cases, the respondents described job activities that had occurred over a long period of time.

Although the list of criticisms for Herzberg's model is long, the impact of the theory on practicing managers should not be underestimated. Many managers feel very comfortable about many of the things Herzberg includes in his two-factor discussion. From a scientific vantage point, this satisfaction presents some dangers of misuse, but from a very important, organizational-world perspective, it is appealing to managers and has been implemented in numerous organiza-

---

[15]Karen Roberts, Ellen Ernst Kossek, and Cynthia Ozeki, "Managing the Global Workforce: Challenges and Strategies," *Academy of Management Executive,* 1998, pp. 93–106.

Ethics Encounter 4.1

Whatever It Takes!

A well-known financial institution advertises that its employees do "whatever it takes" to please customers. They imply that employees regularly go above-and-beyond the call of duty in performing their jobs. The idea of doing more than is expected has become an important one as service organizations dominate our economy. In fact, it may be difficult if not impossible for a manufacturing assembly-line employee to go above and beyond the call of duty. But for a customer-contact employee in a retail store, financial institution, airline, or other service business, the opportunity to do more than what is expected may occur several times a day.

These out-of-role activities are called *organizational citizenship behaviors* (OCBs), and are important because they are often cited by customers, clients, and students when praising exemplary service or switching service providers. An important question for managers in service organizations is "Why do employees engage in OCBs, and what can be done to encourage them?" Research has provided some explanations.

First, no clear relationships with most personality characteristics have been found. But a higher frequency of OCBs has been found among those employees with a higher collectivist orientation than among those who have a more individualistic perspective.

Second, certain situational factors seem to be related to OCBs. One of these factors relates to what employees and managers define as part of the job and what is "out-of-role." Employees will often define their jobs quite broadly and will include activities as part of their duties that their managers perceive as "extra." These OCBs also are likely to influence managerial evaluations of employees, but sometimes they may be interpreted as attempts to influence these evaluations rather than efforts to do something good for the company and the customer.

Finally, a major influence on OCBs is the leadership that employees receive from their managers. Specifically, trust between an employee and a manager and a management style that encourages the development of leadership skills among employees have been found to encourage the expression of OCBs.

Sources: Dennis W. Organ, "Personality and Organizational Citizenship Behavior," *Journal of Management*, Summer 1994, pp. 465–78; Mary A. Konovsky and S. Douglas Pugh, "Citizenship Behavior and Social Exchange," *Academy of Management Journal*, June 1994, pp. 656–69; and Jill W. Graham, "Leadership, Moral Development, and Citizenship Behavior," *Business Ethics Quarterly*, January 1995, pp. 43–54.

www.hp.com

tions. Hewlett-Packard, for example, has restructured many of its operations along the lines described by Herzberg. They rely on both motivators and hygiene factors to increase satisfaction and decrease the likelihood of dissatisfaction. Examples at Hewlett-Packard include providing resources (time, money, and space) to work on ideas for improving products and processes; instituting flex-time scheduling to increase employee job discretion; and using a profit-sharing plan which may increase satisfaction by providing a source of both achievement and recognition. With the amount of discretion increasing in many jobs, the opportunity also exists for employees to do more than what is expected. Ethics Encounter 4.1 examines this pleasant situation.

McClelland's Learned Needs Theory

McClelland has proposed a theory of motivation that is closely associated with learning concepts. He believes that many needs are acquired from the culture.[16] Three of these learned needs are the need for achievement (n Ach), the need for affiliation (n Aff), and the need for power (n Pow).

McClelland contends that when a need is strong in a person, its effect is to motivate the person to use behavior that leads to its satisfaction. For example, having

[16]David C. McClelland, "Business Drive and National Achievement," *Harvard Business Review*, July-August 1962, pp. 99–112.

a high n Ach encourages an individual to set challenging goals, to work hard to achieve the goals, and to use the skills and abilities needed to achieve them.

Based on research results, McClelland developed a descriptive set of factors that reflect a high need for achievement. These are:

1. The person likes to take responsibility for solving problems.
2. The person tends to set moderate achievement goals and is inclined to take calculated risks.
3. The person desires feedback on performance.

The need for affiliation reflects a desire to interact socially with people. A person with a high need for affiliation is concerned about the quality of important personal relationships, and thus, social relationships take precedence over task accomplishment. A person with a high need for power, meanwhile, concentrates on obtaining and exercising power and authority. He or she is concerned with influencing others and winning arguments. Power has two possible orientations according to McClelland. It can be negative in that the person exercising it emphasizes dominance and submission. Or power can be positive in that it reflects persuasive and inspirational behavior.

The main theme of McClelland's theory is that these needs are learned through coping with one's environment. Since needs are learned, behavior which is rewarded tends to recur at a higher frequency. Managers who are rewarded for achievement behavior learn to take moderate risks and to achieve goals. Similarly, a high need for affiliation or power can be traced to a history of receiving rewards for sociable, dominant, or inspirational behavior. As a result of the learning process, individuals develop unique configurations of needs that affect their behavior and performance.

There are a number of criticisms of McClelland's theory. Not the least of these criticisms is that most of the evidence available which supports the theory has been provided by McClelland or his associates. McClelland's use of projective psychological personality tests has been questioned as being unscientific. Furthermore, McClelland's claim that n Ach can be learned runs counter to a large body of literature that argues that the acquisition of motives normally occurs in childhood and is very difficult to alter in adulthood. Finally, McClelland's theory is questioned on grounds of whether the needs are permanently acquired. Research is needed to determine whether acquired needs last over a period of time. Can something learned in a training-and-development program be sustained on the job? This is an issue that McClelland and others have not been able to clarify.

A Synopsis of the Four Content Theories

Each of the four content theories attempt to explain behavior from a slightly different perspective. None of the theories has been accepted as the sole basis for explaining motivation. Although some critics are skeptical, it appears that people have innate and learned needs and that various job factors result in a degree of satisfaction. Thus, each of the theories provides the manager with some understanding of behavior and performance.

The four approaches are compared in Exhibit 4.8. McClelland proposed no lower-order needs. However, his needs for achievement and power aren't identical with Herzberg's motivators, Maslow's higher-order needs, or Alderfer's growth needs, although there are some similarities. A major difference between the four

EXHIBIT 4.8   **A Graphic Comparison of Four Content Approaches to Motivation**

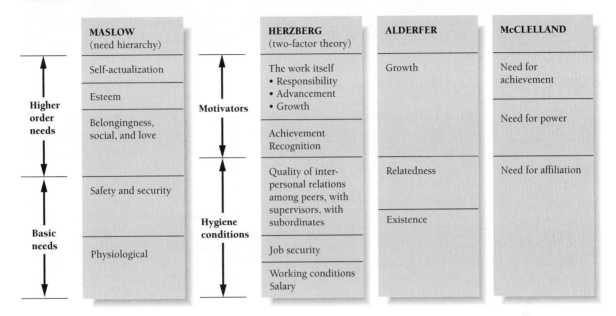

content theories is McClelland's emphasis on socially acquired needs. Also, the Maslow theory offers a static need hierarchy system; Alderfer presents a flexible, three-need classification approach; and Herzberg discusses intrinsic and extrinsic job factors.

Each of the content approaches purports to present the clearest, most-meaningful, and most-accurate explanation of motivation. In reality, each has strengths and limitations that practicing managers need to consider; none is clearly inferior or superior to the others, especially in today's diverse workplace. Smart managers will look to all of these approaches to provide insights that can be applied to specific challenges and problems.

PROCESS APPROACHES

The content theories we have examined focus mainly on the needs and incentives that cause behavior. They are concerned primarily about which specific things motivate people. The process theories of motivation are concerned with answering the questions of how individual behavior is energized, directed, maintained, and stopped. This section examines three process theories: expectancy theory, equity theory, and goal-setting theory. In discussing each of these in the paragraphs that follow, we will show how the motivational process works in organizational settings.

Expectancy Theory   One of the more popular explanations of motivation was developed by Victor Vroom.[17] Numerous studies have been done to test the

---

[17]Victor H. Vroom, *Work and Motivation* (New York: John Wiley & Sons, 1964). For earlier work, see Kurt Lewin, *The Conceptual Representation and the Measurement of Psychological Forces* (Durham, NC: Duke University Press, 1938), and E. C. Tolman, *Purposive Behavior in Animals and Men* (New York: Appleton-Century-Crofts, 1932).

accuracy of expectancy theory in predicting employee behavior, and direct tests have been generally supportive.[18] Vroom defines *motivation* as a process governing choices among alternative forms of voluntary activity. In his view, most behaviors are considered to be under the voluntary control of the person and consequently are motivated. In order to understand expectancy theory, it is necessary to define the terms of the theory and explain how they operate. The four most important terms are: *first-* and *second-level outcomes, instrumentality, valence,* and *expectancy.*

First-Level and Second-Level Outcomes   First-level outcomes resulting from behavior are those associated with doing the job itself and include productivity, absenteeism, turnover, and quality of productivity. The second-level outcomes are those events (rewards or punishments) that the first-level outcomes are likely to produce, such as merit pay increases, group acceptance or rejection, promotion, and termination.

The individual in the expectancy theory approach is asking "If I work hard, I can accomplish a specific performance level (assuming the person has the ability and skill and that the performance is recognized). Then the individual asks: "If my performance is acknowledged (e.g., managers make comments, performance appraisal rating is high) will it lead to rewards (e.g., recognition, pay, opportunities, time off)?"

Instrumentality   Instrumentality is the perception by an individual that first-level outcomes (performance) are associated with second-level outcomes (rewards). It refers to the strength of a person's belief that attainment of a particular outcome will lead to (be instrumental in) attaining one or more second-level outcomes. Instrumentality can be negative, suggesting that attaining a second-level outcome is less likely if a first-level outcome has occurred, or positive, suggesting that the second-level outcome is more likely if the first-level outcome has been attained.

Valence   Valence refers to the preferences for outcomes as seen by the individual. For example, a person may prefer a 10 percent merit raise over a relocation to a new facility. An outcome is positively valent when it is preferred and negatively valent when it is not preferred or is avoided. An outcome has a valence of zero when the individual is indifferent to attaining or not attaining it. The valence concept applies to both first- and second-level outcomes. Thus, a person may prefer to be a high-performing employee (first-level outcome) because she believes this will lead to a desired merit raise in pay (second-level outcome).

Expectancy   Expectancy refers to the individual's belief regarding the likelihood or subjective probability that a particular behavior will be followed by a particular outcome, and it is most easily thought of as a single-probability statement. That is, it refers to a perceived chance of something occurring because of the behavior. Expectancy can take values ranging from 0, indicating no chance that an outcome will occur after the behavior or act, to +1, indicating perceived certainty that a particular outcome will follow a behavior or act.

---

[18]R. M. Lynd-Stevenson, "Expectancy Theory and Predicting Future Employment Status in the Young Unemployed," *Journal of Occupational and Organizational Psychology,* March 1999, pp. 101–106.

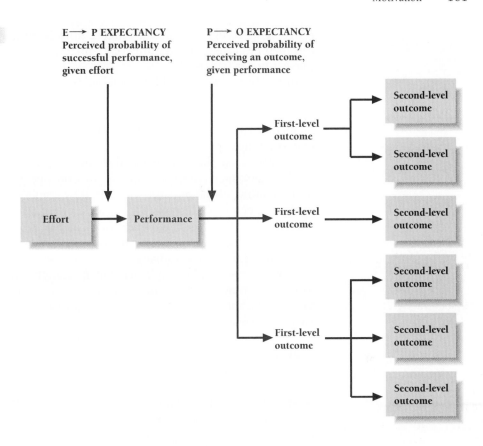

EXHIBIT 4.9
Expectancy Theory

E⟶ P EXPECTANCY
Perceived probability of
successful performance,
given effort

P⟶ O EXPECTANCY
Perceived probability of
receiving an outcome,
given performance

In the work setting, individuals hold an effort-performance expectancy. This expectancy represents the individual's perception of how hard it will be to achieve a particular behavior (say, completing the budget on time) and the probability of achieving that behavior. There is also a performance-outcome expectancy. In the individual's mind, every behavior is associated with outcomes (rewards or punishments). For example, an individual may have an expectancy that if the budget is completed on time, he or she will receive a day off next week. Exhibit 4.9 presents the general expectancy model and includes the two expectancy points (E→P and P→O).

From a managerial perspective, expectancy theory suggests that the manager should develop an awareness of employee thought processes and, based on that awareness, take actions that will influence those processes in a manner that facilitates the attainment of positive organizational outcomes.

Managers at Lucent Technologies' Microelectronics Division in Pennsylvania have designed a successful incentive program that uses expectancy theory concepts. The program was designed to increase employee recognition, achieve cost saving, and produce revenue from ideas provided by employees.[19] Those individuals and teams that are top performers or who generate implemented improvement ideas will be recognized in their performance evaluations. Then, as suggested by expectancy theory, they are rewarded for their performance and

www.lucent.com

[19]Sharon Cauldron, "Spreading out the Carrots," *Industry Week,* May 19, 1997, pp. 20–24.

provided by recognition points ranging from 50 to 250,000 points. The points can then be turned into rewards (e.g., prizes, vacations, time off) that the employees prefer (valence).

In the first year 6,000 ideas were submitted by employees, of which 2,100 were implemented. For example, how to improve the division's e-mail system, create a safer work environment, and decrease recycling scrap were implemented programs. In total in the first year, the division achieved $20,000 worth of cost savings.

Managers, like those at Lucent Technologies, can use the concepts and principles of expectancy theory to improve performance. It is important to acquire an understanding of the outcomes preferred by employees. Listening, talking, and observing, employee responses to various rewards such as compensation, incentives, promotions, praise, gift certificates, and time off are important managerial behaviors. What employees want today is likely to be different tomorrow because needs and goals regularly change.[20]

www.frito-lay.com

Managers also need to implement fair, meaningful, and easy-to-understand performance review and evaluation systems. It is important in applying expectancy theory to be able to recognize and use performance. At Frito-Lay Processing and Packaging Division in Lubbock, Texas, an incentive program has achieved excellent results. Machine operators were involved in reducing the amount of "giveaway" in each bag of chips. Frito-Lay strives to maintain .4 grams in give-away in each bag of chips. If too much is given away, profit margins are reduced. The exact weight of each bag is calculated to the gram. The operator's performance can be specifically pinpointed. Each week the operator who is the best in reducing the give-away waste wins a gift certificate. Since the gift certificate prize was one that operators preferred, this type of reward is significant enough for the operators to be fully involved in trying to win the contest and has significantly reduced waste and improved morale among the operators.[21]

Equity Theory

The essence of *equity* (which also means "fairness") theory is that employees compare their efforts and rewards with those of others in similar work situations. This theory of motivation is based on the assumption that individuals are motivated by a desire to be equitably treated at work. The individual works in exchange for rewards from the organization.

Four important terms in this theory are:

1. *Person.* The individual for whom equity or inequity is perceived
2. *Comparison other.* Any group or persons used by Person as a referent regarding the ratio of inputs and outcomes
3. *Inputs.* The individual characteristics brought by Person to the job. These may be achieved (e.g., skills, experience, learning) or ascribed (e.g., age, sex, race)
4. *Outcomes.* What Person received from the job (e.g., recognition, fringe benefits, pay)

---

[20]Ibid.

[21]Frito-Lay, Annual Report, 1999.

EXHIBIT 4.10   The Equity Theory of Motivation

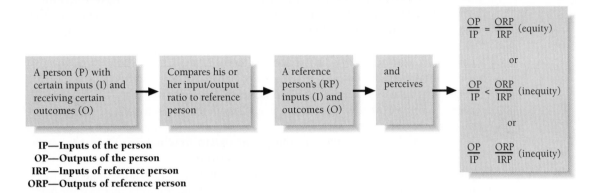

IP—Inputs of the person
OP—Outputs of the person
IRP—Inputs of reference person
ORP—Outputs of reference person

Equity exists when employees perceive that the ratios of their inputs (efforts) to their outputs (rewards) are equivalent to the ratios of other employees. Inequity exists when these ratios are not equivalent; an individual's own ratio of inputs to outcomes could be greater than, or less than, that of others.[22] Exhibit 4.10 illustrates the equity theory of motivation.

Change Procedures to Restore Equity

Equity theory suggests a number of alternative ways to restore a feeling or sense of equity. Some examples of restoring equity are:

1. *Changing inputs.* The employee may decide that he or she will put less time or effort into the job.
2. *Changing outcomes.* The employee may decide to produce more units since a bonus pay plan is being used.
3. *Changing attitudes.* Instead of changing inputs or outcomes, the employee may simply change the attitude he or she has. Instead of actually putting in more time at work, the employee may decide that "I put in enough time" to make a good contribution.
4. *Changing the reference person.* The reference person can be changed by making comparisons with the input/outcome ratios of some other person. This change can restore equity.
5. *Changing the inputs or outcomes of the reference person.* If the reference person is a coworker, it might be possible to attempt to alter his or her inputs or outcomes as a way to restore equity.
6. *Leaving the field.* The employee may decide to simply quit his or her job.

---

[22]J. Stacy Adams, "Toward an Understanding of Equity," *Journal of Abnormal and Social Psychology,* November 1963, pp. 422–36.

Research on Equity

Most of the research on equity theory has focused on pay as the basic outcome.[23] The failure to incorporate other relevant outcomes limits the impact of the theory in work situations. A review of the studies also reveals that the comparison person is not always clarified. A typical research procedure is to ask a person to compare his or her inputs and outcomes with those of a specific person. In most work situations, an employee selects the comparison person after working for some time in the organization. Two issues to consider are whether comparison persons are within the organization and whether comparison persons change during a person's work career.

Several individuals have questioned the extent to which inequity that results from overpayment (rewards) leads to perceived inequity. Locke argues that employees seldom are told they are overpaid. He believes that individuals are likely to adjust their idea of what constitutes an equitable payment to justify their pay.[24] Campbell and Pritchard point out that employer-employee exchange relationships are highly impersonal when compared to exchanges between friends. Perceived overpayment inequity may be more likely when friends are involved. Thus, an individual probably will react to overpayment inequity only when that individual believes that his or her actions have led to a friend's being treated unfairly. The individual receives few signals from the organization that he or she is being treated unfairly.

Despite limitations, equity theory provides a relatively insightful model to help explain and predict employee attitudes about pay. The theory also emphasizes the importance of comparisons in the work situation. The identification of comparison persons seems to have some potential value when attempting to restructure a reward program. The theory has been shown to be a useful framework for examining the growing number of two-tier wage structures.[25] Equity theory also raises the issue of methods for resolving inequity, which can cause problems with morale, turnover, and absenteeism.

Procedural Justice   Equity theory focuses on fairly distributing outcomes to create an atmosphere of high, intense positive motivation. The concept of **procedural justice** states that people when reacting to organizational decisions and processes that affect them are influenced by procedures used to establish the outcomes.[26] That is, employees are concerned with the fairness of the decision-making procedures, or what is referred to as *procedural justice*. This focus on procedural justice is in contrast to distributive justice, which is the basis of equity theory.

---

[23]See, for example, Steve Werner and Neal Mero, "Fair or Foul?: The Effects of External, Internal, and Employee Equity on Changes in Performance of Major League Baseball Players," [Summary] *Proceedings of the 54th Annual Meeting of the Academy of Management*, August 1994, p. 414, and Larry Howard and Janis Miller, "Fair Pay for Fair Play: Estimating Pay Equity in Professional Baseball with Data Envelopment Analysis," *Academy of Management Journal*, August 1993, pp. 882–94.

[24]Edwin Locke, "The Nature and Causes of Job Satisfaction," in *Handbook of Industrial and Organizational Psychology*, M. Dunnette, ed. (Skokie, IL: Rand McNally, 1976), pp. 1297–349.

[25]J. E. Martin and M. M. Peterson, "Two-Tier Wage Structures: Implications for Equity Theory," *Academy of Management Journal*, June 1987, pp. 286–315.

[26]E. A. Lund and T. R. Tyler, *The Social Psychology of Procedural Justice* (New York: Plenum Press, p. 188).

Procedural justice has been shown to have a positive impact on a number of affective and behavioral reactions.[27] These reactions include:

- Organizational commitment
- Intent to stay with organization
- Organizational citizenship
- Trust in supervisor
- Satisfaction with decision outcome
- Work effort
- Performance

Positive consequences of procedural justice have been found in important organizational decision contexts including pay allocation, personnel selection, and performance appraisal. Since procedural justice can provide benefits to organizations, an important issue involves the types of decision-making procedures that people consider to be fair. People are more inclined to interpret decisions to be fair when they have a voice in the decision, there is consistency in decision making, and the process and procedures conform to ethical and moral values.

Two explanations have emerged regarding why procedural justice works. Self-interest theory proposes that people want fair procedures because such fairness enables them to obtain desired extrinsic outcomes. Although a manager may decide not to promote a person, if the process has been fair it will be accepted.[28]

Group value theory suggests that people value fairness as a means of realizing such desired intrinsic outcomes as self-esteem. People have a strong sense of affiliation with groups to which they belong. Fair group procedures are considered to be a sign of respect and an indication that they are valued members of the group. This results in feeling a sense of self-esteem.

Treating employees and customers fairly, respectfully, and in a timely manner is a worthy managerial approach. First, managers must understand the importance of procedural justice. Second, managers can achieve good performance results when procedural justice is widely practiced for decision making. Finally, employee perceptions are extremely critical in identifying procedural justice. Determining these perceptions requires strong interpersonal and observation skills on the part of managers.[29]

Goal Setting

There has been considerable and growing interest in applying goal setting to organizational problems and issues since Locke presented what is now considered a classic paper in 1968.[30] A *goal* is a result that a person, team, or group is

---

[27]D. R. Skarlicki and A. Foyger, "Retaliation in the Workplace: The Roles of Distributive, Procedural, and Interactional Justice," *Journal of Applied Psychology,* August 1997, pp. 434–43.

[28]Daniel P. Skarlicki, John H. Ellard, and Brad R. C. Kelln, "Third-Party Perceptions of Layoff, Procedural, Derogation and Retributive Aspects of Justice," *Journal of Applied Psychology,* February 1998, pp. 119–27.

[29]Stefanie E. Naumann and Nathan Bennett, "A Case for Procedural Justice Climate: Development and Test of a Multilevel Model," *Academy of Management Journal,* October 2000, pp. 881–89.

[30]Edwin A. Locke, "Toward a Theory of Task Motivation and Incentives," *Organizational Behavior and Human Performance,* May 1968, pp. 157–89.

attempting to accomplish through behavior and actions. Locke proposed that **goal setting** is a cognitive process of some practical utility. His view is that an individual's conscious goals and intentions are the primary determinants of behavior.[31] It has been noted that "one of the commonly observed characteristics of intentional behavior is that it tends to keep going until it reaches completion."[32] That is, once a person starts something (e.g., a job, a new project), he or she pushes on until a goal is achieved. Also, goal-setting theory places specific emphasis on the importance of conscious goals in explaining motivated behavior. Locke has used the notion of intentions and conscious goals to propose and provide research support for the thesis that harder conscious goals will result in higher levels of performance if these goals are accepted by the individual.[33]

Descriptions of Goal Setting   For example, the attempt to produce four units on a production line or to cut direct costs by $3,000 or to decrease absenteeism in a department by 12 percent are goals. Locke has carefully described the attributes or the mental (cognitive) processes of goal setting. The attributes he highlights are goal specificity, goal difficulty, and goal intensity.

Goal specificity is the degree of quantitative precision (clarity) of the goal. **Goal difficulty** is the degree of proficiency or the level of performance that is sought. **Goal intensity** pertains to the process of setting the goal or of determining how to reach it. To date, goal intensity has not been widely studied, although a related concept, **goal commitment**, has been considered in a number of studies. Goal commitment is the amount of effort used to achieve a goal.

Exhibit 4.11 presents a model of individual goal setting using available theoretical research, but illustrating a practical framework that managers can apply. The goal-setting model emphasizes that a goal serves as a motivator. It is important for any goal to be clear, meaningful, and challenging. When goals are not accomplished, an individual is faced with a sense of dissatisfaction. Whether there is a relationship between goals and job performance is moderated by a number of factors, including ability, commitment, and feedback.

A person's ability can limit his or her efforts to accomplish goals. If a manager sets a difficult goal and a person lacks the ability to accomplish it, there will not be accomplishment.

A person who is committed to a goal has a drive, intensity, and persistence to work hard. Commitment creates a desire to reach the goal and overcome problems or barriers.

Feedback provides data, information, and facts about progress in goal accomplishment. A person can use feedback to gauge where adjustments in effort need to be made. Without feedback a person operates without guidance or information to make corrections so that goals are accomplished on time and at budgeted levels.

As goals are accomplished and this performance is evaluated, rewards are distributed. If the rewards are preferred as discussed in expectancy theory, employees are likely to be satisfied and motivated.

---

[31]Gary P. Latham, "The Reciprocal Effects of Science on Practice: Insights from the Practice and Science of Goal Setting," *Canadian Psychology* (in press, October 2000), pp. 1–33.

[32]Thomas A. Ryan, *Intentional Behavior* (New York: Ronald Press, 1970), p. 95.

[33]E. A. Locke and G. P. Latham, *A Theory of Goal Setting and Task Performance* (Englewood Cliffs, NJ: Prentice Hall, 1990).

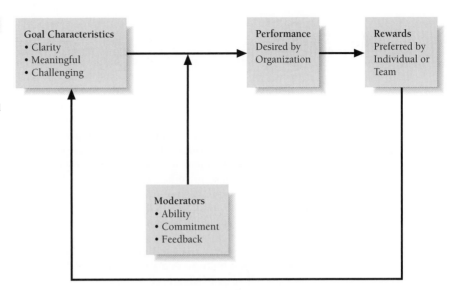

EXHIBIT 4.11
Goal Setting Applied to Organizations
Source: Modified and Based on Edwin A. Locke and Gary P. Locke, "*A Theory of Goal Setting and Task Performance* (Englewood Cliffs, N.J.: Prentice-Hall, 1990).

Goal-Setting Research

Between 1968 and 1998, the amount of research on goal setting increased considerably. Locke's 1968 paper certainly contributed to the increase in laboratory and field research on goal setting. Another force behind the increase in interest and research was the demand of managers for practical and specific techniques that they could apply in their organizations. Goal setting offered such a technique for some managers, and it thus became an important management tool for enhancing work performance.[34]

Empirical research findings from a variety of managerial and student samples have provided support for the theory that conscious goals regulate behavior. Yet a number of important issues concerning goal setting still must be examined more thoroughly. One area of debate concerns the issue of how much subordinate participation in goal setting is optimal. A field experiment conducted by skilled technicians compared three levels of subordinate participation: full (the subordinates were totally involved); limited (the subordinates made some suggestions about the goals the superior set); and none.[35] Measures of performance and satisfaction were taken over a 12-month period. The groups with full- or limited-participant involvement in goal setting showed significantly more performance and satisfaction improvements than did the group that did not participate in goal setting. Interestingly, these improvements began to dissipate six to nine months after the program was started. Some research, however, has failed to find significant relationships between performance and participation in the goal-setting process.[36] Not surprising, the necessity for and effectiveness of participatory

[34]Latham, "Reciprocal Effects of Science on Practice."

[35]John M. Ivancevich, "Different Goal-Setting Treatments and Their Effects on Performance and Job Satisfaction," *Academy of Management Journal,* September 1977, pp. 406–19.

[36]C. Shalley, G. Oldham, and J. Porac, "Effects of Goal Difficulty, Goal-Setting Method, and Expected External Evaluation on Intrinsic Motivation," *Academy of Management Journal,* September 1987, pp. 553–63.

The Ethical Way to Manage?

You Be the Judge

Employee participation has become an integral feature of quality work life, quality circles, employee stock option plans, and workplace design. When used properly, participative management has been effective in improving performance, productivity, and job satisfaction. Employees—as members of a manager-employee team or as part of a group of coworkers—participate in decision making, goal setting, salary determination, and changing the organization's structure.

In fact, there are some who believe that participative management is an ethical imperative. Their argument is that research clearly demonstrates the effectiveness of participative management because it satisfies a basic human need. In other words, it is natural for people to want to participate in those matters which impact them, and to not allow them to do so is ethically wrong. To not allow employee participation frustrates a basic human need and is, therefore, unethical.

Others argue, however, that job satisfaction is not an employee right and that an organization is not duty-bound to provide it. Besides, they note that decades of research do not indicate that participation leads to improved employee morale and job satisfaction in all situations. In fact, they point out that in many cases authoritative methods lead to similar improvements in productivity. So the issue is, is participative management the ethical way to manage? You be the judge.

Sources: The "ethical imperative" idea was first introduced by Marshall Saskin, "Participative Management Is an Ethical Imperative," *Organizational Dynamics,* Spring 1984, pp. 5–22, and elaborated on in "Participative Management Remains an Ethical Imperative," *Organizational Dynamics*, Spring 1986, pp. 62–75. Arguments opposing the ethical imperative view can be found in Edwin A. Locke, David M. Schweiger, and Gary Latham, "Participation in Decision Making: When Should It Be Used," *Organizational Dynamics*, Winter 1986, pp. 65–79.

management styles in any area of management is a much debated topic. You Be the Judge briefly describes the issue.

Research has found that specific goals lead to higher output than do vague goals such as "do your best." Field experiments using clerical workers, maintenance technicians, marketing personnel, engineers, typists, manufacturing employees, and others have compared specific versus do-your-best goal-setting conditions. The vast majority of these studies support—partly or totally—the hypothesis that specific goals lead to better performance than do vague goals. The Weyerhaeuser Corporation, for example, used specific goals to improve an important aspect of the performance of their logging trucks. Traditionally, logging truckers had been operating under the instruction to "do their best" in terms of judging weight loads for their trucks in the field. Management decided that 94 percent of weight capacity was a difficult, yet attainable, specific goal for the drivers. This specific goal worked and became an effective motivator; in less than a full year, the company saved over one-quarter of a million dollars.

Certain aspects of goal setting need to be subjected to scientific examination. One such area centers on individual differences and their impact on the success of goal-setting programs. Such factors as personality, career progression, training background, and personal health are important individual differences that should be considered when implementing goal-setting programs. Goal-setting programs also should be subjected to ongoing examination to monitor attitudinal and performance consequences. Some research has demonstrated that goal-setting programs tend to lose their potency over time, so there is a need to discover why this

── **Management Pointer 4.1** ──

IS GOAL SETTING FOR YOU?

Many successful managers and other successful professionals claim to be goal-setters and believe that it is a key to their success. They continually write down goals and keep track of how they are doing. Is goal setting for you? Here are some questions which, once answered, can be converted into specific goals.

1. Is my knowledge of my job progressing?

2. How developed are my people skills?

3. Have I improved and increased my network of contacts?

4. What other skills should I be working on (e.g., problem solving, managing time, negotiation)?

5. How does this period's performance match up with similar periods of past performance?

6. Out of everything I've done at work in the past three months, of which three things am I the most proud? Least proud?

phenomenon occurs in organizations. Sound evaluation programs would assist management in identifying success, problems, and needs.

Goal setting can be a very powerful technique for motivating employees. When used correctly, carefully monitored, and actively supported by managers, goal setting can improve performance. However, neither goal setting nor any other technique can be used to correct every problem. Is goal setting for you? Management Pointer 4.1 "Is Goal Setting for You?" provides you with some questions to ask and answer.

MOTIVATION AND THE PSYCHOLOGICAL CONTRACT

A conceptual framework that provides a useful perspective for viewing the topic of motivation is *exchange theory*.[37] In a very general sense, exchange theory suggests that members of an organization engage in reasonably predictable give-and-take relationships (exchanges) with each other. For example, an employee gives time and effort in exchange for pay; management provides pleasant working conditions in exchange for employee loyalty. Schein suggests that the degree to which employees are willing to exert effort, commit to organizational goals, and derive satisfaction from their work is dependent on two conditions:[38]

1. The extent to which employee expectations of what the organization will give them and what they owe the organization in return matches the organization's expectations of what it will give and receive.

2. Assuming there is agreement on these expectations, the specific nature of what is exchanged (effort for pay, for example).

These mutual expectations regarding exchanges constitute part of the psychological contract.[39] **The psychological contract** is an unwritten agreement between the individual and the organization which specifies what each expects to give to and receive from the other. While some aspects of an employment relationship, such as pay, may be explicitly stated, many others are not. These implicit agreements which may focus on exchanges involving satisfaction, challenging work, fair treatment, loyalty, and opportunity to be creative may take precedence over written agreements.

In the ideal psychological contract, those contributions the individual was willing to give would correspond perfectly to what the organization wanted to receive; similarly, what the organization wanted to give would correspond totally with what the individual wished to receive. In reality, however, this seldom if ever occurs. Additionally, psychological contracts are not static; either party's

---

[37]P. Ekeh, *Social Exchange Theory* (Cambridge, MA: Harvard University Press, 1974).

[38]H. Schein, *Organizational Psychology,* 2nd ed. (Englewood Cliffs, NJ: Prentice Hall, 1980).

[39]Sandra Robinson, Matthew Kraatz, and Denise Rousseau, "Changing Obligations and the Psychological Contract: A Longitudinal Study," *Academy of Management Journal,* February 1994, pp. 137–52.

expectations can change as can either party's ability or willingness to continue meeting expectations.

When there are few or a decreasing number of matches between what each party expects to give and receive in the contract, work motivation suffers. The psychological contract provides a perspective for why this is true. Looking at motivation from a content theory approach, the psychological contract suggests that in return for time, effort, and other considerations, individuals desire to receive need gratification. Using Maslow's need hierarchy as an example, if an employee is operating at the self-actualization level and fails to receive a challenging job which allows for the application of all the capabilities that employee has, motivation will suffer. In other words, the satisfaction of needs is part of the contract; when the expectation of need satisfaction is not matched with the opportunity to achieve such satisfaction, the contract is violated and motivation is negatively affected.

The perspective on motivation provided by the concept of the psychological contract is not limited to content approaches to motivation, however; it is equally applicable to process explanations as well. Adam's equity theory is, in fact, a form of exchange theory. The notion of inputs and outcomes within equity theory is very similar to expectations of giving and receiving in the psychological contract. In the context of an expectancy approach to motivation, performance-outcome expectancies relate directly to the exchange of performance for pay, advancement, satisfaction, or other outcomes in the psychological contract; likewise, the desire to receive certain considerations in the context of the contract is analogous to positively valent outcomes in expectancy theory.

Managing the psychological contract successfully is one of the more important and challenging aspects of most managers' jobs.[40] The more attuned the manager is to needs and expectations of subordinates, the greater the number of matches that are likely to exist and be maintained in the psychological contract. This, in turn, can positively impact the direction, intensity, and persistence of motivation in the organization.

REVIEWING MOTIVATION

In this chapter, a number of popular theories of motivation are portrayed. The theories typically are pitted against one another in the literature. This is unfortunate since each approach can help managers better understand workplace motivation. Each approach attempts to organize, in a meaningful manner, major variables associated with explaining motivation in work settings. The content theories are individual-oriented in that they place primary emphasis on the characteristics of people. Each of the process theories has a specific orientation. Expectancy theory places emphasis on individual, job, and environmental variables. It recognizes differences in needs, perceptions, and beliefs. Equity theory primarily addresses the relationship between attitudes toward inputs and outputs and reward practices. Goal-setting theory emphasizes the cognitive processes and the role of intentional behavior in motivation.

If anything, this chapter suggests that instead of ignoring motivation, managers must take an active role in motivating their employees. Four specific conclusions are offered here:

---

[40]Thomas O. Davenport, *Human Capital: What It Is and Why People Invest in It* (San Francisco: Jossey-Bass, 1999).

1. Managers can influence the motivation state of employees. If performance needs to be improved, then managers must intervene and help create an atmosphere that encourages, supports, and sustains improvement.

2. Managers should be sensitive to variations in employees' needs, abilities, and goals. Managers also must consider differences in preferences (valences) for rewards.

3. Continual monitoring of needs, abilities, goals, and preferences of employees is each individual manager's responsibility and is not the domain of personnel/human resources managers only.

4. Managers need to work on providing employees with jobs that offer task challenge, diversity, and a variety of opportunities for need satisfaction.

In simple terms, the theme of our discussion of motivation is that the *manager needs to be actively involved.* If motivation is to be energized, sustained, and directed, managers must know about needs, intentions, preferences, goals, and comparisons, and they must act on that knowledge. Failure to do so will result in many missed opportunities to help motivate employees in a positive manner.

Summary of Key Points

- Motivation is made up of at least three distinct components. *Direction* refers to what an individual chooses to do when presented with a number of possible alternative courses of action. *Intensity* relates to the strength of the individual's response once the choice (direction) is made. Finally, *persistence* refers to the staying power of behavior, or how long a person will continue to devote effort.

- Maslow's theory of motivation suggests that individuals' needs are arranged in a hierarchical order of importance and that people will attempt to satisfy the more basic (lower-level) needs before directing behavior toward satisfying higher-level needs. Maslow's five need levels, from lowest to highest, are (1) physiological, (2) safety and security, (3) belongingness, social, and love, (4) esteem, and (5) self-actualization.

- Alderfer's ERG theory is a need hierarchy comprised of three sets of needs: *existence, relatedness,* and *growth.* In addition to the satisfaction-progression process Maslow describes, Alderfer suggests that if a person is continually frustrated in trying to satisfy one level of need, he or she may regress to the next lowest level need.

- Herzberg's research suggests that there are two important sets of factors. *Motivators* are intrinsic conditions and include achievement, recognition, and responsibility. *Hygienes* are extrinsic conditions and include salary, working conditions, and job security. In Herzberg's view, it is only the motivators that contribute to satisfaction and thus have the power to provide motivation.

- McClelland has developed a descriptive set of factors that reflect a high need for achievement. These are: (1) the person likes to take responsibility for solving problems; (2) the person tends to set moderate achievement goals and is inclined to take calculated risks; and (3) the person desires feedback on performance.

- Key terms in expectancy theory include instrumentality, valence, and expectancy. *Instrumentality* refers to the strength of a person's belief that achieving a specific result or outcome will lead to attaining a secondary outcome. *Valence* refers to a person's preference for attaining or avoiding a particular outcome. *Expectancy* refers to a person's belief regarding the likelihood or subjective probability that a particular behavior will be followed by a particular outcome.

- The essence of equity theory is that employees compare their job inputs and outputs with those of others in similar work situations. *Inputs* are what an individual brings to the job and include skills, experiences, and effort, among others. *Outputs* are what a person receives from a job and include recognition, pay, fringe benefits, and satisfaction, among others.

- The key steps in applying goal setting are: (1) diagnosis for readiness; (2) preparing employees via increased interpersonal interaction, communication, training, and action plans for goal setting; (3) emphasizing the attributes of goals that should be understood by a manager and subordinates; (4) conducting intermediate reviews to make necessary adjustments in established goals; and (5) performing a final review to check the goals set, modified, and accomplished.

- Employee expectations of what the organization will give them, what they owe the organization, and the organization's expectation of what it will give to and receive from employees constitute the psychological contract. A *psychological contract* is an unwritten agreement between the individual and the organization which specifies what each expects to give to and receive from the other.

Review and Discussion Questions

1. Why is it important for a manager to consider the various components of motivation when diagnosing motivation problems? Is any one of the components more or less important than any of the others? Explain.

2. Which of the content theories discussed in the chapter do you believe offers the best explanation of motivation? Which of the process theories? Overall, do you feel the content approach or the process approach best explains motivation?

3. Motivation is just one of several factors that influence productivity. What other factors were discussed in this chapter? What is the relationship between these factors and motivation?

4. What implications does Herzberg's two-factor theory have for the design of organizational reward systems? How can the theory be used to explain differences in the three components of motivation?

5. Describe the sequence of events involved in the individual motivational process. What would happen to this process if no need deficiencies existed?

6. As a manager, would you rather the people for whom you are responsible be extrinsically or intrinsically motivated? Explain.

7. What would it be like to manage an organization where all the employees were self-actualized? What kinds of opportunities and problems would this situation present to management?

8. How important a role does perception play in determining whether an employee is receiving equitable treatment? What kinds of things might a manager do to influence those perceptions?

9. Goal setting can be a difficult system to implement effectively. What kinds of problems might be encountered in attempting to install a goal-setting program in an organization? As a manager, what would you do to minimize the likelihood you would encounter these problems?

10. Is there a psychological contract between the students enrolled in this course and the instructor? What are some of the specifics of this contract? How was the contract determined?

READING 4.1   How to Earn Your Employees' Commitment

MOTIVATING EMPLOYEES IN AN AGE OF EMPOWERMENT

Viacom recently reached agreement to sell its Prentice Hall publishing operations to Pearson plc, for $4.6 billion. In announcing the sale, Prentice Hall's president thanked its employees for their past hard work and dedication, and reminded them that during the transition, "it is more important than ever to focus on our individual responsibilities to ensure that our company performs at the highest levels."[1] His message spotlights a dilemma all managers have today: maintaining employee commitment—an employee's identification with and agreement to pursue the company's or the unit's mission—in the face of downsizings, mergers, and turbulent change.[2]

Managers today have numerous motivation tools they can use, ranging from incentives to job enrichment to participative management: Why, then, go through the trouble of winning commitment at all? For several reasons.

First, today's focus on teamwork, empowerment, and flatter organizations puts a premium of self-control or organizational citizenship behavior, "discretionary contributions that are organizationally related, but are neither explicitly required nor contractually rewarded by the organization, yet nevertheless contribute to its effective functioning,"[3] and studies show commitment can encourage just such behavior. For example, one study concludes that "having a membership that shares the organization's goals and values can ensure that your individuals act instinctively to benefit the organization."[4] Commitment—both to the organization, and to one's team—was positively related to "willingness to help" in another study.[5] And another similarly concluded that organizational commitment was associated with the employees' and organization's ability to adapt to unforeseeable occurrences.[6]

Commitment has other favorable outcomes, too. Committed employees tend to have better attendance records and longer job tenure than less committed employees.[7] Not surprisingly, they also tend to work harder at their jobs and perform better than do those with weak commitment.[8] In summary, there is considerable evidence that committed employees will be more valuable employees than those with weak commitment.[9] The question, then, is "how can a manager foster employee commitment?"

Source: Gary Dessler, How to Earn Your Employees' Commitment," *Academy of Management Executive*, May 1999, pp. 58–67.

[1]Newcomb, J. 1998. Letter to employees, May 17.

[2]A variety of definitions, generally focusing on different facets of commitment, have been proposed. Meyer & Allen, for instance, discuss affective commitment, which "refers to the employees' emotional attachment to, identification with, and involvement in the organization." Porter et al. defined organizational commitment as a strong belief in, and acceptance of, the organization's goals and values, a willingness to exert considerable effort on behalf of the organization, and a strong desire to remain in the organization. See Meyer, J. P. & Allen, J. J. 1997. *Commitment in the Workplace: Theory, Research, and Application.* Thousand Oaks, CA: Sage Publications, Inc., 11, 12. For other definitions see, for instance, Becker, T. 1995. The multidimensional view of commitment and the theory of reasoned action: A comparative evaluation. *Journal of Management,* 21(4), 617–638; Allen, N. 1996. Affective, continuance, and normative commitment to the organization: An examination of construct validity. *Journal of Vocational Behavior,* December, 49(3), 252–276; Cooke, D. 1997. Discriminant validity of the organizational commitment questionnaire. *Psychological Reports,* April, 8(2), 431–441; and Wright, P. M., et al. 1994. On the meaning and measurement of goal commitment. *Journal to Applied Psychology,* 79(6), 795–803. Chris Argyris recently distinguished between two kinds of commitment, internal commitment and external commitment: see Argyris, C. 1998. Empowerment: The Emperor's new clothes, *Harvard Business Review,* May–June, 99–100; Hollenback and Klein, define goal commitment as the determination to try for a goal and the unwillingness to abandon or lower that goal: Hollenback, J. R., & Klein, H. J. 1987. Goal commitment and the goal setting process: Problems, prospects, and proposals for future research. *Journal of Applied Psychology,* 72, 212–220. Porter, L. W., Steers, R., Mowday, R. T., & Boulian, P. V. 1974. Unit performance, situational factors, and employee attitudes in spatially separated work units. *Organizational Behavior and Human Performance,* 15, 87–98.

[3]Meyer and Allen, op. cit., 34.

[4]O'Reilly, C., III & Chatman, J. 1986. Organizational commitment and psychological attachment: The affective compliance, identification, and internalization on pro-social behavior. *Journal of Applied Psychology,* 71, 493.

[5]Bishop, J. W. & Scott, K. D. 1997. How commitment affects team performance. *HRMagazine,* February, 107–111.

[6]angle, H. & Perry, J. 1981. An empirical assessment of organizational commitment and organizational effectiveness. *Administrative Science Quarterly,* March, 26, 1–13.

[7]Mowday, R., Porter, L., & Steers, R. 1982. *Employee-Organization Linkages: The Psychology of Commitment, Absenteeism, and Turnover.* New York: Academic Press, 36–37; Kline, C. & Peters, L. 1991. Behavioral commitment and tenure of new employees: A replication and extension. *The Academy of Management Journal,* 34(1), March, 194–204; Somers, M. J. 1995. Organizational commitment, turnover and absenteeism: An examination of direct and interaction affects. *Journal of Organizational Behavior,* 16, 49–58; Bishop, J. W. & Scott, K. D. 1997. How commitment affects team performance. *HRMagazine,* February, 107–111.

[8]Meyer & Allen, op. cit., 28–29. Keep in mind, though, that the relations between commitment and performance are not always so predictable, and even in this particular case, according to the authors, "Many of these findings are based on employee reports of their own behavior." For further discussion see Benkhoff, B. 1997. Ignoring commitment is costly: New approaches establish the missing link between commitment and performance. *Human Relations,* June, 50(6), 701–726.

[9]Meyer & Allen, op. cit., p. 38.

In determining how companies win employee commitment, researchers have studied organizations ranging from utopian communities to business organizations to law firms to labor unions in America, Europe, and Japan. Our examples of how managers can foster commitment is not exhaustive. Possible precursors of commitment such as money are not included, in part because of their obviousness or because of insufficient research evidence.[10] What follows, however, is a useful overview of the actions required to win commitment and how to implement them.

CLARIFY AND COMMUNICATE YOUR MISSION

A number of years ago, Rosabeth Moss Kanter conducted an investigation of commitment that focused not on businesses, but on Utopian communities such as the Shakers and the Oneida. Most of those communities were formed in the United States in the 1800s, usually with the aim of having people live together cooperatively, create their own governance, and operate according to a higher order of natural and spiritual laws. Communities like these, said Kanter, were held together not by coercion but by commitment. In Utopia, what people want to do is the same as what they have to do, and the interests of the individuals are congruent with those of the group.[11]

Life in these communities was organized to support what Kanter calls "core commitment building processes." Kanter called one of these core processes transcendence, a process whereby someone "attaches his decision making perspective to a power greater than himself, surrendering to the higher meaning contained by the group and submitting to something beyond himself." This permits the person "to find himself anew in something larger and greater."[12] The key to achieving this, said Kanter, is creating a strong linkage between the mission and ideology on the one hand, and the person's understanding of how his or her role in the commune fits with the transcendent mission on the other. The commitment in these communities derived, in other words, in part from the power of their mission and ideology and from their members' willingness to accept the community's aims, both as their own and as part of a greater mission. The members became crusaders.

Is it realistic for business organizations to try to achieve the same commitment to a mission? Not just realistic, but essential. For one thing, having goals without commitment is futile. "It's not just the presence of a goal that stimulates progress, [but] also the level of commitment to the goal," as James Collins and Jerry Porras note in their book *Built to Last*.[13] Conversely, commitment without a cause is meaningless.

In practice, there are several things a firm can do to achieve this feeling among employees that they are part of something larger and greater than themselves: create a shared mission and an ideology that lays out a basic way of thinking and doing things; create institutional charisma by linking their missions and values to a higher calling; and promote the commitment of employees to the mission and ideology, for example through selective hiring and focused, value-based orientation.

Clarify the Mission and Ideology

A clear mission and ideology provides a double benefit: The mission provides a focus to which employees can commit, while the values that make up the firm's ideology provide internalized guidelines for their behaviors.

Saturn Corporation provides a good illustration of how to clarify and communicate a mission and ideology. Each Saturn employee receives a pocket card listing Saturn's mission, philosophy, and values. The Saturn mission— "[to] market vehicles developed and manufactured in the United States that are world leaders in quality, cost and customer satisfaction"—is supported by the more detailed Saturn philosophy—showing how, for example, Saturn will meet its customers' and workers' needs. The pocket card then lists and explains Saturn's basic values, which focus on customer enthusiasm, excelling, teamwork, respect for the individual, and continuous improvement.

Make it Charismatic

While not all business firms would want to emulate the spiritual higher-callings of Kanter's early communes, it is possible to couch a mission so that it evokes a higher, charismatic calling that employees can espouse.[14] Like Medieval crusaders, employees then do their best for the firm, not just because they're paid to do so, but because it is a higher calling.

The mission of Ben & Jerry's Homemade symbolizes the founders' unique idea of what a business should be and provides the firm and its employees with an ideology

---

[10]Demographic variables, organizational factors (including organizational size), management style, and organizational climate are among the other antecedents of commitment that have been studied. See, for example, Sommer, S., Bae, S. H., & Luthans, F. 1996. Organizational commitment across cultures: The impact of antecedents on Korean employees. *Human Relations,* 49(7), 977–993; and Wallace, J. 1995. Corporatist control and organizational commitment among professionals: The case of lawyers working in law firms. *Social Forces,* March, Vol. 73(3), 811–839, for example.

[11]Kanter, R. M. 1972. *Commitment and Community: Communes and Utopias in Sociological Perspective.* Cambridge, MA: Harvard University Press, 1. Copyright 1972 by the President and Fellows of Harvard College. Applying conclusions like hers—based, as they are, on a special type of organization— to a corporate setting is always risky. However, there are some corporate lessons to be learned in what she found.

[12]Kanter, op. cit., 74.

[13]Collins, J. & Porras, J. 1997. *Built to Last.* New York: Harper Business, 100.

[14]Based on Dessler, G. 1992. *Winning Commitment.* New York: McGraw-Hill.

that represents a higher, transcendent calling to which all can commit. The mission statement reads, in part:

> Ben & Jerry's is dedicated to the creation and demonstration of a new corporate concept of linked prosperity. . . .

> Social mission: To operate the company in a way that actively recognizes the central role that business plays in the structure of a society by initiating innovative ways to improve the quality of life of a broad community: local, national, and international. . . .[15]

The company's founders practice what they preach. Ben & Jerry's has "green teams" that are responsible for assessing the firm's environmental impact in all areas of operation. It still purchases many of its raw materials—often at above-market prices—from suppliers so as to benefit indigenous people in Maine or in the Brazilian rain forest.

However, formulating an ideology and a mission, even a charismatic one, isn't enough. Employees then need to be steeped in the ideology and to accept it as their own. In her study of Utopian communities, Kanter found that successful communities achieved this by requiring commitment to the ideology, by expecting recruits to take vows, by enforcing fairly exhaustive procedures for choosing members, and by emphasizing tradition. Modern-day equivalents to these practices in business firms include value-based hiring and orientation, and ceremonials that enhance tradition.

Use Value-Based Hiring Practices

In many firms the process of linking employees to ideology begins before the worker is even hired, with value-based hiring practices. These firms first clarify what their basic values are. Then they enforce procedures for screening new employees, require evidence of commitment to the firms' values by their candidates, and reject large numbers of prospective employees. The net effect is to select employees whose values and skills match the firm's ideology and who are thus well on the road to becoming believers before they are even hired. Value-based hiring screens out those who might not fit.

For example, using tests, interviews, and background checks, Ben & Jerry's screens out managers who don't share the firm's social goals, Toyota Manufacturing USA screens out non-team players, and Goldman Sachs emphasizes integrity. Toyota applicants traverse an extensive five-day testing and interviewing program focused on teamwork, quality orientation, and communications ability—the values Toyota covets.

Stress Values-Based Orientation and Training

Steeping the new employees in the values and culture is also important.[16] For example, the orientation (or, as they call it, "assimilation") program at Toyota covers traditional topics such as company benefits, but is intended mostly to convert new team members to the firm's ideology of quality, teamwork, personal development, open communication, and mutual respect. Combined with continuing team- and quality-oriented training, employees completing the four-day process are steeped in—and, ideally, converted to—Toyota's ideology, mission of quality, and values of teamwork, unending incremental improvement, and problem solving.

Build the Tradition

Tradition-building symbols, stories, rites, and ceremonials can further enhance employees' conversion to cultural believers. One Saturn vice president commented: "Creating a value system that encourages the kind of behavior you want is not enough. The challenge is then to engage in those practices that symbolize those values, and tell people what it's really okay to do—and what not [to do]. Actions, in other words, speak much more loudly than words."[17]

Companies are doing this in a variety of ways. A company where having fun is both a basic value and an inalienable right, Ben & Jerry's has a "joy gang," a voluntary group that meets once or twice a week to create new ways to help employees enjoy their work. The joy gang is a concrete example of Ben & Jerry's ideology, which emphasizes charity, fun, and goodwill toward fellow workers. At the annual JCPenney "HCSC" inauguration meetings, new management associates solemnly swear allegiance to the JCPenney Idea and receive HCSC lapel pins, signifying the firm's basic values of honor, confidence, service, and cooperation.[18]

GUARANTEE ORGANIZATIONAL JUSTICE

Organizational justice—"the extent to which fair procedures and processes are in place and adhered to and the extent to which individuals see their leaders as being fair and sincere and having logic or rationale for what they do"[19]—also plays a role in fostering commitment. One study concluded that "Considerable evidence supports a link between the procedural justice associated with organizational policies and the affective commitment of

---

[15]Ben & Jerry's 1990 Annual Report, 5.

[16]See, for example, Laker, D. 1995. The impact of alternative socialization tactics on self-managing behavior and organizational commitment. *Journal of Social Behavior & Personality*, September, 10(3), 645–660.

[17]Personal interview with Bob Boruff, vice president, Saturn, March 1992.

[18]Dessler, op. cit., 86.

[19]For a discussion of definitions of organizational justice see, for example, Skarlicki, D. & Latham, G. 1996. Increasing citizenship behavior within a labor union: A test of organizational justice theory. *Journal of Applied Psychology*, 81(2), 161–169.

employees."[20] Another found that satisfaction with the two-way communication in the organization contributed to organizational commitment.[21] Another study concluded that discretionary contributions above and beyond those specifically required by the organization increased with increases in perceived organizational justice.[22]

Fair procedures and processes embodied in formal grievance procedures are one obvious source of organizational justice. Involving employees in decisions by getting their input, and ensuring that they understand why decisions were made is another.[23]

Have Comprehensive Grievance Procedures

Federal Express's Guaranteed Fair Treatment Procedure is a good example of the former. As its employee handbook says,

> Perhaps the cornerstone of Federal Express' "people" philosophy is the Guaranteed Fair Treatment Procedure (GFTP). This policy affirms your right to appeal any eligible issue through this process of systematic review by progressively higher levels of management. Although the outcome is not assured to be in your favor, your right to participate within the guidelines of the procedure is guaranteed. At Federal Express, where we have a "people-first" philosophy, you have a right to discuss your complaints with management without fear of retaliation.[24]

In brief, GFTP contains three steps. In step one, management review, a complainant submits a written complaint to a manager, who reviews all relevant information, holds a conference with the employee, and makes a decision either to uphold, modify, or overturn the original supervisor's actions.[25] In step two, officer review, the complainant can then submit a written complaint to a vice president or senior vice president, who reviews the case, conducts an additional investigation, and upholds, overturns, or modifies the manager's actions. In step three, executive appeals review, the complainant can then submit a written complaint to an appeals board comprising the CEO, president, chief personnel officer, and two senior vice presidents. The board reviews all relevant information and upholds or overturns the decision. When there is a question of fact, the appeals board may initiate a board of review.

Provide Extensive Two-Way Communications

Providing for plenty of opportunities for two-way communication is another way to cultivate the feeling that the work experience is a just one. Indeed, a Saturn assembly team, when asked, "What's the first thing you would tell a boss to do to get commitment?" responded, in unison, "Tell them to listen."[26]

Saturn's assemblers get information continuously via the plant's internal television network. FedEx's Survey Feedback Action program lets employees express feelings about the company and their managers. "Hotline" programs are another option. For example, Toyota's handbook states, "Don't spend time worrying about something. Speak up!" The company's "Hotline" gives team members a 24-hour channel for bringing questions or problems to management's attention. Employees can pick up any phone, dial the hotline extension, and leave messages on a recorder. All hotline messages are reviewed by the human resources manager and thoroughly investigated. If it is decided a particular question would be of interest to other Toyota team members, then the questions and Toyota's response is posted on plant bulletin boards. Employees wanting a personal response must leave their names, but no attempt is made to identify anonymous callers.[27]

CREATE A SENSE OF COMMUNITY

Kanter, in her study of Utopian communities, also observed that all the successful communities she studied shared a sense of community, one in which "connection, belonging, participation in a whole, mingling of the self and the group, and an equal opportunity to contribute and to benefit all are part."[28] This sense of community contributed to creating commitment among the communities' members, who developed a strong "we-feeling"—that they were like a family. The result was a "cohesive, emotionally involving, and effectively satisfying community."[29]

Kanter identified several practices through which the communities fostered this sense of community. There was usually some homogeneity of background among members, which made it easier for them to share common experiences and identify with one another and with the community. There was also some communal sharing of both property and work, as members shared to some extent the assets of the community and the output of its efforts. Communal work provided an opportunity for joint

[20]Meyer & Allen, op. sit., 47.

[21]Varona, F. 1995. Communication satisfaction and organizational commitment: A study in three Guatemalan organizations. *Dissertation Abstracts International,* March, 53(9-A), 3048.

[22]Skarlicki, D. & Latham, G. 1996. Increasing citizenship behavior.

[23]Kim, W. C. & Manborgne, R. 1997. Fair process: Managing in the knowledge economy. *Harvard Business Review,* July/August, 65–66.

[24]The Federal Express Employee Handbook, August 7, 1989, 89.

[25]Ibid.

[26]Dessler, op. cit., 87.

[27]Team Member Handbook, Toyota Motor Manufacturing, USA, February 1988, 52–53.

[28]Kanter, op. cit. You should note that the next line in her quote is "The principle is 'from each according to his abilities, to each according to his needs.' " Thus we have to be quite choosy about which practices might be applicable in a corporate setting.

[29]Ibid, 93.

effort, with all members, as far as possible, performing all tasks for equal rewards. Finally, there was regularized group contact, continuing activities that brought the individual into periodic contact with the group as a whole. All these practices have their practical parallels in business organizations today.

Build Value-Based Homogeneity

Hiring a homogeneous workforce in these days of cultural diversity and equal employment opportunity requires focusing on values, skills, and interests rather than on discriminatory traits such as ethnic background. Many firms thus explicitly select employees based on those values that are desirable to the firm. At Goldman Sachs, these values include excellence, creativity and imagination; the ability to assume responsibility rapidly; teamwork and dedication to the firm; intense effort in work; and integrity and honesty.[30] At Toyota, interpersonal skills, reasoning skills, flexibility, and willingness to be team members characterize successful employees (who are always referred to as "team members"). The point is that in firms like these, the people who are hired are already well on their way to fitting in. They are homogeneous, not in the sense of being all-white or all-male or all-Ivy league, but in their potential fit with the firm's values. They are people who by aspirations, values, and skills should fit right in.

Share and Share Alike

Despite significant disparities between the salaries of executives and workers, it's also possible to foster a sense that everyone shares in a firm's fortunes. At FedEx, for instance, chairman Fred Smith has no assigned parking spot and there are no company cars. There is no executive lunchroom and the executives' offices are modest. "We do as much as we can to minimize differences between non-executive levels and ourselves," one top FedEx manager explained.

Profit sharing can play a role too. The legendary number of millionaires at Microsoft is one notable example. Increasingly, substantial bonuses, profit sharing, and pay-for-performance plans enable employees throughout industry to appreciate that not only top managers get a sizable share of the pie.

Emphasize Barnraising, Cross-Utilization, and Teamwork

Getting everyone to work cooperatively on a project and even to share work and jobs also fosters a sense of community. Even today in some Utopian communities, people still get together to build a house or a barn. Much the same applies in business: Delta Airlines airport work teams routinely rotate jobs; reservations clerks fill in at the check-in ramp or in baggage handling if the need arises. The Delta Policy Manual calls the practice cross-utilization.[31] Organizing around teams—especially self-managing teams—is another way to enhance the feeling that the work is shared. The members of self-managing teams at firms from Saturn to American Express often share each other's work and routinely rotate jobs.

Get Together

In many companies, frequent group meetings and other regularized contacts further enhance employees' sense of community. Ben & Jerry's has monthly staff meetings in the receiving bay of the Waterbury, Vermont, plant. Production stops and all employees attend. The firm's joy gangs organize regular "joy events," including Cajun parties, table tennis contests, and manufacturing appreciation days, all aimed at getting employees together.

At Federal Express, daily teleconferenced meetings describe the previous day's accomplishments. Toyota has a TV system called Toyota Network News, and spends about $250,000 annually on a "perfect attendance" meeting to which all high-attendance employees are invited. At Mary Kay Cosmetics, weekly meetings of directors and their sales consultants similarly serve to reinforce the sense of communion and togetherness.

SUPPORT EMPLOYEE DEVELOPMENT

Studies also suggest employees are more committed to employers who are more committed to the employees' long-term career development.[32] For example, managers in eight large U.S. organizations were asked to evaluate whether their firms had fulfilled their promises and met the managers' expectations. Those who answered affirmatively were much more likely to be committed to the organization, results that underscore the role of career satisfaction and success in winning commitment.[33] "The best route to employee commitment," the study concluded, is "for the organization to take the time and the trouble to provide each manager with the experience he or she needs—even craves—at each stage of his or her career."[34]

An analysis of employee commitment among hospital administrators, nurses, service workers, and clerical employees and among scientists and engineers from a research lab concluded that the employer's ability to fulfill the employee's personal career aspirations had a

---

[30]Except as noted, the discussion of "Creating a Sense of Community" is based on Dessler, op. cit., 50–60.

[31]Delta's Personnel Policy Manual, 18.

[32]Wood, S. & Albanese, M. 1995. Can we speak of high commitment management on the shop floor? *Journal of Management Studies*, 32(2), March, 215–247.

[33]Buchanan, B. 1975. To walk an extra mile: The whats, whens, and whys of organizational commitment. *Organizational Dynamics*, Spring, 75.

[34]Ibid.

marked effect on employee commitment. As this study summarized,

> Individuals come to organizations with certain needs, desires, skills, and so forth and expect to find a work environment where they can utilize their abilities and satisfy many of their basic needs. When the organization provides such a vehicle, the likelihood of increasing commitment is apparently enhanced. When the organization is not dependable, however, or where it fails to provide employees with challenging and meaningful tasks, commitment levels tend to diminish.[35]

A study of employees of a manufacturing plant similarly found that internal mobility and promotion from within, company-sponsored training and development, and job security were all correlated with employee commitment. As these researchers concluded,

> commitment is higher among employees who believe they are being treated as resources to be developed rather than commodities to buy and sell. Even controlling for other known antecedents, employees are committed to the extent that they believe the company is providing a long-term developmental employment opportunity.[36]

Anecdotal evidence from the author's studies at Saturn and Federal Express support this idea. In the words of one Saturn assembler,

> I'm committed to Saturn in part for what they did for me; for the 300-plus hours of training in problem solving and leadership that helped me expand my personal horizons; for the firm's "Excel" program that helps me push myself to the limit; and because I know that at Saturn I can go as far as I can go. This company wants its people to be all that they can be. . . .[37]

Similarly, one Federal Express manager explained,

> At Federal Express, the best I can be is what I can be here. I have been allowed to grow [at Federal Express]. People here are not turned on by money. The biggest benefit is that Federal Express made me a man. It gave me the confidence and self-esteem to become the person I had the potential to become.

The net effect is that employees become committed to firms that are committed to them—to their development, to their well being, and to their desire to become the peo-

ple they always hoped they could be. Employers can show such commitment in several ways.

Commit to Actualizing

What companies believe and commit to drives what they do. Employers seeking to actualize their employees must therefore start by committing to do so, and then memorialize that commitment in their literature and management training. A top executive at JCPenney described his company's policy on development this way:

> We have an obligation to develop our people to the fullest. You never know how high is high . . . one of the best measures of a manager's effectiveness is the length of the list of names of those he helped to develop career wise. For me, one of the truest measures of a Penney manager's effectiveness is how many people would put you on the list of those who helped their careers here.

Provide First-Year Job Challenge

Employees bring their needs, aspirations, and hopes to their jobs, and become committed to employers that take concrete steps to help them develop their abilities and achieve their potential. Young graduates or new recruits often start their jobs expecting challenging assignments to help them test and prove their abilities. Providing such challenging first jobs is therefore a practice at many firms. Young professionals at Goldman Sachs are expected to contribute at once and immediately find themselves on teams involved in challenging projects. As one manager there explained,

> Even our young people often start out handling millions of dollars of responsibility. And at a meeting with a client, the partner in charge will often not talk first at the meeting, but the youngest will. At Goldman Sachs, you take the responsibility and you're supported by the team. That's what attracts people to Goldman Sachs—ability to make decisions early.

Enrich and Empower

Behavioral scientists have long encouraged job enrichment—increasing the breadth of responsibility and self-management in the job—as a way to appeal to employees' higher level needs. The effect of such enrichment can, in fact, be almost intoxicating. Here's how one Saturn assembler described the experience of self-managing teams:

> You don't have anyone here who is a supervisor. You don't experience supervision. We are supervised by ourselves. We become responsible to people we work with every day. What I do affects my people. In other firms you're treated like children and here we are treated like adults. We make

[35]Steers, R. M. 1977. Antecedents and outcomes of organizational commitment. *Administrative Science Quarterly,* 22, March, 53.
[36]Gaertner, K. & Nollen, S. 1989. Career experiences, perceptions of employment practices, and psychological commitment in the organization. *Human Relations,* 42(11), 987.
[37]Except as noted, the discussion on "Support Employee Development" is based on Dessler, G. 1992. *Winning Commitment,* 110–138.

up our own work schedule. We do our own budgeting and buying of tools. We decide and improve on the work process by consensus.

Promote from Within

Promotion from within is not always feasible in today's business environment. But there are benefits to letting employees know a firm has fair promotional practices. Here it's important to distinguish between promotion from within programs and policies. Policies such as "open positions are filled, whenever possible, by qualified candidates from within the existing work force" are one thing. The hard part is to breathe life into such policies by organizing your HR processes to support them.

Managers can do several things to create more meaningful promotion from within practices. Career-oriented appraisals are one component. Many employers don't just assess past performance, but link an employee's performance, career preferences, and developmental needs in a formal career plan. As Delta's HR manager explained:

> Our annual evaluations are formal and include an interview. We touch on whether the employee is making progress or not, review his or her past experience, and discuss where that person is going with his or her career. The formal evaluation forces the supervisor and employee to communicate and talk about the person's career path.

An effective career-records/job-posting system can also bolster a firm's program of promotion from within by ensuring that an inside candidate's career goals and skills are matched openly, fairly, and effectively with promotional opportunities. For example, FedEx's electronic Job Change Applicant Tracking System announces new openings every Friday. All employees posting for a position are given numerical scores based on job performance and length of service and are advised whether they have been chosen as candidates.

Provide Developmental Activities

Developmental activities such as career workshops enhance employees' opportunities for promotion from within, appeal to their desire to grow and to learn, provide more opportunities for lateral moves, and give them a chance to move on to another company. Saturn's career-growth workshop uses vocational guidance tools (including a skills-assessment disk) to help employees identify skills they need to develop. "You assess yourself and then your team assesses you," is how one Saturn employee put it. Tuition reimbursement, company-sponsored training and development, and other developmental activities are available to help Saturn employees develop those skills.

The Question of Employee Security

While few firms promise lifetime employment, incurring the costs of value-based hiring, extensive training, empowering, and developing employees without some job security is somewhat self-defeating.

Some companies provide job security while making it clear that their commitment to job security is a commitment to do their best, but not a guarantee. A Federal Express executive emphasized that "No-layoff is a commitment, not a policy. There are no guarantees, but the firm is on record as having a strong commitment to make every effort not to lay off personnel except in the most extreme economic circumstances, as determined by the chief executive officer." Delta Airlines tries to minimize layoffs by keeping a small temporary work force in airport operations and regional offices, that may ebb and flow with seasonal changes.

COMMIT TO PEOPLE-FIRST VALUES

The commitment-building processes—clarifying and communicating a mission, guaranteeing organizational justice, creating a sense of community, and supporting employee development—all rest on one foundation, and that is the employer's commitment to values that put people first.

Studies do suggest that treating employees as important and respected individuals contributes to their commitment.[38] The extent to which employees are made to feel that they are making important contributions to the organization is a "central theme" that emerges from the commitment research.[39] And, the research notwithstanding, it's hard to imagine being serious about organizational justice, creating a sense of community, or supporting employee development if you're not seriously committed to respecting your employees as individuals. Operationally, companies accomplish this in several ways.

Put It In Writing

A good first step is to replace talk with action and to codify and distribute the firm's people-first values. FedEx's Manager's Guide, for instance, states: "I have an inherent right to be treated with respect and dignity and that right should never be violated."[40]

Saturn employees carry pocket cards that lists the firm's values, one of which says:

> Trust and respect for the individual: we have nothing of greater value than our people. We believe that demonstrating respect for the uniqueness of every individual

[38]See, for example, Steers, op. cit., 53.

[39]Meyer & Allen, op. cit., 48.

[40]Except as noted, the discussion of "Commit to People-First Values" is based on Dessler, op. cit., 28–33.

builds a team of confident, creative members possessing a high degree of initiative, self-respect, and self-discipline.

Hire "Right-Kind" Managers

Putting the company's people-first values into practice means that managers must have internalized these values and become committed to them. In many firms, this means hiring the right kind of people in the first place, and then carefully indoctrinating them in the gospel of respect. FedEx's program provides one good example. All FedEx supervisory candidates must enroll in a special leader identification program to prove they have the values and skills to be managers. About 20 percent of these candidates fall out after the first phase of the program—"Is Management for Me?"—a one-day session that familiarizes them with the manager's job. This session is followed by three months of self-evaluations and supervisory assessments of the candidates' values and skills, and a series of peer assessments and panel interviews with senior managers. Management training sessions in the firm's Leadership Institute then reinforce FedEx's values and indoctrinates the new managers in the principles and values of the firm.

Walk the Talk

Similarly, Saturn Corporation translates its people-first values into practice every day. Extensive two-way communication systems (frequent meetings, open-door policies, and so forth), job security, team-centered work groups, and an emphasis on employee self-actualization—giving each employee an opportunity to be all he or she can be through involvement in most job-related decisions, plus promotion from within and extensive career assessment, training, and development programs—all reflect Saturn's people-first values. As one Saturn vice president put it, Saturn's emphasis on igniting employee commitment stems from

> creating a value system that encourages the kind of behavior we knew we wanted. We knew we had to put in an actionable value system that changed how managers thought and how people built cars. If you start with the premise that you trust people and that they will do a good job, it takes

you in a whole new direction. But if you really want to trust people, you have to show that you do and you start by eliminating all those things that say, "I don't trust you." That includes time clocks, gates, and hourly pay, for example.

SUMMING UP: HOW TO EARN YOUR EMPLOYEES' COMMITMENT

Managers today have a dilemma: maintaining employee commitment in the face of downsizings, mergers, and turbulent change. It is, in a very real sense, a paradoxical situation: on the one hand today's focus on teamwork, empowerment, and flatter organizations puts a premium on just the sort of self-motivation that one expects to get from committed employees; on the other hand, environmental forces are acting to diminish the foundations of employee commitment.

Over the past 30 years or so, we've learned quite a bit about how to win commitment. The evidence suggests that winning commitment requires a comprehensive, multifaceted management system, one consisting of an integrated and internally consistent package of concrete actions and policies. The main steps and substeps in implementing such a commitment-oriented management system would include the following:

- Commit to people-first values: Put it in writing; hire right-kind managers; walk the talk.   www. saturncar com
- Clarify and communicate your mission: Clarify the mission and ideology; make it charismatic; use value-based hiring practices; stress values-based orientation and training; build the tradition.
- Guarantee organizational justice: Have a comprehensive grievance procedure; provide for extensive two-way communications.
- Create a sense of community: Build value-based homogeneity; share and share alike; emphasize barnraising, cross-utilization, and teamwork; get together.
- Support employee development: Commit to actualizing; provide first year job challenge; enrich and empower; promote from within; provide developmental activities; provide employee security without guarantees.

Exercises

EXERCISE 4.1   Goal Setting—How to Do It

Each person is to work alone for at least 30 minutes with this exercise. After sufficient time has elapsed for each person to work through the exercise, the instructor will go over each goal and ask for comments from the class or group. The discussion should display the understanding of goals that each participant has and what will be needed to improve his or her goal-writing skills.

Writing and evaluating goals seem simple, but they are often not done well in organizations. The press of time, previous habits, and little concern about the attributes of a goal statement are reasons why goals are often poorly constructed. Actually, a number of guidelines should be followed in preparing goals.

1. A well-presented goal statement contains four elements:
   a. An action or accomplishment verb
   b. A single and measurable result
   c. A date of completion
   d. A cost in terms of effort, resources, or money, or some combination of these factors
2. A well-presented goal statement is short; it is not a paragraph, but should be presented in a sentence.
3. A well-presented goal statement specifies only what and when and doesn't get into how or why.
4. A well-presented goal statement is challenging and attainable. It should cause the person to stretch his or her skills, abilities, and efforts.
5. A well-presented goal statement is meaningful and important. It should be a priority item.
6. A well-presented goal statement must be acceptable to you so that you will try hard to accomplish the goal. The goal statement model should be:

To (action or accomplishment verb) (single result) by (a date—keep it realistic) at (effort, use of what resource, cost).

An example for a production operation:

To reduce the production cost per unit of mint toothpaste by at least 3 percent by March 1, at a changeover of equipment expense not to exceed $45,000.

Examine the next four statements that are presented as goal statements. Below each goal, write a critique of the statement. Is it a good goal statement? Why? Discuss your viewpoints in the class group discussion.

To reduce my blood pressure to an acceptable level.

To make financial investments with a guaranteed minimum return of at least 16 percent.

To spend a minimum of 45 minutes a day on a doctor-approved exercise plan, starting Monday, lasting for six months, at no expense.

To spend more time reading non-work-related novels and books during the next year.

Cases

CASE 4.1   FAB Sweets Limited

ORGANIZATIONAL SETTING

FAB Sweets Limited is a manufacturer of high-quality sweets (candies). The company is a medium-sized, family-owned, partially unionized and highly successful confectionery producer in the north of England. The case study is set within a single department in the factory where acute problems were experienced.

Source: Case prepared by N. Kemp, C. Clegg, T. Wall, *Case Studies in Organizational Behaviour*, ed. C. Clegg, N. Kemp, and K. Legge (London: Harper & Row, 1985).

BACKGROUND TO THE CASE

The department (hereafter called HB) produces and packs over 40 lines of hard-boiled sweets on a batch-production system. It is organized in two adjacent areas, one for production staffed by men and one for packing staffed by women. The areas are separated by a physical barrier, allowing the packing room to be air conditioned and protected from the humidity resulting from production. Management believed this was necessary to stop the sweets from sweating (thus sticking to their wrappers) during storage. Each room has a chargehand and a supervisor who reports to the department manager, who him-

EXHIBIT 4.12   The HB Department: Physical Layout and Work Flow

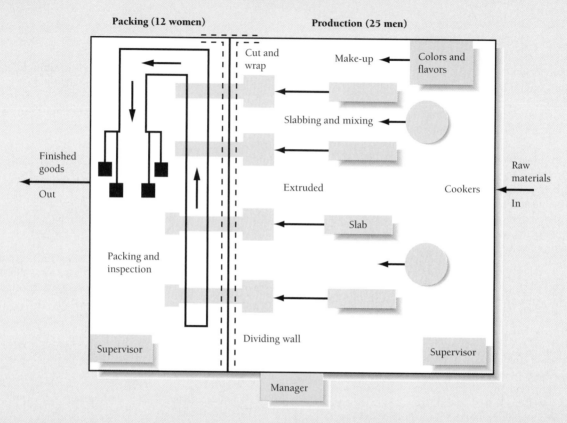

self is responsible to the factory manager. In total, 37 people work in the department (25 in production, 12 in packing), the majority of whom are skilled employees. Training takes place on the job, and it normally takes two years to acquire the skills necessary to complete all the production tasks. Exhibit 4.12 presents an outline of the physical layout of the department and the work flow.

The production process is essentially quite simple. Raw materials, principally sugar, are boiled to a set temperature, with "cooking time" varying from line to line. The resulting batches are worked on by employees who fold and manipulate them so as to create the required texture, while adding coloring and flavorings ("slabbing" and "mixing"). Different batches are molded together to create the flavor mixes and patterns required ("make up"). The batch, which by now is quite cool, is then extruded through a machine which cuts it into sweets of individual size. Some products at this stage are automatically wrapped and then passed by conveyor belt to the packing room where they are inspected, bagged, and boxed ready for dispatch to retail and wholesale outlets. Other products progress unwrapped into the packing room where they are fed into a wrapping machine, inspected, bagged,

and dispatched. Several different product lines can be produced at the same time. The most skilled and critical tasks occur early in the process; these include "cooking" mixtures for different products and "make up" (e.g., for striped mints). These skills are gradually learned until the operator is able to "feel" the correct finish for each of the 40 lines. All the tasks are highly interdependent such that any one individual's performance affects the ease with which the next person down the line can successfully achieve his/her part of the production process. Although the work appears quite simple and the management of the process straightforward, the department nevertheless experienced acute problems. These are outlined below.

THE PROBLEM

In objective terms, the problems in HB were manifest in a high level of labor turnover, six new managers in eight years, production which consistently fell below targets based on work-study standards, and high levels of scrap. The department was known as the worst in the factory, and its problems were variously characterized in terms of "attitude," "atmosphere," and "climate." Moreover, employees had few decision-making responsibilities, low motivation, low job satisfaction, and received little information on their performance. Finally, there were interpersonal problems between the employees in the production and packing rooms, between the two supervisors, and also among the operators, and there were a number of dissatisfactions relating to grading and payment levels.

EXPERIENCE OF THE METHOD OF WORKING

To understand how HB works and how people experienced their work, it is necessary to recognize the strong drive throughout the organization for production. Departmental managers are judged primarily in terms of their production levels (against targets) and the efficiency (against work-study standards) at which they perform. In HB this pressure was transmitted to the two supervisors. In practice, production levels were the numbers of batches of sweets processed, and efficiency was the ratio of batches produced to hours used by direct labor.

The production supervisor responded to the pressure for production in a number of ways. First, in an attempt to maximize production, he always allocated people to the jobs at which they performed best. He also determined the cooker speeds. In effect, this set the pace of work for both production and packing. Buffer stocks were not possible in production because the sweets needed processing before they cooled down. If he was falling behind the target, the supervisor responded by speeding up the pace of work. In addition, he regarded his job purely in terms of processing batches and ignored problems in the packing room which may in fact have resulted directly from his actions or from those of his staff. The supervisory role thus involved allocating people to tasks, setting machine speeds (and hence the pace of work), organizing reliefs and breaks, monitoring hygiene, safety, and quality standards, maintaining discipline, and recording data for the management information systems. The chargehand undertook these responsibilities in the absence of a supervisor, spending the rest of his time on production.

The men in production complained that they were bored with always doing the same jobs, especially as some were physically harder than others (for example, "slabbing" involved manual manipulation of batches of up to 50 kilograms). Several claimed that their greater efforts should receive financial recognition. Furthermore, this rigidity of task allocation was in direct conflict with the grading system which was designed to encourage flexibility. To be on the top rate of pay in the department, an operator had to be capable of performing all the skills for all the lines and hence be able to cover any job. Training schedules matched this. In practice, however, people rarely used more than one or two of their skills. The others decayed through disuse. All the staff recognized that the grading system was at odds with how the department

actually worked and tended to be dissatisfied with both. The production supervisor's strict control over the pace of work also proved suboptimal in other ways. For example, he sometimes pushed the pace to a level regarded as impossible by the staff. Whether this was true or self-fulfilling is a moot point—the net result was an increase in the level of scrap. Also, he ignored the wishes of the staff to work less hard in the afternoon when they were tired: again scrap resulted. In addition, the feeling was widespread among the men in production that management and supervision organized the work badly and would do better if they took advice from the shop floor. Their own perceived lack of control over the job led them to abrogate responsibility when things went wrong ("We told them so!!"). And finally, although the processes of production were highly interdependent, operators adopted an insular perspective and the necessary cooperation between workers was rarely evident, and then only on the basis of personal favors between friends.

The equivalent pressure on the packing supervisor was to pack the sweets efficiently. As her section could pack no more than was produced, her only manipulable variable was hours worked. Thus, to increase her efficiency she could only transfer the packers to "other work" within her room (e.g., cleaning) or to another department.

The packers for their part resented being asked to work flat out when HB was busy, only to be moved elsewhere when things were slacker. As described above, their own work flow was basically controlled by the speed at which the men were producing. When in difficulty, direct appeals to the men to slow down were unsuccessful and so they channeled their complaints through their supervisor. Because of the insular perspective adopted by the production supervisor (in rational support of his own targets), her approaches were usually ignored ("It's my job to produce sweets"), and the resulting intersupervisory conflict took up much of the department manager's time. In addition the packing room was very crowded, and interpersonal conflicts were common.

Finally, production problems throughout the factory were created by seasonal peaks and troughs in the market demand for sweets. These "busy" and "slack" periods differed between production departments. In order to cope with market demands, the production planning department transferred staff, on a temporary basis, between production departments. In HB this typically meant that, when they were busy, "unskilled" employees were drafted in to help, whereas when demand was low, HB employees were transferred to other departments where they were usually given the worst jobs. Both of these solutions were resented by the employees in HB.

This description of the department is completed when one recognizes the complications involved in scheduling over 40 product lines through complex machinery, all of it over 10 years old. In fact, breakdowns and interruptions to smooth working were common. The effects of these on the possible levels of production were poorly understood, and in any case few operators were aware of their targets or of their subsequent performance. More immediately, the breakdowns were a source of continual conflict between the department and the maintenance engineers responsible to an engineering manager. The department laid the blame on poor maintenance, the engineers on abuse or lack of care by production workers in handling the machinery. Much management time was spent in negotiating "blame" for breakdowns and time allowances resulting since this affected efficiency figures. Not surprisingly, perhaps, the factorywide image of the department was very poor on almost all counts, and its status was low.

PARTICIPANTS' DIAGNOSES OF THE PROBLEMS

Shop floor employees, chargehands, supervisors, the department manager, and senior management were agreed that much was wrong in HB. However, there was no co-herent view of the causes and what should be done to make improvements. Many shop floor employees placed the blame on supervision and management for their lack of technical and planning expertise and their low consideration for subordinates. The production supervisor favored a solution in terms of "getting rid of the trouble-makers," by transferring or sacking his nominated culprits. The department manager wanted to introduce a senior supervisor to handle the conflicts between the production and packing supervisors and further support the pressure for production. The factory manager thought the way work was organized and managed might be at the core of the difficulties.

QUESTIONS:

1. Why is turnover often considered a motivation problem?
2. How would you analyze the department problem using expectancy theory?
3. How would you solve the motivation problem? Be specific.

5

Evaluation, Feedback, and Reward of Individual Behavior

After completing Chapter 5, you should be able to:

Learning Objectives

- Describe several purposes of performance evaluation.

- Explain why a 360-Degree Feedback Program is considered more thorough.

- Discuss reinforcement theory.

- Describe the elements in a model of rewards.

- Compare intrinsic and extrinsic rewards.

- Understand the role rewards play in turnover, absenteeism, performance, and commitment.

- Identify several innovative reward systems.

Organizations use a variety of rewards to attract and retain people and to motivate them to achieve their personal and organizational goals. The manner and timing of distributing rewards are important issues that managers must address almost daily. Managers distribute such rewards as pay, transfers, promotions, praise, and recognition. They also can help create the climate that results in more challenging and satisfying jobs. Because these rewards are considered important by employees, they have significant effects on behavior and performance. In this chapter we are concerned with how rewards are distributed by managers. We discuss the reactions of people to rewards and examine the response of employees to rewards received in organizational settings. Additionally, we present the role of rewards in organizational absenteeism, turnover, commitment, and job performance.

Before individuals can be rewarded, there must be some basis for distributing rewards. Some rewards may accrue to all individuals simply by virtue of their employment with the organization. These are what are known as *universal* or *across-the-board rewards*. Other rewards may be a function of tenure or seniority. Many rewards, however, are related to job performance.[1] To distribute these rewards equitably, it is necessary to evaluate employee performance. Thus, we begin this chapter with a look at performance evaluation. Developing effective evaluation systems is just as critical to organizational success as is developing effective reward systems. Both systems represent efforts to influence employee behavior. To achieve maximum effectiveness, it is necessary to carefully link employee evaluation systems with reward systems.

EVALUATION OF PERFORMANCE

Virtually every organization of at least moderate size has a formal employee performance evaluation system. Assessing and providing feedback about performance is considered essential to an employee's ability to perform job duties effectively.[2] In discussing this topic, we will identify the purposes performance evaluation may serve, and examine what the focus of evaluations should be. We will also take a look at a number of different performance evaluation methods, examining their strengths and weaknesses.

Purposes of Evaluation

The basic purpose of evaluation, of course, is to provide information about work performance.[3] More specifically, however, such information can serve a variety of purposes. Some of the major ones are:

1. Provide a basis for reward allocation, including raises, promotions, transfers, layoffs, and so on
2. Identify high-potential employees
3. Validate the effectiveness of employee selection procedures
4. Evaluate previous training programs

---

[1]Shari Caudron, "Spreading Out the Carrots," *Industry Week*, May 19, 1997, pp. 20–25.

[2]Roger E. Herman and Joyce L. Gioia, *Employer of Choice* (Winchester, VA: Oakhall Press, 2000).

[3]Jonathan A. Segal, "86 Your Appraisal Process," *HR Magazine*, October 2000, pp. 199–206.

5. Stimulate performance improvement
6. Develop ways of overcoming obstacles and performance barriers
7. Identify training and development opportunities
8. Establish supervisor-employee agreement on performance expectations

These eight specific purposes can be grouped into two broad categories. The first four have a *judgmental orientation;* the last four have a *developmental orientation.* Evaluations with a judgmental orientation focus on past performance and provide a basis for making judgments regarding which employee should be rewarded and how effective organizational programs—such as selection and training—have been. Evaluations with a developmental orientation are more concerned with improving future performance by ensuring expectations are clear and by identifying ways to facilitate employee performance through training. These two broad categories are, of course, not mutually exclusive. Performance evaluation systems can, and do, serve both general purposes.

The general purpose for which performance evaluations are conducted will also vary across different cultures. So also will the frequency with which evaluations are conducted, who conducts them, and a variety of other components. International Encounter 5.1 illustrates some cultural differences in typical performance evaluations across three different countries.

Focus of Evaluation

Effective performance evaluation is a continuous, ongoing process and, simply stated, involves asking two questions: "Is the work being done effectively?" and "Are employee skills and abilities being fully utilized?" The first question tends toward a judgmental orientation, while the second is more developmental in nature. Generally, evaluations should focus on translating the position responsibilities into each employee's day-to-day activities. Position responsibilities are determined on the basis of a thorough job analysis, a procedure that is discussed in more detail in Chapter 6. Additionally, the evaluation should assist the employee in understanding these position responsibilities, the work goals associated with them, and the degree to which the goals have been accomplished.

Performance evaluations should focus on job performance, not individuals. If a software engineer's work comes to her by electronic communication and she forwards the completed work via e-mail to persons with whom she has no personal contact, should the fact that she cannot express herself well when talking to someone be an important factor in judging her performance? If we focus on her communication ability, we are concerned about her as an individual and are evaluating *her.* But if we look at this in relation to its effect on how well she does her job, we are evaluating her **performance**.

When evaluating employee behavior, it is necessary to ensure not only that the focus of the appraisal remains on job performance, but that it also has proper weighting of relevant behaviors. Relevancy, in the context of performance evaluation, has three aspects: deficiency, contamination, and distortion. *Deficiency* occurs when the evaluation does not focus on all aspects of the job. If certain job responsibilities and activities are not considered, the evaluation is deficient. *Contamination* can be said to be the reverse of deficiency. It occurs when activities *not* part of the job are included in the evaluation. If we evaluate the word processor mentioned in the previous paragraph on her verbal skills, this would

International Encounter 5.1

Cultural Differences in Performance Evaluations

Performance evaluations, like many other management procedures, are not universally the same across all cultures. The primary purpose served by evaluations, the procedures used to conduct evaluations, and the manner in which information is communicated are just a few of the components of performance evaluation that may differ as a function of the culture in which the evaluation is being conducted. Below are a few examples of some of the differences that exist between the United States, Saudi Arabia, and Japan. For each country, the descriptions of the various components reflect usual or typical practice. Clearly within any single country there will be variations between organizations and, less frequently, within organizations.

Component	United States	Saudi Arabia	Japan
Purpose	Fairness, employee development	Placement	Employee development
Who conducts evaluation	Supervisor	Manager several layers higher	Mentor and supervisor
Frequency	Once a year or periodically	Once a year	Developmental appraisal once a month. Evaluation appraisal after 12 years
Assumptions	Objective appraiser is fair	Subjective more important than objective	Objective and subjective equal importance
Manner of communication and feedback	Criticism direct and may be in writing	Criticism subtle and will not be in writing	Criticism subtle and given orally
Rebuttals	Employee will feel free to rebut	Employee will feel free to rebut	Employee will rarely rebut
Praise	Given individually	Given individually	Given to entire group

Sources: Adapted from a report of the Association of Cross-Cultural Trainers in Industry, Southern California, 1984; and from P. R. Harris and R. T. Moran, *Managing Cultural Differences*, 3rd ed. (Houston: Gulf Publishing, 1991).

be a form of contamination. Finally, *distortion* takes place in the evaluation process when an improper emphasis is given to various job elements. If, for example, placing the phones on automatic answering at the close of each business day is only a small element of a secretary's job, making that activity the major factor in evaluating his performance would be distorting that particular job element. Well-focused performance evaluations avoid deficiencies, contaminations, and distortions.

Improving Evaluations

It has been suggested that performance evaluation is the most important human resource function in an organization.[4] Developing an effective performance evaluation system constitutes a critical and challenging task for management. This means, among other things, maximizing the use and acceptance of the evaluations while minimizing dissatisfaction with any aspect of the system. A full treatment of performance evaluation problems and methods of overcoming them is

---

[4]Dick Grote, "Performance Appraisals: Solving Tough Challenges," *HR Magazine,* July 2000, pp. 145–50.

beyond the scope of our discussion here. We offer, however, the following suggestions for improving the effectiveness of virtually any evaluation system.

1. Higher levels of *employee participation* in the evaluation process lead to more satisfaction with the system.
2. Setting *specific performance goals* to be met results in greater performance improvement than discussions of more general goals.
3. Evaluating subordinates' performance is an important part of a supervisor's job; they should *receive training* in the process, and they should be evaluated on *how effectively* they discharge this part of their own job responsibilities.
4. Systematic evaluation of performance does little good if the results are not *communicated* to employees.
5. Performance evaluation feedback should not focus solely on problem areas; good performance should be *actively recognized and reinforced.*
6. Remember that while formal performance evaluation may take place on a set schedule (for example, annually), effective evaluation is a *continuous* ongoing process.

To the extent that performance is linked with the organization's reward system, then performance evaluation represents an attempt to influence the behavior of organizational members. That is, it is an attempt to *reinforce* the continuation or elimination of certain actions. The basic assumption is that behavior is influenced by its consequences and that it is possible to affect behavior by controlling such consequences. Consequently, we begin our discussion of rewarding individual behavior by examining the topic of reinforcement.

PERFORMANCE EVALUATION FEEDBACK

Upon the completion of a performance evaluation, the manager (evaluator) usually is expected to provide feedback. The feedback session provides information concerning the rationale for the evaluation to the individual. If possible, objective information is used to guide the evaluated employee to improve, or sustain performance. The need for feedback among people on and off the job is significant. People want to know how they are doing, how they are being perceived by others, and how they can make adjustments to perform better. Simply telling someone that "you are doing okay," "keep up the good work," or "you're too emotional" is too vague and subjective to be useful to bring about improvement.

One of the most dreaded experiences of managers is delivering feedback to a poor performing employee. Telling a person that you have evaluated their performance as inadequate, poor, or below expectations is difficult. Giving a person bad news is just not a comfortable, enjoyable experience.

www.pwcglobal.com

An illustration of how dreaded providing feedback can be is an exercise used at Price Waterhouse Coopers (PWC). The staff sitting opposite each other in a meeting are told that they are to form over a short period of time an impression of the other person. They are each given a few minutes to formulate their impressions. When the time has expired, the participants are informed that they will not be required to feedback their impressions after all.[5] The exercise is designed

---

[5]Liam O'Brian, "Improving Performance Appraisal Interviews," *Supply Management,* May 2000, pp. 36–37.

to show how fearful people become when they are faced with informing someone about their impressions. Those dreaded feelings are a product of the top-down manner in which appraisal feedback has usually occurred. Managers typically tell subordinates what is wrong or right and how they should improve performance.

Purpose of Evaluation Feedback

Performance evaluation feedback can be instructional and/or motivational to the receiver (the evaluated person). Feedback instructs when it points out areas for improvement and teaches new behavior. For example, a sales associate may be informed that his reporting of expenses is not organized and is not detailed enough. A new program for preparing sales expense reports could improve his reports. Learning how to use the program permits the sales associate to use his laptop and the program to prepare reports that are considered accurate, informative, and timely.

Performance evaluation feedback is motivational when it provides a reward or promises a reward. A supervisor informing a technician that her report is superb and will serve as an example of an outstanding model is a form of reward via recognition. Receiving a complement or sign of excellent work from a valued colleague (e.g., supervisor, peer, or subordinate) can be very motivational and energizing.

A meta-analysis of over 20,000 feedback incidents revealed some interesting results. First, while feedback did have an impact on increasing performance, the actual performance did decline in over 38 percent of the reported feedback incidents.[6] This analysis of multiple studies suggests that managers need to understand how people process feedback. As Exhibit 5.1 illustrates, feedback is emitted from the person (self), others (supervisors, colleagues), and the job itself. This feedback impacts the person who processes the feedback before acting or behaving. Feedback just does not simply lead directly to efforts to improve performance. The cognitive processing that occurs involves many characteristics and factors.

A Feedback Model

Exhibit 5.1 presents a sample of feedback sources, individual characteristics, and cognitive evaluation factors that have an impact on the eventual behavioral outcomes. A person that possesses a high self-efficacy is a candidate for wanting feedback. They want to verify and validate their competency or self-efficacy.

Exhibit 5.1 points out feedback can result in greater effort, a desire to make corrective adjustments, and persistence. These can be very positive behaviors that ultimately result in better or improved performance. There is, however, another possible consequence of feedback, namely disregarding it or simply not accepting it as valid.

Research and the practical implementation of feedback have resulted in numerous samples of using feedback to improve performance.[7] First, feedback should be given frequently, not once a year at a performance evaluation session.

---

[6]A. N. Kluger and A. De Nise, "The Effects of Feedback Interventions on Performance: A Historical Review, a Meta-Analysis, and a Preliminary Feedback Intervention Theory," *Psychological Bulletin,* March 1996, pp. 254–84.

[7]D. M. Herold, C. K. Parsons, and R. B. Rensvold, "Individual Differences in the Generation and Processing of Performance Feedback," *Educational and Psychological Measurement,* February 1996, pp. 5–25.

EXHIBIT 5.1
Cognitive Model of Feedback: Sample of Sources, Characteristics, Cognitive Evaluation, and Behavioral Results

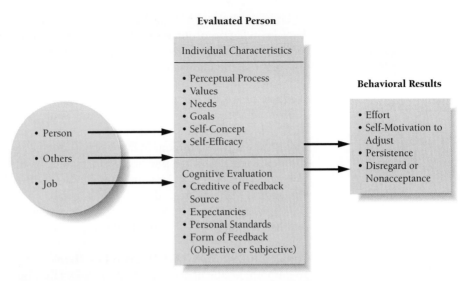

Source: Based on A. N. Kluger and A. De Nisi, "The Effects of Feedback Interventions on Performance: A Historical Review, a Meta-Analysis, and a Preliminary Feedback Invention Theory," *Psychological Bulletin*, March 1996, pp. 254–84, and R. Kreintner and A. Kinicki, *Organizational Behavior* (Burr Ridge, IL: Irwin/McGraw-Hill, 1998), p. 257.

Second, permitting the evaluated person to participate in the feedback sessions is important. This serves as a two-way exchange, problem-solving approach rather than an "evaluator telling" method. When employees participate they are usually more satisfied with the feedback communication. Third, in providing feedback it is advised to not only or solely focus on ineffective performance or problems. Praise, recognition, and encouragement serves as a form of positive reinforcement. Fourth, feedback should address results, goals, and goals accomplished, and not performed characteristics.[8] A golden rule of gaining and maintaining the respect of subordinates (evaluated employees) is to not attack or discuss their personality, attitudes, or values. These four guidelines are not perfect, nor do they always work effectively. They are, however, supported by research and they are not difficult to implement.

Multisource Feedback: A 360-Degree Approach

An increasing number of firms are using multisource feedback, instead of using only a top-down feedback program. A recent survey suggests that 90 percent of *Fortune 1000* firms use some form of multisource program. The increasing use of multisource programs is the result of calls for more fairness, clarity, and credibility in performance improvement programs.

In a 360-degree program, evaluators could include creditors, peers or team members, supervisors, subordinates, and the person. Everyone in the person's full domain (his or her circle or 360-degree range) could serve as an evaluator. It is assumed that this network has a truer picture of a person's performance than just a supervisor or any other category by itself.

www.works911.com/
performance/particles/360.htm

---

[8]M. Hequet, "Giving Good Feedback," *Training*, September 1994, pp. 72–77.

Unfortunately, although the 360-degree program has good face validity, there have been few rigorous research studies of its effectiveness.[9] One study of managers given evaluation and feedback in a public utility firm provided some positive results. The managers being evaluated showed improved performance.[10]

Arguments in Favor of 360-Degree Feedback   There is still not sufficient research evidence to propose the use of a multisource, 360-degree performance feedback program. The constant concern about fairness and credibility in evaluation is the major argument in favor of 360-degree programs. Multiple raters have different viewpoints of a person's performance. A supervisor has a single-person's perspective or overview. It is considered more thorough and credible to have multiple views being expressed.

There appears to be support among evaluated persons for a 360-degree program. Worker acceptance is important in using any management-initiated program.[11]

Arguments against 360-Degree Feedback   When information is being used to pinpoint performance, feedback providers may be reluctant to provide true ratings for fear that negative sources/comments might be used against the person's career progress or salary progression. If feedback sources are concerned about the use of their ratings, they may inflate such ratings. The result is inflation.[12]

Another argument against 360-degree programs involves the frequency of observation of performance. How often does a supplier or even a peer view, first hand, the performance of a person? There are differences in observation frequency across evaluators which results in varying responses based not on actual or regular performance, but on what was observed on a limited number of occasions.[13]

The 360-degree feedback process needs to be more thoroughly researched and fine-tuned. As the Organizational Encounter 5.1 indicates, the 360-degree feedback approach offers promise to managers who are interested and brave enough to receive information on how they are doing.

There are available 360-degree feedback approaches for teams. A software product called TeamWorks/360 focuses on the team as a group, rather than on individuals. Each team member rates the team's performance, then internal or external customers rate the team's performance. The software is used to provide ratings on 31 different behaviors. All team member rates themselves on each of the behaviors. Team members can also evaluate other members of the team.[14]

A summary graph shows the team member how his or her self-rating compares with the views of other evaluators (e.g., other team members, customers). In addition, the report received by a team member indicates the five areas in

---

[9]Richard R. Reilly, James W. Smither, and Nicholas L. Vasilopoulos, A Longitudinal Study of Upward Feedback," *Personnel Psychology*, Autumn 1996, pp. 599–612.

[10]J. F. Hazucka, S. A. Hezlett, and R. J. Schneider, "The Impact of 360-Degree Feedback on Managerial Skills Development," *Human Resource Management*, Summer/Fall 1993, p. 42.

[11]Mark R. Edwards and Ann J. Even, "How to Manage Performance and Pay with 360-Degree Feedback," *Compensation and Benefits Review*, May/June 1996, pp. 41–46.

[12]Mark R. Edwards and Ann J. Ewen, *360 Degree Feedback* (New York: AMACOM, 1996).

[13]Mary N. Vinson, "The Pros and Cons of 360-Degree Feedback: Making It Work," *Training and Development*, April 1996, pp. 11–12.

[14]John Day, "Simple Strong Team Ratings," *HR Magazine*, September 2000, pp. 159–61.

Organizational Encounter 5.1

360-Degree Feedback Helps Develop Quality Managers

General Electric relies on 360-degree feedback for its senior executives, who discuss the results of the candid report in confidentiality with their bosses. Ellen Hart, head of Gemini Consulting leadership practice, notes that 360-degree feedback is most essential for developing upper-level managers because "the higher executives get in an organization, the less direct feedback they get about their behavior." In other words, they drift out of touch with the people who actually produce their organization's goods and services.

Some organizations opt to send their managers "outside" for 360-degree feedback. Sanofi Winthorp Pharmaceuticals is one of them. The company sent C. Richard Truex, the senior director of national accounts, to the Center for Creative Leadership in Greensboro, North Carolina, where he was one of 22 managers to participate in a six-day program designed to evaluate their skills at interacting with other people. The goal of the program, which has "graduated" 38,000 participants in the last 20 years, is to identify and develop creative leaders.

Truex and his classmates, who came from a wide range of professional backgrounds, including an insurance sales director and a maintenance manager for the U.S. Army, were subjected to a battery of exercises and tests, some of which seemed pretty outlandish. In one session, the group was assigned to come up with a list of ideal characteristics for the leader of a new planet. In another, the group had to pretend that they were caught hiking in a blizzard and ultimately stranded with only a few items; they had to figure out which items were most important to their survival.

Perhaps most sobering, however, was the surprise "Valentine from home"—a packet containing evaluations from bosses, peers, and employees—that each manager received. Truex's evaluations came back to a single theme, over and over: "Forcefulness was a question mark in the back of my mind," says Truex. "It's confirmed that I am not forceful, and it is an area that I have to work on." After more group exercises, during which each student anonymously observed and evaluated three others, Truex and his classmates exchanged more feedback. The class feedback also pointed out Truex's problems with decisiveness. Finally, in his session with a clinical psychologist, Truex learned why he had trouble being assertive: "The reason I'm not decisive is that I won't give myself permission to be wrong," he explains. He couldn't bear to make a mistake.

How does all this intensive feedback help develop leaders who enhance their company's competitiveness? It is difficult to quantify the results of a program like the one offered by the Center for Creative Leadership, but Truex vows to take more risks and to try to make more rapid decisions. This may increase the speed at which tasks over which he has control are completed and encourage his employees and colleagues to be more innovative and creative.

Source: Lori Bongiormo, "How'm I Doing?" *Business Week*, October 23, 1995, pp. 72, 74; Stratford Sherman, "How Tomorrow's Best Leaders Are Learning Their Stuff," *Fortune*, November 27, 1995, p. 102.

which the member's performance was most effective and the five areas of least-effective performance.

REINFORCEMENT THEORY

Learning experts believe that reinforcement is the most important principle of learning. Desirable or reinforcing consequences (e.g., recognition in the feedback program of doing an excellent job) will increase the strength of a behavior (e.g., high-quality performance) and increase the probability of being repeated. Undesirable or punishment consequences will decrease the strength of a response and decrease its probability of being repeated.

Attempts to influence behavior through the use of rewards and punishments that are consequences of the behavior are called *operant conditioning.* **Operants** are behaviors that can be controlled by altering the consequences that follow them. Most workplace behaviors such as performing job-related tasks, reading a budget report, or coming to work on time are operants. A number of important principles of operant conditioning can aid the manager in attempting to influence behavior.

EXHIBIT 5.2	Rewards, Reinforcement, and Punishment	
	Desirable	**Undesirable**
Applied	I Positive reinforcement (behavior increases)	II Punishment (behavior decreases)
Withdrawn	III Punishment (behavior decreases)	IV Negative reinforcement (behavior increases)

Reinforcement

Reinforcement is an extremely important principle of conditioning. Managers often use *positive reinforcers* to influence behavior. A positive reinforcer is a stimulus which, when added to the situation, strengthens the probability of a behavioral response. Thus, if the positive reinforcer has value (is desirable) to the person, it can be used to improve performance. This is shown in cell I of Exhibit 5.2. (It should be noted, however, that a positive reinforcer which has value to one person may not have value to another person.) Sometimes *negative reinforcers* may be used. Negative reinforcement refers to an increase in the frequency of a response following removal of the negative reinforcer immediately after the response. As an example, exerting high degrees of effort to complete a job may be negatively reinforced by not having to listen to the "nagging" boss (undesirable). That is, completing the job through increased effort (behavior) minimizes the likelihood of having to listen to a nagging stream of unwanted advice (negative reinforcer) from a superior. This is illustrated by cell IV in Exhibit 5.2.

Reinforcement is different than a reward in that a reward is perceived to be desirable and is provided to a person after performance. All rewards are not reinforcers. Recall that reinforcers are defined as increasing the rate of behavior.

Punishment

Punishment is defined as presenting an uncomfortable or unwanted consequence for a particular behavioral response. It is an increasingly used managerial strategy.[15] Some work-related factors that can be considered punishments include a superior's criticism or being demoted. While punishment can suppress behavior if used effectively, it is a controversial method of behavior modification in organizations. It should be employed only after careful and objective consideration of all the relevant aspects of the situation. The dilemma of using punishment is displayed in cell II and III in Exhibit 5.2. Exhibit 5.2 compares positive and negative reinforcement and punishment when applied or withdrawn in a work setting.

---

[15]Gail Ball, Linda Trevino, and Henry Sims, Jr., "Just and Unjust Punishment: Influences on Subordinate Performance and Citizenship," *Academy of Management Journal*, April 1994, pp. 299–322.

EXHIBIT 5.3	Reinforcement Schedules and Their Effects on Behavior			
Schedule	Description	When Applied to Individual	When Removed by Manager	Organizational Example
Continuous	Reinforcer follows every response	Faster method for establishing new behavior	Faster method to cause extinction of new behavior	Praise after every response, immediate recognition of every response
Fixed interval	Response after specific time period is reinforced	Some inconsistency in response frequencies	Faster extinction of motivated behavior than variable schedules	Weekly, bimonthly, monthly paycheck
Variable interval	Response after varying period of time (an average) is reinforced	Produces high rate of steady responses	Slower extinction of motivated behavior than fixed schedules	Transfers, promotions, recognition
Fixed ratio	A fixed number of responses must occur before reinforcement	Some inconsistency in response frequencies	Faster extinction of motivated behavior than variable schedules	Piece rate, commission on units sold
Variable ratio	A varying number (average) of responses must occur before reinforcement	Can produce high rate of response that is steady and resists extinction	Slower extinction of motivated behavior than fixed schedules	Random checks for quality yield praise for doing good work

Source: Adapted from O. Behling, C. Schriesheim, and J. Tolliver, "Present Theories and New Directions in Theories of Work Effort," *Journal of Supplement Abstract Service of the American Psychological Association,* 1974, p. 57.

Extinction

Extinction reduces unwanted behavior. When positive reinforcement for a learned response is withheld, individuals will continue to practice that behavior for some period of time. However, after a while, if the nonreinforcement continues, the behavior will decrease in frequency and intensity and will eventually disappear. The decline and eventual cessation of the response rate is known as *extinction.* For example, the continual telephone calls from a financial advisor that are not returned are eventually going to stop.

Reinforcement Schedules

It is extremely important to properly time the rewards or punishments used in an organization. The timing of these outcomes is called *reinforcement scheduling* (see Exhibit 5.3). In the simplest schedule, the response is reinforced each time it occurs. This is called **continuous reinforcement.** If reinforcement occurs only after some instances of a response and not after each response, an *intermittent reinforcement* schedule is being used. From a practical viewpoint, it is virtually impossible to reinforce continually every desirable behavior. Consequently, in organizational settings, almost all reinforcement is intermittent in nature.

An intermittent schedule means that reinforcement does not occur after every acceptable behavior. The assumption is that learning is more permanent when

Organizational Encounter 5.2

Reinforcement Theory and the Casino Bottom Line

Reinforcement theory is alive and well among casino owners in Atlantic City, New Jersey, and Las Vegas, Nevada. These owners know how people react to reinforcement.

Most players of slot machines assume that jackpots occur according to some variable ratio schedule. If the casino owners set the machines to pay off on a fixed-ratio schedule, then counting the number of pulls between each jackpot would be a successful technique. If the slots were on a fixed-interval schedule, then the player simply would have to watch the clock and time the occurrence of jackpots. The casino owners know that players are more likely to stay with the machine and feed in coins if there is a random-reinforcement schedule. Then the players have no idea when they will strike it rich. They must keep playing to win, even once or twice. Thus, what we find in Atlantic City and Las Vegas is a program of random reinforcement.

The casino owners also know the value of atmosphere in keeping players at the machine. An atmosphere of excitement is created because people all around seem to be winning. The owners have accomplished this excitement by connecting each slot machine to a central control. Why? So that when any single slot machine hits a jackpot, sirens wail, lights flash, bells sound off, and screams of joy and displays of pleasure are heard and seen by everyone. The sights and sounds inform everyone that it pays to keep playing.

Does it work? Absolutely. Above all else, casino owners are businesspeople. Their objective is to make a profit. They have learned that what keeps the slot machine player coming back more effectively than anything else is a variable ratio schedule of reinforcement.

www.ccsa.
ca/final3.h

correct behavior is rewarded only part of the time. Ferster and Skinner have presented four types of intermittent reinforcement schedules.[16] Briefly, the four are:

1. *Fixed interval.* A reinforcer is applied only when the desired behavior occurs after the passage of a certain period of time since the last reinforcer was applied. An example would be to only praise positive performance once a week and not at other times. The fixed interval is one week.

2. *Variable interval.* A reinforcer applied at some variable interval of time. A promotion is an example.

www.bfskinner.org/index.asp

3. *Fixed ratio.* A reinforcer is applied only if a fixed number of desired responses has occurred. An example would be paying a salesperson for an e-learning firm for each dollar of revenue above $6,000 for which she receives a 12 percent commission.

4. *Variable ratio.* A reinforcer is applied only after a number of desired responses, with the number of desired responses changing from situation to situation, around an average. For a classic example of a variable ratio schedule, consider the casino Encounter. (See Organizational Encounter 5.2.)

Research on reinforcement schedules has shown that higher rates of response usually are achieved with ratio rather than interval schedules. This finding is understandable since high response rates do not necessarily speed up the delivery of a reinforcer in an interval schedule as they do with ratio schedules. Occasionally, however, reinforcement schedule research has produced unexpected findings. For example, one study compared the effects of continuous and variable ratio piece-rate bonus pay plans. Contrary to predictions, the continuous schedule yielded the highest level of performance. One reason cited for the less-than-expected effectiveness of the variable ratio schedules was that some em-

---

[16]C. B. Ferster and B. F. Skinner, *Schedules of Reinforcement* (New York: Appleton-Century-Crofts, 1957).

w.
nchard
ining.com

—— **Management Pointer 5.1** ——

LEARN HOW TO PRAISE OTHERS

Praising the performance of a person is often gratifying. In the *One Minute Manager*, Ken Blanchard and Spencer Johnson provide some straightforward pointers that can be easily implemented by management. Praise is a form of recognition that takes little time to provide. The power of such a reward is knowing that someone took the time to notice the achievement.

- Inform people that you are going to provide them with feedback on how they are doing.
- Praise people immediately.
- Inform people in specific terms what they did that you like.
- Praise people for going out of their way to help others perform their jobs.
- Tell people that the organization is a better place because of their excellent work.
- Remember when offering praise, use the person's name. People like to hear their name.
- If possible, say "thank you" in the praise message.

ployees working on these schedules were opposed to the pay plan. They perceived the plan as a form of gambling, and this was not acceptable to them.[17]

Using a praise program can serve as reinforcement. Management Pointer 5.1 provides some guidelines via how to use a praise program to reinforce desirable performance.

A MODEL OF INDIVIDUAL REWARDS

The main objectives of reward programs are: (1) to attract qualified people to *join* the organization, (2) to *keep* employees coming to work, and (3) to *motivate* employees to achieve high levels of performance. Exhibit 5.4 presents a model that attempts to integrate satisfaction, motivation, performance, and rewards. Reading the exhibit from left to right suggests that the motivation to exert effort is not enough to cause acceptable performance. Performance results from a combination of the effort of an individual and the individual's level of ability, skill, and experience. The performance results of the individual are evaluated either formally or informally by management, and two types of rewards can be distributed: intrinsic or extrinsic.[18] The rewards are evaluated by the individual, and to the extent the rewards are satisfactory and equitable, the individual achieves a level of satisfaction.

A significant amount of research has been done on what determines whether individuals will be satisfied with rewards. Lawler has summarized five conclusions based on the behavioral science research literature. They are:

1. *Satisfaction with a reward is a function both of how much is received and of how much the individual feels should be received.* This conclusion is based on the comparisons that people make. When individuals receive less than they feel they should, they are dissatisfied.

2. *An individual's feelings of satisfaction are influenced by comparisons with what happens to others.* People tend to compare their efforts, skills, seniority, and job performance with those of others. They then attempt to compare rewards. That is, they compare their own inputs with the inputs of others relative to the rewards received. This input-outcome comparison was discussed when the equity theory of motivation was introduced in Chapter 4.

3. *Satisfaction is influenced by how satisfied employees are with both intrinsic and extrinsic rewards.* Intrinsic rewards are valued in and of themselves; they are related to performing the job. Examples would be feelings of accomplishment and achievement. Extrinsic rewards are external to the work itself; they are administered externally. Examples would be salary and wages, fringe benefits, and promotions. There is an ongoing debate among researchers as to whether intrinsic or extrinsic rewards are more important in determining

---

[17]Edward E. Lawler, III, *Rewarding Excellence: Pay Strategies for the New Economy* (San Francisco: Jossey-Bass, 2000).

[18]Jon R. Katzenbach, *Peak Performance: Aligning the Hearts and Minds of Your Employees* (Boston: Harvard Business School Press, 2000).

EXHIBIT 5.4   The Reward Process

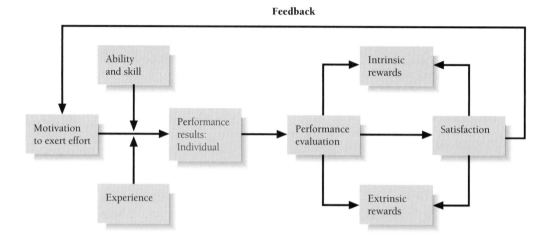

job satisfaction. The debate has not been settled because most studies suggest that both rewards are important. One clear message from the research is that extrinsic and intrinsic rewards satisfy different needs.

4. *People differ in the rewards they desire and in how important different rewards are to them.* Individuals differ on what rewards they prefer. In fact, preferred rewards vary at different points in a person's career, at different ages, and in various situations.

5. *Some extrinsic rewards are satisfying because they lead to other rewards.* For example, a large office or an office that has carpeting or drapes is often considered a reward because it indicates the individual's status and power. Money is a reward that leads to such things as prestige, autonomy and independence, security, and shelter.

The relationship between rewards and satisfaction is not perfectly understood, nor is it static. It changes because people and the environment change. There are, however, some important considerations that managers could use to develop and distribute rewards. First, the rewards available must be sufficient to satisfy basic human needs. Federal legislation, union contracts, and managerial fairness have provided at least minimal rewards in most work settings. Second, individuals tend to compare their rewards with those of others. If inequities are perceived, dissatisfaction occurs. People make comparisons regardless of the quantity of the rewards they receive. Finally, the managers distributing rewards must recognize individual differences. Unless individual differences are considered, invariably the reward process is less effective than desired. Any reward package should (1) be sufficient to satisfy basic needs (e.g., food, shelter, clothing), (2) be considered equitable, and (3) be individually oriented.[19] To these could be added the very important point made by Steven Kerr in his article accompanying this chapter (see Reading 5.1). For rewards to have their desired effect, they must reward the behavior that management wishes to encourage. Too often, as Kerr points out, what actually get rewarded are behaviors which the manager is trying to discourage.

Reading 5.1

On the Folly of Rewarding A,
While Hoping for B

---

[19]Karen Renk, "I Want My TV," *HR Magazine*, October 2000, pp. 153–63.

One aspect of some reward programs that is not considered involves taxation. For example, announcing a $1,000 bonus could be great news by itself. However, if because of taxes the recipients only get $667, the news may be less positive. An important question is to determine, "If it is possible to reward an employee without inflicting the burden of tax liability?" Wilson Group of Concord, Massachusetts, designs reward systems for Amazon.com, Sears Roebuck, and Cigna Corporation. Wilson recommends that firms "gross up" cash incentives—that is, provide the employee full value. Instead of receiving the $1,000 bonus, provide the employee with a check for $1,333. Thus, although the $1,333 is taxed the full $1,000 is received.[20]

www.cigna.com

www.xensi.com/users/wilson/intex.html

www.sears.com

Intrinsic and Extrinsic Rewards

The rewards shown in Exhibit 5.4 are classified into two broad categories, extrinsic and intrinsic. Whether rewards are extrinsic or intrinsic, it is important to first consider the rewards valued by the person since an individual will put forth little effort unless the reward has value. An *intrinsic reward* is defined as one that is self-administered by the person. It provides a sense of satisfaction or gratification. An *extrinsic reward* is initiated from outside the person. Receiving praise from a supervisor is extrinsic or initiated by someone other than the person, a supervisor. Both extrinsic and intrinsic rewards can have value. We will examine both types in the following sections.

Extrinsic Rewards

Financial Rewards: Salary and Wages   Money is a major extrinsic reward. It has been said, "Although it is generally agreed that money is the major mechanism for rewarding and modifying behavior in industry . . . very little is known about how it works."[21] To really understand how money modifies behavior, the perceptions and preferences of the person being rewarded must be understood. Of course, this is a challenging task for a manager to complete successfully. Unless employees can see a connection between performance and merit increases, money will not be a powerful motivator.

Exercise 5.2

Making Choices about Rewards

Many organizations utilize some type of incentive pay plan to motivate employees. Lawler presents the most comprehensive summary of the various pay plans and their effectiveness as motivators.[22] Each plan is evaluated on the basis of the following questions:

1. How effective is it in creating the perception that pay is related to performance?

2. How well does it minimize the perceived negative consequences of good performance?

3. How well does it contribute to the perception that important rewards other than pay (e.g., praise and interest shown in the employee by a respected superior) result in good performance?

---

[20]Lin Grensing-Pophal, "Rewards That Don't Penalize Your Employees," *HR Magazine,* November 1999, pp. 98–104.

[21]R. L. Opsahl and M. D. Dunnette, "The Role of Financial Compensation in Industrial Motivation," *Psychological Bulletin,* August 1966, p. 114.

[22]Edward E. Lawler, III, *Pay and Organizational Effects* (New York: McGraw-Hill, 1971), pp. 164–70.

A controversial issue regarding pay systems centers on whether they are public or private matters. Openness versus secrecy is not an either/or issue; it is a matter of degree. Some organizations will disclose the pay ranges, the pay decision criteria, and a schedule for receiving pay increases. Other organizations may present an entire array of employees and the pay increases each received in a particular performance review period.

Research indicates that a totally open (no secrets) system works best in organizations in which:

1. Worker performance can be measured objectively
2. There is a low amount of interdependence among employees

Research indicates that a totally open (no secrets) system works best in organizations in which:

1. Worker performance can be measured objectively
2. There is a low amount of interdependence among employees
3. Measures are available for all the important aspects of a job
4. Effort and performance are related closely over a short time span

If these four conditions can be met, an open financial reward system can be well received. If, however, these conditions can't be met, the conflict, backlash, and hostility of an open system should be avoided with another system. Management in a less than fully open pay system should work at presenting information on how performance and financial rewards are linked. Illustrating that desirable job assignments, promotions, and results of performance appraisals are linked to improved financial rewards is an approach that takes on greater relevance when the pay system can't be totally open.[23]

Financial Rewards: Employee Benefits   In the United States, organizations spend on average over $14,000 annually on employee benefits. In most cases, what has been referred to as fringe benefits are primarily financial. Calling these benefits fringe is misleading since they represent over 35 percent of a firm's payroll costs. Some fringe benefits, however, such as IBM's recreation program for employees and General Mills's picnic grounds, are not entirely financial. The major financial employee benefit in most organizations is the pension plan, and for most employees, the opportunity to participate in the pension plan is a valued reward. Employee benefits such as pension plans, hospitalization, and vacations usually are not contingent on the performance of employees, but are based on seniority or attendance.

Interpersonal Rewards   The manager has some power to distribute such interpersonal rewards as status and recognition. By assigning individuals to prestigious jobs, the manager can attempt to improve or remove the status a person possesses. However, if coworkers do not believe that a person merits a particular job, it is likely that status will not be enhanced. By reviewing performance, managers can, in some situations, grant what they consider to be job changes to improve status. The manager and coworkers both play a role in granting job status.

---

[23]Michael Zwell, *Creating a Culture of Competence* (New York: John Wiley, 2000).

Lee Memorial Health System in Cape Cod, Florida, found out how powerful a simple recognition program can be. Lee Memorial received an award for being one of the top health care networks. Management wanted to thank its over 5,000 employees for the reward the firm received. The firm decided that a customized key chain for each employee was the answer. The key chains had the words "Valued Employee Since _____", displayed on the top of the brass emblem with the employee's year-of-hire date.

The excitement stirred by the key chains was stunning. Everyone was excited, talking about the key chains, and pleased to be recognized. The employees appreciated the fact that each employee was recognized by the hire date. The time and minimal cost of $4.50 per employee for the "key chain" recognition was well worth the gesture.[24]

Promotions   For many employees, promotion does not happen often; some employees never experience it in their careers. The manager making a promotion reward decision attempts to match the right person with the job. Criteria often used to reach promotion decisions are performance and seniority. Performance, if it can be accurately assessed, is often given significant weight in promotion reward allocations.

INTRINSIC REWARDS

Completion   The ability to start and finish a project or job is important to some individuals. These people value what is called *task completion*. Some people have a need to complete tasks, and the effect that completing a task has on a person is a form of self-reward. Opportunities that allow such people to complete tasks can have a powerful motivating effect.

Achievement   Achievement is a self-administered reward that is derived when a person reaches a challenging goal. McClelland has found that there are individual differences in striving for achievement.[25] Some individuals seek challenging goals, while others tend to seek moderate or low goals. In goal-setting programs, it has been proposed that difficult goals result in a higher level of individual performance than do moderate goals. However, even in such programs, individual differences must be considered before reaching conclusions about the importance of achievement rewards.

Autonomy   Some people want jobs that provide them with the right and privilege to make decisions and operate without being closely supervised. A feeling of autonomy could result from the freedom to do what the employee considers best in a particular situation. In jobs that are highly structured and controlled by management, it is difficult to create tasks that lead to a feeling of autonomy.

Personal Growth   The personal growth of any individual is a unique experience. An individual who is experiencing such growth senses his or her development and can see how his or her capabilities are being expanded. By expanding capabilities, a person is able to maximize or at least satisfy skill potential. Some people often become dissatisfied with their jobs and organizations if they are not

---

[24]Bill Leonard, "The Key to Unlocking an Inexpensive Recognition Program," *HR Magazine,* October 1999, p. 26.

[25]David C. McClelland, *The Achieving Society* (New York: D. Van Nostrand, 1961).

Your Reward Preferences

You Be the Judge

A group of executives (e.g., directors, vice presidents, and presidents) were asked to rank the most valued rewards of their subordinates from the most desired to the least desired. These executives were thinking about people working for them. Does your ranking match the executive rankings? You Be The Judge.

Rewards Desired by My Subordinates

1. More money (pay/incentives)
2. Time off
3. Advancement opportunities
4. Recognition
5. An ownership share in the organization
6. Autonomy
7. Selecting the job to do
8. Personal growth
9. Fun at work
10. Prizes

allowed or encouraged to develop their skills. What is important to you in terms of rewards? The You Be The Judge example asks for your ranking of 10 rewards.

Rewards Interact

The general assumption has been that intrinsic and extrinsic rewards have an independent and additive influence on motivation. That is, motivation is determined by the sum of the person's intrinsic and extrinsic sources of motivation. This straightforward assumption has been questioned by several researchers. Some have suggested that in situations in which individuals are experiencing a high level of intrinsic rewards, the addition of extrinsic rewards for good performance may cause a decrease in motivation.[26] Basically, the person receiving self-administered feelings of satisfaction is performing because of intrinsic rewards. Once extrinsic rewards are added, feelings of satisfaction change because performance is now thought to be due to the extrinsic rewards. The addition of the extrinsic rewards tends to reduce the extent to which the individual experiences self-administered intrinsic rewards.

The argument concerning the potential negative effects of extrinsic rewards has stimulated a number of research studies. Unfortunately, these studies report contradictory results. Some researchers report a reduction in intrinsic rewards following the addition of extrinsic rewards for an activity.[27]

Other researchers have failed to observe such an effect.[28] A review of the literature found that 14 of 24 studies reported the theory that extrinsic rewards re-

[26]E. L. Deci, "The Effects of Externally Mediated Rewards on Intrinsic Motivation," *Journal of Personality and Social Psychology,* 1971, pp. 105–15. Also, E. L. Deci, *Intrinsic Motivation* (New York: Plenum Press, 1975).

[27]B. M. Staw, "The Attitudinal and Behavior Consequences of Changing a Major Organizational Reward," *Journal of Personality and Social Psychology,* June 1974, pp. 742–51.

[28]C. D. Fisher, "The Effects of Personal Control, Competence, and Extrinsic Reward Systems on Intrinsic Motivation," *Organizational Behavior and Human Performance,* June 1978, pp. 273–87. Also, J. S. Phillips and R. G. Lord, "Determinants of Intrinsic Motivation: Locus of Control and Competence Information as Components of Deci's Cognitive Evaluation Theory," *Journal of Applied Psychology,* April 1980, pp. 211–18.

duced intrinsic motivation.[29] However, 10 of the 24 studies found no support for the reducing effect theory. Of the 24 studies reviewed, only two used actual employees as subjects. All of the other studies used college students or grade school students. In studies of telephone operators and clerical employees, the reducing effect theory was not supported.[30] Managers need to be aware that no scientifically based and reported study substantiates that extrinsic rewards have a negative effect on intrinsic motivation.

Administering Rewards

Managers are faced with the decision of how to administer rewards. Three major theoretical approaches to reward administration are: (1) positive reinforcement, (2) modeling and social imitation, and (3) expectancy.

Positive Reinforcement   In administering a positive reinforcement program, the emphasis is on the desired behavior that leads to job performance rather than performance alone. The basic foundation of administering rewards through positive reinforcement is the relationship between behavior and its consequences. This relationship was discussed earlier in the chapter. While positive reinforcement can be a useful method of shaping desired behavior, other considerations concerning the type of reward schedule to use are also important. This relates to the discussion of continuous and intermittent schedules presented earlier. Suffice it to say that management should explore the possible consequences of different types of reward schedules for individuals. It is important to know how employees respond to continuous, fixed-interval, and fixed-ratio schedules.

Modeling and Social Imitation   There is little doubt that many human skills and behaviors are acquired by observational learning or, simply, imitation. Observational learning equips a person to duplicate a response, but whether the response actually is imitated depends on whether the model person was rewarded or punished for particular behaviors. If a person is to be motivated, he or she must observe models receiving reinforcements that are valued. In order to use **modeling** to administer rewards, managers must determine who responds to this approach. In addition, selecting appropriate models is a necessary step. Finally, the context in which modeling occurs needs to be considered. That is, if high performance is the goal and it is almost impossible to achieve that goal because of limited resources, the manager should conclude that modeling is not appropriate.[31]

Expectancy Theory   Some research suggests that expectancy theory constructs provide an important basis for classifying rewards.[32] From a rewards administration perspective, the expectancy approach, like the other two methods of

---

[29]K. B. Boone and L. L. Cummings, "Cognitive Evaluation Theory: An Experimental Test of Processes and Outcomes," *Organizational Behavior and Human Performance,* December 1981, pp. 289–310.

[30]E. M. Lopez, "A Test of Deci's Cognitive Evaluation Theory in an Organizational Setting." Paper presented at the 39th annual convention of the Academy of Management, Atlanta, Georgia, August 1979.

[31]Glenn Parker, Jerry McAdams, and David Zielinski, *Rewarding Teams: Lessons from the Trenches* (San Francisco: Jossey-Bass, 2000).

[32]R. Kanungo and J. Hartwick, "An Alternative to the Intrinsic-Extrinsic Dichotomy of Work Rewards," *Journal of Management,* Fall 1987, pp. 751–66.

Ethics Encounter 5.1

Are Women Receiving Equitable Pay Treatment?

There is no question that, on the average, employed women receive less pay than employed men. This, of course, does not necessarily mean women are being treated inequitably or unethically; it could merely reflect differences in the types of jobs held by women and men. But it most likely doesn't. This is because significant pay differentials exist *within* job categories, as well as across them. For example, based on the same 1990 figures, women's earnings as a percent of men's within job categories included the following: 66 percent for service workers, machine operators, assemblers, and inspectors; 65 percent for transportation workers; 64 percent for executives and managers; and 57 percent for sales. While other gaps are somewhat smaller, they exist for virtually every category of jobs. The gender gap in what are considered the prime earning years of ages 35–44 is even larger; across all full-time workers in that age category, women's pay is equal to only 69 percent of men's.

The 1963 amendment to the Fair Labor Standards Act known as the Equal Pay Act requires equal pay for equal work for men and women. Equal work is defined as work requiring equal skills, effort, and responsibility under similar working conditions. Since the passage of this legislation, the female-male pay gap has clearly narrowed. As the figures cited above indicate, however, just as clearly there is a great deal that remains to be done.

A 1984 Supreme Court ruling permits women to bring suit on the grounds that they are paid less than men holding jobs of comparable worth based on job content evaluation. In this suit, Washington County, Oregon, prison matrons claimed sex discrimination because male prison guards, whose jobs were somewhat different, received substantially higher pay. The county had evaluated the male's jobs as having 5 percent more job content than the female's jobs, but paid the males 35 percent more. That same year, the state of Washington began wage adjustments to approximately 15,000 employees. This was the first of several adjustments aimed at eliminating state pay differentials between predominately female and male jobs by 1993.

While there are frequently legitimate reasons for pay differentials between women and men in comparable jobs (length of service in the position, for example), unfair differences still exist. To reward employees differently based solely on gender is not only unethical and illegal, it is poor business practice as well.

administering rewards, requires managerial action. Managers must determine the kinds of rewards employees desire and do whatever is possible to distribute those rewards. Or they must create conditions so that what is available in the form of rewards can be applied. In some situations, it simply is not possible to provide the rewards that are valued and preferred. Therefore, managers often have to increase the desirability of other rewards.

A manager can, and often will, use principles from each of the three methods of administering rewards—positive reinforcement, modeling, and expectancy. Each of these methods indicates that employee job performance is a result of the application of effort. To generate the effort needed to achieve desirable results, managers can use positive reinforcers, modeling, and expectations.

What combination of methods to use is not, of course, the only issue in administering rewards. Organizational resources, competitive influences, labor market constraints, and government regulations are but a few of the many factors which must be considered in developing and maintaining reward programs. One particular issue which is receiving increasing attention is that of gender equity in reward administration. Ethics Encounter 5.1 illustrates that women's salaries still trail those of men, and to the extent this reflects gender differences within the same jobs, it becomes at least an ethical issue if not a legal one.

REWARDS AFFECT ORGANIZATIONAL CONCERNS

Rewards affect employee perceptions, attitudes, and behavior in a variety of ways. In turn, organizational efficiency and effectiveness are affected. Three important organizational concerns that are influenced by rewards are turnover and absenteeism, performance, and commitment. We will briefly examine each of these.

Turnover and Absenteeism

Some managers assume that high turnover is a mark of an effective organization. This view is somewhat controversial because a high quit rate means more expense for an organization. However, some organizations would benefit if disruptive and low performers quit.[33] Thus, the issue of turnover needs to focus on the *frequency* and on *who* is leaving.

Ideally, if managers could develop reward systems that retained the best performers and caused poor performers to leave, the overall effectiveness of an organization would improve. To approach this ideal state, an equitable and favorably compared reward system must exist. The feeling of *equity* and *favorable comparison* has an external orientation. That is, the equity of rewards and favorableness involve comparisons with external parties. This orientation is used because quitting most often means that a person leaves one organization for an alternative elsewhere.

There is no perfect means for retaining high performers. It appears that a reward system based on *merit* should encourage most of the better performers to remain with the organization. There also has to be some differential in the reward system that discriminates between high and low performers, the point being that the high performers must receive significantly more extrinsic and intrinsic rewards than the low performers.

Absenteeism, no matter for what reason, is a costly and disruptive problem facing managers.[34] It is costly because it reduces output and disruptive because it requires that schedules and programs be modified. It is estimated that absenteeism in the United States results in the loss of more than 500 million workdays per year, about 5 days per employee or $600 per employee.[35] Employees go to work because they are motivated to do so. The level of motivation will remain high if an individual feels that attendance will lead to more valued rewards and fewer negative consequences than alternative behaviors.

Managers appear to have some influence over attendance behavior. They have the ability to punish, establish bonus systems, and allow employee participation in developing plans. Whether these or other approaches will reduce absenteeism is determined by the value of the rewards perceived by employees, the amount of the rewards, and whether employees perceive a relationship between attendance and rewards. These same characteristics appear every time we analyze the effects of rewards on organizational behavior.

---

[33]Carla Johnson, Capturing Turnover Costs," *HR Magazine,* July 2000, pp. 107–19.

[34]Paul Falcone, "Tackling Excessive Absenteeism," *HR Magazine,* April 2000, pp. 138–44.

[35]Ibid.

Job Performance

Behaviorists and managers agree that extrinsic and intrinsic rewards can be used to motivate job performance. It is also clear that certain conditions must exist if rewards are to motivate good job performance: The rewards must be valued by the person, and they must be related to the level of job performance that is to be motivated.

In Chapter 4, expectancy motivation theory was presented. It was stated that, according to the theory, every behavior has associated with it (in a person's mind) certain outcomes or rewards or punishments. In other words, an assembly-line worker may believe that, by behaving in a certain way, he or she will get certain things. This is a description of the *performance-outcome expectancy*. The worker may expect that a steady performance of 10 units a day eventually will result in transfer to a more challenging job. On the other hand, the worker may expect that a steady performance of 10 units a day will result in being considered a rate-buster by coworkers.

Each outcome has a **valence** or value to the person. Outcomes such as pay, promotion, a reprimand, or a better job have different values for different people because each person has different needs and perceptions. Thus, in considering which rewards to use, a manager has to be astute at considering individual differences. If valued rewards are used to motivate, they can result in the exertion of effort to achieve high levels of performance.

Organizational Commitment

There is little research on the relationship between rewards and organizational commitment. **Commitment** to an organization involves three attitudes: (1) a sense of identification with the organization's goals, (2) a feeling of involvement in organizational duties, and (3) a feeling of loyalty for the organization.[36] Research evidence indicates that the absence of commitment can reduce organizational effectiveness.[37] People who are committed are less likely to quit and accept other jobs.[38] Thus, the costs of high turnover are not incurred. In addition, committed and highly skilled employees require less supervision. Close supervision and a rigid monitoring control process are time-consuming and costly. Furthermore, a committed employee perceives the value and importance of integrating individual and organizational goals. The employee thinks of his or her goals and the organization's goals in personal terms.

Intrinsic rewards are especially important for the development of organizational commitment. Organizations able to meet employee needs by providing achievement opportunities and by recognizing achievement when it occurs have a significant impact on commitment. Thus, managers need to develop intrinsic reward systems that focus on personal importance or self-esteem, to integrate individual and organizational goals, and to design challenging jobs.

---

[36]K. R. Moore, "Trust and Relationship Commitment in Logistics Alliances: A Buyer Perspective," *Journal of Purchasing and Materials Management*, February 1998, pp. 24–37.

[37]S. Chow and R. Holden, "Toward an Understanding of Loyalty: The Moderating Role of Trust," *Journal of Management Issues*, Spring 1997, pp. 275–98.

[38]David P. Shadicki, Robert Folger, and Paul Tesluk, "Personality as a Moderator in the Relationship between Fairness and Retaliation," *Academy of Management Journal*, March 1999, pp. 100–08.

INNOVATIVE REWARD SYSTEMS

The typical list of rewards that managers can and do distribute in organizations has been discussed. We all know that pay, fringe benefits, and opportunities to achieve challenging goals are considered rewards by most people. It is also generally accepted that rewards are administered by managers through such processes as reinforcement, modeling, and expectancies. What are some of the newer and innovative, yet largely untested, reward programs that some managers are experimenting with? Seven different approaches to rewards that are not widely tested are skill-based pay, broadbanding, team-based rewards, banking time off, all-salaried team, gain sharing, and employee stock ownership plans.

Skill-Based Pay

Skill-based pay is being used by a growing number of firms. In traditional compensation systems, workers are paid on the basis of their jobs. The hourly wage rate depends primarily on the job performed. In a skill-based plan, employees are paid at a rate based on their personal skills. Typically, employees start at a basic initial rate of pay; they receive increases as their skills develop. Their pay rates are based on skill levels, no matter which jobs they are assigned.

In conventional pay systems, the job determines the pay rate and range. In the skill-based plan, however, the skills developed by employees are the key pay determinants. The skill-based pay plan approximates how professionals are compensated. In many organizations, professionals who do similar work are difficult to separate in terms of contributions made. Thus, surveys of what other firms pay professionals are used to establish pay grades and maturity curves. In skill-based plans, pay increases are not given at any specific time because of seniority. Instead, a raise is granted when employees demonstrate their skills to perform particular jobs.

Skill-based pay systems have at least four potential advantages:[39] (1) Since employees have more skills, the organization increases its flexibility by assigning workers to different jobs; (2) Because pay is not determined on the basis of the classification to which the job is assigned, the organization may need fewer distinct job classifications; (3) Fewer employees are needed because more workers are interchangeable; and (4) The organization may experience reductions in turnover and absenteeism. Skill-based pay has worked well for a division of Rohm and Haas in LaPorte, Texas. At this plant, employees learn all of the jobs to run a particular operation. The training takes about three years, and when it is successfully completed employees make approximately $12,000 a year more than when they started.[40]

A good place to begin the search and identification of key skills to perform well is with the already exceptional performers. At LEGO Systems, Inc., the organization's top performers were identified. The toy maker identified technical skills, team achievement skills, and personal skills. Then, through focus groups and interviews with these top performers, the skills were clarified. LEGO used this in-

---

[39]Frederick Hills, Thomas Bergmann, and Vida Scarpello, *Compensation Decision Making* (New York: The Dryden Press, 1994).

[40]D. K. Denton, "Multi-Skilled Teams Replace Old Work Systems," *HR Magazine,* September 1992, pp. 55–56.

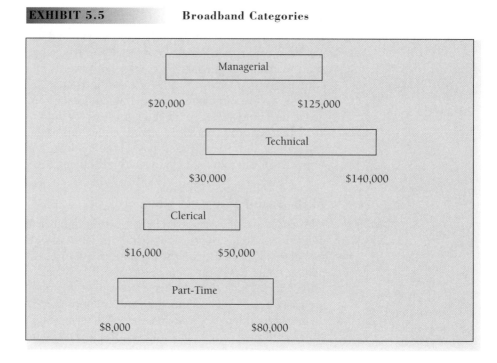

EXHIBIT 5.5   **Broadband Categories**

Managerial

$20,000 $125,000

Technical

$30,000 $140,000

Clerical

$16,000 $50,000

Part-Time

$8,000 $80,000

formation to build a competency model. The model then served as the basis for linking pay to specific skill/competency.[41]

Broadbanding

An element of financial reward that organizations are having problems with is the system of grading. Most systems have a large number of grades. The multiple grade approach is often out of alignment with the flatter, more team-oriented organizational designs institutions are moving toward. To counter this poor alignment, some firms are adopting what is called a banding or broadbanding approach. **Broadbanding** involves reducing numerous pay grades to a relatively few broad band grades.

An example of broadbanding would be placing all managers into one band; all technicians into a second band; all clerical personnel into a third band; and all part-time employees into a fourth band. Broadbanding emphasizes titles, grades, and job descriptions as presented in Exhibit 5.5.

Rather than concentrating on moving up a series of pay grades in a vertical system, employees could spend most, if not all, of their careers in a single-band and move laterally as they acquire new skills or improve their performance. This type of pay system allows a person who needs to develop new skills to be placed in a lower skill, but continue to be paid more.

---

[41]Thomas P. Flannery, David A. Hofrichter, and Paul E. Platten, *People, Performance, and Pay* (New York: Free Press, 1996), pp. 98–99.

How many pay bands are needed? There is no correct answer. Surveys suggest that organizations using broadbanding have from 1 to 18 bands.[42] The number of bands might depend on the levels in the firm's hierarchy, the key areas of accountability, or natural job clusters. General Electric has elected to use five bands for managerial personnel (professional, senior professional, leadership, executive, and senior executive). The results of GE's approach have not been subjected to careful analysis. Some critics of broadbanding at GE claim that it is too gimmicky and is not as good as a well-designed, multiple grade pay system.

At Scottish Bank broadbanding was introduced with changes initiated by the chief executive officer. Fifteen pay grades covering all white-collar staff up to senior management were replaced by five broad bands.[43] Incremental pay progression and cost-of-living reviews were eliminated and totally flexible, merit-based increases were introduced. After about one year under the five broadband system, a number of modifications were made. Four distinct job family bands with levels in each were introduced. Also, pay progression to the band midpoint was guaranteed for effective performers within four years. The band also installed minimum pay increases for a growth in responsibilities and for the development of additional competencies. After these modifications, the broadbands approach is now well received throughout the bank.

Broadbanding can make it easier to pay for skills and simplify the problem of placing employees and/or job into a pay grade. It is easier because there are fewer pay grades. If a firm has 70 pay grades, the differences between each grade is so small. What is the difference between a person being a 42 or a 43 grade? Broadbanding appears to have more flexibility for a person to make a lateral career move without punishing him or her by reducing their pay. Traditional pay systems usually give no credit for the skills a person learned in their previous job. The person is simply paid on the basis of their new job. Why would some be interested in moving laterally when everything is not included in the pay calculation?

Concierge Services

www.aventail.com

In Seattle, a vice president at the high tech company Aventail has a tailor in his office to fit him for a new suit. At Arthur Andersen an accountant has a person track down tickets for a sold-out golf tournament. Do their bosses know about this? Yes, the boss knows and provides these rewards as part of a company program. This kind of employee benefit reward is not new, but it is attracting attention because of labor shortages, the clamor to balance work and life, the evaluation in benefit programs, and the Internet's ability to access services.[44]

www.arthurandersen.com

The Society for Human Resource Management's 2000 Benefits Survey found that only 4 percent of employees report concierge services. Nevertheless, Fortune magazine's 100 best companies to work for found 26 offering concierge services.

www.shrm.org

In many cases employees still have to pay for the most lavish services such as massages, but employers underwrite the location of the concierge. The availability of a concierge service for a wide range of "must do" activities is considered an

---

[42]Ibid.

[43]Duncan Brown, "Broadbanding: A Study of Company Practices in the United Kingdom," *Compensation & Benefits Review,* November–December 1996, pp. 41–49.

[44]Karla Taylor, "May I Help You, Please?" *HR Magazine,* August 2000, pp. 90–96.

attractive part of working for a particular firm. Freeing the employee to concentrate on performance can be considered an employer benefit worth the work and effort.

Team-Based Rewards

www.denning.org

Individual pay-for-performance reward systems do not properly fit an organization that is designed around or uses teams. W. Edwards Denning (an originator of the total quality management approach) and other reward experts have clearly warned against putting individuals, who need to cooperate, under a reward system that fosters competition. Teams need to cooperate within the team structure and process. It is still difficult in a country that prides itself on individualism, such as the United States, to convince employees to work together, to trust each other, and to be committed to group goals above individual work-related goals. People with strong individualism values become worried and skeptical about the so-called freeloader who doesn't perform well, but gets the same rewards as everyone else.[45] It isn't fair. There are ways, however, to encourage poor performers to improve or leave. There are also methods to give special recognition and show respect to outstanding team leaders and performers.[46]

The design of a team-based reward system should follow the groupings in the overall organizational design. In situations where teams are relatively independent and measurable goals can be set and evaluated, rewards can be based on goal accomplishment.

In situations where teams are interdependent on each other, a plant, division, or area reward plan may be the best system. Management must carefully analyze the independence-interdependence conditions.

Providing rewards to project teams is somewhat different. Since project team performance is usually short-team, and a one-time occurrence it seems more appropriate to provide members with bonuses instead of permanent, base-pay merit rewards.

At a division of Unisys, a team-based reward system was carefully developed.[47] In the Bismarck, North Dakota, office 140 people are organized in 10 teams. These teams handle various accounting functions. Each team takes care of an entire process. Unisys selects team members based on their skills to work cooperatively on customer-focused teams. The reward system is a combination of individual base pay and rewards based on team performance.

www.trigon.com

Trigon Blue Cross–Blue Shield of Virginia uses a team-pay plan for an operation team. The team's base salary ranges, and merit increases are 5 percent lower than other employees and groups. In return, the team has an opportunity to earn incentive pay up to 15 percent of base salary. Trigon evaluates the team on two financial measures—administrative expense and enrollment growth. The team members earned more under this system. As the team earns more, others at Trigon are now interested in how they as individuals and as teams can become eligible for the base-plus-team-incentive plan.

Although teams are here to stay, it is not certain how to reward teams. The available research is spotty and a lot of experimentation is occurring. Unisys and

---

[45]E. Neuforne, "Companies Save, But Workers Pay," *USA Today,* February 25, 1997, pp. 1B–2B.

[46]Edward E. Lawler, III, *From the Ground Up* (San Francisco: Jossey-Bass, 1996), pp. 211–13.

[47]Steven E. Gross, "When Jobs become Team Roles, What Do You Pay For?" *Compensation and Benefits Review,* November–December 1996, pp. 48–51.

—— Management Pointer 5.2 ——

**A FEW GUIDELINES TO
CONSIDER BEFORE JUMPING
ON THE TEAM-BASED
REWARD BANDWAGON**

1. Make sure the team is clearly identified.
2. Do the people making up the team get along? If not, you are going to have ongoing problems.
3. Recognize individual contributions even in a team-based reward plan.
4. Be patient for the team-based approach to take hold. It is different than individual-based pay, and it takes time for the culture to change.
5. Clearly set team goals and link rewards to their accomplishment.

Trigon use methods to reward teams that appear to be working. However, a much longer observation of these two companies and the many others using team-based rewards is needed.[48] Some sound advice about team-based rewards systems are offered in the following Management Pointer 5.2.

Part-Time Benefits

The talent shortage has resulted in more employers relying more on people who work part-time. The U.S. Bureau of Labor Statistics defines part-time as working less than 35 hours per week. About 19 million U.S. workers are considered part-timers. About 80 percent of employees provide vacation, holiday, and sick leave benefits, while about 70 percent offer some form of health care benefits.[49] Proving benefits to part-timers can be interpreted as a reward that is not mandatory.

Most employers prorate benefits to their part-time workers. The most common way to calculate the rate for benefits is to divide the employees' average work hours in a full-time week. For example, if the average workweek in a firm is 40 hours, an employee who works 20 hours a week would receive benefits at 50 percent or one-half of the full-time rate.

One fear of smaller firms is that if a firm provides a full range of benefits to part-timers, some portion of full-timers will want to reduce their hours. In firms that are understaffed, having more full-timers opt for part-time status may result in a major crisis of operating the organization.

Gain-Sharing

Gain-sharing plans provide employees with a share of the financial benefits the organization accrues from improved operating efficiencies and effectiveness.[50] Probably the best-known example of gain-sharing is the Scanlon plan, named after its developer, Joseph Scanlon. A typical Scanlon plan measures the labor costs required to produce goods or services during a base period. If future labor costs are less, a portion of the savings realized is shared with the employees responsible for the cost savings. In some companies, bonuses paid to workers under a Scanlon plan can equal or exceed the employee's usual salary. Scanlon plan companies typically rely on elaborate suggestion systems for receiving employee recommendations for operating efficiencies.

In a typical gain-sharing plan, an organization uses a formula to share financial gains with all employees in a single plant or location.[51] The organization establishes a historical base period of performance and uses this to determine

---

[48]C. James Novak, "Proceed with Caution When Paying Teams," *HR Magazine*, April 1997, pp. 73–78.

[49]Bill Leonard, "Recipes for Part Time Benefits," *HR Magazine*, April 2000, pp. 56–62.

[50]Richard Blackburn and Benson Rosen, "Total Quality and Human Resources Management: Lessons Learned from Baldrige Award-Winning Companies," *Academy of Management Executive*, August 1993, pp. 49–66.

[51]Stephanie Y. Wilson, "When Is Compensation Not Enough? Rethinking How to Reward the Workforce," *Compensation and Benefits Review*, September–October 1996, pp. 59–64.

whether or not gains in performance have occurred. Typically, only controllable costs are measured for the purpose of computing the gain. Unless a major change occurs in the organization's products or technology, the historical base figure stays the same over the duration of the plan.[52] The organization's performance is always compared to the time period before it implemented the gain-sharing plan. General Electric, Motorola, Rockwell, 3M, Dana, and TRW are among the thousands of firms using gain-sharing plans. GE has more than 10 gain-sharing plans in use.

Gain-sharing can take many forms. Simple cash awards for suggestions that are implemented is a form of gain-sharing. Virtually any program that shares cost reductions with employees may be considered gain-sharing. For example, Certified Transmissions, a chain of automotive transmission repair shops, was faced with escalating worker compensation costs because of high injury rates to its repairmen (not unusual in the automotive repair business). The company instituted a plan where all employees, including office staff, received a bonus each month there were no injuries. Bonus payments come from the money saved in reduced worker compensation costs, which have dropped to less than half of what the company had been paying prior to implementing the bonus plan.[53]

Successful gain-sharing programs require a strong commitment to operating efficiencies from both management and employees. In turn, such a commitment requires open communications, information sharing, and high levels of trust between all parties.

Goal-sharing is a follow-on to gain-sharing. Gain-sharing rewards employees based on financial performance. Goal-sharing has a broader approach. It refers to group incentive programs that reward employees for meeting specific goals. These goals often reflect job performance, quality, and service within a unit of a firm.[54]

www.wy.com

At Weyerbauser in Federal Way, Washington employees have no direct control over many of the financial aspects of the plant's success. The employees can make a difference in nonfinancial areas such as quality, safety, and efficiency. The employees set goals in these areas. By accomplishing the goals, the Weyerhauser employees earn a bonus. At Corning, Inc., the goal-sharing bonus is paid at the end of the year with a check that is separate from the regular paycheck. Corning has calculated that it receives $7.87 per each goal-sharing dollar it pays to employees.

Sears, Roebuck, and Company has used goal-sharing at various stores. The goal-sharing unit is a specific store. Individual stores set their own goals. The goals relate to customer service and satisfaction.

Employee Stock Ownership Plans

ESOPs, as employee stock ownership plans are commonly called, are a relatively recent development in reward systems. They are somewhat like gain-sharing plans, a form of group incentive. Under ESOPs, companies make contributions of stock (or cash to purchase stock) to employees. Typically, but not always, individual employee allocation is based upon seniority. ESOPs can provide a sub-

---

[52]E. E. Lawler, S. A. Mohrman, and G. E. Ledford, *Creating High Performance Organizations: Practices and Results of Employee Involvement and Quality Management in Fortune 1000 Companies* (San Francisco: Jossey-Bass, 1995).

[53]"These Bonuses Are a Safe Bet," *Business Ethics,* March–April 1994, p. 31.

[54]Charlotte Garvey, "Goalsharing Scores," *HR Magazine,* April 2000, pp. 99–106.

www.polaroid.com

www.avis.com

www.brunswickcorp.com

www.antioch.com

stantial nest egg for employees upon retiring or leaving the company. Organizations can benefit from improved performance from employees who now have a very direct financial stake in the company. An increasing number of organizations have instituted ESOPs, among them being Procter & Gamble, Polaroid, Lockheed, Brunswick Corporation, and Anheuser-Busch. Avis Corporation, one of the country's largest car rental firms, is wholly owned by its employees.

In order to create a more performance-oriented culture, Utili Corp., a Kansas City–based utility, created a stock ownership plan. The goal of the plan is to provide 25 percent employee ownership. The company offers stock at a 15 percent discount and allows employees to buy shares in amounts of up to 20 percent of their base compensation. The 6 percent company match in the organization's 401K program also is awarded as stock. Even part of the annual incentive bonus for key employees is in the form of stock. Company officials report higher levels of satisfaction with the reward system since the time the stock plan has been implemented.[55]

Research on the effectiveness of employee stock ownership plans is mixed. Some companies, such as Brunswick, have attributed significant organizational performance improvements to the plans. Antioch Publishing Company has seen sales increase 13-fold since it instituted its ESOP. Company management reports that the ESOP has been important to that growth by making it easier to attract and retain good employees.[56] Other companies, however, see no apparent benefit from their plans. Like any other reward system, results will vary as a function of how well management introduces and implements the plan. Administering rewards is perhaps one of the most challenging and frustrating tasks that managers must perform.

Line of Sight: The Key Issue

Promotions, increased pay, recognition for a job well done, or the opportunity to own a part of an organization can be motivators if there is a clear line of sight between what the employee is doing and the reward. *Line of sight* means that the employee perceives that there is a "real" linkage between his or her performance and the rewards received. In the case of extrinsic rewards, organizations need to have systems that clearly tie rewards to desired performance.

Gain-sharing, stock options, and other extrinsic systems must be built around the line-of-sight concept. Unfortunately, accomplishing a clear line of sight is difficult. Merit-pay systems claim that they reward performance. Unfortunately, despite the notion of merit, employees do not always see or perceive the connection between rewards and performance. The practice of pay secrecy suggests that line of sight is difficult to achieve. Secret pay actions cloud up any line-of-sight effort.

Intrinsic rewards are personal and come from the employee. However, organizations can influence intrinsic rewards and the employees line of sight of them by providing jobs that are challenging and by providing clear feedback on job performance. The design of a job should be carefully weighed when considering the line-of-sight issue. When jobs are designed with these issues in mind, the intrinsic rewards of working on the job become a top priority. Of course not all jobs can be enriched so that desired intrinsic rewards are provided to the employee.

[55]Shari Caudron, "Employee, Cover Thyself," *Workforce*, April 2000, pp. 34–42.

[56]Lawler, *Pay and Organizational Effectiveness*, pp. 214–16.

www.marykay.com

However, when jobs can be designed and enriched to provide a clear line of sight for matching intrinsic rewards and performance the results have been positive. For example, Mary Kay Cosmetics Company has designed jobs by making them autonomous and responsible. Sales representatives in most cases have found the jobs intrinsically rewarding and have linked their intrinsic rewards with exceptional performance. The line of sight of the job, rewards, and performance is validated constantly at Mary Kay Cosmetics.[57]

---

[57]Ibid., p. 128.

Summary of Key Points

- Among the major purposes which performance evaluation can serve are (1) providing a basis for reward allocation, (2) identifying high-potential employees, (3) validating the effectiveness of employee selection procedures, (4) evaluating previous training programs, and (5) facilitating future performance improvement.

- Feedback sessions should use objective information to help guide the evaluated employee to improve or sustain performance.

- A 360-degree feedback program involves the use of multisources of evaluation information collected from a full circle of evaluators (e.g., supervisors, subordinates, peers, and others).

- Reinforcement theory suggests that behavior is influenced by its consequences and that it is possible to affect behavior by controlling such consequences. Desired behaviors are reinforced through the use of rewards, while undesired behaviors can be extinguished through punishment. The timing of rewards and punishments is extremely critical and is controlled through the use of various *reinforcement schedules.*

- A useful model of individual rewards would include the suggestion that ability, skill, and experience, in addition to motivation, result in various levels of individual performance. The resulting performance is then evaluated by management, which can distribute two types of rewards: intrinsic and extrinsic. These rewards are evaluated by the individual receiving them, and to the extent they result in satisfaction, motivation to perform is enhanced.

- Organizational rewards can be classified as either extrinsic or intrinsic. Extrinsic rewards include salary and wages, fringe benefits, promotions, and certain types of interpersonal rewards. Intrinsic rewards can include such things as a sense of completion, achievement, autonomy, and personal growth.

- An effective reward system would encourage the best performers to remain with the organization, while causing the poorer performers to leave. To accomplish this, the system must be perceived as equitable. Additionally, the reward system should minimize the incidents of absenteeism. Generally, absenteeism will be less if an employee feels that attendance will lead to more valued rewards and fewer negative consequences.

- Both extrinsic and intrinsic rewards can be used to motivate job performance. For this to occur, certain conditions must exist: The rewards must be valued by the employee, and they must be related to the level of job performance that is to be motivated.

- In addition to standard organizational rewards such as pay, fringe benefits, advancement, and opportunities for growth, some organizations are experimenting with more innovative reward programs. Examples of such approaches include cafeteria-style benefits, banking time off, all-salaried teams, skill-based pay, gain-sharing, and employee stock ownership plans.

Review and Discussion Questions

1. Why is providing feedback on poor performance a dreaded but necessary management experience?

2. Who should be included in a person's 360-degree domain when evaluating his/her performance?

3. What intrinsic rewards are important to you personally on a job and as a student?

4. From a managerial perspective, why is it impractical to provide continuous reinforcement in work environments? If it were practical, would it be a good idea? Explain.

5. The degree of employee satisfaction with the organization's reward system will significantly affect how

successful the system is in influencing performance. Based on the research literature, what do we know about what influences whether individuals will be satisfied with the rewards they receive?

6. What are some of the problems that must be overcome to successfully administer a merit pay plan in an organization? What solutions can you offer for these problems?

7. What might be some of the benefits and problems associated with using each of the three approaches to reward administration discussed in this chapter?

8. Why are team-based reward systems becoming more widely used?

9. This chapter discusses a number of innovative reward systems. Can you suggest other innovative approaches organizations might use? Identify potential problems with the approaches you suggest and try to find ways of overcoming them.

10. In what type of work settings would goal-sharing be suitable?

READING 5.1   On the Folly of Rewarding A, While Hoping for B

Steven Kerr

Whether dealing with monkeys, rats, or human beings, it is hardly controversial to state that most organisms seek information concerning what activities are rewarded, and then seek to do (or at least pretend to do) those things, often to the virtual exclusion of activities not rewarded. The extent to which this occurs, of course, will depend on the perceived attractiveness of the rewards offered, but neither operant nor expectancy theorists would quarrel with the essence of this notion.

Nevertheless, numerous examples exist of reward systems that are fouled up in that behaviors which are rewarded are those which the rewarded is trying to *discourage*, while the behavior he desires is not being rewarded at all.

In an effort to understand and explain this phenomenon, this paper presents examples from society, from organizations in general, and from profit-making firms in particular. Data from a manufacturing company and information from an insurance firm are examined to demonstrate the consequences of such reward systems for the organizations involved, and possible reasons why such reward systems continue to exist are considered.

SOCIETAL EXAMPLES

Politics

Official goals are "purposely vague and general and do not indicate . . . the host of decisions that must be made among alternative ways of achieving official goals and the priority of multiple goals. . . ." They usually may be relied on to offend absolutely no one and in this sense can be considered high-acceptance, low-quality goals. An example might be "build better schools." Operative goals are higher in quality but lower in acceptance, since they specify where the money will come from, what alternative goals will be ignored, etc.

The American citizenry supposedly wants its candidates for public office to set forth operative goals, making their proposed programs "perfectly clear," specifying sources and uses of funds, etc. However, since operative goals are lower in acceptance, and since aspirants to public office need acceptance (from at least 50.1 percent of the people), most politicians prefer to speak only of official goals, at least until after the election. They of course would

agree to speak at the operative level if "punished" for not doing so. The electorate could do this by refusing to support candidates who do not speak at the operative level.

Instead, however, the American voter typically punishes (withholds support from) candidates who frankly discuss where the money will come from, rewards politicians who speak only of official goals, but hopes that candidates (despite the reward system) will discuss the issues operatively. It is academic whether it was moral for Nixon, for example, to refuse to discuss his 1968 "secret plan" to end the Vietnam war, his 1972 operative goals concerning the lifting of price controls, the reshuffling of his cabinet, etc. The point is that the reward system made such refusal rational.

It seems worth mentioning that no manuscript can adequately define what is "moral" and what is not. However, examination of costs and benefits, combined with knowledge of what motivates a particular individual, often will suffice to determine what for him is "rational."[1] If the reward system is so designed that it is irrational to be moral, this does not necessarily mean that immorality will result. But is this not asking for trouble?

War

If some oversimplification may be permitted, let it be assumed that the primary goal of the organization (Pentagon, Luftwaffe, or whatever) is to win. Let it be assumed further that the primary goal of most individuals on the front lines is to get home alive. Then there appears to be an important conflict in goals—personally rational behavior by those at the bottom will endanger goal attainment by those at the top.

But not necessarily! It depends on how the reward system is set up. The Vietnam war was indeed a study of disobedience and rebellion, with terms such as *fragging* (killing one's own commanding officer) and *search and evade* becoming part of the military vocabulary. The difference in subordinates' acceptance of authority between World War II and Vietnam is reported to be considerable, and veterans of the Second World War often have been quoted as being outraged at the mutinous actions of many American soldiers in Vietnam.

Consider, however, some critical differences in the reward system in use during the two conflicts. What did the GI in World War II want? To go home. And when did he

Source: Reprinted with permission from *Academy of Management Journal,* December 1975, pp. 764–83.

[1]Chester I. Barnard, *The Functions of the Executive*. Cambridge, MA.: Harvard University Press, 1968. (First published in 1936).

get to go home? When the war was won! If he disobeyed the orders to clean out the trenches and take the hills, the war would not be won and he would not go home. Furthermore, what were his chances of attaining his goal (getting home alive) if he obeyed the orders compared to his chances if he did not? What is being suggested is that the rational soldier in World War II, *whether patriotic or not,* probably found it expedient to obey.

Consider the reward system in use in Vietnam. What did the man at the bottom want? To go home. And when did he get to go home? When his tour of duty was over! This was the case *whether or not* the war was won. Furthermore, concerning the relative chance of getting home alive by obeying orders compared to the chance if they were disobeyed, it is worth noting that a mutineer in Vietnam was far more likely to be assigned rest and rehabilitation (on the assumption that fatigue was the cause) than he was to suffer any negative consequence.

In his description of the "zone of indifference," Barnard stated that "a person can and will accept a communication as authoritative only when . . . at the time of his decision, he believes it to be compatible with his personal interests as a whole." In light of the reward system used in Vietnam, would it not have been personally irrational for some orders to have been obeyed? Was not the military implementing a system which *rewarded* disobedience, while *hoping* that soldiers (despite the reward system) would obey orders?

Medicine

Theoretically, a physician can make either of two types of error, and intuitively one seems as bad as the other. A doctor can pronounce a patient sick when he is actually well, thus causing him needless anxiety and expense, curtailment of enjoyable foods and activities, and even physical danger by subjecting him to needless medication and surgery. Alternatively, a doctor can label a sick person well, and thus avoid treating what may be a serious, even fatal ailment. It might be natural to conclude that physicians seek to minimize both types of error.

Such a conclusion would be wrong.[2] It is estimated that numerous Americans are presently afflicted with iatrogenic (physician-*caused*) illnesses. This occurs when the doctor is approached by someone complaining of a few stray symptoms. The doctor classifies and organizes these symptoms, gives them a name, and obligingly tells the patient what further symptoms may be expected. This information often acts as a self-fulfilling prophecy, with the result that from that day on the patient for all practical purposes is sick.

Why does this happen? Why are physicians so reluctant to sustain a type 2 error (pronouncing a sick person well) that they will tolerate many type 1 errors? Again, a look at the reward system is needed. The punishments for a type 2 error are real: guilt, embarrassment, and the threat of a lawsuit and scandal. On the other hand, a type 1 error (labeling a well person sick) "is sometimes seen as sound clinical practice, indicating a healthy conservative approach to medicine." Type 1 errors also are likely to generate increased income and a stream of steady customers who, being well in a limited physiological sense, will not embarrass the doctor by dying abruptly.

Fellow physicians and the general public therefore are really *rewarding* type 1 errors and at the same time *hoping* fervently that doctors will try not to make them.

GENERAL ORGANIZATIONAL EXAMPLES

Rehabilitation Centers and Orphanages

In terms of the prime beneficiary classification, organizations such as these are supposed to exist for the "public-in-contact," that is, clients. The orphanage therefore theoretically is interested in placing as many children as possible in good homes. However, often orphanages surround themselves with so many rules concerning adoptions that it is nearly impossible to pry a child out of the place. Orphanages may deny adoption unless the applicants are a married couple, both of the same religion as the child, without history of emotional or vocational instability, with a specified minimum income and a private room for the child, etc.

If the primary goal is to place children in good homes, then the rules ought to constitute means toward that goal. Goal displacement results when these "means become ends-in-themselves that displace the original goals."

To some extent these rules are required by law. But the influence of the reward system on the orphanage's management should not be ignored. Consider, for example, that the:

1. Number of children enrolled often is the most important determinant of the size of the allocated budget.
2. Number of children under the director's care also will affect the size of his staff.
3. Total organizational size will determine largely the director's prestige at the annual conventions, in the community, etc.

Therefore, to the extent that the staff size, total budget, and personal prestige are valued by the orphanage's executive personnel, it becomes rational for them to make it difficult for children to be adopted. After all, who wants to be the director of the smallest orphanage in the state?

If the reward system errs in the opposite direction, paying off only for placements, extensive goal displacement again is likely to result. A common example of vocational

---

[2]Peter M. Blau and W. Richard Scott. *Formal Organizations.* San Francisco: Chandler, 1962.

rehabilitation in many states, for example, consists of placing someone in a job for which he has little interest and few qualifications, for two months or so, and then "rehabilitating" him again in another position. Such behavior is quite consistent with the prevailing reward system, which pays off for the number of individuals placed in any position for 60 days or more. Rehabilitation counselors also confess to competing with one another to place relatively skilled clients, sometimes ignoring persons with few skills who would be harder to place. Extensively disabled clients found that counselors often prefer to work with those whose disabilities are less severe.[3]

Universities

Society *hopes* that teachers will not neglect their teaching responsibilities but *rewards* them almost entirely for research and publications. This is most true at the large and prestigious universities. Clichés such as "good research and good teaching go together" notwithstanding, professors often find that they must choose between teaching and research-oriented activities when allocating their time. Rewards for good teaching usually are limited to outstanding teacher awards, which are given to only a small percentage of good teachers and which usually bestow little money and fleeting prestige. Punishments for poor teaching are also rare.

Rewards for research and publications, on the other hand, and punishments for failure to accomplish these, are commonly administered by universities at which teachers are employed. Furthermore, publication-oriented resumes usually will be well received at other universities, whereas teaching credentials, harder to document and quantify, are much less transferable. Consequently, it is rational for university teachers to concentrate on research, even if to the detriment of teaching and at the expense of their students.

By the same token, it is rational for students to act based upon the goal displacement which has occurred within universities concerning what they are rewarded for. If it is assumed that a primary goal of a university is to transfer knowledge from teacher to student, then grades become identifiable as a means toward that goal, serving as motivational, control, and feedback devices to expedite the knowledge transfer. Instead, however, the grades themselves have become much more important for entrance to graduate school, successful employment, tuition refunds, parental respect, etc., than the knowledge or lack of knowledge they are supposed to signify.

It therefore should come as no surprise that information has surfaced in recent years concerning fraternity files for examinations, term-paper writing services, organized cheating at the service academies, and the like. Such activities constitute a personally rational response to a reward system which pays off for grades rather than knowledge.

BUSINESS-RELATED EXAMPLES
Ecology

Assume that the president of XYZ Corporation is confronted with the following alternatives:

1. Spend $11 million for antipollution equipment to keep from poisoning fish in the river adjacent to the plant; or
2. Do nothing, in violation of the law, and assume a 1 in 10 chance of being caught, with a resultant $1 million fine plus the necessity of buying the equipment.

Under this not unrealistic set of choices, it requires no linear program to determine that XYZ Corporation can maximize its probabilities by flouting the law. Add the fact that XYZ's president is probably being rewarded (by creditors, stockholders, and other salient parts of his task environment) according to criteria totally unrelated to the number of fish poisoned, and his probable course of action becomes clear.

Evaluation of Training

It is axiomatic that those who care about a firm's wellbeing should insist that the organization get fair value for its expenditures. Yet it is commonly known that firms seldom bother to evaluate a new GRID, MBO, job enrichment program, or whatever, to see if the company is getting its money's worth. Why? Certainly it is not because people have not pointed out that this situation exists; numerous practitioner-oriented articles are written each year to just this point.

The individuals (whether in personnel, manpower planning, or wherever) who normally would be responsible for conducting such evaluations are the same ones often charged with introducing the change effort in the first place. Having convinced top management to spend the money, they usually are quite animated afterwards in collecting rigorous vignettes and anecdotes about how successful the program was. The last thing many desire is a formal, systematic, and revealing evaluation. Although members of top management may actually *hope* for such systematic evaluation, their reward systems continue to *reward* ignorance in this area. And if the personnel department abdicates its responsibility, who is to step into the breach? The change agent himself? Hardly! He is likely to be too busy collecting anecdotal "evidence" of his own, for use with his next client.

Miscellaneous

Many additional examples could be cited of systems which in fact are rewarding behaviors other than those

[3]Fred E. Fiedler, "Predicting the Effects of Leadership Training and Experience from The Contingency Model," *Journal of Applied Psychology* (February 1972), pp. 114–119.

supposedly desired by the rewarder. A few of these are described briefly below.

Most coaches disdain to discuss individual accomplishments, preferring to speak of teamwork, proper attitude, and a one-for-all spirit. Usually, however, rewards are distributed according to individual performance. The college basketball player who feeds his teammates instead of shooting will not compile impressive scoring statistics and is less likely to be drafted by the pros. The ballplayer who hits to right field to advance the runners will win neither the batting nor home run titles and will be offered smaller raises. It therefore is rational for players to think of themselves first and the team second.

In business organizations where rewards are dispensed for unit performance or for individual goals achieved, without regard for overall effectiveness, similar attitudes often are observed. Under most management by objectives (MBO) systems, goals in areas where quantification is difficult often go unspecified. The organization therefore often is in a position where it *hopes* for employee effort in the areas of team building, interpersonal relations, creativity, etc., but it formally *rewards* none of these. In cases where promotions and raises are formally tied to MBO, the system itself contains a paradox in that it "asks employees to set challenging, risky goals, only to face smaller paychecks and possibly damaged careers if these goals are not accomplished."

It is *hoped* that administrators will pay attention to long-run costs and opportunities and will institute programs which will bear fruit later on. However, many organizational reward systems pay off for shorter-run sales and earnings only. Under such circumstances, it is personally rational for officials to sacrifice long-term growth and profit (by selling off equipment and property, or by stifling research and development) for short-term advantages. This probably is most pertinent in the public sector, with the result that many public officials are unwilling to implement programs which will not show benefits by election time.

As a final, clear-cut example of a fouled-up reward system, consider the cost-plus contract or its next of kin, the allocation of next year's budget as a direct function of this year's expenditures. It probably is conceivable that those who award such budgets and contracts really hope for economy and prudence in spending. It is obvious, however, that adopting the proverb "to him who spends shall more be given," rewards not economy, but spending itself.

TWO COMPANIES' EXPERIENCE

A Manufacturing Organization

A Midwest manufacturer of industrial goods had been troubled for some time by aspects of its organizational climate it believed dysfunctional. For research purposes, interviews were conducted with many employees and a questionnaire was administered on a companywide basis, including plants and offices in several American and Canadian locations. The company strongly encouraged employee participation in the survey, and made available time and space during the workday for completion of the instrument. All employees in attendance during the day of the survey completed the questionnaire. All instruments were collected directly by the researcher, who personally administered each session. Since no one employed by the firm handled the questionnaire, and since respondent names were not asked for, it seems likely that the pledge of anonymity given was believed.

A modified version of the Expect Approval scale was included as part of the questionnaire. The instrument asked respondents to indicate the degree of approval or disapproval they could expect if they performed each of the described actions. A seven-point Likert scale was used, with 1 indicating that the action would probably bring strong disapproval and 7 signifying likely strong approval.

Although normative data for this scale from studies of other organizations are unavailable, it is possible to examine fruitfully the data obtained from this survey in several ways. First, it may be worth noting that the questionnaire data corresponded closely to information gathered through interviews. Furthermore, as can be seen from the results summarized in Exhibit 5.6, sizable differences between various work units, and between employees at different job levels within the same work unit, were obtained. This suggests that response bias effects (social desirability in particular loomed as a potential concern) are not likely to be severe.

Most importantly, comparisons between scores obtained on the Expect Approval scale and a statement of problems which were the reason for the survey revealed that the same behaviors which managers in each division thought dysfunctional were those which lower-level employees claimed were rewarded. As compared to job levels 1 to 8 in Division B (see Exhibit 5.6), those in Division A claimed a much higher acceptance by management of "conforming" activities. Between 31 and 37 percent of Division A employees at levels 1–8 stated that going along with the majority, agreeing with the boss, and staying on everyone's good side brought approval; only once (level 5–8 responses to one of the three items) did a majority suggest that such actions would generate disapproval.

Furthermore, responses from Division A workers at levels 1–4 indicate that behaviors geared toward risk avoidance were as likely to be rewarded as to be punished. Only at job levels 9 and above was it apparent that the reward system was positively reinforcing behaviors desired by top management. Overall, the same "tendencies toward conservatism and apple-polishing at the lower levels" which divisional management had complained about during interviews were those claimed by subordinates to be

EXHIBIT 5.6　Summary of Two Divisions' Data Relevant to Conforming and Risk-Avoidance Behaviors (Extent to Which Subjects Expect Approval)

Dimension	Item	Division and Sample	Total Responses	1, 2, or 3 (Disapproval)	4	5, 6, or 7 Approval
				Percentage of Workers Responding		
Risk avoidance	Making a risky decision based on the best information available at the time, but which turns out wrong.	A, levels 1–4 (lowest)	127	61	25	14
		A, levels 5–8	172	46	31	23
		A, levels 9 and above	17	41	30	30
		B, levels 1–4 (lowest)	31	58	26	16
		B, levels 5–8	19	42	42	16
		B, levels 9 and above	10	50	20	30
Risk	Setting extremely high and challenging standards and goals, and then narrowly failing to make them.	A, levels 1–4	122	47	28	25
		A, levels 5–8	168	33	26	41
		A, levels 9 +	17	24	6	70
		B, levels 1–4	31	48	23	29
		B, levels 5–8	18	17	33	50
		B, levels 9 +	10	30	0	70
	Setting goals which are extremely easy to make and then making them.	A, levels 1–4	124	35	30	35
		A, levels 5–8	171	47	27	26
		A, levels 9 +	17	70	24	6
		B, levels 1–4	31	58	26	16
		B, levels 5–8	19	63	16	21
		B, levels 9 +	10	80	0	20
	Being a "yes man" and always agreeing with the boss.	A, levels 1–4	126	46	17	37
		A, levels 5–8	180	54	14	31
		A, levels 9 +	17	88	12	0
		B, levels 1–4	32	53	28	19
		B, levels 5–8	19	68	21	11
		B, levels 9 +	10	80	10	10
	Always going along with the majority.	A, levels 1–4	125	40	25	35
		A, levels 5–8	173	47	21	32
		A, levels 9 +	17	70	12	18
		B, levels 1–4	31	61	23	16
		B, levels 5–8	18	68	11	21
		B, levels 9 +	10	80	10	10
	Being careful to stay on the good side of everyone, so that everyone agrees that you are a great guy.	A, levels 1–4	124	45	18	37
		A, levels 5–8	173	45	22	33
		A, levels 9 +	17	64	6	30
		B, levels 1–4	31	54	23	23
		B, levels 5–8	19	73	11	16
		B, levels 9 +	10	80	10	10

the most rational course of action in light of the existing reward system. Management apparently was not getting the behaviors it was *hoping* for, but it certainly was getting the behaviors it was perceived by subordinates to be *rewarding*.

An Insurance Firm

The Group Health Claims Division of a large Eastern insurance company provides another rich illustration of a reward system which reinforces behaviors not desired by top management.

Attempting to measure and reward accuracy in paying surgical claims, the firm systematically keeps track of the number of returned checks and letters of complaint received from policyholders. However, underpayments are likely to provoke cries of outrage from the insured, while overpayments often are accepted in courteous silence. Since it often is impossible to tell from the physician's statement which of two surgical procedures, with different allowable benefits, was performed, and since writing for clarifications will interfere with other standards used by the firm concerning "percentage of claims paid within two days of receipt," the new hire in more than one claims section is soon acquainted with the informal norm: "When in doubt, pay it out!"

The situation would be even worse were it not for the fact that other features of the firm's reward system tend to neutralize those described. For example, annual "merit" increases are given to all employees, in one of the following three amounts:

1. If the worker is "outstanding" (a select category, into which no more than two employees per section may be placed): 5 percent.
2. If the worker is "above average" (normally all workers not "outstanding" are so rated): 4 percent.
3. If the worker commits gross acts of negligence and irresponsibility for which he might be discharged in many other companies: 3 percent.

Now, since (a) the difference between the 5 percent theoretically attainable through hard work and the 4 percent attainable merely by living until the review date is small, and (b) since insurance firms seldom dispense much of a salary increase in cash (rather, the worker's insurance benefits increase, causing him to be further over-insured), many employees are rather indifferent to the possibility of obtaining the extra 1 percent reward and therefore tend to ignore the norm concerning indiscriminate payments.

However, most employees are not indifferent to the rule which states that, should absences or lateness total three or more in any six-month period, the entire 4 or 5 percent due at the next "merit" review must be forfeited. In this sense the firm may be described as *hoping* for performance, while *rewarding* attendance. What it gets, of course, is attendance. If the absence-lateness rule appears to the reader to be stringent, it really is not. The company counts "times" rather than "days" absent, and a 10-day absence therefore counts the same as one lasting 2 days. A worker in danger of accumulating a third absence within six months merely has to remain ill (away from work) during his second absence until his first absence is more than six months old. The limiting factor is that at some point his salary ceases, and his sickness benefits take over. This usually is sufficient to get the younger workers to return, but for those with 20 or more years' service, the company provides sickness benefits of 90 percent of normal salary, tax-free! Therefore. . . .

Causes

Extremely diverse instances of systems which reward behavior A although the rewarder apparently hopes for behavior B have been given. These are useful to illustrate the breadth and magnitude of the phenomenon, but the diversity increases the difficulty of determining commonalities and establishing causes. However, four general factors may be pertinent to an explanation of why fouled-up reward systems seem to be so prevalent.

Fascination with an "Objective" Criterion

It has been mentioned elsewhere that:

> Most "objective" measures of productivity are objective only in that their subjective elements are (a) determined in advance, rather than coming into play at the time of the formal evaluation, and (b) well concealed on the rating instrument itself. Thus industrial firms seeking to devise objective rating systems first decide, in an arbitrary manner, what dimensions are to be rated, . . . usually including some items having little to do with organization effectiveness while excluding others that do. Only then does Personnel Division churn out official-looking documents on which all dimensions chosen to be rated are assigned point values, categories, or whatever.

Nonetheless, many individuals seek to establish simple, quantifiable standards against which to measure and reward performance. Such efforts may be successful in highly predictable areas within an organization, but are likely to cause goal displacement when applied anywhere else. Overconcern with attendance and lateness in the insurance firm and with the number of people placed in the vocational rehabilitation division may have been largely responsible for the problems described in those organizations.

Overemphasis on Highly Visible Behaviors

Difficulties often stem from the fact that some parts of the task are highly visible while other parts are not. For example, publications are easier to demonstrate than teaching, and scoring baskets and hitting home runs are more readily observable than feeding teammates and advancing base runners. Similarly, the adverse consequences of pronouncing a sick person well are more visible than those sustained by labeling a well person sick. Team-building and creativity are other examples of behaviors which may not be rewarded simply because they are hard to observe.

Hypocrisy

In some of the instances described, the rewarder may have been getting the desired behavior, notwithstanding claims that the behavior was not desired. This may be true, for example, for management's attitude toward apple-polishing in the manufacturing firm (a behavior which subordinates felt was rewarded, despite management's avowed dislike of the practice). This also may explain politicians' unwillingness to revise the penalties for disobedience of ecology laws, and the failure of top management to devise reward systems which would cause systematic evaluation of training and development programs.

Emphasis on Morality or Equity Rather than Efficiency

Some consideration of other factors prevents the establishment of a system which rewards behaviors desired by the rewarder. The felt obligation of many Americans to vote for one candidate or another, for example, may impair their ability to withhold support from politicians who refuse to discuss the issues. Similarly, the concern for spreading the risks and costs of wartime military service may outweigh the advantage to be obtained by committing personnel to combat until the war is over.

It should be noted that only with respect to the first two causes are reward systems really paying off for other than desired behaviors. In the case of the third and fourth causes, the system is rewarding behaviors desired by the rewarder, and the systems are fouled up only from the standpoints of those who believe the rewarder's public statements (cause 3), or those who seek to maximize efficiency rather than other outcomes (cause 4).

CONCLUSIONS

Modern organization theory requires a recognition that the members of organizations and society possess divergent goals and motives. It therefore is unlikely that managers and their subordinates will seek the same outcomes. Three possible remedies for this potential problem are suggested.

Selection

It is theoretically possible for organizations to employ only those individuals whose goals and motives are wholly consonant with those of management. In such cases the same behaviors judged by subordinates to be rational would be perceived by management as desirable. State-of-the-art reviews of selection techniques, however, provide scant grounds for hope that such an approach would be successful.

Training

Another theoretical alternative is for the organization to admit those employees whose goals are not consonant with those of management and then, through training, socialization, or whatever, alter employee goals to make them consonant. However, research on the effectiveness of such training programs, though limited, provides further grounds for pessimism.

Altering the Reward System

What would have been the result if:

1. Nixon had been assured by his advisors that he could not win reelection except by discussing the issues in detail?
2. Physicians' conduct was subjected to regular examination by review boards for type 1 errors (calling healthy people ill) and to penalties (fines, censure, etc.) for errors of either type?
3. The President of XYZ Corporation had to choose between (a) spending $11 million for antipollution equipment, and (b) incurring a 50-50 chance of going to jail for five years?

Managers who complain that their workers are not motivated might do well to consider the possibility that they have installed reward systems which are paying off for behaviors other than those they are seeking. This, in part, is what happened in Vietnam, and this is what regularly frustrates societal efforts to bring about honest politicians, civic-minded managers, etc. This certainly is what happened in both the manufacturing and the insurance companies.

A first step for such managers might be to find out what behaviors currently are being rewarded. Perhaps an instrument similar to that used in the manufacturing firm could be useful for this purpose. Chances are excellent that these managers will be surprised by what they find—that their firms are not rewarding what they assume they are. In fact, such undesirable behavior by organizational members as they have observed may be explained largely by the reward systems in use.

This is not to say that all organizational behavior is determined by formal rewards and punishments. Certainly it is true that, in the absence of formal reinforcement, some soldiers will be patriotic, some presidents will be ecology-minded, and some orphanage directors will care about children. The point, however, is that in such cases the rewarder is not *causing* the behaviors desired but is only a fortunate bystander. For an organization to *act* upon its members, the formal reward system should positively reinforce desired behaviors, not constitute an obstacle to be overcome.

It might be wise to underscore the obvious fact that there is nothing really new in what has been said. In both theory and practice these matters have been mentioned before. Thus, in many states, Good Samaritan laws have been installed to protect doctors who stop to assist a stricken motorist. In states without such laws, it is commonplace for doctors to refuse to stop for fear of involvement in a subsequent lawsuit. In college basketball, additional penalties have been instituted against players who foul their opponents deliberately. It has long been argued by Milton Friedman and others that penalties should be altered so as to make it irrational to disobey the ecology laws, and so on.

By altering the reward system, the organization escapes the necessity of selecting only desirable people or of trying to alter undesirable ones. In Skinnerian terms,

"As for responsibility and goodness—as commonly defined—no one . . . would want or need them. They refer to a man's behaving well despite the absence of positive reinforcement that is obviously sufficient to explain it. Where such reinforcement exists, 'no one needs goodness.' "

Exercises

EXERCISE 5.1   Diagnosing a Work Performance Problem

BACKGROUND

Proper diagnosis is a critical aspect of effective motivation management. Oftentimes managers become frustrated because they don't understand the causes of observed performance problems. They might experiment with various "cures," but the inefficiency of this trial-and-error process often simply increases their frustration level. In addition, the accompanying misunderstanding adds extra strain to the manager-subordinate relationship. This generally makes the performance problem even more pronounced, which prompts the manager to resort to more drastic responses, and a vicious, downward spiral ensues.

The performance diagnosis model in Exhibit 5.7 offers a systematic way for managers and subordinates to collaboratively pinpoint the cause(s) of dissatisfaction and performance problems. It assumes that employees will work hard and be good performers if the work environment encourages these actions. Consequently, rather than jumping to conclusions about poor performance stemming from deficiencies in personality traits or a bad attitude, this diagnostic process helps managers focus their attention on improving the selection, job design, performance evaluation, and reward allocation systems. In this manner, the specific steps necessary to accomplish work goals and management's expectations are examined to pinpoint why the worker's performance is falling short.

The manager and low-performing subordinate should follow the logical discovery process in the model, step by step. They should begin by examining the current perceptions of performance, as well as the understanding of performance expectations, and then proceed through the model until the performance problems have been identified. The model focuses on seven of these problems.

A. *Perception Problem.* "Do you agree your performance is below expectations?" A perception problem suggests that the manager and subordinate have different views of the subordinate's current performance level. Unless this disagreement is resolved, it is futile to

continue the diagnostic process. The entire problem-solving process is based on the premise that both parties recognize the existence of a problem and are interested in solving it. If agreement does not exist, the manager should focus on resolving the discrepancy in perceptions, including clarifying current expectations (Problem E).

B. *Resources Problem.* "Do you have the resources necessary to do the job well?" (Ability has three components, and these should be explored in the order shown in the model. This order reduces a subordinate's defensive reactions.) Poor performance may stem from a lack of resource support. Resources include material and personnel support as well as cooperation from interdependent work groups.

C. *Training Problem.* "Is a lack of training interfering with your job performance?" Individuals may be asked to perform tasks that exceed their current skill or knowledge level. Typically this problem can be overcome through additional training or education.

D. *Aptitude Problem.* "Do you feel this is the right job/blend of work assignments for you?" This is the most difficult of the three ability problems to resolve because it is the most basic. If the *resupply* (providing additional resources) and *retraining* solutions have been explored without success, then more drastic measures may be required. These include *refitting* the person's current job requirements, *reassigning* him to another position, or, finally, *releasing* him from the organization.

E. *Expectations Problem.* "What are your performance expectations for this position? What do you think my expectations are?" This problem results from poor communications regarding job goals or job requirements. In some cases, the stated goals may be different from the desired goals. In other words, the employee is working toward one goal while the supervisor desires another. This often occurs when subordinates are not sufficiently involved in the goal-

EXHIBIT 5.7   Performance Diagnosis Model

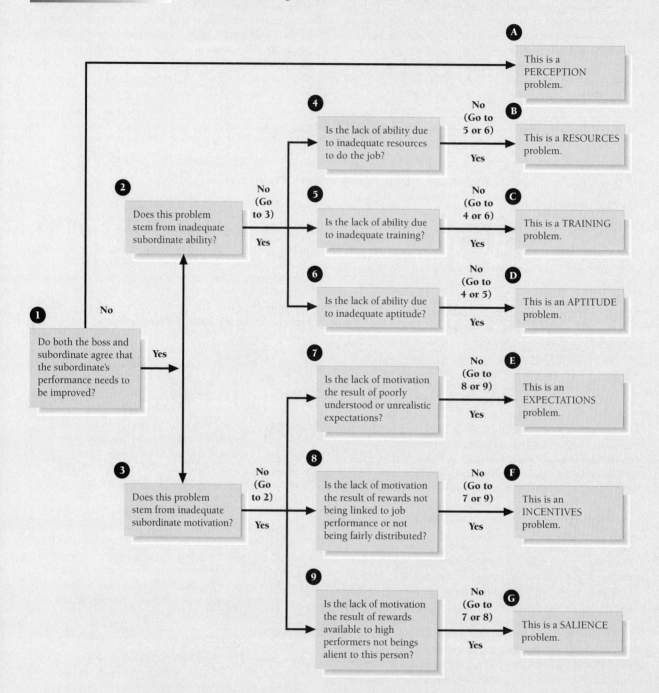

or standard-setting process. When this results in unrealistic, imposed expectations, motivation suffers.

F. *Incentives Problem.* "Do you believe rewards are linked to your performance in this position?" Either the individual does not believe that "performance makes a difference" or insufficient performance feedback and reinforcement have been given. The manager should also ask, "Do you feel rewards are being distributed equitably?" This provides an opportunity to discuss subordinates' criteria for judging fairness. Often, unrealistic standards are being used.

G. *Salience Problem.* "Are the performance incentives attractive to you?" Salience refers to the importance an individual attaches to available rewards. Oftentimes the incentives offered to encourage high performance simply aren't highly valued by a particular individual. The salience problem points out the need for managers to be creative in generating a broad range of rewards and flexible in allowing subordinates to choose among rewards.

ASSIGNMENT

Option 1: Read the case below, "Joe's Performance Problems," and privately use the diagnostic model Exhibit 5.7 to pinpoint plausible performance problems. Next, in small groups discuss your individual assessments, and list the specific questions you should ask Joe in order to accurately identify, from his point of view, the obstacles to his high performance. Finally, brainstorm ideas for plausible solutions. Be prepared to represent your group in role-playing a problem-solving interview with Joe.

JOE'S PERFORMANCE PROBLEMS

Joe joined your architectural firm two years ago as a draftsman. He is 35 years old and has been a draftsman since graduating from a two-year technical school right after high school. He is married and has four children. He has worked for four architectural firms in 12 years.

Joe came with mediocre recommendations from his previous employer, but you hired him anyway because you needed help desperately. Your firm's workload has been extremely high due to a local construction boom. The result is that a lot of the practices that contribute to a supportive, well-managed work environment have tended to be overlooked. For instance, you can't remember the last time you conducted a formal performance review or did any career counseling. Furthermore, the tradition of closing the office early on Friday for a social hour was dropped long ago. Unfortunately, the tension in the office runs pretty high some days due to unbearable time pressures and the lack of adequate staff. Nighttime and weekend work have become the norm rather than the exception.

Overall, you have been pleasantly surprised by Joe's performance. Until recently he worked hard and consistently produced high-quality work. Furthermore, he frequently volunteered for special projects, made lots of suggestions for improving the work environment, and demonstrated an in-depth practical knowledge of architecture and the construction business. However, during the past few months, he has definitely slacked off. He doesn't seem as excited about his work, and several times you have found him daydreaming at his desk. In addition, he has gotten into several heated arguments with architects about the specifications and proper design procedures for recent projects.

After one of these disagreements, you overheard Joe complaining to his officemate, "No one around here respects my opinion; I'm just a lowly draftsman. I know as much as these hotshot architects, but because I don't have the degree, they ignore my input, and I'm stuck doing the grunt work. Adding insult to injury, my wife has had to get a job to help support our family. I must be the lowest-paid person in this firm." In response to a question from a coworker regarding why he didn't pursue a college degree in architecture, Joe responded, "Do you have any idea how hard it is to put bread on the table, pay a Seattle mortgage, work overtime, be a reasonably good father and husband, plus go to night school? Come, on, be realistic!"

Exercises

EXERCISE 5.2   Making Choices about Rewards

OBJECTIVES

1. To illustrate individual differences in reward preferences
2. emphasize how both extrinsic and intrinsic rewards are considered important
3. To enable people to explore the reasons for the reward preferences of others

STARTING THE EXERCISE

Initially individuals will work alone establishing their own lists of reward preferences after reviewing Exhibit 5.8. Then the instructor will set up groups of four to six students to examine individual preferences and complete the exercise.

EXHIBIT 5.8   Some Possible Rewards for Employees

Company picnics	Smile from manager	Vacation trips for performance
Watches	Feedback on performance	Manager asking for advice
Trophies	Feedback on career progress	Informal leader asking for advice
Piped-in music	Larger office	Office with a window
Job challenge	Club privileges	The privilege of completing a job from start to finish
Achievement opportunity	More prestigious job	
Time off for performance	More job involvement	
Vacation	Use of company recreation facilities	
Autonomy		
Pay increase	Participation in decisions	
Recognition	Stock options	

The Facts

It is possible to develop an endless list of on-the-job rewards. Presented in a random fashion in Exhibit 5.8 are some of the rewards that could be available to employees.

Exercise Procedures

Phase I: **25 minutes**

1. Each individual should set up from Exhibit 5.8 a list of extrinsic and intrinsic rewards.
2. Each person should then rank-order from most important to least important the two lists.
3. From the two lists, rank the eight most important rewards. How many are extrinsic, and how many are intrinsic?

Phase II: **30 minutes**

1. The instructor will set up groups of four to six individuals.
2. The two lists in which the extrinsic and intrinsic categories were developed should be discussed.
3. The final rank orders of the eight most important rewards should be placed on a board or chart at the front of the room.
4. The rankings should be discussed within the groups. What major differences are displayed?

Cases

CASE 5.1   The Politics of Performance Appraisal

Every Friday, Max Steadman, Jim Coburn, Lynne Sims, and Tom Hamilton meet at Charley's after work for drinks. The four friends work as managers at Eckel Industries, a manufacturer of arc-welding equipment in Minneapolis. The one-plant company employs about 2,000 people. The four managers work in the manufacturing division. Max, 35, manages the company's 25 quality-control inspectors. Lynne, 33, works as a supervisor in inventory management. Jim, 34, is a first-line supervisor in the metal coating department. Tom, 28, supervises a team of assemblers. The four managers' tenure at Eckel Industries ranges from 1 year (Tom) to 12 years (Max).

The group is close-knit; Lynne, Jim, and Max's friendship stems from their years as undergraduate business students at the University of Minnesota. Tom, the newcomer, joined the group after meeting the three at an Eckel management seminar last year. Weekly get-togethers at Charley's have become a comfortable habit for the group and provide an opportunity to relax, exchange the latest gossip heard around the plant, and give and receive advice about problems encountered on the job.

This week's topic of discussion: performance appraisal, specifically the company's annual review process, which the plant's management conducted in the last week. Each of the four managers completed evaluation forms (graphic rating scales) on all of his or her subordinates and met with each subordinate to discuss the appraisal.

TOM: This was the first time I've appraised my people, and I dreaded it. For me, it's been the worst week of the year. Evaluating is difficult; it's highly subjective and inexact. Your emotions creep into the process. I got angry at one of my assembly workers last week, and I still felt the anger when I was filling out the evaluation forms. Don't tell me that my frustration with the guy didn't bias my appraisal. I think it did. And I think the technique is flawed. Tell me—what's the difference between a five and a six on "cooperation"?

JIM: The scales are a problem. So is memory. Remember our course in human resources in college? Dr. Philips said that according to research, when we sit down to evaluate someone's performance in the past year, we will only be able to actively recall and use 15 percent of the performance we actually observed.

LYNNE: I think political considerations are always a part of the process. I know I consider many other factors besides a person's actual performance when I appraise him.

TOM: Like what?

LYNNE: Like the appraisal will become part of his permanent written record that affects his career. Like the person I evaluate today, I have to work with tomorrow. Given that, the difference between a five and a six on cooperation isn't that relevant, because frankly, if a five makes him mad and he's happy with a six. . . .

MAX: Then you give him the six. Accuracy is important, but I'll admit it—accuracy isn't my primary objective when I evaluate my workers. My objective is to motivate and reward them so they'll perform better. I use the review process to do what's best for my people and my department. If that means fine-tuning the evaluations to do that, I will.

TOM: What's an example of fine-tuning?

MAX: Jim, do you remember three years ago when the company lowered the ceiling on merit raises? The top merit increase that any employee could get was 4 percent. I boosted the ratings of my folks to get the best merit increases for them. The year before that, the ceiling was 8 percent. The best they could get was less than what most of them received the year before. I felt they deserved the 4 percent, so I gave the marks that got them what I felt they deserved.

LYNNE: I've inflated ratings to encourage someone who is having personal problems but is normally a good em-ployee. A couple of years ago, one of my better people was going through a painful divorce, and it was showing in her work. I don't think it's fair to kick someone when they're down, even if their work is poor. I felt a good rating would speed her recovery.

TOM: Or make her complacent.

LYNNE: No, I don't think so. I felt she realized her work was suffering. I wanted to give her encouragement; it was my way of telling her she had some support and that she wasn't in danger of losing her job.

JIM: There's another situation where I think fine-tuning is merited—when someone's work has been mediocre or even poor for most of the year, but it improves substantially in the last two, three months or so. If I think the guy is really trying and is doing much better, I'd give him a rating that's higher than his work over the whole year deserves. It encourages him to keep improving. If I give him a mediocre rating, what does that tell him?

TOM: What if he's really working hard, but not doing so great?

JIM: If I think he has what it takes, I'd boost the rating to motivate him to keep trying until he gets there.

MAX: I know of one or two managers who've inflated ratings to get rid of a pain in the neck, some young guy who's transferred in and thinks he'll be there a short time. He's not good, but thinks he is and creates all sorts of problems. Or his performance is OK, but he just doesn't fit in with the rest of the department. A year or two of good ratings is a sure trick for getting rid of him.

TOM: Yes, but you're passing the problem on to someone else.

MAX: True, but it's no longer my problem.

TOM: All the examples you've talked about involve inflating evaluations. What about deflating them, giving someone less than you really think he deserves? Is that justified?

LYNNE: I'd hesitate to do that, because it can create problems. It can backfire.

MAX: But it does happen. You can lower a guy's ratings to shock him, to jolt him into performing better. Sometimes, you can work with someone, coach him, try to help him improve, and it just doesn't work. A basement-level rating can tell him you mean business. You can say that isn't fair, and for the time being, it isn't. But what if you feel that if the guy doesn't shape up, he faces being fired in a year or two, and putting him in the cellar, ratingswise, will solve his problem? It's fair in the long run if the effect is that he improves his work and keeps his job.

JIM: Sometimes, you get someone who's a real rebel, who always questions you, sometimes even oversteps his bounds. I think deflating his evaluation is merited just to remind him who's the boss.

LYNNE: I'd consider lowering someone's true rating if they've had a long record of rather questionable performance, and I think the best alternative for the person is to consider another job with another company. A low appraisal sends him a message to consider quitting and start looking for another job.

MAX: What if you believe the situation is hopeless, and you've made up your mind that you're going to fire the guy as soon as you've found a suitable replacement. The courts have chipped away at management's right to fire. Today, when you fire someone, you'd better have a strong case. I think once a manager decides to fire, appraisals become very negative. Anything good that you say about the subordinate can be used later against you. Deflating the ratings protects you from being sued and sometimes speeds up the termination process.

TOM: I understand your points, but I still believe that accuracy is the top priority in performance appraisal. Let me play devil's advocate for a minute. First, Jim, you complained about our memory limitations introducing a bias into appraisal. Doesn't introducing politics into the process further distort the truth by introducing yet another bias? Even more important, most would agree that one key to motivating people is providing true feedback—the facts about how they're doing so they know where they stand. Then you talk with them about how to improve their performance. When you distort an evaluation—however slightly—are you providing this kind of feedback?

MAX: I think you're overstating the degree of fine-tuning.

TOM: Distortion, you mean.

MAX: No, fine-tuning. I'm not talking about giving a guy a seven when he deserves a two, or vice versa. It's not that extreme. I'm talking about making slight changes in the ratings when you think that the change can make a big difference in terms of achieving what you think is best for the person and for your department.

TOM: But when you fine-tune, you're manipulating your people. Why not give them the most accurate evaluation and let the chips fall where they may? Give them the facts and let them decide.

MAX: Because most of good managing is psychology. Understanding people, their strengths and shortcomings. Knowing how to motivate, reward, and act to do what's in their and your department's best interest. And sometimes, total accuracy is not the best path. Sometimes, it's not in anybody's best interest.

JIM: All this discussion raises a question. What's the difference between fine-tuning and significant distortion? Where do you draw the line?

LYNNE: That's about as easy a question as what's the difference between a five and a six. On the form, I mean.

QUESTIONS:

1. Based on your view of the objectives of performance evaluation, evaluate the perspectives about performance appraisal presented by the managers.
2. In your opinion, at what point does "fine-tuning" evaluations become unacceptable distortion?
3. Assume you are the vice president of human resources at Eckel Industries and that you are aware that fine-tuning evaluations is a prevalent practice among Eckel managers. If you disagree with this perspective, what steps would you take to reduce the practice?

6

Chapter

Job Design

After completing Chapter 6, you should be able to:

Learning Objectives

- Describe the relationship between job design and quality of work life.

- Identify the key elements linking job design and performance.

- Define the term *job analysis*.

- Compare the job design concepts of range and depth.

- Describe what is meant by perceived job content.

- Identify the different types of job performance outcomes.

- Compare job rotation with job enlargement.

- Discuss several approaches to job enrichment.

We have seen in earlier chapters that a multitude of factors may affect job performance: Skills and abilities, perceptions, attitudes, and personality characteristics are all examples of previously discussed individual differences that play a role in shaping performance. Additionally, the direction, intensity, and persistence of an individual's motivation play a critical role, as does the evaluation and reward system that is used. In this chapter we will examine another critical variable: job design.

The jobs that people perform in organizations are the building blocks of all organization structures. In fact, organizations exist to enable people to do work in assigned jobs. The phrase *Let's get organized!* usually means that we need to clarify what job each individual should be doing. But we are also interested in performing jobs effectively and we need to understand the causes of effective and ineffective job performance.

A major cause of effective job performance is job design—what we get when we clarify what each employee should be doing. In a more technical sense, job design refers to the process by which managers decide individual job tasks and authority. Apart from the very practical issues associated with job design (that is, issues that relate to effectiveness in economic, political, and monetary terms), we can appreciate its importance in social and psychological terms. Jobs can be sources of psychological stress and even mental and physical impairment. On a more positive note, jobs can provide income, meaningful life experiences, self-esteem, esteem from others, regulation of our lives, and association with others. Thus, the well-being of organizations and people relates to how well management designs jobs.

This chapter describes some of the many theories and practices that deal with job design and redesign. We must understand the implication of the term **job redesign** in the context of our discussion. It means that management has decided that it's worthwhile to reconsider what employees are expected to do on the job. In some instances, the redesign effort may be nothing more than requiring the individual to use a computer rather than a calculator to do clerical work. In other instances, the redesign effort may require the individual to work with other employees in a team effort rather than to work alone on the task. The contemporary trend in organizations is to redesign jobs that require individuals to work together in groups. Whether Americans can work effectively in groups is the controversial issue.

In contrast to job redesign, job design refers to the first instance in which management creates a job by specifying its duties and responsibilities. But with the passage of time and the development of new tools and processes, management's expectations for that job will change (i.e., it will be redesigned). We should understand job design to be an ongoing, dynamic process. *Thus we will use the term* job design *to refer to any and all managerial efforts to create jobs whether initially or subsequently.*

We begin the discussion of job design by introducing the issue of quality of work life. As is apparent to anyone who has ever worked, what we do on the job plays a major role in our social, health, and psychological statuses as well as our economic standing. After introducing the relationships between job design and quality of work life, we'll address the more technical aspects of job design.

JOB DESIGN AND QUALITY OF WORK LIFE

The concept of **quality of work life** (QWL) is widely used to refer to "a philosophy of management that enhances the dignity of all workers; introduces changes in an organization's culture; and improves the physical and emotional well-being of employees (e.g., providing opportunities for growth and development)."[1] Indicators of quality of work life include accident rates, sick leave usage, employee turnover, and number of grievances filed.[2] In some organizations, QWL programs are intended to increase employee trust, involvement, and problem solving so as to increase both worker satisfaction and organizational effectiveness.[3] Thus, the concept and application of QWL are broad and involve more than jobs, but the jobs that people do are important sources of satisfaction. It is not surprising to find that the quality of work life concept embodies theories and ideas of the human relations movement of the 1950s and the job enrichment efforts of the 60s and 70s.

The continuing challenge to management is to provide for quality of work life and to improve production, quality, and efficiency through revitalization of business and industry. At present, the trade-offs between the gains in human terms from improved quality of work life and the gains in economic terms from revitalization aren't fully known. Some believe that we must defer quality of work life efforts so as to make the American economy more productive and efficient.[4] Others observe that the sense of urgency to become more competitive in domestic and overseas trade presents opportunities to combine quality of life and reindustrialization efforts.[5] To those ends, job design can play a vital role.

Job design attempts (1) to identify the most important needs of employees and the organization and (2) to remove obstacles in the workplace that frustrate those needs. Managers hope that the results are jobs that (1) fulfill important individual needs and (2) contribute to individual, group, and organizational effectiveness. Managers are, in fact, designing jobs for teams and groups. Some studies have reported that employees who participate in teams get greater satisfaction from their jobs.[6] But other studies report contrary results.[7] So we're left with the uncomfortable, but realistic, conclusion that quality of work life improvements through job design cannot be ensured in specific instances. Obviously, designing jobs is complex. This chapter reviews the important theories, research, and practices of job

---

1Richard E. Kopelman, "Job Redesign and Productivity: A Review of the Evidence," *National Productivity Review,* Summer 1985, p. 239.

2Blake E. Ashforth, Glen E. Kreiner, and Mel Fugate, "All in a Day's Work: Boundaries and Micro Role Transitions," *Academy of Management Review,* July 2000, pp. 472–91.

3Paul Osterman, "How Common Is Workplace Transformation and Who Adopts it?" *Industrial and Labor Relations Review,* January 1994, pp. 173–88; and Harry C. Katz, Thomas A. Kochan, and Mark R. Weber, "Assessing the Effects of Industrial Relations Systems and Efforts to Improve the Quality of Working Life on Organizational Effectiveness," *Academy of Management Journal,* September 1985, pp. 514–15.

4Ed Diener and Don R. Rahtz (eds.), *Advances in Quality of Life Theory and Research* (Boston: Kluiver, 2000).

5Tarek M. Khalil, *Management of Technology: The Key to Competitiveness and Wealth Creation* (New York: McGraw-Hill, 2000).

6Vishwanath V. Baba and Muhammad Jamal, "Routinization of Job Context and Job Content as Related to Employees' Quality of Working Life: A Study of Canadian Nurses," *Journal of Organizational Behavior,* September 1991, pp. 379–86; Barry M. Staw, Robert I. Sutton, and Lisa H. Pelled, "Employee Positive Emotion and Favorable Outcomes at the Workplace," *Organization Science,* February 1994, pp. 51–71.

7Robert T. Goliembiewski and Ben-Chu Sun, "QWL Applications in Public Agencies: Do Success Rates Reflect a Positive-Findings Bias? " *International Journal of Public Administration,* Vol. 15, No. 6 (1992), pp. 1263–79; and Robert T. Goliembiewski and Ben-Chu Sun, "Positive-Findings Bias in QWL Studies: Rigor and Outcomes in a Large Sample," *Journal of Management,* September 1990, pp. 665–74.

design. As will be seen, contemporary management has at its disposal a wide range of techniques that facilitate the achievement of personal and organizational performance.

A CONCEPTUAL MODEL OF JOB DESIGN

The conceptual model in Exhibit 6.1 is based upon extensive research and practical experience. The model includes the various terms and concepts appearing in the current literature. When linked together these concepts describe the important determinants of job performance and organizational effectiveness. The model takes into account a number of sources of complexity. It recognizes that individuals react differently to jobs. While one person may derive positive satisfaction from a job, another may not. It also recognizes the difficult trade-offs between organizational and individual needs. For example, the technology of manufacturing (an environmental difference) may dictate that management adopt assembly-line mass production methods and low-skilled jobs to achieve optimal efficiency. Such jobs, however, may result in great unrest and worker discontent. Perhaps these costs could be avoided by carefully balancing organizational and individual needs.

The ideas reflected in Exhibit 6.1 are the bases for this chapter. We'll present each important cause or effect of job design, beginning with the end result of job design, **job performance**.

JOB PERFORMANCE OUTCOMES

Case 6.1

The Hovey and Beard Company Case

Job performance includes a number of outcomes. In this section we'll discuss performance outcomes that have value to the organization and to the individual.

Objective Outcomes

Quantity and quality of output, absenteeism, tardiness, and turnover are objective outcomes that can be measured in quantitative terms. For each job, implicit or explicit standards exist for each of these objective outcomes. Industrial engineering studies establish standards for daily quantity, and quality control specialists establish tolerance limits for acceptable quality. These aspects of job performance account for characteristics of the product, client, or service for which the jobholder is responsible. But job performance includes other outcomes.

Personal Behavior Outcomes

The jobholder reacts to the work itself. She reacts by either attending regularly or being absent, by staying with the job or by quitting. Moreover, physiological and health-related problems can ensue as a consequence of job performance. Stress related to job performance can contribute to physical and mental impairment; accidents and occupation-related disease can also result.

Intrinsic and Extrinsic Outcomes

Job outcomes include intrinsic and extrinsic work outcomes. The distinction between intrinsic and extrinsic outcomes is important for understanding people's reactions to their jobs. In a general sense, an intrinsic outcome is an object or

EXHIBIT 6.1   **Job Design and Job Performance**

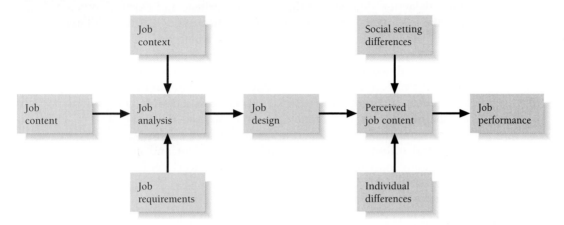

event that follows from the worker's own efforts and doesn't require the involvement of any other person. More simply, it's an outcome clearly related to action on the worker's part. Contemporary job design theory defines *intrinsic motivation* in terms of the employee's "empowerment" to achieve outcomes from the application of individual ability and talent.[8] Such outcomes typically are thought to be solely in the province of professional and technical jobs; yet all jobs potentially have opportunities for intrinsic outcomes. Such outcomes involve feelings of responsibility, challenge, and recognition; they result from such job characteristics as variety, autonomy, identity, and significance.[9]

Extrinsic outcomes, however, are objects or events that follow from the workers' own efforts in conjunction with other factors or persons not directly involved in the job itself. Pay, working conditions, coworkers, and even supervision are objects in the workplace that are potentially job outcomes, but that aren't a fundamental part of the work. Dealing with others and friendship interactions are sources of extrinsic outcomes.

Most jobs provide opportunities for both intrinsic and extrinsic outcomes so we must understand the relationship between the two. It's generally held that extrinsic rewards reinforce intrinsic rewards in a positive direction when the individual can attribute the source of the extrinsic reward to her own efforts. For example, a pay raise (extrinsic reward) increases feeling good about oneself if the cause of the raise is thought to be one's own efforts and competence and not favoritism by the boss. This line of reasoning explains why some individuals get no satisfaction out of sharing in the gains derived from group effort rather than individual effort.[10]

[8]Kenneth W. Thomas and Betty A. Velthouse, "Cognitive Elements of Empowerment: An 'Interpretive' Model of Intrinsic Task Motivation," *Academy of Management Review,* October 1990, pp. 666–81.

[9]Aaron A. Buchko, "Effects of Employee Ownership on Employee Attitudes—A Test of Three Theoretical Perspectives," *Work and Occupations,* February 1992, pp. 59–78.

[10]Jon R. Katzenberg, *Peak Performance: Aligning the Hearts and Minds of Your Employees* (Boston: Harvard Business School Press, 2000).

Job Satisfaction Outcomes

Job satisfaction depends on the levels of intrinsic and extrinsic outcomes and how the jobholder views those outcomes. These outcomes have different values for different people. For some people, responsible and challenging work may have neutral or even negative value depending upon their education and prior experience with work providing intrinsic outcomes.[11] For other people, such work outcomes may have high positive values. People differ in the importance they attach to job outcomes. Those differences alone would account for different levels of job satisfaction for essentially the same job tasks. For example, one company that has initiated management systems intended to provide employees with a great deal of opportunity for exercising judgment and making decisions has found many individuals unable or unwilling to work for it. The company, W. L. Gore & Associates, has been the subject of considerable interest among those who advocate employee empowerment.[12]

www.gore.com

Other important individual differences include job involvement and commitment to the organization.[13] People differ in the extent that (1) work is a central life interest, (2) they actively participate in work, (3) they perceive work as central to self-esteem, and (4) they perceive work as consistent with self-concept. Persons who are not involved in their work or the organizations that employ them cannot be expected to realize the same satisfaction as those who are. This variable accounts for the fact that two workers could report different levels of satisfaction for the same performance levels.

A final individual difference is the perceived equity of the outcome in terms of what the jobholder considers a fair reward.[14] If outcomes are perceived to be unfair in relation to those of others in similar jobs requiring similar effort, the jobholder will experience dissatisfaction and seek means to restore the equity, either by seeking greater rewards (primarily extrinsic) or by reducing effort.

Thus, we see that job performance includes many potential outcomes. Some are of primary value to the organization—the objective outcomes, for example. Other outcomes (such as job satisfaction) are of primary importance to the individual. Job performance is without doubt a complex variable that depends upon the interplay of numerous factors. Managers can make some sense of the issue by understanding the motivational implications of jobs through the application of job analysis.[15]

---

[11]Joan Magretta (ed.), *Managing in the New Economy* (Cambridge, MA: Harvard Business Review Book, 1999).

[12]Frank Shipper and Charles C. Manz, "Employee Self-Management without Formally Designated Teams: An Alternative Road to Empowerment," *Organizational Dynamics,* Winter 1992, pp. 48–61.

[13]S. D. Saleh and James Hosek, "Job Involvement: Concepts and Measurements," *Academy of Management Journal,* June 1976, pp. 213–24; and Robert J. Vandenberg and Charles E. Lance, "Examining the Causal Order of Job Satisfaction and Organizational Commitment," *Journal of Management,* March 1992, pp. 153–67.

[14]Glenn Bassett, "The Case against Job Satisfaction," *Business Horizons,* May/June 1994, pp. 61–68; Jill Kanin-Lovers and Gordon Spunich, "Compensation and the Job Satisfaction Equation," *Journal of Compensation and Benefits,* January–February 1992, pp. 54–57.

[15]Stephen Bach and Keith Sisson (eds.), *Personnel Management: A Comprehensive Guide to Theory and Practice* (Malden, MA: Blackwell, 2000).

JOB ANALYSIS

The purpose of **job analysis** is to provide an objective description of the job itself.[16] The result of a job analysis is a job description. Individuals who perform job analysis gather information about three aspects of all jobs: job content, job requirements, and job context. Many different job analysis methods help managers identify content, requirements, and context. One study suggests that these methods can be classified into four categories (mechanistic, motivational, biological, and perceptual-motor) depending upon the primary focus and intent.[17] Here we'll be concerned only with understanding the three general aspects of all jobs.[18]

Job Content

Job content refers to the activities required of the job. Depending upon the specific job analysis used, this description can be broad or narrow in scope. The description can vary from general statements of job activities down to highly detailed statements of each and every hand and body motion required to do the job. One widely used method, **functional job analysis (FJA)**, describes jobs in terms of:

1. What the worker does in relation to data, people, and jobs
2. What methods and techniques the worker uses
3. What machines, tools, and equipment the worker uses
4. What materials, products, subject matter, or services the worker produces

The first three aspects relate to job activities. The fourth aspect relates to job performance. FJA provides descriptions of jobs that can be the bases for classifying jobs according to any one of the four dimensions. In addition to defining what activities, methods, and machines make up the job, FJA also defines what the individual doing the job should produce. FJA can, therefore, be the basis for defining standards of performance.

FJA is the most popular and widely used of the job analysis methods.[19] In addition, it's the basis for the most extensive available list of occupational titles.[20]

Job Requirements

Job requirements refer to education, experience, licenses, and other personal characteristics that are expected of an individual if he's to perform the job content. In recent years, the idea has emerged that job requirements should also identify skills, abilities, knowledge, and other personal characteristics required

---

[16]Ibid.

[17]Michael A. Campion and Paul W. Thayer, "Job Design: Approaches, Outcomes, and Trade-offs," *Organizational Dynamics*, Winter 1987, pp. 66–79, and Michael A. Campion, "Interdisciplinary Approaches to Job Design: A Constructive Replication with Extensions," *Journal of Applied Psychology*, August 1988, pp. 467–81.

[18]Frank Ostroff, *The Horizontal Organization: What the Organization of the Future Actually Looks Like and How It's Believers Value to Customers* (London: Oxford University Press, 1999).

[19]G. Jonathan Meng, "Using Job Descriptions, Performance and Pay Innovations to Support Quality," *National Productivity Review*, Spring 1992, pp. 247–55.

[20]Ibid.

to perform the job content in the particular setting. One widely used method, **position analysis questionnaire (PAQ)**, takes into account these human factors through analysis of the following job aspects:

1. Information sources critical to job performance
2. Information processing and decision making critical to job performance
3. Physical activity and dexterity required of the job
4. Interpersonal relationships required of the job
5. Reactions of individuals to working conditions[21]

The position analysis questionnaire can be adapted to jobs of all types, including managerial jobs.[22]

Job Context

Job context refers to factors such as the physical demands and working conditions of the job, the degree of accountability and responsibility, the extent of supervision required or exercised, and the consequences of error. Job context describes the environment within which the job is to be performed.

Numerous methods exist to perform job analysis. Different methods can give different answers to important questions such as "How much is the job worth?"[23] Thus, selecting the method for performing job analysis isn't trivial—it's one of the most important decisions in job design.[24] Survey of expert job analysts' opinions bear out the popularity of PAQ and FJA.[25]

Job Analysis in Different Settings

People perform their jobs in a variety of settings—too many to discuss them all. We'll instead discuss two significant job settings: the factory and the office. One has historical significance, the other has future significance.

Jobs in the Factory   Job analysis began in the factory. Industrialization created the setting in which individuals perform many hundreds of specialized jobs.

---

[21]E. J. McCormick, *Job Analysis: Methods and Applications* (New York: AMACOM, 1979); and E. J. McCormick, P. R. Jeanneret, and R. C. Mecham, "A Study of Job Characteristics and Job Dimensions as Based on the Position Analysis Questionnaire (PAQ)," *Journal of Applied Psychology*, August 1972, pp. 347–68.

[22]James Sparrow, "The Utility of PAQ in Relating Job Behaviours to Traits," *Journal of Occupational Psychology* (UK), June 1989, pp. 151–62, and Angelo S. DeNisi, Edwin T. Cornelius III, and Allyn G. Blencoe, "Further Investigation of Common Knowledge Effects on Job Analysis Ratings," *Journal of Applied Psychology*, May 1987, pp. 262–68.

[23]Robert M. Madigan and David J. Hoover, "Effects of Alternative Job Evaluation Methods on Decisions Involving Pay Equity," *Academy of Management Journal*, March 1986, pp. 84–100; Edward H. Lawler III, "What's Wrong with Point-Factor Job Evaluation," *Personnel*, January 1987, pp. 38–4; and Howard W. Risher, "Job Evaluation: Validity and Reliability," *Compensation and Benefits*, January–February, 1989, pp. 22–36.

[24]Philip C. Grant, "What Use Is a Job Description?" *Personnel Journal*, February 1988, pp. 44–65.

[25]Jai V. Ghorpade, *Job Analysis: A Handbook for the Human Resource Director* (Englewood Cliffs, NJ: Prentice-Hall, 1988), and Edward L. Levine, Ronald A. Ash, Hardy Hall, and Frank Sistrunk, "Evaluation of Job Analysis Methods by Experienced Job Analysts," *Academy of Management Journal*, June 1983, pp. 339–48.

Management Pointer 6.1

**ADVICE ON WHAT MANAGERS
SHOULD DO FROM
F. W. TAYLOR**

F. W. Taylor stated that managers should undertake specific activities if they were to be effective. In fact he noted four distinct principles they should adopt as follows:

First: Develop a science for each element of a man's work that replaces the old rule-of-thumb method.

Second: Scientifically select and then train, teach, and develop the workman, whereas in the past he chose his own work and trained himself as best he could.

Third: Heartily cooperate with the men so as to ensure that all of the work is done in accordance with the principles of the science that has been developed.

Fourth: There is almost an equal division of the work and the responsibility between management and workmen. Management takes over all work for which it's better fitted than workmen, while in the past, almost all of the work and the greater part of the responsibility were thrown upon workmen.[27]

These four principles express the theme of scientific management methods. Management should take into account task and technology to determine the best way for each job and then train people to do the job that way.

The earliest attempts to do job analysis followed the ideas advanced by the proponents of scientific management. They were industrial engineers who, at the turn of the 20th century, began to devise ways to analyze industrial jobs. The major theme of scientific management is that objective analyses of facts and data collected in the workplace could provide the bases for determining the one best way to design work.[26] Even though Taylor was writing almost 100 years ago, his advice to managers still has considerable validity as noted in the following Management Pointer 6.1.[27]

Scientific management produced many techniques in current use. Motion and time study, work simplification, and standard methods are at the core of job analysis in factory settings. Although the mechanistic approach to job analysis is widespread, many service organizations as well as manufacturers are discovering some of the negative consequences of jobs that are overly routine as the following Organizational Encounter 6.1 suggests.[28]

Consequently, many organizations are turning away from the idea of one person doing one specialized job. As we'll learn later in the chapter, many manufacturing firms are now analyzing jobs to determine the extent to which content and requirements can be increased to tap a larger portion of the individual's talents and abilities.

Jobs in the Office in the New Economy   In the short space of time since the advent of scientific management, the American economy has shifted from factory-oriented to office-oriented work to what is designated the new economy, service oriented, virtual work, and rapidly changing environment. The fastest growing segment of jobs is secretarial, clerical, and information workers. The growth of these jobs is due to technological breakthroughs in both factory and office settings.

Technological breakthroughs in automation, robotics, and computer-assisted manufacturing have reduced the number of manufacturing jobs. But that same technology has increased the need for office technical, and information technology jobs. Still, the modern office isn't a mere extension of the traditional factory. The modern office reflects new computer technology. Its most striking feature is the replacement of paper with some electronic medium, usually a visual display

---

[26]The literature of scientific management is voluminous. The original works and the subsequent criticisms and interpretations would make a large volume. Of special significance are the works of the principal authors including Frederick W. Taylor, *Principles of Scientific Management* (New York: Harper & Row, 1911); Harrington Emerson, *The Twelve Principles of Efficiency* (New York: Engineering Magazine, 1913); Henry L. Gantt, *Industrial Leadership* (New Haven, CT: Yale University Press, 1916); Frank B. Gilbreth, *Motion Study* (New York: D. Van Nostrand, 1911); and Lillian M. Gilbreth, *The Psychology of Management* (New York: Sturgis & Walton, 1914).

[27]Taylor, *Principles*, pp. 36–37.

[28]Larry D. Grieshaber, Patricia Parker, and Judy Deering, "Job Satisfaction of Nursing Assistants in Long-Term Care," *Health Care Supervisor,* June 1995, pp. 18–28.

Organizational Encounter 6.1

Motorola's Experience with Total Quality Management and Flexible Jobs

Motorola has been a leader in the adoption of less mechanistic jobs. The company learned in the mid-1980s that its products weren't competitive in the global market and that the primary cause for this poor quality was the way the company had traditionally designed jobs. Motorola's search for quality was triggered by its winning an antidumping suit against Japanese manufacturers of cellular phones. But that suit did not solve Motorola's underlying problem of poor quality. The company's product was simply not up to the standards of competition, so product quality improvement became the most important management problem to solve. Management responded by shifting responsibility for quality control from inspectors at the end of the assembly line to individual production workers. Then, to encourage individual workers to learn to understand and do all the jobs on the line so as to recognize potential and actual sources of quality failures, Motorola revised its compensation plan to reward individuals who learned a variety of jobs. The effect was to increase the content and requirements of the production workers' jobs and to decrease the rate of product failure by 77 percent.

These developments were the early evidence of Motorola's commitment to quality and to the ideas of total quality management (TQM). Since 1985, Motorola has invested heavily in employee training and education and has been a national leader in pushing for greater appreciation of TQM. Although Motorola uses modern technology and sophisticated computer applications in its production departments, it maintains that the primary source of its gains is employees who have taken on the responsibility for bigger jobs with greater responsibility.

www.
motorola
com

Source: Robert W. Galvin, "Quality Thinking," *Executive Excellence*, February 1997, pp. 15–16; Bob Carroll, "The Power of Empowered Teams," *National Productivity Review*, Autumn 1996, pp. 85–92; and Boudewijn Bertsch and Roger Williams, "How Multinational CEOs Make Change Programmes Stick," *Long Range Planning*, October 1994, pp. 12–24.

terminal (VDT). One individual interacts with the VDT to do a variety of tasks that in earlier times would have required many individuals. A significant aspect of job analysis in modern offices is the creation of work modules; interrelated tasks that can be assigned to a single individual.

In recent times, managers and researchers have found that human factors must be given special attention when analyzing jobs in the electronic office. VDT operators report that they suffer visual and postural problems such as headaches, burning eyes, and shoulder and backaches.[29] The sources of these problems seem to be in the design of the workplace, particularly the interaction between the individual and the VDT.

Job analysis in the office must pay particular attention to human factors. The tendency is to overemphasize the technological factor—in this case, the computer—and to analyze jobs only as extensions of the technology. As was true of job analysis in factories, it's simply easier to deal with the relatively fixed nature of tasks and technology than to deal with the variable of human nature.[30]

In the new economy, the reliance on job analysis and specific job descriptions may be altered significantly. Today an emphasis on speed, information processing, and the influence of computer technology has resulted in criticisms of pas-

---

[29]Douglas R. May and Catherine E. Schwoerer, "Employee Health by Design: Using Employee Involvement Teams in Ergonomic Job Redesign," *Personnel Psychology*, Winter 1994, pp. 861–76, and Larry Reynolds, "Ergonomic Concerns Stiffen Rules Regarding VDT Use," *Personnel*, April 1991, pp. 1–2.

[30]Rob Cross and Lloyd Baird, "Technology Is Not Enough: Improving Performance by Building Organizational Memory," *Sloan Management Review*, Spring 2000, pp. 69–78.

sive job descriptions or broadly stated descriptions of what a person or team is expected to do to service customers, contribute to the firm's profit, and gain market share. In the new economy thinking a worker will be expected to do what is needed. Adhering to a narrow job description is not going to be sufficient in a world pressed by constant change.[31]

William Bridges, author of *Job Shift*, foresees a shift from narrow job classifications and descriptions to a work environment in which "work" is emphasized.[32] He believes that a continuum exists, with work at one end that needs clear job descriptions (e.g., nuclear power plant technician). The work specifics need to be crystal clear. On the other side of the continuum there are whole industries (e.g., software, dot-com, consulting) in which job descriptions are stifling. Work gets done in cross-functional teams or parts of it are outsourced. The word *job* is too narrow.[33] Many industries in which technology is rendering place and time as less important are moving away from "job" identities to "work," "project," or "team" entities.

JOB DESIGNS: THE RESULTS OF JOB ANALYSIS

Job designs are the results of job analysis. They specify three characteristics of jobs: range, depth, and relationships.

Range and Depth

Job range refers to the number of tasks a jobholder performs. The individual who performs eight tasks to complete a job has a wider job range than a person performing four tasks. In most instances, the greater the number of tasks performed, the longer it takes to complete the job.

A second characteristic is **job depth**, the amount of discretion an individual has to decide job activities and job outcomes. In many instances, job range relates to personal influence as well as delegated authority. Thus, an employee with the same job title who's at the same organizational level as another employee may possess more, less, or the same amount of job depth because of personal influence.

Job range and depth distinguish one job from another not only within the same organization, but also among different organizations. To illustrate how jobs differ in range and depth, Exhibit 6.2 depicts the differences for selected jobs of firms, hospitals, and universities. For example, business research scientists, hospital chiefs of surgery, and university presidents generally have high job range and significant depth. Research scientists perform a large number of tasks and are usually not closely supervised. Chiefs of surgery have significant job range in that they oversee and counsel on many diverse surgical matters. In addition, they aren't supervised closely and they have the authority to influence hospital surgery policies and procedures.

University presidents have a large number of tasks to perform. They speak to alumni groups, politicians, community representatives, and students. They

---

[31]Sharon Leonard, "The Demise of Job Descriptions," *HR Magazine,* August 2000, pp. 184–85.

[32]William Bridges, *Job Shift* (Reading, MA: Addison-Wesley, 1994).

[33]Caitlen P. Williams, "The End of the Job as We Know It," *Training & Development,* January 1999, pp. 52–54.

EXHIBIT 6.2   Job Depth and Range

High Depth

BUSINESS Packaging machine mechanics	HOSPITAL Anesthesiologists	UNIVERSITY College professors	BUSINESS Research scientists	HOSPITAL Chiefs of surgery	UNIVERSITY Presidents

Low Range   **High Range**

BUSINESS Assembly-line workers	HOSPITAL Bookkeepers	UNIVERSITY Graduate student instructors	BUSINESS Maintenance repairmen	HOSPITAL Nurses	UNIVERSITY Department chairpersons

Low Depth

develop, with the consultation of others, policies on admissions, fund raising, and adult education. They can alter the faculty recruitment philosophy and thus alter the course of the entire institution. For example, a university president may want to build an institution that's noted for high-quality classroom instruction and for providing excellent services to the community. This thrust may lead to recruiting and selecting professors who want to concentrate on these two specific goals. In contrast, another president may want to foster outstanding research and high-quality classroom instruction. Of course, yet another president may attempt to develop an institution that's noted for instruction, research, and service. The critical point is that university presidents have sufficient depth to alter the course of a university's direction.

Examples of jobs with high depth and low range are packaging machine mechanics, anesthesiologists, and faculty members. Mechanics perform the limited tasks that pertain to repairing and maintaining packaging machines. But they can decide how breakdowns on the packaging machine are to be repaired. The discretion means that the mechanics have relatively high job depth.

Anesthesiologists also perform a limited number of tasks. They are concerned with the rather restricted task of administering anesthetics to patients. However, they can decide the type of anesthetic to be administered in a particular situation, a decision indicative of high job depth. University professors specifically engaged in classroom instruction have relatively low job range. Teaching involves comparatively more tasks than the work of the anesthesiologist, yet fewer tasks than that of the business research scientist. However, professors' job depth is greater than graduate student instructors' since professors determine how they'll conduct the class, what materials will be presented, and the standards to be used in evaluating students. Graduate students typically don't have complete freedom in the choice of class materials and procedures. Professors decide these matters for them.

Highly specialized jobs are those having few tasks to accomplish by prescribed means. Such jobs are quite routine; they also tend to be controlled by specified rules and procedures (low depth). A highly despecialized job (high range) has many tasks to accomplish within the framework of discretion over means and ends (high depth). Within an organization, there typically are great differences among jobs in both range and depth. Although there are no precise equations that managers can use to decide job range and depth, they can follow this guideline: Given the economic and technical requirements of the organization's mission, goals, and objectives, what is the optimal point along the continuum of range and depth for each job?

Job Relationships

Job relationships are determined by managers' decisions regarding departmentalization bases and spans of control. The resulting groups become the responsibility of a manager to coordinate toward organization purposes. These decisions also determine the nature and extent of jobholders' interpersonal relationships, individually and within groups. As we already have seen in the discussion of groups in organizations, group performance is affected in part by group cohesiveness. And the degree of group cohesiveness depends upon the quality and kind of interpersonal relationships of jobholders assigned to a task or command group.

The wider the span of control, the larger the group and consequently the more difficult it is to establish friendship and interest relationships. Simply, people in larger groups are less likely to communicate (and interact sufficiently to form interpersonal ties) than people in smaller groups. Without the opportunity to communicate, people will be unable to establish cohesive work groups. Thus, an important source of satisfaction may be lost for individuals who seek to fulfill social and esteem needs through relationships with coworkers.

The basis for departmentalization that management selects also has important implications for job relationships. The functional basis places jobs with similar depth and range in the same groups, while product, territory, and customer bases place jobs with dissimilar depth and range. Thus, in functional departments, people will be doing much the same specialty. Product, territory, and customer departments, however, are comprised of jobs that are quite different and heterogeneous. Individuals who work in heterogeneous departments experience feelings of dissatisfaction, stress, and involvement more intensely than those in homogeneous, functional departments. People with homogeneous backgrounds, skills, and training have more common interests than those with heterogeneous ones. Thus, it's easier for them to establish social relationships that are satisfying with less stress, but also with less involvement in the department's activities.

Job designs describe the *objective* characteristics of jobs. That is, through job analysis techniques managers can design jobs in terms of required activities to produce a specified outcome. But yet another factor—perceived job content—must be considered before we can understand the relationship between jobs and performance.

THE WAY PEOPLE PERCEIVE THEIR JOBS

The way people do their jobs depends in part on how they perceive and think of their jobs. Even though Taylor proposed that the way to improve work (that is, to make it more efficient) is to determine (1) the "best way" to do a task (motion study) and (2) the standard time for completion of the task (time study), the actual performance of jobs goes beyond its technical description.

The belief that job design can be based solely on technical data ignores the very large role played by the individual who performs the job. Individuals differ pro-

Exercise 6.1

Job Design Preferences

foundly, as we noted in the chapter on individual differences. They come to work with different backgrounds, needs, and motivations. Once on the job, they experience the social setting in which the work is performed in unique ways. It's not surprising to find that different individuals perceive jobs differently.

Perceived job content refers to characteristics of a job that define its general nature as perceived by the jobholder. We must distinguish between a job's *objective properties* and its *subjective properties* as reflected in the perceptions of people who perform it.[34] Managers can't understand the causes of job performance without considering individual differences such as personality, needs, and span of attention.[35] Nor can managers understand the causes of job performance without considering the social setting in which the job is performed.[36] According to Exhibit 6.1, perceived job content precedes job performance. Thus, if managers desire to increase job performance by changing perceived job content, they can change job design, individual perceptions, or social settings—the causes of perceived job content.

If management is to understand perceived job content, some method for measuring it must exist.[37] In response to this need, organization behavior researchers have attempted to measure perceived job content in a variety of work settings. The methods that researchers use rely upon questionnaires that jobholders complete and that measure their perceptions of certain job characteristics.

Job Characteristics

The pioneering effort to measure perceived job content through employee responses to a questionnaire resulted in the identification of six characteristics: variety, autonomy, required interaction, optional interaction, knowledge and skill required, and responsibility.[38] The index of these six characteristics is termed the Requisite Task Attribute Index (RTAI). The original RTAI has been extensively reviewed and analyzed. One important development was the review by Hackman and Lawler, who revised the index to include six characteristics.[39]

Variety, task identity, and feedback are perceptions of job range. Autonomy is the perception of job depth; dealing with others and friendship opportunities reflect perceptions of job relationships. Employees sharing similar perceptions, job designs, and social settings should report similar job characteristics. Employees with different perceptions, however, report different job characteristics of the

[34]Kent W. Seibert, "Reflection-in-Action: Tools for Cultivating On-the-Job Learning Conditions," *Organizational Dynamics*, Winter 1999, pp. 54–65.

[35]Brett M. Wright and John L. Cordey, "Production Uncertainty as a Contextual Moderator of Employee Reactions to Job Design," *Journal of Applied Psychology*, June 1999, pp. 456–463.

[36]William H. Tuinley and Daniel C. Feldman, "The Impact of Psychological Contract Violations on Exit, Voice, Loyalty and Neglect," *Human Relations*, July 1999, pp. 895–922.

[37]Pere Joan Ferrando, "Likert Scaling using Continuous, Censored, and Graded Response Models: Effects on Criterion-Rated Validity," *Applied Psychological Measurement*, June 1999, pp. 161–75.

[38]Eugene F. Stone and Hal G. Gueuthal, "An Empirical Derivation of the Dimensions along which Characteristics of Jobs Are Perceived," *Academy of Management Journal*, June 1985, pp. 376–96; Arthur N. Turner and Paul R. Lawrence, *Industrial Jobs and the Worker: An Investigation of Response to Task Attributes* (Cambridge, MA: Harvard University Press, 1965), to be the source of contemporary measures of perceived job characteristics.

[39]J. Richard Hackman and Edward W. Lawler, III, "Employee Reactions to Job Characteristics," *Journal of Applied Psychology*, June 1971, pp. 259–86; and J. Richard Hackman and Greg R. Oldham, "Development of the Job Diagnostic Survey," *Journal of Applied Psychology*, April 1975, pp. 159–70.

same job. For example, an individual with a high need for social belonging would perceive "friendship opportunities" differently than another individual with a low need for social belonging.

Individual Differences

Individual differences "provide filters such that different persons perceive the same objective stimuli in different manners."[40] Individual differences in need for strength, particularly the strength of growth needs, have been shown to influence the perception of task variety. Employees with relatively weak higher-order needs are less concerned with performing a variety of tasks than are employees with relatively strong growth needs. Thus, managers expecting higher performance to result from increased task variety would be disappointed if the jobholders did not have strong growth needs. Even individuals with strong growth needs cannot respond continuously to the opportunity to perform more and more tasks. At some point, performance turns down as these individuals reach the limits imposed by their abilities and time. The relationship between performance and task variety (even for individuals with high growth needs) is likely to be curvilinear.[41]

Social Setting Differences

Differences in social settings of work also affect perceptions of job content. Examples of social setting differences include leadership style[42] and what other people say about the job.[43] As more than one research study has pointed out, how one perceives a job is greatly affected by what other people say about it. Thus, if one's friends state their jobs are boring, one is likely to state that his job is also boring. If the individual perceives the job as boring, job performance will no doubt suffer. Job content, then, results from the interaction of many factors in the work situation.

The field of organization behavior has advanced a number of suggestions for improving the motivational properties of jobs. Invariably, the suggestions, termed *job design strategies*, attempt to improve job performance through changes in actual job characteristics.[44] The next section reviews the more significant of these strategies.

DESIGNING JOB RANGE: JOB ROTATION AND JOB ENLARGEMENT

The earliest attempts to design jobs date to the scientific management era. Efforts at that time emphasized efficiency criteria. In so doing, the individual tasks that comprise a job are limited, uniform, and repetitive. This practice leads to narrow

---

[40]Randall B. Dunham, Ramon J. Aldag, and Arthur P. Brief, "Dimensionality of Task Design as Measured by the Job Diagnostic Survey," *Academy of Management Journal*, June 1977, p. 222.

[41]Joseph E. Champoux, "A Three Sample Test of Some Extensions to the Job Characteristics Model of Work Motivation," *Academy of Management Journal*, September 1980, pp. 466–78.

[42]Ricky W. Griffin, "Supervisory Behavior as a Source of Perceived Task Scope," *Journal of Occupational Psychology*, September 1981, pp. 175–82.

[43]Joe Thomas and Ricky W. Griffin, "The Social Information Processing Model of Task Design: A Review of the Literature," *Academy of Management Review*, October 1983, pp. 672–82; Ricky W. Griffin, "Objective and Subjective Sources of Information in Task Redesign: A Field Experiment," *Administrative Science Quarterly*, June 1983, pp. 184–200; and Jeffrey Pfeffer, "A Partial Test of the Social Information-Processing Model of Job Attitudes," *Human Relations*, July 1980, pp. 457–76.

[44]Bridges, *sq. cet.*

job range and, consequently, reported high levels of job discontent, turnover, absenteeism, and dissatisfaction. Accordingly, strategies were devised that resulted in wider job range through increasing the requisite activities of jobs. Two of these approaches are job rotation and job enlargement.

Job Rotation

www.bethsteel.com

www.trw.com

Managers of organizations such as Western Electric, Ford, Bethlehem Steel, TRW Systems, and Greyhound Financial Corporation have utilized different forms of the job rotation strategy.[45] This practice involves rotating managers and non-managers alike from one job to another. In so doing, the individual is expected to complete more job activities since each job includes different tasks.[46] Job rotation involves increasing the range of jobs and the perception of variety in the job content. Increasing task variety should, according to recent studies, increase employee satisfaction, reduce mental overload, decrease the number of errors due to fatigue, improve production and efficiency,[47] and reduce on-the-job injuries.[48] However, job rotation doesn't change the basic characteristics of the assigned jobs. Some relatively small firms have successfully used job rotation.

One relatively small manufacturer, Rohm & Haas Bayport, was founded in 1981 to produce specialty chemicals. The plant is located in LaPorte, Texas, and its 67 employees play active roles in management because their jobs are designed with that activity in mind. The company's philosophy is to provide autonomy and responsibility in each individual's job and, consequently, to enable employees to feel a sense of "ownership" of key decisions and actions. Every person in the organization is trained to be and to act like a manager. The 46 process technicians and 15 engineers and chemists report to one of the two manufacturing unit managers who in turn report to the executive team.

The technicians make operating decisions among themselves while working in teams of four to seven people. The company has no shift foremen or line supervisors in the usual sense of these positions. Rather, technicians are expected to be self-managed. Team members rotate jobs with other team members every 4 to 12 weeks to provide task variety and cross-training. They're also trained to do routine maintenance and repairs of their equipment and not to depend on a separate maintenance team for that support. The company's idea is to give individuals near complete control of the conditions that govern work pace and quality. They evaluate each other's performance and interview applicants for positions. Job designs at Rohm & Haas Bayport contribute to individual performance, according to company spokespersons.[49]

---

[45]Gregory B. Northcraft, Terri L. Griffith, and Christina E. Shalley, "Building Top Management Muscle in a Slow Growth Environment," *Academy of Management Executive,* February 1992, pp. 32–41.

[46]Michael A. Campion, Lisa Cheraskin, and Michael J. Stevens, "Career-Related Antecedents and Outcomes of Job Rotation," *Academy of Management Journal,* December 1994, pp. 1518–42, and Allan W. Farrant, "Job Rotation Is Important," *Supervision,* August 1987, pp. 14–16.

[47]Michael A. Campion and Carol L. McClelland, "Follow-Up and Extension of the Interdisciplinary Costs and Benefits of Enlarged Jobs," *Journal of Applied Psychology,* June 1993, pp. 339–51; Michael A. Campion and Carol L. McClelland, "Interdisciplinary Examination of the Costs and Benefits of Enlarged Jobs: A Job Design Quasi-Experiment," *Journal of Applied Psychology,* April 1991, pp. 186–98.

[48]Lance Hazzard, Joe Mautz, and Denver Wrightman, "Job Rotation Cuts Cumulative Trauma Cases," *Personnel Journal,* February 1992, pp. 29–32.

[49]Don Nichols, "Taking Participative Management to the Limit," *Management Review,* August 1987, pp. 28–32; and Bob Deierlein, "Team Cuts Costs," *Fleet Equipment,* April 1990, pp. 28–30.

Critics state that job rotation often involves nothing more than having people perform several boring and monotonous jobs rather than one. An alternative strategy is job enlargement.

Job Enlargement

The pioneering Walker and Guest study[50] was concerned with the social and psychological problems associated with mass production jobs in automobile assembly plants. They found that many workers were dissatisfied with their highly specialized jobs. In particular, they disliked mechanical pacing, repetitiveness of operations, and a lack of a sense of accomplishment. Walker and Guest also found a positive relationship between job range and job satisfaction. Findings of this research gave early support for motivation theories that predict that increases in job range will increase job satisfaction and other objective job outcomes. Job enlargement strategies focus upon the opposite of dividing work—they're a form of despecialization or increasing the number of tasks that an employee performs. For example, a job is designed such that the individual performs six tasks instead of three.

Although, in many instances, an enlarged job requires a longer training period, job satisfaction usually increases because boredom is reduced. The implication, of course, is that job enlargement will lead to improvement in other performance outcomes.

The concept and practice of job enlargement have become considerably more sophisticated. In recent years, effective job enlargement involves more than simply increasing task variety. In addition, it's necessary to design certain other aspects of job range, including providing worker-paced (rather than machine-paced) control.[51] Each of these changes involves balancing the gains and losses of varying degrees of division of labor. Contemporary applications of job enlargement involve training individuals to perform several different jobs, each requiring considerable skill, whether in manufacturing or service organizations.

www.dhc.com

Lechmere Inc., a 27-store retail chain owned by Dayton Hudson, opened an outlet in Sarasota, Florida, in 1987. It faced an unusual circumstance of being unable to employ its typical workforce of part-timers such as teenagers and homemakers. The unemployment rate in the area was less than 4 percent and entry-level people were in short supply. Retailers such as Lechmere rely on part-time employees because they can use them at times of peak activity. But in the absence of such employees, Lechmere adopted a different approach of designing jobs that included considerable range of activities. They hired full-time employees but then rewarded them for learning and doing many different jobs.

Cashiers learned to sell merchandise; sporting goods salespeople learned to operate forklifts in the warehouse. In this way, management can shift individuals from job to job as the need arises. The Sarasota store's staff is 60 percent full-timers compared to 30 percent for the entire chain. Moreover, the store has higher

---

[50]Charles R. Walker and Robert H. Guest, *The Man on the Assembly Line* (Cambridge, MA: Harvard University Press, 1952).

[51]Jeffrey R. Edwards, Judith A. Scidly, and Mary D. Brtek, "The Measurement of Work: Hierarchical Representation of the Multimethod Job Design Questionnaire," *Personnel Psychology,* Summer 1999, pp. 305–34.

Job Design and Ethics

You Be the Judge

www.johnsoncontrols.com

No manager would dispute that jobs should be designed in a way which eliminates, or at least minimizes, the likelihood that employees may experience adverse physical or health consequences from performing the job. Some jobs, however, even when properly designed, may still be inherently hazardous. For example, it may be impossible to completely eliminate exposure to toxic chemicals or hazardous substances even when jobs have been well designed. Such was the case at the battery manufacturing division of Johnson Controls, an automotive equipment supplier.

By its very nature, battery manufacturing entails possible exposure to high lead levels. Sufficiently high blood lead levels can be dangerous to anyone; even moderately elevated levels, however, can pose a particular risk for pregnant women and their unborn children. Thus, after having designed the manufacturing operation in a manner to minimize exposure, Johnson Controls instituted a policy to provide further safeguards for a particularly susceptible group: Women with childbearing capacity were essentially prohibited from working in high lead exposure positions in its battery facility. Fertile women already employed in such positions when the policy went into effect were permitted to stay as long as they maintained safe blood lead levels; otherwise they were transferred to another job with no loss of pay or benefits.

Most management students, when queried, indicate that this sounds like a reasonable policy, with many suggesting that it would be unethical (and perhaps should be illegal) for the company not to protect a particularly susceptible group of individuals—some of whom (unborn children) are powerless to protect themselves. At the same time, however, virtually all of these students agree that sex discrimination in hiring and employment decisions is clearly unethical (and also illegal). And sex discrimination is what Johnson Controls was charged with as a result of this policy. What do you think the court should have decided in this case?

Source: Caryn L. Beck-Dudley and Edward J. Conry, "Legal Reasoning and Practical Reasonableness," *American Business Law Journal*, Fall 1995, pp. 91–130; Matthew F. Weil, "Protecting Employees' Fetuses from Workplace Hazards: Johnson Controls Narrows the Options," *Berkeley Journal of Employment and Labor Law*, Vol. 14 No. 1 (1993); and G. P. Panaro, *Employment Law Manual* (Boston: Warren, Gorham & Lamont, 1991), pp. 29–30.

productivity records than other stores. The company has increased the job range by increasing content and context.[52]

Some employees can't cope with enlarged jobs because they can't comprehend complexity; moreover, they may not have a sufficiently long attention span to complete an enlarged set of tasks. However, if employees are amenable to job enlargement and have the requisite ability, then job enlargement should increase satisfaction and product quality and decrease absenteeism and turnover. These gains aren't without costs, including the likelihood that employees will demand larger salaries in exchange for performing enlarged jobs. Yet these costs must be borne if management desires to implement the design strategy—job enrichment—that enlarges job depth. Job enlargement is a necessary precondition for job enrichment.

Redesigning jobs is not without ethical and legal implications as suggested in You Be the Judge.

---

[52]Frederick Herzberg, "The Wise Old Turk," *Harvard Business Review*, September–October 1974, pp. 70–80.

DESIGNING JOB DEPTH: JOB ENRICHMENT

The impetus for designing job depth was provided by Herzberg's two-factor theory of motivation. The basis of his theory is that factors that meet individuals' need for psychological growth (especially responsibility, job challenge, and achievement) must be characteristic of their jobs. The application of his theory is termed *job enrichment*.

The implementation of job enrichment is realized through direct changes in job depth.[53] Managers can provide employees with greater opportunities to exercise discretion by making the following changes:

1. *Direct feedback.* The evaluation of performance should be timely and direct.
2. *New learning.* A good job enables people to feel that they are growing. All jobs should provide opportunities to learn.
3. *Scheduling.* People should be able to schedule some part of their own work.
4. *Uniqueness.* Each job should have some unique qualities or features.
5. *Control over resources.* Individuals should have some control over their job tasks.
6. *Personal accountability.* People should be provided with an opportunity to be accountable for the job.

www.ti.com

As defined by the executive in charge of a pioneering job enrichment program at Texas Instruments (TI), job enrichment is a process that (1) encourages employees to behave like managers in managing their jobs and (2) designs the job to make such behavior feasible.[54] The process as implemented in TI is continuous and pervades the entire organization. Every job in TI is viewed as subject to analysis to determine if it can be enriched to include managerial activities. Moreover, as the jobs of nonmanagerial personnel are designed to include greater depth, the jobs of managers must be designed. These managerial jobs emphasize training and counseling of subordinates and deemphasize control and direction.

As the theory and practice of job enrichment have evolved, managers have become aware that successful applications require numerous changes in how work is done. Important changes include giving workers greater authority to participate in decisions, to set their own goals, and to evaluate their (and their work groups') performance. Job enrichment also involves changing the nature and style of managers' behavior. Managers must be willing and able to delegate authority.[55] Given employees' ability to carry out enriched jobs and managers' willingness to delegate authority, gains in performance can be expected. These positive outcomes are the result of increasing employees' expectations that efforts lead to performance, that performance leads to intrinsic and extrinsic rewards, and that these rewards have power to satisfy needs. These significant changes in managerial jobs when coupled with changes in nonmanagerial jobs suggest that a supportive work environment is a prerequisite for successful job enrichment efforts.[56]

---

[53]Blake E. Ashforth, Glen E. Kreiner, and Mel Fugate, "All in a Day's Work: Boundaries and Micro Role Transitions," *Academy of Management Review,* July 2000, pp. 472–91.

[54]M. Scott Myers, *Every Employee a Manager* (New York: McGraw-Hill, 1970), p. xii.

[55]Russ S. Moxley, *Leadership and Spirit: Breathing New Vitality Into Individuals and Organizations* (San Francisco: Jossey-Bass, 2000).

[56]Gerald R. Ferris and David C. Gilmore, "The Moderating Role of Work Context in Job Design Research: A Test of Competing Models," *Academy of Management Journal,* December 1984, pp. 885–92.

EXHIBIT 6.3
The Job
Characteristics Model

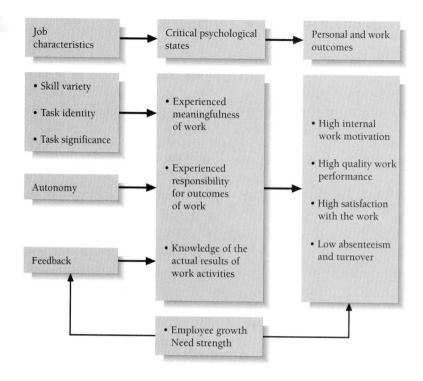

Job characteristics → Critical psychological states → Personal and work outcomes

- Skill variety
- Task identity
- Task significance

→ • Experienced meaningfulness of work

Autonomy → • Experienced responsibility for outcomes of work

Feedback → • Knowledge of the actual results of work activities

- High internal work motivation
- High quality work performance
- High satisfaction with the work
- Low absenteeism and turnover

- Employee growth Need strength

Jobs can be designed on the basis of range and significant depth (called *job specialization*), a moderate amount of range and depth (called *job enlargement*), or significant depth and generally low range.

Job enrichment and job enlargement aren't competing strategies. Job enlargement but not job enrichment may be compatible with the needs, values, and abilities of some individuals. Yet job enrichment, when appropriate, necessarily involves job enlargement. A promising new approach to job design that attempts to integrate the two approaches is the job characteristics model. Hackman, Oldham, Janson, and Purdy devised the approach, basing it on the job diagnostic survey cited in an earlier section.[57]

The model attempts to account for the interrelationships among (1) certain job characteristics, (2) psychological states associated with motivation, satisfaction, and performance, (3) job outcomes, and (4) growth needs strength. Exhibit 6.3 describes the relationships among these variables. Although variety, identity, significance, autonomy, and feedback don't completely describe perceived job content, they, according to this model, sufficiently describe those aspects that management can manipulate to bring about gains in productivity.

Steps that management can take to increase the core dimensions include:

1. Combining task elements
2. Assigning whole pieces of work (i.e., work modules)

---

[57]J. Richard Hackman, Greg Oldham, Robert Janson, and Kenneth Purdy, "New Strategy for Job Enrichment," *California Management Review,* Summer 1975, pp. 57–71; and J. Richard Hackman and Greg Oldham, "Development of the Job Diagnostic Survey," *Journal of Applied Psychology,* April 1975, pp. 159–70.

3. Allowing discretion in selection of work methods
4. Permitting self-paced control
5. Opening feedback channels

These actions increase task variety, identity, and significance; consequently, the "experienced meaningfulness of work" psychological state is increased. By permitting employee participation and self-evaluation and by creating autonomous work groups, the feedback and autonomy dimensions are increased along with the psychological states "experienced responsibility" and "knowledge of actual results."

Implementing the job characteristics model in a particular situation begins with a study of existing job perceptions by means of the job diagnostic survey. Hackman and Oldham have reported numerous applications of the model in a variety of organizations.[58] They have also compiled normative data for a variety of job categories so that managers and practitioners can compare the responses of their own employees to those of a larger population.[59] Although the track record of job design efforts is generally positive, some caveats are warranted.

The positive benefits of these efforts are moderated by individual differences in the strength of employees' growth needs. That is, employees with strong need for accomplishment, learning, and challenge will respond more positively than those with relatively weak growth needs. In more familiar terms, employees with high need for self-esteem and self-actualization are the more likely candidates for job design.[60] Employees who are forced to participate in job design programs but who lack either the need strength or the ability to perform designed jobs may experience stress, anxiety, adjustment problems, erratic performance, turnover, and absenteeism.

The available research on the interrelationships between perceived job content and performance is meager. One survey of 30 applications of job design strategies confirms that failures are as frequent as successes.[61] It's apparent, however, that managers must cope with significant problems in matching employee needs and differences with organizational needs.[62]

Problems associated with job design include:

1. Unless lower-level needs are satisfied, people will not respond to opportunities to satisfy upper-level needs. And even though our society has been rather successful in providing food and shelter, these needs regain importance when the economy moves through periods of recession and high inflation.

2. Job design programs are intended to satisfy needs typically not satisfied in the workplace. As workers are told to expect higher-order need satisfaction, they may raise their expectations beyond what's possible. Dissatisfaction with the program's unachievable aims may displace dissatisfaction with the jobs.

3. Job design may be resisted by labor unions who see the effort as an attempt to get more work for the same pay.

---

[58]J. Richard Hackman and Greg Oldham, *Work Redesign* (Reading, MA: Addison-Wesley, 1980).

[59]Tom D. Taber and Elisabeth Taylor, "A Review and Evaluation of the Psychometric Properties of the Job Diagnostic Survey," *Personnel Psychology*, Autumn 1990, pp. 467–500.

[60]Gary Johns, Jia L. Xie, and Yongqing Fang, "Mediating and Moderating Effects in Job Design," *Journal of Management*, December 1992, pp. 657–76.

[61]Kopelman, "Job Redesign and Productivity."

[62]William E. Zierden, "Congruence in the Work Situation: Effects of Growth Needs, Management Style, and Job Structure on Job-Related Satisfactions," *Journal of Occupational Behavior*, October 1980, pp. 297–310.

4. Job design efforts may not produce tangible performance improvements for some time after the beginning of the effort. One study indicated that significant improvements in effectiveness couldn't be seen until four years after the beginning of the job design program.[63]

Practical efforts to improve productivity and satisfaction through job design have emphasized autonomy and feedback, as described in International Encounter 6.1 featuring the experience of Volvo. Relatively less emphasis has been placed on identity, significance, and variety.[64] Apparently, it's easier to provide individuals with greater responsibility for the total task and increased feedback than to change the essential nature of the task itself. To provide identity, significance, and variety often requires enlarging the task to the point of losing the benefits of work simplification and standardization. But within the economic constraints imposed by the logic of specialization, it's possible to design work so as to give individuals complete responsibility for its completion and at the same time to provide supportive managerial monitoring.

In general, one reaches two conclusions when considering the experience of job design approaches. First, job design approaches are relatively successful in increasing quality of output. This conclusion pertains, however, only if the reward system already satisfies lower-level needs. If it presently doesn't satisfy lower-level needs, employees can't be expected to experience upper-level need satisfaction (intrinsic rewards) through enriched jobs. In particular, managers can't expect individuals with relatively low growth needs to respond as would those with relatively high growth needs.[65]

Successful efforts are the result of the circumstances that initiate the effort and the process undertaken to manage the effort. Organizations under external pressure to change have a better chance of successfully implementing job design than those not under such pressure. Moreover, successful efforts are accompanied by broad-scale participation of managers and employees alike. Since a primary source of organizational effectiveness is job performance, managers should design jobs according to the best available knowledge.[66]

Self-Managed Teams

One approach to job redesign that has placed emphasis on factors such as task significance and identity is the use of self-managed teams. Self-managed teams (SMT) represent a job enrichment approach to redesign at the group level. An SMT is a relatively small group of individuals who are empowered to perform certain activities based on procedures established and decisions

---

[63]Ricky W. Griffin, "Effects of Work Redesign on Employee Perceptions, Attitudes, and Behaviors: A Long-Term Investigation," *Academy of Management Journal*, June 1991, pp. 425–35.

[64]Kopelman, "Job Design and Productivity," p. 253.

[65]Joseph Fiorelli and Richard Feller, "Re-Engineering TQM and Work Redesign: An Integrative Approach to Continuous Organizational Excellence," *Public Administration Quarterly*, Spring 1994, pp. 54–63; Scott A. Snell and James W. Dean, Jr., "Strategic Compensation for Integrated Manufacturing: The Moderating Effects of Jobs and Organizational Inertia," *Academy of Management Journal*, October 1994, pp. 1109–40; James W. Dean, Jr., and Scott A. Snell, "Integrated Manufacturing and Job Design: Moderating Effects of Organizational Inertia," *Academy of Management Journal*, December 1991, pp. 776–804.

[66]Howard W. Oden, *Transforming The Organization: A Social-Technical* (Westport, CT: Quorum, 1999).

Job Redesign at Volvo Corporation

When Pehr Gyllenhammar joined Volvo in 1971 as its managing director, performance indicators such as productivity, absenteeism, and turnover were unsatisfactory. Gyllenhammar took a keen interest in the experiments of Ingvar Barrby, head of the upholstery department, in job rotation (termed *job alternation* in Volvo). The reduction in turnover from 35 percent to 15 percent encouraged the new managing director to adopt other aspects of job redesign. For example, group management and work modules are used at the Torslanda car assembly plant. Employees, in groups, follow the same auto body for seven or eight work stations along the line for a total period of 20 minutes.

Job redesign at Volvo reached a major milestone when the Kalmar, Sweden, assembly plant opened. Gyllenhammar had been personally and visibly behind the design and construction phases of the new plant to assure that opportunities to provide job enrichment were part of the physical and technological layout. The plant incorporates a technology of assembly in which overhead carriers move the auto body, chassis, and subassemblies to assembly team areas. There, work teams of 20 to 25 employees complete major segments of auto assembly: electrical systems, instrumentation, finishing, and so on. Each group is responsible for a whole piece of work; it functions as an autonomous unit much as those at the truck assembly plant.

Source: Ake Sandbery (ed.), *Enriching Production: Perspectives of Volvo's Uddevalla Plant as an Alternative to Lean Production* (New York: Averbury Publishing Co., Inc. 1995); Tomas Engstrom and Lars Medbo, "Intra-Group Work Patterns in Final Assembly of Motor Vehicles," *International Journal of Operations and Production Management*, Vol. 14 No. 3 (1994), pp. 101–13; Paul Adler and Robert E. Cole, "Designed for Learning: A Tale of Two Auto Plants," *Sloan Management Review*, Spring 1993, pp. 85–94; and H. G. Jones, "Motivation for Higher Performance at Volvo," *Long Range Planning*, October 1991, pp. 92–104.

made within the group, with minimum or no outside direction. SMTs can take many forms, including task forces, project teams, quality circles, and new venture teams.[67] Typically, SMTs determine their own work assignments within the team and are responsible for an entire process from inception to completion. It is not unusual for SMTs to select their own members and to evaluate their own performance, activities usually thought of as management functions.

The automotive industry has been particularly interested in the use of self-managed work groups. General Motors is using such teams in its joint venture with Toyota. In a particularly bold new endeavor, the Saturn Corporation, an independent subsidiary of General Motors, is using the team approach to producing a brand new automobile in a state-of-the-art plant in Spring Hill, Tennessee. Prior to plant construction, a team of 99 Saturn workers visited 160 different facilities around the world, traveling over two million miles to find what worked and what didn't.[68] The Saturn plant is organized around nearly 200 SMTs, each of which has the authority to decide how to do its job, including hiring team members. Most even have budgetary responsibilities and can make decisions to change suppliers for parts that team members use. Saturn has one of the most extensive worker training programs found in the automotive industry. Employees spend a minimum of 250 hours in training, with many receiving three times that much. Nor is training restricted to nuts and bolts of assembly. It also includes topics such as awareness, conflict management techniques, consensus–decision making, and group dynamics. Initial indications point to some important successes at Saturn, foremost among them being a level of production quality previously unequaled by a

---

[67]David Barry, "Managing the Bossless Team: Lessons in Distributed Leadership," *Organizational Dynamics,* Summer 1991, pp. 31–47.

[68]S. C. Gwynne, "The Right Stuff," *Time,* October 29, 1990, pp. 74–84.

domestic automobile manufacturer. It remains to be seen, however, if the plant can achieve and maintain profitability.

The difficulty of switching from a traditional hierarchical structure to one in which work teams assume responsibility for their own decisions is not easy. Two notable barriers to SMTs are resistance and misunderstanding. SMTs require not only a new workflow and set of processes, but also new attitudes and behaviors. Team members may not like being responsible for goals that others in the team have not helped to achieve. Managers often fear loss of control and status.[69]

The implementation of SMTs causes changes in thinking about "yourself," leadership, and organization. Understanding how SMTs apply to themselves is hard for employees to grasp. Also, managers are often not clear about what they should be doing under an SMT arrangement.

Simply assuming that SMTs will work is not accurate since resistance and misunderstandings are obvious problems. Team leaders that strike a balance between too much involvement and not enough are needed. As SMTs evolve each member needs to acquire and develop the qualities of a leader and move from "I" to "we" thinking and behavior.

Alternative Work Arrangements

Enriching the content of a job is not the only way to provide enrichment. Enrichment can also be achieved within the context of a job. One aspect of job context relates to when the job is performed, or the work schedule. Giving employees decision-making control over when they perform their work is an approach to job redesign that is becoming increasingly popular. It has led to a variety of innovations which we will collectively refer to as alternative work arrangements.

One of the earliest forms of alternative work arrangements was that of the compressed workweek. In its most popular form, employees are given an opportunity to work four 10-hour days rather than the more standard five 8-hour days. The 4-40 programs allow workers more leisure time, as well as permit them to travel to and from work during nonrush-hour traffic. While some employees may be able to opt for a compressed work schedule with others electing a standard one, typically everyone at the same location is on the same schedule.

An arrangement that provides employees even greater individual control over work scheduling is flextime. In a flextime arrangement, employees can determine, within some limits, when they will go to work. As is shown in the two examples in Exhibit 6.4, employees are required to be present during the "common core" hours. They may make up the rest of their workday in any combination during flextime hours. In most flextime plans, employees may vary their attendance day-to-day, provided they are at work a specific number of hours a week. Some flextime plans allow employees to accumulate extra hours worked and exchange them for an additional day off each month.

Employees concerned about balancing personal and work life report that a flexible work schedule is high on the list of benefits that factor into job satisfaction. Aladdan Equipment of Sarasota, Florida, established a workweek of four 9-hour days and a half-day on Friday. Their result is a 50 percent increase in productivity. In a survey of 6,000 workers by Ranstad, an Atlanta staffing firm, 51 percent said they would stay with the firm even without a pay raise, if Ranstad of-

---

[69]Milam Moravec, "Self-Managed Teams," *Executive Excellence*, October 1999, p. 78.

EXHIBIT 6.4
Two Possible Flextime Schedules

Flextime	Common Core	Flextime
6 AM – 10 AM	10 AM – 4 PM	4 PM – 8 PM

Flextime	Common Core	Flextime	Common Core	Flextime
6 AM – 9 AM	9 AM – 11 AM	11 AM – 2 PM	2 PM – 4 PM	4 PM – 7 PM

fered flexible work hours.[70] Some of the benefits of flextime schedules are presented in the Organizational Encounter 6.2.

Another approach which increases employee discretion is that of job sharing. In job sharing, two or more individuals share one job. One person might work from 8:00 A.M. until noon, and a second person may do the same job from 1:00 P.M. until 5:00 P.M. Or they might each work full, but alternate, days. Job sharing provides maximum flexibility for the employee. The payoff for the employer is being able to draw upon the talents of two individuals in one job. Job sharers Stephanie Kahn and Joan Girardi at American Express are typical examples. Stephanie works on Monday, Tuesday, and Thursday; Joan works on Tuesday, Wednesday, and Friday. Their job is to enroll new cardholders. In addition to splitting days of the week, they also split the job by marketing channels. Joan handles direct mail, while Stephanie concentrates on telemarketing.[71]

Perhaps the ultimate in alternative work arrangements is telecommuting. Telecommuting involves working at home while being linked to the office via a computer and/or fax machine. While telecommuting emphasizes location rather than scheduling, most telecommuting jobs provide a high degree of flexible scheduling as well. Pacific Bell has been a pioneer in the use of telecommuting. In addition to experiencing increased productivity and improved employee morale, the company, with major offices in Los Angeles, has made significant contributions to reducing freeway congestion and smog.

The use of various alternative work arrangements is increasing. As the needs of an increasingly diverse workforce grow, alternative arrangements can have a positive appeal to both employers and employees. While more and better research needs to be conducted to determine the effectiveness of such plans, there seems to be little question that job redesign strategies for the future will include a multitude of these flexible scheduling arrangements.

TOTAL QUALITY MANAGEMENT AND JOB DESIGN

TQM, according to those who espouse and practice it, combines technical knowledge and human knowledge. To deal with the inherent complexity and variability of production and service delivery technology, people must be empowered with authority to make necessary decisions and must be enabled with knowledge to know when to exercise that authority. Aspects of TQM job designs

---

[70]Sarah Boehle, David Stamps, and Jeremy Stratton, "The Increasing Value of Flexible Time," *Training*, July 2000, p. 32.

[71]Alan Deutschman, "Pioneers of the New Balance," *Fortune*, May 20, 1991, pp. 60–68.

Flextime Options and Benefits

Companies compress workweeks in several different ways. The most common schedule is four 10-hour workdays, but even this option has several variations.

At the Tucson, Arizona, office of AVT Document Exchange Software Group, which has 150 employees and provides organizations with e-document software, two separate compressed workweek schedules are operating—one for its general workers and one for some of its information technology (IT) employees.

AVT's general workers are allowed to work four 10-hour days, and they can choose the day they would like to take off. IT workers who are on the swing and midnight shifts work four 9-hour days. IT employees work fewer hours than other employees.

"We polled our tech-support employees about what would make them volunteer to work these two shifts, and they said they wanted an extra day off," says HR Manager Lisa Vervantz, PHR. "And as far as having them work a 9-hour schedule instead of 10 hours, we considered it comparable to offering them a differential pay." That's also a good way to get around high pay scales for IT workers.

The Madison Avenue corporate office of Marcel Dekker also offers two compressed schedules. The main office schedule is Monday through Thursday, and employees start their days between 7:30 A.M. and 9:30 A.M., working a total of 38 hours. The company's IT workers have the option of a schedule from Monday through Thursday or Tuesday through Friday.

Nahan Printing Inc. in St. Cloud, Minnesota, offers an even more unusual flexible schedule. "We work three 12-hour shifts," explains Judy Wehking, HR manager. "But then we also rotate this schedule every three weeks."

For example, half the employees work 12 hours a day Monday through Wednesday for three weeks in a row. After the last Wednesday, they get off seven days—Thursday through Wednesday—before starting a new, three-week

rotation of working Thursday through Sunday. Then the group goes back to working Monday through Wednesday. While the first group is working the Monday-through-Wednesday shift, another group is working the Thursday-through-Sunday shift. So, each group gets seven days off every two months, in addition to their normal days off. Note that employees work 36 hours a week, instead of the traditional 40 hours.

Another advantage for companies using alternative work schedules may be the ability to attract and retain workers. "We would have lost employees who would have found another position where they could have this type of flexibility," says Vervantz.

Windy Henson, a quality assurance test engineer at AVT, proves Vervantz's point. The mother of 11-month-old twin girls, Henson says she probably "would have dropped out of the workforce until the girls were old enough to go to preschool" if the company did not offer compressed workweeks. Henson and her husband, a technical writer for the company, says they feel the company "understands how our family life affects how we perform."

Issues about holidays, vacations and sick leave do not seem to present any real problems, and overtime issues are usually easily handled, although some states require overtime payment for any employees working more than eight hours a day. Employers should check state laws before implementing an alternative work schedule to determine which laws may apply.

The biggest administrative headache appeared to be the supervision of workers. This problem did not arise in companies where it was mandated that everyone in the department or throughout the company work the same schedule. But in companies that allowed their employees a choice of schedules, management concerns surfaced about how to handle supervision.

www. rightfix. com

www. nahan. com

Source: Adapted from Nancy Hatch Woodward, "TGI Thursday," *HR Magazine*, July 2000, pp. 72–76 and V. Borg, T. S. Kristensen and H. Burr, "Work Environment and Change In Self-Related Health: A Five Year Follow-Up Study", *Stress Medicine*, January 2000, pp. 37–48.

have appeared throughout this discussion. We've discussed job enrichment including provision of autonomy, creation of work modules, and development of trust and collaboration. We've seen these job attributes in the practices of organizations discussed throughout this chapter. But even as we close this chapter, we must raise a fundamental question: Can American workers adjust to the requirements for working together in teams and in collaboration with management? Are the ideas of TQM totally applicable to the American worker? Is TQM the wave of the future? Do American managers have the ability and commitment to implement the necessary changes in jobs required by new technologies and new global realities?[72] Many contemporary observers warn us that the answers to all these questions must be yes because no other choice exists.[73]

Job design strategy focuses on jobs in the context of individuals' needs for economic well-being and personal growth. But let's put the strategy in a broader framework and include the issue of the sociotechnical system. Sociotechnical theory focuses on interactions between technical demands of jobs and social demands of people doing the jobs. The theory emphasizes that too great an emphasis on the technical system in the manner of scientific management or too great an emphasis on the social system in the manner of human relations will lead to poor job design. Rather, job design should take into account both the technology and the people who use the technology.

Sociotechnical theory and application of job design developed from studies undertaken in English coal mines from 1948 to 1958.[74] The studies became widely publicized for demonstrating the interrelationship between the social system and the technical system of organizations. The interrelationship was revealed when economic circumstances forced management to change how coal was mined (the technical system). Historically, the technical system consisted of small groups of miners (the social system) working together on "short faces" (seams of coal). But technological advancement improved roof control and safety and made longwall mining possible. The new technical system required a change in the social system. The groups would be disbanded in favor of one-person, one-task jobs. Despite the efforts of management and even the union, miners eventually devised a social system that restored many characteristics of the group system. This experience has been completely described in organizational behavior literature and has stimulated a great deal of research and application.

For example, Citibank extensively changed the ways its employees did their work. According to George E. Seegers, a bank vice president, a customer survey indicated that the bank scored very low on customer service. Upon examining causes of the problem, bank management concluded that the reason was that its employees didn't "feel like somebody." They were dissatisfied with their rather mundane jobs created in part by the bank's decision some time ago to introduce automatic teller machines. Building on the idea that everybody wants to feel like somebody, the bank undertook extensive changes designed to recognize the individuality of employees as well as customers.[75]

There's no contradiction between sociotechnical theory and total quality management. In fact, the two approaches are quite compatible. The compatibility relates to the demands of modern technology for self-directed and self-motivated job behavior. Such job behavior is made possible in jobs designed to provide autonomy and variety. As worked out in practice, such jobs are parts of self-regulating

[72]Cynthia K. West, *Techno-Human Mesh* (Westport, CT: Quorum, 2001).

[73]Russ S. Moxley, *Leadership and Spirit: Breathing New Vitality and Energy into Individuals and Organizations* (San Francisco: Jossey-Bass, 2000).

[74]Eric Trist, "The Evolution of Sociotechnical Systems," *Occasional Paper* (Ontario Quality of Working Life Centre, June 1981); William M. Fox, "Sociotechnical System Principles and Guidelines," *Journal of Applied Behavioral Science,* March 1995, pp. 91–105.

[75]Roy W. Walters, "The Citibank Project: Improving Productivity through Work Design," in Donald L. Kirkpatrick, *How to Manage Change Effectively* (San Francisco: Jossey-Bass, 1985), pp. 195–208.

work teams responsible for completing whole tasks. The work module concept pervades applications of sociotechnical theory.[76]

Numerous applications of sociotechnical design and total quality management are reported in the literature.[77] Some notable American examples include the Sherwin-Williams Paint Factory in Richmond, Kentucky, and the Quaker Oats pet food factory in Topeka, Kansas. Both factories were constructed from the ground up to include and allow for specific types of jobs embodying basic elements of autonomy and empowerment. Firms that don't have the luxury of building the plant from scratch must find ways to renovate both their technology and their job designs to utilize the best technology and people. Some of the most influential industrial and service organizations have confronted the necessity to design jobs to take advantage of the rapid pace of technological advance. In the contemporary global environment, sociotechnical system design has been incorporated in the total quality management approach to management.

---

[76]Fred Emery, "Participative Design: Effective, Flexible and Successful," *Journal of Quality and Participation*, January/February 1995, pp. 6–9.

[77]A. B. Shani and James A. Sena, "Information Technology and the Integration of Change: Sociotechnical System Approach," *Journal of Applied Behavioral Science*, June 1994, pp. 247–270; Louis E. Davis and James C. Taylor (eds.), Design of Jobs (Santa Monica, CA: Goodyear, 1979); Marc Bassin, "A Special Blend of Teamwork," *Personnel Journal*, May 1988, p. 62; and Roger Smith, "The U.S. Must Do What GM Has Done," *Fortune*, February 13, 1989, pp. 70–73.

Summary of Key Points

Job design involves managerial decisions and actions that specify objective job depth, range, and relationships to satisfy organizational requirements as well as the social and personal requirements of jobholders.

- Contemporary managers must consider the issue of quality of work life when designing jobs. This issue reflects society's concern for work experiences that contribute to employees' personal growth and development.

- Strategies for increasing jobs' potential to satisfy the social and personal requirements of jobholders have gone through an evolutionary process. Initial efforts were directed toward job rotation and job enlargement. These strategies produced some gains in job satisfaction, but didn't change primary motivators such as responsibility, achievement, and autonomy.

- During the 1960s, job enrichment became a widely recognized strategy for improving quality of work life factors. This strategy is based upon Herzberg's motivation theory and involves increasing jobs' depth through greater delegation of authority to jobholders. Despite some major successes, job enrichment isn't universally applicable because it doesn't consider individual differences.

- Individual differences are now recognized as crucial variables to consider when designing jobs. Experience, cognitive complexity, needs, values, valences, and perceptions of equity are some of the individual differences influencing jobholders' reactions to the scope and relationships of their jobs. When individual differences are combined with environmental, situational, and managerial differences, job design decisions become increasingly complex.

- The most recently developed strategy of job design emphasizes the importance of core job characteristics as perceived by jobholders. Although measurements of individual differences remain a problem, managers should be encouraged to examine ways to increase positive perceptions of variety, identity, significance, autonomy, and feedback. By doing so, the potential for high-quality work performance and high job satisfaction is increased given that jobholders possess relatively high growth needs strength.

- Many organizations including Volvo, Citibank, General Motors, and General Foods have attempted job design with varying degrees of success. The current state of research knowledge is inadequate for making broad generalizations regarding exact causes of success and failure in applications of job design. Managers must diagnose their own situations to determine the applicability of job design in their organizations.

- Sociotechnical theory combines technological and social issues in job design practice. Sociotechnical theory is compatible with job design strategy and in fact emphasizes the practical necessity to design jobs that provide autonomy, feedback, significance, identity, and variety.

- Total quality management (TQM) combines the ideas of job enrichment and sociotechnical theory. Managers who implement TQM design jobs that empower individuals to make important decisions about product/service quality. The empowerment process encourages participative management, team-oriented task modules, and autonomy.

Review and Discussion Questions

1. Do you believe that American workers will accept the idea that they must work together in groups and receive group-based rewards rather than working as individuals and receiving individual-based rewards? Explain your reasoning.

2. Explain the differences between job rotation and job enrichment and analyze the relative advantages of these two approaches in organizations you have worked for.

3. What is the significance of the idea of quality of work life (QWL)? In particular what would seem to be the tradeoffs between meaningful jobs and productive jobs during periods of declining economic activity and unemployment?

4. There is a distinct move away from a "job" emphasis in some industries. Why is this occurring?

5. What characteristics of jobs can't be enriched? Do you believe that management should ever consider any job to be incapable of enrichment?

6. Explain the relationships between feedback as a job content factor and personal goal setting. Is personal goal setting possible without feedback? Explain.

7. This chapter has described job designs in various service and manufacturing organizations. In which type of organization is job enrichment likely to be more effective as a strategy of increasing motivation and performance? Explain.

8. Explain which core dimension you now value most highly and why.

9. Flexible work schedules are becoming more popular. Why?

10. As you understand the idea and practice of total quality management, do you believe that it's the wave of the future in American organizations? Explain.

READING 6.1   Employees Redesign Their Jobs

Stephen L. Perlman

This unique idea allows workers to be creative in outlining their job responsibilities and forces them to justify how the proposed changes will help them flourish—from an individual and organizational perspective.

Employee-centered work redesign is an innovative concept that may provide a practical solution to the organizational/individual gap by linking the mission and goals of the company with the individual job satisfaction needs of employees. The concept is outlined in Exhibit 6.5.

Without abandoning the successful team methods used in quality circles (QCs), self-directed teams (SDTs), and traditional work redesign, the employee-centered approach allows individuals to practice creative decision making. This is achieved because fundamental work enhancement (from satisfaction and quality improvement perspectives) is placed in the hands of the employees who develop and implement their ideas under the guidance of management. Employee-centered work redesign develops constructive means for employees to become involved in redefining work roles to benefit the organization as well as themselves.

What gives employee-centered work redesign its unique organizational-individual link is its emphasis on total accountability. Although employees are encouraged to be creative in redesigning their jobs, they must be able to justify how their proposed changes will improve quality and support the organization's vision and mission as well as have a positive impact on other employees and systems.

Employees also must be able to justify how their job redesigns will give them greater job satisfaction and provide decision-making control and a degree of autonomy, as well as an opportunity for professional growth. By making employees accountable from an organizational and individual perspective, they become challenged to take the responsibility of thinking, planning, and implementing ideas and to invest themselves in the organization.

Another critical factor in the employee-centered concept is recognizing the contributions of each employee, although individual ideas are part of an overall team mission. This recognition comes from establishing the redesign contribution within the organizational work structure and its daily functioning. Some ways to do this include:

A redesigned job title, created by the employee.

A revised job description, based on the redesign.

A criteria-based performance evaluation in which the employee holds him- or herself accountable for the job.

Recognition in this sense tends to be permanent because the redesigned work role is acknowledged by man-

---

EXHIBIT 6.5   Employee-Centered Work Redesign

Critical Factors	Employee Benefits	Organizational Benefits
• Strong commitment from management to the program to ensure success	• Career and professional growth opportunities realized within the organization	• Greater use of employees
• Teamwork between employees and their managers to redesign work functions	• Increased employee job satisfaction	• Taps into employee skills, knowledge, and creativity
• Organizational benefit in one or more of the following areas: 1)Work productivity 2)Work quality 3)Cost containment	• Employees gain insights into the organization • Opportunity to contribute to organizational goals	• Increased productivity and improved quality • Reduced employee turnover • Employees become stakeholders, not job holders, in the organization
• Demonstrate positive impact on staff and existing systems	• Employees learn to communicate their needs, concerns, and interests • Broadened organization perspective	• Increased accountability leads to cost-effective behavior
• Hands-on problem-solving format	• Promotes career growth opportunities • Access to information • Identify critical skills	• Promotes positive work attitude to discourage employee grievances • Supports cooperative teamwork between employees and management

agement and staff daily. In turn, this sends a clear and powerful message to employees—the company considers their work to be meaningful.

Since employee-centered work redesign was introduced at several Southern California community hospitals in 1985, there has been strong evidence to support its ability to enhance quality of service and quality of work life. From an organizational standpoint, employee-centered groups (during a three- to five-year period) representing 35 programs and involving 482 employees, had a 57 percent lower turnover ratio than nonemployee-centered groups. In addition, department managers consistently say that they've been able to retain valuable employees better through employee-centered work redesign.

Another benefit is that employee-relations problems tend to decline and remain low for staff who participate in employee-centered programs. This may occur for several reasons. Perhaps most significantly, employees learn to be sensitive and appreciate other people's ideas, even if they're inconsistent with their own.

During an employee-centered program, workers have the opportunity to gain a better understanding of process and change. They realize that alterations must benefit the organization as well as their needs, and they recognize that they're accountable for facilitating that change.

Surveys taken after such programs reveal that employees most often increase their awareness of how change takes place and become more receptive to working productively with other individuals.

Similarly, performance scores for the same employee groups during a three- to five-year period (on a 0–100 scale) have averaged a 23 percent improvement during the first year following the program and have remained at approximately 19 percent above nonemployee-centered groups.

There also are numerous examples of previously mediocre performers participating in employee-centered programs and going on to achieve individual recognition. In the area of quality improvement, employee-centered changes have streamlined departmental operations, promoted commitment to organizational ideals and values, and encouraged task-oriented checks and balances.

Employee-generated ideas have resulted in new and/or improved programs and services that have produced additional revenue or contained costs. Of the 482 approved work redesign models, 31 percent saved more than $5,000 during the first year and 15 percent saved more than $13,500. Independent customer satisfaction and quality control surveys also have shown impressive results for groups that have participated in employee-centered programs.

From an individual perspective, employee-centered work redesign has been an effective mechanism to keep creative high performers in the organization by providing them with a work environment where they continually can be challenged and grow. In so doing, it has shown the ability to strengthen an organization's career development activities by facilitating a multitude of professional growth and advancement opportunities where few or none may have existed before. This is because the nature of work redesign allows new or modified jobs to be created based on changing organizational needs.

Employee-centered work redesign has proven to be an excellent method for employees to communicate their needs, concerns, and interests to management as well as to one another. It has been used effectively in helping employees identify skills, knowledge, and work experiences they wish to refine or gain and creates a practical method for incorporating these goals into a plan that also benefits the organization.

With its focus on work-role identification, employee-centered work redesign has produced significant job expansion and modification, allowing greater control of individual work functions and thereby stimulating job accountability.

THE PROCESS STARTS WITH AN ORGANIZATIONAL MISSION

The employee-centered work redesign process begins with individuals learning about the vision and mission of their respective departments through informal yet in-depth discussions with their managers. In cases in which the mission has yet to be created or is undergoing revision (because of organizational or external conditions), ask high-performing employees who have demonstrated company loyalty to participate in mission development.

Workers then complete a needs assessment survey that helps them identify personal job satisfaction and professional development goals that are consistent with the mission and goals of the unit. To ensure consistency, the department manager and work redesign trainer review and discuss each individual goal with the employee (and modify it if necessary) before granting approval. Each employee is asked to specify at least three meaningful personal/professional goals before moving on to the next exercise.

Next, employees learn to identify potential obstacles to their goals and form strategic ways to eliminate or minimize such barriers through communicating concerns with their managers and peers, and by effective planning and intervention. Obstacle identification and intervention is a good form of reality testing that allows the worker to examine his or her goals from a practicality standpoint and to help reduce any anxieties produced in going through the process.

Employees then prepare inventories of their present work, separating major tasks into three distinct areas: work to be retained; work to be modified; and work to be eliminated. Employees also are asked to identify new work to be added to their positions. Where an employee places a current task is based on the need for a better-functioning job as well as to meet job satisfaction and professional development goals better. The same accountability applies to any new tasks identified.

In the next stage, employees must identify preferred work roles for every modified or new task listed in the inventory. This identification should take the form of an action verb (i.e., coordinate, analyze, conduct, process, distribute, and so on). The preferred work role is a key component in the process of making employees accountable for their positions.

For example, an employee may have the general title of clerk, but through employee-centered work redesign he or she actually may coordinate or supervise a particular job function. Employees also must justify their work redesign changes by determining how each alteration will produce some benefit to the department in terms of quality improvement, productivity, and/or cost containment.

Although employees initially are left to come up with their own creative ideas for work redesign, there's the occasional need to provide assistance to facilitate thinking, such as learning how to use guided imagery to visualize or discover new work areas to develop. During this process, some employees will have valid suggestions for improving task functions, but need help from their peers, trainers, or managers as to the mechanics of the redesign.

In addition, employees must identify how their ideas will impact other staff members and the department as a whole. Potentially negative discoveries are discussed candidly in group settings or in individual consultations with the trainer and manager. Modifications in the work redesign model are made accordingly.

During the entire program, employees, trainers, and managers work as a team, sharing the goal of facilitating total quality improvement with inidividual job satisfaction. The trainer's role is to teach the redesign process, help refine ideas, and offer support and guidance. The manager, while allowing ideas to originate with employees, stands ready to support or offer constructive criticism and direction when necessary to ensure a well-thought-out design.

In most cases, employees working in groups will identify common goals and interventions to improve quality. What results may be viewed as a team project or even a team redesign. To retain individuality (and a sense of job accountability), however, each member of the group identifies a permanent role he or she wants to have in the redesign model. Eventually, this is added to the employee's new job description to ensure accountability.

All work redesign proposals must be reviewed carefully by management on a trial basis before implementation. During this time, new systems, tasks, or other changes are monitored for effectiveness and impact on all affected parties. If minor flaws in the design are identified, corrections can be made quickly. Redesign models that successfully pass the trial period are made permanent.

Developing and implementing an employee-centered program within an organization doesn't necessarily mean discarding all other HR strategies. What it does mean is viewing the overall strategy from the concept of building high performance/customer satisfaction together with a high quality of work life.

Strategies that already support the recognition of employees as major contributors to the development of the organization's desired culture should be retained. Firms that pride themselves on being innovative could incorporate the employee-centered approach (with its focus on creativity) and integrate employee-centered outcomes with a pay-for-performance merit plan.

These programs also can be used to help solve other productivity/quality problems and make better use of current talent through job sharing, flex schedules, and so forth, which simultaneously satisfy diverse individual needs.

A well-administered, employee-centered plan can add multiple avenues for professional growth and advancement, and become a vital part of any company's career development effort. In fact, using employee-centered work redesign gives employees a reason to stay in a certain area as opposed to transferring out. Employee-centered ideas, approved by management and incorporated into the mainstream of the work structure and system, only can enhance a firm's recognition program.

Naturally, special care must be taken when designing these programs. Although a major goal of any employee-centered program is worker empowerment, that power must be monitored and channeled to ensure that: (1) there's sufficient organizational benefit in the proposed change; and (2) the change doesn't have an adverse impact on other employees, management, and the system at large.

The process of initiating employee-centered work redesign ideally shoulders a part of a larger process in identifying or redefining the organization's vision, mission, goals, and objectives, so that employees have a clear direction in assessing their roles. Furthermore, the most effective employee-centered programs have occurred when there is full and collaborative management participation.

No matter what change process an organization wants to use for its human resources strategies, it may need to alter its view of employees—perhaps, regarding them less as subordinates and more as partners. In this manner, firms may find practical and realistic ways to deal with and solve their human resources and organizational problems.

Exercises

EXERCISE 6.1   Job Design Preferences

OBJECTIVES

1. To illustrate individual differences in preferences about various job design characteristics.
2. To illustrate how your preferences may differ from those of others.
3. To examine the most important and least important job design characteristics and how managers would cope with them.

STARTING THE EXERCISE

First you will respond to a questionnaire asking about your job design preferences and how you view the preferences of others. After working through the questionnaire individually, small groups will be formed. In the groups, discussion will focus on the individual differences in preferences expressed by group members.

Job design is concerned with a number of attributes of a job. Among these attributes are the job itself, the requirements of the job, the interpersonal interaction opportunities on the job, and performance outcomes. There are certain attributes that individuals prefer. Some prefer job autonomy, while others prefer to be challenged by different tasks. It is obvious that individual differences in preferences would be an important consideration for managers. An exciting job for one person may be a demeaning and boring job for another. Managers could use this type of information in attempting to create job design conditions that allow organizational goals and individual goals and preferences to be matched.

The Job Design Preference form is presented below. Please read it carefully and complete it after considering each characteristic listed. Due to space limitations, not all job design characteristics are included for your consideration. Use only those that are included on the form.

Phase I: 15 minutes

1. Individually complete the A and B portions of the Job Design Preference form.

Phase II: 45 minutes

1. The instructor will form groups of four to six students.
2. Discuss the differences in the rankings individuals made on the A and B parts of the form.
3. Present each of the A rank orders of group members on a flip chart or the blackboard. Analyze the areas of agreement and disagreement.
4. Discuss what implications the A and B rankings would have to a manager who would have to supervise a group such as the group you are in. That is, what could a manager do to cope with the individual differences displayed in steps 1, 2, and 3 above?

JOB DESIGN PREFERENCES

A. Your Job Design Preferences

Decide which of the following is most important to you. Place a 1 in front of the most important characteristic. Then decide which is the second most important characteristic to you and place a 2 in front of it. Continue numbering the items in order of importance until the least important is ranked 10. There are no right answers, since individuals differ in their job design preferences. Do not discuss your individual rankings until the instructor forms groups.

_____ Variety in tasks

_____ Feedback on performance from doing the job

_____ Autonomy

_____ Working as a team

_____ Responsibility

_____ Developing friendships on the job

_____ Task identity

_____ Task significance

_____ Having the resources to perform well

_____ Feedback on performance from others (e.g., the manager, coworkers)

B. Others' Job Design Preferences

In the A section you have provided your preferences. Now number the items as you think others would rank them. Consider others who are in your course, class, or program, that is, those who are also completing this exercise. Rank the factors from 1 (most important) to 10 (least important).

_____ Variety in tasks

_____ Feedback on performance from doing the job

_____ Autonomy

_____ Working as a team

_____ Responsibility

_____ Developing friendships on the job

_____ Task identity

_____ Task significance

_____ Having the resources to perform well

_____ Feedback on performance from others (e.g., the manager, coworkers)

Cases

CASE 6.1   The Hovey and Beard Company Case

PART 1

The Hovey and Beard Company manufactures a variety of wooden toys, including animals, pull toys, and the like. The toys were manufactured by a transformation process that began in the wood room. There, toys were cut, sanded, and partially assembled. Then the toys were dipped into shellac and sent to the painting room.

In years past, the painting had been done by hand, with each employee working with a given toy until its painting was completed. The toys were predominantly two-colored, although a few required more than two colors. Now, in response to increased demand for the toys, the painting operation was changed so that the painters sat in a line by an endless chain of hooks. These hooks moved continuously in front of the painters and passed into a long horizontal oven. Each painter sat in a booth designed to carry away fumes and to backstop excess paint. The painters would take a toy from a nearby tray, position it in a jig inside the painting cubicle, spray on the color according to a pattern, and then hang the toy on a passing hook. The rate at which the hooks moved was calculated by the engineers so that each painter, when fully trained, could hang a painted toy on each hook before it passed beyond reach.

The painters were paid on a group bonus plan. Since the operation was new to them, they received a learning bonus that decreased by regular amounts each month. The learning bonus was scheduled to vanish in six months, by which time it was expected that they would be on their own—that is, able to meet the production standard and earn a group bonus when they exceeded it.

QUESTIONS

1. Assume that the training period for the new job setup has just begun. What change do you predict in the level of output of the painters? Why?

    increase   decrease   stay the same

2. What other predictions regarding the behavior of these painters do you make based upon the situation described so far?

PART 2

By the second month of the training period, trouble developed. The painters learned more slowly than had been anticipated, and it began to look as though their production would stabilize far below what was planned. Many of the hooks were going by empty. The painters complained that the hooks moved too fast and that the engineer had set the rates wrong. A few painters quit and had to be replaced with new ones. This further aggravated the learning problem. The team spirit that the management had expected to develop through the group bonus was not in evidence except as an expression of what the engineers called "resistance." One painter, whom the group regarded as its leader (and the management regarded as the ringleader), was outspoken in taking the complaints of the group to the supervisor. These complaints were that the job was messy, the hooks moved too fast, the incentive pay was not correctly calculated, and it was too hot working so close to the drying oven.

PART 3

A consultant was hired to work with the supervisor. She recommended that the painters be brought together for a general discussion of the working conditions. Although hesitant, the supervisor agreed to this plan.

The first meeting was held immediately after the shift was over at 4 o'clock in the afternoon. It was attended by all eight painters. They voiced the same complaints again: the hooks went by too fast, the job was too dirty, and the room was hot and poorly ventilated. For some reason, it was this last item that seemed to bother them most. The supervisor promised to discuss the problems of ventilation and temperature with the engineers, and a second meeting was scheduled. In the next few days the supervisor had several talks with the engineers. They, along with the plant superintendent, felt that this was really a trumped-up complaint and that the expense of corrective measures would be prohibitively high.

The supervisor came to the second meeting with some apprehensions. The painters, however, did not seem to be much put out. Rather, they had a proposal of their own to make. They felt that if several large fans were set up to circulate the air around their feet, they would be much more comfortable. After some discussion, the supervisor agreed to pursue the idea. The supervisor and the consultant discussed the idea of fans with the superintendent. Three large propeller-type fans were purchased and installed.

The painters were jubilant. For several days the fans were moved about in various positions until they were placed to the satisfaction of the group. The painters seemed completely satisfied with the results, and the relations between them and the supervisor improved visibly.

The supervisor, after this encouraging episode, decided that further meetings might also prove profitable. The painters were asked if they would like to meet and discuss other aspects of the work situation. They were eager to do this. Another meeting was held and the discussion quickly centered on the speed of the hooks. The painters maintained that the engineer had set them at an unreasonably fast speed and that they would never be able to fill enough of them to make a bonus.

The discussion reached a turning point when the group's leader explained that it wasn't that the painters couldn't work fast enough to keep up with the hooks but that they couldn't work at that pace all day long. The supervisor explored the point. The painters were unanimous in their opinion that they could keep up with the belt for short periods if they wanted to. But they didn't want to because if they showed they could do this for short periods then they would be expected to do it all day long. The meeting ended with an unprecedented request by the painters: "Let us adjust the speed of the belt faster or slower depending on how we feel." The supervisor agreed to discuss this with the superintendent and the engineers.

The engineers reacted negatively to the suggestion. However, after several meetings it was granted that there was some latitude within which variations in the speed of the hooks would not affect the finished product. After considerable argument with the engineers, it was agreed to try out the painters' idea.

With misgivings, the supervisor had a control with a dial marked "low, medium, fast" installed at the booth of the group leader. The speed of the belt could now be adjusted anywhere between the lower and upper limits that the engineers had set.

QUESTIONS:

1. What changes do you now expect in the level of output of the painters? Why?

       increase   decrease   stay the same

2. What changes do you expect in the feelings of the painters toward their work situation? Why?

      more positive   more negative   no change

3. What other predictions do you make about the behavior of the painters?

PART 4

The painters were delighted and spent many lunch hours deciding how the speed of the belt should be varied from hour to hour throughout the day. Within a week the pattern had settled down to one in which the first half hour of the shift was run on a medium speed (a dial setting slightly above the point marked "medium"). The next two and a half hours were run at high speed, and the half hour before lunch and the half hour after lunch were run at low speed. The rest of the afternoon was run at high speed with the exception of the last 45 minutes of the shift, which was run at medium.

The constant speed at which the engineers had originally set the belt was actually slightly below the "medium" mark on the control dial; the average speed at which the painters were running the belt was on the high side of the dial. Few, if any, empty hooks entered the oven, and inspection showed no increase of rejects from the paint room.

Production increased, and within three weeks (some two months before the scheduled ending of the learning bonus) the painters were operating at 30 to 50 percent above the level that had been expected under the original arrangement. Naturally, their earnings were correspondingly higher than anticipated. They were collecting their base pay, earning a considerable piece-rate bonus, and still benefiting from the learning bonus. They were earning more now than many skilled workers in other parts of the plant.

QUESTIONS

1. How do you feel about the situation at this point?
2. Suppose that you were the supervisor. What would you expect to happen next? Why?

PART 5

Management was besieged by demands that the inequity between the earnings of the painters and those of other workers in the plant be taken care of. With growing irritation between the superintendent and the supervisor, the engineers and supervisor, and the superintendent and engineers, the situation came to a head when the superintendent revoked the learning bonus and returned the painting operation to its original status: The hooks moved again at their constant, time-studied, designated speed.

Production dropped again and within a month all but two of the eight painters had quit. The supervisor stayed on for several months, but, feeling aggrieved, left for another job.

7
Chapter

Organizational Stress:
An Individual View

After completing Chapter 7, you should be able to:

Learning Objectives

- Define what is meant by the term *stress*.

- Describe the components of the organizational stress model.

- Distinguish between four different categories of stressors.

- Discuss major individual and organizational consequences of stress.

- Identify some of the variables which moderate the stress process.

- Describe several different organizational and individual approaches to stress prevention and management.

The experience of work and life stress is certainly not new. Our cave-dwelling ancestors faced stress every time they left their caves and encountered their enemy, the sabertooth tigers.[1] The tigers of yesteryear are gone, but they have been replaced by other predators—work overload, a nagging boss, computer problems, downsizing, mergers, time deadlines, poorly designed jobs, marital disharmony, financial crises, accelerating rates of change. These work and nonwork predators interact and create stress for individuals on and off the job.

This chapter focuses primarily on the individual at work in organizations and on the stress created in this setting. Much of the stress experienced by people in our industrialized society originates in organizations; much of the stress that originates elsewhere affects our behavior and performance in these same organizations. In the article "Who Beats Stress—and How," which is part of this chapter, the author points out that what we do not understand about stress would fill volumes. His point is well taken. One of the complicating issues in understanding stress is the fact that it has been defined in many ways. We begin this chapter with our definition of stress.

Reading 7.1

Who beats stress best—and how

WHAT IS STRESS?

Stress means different things to different people. From a layperson's perspective, stress can be described as feeling tense, anxious, or worried. Scientifically, these feelings are all manifestations of the stress experience, a complex programmed response to perceived threat that can have both positive and negative results. The term *stress* itself has been defined in literally hundreds of ways in the literature. Virtually all of the definitions can be placed into one of two categories, however; stress can be defined as either a *stimulus* or a *response*.

A stimulus definition treats stress as some characteristic or event that may result in a disruptive consequence. It is, in that respect, an engineering definition of stress, borrowed from the physical sciences. In physics, stress refers to the external force applied to an object, for example a bridge girder. The response is "strain," which is the impact the force has on the girder.

In a response definition, stress is seen partially as a response to some stimulus, called a **stressor**. A stressor is a potentially harmful or threatening external event or situation. Stress is more than simply a response to a stressor, however. In a response definition, stress is the consequence of the interaction between an environmental stimulus (a stressor) and the individual's response. That is, stress is the result of a unique interaction between stimulus conditions in the environment and the individual's predisposition to respond in a particular way. Using a response definition, we will define **stress** as:

> An adaptive response, moderated by individual differences, that is a consequence of any action, situation, or event that places special demands on a person.

We think it is useful to view stress as the response a person makes and to identify stimulus conditions (actions, situations, events) as stressors. This allows us to focus attention on aspects of the organizational environment that are potential stress producers. Whether stress is actually felt or experienced by a particular in-

---

[1]Richard S. DeFrank and John M. Ivancevich, "Stress on the Job: An Executive Update," *Academy of Management Executive*, August 1998, pp. 55–56.

dividual will depend on that individual's unique characteristics. Furthermore, note that this definition emphasizes that stress is an adaptive response. Since the great majority of stimuli in the work environment do not require adaptation, they are not really potential stress sources.

In the context of our definition of stress, it is important to understand that stress is the result of dealing with something placing *special* demands on us. *Special* here means unusual, physically or psychologically threatening, or outside our usual set of experiences. Starting a new job assignment, changing bosses, having a flat tire, missing a plane, making a mistake at work, having a performance evaluation meeting with the boss—all of these are actions, situations, or events that may place special demand on you. In that sense, they are *potential* stressors. We say *potential* because not all stressors will always place the same demands on people. For example, having a performance appraisal meeting with the boss may be extremely stressful for Lynn and not the least stressful for her coworker, Sabrina. Such a meeting makes special demands of Lynn; for Sabrina it does not. For Lynn the meeting is a stressor; for Sabrina it is not.[2]

In order for an action, situation, or event to result in stress, it must be perceived by the individual to be a source of threat, challenge, or harm. If there are no perceived consequences—good or bad—there is no potential for stress. Three key factors determine whether an experience is likely to result in stress. These factors are importance, uncertainty, and duration. *Importance* relates to how significant the event is to the individual. For example, let us suppose that you are facing a job layoff. The more significant that layoff is to you, the more likely you are to find it stressful. If you expect the layoff to be followed by a period of prolonged unemployment, you will probably view it as a more important event than if immediate reemployment is assured.

Uncertainty refers to a lack of clarity about what will happen. Rumors of an impending layoff may be more stressful to some people than knowing for certain they will be laid off. At least in the latter case, they can make plans for dealing with the situation. Frequently, "not knowing" places more demands on people than does knowing, even if the known result is perceived as negative.

Finally, *duration* is a significant factor. Generally speaking, the longer special demands are placed on us, the more stressful the situation. Being given a distasteful job assignment that only lasts a day or two may be mildly upsetting, while the same assignment lasting for six months may be excruciating. Most people can endure short periods of strenuous physical activity without tiring; prolong the duration, however, and even the most fit among us will become exhausted. The same holds true for stressors. Stress of short duration is sometimes referred to as acute stress. It may last a few seconds, a few hours, even a few days. Long duration stress, on the other hand, is sometimes referred to as *chronic stress*. Chronic stress may last for months and years. It is the ongoing tension experienced by the people of the Middle East or the turmoil that ethnic rivalries have brought to the people of Chechnya and Russia. It may also be the unrelenting pressure of a job one finds no satisfaction in performing, the constant demands made by an unreasonable boss, or the never-ending struggle to advance in one's chosen career.

---

[2]Michael T. Matteson and John M. Ivancevich, *Controlling Work Stress* (San Francisco: Jossey-Bass, 1987).

www.gm.com

Is the Organization Responsible for an Employee's Stress?

You Be the Judge

The text refers to stress as an adaptive response that is a result of a situation that places special demands on a person. If those special demands are related to an employee's job, should the employer be responsible? One employee thought so. Here's what happened.

James Carter was an automobile assembly-line worker employed by General Motors Corporation. The problem was, he was having a difficult time keeping up with the speed of the production line. The line moved past his work station faster than he was sometimes able to perform the operations for which he was responsible. Making the situation even more stressful for James was the fact that his supervisor frequently criticized him for his failure to keep up with line speed. Eventually the stress became more than he could cope with and he suffered a psychological breakdown. He wanted to be compensated for his "mental injury" and receive worker's disability payments. GM argued that it wasn't the job that caused the problem; thousands of workers perform essentially the same job in assembly plants without problems; it was Carter's reaction to the job, they said, and thus they were not responsible.

Was Carter's stress an injury? Was GM liable? You be the judge!

ORGANIZATIONAL STRESS: A MODEL

For most employed people, work and work-related activities and preparation time represent much more than a 40-hour-a-week commitment. Work is a major part of our lives, and work and nonwork activities are highly interdependent. The distinction between stress at work and stress at home has always been an artificial one at best. With the explosive increase of dual-career couples in the latter part of the 20th century, even this artificial distinction has become blurred. Our primary concern here, however, is with direct work-related stressors.

The model shown in Exhibit 7.1 is designed to help illustrate the link among organizational stressors, stress, and outcomes. Recall from our earlier definition that stress is a response to an action, situation, or event that places special demands on an individual. These occurrences are represented in Exhibit 7.1 as *stressors.* We have divided these stressors into main categories: individual, group, organizational, and extra organizational. The first three stressor categories are work-related.

The experience of work-related and extraorganizational stress produces outcomes behavioral, cognitive, and physiological. The model suggests that the relationship between stress and outcomes (individual and organizational) is not necessarily direct; similarly neither is the relationship between the stressors and stress. These relationships may be influenced by stress moderators. Individual differences such as age, social support mechanisms, and personality are introduced as potential moderators. A **moderator** is a valuable attribute that affects the nature of a relationship. While numerous moderators are extremely important, we focus our attention on three representative ones: personality, Type A behavior, and social support.

This provides managers with a framework for thinking about stress in the workplace. Consequently, it suggests that interventions may be needed and can be effective in improving negative stress consequences. Stress prevention and management can be initiated by individuals or the organization. The intention of most preventive programs is to reduce the occurrence, intensity, and negative impact of stress. The management of stress attempts to eliminate or minimize

EXHIBIT 7.1   A Model of Stressors, Stress, and Outcomes

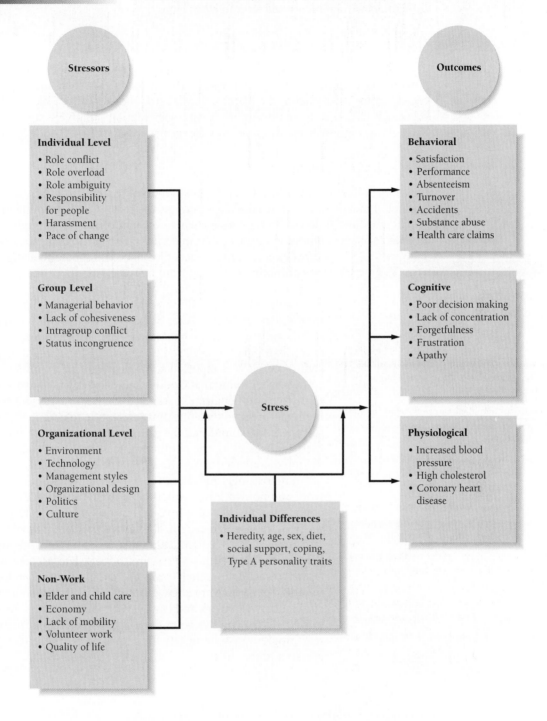

Stressors

Outcomes

Individual Level
- Role conflict
- Role overload
- Role ambiguity
- Responsibility for people
- Harassment
- Pace of change

Group Level
- Managerial behavior
- Lack of cohesiveness
- Intragroup conflict
- Status incongruence

Organizational Level
- Environment
- Technology
- Management styles
- Organizational design
- Politics
- Culture

Non-Work
- Elder and child care
- Economy
- Lack of mobility
- Volunteer work
- Quality of life

Stress

Individual Differences
- Heredity, age, sex, diet, social support, coping, Type A personality traits

Behavioral
- Satisfaction
- Performance
- Absenteeism
- Turnover
- Accidents
- Substance abuse
- Health care claims

Cognitive
- Poor decision making
- Lack of concentration
- Forgetfulness
- Frustration
- Apathy

Physiological
- Increased blood pressure
- High cholesterol
- Coronary heart disease

negative consequences of stress. Prevention and the management of stress are difficult as will be illustrated later in this chapter.

WORK STRESSORS: INDIVIDUAL, GROUP, AND ORGANIZATIONAL

Stressors are those actions, situations, or events that place special demands on a person. Since, in the right circumstances, virtually any occurrence can place special demands on a person, the list of potential stressors is infinite. We will limit our examination to a small number of stressors that are relatively common in each of our model's three work-specific categories.

Individual Stressors

Stressors at the individual level have been studied more than any other category presented in *Exhibit 7.1*. Role conflict is perhaps the most widely examined individual stressor.[3] **Role conflict** is present whenever compliance by an individual to one set of expectations about the job is in conflict with compliance to another set of expectations. Facets of role conflict include being torn by conflicting demands from a supervisor about the job and being pressured to get along with people with whom you are not compatible. Regardless of whether role conflict results from organizational policies or from other persons, it can be a significant stressor for some individuals. For example, a study at Goddard Space Flight Center determined that about 67 percent of employees reported some degree of role conflict. The study further found that Goddard employees who experienced more role conflict also experienced lower job satisfaction and higher job-related tension.[4] It is interesting to note that the researchers also found that the greater the power or authority of the people sending the conflicting messages, the greater was the job dissatisfaction produced by role conflict.

An increasingly prevalent type of role conflict occurs when work and nonwork roles interfere with one another. The most common nonwork roles involved in this form of conflict are those of spouse and parent. Balancing the demands of work and family roles is a significant daily task for a growing number of employed adults.[5] Pressure to work late, to take work home, to spend more time traveling, and to frequently relocate in order to advance are a few examples of potential sources of conflict between work and family. When both spouses are employed, added conflict potential exists when one partner's career progress may be negatively impacted by the career progression of the other.

www.gsfc.nasa.gov

Management Pointer 7.1

RECOGNIZING THE WARNING SIGNS OF STRESS IN EMPLOYEES

As a manager you should be alert to warning signs of stress in your subordinates. One indicator is change in behavior. Some of the more common changes include:

1. A normally punctual employee develops a pattern of tardiness (or a pattern of absences in a usually reliable worker).

2. A normally gregarious employee becomes withdrawn (or, less typically, a loner suddenly becomes a social butterfly).

3. An employee whose work is normally neat and demonstrates attention to detail submits messy, incomplete, or sloppy work.

4. A good decision maker suddenly starts making bad decisions (or seems to be unable to make decisions).

5. An easygoing employee who gets along well with others becomes irritable and discourteous.

6. A normally well groomed employee neglects his or her appearance.

----

[3]Cary Cooper, "Future Research in Occupational Stress," *Stress Medicine,* March 2000, pp. 63–65.

[4]R. L. Kahan, D. M. Wolfe, R. P. Quinn, J. D. Snoek, and R. A. Rosenthal, *Organizational Stress: Studies in Role Conflict and Ambiguity* (New York: John Wiley & Sons, 1964), p. 94.

[5]Stewart D. Friedman and Jeffrey H. Greenhaus, *Work and Family—Allies or Enemies?* (London, Oxford University Press, 2000).

Case 7.1

No response from monitor 23

Virtually everyone has experienced work overload at one time or another, and the incident rate is increasing.[6] Overload may be of two types: qualitative or quantitative. **Qualitative overload** occurs when people feel they lack the ability needed to complete their jobs or that performance standards have been set too high. Quantitative overload, on the other hand, results from having too many things to do or insufficient time to complete a job. As organizations attempt to increase productivity, while decreasing workforce size, quantitative overload increases (as does stress). The New York law firm of Cleary, Gottlieb, Steen, & Hamilton was sued by the father of an associate at the firm. The associate, unable to cope with the workload, committed suicide by jumping off the roof of the firm's building.[7]

From a health standpoint, numerous studies have established that quantitative overload might cause biochemical changes, specifically elevations in blood cholesterol levels. One study examined the relationship of overload, underload, and stress among 1,540 executives. Those executives in the low and high ends of the stress ranges reported more significant medical problems. This study suggests that the relationships among stressors, stress, and disease may be curvilinear. That is, those who are underloaded and those who are overloaded represent two ends of a continuum, each with a significantly elevated number of medical problems.[8] The underload-overload continuum is presented in Exhibit 7.2. The optimal stress level provides the best balance of challenge, responsibility, and reward. The potential negative effects of overload can be increased when overload is coupled with low ability to control the work demand.[9] Research suggests that when individuals experience high work demands with little or no control over these demands, the physiological changes that occur persist even after the individual has left work.[10]

Perhaps the most pervasive individual stressor of all is the unrelenting pace of change that is part of life today. At no other point in the history of industrialized society have we experienced such rapid change in the world around us. The last third of the 20th century included the advent of such wonders as communications satellites, moon landings, organ transplants, laser technology, nuclear power plants, intercontinental ballistic missiles, supersonic transportation, artificial hearts, and many other space-age developments. The pace of change within organizations has been no less remarkable at the start of the 21st century. Radical restructuring, new technologies, the stunning emergence of dot-com firms, new organizational firms, mergers, acquisitions, downsizings, and renewed emphasis on teams support this commonsense conclusion. On the other hand, many people who experience a great deal of change show absolutely no subsequent health problems. For some reason,

---

[6]P. Cramer, "Defense Mechanisms in Psychology Today: Further Processes for Adaptation," *American Psychologist,* June 2000.

[7]A. Stevens, "Suit over Suicide Raises Issue: Do Associates Work Too Hard?" *Wall Street Journal,* April 15, 1994, pp. B1, B7.

[8]Clinton Weiman, "A Study of Occupation Stressors and the Incidence of Disease/Risk," *Journal of Occupational Medicine,* February 1977, pp. 119–22.

[9]Toby Wall, Paul Jackson, Sean Mullarkey, and Sharon K. Parker, "The Demands-Control Model of Job Strain: A More Specific Test," *Journal of Occupational & Organizational Psychology,* June 1996, pp. 153–66.

[10]Einar M. DeCroon, Allard J. Van Der Beek, Roland W. B. Blonk, and Monique H. W. Frings-Dresen, "Job Stress and Psychosomatic Health Complaints among Dutch Truck Drivers: A Re-Evaluation of Karasik's Interactive Job Demand-Control Model," *Stress Medicine,* March 2000, pp. 101–107.

EXHIBIT 7.2
The Underload
Overload Continuum

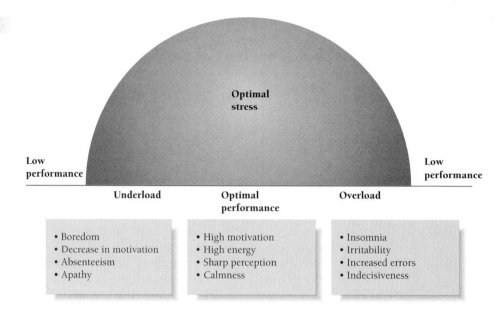

Underload	Optimal performance	Overload
• Boredom • Decrease in motivation • Absenteeism • Apathy	• High motivation • High energy • Sharp perception • Calmness	• Insomnia • Irritability • Increased errors • Indecisiveness

these people are strong enough to withstand the negative consequences of large doses of change that others do not.

Why this is so is an intriguing question. One organizational researcher, Suzanne Kobassa, has proposed that individuals who experience high rates of change without consequently suffering health problems might differ in terms of personality from those who do. She refers to the personality characteristic as "hardiness."[11] People with the hardiness personality trait seem to possess three important characteristics. First, they believe that they can control the events they encounter. Second, they are extremely committed to the activities in their lives. Third, they treat change in their lives as a challenge. In a longitudinal study to test the three-characteristic theory of hardiness, managers were studied over a two-year period. It was found that the more managers possessed hardiness characteristics, the smaller the impact of life changes on their personal health. Hardiness appeared to offset, or buffer, the negative impact of change.

Hardiness is proposed as a factor to reduce stress by changing the way stressors are perceived. The hardy person is able to work through and around stressors, while the less hardy person becomes overwhelmed and unable to cope. The hardy respond by coping, attempting to control, and taking on the stressors as a challenge. This type of response typically results in better behavioral, cognitive, and physiological consequences.[12]

Individual stressors abound. Not only can they cause stress but a number of negative consequences as well. As we will see later in the chapter, stress consequences can affect not only health, but a variety of job performance variables as well. Ethics Encounter 7.1 suggests stress may even be related to unethical behavior.

---

[11]S. R. Maddi and S. C. Kobasa, *The Hardy Executive: Heath under Stress* (Homewood, IL: Dow Jones-Irwin, 1984).

[12]R. Frank, "Coping: The Psychology of What Works," in C. R. Snyder (ed.), *Coping* (New York: Oxford University Press,) pp. vii–ix.

Ethics Encounter 7.1

Are Some Unethical Behaviors Stress Related?

Have you ever:

- Called in sick, when you really weren't?
- Lied to a boss, underling, or customer?
- Taken more time for a break or lunch than you should?
- Taken credit for someone else's idea?
- Overstated how much time you spent on a work assignment?

If you answered "yes" to one or more of these questions, well that makes you like a whole lot of other people. Despite renewed interest in employee and employer ethics in the last several years, dishonesty in the workplace is becoming as common as casual Friday. Nearly half of work-

ers engaged in unethical and/or illegal acts in a recent year, according to a survey completed by the Ethics Officer Association and the Chartered Life Underwriters and Chartered Financial Consultants.

According to the survey results, the high-stress atmosphere in many organizations may be to blame. Faced with demands of overtime, balancing work and family, and downsizing-related job insecurity, workers said they feel more stress than they did five years ago, as well as more pressure to act unethically. "Daily pressures are extreme, and it's those pressures that may be driving unethical practices," according to John Driskill, vice president of the Society of Underwriters and Financial Consultants.

Source: Based in part on an April 5, 1997, Associated Press wire release.

Group and Organizational Stressors

The list of potential group and organizational stressors is a long one. In the next chapter, for example, a number of group characteristics are discussed. These include group norms, leadership, and the status hierarchy. Each of these can be a stressor for some group members, as can the different types of group conflict discussed in Chapter 9. One problem in discussing group and organizational stressors is identifying which are the most important ones. In the paragraphs that follow we will briefly highlight what we feel are the more significant stressors.

Participation   Participation refers to the extent that a person's knowledge, opinions, and ideas are included in the decision-making process. It is an important part of working in organizations for some people. Groups and organizations that do not encourage or allow participation will be a source of frustration to those who value it. Likewise, others will be frustrated by the delays often associated with participative decision making. Others may view shared decision making as a threat to the traditional right of a manager to have the final say. Participation will act as a stressor for these people.

Intra and Intergroup Relationships   Poor relationships within and between groups can be a source of stress. Poor relationships may include low trust, lack of cohesion, low supportiveness, and lack of interest in listening to and dealing with the problems that confront a group or group member. Problem relationships can lead to communication breakdowns and low job satisfaction, further increasing the likelihood of stress.

Organizational Politics   High levels of political behavior in organizations can be a source of stress for many employees. Office politics are consistently cited as a primary stressor in organizations. Political activity, game playing, and power struggles can create friction, heighten dysfunctional competition between individuals and groups, and increase stress.

Friction, stress, and a hard-driving style are exemplified by the actions of Al Dunlap, a designated turnaround chief executive officer. Dunlap was given credit for turning around troubled American Can, Crown Zellenbach, and Scott Paper. On the other hand, he was a failure at Sunbeam and was eventually fired.[13] He had a reputation of being political, gruff, and demeaning. One of the first meetings at Sunbeam was described as follows: "It was like a dog barking at you for hours. He just yelled, ranted, and raved. He was condescending, belligerent, and disrespectful."[14] Many managers left Sunbeam because it became a highly politicized and stressful place to work. Al Dunlap was himself a stressor for many of the managers who wouldn't tolerate his behavior and style.

Organizational Culture   Like individuals, organizations have distinct personalities. The personality of an organization is shaped largely by its top executives. A tyrannical and autocratic executive team is able to create a culture that is filled with fear. Ernest Gallo is credited with being the stress producer at Gallo Winery because of the culture he has established with his hard-driving style, unrelenting insistence on superior performance, and low tolerance for failure.[15]

Lack of Performance Feedback   Most people want to know how they are doing, and how management views their work. All too often, however, meaningful performance evaluation information is lacking. Or, the information is provided in a highly authoritarian or critical manner. Performance feedback information must be provided, and if it is to be provided in a way that minimizes stress, it must take place in an open two-way communication system.

Inadequate Career Development Opportunities   Career development opportunity stressors are those aspects of the organizational environment that influence a person's perception of the quality of his or her career progress. Career variables may serve as stressors when they become sources of concern, anxiety, or frustration. This can happen if an employee is concerned about real or imagined obsolescence, feels that promotion progress is inadequate, or is generally dissatisfied with the match between career aspirations and the current position.

Downsizing   Downsizing is primarily associated with the reduction of human resources by layoffs, attrition, redeployment, or early retirement.[16] As some organizations strive to become "lean and mean," increasing numbers of employees are either downsized or fear being downsized. In either case, it is a potent stressor. It can have negative effects for both individuals and organizations. Studies have shown, for example, that disability claims can increase as much as 70 percent in companies that have recently downsized.[17] This increase comes both from employees who have been dismissed as well as from those who remained. That is

---

[13]Pamela L. Perrewe, Gerald R. Ferris, Dwight D. Frink, and William P. Anthony," Political Skill: An Antidote for Workplace Stressors," *Academy of Management Executive,* August 2000, pp. 115–23.

[14]J. A. Byrne, "Chainsaw: The Notorious Career of Al Dunlap," (New York: Harper Collins, 1999).

[15]M. T. Matteson and J. M. Ivancevich, *Controlling Work Stress,* p. 48.

[16]James B. Shaw, "A Conceptual Framework for Assessing Organization, Work Group, and Individual Effectiveness during and after Downsizing," *Human Relations,* February 1997, pp. 109–27.

[17]Martha H. Peak, "Cutting Jobs? Watch Your Disability Expenses Grow," *Management Review,* March 1997, p. 9.

probably why many companies have followed the lead of ReliaStar Bankers Security Life Insurance Co., who established a program to help employees cope with the stress of reorganizations and layoffs.

Nonwork stressors are those caused by factors outside the organization. Although, the emphasis in the chapter is on work, nonwork stressors should not be ignored. Raising children, caring for elders, volunteering in the community, taking college courses, and balancing family and work life are stressful situations for numerous people. The stress produced outside of work is likely to impact a person's work, behavior in general, and performance. The distinction between work and nonwork is blurred, overlaps, and is significant in any discussion or analysis of stress.

STRESS OUTCOMES

The effects of stress are many and varied. Some effects, of course, are positive, such as self-motivation and stimulation to satisfy individual goals and objectives. Nonetheless, some stress consequences are disruptive, counterproductive, and even potentially dangerous. Additionally, as was discussed earlier (see Exhibit 7.2), there are consequences associated with *too little* stress as well as too much.

Not all individuals will experience the same outcomes. Research suggests, for example, that one of many factors influencing stress outcomes is type of employment. In one study, conducted at the Institute for Social Research at the University of Michigan, a sample of 2,010 employees was chosen from 23 occupations to examine the relationship between stress and stress consequences. The occupations were combined into four specific groups—blue-collar workers (skilled and unskilled) and white-collar workers (professional and nonprofessional).

Blue-collar workers reported the highest subjective effects, including job dissatisfaction; white-collar workers, the lowest. The unskilled workers reported the most boredom and apathy with their job conditions. They specifically identified a number of major stressors that created their psychological state: underutilization of skills and abilities, poor fit of the job with respect to desired amounts of responsibility, lack of participation, and ambiguity about the future. Skilled blue-collar workers shared some of these stressors and consequences with their unskilled counterparts, but not all; they reported above-average utilization of their skills and abilities but had less responsibility and more ambiguity. White-collar professionals reported the fewest negative consequences. In all groups, however, there were indications that job performance was affected.[18]

In examining stress outcomes, the distinction in our model between organizational and individual outcomes is somewhat arbitrary. For example, a decrement in job performance due to stress is clearly an individual outcome, it is the individual's performance that is being affected. Just as clearly, however, the organization experiences important consequences from stress-related performance decrements.

Individual Outcomes

The emergence or evolution of stress outcomes takes time to identify or pinpoint. Eventually, evidence is available upon which to reach a number of conclusions.

---

[18]J. French, W. Rogers, and S. Cobb, "A Model of Person-Environment Fit," in G. Coelho, D. Hamburgh, and J. Adams (eds.), *Coping and Adaptation* (New York: Basic Books, 1974).

International Encounter 7.1

Stress and Death in Japan

Have you ever felt or heard someone else express the feeling, "This job is going to kill me!" Chances are you—or the person you heard—didn't literally believe that. If you were a Japanese worker, however, you might be very serious. Polls indicate that over 40 percent of Japanese workers aged 30 to 60 believe they will die from the stress of overwork, what the Japanese call *Karoshi*. The victims of *Karoshi* are known in their companies as *moretsu shain* (fanatical workers) and *yoi kigyo senshi* (good corporate soldiers).

In spite of recent revisions of the Japanese labor standard law that reduced the length of the average workweek, Japanese workers spend on average about six weeks (or about 250 hours per year) more on the job than most Americans. A Japanese Health Ministry report called *Karoshi* the second leading cause of death among workers (the first is cancer). Fierce competition among employees, as well as a strong sense of responsibility to their companies, lead many workers to stay at the office well into the night. When they do go home they are tense and anxious because they feel that they should really be back at work. Some workers deal with the pressure by disappearing. As many as 10,000 men disappear each year, choosing to drop out rather than face the pressure of their jobs.

There are signs, however, that things are changing. The government has funded a multimillion dollar study of *Karoshi*. Some of Japan's leading firms, such as Sony Corporation, have begun to require employees to take vacations whether they want to or not. Also, more companies are closing on Saturday, part of a national drive toward a five-day workweek. Traditions die hard in Japan, however, and no one believes fear of *Karoshi* will disappear any time soon.

www.sony.com

For example, a promoted employee develops an uncharacteristic pattern of Friday and Monday absence. A salesperson begins to lose repeat business; nonrenewing customers complain that he has become inattentive and curt in his dealings with them. A formerly conscientious nurse forgets to administer medications, with potentially serious patient consequences. An assembly worker experiences a significant increase in the percentage of her production rejected by the quality-control unit. A software designer displays sudden, apparently unprovoked outbursts of anger. Each of these individuals is experiencing the effects, or consequences, of excessive stress.

Stress can produce *psychological consequences*. These would include anxiety, frustration, apathy, lowered self-esteem, aggression, and depression. With respect to depression, a comprehensive survey of American workers concluded that a third of them experienced job stress-related depression.[19] Nor are such consequences restricted to American workers, as International Encounter 7.1 demonstrates.

There is a stigma associated with depression.[20] Part of the stigma is that most people lack an understanding of depression and its frequency. Unfortunately most managers are not aware of these facts:

- According to the National Mental Health Association, the cost of depression is $43 billion a year in medical bills, lost productivity, and absenteeism.[21]
- Depression is the seventh most common cause of adult deaths.[22]

---

[19]C. L. Park and S. Folkman, "The Role of Meaning in the Context of Stress and Coping," *General Review of Psychology,* Spring 1997, pp. 115–44.

[20]Joseph Kline, Jr. and Lyle Sussman, "An Executive Guide to Workplace Depression," *Academy of Management Review,* August 2000, pp. 103–14.

[21]Sharon Johnson, "Depression: Dragging Millions Down," *The New York Times Magazine,* October 29, 2000, pp. 39, 47.

[22]Ibid.

- Depression is difficult to detect, especially within the present health care system.[23]

The Diagnostic and Statistical Manual of Mental Disorders (DSM-IV) is the diagnostic tool used to detect depression. The DSM-IV indicates that the diagnosis of depression requires the presence of either a depressed mood or diminished interest in all or most activities, marked psychomotor retardation, significant appetite or weight change, changes in sleep, fatigue, or loss of energy, problems thinking or concentrating, feelings of worthlessness, excessive feelings of guilt, or thoughts of suicide or death. These signs must be persistent over the course of two weeks.

Managerial understanding of these symptoms can help the organization especially when the manager requests professional counselors to intervene. Managers are not skilled enough to intervene. Mild and moderate cases of depression can be treated over a period of time. It would be unwise for managers to ignore depression or to attempt to counsel workers suspected of being depressed. Being aware of depression symptoms and the situations that precipitate it is the first line of intervention. Unfortunately, the stigma of depression results in a lack of understanding of its pervasiveness, costs, and treatment possibilities.[24]

Some outcomes may be *cognitive.* Cognitive outcomes would include poor concentration, inability to make sound decisions or any decisions at all, mental blocks, and decreased attention spans. Other effects may be *behavioral.* Such manifestations as accident proneness, impulsive behavior, alcohol and drug abuse, and explosive temper are examples. Finally, *physiological outcomes* could include increased heart rate, elevated blood pressure, sweating, hot and cold flashes, increased blood glucose levels, and elevated stomach acid production.

Among the individual outcomes of stress, those classified as physiological are perhaps the most dysfunctional because they can in turn contribute to physical illness. One of the more significant of the physiological consequences and illness relationships is that of coronary heart disease (CHD). Although virtually unknown in the industrialized world a century ago, CHD now accounts for almost two out of every five deaths in the United States. Traditional risk factors such as obesity, smoking, heredity, and high cholesterol can account for no more than about 25 percent of the incidence of CHD. There is growing medical opinion that job and life stress may be a major contributor to the remaining 75 percent.[25] Several studies have found, for example, a relationship between changes in blood pressure and job stress.[26]

Some stress outcomes combine effects from several of the categories of consequences described above. Consider, for example, the following two scenarios:

> Bob is a teacher in an inner-city high school. He barely remembers the time when he could not wait for the start of each school day; now he cannot wait until each day ends. As much as he could use the money, he quit teaching optional summer school three summers ago. He needs that break to recharge his batteries, which seem to run

[23]K. B. Wells, R. Sturm, C. D. Sherbourne, & L. S. Meredith, *Caring for Depression: A Rand Study* (Cambridge, MA: Harvard University Press, 1996).

[24]M. Dewan, "Are Psychiatrists Cost-Effective? An Analysis of Integrated versus Split Treatment," *The American Journal of Psychiatry,* Summer 1999.

[25]D. C. Schwebel and J. Seels, "Cardiovascular Reactivity and Neuroticism: Results from a Laboratory and Controlled Ambulatory Stress Protocol," *Journal of Personality,* January 1999, pp. 67–92.

[26]C. Aldwin, *Stress, Coping, and Development* (New York: Guilford Press, 1994).

EXHIBIT 7.3   Burnout Indicators

Emotional Exhaustion	Depersonalization	Low Personal Accomplishment
Feel drained by work	Have become calloused by job	Cannot deal with problems effectively
Feel fatigued in the morning	Treat others like objects	Do not have a positive influence on others
Frustrated	Do not care what happens to other people	Cannot understand others' problems or identify with them
Do not want to work with other people	Feel other people blame you	No longer feel exhilarated by your job

down earlier with each passing school year. Many of his students are moody, turned off to society, and abusive to others. Bob is beginning to realize that he himself is becoming moody, turned off to society, and abusive to others.

Paula works as an air traffic controller in the second-busiest airport in the country. Every day, the lives of literally thousands of people depend on how well she does her job. Near misses are an everyday occurrence; avoiding disasters requires quick thinking and a cool head. At 31 years of age, Paula is the third oldest controller in the tower. She knows there are few controllers over the age of 40, and she is certain she will never be one. To make matters worse, she is in the final stages of a divorce. Paula was told after her last physical that she had developed a stomach ulcer. She is thinking of going into the nursery business with her sister; having responsibility for the well-being of shrubs and trees, rather than people, is very attractive to her.

Bob and Paula are both experiencing job burnout. Burnout is a psychological process, brought about by unrelieved work stress, that results in emotional exhaustion, depersonalization, and feelings of decreased accomplishment.[27] Exhibit 7.3 displays some of the indicators of these three burnout outcomes. Burnout tends to be a particular problem among people whose jobs require extensive contact with and/or responsibility for other people. Indeed, much of the research that has been conducted on burnout has centered on the so-called helping professions: teachers, nurses, physicians, social workers, therapists, police, and parole officers.[28] Organizational Encounter 7.1 presents some of the myths that surround the burnout concept.

A very important idea implicit in this conceptualization of burnout relates to job involvement. A high degree of involvement in, identification with, or commitment to one's job or profession is a necessary prerequisite for burnout. It is unlikely that one would become exhausted without putting forth a great deal of effort. Thus, the irony of burnout is that those most susceptible are those most committed to their work; all else being equal, lower job commitment equals lower likelihood of burnout. Various individual variables also affect the likelihood of developing burnout. For example, women are more likely to burn out than men, younger employees are more susceptible than older ones (particularly beyond age 50), and unmarried workers are more likely to burn out than married ones.

---

[27]R. J. Burke, "Workalcoholism in Organizations: Psychological and Physical Well-Being Consequences," *Stress Medicine,* January 2000, pp. 11–16.

[28]Ibid.

Myths and Burnout

A study reported in the *Wall Street Journal* involved interviewing dozens of managers in an attempt to understand managerial behavior that seems to push employees over the edge into job burnout. In the process, three myths were uncovered that organizations need to dispel if they are to reduce incidents of burnout among their staff.

Myth One: When a client says jump, the only answer is "How high?"

Lawyers, accountants, and management consultants are particularly vulnerable to believing in this myth even when it appears to result in high levels of burnout and turnover within their staffs. However, the study reported that a few professional firms are taking steps to integrate personal needs and concerns with the work lives of their employees. For example, Deloitte & Touche has implemented a policy that limits their employees' travel time. It is no longer company policy for employees to spend all five working days of the week at clients' offices. At a maximum, employees are to spend only three nights (four working days) away from home and work the fifth day in their own offices each week, even when on lengthy assignments. A Deloitte managing director stated, "Most clients recognize that this policy is a good thing." Among other things, it also limits the amount of time that clients' employees have to be involved with the work that Deloitte is doing for them, thus allowing better control of their own schedules.

Myth Two: Reining in employees' workloads will turn them into slackers.

Managers often behave as though a reduction in work overload will cause productivity to drop. Yet, studies often show the opposite result. Ernst & Young has a committee that monitors its staff accountants' workloads to head off burnout situations. The company says that its policies are raising retention rates and improving client service. A senior manager at Ernst, observed that employees typically won't admit to burning out; thus having some compassionate, objective overview is useful. "About the only time we would find out that someone was suffering from job burnout was during the exit interview, and then it was too late."

Myth Three: If employees are working themselves into the ground, it's their own fault.

Although this attribution may sometimes be true for some people, it is far from true for most. At the International Food Policy Research Institute, a nonprofit research organization in Washington, DC, consultants discovered that a "crisis mentality" was driving scientists and support staff to work incredibly long hours. Management of the institute assumed that either (1) employees wanted to work these hours or (2) employees were managing their time poorly. Neither of these assumptions was valid. Rather, a shift in research focus coupled with an increased emphasis on using research teams allied with groups from other agencies and organizations had created an inefficient pattern of work for many people. Meetings, phone calls, and other forms of coordinated activity were eating up the workday, driving more productive research and writing into the evening hours. Once the institute's management became aware of the inefficient patterns of work behavior, major changes were made in workplace routine. The redesign of activities reduced the amount of time people were having to work, which in turn reduced stress and increased productivity. In this case, management initially viewed the time problems as failures of individuals when, the fact, it was a failure of the organization.

Adapted from Sue Schellenberger, "The Myths That Make Managers Push Staff to the Edge of Burnout," *Wall Street Journal*, March 17, 1999, p. B1.

Organizations contribute to employee job burnout in a variety of ways. Researchers identify four factors that are particularly important contributors to burnout: high levels of work overload, dead-end jobs, excessive red tape and paperwork, and poor communication and feedback, particularly regarding job performance. In addition, factors that have been identified in at least one research study as contributing to burnout include role conflict and ambiguity, difficult interpersonal relationships, and reward systems that are not contingent upon performance.[29]

---

[29]Cynthia L. Cordes and Thomas W. Dougherty, "A Review and an Integration of Research on Job Burnout," *Academy of Management Review*, October 1993, pp. 621–56.

w.us.
oitte.com

w.ey.com

Organizational Consequences

As illustrated in Exhibit 7.1 a number of the behavioral, cognitive, and physiological outcomes that are individually linked also have organizational consequences. While the organizational consequences of stress are many and varied, they share one common feature: Stress costs organizations money. Although precise figures are lacking, based on a variety of estimates and projections from government, industry, and health groups, we place the costs of stress at approximately $150 billion annually. This estimate, which probably is conservative (some estimates are as high as $300 billion annually)[30] attempts to take into account the dollar effects of reductions in operating effectiveness resulting from stress. The effects include poorer decision making and decreases in creativity. The huge figure also reflects the costs associated with mental and physical health problems arising from stress conditions, including hospital and medical costs, lost work time, turnover, sabotage, and a host of other variables that may contribute to stress costs. When you consider that employers pay approximately 80 percent of all private health insurance premiums, and that workers' compensation laws increasingly include provisions for awarding benefits for injuries stemming from stress in the workplace, it is clear that organizational consequences are significant.

Excessive stress increases job dissatisfaction. As we saw in Chapter 3, job dissatisfaction can be associated with a number of dysfunctional outcomes, including increased turnover and absenteeism and reduced job performance. If productivity is reduced just three percent, for example, an organization employing 1,000 people would need to hire an additional 30 employees to compensate for that lost productivity. If annual employee costs are $40,000 per employee including wages and benefits, stress is costing the company $1.2 million just to replace lost productivity. This doesn't include costs associated with recruitment and training. Nor does it consider that decreases in *quality* of performance may be more costly for an organization than quantity decreases. Customer dissatisfaction with lower-quality goods or services can have significant effects on an organization's growth and profitability.

Further examples of organizational costs associated with stress include:

- 60 to 80 percent of worksite accidents are the result of stress.[31]
- Stressed workers smoke more, eat less well, have more problems with alcohol and drugs, have more family problems, and have more problems with coworkers.[32]
- As many as 75 to 90 percent of visits to physicians are stress related, costing industry over $200 billion a year.[33]
- Costs associated with stress may reduce U.S. industry profits by 10 percent.[34]
- Stress explains over 20 percent of the total number of health care claims and 16 percent of the costs.[35]

---

[30]Cooper, "Future Research," p. 63.

[31]P. J. Rosch, "Job Stress: America's Leading Health Problem," *USA Today*, May 1991, pp. 42–45.

[32]Janet Cahill, Paul Landsbergis, and Peter L. Schnall, "Reducing Occupational Stress," Presented at Work Stress and Health Conference, Washington DC, September 12, 1995.

[33]Joseph A. Dear, "Creating Healthier Workplaces," Presented at Work Stress and Health Conference, Washington DC, September 14, 1995.

[34]Richard S. Lazarus, *Stress and Emotion: A New Synthesis* (New York: Spring 1999).

[35]Ibid.

Estimates and projections such as these (including our own estimate of annual stress-related costs) should be treated cautiously. There are simply too many variables to measure costs precisely. There is no doubt however, that the consequences of excessive stress are significant in both individual and organizational terms.

STRESS MODERATORS

Stressors evoke different responses from different people. Some people are better able to cope with a stressor than others. They can adapt their behavior in such a way as to meet the stressor head-on. On the other hand, some people are predisposed to stress; that is, they are not able to adapt to the stressor.

The model presented in Exhibit 7.1 suggests that various factors can moderate the relationships among stressor, stress, and consequences. A moderator is a condition, behavior, or characteristic that qualifies the relationship between two variables. The effect may be to intensify or weaken the relationship. The relationship between the number of gallons of gasoline used and total miles driven, for example, is moderated by driving speed. At very low and very high speeds, gas mileage declines; at intermediate speeds, mileage increases. Thus, driving speed affects the relationship between gasoline used and miles driven.

Many conditions, behaviors, and characteristics may act as stress moderators, including such variables as age, gender, and the hardiness construct discussed earlier in the chapter. In this section, we will briefly examine three representative types of moderators: (1) personality, (2) Type A behavior, and (3) social support.

Personality

As discussed in Chapter 3, the term *personality* refers to a relatively stable set of characteristics, temperaments, and tendencies that shape the similarities and differences in people's behavior. The number of aspects of personality that could serve as stress moderators is quite large. We will confine our attention to those aspects of personality previously identified in Chapter 3: the Big Five Model, locus of control, and self-efficacy.

As you may recall from Chapter 3, the Big Five Model of personality is made up of five dimensions: extroversion, emotional stability, agreeableness, conscientiousness, and openness to experience. Of these, *emotional stability* is most clearly related to stress. Those high on this dimension are most likely to experience positive moods and feel good about themselves and their jobs. While they certainly experience stress, they are less likely to be overwhelmed by it and are in a better position to recover from it. To a somewhat lesser degree, those high on *extroversion* are also more predisposed to experience positive emotional states. Because they are sociable and friendly, they are more likely to have a wider network of friends than their introverted counterparts; consequently, they have more resources to draw upon in times of distress.

If you are low on *agreeableness* you have a tendency to be antagonistic, unsympathetic, even rude, toward others. You are also probably somewhat mistrusting of others. These attributes increase the likelihood you will find other people to be a source of stress, and since others are more likely to find interacting with you stressful as well, an interpersonal relationship environment full of stressful situations is created. *Conscientiousness* is the Big Five dimension most consistently related to job performance and success. To the extent that good performance leads to satisfaction and other rewards, those high on conscientiousness are less likely to experience stress with respect to these aspects of their jobs. Those low on this dimension, however, are more likely to be poorer performers, receive fewer rewards, and generally be less successful in their careers, not a recipe for low stress levels! Finally, those high on *openness to experience* are better prepared to deal with stressors associated with change because they are more likely to view change as a challenge, rather than a threat.

Beliefs people have about where control over their lives resides relates to *locus of control*. As discussed in Chapter 3, "internals" perceive themselves to be in control of the events that shape their lives to a greater extent than "externals," who feel that control is external to them. The traditional assumption is that if people feel they have control in a situation, they will be less likely to assess the situation as threatening or stress causing.

While this assumption may be valid in a general sense, the relationship between locus of control and stress is not always that straightforward. A more inclusive depiction suggests that internals are more likely to experience stress when they are unable to exercise the control they believe they should, while externals will be threatened (and consequently, stressed) in situations where they can exercise some degree of control over what is happening. Viewed from this perspective, the locus of control–stress relationship is a function of personal beliefs and environmental realities: When a person's beliefs about where control resides are congruent with the actual locus of control in a given situation, there is less likelihood stress will result. When beliefs and reality are not the same, the likelihood of experiencing stress increases.

Self-efficacy is another personality attribute that is an important moderator variable. Individuals with high levels of self-efficacy feel confident in their abilities and in their job performance. They are more likely to perceive potential stressors as challenges and opportunities, rather than threats and problems. Those with low levels of self-efficacy, on the other hand, are less confident in their abilities and more likely to assume they will fail. Since they believe they will fail, they will likely exert less effort, and thereby ensuring their assessment of their abilities is correct! Even when a situation is perceived as threatening, those with high self-efficacy are more likely to deal with the threat quickly, effectively, and with fewer negative outcomes.

The relationship between self-efficacy and stress is not confined to one part of the stress process. Self-efficacy may moderate the process from the perception of stressors (workers with low self-efficacy are more likely to experience work overload, for example) to consequences (low self-efficacy has been associated with increased incidence of coronary heart disease risk, for example). Thus, as a moderator, self-efficacy plays a rather pervasive role.

Type A Behavior Pattern

In the 1950s, two medical cardiologists and researchers, Meyer Friedman and Ray Rosenman, discovered what they called the **Type A behavior pattern (TABP)**.[36] They searched the medical literature and found that traditional coronary risk fac-

---

[36]Meyer Friedman and Diane Ulmer, *Treating Type A Behavior and Your Heart* (New York: Alfred A. Knopf, 1984).

tors such as dietary cholesterol, blood pressure, and heredity could not totally explain or predict coronary heart disease (CHD). *Coronary heart disease* is the term given to cardiovascular diseases that are characterized by an inadequate supply of oxygen to the heart. Other factors seemed to the two researchers to be playing a major role in CHD. Through interviews with and observation of patients, they began to uncover a pattern of behavior or traits. They eventually called this the Type A behavior pattern (TABP).

The person with TABP has these characteristics:

Exercise 7.1

Behavior Activity Profile

- Chronically struggles to get as many things done as possible in the shortest time period
- Is aggressive, ambitious, competitive, and forceful
- Speaks explosively, rushes others to finish what they are saying
- Is impatient, hates to wait, considers waiting a waste of precious time
- Is preoccupied with deadlines and is work-oriented
- Is always in a struggle with people, things, events

The converse, Type B individual, mainly is free of the TABP characteristics and generally feels no pressing conflict with either time or persons. The Type B may have considerable drive, wants to accomplish things, and works hard, but the Type B has a confident style that allows him or her to work at a steady pace and not to race against the clock. The Type A has been likened to a racehorse; the Type B, to a turtle.

More recent research into TABP suggests that not all aspects of the behavior pattern are equally associated with negative consequences. Specifically, hostility has been identified as being the TABP subcomponent most predictive of the development of coronary heart disease among Type As.[37] Nor is CHD the only negative outcome. TABP has been associated with a number of health-related consequences including ulcers, insomnia, and depression.[38] As researchers learn more about the individual components that comprise Type A behavior, further refinements in our understanding of this moderator can be expected.

Social Support

Both the quantity and quality of the social relationships individuals have with others appear to have a potentially important effect on the amount of stress they experience and on the likelihood that stress will have adverse effects on their mental and physical health. **Social support** can be defined as the comfort, assistance, or information one receives through formal or informal contacts with individuals or groups. A number of studies have linked social support with aspects of health, illness, and stress.[39]

Social support may take the form of *emotional support* (expressing concern, indicating trust, boosting esteem, listening); *appraisal support* (providing feedback and affirmation); or *informational support* (giving advice, making suggestions,

---

[37]K. Orth-Gomer and N. Schneiderman (eds.), *Behavioral Medicine Approaches to Cardiovascular Disease Prevention* (Mahwah, NJ: Erlbaum, 1996).

[38]Ibid.

[39]See, for example, Fran H. Norris and Krzysztof Kaniasty, "Received and Perceived Social Support in Times of Stress: A Test of the Social Support Deterioration Deterrence Model," *Journal of Personality & Social Psychology*, September 1996, pp. 498–511.

—— **Management Pointer 7.2** ——

SOCIAL SUPPORT

Developing Social Support

As a manager, there are actions you can take to help create a supportive work environment. These include:

1. Set an example by being a source of support for others, particularly subordinates.

2. Encourage open communication and maximum exchange of information.

3. Make certain you provide subordinates with timely performance feedback, presented in an encouraging, nonthreatening manner.

4. Provide for mentoring of the less experienced by more senior members of the work group.

5. Work to maintain and increase work group cohesion (see Chapter 8 for specifics regarding how to do this).

providing direction). People who can serve as sources of social support at work include supervisors, coworkers, subordinates, and customers or other nonorganizational members with whom an employee might have contact. Nonwork support sources include family members (immediate and extended), friends, neighbors, caregivers (ministers, for example), health professionals (physicians, psychologists, counselors), and self-help groups (Alcoholics Anonymous, Weight Watchers).

A coworker listening to a friend who failed to receive a desired promotion, a group of recently laid-off workers helping each other find new employment, or an experienced employee helping a trainee learn a job are all examples of providing support. Social support is effective as a stress moderator because it buffers the negative impact of stressors by providing a degree of predictability, purpose, and hope in upsetting and threatening situations. Most everyone has experienced feeling "better" (calmer, less anxious, or concerned) after having talked about a problem with a spouse, friend, or coworker. Similarly, most everyone has provided support to someone else that has had positive effects for that person. Thus, virtually all of us know from first-hand experience the moderating role support can play.

A number of studies reinforce what we know to be true for our own experiences. Social support has been shown to reduce stress among employed individuals ranging from unskilled workers to highly trained professionals; it is consistently cited as an effective stress coping technique, and it has been associated with fewer health complaints experienced during periods of high stress.[40]

STRESS PREVENTION AND MANAGEMENT

An astute manager never ignores a turnover or absenteeism problem, workplace drug abuse, a decline in performance, hostile and belligerent employees, reduced quality of production, or any other sign that the organization's performance goals are not being met. The effective manager, in fact, views these occurrences as symptoms and looks beyond them to identify and correct the underlying causes. Yet most managers likely will search for traditional causes such as poor training, defective equipment, or inadequate instructions regarding what needs to be done. In all likelihood, stress will not be on the list of possible problems. Thus, the very first step in any attempt to deal with stress so that it remains within tolerable limits is recognition that it exists. Once that is accomplished, a variety of approaches and programs for preventing and managing organizational stress are available.

Exhibit 7.4 presents how organizational stress management programs can be targeted. Programs are targeted to (1) identify and modify work stressors, (2) engage employees in modifying and understanding of stress and its impact, and (3) provide employees support to cope with the negative impact of stress. In a rapidly changing work environment this type of targeting is difficult to accom-

---

[40]C. R. Snyder, "Coping: Where Are You Going?" in C. R. Snyder (ed.), *Copy* (New York: Oxford University Press, 1999), pp. 324–33.

EXHIBIT 7.4   **Organizational Stress Management Program Targets**

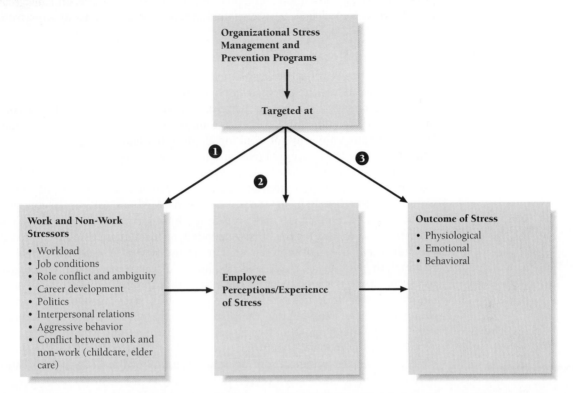

Source: John M. Ivancevich, Michael T. Matteson, Sara M. Freedman, and James S. Phillips, "Worksite Stress Management Interventions," *American Psychologist*, 1990, p. 253.

plish. However a trained, educated, and knowledgeable workforce can make modifications with the help of management in how work is performed. Some of the targeted, corrective programs include:

- Training programs for managing and coping with stress
- Redesigning work to minimize stressors
- Changes in management style to one of more support and coaching to help workers achieve their goals
- More flexible work hours and attention paid to work/life balance with regard to child and elder care
- Better communication and team-building practices
- Better feedback on worker performance and management expectation

These and other efforts are targeted to prevent and/or manage stress. The potential for success of any prevention or management of stress program is good if there is a true commitment to understanding how stressors, stress, and outcomes are linked.

There is a very important distinction between preventing stress and managing it. Stress *prevention* focuses on controlling or eliminating stressors that might provoke the stress response. Stress *management* suggests procedures for helping people cope effectively with or reduce stress already being experienced. In this concluding section of the chapter we will examine organizational programs and individual approaches to stress prevention and management, with the emphasis on *management*. First, however, we will look at a way of thinking about organizational stress *prevention*.

Maximizing Person-Environment Fit

In defining stress earlier in the chapter, we emphasized that stress is the consequence of the interaction between an environmental stimulus (a stressor) and the individual's response. From this perspective, stress may be viewed as a consequence of the relationship between the individual and the work environment. While there are many ways of thinking about individual-organizational relationships and stress, the concept of person-environment fit is the most widely used.[41]

A person-environment fit (P-E fit) approach generally focuses on two dimensions of fit.[42] One is the extent to which work provides formal and informal rewards that meet or match (fit) the person's needs. Misfit on this dimension results in stress. For example, a job may provide too little job security, insufficient compensation and reward for the effort expended, or inadequate recognition to meet the individual's needs or preferences. The second type of fit deals with the extent to which the employee's skills, abilities, and experience match the demands and requirements of the employer. To the extent that the individual's talents are insufficient for or underutilized by job requirements, stress results. By improving the quality of, or maximizing, the fit between the employee and the organizational environment, potential stressors are eliminated and stress is prevented. This P-E fit approach is somewhat similar to—and very consistent with—the concept of the psychological contract that was developed in Chapter 4. Violations of the psychological contract represent breakdowns in P-E fit.

There are numerous strategies for maximizing P-E fit. Ideally, the process begins before an individual even joins the organization. Employee recruitment programs which provide realistic job previews help potential employees determine whether the reality of the job matches their needs and expectations. Selection programs that are effective in ensuring that potential employees possess the requisite skills, knowledge, experience, and abilities for the job are key elements in maximizing fit.

Job skills and knowledge are not the only important factors to consider in employee selection, however. Fit can be maximized by closely linking personal predispositions to relevant aspects of the work environment as well. For example, as was suggested earlier, individuals with a low tolerance for ambiguity who find themselves in jobs or organizational environments in which there is little structure will very likely experience stress. There are many other examples: An individual who is by nature authoritarian will experience stress in a participative organization; those who value intrinsic satisfaction will be frustrated by an environment that provides only extrinsic rewards; those wishing autonomy will be distressed by tight controls; and individuals with a high need for performance feedback will be stressed by supervisors who never communicate performance information.

---

[41]See, for example, Jeffrey R. Edwards, "An Examination of Competing Versions of the Person-Environment Fit Approach to Stress," *Academy of Management Journal,* April 1996, pp. 292–339.

[42]Jeffrey R. Edwards, "An Examination of Competing Versions of the Person-Environment Fit Approach to Stress," *Academy of Management Journal,* April 1996, pp. 292–339.

Once in the organization, a critical variable in maximizing fit and preventing stress is effective socialization. Socialization is the process by which the individual learns and internalizes the values, expected behaviors, and social knowledge that are important for becoming an effective organizational member. The stages and characteristics of effective socialization were discussed in detail in Chapter 2, and you may wish to refer to that discussion in the present context of maximizing P-E fit.

A number of other organizational activities and programs can be helpful in maintaining good fit. For example, effective job design and ongoing redesign efforts have a critical role to play in maximizing fit. So do organizational reward systems, communication processes, effective leadership, and a variety of other variables addressed in previous or coming chapters. All of these activities can serve to eliminate or defuse potential stressors and thus serve to prevent organizational stress.

Organizational Stress Prevention and Management Programs

In addition to the variety of activities that may be undertaken to improve person-environment fit, an increasing number of organizations have developed very specific stress prevention and/or management programs. Some of these programs focus on a specific issue or problem, such as alcohol or drug abuse, career counseling, job relocation, or burnout. The United States Postal Service, for example, has developed a workplace violence prevention program. This program, the most comprehensive one in existence, represents an attempt to reduce the employee-initiated violence that characterized the service in the past.[43]

www.usps.gov

Still other programs may target a specific group within the organization. An example is the Resident Assistance Program in place at Baylor College of Medicine. This program was designed to help medical residents cope successfully with the multitude of stressors they encounter.[44] Some programs may focus on a particular technique, such as developing relaxation skills. (For an example of a somewhat unusual focus, see Organizational Encounter 7.2) Others are more general in nature, using a variety of approaches and geared to a cross-section of employees, such as the Employee Assistance Program at B. F. Goodrich, the Coors Brewing Company Wellness Program, and the Emotional Health Program at Equitable Life. Two specific types of organizational programs have become particularly popular during the last two decades: employee assistance programs and wellness programs.

Employee Assistance Programs (EAPs)   Originally conceived as alcohol abuse programs, most current employee assistance programs (EAPs) are designed to deal with a wide range of stress-related problems, both work and nonwork related, including behavioral and emotional difficulties, substance abuse, family and marital discord, and other personal problems. B. F. Goodrich, IBM, Xerox, and Caterpillar are examples of companies with such programs. EAPs tend to be

Exercise 7.2

Health Risk Appraisal

---

[43]"How the Postal Service Plans to Stop 'Going Postal'," *Government Executive,* December 1996, p. 14.

[44]Iris C. Mushin, Michael T. Matteson, and Edward C. Lynch, "Developing a Resident Assistance Program," *Archives of Internal Medicine,* March 1993, pp. 729–34.

Dealing with Stress Can Be a Laughing Matter

While passengers were preparing to board a Southwest Airlines flight, a Southwest customer service agent came over the public address system to announce, "Southwest Airlines would like to congratulate one of our first-time fliers who is celebrating his eighty-ninth birthday. As you board, be sure to stick your head into the cockpit and say happy birthday to your pilot, Captain John Smith."

The above true anecdote typifies the culture at Southwest Airlines, where they firmly believe that if employees are having fun they are going to do their jobs better and be less likely to experience dissatisfaction, stress, and burnout. Increasingly, companies are turning to humor as a way of improving employee morale and combating stress. A growing number of "humor consultants" are being hired by companies nationwide to lighten up an overworked and anxious workforce. Research supports the conclusion that humor boosts the human immune system,

reduces stress, and helps keep people well. Other research shows decreases in production of stress hormones while people are laughing.

One group of humor consultants is developing a program called Subjective Multidimensional Interactive Laughter Evaluation (SMILE) which will survey humor preferences, coping styles, and help tailor a personalized humor approach to stress reduction. What kind of organization would use such a program, or hire a humor consultant? The answer seems to be companies suffering from low morale, cutbacks, or buyouts. Corporations undergoing downsizing are a major user.

The rationale for these programs is that humor is a set of skills that some people have developed better than others. For those in need of skill development, humor programs can help people increase the tools they have to combat stress.

Source: Based in part on Maggie Jackson, "Firms Use Laughter to Aid Workers," *Houston Chronicle*, April 23, 1977, pp. 1C, 3C.

based on the traditional medical approach to treatment. General program elements include:

- *Diagnosis.* Employee with a problem asks for help; EAP staff attempts to diagnose the problem.
- *Treatment.* Counseling or supportive therapy is provided. If in-house EAP staff are unable to help, employee may be referred to appropriate community-based professionals.
- *Screening.* Periodic examination of employees in highly stressful jobs is provided to detect early indications of problems.
- *Prevention.* Education and persuasion are used to convince employees at high risk that something must be done to assist them in effectively coping with stress.

An increasing number of employers believe that good health among employees is good for the organization. Blue Cross/Blue Shield determined that every dollar spent on the psychological care of employees with breast cancer saved $2.50 to $5.10 in overall medical expenses. The public school system of Orange County, Florida, found that the cost of medical claims dropped by 66 percent over five years for employees who used the EAP. At the end of five years, the same employees were taking 36 percent fewer sick leaves. At McDonnell-Douglas (now called Boeing) workers treated for alcohol and drug problems missed 44 percent fewer days of work after the EAP was set up.[45]

[45]Vijai P. Shaimi, "Take Advantage of Employee Assistance Programs," *Mindpub*, October 2000, p. 225.

EAPs may be internal company-run programs or external efforts in which the organization contracts with a private firm to provide services to company employees. The previously cited Emotional Health Program at Equitable Life is typical of such programs. It is concerned with prevention, treatment, and referral of employees. Staffed with a clinical psychologist, a physician, a psychology intern, and a counselor, it focuses on individual intervention. Offered are biofeedback, relaxation training, and counseling. When appropriate, referrals are made to external health practitioners and hospitals.

Crucial to the success of any EAP is trust. Employees must trust that (1) the program can and will provide real help, (2) confidentiality will be maintained, and (3) use of the program carries no negative implications for job security or future advancement. If employees do not trust the program or company management, they will not participate. EAPs with no customers cannot have a positive effect on stress prevention and management.

Wellness Programs   **Wellness programs**, sometimes called Health Promotion Programs, focus on the employee's overall physical and mental health. Simply stated, any activity an organization engages in that is designed to identify and assist in preventing or correcting specific health problems, health hazards, or negative health habits can be thought of as wellness-related. This includes not only disease identification but lifestyle modification as well. Among the most prevalent examples of such programs are those emphasizing hypertension identification and control, smoking cessation, physical fitness and exercise, nutrition and diet control, and job and personal stress management.

It might appear strange that we would include wellness programs in a discussion of stress management. There are several reasons we do. First, stress prevention and management is a vital part of wellness, and, as we have already noted, it is frequently a component of wellness programs. Second, many of the concerns of wellness programs are at least partially stress related. Stress has been cited as the greatest cause of poor health habits,[46] and poor health habits are what wellness programs attempt to change. Third, a major reason organizations are interested in stress management is that it contributes to healthier, more productive, and more effective employees, and consequently to healthier, more productive, and more effective organizations. Corporate wellness programs simply extend these payoffs. Fourth, it is impossible to divorce the topic of stress from health. In a sense, wellness programs represent a broad-based, contemporary extension of stress programs; their focus is concern for employee health and quality-of-life issues.

Examples of well-established wellness programs (all of which include a stress reduction component) include Mass Mutual's Wellness Partnership, 3M's Lifestyle 2000 program, Warner-Lambert's LifeWise program, and Control Data's StayWell program. StayWell has been so successful that it is now marketed to other companies. Wellness programs, however, are not restricted to large companies like those just cited. Over 60 percent of firms with fewer than 250 employees provide some form of wellness program for their workers.[47]

www.3m.com

www.warner-lambert.com

---

[46]Ernesto A. Randolfi, "Stressed Out about Stress Management Program Evaluation?" Presented at Outcome of Preventive Health Programs Conference (Atlanta, Georgia), December 12, 1996.

[47]Laura M. Litvan, "Preventive Medicine," *Nation's Business*, September 1995, pp. 32–36.

www.roche.com

Roche Pharmaceutical of Nutley, New Jersey, found that it spent only 3 percent of medical benefit dollars on preventive health measures. This small expenditure was in spite of the fact that 39 percent of the health claims submitted were the result of preventable conditions. Roche management concluded that focusing on prevention would mean healthier, more productive, less stressed, more creative, and less absent employees. Roche named its wellness program "Choosing Health."[48]

Choosing Health starts at the individual level by assessing employee health risks via a 76-item survey. The form takes 15 minutes to complete. A health profile is provided and sent directly to the employee's home. All employee responses and profiles are confidential and not released to a third party. The company also provides on-site screening for such ailments as high blood pressure, high cholesterol, and breast and skin cancers. Roche's Human Resource Management (HRM) group receives only aggregated data showing risks within the general population. HRM then patterns preventive health programs after the health risks and education needs of employees as a group. Almost 100 percent of Roche employees participate in Choosing Health.

The Roche program provides a $100 incentive for completing 100 sessions at a fitness facility or in a group exercise program. In the second year of the program, 23 percent of Choosing Health participants have reduced their health risks.

A part of Choosing Health is an evaluation process to evaluate the impact of the program. In two years, the average lifestyle score has increased from 63 to 68 (100 is the optimal score). Roche is constantly working to align prevention, intervention, employee health, and productivity.

Simply offering an EAP or wellness program does not guarantee positive results for either employers or the sponsoring organization. While many factors determine how successful any particular program will be, a number of recommendations, if followed, will increase the likelihood of achieving beneficial outcomes. Among the more important are:

1. Top-management support, including both philosophical support and support in terms of staff and facilities, is necessary.
2. Unions should support the program and participate in it where appropriate. This can be particularly difficult to accomplish. Many unions take the position that instead of helping employees deal with stress, management should focus on eliminating those conditions that contribute to the stress in the first place.
3. The greatest payoff from stress prevention and management comes not from one-shot activities, but from ongoing and sustained effort; thus, long-term commitment is essential.
4. Extensive and continuing employee involvement would include involvement not only in the initial planning but in implementation and maintenance as well. This is one of the most critical factors for ensuring representative employee participation.
5. Clearly stated objectives lay a solid foundation for the program. Programs with no or poorly defined objectives are not likely to be effective or to achieve sufficient participation to make them worthwhile.

---

[48]Kelly Dunn, "Rocke Chooses Health by Promoting Prevention," *Workforce,* April 2000, pp. 82–84.

6. Employees must be able to participate freely, without either pressure or stigma.

7. Confidentiality must be strictly adhered to. Employees must have no concerns that participation will in any way affect their standing in the organization.

www.dupont.com

Du Pont Corporation has for years been dedicated to health promotion.[49] Cost effectiveness studies at Du Pont indicate that fitness programs work. Du Pont estimates that for every dollar invested in the health promotion program, at least two dollars is received in return. One analysis at Du Pont indicates that the annual company costs per person at risk are as follows:

Smokers	$960
Overweight	$401
Excess alcohol use	$389
High cholesterol	$370
High blood pressure	$343

Du Pont also determined that reducing absenteeism annually by about 6.8 percent would pay for the firm's entire health promotion effort.

Individual Approaches to Stress Prevention and Management   Organization members do not have to—nor should they—rely on formal organizational programs to assist in stress prevention and management. There are many individual approaches to dealing with stressors and stress. To see this, all you have to do is visit any bookstore on-site or online (*www.amazon.com, www.fatbrain.com*) and look at the self-improvement section. It will be stocked with numerous how-to books for reducing stress. Below, we will briefly examine a few of the more popularly cited and frequently used approaches for individual stress prevention and management. It is not unusual for any of these approaches to be included in the range of options available within an organizational stress management or wellness program. It should also be noted that there is a great deal of variation in the effectiveness of these techniques. What one person finds useful, another may not. There is still a great deal we do not know regarding the effects of individual differences on stress management outcomes.[50]

Cognitive Techniques   The basic rationale for some individual approaches to stress management, known collectively as cognitive techniques, is that a person's response to stressors is mediated by cognitive processes, or thoughts. The underlying assumption of these techniques is that people's thoughts, in the form of expectations, beliefs, and assumptions, are labels they apply to situations, and these labels elicit emotional responses to the situation. Thus, for example, if an individual labels the loss of a promotion a catastrophe, the stress response is to the label, not to the situation. Cognitive techniques of stress management focus on changing labels or cognitions so that people appraise situations differently. This reappraisal typically centers on removing cognitive distortions such as

---

[49]Discussion with Du Pont Health and Wellness Services manager on October 16, 18, and 20, 2000.

[50]David Bunce, "What Factors Are Associated with the Outcome of Individual-Focused Worksite Stress Management Interventions?" *Journal of Occupational and Organizational Psychology,* March 1997, pp. 1–17.

magnifying (not getting the promotion is the end of the world for me), over-generalizing (not getting promoted means my career is over; I'll never be promoted in any job, anywhere), and personalization (since I didn't get the promotion it's clear I'm a terrible person). All cognitive techniques have a similar objective: to help people gain more control over their reactions to stressors by modifying their cognitions.

Evaluative research of cognitive techniques to stress management is not extensive, although the studies reported are generally positive. Representative occupational groups where research has indicated positive outcomes with the use of cognitive approaches include nurses, teachers, athletes, and air traffic controllers.[51] The positive research, coupled with the wide range and scope of situations and stressors amenable to such an approach, make cognitive techniques particularly attractive as an individual stress management strategy.

Relaxation Training   The purpose of this approach is to reduce a person's arousal level and bring about a calmer state of affairs, both psychologically and physiologically. Psychologically, successful relaxation results in enhanced feelings of well-being, peacefulness and calm, a clear sense of being in control, and a reduction in tension and anxiety; physiologically, decreases in blood pressure, respiration, and heart rate should take place. Relaxation techniques include breathing exercises; muscle relaxation; autogenic training, which combines elements of muscle relaxation and meditation; and a variety of mental relaxation strategies, including imagery and visualization.

Conditions conducive to achieving relaxed states include a quiet environment, a comfortable physical position, and closed eyes. Simply taking a few moments of "mental rest" from job activities can be an effective relaxation activity. Short, more frequent breaks of this sort are more relaxing than fewer, longer breaks.[52]

Meditation   Many of the meditative forms that have achieved some degree of popularity in this country are derivatives of Eastern philosophies. Included in this category are Zen Meditation and Nam Sumran, or Sikh meditation. Perhaps the most widely practiced in the United States is transcendental meditation, or TM. Its originator, Maharishi Mahesh Yogi, defines TM as turning the attention toward the subtler levels of thought until the mind transcends the experience of the subtlest state of thought and arrives at the source of thought.[53] The basic procedure used in TM is simple, but the effects claimed for it are extensive. One simply sits comfortably with closed eyes and engages in the repetition of a special sound (a mantra) for about 20 minutes twice a day. Studies indicate that TM practices are associated with reduced heart rate, lowered oxygen consumption, and decreased blood pressure.[54]

Not everyone who meditates experiences positive payoffs. A sufficiently large number of people report meditation to be effective in managing stress. A number of organizations have started, supported, or approved of meditation programs for

---

[51]Donald Meichenbaum, *Stress Inoculation Training* (New York: Pergamon Press, 1985).

[52]Julia von Onciul, "Stress at Work," *British Medical Journal*, September 1996, pp. 745–48.

[53]E. E. Solberg, R. Halrorsen, and H. H. Holen, "Effect of Meditation on Immune Cells," *Stress Medicine*, April 2000, pp. 185–200.

[54]Ibid.

employees. They include Coors Brewing, Monsanto Chemicals, Xerox, Connecticut General Life Insurance Company, and the U.S. Army.

Biofeedback   Individuals can be taught to control a variety of internal body processes by using a technique called *biofeedback*. In biofeedback, small changes occurring in the body or brain are detected, amplified, and displayed to the person. Sophisticated recording and computer technology make it possible for a person to attend to subtle changes in heart rate, blood pressure, temperature, and brain-wave patterns that normally would be unobservable. Most of these processes are affected by stress.

The potential role of biofeedback as an individual stress management technique can be seen from the bodily functions that can, to some degree, be brought under voluntary control. These include brain waves, heart rates, muscle tension, body temperature, stomach acidity, and blood pressure. Most if not all of these processes are affected by stress. The potential of biofeedback is its ability to help induce a state of relaxation and restore bodily functions to a nonstressed state. One advantage of biofeedback over nonfeedback techniques is that it gives precise data about bodily functions. By interpreting the feedback, individuals know how high their blood pressure is, for example, and discover, through practice, means of lowering it. When they are successful, the feedback provides instantaneous information to that effect.

Biofeedback training has been useful in reducing anxiety, lowering stomach acidity (and thus reducing the likelihood of ulcer formation), controlling tension and migraine headaches, and, in general, reducing negative physiological manifestations of stress. Despite these positive results, people looking to biofeedback for stress control should understand that success requires training and the use of equipment that may be very expensive.

Summary of Key Points

- Stress may be viewed as either a stimulus or a response. We view it as an adaptive response moderated by individual differences, that is, a consequence of any action, situation, or event that places special demands on a person.

- Major variables in the model of organizational stress presented in this chapter are: (1) work stressors (work environment, individual, and group and organizational); (2) stress itself; (3) stress consequences (organizational and individual); (4) stress moderators (personality, Type A behavior, and social support); and (5) stress prevention and management (maximizing person-environment fit, organizational programs, and individual approaches).

- Stressors are actions, situations, or events that place special demands on a person. Three important categories of stressors are: (1) work environment (e.g., chemicals, radiation, temperature); (2) individual stressors (e.g., role conflict, work overload, change);

and (3) group and organizational stressors (e.g., politics, culture, interpersonal relationships, downsizing).

- While some consequences of stress are positive, many are dysfunctional. Negative individual consequences include accident proneness, poor concentration, drug and alcohol abuse, and burnout. Organizational consequences may include absenteeism, turnover, increased health and medical costs, and quantitative and qualitative decrements in productivity.

- Some factors affect the nature of the stress response. These are called *stress moderators*. Three important moderators are personality (e.g., locus of control and self-esteem), Type A behavior, and social support.

- Stress prevention and management strategies include (1) maximizing person-environment fit, (2) organizational programs such as employee assistance and wellness, and (3) individual approaches such as cognitive techniques, relaxation training, meditation, and biofeedback.

Review and Discussion Questions

1. It has been suggested that "stress is in the eyes of the beholder." What does this mean? Do you agree?

2. Why should managers not even attempt to counsel or provide advice to any employee suspected of being depressed?

3. The issue of who should be responsible for dealing with work stress—the individual or the organization—is an important one. What do you think? What are the arguments for and against each position?

4. Do you think some types of jobs or organizations attract Type A individuals? Do some attract Type B individuals? Why?

5. What is the relationship between work stress and work motivation? If we could eliminate all stress, what effect would this have on motivation?

6. Work underload may be every bit as dysfunctional as work overload. Can you think of other work variables where "too little" may be as counterproductive as "too much?"

7. What kinds of things could an organization do to better maximize employee-environment fit?

8. What is the relationship between stress and personality? What aspects of personality might tend to increase stress? Decrease it?

9. Why are people in certain occupations more susceptible to burnout? What kinds of things might organizations do to reduce the likelihood their members will experience burnout?

10. Increasingly, American workers are being sent on overseas assignments. What stressors might be unique to such assignments? What might organizations do to minimize their impact?

READING 7.1   Who Beats Stress Best—And How

In a faster-spinning world, managers are finding new ways to ease stress in workers and themselves. Wisdom comes from surprising sources—like the Army—and pays off.

What we don't understand about stress could fill volumes. And it does. Some books say stress is an invigorating tonic; others, that it's lethal. Stress stands implicated in practically every complaint of modern life, from equipment downtime to premature ejaculation, from absenteeism to sudden death. Some workers in high-stress occupations—bomb deactivators, for example—suffer its effects hardly at all. Yet a man who tastes port for a living lies awake some nights worried that "the whole business is riding on my palate." There's enough apparently contradictory information about stress to make any honest seeker after truth, well, anxious.

Isn't there more stress today than ever before? There might be. There might be more love. But neither condition is quantifiable. Diseases to which stress contributes—hypertension, heart attack, ulcers, the common cold—are quantifiable, but since stress isn't their only cause, an increase in them doesn't necessarily signal an increase in stress.

Ask people if they *feel* more stressed, and, of course, they say yes. Who would admit, even if it were true, that he feels *less* stressed than he did a year ago? Inner peace is seen to be the prerogative of dweebs. It's hip to be stressed. Earlier this year, Northwestern National Life Insurance questioned a random sample of 600 U.S. workers. Almost half (46 percent) said their jobs were highly stressful; 34 percent said they felt so much stress they were thinking of quitting.

Some of them were telling the truth. Commutes really are growing longer, highways more congested. In more families, both husbands and wives have jobs. And with upsizings, downsizings, rightsizings, takeovers, and mergers, the corporate world in recent years has turned upside down more times than James Dean's roadster.

The number of stress-related workers' compensation claims has ballooned in states such as California that compensate for so-called mental-mental injuries. In these, an intangible (mental) injury results from an intangible (mental) cause, such as stress. California courts have awarded compensation to workers who just say they feel hurt.

Judith Bradley, a former cake decorator with Albertson's, a supermarket chain, won compensation in part because she said her supervisor had been "very curt" with her. He had told her to "get the lead out" and to "get your butt in high gear," and had reprimanded her for leaving cakes out of the freezer. She was distressed, sued, and won.

Though recently the number of stress-related claims has begun to decline in California, dollar costs nationally continue to rise. Donna Dell, manager of employee relations for Wells Fargo Bank, says workers suffering from stress "typically are out a long, long time, and they need lots of rehabilitation," including costly visits to psychiatrists. In medical treatment and time lost, stress cases cost, on average, twice as much as other workplace injuries: more than $15,000 each.

Perhaps the most telling sign of stress's apparent rise: strong business for purveyors of relief. Psychologist Stanley Fisher, a Manhattan hypnotist, says the demise of New York's boom-boom real estate market has sent many relief-seeking former brokers and developers his way. Gene Cooper, a partner at Corporate Counseling Associates (a supplier of corporate employee assistance programs), says, "It used to be, 3 percent to 5 percent of our calls for counseling were stress related. Now, more like 8 percent to 14 percent." They come from all levels, clerks to VPs.

There are stress-fighting tapes, goggles that send pulses of white light into your head, vibrating music beds ("not quite like the first time you had sex," says one manufacturer, "but maybe the second"). Morgan Fairchild has a video out (*Morgan Fairchild Stress Management*, $19.95).

Whenever the status quo gets a good shaking—even where the shaking eventually results in greater opportunity and freedom of choice—stress goes up as people scramble to adapt. Yet if change is a constant, and if everyone is susceptible to stress, why doesn't everyone suffer from it equally? Why do some maddeningly healthy people appear not to suffer from it at all?

Not everyone finds the same event stressful. Drop a scorpion into a box of puppies, and you get stressed puppies. But drop it into a box of elf owls, which eat scorpions, and you get satisfaction. If a tree falls in the rain forest and nobody from Ben & Jerry's hears it, is there stress? No. Perhaps you think drinking port is fun. Peter Ficklin, wine master of Ficklin Vineyards, a California portmaker, says, "Sure, it's a pleasure to taste port. But the fortified wine category is down. There's increased competition. In

Source: "Who Beats Stress Best—And How," *Fortune*, October 7, 1991, pp. 71–86.

295

the busy season, sometimes, I have trouble sleeping. The whole business is riding on my palate."

Some people are protected from stress by buffers. For example, the more mastery or control a person feels he has over circumstances, the less stress he's apt to feel, even if his control extends no further than the power to decide how he's going to feel about change. A surefire recipe for creating stress is to put someone in a job that affords him little decision-making power but carries great responsibility or imposes heavy psychological demands.

Rare is the job where an employee has complete control. Wally Goelzer, a flight attendant for Alaska Airlines, has plenty of control over his schedule—he's got 11 years' seniority. But the workplace limits his freedom: "Probably the worst incident in the last six months was an alcohol situation. The plane was full of a mixture of tourists and commercial fishermen. I had to tell this guy, one of the fishermen, that we wouldn't serve him any more alcohol. Now these fishermen are out on their boat sometimes six or eight weeks. He wasn't pleased. Yelling. Profanities. People around him were not having an ideal travel experience. 'What you're doing,' I told him, 'is you're being loud now.' I didn't want to stir him up too much, since we're all trapped in a tube at 29,000 feet."

The most potent buffer against stress may well be membership in a stable, close-knit group or community. Example: the town of Roseto, Pennsylvania. Stress researcher Dr. Stewart Wolf wondered 25 years ago why Roseto's residents, though they smoked, drank, ate fat, and otherwise courted doom, lived free from heart disease and other stress-related ills. He suspected their protection sprang from the town's uncommon social cohesion and stability: It was inhabited almost entirely by descendants of Italians who had moved there 100 years previously from Roseto, Italy. Few married outside the community; the firstborn was always named after a grandparent; ostentation or any display of superiority was avoided, since that would invite "the evil eye" from one's neighbor.

Wolf predicted Rosetians would start dying like flies if the modern world intruded. It did. They did. By the mid-1970s, Rosetians had Cadillacs, ranch-style homes, mixed marriages, new names, and a rate of coronary heart disease the same as any other town's.

The U.S. Army tries to instill a Rosetian cohesion prophylactically. Says Dr. David Marlowe, chief of the department of military psychiatry at the Walter Reed Army Institute of Research: "If a bond trader feels stress, he can go meditate for 20 minutes. A soldier facing enemy fire can't. So we have to give him the maximum protection ahead of time." Marlowe says that where stress is concerned, Army research shows the primary issues are organizational. "You want to build cohesion into a group, by making sure soldiers have good information, that they aren't faced with ambiguity, that they have solid relationships with leaders. If a man feels his squad is listening to him, if he can talk to it about his hopes, fears, anxieties, he's not likely to experience stress." The Army's No. 1 psychological discovery from World War II, he says, was "the strength imparted by the small, primary work group."

Keeping group cohesion strong *after* battle is crucial, too, since members, by collectively reliving their experience and trying to put it in perspective, get emotions off their chests that otherwise might leave them stressed out for months or years. The process is called debriefing. Squad members, for example, are encouraged to use travel time en route home from a war zone to talk about their battlefield experience. "It helps them detoxify," says Marlowe. "That's why we brought them back in groups from Desert Storm. Epidemiologically, we know it works." Thus, the group emerges both as the primary protection against stress and as the means for relief after a stressful event.

In light of the Army's approach, much of what passes for stress management in U.S. industry looks superficial. Most Fortune 500 companies offer employees either an employee assistance program (EAP), a wellness promotion program, or both. Some of these emphasize stress management. At Liz Claiborne, for example, well-attended lunchtime seminars explain how workers can relax by using mental imagery, muscle relaxation, and a variety of other proven techniques. Why the big turnout? "Misery loves company," says Sharon Quilter, Claiborne's director of benefits. Honeywell has offered a 45-minute program called Wellness and Your Funny Bone, taught by Sister Mary Christelle Macaluso, R. S. M. (Religious Sister of Mercy), Ph.D., "a lecturer/humorist with a Ph.D. in anatomy."

Ted Barash, president of a company that provides wellness programs, dismisses such approaches to stress reduction as "Band-Aid happy hours and traveling humor shows." Professor Paul Roman, a University of Georgia expert on behavioral health who has surveyed EAP programs, says most "never address the source of the stress. They blame the victim. Our studies at Southwestern Bell and other companies show the single biggest source of stress is poorly trained and inept supervisors."

External suppliers of EAP programs, such as Corporate Counseling Associates, purveyors of counseling to Time Warner, Digital Equipment, Liz Claiborne, and others, are understandably reluctant to tell clients how to run their own businesses. Says CAA Partner Gene Cooper: "We help employees develop coping mechanisms. We don't reduce the stress itself." One of Cooper's counselors, asked if she ever suggests stress-relieving organizational changes to employers, says no, "that would be presumptuous."

Stress experts who advocate a more interventionist approach ask how it can possibly make sense for a company to soothe employees with one hand—teaching them relaxation through rhythmic breathing—while whipping

www.fick
com

them like egg whites with the other, moving up deadlines, increasing overtime, or withholding information about job security. Any company serious about stress management should consider the following steps:

- **Audit stress.** Dr. Paul J. Rosch, president of the American Institute of Stress, thinks any intelligent program must begin and end with a stress audit. Questionnaires typically ask workers and managers to list conditions they find most stressful. Answers can illuminate areas where workers are stressed by boredom, as well as those where they are stressed by overwork. (Rustout, stressmeisters are fond of saying, can be as anxious-making as burnout.) Rosch says, "An audit may show a need for programs not generally thought of as stress reducing, though they serve that function." Examples: child care and flextime. Follow-up audits show results.

- **Use EAPs aggressively.** Try to catch stress before it blooms. At McDonnell Douglas, EAP director Daniel Smith uses a program called Transitions to prepare workers for potentially traumatic organizational changes. "You tell people what they're going to feel before they feel it," he says. "It prevents more significant problems downstream."

    Case in point: Pete Juliano, head of McDonnell Douglas's 2,000-person facilities management operation, knew he would have to flatten and streamline his division to make it more responsive. Specifically, he would have to strip five levels of management with 260 managers down to three levels with 170.

    "Nobody was going out the door," he says, "and nobody was getting a pay cut. They'd all be staying on, though not all as managers. Still, that's a tough nut to crack: One day you're a manager. The next, you're carrying tools. How do you tell your wife and kids? How do you go to work each day and face not being a manager?"

    Juliano called in the Transitions team, whose members made a two-hour presentation to the department. They covered such topics as how to face your spouse and peers if you don't continue as a manager, how to recognize denial, how to cope with anger. The counselors also told listeners about career options if they decided to leave the division or McDonnell Douglas. "It gave them a chance to vent," says Juliano. "There have been cases of guys committing suicide when they had to go back to carrying tools. But we didn't have any serious problems."

- **Examine EAP usage.** If you've got an EAP program, study the usage data that counselors collect: How many employees from what departments are requesting help, and for what? For example, if you know that (1) in the past five years nobody from your tax department has ever used the EAP program, (2) half the accountants signed up for stress counseling last week, and (3) it's not mid-April, then you might be seeing evidence of a problem.

- **Give employees information.** They can't feel in control of circumstances if they lack it. When Donna Dell became manager of employee relations at Wells Fargo Bank last November, she saw there were about 3,000 workers' compensation cases outstanding. Accidents accounted for 80 percent; another 10 percent were from workers claiming various injuries from working at video display terminals; and 10 percent were from stress. She wanted to know where the stress claims came from. Were they, for instance, from employees who had been laid off or who had just been through a performance review? There was no correlation to either event. "I was surprised," says Dell. "Vengeance, apparently, was not the issue."

    Asbestos was. "We don't have any claims for asbestosis per se," she says, "but we get stress claims from people who *fear* they may have been exposed. You don't have to prove you were exposed to get workers' comp. The fear is enough. Now we provide instruction at sites where toxic material construction has been scheduled. We go in, in advance, with trainers and explain to the employees what's going to happen. Since we implemented this program about a year and a half ago, we haven't had any more such claims."

- **Match employees with jobs they can master.** In his bestselling book, *Flow,* Mihaly Csikszentmihalyi, a psychology professor at the University of Chicago, points out that the least-stressed people often are those who are working flat out on some task that *they* have selected—something they really love to do. They give themselves so completely that they achieve a kind of precision and grace—what the author calls "flow." The chance of your getting such performance from workers goes up, and their stress down, the more choice you give them over assignments.

- **Be prepared for trauma.** It's easy to forget that stress isn't always the result of a thousand tiny cuts. "Having a gun put to your head can be upsetting," says Chris Dunning, a trauma expert at the University of Wisconsin at Milwaukee. She ought to know. Her business is de-stressing shot cops, crews of crashed airliners, and, at this writing, the forensic examiners in the Jeffrey Dahmer case ("they're having trouble eating meat").

    Abrupt and upsetting things happen in offices. Homicide and suicide—not accidents—now account for 14 percent of male on-the-job deaths and 46 percent of female, reports psychologist James Turner, an expert on workplace mayhem. At the emergency department of Oakland's Highland Hospital, says Chief Resident Linda Jenks, mounting stress—with no end in sight—precipitated two suicides. "A young intern got into her car, numbed up her neck with lidocaine, took out a scalpel, and dissected herself in her rearview mirror. Within a week, a night nurse started an IV on herself—injected potassium, which stopped her heart immediately. After that, the hospital said, 'Okay, we're ignoring a problem here.' It's as if to admit it is a sign of failure." A suicide, an industrial accident, or any other traumatic event, says Dunning, leaves a lingering psychological strain on survivors: "It usually takes a good three months to get an organization back on track."

But, says Mark Braverman, president of Crisis Management Group, a Massachusetts consulting firm, these traumas present management with opportunities as well as problems. "Management sometimes won't talk about the event or face up to it directly," he says. "We try to tell them that if they do face up to it and answer workers' questions, they can build a bond that lasts longer afterward." Even if you can't talk, he says, talk: "If you can't tell them much because OSHA is still completing an investigation, tell them that."

Braverman cites an example of trauma handled right: "A computer company had had a helicopter crash. They'd also had a work site shooting. So they decided, within the structure of their EAP, to create a protocol for dealing with traumatic stress. Later a safety system failed in a plant with 2,000 people, killing one. Every work group got together. The international manager of facilities was flown in to answer questions, including the ones on everybody's minds: "Why did the system fail? Could it happen again?" EAP counselors were available, but it was the information itself that was most stress-relieving."

Traumatic stress tends to be infectious. Since large numbers of employees are involved, clusters of stress-based workers' comp suits can result. In court, the cases are much harder to defend against than less-dramatic stress cases. Says Jim Turner: "It behooves you greatly to go in early with counselors, since this will reduce your overall long-term cost."

At Wells Fargo, where bank robberies rose 37 percent in this year's first quarter, tellers have been traumatized. "We do get stress claims from robbery incidents, and we don't dispute them," says Donna Dell. Instead, the bank dispatches EAP counselors to affected branches, where they conduct group debriefings, much the way the Army does.

Bryan Lawton, head of Wells Fargo's debriefing program, explains how it works: "The professional asks them things like, where were you when the incident happened, how did you respond, how did the others act? When the employees start to talk, they find out they're not alone, not the only ones who feel the way they do. Everybody else feels guilty or angry over the event. They're told these are normal emotions." The professional then tells them how they can expect to feel weeks later."

Nobody is sure why debriefings work, but they do. And they are cost-effective. "All it takes," says Lawton, "is one case to lead to a significant expense. One person's trauma can lead to a significant expense. One person's trauma can wind up costing the bank $100,000." The figure includes lost time, medical treatment, and retraining cost.

O'Dell Williams, with the bank 16 years, has survived ten robbery situations, the most recent one as a branch manager in Vallejo, California, on May 20. The robbery attempt scared more than 20 of his employees. "I was afraid we'd lose some afterward," he says. But EAP counselors intervened quickly, and so far nobody has quit. And nobody has filed a workers' comp claim.

- **Don't forget the obvious.** Managers who want to reduce stress should make sure workers have the tools and training they need to get the job done. Says John Murray, a police bomb deactivator in Florida: "I'm lucky. I've got the best equipment and the best training. There are departments where all they used to give you was a mattress and a fishhook." Managers should set realistic deadlines and go out of their way not to change deadlines, once set. What works well for the Army works just as well in the office: Build cohesion through communication. Straighten out managers who like to play the Charles Boyer part from *Gaslight*—who hold sway over subordinates by keeping them confused, by withholding information, or by keeping roles and responsibilities ill-defined.

Do all these things, behave flawlessly, and your exposure to stress-based lawsuits still remains almost unimaginably broad. Chris Dunning cites a case where an employee, as part of some lunchroom high jinks, got silly and taped a co-worker's arm to a chair—very lightly, not so it restrained her. She started screaming. Other workers looked at each other in disbelief: What was the woman's problem? It turned out that, as a child, she had been forcibly restrained and raped. The taping of the arm caused her to reexperience the trauma of that, and her subsequent disability was judged to be 100 percent the employer's responsibility.

At least this worker's distress was real. Some employees undoubtedly abuse the system, and there are lawyers and doctors eager to help them. Listen to Joseph Alibrandi, chairman of Whittaker Corp., an aerospace manufacturer: "We try to minimize the problems in the physical workplace, to do all we can to reduce *true* stress.

But a lot of that seems frustratingly irrelevant. There's always an epidemic of 'sore back' after a layoff. Or they say they can't perform sexually. How the hell are you going to defend against that?"

It's almost impossible, of course, but you can try to flag potential claimants early on. New hires can be asked, as part of their medical evaluation, "Have you ever been off work due to a stress-related illness?" A "yes" may indicate to the doctor that the employee's assignment should be changed.

Performing a periodic stress audit, or making stress management part of your EAP or wellness program, can pay off in court. Says John M. Ivancevich, dean of the business school at the University of Houston: "Even a sloppy attempt at stress management can be a legal defense."

Finally: you. Feeling stressed? Not sure what to do? The first rule, says Dr. James Turner, is, Don't quit your job. "They build these fantasies," he says of stressed-out executives. "They'll go sailing. They'll open a copy center. Lately, for some reason, they all want to open copy centers." But sooner or later everyone wants to come back.

Instead of quitting, learn the techniques of coping. You'll find plenty of experts willing to teach them to you for a price, but they're not too complex, and many stressed workers have discovered them without help. Flight attendant Wally Goelzer and plenty of other people use them daily without knowing it. "Sometimes I put my hands out like a scale," he says. "I ask myself: How much does this problem matter? I think of a friend of mine who was killed in a plane crash. 'Life is too short,' I can hear her say. She used to say that, and I can see her face."

Emergency room resident Jenks and bomb deactivator Murray know the stress-relieving power of humor, even when it's of the gallows type. Says Murray: "Yeah, I get a certain amount of kidding. I've got three daughters, and when Father's Day comes around they give me a card with a fuse in it." Says Jenks: "We use black humor at work so much that it's gotten so I have to remember to clean up my act when I'm around normal people."

Then again, you might want to put aside the tricks and strategies, since these change like frocks. You might think about your life. Is it the way you wanted? If not, all the perspective and joking in the world will get you only so far. Mihaly Csikszentmihalyi, who lectures occasionally to 40-ish managers, notes that those who insist on regaining control of their lives, even at what temporarily may seem the peril of their careers, often see an unexpected payoff down the line. "There comes a point where they're working 70 hours a week, and they're not sure why. Their family lives are suffering. Maybe they've never given any thought to setting priorities. Some decide they can't do everything—that they have to step off the fast track to get back their family life or take better care of their health. And then a most interesting thing happens: The ones who do it, most of them, in a year or two, they get promoted." Dare to be second-rate, if that's how you have to think of it. It may not be what you imagine.

Exercises

EXERCISE 7.1   Behavior Activity Profile—A Type A Measure

Each of us displays certain kinds of behaviors, thought patterns of personal characteristics. For each of the 21 sets of descriptions below, circle the number which you feel best describes where you are between each pair. The best answer for each set of descriptions is the response that most nearly describes the way you feel, behave, or think. Answer these in terms of your regular or typical behavior, thoughts, or characteristics.

1. I'm always on time for appointments.	7 6 5 4 3 2 1	I'm never quite on time.
2. When someone is talking to me, chances are I'll anticipate what they are going to say, by nodding, interrupting, or finishing sentences for them.	7 6 5 4 3 2 1	I listen quietly without showing any impatience.
3. I frequently try to do several things at once.	7 6 5 4 3 2 1	I tend to take things one at a time.

Copyright © 1982 by Michael T. Matteson and John M. Ivancevich.

4. When it comes to waiting in line (at banks, theaters, etc.), I really get impatient and frustrated.   7 6 5 4 3 2 1   It simply doesn't bother me.

5. I always feel rushed.   7 6 5 4 3 2 1   I never feel rushed.

6. When it comes to my temper, I find it hard to control at times.   7 6 5 4 3 2 1   I just don't seem to have one.

7. I tend to do most things like eating, walking, and talking rapidly.   7 6 5 4 3 2 1   Slowly

TOTAL SCORE 1–7 _____ = S

8. Quite honestly, the things I enjoy most are job-related activities.   7 6 5 4 3 2 1   Leisure-time activities.

9. At the end of a typical work day, I usually feel like I needed to get more done than I did.   7 6 5 4 3 2 1   I accomplished everything I needed to.

10. Someone who knows me very well would say that I would rather work than play.   7 6 5 4 3 2 1   I would rather play than work.

11. When it comes to getting ahead at work, nothing is more important.   7 6 5 4 3 2 1   Many things are more important.

12. My primary source of satisfaction comes from my job.   7 6 5 4 3 2 1   I regularly find satisfaction in non-job pursuits, such as hobbies, friends, and family.

13. Most of my friends and social acquaintances are people I know from work.   7 6 5 4 3 2 1   Not connected with my work.

14. I'd rather stay at work than take a vacation.   7 6 5 4 3 2 1   Nothing at work is important enough to interfere with my vacation.

TOTAL SCORE 8–14 _____ = J

15. People who know me well would describe me as hard driving and competitive.   7 6 5 4 3 2 1   Relaxed and easygoing.

16. In general, my behavior is governed by a desire for recognition and achievement.   7 6 5 4 3 2 1   What I want to do—not by trying to satisfy others.

17. In trying to complete a project or solve a problem, I tend to wear myself out before I'll give up on it.   7 6 5 4 3 2 1   I tend to take a break or quit if I'm feeling fatigued.

18. When I play a game (tennis, cards, etc.) my enjoyment comes from winning.   7 6 5 4 3 2 1   The social interaction.

19. I like to associate with people who are dedicated to getting ahead.   7 6 5 4 3 2 1   Easygoing and take life as it comes.

20. I'm not happy unless I'm always doing something.   7 6 5 4 3 2 1   Frequently, "doing nothing" can be quite enjoyable.

21. What I enjoy doing most are competitive activities.   7 6 5 4 3 2 1   Noncompetitive pursuits.

TOTAL SCORE 15–21 _____ = H

Impatience (S)	Job Involvement (J)	Hard Driving and Competitive (H)	Total Score (A) − S + J + H

The Behavior Activity Profile attempts to assess the three Type A coronary-prone behavior patterns, as well as pro- vide a total score. The three a priori types of Type A coro- nary-prone behavior patterns are shown:

Items	Behavior Pattern	Characteristics
1–7	Impatience (S)	Is anxious to interrupt Fails to listen attentively Gets frustrated by waiting (e.g., in line, for others to complete a job)
8–14	Job Involvement (J)	Focal point of attention is the job Lives for the job Relishes being on the job Gets immersed in job activities
15–21	Hard driving/Competitive (H)	Is hardworking, highly competitive Is competitive in most aspects of life, sports, work, etc. Races against the clock
1–21	Total score (A)	Total of S + J + H represents your global Type A behavior

Score ranges for total score are:

Score	Behavior Type
122 and above	Hard-core Type A
99–121	Moderate Type A
90–98	Low Type A
80–89	Type X
70–79	Low Type B
50–69	Moderate Type B
40 and below	Hard-core Type B

Percentile Scores

Now you can compare your score to a sample of over 1,200 respondents.

Percentile Score	Raw Score	
Percent of Individuals Scoring Lower	Males	Females
99%	___140	___132
95%	___135	___126
90%	___130	___120
85%	___124	___112

Percentile Score	Raw Score	
Percent of Individuals Scoring Lower	Males	Females
80%	___118	___106
75%	___113	___101
70%	___108	___95
65%	___102	___90
60%	___97	___85
55%	___92	___80
50%	___87	___74
45%	___81	___69
40%	___75	___63
35%	___70	___58
30%	___63	___53
25%	___58	___48
20%	___51	___42
15%	___45	___36
10%	___38	___31
5%	___29	___26
1%	___21	___21

Exercises

EXERCISE 7.2   Health Risk Appraisal

The Health Risk Appraisal form was developed by the Department of Health and Welfare of the Canadian government. Their initial testing program indicated that approximately one person out of every three who completed the form would modify some unhealthy aspects of lifestyle for at least a while. Figuring the potential payoff was worth it, the government mailed out over 3 million copies of the questionnaire to Canadians who were on social security.

Subsequent checking indicated that their initial projections of the number of recipients altering their behavior was correct. Perhaps you will be among the one-third.

Choose from the three answers for each question the one answer which most nearly applies to you. The plus and minus signs next to some numbers indicate more than $(+)$ and less than $(-)$. Note that a few items have only two alternatives.

Exercise

_____ 1. Physical effort expended during the workday: mostly?
(a) heavy labor, walking, or housework;
(b) —; (c) deskwork

_____ 2. Participation in physical activities—skiing, golf, swimming, etc., or lawn mowing, gardening, etc.?
(a) daily; (b) weekly; (c) seldom

_____ 3. Participation in vigorous exercise program?
(a) three times weekly; (b) weekly;
(c) seldom

_____ 4. Average miles walked or jogged per day?
(a) one or more; (b) less than one;
(c) none

_____ 5. Flights of stairs climbed per day?
(a) 10+; (b) 10−; (c) —

Nutrition

_____ 6. Are you overweight?
(a) no; (b) 5 to 19 lbs; (c) 20+ lbs.

_____ 7. Do you eat a wide variety of foods, something from each of the following five food groups: (1) meat, fish, poultry, dried legumes, eggs, or nuts; (2) milk or milk products; (3) bread or cereals;
(4) fruits; (5) vegetables?
(a) each day; (b) three times weekly;
(c) —

Alcohol

_____ 8. Average number of bottles (12 oz.) of beer per week?
(a) 0 to 7; (b) 8 to 15; (c) 16 +

_____ 9. Average number of hard liquor (1 ½ oz.) drinks per week?
(a) 0 to 7; (b) 8 to 15; (c) 16+

_____ 10. Average number of glasses (5 oz.) of wine or cider per week?
(a) 0 to 7; (b) 8 to 15; (c) 16+

_____ 11. Total number of drinks per week including beer, liquor, or wine?
(a) 0 to 7; (b) 8 to 15; (c) 16+

Drugs

_____ 12. Do you take drugs illegally?
(a) no; (b) —; (c) yes

_____ 13. Do you consume alcoholic beverages together with certain drugs (tranquilizers, barbiturates, illegal drugs)?
(a) no; (b) —; (c) yes

_____ 14. Do you use painkillers improperly or excessively?
(a) no; (b) —; (c) yes

Tobacco

_____ 15. Cigarettes smoked per day?
(a) none; (b) 10—; (c) 10+

_____ 16. Cigars smoked per day?
(a) none; (b) 5—; (c) 5+

_____ 17. Pipe tobacco pouches per week?
(a) none; (b) 2—; (c) 2+

Personal Health

_____ 18. Do you experience periods of depression?
(a) seldom; (b) occasionally;
(c) frequently

_____ 19. Does anxiety interfere with your daily activities?
(a) seldom; (b) occasionally;
(c) frequently

_____ 20. Do you get enough satisfying sleep?
(a) yes; (b) no; (c) —

_____ 21. Are you aware of the causes and danger of VD?
(*a*) yes; (*b*) no; (*c*) —

_____ 22. Breast self-examination? (*if not applicable, do not score*)
(*a*) monthly; (*b*) occasionally; (*c*) —

Road and Water Safety

_____ 23. Mileage per year as driver or passenger?
(*a*) 10,000−; (*b*) 10,000+; (*c*) —

_____ 24. Do you often exceed the speed limit?
(*a*) no; (*b*) by 10 mph+;
(*c*) by 20 mph+

_____ 25. Do you wear a seat belt?
(*a*) always; (*b*) occasionally; (*c*) never

_____ 26. Do you drive a motorcycle, moped, or snowmobile?
(*a*) no; (*b*) yes; (*c*) —;

_____ 27. If yes to the above, do you always wear a regulation safety helmet?
(*a*) yes; (*b*) —; (*c*) no

_____ 28. Do you ever drive under the influence of alcohol?
(*a*) never; (*b*) —; (*c*) occasionally

_____ 29. Do you ever drive when your ability may be affected by drugs?
(*a*) never; (*b*) —; (*c*) occasionally

_____ 30. Are you aware of water safety rules?
(*a*) yes; (*b*) no; (*c*) —

_____ 31. If you participate in water sports or boating, do you wear a life jacket?
(*a*) yes; (*b*) no; (*c*) —

General

_____ 32. Average time watching TV per day (*in hours*)?
(*a*) 0 to 1; (*b*) 1 to 4; (*c*) 4+

_____ 33. Are you familiar with first-aid procedures?
(*a*) yes; (*b*) no; (*c*) —

_____ 34. Do you ever smoke in bed?
(*a*) no; (*b*) occasionally; (*c*) regularly

_____ 35. Do you always make use of equipment provided for your safety at work?
(*a*) yes; (*b*) occasionally; (*c*) no

To Score: Give yourself 1 point for each *a* answer; 3 points for each *b* answer; 5 points for each *c* answer.

Total Score:

—A *total score* of 35–45 is *excellent*. You have a commendable lifestyle based on sensible habits and a lively awareness of personal health.

—A total score of 45–55 is *good*. With some minor change, you can develop an excellent lifestyle.

—A total score of 56–65 is *risky*. You are taking unnecessary risks with your health. Several of your habits should be changed if potential health problems are to be avoided.

—A total score of 66 and over is *hazardous*. Either you have little personal awareness of good health habits or you are choosing to ignore them. This is a danger zone.

Cases

CASE 7.1   No Response From Monitor 23

LOUDSPEAKER: IGNITION MINUS 45 MINUTES

Paul Keller tripped the sequence switches at control monitor 23 in accordance with the countdown instruction book just to his left. All hydraulic systems were functioning normally in the second stage of the spacecraft booster at checkpoint 1 minus 45. Keller automatically snapped his master control switch to GREEN and knew that his electronic impulse along with hundreds of others from similar consoles within the Cape Canaveral complex signaled continuation of the countdown.

Free momentarily from data input, Keller leaned back in his chair, stretched his arms above his head, and then rubbed the back of his neck. The monitor lights on console 23 glowed routinely.

It used to be an incredible challenge, fantastically interesting work at the very fringe of man's knowledge about himself and his universe. Keller recalled his first day in Brevard County, Florida, with his wife and young daughter. How happy they were that day. Here was the fu-

Source: Robert D. Joyce, *Encounter in Organizational Behavior* (New York: Pergamon Press, 1972). pp, 168–72.

ture, the good life . . . forever. And Keller was going to be part of that fantastic, utopian future.

LOUDSPEAKER: IGNITION MINUS 35 MINUTES

Keller panicked! His mind had wandered momentarily, and he lost his place in the countdown instructions. Seconds later he found the correct place and tripped the proper sequence of switches for checkpoint 1 minus 35. No problem. Keller snapped master control to GREEN and wiped his brow. He knew he was late reporting and would hear about it later.

Damn!, he thought, I used to know countdown cold for seven systems monitors without countdown instructions. But now . . . you're slipping Keller . . . you're slipping, he thought. Shaking his head, Keller reassured himself that he was overly tired today . . . just tired.

LOUDSPEAKER: IGNITION MINUS 30 MINUTES

Keller completed the reporting sequence for checkpoint I minus 30, took one long last drag on his cigarette, and squashed it out in the crowded ashtray. Utopia? Hell: It was one big rat race and getting bigger all the time. Keller recalled how he once naively felt that his problems with Naomi would disappear after they left Minneapolis and came to the Cape with the space program. Now, 10,000 arguments later, Keller knew there was no escape.

Only one can of beer left, Naomi? One stinking lousy can of beer, cold lunchmeat, and potato salad? Is that all a man gets after 12 hours of mental exhaustion?

Oh, shut up, Paul! I'm so sick of you playing Mr. Important. You get leftovers because I never know when you're coming home . . . your daughter hardly knows you . . . and you treat us like nobodies . . . incidental to your great personal contribution to the Space Age.

Don't knock it, Naomi. That job is plenty important to me, to the Team, and it gets you everything you've ever wanted . . . more! Between this house and the boat, we're up to our ears in debt.

Now don't try to pin our money problems on me, Paul Keller. You're the one who has to have all the same goodies as the scientists earning twice your salary. Face it, Paul. You're just a button-pushing technician regardless of how fancy a title they give you. You can be replaced, Paul. You can be replaced by any S.O.B. who can read and punch buttons.

LOUDSPEAKER: IGNITION MINUS 25 MINUTES

A red light blinked ominously indicating a potential hydraulic fluid leak in subsystem seven of stage two. Keller felt his heartbeat and pulse rate increase. Rule 1 . . . report malfunction immediately and stop the count. Keller punched POTENTIAL ABORT on the master control.

LOUDSPEAKER: THE COUNT IS STOPPED AT IGNITION MINUS 24 MINUTES 17 SECONDS

Keller fumbled with the countdown instructions. Any POTENTIAL ABORT required a cross-check to separate an actual malfunction from sporadic signal error. Keller began to perspire nervously as he initiated standard cross-check procedures.

"Monitor 23, this is Control. Have you got an actual abort, Paul?" The voice in the headset was cool, but impatient, "Decision required in 30 seconds."

"I know, I know," Keller mumbled, "I'm cross-checking right now."

Keller felt the silence closing in around him. Cross-check one proved inconclusive. Keller automatically followed detailed instructions for cross-check two.

"Do you need help, Keller?" asked the voice in the headset.

"No, I'm O.K."

"Decision required," demanded the voice in the headset. "Dependent systems must be deactivated in 15 seconds."

Keller read and reread the console data. It looked like a sporadic error signal . . . the system appeared to be in order.

"Decision required," demanded the voice in the headset.

"Continue count," blurted Keller at last. "Subsystem seven fully operational." Keller slumped back in his chair.

LOUDSPEAKER: THE COUNT IS RESUMED AT IGNITION MINUS 24 MINUTES 17 SECONDS

Keller knew that within an hour after liftoff, Barksdale would call him in for a personal conference. "What's wrong lately, Paul?" he would say. "Is there anything I can help with? You seem so tense lately." But he wouldn't really want to listen. Barksdale was the kind of person who read weakness into any personal problems and demanded that they be purged from the mind the moment his men checked out their consoles.

More likely Barksdale would demand that Keller make endless practice runs on cross-check procedures while he stood nearby . . . watching and noting any errors . . . while the pressure grew and grew.

Today's performance was surely the kiss of death for any wage increase too. That was another of Barksdale's methods of obtaining flawless performance . . . which would surely lead to another scene with Naomi . . . and another sleepless night . . . and more of those nagging stomach pains . . . and yet another imperfect performance for Barksdale.

LOUDSPEAKER: IGNITION MINUS 20 MINUTES

The monitor lights at console 23 blinked routinely.

"Keller," said the voice in the earphone. "Report, please."

"Control, this is Wallace at monitor 24. I don't believe Keller is feeling well. Better send someone to cover fast!"

LOUDSPEAKER: THE COUNT IS STOPPED AT 19 MINUTES 33 SECONDS

"This is Control, Wallace. Assistance has been dispatched and the count is on temporary hold. What seems to be wrong with Keller?"

"Control, this is Wallace, I don't know. His eyes are open and fixed on the monitor, but he won't respond to my questions. It could be a seizure or . . . a stroke."

QUESTIONS

1. Is there any way of avoiding the more serious manifestations (as with Paul Keller) of pressure on the job? Explain.
2. Are there any early warning signs given by employees under stress? If so, what are they?
3. What is the proper role of the supervisor here? Should he refer Keller to a professional counselor?

Video Case

JOB SHARING, RHINO FOODS, AND JOB PRESSURE AND ETHICS

The videos "Job Sharing at Rhino Foods" and "Job Pressure and Ethics" illustrate the positive power of distributive and procedural justice and the negative consequences when managers fail to treat employees fairly. Rhino Foods, the Burlington, Vermont, maker of cheesecakes and cookies that employs 60 people, faced a serious challenge. A sales slump left the company with the need to temporarily downsize its workforce by laying off 11 workers.

Rhino President Ted Castle communicated the problem to his employees and asked them for possible solutions. The employees themselves proposed the solution: Find temporary jobs for these 11 workers. It also was proposed that employees be allowed to volunteer for the temporary jobs. Castle agreed and placed five workers at Ben and Jerry's Ice Cream, four workers at a mail-order gardening supply business, and two workers in community service. From the beginning, employees had strong perceptions of procedural justice. They thought that Rhino management valued their input, and they perceived the decision-making process to be a fair one.

The displaced Rhino Foods employees were paid the same wages at their temporary jobs as they received at Rhino, and Rhino provided them with uninterrupted health benefits. Rhino Foods employees therefore also had strong perceptions of distributive justice. In other words, the employees felt that the distribution of salary and benefits was fair. No employee, whether temporarily displaced or not, lost or gained anything relative to any other employee.

Rhino employees' strong sense of equity ultimately paid off for Rhino Foods. As Ted Castle says, "What we gained out of this is an incredible trust from our employees, I feel. They know that we're willing to do whatever it takes before we lay them off."

"Job Pressure and Ethics" shows what can happen when employees do not perceive fairness in procedures and outcomes. Ed Petrie, member of the Ethics Officers Association, reported the results of a survey that found that almost half of the respondents admitted to illegal or unethical actions in the past year. As Petrie says, "Even good people can be tempted to cut a few corners, misrepresent some data, lie about what they've done and do everything they can to cover it up."

What is the cause of this behavior? One cause is unrelenting job pressure, which has increased in the workplace. According to the survey, top contributors to workplace pressure include poor leadership, poor internal communication, too much work, and lack of management support. These factors represent some of the organizational influences that determine unethical behavior, particularly poor role models and perceived pressure for results (see the Model of Ethical Behavior in Chapter 3). This type of organizational climate can lead employees to feel inequity: their inputs are too great relative to the outputs received. If workers feel they are being overworked, one solution may be to engage in unethical activity to strike a balance between their own needs and those of the employer.

In addition, employees feel that poor communication is one of the leading causes of pressure. If employees do not feel that managers are communicating all information concerning their roles in the organization and they do not perceive they have a voice in organizational outcomes, they may perceive that decision-making procedures are unfair. This can lead to lower satisfaction, low organizational commitment, and decreased trust in management, ultimately resulting in unethical behavior. Solutions to this problem, according to survey respondents, include better organizational communication, more commitment by management, and greater job security.

These two examples show the positive results when employees perceive outcomes and procedures to be fair, and the negative consequences when employees do not believe they are treated fairly. Managers should make every effort to communicate with their employees and attempt to manage perceptions of fairness.

QUESTIONS:

1. According to Adams' Equity Theory, what inputs and outcomes were important to Rhino Foods employees when making equity comparisons?
2. How might perceptions of inequity lead employees to commit illegal and unethical acts?
3. What can managers do to improve the organization's ethical climate and reduce the likelihood that their employees will engage in unethical activity?
4. How does providing employees a "voice" in organizational procedures and outcomes lead to perceptions of equity?
5. Review the Model of Ethical Behavior from Chapter 3. Which influences that contribute to unethical employee behavior are likely present in organizations that are downsizing?

Video Case

WORKPLACE PERKS AND MORE COMPANIES PROVIDE FITNESS

Have you ever considered bringing your laundry to work or taking home dinner prepared by the company chef? These are just a few workplace perks offered by today's companies. Until recently, most organizations rewarded their employees in the traditional way: with paychecks, overtime pay, and standard benefits such as medical coverage and retirement programs. However, with workers today working longer, harder, and with less job security, managers are seeing the benefit of creative perks to keep their employees satisfied and motivated.

At CIGNA, employees can place take home orders with the company chef; at Salamon Brothers, employees are able to see their own physician and even get prescription drugs delivered at the office! Anderson Consulting subsidizes a concierge to run any type of errand for employees, and still other companies provide on-site dry-cleaning and laundry services so that employees can enjoy more of their off-work time for leisure activities.

Are all of these perks purely for the benefit of the employees? Not at all, according to one manager who says, "Treat people as if they are human beings with needs and concerns and you'll get back loyalty and good work." In other words, providing these services to workers is just good business. This is evidenced by one worker at a Charlotte, North Carolina, packaging plant with subsidized day care who refers to her boss: "We try to make him happy in every way we can because he's been very good to us." Though these perks have a short-term cost for companies, ultimately managers believe that they will get a long-term return on their investment from happier, more productive workers.

Another way organizations save money in the long run is by making their employees healthier. Many corporations, including Home Depot, Coca-Cola, and the Centers for Disease Control and Prevention, understand that by providing on-site fitness centers for employees, their long-term health costs can be drastically reduced because employees are more fit. Coca-Cola estimates that participants in its fitness center have over $500 less in health care costs per year. This results in a total savings at corporate headquarters of $1.2 million each year. In addition to savings due to reduced health costs, corporate fitness centers are also thought to reduce stress and absence and lead to greater productivity.

Though American workers will likely never give up traditional extrinsic rewards such as bonuses and vacation time, companies are proving that a little creativity in providing employee perks can achieve long-term benefits for both employees and companies.

QUESTIONS:

1. Explain how providing such perks as day care and fitness centers can lead to increased organizational productivity.
2. Is it best to offer workplace perks to all employees or just those that are good performers? Why or why not?
3. What are some potential negative effects of workplace perks?

Video Case

FIGHTING STRESS

According to one survey, 46 percent of American workers suffer some form of work-related stress. The causes include too much work, uncertainty, monotony, and too little control over things that impact them at work. Unfortunately, corporate America as a whole does not seem to be willing to address the problems of workplace stress.

Stress can lead to indirect costs to organizations such as absenteeism, turnover, lower productivity, and quality problems. Employee stress can also cause direct costs to organizations. Kemper Insurance had to pay $300,000 to Francis Dunlavey, an insurance claims adjuster, who sued the company arguing that workplace stress caused his depression. Managers should be aware of the causes and effects of stress for these reasons, as well as for the sake of employees' physical and mental health.

Some companies understand that work-related stress impacts employees and organizational productivity and thus have developed creative ways to tackle stress. CIGNA Corporation helps its employees cope with stress by providing employees access to an exercise physiologist, who provides massages and teaches stress-management techniques. Employees in the customer service department at S. C. Johnson in Racine, Wisconsin, are allowed to engage in squirt gun fights in the office to reduce job-induced stress. Both of these techniques are symptom-management strategies—targeting the consequences of stress after it occurs. These work environments just make good business sense by helping reduce stress, says one executive. However, managers should remember that it is always best to address organizational sources of stress, such as role overload, before symptom management becomes necessary.

When one must deal with stress symptoms, it is important to remember that coping with stress is an individual matter. Shooting one's supervisor with a water pistol may not be effective for every employee or appropriate in every office. Coping effectively with stress must take into account both situational and personal factors.

QUESTIONS:

1. Relatively few companies employ stress-management programs despite the high costs of stress. Why do you think this is the case?
2. Are there potential negative consequences of allowing workers to cope with stress in such ways as having water pistol fights?
3. How can organizations help workers combat stress by enabling them to use the control strategy of stress reduction?

Group Behavior and Interpersonal Influence

*Coming together is a beginning; keeping together is progress;
working together is success.*

Henry Ford

8
Chapter

Group Behavior and Work Teams

After completing Chapter 8 you should be able to:

Learning Objectives

- Understand that the term *group* can be viewed from a number of perspectives.

- Identify the elements in the process of group formation and development.

- Compare formal and informal groups.

- Discuss the reasons why people form groups.

- Describe the stages of group formation.

- Identify several important characteristics of groups.

- Discuss relevant criteria for group effectiveness.

- Describe the different types of teams and the factors important to team success.

This chapter examines groups and teams in organizations. The existence of groups can alter a person's motivation or needs and can influence the behavior of people in an organizational setting. Organizational behavior is more than simply the logical composite of the behavior of separate individuals. It is not their sum or product but rather a much more complex phenomenon, a very important part of which is the group. The chapter provides a model for understanding the nature of groups in organizations. It explores various types of groups, the reasons for their formation, their characteristics, and some end results of group membership. It also focuses on a special form of groups—teams—that is playing an increasingly larger role in current organizational processes. The current understanding of teams builds on theories, research findings, and applications of groups and their formation, maturity, and effectiveness.

Groups and teams are not the same. A **group** is two or more individuals interacting with each other to accomplish a common goal. **Teams** are mature groups with a degree of member interdependence and motivation to achieve a common goal. Teams start out as groups, but not all groups become mature and interdependent or teams. Teams and groups have many common characteristics: two or more who interact, a structure for work and interaction, members who perform specific technical, leadership, problem-solving, and emotional roles, and a common goal or set of goals.

Exhibit 8.1 in a concise manner presents characteristics comparing groups and teams. Groups work together on common goals, while teams work together and are fully committed. In this case the depth of commitment distinguishes groups and teams. Groups are accountable to a manager and are often randomly formed resulting in a varied mix of skills. Teams are internally accountable to each member and the skills directed toward goals complement each other. Group members create and share norms of performance and behavior. On the other hand, teams share culture, the rituals, processes, and philosophy of working together.

Teams over a period of time develop synergy or a special energy by combining the actions and behaviors of members. A team's work and performance is said to be synergistic or greater than the work and performance of individuals working alone on the team. For example, work and performance of the trauma team at Ben Taub Hospital, Houston's busiest emergency room, is synergistic.[1] Physicians, nurses, aides, technicians, and specialists work on teams to treat life and death cases. Trauma teams are committed to saving lives under serious circumstances. Each member brings a special set of skills to the trauma patient. There is no time for conflict, since collaboration of everyone is essential for lives to be saved. Members of the trauma team depend on each other and are accountable to each other.

As a team the Ben Taub unit has acquired a local and national reputation of accomplishing exceptional results in saving patients. The synergistic results could only be accomplished by a committed and dedicated team of professionals.[2] The trauma team is an actual example of the distinct characteristics and differences presented in Exhibit 8.1. Not all teams have such crucial life and death circum-

---

[1] An excellent example of trauma teams which triggered the use of Ben Taub's world-renouned emergency room is found in Afsaneh, and in Ali R. Malekzadeh, *Organizational Behavior* (Englewood Cliffs, NJ: Prentice-Hall, 1999), pp. 267–68.

[2] Jon R. Katzenbach and Jason A. Santemaria, "Firing Up the Front Line," *Harvard Business Review*, May–June 1999, pp. 107, 117.

EXHIBIT 8.1 Comparison of Groups and Teams	
Formal Work Group	**Team**
Works on common goals	Total commitment to common goals
Accountable to manager	Accountable to team members
Skill levels are often random	Skill levels are often complementary
Performance is evaluated by leader	Performance is evaluated by members as well as leaders
Culture is one of change and conflict	Culture is based on collaboration and total commitment to common goals
Performance can be positive, neutral, or negative	Performance can be greater than the sum of members' contribution or synergistic (e.g., $1 + 1 + 1 = 5$)
Success is defined by the leader's aspirations	Success is defined by the members' aspirations

stances regularly facing them. Also, to effectively utilize teams in organizations, managers and leaders will need to understand the distinctions illustrated in Exhibit 8.1.

THE NATURE OF GROUPS

Groups are a pervasive part of modern life. All of us have been—and are—members of many different groups. There are school groups, work groups, family groups, social groups, religious groups. There are small groups and large groups, permanent groups and temporary groups, formal groups and informal groups. Some groups are successful, some are not. Some groups bring out the best in their members, while others may bring out the worst. These are just a few of the multitude of ways in which groups may be characterized.

As indicated earlier, the following definition of groups will be used throughout this chapter:

> Two or more individuals interacting with each other in order to accomplish a common goal.

One way of viewing this definition is to think of it in terms of specifying three minimum requirements that must be met for a group to exist. The first requirement deals with size. There must be *two or more individuals* for there to be a group. One person does not constitute a group. Note that in this definition, while there is a minimum size requirement, there is no maximum.

The second requirement specifies that there must be some form of exchange or communication between these individuals. That is, they must *interact with each other* in some manner. We usually think of interaction between group members as occurring in a face-to-face verbal exchange, but that does not have to be the case. In nominal groups (discussed in Chapter 14), for example, the members might never speak with one another; their only interactions are typically in writing. At a noisy construction site, the communication between supervisor and an ironworker may only come in the form of gestures, yet no one would suggest there was no important interaction taking place. It is certainly true that you can

EXHIBIT 8.2   **A Model of Group Formation and Development**

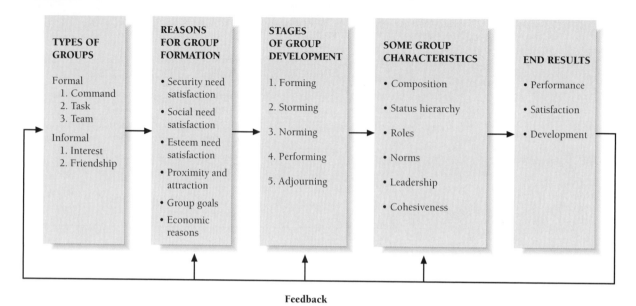

Feedback

have a collection of individuals who do not interact with one another. They are, however, just that: a collection of individuals, not a group.

The final requirement in our definition of groups is that of attempting to *accomplish a common goal.* If there is no common goal or purpose, there is no group by our definition. A common goal is a goal toward which individual members are willing to work. It is different from an individual goal that happens to be shared in common by a number of people. For example, everyone sitting in a physician's reception area may be waiting to see the doctor. Thus, seeing the doctor may be a goal that everyone in the room shares in common, but that is decidedly different from it being a common goal of the group. Each person wants to see the doctor for his and her own individual purposes, not for a common group purpose. Thus, the people in the reception area, even if they are interacting with each other, do not constitute a group by our definition.

AN INTEGRATED MODEL OF GROUP FORMATION AND DEVELOPMENT

Although every group is different, possessing its own unique attributes and dynamics, it is also true that in many important ways groups tend to display similar patterns of evolution. Exhibit 8.2 presents a model of group formation and development that we will follow in discussing this important organizational behavior and management topic. The model suggests that the end results of group activity are shaped by a number of antecedent variables, each category of which we will examine in this chapter. Indeed, each segment of the model can (and, in reality, does) influence each of the other segments.

TYPES OF GROUPS

An organization has technical requirements that arise from its stated goals. The accomplishment of these goals requires that certain tasks be performed and that employees be assigned to perform these tasks. As a result, most employees will be members of a group based on their position in the organization. These are **formal groups**. On the other hand, whenever individuals associate on a fairly continuous basis, there is a tendency for groups to form whose activities may be different from those required by the organization. These are **informal groups**. Both formal groups and informal groups, it will be shown, exhibit the same general characteristics.

Formal Groups

The demands and processes of the organization lead to the formation of different types of groups. Specifically, at least two types of formal groups exist: command and task.

Command Group   The **command group** is specified by the organization chart and is made up of the subordinates who report directly to a given supervisor. The authority relationship between a department manager and the supervisors, or between a senior nurse and her subordinates, is an example of a command group.

Task Group   A **task group** comprises the employees who work together to complete a particular task or project. For example, the activities of clerks in an insurance company when an accident claim is filed are required tasks. These activities create a situation in which several clerks must communicate and coordinate with one another if the claim is to be handled properly. These required tasks and interactions facilitate the formation of a task group.[3] The nurses assigned to duty in the emergency room of a hospital usually constitute a task group, since certain activities are required when a patient is treated.

Informal Groups

Informal groups are natural groupings of people in work environments in response to social needs. In other words, informal groups are not deliberately created; they evolve naturally. Two specific types of informal groups are *interest* and *friendship*.

Interest Groups   Individuals who may not be members of the same command, task group, or team may come together to achieve some mutual objective. Examples of **interest groups** include employees grouping together to present a unified front to management for more benefits and waitresses "pooling" their tips. Note that the objectives of such groups are not related to those of the organization, but are specific to each group.

Friendship Groups   Many groups form because the members have something in common such as age, political beliefs, or ethnic background. These **friendship groups** often extend their interaction and communication to off-the-job activities.

---

[3]Bill Parcells, "The Tough Work of Turning Around a Team," *Harvard Business Review,* November–December 2000, pp. 179–86.

A distinction has been made between two broad classifications of groups—formal and informal. The major difference between them is that formal command and task groups and teams are designated by the formal organization as a means to an end. Informal interest and friendship groups are important for their own sake. They satisfy a basic human need for association. If employees' affiliation patterns were documented, it would become rapidly apparent that they belong to numerous and often overlapping groups. Why so many groups exist is the question to which we turn next.

WHY PEOPLE FORM GROUPS

Formal and informal groups form for various reasons.[4] Some of the reasons involve need satisfaction, proximity, attraction, goals, and economics.

One of the most compelling reasons why people join groups is because they believe membership in a particular group will help them to satisfy one or more important needs. *Social needs,* for example, can be satisfied through groups that provide a vehicle for members to interact with one another. Indeed, it is difficult to imagine being able to fulfill general social needs without participating in at least some groups. *Security needs* may be partially met by membership in a group that acts as a buffer between employees and the organizational system. Without such a group, an individual may feel alone in facing organizational demands. This "aloneness" leads to a degree of insecurity that can be offset by group membership. *Esteem needs* may be partially met by belonging to a high-status or prestige group in which membership is difficult to obtain. An example would be the million-dollar round table in the life insurance business, or an honors organization in college.

Proximity and attraction are two related reasons people form groups. *Proximity* involves the physical distance between employees performing a job. Walking distance, rather than straight-line distance, is a better predictor of the amount of interaction that will occur. It is much easier to interact with a coworker 10 yards away and separated by two desks than it is to interact with someone 1 yard away but separated by a wall. *Attraction* designates the attraction of people to each other because of perceptual, attitudinal, performance, or motivational similarity. Proximity makes it easier to determine areas of common attraction. Thus, both of these factors work together to facilitate group formation.

Group goals, if clearly understood, can be reasons why people are drawn to a group. For example, an individual may join a group that meets after work to become familiar with a new personal computer system. Assume that this system is to be implemented in the work organization over the next year. The person who voluntarily joins the after-hours group believes that learning the new system is a necessary and important goal for employees.

Finally, in many cases groups form because individuals believe they can derive greater *economic benefits* from their jobs if they organize. For example, individuals working at different points on an assembly line may be paid on a group-incentive basis where the production of the group determines the wages of each member. By working and cooperating as a group, the workers may obtain higher economic benefits. Or executives in a corporation may form a group to review executive compensation in hopes of increasing their own economic payoffs.

---

[4] Susan Nash, *Turning Team Performance Inside Out* (Palo Alta, CA: Davies-Black, 2000).

Whatever the circumstances, the group members have a common interest—increased economic benefits—that lead to group affiliation.

STAGES OF GROUP DEVELOPMENT

Groups learn just as individuals do. The performance of a group depends both on individual learning and on how well the members learn to work with one another. For example, a new product committee formed for the purpose of developing a response to a competitor may evolve into a very effective team, with the interests of the company being most important. However, it may also be very ineffective if its members are more concerned about their individual departmental goals than about developing a response to a competitor. This section describes some general stages through which groups evolve and points out the sequential development process involved.[5]

One widely cited model of group development assumes that groups proceed through as many as five stages of development: (1) forming, (2) storming, (3) norming, (4) performing, and (5) adjourning.[6] Although identifying the stage a group is in at a specific time can be difficult, it is nonetheless important to understand the development process. At each stage group behaviors differ, and, consequently, each stage can influence the group's end results.

Forming

The first stage of group development is *forming,* and it is characterized by uncertainty (and, frequently, confusion) about the purpose, structure, and leadership of the group. Activities tend to focus on group members' efforts to understand and define their objectives, roles, and assignments within the group. Patterns of interaction among group members are tried out and either discarded or adopted, at least temporarily. The more diverse the group is, the more difficult it is to maneuver through this stage and the longer it takes. That is why this is a particularly sensitive stage in the formation of multicultural groups. Generally, this stage is complete when individuals begin to view themselves as part of a group.

Storming

The *storming* stage of group development tends to be marked with conflict and confrontation. This generally emotionally intense stage may involve competition among members for desired assignments and disagreements over appropriate task-related behaviors and responsibilities. A particularly important part of storming can involve redefinition of the groups' specific tasks and overall goals.

Individually, group members are likely to begin to decide the extent to which they like the group tasks and their degree of commitment to them. While members may accept the group at one level, at another level there may be resistance to the control the group imposes on them. Some group members may begin to

---

[5]For a review of group development stages, see K. L. Bettenhausen, "Five Years of Group Research: What We Have Learned and What Needs to Be Addressed," *Journal of Management,* June 1991, pp. 345–81.

[6]B. W. Tuckman, "Developmental Sequence in Small Groups," *Psychological Bulletin,* November 1965, pp. 384–99; and B. W. Tuckman and M. Jensen, "Stages of Small Group Development Revisited," *Groups and Organization Studies,* 1977, pp. 419–27.

withdraw during storming, making this stage a particularly critical one for group survival and effectiveness. It is essential that the conflict that typifies storming be managed, as opposed to being suppressed. Suppression of conflict at this point is likely to create negative effects that can seriously hinder group functioning in later stages.

Norming

While storming is marked by conflict and confrontation, *norming* is characterized by cooperation and collaboration. It is also the stage where group cohesion begins significant development. There tends to be an open exchange of information, acceptance of differences of opinion, and active attempts to achieve mutually agreed-upon goals and objectives. There is a strong degree of mutual attraction and commitment and feelings of group identity and camaraderie. Behavioral norms are established and accepted by the completion of this stage, as are leadership and other roles in the group. The specific important impact of norms on group functioning is addressed in a subsequent section on group characteristics.

Performing

The fourth, and what may be the final stage, is performing. *Performing* is that stage where the group is fully functional. The group structure is set, and the roles of each member are understood and accepted. The group focuses its energies, efforts, and commitments on accomplishing the tasks it has accepted.

For some groups, this stage marks the attainment of a level of effectiveness that will remain more or less constant. For others, the process of learning and development will be ongoing so that group effectiveness and efficiency continue. In the former case, group performance will be maintained at a level sufficient to ensure survival; in the latter case, the group will record increasingly higher levels of achievement. Which way any particular group will go will depend on a number of variables, particularly how successfully the group completed earlier development stages.

Adjourning

The *adjourning* stage involves the termination of group activities. Many groups, of course, are permanent and never reach the adjourning stage. For temporary groups, however, such as committees, project groups, task forces, and similar entities, this stage includes disbandment. Customary task activities are complete and the group focuses on achieving closure. This stage can be marked by very positive emotions centering on successful task accomplishment and achievement. It may also be a source of feelings of loss, disappointment, or even anger. The latter may be especially true in the case of permanent groups which fail to survive because of organizational downsizing, merging, or bankruptcy. Increasingly, adjournment is becoming an expected stage of group development, however. Many organizations are relying on temporary groups for problem-solving tasks and product development. Hewlett-Packard and 3M are two examples of companies using temporary groups. At these organizations, project teams may have a life cycle ranging from less than a month to several years.

Of course, not all groups progress smoothly and predictably through these stages. Numerous factors can either hinder or facilitate the process. For example, if new members are constantly entering the group while others are leaving, the group may never complete the performing stage. Other factors that may influence the pattern of group development include the context or environment in which the group operates and group members' awareness of time and deadlines.

CHARACTERISTICS OF GROUPS

As groups evolve through their various stages of development they begin to exhibit certain characteristics. To understand group behavior, you must be aware of these general characteristics. Some of the more important ones are composition, status hierarchy, roles, norms, leadership, and cohesiveness.

Composition

Group composition relates to the extent to which group members are alike. Members of a *homogeneous group* share a number of similar characteristics. Characteristics may be demographic (race, gender, socioeconomic background, education, age, or cultural origin), personality, skills and abilities, or work experience, to name just a few. A *heterogeneous group*, on the other hand, is composed of individuals who have few or no similar characteristics.

Group composition can be extremely important because it can influence a number of other characteristics and outcomes. All else being equal, for example, homogeneous groups are likely to be more cohesive than heterogeneous ones. On the other hand, heterogeneous groups may outperform homogeneous ones in certain situations because they have a richer variety of knowledge and experiences to draw upon. As organizational diversity increases, at least with respect to demographic characteristics, groups will become more heterogeneous in composition. While this offers numerous opportunities for increasing group performance, it also makes the effective management of groups a more challenging task.[7] Sometimes explicit decisions to include individuals with certain characteristics in the composition of a group can have unintended consequences, as this chapter's You Be the Judge demonstrates.

Status Hierarchy

Status and *position* are so similar that the terms often are used interchangeably. The status assigned to a particular position is typically a consequence of certain characteristics that differentiate one position from other positions. In some cases, a person is given status because of such factors as job seniority, age, or assignment. For example, the oldest worker may be perceived as being more technically proficient and is attributed status by a group of technicians. Thus, assigned status may have nothing to do with the formal status hierarchy.

The status hierarchy, and particularly the deference paid to those at the top of the hierarchy, may sometimes have unintended—and undesirable—effects on performance. A vivid example occurred several years ago when a commercial jetliner ran out of fuel and crash-landed short of the runway in Portland, Oregon, killing 10 of the 189 persons aboard. The plane ran out of fuel while flight members were preoccupied with a landing-gear problem that had forced them to circle Portland for some time. The Air Transportation Safety Board's report of the

---

[7]Margaret M. Gootnick and David Gootnick, *Action Tools for Effective Managers* (New York: Amacom, 2000).

Can Organizations Use Gender to Increase Work Group Composition Diversity?

You Be the Judge

Southwood Psychiatric Hospital is a treatment facility with an emphasis on the treatment of emotionally disturbed and sexually abused children. When hospital management reassigned a female child care specialist to the night team, she charged sexual discrimination. She characterized her new assignment as less desirable than being part of the day-treatment team, and claimed it was made on the basis of her gender.

Hospital management readily conceded the charge was true: The hospital had assigned her to the night team because she was a female employee. Ordinarily, making any kind of personnel decision on the basis of gender is illegal—unless gender is a bona fide occupational qualification (such as in selecting attendants for restroom facilities). The hospital argued that it attempted to provide gender diversity within its treatment teams in order to provide better care to female patients who might feel more comfortable when talking to female staff members or to male patients who might relate better to male staff members.

Is this a legitimate exception to the law prohibiting job assignments from being made on the basis of gender? You be the judge!

accident showed that both the copilot and the flight engineer knew the fuel situation was becoming critical, but they did not do enough to warn the captain. A study of the transcript of the cockpit conversation that took place prior to the crash confirms that warnings were made but were subtle, gentle, and extremely deferential to the senior captain in his position at the top of the status hierarchy.[8]

Roles

Each position in the group structure has an associated role that consists of the behaviors expected of the occupant of that position.[9] For example, the director of nursing services in a hospital is expected to organize and control the department of nursing. The director is also expected to assist in preparing and administering the budget for the department. A nursing supervisor, on the other hand, is expected to supervise the activities of nursing personnel engaged in specific nursing services such as obstetrics, pediatrics, and surgery. These expected behaviors generally are agreed on not only by the occupants, the director of nursing, and the nursing supervisor, but by other members of the nursing group and other hospital personnel.

In addition to an *expected role* are also a perceived role and an enacted role. The *perceived role* is the set of behaviors that a person in a position believes he or she should enact. As discussed in Chapter 3, perception can, in some instances, be distorted or inaccurate. The *enacted role,* on the other hand, is the behavior that a person actually carries out. Thus, three possible role behaviors can result.

---

[8]Douglas B. Feaver, "Pilots Learn to Handle Crises—and Themselves," *Washington Post,* September 12, 1982, p. A6.

[9]For an excellent discussion of this and related topics, see Dennis Organ, *Organizational Citizenship Behavior: The Good Citizen Syndrome* (Lexington, MA: Lexington Books, 1988).

Ethics Encounter 8.1

The Ethics of Role Conflict: Using Employees as Informants

Is it ethical for an organization to create role conflict by using employees as paid informants? Law enforcement agencies rely on paid informants routinely. These snitches (as they are known in the business) frequently provide information essential to solving a crime. But while their use by the police is not unusual, the use by management of employees in the role of paid informants is most unusual.

A California department store decided to do just that, however. Emporium-Capwell offered a "bounty" to store employees. One pay period when employees opened their pay envelopes they found a second check in the amount of $300. A close inspection revealed the check to be non-negotiable. An attached note from management, however, promised to reward employees for reporting coworkers who shoplift or commit other dishonest acts.

"Would you like to have this check?" read the note. "If so, simply provide the loss prevention department with information which leads to the termination of a dishonest employee. All information is treated with strict confidence and thoroughly investigated before any action is taken."

When asked, many Emporium employees indicated that they resented the move and definitely would not co-operate with management. "I've worked here 18 years, and this is the lousiest thing I've ever seen here," said one distressed employee. "Everyone was mad. On the one hand, they want you to work as a team and respect your coworkers. On the other, they want you to stab them in the back. I just think it's lousy."

Richard Hedges, president of the union which represents many of the Emporium-Capwell employees, agreed most emphatically. Hedges was quoted as saying, "It's one thing to say, 'If you have knowledge that someone is violating the law, contact us.' It's another to put out a bounty and encourage people to call with their suspicions. I think this may backfire. It will create ill will and paranoia."

Paying informants as the Emporium-Capwell plan did is different from programs such as those at Nynex and Pacific Bell, where whistle-blower hotlines have been set up to facilitate transmission of information regarding illegal activities. No cash rewards are offered, however. While role conflict may be engendered in these latter examples as well, the absence of a "bounty hunter" feature raised far fewer ethical questions.

Source: Based in part on articles appearing in the *Houston Chronicle*. November 9, 1985, sec. 1, p. 4; *Business Week*, September 23, 1991, p. 65.

Conflict and frustration may arise from differences in these three role types. In fairly stable or permanent groups, there typically is a good agreement between expected and perceived roles. When the enacted role deviates too much from the expected role, the person either can become more like the expected role or leave the group.

Through membership in different groups, individuals perform multiple roles. For example, first-line supervisors are members of the management team but also are members of the group of workers they supervise. These multiple roles result in a number of expected role behaviors. In many instances, the behaviors specified by the different roles are compatible. When they are not, however, the individual may experience role conflict. In the case of first-line supervisors, for example, top management has a set of expectations that stresses the supervisor's role in the management group. However, the supervisor is part of the group she is supervising and may have close friendship ties with the other members of the group, who may be former working peers. Similarly, a scientist in a chemical plant who also is a member of a management group might experience role conflict. In such a situation, the scientist may be expected to behave in accordance with the expectations of management as well as the expectations of professional chemists. A physician placed in the role of hospital administrator also may experience this type of role conflict. Sometimes, the conflict is between the individual's role as a work group member on the one hand and a member of the larger organizational group on the other. Ethics Encounter 8.1 is a case in point.

Norms

Norms are the standards shared by members of a group, and they have certain characteristics that are important to group members. First, norms are formed only with respect to things that have significance for the group. They may be written, but very often they can be verbally communicated to members. In many cases they may never be formally stated but somehow are known by all group members. If production is important, then a production norm will evolve. If helping other group members complete a task is important, then an assistance norm will develop. Conversely, if these are not important concerns to the group, no standards for appropriate behavior in these areas will evolve; group members will be free to behave in whatever manner seems reasonable to them.

Second, norms are accepted in various degrees by group members. Some norms are completely accepted by all members, while other norms are only partially accepted. Third, norms may apply to every group member, or they may apply to only some group members. For example, every member may be expected to comply with the production norm, while only group leaders may be permitted to disagree verbally with a management directive.

Groups develop norms for regulating many different aspects of their members' behavior.[10] In work groups, however, the most common norm relates to productivity, and group productivity norms specify "acceptable" production behavior. It is important to understand that the group's perception of what is an acceptable level of production may be significantly different from management's perception. The group's production norm may differ from management's for a number of reasons including a fear of rate-cutting if production is too high or a fear of reprisal if production falls too low.

Exhibit 8.3 illustrates where a group's production norm might fall on a productivity continuum. The zone of acceptance depicted in the exhibit represents minor deviations above and below the norm which would be deemed acceptable to the group. Group members greatly exceeding the norm might be referred to as rate-busters, while those producing well below group expectations might be known as slackers.

Norm Conformity   An issue of concern to managers is why employees conform to group norms.[11] This issue is especially important when a person with skill and capability is performing significantly below his or her capacity so that group norms are not violated. A number of variables may influence conformity to group norms. The *personal characteristics* of the individual play a role. For example, research indicates that persons of high intelligence are less likely to conform than less intelligent individuals, and authoritarian personality types conform more than do nonauthoritarians.[12] *Situational factors,* such as group size and structure, may influence conformity. For example, conformity may become more difficult in larger groups or in those whose members are geographically separated. *Intergroup relationships,* which include such factors as the kind of pressure

---

[10]K. L. Bettenhausen and J. K. Murnighan, "The Development and Stability of Norms in Groups Facing Interpersonal and Structural Change," *Administrative Science Quarterly,* 1991, pp. 20–35.

[11]Daniel C. Feldman, "The Development and Enforcement of Group Norms," *Academy of Management Review,* January 1984, pp. 47–53.

[12]Salvatore R. Maddi, *Personality Theories: A Comparative Analysis* (Homewood, IL: Dorsey Press, 1980), Chap. 7.

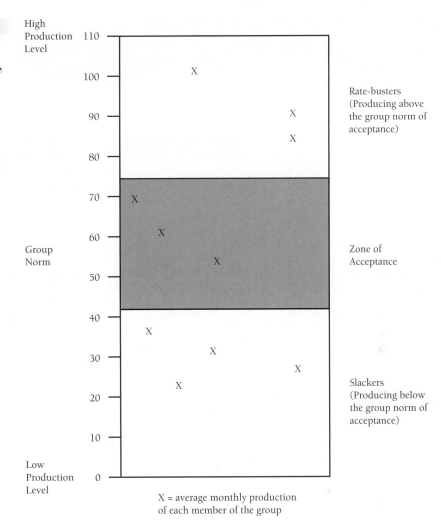

EXHIBIT 8.3
Hypothetical Production Norm and Its Zone of Acceptance

High Production Level

Rate-busters (Producing above the group norm of acceptance)

Group Norm

Zone of Acceptance

Slackers (Producing below the group norm of acceptance)

Low Production Level

X = average monthly production of each member of the group

the group exerts and the degree to which the member identifies with the group, are another potentially important variable.

The degree of conformity with group norms may also be influenced by cultural factors. Some cultures with a more collective tradition may place greater emphasis on the group, and on conformity with norms, than might cultures with a more individualistic orientation. Typical examples of these two orientations are Japan and the United States. Groups have traditionally played a far greater role in Japanese society than in American.

Leadership

The leadership role is an extremely crucial characteristic of groups as the leader exerts influence over the other members of the group.[13] In the formal group the leader can exercise legitimately sanctioned power. That is, the leader can reward

---

[13]*Leadership and Self-Deception* (San Francisco, Berrett-Koehher, 2000).

No Bosses Left at Texas Instruments Malaysia

Because of the demographics of Malaysia and the shortage of highly skilled professional workers, Texas Instruments Malaysia (called TIM for short) needed to find a new way of recruiting, rewarding, and retaining staff. Their answer was to push job responsibility to the lowest level. The move to do so quite literally eliminated group leaders.

Since TIM was formed in 1972 to produce integrated circuits (it now produces more than three million a day) it has relied heavily on group and team structures. Early manifestations of this took the form of Quality Improvement Teams as TIM adopted Total Quality Management practices. By the late 1980s TIM managers began to put operator self-control into practice. They did this in two ways: first by teaching operators how to recognize problems and arrive at solutions; and second by giving them the responsibility, discretion, and authority to do something about a problem when they discovered one.

From there it became a logical progression to move toward eliminating group leaders. By 1992 nearly 90 percent of TIM workers were members of self-managed teams. Today that figure is virtually 100 percent. All day-to-day responsibility for business operating decisions such as stock control, quality, cost, delivery, and service is in the hands of the teams. Line managers have become a thing of the past. Indeed, the only formal leaders left at TIM are senior executives in control of strategy and finance.

Getting rid of the bosses has saved TIM $50 million in quality improvements over 10 years; productivity per employee has gone through the roof; production cycle time has been reduced by half; and absenteeism and tardiness records have dramatically improved. With increased productivity, increased profitability, and decreased organizational bureaucracy TIM seems to be both a worker's and a management's paradise.

www.ti.co

Source: Based in part on "Bosses Not Instrumental at Texas Instruments," *Journal of Management Development*, September 1995, pp. 29–31.

Reading 8.1

What Team Leaders Need to Know

www.volvo.com

or punish members who do not comply with the orders or rules. Sometimes, however, there is no single formal leader, even in a formal group. Such a condition may exist in the case of autonomous work groups. Self-managed teams, for example, may collectively share leader duties among the group members. At Volvo's plant in Uddevalla, Sweden, for example, production of the Volvo 940 luxury sedan is carried out by teams that do not have a supervisor. Each team handles its own production scheduling and quality control operations. Even hiring decisions are made by the team as a whole. International Encounter 8.1 describes a similar situation at Texas Instruments Malaysia.

The leadership role also is a significant factor in an informal group. The person who becomes an informal group leader generally is viewed as a respected and high-status member who embodies the values of the group, aids the group in accomplishing its goals, and enables members to satisfy needs. Additionally, the leader is the choice of group members to represent their viewpoint outside the group and usually is concerned with maintaining the group as a functioning unit.

Cohesiveness

Formal and informal groups seem to possess a closeness or commonness of attitude, behavior, and performance. This closeness has been referred to as *cohesiveness*. Cohesiveness typically is regarded as a force. It acts on the members to remain in a group and is greater than the forces pulling the members away from the group. A cohesive group, then, comprises individuals who are attracted to one another. A group that is low in cohesiveness does not possess interpersonal attractiveness for the members.

Since highly cohesive groups are composed of individuals who are motivated to be together, there is a tendency on the part of management to expect effective

Exercise 8.1

Participating in and
Observations of Group
Processes

group performance. This logic is not supported conclusively by research evidence. In general, as the cohesiveness of a work group increases, the level of conformity to group norms also increases. But these norms may be inconsistent with those of the organization.

There are, of course, numerous sources of attraction to a group. These might include:

1. The goals of the group and the members are compatible and clearly specified.
2. The group has a charismatic leader.
3. The reputation of the group indicates that the group successfully accomplishes its tasks.
4. The group is small enough to permit members to have their opinions heard and evaluated by others.
5. The members are attractive in that they support one another and help one another overcome obstacles and barriers to personal growth and development.[14]

Cohesiveness and Performance   The concept of cohesiveness is important for understanding groups in organizations.[15] The degree of cohesiveness in a group can have either positive or negative effects, depending on how group goals match up with those of the formal organization.[16] In fact, four distinct possibilities exist, as illustrated in Exhibit 8.4.

Exhibit 8.4 indicates that if cohesiveness is high and the group accepts and agrees with formal organizational goals, then group behavior probably will be positive from the formal organization's standpoint. However, if the group is highly cohesive but has goals that are not congruent with those of the formal organization, then group behavior probably will be negative from the formal organization's perspective.

Exhibit 8.4 also indicates that if a group is low in cohesiveness and the members have goals that are not in agreement with those of management, then the results probably will be negative from the standpoint of the organization. Behaviors will be more on an individual basis than on a group basis because of the low cohesiveness. On the other hand, it is possible to have a group low in cohesiveness, where the members' goals agree with those of the formal organization. Here, the results probably will be positive, although again more on an individual basis than on a group basis.

From a managerial perspective, it may sometimes be desirable to alter the cohesion of a work group. If the group has high productivity norms, for example, but is not particularly cohesive, increasing cohesiveness can have very beneficial effects. Increasing cohesion may bring about increased performance, as well as contribute to group members' satisfaction.

---

[14]C. Cartwright and A. Zander, *Group Dynamics: Research and Theory* (New York: Harper & Row, 1968).

[15]Richard A. Guzzo and Marcus W. Dickson, "Teams in Organizations: Recent Research on Performance and Effectiveness," *Annual Review of Psychology*, 1996, pp. 307–38.

[16]It should be noted that cohesiveness is not the only factor which may influence performance. For just one example, see Glenn Littlepage, William Robison, and Kelly Reddington, "Effects of Task Experience and Group Experience on Group Performance," *Organizational Behavior and Human Decision Processes*, February 1997, pp. 133–47.

EXHIBIT 8.4   The Relationship between Group Cohesiveness and Organizational Goals

		Agreement with Organizational Goals	
		Low	**High**
Degree of Group Cohesiveness	**Low**	Performance probably oriented away from organizational goals	Performance probably oriented toward organizational goals
	High	Performance oriented away from organizational goals	Performance oriented toward organizational goals

There may also be times, of course, when *decreasing* cohesion may be in the best interest of the organization. A group whose goals are counter to those of the larger organization would be an example. This could occur during periods of labor unrest or while the organization is experiencing an external threat such as a hostile takeover. Or, it may simply be a need to offset the negative effects of groupthink (discussed below). Management Pointer 8.1 suggests some ways group cohesion may be altered.

It should be noted that attempts to alter the cohesiveness of any group may not work. Indeed, an effect just the opposite of what was intended may be the result. This is particularly true when the attempt is being made to reduce cohesion. The group may see the attempt as a threat, which may have the effect of actually increasing cohesiveness as the group unites to defend itself. Managers should exercise great care in making decisions about attempting to influence the cohesion of work groups.

Groupthink   Highly cohesive groups are important forces in influencing organizational behavior. One author has provided a provocative analysis of highly cohesive groups.[17] In his book, Irving Janis analyzed foreign policy decisions by a number of presidential administrations and concluded that those made by such groups often included a decision-making process he called *groupthink*. Janis defines **groupthink** as the "deterioration of mental efficiency, reality testing, and moral judgment" in the interest of group solidarity.[18] According to Janis, groups suffering from groupthink tend to display a number of common characteristics. Among these characteristics are the following:

Illusion of invulnerability. Group members collectively believe they are invincible.

Tendency to moralize. Opposition to the group's position is viewed as weak, evil, or unintelligent.

Feeling of unanimity. All group members support the leader's decisions. Members may have reservations about decisions

─── **Management Pointer 8.1** ───

ALTERING GROUP COHESION

As a manager, you may sometimes want to alter the cohesion level of a group. Strategies for *increasing* cohesion include:

1. Inducing agreement on group goals.

2. Making the group more homogeneous in its composition.

3. Increasing the frequency of interaction among group members.

4. Making the group smaller (decrease number of members).

5. Physically and/or socially isolating the group from other groups.

6. Allocating rewards to the group rather than to individuals.

To *decrease* group cohesion, do the opposite of the strategies above (e.g., induce disagreement on group goals, make the group more heterogeneous, etc.).

---

[17]Irving Janis, *Victims of Groupthink: A Psychological Study of Foreign Policy Decisions and Fiascos*, 2nd ed. (Boston: Houghton Mifflin, 1982).

[18]Ibid. p. 9.

but do not share these views. Rather than appearing weak, members keep dissenting views to themselves. This indicates how the pressure toward group solidarity can distort the judgment of individual members.

Pressure to conform. Formal and informal attempts are made to discourage discussion of divergent views. Groups exert significant pressure on individual members to conform.

Opposing ideas dismissed. Any individual or outside group that criticizes or opposes a decision receives little or no attention from the group. Group members tend to show strong favoritism toward their own ideas in the manner by which information is processed and evaluated, thereby ensuring that their own ideas will win out.

Certainly, some level of group cohesiveness is necessary for a group to tackle a problem. If seven individuals from seven different organizational units are responsible for a task, the task may never be completed effectively.[19] The point, however, is that more cohesiveness may not necessarily be better. While members of task groups may redefine solving a problem to mean reaching agreement rather than making the best decision, members of cohesive groups may redefine it to mean preserving relations among group members and preserving the image of the group. Some research suggests that, even among highly cohesive work groups, groupthink is not a factor if the group is composed of highly dominant individuals.[20]

END RESULTS

> **Exercise 8.2**
>
> What to Do with Johnny Rocco

Groups exist to accomplish objectives. In the case of work groups, those objectives are generally related to the performance of specific tasks which in turn are designed to result in attainment of formal organizational outcomes. Measurable production (e.g., number of units assembled, percent of market captured, number of customers served) is perhaps the most obvious, but certainly not the only, end result of work group activities.

While some form of production output (goods, services, ideas, etc.) is typically an important measure of group performance and effectiveness, it is not the only consideration. Organizational researcher Richard Hackman identifies three important criteria of group effectiveness:[21]

1. *The extent to which the group's productive output meets the standard of quantity, quality, and timeliness of the users of the output.* For example, a group which produced a product that was unacceptable to a customer could not be considered effective no matter what the group or others thought about the product.

---

[19]Group performance is frequently, but not always, better than individual performance. See Daniel Gigone and Reid Hastie, "Proper Analysis of the Accuracy of Group Judgments," *Psychological Bulletin,* January 1997, pp. 149–67.

[20]Michael Callaway, Richard Marriott, and James Esser, "Effects of Dominance on Group Decision Making: Toward a Stress-Reduction Explanation of Groupthink," *Journal of Personality and Social Psychology,* October 1985, pp. 949–52. For further discussion of the relationship between cohesiveness and groupthink, see P. R. Bernthal and C. A. Insko, "Cohesiveness without Groupthink," *Group and Organizational Management,* March 1993, pp. 66–87.

[21]J. Richard Hackman (ed.), *Groups That Work (and Those That Don't)* (San Francisco: Jossey-Bass Publishers, 1990), pp. 6–7.

2. *The extent to which the group process of actually doing the work enhances the capability of group members to work together interdependently in the future.* This suggests that even though the group might produce a product meeting the standards mentioned in the first criterion, if that end result was obtained in a manner destructive to future working relationships, the group is not effective. The fact that a group is a temporary one, such as a task force or project team, does not negate the importance of this criterion of effectiveness.

3. *The extent to which the group experience contributes to the growth and well-being of its members.* This criterion relates to the end results of development and satisfaction which were specified in Exhibit 8.2 at the beginning of the chapter. Note that it is not necessary for a group to have member development and satisfaction as a stated objective for this to be a legitimate test of group effectiveness. When group participation does not contribute to personal or professional development and/or does not lead to any personal need satisfaction, this may have negative consequences. It suggests group productivity may not continue over an extended period of time, and it may have implications for the quality of group members' participation in subsequent groups.

These criteria are important ones for virtually any work group. However, they are particularly relevant for assessing the effectiveness of self-managed teams. It is critical that SMTs enhance the capabilities of their members to work together interdependently in the future. Similarly, team member growth and well-being are equally necessary ingredients for SMT success.

TEAMS

As we indicated at the start of this chapter, a team is viewed as a mature group comprising people with interdependence, motivation, and a shared commitment to accomplish agreed-upon goals. Admittedly, the distinction between a team and a group can be arbitrary and is sometimes vague. A total commitment to common goals and accountability to the team is what makes a team stand out and distinct from immature, developing groups.

There are a number of reasons why the use of teams has increased so significantly in U.S. organizations. To a certain extent it has been triggered by Japan's economic accomplishments and the fact that teams are thought to be an important contributor to that success.[22] Additional reasons have to do with specific perceived benefits derived from using teams. These include potential quality improvements; enhanced productivity gains from bringing individuals with complementary skills together; and organizational restructuring efforts, particularly those with the objective of flattening the structure. Finally, many companies are moving to teams in response to other firms' teams success stories. The phenomenal success of Microsoft Corporation is attributed in part to its extensive use of software research and development teams, a point not lost on other firms in the industry that have implemented the same practice. Saturn Corporation's success with teams has been emulated by others in the automobile industry, with Chrysler's Neon facility being a recent example.

---

[22]Afsaneh Nahavandi, *The Art and Science of Leadership* (Upper Saddle River, NJ: Prentice Hall, 1997).

Types of Teams

There is no standard classification system in use for describing different types of teams. Distinctions among teams can be made on the basis of size, composition, organizational level, duration (temporary versus permanent), objectives, and potential contribution to organizational performance, to name only a few possibly distinguishing characteristics. We will use a number of these to categorize important types of teams in organizations today; problem-solving teams, research and development teams, and the previously mentioned self-managed teams (SMT).

Problem-Solving Teams   As the name implies, problem-solving teams are formed to deal with problems. The problem may be very specific and known, or the team may be set up to deal with potential future problems that have not yet been identified. In the former case, the team is usually of temporary duration. It is put together to deal with a current problem and then dissolved. The life span of such teams may vary from a few days to many months, occasionally a year or longer.

Quality circles are examples of permanent problem-solving teams. A **quality circle** is a team of employees committed to recommending and implementing work and product improvements and solving quality-related problems. Circles typically comprise 6 to 12 employees who perform related jobs. Circle members are usually trained in group processes (for example, structured techniques for diagnosing problems and brainstorming).[23] Temporary or permanent problem-solving teams are increasingly being used by organizations who realize that teams can significantly outperform individuals in many situations.[24] AT&T, for example, has effectively used problem-solving teams to address customer needs, resulting in quicker response time and increased customer satisfaction.

Cross-Functional Teams   A cross-functional team is one consisting of members from different functional departments (e.g., engineering, accounting, human resources, marketing). This type of team forms to address a specific problem. In most cases team members come from different departments and different levels (managers and nonmanagers). Organizations have used cross-functional, boundary-spanning teams for years. For example, at Caterpillar's tractor division, cross-functional teams working on product design and testing include a product designer, engineers, purchasing and marketing members, assembly workers, and even suppliers.[25]

At Xerox a cross-functional team works on the firm's Intranet project so that all employees can access a firewall network. Individuals from management, advanced business services, and information technology have worked on creating Web Board, the Xerox communication system.[26]

Using the skills, competencies, and experience of individuals from diverse areas within a firm can increase understandably, camaraderie, trust, and performance. A word of caution, however, is that effective cross-functional teams may take time to become effective. Building trust and commitment in cross-functional

www.saturn.car.com

www.cat.com

www.xerox.com

---

[23]Guzzo and Dickson, "Teams in Organizations," p. 325.

[24]J. R. Katzenbach and D. K. Smith, *The Wisdom of Teams* (Boston: Harvard Business School Press, 1993).

[25]Discussion with human resources representative in Peoria, Illinois (October 23, 2000), and G. Taninecz, "Team Players," *Industry Week,* July 15, 1996, pp. 28–32.

[26]M. Warshaw, "The Good Guys Guide to Office Politics," *Fast Company,* April/May 1998, p. 168.

teams is challenging because of previous impressions, attitudes, and relationships that are formed before the team is assembled.

Virtual Teams   A popular response to increasing competition, the need for faster decisions, and technological advancements has been the creation of virtual teams. Working across distances via e-mail, desktop and real-time conferencing, video conferencing, electronic bulletin boards, and other technologies is challenging for leaders. Virtual teams can be connected via computer and telecommunications technology. A **virtual team** is defined as a number of people geographically separated that are assembled by using various technologies to accomplish specific goals. A virtual team's membership rarely meets face-to-face.

Virtual teams can meet without concern for space, time, or physical presence. Team members use communications links to perform their work, individual and team tasks, and roles. Companies such as Hewlett-Packard, IBM, Compaq, and Procter and Gamble have partially or fully eliminated traditional offices for providing customer services. Virtual teams work together to service customer requests, complaints, and suggestions.[27]

www.ibm.com

John Patrick, an IBM senior strategist, in an internal memo convinced the firm to establish virtual teams. He wrote a memo entitled, Getting Connected, that explained how technology could be used to improve performance. IBM began using e-mail as a discussion approach to communicating. Eventually, IBM established Patrick and others as a virtual team. The team's first project was to design IBM's corporate Web site. Patrick's virtual team works on other internal communication projects. The team interacts electronically and continues working on developing innovative Internet applications that benefit IBM and its customers.[28]

The efficient and successful use of technology is one of a number of important factors contributing to the success of virtual teams. Included as possible technology to use with virtual teams is desktop video-conferencing systems, collaborative software systems, and Internet/intranet systems.[29] Each technology needs to be evaluated in terms of its effectiveness and cost benefits regarding the generation of ideas and plans, solving routine and complex problems, and negotiating interpersonal or other forms of conflict.

As virtual team members interact it is important for leaders to coach, build trust, evaluate performance, and provide feedback. Since the virtual team is geographically dispersed and uses technology links, leaders are challenged in performing their motivational team building supportive roles. Virtual team members performing work anytime, anyplace are difficult to lead and manage in the traditional sense. Those charged with leading virtual teams must be technologically linked themselves to members and must be willing to permit a great deal of autonomy and decision-making independence to members.[30] The hierarchical command and control process is minimized when using virtual teams. Virtual team members must be self-reliant but remain connected to and knowledgeable about the goals of the organization.

---

[27]Thomas H. Davenport and Keri Pearlson, "Two Cheers for the Virtual Office," *Sloan Management Review,* Summer 1998, pp. 51–65.

[28]Anthony R. Hendrickson, "Virtual Teams: Technology and the Workplace of the Future," *Academy of Management Executive,* August 1998, pp. 17–29.

[29]Amy Oringel, "John Patrick Reinventing By Blue," Developer.com (March 2, 1998) (www.developer.com/news/profiles/022598-patrick).

[30]Deborah L. Duarte and Nancy Tennant, *Mastering Virtual Teams* (San Francisco: Jossey-Bass, 1999).

Virtual Team Technologies: A Brief Primer

A brief look at technologies that have aided the growth of virtual work arrangements is presented. Each year new technologies are emerging that will improve the effectiveness of virtual teams, teleworkers, and virtual office employees.

Desktop Video Conferencing Systems (DVCS) is a small camera mounted atop a computer monitor providing the video feed while voice transmission can be fed by use of a speakerphone or an earpiece. Connection to other virtual team members is managed through software on the user's computer.

This allows team members to interact and see each other. The audio and video connection results in sharing information, talking to each other, and working on assignments.

Collaborative Software Systems allows team members to work independently or together. Lotus Notes permits team members to share data and communicate. Electronic messaging, scheduling, and analysis can occur with the software.

Internet and intranet technologies are also useful for virtual work arrangements. The Internet is a network of many smaller computer networks that exist all over the world. The Internet's organization is as invisible to the user as the telephone companies who provide local and long-distance service. An intranet is an internal, secure system within an organization that allows company members to use Internet technology to disseminate and aggregate organizational information and encourage employee interaction. Internet and intranet connectivity provide virtual team members with methods to communicate, share data, and solve problems together.

Source: For a concise and excellent discussion of these three technologies, see Anthony M. Townsend, Samuel De Marie, and Anthony R. Hendrickson, "Virtual Teams: Technology and the Workplace of the Future," *Academy of Management Executive*, August 1998, pp. 17–29.

www.lotus.com

The dispersion of virtual team members creates a challenge for leaders in terms of creating a sense of team.[31] Something intangible is lost when team members do not have the opportunity to work and meet face-to-face. The use of Lotus Notes as a collaborative tool is an attempt to bring about a team feeling. Team members connect to electronic discussions to learn about policies, strategies, and expertise. Whether Lotus Notes can address the loss of personal contact is subject to debate and empirical study.[32]

An empirical study of the development of trust in 29 global virtual teams that were connected via e-mail provided some interesting findings. The highest level of trust among virtual teams pointed to three traits. First, members began their interactions with nonwork social interactions providing personal background information. Second, each member had a set of clear task roles. Third, all team members demonstrated positive attitudes. The study also illustrated that low-trust virtual teams were less productive than high-trust virtual teams.

The new competitive pressures and challenges for increased worker autonomy and empowerment suggest that virtual teams and telework (work carried out in a remote location away from a main office, factory, or plant) are a reality. The use of computers and telecommunication technology are likely to increase the dispersion and connectivity of employees. About 40 million employers already telework on a

[31]Wayne F. Cascio, "Managing a Virtual Workplace," *Academy of Management Executive,* August 2000, pp. 81–90.

[32]S. L. Jarvenpaa, K. Knoll, and D. E. Leidner, "Is Anybody Out There? Antecedents of Trust in Global Virtual Teams," *Journal of Management Information Systems,* 1998, pp. 29–64.

global basis.[33] Virtual teams and virtual offices (usually at home) are very likely to become even more significant. New ways to effectively manage and lead organizations with virtual-work arrangements need to be examined and studied. Ford Motor Company and Delta Airlines in February 2000 announced that any employee wanting one would be provided a personal computer for home use. These two firms believe that computer use, wherever it occurs, can benefit the work performance of individuals working in the traditional setting or in a virtual arrangement.[34]

Organizational Encounter 8.2 indicates that teleworking is not always easy or successful. A few issues to consider are raised in the Encounter.

www.delta-air.com

www.ford.com

Research and Development Teams   Research and development (R&D) teams are used to develop new products. Their use is most extensive in high-tech industries such as aviation, electronics, and computers. R&D teams are usually composed of representatives of many different departments or functions in the organization, making them cross-functional in nature. For example, a computer company may form a cross-functional R&D team made up of representatives from marketing, sales, engineering, purchasing, and finance to develop plans for a new product. Such a team, representing expertise from all the relevant areas of the company, can significantly reduce the amount of time required to bring a new product to the marketplace.

In some organizations, R&D teams have been set up to expedite innovation and creative new product design. Such groups are referred to as *skunk works.* Such teams often have their own facilities, somewhat isolated from the rest of the organization. This may facilitate prolonged team interaction without interruption by day-to-day routines and problems. Skunk works team members often become almost fanatical in the extent to which they identify with their products. Hewlett-Packard and 3M are examples of companies with well-established skunk works. When Ford Motor Company almost abandoned development of a new Mustang coupe because of cost considerations, it was a skunk works team that over an eight-week period (with team members sleeping on the workplace floor in shifts) solved the engineering and related cost problems.[35]

www.cocacola.com

www.chevron.com

Self-Managed Teams   As discussed in Chapter 6, self-managed teams (SMTs) are small groups of individuals who are empowered to perform certain activities based on procedures established and decisions made within the team, with minimum or no outside direction. Organizations using SMTs include such industry leaders as AT&T, Campbell Soups, Chevron Chemical, Coca-Cola, Federal Express, General Electric, General Mills, Honeywell, Motorola, Procter & Gamble, Texas Instruments, and Xerox. As a result of global competition, multinational firms increasingly are using SMTs in their foreign affiliates as well.[36]

---

[33]C. Anderson, J. Girard, S. Payne, J. Pultz, M. Zboray, and C. Smith, "Implementing a Successful Remote Access Project: From Technology to Management," New York: Gartner Group, Report R-06-6639, November 18, 1998.

[34]"The New World of Work: Flexibility Is the Watchword" *Business Week,* January 10, 2000, p. 36; and L. Rivenbark, "Employees Want More Opportunities to Telecommunicate," *HR News,* April 2000, pp. 14–16.

[35]J. B. White and O. Suris, "How a 'Skunk Works' Kept the Mustang Alive—On a Tight Budget," *Wall Street Journal,* September 21, 1993, pp. A1, A12.

[36]Bradley L. Kirkman and Debra L. Shapiro, "The Impact of Cultural Values on Employee Resistance to Teams: Toward a Model of Globalized Self-Managing Work Team Effectiveness," *Academy of Management Review,* July 1997, pp. 730–57.

Virtual Work Arrangement Issues to Consider

Virtual employees? They're part of the mainstream now. But working from home hasn't been the panacea for work-life balance that many of us thought it was going to be. In fact, says Christena Nippert-Eng, an associate professor of sociology, "the anxiety level has increased," she says. "We feel less able than ever to place appropriate boundaries around the workday, while at the same time, we realize the need for those boundaries more than ever before."

Fascinated by the rituals of today's overwired and underrested workers, Nippert-Eng, has been exploring the boundaries—or the lack thereof—of the American workplace. She has come up with a couple of new species. Are you an integrator? They're the ones who have a single date book for their business and personal appointments and have desks littered with family snapshots. A segmenter? They'd rather be tortured than disclose the name of their cat to an office worker or have their work keys on the same ring as their home keys.

Overall, though, the new world of work is becoming more integrationist, and that will have implications for people and companies. In an interview with *Fast Company*, Nippert-Eng talked about the future of the virtual workplace.

WHY DON'T MORE PEOPLE FEEL BETTER ABOUT WORKING AT HOME?

Telecommuting is a move toward integration: the home broadband hookup to the office network, the wireless remote access to the e-mail server. But we are still a heavily segmenting culture. People are glad they are home when the kids get home, but few say that they are more comfortable with the work-life balance today than they were five or six years ago. The only people I've talked to who don't have these "boundary" issues are the ones who don't own a home or who aren't married, or whose spouse works in the same kind of environment that they do.

WHAT ARE SOME OF THE SPECIFIC SOURCES OF ANXIETY?

When you're in the office, no one ever doubts whether you're working or not. You could be balancing your checkbook, but the fact that you're there is a reassurance. When you work at home, people don't really be-

lieve that you're working. So a common reaction is to say, "I will respond to every e-mail within 30 seconds. I will be on my computer again at the end of the evening, so that when people come in they will see stuff waiting for them." It becomes another source of stress.

Another source of anxiety is that there's no independent way for a manager to assess whether or not you're doing a good job. "Being there when I need you" is pretty much still the standard. I know managers who actually up the productivity ante for people who work from home.

At the same time, how do you establish an appropriate boundary between home and work? Most people have no idea when they should start and end the workday. Their day turns into this incredible frantic, highly insecure, fast-paced mode where all time is work time and every day is a workday. There's no such thing as vacation anymore.

WHAT WILL IT TAKE FOR THESE ARRANGEMENTS TO WORK BETTER?

From the point of view of the person working at home, do not ask your colleagues to do anything for you that they wouldn't normally do if you were there in the office. I'm hearing about colleagues who actually sabotage the work of teleworkers. These are people who choose not to do this boundary-blurring stuff and who resent office mates who do. Interview colleagues once a week early on, and keep asking them how it is working out for them.

For an organization to be effective with people who work from home, supervisors must create arrangements that are as flexible as possible—but they must also make sure that the workday ends. Companies also need to look closely at the norms and at the expectations they have for their workers. Some supervisors are uncomfortable managing home-work integrators. Plenty of managers still want instantaneous hand-holding from their subordinates. They need to understand their own home-work boundaries and how they assess who's worthy of promotion.

There's one last thing that both sides need to understand: Yes, you are going to lose time that could be spent working on other matters while you are duking out these issues. But if you don't you'll run into bigger problems down the road.

Source: Jennifer Reingold, "There's No Place (to Work) Like Home," *Fast Company*, November 2000, pp. 76–77.

SMTs are not for everyone, nor have they been successful in every organization. When US West first formed its teams, for example, the company sold the concept to employees promising teamwork, empowerment, and no loss of jobs. Many employees later felt that was just a cover for downsizing. As one ex-employee put it, "We showed them how to streamline the work, and now 9,000 people are gone. It makes you feel used."[37]

Before implementing SMTs organizations should make certain that such teams are consistent with the organization's: (1) business requirements; (2) values and goals; and (3) competencies. Once implemented, success depends on management commitment, receptivity to change, and employee trust in management. Without all of these, both individuals and organizations are likely to find the effort unsatisfactory.[38]

Team Effectiveness

Teams represent one form or type of group. As such, factors influencing the effectiveness of any group are important in determining team effectiveness. Previously discussed group characteristics such as composition, norms, leadership, and cohesion are examples. There are some issues, however, that are particularly important when it comes to developing effective teams. We will briefly examine four: training, communications, empowerment, and rewards. (Management Pointer 8.2 suggests some additional considerations).

Training   Effective teams don't just happen. In addition to their individual task-related skills and abilities, team members must also know how to function effectively as team members. This almost always suggests training. Depending on the type and purpose of the team, training may be needed in problem-solving skills, creative thinking, or interpersonal skills. Certainly, at the very least, team members must be well-versed in the company's philosophy regarding teams, the team mission, and new roles and responsibilities individuals will have as a consequence of being part of the team. It has been suggested that without proper training the only thing management gets from creating teams is a guarantee that more time will be spent making worse decisions.

Communications   One of the more significant effects creating teams has on an organization's management is an increased need for information. Team members need information in order to accomplish their objectives. Much of this is information that has traditionally been management's exclusive domain. If teams are to be effective, however, full disclosure of formerly restricted information may be necessary. Management—particularly middle management—is often threatened by this, fearing a loss of their own decision-making power. The failure of many team efforts can be traced directly to management's unwillingness to share information with the teams it has created.

Management Pointer 8.2

HOW TO HELP ENSURE TEAMS WORK

As a manager, here are some steps you can take to increase the likelihood that teams for which you are responsible work.

1. Keep the team size as small as is possible. The larger the size, the greater the potential problems in interacting and making decisions.

2. Make certain that a sufficient range of skills, information, and/or experience to do the task exists among the team members.

3. Instill in the team a sense of common purpose.

4. Give the team leeway to develop its own set of work procedures without outside interference.

5. Help develop a sense of mutual accountability. "We're all in this together" thinking helps develop teamwork and improves team outcomes.

---

[37]Brian Dumaine, "The Trouble with Teams," *Fortune*, September 5, 1994, pp. 86–92.

[38]Edward Ward, "Autonomous Work Groups: A Field Study of Correlates of Satisfaction," *Psychological Reports*, February 1997, pp. 60–62.

Empowerment   Along with information, teams must have the authority to make decisions and act autonomously. Whether a problem-solving team, an R&D team, or a SMT, teams that lack authority are generally less effective. In addition to hindering taking action, lack of authority suggests to team members that management doesn't really trust them in the first place, further reducing team effectiveness.

Being given insufficient authority is typically the root of team empowerment problems. It should be noted, however, that sometimes teams may be given *too much* authority. This is particularly a danger in the early stages of team involvement. Team members may be unaccustomed to making decisions and be overwhelmed by the degree of authority they suddenly possess. This is another reason why training is such an important factor in team success.

Rewards   The reward system in most organizations is individually based. That is, organizational members are rewarded based on evaluation of their individual performance. While the individual's contribution to team success is a legitimate part of the reward system, team success must also be factored in. To the extent that teams perform well, the team should be rewarded. Distribution of that reward to individual team members is an important, but separate issue. There are a number of ways in which rewards can be allocated to teams. With problem-solving teams, for example, an incentive system is frequently used, wherein the team receives a percentage of the savings realized by the organization. Many organizations using SMTs have modified their reward structure to include some form of profit-sharing. Regardless, it is important that teams be rewarded for their contribution to organizational objectives.

As we noted at the start of this chapter, the use of work groups in organizations is rapidly increasing. Groups hold the potential for simultaneously increasing both the productivity and satisfaction of group members. As organizations move through the first decade of the 21st century, it is difficult to overstate the importance of the role groups and teams are assuming in organizational life. Organizational structure, the design of work, performance feedback and reward systems, decision-making procedures, and organizational development strategies, to name a few, are all being profoundly affected by groups and teams. As we will see in the next chapter, group effects are not always positive.

Summary of Key Points

- Groups can be viewed from a number of perspectives, including perception, organization, and motivation. For our purposes, a group may be thought of as two or more individuals interacting with each other to accomplish a common goal.

- Formal groups are created to facilitate the accomplishment of an organization's goals. Command groups, specified by the organization chart; task groups, comprising employees working together to complete a specific project; and teams, comprised of people interacting very closely together with a shared commitment, are three types of formal groups. Informal groups are associations of individuals in the work situation in response to social needs. Interest groups and friendship groups are two types of informal groups.

- Formal and informal groups exist for a number of reasons. Need satisfaction may be a compelling reason to join a group. Security, social, and esteem needs are typical examples. Proximity and attraction may be another reason. That is, people may form groups because their physical location encourages interaction they enjoy. People may also form groups to facilitate the accomplishment of common goals. Finally, some groups form because individuals believe they can derive economic benefits from group membership.

- As groups form and develop, they tend to go through several sequential stages. These are: (1) *forming,* characterized by uncertainty and confusion; (2) *storming,* marked by conflict and confrontation; (3) *norming,* where group cohesion begins significant development; (4) *performing,* where the group becomes fully functional; and (5) *adjourning,* which involves the termination of group activities.

- The model of the process of group formation and development presented in the chapter has a number of elements. These include the different types of groups, the reasons why groups are formed, stages in group development, important characteristics of groups, and end results of group activity.

- To understand group behavior, it is essential to be aware that formal and informal groups exhibit certain characteristics. These include the composition of the group; the status hierarchy that exists and the basis used for determining member status; the norms or behaviors the group expects its members to adhere to; the type of leadership in the group; and the degree of cohesiveness that exists within the group.

- Relevant criteria for group effectiveness include (1) the extent to which group output meets expected standards of quantity, quality, and timeliness; (2) the extent to which the group process enhances the capability of group members to work together interdependently in the future; and (3) the extent to which the group experience contributes to the growth and well-being of the group.

- A team is a special kind of unit. Different types of teams include problem-solving teams, cross-functional teams, virtual teams, research and development teams, and self-managed teams.

Review and Discussion Questions

1. Think of a formal group to which you belong. Describe the group in terms of the characteristics of groups discussed in this chapter.

2. Why is it very likely that virtual work arrangements (teams, offices, telework) are here to stay?

3. Why is it important for managers to be familiar with the concepts of group behavior?

4. In terms of influencing organizational effectiveness, since groups are composed of individuals, is group behavior really any different from individual behavior? Why or why not?

5. Why is groupthink something to be avoided? How might a manager attempt to ensure that groupthink doesn't occur in his or her group?

6. What is the relationship between group norms and group cohesiveness? What roles do both cohesiveness and norms play in shaping group performance?

7. Under what circumstances might an organization encourage the formation of informal employee groups? Under what circumstances might they discourage such groups?

8. Is it always important for satisfactory end-results to be achieved with respect to performance, satisfaction, and development? Can you think of a situation where satisfaction and/or development might be more important than performance?

9. Is leadership more or less an important consideration in self-managed teams than it is in other types of groups? Why or why not?

10. If you were creating a research and development team for an organization, what kinds of factors would you take into consideration in deciding the composition of the team? Would these factors be different if you were putting together a problem-solving team?

READING 8.1   What Team Leaders Need to Know
Susan Caminiti

In 1989, J. D. Bryant was perfectly content overseeing a staff of 15 circuit-board assemblers at Texas Instruments' Forest Lane defense plant in Dallas. "Then one day I heard the company was moving to teams and that I was going to become a facilitator," Bryant, 33, recalled in his Southern drawl. "I'm supposed to teach the teams everything I know and then let them make their own decisions." Not sure if something good or bad had just happened, Bryant pressed his boss for more information. "I said, 'This is career enhancing?' and he said, 'Oh, yes. You don't have to do performance reviews anymore. The team will take them on.'" When Bryant asked if that was all, he got hit with the real zinger. "Well, J. D.," explained his boss, "since you won't be a supervisor anymore, you'll have to take a 5 percent pay cut."

Ah, yes, teams. Everyone knows they shoot efficiency and productivity into the stratosphere and reward workers with more control in their jobs. But overlooked in the midst of all this team glee is just how confusing the experience can be. Companies expect middle managers to metamorphose, effective yesterday, into star team leaders ready to coach, motivate, and empower.

The problem is, few managers—and even fewer companies—understand the transformational process. (It is a safe bet, however, that pay cuts do not help it along.) "Corporations underestimate the shift in mind-set and behavioral skills that team leaders need," says David Nadler, chairman of Delta Consulting Group in New York City. "Even the most capable managers have trouble making the transition because all the command- and control-type things they were encouraged to do before are no longer appropriate. There's no reason to expect them to have any skill or sense of this."

Managers thrust into the new role also wonder what long-term effect it will have on their careers. They worry that all the "soft skills" so essential for success as a team leader—communication, conflict resolution, coaching—might not pack much punch on a resume. "When you take away traditional titles, it makes people nervous," explains James Champy, chairman of CSC Consulting Group, a Cambridge, Massachusetts, firm that specializes in helping organizations reengineer. "It's not clear how being an effective team leader translates into, say, a promotion within the company or another position elsewhere."

Does this mean you should bolt for the nearest exit if asked to make the switch yourself? Hardly. The skills you'll need—the patience to share information, the trust to let others make decisions, and the ability to let go of power—do not develop overnight. But as you'll see from the stories of the men and women below, they can be learned. Here's how:

- Don't be afraid to admit ignorance. What if you're a team leader and you don't really know what your teammates do? Don't panic, advises Eric Doremus of Honeywell's defense avionics division in Albuquerque. Doremus, 37, spent seven years in marketing at Honeywell before being asked in 1992 to lead a team developing data storage systems for Northrop Grumman's B2 bomber. Although he claims not to have panicked, Doremus did say he felt as if he had been "dropped into the middle of a swirling, wet cloud." When the cloud lifted, he realized two things: One, he would never have the technical skills of the engineers on the team. Two, he was good at motivating people to do their best. "In marketing I was always given the no-way-we-can-win assignments," says Doremus. "And we always figured out a way to do them."

The first time he met with the 40 members of the B2 bomber team, he admitted he wouldn't be much help with technical problems. What he could do was help the team communicate better with its customer—Northrop Grumman—and see that the project was completed on time and within budget. Says Doremus: "I know they could have gotten a Ph.D. in optical engineering to be the team leader rather than a marketing guy like me. But I think they were looking for someone who could bring a much different perspective to the job, someone who could focus the team on the customer, which is not the way they were used to working."

Doremus quickly learned what would make him succeed: "My most important task was not trying to figure out everybody's job. It was to help this team feel as if they owned the project by getting them whatever information, financial or otherwise, they needed. I knew that if we could all charge up the hill together, we would be successful." He was right. His team shipped the first prototype of the data storage system for the B2 bomber last summer and will deliver a fully functional unit in June.

Source: Susan Caminiti, *Fortune,* © 1995, Time Inc. All rights reserved.

- Know when to intervene. A common misconception about the role of team leader is that it is strictly hands-off. Although it is essential to learn to let others solve problems, it is equally important—and possibly harder—to know when to step in yourself. "Too little help and direction is just as paralyzing as too much," says Jeanne Wilson, a consultant with DDI, a human resources development firm in Pittsburgh.

Two years ago, Reed Breland became a team facilitator for Hewlett-Packard's 180-person financial services center in Colorado Springs; by April the center will handle all general accounting for H-P's factories across the U.S. After several months in his new position, Breland, 35, saw that members of one of his teams were having a hard time working together. "It was a classic case of personality conflict," he says. "They just didn't like each other. But when two people on an eight-person team don't get along, believe me, it's disruptive."

At first Breland let the team try to work things out. "Of course, I spoke to them about the problems, but I was mainly interested in making sure they understood that the work had to get done, regardless of how they got along," he says. Nine months later the team was still squabbling. "I knew I had to do something then, because it was beginning to affect their work," explains Breland. Rather than trying to determine who was right and wrong, he dissolved the team and had its members placed elsewhere. Breland says the team members are doing fine in their other assignments; he compares their dynamics with those of a sports team. "If the chemistry isn't right, it doesn't matter how good or bad the players are. It's not going to work. As a team leader you have to know when it's reached that point. It's more of an art than a science, but that's what makes the job so interesting."

Becoming a team facilitator was never part of Breland's long-range plans. In the summer of 1992, he was interviewing for another finance-related position at H-P when he came across an unusual ad in the company's job listings. "It said the job seeker must enjoy coaching, working with people, and bringing about improvement through hands-off guidance and leadership," recalls Breland. "And this was for an accounts-payable position. It was unlike any job listing I had ever seen."

Breland, who has an MBA in finance, flew to Colorado Springs for an interview. After discussing some of the more technical aspects of the job, he met with a few members of the accounts-payable team he would lead if hired. "Some of them were 20- or 21-year olds doing clerical-level accounting, so I'm thinking, 'How hard is it going to be to impress them?' " Breland recalls. "But I was amazed at how well-prepared they were. They wanted to know about things like how I handled conflict, what kind of time-management skills I had, and how I felt about delegating. It was the strangest interview I've ever had."

Breland's preparation for the new job consisted of little more than a handshake and a pat on the back. However, other facilitators hired before him had put together a survival guide. Says Breland: "They told me, 'Before you open your mouth, read this.' " Because he didn't want to come across as a typical manager, he decided not to call a staff meeting his first day. Instead, he says, "I attended one of the team's meetings and tried to get a feel for how they spoke to each other. When it was my turn, I said, 'Look, I'm not an expert in the nitty-gritty of accounts payable, so you can't come to me with all your technical questions. You'll have to depend on each other for that. But I am going to challenge you to come up with smarter ways of working.' "

And has it been a challenge for him? "This is the hardest job I've ever had," he says. "I go home every night and rethink what I did, how I did it, and whether I should change it." Breland, who would eventually like to become a controller at H-P, says his time as a facilitator is preparing him well. "Many of the management positions at H-P have disappeared as the company has moved to teams," he says. "The traditional career path of an MBA coming in as a supervisor and then working his way up the management ranks to controller is gone. So I see this as a great opportunity for me to get significant management experience that will be invaluable no matter where I go." www.hp. com

- Learn to truly share power. A big mistake for new team leaders is to embrace the job in words only. J. D. Bryant knows, because that's what he did. Says he: "I didn't buy into teams, partly because there was no clear plan on what I was supposed to do." Bryant had been told to turn over more responsibility to the operators who assembled TI's circuit boards. His response was to let his staff tap into the company's E-mail system to call up their own messages; in the past, he had done it for them. It was not, Bryant admits, the most empowering move in the world. "I never let the operators do any scheduling or any ordering of parts because that was mine. I figured as long as I had that, I had a job."

Frustrated and confused in his new role, Bryant applied to become a software writer at TI's defense plant in McKinney, Texas. This plant, too, had switched to teams, but the role of facilitator was rotated within the software group rather than assigned to one person. Says Bryant: "That suited me just fine." He quickly realized that the McKinney workers had taken a much more disciplined approach to teams. He learned from other team leaders about planning, setting milestones, and transferring responsibility. "It became apparent to me that we did things wrong in Forest Lane because we never planned for anything," says Bryant.

As his enthusiasm for team leadership grew (and his skills improved), Bryant became a roving troubleshooter for the defense group. "Teams could call me if they were having trouble," he explains. "I would go see them, sit in on a few meetings, and try to help resolve things. I wasn't there to take the place of the team leader but rather to make recommendations. I found the job very gratifying because I could see that they were solving problems, say, by reducing cycle time or improving quality."

Bryant's skills proved especially useful to other facilitators. "I knew their frustrations and fears because I had been in their shoes," he says. "So I would meet with them and say, 'Okay, what can you transfer to the team today? What can you transfer in the next couple of months?' I could start to back them out of their old mind-set. But in backing them out, I was also telling them that they now had more time to go out and get new contracts and new business—or time to train themselves to do something else."

In October, Bryant and three colleagues took on similar positions in TI's corporate services division, which handles building maintenance, environmental issues, and security. Says Bryant: "Corporate services is serious about making teams work. They know what they need to do to be successful, but they're not sure how to get their hands around it. That's why we're here."

- Worry about what you take on, not what you give up. As managers turn over more responsibilities to teams, it's only natural for them to worry about whether they are empowering themselves right out of a job. James Malone, 45, heard that concern repeatedly last summer when he interviewed prospective team leaders for Dun & Bradstreet's North American shared-transaction service center in Allentown, Pennsylvania. The center, which opened July 1, consolidated most of the company's financial transactions, including accounts payable, purchasing, and payroll.

Early last year, D&B convened the controllers of its major divisions to discuss whether a team-based center made sense. Malone, then the controller of D&B's Reuben H. Donnelley publishing division, was a believer in consolidating the company's financial operations but thought it would take years to accomplish. Furthermore, he wasn't sold on teams as the way to do it. "I had no idea what self-directed teams were," he recalls. "I figured this was just another directive coming down from on high, and I wasn't sure that it would work."

Then he started educating himself. He read books on teams and visited companies like Johnson & Johnson and Hewlett-Packard that were successfully using them. "I began to believe this was the way to go because it allowed the people who do the work to have a say in how to do it," says Malone. Recruiting team leaders was another matter. "While I was interviewing, people said, 'I won't have an office? I won't have a title? What do I say to my wife? How do I tell my friends what I do?' "

Malone tried to assure his colleagues that they would keep busy. "Once the teams were up and running, we expected the leaders to immerse themselves in reengineering and to deliver savings to the company," says Malone. For example, until recently each of D&B's 15 divisions used a different expense account form. Today there is one form, and that will soon be replaced when the company requires reports to be filed electronically. Getting this message out to the divisions is part of team leaders Scot Kuehm and John Trabulsi's jobs. Besides working with their procurement team, the two spend considerable time visiting the divisions' senior managers, explaining the change in reporting, and making sure it happens on time. Back in Allentown, they share what they have learned with their 25 team members and other team leaders, who have a chance to contribute their ideas on how best to make the new system work.

- Get used to learning on the job. Two years ago Honeywell reorganized its defense avionics division after hearing a volley of complaints from customers. "People said they loved our engineers and our contract writers," explained Walter McConnell, the division's general manager. "The problem was that the two groups didn't communicate well with each other, and customers got forced into the role of go-between." McConnell and other senior managers decided to organize multifunctional teams around each customer. But instead of phasing the teams in, as might be expected in an 1,800-person division, the group set a goal of reorganizing within six months. "We took a burn-the-bridge approach because we wanted people to know we were serious," said McConnell. "If we hadn't made a big fuss, this would have died a natural death."

Of 300 supervisors in the old system, 90 were selected to become team leaders; the rest either joined the teams or transferred to other parts of the company. Says McConnell: "During the interview process, it became easy to distinguish the people who really believed in teams from those who just worried about whether they were going to lose their titles."

Barbara Brockett was an early believer. The team she leads develops pilotless aircraft that are used as aerial targets by the U.S. Army and Air Force. Says Brockett, 35, who began working at Honeywell as an engineer 11 years ago: "Although more training would have been helpful, it's hard to teach someone to be a team leader. You really learn how to do it by doing it every day, by making decisions with people, not off by yourself." She says the hardest part of her job is not having all the answers. "I'm getting more comfortable with the fact that I don't need to know everything. But I do need to know where to get the answers."

At best, the job of team leader is an unscientific blend of instinct, on-the-job learning, and patience. Says consultant David Nadler: "Probably 15 percent of managers are natural team leaders; another 15 percent could never lead a team because it runs counter to their personality. Then there's that huge group in the middle: Team leadership doesn't come naturally to them, but they can learn it." These days, can any good manager afford not to?

Exercises

EXERCISE 8.1   Participating in and Observations of Group Processes

OBJECTIVES

1. To provide experience in participating in and observing groups undertaking a specific task.
2. To generate data that can be the focus of class discussion and analysis.

STARTING THE EXERCISE

The Situation

You are appointed to a personnel committee in charge of selecting a manager for the department that provides administrative services to other departments. Before you begin interviewing candidates, you are asked to develop a list of the personal and professional qualifications the manager needs. The list will be used as the selection criteria.

The Procedure

1. Select five to seven members to serve on the committee.
2. Ask the committee to rank the items in the following list in their order of importance in selecting the department head.
3. The students not on the committee should observe the group process. Some should observe the whole group, and others individual members. The observers can use observation guides A and B.
4. The observers should provide feedback to the participants.
5. The class should discuss how the committee might improve its performance.

Selection Criteria

_____ Strong institutional loyalty

_____ Ability to give clear instructions

_____ Ability to discipline subordinates

_____ Ability to make decisions under pressure

_____ Ability to communicate

_____ Stable personality

_____ High intelligence

_____ Ability to grasp the overall picture

_____ Ability to get along well with people

_____ Familiarity with office procedures

_____ Professional achievement

_____ Ability to develop subordinates

Source: Kae H. Chung and Leon C. Megginson, *Organizational Behavior* (New York: Harper & Row, 1981), pp. 241–44. Used by permission.

A. Group Process Observation Guide

Instructions: Observe the group behavior in the following dimensions. Prepare notes for feedback.

Group Behaviors	Description	Impact
Group Goal: Are group goals clearly defined?		
Decision Procedure: Is the decision procedure clearly defined?		
Communication Network: What kind of communication network is used? Is it appropriate?		
Decision Making: What kind of decision process is used? Is it appropriate?		
Group Norm: Observe the degrees of cohesiveness, compatibility, and conformity.		
Group Composition: What kind of group is it?		
Other Behavior: Is there any behavior that influences the group process?		

B. Individual Role Observation Guide

Instructions: Observe one committee member. Tabulate (or note) behaviors that he or she exhibits as the group works.

Initiating Ideas: Initiates or clarifies ideas and issues.	**Confusing Issues:** Confuses others by bringing up irrelevant issues or by jumping to other issues.
Managing Conflicts: Explores, clarifies, and resolves conflicts and differences.	**Mismanaging Conflicts:** Avoids or suppresses conflicts or creates "win-or-lose" situations.
Influencing Others: Appeases, reasons with, or persuades others.	**Forcing Others:** Gives orders or forces others to agree.
Supporting Others: Reinforces or helps others to express their opinions.	**Rejecting Others:** Deflates or antagonizes others.
Listening Attentively: Listens and responds to others' ideas and opinions.	**Showing Indifferences:** Does not listen or brushes off others.
Showing Empathy: Shows the ability to see things from other people's viewpoint.	**Self-Serving Behavior:** Exhibits behavior that is self-serving.
Exhibiting Positive Nonverbal Behaviors: Pays attention to others, maintains eye contact, composure, and other signs.	**Exhibiting Negative Nonverbal Behaviors:** Tense facial expression, yawning, little eye contact, and other behaviors.

Exercises

EXERCISE 8.2   What to Do with Johnny Rocco

OBJECTIVES

1. Participating in a group assignment playing a particular role.
2. Diagnosing the group decision process after the assignment has been completed.

STARTING THE EXERCISE

After reading the material relating to Johnny Rocco, a committee is formed to decide the fate of Johnny Rocco. The chairperson of the meeting is Johnny's supervisor, who should begin by assigning roles to the group members. These roles (shop steward, head of production, Johnny's coworker, director of personnel, and the social worker who helped Johnny in the past) represent points of view the chairperson feels should be included in this

meeting. (Johnny is not to be included.) Two observers should be assigned.

After the roles have been assigned, each role-player should complete the personal preference part of the worksheet, ordering the alternatives according to their appropriateness from the vantage point of his or her role.

Once the individual preferences have been determined, the chairperson should call the meeting to order. The following rules govern the meeting: (1) the group must reach a consensus ordering of the alternatives; (2) the group cannot use a statistical aggregation, or majority vote, decision-making process; (3) members should stay "in character" throughout the discussion. Treat this as a committee meeting consisting of members with different backgrounds, orientations, and interests who share a problem.

Personal Preference	Group Decision	Worksheet
_____	_____	Give Johnny a warning that at the next sign of trouble he will be fired.
_____	_____	Do nothing, as it is unclear that Johnny did anything wrong.
_____	_____	Create strict controls (do's and don'ts) for Johnny with immediate strong punishment for any misbehavior.
_____	_____	Give Johnny a great deal of warmth and personal attention and affection (overlooking his present behavior) so he can learn to depend on others.
_____	_____	Fire him. It's not worth the time and effort spent for such a low-level position.
_____	_____	Talk over the problem with Johnny in an understanding way so he can learn to ask others for help in solving his problems.
_____	_____	Give Johnny a well-structured schedule of daily activities with immediate and unpleasant consequences for not adhering to the schedule.
_____	_____	Do nothing now, but watch him carefully and provide immediate punishment for any future misbehaviors.
_____	_____	Treat Johnny the same as everyone else, but provide an orderly routine so he can learn to stand on his own two feet.
_____	_____	Call Johnny in and logically discuss the problem with him and ask what you can do to help him.
_____	_____	Do nothing now, but watch him so you can reward him the next time he does something good.

After the group has completed the assignment, the two observers should conduct a discussion of the group process using the Group Process Diagnostic Questions as

a guide. Group members should not look at these questions until after the group task has been completed.

JOHNNY ROCCO

Johnny has a grim personal background. He is the third child in a family of seven. He has not seen his father for several years and his recollection is that his father used to

Source: Adapted from David A. Whetton and Kim S. Cameron, *Developing Management Skills* (Glenview, IL: Scott, Foresman and Company, 1984), pp. 450–53.

come home drunk and beat up every member of the family; everyone ran when he came staggering home.

His mother, according to Johnny, wasn't much better. She was irritable and unhappy and she always predicted that Johnny would come to no good end. Yet she worked when her health allowed her to do so in order to keep the family in food and clothing. She always decried the fact that she was not able to be the kind of mother she would like to be.

Johnny quit school in the seventh grade. He had great difficulty conforming to the school routine—misbehaving often, acting as a truant quite frequently, and engaging in numerous fights with schoolmates. On several occasions he was picked up by the police and, along with members of his group, questioned during several investigations into cases of both petty and grand larceny. The police regarded him as "probably a bad one."

The juvenile officer of the court saw in Johnny some good qualities that no one else seemed to sense. This man, Mr. O'Brien, took it upon himself to act as a "big brother" to Johnny. He had several long conversations with Johnny, during which he managed to penetrate to some degree Johnny's defensive shell. He represented to Johnny the first semblance of personal interest in his life. Through Mr. O'Brien's efforts, Johnny returned to school and obtained a high school diploma. Afterwards, Mr. O'Brien helped him obtain a job.

Now at age 20, Johnny is a stockroom clerk in one of the laboratories where you are employed. On the whole Johnny's performance has been acceptable, but there have been glaring exceptions. One involved a clear act of insubordination on a fairly unimportant matter. In another Johnny was accused, on circumstantial grounds, of destroying some expensive equipment. Though the investigation is still open, it now appears that the destruction was accidental.

Johnny's supervisor wants to keep him on for at least a trial period, but he wants "outside" advice as to the best way of helping him grow into greater responsibility. Of course, much depends on how Johnny behaves in the next few months. Naturally, his supervisor must follow personnel policies that are accepted in the company as a whole. It is important to note that Johnny is not an attractive young man. He is rather weak and sickly and shows unmistakable signs of long years of social deprivation.

A committee is formed to decide the fate of Johnny Rocco. The chairperson of the meeting is Johnny's supervisor, and should begin by assigning roles.

GROUP PROCESS DIAGNOSTIC QUESTIONS

Communications

1. Who responded to whom?
2. Who interrupted? Was the same person interrupted consistently?
3. Were there identifiable "communication clusters"? Why or why not?

4. Did some members say very little? If so, why? Was level of participation ever discussed?
5. Were efforts made to involve everyone?

Decision Making

1. Did the group decide how to decide?
2. How were decisions made?
3. What criterion was used to establish agreement?
   a. Majority vote?
   b. Consensus?
   c. No opposition interpreted as agreement?
4. What was done if people disagreed?
5. How effective was your decision-making process?
6. Does every member feel his or her input into the decision-making process was valued by the group, or were the comments of some members frequently discounted? If so, was this issue ever discussed?

Leadership

1. What type of power structure did the group operate under?
   a. One definite leader?
   b. Leadership functions shared by all members?
   c. Power struggles within the group?
   d. No leadership supplied by anyone?
2. How does each member feel about the leadership structure used? Would an alternative have been more effective?
3. Did the chairperson provide an adequate structure for the discussion?
4. Was the discussion governed by the norms of equity?
5. Was the chairperson's contribution to the content of the discussion overbearing?

Awareness of Feelings

1. How did members in general react to the group meetings? Were they hostile (toward whom or what?), enthusiastic, apathetic?
2. Did members openly discuss their feelings toward each other and their role in the group?
3. How do group members feel now about their participation in this group?

Task Behavior

1. Who was most influential in keeping the group task oriented? How?
2. Did some members carry the burden and do most of the work, or was the load distributed evenly?
3. If some members were not contributing their fair share, was this ever discussed? If so, what was the outcome? If not, why?
4. Did the group evaluate its method of accomplishing a task during or after the project? If so, what changes were made?
5. How effective was our group in performing assigned tasks? What improvements could have been made?

Cases

CASE 8.1 Banana Time Case

This paper undertakes description and explanatory analysis of the social interaction which took place within a small work group of factory machine operatives during a two-month period of participant observation.

My fellow operatives and I spent our long days of simple, repetitive work in relative isolation from other employees of the factory. Our line of machines was sealed off from other work areas of the plant by the four walls of the clicking room. The one door of this room was usually closed. Even when it was kept open during periods of hot weather, the consequences were not social; it opened on an uninhabited storage room of the shipping department. Not even the sounds of work activity going on elsewhere in the factory carried to this isolated workplace. There were occasional contacts with outside employees, usually on matters connected with the work; but, with the exception of the daily calls of one fellow who came to pick up finished materials for the next step in processing, such visits were sporadic and infrequent.

The clickers were of the genus punching machines, of mechanical construction similar to that of the better-known punch presses; their leading features were hammer and block. The hammer, or punching head, was approximately 8 inches by 12 inches at its flat striking surface. The descent upon the block was initially forced by the operator, who exerted pressure on a handle attached to the side of the hammer head. A few inches of travel downward established electrical connection for a sharp power-driven blow. The hammer also traveled by manual guidance in a horizontal plane to and from, and in an arc around, the central column of the machine. Thus, the operator, up to the point of establishing electrical connections for the sudden and irrevocable downward thrust, had flexibility in maneuvering his instrument over the larger surface of the block. The latter, approximately 24 inches wide, 18 inches deep, and 10 inches thick, was made, like a butcher's block, of inlaid hardwood; it was set in the machine at a convenient waist height. On it the operator placed his materials, one sheet at a time if leather, stacks of sheets if plastic, to be cut with steel dies of assorted sizes and shapes. The particular die in use would be moved, by hand, from spot to spot over the materials each time a cut was made; less frequently, materials would be shifted on the block as the operator saw need for such adjustment.

Introduction to the new job, with its relatively simple machine skills and work routines, was accomplished with what proved to be, in my experience, an all-time minimum of job training. The clicking machine assigned to me was situated at one end of the row. Here the superintendent and one of the operators gave a few brief demonstrations, accompanied by bits of advice, which included a warning to keep hands clear of the descending hammer. After a short practice period, at the end of which the superintendent expressed satisfaction with progress and potentialities, I was left to develop my learning curve with no other supervision than that afforded by members of the work group. Further advice and assistance did come from time to time from my fellow operatives, sometimes upon request, sometimes unsolicited.

THE WORK GROUP

Absorbed at first in three related goals of improving my clicking skill, increasing my rate of output, and keeping my left hand unclicked, I paid little attention to my fellow operatives save to observe that they were friendly, middle-aged, foreign born, full of advice, and very talkative. Their names, according to the way they addressed each other, were George, Ike, and Sammy. George, a stocky fellow in his late 50s, operated the machine at the opposite end of the line; he, I later discovered, had emigrated in early youth from a country in southeastern Europe. Ike, stationed at George's left, was tall, slender, in his early 50s, and Jewish; he had come from eastern Europe in his youth. Sammy, number-three man in the line and my neighbor, was heavyset, in his late 50s, and Jewish; he had escaped from a country in eastern Europe just before Hitler's legions had moved in. All three men had been downwardly mobile in occupation in recent years. George and Sammy had been proprietors of small businesses; the former had been "wiped out" when his uninsured establishment burned down; the latter had been entrepreneuring on a small scale before he left all behind him to flee the Germans. According to his account, Ike had left a highly skilled trade which he had practiced for years in Chicago.

THE WORK

It was evident to me before my first workday drew to a weary close that my clicking career was going to be a grim process of fighting the clock, the particular timepiece in this situation being an old-fashioned alarm clock that ticked away on a shelf near George's machine. I had struggled through many dreary rounds with the minutes and

Source: Excerpted from Donald F. Roy, " 'Banana Time,' Job Satisfaction and Informal Interaction." Reproduced by permission of the Society for Applied Anthropology from *Human Organization*, 18, no. 4 (Winter 1959–60), pp. 151–68.

hours during the various phases of my industrial experience, but never had I been confronted with such a dismal combination of working conditions as the extra-long workday, the infinitesimal cerebral excitation, and the extreme limitation of physical movement. The contrast with a recent stint in the California oil fields was striking. This was no eight-hour day of racing hither and yon over desert and foothills with a rollicking crew of "roustabouts" on a variety of repair missions at oil wells, pipelines, and storage tanks. Here there were no afternoon dallyings to search the sands for horned toads, tarantulas, and rattlesnakes or to climb old wooden derricks for raven's nests with an eye out, of course, for the telltale streak of dust in the distance which gave ample warning of the approach of the boss. This was standing all day in one spot beside three old codgers in a dingy room looking out through barred windows at the bare walls of a brick warehouse, leg movements largely restricted to the shifting of body weight from one foot to the other, hand and arm movements confined, for the most part, to a simple repetitive sequence of place the die—punch the clicker—place the die—punch the clicker, and intellectual activity reduced to computing the hours to quitting time. It is true that from time to time a fresh stack of sheets would have to be substituted for the clicked-out old one; but the stack would have been prepared by someone else, and the exchange would be only a minute or two in the making. Now and then a box of finished work would have to be moved back out of the way, and an empty box brought up, but the moving back and the bringing up involved only a step or two. And there was the half hour for lunch and occasional trips to the lavatory or the drinking fountain to break up the day into digestible parts. But after each momentary respite, hammer and die were moving again: click—move die—click—move die.

I developed a game of work. The game developed was quite simple, so elementary, in fact, that its playing was reminiscent of rainy-day preoccupations in childhood when attention could be centered by the hour on colored bits of things of assorted sizes and shapes. But this adult activity was not mere pottering and piddling; what it lacked in the earlier imaginative content, it made up for in clean-cut structure. Fundamentally involved were: (*a*) variation in color of the materials cut, (*b*) variation in shapes of the dies used, and (*c*) a process called "scraping the block." The basic procedure which ordered the particular combination of components employed could be stated in the form: "As soon as I do so many of these, I'll click some brown ones." And with success in attaining the objective of working with brown materials, a new goal of "I'll get to do the white ones" might be set. Or the new goal might involve switching dies.

INFORMAL SOCIAL ACTIVITY OF THE WORK GROUP: TIMES AND THEMES

I began to take serious note of the social activity going on around me; my attentiveness to this activity came with growing involvement in it. What I heard at first, before I started to listen, was a stream of disconnected bits of communication that did not make much sense. Foreign accents were strong, and referents were not joined to coherent contexts of meaning. It was just "jabbering." What I saw at first, before I began to observe, was occasional flurries of horseplay that were so simple and unvarying in pattern and so childish in quality that they made no strong bid for attention. For example, Ike would regularly switch off the power at Sammy's machine whenever Sammy made a trip to the lavatory or the drinking fountain. Correlatively, Sammy invariably fell victim to the plot by making an attempt to operate his clicking hammer after returning to the shop. And as the simple pattern went, this blind stumbling into the trap was always followed by indignation and reproach from Sammy, smirking satisfaction from Ike, and mild paternal scolding from George. My interest in this procedure was at first confined to wondering when Ike would weary of his tedious joke or when Sammy would learn to check his power switch before trying the hammer.

Most of the breaks in the daily series were designated as "times" in the parlance of the clicker operators, and they featured the consumption of food or drink of one sort or another. There was coffee time, peach time, banana time, fish time, Coke time, and, of course, lunch time. Other interruptions that formed part of the series but were not verbally recognized as times were window time, pickup time, and the staggered quitting times of Sammy and Ike. These latter unnamed times did not involve the partaking of refreshments.

My attention was first drawn to this times business during my first week of employment when I was encouraged to join in the sharing of two peaches. It was Sammy who provided the peaches; he drew them from his lunch box after making the announcement, "Peach time!" On this first occasion I refused the proffered fruit but thereafter regularly consumed my half peach. Sammy continued to provide the peaches and to make the "Peach time!" announcement, although there were days when Ike would remind him that it was peach time, urging him to hurry up with the midmorning snack. Ike invariably complained about the quality of the fruit, and his complaints fed the fires of continued banter between peach donor and critical recipient. I did find the fruit a bit on the scrubby side but felt, before I achieved insight into the function of peach time, that Ike was showing poor manners by looking a gift horse in the mouth. I wondered why Sammy continued to share his peaches with such an ingrate.

Banana time followed peach time by approximately an hour. Sammy again provided the refreshments—namely, one banana. There was, however, no four-way sharing of Sammy's banana. Ike would gulp it down by himself after surreptitiously extracting it from Sammy's lunch box, kept on a shelf behind Sammy's work station. Each morning, after making the snatch, Ike would call out, "Banana time!" and proceed to down his prize while Sammy made futile protests and denunciations. George would join in with mild remonstrances, sometimes scolding Sammy for making so much fuss. The banana was one that Sammy brought for his own consumption at lunch time; he never did get to eat his banana but kept bringing one for his lunch. At first this daily theft startled and amazed me. Then I grew to look forward to the daily seizure and the verbal interaction which followed.

Window time came next. It followed banana time as a regular consequence of Ike's castigation by the indignant Sammy. After "taking" repeated references to himself as a person badly lacking in morality and character, Ike would "finally" retaliate by opening the window that faced Sammy's machine to let the "cold air" blow in on Sammy. The slandering which would, in its echolalic repetition, wear down Ike's patience and forbearance usually took the form of the invidious comparison: "George is a good daddy. Ike is a bad man! A very bad man!" Opening the window would take a little time to accomplish and would involve a great deal of verbal interplay between Ike and Sammy, both before and after the event. Ike would threaten, make feints toward the window, then finally open it. Sammy would protest, argue, and make claims that the air blowing in on him would give him a cold; he would eventually have to leave his machine to close the window. Sometimes the weather was slightly chilly, and the draft from the window unpleasant, but cool or hot, windy or still, window time arrived each day. (I assume that it was originally a cold-season development.) George's part in this interplay, in spite of the "good daddy" laudations, was to encourage Ike in his window work. He would stress the tonic values of fresh air and chide Sammy for his unappreciativeness.

THEMES

To put flesh, so to speak, on this interactional frame of times, my work group had developed various "themes" of verbal interplay, which had become standardized in their repetition. These topics of conversation ranged in quality from an extreme of nonsensical chatter to another extreme of serious discourse. Unlike the "times," these themes flowed one into the other in no particular sequence of predictability. Serious conversation could suddenly melt into horseplay, and vice versa. In the middle of a serious discussion on the high cost of living, Ike might

drop a weight behind the easily startled Sammy or hit him over the head with a dusty paper sack. Interaction would immediately drop to a low comedy exchange of slaps, threats, guffaws, and disapprobations, which would invariably include a 10-minute echolalia of "Ike is a bad man, a very bad man! George is good daddy, a very fine man!" Or, on the other hand, a stream of such invidious comparisons as followed a surreptitious switching-off of Sammy's machine by the playful Ike might merge suddenly into a discussion of the pros and cons of saving for one's funeral.

"Kidding themes" were usually started by George or Ike, and Sammy was usually the butt of the joke. Sometimes Ike would have to "take it," seldom George. One favorite kidding theme involved Sammy's alleged receipt of $100 a month from his son. The points stressed were that Sammy did not have to work long hours or did not have to work at all, because he had a son to support him. George would always point out that he sent money to his daughter; she did not send money to him. Sammy received occasional calls from his wife, and his claim that these calls were requests to shop for groceries on the way home were greeted with feigned disbelief. Sammy was ribbed for being closely watched, bossed, and henpecked by his wife, and the expression, "Are you man or mouse?" became an echolalic utterance, used both in and out of the original context.

Serious themes included the relating of major misfortunes suffered in the past by group members. George referred again and again to the loss by fire of his business establishment. Ike's chief complaints centered around a chronically ill wife who had undergone various operations and periods of hospital care. Ike spoke with discouragement of the expenses attendant upon hiring a housekeeper for himself and his children; he referred with disappointment and disgust to a teenage son, an inept lad who "couldn't even fix his own lunch. He couldn't even make himself a sandwich!" Sammy's reminiscences centered on the loss of a flourishing business when he had to flee Europe ahead of the Nazi invasion.

There was one theme of especially solemn import, the "professor theme." This theme might also be termed "George's daughter's marriage theme," for the recent marriage of George's only child was inextricably bound up with George's connection with higher learning. The daughter had married the son of a professor, who instructed in one of the local colleges. This professor theme was not in the strictest sense a conversation piece; when the subject came up, George did all the talking. The two Jewish operatives remained silent as they listened with deep respect, if not actual awe, to George's accounts of the Big Wedding, which, including the wedding pictures, entailed an expense of $1,000. It was monologue, but there was listening, there was communication, the sacred communication of a temple, when George told of going for Sunday afternoon walks on the Midway with the professor or of joining the professor for a Sunday dinner. Whenever he spoke of the professor, his daughter, the wedding, or even of the new son-in-law, who remained for the most part in the background, a sort of incidental like the wedding cake, George was complete master of the interaction. His manner, in speaking to the rank-and-file of clicker operators, was indeed that of master deigning to notice his underlings. I came to the conclusion that it was the professor connection, not the straw-boss-ship or the extra nickel an hour, that provided the fount of George's superior status in the group.

QUESTIONS:

1. What type of group has evolved and is reported in the "Banana Time case"?
2. Describe what you consider to be important group characteristics observed in this work group.
3. Is this work group cohesive? Explain.

9
Chapter

Intergroup Conflict and Negotiations

After completing Chapter 9 you should be able to:

Learning Objectives

- Explain the contemporary perspective on conflict.

- Distinguish between functional and dysfunctional conflict.

- Discuss why intergroup conflict occurs.

- Identify several consequences of dysfunctional intergroup conflict.

- Describe five approaches for managing conflict through resolution.

- Discuss how increased globalization has changed negotiating tactics.

- Distinguish between win-win and win-lose negotiation.

- Identify the major types of third-party negotiations.

For any organization to perform effectively, interdependent individuals and groups must establish working relationships across organizational boundaries, between individuals, and among groups. Individuals or groups may depend on one another for information, assistance, or coordinated action. But the fact is that they are interdependent. Such interdependence may foster either cooperation or conflict.

For example, the production and marketing executives of a firm may meet to discuss ways to deal with foreign competition. Such a meeting may be reasonably free of conflict. Decisions get made, strategies are developed, and the executives return to work. Thus, there is intergroup cooperation to achieve a goal. However, this may not be the case if sales decline because the firm is not offering enough variety in its product line. The marketing department desires broad product lines to offer more variety to customers, while the production department desires narrow product lines to keep production costs at a manageable level and to increase productivity. Conflict is likely to occur at this point because each function has its own goals that, in this case, conflict. Thus, groups may cooperate on one point and conflict on another.

The focus of this chapter is on conflict that occurs between groups in organizations. Intergroup problems are not the only type of conflict that can exist in organizations. Conflict between individuals (interpersonal conflict), however, usually can be more easily resolved through existing mechanisms. Troublesome employees can be counseled, transferred, terminated, or given different work assignments or schedules, or a variety of other alternatives may be implemented.

A CONTEMPORARY PERSPECTIVE ON INTERGROUP CONFLICT

In the past many organizational practitioners operated on the assumption that any and all conflict was bad and thus should be eliminated. Today we understand that is not the case. A more accurate and enlightened view is that conflict is neither inherently good nor bad, but is inevitable. It is true that too much conflict can have negative consequences because it requires time and resources to deal with it and because it diverts energy that could more constructively be applied elsewhere. Too little conflict, on the other hand, can also be negative in that such a state can lead to apathy and lethargy and provide little or no impetus for change and innovation. If everything is going smoothly, people may become too comfortable to want to make changes that could improve organizational effectiveness.

It is true, of course, that some conflict situations produce nothing positive. Other conflict situations, however, may be beneficial if they are used as instruments for change or innovation. For example, evidence suggests conflict can improve the quality of decision making in organizations.[1] Thus in dealing with conflict the critical issue is not so much the conflict itself but how it is managed. Using this perspective, we can define conflict in terms of the effect it has on the organization. In this respect, we shall discuss both *functional* and *dysfunctional* conflict.[2]

---

[1]Donald E. Conlon and Daniel P. Sullivan, "Examining the Actions of Organizations in Conflict: Evidence From The Delaware Court of Chancery," *Academy of Management Journal,* June 1999, pp. 319–29.

[2]S. P. Robbins, *Essentials of Organizational Behavior* (Englewood Cliffs, NJ: Prentice Hall, 1998).

Functional Conflict

A **functional conflict** is a confrontation between groups that enhances and benefits the organization's performance. For example, two departments in a hospital may be in conflict over the most efficient and adaptive method of delivering health care to low-income rural families. The two departments agree on the goal but not on the means to achieve it. Whatever the outcome, low-income rural families probably will end up with better medical care once the conflict is settled. Without this type of conflict in organizations, there would be little commitment to change, and most groups likely would become stagnant. Functional conflict can lead to increased awareness of problems that need to be addressed, result in broader and more productive searches for solutions, and generally facilitate positive change, adaptation, and innovation.

Dysfunctional Conflict

A **dysfunctional conflict** is any confrontation or interaction between groups that harms the organization or hinders the achievement of organizational goals. Management must seek to eliminate dysfunctional conflict.

Beneficial conflicts can often turn into harmful ones. In most cases, the point at which functional conflict becomes dysfunctional is impossible to identify precisely. The same level of stress and conflict that creates a healthy and positive movement toward goals in one group may prove extremely disruptive and dysfunctional in another group (or at a different time for the same group). A group's tolerance for stress and conflict can also depend on the type of organization it serves. Auto manufacturers, professional sports teams, and crisis organizations such as police and fire departments would have different points where functional conflict becomes dysfunctional than would organizations such as universities, research and development firms, and motion-picture production firms.

An 11-year conflict between Arthur Andersen (accounting firm) and its offshoot, Andersen Consulting, finally came to an end in August 2000. The conflict between the units was certainly dysfunctional. Andersen Consulting was created to provide management strategy, business process, change management, and technology consulting services, while Arthur Andersen provided audit, tax, and accounting services. Both units agreed that the more profitable business unit would transfer up to 15 percent of its new income annually to the less-profitable unit. The result was Andersen Consulting, the more profitable unit, making transfer payments to Arthur Andersen each year.[3]

There was also conflict created by Andersen Consulting's claim that Arthur Andersen was building similar consulting skills and competing for the same customers. Andersen Consulting asked the firm's coordinating body, Anderson Worldwide, to intercede in the conflict. The conflict continued and in 1997 Andersen Consulting filed for arbitration, arguing that the steady movement of Arthur Andersen into consulting practices violated the agreement of the units and resulted in dysfunctional conflict and marketplace confusion.[4]

In August 2000, an arbitrator from the International Chamber of Commerce ruled to separate the two units. Andersen Consulting had to relinquish its name (the name belongs to Andersen Worldwide). As of January 1, 2001, Andersen

www.ac.com

---

[3]"Independence Day for Andersen Consulting," www.gartner11.gartnerweb.com, November 4, 2000.

[4]See Anthony Downs, *Inside Bureaucracy* (Boston: Little, Brown, 1968).

www.arthurandersen.com

Consulting will be called Accenture. The arbitrator also ruled that Andersen Consulting must pay more than $1 billion to Andersen Worldwide for distribution to Arthur Andersen and its member firms. The ICC's decision cannot be appealed. Both sides, of course, claim victory and freedom from blame. The 11 years of dysfunctional conflict is finally over as Andersen Consulting becomes Accenture. The new firm Accenture is independent and free to compete in the marketplace with any consulting firm.

Conflict and Organizational Performance

As previously indicated, conflict may have either positive or negative consequences for the organization, depending on how much exists and how it is managed. Every organization has an optimal level of conflict that can be considered highly functional—it helps generate positive performance. When the conflict level is too low, performance can also suffer. Innovation and change are less likely to take place, and the organization may have difficulty adapting to its changing environment. If a low conflict level continues, the very survival of the organization can be threatened. On the other hand, if the conflict level becomes too high, the resulting chaos also can threaten the organization's survival. An example is the popular press coverage of the results of "dissension" in labor unions and its impact on performance. If fighting between rival factions in the union becomes too great, it can render the union less effective in pursuing its mission of furthering its members' interests. The relationship between the level of intergroup conflict and organizational performance that is consistent with a contemporary perspective is presented in Exhibit 9.1 for three hypothetical situations.

Stages of Conflict

Although some conflicts can become intense and full-blown virtually instantaneously, it is more often the case that intergroup conflicts develop over a period of time. When this happens, there are typically several stages of evolution through which the conflict passes. **Perceived conflict** exists when there is a cognitive awareness on the part of at least one group that events have occurred or that conditions exist favorable to creating overt conflict. For example, two units in the same organization both may want to be assigned the same space in the company's new office facility. Or perceived conflict may be part of a company's annual budget planning process, when each department attempts to maximize the resources it receives, potentially at the expense of every other department.

Perceived conflict may or may not lead to **felt conflict**. The felt stage of conflict represents an escalation that includes emotional involvement. It is "felt" in the form of anxiety, tension, and/or hostility. Because such feelings are generally a source of discomfort, the parties involved may be motivated to try to reduce the negative emotions. This, in turn, can lead to positive or negative attempts to deal with the conflict. Typically, all parties to a conflict need to experience both perceived and felt conflict in order to be sufficiently motivated to attempt resolution.

The final stage is that of **manifest conflict**. Manifest conflict is not only perceived and felt, it is acted upon. That is, at the manifest stage the conflicting groups are actively engaging in conflict behavior. There may be verbal, written, even physical attacks. In manifest conflict, it is usually very apparent to noninvolved parties that problems exist. Although it is still possible to successfully resolve manifest conflict, it is far better to deal with conflict at an earlier stage.

EXHIBIT 9.1	Relationship between Intergroup Conflict and Organizational Performance			
	Level of Intergroup Conflict	Probable Impact on Organization	Organization Characterized By	Level of Organizational Performance
Situation I	Low or none	Dysfunctional	• Slow adaptation to environmental changes • Few changes • Little stimulation of ideas • Apathy • Stagnation	Low
Situation II	Optimal	Functional	• Positive movement toward goals • Innovation and change • Search for problem solutions • Creativity and quick adaptation to environmental changes	High
Situation III	High	Dysfunctional	• Disruption • Interference with activities • Coordination difficult • Chaos	Low

Additionally, manifest conflict is more likely to have longer-lasting effects than either perceived or felt conflict.

Every conflict situation leaves a conflict aftermath that affects the way both groups perceive and act upon subsequent conflicts. Generally the earlier conflicts can be resolved, the more likely the aftermath will facilitate positive future interactions between the conflicting groups. While manifest conflicts can have functional aftermaths, the likelihood of dysfunctional outcomes increases as conflict moves from perceived to felt to manifest.

WHAT CAUSES INTERGROUP CONFLICT?

Every group comes into at least partial conflict with every other group with which it interacts. This tendency is known as "the law of interorganizational conflict."[5] In this section we examine three of the more important factors that contribute to group conflict: work interdependence, goal differences, and perceptual differences.

Work Interdependence

Work interdependence occurs when two or more organizational groups must depend on one another to complete their tasks. The conflict potential in such situations ranges from relatively low to very high, depending on the nature of the interdependence. Three distinct types of interdependence among groups have been identified: pooled, sequential, and reciprocal. Exhibit 9.2 provides a visual representation of these three types.

---

[5]J. Thompson, *Organizations in Action* (New York: McGraw-Hill, 1967).

EXHIBIT 9.2
Types of
Interdependence

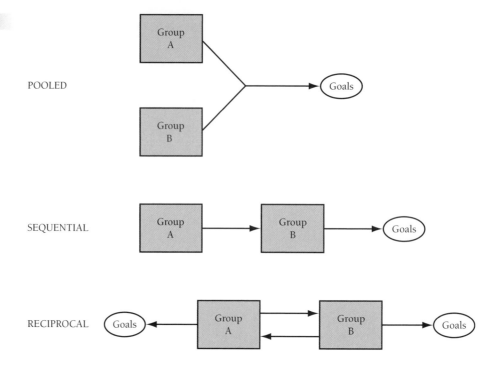

POOLED

SEQUENTIAL

RECIPROCAL

Pooled interdependence requires no interaction among groups because each group, in effect, performs separately. However, the pooled performances of all the groups determine how successful the organization is. For example, the staff of an IBM sales office in one region may have no interaction with its peers in another region. Similarly, two bank branches will have little or no interaction. In both cases, however, the groups are interdependent because the performance of each must be adequate if the total organization is to thrive. The conflict potential in pooled interdependence is relatively low, and management can rely on standard rules and procedures developed at the main office for coordination.

Sequential interdependence requires one group to complete its task before another group can complete its task. Tasks are performed in a sequential fashion. In a manufacturing plant, for example, the product must be assembled before it can be painted. Thus, the assembling department must complete its task before the painting department can begin painting.

Under these circumstances, since the output of one group serves as the input for another, conflict between the groups is more likely to occur. Coordinating this type of interdependence involves effective use of the management function of planning.

Reciprocal interdependence requires the output of each group to serve as input to other groups in the organization. Consider the relationships that exist between the anesthesiology staff, nursing staff, technician staff, and surgeons in a hospital operating room. This relationship creates a high degree of reciprocal interdependence. The same interdependence exists among groups involved in space launchings. Another example is the interdependence among airport control towers, flight crews, ground operations, and maintenance crews. Clearly, the potential for conflict is great in any of these situations. Effective coordination involves management's skillful use of the organizational processes of communication and decision making.

All organizations have pooled interdependence among groups. Complex organizations also have sequential interdependence. The most complicated organizations experience pooled, sequential, and reciprocal interdependence among groups. The more complex the organization, the greater are the potentials for conflict and the more difficult is the task facing management.

Goal Differences

Ideally, interacting groups will always view their goals as mutually compatible and behave in such a way as to contribute to the attainment of both sets of goals. Realistically, however, this is frequently not the case. Several problems related to differences in goals can create conflicts.

Groups with *mutually exclusive goals* can find themselves in conflict. For example, marketing departments usually have a goal of maximizing sales. On the other hand, credit departments seek to minimize credit losses. Depending on which department prevails, different customers might be selected. Or, a production department goal may be to minimize defective products. The purchasing unit, however, in trying to meet its goal of lowering materials cost, may contract with vendors supplying parts of questionable quality. Some incompatible goals may be more apparent than real; what is needed in these situations is for the conflicting groups to refocus on larger organizational objectives.

When *limited resources* must be allocated between groups, mutual dependencies increase and any differences in goals become more apparent. If money, space, the labor forces, and materials were unlimited, every group could pursue its own goals. But in virtually all cases, resources must be allocated or shared. When groups conclude that resources have not been allocated in an equitable manner, pressures toward conflict increase.[6] When the limited resource is money, conflict potential is particularly strong. In some such conflicts there is a moral or ethical dimension involved, such as that described in **Ethics Encounter 9.1 about CEO rewards.**

Finally, the *different time horizons* needed by groups to achieve their goals can be a source of conflict. Research scientists working for a chemical manufacturer may have a time perspective of several years, while the same firm's manufacturing engineers may work within time frames of several months. A bank president might focus on 5- and 10-year time spans, while middle managers of the bank may concentrate on much shorter periods. With such differences in time horizons, problems and issues deemed critical by one group may be dismissed as unimportant by another, and conflicts may erupt.

Perceptual Differences

Goal differences can be accompanied by differing perceptions of reality, and disagreements over what constitutes reality can lead to conflict. For instance, a problem in a hospital may be viewed in one way by the medical staff and in another

Case 9.1

L.E.S., Inc.

---

[6]B. Kabanoff, "Equity, Equality, Power, and Conflict," *Academy of Management Review* April 1991, pp. 416–41.

Ethics Encounter 9.1

Are Company CEOs Rewarded for Laying Off Workers?

Increasingly, the large amounts of compensation received by a handful of top executives in many large corporations have come under fire. Critics have charged that executive performance does not warrant such lofty rewards, and there is growing unrest among organizational members who receive far, far less compensation for their services. Now, it appears, many executives are being rewarded for laying off more employees. The result is that executives may be adding to their salaries by eliminating the salaries (through layoffs) of lower-level organizational members.

The Institute for Policy Studies reports it has found the same trend for four straight years: CEOs at the corporations with the biggest layoffs received compensation increases that were greater than CEOs at similar-sized companies with fewer—or no—layoffs. "Such excessive pay should garner even less respect when the beneficiary is a leading job-slasher," the study said. Among what the Institute for Policy Studies dubbed the "layoff leaders" and the total compensation they received last year were:

- Lockheed Martin CEO Norman Augustine: $23 million, 3,100 layoffs.
- AlliedSignal CEO Lawrence Bossidy: $11.8 million, 3,250 layoffs.
- Alcoa CEO Paul O'Neill: $7.7 million, 3,975 layoffs.

When top management groups are compensated this well—particularly at the expense of workers who actually made the profits—the stage is set for conflict. There are also clear ethical issues as well. Increasingly, even top executives are coming to view these kinds of pay practices as excessive and unfair. Nearly half of 400 top executives surveyed said they think CEO pay practices have surpassed acceptable limits. Moreover, over half said top managers should take salary cuts if their companies' performance lags.

www.lock
martin.c

www.allie
signal.co

www.alco
com

Source: Based, in part, on Marcy Gordon, "Study Says CEOs Rewarded for Layoffs, *Houston Chronicle*, May 2, 1997, p. 3C.

way by the nursing staff. Alumni and faculty may have different perceptions concerning the importance of a winning football program. Many factors cause organizational groups to form differing perceptions of reality.[7] Major factors include status incongruency, inaccurate perceptions, and different perspectives.

Status incongruency conflicts concerning the relative status of different groups are common. Usually, many different status standards are found in an organization, rather than an absolute one. The result is many status hierarchies. For example status conflicts often are created by work patterns—which group initiates the work and which group responds. A production department, for instance, may perceive a change as an affront to its status because it must accept a sales group's initiation of work. This status conflict may be aggravated deliberately by the sales group. Academic snobbery is certainly a fact of campus life at many colleges and universities. Members of a particular academic discipline may perceive themselves, for one reason or another, as having a higher status than those of another discipline.

Inaccurate perceptions often cause one group to develop stereotypes about other groups. While the differences between groups may actually be quite small, each group will tend to exaggerate them. Thus, you will hear that "all women executives are aggressive," or "all bank trust officers behave alike," or "all professors think their course is the only important one." When the differences between the groups are emphasized, the stereotypes are reinforced, relations deteriorate, and conflict develops.

---

[7]M. J. Gelfand and S. Christakopolon, "Culture and Negotiator Cognition: Judgment Accuracy and Negotiation Processes in Individualistic and Collectivistic Cultures," *Organizational Behavior and Human Decision Processes*, April 1999, pp. 248–69.

The example given earlier of alumni and faculty having different perceptions concerning the importance of a winning football program is an example of *different perspectives*. Alumni may wish for a winning football season because that shows a form of institutional success in a very visible public manner. Faculty, on the other hand, may see the football program as a distraction from the school's primary objective of creating and disseminating knowledge. The two groups simply may have a different view of what is most important. Group goals, experience, values, and culture are all factors that may contribute to different ways of seeing the world. The different perspectives growing out of different organizational cultures can explain why conflict frequently results when companies are merged.

Management Pointer 9.1 provides some suggestions for minimizing the role perceptual differences may play in causing conflict.

Management Pointer 9.1

MINIMIZING PERCEPTUAL BASES FOR CONFLICT

Perceptual differences can lead to conflict. To reduce the likelihood this will happen:

1. Communicate effectively! Reduce inaccurate perceptions by ensuring that groups have sufficient information to make accurate judgments.

2. Help develop a group's social sensitivity, that is, help the group understand the basis for another group's perspective (understanding does not necessarily mean agreeing with).

3. Emphasize behavioral flexibility, that is, engage in actions based upon an understanding of the other group's perspective.

4. Communicate effectively! This is so important it bears repeating.

THE CONSEQUENCES OF DYSFUNCTIONAL INTERGROUP CONFLICT

Behavioral scientists have spent more than four decades researching and analyzing how dysfunctional intergroup conflict affects those who experience it.[8] They have found that groups placed in a conflict situation tend to react in fairly predictable ways. We shall examine a number of the changes that can occur *within groups* and *between groups* as a result of dysfunctional intergroup conflict.

Changes within Groups

Many changes are likely to occur within groups involved in intergroup conflict. Unfortunately, these changes generally result in either a continuance or an escalation of the conflict.

Increased Group Cohesiveness   It is clear that when groups are engaged in a conflict, their cohesion tends to increase. Competition, conflict, or perceived external threat usually result in group members putting aside individual differences and closing ranks. Members become more loyal to the group, and group membership becomes more attractive. This increase in cohesion is necessary to mobilize group resources in dealing with the "enemy" and tends to result in the suppression of internal disagreements. This tendency toward increased cohesion in the face of threat was seen in Kosovo. Ethnic groups in the former Yugoslavia have historically had difficulties getting along with each other.

Emphasis on Loyalty   The tendency of groups to increase in cohesiveness suggests that conformity to group norms becomes more important in conflict situations. In reality, it is not unusual for groups to overconform to group norms in

---

[8]The classic work is M. Sherif and C. Sherif, *Groups in Harmony and Tension* (New York: Harper & Row, 1953). Their study was conducted among groups in a boys' camp. They stimulated conflict between the groups and observed the changes that occurred in group behavior. Also see their "Experiments in Group Conflict," *Scientific American,* March 1956, pp. 54–58.

conflict situations. This may take the form of blind acceptance of dysfunctional solutions to the conflict and result in groupthink, as discussed in the previous chapter. In such situations, group goals take precedence over individual satisfaction as members are expected to demonstrate their loyalty. In major conflict situations, interaction with members of "the other group" may be completely outlawed.

Rise in Autocratic Leadership   In extreme conflict situations where threats are perceived, democratic methods of leadership are likely to become less popular. Group members want strong leadership. This was true in the air-traffic controller's strike, discussed in the next chapter. Professional sports offer a number of examples, including the National Football League players' strike in 1987 and the Major League Baseball Players Association strike in 1994, which led to cancellation of the World Series for the first time in 90 years. In this strike, Union President Donald Fehr had tremendous authority from the players to do what he believed was best.

Focus on Activity   When a group is in conflict, its members usually emphasize doing what the group does and doing it very well. The group becomes more task-oriented. Tolerance for members who "goof off" is low, and there is less concern for individual member satisfaction. The emphasis is on accomplishing the group's task and defeating the "enemy" (the other group in the conflict).

Changes between Groups

During conflicts, certain changes will probably occur between the groups involved.

Distorted Perceptions   During conflicts, the perceptions of each group's members become distorted. Group members develop stronger opinions of the importance of their units. Each group sees itself as superior in performance to the other and as more important to the survival of the organization than other groups. In a conflict situation, nurses may conclude that they are more important to a patient than physicians, while physicians may consider themselves more important than hospital administrators. The marketing group in a business organization may think, "Without us selling the product, there would be no money to pay anyone else's salary." The production group, meanwhile, will say, "If we don't make the product, there is nothing to sell." Ultimately, none of these groups is more important, but conflict can cause their members to develop gross misperceptions of reality.

Negative Stereotyping   As conflict increases and perceptions become more distorted, all of the negative stereotypes that may have ever existed are reinforced. A management representative may say, "I've always said these union guys are just plain greedy. Now they've proved it." The head of a local teacher's union may say, "Now we know that what all politicians are interested in is getting reelected, not the quality of education." When negative stereotyping is a factor in a conflict, the members of each group see less differences within their unit and greater differences between the groups than actually exist.

Decreased Communication   Communications between the groups in conflict usually break down. This can be extremely dysfunctional, especially where sequential interdependence or reciprocal interdependence relationships exist be-

www.nflplayers.com

www.kscourts.org/caio/cases/
2000/04/98-5061.htm

tween groups. The decision-making process can be disrupted, and the customers or others whom the organization serves can be affected. Consider the possible consequences to patients, for instance, if a conflict between hospital technicians and nurses continues until it lowers the quality of health care.

While these are not the only dysfunctional consequences of intergroup conflict, they are the most common, and they have been well documented in the research literature. Other consequences, such as violence and aggression, are less common but also occur.

There is also occasionally a tension that results in creativity among individuals and groups. Michael Eisner, chairman of Walt Disney, suggests that creative tension has produced a steady stream of ideas.[9] He indicates that, at Disney, common sense and conflict yield the needed creativity. Without conflict and common sense Eisner believes the creative sparks needed to keep coming up with new ideas would be lost. When intergroup conflicts take place, some form of managerial intervention is usually necessary. How managers can deal with these situations is the subject of the next section.

Exercise 9.1

Third-Party Conflict
Resolution

www.disney.com

MANAGING INTERGROUP CONFLICT THROUGH RESOLUTION

Since managers must live with intergroup conflict, they must confront the problem of managing it.[10] In this section we will examine several different approaches to managing conflict. Exhibit 9.3 provides a framework, in the form of a conflict-resolution grid, for examining these various approaches.[11] As the exhibit suggests, one way of viewing conflict-resolution efforts between groups is to examine the extent to which a conflicting group has an internal and external focus with respect to resolution strategies. An *internal focus* represents the extent to which a group is intent upon addressing its own concerns in a conflict situation. An *external focus* reflects the extent to which a group is intent on addressing the concerns of the other group (or groups) involved in the conflict. From this perspective, internal and external foci are not opposite ends of the same dimension. Rather, they are two separate dimensions. Varying degrees of focus on these two dimensions lead to five different approaches to resolving intergroup conflict. Depending upon the nature and conditions of the conflict, each of these five approaches can represent an effective approach for conflict-resolution management. We will examine each of these approaches separately.

Dominating

A dominating approach by a group to conflict resolution represents a maximum focus on meeting its own concerns, coupled with a minimal focus on meeting the

---

[9]Susy Wetlaufer, "Common Sense and Conflict," *Harvard Business Review,* January–February 2000, pp. 114–24.

[10]For an examination of specific devices for assessing how managers manage conflict, see E. van de Vlert and B. Kabanoff, "Toward Theory-Based Measures of Conflict Management," *Academy of Management Journal,* March 1990, pp. 199–209.

[11]The conflict-resolution grid represents a melding of conflict-management concepts found in R. R. Blake and J. S. Mouton, *The Managerial Grid* (Houston, TX: Gulf Publishing, 1964); K. W. Thomas, "Conflict and Conflict Management," in M. D. Dunnette (ed.) *Handbook of Industrial and Organizational Psychology,* (Chicago: Rand McNally, 1976), pp. 889–935; and M. A. Rahim, *Managing Conflict in Organizations* (New York: Praeger, 1986).

EXHIBIT 9.3
Conflict-Resolution
Grid

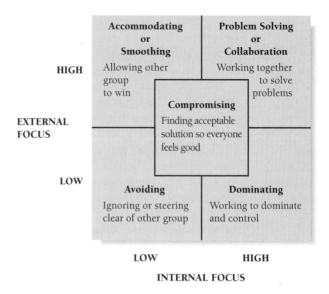

concerns of the other group. Dominating tends to be a power-oriented approach. That is, to be successful it requires that the using group have sufficient power to "force" their resolution on the other group. A group may hold the balance of power because they are higher up in the organizational hierarchy (that is, they have more authority), they control critical resources (for example, budgets, personnel, or important knowledge), they have allied with powerful groups, or for a variety of other reasons.

It is not unusual for both groups in a conflict to attempt a dominating approach to resolving their differences. Frequently in such cases, this means that one of the groups has overestimated its own power relative to that of the other group. In such cases, the outcome can have negative consequences for one or both groups. In labor disputes, for example, both management and the union may adopt a dominating approach to resolving their differences. The end result of this kind of power play may be a prolonged strike that is costly to both sides. Organizational Encounter 9.1 describes how a dominating approach at American Airlines has resulted in intensifying labor-management conflicts.

In spite of the potential problems associated with the use of domination as a means of resolving conflict, there are instances when it may be very appropriate and useful. There are times (for example, emergency situations) when differences must be settled quickly. When rapid and decisive action is important, dominating can represent the most time-effective means of resolution. Or, dominating may be the best approach in resolving important issues when unpopular courses of action must be taken, such as layoffs, implementing new schedules, or enforcing unpopular policies and procedures.

Accommodating

In many respects, accommodating is just the opposite approach from dominating. An accommodating party places maximum emphasis on meeting the needs of the other group, while minimizing its own concerns. Although accommodation may appear to be "giving in," there are situations in which this may be an extremely beneficial approach for a conflicting group to use. For example, issues over which

American Airlines' Dominating Approach to Labor Conflict Creates More Problems

American Airlines' top management—particularly CEO Bob Crandall—has been at war with various employee groups—most notably, American's pilots—for years. While the causes of the problem are many and varied, the basic issue revolves around distrust. The pilots (and other employee groups) distrust management because of the heavy-handed, dominating approach it has used in trying to resolve labor disputes. Crandall is the lightening rod. Among other actions, Crandall:

- Forced institution of a despised two-tier wage system
- Publically belittled employees to Wall Street analysts and to the press
- Threatened to shut down the airline unless the pilots agreed to further concessions
- Has let his combative personality become the focus of labor talks with the unions

American Airlines estimates (probably conservatively) that the most recent labor dispute has so far cost it at least $100 million in lost bookings as fliers, worried about various threatened walkout dates, have elected to fly on rival carriers.

According to one ex-American employee, "Whatever the facts, there's been a growing feeling among American employees that the competitiveness Crandall employed so effectively against other airlines is now being turned toward them." This attitude helps explain why it is taking so long to reach agreement on a new contract. Ray Friedman, a professor of labor relations at Vanderbilt University, seems to sum up the employees' feelings when he says, "It's hard to negotiate . . . with someone who you think will screw you every which way once something comes up a year later."

The pilots are just part of the problem. Even if an agreement is reached with them this year, the flight attendants' contract expires next year—and they don't trust Crandall any more than the pilots do.

Source: Ronald B. Lieber, "Bob Crandall's Boo-Boos," *Fortune*, April 28, 1997, pp. 78, 81.

groups might conflict are not always of equal importance to each group. If the issue is critical to one group and of little importance to the other, obliging the first group through accommodating costs the second group little and may be seen as a goodwill gesture which helps maintain a cooperative relationship. Accommodating may also purchase "credits" which can be used in subsequent conflicts when the issues are more important to the obliging group. Finally, there may be instances when preserving the peace and avoiding disharmony are more important than reaching a resolution that maximizes a particular group's concerns.

Problem Solving

Problem solving represents what might appear to be the theoretically ideal or best approach to conflict resolution. However, it can be an extremely difficult approach to implement effectively. Problem solving, sometimes called collaborating or integrating, seeks to resolve conflict by placing maximum focus on both groups' concerns. Successful problem solving requires that conflicting groups display a willingness to work collaboratively toward an integrative solution that satisfies the needs of all concerned. The greatest obstacle which must be overcome is the win-lose mentality that so often characterizes conflicting groups. Unless the parties involved can rise above that kind of thinking, problem solving is not likely to be successful.

The potential benefits of using a problem-solving approach are significant. When conflicting parties truly collaborate, this can result in a merger of insight, experience, knowledge, and perspective which leads to higher-quality solutions than would be obtained by any other approach. Additionally, because both parties' concerns are incorporated into the resolution, commitment to the effective implementation of the solution is high. Sometimes the problem-solving process is aided by

361

focusing on a superordinate goal. A **superordinate goal** is one that cannot be attained by one group singly and supersedes all other concerns of any of the individual groups involved in the conflict. For example, several unions in the automobile and steel industries have, in recent years, agreed to forego wage increases, and in some cases to accept pay reductions, because the survival of their firms or industries was threatened.[12] Once the crisis is over, demands for higher wages undoubtedly will return, as they have at once-struggling Chrysler Corporation.

Avoiding

Exercise 9.2

World Bank: An Exercise in Intergroup Negotiation

Frequently, some way can be found to avoid conflict. While avoiding may not bring any long-run benefits, it can be an effective and appropriate strategy in some conflict situations. Foremost among these is when avoiding is used as a temporary alternative. When the conflict is a particularly heated one, for example, temporary avoidance gives the involved parties an opportunity to cool down and regain perspective. Avoiding may also buy time needed by one or more of the groups to gather additional information necessary for a longer-range solution. Avoiding may also be appropriate when other parties are in a better position to resolve the conflict or when other matters that are more important need to be addressed. Unfortunately, people have a great temptation to overuse an avoiding approach; the number of situations where avoiding is the most-effective strategy for dealing with a conflict is typically less than we would like them to be. Nonetheless, as a temporary expedient, avoiding can be a useful prelude to the implementation of a longer-range strategy.

Management Pointer 9.2

WHEN TO USE THE DIFFERENT CONFLICT-RESOLUTION APPROACHES

While there are many different situations in which each of the approaches is valid, keep these general points in mind:

- Use a *dominating* approach on important issues where you are certain you are right and where the benefit of a resolution outweighs the drawback of possible negative feelings by the dominated group.
- Use an *accommodating* approach in disputes that are of far greater importance to the other group than they are to your group.
- Use a *problem-solving* approach when both groups are willing to invest time and effort to reach a resolution that maximizes everyone's outcome.
- Use an *avoiding* approach primarily as a temporary expedient to buy more time.
- Use a *compromising* approach as a middle ground. It is a good backup approach when other approaches (mainly dominating and problem solving) fail to resolve the issue.

Compromising

Compromising is a traditional method for resolving intergroup conflicts. With compromise, there is no distinct winner or loser, and the resolution reached probably is not ideal for either group. Compromising can be used very effectively when the goal sought (for example, money) can be divided equitably. If this is not possible, one group must give up something of value as a concession.

Compromising might be useful when two conflicting parties with relatively equal power are both strongly committed to mutually exclusive goals. It may also represent a way of gaining a temporary settlement to particularly complex and difficult issues. We saw earlier that problem solving was a desirable but difficult approach to conflict resolution. Compromise is a good "backup" strategy which conflicting parties can fall back on if their attempts at problem solving are unsuccessful. Sometimes, compromising may involve third-party interventions.[13] Such intervention may take the form of appealing to a managerial

---

[12]J. B. Arthur and J. B. Dworkin, "Current Issues in Industrial and Labor Relations," *Journal of Management,* September 1991, pp. 515–52.

[13]Rupert Brown and Samuel L. Gaertner (eds.), *Blackwell Handbook of Social Process: Intergroup Handbook of Social Psychology,* (New York: Blackwell, 2001).

EXHIBIT 9.4   **An Overview of Intergroup Conflict**

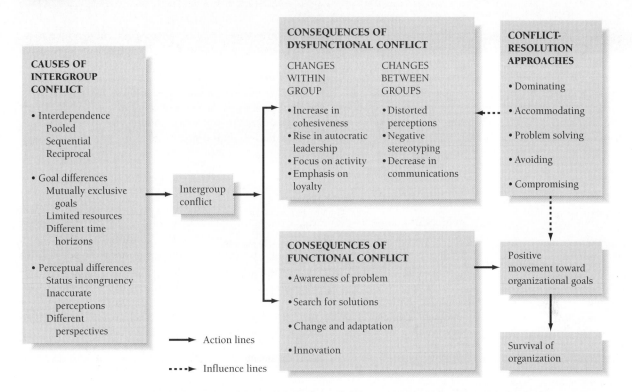

higher authority or a decision to submit the conflict to some form of mediation or arbitration.

Compromising is a middle-of-the-road approach. It typically involves giving up more than dominating, but less than accommodating. Additionally, it addresses issues more directly than avoiding, but with less depth than problem solving.

Each of these five approaches just discussed has assets and liabilities, and each is effective or ineffective in different situations. Management Pointer 9.2 highlights when each might be most appropriate.

What this chapter has said thus far about intergroup conflict is summarized in Exhibit 9.4. The exhibit illustrates the relationship between causes and types of conflict, the consequences of conflict, and approaches to conflict resolution. It is also important to keep in mind that views of conflict and approaches to conflict resolution will vary across cultures. Important aspects of conflict are viewed and experienced differently in different nations. International Encounter 9.1 provides an illustration of this.

STIMULATING CONSTRUCTIVE INTERGROUP CONFLICT

Throughout this chapter we have stressed that some conflict is beneficial. This point was first made in the discussion on the contemporary perspective on conflict and is noted again in Exhibit 9.4, which details some of the functional consequences of intergroup conflict. We have already examined the situation where conflict is dysfunctional because it is too high; we have said little, however, regarding situations in which there is an insufficient amount of conflict. If groups become too complacent because everything always operates smoothly, management might benefit from

Conflict Resolution: How Japanese and Americans Differ

Rensis Likert, the renowned social scientist and management expert, once observed that the strategies used by a society and its organizations for dealing with conflict reflect the basic values and philosophy of that society. In ideal circumstances, conflicts can be difficult to resolve; once the confounding variable of intercultural differences is added, conflict resolution becomes even more complex. Consider, for example, Japanese and American differences.

Of course, these are broad generalizations which may well not apply in specific situations or with specific individuals or groups. Nonetheless, they serve to point out the fact that intercultural conflicts—and successful intercultural conflict resolution—are affected by differing cultural perspectives, values, and styles of interacting. All of these are significant factors which cannot be ignored in the conflict-resolution process.

Japanese	American	Japanese	American
Resolution involves long-term perspective	Short-term perspective	Takes time, process is important; win-win approach	Time is money; win-lose approach
Cooperation based on team spirit	Spirit of competition and rivalry	Emotional sensitivity highly valued	Emotional sensitivity not highly valued
Disagreement with superior often, but polite	Disagreement with superior seldom, but violent	Good of the group is ultimate aim	Profit motive or good of individual ultimate aim
Disputes settled through conferral and trust	Disputes settled through contracts and bringing arbitration	Face-saving crucial; decisions often made to save someone from embarrassment	Decision made on cost-benefit basis; face-saving not always important

Source: Based on materials from P. Casse, *Training for the Multicultural Manager: A Practical and Cross-Cultural Approach to the Management of People* (Washington DC: Society of Intercultural Education, Training, and Research, 1982); and B. J. Punnett, *Experiencing International Management* (Boston: PWS-Kent, 1989).

stimulating conflict. Lack of any disagreement can lead to suboptimum performance, including inferior decision making.

A variety of research supports this conclusion. In one study, experimental and control groups were formed to solve a problem. The experimental groups had a member, a confederate of the researcher, whose job was to challenge the majority view of the groups he or she had been planted in as the group attempted to solve the problem. The control groups had no such member. In every case, the experimental groups outperformed the control groups.[14]

While lack of conflict may prove beneficial in the short run, it can lead to situations where one group holds tremendous influence over another. For example, observers of the Japanese style of participatory management question whether the lack of conflict between managers and employees in Japanese firms is healthy.[15]

---

[14]M. A. Neale and M. H. Bazerman, "The Effects of Framing and Negotiator Overconfidence on Bargaining Behavior and Outcomes," *Academy of Management Journal*, March 1985, pp. 34–49.

[15]R. M. Marsh, "The Difference between Participation and Power in Japanese Factories," *Industrial and Labor Relations Review*, January 1992, pp. 250–57.

There can be a number of benefits from increasing conflict levels. Some conflict is probably necessary to stimulate the critical evaluation of organizational policies and processes and to lay the groundwork for change. Lack of conflict leads to acceptance of the status quo and discourages innovation. Increasing conflict can be an effective antidote for groupthink (discussed in the previous chapter). As was suggested in Exhibit 9.1, organizational performance suffers not only when conflict levels are too high but also when they are too low.

What can management do to increase conflict in order to achieve functional consequences? Four possible strategies are discussed below.

Bringing Outside Individuals into the Group

A technique widely used to "bring back to life" a stagnant organization or subunit of an organization is to hire or transfer in individuals whose attitudes, values, and backgrounds differ from those of the group's present members. Many college faculties consciously seek new members with different backgrounds and often discourage the hiring of graduates of their own programs. This is to ensure a diversity of viewpoints on the faculty.

The technique of bringing in outsiders is also used widely in government and business. Recently, a bank president decided not to promote from within for a newly created position of marketing vice president. Instead, he hired a highly successful executive from the very competitive consumer products field. The bank president felt that, while the outsider knew little about marketing financial services, her approach to, and knowledge of, marketing was what the bank needed to become a strong competitor.

Sears, Roebuck is an example of an organization that could have benefited by stimulating conflict through bringing in outsiders. For decades, Sears was the nation's leading retailing organization. It became complacent in its belief that it was invulnerable. In the 1980s, it became apparent Sears had lulled itself to sleep. Wal-Mart and Kmart overtook Sears, and numerous other retailers were moving up fast. An examination of Sears' organizational chart would have revealed that senior management were all long-time employees, the majority of whom had been at Sears for over a quarter of a century. They were very similar in values and management style. While the nature of retailing was undergoing rapid change, they were trying to maintain the status quo.

Altering the Organization's Structure

Changing the structure of the organization can not only help resolve intergroup conflict, it is also excellent for *creating* conflict. For example, a school of business typically has several departments. One, named the Department of Business Administration, includes all of the faculty members who teach courses in management, marketing, finance, production management, and so forth. Accordingly, the department is rather large, with 32 members under one department chairman, who reports to the dean. A new dean recently has been hired, and he is considering dividing the business administration unit into several separate departments (e.g., departments of marketing, finance, management), each with five or six members and a chairperson. The reasoning is that reorganizing in this manner will create competition among the groups for resources, students, faculty, and so forth, where none existed before because there was only one group. Whether this change will improve performance remains to be seen.

Stimulating Competition

Many managers utilize various techniques to stimulate competition among groups. The use of a variety of incentives, such as awards and bonuses for outstanding performance, often stimulates competition. If properly utilized, such incentives can help maintain a healthy atmosphere of competition that may result in a functional level of conflict. Incentives can be given for least-defective parts, highest sales, best teacher, greatest number of new customers, or in any area where increased conflict is likely to lead to more-effective performance.

Making Use of Programmed Conflict

Increasingly, organizations are turning to programmed conflict to increase creativity and innovation and to improve decision making. Programmed conflict is conflict that is deliberately and systematically created even when no real differences appear to exist. It is "conflict that raises different opinions regardless of the personal feelings of the managers."[16] One popular form of programmed conflict is devil's advocacy. In **devil's advocacy,** someone or some group is assigned the role of critic with the job of uncovering all possible problems with a particular proposal. The role of the devil's advocate is to ensure that opposing views are presented and taken into consideration before any sort of final decision is made.

Numerous organizations use some form of programmed conflict. Royal Dutch Petroleum regularly uses a devil's advocacy approach. Before Anheuser-Busch makes a major decision, such as entering a market or building a plant, it assigns groups the job of making the case for each side of the question. IBM has a system that encourages employees to disagree with their bosses. All of these companies have the same goal: improve organizational performance by stimulating conflict.

NEGOTIATIONS

Frequently, an important part of the process of conflict resolution involves negotiations. Negotiations may be viewed as a process in which two or more parties attempt to reach acceptable agreement in a situation characterized by some level of disagreement. In an organizational context, negotiation may take place (1) between two people (as when a manager and subordinate decide on the completion date for a new project the subordinate has just received, (2) within a group (most group decision-making situations), (3) between groups (such as the purchasing department and a supplier regarding price, quality, or delivery date), which has been the focus in this chapter, and (4) over the Internet. The Internet now serves as a place to negotiate jobs, consulting projects, training program prices, and supplier product prices. The one difference in negotiating on the Internet is that it is done with written communication only. Many of the skills discussed in this section apply to both face-to-face negotiations and Internet transactions.

Regardless of the setting or the parties involved, negotiations usually have at least four elements.[17] First, some disagreement or *conflict* exists. This may be perceived, felt, or manifest. Second, there is some degree of *interdependence* be-

---

[16] Joel Lefowitz, "Sex-Related Differences in Job Attitudes and Dispositional Variables: Now You See Them, . . . ," *Academy of Management Journal,* April 1994, pp. 323–49.

[17] Roy J. Lewicki, David M. Saunders, and John W. Minton, *Negotiations* (Burr Ridge, IL: McGraw-Hill, 1999).

Can Entering a Rehabilitation Program Cost You Your Job?

You Be the Judge

When a hotel and restaurant supply company in Pennsylvania hired a new salesperson, it was unaware he was an alcoholic. Once on the job, the salesperson's drinking grew progressively worse. Before the end of the first year, the salesperson's consumption reached a fifth of rum a day (after which he would usually fall asleep in his car). Ultimately, he realized he had a problem, joined Alcoholics Anonymous, and voluntarily entered a rehabilitation program.

When the company learned that he was in an alcohol rehabilitation program, they fired him. The salesperson, contending that his alcoholism was a disability, filed an Americans with Disabilities Act (ADA) lawsuit. Over a period of time prior to the court date the company attempted to negotiate a settlement, finally offering to rehire him on a probationary basis (at a lower salary) after he completed his rehabilitation program. The salesperson, however, rejected this final offer and elected to go to trial.

Would he have been better off accepting the offer rather than going to trial? You be the judge!

tween the parties. Third, the situation must be conducive to *opportunistic interaction*. This means that each party has both the means and inclination to attempt to influence the other. Finally, there exists some *possibility of agreement*. In the absence of this latter element, of course, negotiations cannot bring about a positive resolution.

When negotiations are successful, each party feels that it has significantly benefited from the resolution. When they fail, however, the conflict often escalates. Such a situation is the basis for this chapter's You Be the Judge.

Win-Lose Negotiating

The classical view suggests negotiations are frequently a form of a zero-sum game. That is, to whatever extent one party wins something, the other party loses. In a zero-sum situation there is an assumption of limited resources, and the negotiation process is to determine who will receive these resources. This is also known as *distributive negotiating*. The term refers to the process of dividing, or "distributing," scarce resources. Such a win-lose approach characterizes numerous negotiating situations. Buying an automobile is a classic example. As the buyer, the less you pay the less profit the seller makes; your "wins" (in the form of fewer dollars paid) are the seller's "losses" (in the form of fewer dollars of profit). Note that in win-lose negotiating, one party does not necessarily "lose" in an absolute sense. Presumably the party selling the car still made a profit, but to the extent the selling price was lowered to make the sale, the profit was lower.

In organizations, win-lose negotiating is quite common. It characterizes most bargaining involving material goods, such as the purchase of supplies or manufacturing raw materials. Win-lose negotiating can be seen in universities where each college attempts to negotiate the best budget for itself, invariably at the expense of some other college. Frequently, the most variable examples of distributive negotiations in organizations are those that take place between labor and management. Issues involving wages, benefits, working conditions, and related matters are seen as a conflict over limited resources.

Win-Win Negotiating

Win-win, or integrative, negotiating brings a different perspective to the process. Unlike the zero-sum orientation in win-lose, win-win negotiating is a positive-sum approach. Positive-sum situations are those where each party gains without a corresponding loss for the other party. This does not necessarily mean that everyone gets everything they wanted, for seldom does that occur. It simply means that an agreement has been achieved which leaves all parties better off than they were prior to the agreement.

It may seem as if a win-win approach is always preferable to a win-lose one. Why should there be a winner and a loser if instead there can be two winners? Realistically, however, not every negotiating situation has an integrative payoff. Some situations really are distributive; a gain for one side must mean an offsetting loss for the other. In the automobile purchase example cited earlier, it is true that both the purchaser and the seller can "win" in the sense that the purchaser obtains the car and the seller makes a profit. Nonetheless, this is essentially a distributive situation. The purchaser can obtain a better deal *only* at the loss of some profit by the seller. There is simply no way the purchaser can get the lowest price while the seller obtains the highest profit.

Even if the nature of what is being negotiated lends itself to a win-win approach, the organization of the negotiators may not. Win-win, or integrative, negotiating can work only when the issues are integrative in nature and all parties are committed to an integrative process. Typically, union and management bargaining includes issues that are both distributive and integrative in nature. However, because negotiators for both sides so frequently see the total process as distributive, even those issues which truly may be integrative become victims of a win-lose attitude, to the detriment of both parties.

INCREASING NEGOTIATION EFFECTIVENESS

Just as there is no one best way to manage, neither is there one best way to negotiate. The selection of specific negotiation strategies and tactics depend on a number of variables. The nature of the issues being negotiated is a critical consideration. For example, how one approaches negotiating distributive issues may be quite different than the strategy employed for negotiating integrative ones. The context or environment in which the negotiations are taking place may also be an important consideration, as may be the nature of the outcomes that are desired from the negotiating process. In many negotiating situations this last consideration may be the most important.

One useful way to think about desired outcomes is to distinguish between *substantive* and *relationship* outcomes.[18] *Substantive outcomes* have to do with how the specific issue is settled. To strive to end up with a bigger piece of the pie than the other party is to focus on a substantive outcome. On the other hand, to negotiate in a manner designed primarily to maintain good relations between the parties—irrespective of the substantive result—is to focus on *relationship outcomes*. While the two concerns are not mutually exclusive, the relative importance assigned them will affect a manager's choice of negotiation strategies.

---

[18]G. T. Savage, J. D. Blair, and R. L. Sorenson, "Consider Both Relationships and Substance When Negotiating Strategically," *Academy of Management Executive,* February 1989, pp. 37–48.

One model for increasing negotiating effectiveness is found in the work of the Dutch management practitioner Willem Mastenbroek. Although the model is extremely comprehensive, the key focus is on four activities.[19]

1. *Obtaining substantial results.* This refers to activities which focus on the content of what is being negotiated. Desirable outcomes cannot be achieved if the negotiations do not stay constructively focused on the real issues. A judicious exchange of information regarding goals and expectations of the negotiating process is an example of this type of activity.

2. *Influencing the balance of power.* The final outcome of negotiations is almost always directly related to the power and dependency relationships between the negotiators. Neither attempts to increase your power through dominance, nor responding with total deference to the other party's attempt to increase their power, represent the most effective means of dealing with power issues. Achieving subtle shifts in the balance of power through the use of persuasion, facts, and expertise are almost always more effective.

3. *Promoting a constructive climate.* This relates to activities which are designed to facilitate progress by minimizing the likelihood that tension or animosity between the parties becomes disruptive. Specific activities might include attending to each party's opinions, acting in a predictable and serious manner, treating each party with respect, and showing a sense of humor. Being on different sides of an issue does not have to mean being at odds personally.

4. *Obtaining procedural flexibility.* These are activities which allow a negotiator to increase negotiating effectiveness through increasing the type and number of options available for conducting the negotiations. The longer a negotiator can keep the widest variety of options open, the greater the likelihood of reaching a desirable outcome. Examples include judicious choice of one's initial position, dealing with several issues simultaneously, and putting as many alternatives on the table as possible.

Using Third-Party Negotiations

Negotiations do not always take place only between the two parties directly involved in the disagreement. Sometimes third parties are called in when negotiations between the main parties have broken down or reached an impasse. At other times, third parties may be part of the negotiations process from the beginning. In some instances, third-party involvement is imposed on the disputing parties; in others, the parties themselves voluntarily seek out third-party assistance. In any event, the instances of third-party negotiations appear to be increasing.

There are different kinds of third-party interventions, and third-party involvement has been characterized in many different ways. One such typology suggests there are four basic kinds of interventions.[20] *Mediation,* where a neutral third party acts as a facilitator through the application of reasoning, suggestion, and persuasion. Mediators facilitate resolution by affecting how the disputing parties interact. Mediators have no binding authority; the parties are free to ignore mediation efforts and recommendations. *Arbitration* is where the third

---

[19]W. Mastenbroek, *Negotiate* (Oxford, United Kingdom: Basil Blackwell, 1989).

[20]R. J. Fisher, *The Social Psychology of Intergroup and International Conflict Resolution* (New York: Springer-Verlag, 1990).

party has the power (authority) to impose an agreement. In conventional arbitration, the arbitrator selects an outcome that is typically somewhere between the final positions of the disputing parties. In final-offer arbitration, the arbitrator is mandated to choose one or the other of the parties' final offers, and thus has no real control over designing the agreement.[21] *Conciliation* occurs where the third party is someone who is trusted by both sides and serves primarily as a communication link between the disagreeing parties. A conciliator has no more formal authority to influence the outcome than does a mediator. Finally, *consultation* is where a third party trained in conflict and conflict-resolution skills attempts to facilitate problem solving by focusing more on the relations between the parties than on the substantive issues. The chief role of the consultant is to improve the negotiating climate so that substantive negotiations can take place at some point in the future.

It is not uncommon for managers to serve as third parties in negotiations. Situations in which this could occur would include two subordinates who are having a disagreement, an employee and a dissatisfied customer, or disputes between two departments, both of which report to the manager. As a third party, the manager could be called upon to assume any and all of these four types of roles.

Negotiating Globally

The number of global negotiations is increasing rapidly. The global deals, markets, and relationships that organizations are forming require careful attention to culture's impact on style.[22] Individual steeped in specific culture negotiates differently. Labeling any culture's negotiating style is too general and constraining. However, there are general characteristics and tendencies that have been observed and noted. The former ambassador from Singapore to the United States noted that American negotiators generally (1) are prepared, (2) are plain speaking, (3) are pragmatic, (4) understand that concessions may be required, and (5) are very specific and candid. Others have described American negotiators as blunt, arrogant, and rushed.[23] The weaknesses of American negotiators appear to center on impatience, legalism, and poor listening skills. The strengths of American negotiators focus on friendliness, fairness, and flexibility.

Exhibit 9.5 provides a description of over 300 negotiators from 12 different countries.[24] The Japanese emphasized a win-win or integrative approach more than any other countries' negotiators. The results also indicate the direct communication styles used by Argentinean, American, and German negotiators.

The differences in negotiating style are extensive. However, political systems, legal policies, ideology, traditions, and culture certainly play a role. The international experience of the negotiators also has an impact on the style utilized. Being familiar with the communication style, time orientation, group versus individual orientation, religious orientation, and customs of the culture of the counterpart

[21]M. H. Bazerman and M. A. Neale, *Negotiating Rationally* (New York: The Free Press, 1992).

[22]Lewicki, Saunders, and Minton,

[23]T. T. B. Koh, "American Strengths and Weaknesses," *Negotiation Journal*, August 1996, pp. 313–17.

[24]J. W. Salacuse, "Ten Ways That Culture Affects Negotiating Style: Some Survey Results," *Negotiation Journal*, July 1998, pp. 221–40.

EXHIBIT 9.5
Cultural Effects on Negotiating Style

NEGOTIATING ATTITUDE: WIN-WIN OR WIN-LOSE?

	Japan	China	Argentina	France	India	USA	UK	Mexico	Germany	Nigeria	Brazil	Spain
Win-Win (%)	100	82	81	80	78	71	59	50	55	47	44	37

PERSONAL STYLE: FORMAL OR INFORMAL?

	Nigeria	Spain	China	Mexico	UK	Argentina	Germany	Japan	India	Brazil	France	USA
Formal (%)	53	47	46	42	35	35	27	27	22	22	20	17

COMMUNICATION STYLE: DIRECT OR INDIRECT?

	Japan	France	China	UK	Brazil	India	Germany	USA	Argentina	Spain	Mexico	Nigeria
Indirect (%)	27	20	18	12	11	11	9	5	4	0	0	0

AGREEMENT FORM: GENERAL OR SPECIFIC?

	Japan	Germany	India	France	China	Argentina	Brazil	USA	Nigeria	Mexico	Spain	UK
General (%)	46	45	44	30	27	27	20	22	20	17	16	11

Source: Adapted from J. W. Salacuse, Ten ways that culture affects negotiating style: Some survey results. *Negotiation Journal*, July 1998, 221–40.

negotiator would be an important step to take in preparing for negotiations.[25] Knowing something about another person's culture is a sign of respect that is appreciated at the negotiating table.

Improving Negotiations

Reading 9.1

Negotiating Rationally: The Power and Impact of the Negotiator's Frame

In one form or another, negotiation is becoming an increasingly important part of the manager's job. A review of the topic of negotiation concluded with a set of recommendations for managers on how to improve the negotiations process. The following suggestions were offered.[26]

1. Begin the bargaining with a positive overture—perhaps a small concession—and then reciprocate the opponent's concessions.

[25]M. J. Gelfand and A. Realo, "Individualism-Collectivism and Accountability In Intergroup Negotiations," *Journal of Applied Psychology*, October 1999, pp. 721–36.

[26]J. A. Wall and M. W. Blum, "Negotiations," *Journal of Management*, June 1991, p. 296.

2. Concentrate on the negotiation issues and the situational factors, not on the opponent or his or her characteristics.
3. Look below the surface of your opponent's bargaining and try to determine his or her strategy.
4. Do not allow accountability to your constituents or surveillance by them to spawn competitive bargaining.
5. If you have power in a negotiation, use it—with specific demands, mild threats, and persuasion—to guide the opponent toward an agreement.
6. Be open to accepting third-party assistance.
7. In a negotiation, attend to the environment and be aware that the opponent's behavior and power are altered by it.

Summary of Key Points

- A contemporary perspective on conflict recognizes that conflict is neither inherently good or bad but can be either depending on how it is dealt with. Rather than eliminating conflict, this view stresses that what is important is that conflict be effectively managed.

- A functional conflict is a confrontation between groups that enhances and benefits the organization's performance. Functional conflict can contribute to creativity, innovation, and improved decision making, among other benefits. Dysfunctional conflict, on the other hand, is that which harms the organization or hinders the achievement of organizational goals.

- Levels of conflict can be related to overall organizational performance. Too much conflict can be disruptive, creating chaos and damaging interpersonal relations. Too little conflict can also detract from performance. If conflict levels are too low, innovation and change are less likely to take place. Each organization has an optimal level of conflict that can be extremely functional.

- Conflict is inevitable. Every group will sometimes come into conflict with one or more other groups. Numerous factors contribute to intergroup conflict. Three particularly important ones are (1) the interdependent nature of the relationship between work groups, (2) differences in goals, and (3) differences in perceptions.

- Groups involved in dysfunctional conflict tend to react in fairly predictable ways. Some changes occur *within* the groups involved in conflict; others take place *between* the groups. Within-group changes include in- creased cohesiveness, emphasis on group loyalty, a rise in autocratic leadership, and a focus on task-oriented activity. Between-group changes include an increase in perceptual distortion, negative stereotyping of the other group, and decreased communication.

- One way of viewing conflict resolution is from the perspective of a conflict-management grid. Such a grid points out five distinct approaches to group conflict resolution: dominating, accommodating, problem solving, avoiding, and compromising.

- Sometimes conflict levels are too low, and the objective becomes stimulating functional conflict between groups. Techniques available for stimulating conflict include bringing outsiders into the group, altering the organization's structure, creating competition between groups, and making use of programmed conflict.

- Win-lose negotiating is a form of a zero-sum game. That is, to the extent one party wins something, the other party loses. Win-win negotiating is a positive-sum approach, wherein each party gains without a corresponding loss for the other party.

- There is an increasing use of third parties in negotiations. In some cases, third parties may be part of the entire process; in others, they may be called in only when an impasse is reached. Different types of third-party negotiations include mediation, arbitration, conciliation, and consultation.

- Negotiating with individuals from different countries and cultures poses a number of issues. Showing knowledge about a person's culture is one way to establish rapport and respect with another negotiator.

Review and Discussion Questions

1. What is the difference between functional and dysfunctional conflict? Can conflict that starts off as functional become dysfunctional? Can dysfunctional conflict be changed to functional?

2. Can you think of situations with which you are familiar that would have benefited from more intergroup conflict? How could additional conflict have improved the situation?

3. When intergroup conflict occurs, changes take place within and between conflicting groups. What are these changes? Which changes generally are positive? Which negative?

4. Is there a relationship between the level of intergroup conflict and organizational performance? How can an organization achieve optimal conflict levels?

5. What are some of the major reasons why intergroup conflict occurs? In your personal experience, what is the most frequent reason?

6. If you were about to begin negotiating with a person from Brazil, what would you want to know about his cultural background? Would it make a difference in the knowledge you seek if the Brazilian negotiator were a woman? Discuss.

7. There are a number of possible consequences of dysfunctional conflict. What are these? Are some of these consequences more or less likely to occur in organizational conflict situations?

8. What are the major differences between resolution and stimulation in managing conflict? Could both be appropriate with the same groups at the same time? Explain.

9. What are the four elements that are typically part of all negotiations? Are there likely to be differences in these elements depending on whether the negotiations are of a win-win or a win-lose nature?

10. How might you apply some of the conflict-management strategies from this chapter to improving union-management relations during contract negotiations?

READING 9.1   Negotiating Rationally: The Power and Impact of the Negotiator's Frame

M. H. Bazerman and M. A. Neale

Everyone negotiates. In its various forms, negotiation is a common mechanism for resolving differences and allocating resources. While many people perceive negotiation to be a specific interaction between a buyer and a seller, this process occurs with a wide variety of exchange partners, such as superiors, colleagues, spouses, children, neighbors, strangers, or even corporate entities and nations. Negotiation is a decision-making process among interdependent parties who do not share identical preferences. It is through negotiation that the parties decide what each will give and take in their relationship.

The aspect of negotiation that is most directly controllable by the negotiator is how he or she makes decisions. The parties, the issues, and the negotiation environment are often predetermined. Rather than trying to change the environment surrounding the negotiation or the parties or issues in the dispute, we believe that the greatest opportunity to improve negotiator performance lies in the negotiator's ability to make effective use of the information available about the issues in dispute, as well as the likely behavior of an opponent to reach more rational agreements and make more rational decisions within the context of negotiation.

To this end, we offer advice on how a negotiator should make decisions. However, to follow this advice for analyzing negotiations rationally, a negotiator must understand the psychological forces that limit a negotiator's effectiveness. In addition, rational decisions require that we have an optimal way of evaluating the behavior of the opponent. This requires a psychological perspective for anticipating the likely decisions and subsequent behavior of the other party. Information such as this can not only create a framework that predicts how a negotiator structures problems, processes information, frames the situation, and evaluates alternatives but also identifies the limitations of his or her ability to follow rational advice.

Rationality refers to making the decision that maximizes the negotiator's interests. Since negotiation is a decision-making process that involves other people that do not have the same desires or preferences, the goal of a negotiation is not simply reaching an agreement. The goal of negotiation is to reach a *good* agreement. In some cases, no agreement is better than reaching an agreement that is not in the negotiator's best interests. When negotiated agreements are based on biased decisions, the chances of getting the best possible outcome are significantly reduced and the probabilities of reaching an agreement when an impasse would have left the negotiator relatively better off are significantly enhanced.

A central theme of our work is that our natural decision and negotiation processes contain biases that prevent us from acting rationally and getting as much as we can out of a negotiation. These biases are pervasive, destroying the opportunities available in competitive contexts and preventing us from negotiating rationally. During the last 10 or so years, the work that we and our colleagues have done suggests that negotiators make the following common cognitive mistakes: (1) negotiators tend to be overly affected by the frame, or form of presentation, of information in a negotiation; (2) negotiators tend to nonrationally escalate commitment to a previously selected course of action when it is no longer the most reasonable alternative; (3) negotiators tend to assume that their gain must come at the expense of the other party and thereby miss opportunities for mutually beneficial trade-offs between the parties; (4) negotiator judgments tend to be anchored upon irrelevant information—such as an initial offer; (5) negotiators tend to rely on readily available information; (6) negotiators tend to fail to consider information that is available by focusing on the opponent's perspective; and (7) negotiators tend to be overconfident concerning the likelihood of attaining outcomes that favor the individual(s) involved.

Describing the impact of each of these biases on negotiator behavior is obviously beyond the scope of this article. What we will attempt to do, however, is to focus on one particular and important cognitive bias, *framing,* and consider the impact of this bias on the process and outcome of negotiation. The manner in which negotiators frame the options available in a dispute can have a significant impact on their willingness to reach an agreement as well as the value of that agreement. In this article, we will identify factors that influence the choice of frame in a negotiation.

THE FRAMING OF NEGOTIATIONS

Consider the following situation adapted from Russo and Shoemaker.[1]

Source: *Academy of Management Executive* (no. 3), August 1992, pp. 42–45.

This article is based on the book by M. H. Bazerman, and M. A. Neale, *Negotiating Rationally* (New York: Free Press, 1992).

[1]Adapted from J. E. Russo and P. J. Shoemaker, *Decision Traps* (New York: Doubleday, 1989).

You are in a store about to buy a new watch which costs $70. As you wait for the sales clerk, a friend of yours comes by and remarks that she has seen an identical watch on sale in another store two blocks away for $40. You know that the service and reliability of the other store are just as good as this one. Will you travel two blocks to save $30?

Now consider this similar situation:

You are in a store about to buy a new video camera that costs $800. As you wait for the sales clerk, a friend of yours comes by and remarks that she has seen an identical camera on sale in another store two blocks away for $770. You know that the service and reliability of the other store are just as good as this one. Will you travel two blocks to save the $30?

In the first scenario, Russo and Shoemaker report that about 90 percent of the managers presented this problem reported that they would travel the two blocks. However, in the second scenario, only about 50 percent of the managers would make the trip. What is the difference between the two situations that makes the $30 so attractive in the first scenario and considerably less attractive in the second scenario? One difference is that a $30 discount on a $70 watch represents a very good deal; the $30 discount on an $800 video camera is not such a good deal. In evaluating our willingness to walk two blocks, we frame the options in terms of the percentage discount. However, the correct comparison is not whether a percentage discount is sufficiently motivating, but whether the savings obtained is greater than the expected value of the additional time we would have to invest to realize those savings. So, if a $30 savings were sufficient to justify walking two blocks for the watch, an opportunity to save $30 on the video camera should also be worth an equivalent investment of time.

Richard Thaler illustrated the influence of frames when he presented the following two versions of another problem to participants of an executive development program:[2]

You are lying on the beach on a hot day. All you have to drink is ice water. For the last hour you have been thinking about how much you would enjoy a nice cold bottle of your favorite brand of beer. A companion gets up to make a phone call and offers to bring back a beer from the only nearby place where beer is sold: a fancy resort hotel. She says that the beer might be expensive and asks how much you are willing to pay for the beer. She will buy the beer if it costs as much as or less than the price you state. But if it costs more than the price you state, she will not buy it. You trust your friend and there

is no possibility of bargaining with the bartender. What price do you tell your friend you are willing to pay?

Now consider this version of the same story:

You are lying on the beach on a hot day. All you have to drink is ice water. For the last hour you have been thinking about how much you would enjoy a nice cold bottle of your favorite brand of beer. A companion gets up to make a phone call and offers to bring back a beer from the only nearby place where beer is sold: a small, run-down grocery store. She says that the beer might be expensive and asks how much you are willing to pay for the beer. She will buy the beer if it costs as much as or less than the price you state. But if it costs more than the price you state, she will not buy it. You trust your friend and there is no possibility of bargaining with the store owner. What price do you tell your friend you are willing to pay?

In both versions of the story, the results are the same: You get the same beer and there is no negotiating with the seller. Also you will not be enjoying the resort's amenities since you will be drinking the beer on the beach. Recent responses of executives at a Kellogg executive training program indicated that they were willing to pay significantly more if the beer were purchased at a "fancy resort hotel" ($7.83) than if the beer were purchased at the "small, run-down grocery store" ($4.10). The difference in price the executives were willing to pay for the same beer was based upon the frame they imposed on this transaction. Paying over $5 for a beer is an expected annoyance at a fancy resort hotel; however, paying over $5 for a beer at a run-down grocery store is an obvious "rip-off!" So, even though the same beer is purchased and we enjoy none of the benefits of the fancy resort hotel, we are willing to pay almost a dollar more because of the way in which we frame the purchase. The converse of this situation is probably familiar to many of us. Have you ever purchased an item because "it was too good of a deal to pass up," even though you had no use for it? We seem to assign a greater value to the quality of the transaction over and above the issue of what we get for what we pay.

Both of these examples emphasize the importance of the particular frames we place on problems we have to solve or decisions we have to make. Managers are constantly being exposed to many different frames, some naturally occurring and others that are purposefully proposed. An important task of managers is to identify the appropriate frame by which employees and the organization, in general, should evaluate its performance and direct its effort.

THE FRAMING OF RISKY NEGOTIATIONS

The way in which information is framed (in terms of either potential gains or potential losses) to the negotiator

[2]R. Thaler, "Using Mental Accounting in a Theory of Purchasing Behavior," *Marketing Science* 4 (1985), pp. 12–13.

can have a significant impact on his or her preference for risk, particularly when uncertainty about future events or outcomes is involved. For example, when offered the choice between gains of equal expected value—one for certain and the other a lottery, we strongly prefer to take the *certain* gain. However, when we are offered the choice between potential losses of equal expected value, we clearly and consistently eschew the loss for certain and prefer the risk inherent in the *lottery*.

There is substantial evidence to suggest that we are not indifferent toward risky situations and we should not necessarily trust our intuitions about risk. Negotiators routinely deviate from rationality because they do not typically appreciate the transient nature of their preference for risk; nor do they take into consideration the ability of a particular decision frame to influence that preference. Influencing our attitudes toward risk through the positive or negative frames associated with the problem is the result of evaluating an alternative from a particular referent point or base line. A referent point is the basis by which we evaluate whether what we are considering is viewed as a gain or a loss. The referent point that we choose determines the frame we impose on our options and, subsequently, our willingness to accept or reject those options.

Consider the high-performing employee who is expecting a significant increase in salary this year. He frames his expectations on the past behavior of the company. As such, he is expecting a raise of approximately $5,000. Because of the recession, he receives a $3,500 salary increase. He immediately confronts his manager, complaining that he has been unfairly treated. He is extremely disappointed in what his surprised manager saw as an exceptional raise because the employee's referent point is $1,500 higher. Had he known that the average salary increase was only $2,000 (and used that as a more realistic referent point), he would have perceived the same raise quite differently and it may have had the motivating force that his manager had hoped to create.

The selection of which relevant frame influences our behavior is a function of our selection of a base line by which we evaluate potential outcomes. The choice of one referent point over another may be the result of a visible anchor, the status quo, or our expectations. Probably one of the most common referent points is what we perceive to be in our current inventory (our status quo)—what is ours already. We then evaluate offers or options in terms of whether they make us better off (a gain) or worse off (a loss) from (what we perceive to be) our current resource state.

Interestingly, what we include in our current resource state is surprisingly easy to modify. Consider the executive vice president of a large automobile manufacturing concern that has been hit by a number of economic difficulties because of the recession in the United States. It appears as if she will have to close down three plants and the employee rolls will be trimmed by 6,000 individuals. In exploring ways to avoid this alternative, she has identified two plans that might ameliorate the situation. If she selects the first plan, she will be able to save 2,000 jobs and one of the three plants. If she implements the second plan, there is a one-third probability that she can save all three plants and all 6,000 jobs, but there is a two-thirds probability that this plan will end up saving none of the plants and none of the jobs. If you were this vice president, which plan would you select (Plan 1 or Plan 2)?

Now consider the same options (Plan 1 or Plan 2) framed as losses: If the vice president implements Plan 1, two of the three plants will be shut down and 4,000 jobs will be lost. If she implements Plan 2, then there is a two-thirds probability of losing all three plants and all 6,000 jobs, but there is a one-third probability of losing no plants and no jobs. If you were presented with these two plans, which would be more attractive, Plan 1 or Plan 2?

It is obvious that, from a purely economic perspective, there is no difference between the two choices. Yet managers offered the plans framed in terms of gains select the first plan about 76 percent of the time. However, managers offered the choice between the plans framed in terms of losses only select the first plan about 22 percent of the time. When confronted with potential losses, the lottery represented by Plan 2 becomes relatively much more attractive.

An important point for managers to consider is that the way in which the problem is framed, or presented, can dramatically alter the perceived value or acceptability of alternative courses of action. In negotiation, for example, the more risk-averse course of action is to accept an offered settlement; the more risk-seeking course of action is to hold out for future, potential concessions. In translating the influence of the framing bias to negotiation, we must realize that the selection of a particular referent point or base line determines whether a negotiator will frame his or her decision as positive or negative.

Specifically, consider any recurring contract negotiation. As the representative of Company "A," the offer from Company "B" can be viewed in two ways, depending on the referent point I use. If my referent point were the current contract, Company "B's" offer can be evaluated in terms of the "gains" Company "A" can expect relative to the previous contract. However, if the referent point for Company "A" is an initial offer on the issues under current consideration, then Company "A" is more likely to evaluate Company "B's" offers as losses to be incurred if the contract as proposed is accepted. Viewing options as losses or as gains will have considerable impact on the negotiator's willingness to accept side "B's" position—even though the same options may be offered in both cases.

Likewise, the referent points available to an individual negotiating his salary for a new position in the company include: (1) his current salary; (2) the company's initial offer; (3) the least he is willing to accept; (4) his estimate of the most the company is willing to pay; or (5) his initial salary request. As his referent moves from 1 to 5, he progresses from a positive to a negative frame in the negotiation. What is a modest *gain* compared to his current wage is perceived as a loss when compared to what he would like to receive. Along these same lines, employees currently making $15/hour and demanding an increase of $4/hour can view a proposed increase of $2/hour as a $2/hour gain in comparison to last year's wage (Referent 1) or as a $2/hour loss in comparison to their stated or initial proposal of $19/hour (Referent 5). Consequently, the location of the referent point is critical to whether the decision is positively or negatively framed and affects the resulting risk preference of the decision maker.

In a study of the impact of framing on collective bargaining outcomes, we used a five-issue negotiation with participants playing the roles of management or labor negotiators.[3] Each negotiator's frame was manipulated by adjusting his or her referent point. Half of the negotiators were told that any concessions they made from their initial offers represented losses to their constituencies (i.e., a negative frame). The other half were told that any agreements they were able to reach which were better than the current contract were gains to their constituencies (i.e., the positive frame). In analyzing the results of their negotiations, we found that negatively framed negotiators were less concessionary and reached fewer agreements than the positively framed negotiators. In addition, negotiators who had positive frames perceived the negotiated outcomes as more fair than those who had negative frames.

In another study, we posed the following problem to negotiators:

> You are a wholesaler of refrigerators. Corporate policy does not allow any flexibility in pricing. However, flexibility does exist in terms of expenses that you can incur (shipping, financing terms, etc.), which have a direct effect on the profitability of the transaction. These expenses can all be viewed in dollar-value terms. You are negotiating an $8,000 sale. The buyer wants you to pay $2,000 in expenses. You want to pay less expenses. When you negotiate the exchange, do you try to minimize your expenses (reduce them from $2,000) or maximize net profit, i.e., price less expenses (increase the net profit from $6,000)?

From an objective standpoint, the choice you make to reduce expenses or maximize profit should be irrelevant. Because the choice objectively is between two identical options, selecting one or the other should have no impact on the outcome of the negotiation. What we did find, in contrast, is that the frame that buyers and sellers take into the negotiation can systematically affect their behavior.[4]

In one study, negotiators were led to view transactions in terms of either (1) net profit or (2) total expenses deducted from gross profits. These two situations were objectively identical. Managers can think about maximizing their profits (i.e., gains) or minimizing their expenses (i.e., losses). These choices are linked; if one starts from the same set of revenues, then one way to maximize profits is to minimize expenses, and if one is successful at minimizing expenses, the outcome is that profit may be maximized. That is, there is an obvious relationship between profits and expenses. So, objectively, there is no reason to believe that an individual should behave differently if given the instructions to minimize expenses or to maximize profits. However, those negotiators told to maximize profit (i.e., a positive frame) were more concessionary. In addition, positively framed negotiators completed significantly more transactions than their negatively framed (those told to minimize expenses) counterparts. Because they completed more transactions, their overall profitability in the market was higher, although negatively framed negotiators completed transactions of greater mean profit.[5]

THE ENDOWMENT EFFECT

The ease with which we can alter our referent points was illustrated in a series of studies conducted by Daniel Kahneman, Jack Knetsch, and Richard Thaler.[6] In any exchange between a buyer and a seller, the buyer must be willing to pay at least the minimum amount the seller is willing to accept for a trade to take place. In determining the worth of an object, its value to the seller may, on occasion, be determined by some objective third party such as an economic market. However, in a large number of transactions, the seller places a value on the item—a value that may include not only the market value of the item but also a component for an emotional attachment to or unique appreciation of the item. What impact might such an attachment have on the framing of the transaction?

[3]M. A. Neale and M. H. Bazerman, "The Effects of Framing and Negotiator Overconfidence," *Academy of Management Journal* 28 (1985), pp. 34–49.

[4]M. H. Bazerman, T. Magliozzi, and M. A. Neale, "The Acquisition of an Integrative Response in a Competitive Market Simulation," *Organizational Behavior and Human Performance* 34 (1985), pp. 294–313.

[5]See, for example, Bazerman, Magliozzi, and Neale (1985), op. cit.; Neale and Bazerman (1985), op. cit.; or M. A. Neale and G. B. Northcraft, "Experts, Amateurs and Refrigerators: Comparing Expert and Amateur Decision Making on a Novel Task," *Organizational Behavior and Human Decision Processes* 38 (1986), pp. 305–317; and M. A. Neale, V. L. Huber, and G. B. Northcraft, "The Framing of Negotiations: Context versus Task Frames," *Organizational Behavior and Human Decision Processes* 39 (1987), pp. 228–41.

[6]D. Kahenman, J. L. Knetsch, and R. Thaler, "Experimental Tests of the Endowment Effect and Coarse Theorem," *Journal of Political Economy,* 1990.

Let's imagine that you have just received a coffee mug.[7] (In the actual demonstration, coffee mugs were placed before one third of the participants, the "sellers," in the study.) After receiving the mug, you are told that in fact you "own the object (coffee mug) in your possession. You have the option of selling it if a price, to be determined later, is acceptable to you." Next, you are given a list (see Exhibit 9.6) of possible selling prices, ranging from $.50 to $9.50, and are told that for each of the possible prices, you should indicate whether you would (a) sell the mug and receive that amount in return, or (b) keep the object and take it home with you. What is your selling price for the mug?

Another third of the group (the "buyers") were told that they would be receiving a sum of money and they could choose to keep the money or use it to buy a mug. They were also asked to indicate their preferences between a mug and sums of money ranging from $.50 to $9.50. Finally, the last third of the participants (the "choosers") were given a questionnaire indicating that they would later be given an option of receiving either a mug or a sum of money to be determined later. They in-

dicated their preferences between the mug and sums of money between $.50 to $9.50. All of the participants were told that their answers would not influence either the pre-determined price of the mug or the amount of money to be received in lieu of the mug.

The sellers reported a median value of $7.12 for the mug; the buyers valued the mug at $2.88; and the choosers valued the mug at $3.12. It is interesting that in this exercise, being a buyer or a chooser resulted in very similar evaluations of the worth of the mug. However, owning the mug (the sellers) created a much greater sense of the mug's worth. In this case, it was approximately 40 percent greater than the market (or retail) value of the mug.

The explanation for this disparity lies in the fact that different roles (buyer, seller, or chooser) created different referent points. In fact, what seems to happen in such situations is that owning something changes the nature of the owner's relationship to the commodity. Giving up that item is now perceived as a loss and, in valuing the item, the owner may include a dollar value to offset his or her perceived loss. If we consider this discrepancy in the value of an item common, then the simple act of "owning" an item, however briefly, can increase one's personal attach-

[7]The coffee mugs were valued at approximately $5.00.

EXHIBIT 9.6   The Coffee Mug Questionnaire

For each price listed below, indicate whether you would be willing to sell the coffee mug for that price or keep the mug.

If the price is $0.50, I will sell _____; I will keep the mug _____ .

If the price is $1.00, I will sell _____; I will keep the mug _____ .

If the price is $1.50, I will sell _____; I will keep the mug _____ .

If the price is $2.00, I will sell _____; I will keep the mug _____ .

If the price is $2.50, I will sell _____; I will keep the mug _____ .

If the price is $3.00, I will sell _____; I will keep the mug _____ .

If the price is $3.50, I will sell _____; I will keep the mug _____ .

If the price is $4.00, I will sell _____; I will keep the mug _____ .

If the price is $4.50, I will sell _____; I will keep the mug _____ .

If the price is $5.00, I will sell _____; I will keep the mug _____ .

If the price is $5.50, I will sell _____; I will keep the mug _____ .

If the price is $6.00, I will sell _____; I will keep the mug _____ .

If the price is $6.50, I will sell _____; I will keep the mug _____ .

If the price is $7.00, I will sell _____; I will keep the mug _____ .

If the price is $7.50, I will sell _____; I will keep the mug _____ .

If the price is $8.00, I will sell _____; I will keep the mug _____ .

If the price is $8.50, I will sell _____; I will keep the mug _____ .

If the price is $9.00, I will sell _____; I will keep the mug _____ .

If the price is $9.50, I will sell _____; I will keep the mug _____ .

ment to an item—and, typically, its perceived value. After such an attachment is formed, the cost of breaking that attachment is greater and is reflected in the higher price the sellers demand to part with their mugs as compared to the value the buyers or the choosers place on the exact same commodity. In addition, we would expect that the endowment effect intensifies to the extent that the value of the commodity of interest is ambiguous or subjective, or the commodity itself is unique or not easily substitutable in the marketplace.

FRAMING, NEGOTIATOR BIAS, AND STRATEGIC BEHAVIOR

In the previous discussion, we described the negotiator behaviors that may arise from positive and negative frames within the context of the interaction. In this section, we identify some of the techniques for strategically manipulating framing to direct negotiator performance.

As our research suggests, simply posing problems as choices among potential gains rather than choices among potential losses can significantly influence the negotiator's preferences for specific outcomes.

Framing can also have important implications for how managers choose to intervene in disputes among their peers or subordinates. Managers, of course, have a wide range of options to implement when deciding to intervene in disputes in which they are not active principals. If the manager's goal is to get the parties to reach an agreement rather than having the manager decide what the solution to the dispute will be, he or she may wish to facilitate both parties' viewing the negotiation from a positive frame. This is tricky, however, since the same referent that will lead to a positive frame for one negotiator is likely to lead to a negative frame for the other negotiator if presented simultaneously to the parties. Making use of the effects of framing may be most appropriate when a manager can meet with each side separately. He or she may present different perspectives to each party to create a positive frame (and the subsequent risk-averse behavior associated with such a frame) for parties on both sides of the dispute. Again, if the manager is to affect the frame of the problem in such a way as to encourage agreement, he or she may also emphasize the possible losses inherent in continuing the dispute. Combining these two strategies may facilitate both sides' preference for the certainty of a settlement.

Being in the role of buyer or seller can be a naturally occurring frame that can influence negotiator behavior in systematic ways. Consider the curious, consistent, and robust finding in a number of studies that buyers tend to outperform sellers in market settings in which the balance of power is equal.[8] Given the artificial context of the lab-

[8]Bazerman, et al. (1985), op. cit.; and M. A. Neale, V. L. Huber, and G. B. Northcraft (1987), op. cit.

oratory settings and the symmetry of the design of these field and laboratory markets, there is no logical reason why buyers should do better than sellers. One explanation for this observed difference may be that when the commodity is anonymous (or completely substitutable in a market sense), sellers may think about the transaction in terms of the dollars exchanged. That is, sellers may conceptualize the process of selling as gaining resources (e.g., how many dollars do I gain by selling the commodity); whereas buyers may view the transaction in terms of loss of dollars (e.g., how many dollars do I have to give up). If the dollars are the primary focus of the participants' attention, then buyers would tend to be risk seeking and sellers risk averse in the exchange.

When a risk-averse party (i.e., the seller, in this example) negotiates with a risk-seeking party (i.e., the buyer), the buyer is more willing to risk the potential agreement by demanding more or being less concessionary. To reach agreement, the seller must make additional concessions to induce the buyer, because of his or her risk-seeking propensity, to accept the agreement. Thus, in situations where the relative achievements of buyers and sellers can be directly compared, buyers would benefit from their negative frame (and subsequent risk-averse behavior). The critical issue is that these naturally occurring frames, such as the role demands of being a "buyer" or "seller," can easily influence the way in which the disputed issues are framed—even without the conscious intervention of one or more of the parties.

It is easy to see that the frames of negotiators can result in the difference between impasse and reaching an important agreement. Both sides in negotiations typically talk in terms of a certain wage, price, or outcome that they must get—setting a high referent point against which gains and losses are measured. If this occurs, any compromise below (or above) that point represents a loss. This perceived loss may lead negotiators to adopt a negative frame to all proposals, exhibit risk-seeking behaviors, and be less likely to reach settlement. Thus, negotiators, similar to the early example involving the beach and the beer, may end up with no beer (or no agreement) because of the frame (the amount of money I will pay for a beer from a run-down grocery store) that is placed on the choices rather than an objective assessment of what the beer is worth to the individual.

In addition, framing has important implications for the tactics that negotiators use. The framing effect suggests that, to induce concessionary behavior from an opponent, a negotiator should always create anchors or emphasize referents that lead the opposition to a positive frame and couch the negotiation in terms of what the other side has to gain.

In addition, the negotiator should make the inherent risk salient to the opposition while the opponent is in a risky situation. If the sure gain that is being proposed is rejected, there is no certainty about the quality of the next offer. Simultaneously, the negotiator should also not be persuaded by similar arguments from opponents. Maintaining a risk-neutral or risk-seeking perspective in evaluating an opponent's proposals may, in the worst case, reduce the probability of reaching an agreement; however, if agreements are reached, the outcomes are more likely to be of greater value to the negotiator.

An important component in creating good negotiated agreements is to avoid the pitfalls of being framed while, simultaneously, understanding the impact of positively and negatively framing your negotiating opponent. However, framing is just one of a series of cognitive bi-ases that can have a significant negative impact on the performance of negotiators. The purpose of this article was to describe the impact of one of these cognitive bi-ases on negotiator behavior by considering the available research on the topic and to explore ways to reduce the problems associated with framing. By increasing our un-derstanding of the subtle ways in which these cognitive biases can reduce the effectiveness of our negotiations, managers can begin to improve not only the quality of agreements for themselves but also fashion agreements that more efficiently allocate the available resources— leaving both parties and the communities of which they are a part better off.

Exercises

EXERCISE 9.1   Third-Party Conflict Resolution

PURPOSE

1. To understand the criteria that third parties use when they intervene and attempt to resolve others' con-flicts.

INTRODUCTION

In addition to being involved in their own conflicts, man-agers are often called upon to intervene and to settle con-flicts between other people. The two activities in this sec-tion are designed to explore how third parties may enter conflicts for the purpose of resolving them and to practice one very effective approach to intervention. In the exer-cise, you will read about a manager who has a problem de-ciding how to intervene in a dispute, and you will discuss this case in class.

Step 1: 5 Minutes

Read "The Seatcor Company" case.

The Seatcor Manufacturing Company

You are senior vice president of operations and chief operating officer of Seatcor, a major producer of office fur-niture. Joe Gibbons, your subordinate, is vice president and general manager of your largest desk assembly plant. Joe has been with Seatcor for 38 years and is two years away from retirement. He worked his way up through the ranks to his present position and has successfully operated his division for five years with a marginally competent staff. You are a long-standing personal friend of Joe's and

respect him a great deal. However, you have always had an uneasy feeling that Joe has surrounded himself with min-imally competent people by his own choice. In some ways, you think he is threatened by talented assistants.

Last week you were having lunch with Charles Stewart, assistant vice president and Joe's second in com-mand. Upon your questioning, it became clear that he and Joe were engaged in a debilitating feud. Charles was hired last year, largely at your insistence. You had been con-cerned for some time about who was going to replace Joe when he retired, especially given the lack of really capa-ble managerial talent on Joe's staff. Thus, you prodded Joe to hire your preferred candidate—Charles Stewart. Charles is relatively young, 39, extremely tenacious and bright, and a well-trained business school graduate. From all reports, he is doing a good job in his new position.

Your concern centers around a topic that arose at the end of your lunch. Charles indicated Joe Gibbons is in the process of completing a five-year plan for his plant. This plan is to serve as the basis for several major plant rein-vestment and reorganization decisions that would be pro-posed to senior management. According to Charles, Joe Gibbons has not included Charles in the planning process at all. You had to leave lunch quickly and were unable to get much more information from Charles. However, he did admit that he was extremely disturbed by this exclu-sion and that his distress was influencing his work and probably his relationship with Joe.

You consider this a very serious problem. Charles will probably have to live with the results of any major deci-sions about the plant. More important, Joe's support is es-sential if Charles is to properly grow into his present and/or future job. Joe, on the other hand, runs a good ship

Source: Developed by Roy J. Lewicki, The Ohio State University. Used with per-mission.

and you do not want to upset him or undermine his authority. Moreover, you know Joe has good judgment; thus, he may have good reason for what he is doing. How would you proceed to handle this issue?

Step 2: 5 Minutes

Before discussing this case with anyone else, answer the following two questions:
1. Assume you were the senior vice president of operations. Exactly what would you do in this situation regarding the conflict between Joe and Charles?

2. Why would you take this action—i.e., what are your primary objectives by intervening in this way?

Step 3: 20–30 Minutes

The instructor will discuss this case with the entire class.

Step 4: 10–15 Minutes

The instructor will summarize the case discussion and present a framework for understanding how participants analyzed the case and decided to intervene.

Exercises

EXERCISE 9.2   World Bank: An Exercise in Intergroup Negotiation

Step 1   The class is divided into two groups. The size of each of the groups should be no more than 10. Those not in one of the two groups are designated as observers. However, groups should not have fewer than six members each. The instructor will play the role of the referee/banker for the World Bank.

Step 2   Read the World Bank Instruction Sheet.

Step 3   Each group or team will have 15 minutes to organize itself and plan strategy before beginning. Before the first round, each team must choose (*a*) two negotiators, (*b*) a representative, (*c*) a team recorder, and (*d*) a treasurer.

Step 4   The referee/banker will signal the beginning of round one and each following round and also end the exercise in about one hour.

Step 5   Discussion. In small groups or with the entire class, answer the following questions.

1. What occurred during the exercise?
2. Was there conflict? What type?
3. What contributed to the relationships among groups?
4. Evaluate the power, leadership, motivation, and communication among groups.
5. How could the relationships have been more effective?

WORLD BANK GENERAL INSTRUCTION SHEET

This is an intergroup activity. You and your team are going to engage in a task in which money will be won or lost. *The objective is to win as much as you can.* There are two teams

involved in this activity, and both teams receive identical instructions. After reading these instructions, your team has 15 minutes to organize itself and plan its strategy.

Each team represents a country. Each country has financial dealings with the World Bank. Initially, each country contributed $100 million to the World Bank. Countries may have to pay further monies or may receive money from the World Bank in accordance with regulations and procedures described below under sections headed Finances and Payoffs.

Each team is given 20 cards. These are your *weapons*. Each card has a marked side (X) and an unmarked side. The marked side of the card signifies that the weapon is armed. Conversely, the blank side shows the weapon to be unarmed.

At the beginning, each team will place 10 of its 20 weapons in their armed positions (marked side up) and the remaining 10 in their unarmed positions (marked side down). These weapons will remain in your possession and out of sight of the other team at all times.

There will be *rounds* and *moves*. Each round consists of seven moves by each team. There will be two or more rounds in this simulation. The number of rounds depends on the time available. Payoffs are determined and recorded after each round.

1. A move consists of turning two, one, or none of the team's weapons from armed to unarmed status, or vice versa.
2. Each team has two minutes to move. There are 30-second periods between moves. At the end of two minutes, the team must have turned two, one, or none of its weapons from armed to unarmed status, or from unarmed to armed status. If the team fails to move in the allotted time, no change can be made in weapons status until the next move.

Source: Adapted from John E. Jones and J. William Pfeiffer (eds.), *The 1975 Annual Handbook for Group Facilitators* (San Diego, CA: University Associates, 1975).

3. The length of the 2 1/2-minute periods between the beginning of one move and the beginning of the next is fixed and unalterable.

Each new round of the experiment begins with all weapons returned to their original positions, 10 armed and 10 unarmed.

FINANCES

The funds you have contributed to the World Bank are to be allocated in the following manner:

$60 million will be returned to each team to be used as your team's treasury during the course of the decision-making activities.

$40 million will be retained for the operation of the World Bank.

PAYOFFS

1. *If there is an attack:*
   a. Each team may announce an attack on the other team by notifying the referee/banker during the 30 seconds following *any* 2-minute period used to decide upon the move (including the seventh, or final, decision period in any round). The choice of each team during the decision period just ended counts as a move. An attack may not be made during negotiations.
   b. If there is an attack (by one or both teams), two things happen: (1) the round ends, and (2) the World Bank levies a penalty of $5 million for each team.
   c. The team with the greater number of armed weapons wins $3 million for each armed weapon it has over and above the number of armed weapons of the other team. These funds are paid directly from the treasury of the losing team to the treasury of the winning team. The referee/bankers will manage this transfer of funds.
2. *If there is no attack:* At the end of each round (seven moves), each team's treasury receives from the World Bank $2 million for each of its weapons that is at that point unarmed, and each team's treasury pays to the World Bank $2 million for each of its weapons remaining armed.

NEGOTIATIONS

Between moves, each team has the opportunity to communicate with the other team through its negotiators.

Either team may call for negotiations by notifying the referee/bankers during any of the 30-second periods between decisions. A team is free to accept or reject any invitation to negotiate.

Negotiators from both teams are *required* to meet after the third and sixth moves (after the 30-second period following that move, if there is no attack).

Negotiations can last no longer than three minutes. When the two negotiators return to their teams, the two-minute decision period for the next move begins once again.

Negotiators are bound only by: (*a*) the three-minute time limit for negotiations, and (*b*) their required appearance after the third and sixth moves. They are otherwise free to say whatever is necessary to benefit themselves or their teams. The teams similarly are not bound by agreements made by their negotiators, even when those agreements are made in good faith.

SPECIAL ROLES

Each team has 15 minutes to organize itself to plan team strategy. During this period before the first round begins, each team must choose persons to fill the following roles. (Each team must have each of the following roles, which can be changed at any time by a decision of the team.)

- *Negotiators*—activities stated above.
- A *representative*—to communicate team decisions to the referee/bankers.
- A *recorder*—to record the moves of the team and to keep a running balance of the team's treasury.
- A *treasurer*—to execute all financial transactions with the referee/bankers.

Cases

CASE 9.1   L. E. S., Inc.

BACKGROUND

L. E. S., Inc., is a large U.S. company engaged in the manufacture and sales of a wide range of electrical products. Headquarters are in Ohio, with five regional sales and marketing offices. L. E. S. has 17 manufacturing fa-

Source: © Ann Cunliffe, March 1991. Reproduced with permission.

cilities mainly concentrated in the Northeast, with newer plants in the Southwest. There is a national network of warehouses to service the U.S. market. The manufacturing operations are organized on a divisional basis: power and transmission, electrical components, and small appliances. There are three plants manufacturing electrical components, such as switches, sockets, and relays. One of these plants is L. E. S. (Worcester).

EXHIBIT 9.7   **Organization Chart, L. E. S., Inc. (Worcester): 236 Employees**

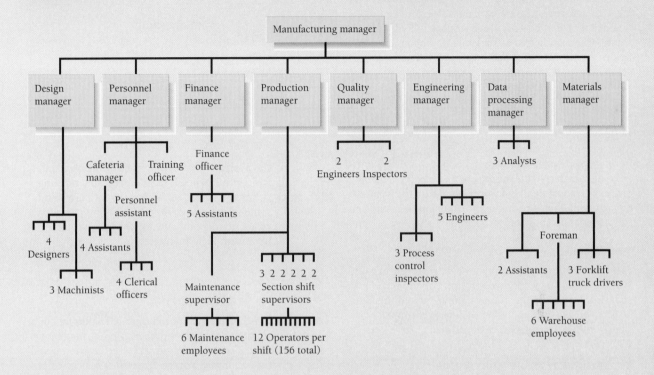

The site of Worcester consists of a manufacturing plant where low-cost, high-volume electrical components are assembled for the computer and electrical industry. Over the last three years, Worcester Plant has doubled its workforce in response to rapid sales growth. (See organization chart in Exhibit 9.7.)

There are six production sections:

Section 1—connector and cable assemblies

Sections 2 and 3—switches, relays, and timers

Sections 4 and 5—circuit board components

Section 6—circuit breaker assemblies

Sections 2 through 6 work two shifts, Section 1 operates three shifts, and each shift has its own supervisor. Half of the production operators have less than one year with the company. Only four section shift supervisors have more than two years' service, and only two of these have had any supervisory training.

KEY CHARACTERS

Manufacturing Manager

Martin Collins; M.B.A.; age 44. Overall responsibility for Worcester Plant. Reports to the divisional vice president in Ohio. Martin has been manufacturing manager for six years, having been appointed to the position from a job at headquarters.

Production Manager

John Drummond; no formal qualifications; age 49. John has worked in the plant for 15 years, 4 as a supervisor, and the last 11 as a production manager. Responsible for the six production sections and their maintenance. This involves planning work schedules, dealing with day-to-day production issues, and the maintenance of equipment and a workshop to build and modify equipment according to plans drawn by the design department.

Quality Manager

Mike Peterson; degree in electrical engineering; age 43. Mike has worked in quality in the plant for the last 12 years, and he insures that products meet quality standards by the inspection of finished products prior to dispatch to the warehouse. He also is responsible for the inspection of incoming new materials.

Engineering Manager

Chris Brooks; degree in electrical engineering; M.B.A.; age 35. The only woman on the management team, she was recruited by the manufacturing manager, three years ago, from outside the company. She is responsible for the development of new products, the improvement of existing manufacturing methods, and technical problem solving in the production departments. There is also a responsibility for process control. Most of the projects relating to the former two activities are self-generated and important in maintaining the competitiveness of L. E. S. The production department relies heavily on the technical expertise of the engineering department in maintaining a smooth flow of operations.

Materials Manager

Rich Sweeney; experience; age 39. He has spent six years in this job. He plans production and insures the required amount of materials are in stock to manufacture customer orders. Responsible also for implementing the manufacturing requirements planning (MRP) to optimize and control material inventories.

Design Manager

Bob Lemire; degree in mechanical engineering; age 30. Worked for L. E. S. (Worcester) for one year. He is responsible for the design of new equipment and the modification of existing equipment. This department works closely with the maintenance department.

TEAM OBJECTIVES

Objectives for each year are set at an annual seminar for the management team listed above. These objectives were identified by the manufacturing manager and agreed to by the team after a brief discussion. Extracts from the annual plan show the main priorities of the company this year:

We are in a very competitive era in which we must reduce costs to survive. Part of this activity is increasing productivity through the introduction of more efficient manufacturing activity. Specifically, this involves the introduction of new equipment and processes, the modification of existing equipment, and the more effective use of that equipment to improve output, quality, and reduce wastage.

It is extremely important to our overall success that we carry out our activities on a team basis. The company will only maintain and improve its product leadership through commitment to a team effort.

Currently, a number of production problems exist in the plant, resulting in late deliveries to customers. These problems have been identified by the management team as:

1. A high scrap rate: 15 percent of wasted products and materials over all sections.
2. Section 1 being fully utilized, 24 hours a day. This results in no leeway in meeting excess demands.
3. Quality problems, requiring products to be reworked to meet quality standards.

Last week, the following memorandum was sent:

Memorandum

From: M. Collins
To: J. Drummond
         M. Peterson
         C. Brooks
         R. Sweeney
         B. Lemire

MANUFACTURING MEETING

As you are aware, we have a number of problems affecting plant performance. I have organized a meeting for next Monday, 2 P.M., to assess the situation and identify some solutions to our problems. This situation is reaching a critical point and we need to take action fast. Please ensure that you attend.

THE MANAGEMENT MEETING

Martin Collins (manufacturing manager): "Thanks for coming. As you know, we have a number of problems that we need to resolve if we are to improve productivity levels and meet current and future market demands. We need to improve manufacturing efficiency, and there are two main problems we need to consider: One, productivity is falling. We have more people but they seem to be less effective. Second, there are a number of projects that have not and will not be completed in the time scale we would like them to be.

"In today's climate, we cannot afford to continue like this. We need to address these issues—and fast! Perhaps we can start by assessing the current situation."

"The problem is, we've just got too much to do," said John (production manager). "We've got to produce more and more with the same number of sections. Section 1 is running to capacity, 24 hours a day, seven days a week. We need more equipment. Maintenance and design are working on improving our existing equipment, but it's a slow job with the breakdowns they keep having to deal with. Bob and I have discussed this and agree it would help us both."

Bob (design manager) nodded in agreement.

"I don't think it's only that, John; we have got quality problems as well, which need to be ironed out," said Chris (engineering manager).

"We can't afford to buy more equipment until we've dealt with our existing problems," said Martin. "The emphasis is on cost reduction as well as on maintaining our market share."

John replied, "The other problem is that half the employees only started with us less than a year ago, so they haven't much experience. The supervisors haven't much idea about work scheduling, as most of them have had no training in supervision. I have to keep on their backs all the time to make sure they get the job done."

"Why don't we get the personnel department down to look at the possibility of training those who need it?" asked Chris. "We could use training as a base for increasing individual efficiency."

"When do you think we have time to take them off production?" John replied. "We have enough trouble meeting targets with everyone working."

"That's true," said Martin.

"Give me some more operators and I might have the time," added John.

"I think it would be worthwhile looking at equipment and staffing implications, as well as at operator and supervisor competence," said Chris. "It's no use saying we need more operators until we know we are utilizing the people and equipment we've got—effectively."

"It's an idea. I'll get personnel to look into the possibilities; after all, its job is to assess staffing needs," said Martin.

"The other problem is that we are not focusing on quality and volume of output for each particular product." Chris paused. "The operators do, but no one else does. We are all more concerned with our own individual functions—we see things in a compartmentalized way, rather than focusing on the product as a whole."

"Yes," agreed Mike (quality manager). "Take quality. Chris and I provided a procedure and control chart for supervisors to work to—but it won't work unless we have some formal mechanism for the engineer, the process control technician, and the supervisor to modify it for each line. There seems to be a lack of communication between these people at the shop floor level, no matter how we try to encourage it."

"I agree," added Chris. "There seem to be a number of solutions to problems that have been improvised or implemented by various people—supervisors, maintenance, quality engineers, and engineers who just happened to get involved. Because these aren't documented, the next person to deal with the problem is unaware of them and has to start dealing with the problem from scratch. We need some formalization of procedures and problem solving."

"It would certainly help," said Mike.

"Look, I've said before that we need to be more flexible in production," said John firmly. He turned to Mike. "You know what it was like when we first started: there were no written job descriptions, everyone knew what they were doing, and did it—we had no problems then."

"But things have changed," said Mike.

"We just got bigger," replied John. "So we need to be more flexible—I'm sure Rick would agree, we were talking about it yesterday."

"Sure," said Rick (materials manager), "and Martin is always saying we need to be more flexible."

"I accept that in our business we need to be able to adapt quickly to customer demands, if we are to remain competitive; but we can still have structure and flexibility. . . ." began Chris.

"Is that what you learned in your business course?" interrupted John. "Well, Mike knows that production can only be effective if we've got that space to maneuver. He's worked with us for 12 years and knows we've had some very good workers who have come up with some creative solutions."

"Well . . . I suppose so," Mike reluctantly agreed.

"That's fine," said Chris. "But because those solutions aren't documented or formalized, we get changes on changes that can mask the original problem. One of the supervisors was telling me yesterday that they rarely get the same maintenance person dealing with problems in her section. When they eventually arrive, they do something—go away—and no one is any the wiser. When the next problem occurs, it's a different maintenance employee who starts again. She says it's the same on other sections, and that the maintenance people can't wait to get back to their workshop to get on with their job there. That is one area that would benefit from formalization. . . ."

"My maintenance department people do their jobs!" interrupted John.

"They do see themselves as a 'cut above the rest,' John," said Mike.

"They have an important job to do," replied John. "They like things as they are."

"But it takes them time to deal with any problems because they are not thoroughly familiar with the detail of that particular section," said Chris. "They've no allegiance to a product."

"Look, I'll say it again—we need to be flexible," said John.

"Well, there is something in that. What about the problem we have with the overrunning of projects?" asked Martin. "It's particularly a problem in engineering and in quality."

"I'm glad to hear it's not only production having problems!" said John, in a loud aside to Rick. "Guess an M.B.A. doesn't give you all the answers!" Ignoring this comment, Chris began, "My engineers are just as frustrated as we are that they aren't meeting the deadlines. Their jobs are becoming fragmented, and they are having to move from one task to another because of the day-to-day problems that arise. This obscures the more long-term projects, and it's only the urgent jobs that get attention. The conflict arises because the same people are dealing with long-term improvement projects and day-to-day problems, and the latter have to take precedence. What do you think, Mike?"

"I agree. We have the same problems and for basically the same reasons," replied Mike. "We can't concentrate on long-term quality problems because of the day-to-day ones . . ."

"We are here to get the product out, Mike," interrupted John. "That's got to be our priority. We need to meet customer orders."

"Yes, but don't forget we also have to retain those customers and meet the quality specifications. We need to consider the medium-to long-term, as well," said Martin.

"We really need to look at how to balance the two and minimize the conflicting demands. Mike and I have been discussing the problem and think it may be useful to separate development and day-to-day problems." Chris looked at Mike for support.

"That's impossible!" retorted John.

"It can be done," replied Chris. "We need to develop a team approach. A small development group could be established to deal with medium- to long-term projects. We could organize production on a team basis, each section having a team consisting of the appropriate shift supervisor or supervisors, someone from maintenance who would have a permanent assignment to that section, an engineer, and quality input."

"One quality inspector could cover each product group," added Mike.

"We would need more staff for that," said Rick, "and John and I have more than enough problems to deal with without trying to get a team to work together!"

"Anyway, we need more operators, not engineers and quality people—it's *producers* we need," said John.

"It would give us more time to study our quality problems. . . ." began Mike.

Martin said, "It would also need more money and an immediate cost increase."

Mike looked around the group. "Well, maybe it is a nonstarter." He looked apologetically at Chris.

Chris tried again. "I believe we should be looking at the way we are organized and staffed. We are obviously going wrong somewhere, and I don't believe it's all based on technical problems. I'm sure we could run more efficiently, even if we only reorganized our existing resources. We also need to stress the importance of quality; the operators can't be very motivated when they see such a high scrap rate—that we are doing little about."

"The only way I'll produce more is with more operators," said John.

Chris gave up, feeling frustrated that no one was open to the points she was making.

"Okay," said Martin. "I'll get personnel to look at staffing levels. Can you liaise with them, John, and report back to our next meeting? I'll also get them to look at the supervisors' training needs, although I doubt we'll have time to release them. Meanwhile, let's try and solve some of those quality problems."

The meeting finished.

Chris caught up with Mike outside. "What happened, Mike? I thought we'd agreed to push for the team approach?" "There isn't much you can do when John gets started," said Mike. "Anyway, things aren't going to change."

"Not if we all take the short-term expedient view," replied Chris. "Martin knows we need to do something, but he's not sure what. We could have put forward those alternatives we discussed—I thought you were all for them?"

"I was . . ." said Mike.

QUESTIONS:

1. What are some of the main causes of conflict at L. E. S., Inc.?
2. Why do each of the participants attending the meeting view the problems differently?
3. How should the situation and conflict be resolved?

10

Organizational Power and Politics

After completing Chapter 10, you should be able to:

Learning Objectives

- Distinguish between the terms *influence* and *power*.

- Identify five interpersonal power bases.

- Describe three forms of structural power.

- Discuss the concepts of *powerlessness* and *empowerment*.

- Identify the contingencies that influence subunit power.

- Explain what is meant by the term *illusion of power*.

- Describe several frequently used influence tactics.

- Discuss the criteria for determining ethical behavior.

- Identify the considerations involved in using power effectively.

Power is a pervasive part of the fabric of organizational life.[1] Managers and non-managers use it. They manipulate power to accomplish goals and, in many cases, to strengthen their own positions. A person's success or failure in using or reacting to power is determined largely by understanding power, knowing how and when to use it, and being able to anticipate its probable effects.[2] The purpose of this chapter is to examine power and its uses in organizations. We will look at sources (bases) of power, how power is used, and the relationship between power and organizational politics.

THE CONCEPT OF POWER

The study of power and its effects is important to understanding how organizations operate. It is possible to interpret every interaction and every social relationship in an organization as involving power.[3] How organizational subunits and individuals are controlled is related to the issue of power and influence. The terms **power** and **influence** are frequently used interchangeably in the management literature; however, there is a subtle, yet important, difference between them. **Influence** is a transaction in which person B is induced by person A to behave in a certain way. For example, if an employee works overtime at the boss's request, that employee has been influenced by the boss.

Like influence, power involves a relationship between two people. Robert Dahl, a political scientist, captures this important relational focus when he defines power as saying "A has power over B to the extent that he can get B to do something B would not otherwise do."[4] What is the difference in this definition of power and our earlier definition of influence? **Power** represents the capability to get someone to do something; influence is the exercise of that capability. Another way of stating the distinction is to say that power is the potential to influence, while influence is power in action. Thus you may have power (the capacity to influence) but not use it; on the other hand, you cannot influence anyone (induce certain behavior in another person) without power.

We frequently speak of someone having power over someone else. While this is correct, it is important to stress that power is not an attribute of a particular person. Rather, it is an aspect of the relationship that exists between two (or more) people. No individual or group can have power in isolation; power must exist in relation to some other person or group. If A has power over B, it is, in part, because B is willing for that to be an aspect of the relationship between them. If and when B no longer desires that to be part of the relationship with A, A will no longer have power over B and no longer be able to influence B's behavior. Thus *obtaining, maintaining,* and *using* power are all essential to influencing the behavior of people in organizational settings.

Some power relationships in organizations are *symmetrical.* This means that both parties are equal, or have the same amount of power. Other power relationships are *asymmetrical,* meaning one person in the relationship has more power than the other. Symmetry is a property that can change over time, as a person or

---

[1]M. Kramer Roderick and Margaret A. Neale (eds.), *Power and Influence in Organizations* (Thousand Oaks, CA: Sage, 1998).

[2]Rosebeth Moss Kanter, "A Culture of Innovation," *Executive Excellence,* August 2000, pp. 10–11.

[3]Tom Duffy, "Power Up!" *Network World,* January 3, 2000, pp. 97–98.

[4]Robert Dahl, "The Concept of Power," *Behavioral Science,* July 1957, pp. 202–203.

group gains or loses power.[5] To understand how power can shift, it is important to know where power is obtained.

WHERE DOES POWER COME FROM?

Power is obtained in a variety of ways in an organization. Since power facilitates the organization's adaptation to its environment, the people and groups within the organization that are able to assist in that adaptation are the ones that will hold power. Two important categories of power in an organization are *interpersonal* and *structural*. Within each of these two categories, there are several specific sources of power. Let's look at these in some detail.

Interpersonal Power

In what is considered a classic writing in the management and organizational behavior literature, John French and Bertram Raven suggested five interpersonal sources, or bases, of power: legitimate, reward, coercive, expert, and referent.[6] As we shall see, these sources of power are not equally available to all organizational members.

Legitimate Power

Legitimate power refers to a person's ability to influence others because of the position within the organization that person holds. Legitimate or position power, as it is sometimes called, is derived from the position itself. That is, the organization has given to an individual occupying a particular position the right to influence—command—certain other individuals. This formal power is what we call **authority**. Orders from a manager in an authority position are followed because the manager has the legitimate power to command certain subordinates in lower positions. Not following orders subjects the offender to disciplinary action just as not following society's legal directives subjects one to disciplinary action in the form of arrest and penalty. Organizational authority has the following characteristics:

1. *It is invested in a person's position.* An individual has authority because of the position she holds, not because of any specific personal characteristics.
2. *It is accepted by subordinates.* The individual in a legal authority position exercises authority and can gain compliance because he or she has a legitimate right.
3. *Authority is used vertically.* Authority flows from the top down in the hierarchy of an organization.

Possessing legitimate power, or authority, does not mean that all orders will be followed by those who are subordinate to the individual in authority. For a subordinate to comply with an order from a superior requires that the order fall within the subordinate's zone of indifference. The term *zone of indifference* may

[5]Belle Rose Ragins, "Diversified Mentoring Relationships in Organizations: A Power Perspective," *Academy of Management Review,* April 1997, pp. 482–521.

[6]John R. P. French and Bertram Raven, "The Basis of Social Power," in D. Cartwright (ed.), *Studies in Social Power* (Ann Arbor: Institute for Social Research, University of Michigan, 1959), pp. 150–67.

be explained as follows: If all possible orders which might be directed to an individual from a superior were arranged in the order of their acceptability to the individual, some would be clearly acceptable while others might be clearly unacceptable. For example, a request by a manager that a subordinate complete her expense report might be an acceptable order. It would lie within her zone of indifference; that is, she is relatively indifferent to the request as far as the question of her boss's authority is concerned.

However, if the boss were to request that she record expenses she did not incur, or that she otherwise "pad" the expense report, such a request might well fall outside her zone of indifference. She may elect not to comply because she is no longer indifferent with respect to such an order. A person's zone of indifference may be wider or narrower depending on a number of factors such as the extent to which the boss has a source of power other than authority.

Reward Power

This type of power is based on a person's ability to reward a follower for compliance. It occurs when someone possesses a resource that another person wants and is willing to exchange that resource in return for certain behavior. **Reward power** is used to back up the use of legitimate power. If followers value the rewards or potential rewards the manager can provide (recognition, a good job assignment, a pay raise, opportunity to attend a training program, etc.), they may respond to orders, requests, and directions. Note, however, that if what a manager is offering as a reward has no value to an individual, it will not likely influence behavior.

Coercive Power

The opposite of reward power is **coercive power,** power to punish. Followers may comply out of fear. A manager may block a promotion or criticize a subordinate for poor performance. These practices and the fear they will be used are coercive power. Of course, one need not be in a position of authority to possess coercive power. For example, fear of rejection by coworkers for not complying with what they want represents coercive power even though one's coworkers have no formal authority.

Expert Power

A person has **expert power** when he or she possesses special expertise that is highly valued. Experts have power even when their formal position in the organizational hierarchy is low. A person may possess expertise on technical, administrative, or personal matters. The salesperson who has a knack for landing new accounts, the software developer who always has an elegant solution for a program's bugs, the college dean who consistently raises the most money—all have enhanced ability to influence others because of their special expertise. The more difficult it is to replace the expert, the greater degree of expert power he or she possesses. Expert power is not unlimited, however; occasionally, individuals' expertise does not bestow upon them as much power as they believe it does. This is vividly illustrated in the Organizational Encounter 10.1 involving the Professional Air Traffic Controller Organization and the President of the United States.

A Miscalculation of Power

Correctly assessing who holds the balance of power in a relationship between two parties can be difficult. Even seemingly objective measures may in fact be quite subjective, and that makes it very easy to over- or underestimate either one's own power or that of another person or group. In a power struggle, misjudging how much power you have relative to your opponent can have consequences ranging from insignificant to catastrophic. In what some have called the greatest miscalculation of power in modern times, the consequences were catastrophic for over 11,000 people who ended up not only being fired but effectively permanently barred from their profession as well.

Here is what happened: On August 31, 1981, 11,500 air traffic controllers, members of the Professional Air Traffic Controller Organization (PATCO), walked off the job. Conflicts between PATCO and the Federal Aviation Administration had reached their peak during the summer. Despite the fact that the controllers were legally prohibited from striking, the vast majority of PATCO members took a walk.

When President Reagan announced that, after a 48-hour grace period, all remaining striking controllers would be fired, only a handful returned to work. The same assessment of their degree of "expert power," which had led them to strike in the first place, led the vast majority to call the president's bluff. PATCO felt its members, because of their specialized knowledge and skill and the essential role they played in aviation, held the balance of power. Their assumption appeared to be that with no controllers, air traffic in the United States would come to a standstill and no president (especially one who had been on the job for only seven months) could afford to let that happen.

It was clearly a miscalculation. The president carried out his intentions, and more than 11,000 controllers lost their jobs. PATCO lost its right to represent the controllers, and simply ceased to exist. Since the federal government employs all but a handful of air traffic controllers in this country, alternative employment as controllers was not available. In a case of legitimate power versus expert power, the expert power side not only lost but was totally destroyed.

Expert power is a personal characteristic, while legitimate, reward, and coercive power are largely prescribed by the organization.

Referent Power

Many individuals identify with and are influenced by a person because of the latter's personality or behavioral style. The charisma of the person is the basis of **referent power**. A person with charisma is admired because of his or her characteristics. The strength of a person's charisma is an indication of his or her referent power. *Charisma* is a term that is often used to describe politicians, entertainers, or sports figures. However, some managers are regarded as extremely charismatic by their subordinates. A charismatic leader, such as Jack Welch at General Electric or Herb Kelleher at Southwest Airlines, can ignite an entire organization. Certain aspects of charismatic leadership will be discussed in more detail in Chapter 12.

The five sources of interpersonal power can be divided into two major categories: organizational and personal. Legitimate, reward, and coercive power are primarily prescribed by the organization, the position, or specific interaction patterns. A person's legitimate power can be changed by transferring the person, rewriting the job description, or reducing the power by restructuring the organization. On the other hand, expert and referent power are very personal. They are the result of an individual's personal expertise or style and, as such, are grounded in the person and not the organization.

These five types of interpersonal power are not independent of each other. On the contrary, a person can use these power sources effectively in various combinations. Some research has suggested, for example, that when subordi-

Case 10.1

Missouri Campus Bitterly
Divided over How to
Reallocate Funds

nates believe a manager's coercive power is increasing, they also perceive a drop in reward, referent, and legitimate power. Finally, different power sources are not always equally well received. Some types of power are more likely to engender positive responses than are others. Management Pointer 10.1 provides further information.

Structural Power

Power is frequently prescribed by structure within the organization. Structural sources of power result from the nature of the organizational social system rather than from attributes of an individual.[7] The structure of an organization is the control mechanism by which the organization is governed. In the organization's structural arrangements, decision-making discretion is allocated to various positions. Also, the structure greatly affects the patterns of communication and the flow of information within the system. Thus, organizational structure creates formal power and authority by specifying certain individuals to perform specific tasks and make certain decisions. Structure also significantly impacts informal power through its effect on information and communication flows within the system.

We have already discussed how formal position is associated with power and authority. Certain rights, responsibilities, and privileges accrue from a person's position. Other forms of structural power exist, however, because of resources, decision making, and information.[8]

Management Pointer 10.1

**SUBORDINATE RESPONSES
TO DIFFERENT POWER
SOURCES**

All things being equal, subordinates respond differently to different types of power. When using power, keep the following generalizations about the five sources of interpersonal power in mind:

1. The use of *legitimate* or *reward* power will typically result in compliance. Compliance means that subordinates will obey your requests, but are unlikely to exert more than the minimal effort necessary.

2. The use of *coercive* power may result in resistance. Resistance means that subordinates may only pretend to comply with your requests, and they may openly resist.

3. The use of *expert* or *referent* power frequently results in commitment. Commitment means subordinates are likely to exert high levels of effort to accomplish what you ask, perhaps even exceeding what you requested.

Remember these are general findings, and each situation is different. Nonetheless, this suggests that even when you have the authority (legitimate power) to order something done, an expert- or referent-based influence attempt is likely to achieve better results.

Resources

Kanter argues quite convincingly that power stems from (1) access to resources, information, and support, and (2) the ability to get cooperation in doing necessary work.[9] Power occurs when a person has open channels to resources—money, human resources, technology, materials, customers, and so on. In organizations, vital resources are allocated downward along the lines of the hierarchy. The top-level manager has more power to allocate resources than do other managers further down in the managerial hierarchy. The lower-level manager receives resources that are granted by top-level managers. In order to ensure compliance with goals, top-level managers (e.g., presidents, vice presidents, directors) allocate resources on the basis of performance and compliance. Thus, a top-level manager usually has power over a lower-level manager because the lower-level manager must receive resources from above to accomplish goals.

[7]Daniel J. Brass and Marlene E. Burkhardt, "Potential Power and Power Use: An Investigation of Structure and Behavior," *Academy of Management Journal*, June 1993, pp. 441–70.

[8]Jeffrey Pfeffer, "Understanding Power in Organizations," *California Management Review*, Winter 1992, pp. 29–50.

[9]Kanter, *op. cit.*

Decision-Making Power

The degree to which individuals or subunits (e.g., a department or a special project group) can affect decision making determines the amount of power acquired. A person or subunit with power can influence how the decision-making process occurs, what alternatives are considered, and when a decision is made.[10] For example, when Richard Daley was mayor of Chicago, he was recognized as a power broker. He not only influenced the decision-making process, but he also had the power to decide which decisions would be given priority in the city council and when decisions would be made. He was a powerful politician because he was considered to be an expert at controlling each step in important decisions. Another example of a power broker in action involves Hyundai's founder and chairman Chung Ju-Yung and his two sons (Organizational Encounter 10.2).

Information Power

Knowledge is considered by some experts to be more powerful than any part or structure of an organization. **Knowledge** is defined as a conclusion or analysis derived from data and information.[11] Data are facts, statistics, and specifics. Information is the context in which data are placed.

www.hmc.co.hc

www.wal-mart.com

www.nestle.com

www.fedex.com

Microsoft, Dell, Wal-Mart, Cisco Systems, Nestles, and Nortel did not become prominent, profitable companies because they were richer than Apple, General Foods, or Sears. They were able to utilize and leverage more effectively their intellectual capital. That is, these firms used the knowledge, information, experience, and creativity possessed by employees to gain a competitive advantage in their industries.

An excellent Federal Express television commercial illustrates how knowledge and information have become valued assets in organizations. In the commercial a ranting, scowling boss rushes into a room to reprimand an employee about a package that he has been informed has not arrived on time. A complaining customer triggered off the ranting. The boss continues blasting the employee as she taps on her computers keyboard. The employee finally announces that her screen shows the package arrived and was signed for at a specific time. All of the employee's colleagues cheer her result. She had knowledge and information that disputed the boss's ranting. Employees and customers at Federal Express were able to track the package to the minute. The tracking (information) provides the knowledge about when the package was delivered.[12]

www.kraftfoods.com

Having access to relevant and important knowledge information is power. Accountants generally do not have a particularly strong or apparent interpersonal power base in an organization. Rather, accountants have power because they control important information. Information is the basis for making effective decisions. Thus, those who possess information needed in order to make optimal decisions have power. The accountant's position in the organization structure may

---

[10]For an excellent discussion of structural and situationally oriented sources of power, see Don Hellriegal, John W. Slocum, Jr., and Richard W. Woodman, *Organizational Behavior* (St. Paul, MN: West Publishing, 2000), pp. 465–68.

[11]Thomas A. Stewart, *Intellectual Capital* (New York: Doubleday, 1997).

[12]Ibid.

Power Broker and Power Struggles at Hyundai

A family feud at Hyundai Group, the largest conglomerate in Korea, has ended in a victory for Chung Mong-Hun, who has been running Hyundai Electronics Industries and Hyundai Engineering & Construction.

Hyundai's founder and honorary chairman Chung Ju-Yung appointed Mong-Hun, his fifth son, as successor of the group, while Mong-Hun's elder brother Chung Mong-Koo runs the automotive unit of the group, which includes Hyundai Motors, Kia Motors, and Hyundai Precision.

However, the infighting between Chung's two sons over the control of the conglomerate has tarnished the image of the group. Observers say that Hyundai Group virtually is divided into two smaller conglomerates with the power struggle. Any compromise between Mong-Koo and Mong-Hun is unlikely, although the power struggle has been settled temporarily by the so-called king chairman, founder Chung Ju-Yung.

Observers say that the dispute is a prelude to a tragedy in the Hyundai family. In a worst-case scenario, a legal battle could take place after the death of the 85-year-old founder, some observers predict.

According to the restructuring plan the group submitted to the government and its creditor banks, Hyundai will separate from the automotive division during the first half of this year. That will be followed by weaning of the conglomerate's heavy industries division and the electronics division.

Chung's sixth son, Mong-Joon, will take over Hyundai Heavy Industries, while the electronics and financial units will be controlled by Mong-Hun, the official chairman of the group.

The fight between the two brothers was triggered by their struggle to control the financial units. It is unclear whether Mong-Hun will be able to control the financial businesses because there is enough time for Mong-Koo to recapture the attractive units before 2003, when they will separate from the group.

Some observers speculate that the king chairman intentionally has allowed the two sons to compete with each other for ownership of the financial businesses. Chung's physical condition is healthy enough for his age, but there is a growing presumption that something is wrong with his judgment. And that could drive the group into a critical situation. Hyundai's financial division is strong.

Until three or four years ago, the conglomerate's financial companies were second-string players. Now, Hyundai controls nine financial institutions, including Hyundai Securities, Hyundai Investment Trust & Securities, Hyundai Life Insurance, Hyundai Futures and Hyundai Technology Financing.

Hyundai Securities, Hyundai Investment & Securities, and Hyundai Finance Corporation are leaders in their respective fields. In addition, Hyundai Life Insurance is expanding its businesses in anticipation of the fierce competition among domestic insurers. Industry sources say that the ownership of the financial units will remain unclear until 2003.

New group chairman Mong-Hun's supporters include Hyundai Securities Chairman Lee Ik-Chi, Hyundai Engineering and Construction President Kim Yoon-Kyu, and Hyundai Group's restructuring team head, Kim Jae-Soo. All of them are former secretaries of honorary chairman Chung. Insiders say that Lee has played a decisive role in changing the balance of the group's control from Mong-Koo to Mong-Hun. On the other hand, Kim Yoon-Kyu is the man who controls Hyundai's North Korean economic cooperation project on behalf of Chung Ju-Yung.

In the midst of the battle between the two brothers, Hong-Hun, who has a 13.44 percent stake in Hyundai Merchant Marine, was not appointed as one of the company's directors. That is noteworthy because Hyundai Merchant Marine is the largest shareholder of Hyundai Securities with a 16.63 percent stake.

When inaugurated as chairman of Hyundai Group, Mong-Koo expressed his strong intention to build up the financial units. He might need the support of the financing units to propel Hyundai Motors into one of the world's top five automakers, his stated goal.

For this reason, there could be a second round of a showdown between Mong-Koo and Mong-Hun over ownership of the financial division. There is a possibility that the financial units will be operated independently by professional managers, while Mong-Koo runs the automotive units and Mong-Hun controls the construction and electronics businesses.

Anyway, it is certain that Hyundai's image will be spoiled further as long as such a power struggle continues. Observers say that the loss of the group's prestige will affect other family-owned chaebols such as Samsung, SK, and LG, and their positions are linked to the overall credit standing of Korea.

Source: Adapted from "Brother's Battle for Control Is Costly to Conglomerate," *Business Korea*, April 2000, pp. 12–13.

EXHIBIT 10.1   Symptoms and Sources of Powerlessness

Position	Symptoms	Sources
First-line supervisors (e.g., manager)	Supervise too closely; fail to train subordinates; not sufficiently oriented to the management team; inclined to do the job themselves	Routine, rule-minded jobs: limited lines of communication; limited advancement opportunities for themselves and their subordinates
Staff professionals (e.g., corporate lawyer, personnel/human resources specialist)	Create islands and set themselves up as experts; use professional standards as basis for judging work that distinguishes them from others; resist change and become conservative risk takers	Their routine tasks are only adjuncts to real line job; blocked career advancement replaced by outside consultants for nonroutine work
Top-level managers (e.g., chief executive officer, vice president)	Short-term horizon; top-down communication systems emphasized; reward followers to think like the manager, do not welcome bearers of bad news	Uncontrollable lines of supply; limited or blocked lines of information about lower managerial levels; diminished lines of support because of challenges to legitimacy

Source: Reprinted by permission of the *Harvard Business Review.* Adapted from "Power Failures in Management Circuits," by Rosabeth Moss Kanter (July–August 1979), p. 73. Copyright © 1979 by the President and Fellows of Harvard College; all rights reserved.

not accurately portray the amount of power that he or she wields. A true picture of a person's power is provided not only by the person's position but also by the person's access to relevant information.

A number of organizational situations can serve as the source of either power or powerlessness (not acquiring power). The powerful manager exists because he or she allocates required resources, makes crucial decisions, and has access to important information.[13] He or she is likely to make things happen. The powerless manager, however, lacks the resources, information, and decision-making prerogatives needed to be productive. Exhibit 10.1 presents some of the common symptoms and sources of powerlessness of first-line supervisors, staff professionals, and top-level managers. This exhibit indicates that a first-line manager, for example, may display a number of symptoms of powerlessness such as supervising very closely and not showing much concern about training or developing subordinates. If these symptoms persist, it is likely that the individual is powerless.

EMPOWERMENT

www.ci.nyc.us/html/nypd/home.html

The New York City police commissioner commands 44,000 armed men and women. By any definition it is a powerful position. During his two years in the job, William Bratton reduced crime in New York by an extraordinary 38 percent. He didn't accomplish that, however, because he had amassed a great deal of power; rather, he accomplished it because he gave a great deal of his power away by pushing decision-making authority far down the organizational hierarchy. He *empowered* officers at the precinct to take actions that previously could only be

---

[13]Anthony T. Cobb, "An Episodic Model of Power: Toward an Integration of Theory and Research," *Academy of Management Review,* July 1984, pp. 482–93.

Reading 10.1

Create an Empowering
Environment

done at the commissioner's office level.[14] **Empowerment** has been defined by Conger and Kanungo as "a process of enhancing feelings of self-efficacy among organizational members through the identification of conditions that foster powerlessness and through their removal by both formal organizational practices and informal techniques of providing efficacy information.[15]

Despite a commonsense appeal of empowering employees, there are a number of reasons that empowerment is not universally embraced, such as:

1. Managers fear the loss of power, control, and authority.
2. Employees are not able to make responsible decisions.
3. Empowering employees was attempted before and it failed.
4. Sharing proprietary information means leaking ideas, plans, and knowledge to competitors.
5. Not everyone wants to be empowered. Those resisting empowerment become isolates, misfits, and not team players in the minds and perceptions of advocates of empowerment.[16]

Despite the skepticism and resistance portrayed by the five reasons cited above, empowerment continues to be an attractive way to operate. The empowerment process is presented in a staged sequence within organizations. The first stage involves identifying the conditions existing in the organization that lead to feelings of powerlessness on the part of organizational members. These conditions could find their origin in organizational factors (such as poor communications or highly centralized resources), management styles (such as authoritarianism), reward systems (nonmerit-based rewards, low incentive value rewards), or the nature of the jobs (low task variety, unrealistic performance goals).

Exercise 10.1

Empowerment Profile

The diagnoses completed in the first stage lead to the implementation of empowerment strategies and techniques in the second stage. Use of participative management, establishing goal-setting programs, implementing merit-based pay systems, and job enrichment through redesign are examples of possible empowerment activities. The use of these programs is designed to accomplish two objectives in the third stage. One is simply to remove the conditions identified in the first stage as contributing to powerlessness. The second, and more important, is to provide self-efficacy information to subordinates. Self-efficacy describes a belief in one's effectiveness. Individuals high in self-efficacy tend to be confident and self-assured and feel they are likely to be successful in whatever endeavors they undertake.

Receiving such information results in feelings of empowerment in the fourth stage. This is because increasing self-efficacy strengthens effort-performance expectancies. You will recall from the discussion of expectancy theory in Chapter 4 that this means increasing the perceived probability of successful performance, given effort. Finally, the enhanced empowerment feelings from stage four are translated into behaviors in the fifth and final stage. These behavioral consequences of empowerment include increased activity directed toward task accomplishment.

---

[14]Thomas A. Stewart, "Get with the New Power Game," *Fortune,* January 13, 1997, pp. 58–62.

[15]J. A. Conger and R. N. Kanungo, "The Empowerment Process: Integrating Theory and Practice," *Academy of Management Review,* July 1988, p. 474.

[16]Eileen Brownell, "Empowerment, the Key to Exceptional Service," *American Salesman,* August 2000, pp. 20–24.

Thus, by helping organizational members feel more assured of their capability to perform well, and by increasing the linkages between effort and performance, empowerment can lead to what has been described as a "culture of contribution."[17] Such a culture can be found, for example, in Newfield Exploration, a New York Stock Exchange–listed oil and gas exploration company, where there are only two levels of management in the entire company. Because each employee has critical decision-making authority, everyone understands that the success of the company is in large measure dependent on the contribution they make. The company's success, in turn, directly affects the employees, since each employee is also an owner.

www.nyse.com

As we have already noted in previous chapters, organizations are increasingly relying on a variety of team structures to complete many work tasks. One of the benefits of team approaches is the increased empowerment of team members. In the case of self-managed teams, for example, empowerment is fostered in at least two ways. First, additional formal decision-making control is delegated to the team. This empowers the team to make decisions and take actions that previously were reserved for—or at least required the approval of—a higher level. Second, because team members usually have broader responsibilities, they acquire additional skills, knowledge, and experiences. This increased expertise makes them more valuable to the organization, effectively increasing their influence.

When Chrysler Corporation brought its new, inexpensive Neon model to the market a few years ago, it was one of the most successful new-model introductions in years. A key factor in that success was Chrysler's decision to combine all of the disciplines needed to bring a new car to market in one location. Their "small-car platform team" comprised designers, engineers, purchasing personnel, plant assembly-line workers, and external suppliers. The team was empowered by having available the broad range of different knowledge and perspectives present among the various team members. It was in a position to make higher-quality decisions more rapidly than typically had been possible. The Neon was launched at a cost of $1.3 billion, compared to a typical new-model introduction cost of $3 billion. Clearly, Chrysler's decision to empower employees involved in the start-up process paid large dividends. Management Pointer 10.2 provides some suggestions for successfully empowering subordinates.[18]

Management Pointer 10.2

INCREASING YOUR EFFECTIVENESS IN EMPOWERING OTHERS

1. When you delegate responsibility, make certain you are also delegating authority to go along with it.

2. Be prepared to give up your managerial "parent" role and assume a "partner" role.

3. Assure your subordinates through words and deeds that it is OK to make mistakes.

4. Information sharing is important. Empowered employees must have sufficient information to be able to see the "big picture."

5. Provide training opportunities so employees can develop skills to successfully perform new job responsibilities.

6. Performance feedback is always important; it is particularly important for newly empowered employees. Feedback enhances learning and can provide needed assurance that the job is being mastered.

INTERDEPARTMENTAL POWER

The primary focus to this point has been on individual power and how it is obtained. However, it is also important to consider subunit or interdepartmental power. Subunit power is the focus of the strategic contingency theory developed by Hickson. A **strategic contingency** is an event that is extremely important for

---

[17]James R. Fisher, Jr., "A Culture of Contribution," *Executive Excellence,* January 1997, p. 16.

[18]Thomas W. Malone, "Is Empowerment Just a Fad? Control, Decision Making, and IT," *Sloan Management Review,* Winter 1997, pp. 23–35.

accomplishing organizational goals.[19] Crozier, a French sociologist, provided insight into the idea of strategic contingencies. He studied the relationships between workers in the production and maintenance departments of French tobacco-processing plants. Crozier found that the production workers enjoyed job security because of tenure, were protected against unfair disciplinary action, and were not replaced or transferred arbitrarily. The production workers were less skilled than the maintenance workers. The maintenance workers were highly skilled and were recruited and selected only after going through a rigorous screening process.

The production workers were dependent on the maintenance workers. This power differential was explained in terms of the control exercised by the maintenance workers over an important contingency. If machines were shut down, the entire plant came to a halt. Efficiently functioning machines were needed to accomplish output goals. Since the maintenance workers, at the request of the production workers, repaired machines that were down, they possessed significant power.

When machines were down, the job performance of the production workers suffered. Stoppages totally disrupted the workflow and the output of the production workers. Crozier proposed that the maintenance workers controlled a strategically contingent factor in the production process. Crozier's study provided clear evidence of subunit power differences. The study also stimulated other studies that eventually resulted in a strategic contingencies explanation of power differences.[20]

Using the work of Crozier and Hickson and his associates, it is possible to develop a concise explanation of strategic contingencies. The model presented in Exhibit 10.2 suggests that subunit power, the power differential between subunits, is influenced by (1) the degree of ability to cope with uncertainty, (2) the centrality of the subunit, and (3) the substitutability of the subunit.

Coping with Uncertainty

Unanticipated events can create problems for any organization or subunit. It is, therefore, the subunits most capable of coping with uncertainty that typically acquire power. There are three types of coping activities. First is *coping by prevention*. Here a subunit works at reducing the probability that some difficulty will arise. One example of a coping technique is designing a new product to prevent lost sales because of new competition in the marketplace.

Second is *coping by information*. The use of forecasting is an example. Possessing timely forecasting information enables a subunit to deal with such events as competition, strikes, shortages of materials, and consumer demand shifts. Planning departments conducting forecasting studies acquire power when their predictions prove accurate.

---

[19]Michael Crozier, *The Bureaucratic Phenomenon* (Chicago: University of Chicago Press, 1964).

[20]It should be noted the strategic contingency theory was developed by D. J. Hickson and his colleagues. Other theorists and researchers have modified and discussed this approach. However, the reader is urged to use the original sources for a discussion of the complete and unmodified theory. See D. J. Hickson, C. R. Hinnings, C. A. Lee, R. E. Schneck and J. M. Pennings, "A Strategic Contingency Theory of Intraorganizational Power," *Administrative Science Quarterly,* June 1971, pp. 216 29; and C. R. Hinnings, D. J. Hickson, J. M. Pennings, and R. E. Schneck, "Structural Conditions of Intraorganizational Power," *Administrative Science Quarterly,* March 1974, pp. 22–44.

EXHIBIT 10.2
A Strategic
Contingency Model
of Subunit Power

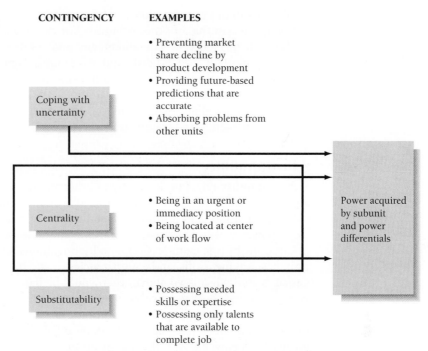

CONTINGENCY

Coping with uncertainty

EXAMPLES

• Preventing market share decline by product development
• Providing future-based predictions that are accurate
• Absorbing problems from other units

Centrality

• Being in an urgent or immediacy position
• Being located at center of work flow

Substitutability

• Possessing needed skills or expertise
• Possessing only talents that are available to complete job

Power acquired by subunit and power differentials

This figure is based on the detailed research work conducted by D. J. Hickson, C. R. Hinnings, C. A. Lee, R. E. Schneck, and J. M. Pennings, "A Strategic Contingency Theory of Intraorganizational Power," *Administrative Science Quarterly,* June 1971, pp. 216–29; and C. R. Hinnings, D. J. Hickson, J. M. Pennings, and R. E. Schneck, "Structural Conditions of Intraorganizational Power," *Administrative Science Quarterly,* March 1974, pp. 22–44.

Third is *coping by absorption.* This coping approach involves dealing with uncertainty as it impacts the subunit. For example, one subunit might take a problem employee from another subunit and attempt to retrain and redirect that employee. This is done as a favor so that the other subunit will not have to go through the pain of terminating or continuing to put up with the employee. The subunit that takes in the problem employee gains the respect of other subunits, which results in an increase in power.

The relation of coping with uncertainty to power was expressed by Hickson as follows: "The more a subunit copes with uncertainty, the greater its power within the organization."[21]

Centrality

The findings of a number of research studies strongly suggest that centrality can be a significant source of subunit power.[22] The subunits that are most central to the flow of work in an organization typically acquire power. No subunit has zero centrality since all subunits are somehow interlinked with other subunits. A measure of centrality is the degree to which the work of the subunit contributes to the final output of the organization. Since a subunit is in a position to affect other subunits, it has some degree of centrality and therefore power.

[21]Hickson, et al., "Strategic Contingency Theory."

[22]Herminia Ibarra, "Network Centrality, Power, and Innovation Involvement: Determinants of Technical and Administrative Roles," *Academy of Management Journal,* June 1993, pp. 471–501.

Also, a subunit possesses power if its activities have a more immediate or urgent impact than that of other subunits. For example, Ben Taub is a major public hospital in Houston. The emergency and trauma treatment subunit is extremely important and crucial, and it contains significant power within the hospital. Failures in this subunit could result in the death of emergency victims. On the other hand, the psychiatric subunit does important work but not of the crucial and immediate type. Therefore, it has significantly less subunit power than the emergency and trauma treatment subunit.

Substitutability

Substitutability refers to the ability of other subunits to perform the activities of a particular subunit. If an organization has or can obtain alternative sources of skill, information, and resources to perform the job done by a subunit, the subunit's power will be diminished. Training subunits lose power if training work can be done by line managers or outside consultants. On the other hand, if a subunit has unique skills and competencies (e.g., the maintenance workers in Crozier's study discussed above) that would be hard to duplicate or replace, this would tend to increase the subunit's power over other subunits.

Hickson, et al., capture the importance of substitutability power when they propose that the lower the substitutability of the activities of a subunit, the greater is its power within the organization.[23]

THE ILLUSION OF POWER

Admittedly, some individuals and subunits have vast amounts of power to get others to do things the way they want them done. However, there are also illusions of power. Imagine that one afternoon your supervisor asks you to step into his office. He starts the meeting: "You know we're really losing money using that Beal stamping machine. I'd like you to do a job for the company. I want you to destroy the machine and make it look like an accident." Would you comply with this request? After all, this is your supervisor, and he is in charge of everything—your pay, your promotion opportunities, your job assignments. You might ask yourself, "Does my supervisor have this much power over me?"

Where a person or subunit's power starts and stops is difficult to pinpoint. You might assume that the supervisor in the hypothetical example has the specific power to get someone to do this unethical and illegal "dirty work." However, even individuals who seemingly possess only a little power can influence others. A series of studies conducted by Milgram focused on the illusion of power. In these studies, subjects who had been voluntarily recruited thought they were administering electrical shocks of varying intensity to other subjects.[24] Ostensibly the experiment was designed to study the effects of punishment on learning. In reality, the studies focused on obedience to authority. Exhibit 10.3 displays the surprising results.

---

[23]Ibid., p. 40.

[24]S. Milgram, "Behavioral Study of Obedience," *Journal of Abnormal and Social Psychology*, October 1963, pp. 371–78; and S. Milgram, *Obedience to Authority* (New York: Harper & Row, 1974).

EXHIBIT 10.3
Results of Milgram's Classic Experiment on Obedience

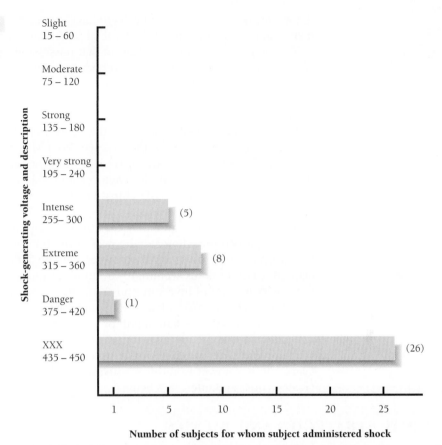

Source: Based on descriptions and data presented in S. Milgram, "Behavioral Study of Obedience," *Journal of Abnormal and Social Psychology,* October 1963, pp. 371–78.

At the experimenter's direction, 26 of 40 subjects, or 65 percent, continued to increase the intensity of the shocks they thought they were administering to another person all the way to the maximum voltage. This was in spite of the fact that the control panel indicated increasing voltage dosages as "intense," "extreme," "danger," and "severe shock." Additionally, screams could be heard coming from the booth, and the subject allegedly receiving the shock begged the experimenter to stop the project. In spite of this, and even though the subjects were uncomfortable administering the shocks, they continued. Milgram stated:

> I observed a mature and initially poised businessman enter the laboratory, smiling and confident; within 20 minutes he was reduced to a twitching, stuttering wreck, who was rapidly approaching a point of nervous collapse . . . yet he continued to respond to every word of the experimenter and obeyed to the end.[25]

Why did the subjects obey the experimenter? Although the experimenter possessed no specific power over the subjects, he appeared to be a powerful person. He created an illusion of power. The experimenter, dressed in a white lab coat, was addressed by others as "doctor" and was very stern. The subjects perceived

[25]Milgram, "Behavioral Study of Obedience," p. 377.

the experimenter as possessing legitimacy to conduct the study. The experimenter apparently did an excellent job of projecting the illusion of having power.

The Milgram experiments indicate that possessing power in a legitimate way is not the only way power can be exerted. Individuals who are perceived to have power may also be able to significantly influence others. Power is often exerted by individuals who have only minimum or no actual power. The "eye of the beholder" plays an important role in the exercise of power.

www.netscape.com

www.sgi.co

Jim Clark has created almost a cultlike power of illusion in Silicon Valley. His ideas and his involvement with Netscape, Web MD, and Silicon Graphics have helped reshape entire industries. He was the idea person behind each of these three companies. For example, engineer and Stanford professor Jim Clark at Silicon Graphics invented 3-D chips which gave the firm a technological lead over other makers of high-priced workstations.[26] The chips allowed for the creation of the digital dinosaurs in the Oscar-winning hit movie *Jurassic Park*.

Clark grasped the commercial power of the Internet ahead of other geniuses. Few people had heard of a Web browser, which Clark's firm Netscape commercialized. Clark took his seemingly far out ideas and has converted them into billions, making a lot of investors and employees very wealthy. His commercialization of ideas has created a halo aura about Clark. The illusion is that he has the midas touch. A closer examination of Clark's history and background illustrates a mystique and some myth surround Jim Clark. The financial records of Clark's start-ups and ideas over a period of time show some fading out and trouble. Yet, Clark still has power to influence investors. The mention of his name in a deal creates a buzz and interest in being a part of the next Jim Clark idea and business.

POLITICAL STRATEGIES AND TACTICS

Individuals and subunits continually engage in politically oriented behavior.[27] By politically oriented behavior we mean a number of things:

Exercise 10.2

How Political Are You?

1. Behavior that usually is outside the legitimate, recognized power system
2. Behavior that is designed to benefit an individual or subunit, often at the expense of the organization in general
3. Behavior that is intentional and is designed to acquire and maintain power

As a result of politically oriented behaviors, the formal power that exists in an organization often is sidetracked or blocked. In the language of organizational theory, political behavior results in the displacement of power.

Research on Politics

A number of studies have been conducted to explore political behavior and perceptions in organizations. A study of 142 purchasing agents examined their political behavior. The job objective of the purchasing agents was to negotiate and fill orders in a timely manner. However, the purchasing agents also viewed their jobs as being a crucial link with the environment—competition, price changes,

[26]Ralph King, "Do You Believe in Jim Clark?" www.ecompany.com, December 2000, pp. 123–30.

[27]Russel Cropanzano, John Hughes, Alicia Grandey, and Paul Toth, "The Relationship of Organizational Politics and Support to Work Behaviors, Attitudes, and Stress," *Journal of Organizational Behavior,* March 1997, pp. 159–80.

market shifts.[28] Thus, the purchasing agents considered themselves information processors. The vital link of the purchasing agents with the external environment placed them in conflict with the engineering department. As a result of the conflict, attempts to influence the engineering subunit were a regular occurrence.

A variety of political tactics used by the purchasing agents were discovered in this study. They included:

1. *Rule evasion.* Evading the formal purchase procedures in the organization
2. *Personal-political.* Using friendships to facilitate or inhibit the processing of an order
3. *Educational.* Attempting to persuade engineering to think in purchasing terms
4. *Organizational.* Attempting to change the formal or informal interaction patterns between engineering and purchasing

These political tactics, used by the purchasing agents to accomplish their goals, (1) were outside the legitimate power system, (2) occasionally benefited the purchasing agent at the expense of the rest of the organization, and (3) were intentionally developed so that more power was acquired by the purchasing agent.

Another study of political behavior was conducted in the electronics industry in southern California. A total of 87 managers (30 chief executive officers, 28 higher-level staff managers, and 29 supervisors) were interviewed and asked about a number of aspects of organizational political behavior.[29] Among other questions, the managers were asked to describe the personal characteristics of organizational members who were effective "politicians." These characteristics are presented in Exhibit 10.4, along with the percentage of each group of managers who thought the characteristic was associated with effective political behavior.

A total of 13 characteristics were identified as being important, headed by articulateness, sensitivity, and social adeptness. As Exhibit 10.4 shows, there was a fairly high level of agreement between the three levels of managers on what characteristics were regarded as important. There were, however, some exceptions. For example, supervisors saw *ambitiousness* as being far less-often associated with effective political behavior (4 percent) than did CEOs (20 percent) and staff managers (25 percent). On the other hand, many more staff managers (21 percent) than CEOs (3 percent) or supervisors (7 percent) thought being *logical* was characteristic of effective political players. It is probably reasonable to conclude that some of the differences between the groups were attributable to different perspectives. It is also probably the case that different political behaviors were used at different levels within the organization.

Playing Politics

The managers in the study described above were aware of political behavior because it was a part of their organizational experiences. As the researchers noted, the study was not designed to either praise or criticize organizational political behavior. Instead, it was intended to show that politics is a fact of organizational

---

[28]George Strauss, "Tactics of the Lateral Relationship: The Purchasing Agent," *Administrative Science Quarterly,* 1962, pp. 161–86.

[29]Robert W. Allen, Dan L. Madison, Lyman W. Porter, Patricia A. Renwick, and Bronston T. Mayes, "Organizational Politics: Tactics and Characteristics of Its Actors," *California Management Review,* 1979, pp. 77–83.

EXHIBIT 10.4   Personal Characteristics of Effective Organizational Politicians

Personal Characteristics	Combined Groups	Chief Executive Officers	Staff Managers	Supervisors
Articulate	30%	37%	39%	13%
Sensitive	30	50	21	17
Socially adept	20	10	32	17
Competent	17	10	21	21
Popular	17	17	11	24
Extroverted	16	17	14	17
Self-confident	16	10	21	17
Aggressive	16	10	14	24
Ambitious	16	20	25	4
Devious	16	13	14	21
Organization person	13	20	4	14
Highly intelligent	12	20	11	3
Logical	10	3	21	7

Source: Adapted from R. W. Allen, D. L. Madison, L. W. Porter, P. A. Renwick, and B. T. Mayers, "Organizational Politics: Tactics and Characteristics of Its Actors," *California Management Review,* December 1979, p. 78.

life. Politics and political behavior exist in every organization. In this section, we will briefly examine a couple of different ways that the study of political behavior, or "playing politics," has been approached in organizations. We will close the section with a look at one specific political strategy that is receiving a great deal of attention currently, *impression management.*

Game Playing

Political behavior in organizations has been described by many researchers in terms of game playing. Henry Mintzberg has identified 13 types of political games played in organizations.[30] These games, played at all organizational levels by both managers and nonmanagers, are intended to accomplish a variety of purposes. Games are played to (1) resist authority (the insurgency game), (2) counter the resistance to authority (the counterinsurgency game), (3) build power bases (the sponsorship game and coalition-building game), (4) defeat rivals (the line-versus-staff game), and bring about organizational change (the whistle-blowing game).

Let's look at one of Mintzberg's games. The insurgency game is played to resist authority, and there are many different ways to play it. For example, suppose that a plant foreman is instructed to reprimand a particular worker for violating company policies. The reprimand can be delivered according to the foreman's feelings and opinions about its worth and legitimacy. If the reprimand is delivered in a half-hearted manner, accompanied by a sly wink, it will probably have an effect very different from what was expected. Insurgency in the form of not delivering

---

[30]This discussion of games relies on the presentation in Henry Mintzberg, *Power in and around Organizations* (Englewood Cliffs, NJ: Prentice Hall, 1983), chap. 13, pp. 171–271. Please refer to this source for a complete and interesting discussion of political games.

the reprimand as expected by a higher authority would be difficult for that authority to detect and correct. Technically, the foreman followed orders. Practically, however, he resisted those orders.

Insurgency, along with the rest of Mintzberg's games, is practiced in all organizations. Games are played within and between subunits, and they are played by individuals who are sometimes representing themselves and sometimes representing their units. It is unrealistic to assume that game playing can be eliminated. Even in the most efficient, profitable, productive, and responsible organizations, political games are being played.

Political Influence Tactics

Influence is what playing politics is all about. Individuals and groups engage in political behavior in order to influence the perceptions or behaviors of other individuals and groups. Accordingly, the means or tactics used to accomplish this have been the focus of much research. One particularly interesting approach has been refined over a period of many studies by several different researchers.[31] This research stream has identified nine specific tactics used by individuals to influence their superiors, coworkers, and subordinates to do what they wanted them to do. These tactics are:

1. *Consultation.* Used to gain your support for a course of action by letting you participate in the planning for the action
2. *Rational persuasion.* Used to convince you that a particular course of action is "logically" the best course because it is in your best interest
3. *Inspirational appeals.* Used to gain support by appealing to your values or ideals, or by increasing your confidence that the desired course of action will be successful
4. *Ingratiating tactics.* Used to create a sense of obligation because someone is doing something nice for you. Designed to make it difficult for you not to support the course of action desired by the ingratiator
5. *Coalition tactics.* Used to gain your support by seeking the help of others to persuade you, or by using the support of others as an argument for you to also give your support
6. *Pressure tactics.* The use of demands, intimidation, or threats to gain your support for a particular course of action
7. *Legitimating.* Used to gain your support by claiming the authority to ask for your support, or by claiming that such support is consistent with organizational policies or rules
8. *Personal appeals.* Used to appeal to your feelings of loyalty and friendship in order to gain your support

---

[31]See, for example, David Kipnis, Stuart Schmidt, and Ian Wikinson, "Interorganizational Influence Tactics: Explorations in Getting One's Way," *Journal of Applied Psychology,* August 1980, pp. 440–52; Gary Yukl and Cecilia Falbe, "Influence Tactics and Objectives in Upward, Downward, and Lateral Influence Attempts," *Journal of Applied Psychology,* April 1990, pp. 132–40; Cecilia Falbe and Gary Yukl, "Consequences for Managers of Using Single Influence Tactics and Combinations of Tactics," *Academy of Management Journal,* April 1992, pp. 638–52; and Gary Yukl, Patricia Guinan, and Debra Scottolano, "Influence Tactics Used for Different Objectives with Subordinates, Peers, and Superiors," *Group and Organizational Management,* September 1995, pp. 272–96.

EXHIBIT 10.5   Frequency of Outcomes for the Use of Political Influence Tactics

Influence Tactic	Outcomes		
	Resistance	Compliance	Commitment
1. Consultation	18%	27%	55%
2. Rational persuasion	47	30	23
3. Inspiration	O	10	90
4. Ingratiation	41	28	31
5. Coalition	53	44	3
6. Pressure	56	41	3
7. Legitimating	44	56	0
8. Personal appeals	25	33	42
9. Exchange	24	41	35

Source: Adapted from Cecilia M. Falbe and Gary Yukl, "Consequences for Managers of Using Single Influence Tactics and Combinations of Tactics," *Academy of Management Journal,* August 1992, p. 647.

9. *Exchange tactics.* Used to gain your support by the promise that you will receive a reward or benefit if you comply, or by reminding you of prior favors which you must now reciprocate

Not all of these tactics are necessarily equally effective in bringing about desired results. Exhibit 10.5 shows the results found in one study where the effectiveness of each tactic was assessed. Over 500 cases involving the use of influence tactics were analyzed in terms of leading to one of three outcomes:

1. **Commitment** results when you agree internally with the decision, action, or request, are enthusiastic about it, and are likely to exert unusual effort to carry out the request.

2. **Compliance** occurs when you carry out the request but are apathetic about it and make only a minimal effort to do it.

3. **Resistance** results when you are opposed to the request and try to avoid doing it.[32]

As can be seen from the exhibit, inspirational appeals and consultation were more effective than the rest of the tactics, with inspiration resulting in commitment 90 percent of the time it was used. On the other hand, legitimating, coalition, and pressure were less effective than the other tactics. It is important to keep in mind that variables other than the type of influence tactic used can impact the success of the influence attempt. Even the use of a tactic such as pressure can sometimes result in commitment. Likewise, any tactic may result in resistance if it is used in an unskillful manner or if the request being made is clearly objectionable.[33]

[32]Falbe and Yukl, "Consequences for Managers," pp. 645–46.

[33]For additional discussion of the effectiveness of various tactics, see Steven M. Farmer, John M. Maslyn, Donald B. Dedor, and Jodi S. Goodman, "Putting Upward Influence Strategies in Context," *Journal of Organizational Behavior,* January 1997, pp. 17–42.

Impression Management

Impression management refers to the actions individuals take to control the impressions that others form of them.[34] Impression management is universal. Employers do it, as do employees; students do it with professors and professors do it with students; parents and children do it with each other. Research suggests that a significant part of behavior in organizations is motivated by the desire of organization members to be perceived by others in certain ways.[35] Virtually everyone makes a deliberate effort in some situations to create a desirable impression. Some of the political influence tactics discussed in the previous section represent attempts at impression management. Consultation, for example, is used to create the impression that you are participative and that you want, value, and respect input from the person you are trying to influence. Ingratiation is designed to project an impression of you as a nice, thoughtful, or friendly person.

Impression management has only fairly recently gained the attention of organizational researchers. Because of its universality, however, it is an important area. Effective impression management can be quite useful. An obvious example is the employment interview. It could be argued, in fact, that at no time is successful impression management more important; if you fail to create a favorable impression, you are not likely to be offered the job!

It should be noted that impression management does not necessarily imply that a *false* impression is being conveyed. Clearly, some impressions are designed to mislead. Creating blatantly false impressions, however, can be costly in terms of damage to your credibility and reputation.

Many impression-management tactics are designed to emphasize the positive. Self-promotion, such as acclaiming your accomplishments, is an example. Flattering others is another example. Other impression-management tactics may be aimed at reducing negatives. Providing an excuse for why you made a mistake, for example, may be designed to further the impression that the error was beyond your control. Or simply admitting responsibility for the mistake may be designed to demonstrate willingness to take responsibility. When Attorney General Janet Reno accepted responsibility for the decision to launch the disastrous raid on the Branch Davidian complex in Waco, Texas, her stock soared because the public found it refreshing that someone in Washington was taking responsibility instead of blaming somebody else.

One very effective impression-management technique, self-handicapping, is designed to make the best of an as yet undetermined outcome. **Self-handicapping** refers to any action taken in advance of an outcome that is designed to provide either an excuse for failure or a credit for success. A self-handicap provides a persuasive causal explanation for potential failure, while setting the stage for the individual to receive more credit for success than would otherwise be the case.[36] For example, a quarterback who lets everyone know about his sore arm is not expected to have a good game. If in fact he does poorly, everyone attributes it to his

---

[34]M. R. Leary and R. M. Kowalski, "Impression Management: A Literature Review and Two-Component Model," *Psychological Bulletin,* January 1990, pp. 34–47.

[35]Dennis P. Bozeman and Michele K. Kacmar, "A Cybernetic Model of Impression Management Processes in Organizations," *Organizational Behavior & Human Decision Processes,* January 1997, pp. 9–30.

[36]J. Michael Crant and Thomas S. Bateman, "Assignment of Credit and Blame for Performance Outcomes," *Academy of Management Journal,* February 1993, pp. 7–27.

sore arm rather than his ability or lack of effort; if he does well, he did so in spite of his handicap, suggesting truly extraordinary ability or effort. The employee who reports being up all night with a sick child the day of a scheduled presentation to management is another example. If the presentation goes poorly, there is a reason beyond the employee's reasonable control; if it goes well, the employee excelled under adverse conditions.

ETHICS, POWER, AND POLITICS

Issues of power and politics often involve ethical issues as well. For example, if power is used within the formal boundaries of a manager's authority and within the framework of organizational policies, job description, procedures, and goals, it is really nonpolitical power and most likely does not involve ethical issues. When the use of power is outside the bounds of formal authority, policies, procedures, job descriptions, and organizational goals, it is political in nature. When this occurs, ethical issues are likely to be present. Some examples might include bribing government officials, lying to employees and customers, polluting the environment, and a general "ends justify the means" mentality. You Be the Judge describes a situation in which a possible invasion-of-privacy issue arose from the use of power.

Managers confront ethical dilemmas in their jobs because they frequently use power and politics to accomplish their goals. Each manager, therefore, has an ethical responsibility. Researchers have developed a framework that allows a manager to integrate ethics into political behavior. These researchers recommend that a manager's behavior must satisfy certain criteria to be considered ethical.[37]

1. *Criterion of utilitarian outcomes.* The manager's behavior results in optimization of satisfaction of people inside and outside the organization. In other words, it results in the greatest good for the greatest number of people.
2. *Criterion of individual rights.* The manager's behavior respects the rights of all affected parties. In other words, it respects basic human rights of free consent, free speech, freedom of conscience, privacy, and due process.
3. *Criterion of distributive justice.* The manager's behavior respects the rules of justice. It does not treat people arbitrarily but rather equitably and fairly.

What does a manager do when a potential behavior cannot pass the three criteria? The behavior may still be considered ethical in the particular situation if it passes the *criterion of overwhelming factors.* To justify the behavior, it must be based on the tremendously overwhelming factors in the nature of the situation, such as conflicts among criteria (e.g., the manager's behavior yields both positive and negative results), conflicts within the criteria (e.g., a manager uses questionable means to achieve a positive result), or an inability to employ the first three criteria (e.g., the manager acts with incomplete or inaccurate information.) Ethics Encounter 10.1 presents a decision-tree approach to the application of these criteria.

In closing this section it should be noted that with the previously discussed increased emphasis on empowerment, ethical issues are even more prevalent. In an empowered organization where decisions are forced down to the lowest levels,

---

[37]G. E. Cavanagh, D. J. Moberg, and M. Velasquez, "The Ethics of Organizational Politics," *Academy of Management Review,* July 1981, pp. 363–74; and M. Velasquez, D. J. Moberg, and G. F. Cavanagh, "Organizational Statesmanship and Dirty Politics: Ethical Guidelines for the Organizational Politician," *Organizational Dynamics,* Autumn 1983, pp. 65–79.

Is Continuous Video Surveillance of Employees an Abuse of Management's Power?

You Be the Judge

Imagine that a permanent videotape record is made of every single move you make in your work area during the course of a day. Not a second elapses when the camera is not filming. In addition to your work activities, every yawn, every scratch, every facial expression is recorded. You cannot turn your back to the camera, because there are multiple cameras recording from each direction. If this happened to you, would you feel that management had gone too far? That your privacy was being invaded?

To a number of employees of the Puerto Rico Telephone Company (PRTC) the answer to these questions was yes. PRTC maintains a communication center where employees monitor computer banks to detect signals emanating from alarm systems at PRTC facilities throughout Puerto Rico. They then alert appropriate authorities if an alarm sounds. The work area is completely open, and no employee has an assigned office, cubicle, workstation, or desk. Four cameras continually record the activities in the work area. The surveillance is visual; the cameras have no microphones.

The company maintained the surveillance system was desirable for security reasons. The unhappy employees concede that they should expect to be under a supervisor's watchful eyes while at work. But at some point, they argued, surveillance becomes unreasonable. They argue that when surveillance is electronic it is unremitting because the camera, unlike the human eye, never blinks, PRTC employees sued the company, maintaining their right to reasonable privacy had been violated by management's overzealous exercise of power. Were they right? You be the judge!

employees need to understand the importance of being constantly aware of the ethical implications of what they do.[38] Many companies are instituting ethics training programs to assist newly empowered employees in making ethical decisions. Texas Instruments, for example, uses interactive case studies to educate employees about the company's ethics code. In addition they publish a series of booklets, each one covering a single ethics topic. They have booklets covering personal rights, gifts, travel and entertainment, and conducting business with the U.S. government. An online ethics newspaper provides Texas Instruments employees with further reinforcement.[39]

USING POWER TO MANAGE EFFECTIVELY

Nothing gets done in any organization until someone makes it happen. Making the right things happen is what a manager's job is all about.[40] To be effective a manager must successfully influence the activities of other organizational members. As we pointed out at the start of this chapter, influence requires the exercise of power. To influence successfully, power must be used effectively. Organizational theorist and researcher Jeffrey Pfeffer has identified several considerations that are important in using power to manage effectively. We close this chapter with a look at Pfeffer's conclusions in this regard.[41]

---

[38]Suzy Wetluufer, "Organizing for Empowerment: An Interview with AES's Roger Sant and Dennis Bakke," *Harvard Business Review,* January–February 1999, pp. 110–23.

[39]Gillian Flynn, "Make Employee Ethics Your Business," *Personnel Journal,* June 1995, pp. 30–41.

[40]Christopher L. Tyner, "Technitrol's James Papada," *Investor's Business Daily,* September 7, 2000, p. A4.

[41]Jeffrey Pfeffer, *Managing with Power* (Boston: Harvard Business School Press, 1992). This section is based primarily on pp. 337–45.

Using an Ethical Decision Tree

Political behavior is pervasive. As the text indicates, such behavior is inherently neither good nor bad. In determining whether a particular choice of behaviors is ethical or unethical, based on the criteria discussed in the text, a manager might find the following decision tree useful.

Application of this decision tree approach is certainly not a panacea. There may be situations in which one or more of these criteria cannot be employed or in which there is a conflict among criteria. Making the ethically correct political behavior choice is neither always easy nor possible. However, models such as this one can be of assistance to managers in their decision making.

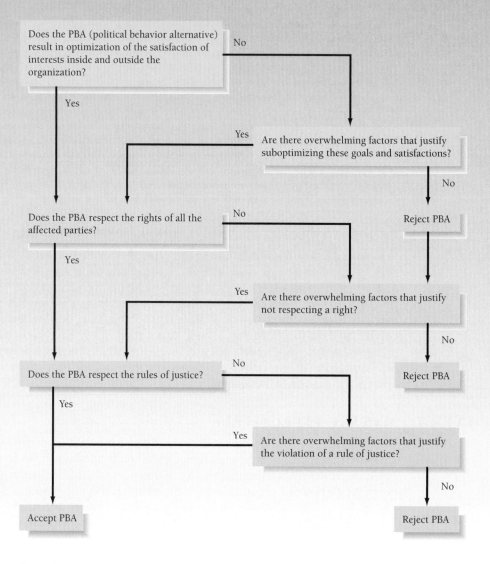

Source: Adapted from G. F. Cavanagh, D. J. Moberg, and M. Valesquez, "The Ethics of Organizational Politics," *Academy of Management Review*, July 1981, p. 368.

Recognize that there are multiple interests in virtually every organization. Not everyone has the same interests, and not everyone's interests are necessarily compatible with yours. It is important to understand the organization's political landscape by knowing what interests exist and to whom they belong.

Know what position relevant individuals and groups hold with respect to issues important to you. When this perspective is different than yours it is also important to understand the basis for the difference. It is much easier to influence those who agree with us than it is to affect the behavior of those who do not. Knowing why someone's perspective is different from yours makes the task of exercising influence easier. Understanding why subordinates dislike a new incentive pay plan, for example, affords you a better opportunity to diagnose how they are likely to respond to different attempts you might make to selling them on its merits.

Understand that to get things done you must have power, and in the case of those who oppose you, you must have more power than they do. This means it is essential that you know where power comes from and how these sources of power can be nurtured. It is important to recognize that there is nothing wrong with the acquisition and use of power if it is done in a professional and ethical manner. However effective you are as a manager, increasing your influence will further increase your effectiveness.

Finally, *recognize the strategies and tactics through which organizational power is developed and used.* This includes understanding the importance of timing, the use of the organization's structure, and the various forms of interpersonal power. As Pfeffer concludes, "We need to understand strategies and tactics of using power so that we can consider the range of approaches available to us, and use what is likely to be effective."[42]

An organizational member does not have to be in a formal leadership position to possess or use power. Having and using power, however, is an integral part of leadership. Now that we have examined the relevant aspects of power, in the next two chapters we turn to the all-important topic of leadership.

---

[42]Ibid, p. 341.

Summary of Key Points

- Power is the capability one party has to affect the actions of another party. Influence is a transaction in which one party induces another party to behave in a certain way. Another way of making the distinction is to think of power as the potential to influence, and influence as power in action.

- French and Raven introduced the notion of five interpersonal power bases: legitimate (position based), reward, coercive (punishment based), expert, and referent (charismatic). These five bases can be divided into two major categories: organizational and personal. Legitimate, reward, and coercive power are primarily prescribed by an organization, while expert and referent power are based on personal qualities.

- Organizational structure creates power by specifying certain individuals to perform certain tasks. Three important forms of structural power include (1) access to resources, (2) ability to affect decision-making processes, and (3) having access to relevant and important information.

- Powerlessness occurs when an individual has little or no access to the bases of interpersonal or structural power. Empowerment refers to a process whereby conditions that contribute to powerlessness are identified and removed. Two important factors in empowerment are helping organizational members feel confident of their ability to perform well and increasing the linkages between effort and performance.

- The strategic contingency approach addresses subunit power. A strategic contingency is an event or activity that is extremely important for accomplishing organizational goals. The strategic contingency factors that have been disclosed by research include coping with uncertainty, centrality, and substitutability.

- Individuals with very little or no real power may still influence others because they *appear* to be powerful. This is the illusion of power that was clearly illustrated in the Milgram experiments on obedience.

- Frequently used influence tactics include consultation, rational persuasion, inspirational appeals, ingratiating tactics, coalition building, use of pressure, legitimating, personal appeals, and exchange tactics. A particu-

larly important and frequently used tactic is that of impression management.

- A manager's behavior should satisfy certain criteria to be considered ethical. These include the (1) *criterion of utilitarian outcomes* (the greatest good for the greatest number), (2) *criterion of individual rights* (respecting rights of free consent, speech, privacy, and due process), and (3) *criterion of distributive justice* (respecting the rules of justice).

- Using power to manage effectively means (1) recognizing that there are multiple interests in every organization, (2) knowing what position others hold with respect to issues important to you, (3) understanding that getting things done requires having and using power, and (4) recognizing the strategies and tactics through which organizational power is developed and used.

Review and Discussion Questions

1. Power is an aspect of a relationship between two or more persons. What implication does this fact have for organizational members who wish to increase their power? Decrease the power of others?

2. What is meant by the term *empowerment?* Does empowering a subordinate necessarily mean that the person granting power is losing power? Can an act of empowerment increase a manager's power? Explain.

3. Why would it be concluded that knowledge in an organization is the most powerful part of a firm?

4. What changes in an organization's or department's environment would bring about changes in strategic contingencies? How might changes in these contingencies affect power relationships in the unit?

5. How the illusion of power can be just as effective as actual power was clearly illustrated in the "obedience to authority" experiments conducted by Milgram. Can you think of other examples where people have responded to the illusion of power? Does this happen in organizations?

6. Sometimes "playing politics" is a very effective way to achieve objectives. Why is this the case? Should organizations be concerned about it?

7. A number of frequently used influence tactics were discussed in the text. How many have you witnessed being played in organizations of which you were a member? What other tactics have you seen used?

8. The use of power and politics often involves ethical issues. What are the criteria that may be used to determine the extent to which a manager's behavior is ethical? Are there ever legitimate exceptions to these criteria?

9. Is it realistic to think that power ever flows upward in an organization? How might this happen? Is this direction of power flow good or bad from management's perspective?

10. When was the last time you engaged in impression management? Was it effective? Why or why not? How might you use impression management to get a promotion? To receive a better grade in a course?

READING 10.1 Create An Empowering Environment

By Shari Caudron

em-pow-er-ment: When employees "own" their jobs; when they are able to measure and influence their individual success as well as the success of their departments and their companies. Empowered employees are energetic and passionate. They want to do a better job because they feel personally rewarded for doing so.

It's hard to imagine any group of employees being less empowered than those who worked in communist enterprises behind the Iron Curtain. The communist "management" style was blatantly authoritarian: Employees simply did what they were told, no questions asked. Forget creativity and innovation. Employees were seen as bodies, not minds, and any thinking that needed to be done would be done by supervisors, thank you very much. The communist regime destroyed employee initiative, eliminated trust and created legions of workers who weren't lazy so much as they were uninspired.

This was the kind of work force New York City–based Colgate-Palmolive Corp. confronted when the company began to open manufacturing plants in Central Europe three years ago. The HR challenge? How to get the best from employees in countries such as Czechoslovakia, Romania and Poland, employees who were used to doing only what was required—no more, no less. "We wanted employees to believe in the business, to understand what needed to be done and to be willing to give us their good ideas," explains Philip Berry, the company's director of HR for Central Europe, Middle East and Africa. In short, the company wanted empowered employees. Managers knew, however, that the idea was antithetical to the workers' way of thinking. Creating a truly empowered work force would require patience and an extraordinary HR effort.

"We could have brought in strong expatriate managers to go with the grain, to continue the authoritarian management style," Berry says. Instead, the company chose to emphasize its own culture, the Colgate-Palmolive managerial style that's consistent around the world. The company encouraged employees to share their ideas about how to run the business and then rewarded them for doing so. To help them generate ideas, managers gave employees information about the business, invested in new skills training, set goals for employees and gave them on-

going feedback on how they were meeting those goals. "In short," Berry says, "we treated them like adults."

Just a few years later, the results are nothing short of amazing. Workers have blossomed—they're finding skills they didn't know they had, and the majority of the work force is operating at a capacity never before thought possible. Job satisfaction is high, most employees appear to trust management, and when you ask Berry if he thinks workers have become empowered, he answers with an emphatic "Yes." Now, if Colgate can get these kinds of results from employees used to working in autocracies, imagine what companies can achieve by empowering their U.S. work forces.

Unfortunately, this is no easy task. True empowerment doesn't provide immediate gratification. Bill Byham, president and CEO of Pittsburgh-based Development Dimensions Int'l., and author of *Zapp! The Lightning of Empowerment,* says the length of the learning curve is the greatest challenge to most empowerment programs. "It takes longer for employees to figure out how to make improvements on their own than it does to just tell them what to do," he says. "The cost of empowerment is in the time it takes, not in the cost of training or anything else."

It also takes time for workers to understand managers really do want more input on how to run the business. "Empowerment is a very agile process," says Jerry Pfundtner, quality assurance manager at Stamford, Connecticut–based Xerox Corp. "It's subject to a great many influences, including changes in managers, employees, priorities and job requirements."

In addition to the patience many companies lack, a lot of so-called empowerment programs fail because HR initiates the process the wrong way. As Colgate discovered, empowerment isn't something you do to people. It's something HR must nurture and encourage by creating a empowering environment—one in which employees are given goals, information, feedback, training, and perhaps most importantly, positive reinforcement.

Work teams and information sharing are the building blocks of an empowering environment. "Empowerment programs tend to fail when management doesn't deal with the environment that influences employee behavior," explains Byham, considered one of the country's foremost authorities on employee empowerment. The only way to capture employees' hearts and get them psychologically involved in work, he says, is by changing how they view that work.

Source: "Create an Empowering Environment," by Shari Caudron, copyright July 1998. Used with permission or ACC Communications Inc./Workforce Costa Mesa, CA. All rights reserved.

Companies in which employees are most likely to consider themselves empowered are those that rely heavily on teams and teamwork. That's because by working in teams, employees not only find greater meaning in their work but also have more ability to influence its outcome. As a result, teams change how work is viewed, setting the stage for more important and longer-lasting changes in attitude.

"Empowerment programs won't work unless employees work in teams," agrees Russell Justice, technical associate and quality consultant for Eastman Chemical Co. in Kingsport, Tennessee, a 1993 Malcolm Baldrige National Quality Award winner. Team members get ongoing positive feedback from each other in a way they never could working independently and relying on a single supervisor for support and direction. For this reason, HR professionals who want employees to feel empowered should start by reorganizing their work force into teams. Only then can they start making the environmental changes needed to support those teams.

The first of these changes is information sharing. Give employees information about the business and demonstrate how their work fits in. One of the most important measures of job satisfaction is whether employees find meaning in their work—if they know what they're working toward and understand how their work affects other employees and the company as a whole. Surprisingly few organizations take the time to share this kind of information. HR needs to take special care that employees aren't left in the dark.

"Employees tend to resist empowerment programs when they don't understand what it is they're working toward," says Richard Harris, senior vice president of the Forum Corp., a global training company based in Boston. "Employees need strategic goals, and they need to understand the impact their work has on the achievement of those goals." This kind of information creates the buy-in necessary to generate dramatic and ongoing improvements in the business.

Take the Central European employees hired by Colgate. These people had spent their careers working in a vacuum. They had no information about organizational goals. They knew nothing about sales. They had no idea what it cost to produce products. And because they were used to working in a communist system, they had no understanding of marketing or free enterprise.

To help employees understand their new jobs, Colgate's HR managers gave them information about the company and explained what the free-enterprise system is all about. They shared sales and cost figures, they talked about their products and their competitors' products, and they described company initiatives in a way that made employees understand how their work fit into the big picture. Not accustomed to being given this kind of information, employees were skeptical at first. But as Berry says,

"Everyone wants to feel they do something of value. When you demonstrate the value individuals bring to the business, people want to grow."

As employees began to understand the business, the individual and team goals that they were working toward and how their contributions fit into the company's larger business goals, they began to find greater meaning in their work, and productivity improved.

Information sharing is also key to employee empowerment at Eastman Chemical, where every employee works on teams that are challenged to find ways to improve the business. "Teams are regarded as the board of directors for their particular business," Justice says, "because no one knows how to improve the work better than the people who do it every day."

Like any board of directors, however, those team members need information to make decisions about how to improve the work. For this reason, Eastman Chemical, like Colgate, shares information about sales results, quality improvements, cost reductions and anything else employees need to understand their jobs better.

The company also spends a lot of time talking about goals and explaining why those goals are important to customers, to the company and to individual employees. Each goal is accompanied by a timeline and a description of what management will do to help employees achieve it.

This information helps employees focus on things that need improving, Justice says. It helps team members become like-minded. "Without focus, employees are like an orchestra that's warming up," he adds. "Individually, they may be very talented, but if they don't know what they're working toward, no common sound will emerge."

Provide the training and resources needed to do a good job. Once employees understand what needs to be done to improve the company, they must have the skills and resources necessary to be able to accomplish those improvements. Nothing is more demotivating or disempowering than being stopped in your tracks because you either don't know how to proceed or lack the tools necessary to do a good job.

"Having the skills and ability to do a job well is one of the most important dimensions of empowerment," says Justice. That's why at Eastman Chemical—as with most other companies with successful empowerment initiatives—training is an important part of the process. There, team members attend training together, bringing an actual problem that needs solving to the training program. Legal teams, for example, are working on ways to cut down on legal jargon so it's easier to do business with Eastman. Sales teams are working on how to better ensure sales orders are completed with the correct information. "This way, employees acquire skills they need when they need them," Justice says.

Pfundtner agrees that employee development is key to an empowered work force. If you want to make significant changes in the business, you have to make significant changes in how you do things, he says. And you do this by showing employees how to do things differently through continuous education and skills upgrading.

Team training and interpersonal-skills training are especially important because empowered employees rarely, if ever, work independently. "Empowerment is about interdependence," says Byham. " A good idea doesn't mean anything unless other people can help you put it to work."

After employee training, the second half of empowerment training is aimed at helping management learn to empower others. This kind of training, by necessity, is less about management and more about coaching and creating an environment open to new ways of doing things. For employees to truly be empowered, managers have to give up control—and that's not easy. They have to learn less hands-on, more supportive management styles. Managers also have to learn how to nurture and reward good ideas, and know what kind of challenges to give employees.

"A lot of managers make the mistake of giving employees too great a challenge in the early days of empowerment," Byham says. Then, the employees fail and are unwilling to take the initiative again. As Aubrey Daniels, author of *Bringing Out the Best in People,* writes in his book: "The best way to empower team members is gradually and systematically. You can't say to people, 'Okay, after all these years of reporting to your boss, getting everything approved and working within limited boundaries, you are now free! You're on your own! Start taking responsibility and making decisions!' Responsibilities for self-management and decision making should be turned over to employees on an as-ready basis, and the responsibilities given initially should be limited in scope."

Managers must also accept the fact that not all employees want to be empowered. Many workers just work better in jobs that are clearly defined and closely supervised. Even at Colgate's Central European plants, a full 25 percent of the employees have resisted the notion of empowerment, Berry says, adding that those employees tend to be older and more resistant to the idea of change in general.

"Usually employees uncomfortable with empowerment leave the company on their own," adds Justice. "The peer pressure to get involved is so great that either they do or they opt out."

Once both employees and managers have received proper training, the next step is to give employees control of the resources needed to make improvements. A team formed at Allied Systems Inc., based in Decatur, Georgia, for example, was empowered to find ways of reducing on-the-job injuries by 50 percent within one year. Managers gave the team a goal and information about the current in-

jury rate (team building and information sharing being the important first steps mentioned earlier). Then, the group was given a budget and told to find ways to improve safety awareness.

"The employees were in total control of the budget and in determining how to spend it," says Jim Gage, terminal manager at the St. Louis facility where the team was formed. Armed with the necessary information, a clear sense of direction and resources to work with, the team reduced injuries by 71 percent, well above the stated goal.

Provide measurements, feedback and reinforcement. Once employees have devised ways to improve their jobs, departments or the business as a whole, managers must allow employees to measure those improvements. If, for example, employees find a method they believe will reduce scrap in the manufacturing process, they need to know on a regular basis if scrap is indeed being reduced. After all, why would they continue to seek improvements when they don't know whether their previous suggestions are working?

"The secret of empowerment is [having] measurements that people can control," Byham says. Ideally, employees should come up with their own goals and ways of measuring achievement of those goals. But this may not always be possible, as information is often collected and managed by other departments within a company. Therefore, managers must find ways to gather and disseminate measurements and provide feedback on them.

At Eastern Chemical, for example, managers are in the process of devising a "sale-o-meter," in which sales figures will be transferred immediately from the computers on which orders were placed to an electronic display in the employee lunchroom. Employees will eventually see a running tally of sales made each day, with the top 10 sales highlighted. Knowing daily sales figures gives employees a shared sense of accomplishment and pride in the company, Justice says. "The whole idea is to make performance visible."

Employee empowerment requires ongoing positive reinforcement. Just as important as providing progress measurement is providing continued, positive reinforcement, says Daniels, president of management-consulting firm Aubrey Daniels and Associates in Tucker, Georgia. "You have to make empowerment something employees want to do, and you do this by celebrating their successes," he explains. "Change requires many reinforcers for the new behaviors before new habits can be established." Motivational experts suggest managers give positive reinforcement often and immediately after a job well done. Employees want to be recognized individually for good work from their supervisors. They also want to be publicly recognized because it tells them their achievements are worth everyone's attention. But groups also want to celebrate their successes.

At Eastman Chemical, managers create very elaborate plans for positively reinforcing group achievement. The company doesn't spend a lot of money on these celebrations. Instead, it spends a lot of creativity. For example, a group of mechanics who met an important goal were treated to a car wash conducted by top managers. Employees whose ideas generated $1 million in cost savings were invited to come view $1 million in $20 bills. "We went to the bank, got a million dollars and invited employees to come up and see what their savings looked like," Justice says.

Another expression that's often used to refer to the positive reinforcement process is "performance management," and companies whose employees demonstrate great initiative are those in which performance management is an established part of doing business. At *The Orange County Register* in Santa Ana, California, performance management has been implemented on a companywide basis for more than two years. The goal? To encourage employees to continually improve customer service, then reward them for doing so.

An important part of the company's performance-management process is its system of positive reinforcement through celebrations. Managers solicited ideas for successful celebrations from everyone in the company and then developed a "cookbook" that includes recipes for a variety of celebrations. Included were "fast-food recipes," which are quick and economical celebrations used in the early stages of employee empowerment and goal setting; "main meals" designed for observing a group or departmental subgoal; and "gourmet meals" which are elaborate celebrations for achievement of a major goal.

The company's emphasis on positive reinforcement has created dramatic improvements in the business—improvements that resulted from employees taking the initiative to get things done. After suffering through a departmental downsizing that affected 100 employees, for instance, the circulation department still managed to improve productivity and customer service. A program to reduce newsprint waste ended up also reducing errors, saving film, saving printing plates and improving print quality and department productivity. "The results have been nothing short of phenomenal," says John Schueler, president and chief operating officer.

By giving employees information, resources and training, and by following up with measurements and reinforcement, HR can create an empowered environment. But remember, empowering employees is a continual process–like quality improvement, it's a race without a finish line. Those companies that take the first step by creating an environment conducive to empowerment will be at the head of the pack.

Exercises

EXERCISE 10.1   Empowerment Profile

Step 1:   Complete the following questionnaire.
For each of the following items, select the alternative with which you feel more comfortable. While for some items you may feel that both a and b describe you or neither is ever applicable, you should select the alternative that better describes you most of the time.

1. When I have to give a talk or write a paper, I . . .
   ___ a. Base the content of my talk or paper on my own ideas.
   ___ b. Do a lot of research, and present the findings of others in my paper or talk.
2. When I read something I disagree with, I . . .
   ___ a. Assume my position is correct.
   ___ b. Assume what's presented in the written word is correct.

3. When someone makes me extremely angry, I . . .
   ___ a. Ask the other person to stop the behavior that is offensive to me.
   ___ b. Say little, not quite knowing how to state my position.
4. When I do a good job, it is important to me that . . .
   ___ a. The job represents the best I can do.
   ___ b. Others take notice of the job I've done.
5. When I buy new clothes, I . . .
   ___ a. Buy what looks best on me.
   ___ b. Try to dress in accordance with the latest fashion.
6. When something goes wrong, I . . .
   ___ a. Try to solve the problem.
   ___ b. Try to find out who's at fault.
7. As I anticipate my future, I . . .
   ___ a. Am confident I will be able to lead the kind of life I want to lead.
   ___ b. Worry about being able to live up to my obligations.

Source: "The Empowerment Profile" from *The Power Handbook* by Pamela Cuming. Copyright © 1980 by CBI Publishing. Reprinted by permission by Van Nostrand Reinhold Co., Inc.

8. When examining my own resources and capacities, I . . .
   ___ a. Like what I find.
   ___ b. Find all kinds of things I wish were different.
9. When someone treats me unfairly, I . . .
   ___ a. Put my energies into getting what I want.
   ___ b. Tell others about the injustice.
10. When someone criticizes my efforts, I . . .
    ___ a. Ask questions in order to understand the basis for the criticism.
    ___ b. Defend my actions or decisions, trying to make my critic understand why I did what I did.
11. When I engage in an activity, it is very important to me that . . .
    ___ a. I live up to my own expectations.
    ___ b. I live up to the expectations of others.
12. When I let someone else down or disappoint them, I . . .
    ___ a. Resolve to do things differently next time.
    ___ b. Feel guilty, and wish I had done things differently.
13. I try to surround myself with people . . .
    ___ a. Whom I respect.
    ___ b. Who respect me.
14. I try to develop friendships with people who . . .
    ___ a. Are challenging and exciting.
    ___ b. Can make me feel a little safer and a little more secure.
15. I make my best efforts when . . .
    ___ a. I do something I want to do when I want to do it.
    ___ b. Someone else gives me an assignment, a dead-line, and a reward for performing.

16. When I love a person, I . . .
    ___ a. Encourage him or her to be free and choose for himself or herself.
    ___ b. Encourage him or her to do the same thing I do and to make choices similar to mine.
17. When I play a competitive game, it is important to me that I . . .
    ___ a. Do the best I can.
    ___ b. Win.
18. I really like being around people who . . .
    ___ a. Can broaden my horizons and teach me something.
    ___ b. Can and want to learn from me.
19. My best days are those that . . .
    ___ a. Present unexpected opportunities.
    ___ b. Go according to plan.
20. When I get behind in my work, I . . .
    ___ a. Do the best I can and don't worry.
    ___ b. Worry or push myself harder than I should.

Step 2: Score your responses as follows:
Total your a responses: ___
Total your b responses: ___

Step 3: Discussion. In small groups or with the entire class, answer the following questions:
1. What did you learn about yourself?
2. Would your closest friend agree with the scores or the scoring for a and b?
3. How could an organization use information gathered from this type of empowerment profile?

--- **Exercises** ---

EXERCISE 10.2   How Political Are You?

Mark each of the following statements either mostly true or mostly false. In some instances, "mostly true" refers to "mostly agree," and "mostly false" refers to "mostly disagree." We are looking for general tendencies, so don't be concerned if you are uncertain as to the more accurate response to a given statement.

	Mostly True	Mostly False
1. I would stay late in the office just to impress my boss.	___	___
2. Why teach your subordinates everything you know about your job? One of them could then replace you.	___	___
3. I have no interest in using gossip to personal advantage.	___	___
4. Be extra careful about ever making a critical comment about your firm, even if it is justified.	___	___

Source: A. J. DuBrin, *Winning Office Politics* (Englewood Cliffs, NJ: Prentice Hall, 1990), pp. 19–27. Used by permission of the publisher, Prentice Hall/A. Simon & Schuster Company, Englewood Cliffs, NJ.

5. I would go out of my way to cultivate friendships with powerful people.   _____   _____
6. I would never raise questions about the capabilities of my competition.
   Let his or her record speak for itself.   _____   _____
7. I am unwilling to take credit for someone else's work.   _____   _____
8. If I discovered that a coworker was looking for a job, I would inform my boss.   _____   _____
9. Even if I made only a minor contribution to an important project,
   I would get my name listed as being associated with that project.   _____   _____
10. There is nothing wrong with tooting your own horn.   _____   _____
11. My office should be cluttered with personal mementos, such as pencil holders
    and decorations, made by my friends and family.   _____   _____
12. One should take action only when one is sure that it is ethically correct.   _____   _____
13. Only a fool would publicly correct mistakes made by the boss.   _____   _____
14. I would purchase stock in my company even though it might not be a
    good financial investment.   _____   _____
15. Even if I thought it would help my career, I would refuse a
    hatchetman assignment.   _____   _____
16. It is better to be feared than loved by your subordinates.   _____   _____
17. If others in the office were poking fun at the boss, I would decline to join in. _____   _____
18. In order to get ahead, it is necessary to keep self-interest above the
    interests of the organization.   _____   _____
19. I would be careful not to hire a subordinate who might outshine me.   _____   _____
20. A wise strategy is to keep on good terms with everybody in your office
    even if you don't like everyone.   _____   _____

Cases

CASE 10.1   Power Abuse: Yes or No?

There are some experts who suggest that many sexual harassment cases in organizations involve the misuse and abuse of power. The following case involves a sexual harassment lawsuit filed by two female police officers, Andrews and Conn, under the jurisdiction of Title VII of the Civil Rights Act.

While employees were assigned to the Auto Investigation Division (AID) of the Philadelphia police department, males dominated the division and according to Andrews, the AID squadroom was charged with sexism. Women were regularly referred to in an offensive and obscene manner and they personally were addressed by obscenities. There was evidence that the language was commonplace in police headquarters, but also testimony that one of the plaintiffs, a twelve-year police veteran, "had never been called some of the names that [she] was called in AID." There was also evidence of pornographic pictures of women displayed in the locker room on the inside of a locker which most often was kept open. Plaintiffs contend that the language and pictures embarrassed, humiliated, and harassed them.

Both employees further claimed that their files often disappeared from their desks, or were ripped or sabotaged. When Conn reported the sabotage, she was told by her supervisor, "You know, you're no spring chicken. You have to expect this working with the guys." Male officers who were to assist them in their work often hindered them or refused to help, although the men would help each other. The women experienced vandalism of their personal property, with Andrews having her car thrice vandalized while parked on the AID lot, with tires slashed, car scratched and windshield wipers removed; soda was poured into her typewriter: someone tore the cover off Andrew's book needed to keep track of investigations. Someone spit on Conn's coat, cut the band off her hat, and scratched her car. A roll of film Conn was using in an investigation disappeared before it was dispatched for developing.

Both employees also received obscene phone calls at their unlisted home phone numbers which AID had access to. One of the time periods for the calls was after the lawsuit was filed.

During one of the conversations Andrews heard someone say "Yoh, sarge" in the background. Conn testified that the calls made her very scared and nervous and un-

Source: Adapted from *Andrew v. City of Philadelphia* 895 F.2d 1469 (3rd Cir. 1990).

able to function emotionally. She was also harassed by co-workers placing sexual devices and pornographic magazines in her desk drawer and gathering around and laughing at her reaction. When she reported this to her superior, he remained unresponsive. Another time a caustic substance was placed inside Andrews' shirt in her locker in the women's locker room. Andrews' back was severely burned by what was later determined to be a lime substance. Lime was found in other clothing in the locker and on the handle. Andrews also says that lewd pictures were posted on the walls and that she was embarrassed by pornographic pictures placed in her personal desk drawer.

Some of Conn and Andrews' complaints were investigated, others were not, but nothing significant came of any investigations. In both cases there was some sexually based activity directed toward the women, such as suggestive remarks or tones used in connection with them.

We believe that the trial court too narrowly construed what type of conduct can constitute sexual harassment. Great emphasis was put on the lack of sexual advances, innuendo, or contact. In the lower court's opinion, evidence was extremely minimal and would not, standing alone, support a finding of a sexually hostile work environment, noting the lack of evidence of direct sexual harassment. To the extent that the court ruled that overt sexual harassment is necessary to establish a sexually hostile environment, we are constrained to disagree.

To make out a case under Title VII it is only necessary to show that gender is a substantial factor in the discrimination, and that if the plaintiff had been a man she would not have been treated in the same manner. To constitute impermissible discrimination, the offensive conduct is not necessarily required to include sexual overtones in every instance or that each incident be sufficiently severe to detrimentally affect a female employee. Intimidation and hostility toward women because they are women can obviously result from conduct other than explicitly sexual advances. *Meritor* appears to support this proposition as

well, "Title VII affords employees the right to work in an environment free from discriminatory intimidation, ridicule and insult." The Supreme Court in no way limited this concept to intimidation or ridicule of an explicitly sexual nature.

More specifically, we hold that the pervasive use of derogatory and insulting terms relating to women generally and addressed to female employees personally may serve as evidence of a hostile environment. Similarly, so may the posting of pornographic pictures in common areas and in the plaintiff's personal work spaces.

Although the employer's attorney argues vigorously that a police station need not be run like a day care center, it should not, however, have the ambience of a nineteenth century military barracks. We realize that it is unrealistic to hold an employer accountable for every isolated incident of sexism; however, we do not consider it an unfair burden of an employer of both genders to take measures to prevent an atmosphere of sexism to pervade the workplace.

On remand, the trial judge should look at all incidents to see if they produce a work environment hostile and offensive to women of reasonable sensibilities. The evidence in this case includes not only name calling, pornography, displaying sexual objects in desks, but also the recurrent disappearance of plaintiffs' case files and work products, anonymous phone calls, and destruction of other property. The court should view this evidence in its totality, as described above, and then reach a determination. VACATED and REMANDED.

QUESTIONS:

1. Is this a warranted claim against the Philadelphia Police Department?
2. Is this case one that involves the creation of a hostile environment for Andrews and Conn?
3. If you were the manager/supervisor (legitimate power position), what action would you have undertaken?

Video Case

SATURN AND AT&T WORKERS BEAT MEXICAN PLANT

Both Saturn and AT&T have discovered what researchers have known for some time: Cooperation is better than competition. Both the Saturn auto plant and AT&T workers in the Atlanta Consumer Repair Center have experienced success because of cooperation between management and labor. Most of General Motors divisions were experiencing record losses and several plant closures, with the exception of Saturn, located in Tennessee. Saturn employees attend classes on how to break down the traditional barriers between management and workers. The vice president of production and the president of the UAW local have learned to work together to solve problems. Instead of a combative relationship between union and management, the UAW local president reports that he "does 200% more managing than in the old world" of GM. Ninety-eight percent of the union leader's job involves helping to manage the business "with the voice of the worker in the process."

AT&T also benefitted from cooperation between union and management. The AT&T Consumer Repair Center was given 18 months to cut costs or be shut down. The problem was that this AT&T plant could not compete with the cheaper labor in Mexico. The plant manager realized that "there was no chance of success if we maintained an adversarial relationship." Working together, managers and production employees sped up production, reduced inventory, and minimized defects, making the plant more cost effective.

Organizations that have the right organizational culture and provide administrative support and training, as do Saturn and AT&T, provide the best environment in which self-directed work teams can thrive. Saturn's man-

agement provides a trusting and supportive culture. As Saturn's VP of production reports, "Potential has always been in the workforce, but you have to create the environment for that potential to come out." One member of the Saturn dashboard team says, "Team members are willing to do whatever it takes to get the job accomplished." The dashboard production team even hires its own members, a factor that can lead to increased team cohesiveness. The team also boasts a 99% attendance ratio, which would never have been the case at a GM plant with a traditional management style and adversarial culture. Saturn workers are entrusted with making important decisions and are even empowered to stop the production line if there is a problem.

These examples show that for self-directed work teams to help an organization increase its productivity, teams must be supported from the top. The cooperation at top levels of management trickles down to production teams, who respond with trust in management, commitment, and a strong sense of responsibility. As proof, the AT&T Consumer Repair Center became so efficient that despite their $16 an hour wages they took work away from the Mexican plants, where workers made only about $1 an hour!

DISCUSSION QUESTIONS:

1. What are some positive effects of mutual trust between management and workers as shown by Saturn and AT&T?
2. What behaviors were exhibited by management at Saturn to make their employees effective team players?

IV

Part

Organizational Processes

The real leader has no need to lead—he is content to point the way.

Henry Miller, The Wisdom Of The Heart (1941)

11
Chapter

Leadership: An Overview

After completing Chapter 11, you should be able to:

Learning Objectives

- Define the term *leadership*.

- Discuss the trait approach to leadership.

- Describe two major behavior approaches to leadership.

- Explain what situational approaches are and describe several significant ones.

- Identify a number of substitutes for leadership.

www.ge.com

www.ibm.com

www.intel.com

www.cisco.com

Leadership has been a topic of interest, speculation, and debate since the time of Plato. In organizations around the world, from massive conglomerates to new economy dot-coms, the same lament emerges: Where are the leaders. Jack Welch at General Electric, Lou Gerstner of IBM, Andy Grove at Intel, and John Chambers of Cisco Systems are cited so many times as leadership role models that their stories are becoming boring and repetitive. Certainly, not everyone can become an effective leader such as Welch or Chambers. The measure of effectiveness in leading that no one is tired of reading and reflecting about is results achieved.[1]

During the course of history and study we have learned a great deal about what leadership is—and about what it isn't. For all the thousands of studies that have been conducted, however, there is still a great deal we do not know. In this and the chapter that follows we will examine some of what we do know about leadership. We will provide a general historical and contemporary overview of leadership in this chapter, and in the following chapter, we will focus on some very current and emerging leadership concepts and applications.

While a great many aspects of leadership have been studied, most organizational researchers and behavioral scientists have focused on two important leadership issues: (1) why some organizational members become leaders while others do not, and (2) why some leaders are successful while others are not. Both of these issues are thought to be important because *leadership* is thought to be important. It has been suggested that when groups or organizations are successful their leadership receives too much credit, and when they fail their leadership gets too much of the blame. Nonetheless, leaders do make a difference, and leadership is a critical variable in shaping organizational effectiveness.

WHAT IS LEADERSHIP?

www.patagonia.com

With so much interest in leadership, it might be assumed that everyone is in general agreement about what constitutes leadership. Such is not the case, however, and there are some very good reasons why. When Patagonia Incorporated, a leading manufacturer of outdoor wear, and its sister company, Lost Arrow Corporation, were searching for a new chief executive officer, they ran the following advertisement:

> $120 million companies which produce high quality functional outdoor clothing and sportswear, seek CEO able to lead 5.10 in the mountains, kayak Class 5 or surf Pipeline in February. Must be immune to jetlag in order to inspire employees and independent contractors throughout the world: wholesale, retail, and mail order on four continents. A commitment to slow growth and the reduction of environmental impact. These slow growth, high profit companies pledge 1% of sales to controversial environmental and social causes. Must be comfortable working in an open, casual work environment where women hold a significant amount of senior management positions. Requires dedication to open communication throughout the organization, and never, ever, compromising quality. Foreign language and diversity valued. If you have successfully led a company through a transition from an entrepreneurial to an employee owned entity, or have led a more traditional company and believe there is a better way than wanting to be in the Fortune 500, send your cover letter and resume. . . .[2]

---

[1]Daniel Goleman, "Leadership That Gets Results," *Harvard Business Review,* March–April 2000, pp. 78–90.

[2]This advertisement appeared in *Outside Magazine,* November 1993, p. 184.

www.chase.com

www.levi.com

www.motel6.com

Patagonia was looking for a certain kind of person to provide what they were seeking in a leader. Leadership qualities important in one situation may be different from those required in another.[3] It is unlikely that the same people who applied for Patagonia's CEO position would have applied for a similar position at Chase Manhattan Bank, E. F. Hutton, Levi Strauss, or Motel 6. This is because what Chase, Hutton, Levi, and Motel 6 look for in a leader will be as unique to each of them as it was to Patagonia. Leadership does not take place in a vacuum. There are three important variables with which every leader must deal: the *people* who are being led, the *task* that the people are performing, and the *environment* in which the people and the task exist. Because these three variables are different in every situation, what is expected and needed from a leader will be different in every situation. The fact that the best leader for Patagonia may not be the best leader for Chase Manhattan Bank helps to illustrate why there is a lack of general agreement about what constitutes leadership.

The fact that leaders and leadership situations differ has led to a multitude of leadership definitions. Some definitions of leadership are based on leader characteristics, some on leader behaviors, still others on outcomes or end results. A good definition of leadership needs to be sufficiently broad to accommodate different theories, research findings, and applications. We define **leadership** as the process of influencing others to facilitate the attainment of organizationally relevant goals.[4] Note that by this definition you do not have to be in a formal leadership position in order to exert leadership. The role of informal leader can be every bit as important to a group's success as is that of the formal leader.

Differences in definitions, leadership expectations, and the three significant variables that are a part of all leadership situations (people, task, environment) notwithstanding, there are some leadership commonalities. For example, Warren Bennis, who has devoted decades to researching leadership issues, concludes that virtually all leaders of effective groups share four characteristics in common:

1. They provide direction and meaning to the people they are leading. This means they remind people what is important and why what they are doing makes an important difference.

2. They generate trust.

3. They favor action and risk taking. That is, they are proactive and willing to risk failing in order to succeed.

4. They are purveyors of hope. In both tangible and symbolic ways they reinforce the notion that success will be attained.[5]

Organizational Encounter 11.1 illustrates that the most unlikely person can display leadership. As the Encounter illustrates, some individuals obviously possess characteristics that are so attractive to others that they are considered leaders without even attempting to lead.

---

[3]Jennifer Laabs, "Mixing Business with Passion," *Workforce,* March 2000, pp. 80–87, and Richard Barker, "How Can We Train Leaders if We Do Not Know What Leadership Is?" *Human Relations,* April 1997, pp. 343–62.

[4]See Frank E. Saal and Patrick A. Knight, *Industrial/Organizational Psychology* (Pacific Grove, CA: Brooks/Cole, 1995), pp. 321–24, for an excellent discussion of the influence interpretation of leadership.

[5]Warren Bennis, *Organizing Genius: The Secrets of Creative Collaboration* (Reading, MA: Addison-Wesley, 1997).

An Unexpected Leader

An interesting type of leader who provided direction, generated trust, took risks, and was a role model for fostering hope is the lead character in the movie *Rudy*. The movie is a true story about an undersized, nonathletic football player who had a dream and aspiration to go to Notre Dame and be on the football team. Rudy was slated to follow his father and brother into the steel mill. Anyone who looked at Rudy as a football player wannabe saw a small, slow, lightweight individual. He possessed few football skills and was not a good student. Playing football for Notre Dame may have been a dream, but it was not a reality with Notre Dame's stiff academic entrance requirements and national football power reputation.

One of Rudy's friends was killed in a steel mill accident, and this pushed him to make the trek to South Bend, Indiana. Rudy found he didn't meet the academic requirements, so he attended another school to work on his studies and improve his grades. A priest helped guide him and offered some encouragement, which finally paid off. Rudy was admitted to Notre Dame as a junior.

Rudy finally became a member of Notre Dame's practice squad. He practiced hard and won the respect of Notre Dame's regular team players. His grit, determination, attitude, and spirit served as an example of never quitting. Finally, Notre Dame Coach Dan Devine on the last play of the last game of Rudy's senior year decided to put him into the game. The Notre Dame team and the entire stadium were excited when Rudy made a tackle to end the game. He is carried off the field by his admiring and cheering Notre Dame teammates.

Rudy shared the characteristics of effective leaders in spite of his athletic limitations. The Notre Dame "Fighting Irish" football team had accepted Rudy as a leader. His spirit, self-motivation, persistence, passion, and work ethic were models for superior athletes. The team respected Rudy, not because of his football ability, but because he never quit and he worked harder than anyone else.

The trait approach to leadership suggests that there are some common personal **traits** shared by effective leaders. Later in the chapter we will consider whether there are common **behaviors** in which successful leaders engage. As we will see, the search for common threads in the leadership tapestry has been an elusive one.

Is Leadership Important?

Leaders like Jack Welch can make a difference in end results in categories such as performance, goal attainment, and individual growth and development. However, the degree of difference to best use and the process of using leadership to make a difference are somewhat ambiguous.

Empirical evidence of the magnitude of the effects of leadership on performance is modest. Several reasons have been cited to explain these modest effects.[6] First, those selected as leaders are similar in background, experience, and qualifications. The similarity across selected individuals reduces the range of characteristics exhibited by leaders. Second, leaders at even the highest levels do not have unilateral control over resources. Major decisions require approval, review, and suggested modifications by others. Third, many factors cannot be controlled by a leader. Labor markets, environmental factors, and policies are often outside a leader's direct control. External factors may be overwhelming and uncontrollable, no matter how astute, insightful, and influential a leader may be.

Some research has specified only a modest effect of leadership on performance. One study of 167 firms in 13 industries over a 20-year period found that the ad-

---

[6]Robert Goffee and Gareth Jones, "Why Should Anyone Be Led by You?" *Harvard Business Review,* September–October 2000, pp. 63–70.

ministration factor (i.e., a combination of leadership and managership) had a limited effect on sales, profits, and profit margins.[7] Reanalysis of the same data found that leadership accounted for more variance in performance than did many of the other variables studied.[8]

A report by Semler on Brazilian managers again raises doubts about the effect of leaders.[9] Semler believes that democracy, profit sharing, and information are more important than a management hierarchy, a power base headed by a leader, or the specialization of work. Instead, employee involvement, salaries instead of wages, circles instead of management hierarchies, and job rotation makes leaders almost unnecessary. Semler refers to the organization of Brazil's largest marine and food-processing machinery manufacturer which manages to be profitable without managers.

Manz and Sims have clearly pointed out another wave of thinking that emphasizes the replacement of "bosses" with teams of employees who serve as their own bosses.[10] The concept has been labeled variously as *self-managing teams, empowerment teams,* and *autonomous work groups.* Manz and Sims have described "superleaders," individuals who lead others to lead themselves to higher levels of performance.

The teams described by Sims and Manz may not have bosses, but they do have leaders. As the researchers state, "No successful team is without leadership." Team leaders sometimes emerge or are sometimes appointed. They can be called coordinator, facilitator, or coach. They exert influence from a position of respect or expertise that is accepted by the other team members.

Bosses are being replaced with leaders or superleaders who exert the type of influence needed to accomplish goals. Using Sims and Manz's concept helps explain Semler's approach. Semler is replacing bosses with leaders, just as Sims and Manz suggest in their research and books.

Trait Approaches

The thinking and discussion of leadership has evolved over the years from a trait-based approach to the concept of teams without bosses. In order to examine the various views of leadership, it is necessary to trace some of the historical foundations of a number of approaches. Some of the foundation is considered today to be rather simplistic. On the other hand, some of the foundation is so complex that practitioners find little value in what is offered.

Much early discussion and research on leadership focused on identifying intellectual, emotional, physical, and other personal traits of effective leaders. This approach assumed that a finite number of individual traits of effective leaders could be found. To a significant extent, the personnel testing component of scientific management supported the trait theory of leadership.[11] In addition to be-

---

[7]S. Lieberson and J. F. O'Connor, "Leadership and Organization Performance: A Study of Large Corporations," *American Sociological Review,* 1972, pp. 117–30.

[8]Nan Weiner and Thomas Mahoney, "A Model of Corporate Performance as a Function of Environmental, Organizational and Leadership Influences," *Academy of Management Journal,* June 1981, pp. 453–70.

[9]Richardo Semler, "Managing without Managers," *Harvard Business Review,* September–October 1989, pp. 76–84.

[10]Charles C. Manz and Henry P. Sims, Jr., *Business without Bosses* (New York: Berkley Books, 1990).

[11]Cheryl Dahl, "Natural Leader," *Fast Company,* December 2000, pp. 268–80.

ing studied by personnel testing, the traits of leaders have been studied by observation of behavior in group situations, by choice of associates (voting), by nomination or rating by observers, and by analysis of biographical data.

Intelligence   In a review of 33 studies, Ralph Stogdill found that leaders were more intelligent than followers.[12] One significant finding was that extreme intelligence differences between leaders and followers might be dysfunctional. For example, a leader with a relatively high IQ attempting to influence a group whose members have average IQs may be unable to understand why the members don't comprehend the problem. In addition, such a leader may have difficulty in communicating ideas and policies. Being too intelligent would be a problem in some situations.

Personality   Some research results suggest that such personality traits as alertness, originality, personal integrity, and self-confidence are associated with effective leadership. Edwin Ghiselli reported several personality traits associated with leader effectiveness.[13] For example, he found that the ability to initiate action independently was related to the respondent's level in the organization. The higher the person went in the organization, the more important this trait became. Ghiselli also found that self-assurance was related to hierarchical position in the organization. Finally, he found that persons who exhibited individuality were the most effective leaders.

Physical Characteristics   Studies of the relationship between effective leadership and physical characteristics such as age, height, weight, and appearance provide contradictory results. Being taller and heavier than the group average is certainly not advantageous for achieving a leader position. However, there are some organizations that believe a physically large person is needed to secure compliance from followers. This notion relies heavily on coercive power. Nonetheless, Truman, Gandhi, Napoleon, and Stalin are examples of individuals of small stature who rose to powerful positions of leadership.

Supervisory Ability   Using the leaders' performance ratings, Ghiselli found a positive relationship between supervisory ability and level in the organizational hierarchy.[14] The supervisor's ability is defined as the "effective utilization of whatever supervisory practices are indicated by the particular requirements of the situation."[15] Once again, a valid measurement of the concept is needed—a difficult problem to resolve.

Exhibit 11.1 summarizes a number of the most-researched traits of leaders (traits found most likely to characterize successful leaders). Some studies have reported that these traits contribute to leadership success. However, leadership success is neither primarily nor completely a function of these or other traits.

Although in some studies traits such as those in Exhibit 11.1 have differentiated effective from ineffective leaders, research findings are still contradictory for

---

[12]Ralph M. Stogdill, *Handbook of Leadership* (New York: Free Press, 1974), pp. 43–44.

[13]Edwin E. Ghiselli, "The Validity of Management Traits in Relation to Occupational Level," *Personnel Psychology*, Summer 1963, pp. 109–13.

[14]Edwin E. Ghiselli, *Explorations in Managerial Talent* (Santa Monica, CA: Goodyear, 1971).

[15]Ibid., p. 19.

EXHIBIT 11.1	Traits Associated with Leadership Effectiveness	
Intelligence	**Personality**	**Abilities**
Judgment	Adaptability	Ability to enlist cooperation
Decisiveness	Alertness	Cooperativeness
Knowledge	Creativity	Popularity and prestige
Fluency of speech	Personal integrity	Sociability (interpersonal skills)
	Self-confidence	Social participation
	Emotional balance and control	Tact, diplomacy
	Independence (noncomformity)	

Source: Adapted from Bernard M. Bass, *Stogdill's Handbook of Leadership* (New York: Free Press, 1982), pp. 75–76.

a number of possible reasons. First, the list of potentially important traits is endless. Every year, new traits—such as the sign under which a person is born, handwriting style, and order of birth—are added to personality, physical characteristics, and intelligence. This continual "adding on" results in more confusion among those interested in identifying leadership traits. Second, trait test scores aren't consistently predictive of leader effectiveness. Leadership traits don't operate singly to influence followers, but act in combination. This interaction influences the leader-follower relationship. Third, patterns of effective behavior depend largely on the situation: Leadership behavior that's effective in a bank may be ineffective in a laboratory. See Ethics Encounter 11.1 for more on leadership behavior. Finally, the trait approach fails to provide insight into what the effective leader does on the job. Observations are needed that describe the behavior of effective and ineffective leaders.

Despite its shortcomings, the trait approach is not completely invalid. Kirkpatrick and Locke find evidence that effective leaders are different from other people.[16] Their review of the literature suggests that drive, motivation, ambition, honesty, integrity, and self-confidence are key leadership traits. Kirkpatrick and Locke believe that leaders don't have to be great intellects to succeed. However, leaders do need to have the "right stuff" or traits to have a good chance to be effective.

Nonetheless, after years of speculation and research on leadership traits, we're not even close to identifying a specific set of such traits. Thus, the trait approach appears to be interesting but not very effective for identifying and predicting leadership potential.

BEHAVIORAL APPROACHES

In the late 1940s, researchers began to explore the notion that how a person acts determines that person's leadership effectiveness. Instead of searching for traits, these researchers examined leader behaviors and their impact on the performance and satisfaction of followers. We will examine two such behavioral approaches that have contributed to subsequent leadership research and practice.

---

[16]Shelly A. Kirkpatrick and Edwin A. Locke, "Leadership: Do Traits Matter?" *Academy of Management Executive*, May 1991, pp. 48–60.

Job-Centered and Employee-Centered Leadership

In 1947, Rensis Likert began studying how best to manage the efforts of individuals to achieve desired performance and satisfaction objectives. The purpose of most leadership research of the Likert-inspired team at the University of Michigan (UM) was to discover the principles and methods of effective leadership. The effectiveness criteria used in many of the studies included:

Productivity per work hour, or other similar measures of the organization's success in achieving its production goals.

Job satisfaction of members of the organization.

Turnover, absenteeism, and grievance rates.

Costs.

Scrap loss.

Employee and managerial motivation.

Studies were conducted in a wide variety of organizations: chemical, electronics, food, heavy machinery, insurance, petroleum, public utilities, hospitals, banks, and government agencies. Data were obtained from thousands of employees doing different job tasks, ranging from unskilled work to highly skilled research and development work.

Through interviewing leaders and followers, researchers identified two distinct styles of leadership, referred to as *job-centered* and *employee-centered*. The *job-centered leader* focuses on completing the task and uses close supervision so that subordinates perform their tasks using specified procedures. This kind of leader relies on coercion, reward, and legitimate power to influence the behavior and performance of followers. Leaders who exhibited this leadership style seemed to view concern for people as an important luxury that they couldn't always afford.

The *employee-centered leader* focuses on the people doing the work and believes in delegating decision making and aiding followers in satisfying their needs by creating a supportive work environment. The employee-centered leader is concerned with followers' personal advancement, growth, and achievement. Such leaders emphasized individual and group development with the expectation that effective work performance would naturally follow.

While providing new insights into the art and science of leadership, the UM series of studies suggest that a leader must be either job-centered or employee-centered, but he or she cannot be both. This seeming inability to be both job- and employee-centered, and still be an effective leader, stimulated other research to further test this conclusion.

Management Pointer 11.1

INCREASING EMPLOYEE-CENTERED BEHAVIORS

Managers can increase employee-centered behaviors in a variety of ways. Some possibilities include:

1. Whenever possible, use rewards rather than punishments for reinforcing and modifying subordinate behaviors.

2. Keep lines of communication open at all times. Share information in a manner that contributes to building and maintaining trust.

3. Listen. Employees want to feel that what they have to say matters.

4. Try to obtain positive outcomes for subordinates (e.g., special bonuses, attractive work assignments, time off).

5. Provide opportunities when possible for employees to accomplish personal career objectives.

6. Don't be afraid to admit mistakes. It not only demonstrates to employees that you are human, it adds to creating a more supportive environment.

Exercise 11.1

Task and people orientations

Initiating Structure and Consideration

One of the more significant leadership research programs that developed after World War II was lead by Edwin Fleishman and his associates at Ohio State University (OSU). This important research program yielded a two-factor theory

Ethics Encounter 11.1

Is Management Becoming Feminized?

Is there a feminization of management and leadership that is taking place in the United States? Consider the following:

- A new model of leadership, one that emphasizes persuasion over power, cooperation over competition, collectivism over individualism, and inclusion over exclusion, is in ascendance. Our archetype of the effective leader as one who is autocratic and ruthlessly competitive is evolving into the leader as selfless steward, according to Patricia Smith and Stanley Smits in a study of the feminization of leadership funded by the Society of Human Resource Management. "Popular notions of successful leadership now encompass characteristics traditionally associated with women," they note.

- More caring workplace policies and practices reflect this nurturing leadership model. Laura Nash, senior research coordinator at Boston University, dubbed the phenomenon "the nanny corporation." Corporate human resources programs now try to develop the "whole employee," she writes, by addressing "nearly every social, physical, psychological, and intellectual need, from day care to dental work to depression to dieting plans, all the way to—no kidding—on-site meditation and massage programs and weekend firewalking and whitewater rafting."

- The current emphasis on valuing diversity has allowed us to drop "gender-neutral" pretenses. In theory, at least, we are learning to acknowledge differences among people in general, without labeling them strengths or weaknesses, good or bad. To some, that means if we call these softer leadership attributes "feminine," we no longer invite accusations of discrimination and negative stereotyping.

Taken together, these trends look like evidence of a gathering momentum in the workplace. We're witnessing a confluence of shifting values and economic necessity—the conditions required for significant change, according to many trend watchers. But are we really?

One very direct indicator that we are witnessing a feminization of management would be significant increases in the number of women in high-level leadership positions. While women's numbers are increasing, few top executives and directors are female. For example, 417 *Fortune 500* companies have at least one woman on their corporate boards. Although this represents almost 85 percent of the Fortune 500 companies, the vast majority of these have only one or two female members. Only 31 companies have three or more female board members. Overall, men hold almost 90 percent of the seats on these boards. Nonetheless, women's numbers are increasing. Over the last several years women's numbers in upper-level executive positions and on corporate boards have been increasing at a rate of 7 to 9 percent a year.

There are indications, however, that the rate of increase may itself be increasing. One of the reasons why there have been so few women in these positions historically is that there were few women who had managerial experience at lower levels who could be promoted. This is definitely changing as the number of women in middle management positions has increased dramatically in recent years.

Source: Adapted in part from Chris Lee, "The Feminization of Management," *Training*, November 1994, pp. 25–31; "Women Directors and Top Executives Are Still Rare at Many Big Companies," *Houston Chronicle*, December 12, 1996, p. 3c; and "More Women Hold Seats on Fortune 500 Boards," *Houston Chronicle*, October 1, 1997, p. 2c.

of leadership.[17] A series of studies isolated two leadership factors, referred to as *initiating structure* and *consideration*. **Initiating structure** involves behavior in which the leader organizes and defines the relationships in the group, tends to establish well-defined patterns and channels of communication, and spells out ways of getting the job done. The leader with a high initiating structure tendency focuses on goals and results. **Consideration** involves behavior indicating friendship, mutual trust, respect, warmth, and rapport between the leader and the followers. The leader with a high consideration overview supports open communication and participation.

---

[17]For a review of the studies, see Stogdill, *Handbook of Leadership,* Chap. 11. Also see E. A. Fleishman, "The Measurement of Leadership Attitudes in Industry," *Journal of Applied Psychology,* June 1953, pp. 153–58; C. L. Shartle, *Executive Performance and Leadership* (Englewood Cliffs, NJ: Prentice Hall, 1956); E. A. Fleishman, E. F. Harris, and H. E. Burtt, *Leadership and Supervision in Industry* (Columbus: Bureau of Educational Research, Ohio State University, 1955).

These dimensions are measured by two separate questionnaires. The Leadership Opinion Questionnaire (LOQ) assesses how leaders think they behave in leadership roles. The Leader Behavior Description Questionnaire (LBDQ) measures perceptions of subordinates, peers, or superiors.

The original premise was that a high degree of consideration and a high degree of initiating structure (High-High) was most desirable. Since the original research was undertaken to develop the questionnaire, there have been numerous studies of the relationship between these two leadership dimensions and various effectiveness criteria. In a study at International Harvester, researchers began to find some more complicated interactions of the two dimensions. Supervisors who scored high on initiating structure not only had high proficiency ratings from superiors but also had more employee grievances. A high consideration score was related to lower proficiency ratings and lower absences.[18]

Other studies have examined how male and female leaders utilize initiating structure and consideration. A literature review of such studies found that male and female leaders exhibit equal amounts of initiating structure and consideration and have equally satisfied followers.[19]

The OSU personal-behavioral theory has been criticized for simplicity (e.g., only two dimensions of leadership), lack of generalizability, and reliance on questionnaire responses to measure leadership effectiveness. Researchers have cautioned against reliance on questionnaire measures of leadership-initiating factors. One convincing argument is that when raters know about a leader's performance, their ratings of her behavior may be substantially distorted. Hence, correlations between past performance and rated behavior may reflect performance-induced distortions in behavioral ratings as well as real causal effects of past behavior on performance.[20]

The simplicity of the initiating structure and consideration view of leadership is appealing. However, most researchers believe that environmental variables play some role in leadership effectiveness. For example, when successful initiating structure behavior is found, what other variables in the environment are at work? A worker who prefers to have a structured job and needs to have a job is likely to perform effectively under high initiating structure. What situational variables need to be considered? The Ohio State approach doesn't point out environmental factors.

Exhibit 11.2 shows the common bases of the behavior approaches. These approaches have provided practitioners with information on what behaviors leaders should possess. This knowledge has resulted in the establishment of training programs for individuals who perform leadership tasks. Each approach is also associated with highly respected theorists, researchers, or consultants, and each has been studied in different organizational settings. Yet the linkage between leadership and such important performance indicators as production, efficiency, and satisfaction hasn't been conclusively resolved by either of these two behavior approaches.

Case 3.1

Rotating Leaders:
Orpheus Orchestra

---

[18]Fleishman, et al., *Leadership and Supervision.*

[19]G. H. Dobbins and S. J. Platz, "Sex Differences in Leadership: How Real Are They?" *Academy of Management Review,* January 1986, pp. 118–27.

[20]Robert G. Lord, "An Information Processing Approach to Social Perceptions, Leadership, and Behavioral Measurement in Organizations," in Larry L. Cummings and Barry M. Staw (eds.), *Research in Organizational Behavior,* (Greenwich, CT: JAI Press, 1985), p. 117.

EXHIBIT 11.2   A Review of Two Behavioral Leadership Approaches

Leadership Factors	Prime Initiator(s) of the Theory	Method of Measurement	Subjects	Principal Conclusions
Employee-centered and job-centered	Likert	Interview and questionnaire responses of groups of followers	Formal leaders and followers in public utilities, banks, hospitals, manufacturing, food, government agencies	Employee-centered and job-centered styles result in production improvements. However, after a brief period of time, the job-centered style creates pressure that is resisted through absenteeism, turnover, grievance, and poor attitudes. The best style is *employee-centered*.
Initiating structure and consideration	Fleishman, Stogdill, and Shartle	Questionnaire responses of groups of followers, peers, the immediate superior, and the leader	Formal leaders and followers in military, education, public utilities, manufacturing, and government agencies	The combination of initiating structure and consideration behavior that achieves individual, group, and organizational effectiveness depends largely on the situation.

Why Trait and Behavior Approaches Fall Short

Both trait and behavior approaches to leadership have helped us better understand the dynamics of leadership situations. Trait approaches consider personal characteristics of the leader that may be important in achieving success in a leadership role. There is no doubt that certain characteristics may be helpful—even essential—in some situations. These same characteristics, however, may be unimportant—even detrimental—in other situations. Similarly, the behavior approaches attempt to specify which kinds of leader behaviors are necessary for effective leadership. And here again there is no doubt that certain behaviors may be important in some situations but may be irrelevant or damaging in others. Initiating-structure behaviors on the part of the leader, for example, may be critical to successful task completion in some situations; in others, where workers know exactly what needs to be done, such behaviors may detract from subordinate performance and satisfaction.

At the start of the chapter we suggested that leaders needed to deal with three important variables: the people being led, the task being performed, and the environment in which the work was taking place. Trait and behavior approaches fail to take into account this interaction among people, tasks, and environments. All three variables are an important part of the leadership situation, yet trait and behavior approaches ignore task and environment considerations. What constitutes effective leadership for a group of people performing one job may be quite different for those

Reading 11.1

The Nine Dilemmas Leaders
Face

same people performing an entirely different job, or the same job in an entirely different environment. In other words, the nature of the situation in which leadership is being exercised must be considered before we can begin to prescribe what leaders should or should not do. It is approaches that address the nature of the leadership "situation" on which we focus next.

SITUATIONAL APPROACHES

When the search for the "best" set of traits or behaviors failed to discover an effective leadership mix and style for all situations, **situational theories of leadership** evolved that suggest leadership effectiveness is a function of various aspects of the leadership situation. A number of situational approaches have been proposed and studied. We will examine several of the more significant ones.

Only after inconclusive and contradictory results evolved from much of the early trait and behavior research was the importance of the situation studied more closely by those interested in leadership. As the importance of situational factors became more recognized, leadership research became more systematic, and situational models of leadership began to appear in the literature. Each model has its advocates, and each attempts to identify the leader behaviors most appropriate for a series of leadership situations. Also, each model attempts to identify the leader-situation patterns important for effective leadership.

The Contingency Leadership Model

Case 11.1

Rotating Leaders:
Orpheus Orchestra

The contingency model of leadership effectiveness was developed by Fiedler[21] and postulates that the performance of groups is dependent on the interaction between leadership style and situational favorableness. Leadership style is measured by the *Least-Preferred Coworker Scale* (LPC), an instrument developed by Fiedler that assesses the degree of positive or negative feelings held by a person toward someone with whom he or she least prefers to work. Low scores on the LPC are thought to reflect a *task-oriented,* or controlling, structuring leadership style. High scores are associated with a *relationship-oriented,* or passive, considerate leadership style.

Fielder proposes three factors which determine how favorable the leadership environment is, or the degree of situational favorableness. **Leader-member relations** refers to the degree of confidence, trust, and respect the followers have in their leader. This is the most important factor. **Task structure** is the second most important factor and refers to the extent to which the tasks the followers are engaged in are structured. That is, is it clearly specified and known what followers are supposed to do, how they are to do it, when and in what sequence it is to be done, and what decision options they have (high structure)? Or are these factors unclear, ambiguous, unspecifiable (low structure)? **Position power** is the final factor and refers to the power inherent in the leadership position. Generally, greater authority equals greater position power.

Together, these three factors determine how favorable the situation is for the leader. Good leader-member relations, high task structure, and strong position power constitute the most favorable situation. Poor relations, low degree of structure, and weak position power represent the least favorable situation. The vary-

---

[21]Fred E. Fiedler, *A Theory of Leadership Effectiveness* (New York: McGraw-Hill, 1967).

EXHIBIT 11.3

Summary of Fiedler's Situational Variables and Their Preferred Leadership Styles

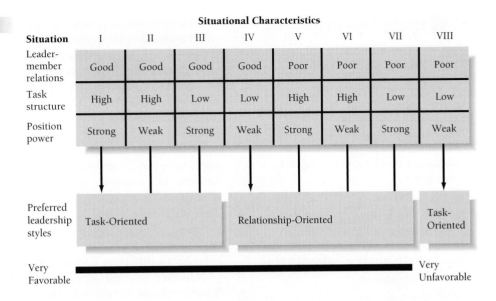

Situational Characteristics

Situation	I	II	III	IV	V	VI	VII	VIII
Leader-member relations	Good	Good	Good	Good	Poor	Poor	Poor	Poor
Task structure	High	High	Low	Low	High	High	Low	Low
Position power	Strong	Weak	Strong	Weak	Strong	Weak	Strong	Weak

Preferred leadership styles: Task-Oriented — Relationship-Oriented — Task-Oriented

Very Favorable ———————————— Very Unfavorable

ing degrees of favorableness and the corresponding appropriate leadership style are shown in Exhibit 11.3.

John Chambers, President and CEO of Cisco Systems, is praised even by his competitors as an exceptional leader. Cisco provides the "plumbing" for the Internet: routers, hubs, and switches. Its networking solutions connect people, computing devises, and computer networks. Chambers through his style has developed strong relationships with his subordinates, works with a high degree of structure, and wields significant power when necessary. Despite his impressive ability and accomplishments, Chamber's takes pride in keeping an eye on the big picture. He believes that Cisco technology must be at all the critical junctures of information flow, moving data from one place or device to the next.[22]

Chambers has a reputation for being a nice man in a cutthroat marketplace. He is considered ethical, polite, humble, and a leader who cares about people. Chambers—using his relationships, power, and technology—wants to lead Cisco into a world in which the Internet is merged with the telephone and cable TV businesses, creating a voice-video-data network worldwide.

Fiedler contends that a permissive, more lenient (relationship-oriented) style is best when the situation is moderately favorable or moderately unfavorable. Thus, if a leader is moderately liked and possesses some power, and the job tasks for subordinates are somewhat vague, the leadership style needed to achieve the best results is relationship-oriented. In contrast, when the situation is highly favorable or highly unfavorable, a task-oriented approach generally produces the desired performance. Fiedler bases his conclusions regarding the relationship between leadership style and situational favorableness on more than two decades of research in business, educational, and military settings.[23] The Management Pointer suggests several steps leaders can take to modify various situations.

---

[22]Michael J. Marquardt and Nancy O. Berger, *Global Leaders for the 21st Century* (Albany, NY: State University of New York Press, 2000), pp. 33–44.

[23]Fred E. Fiedler, "How Do You Make Leaders More Effective? New Answers to an Old Puzzle," *Organizational Dynamics*, Autumn 1972, pp. 3–8.

Management Pointer 11.2

**LEADERSHIP ACTIONS TO
CHANGE SITUATIONS**

To modify leader-member relations:

- Request particular people for work in your group.
- Effect transfers of particular subordinates out of your unit.
- Volunteer to direct difficult or troublesome subordinates.

To modify task structure:

- When possible bring new or unusual tasks or problems to your group (less structure).
- Break jobs down into smaller subtasks that can be more highly structured (more structure).

To modify position power:

- Show subordinates who's boss by exercising fully the authority you have.
- Make sure that information to your group gets channeled through you.
- Let subordinates participate in planning and decision making (lowering power).

Fiedler is not particularly optimistic that leaders can be trained successfully to change their preferred leadership style. Consequently, he sees changing the favorableness of the situation as a better alternative. In doing this, a first step recommended by Fiedler is to determine whether leaders are task- or relationship-oriented. Next, the organization needs to diagnose and classify the situational favorableness of its leadership positions. Finally, the organization must select the best strategy to bring about improved effectiveness. If leadership training is selected as an option, then it should devote special attention to teaching participants how to modify their environments and their jobs to fit their styles of leadership. That is, leaders should be trained to change their leadership situations. Fiedler suggests that when leaders can recognize the situations in which they are most successful, they can then begin to modify their own situations.

Not everyone would agree with Fiedler's contention that leaders cannot be trained to modify their leadership style. Training leaders is a multibillion-dollar business every year. Organizations continue to search for the best candidates and the most effective training programs to prepare leaders. More and more firms are searching for flexibility within the candidates.

Critique of Fiedler's Contingency Model Fiedler's model and research have elicited both support and criticisms.[24] Some researchers have called attention to the questionable measurement of the LPC, finding its reliability and validity to be low. Others have criticized the fact that Fiedler's variables are not precisely defined. For example, at what point does a "structured" task become an "unstructured" task? Still others feel that the model is flawed because it too readily accommodates nonsupportive results.

Despite supporters and detractors, Fiedler's contingency model has made significant contributions to the study and application of leadership principles. Fiedler called direct attention to the situational nature of leadership. His view of leadership stimulated numerous research studies and much-needed debate about the dynamics of leader behavior. Certainly, Fiedler has played one of the most prominent roles in encouraging the scientific study of leadership in work settings. He pointed the way and made others uncomfortably aware of the complexities of the leadership process.

Path-Goal Model

Like the other situational or contingency leadership approaches, the path-goal model attempts to predict leadership effectiveness in different situations.

---

[24]See, for example, L. H. Peters, D. D. Hartke, and J. T. Phlmann, "Fiedler's Contingency Theory of Leadership: An Application of the Meta-Analysis Procedures of Schmidt and Hunter," *Psychological Bulletin,* March 1985, pp. 274–85; C. A. Schriesheim, B. J. Tepper, and L. A. Tetrault, "Least Preferred Co-Worker Score, Situational Control, and Leadership Effectiveness: A Meta-Analysis of Contingency Model Performance Predictions," *Journal of Applied Psychology,* August 1994, pp. 561–73; and R. Ayman, M. M. Chemers, and F. Fiedler, "The Contingency Model of Leadership Effectiveness: Its Levels of Analysis," *Leadership Quarterly,* Summer 1995, pp. 147–67.

According to this model, leaders are effective because of their positive impact on followers' motivation, ability to perform, and satisfaction. The theory is designated path-goal because it focuses on how the leader influences the followers' perceptions of work goals, self-development goals, and paths to goal attainment.[25]

The foundation of path-goal theory is the expectancy motivation theory discussed in Chapter 4. Some early work on the path-goal theory asserts that leaders will be effective by making rewards available to subordinates and by making those rewards contingent on the subordinates' accomplishment of specific goals. It is argued by some that an important part of the leader's job is to clarify for subordinates the kind of behavior most likely to result in goal accomplishment. This activity is referred to as *path clarification*.

The early path-goal work led to the development of a complex theory involving four specific styles of leader behavior (directive, supportive, participative, and achievement) and three types of subordinate attitudes (job satisfaction, acceptance of the leader, and expectations about effort-performance-reward relationships).[26] The *directive leader* tends to let subordinates know what is expected of them. The *supportive leader* treats subordinates as equals. The *participative leader* consults with subordinates and uses their suggestions and ideas before reaching a decision. The *achievement-oriented leader* sets challenging goals, expects subordinates to perform at the highest level, and continually seeks improvement in performance.

Two types of situational or contingency variables are considered in the path-goal theory. These variables are the *personal characteristics of subordinates* and the *environmental pressures and demands* with which subordinates must cope in order to accomplish work goals and derive satisfaction.

An important personal characteristic is subordinates' perception of their own ability. The higher the degree of perceived ability relative to the task demands, the less likely the subordinate is to accept a directive leader style. This directive style of leadership would be viewed as unnecessarily close. In addition, it has been discovered that a person's *locus of control* also affects responses. Individuals who have an internal locus of control (they believe that rewards are contingent on their efforts) are generally more satisfied with a participative style, while individuals who have an external locus of control (they believe that rewards are beyond their personal control) are generally more satisfied with a directive style.[27]

The environmental variables include factors that are not within the control of the subordinate but are important to satisfaction or to the ability to perform effectively.[28] These include the tasks, the formal authority system of the organization, and the work group. Any of these environmental factors can motivate or constrain

---

[25]Robert J. House, "A Path-Goal Theory of Leadership Effectiveness," *Administrative Science Quarterly,* September 1971, pp. 32–39. Also, see Robert J. House and Terence R. Mitchell, "Path-Goal Theory of Leadership," *Journal of Contemporary Business,* Autumn 1974, pp. 81–98, which is the basis for the discussion.

[26]Robert J. House and Gary Dessler, "The Path-Goal Theory of Leadership: Some Post Hoc and A Priori Tests," in James G. Hunt (ed.), *Contingency Approaches to Leadership* (Carbondale: Southern Illinois University Press, 1974).

[27]Gary A. Yukl, *Leadership in Organizations* (Englewood Cliffs, NJ: Prentice-Hall, 1998).

[28]James R. Detert, Roger G. Schoeder, and John J. Mauriel, "A Framework for Linking Culture and Improvement Initiatives in Organizations," *Academy of Management Review,* October 2000, pp 850–63.

EXHIBIT 11.4
The Path-Goal Model

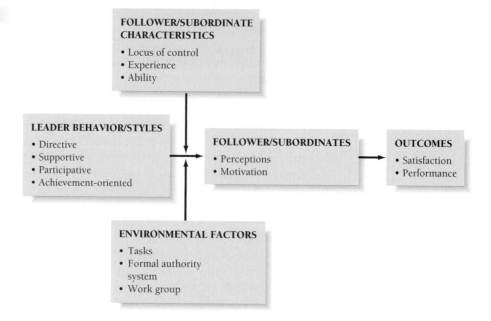

the subordinate. The environmental forces may also serve as a reward for acceptable levels of performance. For example, the subordinate could be motivated by the work group and receive satisfaction from co-workers' acceptance for doing a job according to group norms.

The path-goal theory proposes that leader behavior will be motivational to the extent that it helps subordinates cope with environmental uncertainties. A leader who is able to reduce the uncertainties of the job is considered to be a motivator because he or she increases the subordinate's expectations that their efforts will lead to desirable rewards. Exhibit 11.4 summarizes the basic features of the path-goal approach.

Critique of the Path-Goal Model   The path-goal model warrants further study because some questions remain about its predictive power. One researcher suggested that subordinate performance might be the cause of changes in leader behavior instead of, as predicted by the method, the other way around.[29] A review of the path-goal approach suggested that the model has resulted in the development of only a few hypotheses. These reviewers also point to the record of inconsistent research results associated with the model. Additionally, much of the research to date has involved only partial tests of the model.[30]

On the positive side, however, the path-goal model is an improvement over the trait and personal-behavioral theories. It attempts to indicate which factors affect the motivation to perform. In addition, the path-goal approach introduces both situational factors and individual differences when examining leader behavior and outcomes such as satisfaction and performance. The path-goal approach

[29]C. Green, "Questions of Causation in the Path-Goal Theory of Leadership," *Academy of Management Journal,* March 1979, pp. 22–41.

[30]C. A. Schriesheim and L. L. Neider, "Path-Goal Theory: The Long and Winding Road," *Leadership Quarterly,* Summer 1996, pp. 317–21.

makes an effort to explain why a particular style of leadership works best in a given situation. As more research accumulates, this type of explanation will have practical utility for those interested in the leadership process in work settings.

Hersey-Blanchard Situational Leadership Theory

Managers often complain that esoteric theories don't help them do a better job on the production line, in the office, or in a research and development lab. They request something they can apply and use. Hersey and Blanchard developed a situational leadership theory that has appealed to many managers.[31] Large firms and small businesses have used the situational leadership theory (SLT) and enthusiastically endorse its value.

SLT's emphasis is on followers and their level of maturity. The leader must properly judge or intuitively know followers' maturity level and then use a leadership style that fits the level. Readiness is defined as the ability and willingness of people (followers) to take responsibility for directing their own behavior. It's important to consider two types of readiness: job and psychological. A person high in job readiness has the knowledge and abilities to perform the job without a manager structuring or directing the work. A person high in psychological readiness has the self-motivation and desire to do high-quality work. Again, this person has little need for direct supervision.

Hersey and Blanchard used the Ohio State studies to further develop four leadership styles available to managers:

- *Telling*—the leader defines the roles needed to do the job and tells followers what, where, how, and when to do the tasks.
- *Selling*—the leader provides followers with structured instructions, but is also supportive.
- *Participating*—the leader and followers share in decisions about how best to complete a high-quality job.
- *Delegating*—the leader provides little specific, close direction or personal support to followers.

By determining followers' readiness levels, a manager can choose from among the four leadership styles. Exhibit 11.5 presents characteristics of the SLT.

Application of the model works as follows. Suppose that a manager determines that his recently hired followers are unsure of themselves and insecure about how to perform the job. The followers are at the R1 readiness state. By moving virtually from R1 to the leadership style development curve, the intersection of the vertical line would be at the telling style point. That is, an R1 follower requires a leader who is high on task orientation, gives direct instructions, and is low in support behavior. Task behavior is more needed than supportive behavior. In fact, research is available to support the S1 style over any of the others.[32] Some may as-

---

[31]Originally published in Paul Hersey and Kenneth H. Blanchard, *Management of Organizational Behavior*, in *Utilizing Human Resources* (Englewood Cliffs, NJ: Prentice Hall, 1969), now in 6th edition, which first introduced the concept of readiness. See also Kenneth H. Blanchard and Robert Nelson, "Recognition and Reward," *Executive Excellence*, April 1997, pp. 15–16.

[32]Gary Yukl and Cecilia M. Falbe, "Importance of Different Power Sources in Downward and Lateral Relations," *Journal of Applied Psychology*, June 1991, pp. 416–23.

EXHIBIT 11.5
The Hersey-Blanchard
Situational Leadership
Model

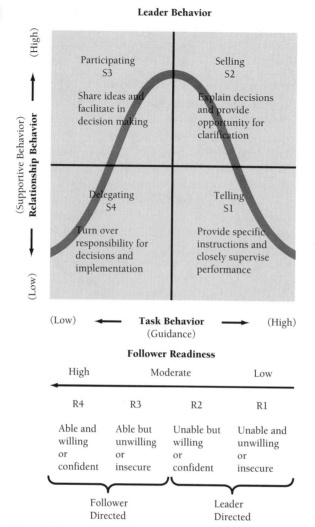

Leader Behavior

(High)

(Supportive Behavior)
Relationship Behavior

Participating
S3

Share ideas and
facilitate in
decision making

Selling
S2

Explain decisions
and provide
opportunity for
clarification

Delegating
S4

Turn over
responsibility for
decisions and
implementation

Telling
S1

Provide specific
instructions and
closely supervise
performance

(Low)

(Low) ← **Task Behavior** → (High)
(Guidance)

Follower Readiness

High		Moderate		Low

R4	R3	R2	R1
Able and willing or confident	Able but unwilling or insecure	Unable but willing or confident	Unable and unwilling or insecure

Follower
Directed

Leader
Directed

Source: P. Hersey and K.H. Blanchard, *Management of Organizational Behavior: Utilizing Human Resources,* 5th ed. (Englewood Cliffs, NJ: Prentice Hall, 1988), p. 171. The original model published in the first edition in 1969 used the label *maturity* instead of *readiness.*

sume that a participative (S3) style is best. However, asking an insecure follower to participate may result in more insecurity about making a mistake or saying something that's considered dumb.

A follower will be more ready to take on more responsibility as other leadership styles become more effective. For example, an R&D lab with expert, experienced scientists who are totally able and willing to do the job would flourish under a delegative (S4) style of leadership. Using the readiness indicator with the four-style model helps the manager conceptualize what's best for followers.

Blanchard has responded to some critics of the SLT by revising the original model.[33] He retitled various terms, calling task behavior *directive behavior* and re-

[33]Kenneth H. Blancard, P. Zigarmi, and D. Zigarmi, *Leadership and the One-Minute Manager* (New York: William Morrow, 1985).

lationship behavior *supportive behavior*. The four leadership styles are now called S1—directing, S2—coaching, S3—supporting, and S4—delegating. Readiness is now called the *development level of followers*. The development level is defined in terms of followers' current competence and commitment to do the job.

Although a number of managers find this model attractive, there are some serious unanswered questions. The most important may be, does it really work? Testing of the model has been very limited. Even the developers, Hersey and Blanchard, have failed to provide significant evidence (1) that predictions can be made from the model, and (2) of which style is best. Another issue revolves around the notion that a leader can change or adapt her style to fit a follower or group. Are people in leadership positions this adaptable? Again, research is needed to validate the flexibility possible among leaders.[34]

Despite the words of caution about limited research and flexibility, many managers like the SLT. It's thought to be practical, meaningful, and useful in training settings. As leadership continues to command attention in organizations, the SLT appears to remain a popular way to express what leaders should be doing at work.

Leader-Member Exchange Approach

For the most part, the leadership approaches we have examined thus far assume that leaders all treat their subordinates in the same way. From your own experience with leaders and groups you probably realize that this is actually seldom the case. The appeal of the leader-member exchange (LMX) approach is its recognition that there is no such thing as consistent leader behavior across subordinates. LMX not only recognizes but emphasizes the differing relationships that leaders develop with different subordinates within a work group.[35] For example, a leader may be very considerate toward one subordinate and very rigid and structured with another. Consequently, a leader with 10 subordinates, for example, will have 10 distinct relationships or leader-member exchanges with each one.[36] It is this one-on-one relationship that determines subordinates' behaviors.

The LMX approach suggests that leaders classify subordinates into *in-group members* and *out-group members*. In-group members have a common bond and value system and interact with the leader. Out-group members have less in common with the leader and don't share much with her. The Leader-Member Exchange Questionnaire partially presented in Exhibit 11.6 measures in-group versus out-group status.[37]

LMX theory suggests that in-group members are likely to receive more challenging assignments and more meaningful rewards. In-group members, in turn, are more positive about the organization culture and have higher job performance and satisfaction than employees in the out-group. An out-group member isn't considered to be the type of person the leader prefers to work with, and this attitude is likely to become a self-fulfilling prophecy. Out-group members receive

---

[34]Jennifer Laabs, "Taking a Stand for Leadership," *Workforce,* May 1999, pp. 23–26.

[35]Elaine M. Engle and Robert G. Lord, "Implicit Theories, Self-Schemas, and Leader-Member Exchange," *Academy of Management Journal,* August 1997, pp. 988–1010.

[36]Tayla N. Bauer and Stephen G. Green, "Development of Leader-Member Exchange: A Longitudinal Test," *Academy of Management Journal,* December 1966, pp. 1538–67.

[37]George Graen, R. Liden, and W. Hoel, "Role of Leadership in the Employee Withdrawal Process," *Journal of Applied Psychology,* December 1982, pp. 868–72.

EXHIBIT 11.6   **Items that Assess Leader-Member Exchange**

1. How flexible do you believe your supervisor is about evolving change in *your* job? 4 = Supervisor is enthused about change; 3 = Supervisor is lukewarm to change; 2 = Supervisor sees little need to change; 1 = Supervisor sees no need for change.

2. Regardless of how much formal organizational authority your supervisor has built into his position, what are the chances that he would be personally inclined to use his power to help you solve problems in your work? 4 = He certainly would; 3 = Probably would; 2 = Might or might not; 1 = No.

3. To what extent can *you* count on your supervisor to "bail you out," at her expense, when *you* really need her? 4 = Certainly would; 3 = Probably; 2 = Might or might not; 1 = No.

4. How often do you take suggestions regarding your work to your supervisor? 4 = Almost always; 3 = Usually; 2 = Seldom; 1 = Never.

5. How would *you* characterize *your* working relationship with your supervisor? 4 = Extremely effective; 3 = Better than average; 2 = About average; 1 = Less than average.

The five items are summed for each participant, resulting in a possible range of scores from 5 to 20.

---

less challenging assignments, receive little positive reinforcement, become bored with their jobs, and may ultimately quit. Viewed from an LMX perspective, the worker described in You Be the Judge was most likely an out-group member.

Research to test various aspects of the LMX model has generally been supportive. The primary contribution that LMX has brought to organizational researchers is found in its basic tenet: Leaders form different types of relationships with subordinates based upon different degrees of emotional support and exchange of resources, and these relationships are pivotal in determining the subordinates' success in the organizations.[38]

SUBSTITUTES FOR LEADERSHIP

Leadership substitutes have been identified as task, organizational, or subordinate characteristics that render relationship- and/or task-oriented leadership as not only impossible but also unnecessary. A related concept is called a *leadership neutralizer*—something that makes it impossible for leadership to make a difference.[39]

Researchers have identified a wide variety of individual, task, environmental, and organizational characteristics as leadership substitute factors that influence relationships between leader behavior and follower satisfaction and performance. Some of these variables (e.g., follower expectations of the leader behavior) appear to influence which leadership style will enable the leader to motivate the direct followers. Others, however, function as *substitutes for leadership*. Substitute variables tend to negate the leader's ability to either increase or decrease follower satisfaction or performance.

---

[38]Raymond T. Sparrowe and Robert C. Liden, "Process and Structure in Leader-Member Exchange," *Academy of Management Review,* April 1997, pp. 522–52.

[39]P. M. Podsakoff, S. B. MacKenzie, and W. H. Bommer, "Meta-Analysis of the Relationships between Kerr and Jermier's Substitutes for Leadership and Employee Job Attitudes, Role Perceptions, and Performance," *Journal of Applied Psychology,* May 1996, pp. 380–99.

If Your Boss Makes You Sick Can You Get a New One?

You Be the Judge

It is clearly illegal for anyone in a managerial or leadership role to discriminate against employees on the basis of such factors as gender, race, religion, age, disabilities, or national origin. Nor can leaders harass their employees in ways that contribute to a hostile work environment. But what if simply working for a particular boss makes an employee sick? Does the company have a legal obligation to get you a new boss? One employee of the New York Federal Reserve Bank (Fed) thought so.

A manager at the Fed suffered a back injury, unrelated to work, and was given two medical leaves at full pay, each about six months long. In between, she worked about six months on a part-time schedule, also at full pay. At various times during this period she expressed dissatisfaction with her boss. While on her second leave her physician and her psychologist both wrote the Fed recommending that she return to work but that certain accommodations be made for her because of her back injury. One of these accommodations was that she be given a new boss because she found working for her current one aggravated her back problem.

The Fed gave her two choices: (1) return to work under her current manager, receive ergonomic furniture, have flexibility to get up and move around periodically, and receive assistance from the personnel office in seeking a new position elsewhere in the Fed, or (2) resign, receive assistance in finding work elsewhere, and receive 26 weeks of severance pay and six months of medical benefits. When she failed to show up for work and did not accept the severance package, she was fired. She sued claiming the Fed discriminated against her because of her disability and failed to make a reasonable accommodation for her as required by the Americans with Disabilities Act. What was the outcome? You be the judge!

Substitutes for leadership are claimed to be prominent in many organizational settings. However, the dominant leadership approaches fail to include substitutes for leadership in discussing the leader behavior–follower satisfaction and performance relationship.

Exhibit 11.7, based on previously conducted research, provides substitutes for only two of the more popular leader behavior styles: relationship-oriented and task-oriented. For each of these styles, Kerr and Jermier present substitutes (characteristics of the subordinate, the task, or the organization) that neutralize the style.[40] For example, an experienced, well-trained, knowledgeable employee doesn't need a leader to structure the task (e.g., a task-oriented leader). Likewise, a job (task) that provides its own feedback doesn't require a task-oriented leader to inform the employee how he's doing. Also, an employee in a close-knit, cohesive group doesn't need a supportive, relationship-oriented leader. The group substitutes for this leader.

Admittedly, we don't fully understand the leader-follower relationship in organizational settings. We need to continue searching for guidelines and principles. Such searching now seems to be centered on more careful analysis of a situational perspective of leadership and on issues such as the cause-effect question,

---

[40]Steven Kerr and John M. Jermier, "Substitutes for Leadership: Their Meaning and Measurement," *Organizational Behavior and Human Performance,* December 1978, pp. 376–403.

EXHIBIT 11.7   Substitutes for Leadership

Characteristic	Neutralizes	
	Relationship-Oriented Leadership	**Task-Oriented Leadership**
Of the subordinate:		
1. Ability, experience, training, knowledge		X
2. Need for independence	X	X
3. "Professional" orientation	X	X
4. Indifference toward organizational rewards	X	X
Of the task:		
5. Unambiguous and routine		X
6. Methodologically invariant		X
7. Provides its own feedback concerning accomplishment		X
8. Intrinsically satisfying	X	
Of the organization:		
9. Formalization (explicit plans, goals, and areas of responsibility)		X
10. Inflexibility (rigid, unbending rules and procedures)		X
11. Highly specified and active advisory and staff functions		X
12. Close-knit, cohesive work groups	X	X
13. Organizational rewards not within the leader's control	X	X
14. Spatial distance between superior and subordinates	X	X

Source: Adapted from Steven Kerr and John M. Jermier, Substitutes for Leadership: Their Meaning and Measurement, *Organizational Behavior and Human Performance,* December 1978, p. 378.

the constraints on leader behavior, and substitutes for leadership. We feel that it's better to study leaders and substitutes for leaders than to use catchy descriptions to identify leaders. Such study and analysis can result in developing programs to train, prepare, and develop employees for leadership roles.

COMPARING THE SITUATIONAL APPROACHES

The four models for examining situation leadership have some similarities and some differences. They are similar in that they (1) focus on the dynamics of leadership, (2) have stimulated research on leadership, and (3) remain controversial because of measurement problems, limited research testing, or contradictory research results.

The themes of each model are summarized in Exhibit 11.8. Fiedler's model, the most tested, is perhaps the most controversial. His view of leader behavior centers on task- and relationship-oriented tendencies and how these interact with task and position power. The path-goal approach emphasizes the instrumental actions of leaders and four styles for conducting these actions (directive, supportive, participative, and achievement-oriented).

The situational variables discussed in each approach differ somewhat. There is also a different view of outcome criteria for assessing how successful the leader behavior has been: Fiedler discusses leader effectiveness, and the path-goal approach focuses on satisfaction and performance.

EXHIBIT 11.8   Summary Comparison of Four Important Situational Models of Leadership

	Fiedler's Contingency Model	House's Path-Goal Model	Hersey-Blanchard Situational Leadership Theory	Leader-Member Exchange (LMX) Approach
Leadership qualities	Leaders are task- or relationship-oriented. The job should be engineered to fit the leader's style.	Leaders can increase followers' effectiveness by applying proper motivational techniques.	Leader must adapt style in terms of task behavior and relationship behavior on the basis of followers.	Leader must be adaptive since there is no such thing as consistent leader behavior across subordinates.
Assumptions about followers	Followers prefer different leadership styles, depending on task structure, leader-member relations, and position power.	Followers have different needs that must be fulfilled with the help of a leader.	Followers' maturity (readiness) to take responsibility and ability to influence the leadership style that is adopted.	Followers are categorized as in-groups (which share a common bond and value system, and interact with the leader) and out-groups (which have less in common with the leader).
Leader effectiveness	Effectiveness of the leader is determined by the interaction of environment and personality factors.	Effective leaders are those who clarify for followers the paths or behaviors that are best suited.	Effective leaders are able to adapt directing, coaching, supporting, and delegating style to fit the followers' levels of maturity.	The perceptive leader is able to adapt her style to fit followers' needs.
History of research: problems	If investigations not affiliated with Fiedler are used, the evidence is contradictory on the accuracy of the model.	Model has generated very little research interest in past two decades.	Not enough research is available to reach a definitive conclusion about the predictive power of the theory.	Approach has generated a limited amount of research to support its assumptions and predictions.

Summary of Key Points

- Leadership is the process of influencing others to facilitate the attainment of organizationally relevant goals. Exercising leadership does not require that one be in a formal leadership position. Three important variables present in all leadership situations are people, task, and environment.

- A trait approach to leadership focuses on identifying the intellectual, emotional, physical, or other personal traits of effective leaders. Traits that have been identified include intelligence, personality, height, and supervisory ability. Trait approaches have failed to identify any universally accepted characteristics.

- Behavior approaches to leadership focus on the *behavior* of the leader. Job-centered and employee-centered leadership and initiating structure and consideration are examples of what has been identified as important leader behavior. Behavior approaches and trait approaches both fail to include the nature of the leadership situation in attempting to prescribe effective leadership approaches.

- Situational approaches emphasize the importance of taking into account the nature of the environment, or situation, in which leadership is exercised. Important situational approaches include Fiedler's contingency model, the path-goal model, Hersey and Blanchard's situational leadership theory, and the leader-member exchange (LMX) approach. Each of these approaches emphasizes a different aspect of the leadership situation that should be considered.

- A leadership substitute is a factor that renders leadership unnecessary or even impossible. Leadership substitutes negate the leader's ability to either increase or decrease follower satisfaction or performance. Substitutes can include cohesive work groups, intrinsically satisfying tasks, and high levels of subordinate ability, experience, and knowledge.

Review and Discussion Questions

1. Why do different organizations look for different characteristics in their leaders? Does it make sense that this should be the case?

2. What aspects of a leadership situation might be important that haven't been identified by the situational leadership approaches already discussed in this chapter?

3. Over time, the many different approaches used to explain leadership have become increasingly involved and complex. Why do you think this has happened?

4. Organizations annually spend a great deal of money on leadership training. Is this a wise investment? Are there other less costly ways of improving leadership effectiveness?

5. Why is it accurate to state that "bosses" may be replaced on teams, but that leaders are not replaceable on any team?

6. Most behavior approaches to leadership focus on two aspects of a leader's behavior: behaviors relating to getting the job done, and behavior relating to building and maintaining good relationships with followers. Can you think of any additional areas of leader behavior that might be important?

7. Realistically, how much control does a leader have over situational favorableness? How might a leader go about trying to improve favorableness? Does it really make sense for a leader to try to *decrease* favorableness?

8. It has been suggested that good leadership is knowing when to take charge and when to delegate. How consistent is this with the various situational approaches discussed in this chapter?

9. Is there a cause-and-effect relationship between leader behavior and follower performance? What is the nature or direction of the relationship? How strong is the relationship?

10. What substitutes for leadership exist for a student preparing to take a final examination in a course offered as part of a firm's educational fringe-benefit program?

READING 11.1   The Nine Dilemmas Leaders Face

by Thomas A. Stewart

Sheree R. Curry

"Management"—the word—traces its origins to the arts of horsemanship—from the Latin *manus*, "hand," via the Italian *maneggiare*, "to train horses." But since most of us call down to the stable to have the coach and four readied even less often than we wear white tie, let's talk cars. When you're driving, you do several potentially contradictory things at once. You want to get to your destination quickly, and also safely. You must watch the road and also look behind and around you. You can do one—you can do the other—but you want to do both. These are dilemmas: a word from the Greek, "two assumptions or premises." Dilemmas are what your boss talks about when he says, "You're in charge, Fosdick, but make sure Susannah is on board."

Managing dilemmas is what you do.

However, you cannot manage what you cannot name. That's why, when God gave Adam dominion over the fish of the sea and the birds of the air and every living thing that moves upon the earth, He brought the creatures before Adam, and had him name them.

A couple of years ago, an opportunity to define the dilemmas of management presented itself when Canadian Imperial Bank of Commerce decided to build an Edenic leadership center for its managers and employees on a rolling 100-acre site 45 minutes north of its Toronto headquarters. When Al Flood, the CEO of the bank (North America's eighth largest, with 1995 assets of $132 billion), okayed the plans, he did what any good banker would: He told Michele Darling, head of human resources, and Hubert Saint-Onge, who was to run the center, to make sure that this asset performed.

Thus challenged, Darling and Saint-Onge responded with an extraordinary act of in-house journalism. To create a mission and a curriculum for the center, Saint-Onge interviewed CIBC's 27 most senior executives, one on one. He asked each of them five open-ended questions: What factors in the business environment most affect CIBC's leaders? What cultural changes does the bank need to be more successful? What organizational capabilities does it need to build? What are the most pressing management-development needs? What features should leadership-center programs include? Those questions elicited a wealth of ideas.

Though some were predictable—what company's leaders don't feel they should "be more customer-driven"?—together they helped Darling and Saint-Onge define their mission. But there was more: The pages upon pages of notes made for an unusual chance to learn how leaders think and what they think about.

Poring over the interviews, Saint-Onge began highlighting phrases like "we must do a . . . but also b," or "in going after x, we must not lose sight of y." When he was done, he found nine "core leadership dilemmas." They fit any business and any manager, though they may be felt most keenly at the top.

Broad-based leadership vs. high-visibility leaders. The bankers acutely felt the need for top executives to get out front, to rally the troops personally and even charismatically. With equal fervor they saw a requirement to foster leadership throughout the company. If top management dominates the airwaves, it will silence others; if it is too reticent, the others will fret and wither for lack of support. For example, experts say reengineering will fail if the CEO doesn't take a strong role, but add that its success depends on a broad cadre of leaders among middle managers, team members, and others.

Independence vs. interdependence We want entrepreneurship, a sense of ownership, and P&L responsibility, but we don't want one division badmouthing another, hogging shared resources, or refusing to take advantage of what the company has to offer. I was gored by the horns of this dilemma once: My then boss told me and a couple of peers that we had authority to make ad-budget decisions; we should consult with the marketing director but feel free to overrule her. When a few months later I felt it was necessary to do precisely that, he rapped my knuckles and said I should be more of a team player.

Long term vs. short term The oldest dilemma in the book, but that doesn't make it easy to resolve. Several years back, I interviewed David Kearns, then CEO of Xerox. The topic: lessons learned from Xerox's failure to make successful businesses out of some of its inventions, like the desktop fax machine and the personal computer. Kearns had been wrestling with the problem of

Source: Thomas A. Stewart, "The Nine Dilemmas Leaders Face," *Fortune*, © Time Inc. All rights reserved.

bc.com

erox.com

how to link labs more closely to the commercial needs of the business—while not gutting their talent for imagining and inventing a faraway future. As he showed me out at the end of our talk, he took a deep breath, shook his head, and settled his shoulders. He said: "We've been talking about five and ten years ago, and five and ten years from now. Waiting outside are a couple of security analysts, and the only thing they care about is the next quarter." What struck me most was the almost physical effort he needed to rearrange his mind.

Creativity vs. discipline You encourage all those entrepreneurial leaders to benefit from freethinking, but they still have to make budget and adhere to company policy. It's as if Mao Zedong had said, "Let a thousand flowers bloom—in a topiary garden."

Trust vs. change At first blush, trust and change don't seem to pull in opposite directions, but they do: Implementing organizational change—whether it's moving offices around or massive reengineering—can damage trust and commitment. Old work groups are sundered, new bosses have new standards, the world's in flux, and it's look out for No. 1. Even positive change can weaken trust: It was those wedding bells, after all, that broke up that old gang of mine. Yet without trust, change is impossible.

Bureaucracy busting vs. economies of scale Let's centralize purchasing to leverage our size to get a better price. Let's also destroy the costly bureaucracies that clog the corporate coronary arteries when they, for example, force me to buy stuff that doesn't fit the needs of my business unit. (If you're not noticing that these dilemmas fall into a pattern, you're not reading closely enough.)

People vs. productivity Another chestnut, but one that's really in the fire these days: The need to maximize productivity, to get everybody contributing 110 percent, must be balanced against the demands of personal life and the realization that, in the long run, all work and no play makes Jack a sitting duck.

Leadership vs. capability The managerial and technical skills that enhance operations are quite different from the people-and-vision skills that produce leadership. The best strategy in the world won't work if it is poorly executed, but superb implementation of the wrong strategy simply means that Armageddon will come sooner than it otherwise would.

Revenue growth vs. cost containment Once, in a hotel lobby, I saw a man carrying a coffee mug on which was printed BUDGETS ARE FOR WIMPS. "Where'd you get that?" I asked, hoping he would tell me a nearby shop had them.

But no: "My boss had them made for us." "He a marketing guy?" I asked.

He said: "How did you know?"

Nine Dilemmas that describe your job. What do you do with them? First, notice that pattern. Says Saint-Onge: "These are all different, but they form a single, central dilemma." Its name: empowerment vs. alignment, the never-ending balancing act of managerial Bongo Board in which you try to give people independence and authority while making sure they use it in a way you'd approve of if they asked, which you don't want them to do except, of course, when you do want them to. Lee Iacocca sent the wrong message in that TV ad. The right one is: "Lead, follow, and get out of the way."

Second, you can make charts—always a good use of managerial time. Take each dilemma, and put one horn on a vertical axis and one on the horizontal. Draw a 45 [degree] diagonal to represent a balance between the two. Then on a scale of 1 to 10, 10 being best, locate your outfit (or yourself or your boss) on the grid. This chart shows a company that pursues revenue growth aggressively but doesn't mind costs well.

Set these up with all the "empowerment" tendencies (broad-based leadership, independence, long-termism, creativity, etc.) on the vertical axis and the "alignment" group on the horizontal. What do you see? Are you usually below the diagonal (too controlling) or above it (too loosey-goosey)?

You want to be spot on the diagonal line, and as far out toward the upper-right-hand corner as possible. This is because both sides of each dilemma are good: You want creativity and you want discipline; in fact, to get the greatest benefit of creativity, you need to temper it with discipline, and vice versa. The goal is to manage better in both directions—you want maximum empowerment and maximum alignment, just as a figure skater wants perfect scores for both artistic impression and technical merit.

For the folks at CIBC, the most important lesson of the nine dilemmas was seeing that, fundamentally, leadership is about ambiguities, not certainties. Says Michele Darling: "The dilemmas helped us come to a different understanding of the roles a leader plays."

One role she calls "polarity management." Leaders often are mesmerized by the virtues of one side of a dilemma, and ignore its worthy alternative. "Successful leaders," says Darling, "explore both ends." If you get your jollies from bureaucracy busting, force yourself to love economies of scale: Who better to reap its benefits than an honest skeptic? Polarities can also help you diagnose and deal with a group's resistance to change—chances are they're hung up on one horn of a dilemma, and you can help by showing them that they are right, but only half right.

Twinned with polarity management is ambiguity management. Too much thinking about leadership has a hortatory "set a vision and march on toward it" feel. But big strategic facts aren't always so clear—something that both leaders and their followers have to understand. Embracing ambiguities can be a powerful way to learn about a changing world.

A third role emerges from polarities and ambiguities: Making meaning. Says Darling: "The defining role of a leader is to sort out a message" from these mixed signals and cross-purposes. The new customer-satisfaction scores have just come in, and they show problems, but you also just received a market-segmentation analysis that shows that some customers demand so much service they are actually unprofitable. Your job is to take those dilemmas and make sense—and sensible plans—out of them. Otherwise it's all Greek.

Exercises

EXERCISE 11.1   Task and People Orientations

Are you task or people oriented? Or do you have a balanced style of leading? The following items describe the people- or task-oriented aspects of leadership. Use any past or present experience in leading a group of people as you complete the 34-item scale. Circle whether you would most likely behave in the described way: always (A), frequently (F), occasionally (O), seldom (S), or never (N).

Source: The T/P Leadership Questionnaire was adapted by J. B. Ritchie and P. Thompson, *Organization and People* (New York: West, 1984). Copyright 1969 by the American Educational Research Association.

A	F	O	S	N	1. I would most likely act as the spokesperson of the group.
A	F	O	S	N	2. I would encourage overtime work.
A	F	O	S	N	3. I would allow employees complete freedom in their work.
A	F	O	S	N	4. I would encourage the use of uniform procedures.
A	F	O	S	N	5. I would permit employees to use their own judgment in solving problems.
A	F	O	S	N	6. I would stress being ahead of competing groups.
A	F	O	S	N	7. I would speak as a representative of the group.
A	F	O	S	N	8. I would encourage members for a greater effort.
A	F	O	S	N	9. I would try out my ideas in the group.
A	F	O	S	N	10. I would let members do their work the way they think best.
A	F	O	S	N	11. I would be working hard for a promotion.
A	F	O	S	N	12. I would tolerate postponement and uncertainty.
A	F	O	S	N	13. I would speak for the group if there were visitors present.
A	F	O	S	N	14. I would keep the work moving at a rapid pace.
A	F	O	S	N	15. I would turn the members loose on a job and let them go to it.
A	F	O	S	N	16. I would settle conflicts when they occur in the group.
A	F	O	S	N	17. I would get swamped by details.
A	F	O	S	N	18. I would represent the group at outside meetings.
A	F	O	S	N	19. I would be reluctant to allow the members any freedom of action.
A	F	O	S	N	20. I would decide what should be done and how it should be done.
A	F	O	S	N	21. I would give some members some of my authority.
A	F	O	S	N	22. Things would usually turn out as I had predicted.
A	F	O	S	N	23. I would allow the group a high degree of initiative.
A	F	O	S	N	24. I would assign group members to particular tasks.
A	F	O	S	N	25. I would be willing to make changes.
A	F	O	S	N	26. I would ask the members to work harder.
A	F	O	S	N	27. I would trust the group members to exercise good judgment.
A	F	O	S	N	28. I would schedule the work to be done.
A	F	O	S	N	29. I would refuse to explain my actions.
A	F	O	S	N	30. I would persuade others that my ideas are to their advantage.

A	F	O	S	N		31. I would permit the group to set its own pace.
A	F	O	S	N		32. I would urge the group to beat its previous record.
A	F	O	S	N		33. I would act without consulting the group.
A	F	O	S	N		34. I would ask that group members follow standard rules and regulations.

T _____ P _____

The T/P Leadership Questionnaire is scored as follows:

a. Circle the item numbers for statements 8, 12, 17, 18, 19, 29, 33, and 34.

b. Write the number 1 in front of a *circled item number* if you responded S (seldom) or N (never) to that statement.

c Also write a number 1 in front of *item numbers not circled* if you responded A (always) or F (frequently).

d. Circle the numbers that you have written in front of the following statements: 3, 5, 8, 10, 15, 18, 19, 21, 23, 25, 27, 29, 31, 33, and 34.

e. Count the *circled number 1s*. This is your score for concern for people. Record the score in the blank following the letter P.

f. Count the *uncircled number 1s*. This is your score for concern for task. Record this number in the blank following the letter T.

Cases

CASE 11.1   Rotating Leaders: Orpheus Orchestra

The second week of January at Baruch High School in Manhattan: Teenagers are noisily making their way to and from class. On the street below, a siren blares through Union Square. And in a classroom on one of the floors of the high school, musicians are sight-reading a piece of music. After several frustrating attempts, cellist Melissa Meell finally stops and shrugs her shoulders. "We're a long way from Carnegie Hall," she quips.

That kind of wisecrack would be typical of a clever 12th-grader who's struggling through her first Mozart symphony, hoping to ace her audition for all-city orchestra and get a crack at playing on the stage of that revered concert hall. But, in fact, Meell is 44, a professional musician, and a member of Orpheus—a Grammy-nominated chamber orchestra that's widely considered one of the best of its kind on the planet. Although she and her fellow musicians are just 19 days away from their next Carnegie Hall performance, they still sound as if they're playing rubber bands.

With such an imposing deadline at hand, why is this prestigious group of musicians rehearsing in such noisy surroundings? The school, it turns out, is its home. Orpheus has been the orchestra in residence at Baruch High School for more than three years and at Zicklin School of Business, which is affiliated with New York City's university system, since September 1999. Orpheus is a conductorless orchestra, and it was for that very reason that Baruch wanted the orchestra to take up residence

there—so that students could watch Orpheus rehearse and observe firsthand how it uses collaboration and consensus-building to settle its creative differences. High school students would get a living lesson in conflict resolution. And business students, who would soon be working in a world where few people believe that a CEO has—or should have—all of the answers, would learn that self-governance makes a worthwhile model and that leadership is most effective when all levels of an organization have input.

Its self-governing and leadership abilities have made Orpheus more than just a group of gifted musicians. Orpheus has actually become a metaphor for structural change—the kind of change that has bedeviled so many big companies and exasperated so many big-company CEOs. Orpheus's founder, Julian Fifer, 49, first became aware of the group's metamorphosis when a chairman of a large Japanese publishing company approached him several years ago. "He told me how much he had enjoyed our concert," Fifer recalls. "But then he confided that he didn't want his employees to discover us." Fifer was amused—and intrigued: If old-line business leaders resisted their self-governing process, presumably there were corporate mavericks who would find it compelling. That assumption proved to be correct: During the past two years, several large companies, including Kraft Foods and Novartis AG, have hired Orpheus to demonstrate its process to their executives.

What do these executives find so compelling about Orpheus's sound and system? To them, the group is a radical, ongoing experiment to find out whether grassroots

Source: Adapted from Ron Lieber, "Leadership Ensemble," *Fast Company,* May 2000, p. 286, used by permission.

democracy and commitment to consensus can lead to transcendental performance—or whether it will all end in organizational chaos and muddled results. So what is the key to the orchestra's continued success? A set of insights about motivation, decision making, performance, and work that are as relevant in conference rooms as they are in concert halls.

MOTIVATION: THE SWEET SOUND OF SATISFACTION

Those who aspire to a career as a classical musician and who are studying at a top conservatory have a few obvious career paths: Clearly, the more talented you are, the more options you have. Those who win or place well in big competitions can go on to sign recording contracts and to enjoy solo careers. They can also choose to join chamber-music groups, as do many of their other colleagues. Virtually all—no matter how successful or well-known—teach. Some, however, are forced to do so to support themselves financially. Most orchestra musicians who want to perform full-time join symphony orchestras.

Those jobs offer relative stability and a decent income, but they are hard to come by. Even so, back in the early 1970s, when Orpheus's founding members were trickling out of music schools and into the New York freelance scene, taking such a job was not high on their list of career goals. "Many of us believed that joining a traditional orchestra would lead to a creative dead end," says Ronnie Bauch, 47, a violinist with Orpheus since 1974, "because you'd be under the thumb of its conductor for the next 30 or 40 years."

"Ironically, your conservatory training leaves you ill-equipped to play in large orchestras," adds Frank Morelli, 49, a bassoonist who joined Orpheus in the late 1970s but sometimes also plays in conductor-led groups. "Presumably, you've devoted so much time to studying music because you have a need for self-expression. If you've studied at a top school for the past four or so years, you've also got a certain amount of pride and ego invested in your career. And you're self-motivated because the competition is so steep. But all of those things can get in the way when you're sitting in an orchestra with a conductor telling you what to do."

Some observers of the orchestra scene today believe that the moral righteousness of Orpheus's early members was prophetic. "The climate in most conductor-led orchestras is appalling," says Harvey Seifter, 46, Orpheus's executive director, who left the theater world about two years ago to take on the delicate task of administering to the needs of this self-governing enterprise. "Orchestras take a lot of very smart people, many of whom learned to read music before they learned to read words, and, if they're violinists, sit them in the last row of the second-violin section, where they must unquestioningly follow someone who's waving a stick at them. Success is defined as how good you are at getting your bow to leap off your violin at the exact same nanosecond as all of the other violinists' bows."

That interpretation is in keeping with the results of a study conducted by Harvard psychology professor Richard Hackman. In the early 1990s, Hackman looked at job satisfaction among symphony musicians in 78 orchestras in four countries and found widespread discontent. Indeed, in this now well-known study, symphony members experienced the same levels of job satisfaction as the federal prison guards whom Hackman had studied earlier. Symphony musicians were, however, happier than professional hockey players.

"Most of them adapt," explains Hackman. "But they often do that by finding other ways to develop musically. One person said that he had to be very careful not to let his symphony job get in the way of making music."

For Fifer, the inspiration for Orpheus came from his chamber-music experiences back at Juilliard. He found the sense of intimacy and connectedness that he felt with other musicians in those groups exciting and inspiring, and he longed to find a way to re-create that experience on a larger scale. "I loved chamber music's clarity of sound and flexibility of temperament," he says. "I wanted to bring that camaraderie and spirit into a larger setting. And in order for everyone to be able to communicate more effectively, it seemed necessary to do without a conductor."

So Fifer invited a select group of musicians to that first rehearsal, carefully choosing among those who he knew could take—as well as give—criticism. He named the group Orpheus, for the Greek god who created music so powerful that stones rose up and followed him. "We had no particular method for presenting interpretations and ideas on a piece, but our spirits were high, and we had a great deal of enthusiasm," he recalls. "It was as if we were calling out to anyone who would listen, 'Look Ma, no hands!' "

DECISION MAKING: EVERYONE'S A LEADER (JUST NOT ALL AT ONCE)

But could they do it? When Fifer's idea first took shape, he knew of no preexisting model for a conductorless group of Orpheus's size—anywhere. So his idea was an ambitious one: assembling a number of renegade musicians and building a sustainable enterprise fueled only (at least at first) by idealism and satisfaction. Still, the group pressed on, meeting at Chinese restaurants, rehearsing in churches, and performing at public libraries and housing projects, because city-owned property cost nothing to rent. Eventually, the group got a few annual grants from New York's arts commission, created a demo tape, and, in 1974, booked a small hall at Lincoln Center for its debut performance. In 1979, Orpheus made its first concert tour of Europe, and five years later, it signed a recording contract with the prestigious Deutsche Grammaphon label.

Even as performances gained recognition and attracted larger audiences, rehearsals remained a work in progress. At first, all 27 members of the group participated in every decision that had to be made for each piece—hundreds of tiny details involving dynamics, phrasing, and tempo. So that Orpheus wouldn't sound like dueling stereos, each decision had to be unanimous. And that could take a while, especially when 27 strong-willed musicians were involved, and the buck stopped with all of them. "Rehearsals were becoming free-for-alls," says Martha Caplin, 48, a violinist with the group since 1982. "We needed twice as many rehearsals just to try all of the ideas."

Any organization that operates on consensus risks the possibility of arriving at utterly wishy-washy decisions. If the agreement process is itself chaotic, that risk is even greater. To combat that problem, Orpheus decided to experiment with a new rehearsal method. Instead of just giving the floor to anyone who had an interpretation to offer, Orpheus formed smaller core groups, whose members would change regularly, that would rehearse each piece before the entire group began working on it.

"These core groups formulate one interpretation of a piece," Bauch emphasizes. "It's not necessarily the interpretation. Sometimes it's just a starting point." A core group does the same sort of preparation that a good conductor would do—researching the composer's other works, learning the history of the particular work that will be performed, and listening to recordings of that piece of music. Then the core group presents its ideas to the entire ensemble during the first read through.

Another unusual aspect of Orpheus is the role that its concertmaster plays. In conductor-led orchestras, the concertmaster is usually more of a team captain. But in Orpheus, that function (which rotates regularly) is similar to that of a player-coach on a soccer team. Orpheus's concertmasters are responsible for actually running its rehearsals, moderating debates among members, suggesting resolutions to those debates, and making sure that such discussions don't get too bogged down. Although the core group exerts its influence mostly in the early stages of rehearsing a piece, the concertmaster has more influence as performance dates near.

According to Fifer, having different people be concertmaster seemed the only logical way to run a group fueled by 1960s idealism. The decision to rotate core-group members was, however, more pragmatic: "That rotation method actually alleviates some of the pressure to try to get your way all of the time," admits Bauch. "Having to modulate our personalities and to take on different roles gives us an opportunity to develop leadership skills as well as a chance to be supportive." At first, the entire

group voted on who would be the concertmaster for each piece. Eventually, Orpheus elected an executive committee that appoints a concertmaster according to an individual's particular musical expertise.

Not only do core groups and concertmasters change from concert to concert, but they also change from piece to piece. Such frequent changes in leadership require some preperformance planning. At the conclusion of every piece, Orpheus musicians bow and walk off stage. When they return for the next selection on the program, they take different seats, according to their part in that piece. This maneuvering is similar to that of the small chamber groups that Fifer envisioned when he formed Orpheus.

And also like those small chamber-music groups, different members of Orpheus give one another musical cues. Alert audience members will notice a musician use a nod of a head or a gesture of a bow, in a way inviting a fellow musician to join the "conversation" by offering that person a chance to pick up a musical thought. "At any time, you can be leading or following." " 'Supporting' is the word that we like to use," says Bauch. "When I'm about to get a cue, I often find myself moving with the musician who's playing." That physical style of playing is usually not experienced in a standard symphony orchestra. It's as if members of Orpheus are all breathing with the same set of lungs.

For performances, Orpheus sits in a semicircle, with the center space (which is normally reserved for a conductor) empty. As a result, casual observers and some critics have erroneously referred to the ensemble as being "leaderless." In fact, "Orpheus exerts more leadership than any other orchestra I've examined," says Harvard's Hackman.

PERFORMANCE: PRACTICE RANDOM ACTS OF LEADERSHIP

Soloists often adjust how loud they play a piece and how long they hold a note to the acoustics of a particular recital hall. Orpheus does the same. Those who have never worked with the group may find its methods fascinating. "One of the neatest things about Orpheus is that one of its musicians will go down and sit in the audience to hear how each piece sounds to a concertgoer's ears," says Susan Botti, 38, a singer and composer who wrote a piece that Orpheus premiered during its series of concerts in late January. "I come from the theater, so I'm used to having people out where the audience sits taking notes and giving feedback during a run-through, but I've never seen that happen in an orchestra before."

Whether or not the concertmaster for a piece is particularly vocal, or the core group unusually opinionated, Orpheus's members all demonstrate great faith in the feedback from the colleague who's doing a sound check. "It's a crucial part of what we do," says Bauch. "On stage, you can't hear how a piece of music sounds to an audience, so you have to trust your colleague's ear. We used to vote on that kind of stuff at the last minute. Now that our listening skills are more refined, I think we trust one another more." (Bauch also has had an opportunity to hone another of his senses—just in case he'll need it on the concert stage: He helped taste-test New York Super Fudge Chunk ice cream for his childhood friends, Ben and Jerry.)

Bauch notes that changing core-group participants and the concertmaster position has given each orchestra member an intensive course in leadership training. "I've always been a quiet person, but in this group, speaking up is a matter of survival," says Susan Palma-Nidel, 53, a flutist with Orpheus since 1980. "This experience has allowed me to discover strengths that I didn't know I had. Not only have I helped lead the group, but I've also been interviewed by the media—something I never thought I'd do. If I hadn't been forced to do those things, I'm not sure that I ever would have."

QUESTIONS:

1. What would business organizations such as Kraft Foods gain from observing Orpheus in action?
2. Orpheus rotates the concertmaster among core-group members. What is the logic of rotating the leader?
3. What are some of the substitutes for permanent leadership that exist within Orpheus?

12

Chapter

Leadership: Developing Applications

After completing Chapter 12, you should be able to:

Learning Objectives

- Describe the Vroom-Jago leadership model.

- Discuss the attribution theory approach to leadership.

- Describe what constitutes charismatic leadership.

- Compare transactional and transformational leadership.

- Identify the major issues in multicultural leadership.

In Chapter 11 we took an overview of leadership, focusing on what the term *leadership* means and examining some of the approaches to studying leadership that have contributed to our current level of knowledge about this important management topic. In the current chapter, we shall examine some developing concepts and applications. The term *development* designates an approach that is still generating theoretical, research, and/or application interest. Some of the leadership explanations in this chapter are not new. They are, however, vibrant, insightful, and offer theorists, researchers, and practicing managers an opportunity to debate, study, and experiment.

As we begin the new millennium, the pace of organizational change is rapidly accelerating. As organizations seek to survive and prosper in a global marketplace, what worked even a decade ago in the form of operating policies, procedures, and planning may no longer be appropriate.[1] The same may be said of leaders and leadership practices. What worked in the past may no longer be ideally suited for the present and future. It has been suggested, for example, that effective leadership for tomorrow's organizations will be built around three dimensions: processing knowledge, building trust, and using power sensitively.[2]

According to this perspective, knowledge is the basis of competitive advantage; finding and disseminating knowledge becomes a key role for a leader. An effective leader builds seamless communication networks and information flows. The second dimension of trust relates to the leader's ability to trust others as well as be trusted by others. Trust relates to the first dimension of processing knowledge; the more reciprocal trust there is, the more information is likely to be shared and the higher the quality of the information is likely to be. The more adept the leader is in understanding the forces that affect trust, the better able he or she will be to build trust. The final dimension of using power sensitively is partly accomplished by effectively accomplishing the first two dimensions of processing knowledge and building trust. The sensitive use of power means appropriately exercising power along a continuum ranging from commanding through consulting, concurring, and consigning.[3]

As we shall see in this chapter, many of the developing approaches to leadership focus less on the operations the leader performs and more on the nature and quality of the atmosphere created by the leader. In this sense, it is important to make a distinction between a manager and a leader. Most managerial positions in organizations come with some authority; thus, most managers perform some leadership roles. But all managers are not leaders, any more than all leaders are managers. Managers perform a number of operations as they "manage" people, materials, capital, and so on. Leaders, on the other hand, create excitement, inspiration, and enthusiasm for setting and reaching organizational goals. Stuart Wells argues that effective leaders assume a number of different roles as part of their leadership responsibilities. For example, *visionaries* push the capacities of followers and inspire them to go beyond what they have previously accomplished. *Magicians* coordinate change by bridging the gap between where the organization is and where it wants to be. *Sages* develop wisdom through expanding

[1]Sarah Boehle, Kevin Dobbs, Sarah Foster, Donna Goldwasser, Jack Gordon, David Stamps, and Ron Zemke, "A New Breed of Visionary," *Training,* November 2000, pp. 44–51.

[2]Dale E. Zand, *The Leadership Triad: Knowledge, Trust, and Power* (New York: Oxford University Press, 1997).

[3]Ibid.

knowledge; they have a capacity to tolerate ambiguity and build strategic possibilities for their organizations.[4]

In this chapter we will examine some approaches and applications that may be associated with helping people become "great" leaders. Among the topics covered include an attribution approach to leadership, charismatic leadership, and transactional and transformational leadership. We begin the chapter with an examination of a normative approach to leadership that focuses on improving the leader's decision-making competencies.

VROOM-JAGO LEADERSHIP MODEL

Victor Vroom and Philip Yetton initially developed a leadership decision-making model that indicated the situations in which various degrees of participative decision making would be appropriate.[5] In contrast to Fiedler's work on leadership (described in the previous chapter), Vroom and Yetton attempted to provide a *normative* model that a leader can use in making decisions. The term *normative* refers to the fact that the model provides norms or guidelines leaders can use for dealing with decision-making situations. Their approach assumed that no one single leadership style was appropriate; rather, the leader must be flexible enough to change leadership styles to fit specific situations. In developing the model, Vroom and Yetton made these assumptions:

1. The model should be of value to managers in determining which leadership styles they should use in various situations.
2. No single style is applicable to all situations.
3. The main focus should be the problem to be solved and the situation in which the problem occurs.
4. The leadership style used in one situation should not constrain the styles used in other situations.
5. Several social processes influence the amount of participation by subordinates in problem solving.

After a number of years of research and application, the original model has been revised by Vroom and Arthur Jago in order to further improve its accuracy.[6] To understand the Vroom-Jago leadership model it is important to consider three elements that are critical components of the model: (1) specification of the criteria by which decision effectiveness is judged, (2) a framework for describing specific leader behaviors or styles, and (3) key diagnostic variables that describe important aspects of the leadership situation.

Decision Effectiveness

Selection of the appropriate decision-making process involves considering two criteria of decision effectiveness: decision quality and subordinate commitment.

---

[4]Stuart Wells, *From Sage to Artisan: The Nine Roles of the Value-Driven Leader* (Palo Alto, CA: Davies-Black Publishing, 1996).

[5]Victor Vroom and Phillip Yetton, *Leadership and Decision Making* (Pittsburgh: University of Pittsburgh Press, 1973).

[6]Victor Vroom and Arthur Jago, *The New Leadership: Managing Participation in Organizations* (Englewood Cliffs, NJ: Prentice-Hall, 1988).

Decision quality refers to the extent to which the decision impacts job performance. For example, deciding whether to paint the stripes in the employee parking lot yellow or white requires low decision quality because it has little or no impact on job performance. On the other hand, a decision regarding at what level to set production goals requires high decision quality. Subordinate commitment refers to how important it is that the subordinates be committed to or accept the decision in order that it may be successfully implemented. Deciding which color paint to use in the parking lot does not really require employee commitment to be successfully implemented; just as clearly, setting production goals at a particular level does require employee commitment if those goals are to be achieved.

In addition to quality and commitment considerations, decision effectiveness may be influenced by time considerations. A decision is not an effective one, regardless of quality and commitment, if it takes too long to make. Even a decision made relatively quickly, if it is a participative one involving a number of people, may be costly in terms of total time spent. Thus, a decision made at a meeting of 15 department members and the department manager that takes two hours has used 32 work hours. In terms of overall organizational effectiveness, this may represent a larger opportunity cost than can be justified.

Decision Styles

The Vroom-Jago model makes a distinction between two types of decision situations facing leaders: individual and group. Individual decision situations are those whose solutions affect only one of the leader's followers. Decision situations that affect several followers are classified as group decisions. Five different leadership styles that fit individual and group situations are available. Described in Exhibit 12.1, these styles are categorized as follows:

1. Autocratic (A): You (the leader) make the decision without input from your subordinates or you (the leader) secure input from subordinates and then make the decision.
2. Consultative (C): Subordinates have some input, but you make the decision.
3. Group (G): The group makes the decision; you (as leader) are just another group member.
4. Delegated (D): You give exclusive responsibility to subordinates.

For group decisions, leaders can choose from styles AI, AII, CI, CII, and GII. For individual decisions, leaders can choose from styles AI, AII, CI, GI, and DI.

Diagnostic Procedure

To determine the most appropriate decision-making style for a given situation, Vroom suggests that leaders perform a situational diagnosis. To accomplish the diagnosis a series of questions can be asked about the situation.[7] These questions that pertain to the model are as follows:

1. How important is the technical quality of the decision?
2. How important is subordinate commitment to the decision?
3. Do you have sufficient information to make a high-quality decision?

---

[7]V. H. Vroom, "Leadership and the Decision Process," *Organizational Dynamics*, Spring 2000.

EXHIBIT 12.1   Vroom-Jago Decision Styles

Individual Level	Group Level
AI. You solve the problem or make the decision yourself, using information available to you at that time.	**AI.** You solve the problem or make the decision yourself, using information available to you at that time.
AII. You obtain any necessary information from the subordinate, then decide on the solution to the problem yourself. You may or may not tell the subordinate what the problem is while getting the information. The role played by your subordinate in making the decision is clearly one of providing specific information that you request, rather than generating or evaluating alternative solutions.	**AII.** You obtain any necessary information from subordinates, then decide on the solution to the problem yourself. You may or may not tell the subordinates what the problem is in getting the information from them. The role played by your subordinates in making the decision is clearly one of providing specific information that you request, rather than generating or evaluating solutions.
CI. You share the problem with the relevant subordinate, getting ideas and suggestions. Then *you* make the decision. This decision may or may not reflect your subordinate's influence.	**CI.** You share the problem with the relevant subordinates individually, getting their ideas and suggestions without bringing them together as a group. Then *you* make the decision. This decision may or may not reflect your subordinates' influence.
GI. You share the problem with one of your subordinates, and together you analyze the problem and arrive at a mutually satisfactory solution in an atmosphere of free and open exchange of information and ideas. You both contribute to the resolution of the problem, with the relative contribution of each being dependent on knowledge rather then formal authority.	**CII.** You share the problem with your subordinates in a group meeting. In this meeting, you obtain their ideas and suggestions. Then *you* make the decision, which may or may not reflect your subordinates' influence.
DI. You delegate the problem to one of your subordinates, providing him or her with any relevant information that you possess, but giving him or her responsibility for solving the problem alone. Any solution the person reaches receives your support.	**GII.** You share the problem with your subordinates as a group. Together, you generate and evaluate alternatives and attempt to reach a consensus on a solution. Your role is much like that of chairperson, coordinating the discussion, keeping it focused on the problem, and making sure that the critical issues are discussed. You do not try to influence the group to adopt "your" solution, and you are willing to accept and implement any solution that has the support of the entire group.

4. Is the problem well-structured?
5. If you were to make the decision by yourself, is it reasonably certain that your subordinates would be committed to the decision?
6. Do subordinates share the organizational goals to be attained in solving this problem?
7. Is conflict among subordinates over preferred solutions likely?
8. Do subordinates have sufficient information to make a high-quality decision?

Each of these questions may be thought of as representing a dichotomy. That is, they may be answered yes or no, or high or low. Within the framework of the model, however, it is possible for responses to fall between dichotomized extremes. Answers of "probably" and "maybe" may reflect subtle differences among situations, particularly those that in some way may be ambiguous or unclear. The capacity of the model to treat these questions as continuous scales is one of the significant additions to the revised Vroom-Jago model.

Application of the Model

Actual application of the Vroom-Jago model can vary significantly in its degree of complexity, sophistication, and specificity, depending on the particular purpose

---

EXHIBIT 12.2   Example Vroom-Jago Rules of Thumb

Rules to improve decision quality:

1. Avoid the use of AI when.

   a. The leader lacks the necessary information.

2. Avoid the use of GII when:

   a. Subordinates do not share the organizational goals.

   b. Subordinates do not have the necessary information.

3. Avoid the use of AII and CI when:

   a. The leader lacks the necessary information.

   b. The problem is unstructured.

4. Move toward GII when:

   a. The leader lacks the necessary information.

   b. Subordinates share the organizational goals.

   c. There is conflict among subordinates over preferred solutions.

Source: Bridged from V. Vroom and A. Jago, *The New Leadership* (Englewood Cliffs, NJ: Prentice-Hall, 1988). Copyright 1987 by V. Vroom and A. Jago. Used with permission of the authors.

Exercise 12.1

Leadership Style Analysis

for which it is used and the needs of the decision maker. In its simplest form, application of the model can be expressed as a set of decision-making rules of thumb. Exhibit 12.2 lists, as an example, four of the rules that apply to the model as discussed here.

In contrast to this simple application, in its most complex form the model requires the use of mathematical formulas too complex to describe here. Using the manager's analysis of the situation represented by his or her responses to the diagnostic questions, the formulas predict the most appropriate way of handling the situation, the second best way, and so forth. This application of the model requires the use of specially developed computer software, however.

Validity of the Model

The Vroom-Jago model lacks complete empirical evidence establishing its validity. Certainly the model is thought to be consistent with what we now know about the benefits and costs of subordinate participation in decision making. Moreover, it represents a direct extension of the original Vroom-Yetton model, for which ample validation evidence does exist.[8] Nonetheless, without additional evidence that the use of the model can improve decision effectiveness and, by extension, leadership success, its value as a theoretical contribution and as a practical tool have yet to be fully determined.

The model also illustrates that leaders make decisions in a linear manner. This is not always the case. For example, a leader's decision with one person or team may not have an immediate impact on others, but over time it may be used as an example. The time element is not a part of this model, and since leadership occurs over a period of time, this can be problematic.

---

[8]Victor H. Vroom and Arthur G. Jago, "Situation Effects and Levels of Analysis in the Study of Leader Participation," *Leadership Quarterly*, Spring, 1995, pp. 45–52.

ATTRIBUTION THEORY OF LEADERSHIP

Since most causes of subordinate, or follower, behaviors are not directly observable, determining causes requires reliance on perception. In attribution theory, individuals are assumed to be rational and concerned about the causal linkages in their environments.

The attributional approach starts with the position that the leader is essentially an *information processor.*[9] In other words, the leader searches for informational cues as to "why" something is happening and then attempts to construct causal explanations that guide her leadership behavior. The process, in simple terms, appears to be follower behavior → leader attributions → leader behavior.

Leader's Attributions

Kelley suggests that the leader's primary attributional task is to categorize the causes of follower, or subordinate, behavior into one of three source dimensions: person, entity, or context. That is, for any given behavior, such as poor quality of output, the leader's job is to determine whether the poor quality was caused by the person (e.g., inadequate ability), the task (entity), or some unique set of circumstances surrounding the event (context).

The leader seeks three types of information when forming attributions about a follower's behavior: distinctiveness, consistency, and consensus. For any behavior, the leader first attempts to determine whether the behavior is *distinctive* to a task—that is, whether the behavior occurs on this task but not on other tasks. Next, the leader is concerned about *consistency,* or how frequently the behavior occurs. Finally, the leader estimates *consensus,* the extent to which others behave in the same way. A behavior unique to one follower has low consensus; if it is common to other followers, this reflects high consensus.

Leader's Perception of Responsibility

The judgment of responsibility moderates the leader's response to an attribution. Clearly, the more a behavior is seen as caused by some characteristic of the follower (i.e., an internal cause) and the more the follower is judged to be responsible for the behavior, the more likely the leader is to take some action toward the follower. For example, an outcome (e.g., poor performance) may be attributed to factors outside the control of a person (such as not having the tools to do the job well) or to internal causes (such as lack of effort).

Attributional Leadership Model

Attribution theory offers a framework for explaining leader behavior more insightfully than either trait or personal-behavioral theories. *Attribution leadership theory* attempts to explain why behaviors are happening;[10] trait and personal be-

---

[9]Emmett C. Murphy and Michael Snell, *Forging the Heroic Organization: A Daring Blueprint for Revitalizing American Businesses* (Englewood Cliffs, NJ: Paramont Publishing, 1995).

[10]Terence R. Mitchell, S. C. Green, and Robert E. Wood, "An Attributional Model of Leadership and the Poor Performing Subordinate: Development and Validation," Barry M. Staw and Larry L. Cummings, (eds.), in *Research in Organizational Behavior* (Greenwich, CT: JAI Press, 1981); and S. G. Green and Terence R. Mitchell, "Attributional Processes of Leaders in Leader-Member Interactions," *Organizational Behavior and Human Performance,* June 1979, pp. 429–58.

EXHIBIT 12.3   An Attributional Leadership Model

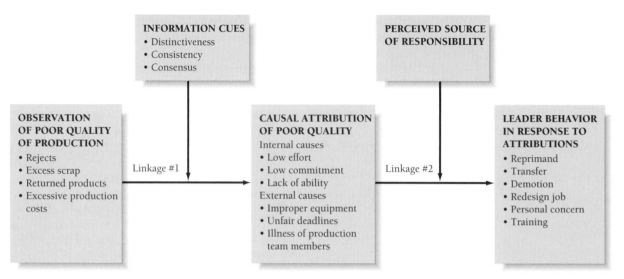

Source: Adapted from Terence R. Michell and Robert E. Wood, "An Empirical Test of an Attributional Model of Leader's Responses to Poor Performance," *Academy of Management Proceedings*, Richard C. Huseman, ed., (1979) p. 94.

havioral theories are more descriptive and don't focus on the *why* issue. Furthermore, attribution theory can offer some predictions about a leader's response to a follower's behavior. Attributions are more likely to be made when failures or problems occur.[11] However, successful outcomes also can trigger the question, "Why did this success occur?"

Exhibit 12.3 presents an attributional leadership model that emphasizes two important linkages. At the first linkage point, the leader attempts to make attributions about poor performance. These attributions are moderated by the three information types: distinctiveness, consistency, and consensus. The second linkage point suggests that the leader's behavior, or response, is determined by the attributions that she makes. This relationship between attribution and leader behavior is moderated by the leader's perception of responsibility. Is the responsibility internal or external?

As discussed previously, distinctiveness, consistency, and consensus influence a leader's attributions. For example, a study of nursing supervisors found that leaders who made attributions of internal causes (e.g., lack of effort) tended to use more punitive behaviors, and leaders tended to make more internal attributions and to respond more harshly when the problems were serious.[12]

[11]Henry P. Sims, Jr., and Peter Lorenzi, *The New Leadership Paradigm* (Newburg Park, CA: Sage, 1992), p. 221.

[12]Terence P. Mitchell and Robert E. Wood, "An Empirical Test of an Attributional Model of Leaders' Responses to Poor Performance," in Richard C. Huseman, (ed.), *Academy of Management Proceedings,* (Athens, GA: University of Georgia, 1979), pp. 94–98.

An interesting research approach has been to include sex effects in the attributional model of leadership. Research regarding the sex of the leader and the sex of the subordinate has been largely neglected. A study of college students examined whether sex of the leader, sex of the subordinate, and the interaction between these two factors would affect both the attributions made for employees' poor performance and the corrective action taken by leaders.[13] The researchers concluded that the sex composition of the leader-subordinate dyad was a critical and neglected variable in attributional research.

Research support for the attributional theory of leadership is limited. There is a need to test the theory in more organizational settings. Understanding the causes of leader behavior, or at least searching for these causes, seems more promising for managerial use than does simply adding another trait or descriptive theory to the leadership literature.

Leader Behavior: Cause or Effect?

Case 12.1

A Leadership Contrast at Ford Motors

We have implied that leader behavior has an effect on the follower's performance and job satisfaction. However, a sound basis exists for proposing that follower performance and satisfaction cause the leader to vary his leadership style. It has been argued that people develop positive attitudes toward objects that are instrumental to satisfying their needs.[14] This argument can be extended to leader-follower relationships. For example, organizations reward leaders (managers) based on the performance of followers (subordinates). Leaders might then be expected to develop positive attitudes toward high-performing followers. Let us say that employee Joe's outstanding performance enables his boss, Mary, to receive the annual $4,000 leadership excellence award. The expectation then is that Mary would think highly of Joe and reward him with a better work schedule or job assignment. In this case, Joe's behavior leads to Mary's being rewarded, and she in turn rewards Joe.

In a field study, data were collected from first-line managers and from two of each manager's first-line supervisors. The purpose of this research was to assess the direction of causal influence in relationships between leader and follower variables. The results strongly suggested that (1) leader consideration behavior caused subordinate satisfaction, and (2) follower performance caused changes in the leader's emphasis on both consideration and the structuring of behavior/performance relationships.[15]

Research on the cause-effect issue is still quite limited. To conclude that all leader behavior or even a significant portion of such behavior is a response to follower behavior would be premature. However, an examination of the leader-follower relationship in terms of **reciprocal causation** is needed. In reciprocal causation, leader behavior causes follower behavior, and follower behavior causes leader behavior.

---

[13]G. H. Dobbins, E. C. Pence, and J. A. Sgro, "The Effects of Sex of the Leader and Sex of the Subordinate on the Use of Organizational Control Policy," *Organizational Behavior and Human Performance,* December 1983, pp. 325–43.

[14]Fred Luthans and Alexander D. Stujkovic, "Reinforce Your Performance: The Need to Go Beyond Pay and Even Rewards," *Academy of Management Executive,* May 1999, pp. 68–80.

[15]C. N. Greene, "The Reciprocal Nature of Influence between Leader and Subordinate," *Journal of Applied Psychology,* April 1975, pp. 187–93.

CHARISMATIC LEADERSHIP

Individuals such as John F. Kennedy, Winston Churchill, Warren Buffet, and Walt Disney possessed an attractiveness that enabled them to make a difference with citizens, employees, and followers. Their leadership approach is referred to as *charismatic leadership*. Max Weber suggested that some leaders have a gift of exceptional qualities—a charisma—that enables them to motivate followers to achieve outstanding performance.[16] Such a charismatic leader is depicted as being able to play a vital role in creating change. Individuals who take on hero qualities possess charisma. Others view the charismatic leader as a hero. Organizational Encounter 12.1 about two charismatic "heroes" illustrates how they brought about change. The charismatic leader is one that creates an atmosphere of motivation based on an emotional commitment and identity to his or her vision, philosophy, and style on the part of followers. In the national political arena, President John F. Kennedy was considered by some to be charismatic, while President Gerald Ford was not considered to be charismatic by most citizens.

www.walmart.com

Sam Walton was considered by many to have possessed charismatic qualities. He worked hard to explain his vision of retailing and serving the customer. He would visit Wal-Mart stores to continually inform his associates (the employees) that customer service is the first, second, and third priority that must be accomplished so that the firm can be recognized as the top retailer. As people responded to his vision and goals, Walton kept up a fast pace to meet other people and express his viewpoint. He paid attention to his employees and his customers—the human assets of business. Walton had a "gift" for making other people feel good about working for him and buying his products and services.

www.apple.com

Steven Jobs, cofounder of Apple Computers, provides another example of how charisma works to inspire others. Jobs's impact, attraction, and inspiration when he was with the firm originally were described as follows:

> When I walked through the Macintosh building with Steve, it became clear that he wasn't just another general manager bringing a visitor along to meet another group of employees. He and many of Apple's leaders weren't managers at all; they were impresarios. . . . Not unlike the director of an opera company, the impresario must cleverly deal with the creative temperaments of artists. . . . His gift is to merge powerful ideas with the performance of his artists.[17]

Defining Charismatic Leadership

Charisma is a Greek word meaning "gift." Powers that could not be clearly explained by logical means were called charismatic. It has been suggested that it is a combination of charm and personal magnetism that contribute to a remarkable ability to get other people to endorse your vision and promote it passionately.[18]

What Constitutes Charismatic Leadership Behavior?   What behavioral dimensions distinguish charismatic leaders from noncharismatic leaders? A criticism of the early work on charismatic leadership is that the explanations of it lacked specificity.

---

[16]Max Weber, *The Theory of Social and Economic Organization*, A. M. Henderson and T. Parsons (trans.), (New York: Free Press, 1947, originally published 1924).

[17]John Sculley, "Sculley's Lessons from Inside Apple," *Fortune*, September 14, 1987, pp. 108–11.

[18]Patricia Sellers, "What Exactly Is Charisma?" *Fortune,* January 15, 1996, pp. 68–75.

Business Leaders as Heroes

Americans love their heroes, be they astronauts, great scientists, poets, or athletes. Courage, intellect, talent, and skill are associated with heroes and their great accomplishments. When searching for heroes, few people think to look at business leaders, which is surprising, considering the U.S. culture is built upon a foundation of free enterprise. A picture of a few business leaders may suggest that heroes also work in companies.

Willie T. Kearney, Jr., believes that any loss of America's competitive edge is not the result of what companies did, but is more likely the result of what they did not do—namely, invest in human capital. At Pratt & Whitney's Turbine Airfoils Division—a $1 billion business with 1,500 employees—"Willie T.," as he is known to co-workers, is doing everything he can to change that.

Regarded as the busiest, friendliest, and downright happiest person at the company, Mr. Kearney, 41, is sort of an evangelist for learning. In a division where 15 percent of the workforce falls below the fourth-grade reading level and another 5 percent speak English as a second language, the learning needs might appear overwhelming. But not to Mr. Kearney.

Under his guidance, the company has implemented a comprehensive literacy training program that goes well beyond reading, writing, and arithmetic. Training in those skills is available and encouraged, but, at Pratt & Whitney, literacy education also includes training in communication, job skills, empowerment, teamwork, company finances, and cross-training for flexibility in job assignments.

In the history of the U.S. civil rights movement, any advances made by women and minorities have typically involved a white male willing to risk his reputation to challenge the status quo. At Inland Steel, Steven J. Bowsher, Vice President of Sales and Marketing, was such a person.

In 1987, four young African-American employees at Inland were discouraged by the lack of opportunity they felt existed at the company. At the time, 88.6 percent of Inland's officers and managers were white, 6.1 percent were African-American, 4.7 percent were Hispanic, 0.6 percent were Asian, and 4.8 percent were female.

After meeting privately for several months to discuss possible strategies for making the company aware of barriers that existed for minorities, the group realized they needed to take their concerns to someone who was sensitive enough to listen and try to understand, but who also possessed the power to take action. "We sought out a white male," explains group member Vivian Cosey, "because it was representative of the power structure." Mr. Bowsher, then a general manager of sales, was chosen because he had a reputation as an innovator and risk-taker, and he was well-established in the company.

The group spent four hours one evening dumping their frustrations on him. Mr. Bowsher listened closely, took copious notes, then went home exhausted and confused. He just didn't get it. By his own admission, his experiences in life had not been oppressed, so he had no way of relating to the group.

After several more meetings that resulted in the same lack of understanding, the group started to funnel articles and brochures about diversity to Mr. Bowsher. One of the brochures was for workshops sponsored by the Urban Crisis Center in Atlanta. On his own time, with his own money, Mr. Bowsher attended the two-day workshop in which he was the only white upper manager in attendance. The group, which was half African-American and predominately female, basically ignored him, putting him in a position that women and minorities find themselves in every day. He finally understood what the group was saying and vowed to do something about their complaints.

He mandated diversity-awareness training for all members of his management staff. He established an aggressive affirmative-action plan for the sales department. Five-year career plans were drawn up for all 300 employees in the department. Diversity objectives were made a part of the business plan and a requisite part of annual reviews and evaluations. He took the diversity message to his peers in other divisions. And, along with the affirmative-action focus group—composed of the four employees who originally approached Mr. Bowsher—he initiated hiring plans for minorities and females, recruiting efforts, and a summer intern program for the sales department. Over a two-year period, minority hires in his group increased to 64 percent from 10 percent of the total hired.

www.inland.
m

Source: Adapted from "Industry's Unsung Heroes," *Industry Week*, December 5, 1994, pp. 20–24.

EXHIBIT 12.4	Behavioral Components of Charismatic and Noncharismatic Leaders	
Component	**Charismatic Leader**	**Noncharismatic Leader**
Relation to status quo	Essentially opposed to status quo and strives to change it (Steve Jobs at Apple)	Essentially agrees with status quo and strives to maintain it
Future goal	Idealized vision highly different than status quo (Tom Monaghan with the Domino's Pizza concept)	Goal not too discrepant from status quo
Likableness	Shared perspective and idealized vision make him or her a likable and honorable hero worthy of identification and imitation (Lee Iacocca in first three years at Chrysler)	Shared perspective makes him or her likable
Expertise	Expert in using unconventional means to transcend the existing order (Al Davis, owner of the Los Angeles Raiders)	Expert in using available means to achieve goals within the framework of the existing order
Environmental sensitivity	Expert in using unconventional means to transcend the existing order (Warren Buffet, CEO of Berkshire Hathaway)	Low need for environmental sensitivity to maintain status quo
Articulation	Strong articulation of future vision and motivation to lead (Jim Clark, CEO of Netscape)	Weak articulation of goals and motivation to lead
Power base	Personal power based on expertise, respect, and admiration for a unique hero (Colin Powell, secretary of state)	Position power and personal power (based on reward, expertise, and liking for a friend who is a similar other)
Leader-follower relationship	Elitist, entrepreneur, an exemplary (Mary Kay Ash of Mary Kay Cosmetics) Transforms people to share the radical changes advocated (Edward Land, inventor of Polaroid camera)	Egalitarian, consensus seeking, or directive Nudges or orders people to share his or her views

Source: Adapted from Jay A. Conger and Rabindra Kanungo, "Toward a Behavioral Theory of Charismatic Leadership in Organizational Settings," *Academy of Management Review,* October 1987, pp. 637–47.

A number of empirical studies have examined behavior and attributes of charismatic leaders, such as ability to inspire, dominating personality, vision, and communication ability.[19] However, no specific set of behaviors and attributes is universally accepted by researchers and practitioners. A descriptive behavioral framework that builds upon empirical work has been offered. The framework, presented in Exhibit 12.4, assumes that charisma must be viewed as an attribution made by followers within the work context.

Many leaders, of course, are not charismatic. These leaders exhibit behavioral components similar to those described in Exhibit 12.4 as "noncharismatic." This does not necessarily mean, however, that they are ineffective. Outstanding administrative skills or keen analytical abilities, for example, can contribute to effectiveness in noncharismatic leaders. Bill Gates of Microsoft is not usually classified as a charismatic leader. He has been, however, very analytical, innovative, and efficient. Gates has used his somewhat noncharismatic style and helped build Microsoft into a powerful organization.

[19]See for example, Shelley A. Kirkpatrick and Edwin A. Locke, "Direct and Indirect Effects of Three Core Charismatic Leadership Components on Performance and Attitudes," *Journal of Applied Psychology,* February 1996, pp. 36–51.

*This Leader's Behavior May Not Be Charismatic,
But Is It Illegal?*

You Be the Judge

www.forkliftsystems.com

Teresa Harris worked as a manager at Forklift Systems, Inc., an equipment rental company, for approximately 30 months. During that time, Charles Hardy was Forklift's president. Throughout her employment period, Hardy often insulted Harris because of her gender and often made her the target of unwanted sexual innuendoes. Hardy told her on several occasions—in the presence of other employees—"You're a woman, what do you know?" and "We need a man as the rental manager"; at least once he told her she was "a dumb-ass woman." Once, in front of others, he suggested that the two of them "go to the Holiday Inn to negotiate [your] raise."

When Harris complained to Hardy about his conduct, Hardy expressed surprise that Harris was offended, claimed to be only joking, apologized, and promised he would stop. Based on this assurance Harris stayed on the job. Within a couple of weeks, however, Hardy began anew. For example, while Harris was arranging a deal with one of Forklift's customers, he asked her—again in front of other employees—"What did you do, promise the guy some sex Saturday night?" Within a few weeks, Harris collected her paycheck and quit.

Harris then sued Forklift under Title VII of the Civil Rights Act, claiming that Hardy's conduct had created an abusive work environment for her because of her gender. Was Hardy's behavior a violation of Title VII? If so, should an employer be held liable for behavior committed by one of its employees? You be the judge!

A few leaders are not only noncharismatic, they seem to display "anticharismatic" qualities. Rather than inspiring followers, they discourage them; rather than building a climate of trust, they erect one based on fear; or, rather than respecting and valuing their followers, they demean and discount them. The You Be the Judge episode describes a situation in which the leader involved seems to have some of these anticharismatic attributes.

Two Types of Charismatic Leaders

Charismatic leaders may be characterized in different ways. Two such ways, or types, are visionary and crisis-based. Most discussions of charismatic leadership emphasize *visionary* leadership. It's argued that the first requirement for exercising charismatic leadership is expressing a shared vision of what the future could be. Through communication ability, the visionary charismatic leader links followers' needs and goals to job or organizational goals. Linking followers with the organization's direction, mission, and goals is easier if they're dissatisfied or unchallenged by the current situation. Visionary charismatic leaders have the ability to see both the big picture *and* the opportunities the big picture presents.[20]

An example of a visionary charismatic leader is Felipe Alfonso, who headed the Asian Institute of Management (AIM) while also serving as the CEO of Manila Electric Company (MERALCO). He is considered a tireless and charismatic

www.meralco.com

---

[20]Barbara Mackoff and Gary Wenet, *The Inner Work of Leaders: Leadership As A Habit of Mind.* New York: AMACOM, 2001.

leader who formulates a vision of the future, while bringing people together to seize opportunities.

AIM has trained and developed many of the top professional, entrepreneurial, and socially responsible leaders of Asia and the rest of the world. It has graduated over 20,000 students from 68 countries.[21]

The Manila Electric Company provides more than half of the Philippines' total electric consumption, and its franchise area produces 50 percent of the country's gross domestic product. Under Alfonso's leadership, both AIM and the Manila Electric Company have clarified their vision, attracted the best talent, and utilized the most advanced information technology. Earning the trust of people through serving them with integrity is one of Alfonso's major axioms. He prides himself on having visions of the future that are inspirational, ethical, and innovative.

Crisis-based charismatic leaders have an impact when the system must handle a situation for which existing knowledge, resources, or procedures are not adequate.[22] The crisis-produced charismatic leader communicates clearly what actions need to be taken and what their consequences will be.

Crisis management is a growing field of study and inquiry.[23] The crises managers face enable charismatic leadership to emerge. First, under conditions of stress, ambiguity, and chaos, followers give power to individuals who have the potential to correct the crisis situation. The leader is empowered to do what's necessary to correct the situation or solve the problem. In many cases, the leader is unconstrained and is allowed to use whatever she thinks is needed.

A crisis also permits the leader to promote nontraditional actions by followers. The crisis-based charismatic leader has greater freedom to encourage followers to search for ways to correct the crisis. Some methods, procedures, and tactics adopted by followers may be disorderly, chaotic, and outside the normal boundary of actions. However, the charismatic leader in a crisis situation encourages, supports, and usually receives action from followers.

One of the most publicized and respected examples of crisis management leadership was James Burke, CEO of Johnson & Johnson in 1982. He received word of deaths in Chicago associated with a company product, Extra-Strength Tylenol capsules.[24] Five Chicago-area residents had purchased Tylenol and passed away within a few days. Medical examiners retrieved bottles from the victims' homes and found capsules laced with cyanide. Johnson & Johnson, under Burke's direction and leadership, recalled the product and advised consumers not to take any of the capsules. The Food and Drug Administration (FDA) suspected someone not connected with Johnson & Johnson had inserted cyanide in some capsules and returned the bottles to stores.

Burke led the company effort in a three-phase approach: (1) determine what happened, (2) assess the damage, and (3) try to restore Tylenol back into the market. Despite an FBI and Illinois investigation, the perpetrator was never found. Burke showed decisiveness in immedia tely recalling the product and informing

www.jnj.com

[21]Marquardt and Nancy O. Berger, *Global Leaders for the 21st Century*, (Albany: State University of New York Press, 2000), pp. 99–109.

[22]Jack A. Gottschalk, *Crisis Response* (Detroit: Visible Ink Press, 1993).

[23]Christine M. Pearson and Judith A. Clair, "Reframing Crisis Management," *Academy of Management Review*, January 1998, pp. 59–76.

[24]Robert F. Hartley, *Management Mistakes and Successes* (New York: John Wiley, 2000), pp. 312–26.

the public. He didn't know the problem, but he communicated quickly and clearly. Under Burke's leadership, a more widespread tragedy was averted. He also helped rebuild the Tylenol brand, and he regained regular user confidence. The firm ran television commercials informing the public that it was doing everything possible to regain their trust. Also, Johnson & Johnson designed a tamper-resistant package to prevent the tragedy. Tylenol was sold only in a new triple-sealed package. Customers were asked to throw away their Tylenol, call a toll-free number, receive a coupon, and receive a free triple-sealed package.

Our knowledge about charismatic leadership is still relatively abstract and ambiguous. Despite Weber's concept of charismatic authority, Conger's framework of how charismatic leadership evolves, and some limited research results, show much more theoretical and research work needs to be done. There is a void in understanding about whether charismatic leaders can be harmful in expressing visions that are unrealistic or inaccurate or in the way they attack a situation. Adolf Hitler and Joseph Stalin were charismatic leaders who had a negative impact on their followers. The attributes of charismatic leaders are presented in the Management Pointer.

TRANSACTIONAL AND TRANSFORMATIONAL LEADERSHIP

Each of the leadership approaches discussed emphasizes the point that leadership is an exchange process. Followers are rewarded by the leader when they accomplish agreed-upon objectives. The leader serves to help followers accomplish the objectives.

Transactional Leadership

The exchange role of the *leader has been referred to as transactional*. Exhibit 12.5 presents the *transactional leadership* roles. The leader helps the follower identify what must be done to accomplish the desired results: better-quality output, more sales or services, reduced cost of production. In helping the follower identify what must be done, the leader takes into consideration the person's self-concept and esteem needs. The transactional approach uses the path-goal concepts as its framework.

In using the transactional style, the leader relies on contingent reward and on management by exception. Research shows that when contingent reinforcement is used, followers exhibit an increase in performance and satisfaction;[25] followers believe that accomplishing objectives will result in their receiving desired rewards. Using management by exception, the leader won't be involved unless objectives aren't being accomplished.

Transactional leadership is not often found in organizational settings. One national sample of U.S. workers showed that only 22 percent of the participants perceived a

---

Management Pointer 12.1

ATTRIBUTES OF CHARISMATIC LEADERS

Want to become more charismatic? Focus on developing as many of these attributes as you can.

1. *Develop visionary thinking.* Establish idealized goals that represent significant improvement over the status quo.

2. *Communicating the vision.* Visions must be articulated in a manner that is consistent with follower's needs.

3. *Conviction.* Charismatic leaders are perceived as being strongly committed to their visions and willing to sacrifice and take significant personal risk to achieve them.

4. *Extraordinary behaviors.* Engage in behaviors that are unconventional and counter to established norms. Such behaviors should be related to obtaining objectives, not just for show.

5. *Develop self-confidence.* Successful charismatic leaders have total confidence in their abilities to overcome obstacles and get things accomplished.

---

[25]See, for example, Francis J. Yammarino, Alan J. Dubinsky, Lucette B. Comer, and Marvin A. Jolson, "Women and Transformational and Contingent Reward Leadership: A Multiple-Levels-of-Analysis Perspective," *Academy of Management Journal,* February 1997, pp. 205–22.

EXHIBIT 12.5
Transactional
Leadership

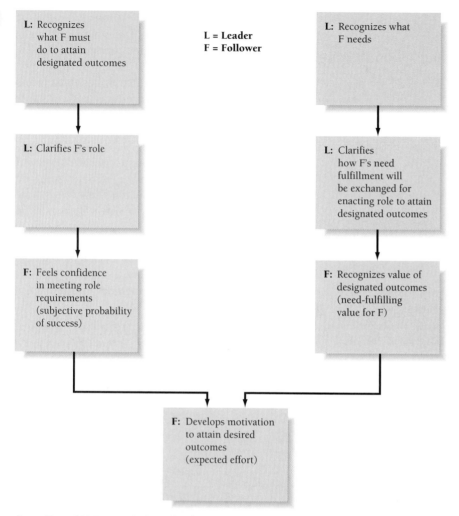

Source: Bernard M. Bass, *Leadership and Performance beyond Expectations* (New York: Free Press, 1985), p. 12.

direct relationship between how hard they worked and how much pay they received.[26] That is, the majority of workers believed that good pay was not contingent on good performance. Although workers prefer a closer link between pay and performance, it was not present in their jobs. Why? There are probably a number of reasons, such as unreliable performance appraisal systems, subjectively administered rewards, poor managerial skills in showing employees the pay-performance link, and conditions outside the manager's control. Also, managers often provide rewards that aren't perceived by followers to be meaningful or important.

A small pay increase, a personal letter from the boss, or a job transfer may not be what employees want in the form of a contingent reward. Until managers understand what the employee wants, administer rewards in a timely manner, and emphasize the pay-performance link, there's likely to be confusion, uncertainty, and minimal transactional impact in leader-follower relationships.

_____

[26]D. Yankelovich and J. Immerivoki, *Putting the Work Ethic to Work* (New York: Public Agenda Foundation, 1983).

The Transformational Theme

Another type of leader, referred to as the *transformation leader,* motivates followers to work for transcendental goals instead of short-term self-interest and for achievement and self-actualization instead of security.[27] In *transformational leadership,* viewed as a special case of transactional leadership, the employee's reward is internal. By expressing a vision, the transformational leader persuades followers to work hard to achieve the goals envisioned. The leader's vision provides the follower with motivation for hard work that is self-rewarding (internal).

Transactional leaders will adjust goals, direction, and mission for practical reasons. Transformational leaders, on the other hand, make major changes in the firm's or unit's mission, way of doing business, and human resources management to achieve their vision. The transformational leader will overhaul the entire philosophy, system, and culture of an organization. The transformational leader uses and expounds upon attitudinal, charismatic, and transitive methods of leadership.

One name that exemplifies a transformational leader is Michael Eisner. Under Michael Eisner's leadership, Walt Disney has moved into live-action movies (including some R-rated), syndicated a new business show for television, introduced a TV channel, developed new cartoon characters, and licensed new apparel products.[28] Eisner took risks and pushed the company along a path that was unheard of for 40 years. He transformed Walt Disney Company from a conservative firm into an assertive, proactive one. Eisner brought in a work ethic, a style, and a vision that has helped put Disney back into the forefront of entertainment.[29]

The development of transformational leadership factors has evolved from research by Bass.[30] He identified five factors (the first three apply to transformational and the last two apply to transactional leadership) that describe transformational leaders. They are:

Charisma. The leader is able to instill a sense of value, respect, and pride and to articulate a vision.

Individual attention. The leader pays attention to followers' needs and assigns meaningful projects so that followers grow personally.

Intellectual stimulation. The leader helps followers rethink rational ways to examine a situation. He encourage followers to be creative.

Contingent reward. The leader informs followers about what must be done to receive the rewards they prefer.

Management by exception. The leader permits followers to work on the task and doesn't intervene unless goals aren't being accomplished in a reasonable time and at a reasonable cost.

One of the most important characteristics of the transformational leader is charisma. However, charisma by itself isn't enough for successful transformational leadership, as Bass clearly states:

The deep emotional attachment which characterizes the relationship of the charismatic leader to followers may be present when transformational leadership occurs, but we can distinguish a class of charismatics who are not at all transformational in

---

[27]Bernard M. Bass, "From Transactional to Transformational Leadership: Learning to Share the Vision," *Organizational Dynamics,* Winter 1990, pp. 19–31.

[28]Hartley, *Management Mistakes,* pp. 75–90.

[29]Ross Groves, *The Disney Touch* (Homewood, IL: Business One Irwin, 1991).

[30]Bernard M. Bass, *Leadership Performance beyond Expectations* (New York: Academic Press, 1985).

their influence. Celebrities may be identified as charismatic by a large segment of the public. Celebrities are held in awe and reverence by the masses who are developed by them. People will be emotionally aroused in the presence of celebrities and identify with them in their fantasy, but the celebrities may not be involved at all in any transformation of their public. On the other hand, with charisma, transformational leaders can play the role of teacher, mentor, coach, reformer, or revolutionary. Charisma is a necessary ingredient of transformational leadership, but by itself it is not sufficient to account for the transformational process.[31]

In addition to charisma, transformational leaders need assessment skills, communication abilities, and a sensitivity to others. They must be able to articulate their vision, and they must be sensitive to the skill deficiencies of followers.

Coaching

Coaching is the everyday interaction of helping another employee improve his or her understanding of the work and improve performance. In Chapter 2, mentoring and socialization were discussed. Mentors are usually senior employees and are often similar in background, religion, ethnicity, and gender to protégés. Coaches come in all varieties and aren't always linked to seniority. Coaches possess skills, experience, and ability that leaders display. Included in the arsenal of exceptional coaches are a talent for observing, decisive decision making, exceptional communication ability, a good understanding of the reward-performance feedback that makes sense, and refrainment from being judgmental.[32]

Doug Blevins is a coach and a leader for the Miami Dolphins football team. He serves as the Dolphins' kicking coach. This is remarkable since he has never attempted to kick a football in his life. Doug was born with cerebral palsy and has never walked.

Doug has exceptional observational and coaching skills. He breaks each kicking motion down to its component parts. He studies the behavior, motions, and mechanics of the kickers and then develops a practice plan for each kicker (putter, field goals, kick-offs) and drills them.

Doug Blevin's offers a few hints on how to coach and lead that can be used in the organization.

1. Observe the detail.
2. Develop the person's strengths.
3. Work to improve people, not change them.
4. Require continual improvement.
5. Pace the person. Don't wear them out by working so hard all the time.
6. Believe that you can be the best.[33]

Blevin's coached kickers are scattered throughout the NFL. Many of these players marvel at Blevin's knowledge, communication and motivational skills, and his work ethic. He has taken a different journey, but Doug Blevins is considered a consummate coach and leader.

---

[31]Ibid., p. 31.

[32]Dorothy Leonard and Walter Swap, "Gurus in the Garage," *Harvard Business Review,* November–December 2000, pp. 71–82.

[33]Todd Shapera, "This Coach Helps the Best to Hit Their Stride," *Fast Company,* September 2000, pp. 48–49.

Coaches, like Doug Blevins, adopt the approach of teacher, not competitor, of being helpful without being judgmental. The coach observes to understand fully what the pupil is doing. In organizations the objective of coaching is to improve performance. However, the focus is more long-term than that of the immediate work, role, or task. Coaching requires confronting the fact that a person is not skilled or talented enough at present to perform well. The buildup of skills to perform well often takes a lot of time and patience. Coaches need to be committed for the long-term to be able to see results.

Practicing a number of coaching techniques is recommended for long-term success.[34] Included in the recommended set are:

- Practice active listening. Play back to the person what was heard.
- Support learning through action and reflection.
- Move from easy to hard skills.
- Set goals.
- Provide tactful feedback, positive and negative. Focus more on successes, but point out failures.

The essence of coaching and leading is to be creative and to look for positives. It may take a long time to observe successes, but a steady course can be very rewarding to both the coach and the pupil.

MULTICULTURAL LEADERSHIP

As each theory or approach to leadership is presented, perhaps it is necessary to ask: To what extent do particular leadership (influence) styles vary around the world? Effective leaders in a Nigerian manufacturing facility may be totally ineffective if transferred to the same type of manufacturing plant in South Africa. The leader's role is performed in a context (e.g., political, cultural). A leader's personality, efforts, or style may emerge from or be in conflict with the context. A leader in a specific national culture may need to apply various attitudes and behaviors to exercise the right blend of influence to accomplish relevant goal achievement.[35] In the global context, there is an inability to generalize the leadership needed to be effective. International Encounter 12.1 looks at one important aspect of global leadership.

Cross-Cultural Research

A study by Bass et al. found that leadership attributes associated with effective leadership results vary across cultures. A considerable amount of research directly or indirectly supports the notion of cultural contingency in leadership. For example, Hofstede's four cultural dimensions (discussed in Chapter 2) provide a good starting point to study cross-country leadership effectiveness characteristics. Employees who rank high on power distance (e.g., India, East Africa, Indonesia) are more likely to prefer an autocratic style of leadership because they are more comfortable with a clear distinction between managers and subordinates. On the other hand, employees in countries that rank low on power distance (e.g., Austria,

[34]James Waldroop and Timothy Butler, "The Executive as Coach," *Harvard Business Review,* November–December, 1996, pp. 111–17.

[35]Richard D. Lewis, "How to Lead in Another Language," *Management Today,* March 1996, pp. 82–84.

International Encounter 12.1

American "International Executive" Ranks Declining

Never before in history has it been so apparent, in so many ways, that we are part of a global economy. While you might think that this would mean more and more "international executives" would be found in U.S. companies, you would be mistaken. Over half of the international companies surveyed in a recent study report that they are increasingly unsuccessful in filling key overseas posts.

Three-fourths of these companies plan to fill these positions with foreign nationals rather than Americans. One reason for this is cost. Relocation costs for an American executive and his or her family are upward of $300,000, excluding training and development. But monetary considerations are only part of the problem. "The demand is definitely greater than the supply when it comes to managers with international experience," said Janice McCormick, the researcher who conducted the study.

The answer? Companies need to create sophisticated career-development paths geared to take younger employees and groom them for overseas assignments. According to McCormick, at most companies overseas assignments become a matter of "survival of the fittest" as managers are sent abroad with little or no cultural and language training. Indeed, only 33 percent of American companies surveyed provided opportunities for language training. By contrast, virtually all Japanese companies provide language and cultural training, as well as highly developed "re-entry" programs designed to take advantage of an executive's international experience.

American companies frequently blunder in their efforts to create strong international divisions because they fail to plan a career path that takes managers' international experience into consideration, says McCormick. Many executives refuse overseas assignments for fear they will be away from the home office and thus out of the "power-loop." The number one reason, however, was family-related. Families must be mobile, accommodating, and flexible enough to adapt to new surroundings and cultures. Not enough American families fit that profile.

Source: Ronald E. Yates, "Fewer U.S. Executives Have Global Outlook," *Houston Chronicle*, March 20, 1996, p. 10F.

Finland) prefer a more participative style of leadership.[36] Hofstede does conclude that participative management approaches that are highly recommended by many American researchers can be counterproductive in many cultures. He further suggests that American researchers tend to concentrate much of their analysis on leaders and not enough on subordinates and their attitudes toward leaders.

Other research points to additional differences in various aspects of leaders and leadership across cultures. Research has shown, for example, that in Nigeria and Taiwan (1) economic success is more likely to result from severe autocratic leadership styles, and (2) success decreases with increasing consideration for employees and their families.[37] As a further example, a recent study reported important differences in how U.S. and People's Republic of China managers dealt with uncertainty and made decisions in ambiguous situations.[38] Studies such as these have important implications, particularly as the number of joint ventures among these countries increase.[39]

The effective multicultural leader in different settings around the world apparently needs various leadership skills that are not always so obvious. Bass[40] has

---

[36]Geert Hofstede, *Cultures and Organizations* (New York: McGraw-Hill, 1991).

[37]Diether Gebert and Thomas Steinkamp, "Leadership Style and Economic Success in Nigeria and Taiwan," *Management International Review*, 1991–92, pp. 161–71.

[38]Peter B. Smith, Mark F. Peterson, and Zhong Ming Wang, "The Manager as Mediator of Alternative Meanings: A Pilot Study from China, the USA and U.K.," *Journal of International Business Studies*, January 1996, pp. 115–37.

[39]Ann S. Davis, "Handling Uncertainty: Do Managers in the People's Republic of China, the US, and the UK Differ?" *Academy of Management Executive*, February 1997, pp. 121–22.

[40]Richard M. Bass and P. C. Burger, *Assessment of Managers: An International Comparison* (New York: Free Press, 1979).

proposed that cross-cultural studies of managers have identified seven factors that are linked to leadership effectiveness:

1. Preferred awareness (willingness to be aware of others' feelings).
2. Actual awareness (actual understanding of oneself and others).
3. Submissiveness (to rules and authority).
4. Reliance on others (in problem solving).
5. Favoring of group decision making.
6. Concern for human relations.
7. Cooperative peer relations.

The skills and other competencies of the leader, however, comprise only one variable in the leadership context. Other factors to consider include the subordinates, the peers, the superiors, the task, and the task environment. Leadership in a multicultural situation, whether the management of a joint venture, a diverse work group in the United States, or a subsidiary abroad, poses many challenging tasks. Researchers have considerable doubts about the generalizability of what is good leadership across national and cultural boundaries. The transferability of leadership practices must be carefully analyzed. Beyond broad generalizations, managers should conduct their own research and consult with others to develop the appropriate leadership style for each unique context and content mix.

The complexity of global joint ventures or of leading a foreign subsidiary requires the careful study of the culture, history, expectations, and working environments that face the leader. There is no right or "universal" way to lead. However, there are differences in style and preferences that, if known, can make the job of leading less frustrating. Influential leaders in any country carefully examine the entire leadership context and their own competencies and then act to achieve relevant organizational goals.

Summary of Key Points

- Vroom and Jago have proposed a leadership model to select the amount of group decision-making participation needed in a variety of problem situations. The model suggests that the amount of subordinate participation depends on the leader's skill and knowledge, whether a quality decision is needed, the extent to which the problem is structured, and whether acceptance by subordinates is needed to implement the decision.

- The attribution theory of leadership suggests that a leader's ability to predict how followers will react is enhanced by knowing how followers explain their behavior and performance. Leaders attribute followers' behaviors to either the person, the task, or a unique set of circumstances called the *context*.

- The ability to influence people that can't be clearly explained by logical means is called *charisma*. Charisma evolves over a period of time. By assessing, adapting, and formulating goals and actions, articulating a vision, and building and reinforcing commitment, the leader builds her charismatic profile. Two types of charismatic leaders have been suggested: one who articulates a vision and one who exercises leadership in a crisis situation.

- Transactional leadership involves engaging in an exchange role in which the leader helps followers accomplish meaningful objectives to achieve satisfactory rewards. The transactional approach is involved in the more expansive transformational leadership framework. Three main characteristics of transformational leadership are charisma, individual attention to followers, and intellectual stimulation of followers.

- Coaching is a form of leadership that is considered important on a day-to-day basis. Coaches are slightly different than mentors, who were discussed in Chapter 3.

- A leader in a specific national culture may need to apply various attitudes and behaviors to exercise the right blend of influence. This blend may be different in different cultural settings. Hofstede's four cultural dimensions provide a starting point for studying cross-cultural leadership effectiveness. The complexities of leading in global environments require the careful study of the culture, history, expectations, and working environments that face the leader.

Review and Discussion Questions

1. Identify individuals whom you believe to be charismatic. Compare your list with those of your classmates. Are there similarities? Why?

2. What skills appear to be important for coaches to be successful?

3. James Burke, CEO of Johnson & Johnson, is used to illustrate a crisis-based charismatic leader. What ability did he display in the Tylenol tragedy?

4. Compare the available research on the Vroom-Jago model of leadership to the transactional explanation of leadership. What additional research is needed in both leadership theories?

5. Can you explain how leaders such as Adolf Hitler were able to attract such large and avid followings in spite of the clearly negative outcomes of their leadership?

6. Which of the theories in this chapter would be most useful in explaining to someone from Russia what leadership approaches will be needed to make Russia more competitive in the international marketplace?

7. It has been said that transactional leadership is not very common in today's organizations. Do you agree or disagree? If you agree, what would it take for the number of transactional leaders to increase?

8. Why is it so difficult, if not impossible, to generalize effective leadership behaviors across different nations? Are there some dimensions of effective leadership that are easier to generalize than others?

9. Hillary Clinton is considered by some to be charismatic. Do you agree? Why?

10. Why is communication such an important skill in charismatic, transactional, transformational, and coaching explanations of leadership?

READING 12.1   Leading Learning

Michael E. McGill

John W. Slocum, Jr.

1993 was a very good year for the Associates Corporation of North America, the nineteenth consecutive year of increased earnings, growing to total assets of $30 billion. In large part, 1993 was successful because of the contributions of the Consumer Financial Services Division of The Associates, a confederation of consumer lending businesses with branches throughout the U.S. To recognize the successful efforts of the branch managers, a gala year-end meeting was held in Dallas. Along with the awards banquets, entertainment, and recreational activities, managers and their spouses also were presented with some learning opportunities. Workshops on marketing, managing diversity, benefits, and managing relationships were provided. At many company meetings such as this, especially where spouses are included, attendance at workshops is often sparse at best. This is not the case at The Associates, where the workshops are packed, people take notes, and informal discussions carry topics far beyond the allotted time. There is a genuine and visible involvement in learning.

One reason employees at The Associates are so involved in learning can be found in the behavior of a workshop attendee, Reece A. Overcash, Jr., the 68-year-old chairman and chief executive officer of The Associates. The leader of learning at The Associates, Overcash is adamant about the need for continual learning. He is fond of quoting G.E.'s Jack Welch: "Are you regenerating? Are you dealing with new things? When you find yourself in a new environment, do you come up with a fundamentally different approach? That's the test. When you flunk, you leave." Overcash's commitment to learning goes far beyond talking about learning. He leads learning at The Associates in direct and tangible ways. He is a *model* for learning. Overcash has a seemingly insatiable appetite for new ideas and perspectives. He willingly and frequently puts himself in the role of student and prods other managers to do likewise. At the consumer lenders' meeting he attended workshops, took notes, asked questions—he set an example. Overcash is a revered *mentor;* he is constantly teaching. Asking questions, sparking interactions, he seems always to be working toward creating a learning environment. Keith Hughes, president and chief operating officer of The Associates and heir apparent to the top spot upon Overcash's retirement, talks about his relationship

with Overcash as a "tutorial in how to be a CEO." Like Hughes, every executive in The Associates' hierarchy can point to lessons they've learned from Overcash.

Overcash's leadership of learning at The Associates is not as casual as it may seem. His modeling is personal but purposeful as well. His mentoring follows an agenda. In short, he *manages* learning at The Associates. Management of learning is seen in the assignment of tasks and responsibilities, the rotation of key individuals through challenging assignments, the use of every opportunity to urge one group or division within the company to look at what another group is doing and learn from their experience.

Finally, Overcash leads learning by *monitoring* the learning going on at The Associates. Like most successful CEOs, Overcash knows the numbers of each of The Associates' businesses backwards and forwards. It is not uncommon for Overcash to ask a division vice president a question about some small detail of his operation. He closely tracks new programs and new pursuits at The Associates, measuring them against their plan and their potential. Beyond the numbers and new ventures, Overcash monitors relationships. It is his belief that the lending business is a relationship business. On vacations, it is his practice to stop in at branches, greet people by name, ask them about themselves, their business, and what they have learned. Overcash does not micromanage, but instead builds close relationships that help him understand all facets of the business.[1]

As the pace of change in the business world has accelerated, it is apparent that yesterday's accomplishments and even today's successes are no guarantees of tomorrow's success. What managers have known to work in the past, understood to be true, or thought to solve problems is called into question as business conditions differ from one day to the next. Change, the modern-day manager's mantra, has in recent years proven to be an inadequate response. A decade and a half of the pursuit of change has left many organizations scarcely better equipped to deal with their dynamic competitive environments than if they had never changed at all. Smarter organizations learn *to* change and learn *from* change.[2] Smart organizations actively manage

---

[1] Conversation with Reece Overcash and Keith Hughes, March 18, 1993.

[2] M. McGill and J. Slocum, *The Smarter Organization* (New York: John Wiley & Sons, 1994).

Source: *The Journal of Leadership Studies* 1, no. 3, June 1994.

the learning process to ensure that it occurs by design rather than by chance. Smarter organizations are learning organizations, able to process their experiences—with customers, competitors, partners, and suppliers—in ways that allow them to create environments in which they can be successful. Learning is their sustainable competitive advantage; leadership makes learning happen.

The purpose of this paper is to capture the behaviors of leaders of learning organizations and, from those behaviors, to outline how to lead learning. Leading learning requires modeling, mentoring, managing, and monitoring learning. We believe that these are the most powerful ways that leaders can influence the behavior of people in their organizations. Leading learning provides a very different perspective on leadership than the styles theory so popular in years past and transformational leadership that currently is in vogue. In order to learn these behaviors, leaders and followers must unlearn much of what they have believed to be true about leadership.

LEADERS MODEL LEARNING

One of the most powerful dynamics at work in leadership is what Arnold Toynbee called "mimesis," literally the process by which people mimic their leaders. When employees look to leaders, however, they often see little change or learning modeled. Those who have reached positions of influence *argue* the need for individual and organizational learning in the face of increasing turbulent environmental conditions. These same leaders often *act* as though their experiences from the past will be an adequate guide. Reflecting in 1987 on his handling of early crises at Apple—the departure of Steve Jobs, 20 percent layoffs, a drop in stock price, bad press—John Sculley described how he responded: "Well, I found it most useful to be able to fall back on things that I already understood, to define problems in such a way that would let me use solutions that I already had some experience with."[3] At the same time that Sculley was trying to convince Apple employees that events in the personal computer industry required that they needed dramatically different understandings and actions, Sculley himself was drawing upon a repertoire anchored in his own experience at PepsiCo—acting to establish control, eliminate chaos, maintain distance, in short, to bring the lessons of professional management to Apple. Many managers view it as their job to be a model for learning. G.E.'s Jack Welch says, "My job is to listen to, search for, think of, and spread ideas, to expose people to good ideas and role models. I'm almost a maitre'd, getting the crowd to come sit at this table: 'Enjoy the food here. Try it. See if it tastes good.' And they do."[4]

Leaders of learning recognize the importance of reflecting on their own experience and the need to periodically retreat from the pace of their office to engage in self-renewal so that they might return reenergized and better able to be a catalyst for others. The notion of renewal or reinvention characterizes the leaders of learning organizations who hold themselves to the same standard that they hold their organizations—"Are you regenerating?"

LEADERS MENTOR LEARNING

The most effective leaders of learning not only inspire others by their example, they also take a personal interest in the learning of others; they serve as mentors. Borrowing from Greek legend and lexicon where Homer's "faithful and wise" mentor advised Odysseus and was entrusted with the education of Telemachus, *mentor* has been broadly used to describe the teachers, guides, coaches, helpers, et al., who contribute to an individual's development. Where learning is concerned, the mentoring behaviors of leaders are quite specific: (1) they set learning agendas, targeting particular kinds of learning; (2) they create a learning environment with challenging assignments, assignments in which there is a great deal to be learned, assignments which entail risk-taking; and (3) they help process the learning experience, they debrief *what* was learned and *how* it was learned.

The nature of the mentor relationship—interpersonal and intimate—and the dynamics of the mentoring process—intentional and involved—are such that leaders must be very selective in whom they choose to mentor. Leaders set an example for the rest of the organization about the value of mentoring. James E. Burke, former chairman and CEO of Johnson & Johnson, often retells of being mentored early in his career. Six years after Burke went to work for Johnson & Johnson in 1949, he was named director of new products. Burke recalls that, in those days, coming up with new products wasn't the science that it is today. "We found that only 3 out of 10 new products which reached the marketplace succeeded." Among Burke's early new products was a children's chest rub promoted as safer and easier to use than those already on the market. The chest rub was designed like today's stick deodorants. It failed, along with new nose drops and cough medicine, and Burke was told to report to the chairman's office. At that time, Robert Wood Johnson, "the General," son of the founder, was chairman of Johnson & Johnson. "I was certain that I was going to be fired. I decided to defend myself and was mentally prepared for a good fight. The chairman said to me, 'I understand that your product failed.' I said, 'Yes, sir, that's true.' Picking up a piece of blue paper, he said, 'Furthermore, I understand it cost this corporation $865,000.' I said, 'Yes, sir, that's right.' He stood up, held out his hand and said, 'I just wanted to congratulate you. Nothing happens unless peo-

---

[3]"John Sculley," *INC.*, October 1987, pp. 49–60.

[4]S. Sherman, "A Master Class in Radical Change," *Fortune*, December 13, 1993, pp. 82–90.

ple are willing to make decisions, and you can't make decisions without making mistakes.' "

Burke recalls, "It was during that period that I began to understand the necessity for risk and the realization that you can't grow without it. You simply have to create an environment that encourages risk taking."[5] Mentored by Johnson in the lessons of risk-taking, it is not surprising that when Burke became CEO he passed these same lessons on to his own protégé, Ralph S. Larsen, who took over the reins from Burke. Asked what he had learned from Burke, Larsen responded, "Jim has created a culture based on intelligent risk-taking, on not being afraid to fail, on getting everything on the table and arguing if you have to. I love it—it works."[6]

Through active and purposeful mentoring, leaders enhance the learning of others, helping them to develop their own initiative, strengthening them in the use of their own judgment, and enabling them to grow and to become better contributors to the organization. These learners, by virtue of their learning, then become leaders and mentor to others. In the most effective learning organizations, everyone feels as though they have a mentor, and everyone, in turn, mentors. It starts at the top.

LEADERS MANAGE LEARNING

Leaders in learning organizations must do more than set a good example and be a mentor. If the message of learning is to permeate the organization, leaders must also *manage* learning. Managing learning means leaders must continually focus attention on the learning agenda and institutionalize the learning process.

Employees respond to what leaders attend to and reward. At DuPont, the entire organization became safety conscious when lost-time accidents were written up and given to the chairman daily. At Dell Computer Corporation, customer complaints that aren't fixed in a week go directly to the CEO, Michael S. Dell. This attention assures that employees understand Dell's vision that every customer "must have a quality experience and must be pleased, not just satisfied." When leaders focus attention on the learning agenda, employees respond.

At Home Depot, learning sustains their competitive advantage. The dramatic success of Home Depot is due to the training employees receive, training designed and delivered by the leader and CEO, Bernard Marcus. Home Depot's sales staff can offer on-the-spot lessons in tile laying, electrical installations, and other projects. New hires, who are often experienced electricians or carpenters, start with five days of classes that include lessons on everything from company history to how to greet a customer. After

class, new staffers spend three weeks tethered to a department manager learning how to order, stock, and sell. Employees then learn about the rest of the store, which stocks some 30,000 items of hardware, lumber, tools, lighting, and plumbing supplies. Salespeople regularly attend seminars on paint, tile, and other merchandise that help them answer customer questions. Nonstop questions from customers are what anyone wearing an orange Home Depot apron can expect. To see to it that they have the answers, the company focuses on nonstop learning.[7]

One way for leaders to effectively and continuously focus attention on learning is to institutionalize the organization's commitment to learning. It is ironic that, faced with a dramatic and dynamic environment that demands change, many managers choose to cut back on the very educational programs that might better prepare their employees to learn. Training and management development programs are often early targets for cost cutting. Such moves may speak ill of a company's commitment to learning, but they might just as well reflect the perceived connection (or lack thereof) between training and development and learning. In learning organizations, both the commitment to learning and the connection are clear.

Since its inception in 1956, G. E. Crotonville, G. E.'s Management Development Institute, has been used as a direct lever for change. When Jack Welch began to transform G. E. in 1981, he told then Crotonville manager James Baughman, "I want a revolution to start at Crotonville. I want it to be part of the glue that holds G. E. together." Today Welch uses Crotonville to touch every part of G. E. Since 1989, the energies of Crotonville have been directed toward involving nearly 40,000 G. E. middle managers in learning the workout/reengineering process.[8] Reengineering and workout programs are learning processes particularly applicable to administrative, operating, and human resource systems. By institutionalizing workout in the Crotonville curriculum, Welch has assured that the learning will go on long after managers have left the Crotonville campus.

At Hitachi, the Japanese electronics giant, there can be no mistaking leadership's commitment to learning. Years ago, Hitachi founded the Institute of Management Development, the first in-house institute created in Japan for management education. To maintain Hitachi's traditions, approximately 70 percent of the instructors at the institute are Hitachi employees. Education is provided for all levels of employees, from recruits to top-level managers.

Programs offered by the institute last one to two weeks and host groups of 16 to 20 employees. All share five objectives for their courses. The first objective is to give

[5]T. Horton, *What Works for Me* (New York: Random House, 1987), pp. 119–120.

[6]C. H. Deutsch, "Taking the Reins from a Legend," *New York Times*, October 30, 1988, p. 24.

[7]W. Konrad, "Cheerleading and Clerks Who Know Awls from Augers," *Business Week*, August 3, 1992, p. 51.

[8]N. M. Tichy, "G.E.'s Crotonville: A Staging Ground for Corporate Revolution," *Academy of Management Executive*, May 1989, pp. 99–106.

managers a clear understanding of Hitachi's management concepts. Managers must understand the company's three maxims—harmony, sincerity, and pioneering spirit—and recognize that the customer comes first. Managers must also be able to lead and develop the employees under them.

The second objective is to acquire an entrepreneurial spirit and innovative thinking since Hitachi relies on creative products to stay ahead of its competition. Managers must grasp the difference between being a "technology-oriented" business and a "marketing-oriented" industry.

The third objective is to give managers a broad awareness of the world in order to aid Hitachi's international businesses. Politics, culture, religion, as well as international economics are in the curriculum. This knowledge helps Hitachi conduct harmonious business activities in the global marketplace.

The fourth objective is to unify managers' opinions and sense of direction in order to maintain a common, cohesive outlook. This is especially important for Hitachi since a large number of its group companies and subsidiaries are encouraged to be independent. The intricate web of financial, manufacturing, and distribution relationships make it imperative that relationships be strong.

Finally, the fifth objective is to improve overall business skills: management, marketing, financial management, human resource management, and so on.

To meet the needs of management in a variety of fields, Hitachi's programs are diverse. But some common threads run through all the courses. For example, company executives are available during the courses to engage in dialogue with the managers. The president attends any course for department managers and above, and the vice presidents attend courses for section managers. Occasionally, presidents of some of Hitachi's group companies serve as instructors. All courses have some of the board officers in attendance as well. Hitachi believes that people make the business and that to respect, develop, and make the most of each individual is the road to success.[9]

LEADERS MONITOR LEARNING

Many fine ideas go unrealized in organizations because no one feels personally responsible for seeing to it that platitudes and pledges are translated into performance and rewards. Managers who are serious about leading learning in their organizations *monitor* learning and, in so doing, make learning everyone's responsibility. Unfortunately, it is not as easy to monitor learning as it is to track production or sales. A leader cannot simply call up on a computer screen the monthly learning figures the way he or she might access production numbers or sales or any one of a number of important financial indicators. To date there is

no Lotus 1-2-3 or Windows program for learning. Learning is difficult to monitor because learning is a process, not a product. As such, measurement must be at once more immediate and more intimate. The process must be assessed as it is delivered by those involved. Monitoring organization learning must be built in to the organization's learning. There are two leader behaviors that result in effective monitoring and simultaneously promote learning: (1) leaders establish routines for receiving undistorted feedback, and (2) leaders encourage *new* failures.

Without feedback there can be no learning. It is feedback that allows us to adjust our behavior to better attain our goals. In modern organizations, feedback is plentiful, but it is often difficult to get the truth. One significant measure of a learning organization is how much truth the leader hears. There are several dynamics at work in organizations that act to distort feedback to leaders and, therefore, frustrate learning. First, over time there is a tendency for everyone in an organization—especially those at the top—to look alike and think alike. This contributes to "groupthink," where fitting in and gaining the leader's approval becomes more important than making a meaningful difference. When Ed Whitacre took over as CEO at Southwestern Bell Corporation, he remarked that a habit SBC needed to break was having everyone "molded into our very image."[10] Learning organizations value the contribution diversity can make to undistorted feedback. Bill Kaufman, manager of New Areas for Oryx Energy Company, comments on the composition of his group, "I like to have the lawyer and the marketing guy involved; they bring a different perspective. We're dealing in some parts of the world (Kazakhstan) where 'business as usual just isn't going to cut it.' The rest of us have been together for a long time and we've been doing what we're doing for a long time. We need somebody to challenge our thinking."[11]

These remarks suggest the second organizational impediment to undistorted feedback. Many leaders will not harbor dissent, choosing instead to "shoot the messenger." The legendary moviemaker, Samuel Goldwyn, presented his key advisors with an unenviable choice when, after a succession of box office bombs, he called them together and demanded, "I want you to tell me exactly what's wrong with me and MGM, even if it means losing your job."[12] Many a manager has been faced with the same dilemma—tell the boss what's wrong and risk being fired, or don't tell and risk being fired because what's wrong doesn't get fixed! Leaders in learning organizations encourage dissent, recognizing that dissent promotes

---

[9]T. Tanaka, "Developing Managers in the Hitachi Institute of Management Development," *Journal of Management Development,* Fall 1989, pp. 27–39.

[10]J. D. Judy, "New Man at the Helm," *Enterprise,* no. 1 (1990), p. 12.

[11]Conversation with Bill Kaufman, December 19, 1993.

[12]As retold by Warren Bennis, "Followers Make Good Leaders Good," *New York Times,* December 31, 1989, p. 24.

learning by forcing people to look at a wider range of possibilities. Some learning leaders even go so far as to structure dissent into the decision-making process and to reward dissenters.

Six months after Apple chairman John Sculley gave the Newton project the go-ahead, Donna Auguste was named software engineering manager. She joined an insulated group. "There weren't any people who didn't already know people on the Newton team when they joined the group. I didn't think it was healthy." Auguste set out to increase the diversity and dissent in the Newton group. She began hiring engineers from outside the small circle, bringing in blacks and women in the process. She refined the interviewing process to reach beyond the usual applicants, and looked much farther afield than Apple typically does. With this diversity came dissent which Auguste did not try to smooth away; she used dissent to move the project forward. One of the Newton designers who worked with Auguste recalls, "She was a lousy diplomat. But this is obviously preferable to the inverse approach that is taken by most managers. They'd much rather think everybody likes them than actually get anything done." When leaders *use* diversity and dissent, the group learns and things get done.[13]

Some learning organizations have instituted routines for systematically debriefing their management practices. The concept of upward evaluation or 360-degree feedback has become popular in some of America's most admired companies as a mechanism for debriefing employees' experience and giving feedback to leadership. Alcoa, Burlington, General Mills, Hewlett-Packard, Herman Miller, Whirlpool, British Petroleum, 3M, and UPS are all companies that use upward and lateral evaluations along with more traditional downward performance appraisals. The learning potential is tremendous. At UPS, the company learned that its 35,000 managers were not doing a satisfactory job of helping workers to develop their technical and communication skills. Only 48 percent of workers gave their managers satisfactory marks on employee development. Having learned, UPS is now acting to improve the teaching skills of its managers.[14] At Hoechst Celanese Corporation, a key component of the Middle Management Leadership Program is "Leadership Feedback." Managers are presented with 360-degree feedback elicited from their boss, their peers, and their subordinates. Reviewing this feedback, they develop action plans for improving their own leadership. These action plans are tracked for the individuals and also used as input into curriculum development for future leadership programs. The individual leaders learn from the 360-de-

gree feedback and the organization learns. This kind of learning is possible only because leaders are willing to debrief their own behavior.

Leaders can effectively monitor learning by noting the diversity, dissent, and debriefings present in their own organizations. More of each means, in all probability, more learning. The same is true of failures. The more you have, the more you can learn.

One company that has had a difficult time learning from its failures in recent years is Eastman Kodak Company. Early in the 1970s, Kodak management decided that the future of silver halide technology, the proprietary film coating on which Kodak was founded, was limited. A 20-year period of mostly failed experiments ensued. Then there was Kodak's entry into instant photography in 1976. This was done by stealing Polaroid's technology. The result: heavy losses, a find of $900 million paid to Polaroid in 1991, and a tarnished reputation. That debacle was followed by Kodak's entry into reprographics. Kodak's first copying machine was far better than anything Xerox had at the time. But Kodak failed to exploit its competitive advantage, and Xerox regained the edge. In 1991 and 1992, Kodak lost money on its $4 billion (revenues) copier and information systems business.

During the 1980s, Kodak set itself up as a venture capitalist for a number of new technologies. Most did not pay off. It purchased a number of publishing and prepublishing companies. For example, Atex was the premier copy processing system for the publishing industry when Kodak bought the company in 1981. Atex's founders, stifled by Kodak, left; and, 10 years later, Kodak sold Atex. A larger failure by far was Kodak's entry into pharmaceuticals.

Failing to learn the lessons of prior experiences, Kodak purchased Sterling Drug in 1988 for $5.1 billion. Kodak reasoned that its extensive background and knowledge of different chemical-based lab processes would instantly make it a formidable player in the profitable pharmaceutical industry. Because Kodak's blood analyzer, diagnostic equipment, chemical substrates, and film products were already widely used in medical laboratories, its managers thought that Sterling would provide them with an easy entry into a new industry that would not face the same kind of intense competitive pressures that characterized the photographic film industry. Unfortunately, these expectations never materialized. The ability to leverage technologies used in films and imaging did not fit well with the skills required for smooth integration and mastery of the pharmaceutical industry. Kodak eventually placed a major part of its Sterling Drug acquisition into a joint venture with French pharmaceutical giant Sanofi.

Analysts suggest that Kodak's repeated failures have been the result of its own ponderous bureaucracy and the fact that it had neither the skill to manage entrepreneurial companies nor the willingness to admit its own managerial

[13]J. Markoff, "Reprogramming the Hacker Elite," *New York Times,* January 2, 1994, p. 6F.

[14]B. Dumain, "Payoff from the New Management," *Fortune,* December, 1993, p. 110.

shortcomings. Much of this failure to learn has been laid at the feet of Kodak's CEOs over the last 20 years, all veterans of the Rochester corporate bureaucracy.

George Fisher, of Motorola, has brought new perspectives to Kodak. Instead of seeking external diversification opportunities, Kodak has refocused its efforts to build a strong presence in new digital-imaging technologies. Now wary of how peripheral businesses can distract the company from its core imaging businesses, Kodak is investing in new products and strategic alliances to extend and renew its imaging-based competencies.[15]

The relevant criticism of Kodak is not that they made mistakes, but that they initially failed to learn from the mistakes they made. Of course, leaders of learning don't actually encourage failures. What they do is encourage experiments by making it clear that it is okay to fail. In most organizations, the costs of failure are so high (often career-ending) that whatever cheerleading managers do on behalf of creativity and risk-taking is not enough to turn employees from the safe and narrow path of making no mistakes. To thwart this inherent conservatism, leaders must often go to the other extreme of seeming to celebrate failures. Ralph C. Stayer, CEO of Johnsonville Foods, used mistakes to stimulate learning. "Mistakes are road signs along the journey which read 'Learning opportunity ahead.' Mistakes are the servomechanisms of life. I used to fight or fear them. When I learned to use them to trigger my own learning, both I and my company made progress. I even formed a 'Mistake of the Month Club' to stimulate discussions about mistakes made and learn from them. I offered a 'Shot in the Foot Award' for the person who made the biggest mistake from which he/she learned the most. It was a coffee cup cast in the form of a foot with a hole in it. I was determined to have individuals see mistakes as an opportunity to learn and try again, not as an act against God's law."[16]

CONDITIONS FOR LEADING LEARNING

Modeling, mentoring, managing, and monitoring are key leader behaviors that promote learning. Here we've described these behaviors as exercised primarily by CEOs, people who have both the position and often the personae of leaders. But nothing about these behaviors makes them the province of members of the executive suite. These leaders may be more visible, but their examples are no more viable than modeling, mentoring, managing, and monitoring done by others elsewhere in the organization. People at every level of an organization have opportunities to model learning, to mentor others' learning, to manage learning, and to monitor learning. In the most effec-

tive learning organizations, everyone acts as a learning leader because everyone is learning.

This is not to suggest that these behaviors are easily come by. Leading learning at any level is a challenging task made all the more so because it is an ongoing process. Today it is common to talk of the leadership challenges presented by crises and dramatic changes, where organizations and individuals need to be 'transformed.' Leadership may actually be easier in these critical times because the need for change is so obvious and people are looking for lessons to learn.

In 1991, Lawrence Bossidy left his position as vice chairman at G.E. to take over the helm of Allied Signal, the then-troubled $12-billion-a-year manufacturer of aerospace equipment and auto parts. "The transformation here has been easier than at G.E. because the people of Allied Signal obviously were on a burning platform and they knew from newspaper reports about the struggles of IBM and Sears. They knew Allied Signal would have to be successful to provide them with job security and opportunities."[17] So much of leadership has come to be associated with fire fighting that some see the role of a leader as creating, if not crisis, at least the awareness of crisis. Bossidy believes, "To inaugurate large-scale change, you may have to create the burning platform. You have to give people a reason to do something differently."

Crises certainly provide an arena for leadership and can test the mettle of any leader. But, in a learning organization, the appropriate measure of leadership is how much learning is going on when things are going well. As difficult as it may be to teach smart people how to learn, it is still more difficult for successful organizations to learn when the platform is not burning.

Ernesto Martens-Rebolledo is the CEO of Vitro, Sociedad Anonima, an 84-year-old Mexican company with over $3 billion in sales and 44,000 employees. One of the largest and most successful of Mexican companies, Vitro, through its subsidiaries such as Anchor Glass Container Corporation and joint ventures with Ford, Corning, Samsonite, and Whirlpool, manufactures everything from glass bottles to washing machines. Martens became Vitro's first nonfamily CEO in 1985. He sees the major challenge before his company now: "One of the most difficult things to do in a successful company is to convince people that they must change." He describes specifically the need to change the mind-set of managers from one of complacency to one of continuous improvement. "The most difficult and probably the most crucial thing we needed to do was change the mind-set of the managers, which is next to impossible to do in a successful company."[18]

[15]S. N. Chakravarty and A. Feldman, "The Road Not Taken," *Forbes*, August 30, 1993, p. 40.

[16]J. A. Belasco and R. C. Stayer, *Flight of the Buffalo* (New York: Warner, 1992), p. 321.

[17]Sherman, *op. cit.*, p. 84.

[18]N. A. Nichols, "From Complacency to Competitiveness," *Harvard Business Review*, September–October 1993, pp. 163–71.

In Martens' view, the problem leaders face is less one of motivation—traditional leadership—than it is one of changing the way the organization reflects upon its own experience—learning. Leaders must help their organization find learning from the commonplace as well as from the critical, from the failures as well as from the successes, and especially from those moments when it seems as though there is nothing to be learned.

UNLEARNING LEADERSHIP

In what ways are modeling learning, mentoring learning, managing learning, and monitoring learning different from the kinds of behaviors that leaders typically do? Leading an organization toward learning poses a fundamentally different way of thinking about leadership. It is more concerned with process than with product, aiming more toward commitment and creativity than compliance, intending not to prove, but to improve. The leader as learner and the responsibility of leading an organization's learning mandate new ways of thinking about a leader's role. In order to assume this perspective, leaders and those who would be leaders need to disabuse themselves of certain widely held notions about leadership.

It is popular today to speak of the role of the leader as though *what the leader does*—leader behaviors—can be separated from *who the leader is*—the leader as a person. Most contemporary views of leadership are based upon identifying certain leader behaviors that are appropriate for certain situations. The popular "leadership styles," "situational leadership," and "transactional" approaches of recent years are typical of this view. In each, aspiring leaders are taught how to diagnose organizational situations and how to draw from their repertoire the indicated leader actions. Viewed in this way, leadership is purely an instrumental activity, a study in means. Leaders, thus trained, are not much concerned about modeling behavior. They do not see the way they lead as a reflection of who they are—it is simply a tool they use, a role that they play to achieve specific results. These leaders often are blind to the impact of their own behavior on others and ignorant of how discongruity between their actions and their words may detract from their leadership.

Learning leaders take a more holistic view of leadership. They understand that learning is not just something a person does, it is the way a person is. Leading learning is not a role one plays, it is the way one looks at oneself and the way one processes one's organizational experience. Given this perspective, learning leaders recognize the importance of modeling. They attach much greater importance to congruity between who they are and what they do as perceived by others. They lead learning in large part by learning—not by telling others they *need* to learn, but by showing in their own behavior the value of learning.

Many leaders today pride themselves on their personal detachment. They argue that tough times demand tough people who are able to set aside their personal agendas in favor of fact-finding, objective analysis, and decision making. We believe that learning occurs through *relational activities*. The effectiveness of learning and of leading learning is, in large part, a function of the effectiveness of the leader's relationships with others in the organization. Nowhere is this more apparent than in mentoring. Mentor/protégé relationships are intensely personal. Who leaders mentor and how they mentor them are choices that have profound effects on learning for individuals and for the organization. Leaders who are "distant" in an effort to be detached and objective diminish the learning possibilities that could come from their own personal immersion in the process. Many leaders, though distant, are able by virtue of their personalities to evoke an emotional attachment from followers. These charismatic leaders remain detached. They may be the object of a relationship, but they are not involved in the way that leading learning requires.

The personal involvement of the leader serves several learning agendas. It makes the model of learning that the leader presents richer and more reachable for others. The relationships that develop become an important source of honest and thoughtful feedback. The leader's personal involvement with others in learning opens him or her to learning *from* others. Recognizing the need for a personal investment in learning and in others emphasizes that leadership is not something done to others, but rather a relationship that one enters into *with* others. As much as what the leader does cannot be separated from who the leader is, learners cannot stand apart from their relationships with others. Learning and leading require a personal involvement with others.

Popular approaches present leadership as event-focused, episodic behaviors engaged in at a time and a manner dictated by the situation. Some even speak of "leader/shipping" as though leadership were a skill to be exercised much like planning or budgeting. This perspective comes from our tendency to put the microscope to leadership only when it seems most needed. Crises provide leaders with opportunities to take bold actions. We know that crises are more likely to give rise to charismatic leaders and leaders who are seen as transformational or visionary, in part because at these times followers see a heightened need for leadership and "sense making."[19] Many leaders seek out these opportunities to "be bold." Who leaders are and what leaders do may be most evident in times of crisis, but the opportunities for learning are not limited to organizational emergencies. Leaders of

[19] R. J. House, W. D. Spangler, and J. Woycke, "Personality and Charisma in the U.S. Presidency: A Psychological Theory of Leader Effectiveness," *Administrative Science Quarterly* 36 (1991) pp. 364–96.

learning manage learning as an on-going organizational process, not an occasional, extraordinary event. They are *always* looking for the learning opportunity.

Leaders manage learning with: (1) a focus on improving processes over proving performances; (2) an intensity of focus that is always greater than what is sufficient, but less than would be stressful or to the point of distress; (3) a processing of experience close enough in time to correct any problems; (4) an appreciation for individual differences as a means to clarify values. Each of these benchmarks for managing learning underscores the observation that leading learning is a full-time, full-service activity, not a some-time situational option which leaders may or may not exercise.

There is a belief shared by most leaders and all too many followers that the leader is infallible. The practical (political) corollary to this belief is, "If the leader does do wrong, he or she should not be confronted with the fact." Leaders who effectively monitor learning will put into place people and processes to generate valid feedback. One of the unintended consequences of effective reengineering programs has been the revelation of the tremendous number of processes and procedures present in organizations, the purpose of which is to prove who or what is right. The majority of these exist at the privilege of leaders at all levels. Ostensibly monitoring mechanisms, these processes and procedures are more commonly used to promote the party line and prompt conformity. The standard defense leaders proffer is, "I don't want to be surprised." The pragmatic translation is, "I don't want to be surprised with feedback which shows me to be wrong." Learning leaders are serious enough about learning to monitor learning in such a way that all valid information is revealed and reflected upon, *even* if it shows the leader to be wrong, *especially* if it shows the leader to be wrong.

The presumption of leader infallibility presents a particular problem for today's "transformational" leaders. These leaders, by virtue of their compelling vision, their personal conviction, and their persuasive communication skills, may foster an almost cult-like devotion from employees. Any questioning of the transformational leader's purpose, programs, or processes may be viewed by the leader and by the organization as disloyal. So strong is this feeling that many in these organizations engage in a kind of self-censorship, withholding critical feedback even when it would best serve the leader and the organization to be forthcoming. Leaders blessed with transformational skills must make a special effort to disabuse themselves and their followers of any semblance of leader infallibility. In a learning organization, everyone acknowledges failures—their own, others', and those of the organization. And, because everyone can fail, everyone can learn.

THE LESSON FOR LEADERS

Over 60 years ago, Fritz Roethlisberger, conducting his legendary Hawthorne studies, observed that leaders are characterized by "A willingness to accept new ideas and a desire to verify them by experience."[20] How can a leader's willingness and desire be discerned? To our mind, there are four simple tests: (1) Is the leader learning? (2) Is the leader involved? (3) Is the learning and leading constant? (4) Is it okay to say the leader was wrong? The most effective leaders have always been and will always be learners. They lead their organizations by modeling, mentoring, managing, and monitoring learning. To come to this point, leaders at all levels and those engaged in leadership relationships must unlearn certain contemporary conventional ideas about who leaders are and what leaders do; they must unlearn the role of the leader, personal detachment, leadershipping, and leader infallibility.

Organizations cannot learn unless leaders are learners. The development of a learning organization must begin with development of individual learners who institutionalize learning processes in organizations which, in turn, promote learning communities and a learning society. This seemingly grand, even grandiose, scheme has implications for each of us. Each of us can act to learn and, in so doing, lead the learning of others, whatever our sphere of activity.

[20]F. Roethlisberger, "Data Concerning the Research Group in Supervisory Training Methods," Section 4.1, 1932 Hawthorne Studies Collection, Harvard University, as reported by Ronald G. Greenwood, "Leadership Theory: A Historical Look," *The Journal of Leadership Studies* 1, no. 1 (1993), p. 10.

Exercises

EXERCISE 12.1   Leadership Style Analysis

OBJECTIVES

1. To learn how to diagnose different leadership situations using the Vroom-Jago model
2. To learn how to apply a systematic procedure for analyzing situations
3. To improve understanding of how to reach a decision

STARTING THE EXERCISE

The instructor will form groups of four to five people to analyze each of the following three cases. Try to reach a group consensus on which decision style is best for the particular case. Each case should take a group between 30 and 45 minutes to analyze.

EXERCISE PROCEDURES

Phase I (10–15 minutes):   Individually read a case and select what you consider to be the best decision style.

Phase II (30–45 minutes):   Join a group appointed by instructor and reach a group consensus.

Phase III (20 minutes):   Each group spokesperson presents the group's response and rationale to other groups.

These phases should be used for each of the cases.

Case I

Setting: Corporate headquarters
Your position: Vice president
As marketing vice president, you frequently receive nonroutine requests from customers. One such request, from a relatively new customer, is for extended terms on a large purchase ($2.5 million) involving several of your product lines. The request is for extremely favorable terms that you would not consider except for the high inventory level of most product lines at the present time due to the unanticipated slack period that the company has experienced over the last six months.

You realize that the request is probably a starting point for negotiations, and you have proved your abilities to negotiate the most favorable arrangements in the past. As preparation for these negotiations, you have familiarized yourself with the financial situation of the customer, using various investment reports that you receive regularly.

Reporting to you are four sales managers, each of whom has responsibility for a single product line. They

know of the order, and, like you, they believe that it is important to negotiate terms with minimum risk and maximum returns to the company. They are likely to differ on what constitutes an acceptable level of risk. The two younger managers have developed a reputation of being "risk takers," whereas the two more senior managers are substantially more conservative.

Case II

Setting: Toy manufacturer
Your position: Vice president, engineering and design
You are a vice president in a large toy manufacturing company, and your responsibilities include the design of new products that will meet the changing demand in this uncertain and very competitive industry. Your design teams, each under the supervision of a department head, are therefore under constant pressure to produce novel, marketable ideas.

At the opposite end of the manufacturing process is the quality control department, which is under the authority of the vice president, production. When quality control has encountered a serious problem that may be due to design features, its staff has consulted with one or more of your department heads to obtain their recommendations for any changes in the production process. In the wake of consumer concern over the safety of children's toys, however, the responsibilities of quality control have recently been expanded to ensure not only the quality but also the safety of your products. The first major problem in this area has arisen. A preliminary consumer report has "blacklisted" one of your new products without giving any specific reason or justification. This has upset you and others in the organization since it was believed that this product would be one of the most profitable items in the coming Christmas season.

The consumer group has provided your company with an opportunity to respond to the report before it is made public. The head of quality control has therefore consulted with your design people, but you have been told that they became somewhat defensive and dismissed the report as "overreactive fanatic nonsense." Your people told quality control that, while freak accidents were always possible, the product was certainly safe as designed. They argued that the report should simply be ignored.

Since the issue is far from routine, you have decided to give it your personal attention. Because your design teams have been intimately involved in all aspects of the development of the item, you suspect that their response was extreme and was perhaps governed more by their emotional reaction to the report than by the facts. You are not convinced that the consumer group is totally irresponsible, and you are anxious to explore the problem in detail and to recommend to quality control any changes that may be required from a design standpoint. The firm's image as a producer of high-quality toys could suffer a serious blow if the report were made public and public confidence were lost as a result.

You will have to depend heavily on the background and experience of your design teams to help you in analyzing the problem. Even though quality control will be responsible for the decision to implement any changes that you may ultimately recommend, your own subordinates have the background of design experience that could enable you to set standards for what is "safe" and to suggest any design modifications that would meet these standards.

Case III

Setting: Corporate headquarters
Your position: Vice president
The sales executives in your home office spent a great deal of time visiting regional sales offices. As marketing vice president, you are concerned that the expenses incurred on these trips are excessive—especially now, when the economic outlook seems bleak and general belt-tightening measures are being carried out in every department.

Having recently been promoted from the ranks of your subordinates, you are keenly aware of some cost-saving measures that could be introduced. You have, in fact, asked the accounting department to review a sample of past expense reports, and it has agreed with your conclusion that several highly favored travel "luxuries" could be curtailed. For example, your sales executives could restrict first-class air travel to only those occasions when economy class is unavailable, and airport limousine service to hotels could be used instead of taxis where possible. Even more savings could be made if your personnel carefully planned trips such that multiple purposes could be achieved where possible.

The success of any cost-saving measures, however, depends on the commitment of your subordinates. You do not have the time (or the desire) to closely review the expense reports of these sales executives. You suspect, though, that they do not share your concerns over the matter. Having once been in their position, you know that they feel themselves to be deserving of travel amenities.

The problem is to determine which changes, if any, are to be made in current travel and expense account practices in light of the new economic conditions.

Cases

CASE 12.1   A Leadership Contrast at Ford Motors

THIS FORD IS DIFFERENT. Can Bill Ford Jr., chairman of The Ford Motor Company Board of Directors, jump-start his old-world auto company and keep employees, customers, and investors—not to mention environmentalists—happy? Or will he turn out to be a Model T leader in a Jaguar age?

Bill Ford Jr. heard the bad news after lunch on a sleety February afternoon a year ago. There had been an explosion at Ford Motor's Rouge plant, the historic complex of belching smokestacks and towers that Ford could see against the skyline from his office. Nobody knew how many people had been hurt. At that moment, Bill Ford, the brand-new chairman of Ford Motor, had a distinctly unchairmanlike reaction: He decided to leave his office for the scene of the accident.

All sorts of well-meaning lieutenants tried to stop him. "You can't go," said one.

"What do you mean, I can't go?" asked Ford.

"Well, we don't have any information."

"Fine," Ford replied. "I'll go over and get some."

"You don't understand," said another. "It could be dangerous."

"Why should I be in any less danger than anybody else?" asked Ford.

"The media will be there," said yet another. "You might say the wrong thing."

Finally, one said in exasperation: "You don't understand. Generals don't go to the front."

"Really," replied Ford. "Well, bust me down to private then, because I'm out of here."

By the end of the day, Bill Ford had visited the plant's triage center. He had been on TV in his windbreaker say-

Source: Betsy Morris, "Idealist on Board," *Fast Company*, April 2000, pp. 122–26. Used by permission.

ing, "This has to be the worst day of my life." Without an entourage, he visited area hospitals late into the night consoling families of the injured and dying (six men were killed). And in that defining day, he made it perfectly clear that he did not intend to be a buttoned-down executive.

Roll over, Business Roundtable. Here comes an entirely new old-economy boss. Bill Ford Jr., 42, is a nice guy with a politician's keen instinct. He is an unapologetic environmentalist. He is a family man who would rather spend Saturday nights eating pizza with his four children than eating hors d'oeuvres with movers and shakers. He is an iconoclast. He prefers ice hockey to golf—he does not do business on the golf course—and he's working on his black belt in tae kwon do. He says what he thinks and does what he thinks he should. "Greenpeace has asked me to speak. I think I'm going to do it," he mused recently in his office. "Yeah, why not? Maybe I should wear a flak jacket."

He is that rare corporate executive who says boldly that his company will do best for its shareholders if it takes care of its employees, its community, and the environment—all of which, he says, will enable Ford Motor to attract better talent, develop loyal customers, enhance its brand, sell more cars and services, and, over time, boost its share price. When Bill refers to Ford's workers as his "extended family," even some of his union bosses believe that he's sincere.

Can someone actually combine an industrialist's pedigree and an idealist's sensibility to steer a Big Three automaker? Can the chairman of America's second-largest industrial company really do well by doing good? It's a radical notion. "There are people who think I'm a Bolshevik, and that this is all a major distraction at best and heresy at worst," says Ford. "But I really don't care. I'm in this for my children and my grandchildren. I want them to inherit a legacy they're proud of. I don't want anybody, whether it's my grandchildren or any of our employees' grandchildren, to have to apologize for working for Ford Motor Co. In fact, I want the opposite. I want them to look and say, 'What a difference we made!' "

Such sentiments sound practically suicidal now, as Wall Street bludgeons stalwarts like Ford. Along with the stocks of other old-economy blue chips, its share price has been slammed. It is trading in the low 40s, having lost more than 25% of its value in the last year, even though Ford—unlike, say, Amazon.com—had a terrific 1999, with record revenues and strong gains in most of its operations. It also bought Volvo's car business and established e-commerce partnerships with Yahoo and Microsoft's CarPoint, an online car-buying service. No matter. Ford Motor is cyclical, not high tech. It has problems in Europe and Latin America. And—eat your hearts out, dot-coms— it has big problems with Wall Street because it has $24 billion in cash. Analysts love Bill Ford, really they do, and

they think social responsibility is nice, yadda, yadda. But what they really want is a stock buyback.

Meanwhile, what older traditional auto industry executives want is for Bill Ford to please shut up. "The part I don't understand is his infatuation with the environmental movement," says one. "Those are groups that would really just like the [auto] industry to go away. I think it's a little naive and disingenuous to say we're so environmentally responsible we want to be the car company everybody loves, when the clear profit motive is to sell more sport utilities and pickup trucks."

Today the intrigue is mostly about Bill's relationship with Ford's CEO Jacques Nasser. Many people believe it's rocky, and the rumors are wild: that they had a shouting match in the lobby of the Dearborn Ritz-Carlton, that they had to be separated by security during an argument at world headquarters. Both men say the rumors are ludicrous. They get along. But they do make an odd couple. Nasser, 10 years Ford's senior, has more operating experience and global depth. As passionately as Bill Ford cares about the environment, Nasser cares about brands and consumers. One of the auto industry's stars, he is just as opinionated as Bill Ford. Their success as partners depends on whether their distinctive views and styles will, over time, mesh or clash. "I think it'll be a miracle if they last two years" says Bob Lutz, a former executive at both Ford Motor and Chrysler. "One wants to be the hero of the environment. The other wants to be the hero of the shareholders."

But the real question about Bill Ford Jr. is not whether he can get along with Jac Nasser. It's whether he can create a new kind of leadership to arouse and fight embattled old-economy corporations. Their shareholders and their managers have deserted in droves for the dot-coms. Their credibility, on matters from genetic engineering to teen smoking to passenger bumping, is about as bad as, well, a used-car salesman's. Now, at the very time Wall Street and Main Street are fed up with the Organization Man, here comes Bill Ford Jr., the antithesis of the Organization Man.

William Clay Ford Jr. was born during the baby boom, on May 3, 1957. He grew up in the rarefied air of Grosse Pointe, a suburban enclave of wealth along Lake St. Clair where most of the Fords have historically lived. Bill Jr. spent many a day riding his Stingray bicycle up and down private Provencal Road, trying to make it sound like a Harley. He wiled away afternoons in the woods of his grandmother's estate at Gaukler Pointe (now a museum) and looked forward to Sundays with his father in the owner's box at Detroit Lions football games.

Because of his personality and the times—in the '70s it was not cool to be rich or have lineage—Bill Ford grew up trying to prove himself separate and apart from being a Ford. "I loved academics and sports because they were great equalizers," he says. When he went to Princeton, a friend chewed him out after discovering, two weeks into their friendship, that Bill Ford had neglected to mention exactly which Ford he was. "What difference does it make?" Ford asked with frustration.

At Princeton, Ford began a struggle that would last for two decades: What, exactly, should he do with his life? Characteristically, his father had never pushed him to join the company. For a while he was tempted to work on Wall Street. But legacy weighed heavily. His history thesis at Princeton, "Henry Ford and Labor: A Reappraisal," reads like a private attempt to reconcile how his great-grandfather could have identified with the working man—he was so generous with wages that he was called a socialist—yet at the same time have become so anti-union. The debate continued at MIT, where Ford got a master's degree in management. Tom Barocci, his professor and thesis adviser, recalls frequent discussions with Bill about "how to balance the legitimate interests of trade unions and workers with shareholder interests. Bill wouldn't buy that these things couldn't be accomplished in tandem."

As Bill's friends left Princeton to spend the roaring '80s in New York, he returned to Detroit. In 1979, Ford Motor, like Chrysler and GM, was struggling to deal with the high oil prices and interest rates caused in part by the Iran hostage crisis; small, cheap Japanese cars were about to start crowding U.S. highways. "Everything in my life had come from Ford Motor Co.," he says. "If I could have any kind of positive impact, I owed it to the company to do that." If Ford Motor hadn't been in trouble, Bill says he might not have gone home: "I didn't want the finality of thinking: Here I am at 21, and I'll be here until 65 or beyond, and my life is all mapped out." Three months after graduation he was a product-planning analyst. Next he moved to the Wayne assembly plant for the launch of the Ford Escort. He used the pseudonym "Bill Clay" at first because "I didn't want people making a big deal out of the thing." Over the next two decades he rotated through 17 jobs, lasting in some just several months, never sure whether he was on the fast track or the track to oblivion. He worked as a marketing analyst, ad specialist, international finance specialist, product development planning manager, truck marketing manager for Europe, head of Switzerland, head of climate control. Despite his pedigree and his ownership, he asked himself, many times over, the question so common to his generation: Is the long, backbiting climb up the ladder worth it?

He impressed people along the way with his hard work and humility. Adds Frank Croskey, a manager who worked with Bill at the climate-control division: "He treats everybody the way he'd like to be treated, whether he's talking to the mechanic in the garage or the President of the U.S. [in this case, George H. W. Bush, a Yale classmate and close friend of his father's."] Over time, word got around: This Ford is different.

He walked into new situations, admitted what he didn't know, and enlisted everybody's help. He explained that he was there to learn and to make sure Ford Motor was around for his great-grandchildren. Then he'd roll up his sleeves and start working. When he became general manager of the climate control division, its internal compressors were failing, it was overwhelmed by bureaucracy—endless meetings, endless reports—and it was losing money. "Bill's patience is not one of his attributes," says Croskey. "I learned his limit was about 30 minutes. He'd get fidgety." He wanted reports on one piece of paper. Croskey recalls Bill telling workers, "I'm here to take the roadblocks out, to get the problem solved"—which it was within six months at climate control.

William Clay Ford's decision to retire as head of the board's finance committee in January 1995 forced Bill into a pivotal decision. Should he stay in his management job, or should he take the powerful board job that had almost always been held by a family member? The latter was no sure ticket to the top, but it would help protect the family's interests. It would also remove what Bill called "a noose around my neck—[the feeling] that management could always forestall the day they would have to make this decision [about naming me chairman or CEO]. One more job. One more experience. And if they were skillful, I could be 65 by the time [they thought I] was ready to take over."

Ford and Nasser couldn't be more different. Ford is heir to an American fortune. Nasser, 52, was born in a Lebanese mountain village to a man who was, he says, "essentially a soldier of fortune." His father, Abdo, lived in France, Cuba, and the U.S. before returning to Lebanon at the beginning of World War II. Abdo worked for the Allies and got to know some Australian soldiers. He decided to move his family to Australia when Jac was 4. While Ford grew up in cloistered Grosse Pointe, surrounded by family, Nasser's family "knew no one, absolutely no one." His father had enough money either to buy a house or start a business. He chose the house and then set out to earn a living by working three or four jobs at a time, one of them chopping wood.

If Ford's parents tried to protect him from the vagaries of wealth, Nasser's parents could do little to shield their son from the racism of 1950s Australia. Nasser remembers being the only non-Anglo child in his class. He says he was teased so badly about the tabbouleh his mother packed for lunch that he hid it—but still went home and told her, "Great lunch." "My brother and I [went] to school together, and we'd be in a fight almost every day," says Nasser. "And if we weren't, we got to the point where we would start to look for one." Nasser says the experience "taught me to read people pretty quickly. You're genuine, or you're not. You're on my team, or you're not on my team. I'll beat the hell out of you, or you're going to beat the hell out of me."

Australia changed greatly during Nasser's time there. His father eventually got into real estate, construction, food services, and transportation. Nasser, who graduated with a degree in business studies from the Royal Melbourne Institute of Technology, joined Ford Motor in 1968 as a financial analyst in Australia. Over the next 30 years he, like Bill Ford, held many jobs. Nasser's were higher octane. He was an executive in Asia and Latin America, and he ran Ford Motor's operations in Australia and Europe. In 1994 he became group vice president of product development and two years later, president of automotive operations.

Nasser is known for his energy, his brainstorming, and his speedy decisions, what a colleague calls "paperless decisions." He is also known for tough decisions. His move to kill the sentimental but unprofitable old Thunderbird, along with lots of other cost-cutting, won him the nickname "Jac the Knife." Just as Ford is passionate about the environment, Nasser is passionate about cars. He loves to visit the design center, to touch the clay.

The obvious differences between Nasser and Bill Ford, along with the history of infighting at the company, undoubtedly fuel suspicions that the men don't get along. "Jac Nasser is from a working-class background, struggling to make this the best car company there is," says a former Ford executive. "His whole life, he never had anything handed to him on a silver platter. If Billy Ford starts saying you can't do this and you can't do that, Jac Nasser is going to be nuts."

That's Bill, not Billy. And so far, Bill has not been telling Jac he can't do this and he can't do that. In fact, for all their differences, the two men share some important similarities. Both are impatient. Both want to make Ford Motor a prototype for New Economy industrial companies. Both want to avoid the backbiting that has been so much a part of Ford Motor. In the beginning, Bill Ford concedes, the relationship was awkward. When he and Nasser began the board-ordered deliberations about how to split their jobs, Bill says, "we had some pregnant pauses" whenever he and Jac got too specific about who would do what. Bill says people told him, "Look, Jac's a tough guy, and you've got to make sure you really carve out your ground up front." At the same time, he says, people told Nasser, "Boy, if this family member gets a foot in the door and you don't delineate right up front what the limits are, you're going to get steamrollered."

Eventually they listened to their own counsel. "We decided early on that this was going to be about working together," says Nasser. "It wasn't going to be about egos. It wasn't going to be about you do this and I do that." They reached some general agreements. Bill would not become involved in the operations, but he could talk to anybody in the company. Board business would go through Bill, but Nasser could talk to any of the directors. "Big decisions,

or even semi-big decisions, we'd talk about," says Bill. They decided not to create separate support staffs to avoid the problem of having different camps vying against each other.

All that took getting used to. If Bill said he was making a speech, people would scurry into Nasser's office to see what he thought. Bill admits he was alarmed by reports he had heard about possible acquisitions: "I thought, my goodness, Jac's never seen a deal he doesn't want to do." (Historically, Ford Motor executives did not study a deal unless they intended to do it.) At first Bill questioned the acquisition of Volvo's car operations, which Nasser pursued soon after they began their new jobs. Bill wanted to be certain they weren't jumping at it "just to start with a big splash." When Nasser outlined how Volvo would fit with his plans for a premier automotive group that would also include the Jaguar and Aston Martin brands, Bill turned around completely.

Now Bill knows that Nasser likes to kick tires on all sorts of deals. Now Bill, too, meets with the investment bankers. Now he and Nasser talk regularly over tea or coffee (both have espresso machines in their offices). The two can move very quickly, as they did when they recently struck a deal to buy Land Rover from BMW. Ford says he's careful not to meddle in operations. "But by the same token, I feel very free, whether it's a dividend policy, a share buyback, an acquisition, a human-rights platform, a product design—I feel very free to get into all of it, and Jac would never discourage me from that," says Ford. "And we do disagree; we do. But . . . if one of us feels really strongly about something, the other tends to say okay."

Nasser says the traditional way of looking at a power-sharing arrangement is "the CEO runs the company and the chairman runs the board." Then he adds, "That's more or less what happens here right now." But "more or less" covers a lot of ground, ground that could some day shift and alter the relationship between CEO and chairman, perhaps over how to deploy Ford Motor's cash—in ways that would better please family members (dividends) or Wall Street (buybacks)—perhaps over the wisdom of an acquisition. Nasser is well aware that Bill Ford did not spend 20 years at the family company to end up as a figurehead. "No," he says adamantly. "That would be demeaning to him and to me."

When the company and the UAW opened contract negotiations last year, Bill arrived wearing the union's button: BARGAINING FOR FAMILIES. "Why not?" he says. "I always hated this us vs. them." Nasser was Ford Motor's chief negotiator, but the perception among employees was that Bill Ford knew exactly what was happening and may have had a role in the sweet deal the contract gave workers at Visteon, the parts business Ford Motor plans to spin off. (A strike threat may also have had something to do with it.) Bill says he wasn't involved in the negotiations. "I suppose everybody knew how I felt. I obviously wanted to make sure the employees were well taken care of."

With his disarming smile and his earnestness, he has charmed some of Ford Motor's most ardent adversaries. He talks on the phone and occasionally lunches with Jerry Sullivan, president of UAW Local 600. Says Sullivan: "His concern for the people, for the community, for the environment—those are things you just don't see in industrialists." Adds Robert Massie, head of a coalition of environmental, labor, and investment groups: "I think Bill Ford has the potential for being a really thrilling corporate leader." Then Massie pauses and adds, "It's funny for me to talk like this. Ralph Nader would say to me, 'What did he [Bill Ford] put in your coffee?' "

Three months after the Rouge disaster, Bill ordered an environmental makeover of the complex, which had been built by Henry Ford. He hired William McDonough, an architect known for environmentally friendly designs, to direct the project. In December he pulled the company out of the Global Climate Coalition, a lobbying group that challenges theories of global warming; since then DaimlerChrysler, GM, and Texaco have also withdrawn.

QUESTIONS:

1. Under what leadership model (transactional, transformational, charismatic, or coach) would you place Bill Ford Jr? Jacques Nasser? Why?
2. In the long run is it possible for two powerful leaders such as Ford and Nasser to work effectively together? Why?
3. Ford's emphasis on environmental issues is still controversial in the company. How can he convince other Ford executives that his views can be beneficial to the firm?

13
Chapter

Communication

After completing Chapter 13, you should be able to:

Learning Objectives

- Explain the elements in the communication process.

- Compare the four major directions of communication.

- Describe the role played by interpersonal communication in organizations.

- Discuss multicultural communication.

- Identify significant barriers to effective communication.

- Describe ways in which communication in organizations can be improved.

The focus of this chapter is the process of organizational communication. Communicating, like the process of decision making discussed in the next chapter, pervades everything that all organizational members—particularly managers—do. The managerial functions of planning, organizing, leading, and controlling all involve communicative activity. In fact, communication is an absolutely essential element in all organizational processes.

THE IMPORTANCE OF COMMUNICATION

Communication is the glue that holds organizations together. Communication assists organizational members to accomplish both individual and organizational goals, implement and respond to organizational change, coordinate organizational activities, and engage in virtually all organizationally relevant behaviors. Yet, as important as this process is, breakdowns in communication are pervasive. The anonymous wit who said, "I know you believe you understand what you think I said, but I am not sure you realize that what you heard is not what I meant," was being more than humorous; she or he was describing what every one of us has experienced: a failure to communicate.

To the extent that organizational communications are less effective than they might be, organizations will be less effective than they might be. For example, in many companies, new-employee orientation programs represent the first important opportunity to begin the process of effective communication with employees. At Marriott International, the worldwide hotel and resort chain, 40 percent of new employees who leave the organization do so during the first three months on the job. At least that had been true historically. Recently, the rate of departures has been significantly reduced because Marriott has embarked on a concerted effort to improve the content and manner in which it communicates with new employees during orientation. In addition to formally providing more information, each new employee is assigned a "buddy" who serves as a vital communication link to which the newcomer has unrestricted access. Marriott helps ensure that its frontline service personnel communicate effectively with their guests by first ensuring that Marriott communicates effectively with its employees, starting from their very first day on the job.

It would be extremely difficult to find an aspect of a manager's job that does not involve communication. Serious problems arise when directives are misunderstood, when casual kidding in a work group leads to anger, or when informal remarks by a top-level manager are distorted. Each of these situations is a result of a breakdown somewhere in the process of communication.

Accordingly, the pertinent question is not whether managers engage in communication because communication is inherent to the functioning of an organization. Rather, the pertinent question is whether managers will communicate well or poorly. In other words, communication itself is unavoidable in an organization's functioning; only *effective* communication is avoidable. *Every manager must be a communicator.* In fact, everything a manager does communicates something in some way to somebody or some group. The only question is: "With what effect?" While this may appear an overstatement at this point, it will become apparent as you proceed through the chapter. Despite the tremendous advances in communication and information technology, communication among people in organizations leaves much to be desired.[1] It is a process that occurs within people.

---

[1]James M. Kouzes, "Link Me to Your Leader," *Business 2.0*, October 10, 2000, pp. 292–95.

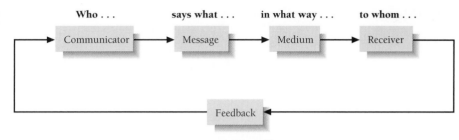

EXHIBIT 13.1
The Communication
Process

THE COMMUNICATION PROCESS

The general process of communication is presented in Exhibit 13.1. The process contains five elements—the communicator, the message, the medium, the receiver, and feedback. It can be simply summarized as: Who . . . says what . . . in what way . . . to whom . . . with what effect?[2] To appreciate each element in the process, we must examine how communication works.

How Communication Works

Communication experts tell us that effective communication is the result of a common understanding between the communicator and the receiver. In fact, the word *communication* is derived from the Latin *communis,* meaning "common." The communicator seeks to establish a "commonness" with a receiver. Hence, we can define **communication** as the *transition of information and understanding through the use of common symbols from one person or group to another.* The common symbols may be verbal or nonverbal. You will see later that in the context of an organizational structure, information can flow up and down (vertical), across (horizontal), and down and across (diagonal).

The most widely used contemporary model of the process of communication has evolved mainly from the work of Shannon and Weaver and Schramm.[3] These researchers were concerned with describing the general process of communication that could be useful in all situations. The model that evolved from their work is helpful for understanding communication. The basic elements include a communicator, an encoder, a message, a medium, a decoder, a receiver, feedback, and noise. The model is presented in Exhibit 13.2. Each element in the model can be examined in the context of an organization.

www.nestle.com

The communication process works extremely well at the world's largest food producer, Nestlé. The company has entered the e-revolution by using the Web for continuous communication. Nestlé provides store owners the option of ordering its chocolates and other products via a Web site: Nestlé EZ Order. The system will eliminate most of the 100,000 phoned or faxed orders a year from mom-and-pop

---

[2]These five questions were first suggested in H. D. Lasswell, *Power and Personality* (New York: W. W. Norton, 1948), pp. 37–51.

[3]Claude Shannon and Warren Weaver, *The Mathematical Theory of Communication* (Urbana: University of Illinois Press, 1948); and Wilbur Schramm; "How Communication Works," in Wilbur Schramm (ed.), *The Process and Effects of Mass Communication,* (Urbana: University of Illinois Press, 1953), pp. 3–26.

EXHIBIT 13.2   A Communication Model

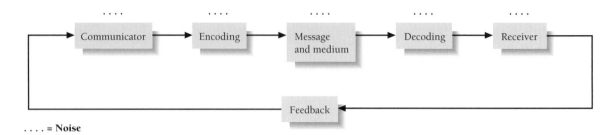

.... = Noise

shops.[4] Nestlé buyers have purchased cocoa beans and other raw ingredients on a country-by-country basis with little information about how colleagues were buying the same products. Now they share price information via the Net and pick suppliers offering the best deals.

Nestlé has traditionally processed its own cocoa butter and powder and manufactured most of its own chocolate. The Web now lets Nestlé communicate regularly with suppliers, making outsourcing a viable option.

In the past, Nestlé guessed at how many Kit Kat Crunch bars it might be able to sell in a promotion. Today, electronic links with supermarkets and other partners provides it with real-time feedback and information.

The Nestlé approach involves each of the elements in the communication process. The difference with Nestlé today and Nestlé yesterday is that some of the firm's exchanges of messages and feedback are performed electronically. Nestlé believes that face-to-face and electronic communicators are needed to operate a profitable business around the world.

The Elements of Communication

Communicator   In an organizational framework, the communicator is an employee with ideas, intentions, information, and a purpose for communicating.

Encoding   Given the communicator, an encoding process must take place that translates the communicator's ideas into a systematic set of symbols—into a language expressing the communicator's purpose. For example, a manager often takes accounting information, sales reports, and computer data and translates them into one message. The function of encoding, then, is to provide a form in which ideas and purposes can be expressed as a message.

Message   The result of the encoding process is the message. The purpose of the communicator is expressed in the form of the message—either *verbal* or *nonverbal*. Managers have numerous purposes for communicating, such as to have others understand their ideas, to understand the ideas of others, to gain acceptance of themselves or their ideas, or to produce action. The message, then, is what the individual hopes to communicate to the intended receiver, and the exact form it

---

[4]William Echikson, "Nestlé: An Elephant Dances," *Business Week,* December 11, 2000, pp. EB44–EB48.

takes depends, to a great extent, on the medium used to carry the message. Decisions relating to the two are inseparable.

Not as obvious, however, are *unintended messages* that can be sent by silence or inaction on a particular issue as well as decisions of which goals and objectives not to pursue and which method not to utilize. For example, a decision to utilize one type of performance evaluation method rather than another may send a "message" to certain people. Messages may also be designed to appear on the surface to convey certain information, when other information is what is really being conveyed. Related to this are messages designed to protect the sender, rather than to facilitate understanding by the receiver. Organizational Encounter 13.1 provides some examples of these latter types of messages.

Medium   The *medium* is the carrier of the message. Organizations provide information to members in a variety of ways, including face-to-face communications, telephone, group meetings, memos, policy statements, reward systems, production schedules, and sales forecasts. The arrival of electronic media based upon the computer and telecommunication technologies has increased interest in the role of the medium in various aspects of organizational communications.[5]

Decoding-Receiver   For the process of communication to be completed, the message must be decoded in terms of relevance to the receiver. Decoding is a technical term for the receiver's thought processes. Decoding, then, involves interpretation. *Receivers* interpret (decode) the message in light of their own previous experiences and frames of reference. Thus, a salesperson is likely to decode a memo from the company president differently than a production manager will. A nursing supervisor is likely to decode a memo from the hospital administrator differently than the chief of surgery will. The closer the decoded message is to the intent desired by the communicator, the more effective is the communication. This underscores the importance of the communicator being "receiver-oriented."

Feedback   Provision for feedback in the communication process is desirable. *One-way* communication processes are those that do not allow receiver-to-communicator feedback. This may increase the potential for distortion between the intended message and the received message. A feedback loop provides a channel for receiver response that enables the communicator to determine whether the message has been received and has produced the intended response. *Two-way* communication processes provide for this important receiver-to-communicator feedback.[6]

For the manager, communication feedback may come in many ways. In face-to-face situations, *direct* feedback through verbal exchanges is possible, as are such subtle means of communication as facial expressions of discontent or misunderstanding. In addition, *indirect* means of feedback (such as declines in productivity, poor quality of production, increased absenteeism or turnover, and lack of coordination and/or conflict between units) may indicate communication breakdowns.

---

[5]Carol Saunders and Jack Jones, "Temporal Sequences in Information Acquisition for Decision Making: A Focus on Source and Medium," *Academy of Management Review*, January 1990, pp. 29–46.

[6]Thad B. Green and Jay T. Knippen, *Breaking the Barrier to Upward Communication* (Westport, CT: Quorim, 1999).

Organizational Encounter 13.1

Confusing the People and Clouding the Issue

Unfortunately, not all organizational communications are meant to clarify; sometimes they are designed to confuse. At other times, protecting the communicator may be the primary objective. Some words and phrases are so frequently used to convey a meaning other than the apparent one that their use has become institutionalized. Below are some humorous examples of alternative interpretions to what otherwise appear as straightforward words or messages.

It is in process—It's so wrapped up in red tape that the situation is hopeless.

We will look into it—By the time the wheel makes a full turn, we assume you will have forgotten about it.

Under consideration—Never heard of it.

Under active consideration—We're looking in our files for it.

We are making a survey—We need more time to think of an answer.

Let's get together on this—I'm assuming you're as confused as I.

For appropriate action—Maybe you'll know what to do with this.

Note and initial—Let's spread the responsibility for this.

It is estimated—This is my guess.

We are aware of it—We had hoped that the person who started it would have forgotten about it by now.

We will advise you in due course—If we figure it out, we'll let you know.

Give us the benefit of your thinking—We'll listen to you as long as it doesn't interfere with what we have already decided to do.

She is in conference—I don't have any idea where she is.

We are activating the file—We're faxing it to as many people as we can think of.

Let me bring you up to date—We didn't like what you were going to do, so we already did something else.

A reliable source—The person you just met.

An informed source—The person who told the person you just met.

An unimpeachable source—The person who started the rumor to begin with.

Noise   In the framework of human communication, noise can be thought of as those factors that distort the intended message. Noise may occur in each of the elements of communication. For example, a manager who is under a severe time constraint may be forced to act without communicating or may communicate hastily with incomplete information. Or a subordinate may attach a different meaning to a word or phrase than was intended by the manager.

The elements discussed in this section are essential for communication to occur. They should not, however, be viewed as separate. They are, rather, descriptive of the acts that have to be performed for any type of communication to occur. The communication may be vertical (superior-subordinate, subordinate-superior) or horizontal (peer-peer). Or it may involve one individual and a group. But the elements discussed here must be present.

Nonverbal Messages

The information sent by a communicator that is unrelated to the verbal information—that is, nonverbal messages or **nonverbal communication**—is a relatively recent area of research among behavioral scientists. The major interest has been in the *physical cues* that characterize the communicator's physical presentation. These cues include such modes of transmitting nonverbal messages as head, face, and eye movements, posture, distance, gestures, voice tone, and clothing and dress choices.[7] Nonverbal messages themselves are influenced by factors such as the gender of the communicator.[8]

Some nonverbal messages are spontaneous and unregulated expressions of emotion, while others are conscious and deliberately presented.[9] Through nonverbal behavior, particularly body movements, we say, "Help me, I'm lonely. Take me, I'm available. Leave me alone, I'm depressed." We act out our state of being with nonverbal body language. We lift one eyebrow for disbelief. We rub our noses for puzzlement. We clasp our arms to isolate ourselves or to protect ourselves. We shrug our shoulders for indifference, wink one eye for intimacy, tap our fingers for impatience, slap our forehead for forgetfulness.[10]

Nonverbal messages may differ from other forms of communication behavior in several ways. For example, nonverbal behavior can be difficult to suppress (e.g., an involuntary frown indicating displeasure). Such unconscious behavior can contradict the message the communicator is sending verbally. Another way in which nonverbal messages differ from other forms is that they are more apparent to the people who observe them than they are to the people who produce them. This can make it very difficult for the sender to know how successfully she or he produced the nonverbal message that was intended. Finally, many nonverbal messages are susceptible to multiple interpretations. Even something as common as a smile may have many different meanings. Smiles may indicate genuine happiness, contempt, deceit, fear, compliance, resignation—even, on occasion, anger.

Research indicates that facial expressions and eye contact and movements generally provide information about the *type* of emotion, while such physical cues as distance, posture, and gestures indicate the *intensity* of the emotion. These conclusions are important to managers. They indicate that communicators often send a great deal more information than is obtained in verbal messages. To increase the effectiveness of communication, a person must be aware of the nonverbal as well as the verbal content of the messages.

When verbal and nonverbal messages conflict, receivers tend to place more faith in nonverbal cues. When this type of conflict occurs, a judgment on what message to decipher is going to be made. Thus, examining nonverbal and verbal cues is constantly occurring. Some of the most common nonverbal cues people study include eye contact, facial expressions (the human face displays over 250,000), posture, and gestures. Being aware of these main cue initiators is important. For example, sustained eye contact in some cultures is considered impolite. While the thumbs up for a successful effort is a cue in the United States for a "job well done," it is an "obscene" gesture in Spain and parts of Latin America.

Being aware of nonverbal messages requires an awareness of their existence and importance. A good way to examine your own nonverbal impression and presence is to videotape yourself making a formal presentation. The review of the videotape will help determine the alignment of verbal and nonverbal messages.

---

[7]E. Kiritani, *Body Language, Journal of Japanese Trade & Industry,* January–February 1999, pp. 50–52.

[8]Dorothy Leeds, "Body Language: Actions Speak Louder Than Words," *National Underwriter,* May 1995, pp. 18–19.

[9]G. Hofstede, "The Universal and the Specific in 21st Century Management," *Organizational Dynamics,* Summer 1999, pp. 34–44.

[10]Leeds, "Body Language."

COMMUNICATING WITHIN ORGANIZATIONS

The design of an organization should provide for communication in four distinct directions: downward, upward, horizontal, and diagonal. Since these directions of communication establish the framework within which communication in an organization takes place, let us briefly examine each one. This examination will enable you to better appreciate the barriers to effective organizational communication and the means to overcome them.

Downward Communication

This type of communication flows downward from individuals in higher levels of the hierarchy to those in lower levels. The most common forms of **downward communication** are job instructions, official memos, policy statements, procedures, manuals, and company publications. In many organizations, downward communication often is both inadequate and inaccurate, as evidenced in the often-heard statement among organization members that "we have absolutely no idea what's happening." Such complaints indicate inadequate downward communication and the need of individuals for information relevant to their jobs. The absence of job-related information can create unnecessary stress among organization members.[11] A similar situation is faced by a student who has not been told the requirements and expectations of an instructor.

Upward Communication

An effective organization needs **upward communication** as much as it needs downward communication. In such situations, the communicator is at a lower level in the organization than the receiver. Some of the most common upward communication flows are suggestion boxes, group meetings, and appeal or grievance procedures. In their absence, people somehow find ways to adopt nonexistent or inadequate upward communication channels. This has been evidenced by the emergence of "underground" employee publications in many large organizations.

Upward communication serves a number of important functions. Organizational communication researcher Gary Kreps identifies several:[12]

1. It provides managers with feedback about current organizational issues and problems, and information about day-to-day operations that they need for making decisions about directing the organization.
2. It is management's primary source of feedback for determining the effectiveness of its downward communication.
3. It relieves employees' tensions by allowing lower-level organization members to share relevant information with their superiors.
4. It encourages employees' participation and involvement, thereby enhancing organizational cohesiveness.

---

[11]J. R. Carlson and R. W. Zmud, "Channel Expansion Theory and the Experimental Nature of Media Richness Perceptions," *Academy of Management Journal*, 1999, pp. 153–70.

[12]Gary L. Kreps, *Organizational Communication* (New York: Longman, 1990), p. 203.

Horizontal Communication

Often overlooked in the design of most organizations is provision for **horizontal communication**. When the chairperson of the accounting department communicates with the chairperson of the marketing department concerning the course offerings in a college of business administration, the flow of communication is horizontal. Although vertical (upward and downward) communication flows are the primary considerations in organizational design, effective organizations also need horizontal communication. Horizontal communication—for example, communication between production and sales in a business organization and among the different departments or colleges within a university—is necessary for the coordination and integration of diverse organizational functions.

Since mechanisms for ensuring horizontal communication ordinarily do not exist in an organization's design, its facilitation is left to individual managers. Peer-to-peer communication often is necessary for coordination and also can provide social need satisfaction.

Diagonal Communication

While it is probably the least-used channel of communication in organizations, **diagonal communication** is important in situations where members cannot communicate effectively through other channels. For example, the comptroller of a large organization may wish to conduct a distribution cost analysis. One part of that task may involve having the sales force send a special report directly to the comptroller rather than going through the traditional channels in the marketing department. Thus, the flow of communication would be diagonal as opposed to vertical (upward) and horizontal. In this case, a diagonal channel would be the most efficient in terms of time and effort for the organization.

Communicating Externally

Organizations are involved in communicating externally to present products and services, to project a positive image, to attract employees, and to gain attention. The typical external communication program includes four distinct programs:

- *Public relations* which involves the communication of a positive image, exemplary corporate/organization citizenship, and promotion of an identity as a contributor to society and the immediate community. If a full-time public relations staff is not used, some type of arrangement with a professional firm may be used.
- *Advertising* involves illustrating products or services in a positive manner. This form of communication is designed to attract customers, clients, or patients.
- *Promoting* the culture and opportunities available to prospective employees. This communication is designed to attract employee talent to sustain and grow the organization.
- *Customer/Client/Patient surveys* to gather feedback about the experience of external constituents with the organization. This information is used to make modifications or changes in service, products, or relationships.

Each of these four communication programs is used to collect or disseminate information. The internal and external communication programs provide ideas, information, connections, and insight into what individuals and groups are saying, what is important, and what needs modification.

INFORMATION RICHNESS AND INFORMATION TECHNOLOGIES

There are many different ways to communicate within an organization and externally to various constituents. Communication media differ in their **information richness**. The richness of communication involves how much information can be effectively transmitted.[13] A media that enables high richness, such as face-to-face interaction, is more likely to result in common understanding between individuals or a group when compared to a low-in-richness media, such as a standard written memo.

Face-to-face communication is high in richness because verbal and nonverbal cues can be exchanged and observed. This form of communication is also in "real time" and consequently permits on-the-spot feedback. If a person fails to understand a communication, request for clarification can immediately be presented.

Information richness is low in the case of a memo to a general population (e.g., a department, the entire project team, a subsidiary company). The impersonal nature of this type of communication is obvious. A specific individual is not being addressed, so feedback is not likely to occur in this type of communication.

The Internet

The Internet has its origins in a late 1960s Department of Defense program to devise communications capable of surviving a military attack. In 1969, the first version of the Internet, then referred to as the Advanced Research Project Agency network (ARPA net), connected four host computers. The Internet body is run by the Internet Society Operating Committee. The average U.S. user has six sessions, surfs about 32 minutes each time, and looks at about 232 pages per week. There were in January 2001 over 144 million Internet users in the United States.[14]

The term *Internet* is used to cover many services and information technologies. The World Wide Web (www) is the service that currently has the most applicable communication protocols and technology for business on the Internet. Internet services include electronic mail (e-mail), newsgroups, and chat rooms. The Web brings graphics, interaction, and hyperlinking capabilities to the Internet and allows for multimedia content such as voice and video. A common mistake is to think that the Internet and the Web are the same.

An **intranet** is a private protected electronic communication system within an organization. If it is connected to the Internet, it has its privacy protected by what are called *firewalls*. A firewall is a network mode set up internally to prevent traffic to cross into the private domain. Intranets are used to communicate such things as proprietary organizational information, company plans, confidential medical records, training programs, compensation data, and company records.

---

[13]G. S. Russ, R. L. Deft, and R. H. Lengel, "Media Selection and Managerial Characteristics in Organizational Communications," *Management Communication Quarterly,* 1990, pp. 151–75.

[14]"Internet at a Glance," *Business 2.0,* October 10, 2000, p. 282.

E-Mail Netiquette Suggestions

Practicing some simple procedures can improve the effectiveness and quality of e-mail communications in an organization. Consider these rules as just a start of sound e-mail practices.

- Reading other people's e-mail is unethical and should be avoided.
- If an e-mail has an attachment, do not open it if the sender is unknown. Viruses (software that can infect, freeze, or destroy programs) can be included in the attachment.
- Don't send an e-mail you wouldn't want to have published.

- Keep it short, to the point, and free of any vulgarity.
- Don't send a single personal message on a company computer.
- Use grammatically correct, properly formatted, and concise messages.
- Respond as soon as possible in a courteous way to e-mails.
- Never respond to an e-mail when you are angry.
- Avoid forwarding an e-mail sent to you without receiving permission from the original sender.

Electronic Mail (e-mail)

Communication that is transmitted through personal computers is referred to as **e-mail** or **messaging**. Senders transmit messages by typing the message on their computer and sending it to a receiver's electronic address. It is estimated that 94 million users sent over 5.5 trillion e-mail messages in 1999.[15]

A few years ago e-mail users sent out unedited, poorly written messages on the fly. This type of sloppiness has been attacked and is discouraged in organizations. The privacy of e-mail is another serious issue. Supervisors, colleagues, and others can access e-mail messages. Consequently, care must be exercised in properly using e-mails as a communication approach. E-mail etiquette suggestions are spelled out in Organizational Encounter 13.2. These are only a few suggestions that should be considered before preparing and sending e-mails.

www.webcom.com/pinknoiz/
covert/summary.html

Astute users of e-mail communications have learned about the dangers. Messages can travel anywhere so they must be carefully written. Also, even erased messages can remain on disk drives. Colonel Oliver North during the Iran Contra hearings found that "deleted files" could be extracted from computers.

Websense Inc. is a maker of employee monitoring software. This software identifies improper use of the Internet and personal (not work-related) e-mails. Nearly one-third of those companies polled by Websense had fired workers for improper use of the Internet. Nearly three-quarters of major U.S. companies are now recording and reviewing employees' communications, including e-mail, telephone calls, and Internet connections. For example, Chevron and Microsoft both settled sexual harassment lawsuits for $2.2 million apiece as a result of internally circulated e-mails that could have created hostile work environments.[16]

E-mail is an effective way of communicating simple messages. Complex data and information should probably be sent in hard copy documents. Think simple. Secure your e-mails. Always use correct and professional language in preparing and sending e-mails.

---

[15]Richard Gibson, "Merchants Mull the Long and the Short of Lines," *Wall Street Journal,* September 1998, B11.
[16]Michelle Conlin, "Workers, Surf at Your Own Risk," *Business Week,* June 12, 2000, pp. 105–06.

Voice Mail

Voice mail links a telephone system to a computer that digitizes and stores incoming messages. Some systems use automated means, allowing callers to reach any associated extension by pushing specific touch-tone telephone buttons. Interactive systems allow callers to receive information from a database. For example, a golf resort in California uses voice mail to answer questions about its five courses. You touch numbers that answer questions, provide tee times, and provide golf tips.

Voice mail serves many functions, but one of the most important is message storage. Incoming messages are delivered without interrupting receivers and allow for communicators to focus on the reason for the call. Voice mail minimizes inaccurate message-taking and time-zone difference barriers.

Videoconferencing and Teleconferencing

www.kn.pachell.com/wired/
vidconf

Videoconferencing refers to technologies associated with viewing, and *teleconferencing* refers to technologies primarily associated with speaking. Often the terms are used interchangeably. Both technologies enable individuals to conduct meetings without getting together face to face.

Some technologies enable participants to interact at the same time even when they are in different places. HighTech Campus, a Dallas and Houston e-learning training company, conducts 80 percent of its executive operating meetings through videoconferencing. The remainder of times, executives meet in either Dallas or Houston. Travel expenses and travel time have been greatly reduced since HighTech Campus began using videoconferencing in June 2000.[17]

Electronic Meetings

Electronic meeting software (EMS) uses networked computers to automate meetings. A large screen at the front of the room is the focal point. The screen serves as an electronic flip chart displaying comments, ideas, and responses of participants. Meetingware allows facilitators to poll meeting participants, analyze voting results, and create detailed reports.

Meetingware is helpful when large groups must reach decisions quickly. Meeting participants can simultaneously instead of one-by-one provide a vote, an opinion, or an idea. At Hewlett-Packard, meetingware has accelerated new product development by 30 percent.[18] Structured electronic meetings are 20 to 30 percent shorter than face-to-face meetings.

Advancements in information technologies are continuing and are providing organizational members with additional ways to communicate. Technologies, however, will not solve all communication problems. Overloading employees with new "toys," additional information, and technologies to learn can result in less efficiency. There is also the social interaction and personal touch that can be lost by relying solely on electronic technologies for communication. Electronic communication omits many verbal and most nonverbal cues that people use to acquire feedback. Guarding against anonymity and depersonalization are con-

---

[17]See *www.hightechcampus.com* for a look at this e-learning company and its products and services.

[18]See *www.hp.com* and annual report 1997 of Hewlett-Packard.

cerns when using many of the information technologies such as e-mail, video-conferencing, and electronic meetings.

INTERPERSONAL COMMUNICATIONS

Exercise 13.1

Your Communication Style

Within an organization, communication flows from individual to individual in face-to-face and group settings. Such flows are termed **interpersonal communications** and can vary from direct orders to casual expressions. Interpersonal behavior could not exist without interpersonal communication. In addition to providing needed information, interpersonal communication also influences how people feel about the organization. For example, research indicates that satisfaction with communication relationships affects organizational commitment.[19]

The problems that arise when managers attempt to communicate with other people can be traced to *perceptual differences* and *interpersonal style differences*. We know from Chapter 3 that each manager perceives the world in terms of his or her background, experiences, personality, frame of reference, and attitude. The primary way in which managers relate to and learn from the environment (including the people in that environment) is through information received and transmitted. And the way in which managers receive and transmit information depends, in part, on how they relate to two very important *senders* of information—*themselves* and *others*.

In research involving interpersonal communications, it has been found that only 7 percent of the "attitudinal" meaning of a message comes from words spoken. Over 90 percent of meaning results from nonverbal cues.[20] These silent signals exert a strong influence on the receiver. However, interpreting them is by no means scientifically based. For example, does a downward glance during a brief encounter in an office mean modesty, embarrassment, a lack of respect, or fatigue?

MULTICULTURAL COMMUNICATION

Case 13.1

The Road to Hell

An often-repeated and much-enjoyed joke in Latin America and Europe poses this question: "If someone who speaks three languages is called *trilingual,* and someone who speaks two languages is called *bilingual,* what do you call someone who speaks only one language?" The answer is "an American." Although certainly not universally true, nonetheless, this story makes a telling point. While the average European speaks several languages, the typical American is fluent only in English. A review of practices indicates that 23,000 American college students study Japanese; in the same year, 20 million Japanese were studying English.[21]

In the international business environment of today—and even more so, of tomorrow—foreign language training and fluency is a business necessity. It is true that English is an important business language and that many foreign businesspeople speak it fluently. The fact remains, however, that the vast majority of the world's population neither speaks nor understand English. Nor is language per se the only barrier to effective cross-cultural communications; in fact, it may be one of the easiest

---

[19]J. M. Putti, S. Aryee, and J. Phua, "Communication Relationship Satisfaction and Organizational Commitment," *Group and Organizational Studies,* March 1990, pp. 44–52.

[20]Mary Ellen Guffey, *Business Communication* (Cincinnati, OH: South-Western, 2000), p. 50.

[21]Phillip Harris and Robert Moran, *Managing Cultural Differences,* 3rd ed. (Houston: Gulf Publishing, 1991).

difficulties to overcome. There are numerous cultural-related variables that can hinder the communication process, not the least of which is *ethnocentrism*.

Ethnocentrism is the tendency to consider the values, norms, and customs of one's own country to be superior to those of other countries. Ethnocentrism need not be explicit to create communication problems. Implicit assumptions based on an ethnocentric view make it less likely that we will have sufficient cultural sensitivity even to be aware of possible differences in points of view, underlying assumptions, interpretation, or other factors that may create communication difficulties. Consider the following true incident involving an Indian and an Austrian.

> When asked if his department could complete a project by a given date, a particular Indian employee said, "yes" even when he knew he could not complete the project, because he believed that his Austrian supervisor wanted "yes" for an answer. When the completion date arrived and he had not finished the project, his Austrian supervisor showed dismay. The Indian's desire to be polite—to say what he thought his supervisor wanted to hear—seemed more important than an accurate assessment of the completion date.[22]

Both of the individuals depicted in this incident were operating from their own cultural frame of reference. The Austrian valued accuracy; for the Indian, politeness was the central value. By not being sensitive to the possibility of cultural differences, both contributed to the unfortunate misunderstanding.

Numerous other examples are possible. Words and phrases do not mean the same to all people. If, during an attempt to work out a business deal, for example, an American were to tell another American, "That will be difficult," the meaning is entirely different than if a Japanese were to use that phrase. To the American it means the door is still open, but perhaps some compromise needs to be made. To the Japanese it clearly means "no"; the deal is unacceptable.[23] As another example, consider eye contact. Americans are taught to maintain good eye contact, and we may unconsciously assume those who do not look us in the eye are dishonest, or at least rude. In Japan, however, when speaking with a superior it is customary to lower ones' eyes as a gesture of respect. The following Organizational Encounter describes further examples of language and other problems in cross-cultural communication contexts.

In spite of innumerable differences, multicultural communication can be successful. Businesspeople from different cultures effectively and efficiently communicate with each other hundreds, perhaps thousands, of times every business day. By and large, the senders and receivers of those successful communications exhibit some, or all, of the following attributes:

1. They have made it a point to familiarize themselves with significant cultural differences that might affect the communication process. They do this through study, observation, and consultation with those who have direct or greater experience with the culture than do they.
2. They make a conscious, concerted effort to lay aside ethnocentric tendencies. This does not mean they must agree with values, customs, interpretations, or perspectives different from their own; awareness, not acceptance, is what is required to facilitate communications.

---

[22]Nancy Adler, *International Dimensions of Organizational Behavior,* 2nd ed. (Boston PWS-Kent, 1991), p. 131.

[23]Jeswald Salacuse, *Making Global Deals* (Boston: Houghton Mifflin, 1991).

Cross-Cultural Communication Problems

Communicating exactly what you want to communicate, rather than more, less, or something altogether different, can be a challenge when the communication takes place within a single culture. Achieving the desired results cross-culturally can present special problems.

Many of the difficulties encountered with cross-cultural communications stem from the fact that there are different languages involved and direct translation is not always feasible. American automobile manufacturers have learned this lesson. When Ford Motor Company introduced its Fiera truck line in some developing countries, it discovered that *Fiera* is a Spanish slang word meaning "ugly woman." Chevrolet discovered that in Italian Chevrolet Nova translates as "Chevrolet no go." Similarly, GM's "Body by Fisher" logo translates in at least one language into "Corpse by Fisher." Such problems are, of course, not restricted to car makers. Coca-Cola, for example, has had its share of translation problems. In Chinese, Coca-Cola becomes "Bite the head of a dead tadpole." In some parts of Asia the familiar Coke advertising slogan "Coke adds life" is translated as "Coke brings you back from the dead."

Language translation problems are not the only source of problems. Head, hand, and arm gestures may mean different things in different cultures. In some countries, for example, moving one's head from side to side means "yes," while bobbing it up and down means "no." Just the reverse of U.S. meaning. Or take the familiar A-OK hand gesture. In the United States it means things are fine, or everything is working. In France it has no such meaning; it simply means "zero." In Japan, on the other hand, it is a symbol representing money. There it may be used to indicate that something is too expensive. And in Brazil, the gesture is interpreted as obscene.

Many other aspects of the communication process can cause difficulties. Different cultural interpretations of the significance of eye contact, the physical distance maintained between two people talking with one another, and differences in accepted forms of address are but a few examples. Effective cross-cultural communications require that we become less ethnocentric and more culturally sensitive.

3. Perhaps most importantly, despite their efforts at doing what is described in the above two points, they maintain a posture of "knowing they do not know." This simply means that in the absence of direct, usually extensive, ongoing exposure to another culture, there will be nuances in the communication process of which they may well be unaware. Rather than assuming understanding is complete unless demonstrated otherwise, they assume it is *in*complete until shown otherwise.

In the two chapter sections that follow, you will be able to identify barriers to effective communications, which may be especially relevant in multicultural contexts, as well as find techniques for improving communications, which are particularly important in the same contexts.

www.fourseasons.com

Four Seasons, the luxury hotel chain, understands multicultural communication very well. In recruiting and selecting overseas managers, Four Seasons's profile includes strong listening skills, alertness to body language, and open minds.[24] Four Seasons believes that culture is learned and that open-mindedness allows managers to learn new attitudes to deal with diversity of customers.

BARRIERS TO EFFECTIVE COMMUNICATION

A good question at this point is: "Why does communication break down?" On the surface, the answer is relatively easy. We have identified the elements of communication as the communicator, encoding, the message, the medium, decoding, the receiver, and feedback. If noise exists in these elements in any way, complete

---

[24]See *www.fourseasons.com.*

clarity of meaning and understanding will not occur. A manager has no greater responsibility than to develop effective communications. In this section, we discuss several barriers to effective communication that can exist both in organizational and interpersonal communications.

Frame of Reference

Different individuals can interpret the same communication differently depending on their previous experiences. This results in variations in the encoding and decoding process. Communication specialists agree that this is the most important factor that breaks down the "commonness" in communications. When the encoding and decoding processes are not alike, communication tends to break down. Thus, while the communicator actually is speaking the "same language" as the receiver, the message conflicts with the way the receiver "catalogs" the world. If a large area is shared in common, effective communication is facilitated. If a large area is not shared in common—if there has been no common experience—then communication becomes impossible or, at best, highly distorted. The important point is that communicators can encode and receivers can decode only in terms of their experiences. As a result, distortion often occurs because of differing frames of reference. People in various organizational functions interpret the same situation differently. A business problem will be viewed differently by the marketing manager than by the production manager. An efficiency problem in a hospital will be viewed by the nursing staff from its frame of reference and experiences, which may result in interpretations different from those of the physician staff. Different levels in the organization also will have different frames of reference. First-line supervisors have frames of reference that differ in many respects from those of vice presidents. They are in different positions in the organization structure, and this influences their frames of reference. As a result, their needs, values, attitudes, and expectations will differ, and this difference will often result in unintentional distortion of communication. This is not to say that either group is wrong or right. All it means is that, in any situation, individuals will choose the part of their own past experiences that relates to the current experience and is helpful in forming conclusions and judgments.

Selective Listening

A vital part of the communication process involves listening. In fact about 75 percent of communication is listening. Most people only spend between 30 and 40 percent of their time listening.[25] This means that there are a lot of listening errors and deficiencies. Most speakers talk at a rate of about 150 words per minute. A good listener can process and understand oral communication at a rate of about 400 words per minute.

Listening takes place in four phases—perception, interpretation, evaluation, and action. Barriers can obstruct and block the listening process. The meaning attached to a manager's request is colored by a person's cultural, educational, and social frames of reference. Thus, **interpretation** of the manager's meaning may be different because of frame-of-reference differences.

The method of **evaluation** used is influenced by attitudes, preferences, and experience. The type of **action** taken involves memory and recall. Sometimes memory failures do not permit the best actions.

---

[25]M. P. Nichols, *The Lost Art of Listening* (New York: Guilford, 1995).

Selective listening is a form of selective perception in which we tend to block out new information, especially if it conflicts with what we believe. When we receive a directive from management, we notice only those things that reaffirm our beliefs. Those things that conflict with our preconceived notions we either do not note at all or we distort to confirm our preconceptions.

For example, a notice may be sent to all operating departments that costs must be reduced if the organization is to earn a profit. The communication may not achieve its desired effect because it conflicts with the "reality" of the receivers. Thus, operating employees may ignore or be amused by such information in light of the large salaries, travel allowances, and expense accounts of some executives. Whether they are justified is irrelevant; what is important is that such preconceptions result in breakdowns in communication.

www.oprah.com

A few worthwhile listening pointers are apparent in observing Oprah Winfrey, the celebrated talk show host. Oprah blocks out distractions and focuses on the talker (guest, audience member); she is always actively involved with great eye contact, listens emphatically without interrupting, and paraphrases her guest's comments and ideas. She is a master at making sure the speaker is understood. Managers could learn a lot about listening in general, selective listening, and emphatic listening from Oprah. Her style and approach make guests feel important, welcomed, and understood.

Value Judgments

In every communication situation, *value judgments* are made by the receiver. This basically involves assigning an overall worth to a message prior to receiving the entire communication. Value judgments may be based on the receiver's evaluation of the communicator or previous experiences with the communicator, or on the message's anticipated meaning. For example, a hospital administrator may pay little attention to a memorandum from a nursing supervisor because "she's always complaining about something." A college professor may consider a merit evaluation meeting with the department chairperson as "going through the motions" because the faculty member perceives the chairperson as having little or no power in the administration of the college. A cohesive work group may form negative value judgments concerning all actions by management.

Source Credibility

Source credibility is the trust, confidence, and faith that the receiver has in the words and actions of the communicator. The level of credibility the receiver assigns to the communicator in turn directly affects how the receiver views and reacts to words, ideas, and actions of the communicator.

Thus, how subordinates view a communication from their manager is affected by their evaluation of the manager. This, of course, is heavily influenced by previous experiences with the manager. Again we see that everything done by a manager communicates. A group of hospital medical staff who view the hospital administrator as less than honest, as manipulative, and as not to be trusted are apt to assign nonexistent motives to any communication from the administrator. Union leaders who view management as exploiters and managers who view union leaders as political animals are likely to engage in little real communication.

Filtering

Filtering, a common occurrence in upward communication in organizations, refers to the manipulation of information so that the receiver perceives it as positive. Subordinates cover up unfavorable information in messages to their superiors. The reason for filtering should be clear; this is the direction (upward) that carries control information to management. Management makes merit evaluations, grants salary increases, and promotes individuals based on what it receives by way of the upward channel. The temptation to filter is likely to be strong at every level in the organization.

At General Electric, under the strong leadership of Jack Welch, filtering has sometimes been a problem. CEO Welch has a reputation for being tough, aggressive, impatient, and intimidating, which has led to his being both highly admired and feared.[26] When GE senior executives (or anyone else) are apprehensive about communicating information to a superior, filtering can and does occur.

In-Group Language

Each of us undoubtedly has had associations with experts and has been subjected to highly technical jargon, only to learn that the unfamiliar words or phrases described very simple procedures or familiar objects. Many students are asked by researchers to "complete an instrument as part of an experimental treatment." The student soon learns that this involves nothing more than filling out a paper-and-pencil questionnaire.

Often, occupational, professional, and social groups develop words or phrases that have meaning only to members. Such special language can serve many useful purposes. It can provide members with feelings of belonging, cohesiveness, and, in many cases, self-esteem. It also can facilitate effective communication *within* the group. The use of *in-group language* can, however, result in severe communication breakdowns when outsiders or other groups are involved. This is especially the case when groups use such language in an organization, not for the purpose of transmitting information and understanding, but rather to communicate a mystique about the group or its function.

Status Differences

Organizations often express hierarchical rank through a variety of symbols—titles, offices, carpets, and so on. Such *status differences* can be perceived as threats by persons lower in the hierarchy, and this can prevent or distort communication. Rather than look incompetent, a nurse may prefer to remain quiet instead of expressing an opinion or asking a question of the nursing supervisor.

Many times superiors, in an effort to utilize their time efficiently, make this barrier more difficult to surmount. The governmental administrator or bank vice president may be accessible only by making an advance appointment or by passing the careful quizzing of a secretary. This widens the communication gap between superior and subordinates.

---

[26]Amy Barrett, "Jack's Risky Last Act," *Business Week*, November 6, 2000, pp. 40–45.

Time Pressures

The pressure of time is an important barrier to communication. An obvious problem is that managers do not have the time to communicate frequently with every subordinate. However, time pressures often can lead to far more serious problems than this. *Short-circuiting* is a failure of the formally prescribed communication system that often results from time pressures. What it means simply is that someone has been left out of the formal channel of communication who normally would be included.

For example, suppose a salesperson needs a rush order for a very important customer and goes directly to the production manager with the request since the production manager owes the salesperson a favor. Other members of the sales force get word of this and become upset over this preferential treatment and report it to the sales manager. Obviously, the sales manager would know nothing of the deal, since he or she has been short-circuited. In some cases, however, going through formal channels is extremely costly or is impossible from a practical standpoint. Consider the impact on a hospital patient if a nurse had to report a critical malfunction in life-support equipment to the nursing team leader, who in turn had to report it to the hospital engineer, who would instruct a staff engineer to make the repair.

Communication Overload

One of the vital tasks performed by a manager in decision making, and one of the necessary conditions for effective decisions, is *information.*[27] Because of the advances in communication technology, the difficulty is not in generating information. In fact, the last decade often has been described as the "Information Era" or the "Age of Information." Managers often feel buried by the deluge of information and data to which they are exposed, and they cannot absorb or adequately respond to all of the messages directed to them. They "screen out" the majority of messages, which in effect means that these messages are never decoded. Thus, the area of organizational communication is one in which more is not always better. When Connecticut Bank and Trust Company surveyed its employees, it discovered that 40 percent of them were dissatisfied with the bank's internal communications. One major problem was communication overload in the form of too many memos. New guidelines were adopted which significantly improved employee satisfaction with communications while decreasing the number of memos sent by 57 percent.

The barriers to communication that have been discussed here, while common, are by no means the only ones. Examining each barrier indicates that they are either *within individuals* (e.g., frame of reference, value judgments) or *within organizations* (e.g., in-group language, filtering). This point is important because attempts to improve communication must, of necessity, focus on changing people and/or changing the organizational structure.

---

[27]For a review of developments in decision making and communication, see Janet Fulk and Brian Boyd, "Emerging Theories of Communication in Organizations," *Journal of Management,* June 1991, pp. 407–46.

The Company Talk Show

It's 11 A.M. on a Wednesday, and Dan Hunt, president of Caribbean and Latin American operations for Nortel Networks, is live and on the air! Seated behind a stage-prop desk in the company's South Florida TV studio, the slender, articulate executive stares into a camera as he fields questions from Nortel employees—an audience every bit as tough as any that shows up for a taping of *The Tonight Show*. A caller from Mexico wants to know the implications of a joint venture between Nortel rivals Motorola and Cisco. Hunt delivers a detailed answer. Someone asks about the new competitive threat posed by Lucent Technologies. After taking a breath, Hunt answers. Next comes a query about Nortel's new branding strategy. Hunt smiles and defers to the host of this corporate talk show, Emma Carrasco, vice president of marketing and communications, whom Hunt laughingly introduces as "the mistress of all branding."

Hunt isn't your standard talk-show guest. And this isn't your standard TV talk show. But it is an important corporate conversation. Once a month, Hunt and Carrasco broadcast the "Virtual Leadership Academy," an hour-long program that presents company spin and in-depth, highly usable information in an interactive, talk-show format. This morning's audience, consisting of 2,000 employees in 40 countries, has been treated to a conversational stew featuring industry news, a surprisingly interesting discussion of international tax strategy, and a chance to pepper Hunt and other Nortel executives with direct questions about the company and its competitors—all from the comfort of their regional offices. "We're always looking for ways to break down barriers in the company, and people are comfortable with the talk-show format," says Carrasco, who designed the program to tap into what she calls the "talk-show culture" of her audience. "People watch talk shows in every country in the region, and they've learned that it's okay to say what's on their minds. In fact, it's expected."

Nortel isn't the only company that is borrowing from talk-show culture to improve internal communication. Breaking the centuries-old convention of one-way, top-down, rigidly formulaic corporate monologues, smart organizations are experimenting with new, more interactive, less formal modes of talking to—and listening to—employees and customers. Not every company takes the talk-show model as literally as Nortel does—with its set, its TelePrompTers, and its commercial breaks. But at a time when all kinds of other boundaries in business are being bent, blended, and broken, the new metaphor for corporate communication is best described as "edutainment": the company as talk show.

Think about it. In the Information Age, organizations that succeed are those that can quickly and effectively communicate critical knowledge to their constituents. And the best way to do that? Traditional top-down communication techniques—from shotgun memos to routinized meetings to heavily touted "knowledge management" systems—seem either heavily bureaucratic or unnecessarily technocentric. In the new workplace, rigid hierarchies are giving way to informality and networks—which is another way of saying that the most important elements of any organization are personal relationships: between management and workers, between colleagues, and, of course, between a company and its customers. And how do you build deep, valuable, personal relationships? Not through formal memos and structured meetings, but through repeated personal contact. Through informal contact. Through talk.

Source: Adapted from Paul Roberts, "Live! From Your Office! It's . . .," *Fast Company*, October 1999, pp. 150–70.

www.nortel networks.c

IMPROVING COMMUNICATION IN ORGANIZATIONS

Managers striving to become better communicators have two separate tasks they must accomplish. First, they must improve their *messages*—the information they wish to transmit. Second, they must seek to improve their own *understanding* of what other people are trying to communicate to them. As organizations become increasingly diverse, the opportunities for communication breakdowns will most likely increase. Before examining the general means that managers can use to improve communication, consult Management Pointer 13.1, which presents some very specific ways to improve communication in diverse organizations. The bottom line of this final section of the chapter is that managers must become better encoders and decoders. They must strive not only to be understood but also

Management Pointer 13.1

**IMPROVING
COMMUNICATIONS IN
DIVERSE ORGANIZATIONS**

Take a proactive approach to improve
communications in a diverse organization. The
following are ideas that have been implemented
successfully in such organizations as Avon, Apple
Computer, Digital Equipment, and Prudential
Insurance.

1. Encourage employees to organize cultural
    communication networks. These networks help
    new employees adjust, arrange cultural events,
    and provide feedback to management.

2. Consider establishing a managerial position, the
    responsibility of which includes developing and
    overseeing multicultural and affirmative action
    programs.

3. Institute a mentor program whereby new
    minority employees are introduced to the
    company culture.

4. Celebrate cultural events such as Black History
    Month and Hispanic Heritage Week.

5. Conduct diversity-management workshops which
    allow managers to explore the meaning of being
    a minority in a majority society.

to understand. The techniques discussed here can contribute
to accomplishing these two important tasks.

Organizational Encounter 13.4 on organizational communications illustrates that the company talk show can help employees identify more strongly with the firm.

Following Up

Following up involves assuming that you are misunderstood
and, whenever possible, attempting to determine whether
your intended meaning actually was received. As we have
seen, meaning often is in the mind of the receiver. An accounting unit leader in a government office passes on to staff
members notices of openings in other agencies. While long-
time employees may understand this as a friendly gesture, a
new employee might interpret it as an evaluation of poor performance and a suggestion to leave.

Regulating Information Flow

The regulation of communication can ensure an optimum flow
of information to managers, thereby eliminating the barrier of
"communication overload." Communication is regulated in
terms of both quality and quantity. The idea is based on the *exception principle* of management, which states that only significant deviations from policies and procedures should be brought
to the attention of superiors. In terms of formal communication, then, superiors should be communicated with only on
matters of exception and not for the sake of communication.

Utilizing Feedback

Earlier in the chapter, feedback was identified as an important element in effective two-way communication. It provides a channel for receiver response that enables the communicator to determine whether the message has been received and
has produced the intended response.[28]

In face-to-face communication, direct feedback is possible. In downward communication, however, inaccuracies often occur because of insufficient opportunity for feedback from receivers. A memorandum addressing an important policy
statement may be distributed to all employees, but this does not guarantee that
communication has occurred. You might expect that feedback in the form of upward communication would be encouraged more in organic organizations, but
the mechanisms discussed earlier that can be utilized to encourage upward communication are found in many different organization designs.

Empathy

Empathy involves being receiver-oriented rather than communicator-oriented.
The form of the communication should depend largely on what is known about

---

[28]C. D. Mortenson, *Miscommunication* (Thousand Oaks, CA: Sage, 1997).

the receiver. Empathy requires communicators to place themselves in the shoes of the receiver in order to anticipate how the message is likely to be decoded. Empathy is the ability to put oneself in the other person's role and to assume that individual's viewpoints and emotions. Remember that the greater the gap between the experiences and background of the communicator and the receiver, the greater is the effort that must be made to find a common ground of understanding—where there are overlapping fields of experience.

Repetition

Repetition is an accepted principle of learning. Introducing repetition or redundancy into communication (especially that of a technical nature) ensures that if one part of the message is not understood, other parts will carry the same message. New employees often are provided with the same basic information in several different forms when first joining an organization. Likewise, students receive much redundant information when first entering a university. This is to ensure that registration procedures, course requirements, and new terms such as *matriculation* and *quality points* are communicated.

Encouraging Mutual Trust

We know that time pressures often negate the possibility that managers will be able to follow up communication and encourage feedback or upward communication every time they communicate. Under such circumstances, an atmosphere of mutual confidence and trust between managers and their subordinates can facilitate communication. Managers who develop a climate of trust will find that following up on each communication is less critical and that no loss in understanding will result among subordinates from a failure to follow up on each communication. This is because they have fostered high "source credibility" among subordinates.

Effective Timing

Individuals are exposed to thousands of messages daily. Many of these messages are never decoded and received because of the impossibility of taking them all in. It is important for managers to note that, while they are attempting to communicate with a receiver, other messages are being received simultaneously. Thus, the message that managers send may not be "heard." Messages are more likely to be understood when they are not competing with other messages.[29] On an everyday basis, effective communication can be facilitated by properly timing major announcements. The barriers discussed earlier often are the result of poor timing that results in distortions and value judgments.

Simplifying Language

Complex language has been identified as a major barrier to effective communication. Students often suffer when their teachers use technical jargon that transforms simple

---

[29]D. T. Hall, K. L. Otazo, and G. P. Hollenbeck, "Behind Closed Doors: What Really Happens in Executive Coaching," *Organizational Dynamics,* Winter 1999, pp. 39–53.

Reading 13.1

Active Listening

concepts into complex puzzles. Universities are not the only place where this occurs, however. Government agencies are also known for their often-incomprehensible communications. We already have noted instances where professional people use in-group language in attempting to communicate with individuals outside their group. Managers must remember that effective communication involves transmitting *understanding* as well as information. If the receiver does not understand, then there has been no communication. Managers must encode messages in words, appeals, and symbols that are meaningful to the receiver.

Using the Grapevine

The grapevine is an important information communication channel that exists in all organizations. It basically serves as a bypassing mechanism, and in many cases it is faster than the formal system it bypasses. The grapevine has been aptly described in the following manner: "With the rapidity of a burning train, it filters out of the woodwork, past the manager's office, through the locker room, and along the corridors." Because it is flexible and usually involves face-to-face communication, the grapevine transmits information rapidly. The resignation of an executive may be common knowledge long before it is officially announced.

On the other hand, the grapevine is not a formal channel of communications. Thus, there are those who believe that managers should avoid using the grapevine because to not do so borders on being unethical as well as potentially dangerous. The You Be the Judge examines the very real issue of what to do about the grapevine.

Promoting Ethical Communications

It is incumbent upon organizational members to deal ethically with one another in their communication transactions. Kreps postulates three broad principles which are applicable to internal organizational communications.[30] The first is that organizational members should not intentionally deceive one another. This may not be as simple a principle to conform to as it may seem. While lying clearly violates it, is communicating less than you know to be true a breach of ethics? There is no hard and fast answer. The second principle is that organization members' communication should not purposely harm any other organization member. This is known as nonmalfeasance, or refraining from doing harm. Finally, organization members should be treated justly. This too can be difficult, for justice is a relative principle that must be evaluated in a specific context.

Gathering information, data, and ideas from competitors has become a big business. Is it ethical? Spying on someone or another business is distasteful to some, but the price of surviving is necessary to others. Some managers propose that if the law is not broken, gathering intelligence through reviewing memos, posing as a customer, surfing a competitor's Web site, listening carefully to comments, attending trade shows, and talking to loose-lipped employees is all about business.

There is no one method of gathering intelligence, but a number of tools are available. Web monitoring services (*www.knowx.com*), books, Internet links, and books provide communication that might be useful.[31]

---

[30]Kreps, *Organizational Communication,* pp. 250–51.

[31]Carole Ashfinaze, "Spies Like Us," *Business Week,* June 12, 2000, pp. F24–F32.

What to Do about the Grapevine!

You Be the Judge

There are those who believe that the grapevine—the gossip chain—is the speediest, most efficient channel of communication in an organization. Research also points out that it is accurate. At least 75 percent of the gossip that travels through the grapevine is said to be true. Thus, many believe that the grapevine is a very useful channel of communication and should, therefore, be utilized by managers. It can serve as an early warning system for employees, serving up bad news long before any formal announcements are made. It can promote closeness among employees, allowing them to let off steam and alleviate stress. It provides managers the opportunity to float trial balloons (e.g., concerning a plan they're considering putting into action) and thus receive early indications of peoples' reactions. Finally, it can serve as a medium for building and maintaining a firm's culture. Via gossip, the company war stories and those stories that communicate the firm's values can be told.

On the other hand, there are those who believe that the grapevine carries a very costly downside—a negative impact on productivity. The argument is that gossip takes time and saps employee morale. While 75 percent of the grapevine gossip may be true, it is the remaining 25 percent that carries false and destructive rumors that employees spend costly time worrying about. As a result, managers spend a disproportionate amount of time dealing with situations caused by rumor and gossip, not reality. Managers may also be held personally liable for defamation as a result of workplace conversations that may disclose confidential information or start rumors. Finally, while managers have used the grapevine for years as an early warning system or break-it-to-them gently tool, it can no longer even serve in this capacity in many organizations because younger employees disbelieve all company communication, whether by official memo or gossip.

Because the grapevine is not likely to go away, it is important for management not to ignore it. What things can management do to curb gossip?

Source: "Who Pruned the Grapevine?" *Across the Board,* March 1997, pp. 55–56; M. K. Zackary, "The Office Grapevine: A Legal Noose?" *Getting Results,* August 1996, pp. 6–7; M. M. Kennedy, "The Unkindest Cut," *Across the Board,* June 1996, pp. 53–54; and G. J. Modic, "Grapevine Rated Most Believable," *Industry Week,* May 15, 1989, pp. 11–12.

Competitive intelligence—a system for gathering information (all forms of communication) that affects a firm, analyzing the data, and taking action—is becoming an accepted practice. Used properly and with concern for ethical behavior, competitive intelligence can speed a firm's reaction to changes, help outmaneuver competitors, and protect a firm's own secrets.

An example of an unethical practice of competitive intelligence was discovered by the Granite Island Group in Gloucester, Massachusetts. The firm sweeps offices for technical surveillance devices. The firm found a videoconferencing camera that timed itself on and recorded a board meeting of a client. The investigators found that a rival competitor had set up a system to activate the camera remotely and look and listen in on the discussion.[32]

www.tscm.com

Competitive intelligence does not have to involve turning on cameras from a remote area. Listening to a rival's public statements, which is perfectly ethical,

---

[32]Ibid.

EXHIBIT 13.3
Improving Communications in Organizations (Narrowing the Communication Gap)

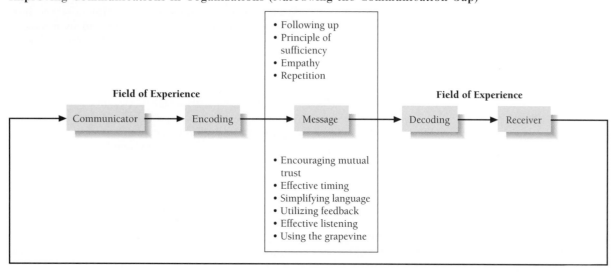

could reveal protected information. A West Coast provider of insurance in an interview gave information about a new wellness product. A Web-based monitoring service picked this information up. Competitors seized on the information and got to the market first with their own wellness protection policies.

In conclusion, it would be hard to find an aspect of a manager's job that does not involve communication. If everyone in the organization had common points of view, communicating would be easy. Unfortunately, this is not the case. Each member comes to the organization with a distinct personality, background, experience, and frame of reference. The structure of the organization itself influences status relationships and the distance levels between individuals, which in turn influence the ability of individuals to communicate.

In this chapter we have tried to convey the basic elements in the process of communication and what it takes to communicate effectively. These elements are necessary whether the communication is face-to-face or written and communicated vertically, horizontally, or diagonally within an organizational structure.

We discussed several common communication barriers and several means to improve communication. Exhibit 13.3 illustrates the means that can be used to facilitate more effective communication. We realize that often there is not enough time to utilize many of the techniques for improving communication, and that skills such as empathy and effective listening are not easy to develop. The exhibit does, however, illustrate the challenge of communicating effectively, and it suggests what is required. Exhibit 13.3 shows that communicating is a matter of transmitting and receiving. Managers must be effective at both. They must understand as well as be understood.

Summary of Key Points

- Communication is one of the vital processes that breathes life into an organizational structure. The process contains five elements: the *communicator* who initiates the communication; the *message,* which is the result of encoding and which expresses the purpose of the communicator; the *medium,* which is the channel or carrier used for transmitting the message; the *receiver* for whom the message is intended; and *feedback,* a mechanism that allows the communicator to determine whether the message has been received and understood.

- Communication flow moves in one of four directions. Downward communications are the most common and include job instructions, procedures, and policies. An upward flow can be just as important and may involve the use of suggestion boxes, group meetings, or grievance procedures. Horizontal and diagonal communications serve an important coordinative function.

- Information technologies such as e-mails, voice mails, videoconferencing, and electronic meetings are becoming common in organizations of all sizes. Caution must be taken in how, when, and where these technologies are used.

- Interpersonal communication is that which flows from individual to individual in face-to-face and group settings. In addition to providing needed information, interpersonal communication can also influence how people feel about the organization and its members. *Interpersonal style* is a term used to describe the way an individual prefers to relate to others in interpersonal communication situations.

- In the international business environment, needing to communicate with members of other cultures is becoming commonplace. In addition to obvious language problems, different cultural customs, values, and perspectives can serve to complicate effective communications. A significant barrier is *ethnocentrism,* which is the tendency to consider the values of one's own country superior to those of other countries.

- There are numerous barriers to effective communication. Among the more significant are frame of reference, selective listening, value judgments, source credibility, filtering, in-group language, status differences, time pressures, and communication overload.

- Improving organizational communications is an ongoing process. Specific techniques for doing this include following up, regulating information flow, utilizing feedback, empathy, repetition, encouraging mutual trust, effective timing, simplifying language, effective listening, using the grapevine, and promoting ethical communications.

Review and Discussion Questions

1. Can you think of a communication transaction you have been part of when an encoding or decoding error was made? Why did it happen, and what could have been done to avoid it?

2. Why do you think that downward communication is much more prevalent in organizations than upward communication? How easy would it be to change this?

3. Some claim that e-mail can take so much time reading and replying to that they are actually a drain on productivity. Do you agree? Why?

4. In your experience, which of the barriers to effective communication discussed in the chapter is responsible for the most communication problems? Which barrier is the hardest to correct?

5. Similarly, in your experience, which of the techniques for improving communication discussed in the chapter would solve the greatest number of problems? Which technique is the most difficult to put into practice?

6. Can you think of reasons why some individuals might prefer one-way communications when they are the sender, and two-way when they are the receiver? Explain.

7. A study once revealed that 55 percent of our communication time is spent transmitting and 45 percent is spent receiving. If true, what are the implications of this finding?

8. "Organizations should be less concerned with improving communication than with reducing the volume of information they disseminate to employees." Do you agree or disagree with this statement? Explain.

9. How does communication affect the interpersonal influence topics discussed in Chapters 7–9?

10. Have you ever been in a cross-cultural communication situation? How effective was it? What was the most difficult aspect of the situation?

READING 13.1 Active Listening

Carl B. Rogers and Richard E. Farson

THE MEANING OF ACTIVE LISTENING

One basic responsibility of the supervisor or executive is the development, adjustment, and integration of individual employees. He tries to develop employee potential, delegate responsibility, and achieve cooperation. To do so, he must have, among other abilities, the ability to listen intelligently and carefully to those with whom he works. There are, however, many kinds of listening skills. The lawyer, for example, when questioning a witness, listens for contradictions, irrelevancies, errors, and weaknesses. But this is not the kind of listening skill we are concerned with. The lawyer usually is not listening in order to help the witness adjust or cooperate or produce. On the other hand, we will be concerned with listening skills which *will help* employees gain a clearer understanding of their situations, take responsibility, and cooperate with each other.

TWO EXAMPLES

The kind of listening we have in mind is called active listening. It is called active because the listener has a very definite responsibility. He does not passively absorb the words which are spoken to him. He actively tries to grasp the facts and the feelings in what he hears, and he tries, by his listening, to help the speaker work out his own problems.

To get a fuller picture of what is meant by active listening, let us consider two different approaches to the same work problem.

Example No.1

FOREMAN: Hey, Al, I don't get this production order. We can't handle this run today. What do they think we are?

SUPERVISOR: But that's the order. So get it out as soon as you can. We're under terrific pressure this week.

FOREMAN: Don't they know we're behind schedule already because of that press breakdown?

SUPERVISOR: Look, Kelly, I don't decide what goes on upstairs. I just have to see that the work gets out, and that's what I'm gonna do.

FOREMAN: The guys aren't gonna like this.

SUPERVISOR: That's something you'll have to work out with them, not me.

Example No.2

FOREMAN: Hey, Ross, I don't get this production order. We can't handle this run today. What do they think we are?

SUPERVISOR: Sounds like you are pretty sore about it, Kelly.

FOREMAN: I sure am. We were just about getting back to schedule after that press breakdown. Now this comes along.

SUPERVISOR: As if you didn't have enough work to do, huh?

FOREMAN: Yeah, I don't know how I'm gonna tell the guys about this.

SUPERVISOR: Hate to face 'em with it now, is that it?

FOREMAN: I really do. They're under a real strain today. Seems like everything we do around here is rush, rush.

SUPERVISOR: I guess you feel like it's unfair to load anything more on them.

FOREMAN: Well, yeah, I know there must be plenty of pressure on everybody up the line, but—well, if that's the way it is—guess I'd better get the word to 'em.

There are obviously many differences between these two examples. The main one, however, is that Ross, the supervisor in the second example, is using the active-listening approach. He is listening and responding in a way that makes it clear that he appreciates both the meaning and the feeling behind what Kelly is saying.

Active listening does not necessarily mean long sessions spent listening to grievances, personal or otherwise. It is simply a way of approaching those problems which arise out of the usual day-to-day events of any job.

To be effective, active listening must be firmly grounded in the basic attitudes of the user. We cannot employ it as a technique if our fundamental attitudes are in conflict with its basic concepts. If we try, our behavior will be empty and sterile, and our associates will be quick to recognize this. Until we can demonstrate a spirit which genuinely respects the potential worth of the individual, which considers his rights and trusts his capacity for self-direction, we cannot begin to be effective listeners.

Source: Reprinted by permission of the Industrial Relations Center, The University of Chicago.

WHAT WE ACHIEVE BY LISTENING

Active listening is an important way to bring about changes in people. Despite the popular notion that listening is a passive approach, clinical and research evidence clearly shows that sensitive listening is a most effective agent for individual personality change and group development. Listening brings about changes in people's attitudes toward themselves and others; it also brings about changes in their basic values and personal philosophy. People who have been listened to in this new and special way become more emotionally mature, more open to their experiences, less defensive, more democratic, and less authoritarian.

When people are listened to sensitively, they tend to listen to themselves with more care and to make clear exactly what they are feeling and thinking. Group members tend to listen more to each other, to become less argumentative, more ready to incorporate other points of view. Because listening reduces the threat of having one's ideas criticized, the person is better able to see them for what they are and is more able to feel that his contributions are worthwhile.

Not the least important result of listening is the change that takes place with the listener himself. Besides providing more information than any other activity, listening builds deep, positive relationships and tends to alter constructively the attitudes of the listener. Listening is a growth experience.

These, then, are some of the worthwhile results we can expect from active listening. But how do we go about this kind of listening? How do we become active listeners?

HOW TO LISTEN

Active listening aims to bring about changes in people. To achieve this end, it relies upon definite techniques—things to do and things to avoid doing. Before discussing these techniques, however, we should first understand why they are effective. To do so, we must understand how the individual personality develops.

The Growth of the Individual

Through all of our lives, from early childhood on, we have learned to think of ourselves in certain very definite ways. We have built up pictures of ourselves. Sometimes these self-pictures are pretty realistic, but at other times they are not. For example, an overage, overweight lady may fancy herself as a youthful, ravishing siren, or an awkward teenager regards himself as a star athlete.

All of us have experiences which fit the way we need to think about ourselves. These we accept. But it is much harder to accept experiences which don't fit. And sometimes, if it is very important for us to hang on to this self-picture, we don't accept or admit these experiences at all.

These self-pictures are not necessarily attractive. A man, for example, may regard himself as incompetent and worthless. He may feel that he is doing his job poorly in spite of favorable appraisals by the company. As long as he has these feelings about himself, he must deny any experiences which would seem not to fit this self-picture—in case any might indicate to him that he is competent. It is so necessary for him to maintain this self-picture that he is threatened by anything which would tend to change it. Thus, when the company raises his salary, it may seem to him only additional proof that he is a fraud. He must hold on to this self-picture because, bad or good, it's the only thing he has by which he can identify himself.

This is why direct attempts to change this individual or change his self-picture are particularly threatening. He is forced to defend himself or to completely deny the experience. This denial of experience and defense of the self-picture tend to bring on rigidity of behavior and create difficulties in personal adjustment.

The active-listening approach, on the other hand, does not present a threat to the individual's self-picture. He does not have to defend it. He is able to explore it, see it for what it is, and make his own decision about how realistic it is. And he is then in a position to change.

If I want to help a man reduce his defensiveness and become more adaptive, I must try to remove the threat of myself as his potential changer. As long as the atmosphere is threatening, there can be no effective communication. So I must create a climate which is neither critical, evaluative, nor moralizing. It must be an atmosphere of equality and freedom, permissiveness and understanding, acceptance and warmth. It is in this climate and this climate only that the individual feels safe enough to incorporate new experiences and new values into his concept of himself. Let's see how active listening helps to create this climate.

What to Avoid

When we encounter a person with a problem, our usual response is to try to change his way of looking at things—to get him to see his situation the way we see it or would like to see it. We plead, reason, scold, encourage, insult, prod—anything to bring about a change in the desired direction, that is, in the direction we want him to travel. What we seldom realize, however, is that, under these circumstances, we are usually responding to *our own* needs to see the world in certain ways. It is always difficult for us to tolerate and understand actions which are different from the ways in which *we* believe *we* should act. If, however, we can free ourselves from the need to influence and direct others in our own paths, we enable ourselves to listen with understanding and thereby employ the most potent available agent of change.

One problem the listener faces is that of responding to demands for decisions, judgments, and evaluations. He is constantly called upon to agree or disagree with someone or something. Yet, as he well knows, the question or challenge frequently is a masked expression of feelings or needs which the speaker is far more anxious to communicate than he is to have the surface questions answered. Because he cannot speak these feelings openly, the speaker must disguise them to himself and to others in an acceptable form. To illustrate, let us examine some typical questions and the types of answers that might best elicit the feelings beneath them.

These responses recognize the questions but leave the way open for the employee to say what is really bothering him. They allow the listener to participate in the problem or situation without shouldering all responsibility for decision making or actions. This is a process of thinking *with* people instead of *for* or *about* them.

Passing judgment, whether critical or favorable, makes free expression difficult. Similarly, advice and information are almost always seen as efforts to change a person and thus serve as barriers to his self-expression and the development of a creative relationship. Moreover, advice is seldom taken and information hardly ever utilized. The eager young trainee probably will not become patient just because he is advised that "the road to success in business is a long, difficult one, and you must be patient." And it is no more helpful for him to learn that "only one out of a hundred trainees reaches a top management position."

Interestingly, it is a difficult lesson to learn that positive *evaluations* are sometimes as blocking as negative ones. It is almost as destructive to the freedom of a relationship to tell a person that he is good or capable or right, as to tell him otherwise. To evaluate him positively may make it more difficult for him to tell of the faults that distress him or the ways in which he believes he is not competent.

Encouragement also may be seen as an attempt to motivate the speaker in certain directions or hold him off, rather than as support. "I'm sure everything will work out O.K." is not a helpful response to the person who is deeply discouraged about a problem.

In other words, most of the techniques and devices common to human relationships are found to be of little use in establishing the type of relationship we are seeking here.

WHAT TO DO

Just what does active listening entail, then? Basically, it requires that we get inside the speaker, that we grasp, *from his point of view*, just what it is he is communicating to us. More than that, we must convey to the speaker that we are seeing things from his point of view. To listen actively, then, means that there are several things we must do.

Listen for Total Meaning

Any message a person tries to get across usually has two components: the *content* of the message and the *feeling* or attitude underlying this content. Both are important; both give the message *meaning*. It is this total meaning of the message that we try to understand. For example, a ma-

chinist comes to his foreman and says, "I've finished that lathe setup." This message has obvious content and perhaps calls upon the foreman for another work assignment. Suppose, on the other hand, that he says, "Well, I'm finally finished with that damned lathe setup." The content is the same, but the total meaning of the message has changed—and changed in an important way for both the foreman and the worker. Here, sensitive listening can facilitate the relationship. Suppose the foreman were to respond by simply giving another work assignment. Would the employee feel that he had gotten his total message across? Would he feel free to talk to his foreman? Will he feel better about his job, more anxious to do good work on the next assignment?

Now, on the other hand, suppose the foreman were to respond with, "Glad to have it over with, huh?" or "Had a pretty rough time of it?" or "Guess you don't feel like doing anything like that again," or anything else that tells the worker that he heard and understands. It doesn't necessarily mean that the next work assignment need be changed or that he must spend an hour listening to the worker complain about the setup problems he encountered. He may do a number of things differently in the light of the new information he has from the worker—but not necessarily. It's just that extra sensitivity on the part of the foreman which can transform an average working climate into a good one.

Respond to Feelings

In some instances, the content is far less important than the feeling which underlies it. To catch the full flavor or meaning of the message, one must respond particularly to the feeling component. If, for instance, our machinist had said, "I'd like to melt this lathe down and make paper clips out of it," responding to content would be obviously absurd. But to respond to his disgust or anger in trying to work with his lathe recognizes the meaning of this message. There are various shadings of these components in the meaning of any message. Each time, the listener must try to remain sensitive to the total meaning the message has to the speaker. What is he trying to tell me? What does this mean to him? How does he see this situation?

Not All Cues

Not all communication is verbal. The speaker's words alone don't tell us everything he is communicating. And hence, truly sensitive listening requires that we become aware of several kinds of communication besides verbal. The way in which a speaker hesitates in his speech can tell us much about his feelings. So, too, can the inflection of his voice. He may stress certain points loudly and clearly and may mumble others. We should also note such things as the person's facial expressions, body posture, hand movements, eye movements, and breathing. All of these help to convey his total message.

WHAT WE COMMUNICATE BY LISTENING

The first reaction of most people when they consider listening as a possible method for dealing with human beings is that listening cannot be sufficient in itself. Because it is passive, they feel, listening does not communicate anything to the speaker. Actually, nothing could be farther from the truth.

By consistently listening to a speaker, you are conveying the idea that: "I'm interested in you as a person, and I think that what you feel is important. I respect your thoughts, and even if I don't agree with them, I know that they are valid for you. I feel sure that you have a contribution to make. I'm not trying to change or evaluate you. I just want to understand you. I think you're worth listening to, and I want you to know that I'm the kind of a person you can talk to."

The subtle but most important aspect of this is that it is the *demonstration* of the message that works. While it is most difficult to convince someone that you respect him by *telling* him so, you are much more likely to get this message across by really *behaving* that way—by actually *having* and *demonstrating* respect for this person. Listening does this most effectively.

Like other behavior, listening behavior is contagious. This has implications for all communication problems, whether between two people or within a large organization. To ensure good communication between associates up and down the line, one must first take the responsibility for setting a pattern of listening. Just as one learns that anger is usually met with anger, argument with argument, and deception with deception, one can learn that listening can be met with listening. Every person who feels responsibility in a situation can set the tone of the interaction, and the important lesson in this is that any behavior exhibited by one person will eventually be responded to with similar behavior in the other person.

It is far more difficult to stimulate constructive behavior in another person but far more profitable. Listening is one of these constructive behaviors, but if one's attitude is to "wait out" the speaker rather than really listen to him, it will fail. The one who consistently listens with understanding, however, is the one who eventually is most likely to be listened to. If you really want to be heard and understood by another, you can develop him as a potential listener, ready for new ideas, provided you can first develop yourself in these ways and sincerely listen with understanding and respect.

TESTING FOR UNDERSTANDING

Because understanding another person is actually far more difficult than it at first seems, it is important to test constantly your ability to see the world in the way the speaker sees it. You can do this by reflecting in your own words what the speaker seems to mean by his words and actions. His response to this will tell you whether or not he feels understood. A good rule of thumb is to assume that you never really understand until you can communicate this understanding to the other's satisfaction.

Here is an experiment to test your skill in listening. The next time you become involved in a lively or controversial discussion with another person, stop for a moment and suggest that you adopt this ground rule for continued discussion: Before either participant in the discussion can make a point or express an opinion of his own, he must first restate aloud the previous point or position of the other person. This restatement must be in his own words (merely parroting the words of another does not prove that one has understood but only that he has heard the words). The restatement must be accurate enough to satisfy the speaker before the listener can be allowed to speak for himself.

This is something you could try in your own discussion group. Have someone express himself on some topic of emotional concern to the group. Then, before another member expresses his own feelings and thought, he must rephrase the *meaning* expressed by the previous speaker to that individual's satisfaction. Note the changes in the emotional climate and in the quality of the discussion when you try this.

PROBLEMS IN ACTIVE LISTENING

Active listening is not an easy skill to acquire. It demands practice. Perhaps more important, it may require changes in our own basic attitudes. These changes come slowly and sometimes with considerable difficulty. Let us look at some of the major problems in active listening and what can be done to overcome them.

The Personal Risk

To be effective at all in active listening, one must have a sincere interest in the speaker. We all live in glass houses as far as our attitudes are concerned. They always show through. And if we are only making a pretense of interest in the speaker, he will quickly pick this up, either consciously or unconsciously. And once he does, he will no longer express himself freely.

Active listening carries a strong element of personal risk. If we manage to accomplish what we are describing here—to sense deeply the feeling of another person, to understand the meaning his experiences have for him, to see the world as he sees it—we risk being changed ourselves. For example, if we permit ourselves to listen our way into the psychological life of a labor leader or agitator—to get the meaning which has life for him—we risk coming to see the world as he sees it. It is threatening to give up, even momentarily, what we believe and start thinking in someone else's terms.

It takes a great deal of inner security and courage to be able to risk one's self in understanding another.

For the supervisor, the courage to take another's point of view generally means that he must see *himself* through another's eyes—he must be able to see himself as others see him. To do this may sometimes be unpleasant, but it is far more *difficult* than unpleasant. We are so accustomed to viewing ourselves in certain ways—to seeing and hearing only what we want to see and hear—that it is extremely difficult for a person to free himself from his needs to see things these ways.

Developing an attitude of sincere interest in the speaker is thus no easy task. It can be developed only by being willing to risk seeing the world from the speaker's point of view. If we have a number of such experiences, however, they will shape an attitude which will allow us to be truly genuine in our interest in the speaker.

Hostile Expressions

The listener will often hear negative, hostile expressions directed at himself. Such expressions are always hard to listen to. No one likes to hear hostile words. And it is not easy to get to the point where one is strong enough to permit these attacks without finding it necessary to defend oneself or retaliate.

Because we all fear that people will crumble under the attack of genuine negative feelings, we tend to perpetuate an attitude of pseudo peace. It is as if we cannot tolerate conflict at all for fear of the damage it could do to us, to the situation, to the others involved. But of course the real damage is done to all these by the denial and suppression of negative feelings.

Out-of-Place Expressions

There is also the problem of out-of-place expressions—expressions dealing with behavior which is not usually acceptable in our society. In the extreme forms that present themselves before psychotherapists, expressions of sexual perversity or homicidal fantasies are often found blocking to the listener because of their obvious threatening quality. At less extreme levels, we all find unnatural or inappropriate behavior difficult to handle. That is, anything from an off-color story told in mixed company to a man weeping is likely to produce a problem situation.

In any face-to-face situation, we will find instances of this type which will momentarily, if not permanently, block any communication. In business and industry, any expressions of weakness or incompetency will generally be regarded as unacceptable and therefore will block good two-way communication. For example, it is difficult to listen to a supervisor tell of his feelings of failure in being able to "take charge" of a situation in his department, because *all* administrators are supposed to be able to "take charge."

Accepting Positive Feelings

It is both interesting and perplexing to note that negative or hostile feelings or expressions are much easier to deal with in any face-to-face relationship than are truly and deeply positive feelings. This is especially true for the businessman, because the culture expects him to be independent, bold, clever, and aggressive and manifest no feelings of warmth, gentleness, and intimacy. He therefore comes to regard these feelings as soft and inappropriate. But no matter how they are regarded, they remain a human need. The denial of these feelings in himself and his associates does not get the executive out of the problem of dealing with them. They simply become veiled and confused. If recognized, they would work for the total effort; unrecognized, they work against it.

EMOTIONAL DANGER SIGNALS

The listener's own emotions are sometimes a barrier to active listening. When emotions are at their height, which is when listening is most necessary, it is most difficult to set aside one's own concerns and be understanding. Our emotions are often our own worst enemies when we try to become listeners. The more involved and invested we are in a particular situation or problem, the less we are likely to be willing or able to listen to the feelings and attitudes of others. That is, the more we find it necessary to respond to our own needs, the less we are able to respond to the needs of another. Let us look at some of the main danger signals that warn us that our emotions may be interfering with our listening.

Defensiveness

The points about which one is most vocal and dogmatic, the points which one is most anxious to impose on others—these are always the points one is trying to talk oneself into believing. So one danger signal becomes apparent when you find yourself stressing a point or trying to convince another. It is at these times that you are likely to be less secure and consequently less able to listen.

Resentment of Opposition

It is always easier to listen to an idea which is similar to one of your own than to an opposing view. Sometimes, in order to clear the air, it is helpful to pause for a moment when you feel your ideas and position being challenged, reflect on the situation, and express your concern to the speaker.

Clash of Personalities

Here again, our experience has consistently shown us that the genuine expression of feelings on the part of the listener will be more helpful in developing a sound relationship than the suppression of them. This is so whether the feelings be resentment, hostility, threat, or admiration. A basically honest relationship, whatever the nature of it, is the most productive of all. The other party becomes secure when he learns that the listener can express his feelings honestly and openly to him. We should keep this in mind when we begin to fear a clash of personalities in the listening relationship. Otherwise, fear of our own emotions will choke off full expression of feelings.

LISTENING TO OURSELVES

To listen to oneself is a prerequisite for listening to others. And it is often an effective means of dealing with the problems we have outlined above. When we are most aroused, excited, and demanding, we are least able to understand our own feelings and attitudes. Yet, in dealing with the problems of others, it becomes most important to be sure of one's own position, values, and needs.

The ability to recognize and understand the meaning which a particular episode has for you, with all the feelings which it stimulates in you, and the ability to express the meaning when you find it getting in the way of active listening will clear the air and enable you once again to be free to listen. That is, if some person or situation touches off feelings within you which tend to block your attempts to listen with understanding, begin listening to yourself. It is much more helpful in developing effective relationships to avoid suppressing these feelings. Speak them out as clearly as you can and try to enlist the other person as a listener to your feelings. A person's listening ability is limited by his ability to listen to himself.

ACTIVE LISTENING AND COMPANY GOALS

How can listening improve production?

We're in business, and it's a rugged, fast, competitive affair. How are we going to find time to counsel our employees?

We have to concern ourselves with organizational problems first.

We can't afford to spend all day listening when there's a job to be done.

What's morale got to do with production?

Sometimes we have to sacrifice an individual for the good of the rest of the people in the company.

Those of us who are trying to advance the listening approach in industry hear these comments frequently. And because they are so honest and legitimate, they pose a real problem. Unfortunately, the answers are not so clear-cut as the questions.

INDIVIDUAL IMPORTANCE

One answer is based on an assumption that is central to the listening approach. That assumption is: The kind of behavior which helps the individual will eventually be the best thing that could be done for the group. Or saying it another way: The things that are best for the individual are best for the company. This is a conviction of ours, based on our experience in psychology and education. The research evidence from industry is only beginning to come in. We find that putting the group first, at the expense of the individual, besides being an uncomfortable individual experience, does *not* unify the group. In fact, it tends to make the group less a group. The members become anxious and suspicious.

We are not at all sure in just what ways the group does benefit from a concern demonstrated for an individual, but we have several strong leads. One is that the group feels more secure when an individual is being listened to and provided for with concern and sensitivity. And we assume that a secure group will ultimately be a better group. When each individual feels that he need not fear exposing himself to the group, he is likely to contribute more freely and spontaneously. When the leader of a group responds to the individual, puts the individual first, the other members of the group will follow suit and the group will come to act as a unit in recognizing and responding to the needs of a particular member. This positive, constructive action seems to be a much more satisfying experience for a group than the experience of dispensing with a member.

LISTENING AND PRODUCTION

Whether listening or any other activity designed to better human relations in an industry actually raises production—whether morale has a definite relationship to production—is not known for sure. There are some who frankly hold that there is no relationship to be expected between morale and production—that the production often depends upon the social misfit, the eccentric, or the isolate. And there are some who simply choose to work in a climate of cooperation and harmony, in a high-morale group, quite aside from the question of increased production.

A report from the Survey Research Center[1] at the University of Michigan on research conducted at the Prudential Life Insurance Company lists seven findings relating to production and morale. First-line supervisors in high-production work groups were found to differ from those in low-production work groups in that they:

1. Are under less close supervision from their own supervisors

[1]"Productivity, Supervision, and Employee Morale." *Human Relations*, Series I, Report 1 (Ann Arbor: Survey Research Center, University of Michigan).

2. Place less direct emphasis upon production as the goal
3. Encourage employee participation in the making of decisions
4. Are more employee-centered
5. Spend more of their time in supervision and less in straight production work
6. Have a greater feeling of confidence in their supervisory roles
7. Feel that they know where they stand with the company

After mentioning that other dimensions of morale, such as identification with the company, intrinsic job satisfaction, and satisfaction with job status, were not found significantly related to productivity, the report goes on to suggest the following psychological interpretation:

People are more effectively motivated when they are given some degree of freedom in the way in which they do their work than when every action is prescribed in advance. They do better when some degree of decision making about their jobs is possible than when all decisions are made for them. They respond more adequately when they are treated as personalities than as cogs in a machine. In short, if the ego motivations of self-determination, or self-expression, of a sense of personal worth can be tapped, the individual can be more effectively energized. The use of external sanctions or pressuring for production may work to some degree, but not to the extent that the more internalized motives do. When the individual comes to identify himself with his job and with the work of his group, human resources are much more fully utilized in the production process.

The Survey Research Center has also conducted studies among workers in other industries. In discussing the results of these studies, Robert L. Kahn writes:

In the studies of clerical workers, railroad workers, and workers in heavy industry, the supervisors with the better production records gave a larger proportion of their time to supervisory functions, especially the interpersonal aspects of their jobs. The supervisors of the lower-producing sections were more likely to spend their time in tasks which the men themselves were performing, or in the paperwork aspects of their jobs.[2]

MAXIMUM CREATIVENESS

There may never be enough research evidence to satisfy everyone on this question. But speaking from a business point of view, in terms of the problem of developing resources for production, the maximum creativeness and productive effort of the human beings in the organization are the richest untapped source of power still existing. The difference between the maximum productive capacity of people and that output which industry is now realizing is immense. We simply suggest that this maximum capacity might be closer to realization if we sought to release the motivation that already exists within people rather than try to stimulate them externally.

This releasing of the individual is made possible, first of all, by sensitive listening, with respect and understanding. Listening is a beginning toward making the individual feel himself worthy of making contributions, and this could result in a very dynamic and productive organization. Competitive business is never too rugged or too busy to take time to procure the most efficient technological advances or to develop rich raw-material resources. But these in comparison to the resources that are already within the people in the plant are paltry. This is industry's major procurement problem.

G. L. Clemens, president of Jewel Tea Co., Inc., in talking about the collaborative approach to management, says:

We feel that this type of approach recognizes that there is a secret ballot going on at all times among the people in any business. They vote for or against the supervisors. A favorable vote for the supervisor shows up in the cooperation, teamwork, understanding, and production of the group. To win this secret ballot, each supervisor must share the problems of his group and work for them.[3]

The decision to spend time listening to his employees is a decision each supervisor or executive has to make for himself. Executives seldom have much to do with products or processes. They have to deal with people who must in turn deal with people who will deal with products or processes. The higher one goes up the line, the more one will be concerned with human relations problems, simply because people are all one has to work with. The minute we take a man from his bench and make him a foreman, he is removed from the basic production of goods and now must begin relating to individuals instead of nuts and bolts. People are different from things, and our foreman is called upon for a different line of skills completely. His new tasks call upon him to be a special kind of person. The development of himself as a listener is a first step in becoming this special person.

[2]Robert L. Kahn, "The Human Factors Underlying Industrial Productivity." *Michigan Business Review*, November 1952.

[3]G. L. Clemens, "Time for Democracy in Action at the Executive Level" (Address given before the AMA Personnel Conference, February 28, 1951).

Exercises

EXERCISE 13.1   Your Communication Style

To determine your preferred communication style, select the one alternative that most closely describes what you would do in each of the 12 situations below. Do not be concerned with trying to pick the correct answer; select the alternative that best describes what you would actually do. Circle the letter *a, b, c,* or *d*.

1. Wendy, a knowledgeable person from another department, comes to you, the engineering supervisor, and requests that you design a special product to her specifications. You would:
   a. Control the conversation and tell Wendy what you will do for her.
   b. Ask Wendy to describe the product. Once you understand it, you would present your ideas. Let her realize that you are concerned and want to help with your ideas.
   c. Respond to Wendy's request by conveying understanding and support. Help clarify what is to be done by you. Offer ideas, but do it her way.
   d. Find out what you need to know. Let Wendy know you will do it her way.

2. Your department has designed a product that is to be fabricated by Saul's department. Saul has been with the company longer than you have; he knows his department. Saul comes to you to change the product design. You decide to:
   a. Listen to the change and why it would be beneficial. If you believe Saul's way is better, change it; if not, explain why the original idea is superior. If necessary, insist that it be done your way.
   b. Tell Saul to fabricate it any way he wants to.
   c. You are busy; tell Saul to do it your way. You don't have the time to listen and agree with him.
   d. Be supportive; make changes together as a team.

3. Upper management has a decision to make. They call you to a meeting and tell you they need some information to solve a problem they describe to you. You:
   a. Respond in a manner that conveys personal support and offer alternative ways to solve the problem.
   b. Respond to their questions.
   c. Explain how to solve the problem.
   d. Show your concern by explaining how to solve the problem and why it is an effective solution.

4. You have a routine work order. The work order is to be replaced verbally and completed in three days.

Sue, the receiver, is very experienced and willing to be of service to you. You decide to:
   a. Explain your needs, but let Sue make the other decisions.
   b. Tell Sue what you want and why you need it.
   c. Decide together what to order.
   d. Simply give Sue the order.

5. Work orders from the staff department normally take three days; however, you have an emergency and need the job today. Your colleague Jim, the department supervisor, is knowledgeable and somewhat cooperative. You decide to:
   a. Tell Jim that you need it by three o'clock and return at that time to pick it up.
   b. Explain the situation and how the organization will benefit by expediting the order. Volunteer to help any way you can.
   c. Explain the situation and ask Jim when the order will be ready.
   d. Explain the situation and together come to a solution to your problem.

6. Danielle, a peer with a record of high performance, has recently had a drop in productivity. Her problem is affecting her performance. You know Danielle has a family problem. You:
   a. Discuss the problem; help Danielle realize the problem is affecting her work and yours. Supportively discuss ways to improve the situation.
   b. Tell the boss about it and let him decide what to do about it.
   c. Tell Danielle to get back on the job.
   d. Discuss the problem and tell Danielle how to solve the work situation; be supportive.

7. You are a knowledgeable supervisor. You buy supplies from Peter regularly. He is an excellent salesperson and very knowledgeable about your situation. You are placing your weekly order. You decide to:
   a. Explain what you want and why: Develop a supportive relationship.
   b. Explain what you want and ask Peter to recommend products.
   c. Give Peter the order.
   d. Explain your situation and allow Peter to make the order.

8. Jean, a knowledgeable person from another department, has asked you to perform a routine staff function to her specifications. You decide to:
   a. Perform the task to her specification without questioning her.

Source: Robert N. Lussier, *Human Relations in Organizations: A Skill Building Approach* (Homewood, IL: Irwin, 1993), pp. 153–56.

b. Tell her that you will do it the usual way.

c. Explain what you will do and why.

d. Show your willingness to help; offer alternative ways to do it.

9. Tom, a salesperson, has requested an order for your department's services with a short delivery date. As usual, Tom claims it is a take-it-or-leave-it offer. He wants your decision now, or within a few minutes, because he is in the customer's office. Your action is to:

a. Convince Tom to work together to come up with a later date.

b. Give Tom a yes or no answer.

c. Explain your situation and let Tom decide if you should take the order.

10. As a time-and-motion expert, you have been called in regard to a complaint about the standard time it takes to perform a job. As you analyze the entire job, you realize the one element of complaint should take longer, but other elements should take less time. The end result is a shorter total standard time for the job. You decide to:

a. Tell the operator and foreman that the total time must be decreased and why.

b. Agree with the operator and increase the standard time.

c. Explain your findings. Deal with the operator and/or foreman's concerns, but ensure compliance with your new standard.

d. Together with the operator, develop a standard time.

11. You approve budget allocations for projects. Marie, who is very competent in developing budgets, has come to you. You:

a. Review the budget, make revisions, and explain them in a supportive way. Deal with concerns, but insist on your changes.

b. Review the proposal and suggest areas where changes may be needed. Make changes together, if needed.

c. Review the proposed budget, make revisions, and explain them.

d. Answer any questions or concerns Marie has and approve the budget as is.

12. You are a sales manager. A customer has offered you a contract for your product with a short delivery date. The offer is open for days. The contract would be profitable for you and the organization. The cooperation of the production department is essential to meet the deadline. Tim, the production manager, and you do not get along very well because of your repeated requests for quick delivery. Your action is to:

a. Contact Tim and try to work together to complete the contract.

b. Accept the contract and convince Tim in a supportive way to meet the obligation.

c. Contact Tim and explain the situation. Ask him if you and he should accept the contract, but let him decide.

d. Accept the contract. Contact Tim and tell him to meet the obligation. If he resists, tell him you will go to the boss.

To determine your preferred communication style, in the chart below, circle the letter you selected as the alternative you chose in situations 1–12. The column headings indicate the style you selected.

	Autocratic	Consultative	Participative	LaissezFaire
1.	a	b	c	d
2.	c	a	d	b
3.	c	d	a	b
4.	d	b	c	a
5.	a	b	d	c
6.	c	b	a	b
7.	c	a	b	d
8.	b	c	d	a
9.	b	d	a	c
10.	a	c	d	b
11.	c	a	b	d
12.	d	b	a	c
Total				

Cases

CASE 13.1   The Road to Hell

John Baker, chief engineer of the Caribbean Bauxite Company Limited of Barracania in the West Indies, was making his final preparations to leave the island. His promotion to production manager of Keso Mining Corporation near Winnipeg—one of Continental Ore's fast-expanding Canadian enterprises—had been announced a month before, and now everything had been tidied up except the last vital interview with his successor, the able young Barracanian Matthew Rennalls. It was vital that this interview be a success and that Rennalls leave Baker's office uplifted and encouraged to face the chal-

Source: Reprinted by permission of the Industrial Relations Center, The University of Chicago.

lenge of his new job. A touch on the bell would have brought Rennalls walking into the room, but Baker delayed the moment and gazed thoughtfully through the window, considering just exactly what he was going to say and, more particularly, how he was going to say it.

Baker, an English expatriate, was 45 years old and had served his 23 years with Continental Ore in many different places: the Far East; several countries of Africa; Europe; and, for the last two years, the West Indies. He had not cared much for his previous assignment in Hamburg and was delighted when the West Indian appointment came through. Climate was not the only attraction. Baker had always preferred working overseas in what were called the developing countries because he felt he had an innate knack—more than most other expatriates working for Continental Ore—of knowing just how to get on with regional staff. Twenty-four hours in Barracania, however, soon made him realize that he would need all of his innate knack if he were to deal effectively with the problems in this field that now awaited him.

At his first interview with Glenda Hutchins, the production manager, the whole problem of Rennalls and his future was discussed. There and then it was made quite clear to Baker that one of his most important tasks would be the grooming of Rennalls as his successor. Hutchins had pointed out that not only was Rennalls one of the brightest Barracanian prospects on the staff of Caribbean Bauxite—at London University he had taken first-class honors in the B.Sc. engineering degree—but, being the son of the minister of finance and economic planning, he also had no small political pull.

Caribbean Bauxite had been particularly pleased when Rennalls decided to work for it rather than for the government in which his father had such a prominent post. The company ascribed his action to the effects of its vigorous and liberal regionalization program that, since World War II, had produced 18 Barracanians at the middle-management level and given Caribbean Bauxite a good lead in this respect over all other international concerns operating in Barracania. The success of this timely regionalization policy had led to excellent relations with the government—a relationship that gained added importance when Barracania, three years later, became independent, an occasion that encouraged a critical and challenging attitude toward the role foreign interest would have to play in the new Barracania. Hutchins, therefore, had little difficulty convincing Baker that the successful career development of Rennalls was of the first importance.

The interview with Hutchins was now two years in the past, and Baker, leaning back in his office chair, reviewed just how successful he had been in the grooming of Rennalls. What aspects of the latter's character had helped, and what had hindered? What about his own personality? How had that helped or hindered? The first item to go on the credit side, without question, would be the

ability of Rennalls to master the technical aspects of his job. From the start he had shown keenness and enthusiasm, and he had often impressed Baker with his ability in tackling new assignments and the constructive comments he invariably made in departmental discussions. He was popular with all ranks of Barracanian staff and had an ease of manner that stood him in good stead when dealing with his expatriate seniors.

These were all assets, but what about the debit side? First and foremost was his racial consciousness. His four years at London University had accentuated this feeling and made him sensitive to any sign of condescension on the part of expatriates. Perhaps to give expression to this sentiment, as soon as he returned home from London, he threw himself into politics on behalf of the United Action Party, who were later to win the preindependence elections and provide the country with its first prime minister.

The ambitions of Rennalls—and he certainly was ambitious—did not, however, lie in politics. Staunch nationalist he was, but he saw that he could serve himself and his country best—for was not bauxite responsible for nearly half the value of Barracania's export trade?—by putting his engineering talent to the best use possible. On this account, Hutchins found that he had an unexpectedly easy task in persuading Rennalls to give up his political work before entering the production department as an assistant engineer.

It was, Baker knew, Rennall's well-repressed sense of racial consciousness that had prevented their relationship from being as close as it should have been. On the surface, nothing could have seemed more agreeable. Formality between the two was minimal. Baker was delighted to find that his assistant shared his own peculiar "shaggy dog" sense of humor, so jokes were continually being exchanged. They entertained one another at their houses and often played tennis together—and yet the barrier remained invisible, indefinable, but ever present. The existence of this screen between them was a constant source of frustration to Baker, since it indicated a weakness which he was loath to accept. If successful with people of all other nationalities, why not with Rennalls?

At least he had managed to break through to Rennalls more successfully than had any other expatriate. In fact, it was the young Barracanian's attitude—sometimes overbearing, sometimes cynical—toward other company expatriates that had been one of the subjects Baker raised last year when he discussed Rennall's staff report with him. Baker knew, too, that he would have to raise the same subject again in the forthcoming interview, because Martha Jackson, the senior drafter, had complained only yesterday about the rudeness of Rennalls. With this thought in mind, Baker leaned forward and spoke into the intercom: "Would you come in, Matt, please? I'd like a word with you." Rennalls came in, and Baker held out a box and said, "Do sit down. Have a cigarette."

He paused while he held out his lighter, and then went on. "As you know, Matt, I'll be off to Canada in a few days' time, and before I go, I thought it would be useful if we could have a final chat together. It is indeed with some deference that I suggest I can be of help. You will shortly be sitting in this chair and doing the job I am now doing, but I, on the other hand, am 10 years older, so perhaps you can accept the idea that I may be able to give you the benefit of my long experience."

Baker saw Rennalls stiffen slightly in his chair as he made this point, so he added in explanation, "You and I have attended enough company courses to remember those repeated requests by the personnel manager to tell people how they are getting on as often as the convenient moment arises, and not just the automatic once a year when, by regulation, staff reports have to be discussed."

Rennalls nodded his agreement, so Baker went on, "I shall always remember the last job performance discussion I had with my previous boss back in Germany. She used what she called the 'plus and minus technique.' She firmly believed that when seniors seek to improve the work performance of their staff by discussion, their prime objective should be to make sure the latter leave the interview encouraged and inspired to improve. Any criticism, therefore, must be constructive and helpful. She said that one very good way to encourage a person—and I fully agree with her—is to discuss good points, the plus factors, as well as weak ones, the minus factors. So I thought, Matt, it would be a good idea to run our discussion along these lines."

Rennalls offered no comment, so Baker continued. "Let me say, therefore, right away, that as far as your own work performance is concerned, the pluses far outweigh the minuses. I have, for instance, been most impressed with the way you have adapted your considerable theoretical knowledge to master the practical techniques of your job—that ingenious method you used to get air down to the fifth shaft level is a sufficient case in point. At departmental meetings I have invariably found your comments well taken and helpful. In fact, you will be interested to know that only last week I reported to Ms. Hutchins that, from the technical point of view, she could not wish for a more able person to succeed to the position of chief engineer.

"That's very good indeed of you, John," cut in Rennalls with a smile of thanks. "My only worry now is how to live up to such a high recommendation."

"Of that I am quite sure," returned Baker, "especially if you can overcome the minus factor which I would like now to discuss with you. It is one that I have talked about before, so I'll come straight to the point. I have noticed that you are more friendly and get on better with your fellow Barracanians than you do with Europeans. In point of fact, I had a complaint only yesterday from Ms. Jackson, who said you had been rude to her—and not for the first time, either.

"There is, Matt, I am sure, no need for me to tell you how necessary it will be for you to get on well with expatriates, because until the company has trained up sufficient men of your caliber, Europeans are bound to occupy senior positions here in Barracania. All this is vital to your future interests, so can I help you in any way?"

While Baker was speaking on this theme, Rennalls sat tensed in his chair, and it was some seconds before he replied. "It is quite extraordinary, isn't it, how one can convey an impression to others so at variance with what one intends? I can only assure you once again that my disputes with Jackson—and you may remember also Godson—have had nothing at all to do with the color of their skins. I promise you that if a Barracanian had behaved in an equally peremptory manner, I would have reacted the same way. And again, if I may say it within these four walls, I am sure I am not the only one who has found Jackson and Godson difficult. I could mention the names of several expatriates who have felt the same. However, I am really sorry to have created this impression of not being able to get on with Europeans—it is an entirely false one—and I quite realize that I must do all I can to correct it as quickly as possible. On your last point, regarding Europeans holding senior positions in the company for some time to come, I quite accept the situation. I know that Caribbean Bauxite—as it has been for many years now—will promote Barracanians as soon as their experience warrants it. And, finally, I would like to assure you, John—and my father thinks the same, too—that I am very happy in my work here and hope to stay with the company for many years to come."

Rennalls had spoken earnestly, and Baker, although not convinced by what he had heard, did not think he could pursue the matter further except to say, "All right, Matt, my impression may be wrong, but I would like to remind you about the truth of that old saying 'What is important is not what is true, but what is believed.' Let it rest at that."

But suddenly Baker knew that he did not want to "let it rest at that." He was disappointed once again at not being able to break through to Rennalls and at having again had to listen to his bland denial that there was any racial prejudice in his makeup.

Baker, who had intended to end the interview at this point, decided to try another tack. "To return for a moment to the plus and minus technique I was telling you just now, there is another plus factor I forgot to mention. I would like to congratulate you not only on the caliber of your work, but also on the ability you have shown in overcoming a challenge that I, as a European, have never had to meet.

"Continental Ore is, as you know, a typical commercial enterprise—admittedly a big one—that is a product of the economic and social environment of the United States and western Europe. My ancestors have all been brought up in this environment of the past 200 or 300 years, and I have, therefore, been able to live in a world in which commerce (as we know it today) has been part and parcel of my being.

It has not been something revolutionary and new that has suddenly entered my life. In your case," went on Baker, "the situation is different, because you and your forebears have only had some 50 and not 200 or 300 years. Again, Matt, let me congratulate you—and people like you—on having so successfully overcome this particular hurdle. It is for this very reason that I think the outlook for Barracania—and particularly Caribbean Bauxite—is so bright."

Rennalls had listened intently, and when Baker finished, he replied, "Well, once again, John, I have to thank you for what you have said, and, for my part, I can only say that it is gratifying to know that my own personal effort has been so much appreciated. I hope that more people will soon come to think as you do."

There was a pause, and, for a moment, Baker thought hopefully that he was about to achieve his long-awaited breakthrough. But Rennalls merely smiled back. The barrier remained unbreached. There were some five minutes' cheerful conversation about the contrast between the Caribbean and Canadian climates and whether the West Indies had any hope of beating England in the Fifth Test before Baker drew the interview to a close. Although he was as far from ever knowing the real Rennalls, he was nevertheless glad that the interview had run along in this friendly manner and, particularly, that it had ended on such a cheerful note.

This feeling, however, lasted only until the following morning. Baker had some farewells to make, so he arrived at the office considerably later than usual. He had no sooner sat down at his desk than his secretary walked into the room with a worried frown on her face. Her words came fast. "When I arrived this morning, I found Mr. Rennalls already waiting at my door. He seemed very angry and told me in quite a peremptory manner that he had a vital letter to dictate that must be sent off without any delay. He was so worked up that he couldn't keep still and kept pacing about the room, which is most unlike him. He wouldn't even wait to read what he had dictated. Just signed the page where he thought the letter would end. It has been distributed, and your copy is in your tray."

Puzzled and feeling vaguely uneasy, Baker opened the envelope marked "Confidential" and read the following letter;

FROM: Assistant Engineer

TO: The Chief Engineer
    Caribbean Bauxite Limited

SUBJECT: Assessment of Interview
    Between Messrs. Baker and Rennalls

DATE: 14th August 1982

It has always been my practice to respect the advice given me by seniors, so after our interview, I decided to give careful thought once again to its main points and so make sure that I had understood all that had been said. As I promised you at the time, I had every intention of putting your advice to the best effect.

It was not, therefore, until I had sat down quietly in my home yesterday evening to consider the interview objectively that its main purport became clear. Only then did the full enormity of what you said dawn on me. The more I thought about it, the more convinced I was that I had hit upon the real truth—and the more furious I became. With a facility in the English language which I—a poor Barracanian—cannot hope to match, you had the audacity to insult me (and through me every Barracanian worth his salt) by claiming that our knowledge of modern living is only a paltry 50 years old, while yours goes back 200 to 300 years. As if your materialistic commercial environment could possibly be compared with the spiritual values of our culture! I'll have you know that if much of what I saw in London is representative of your boasted culture, I hope fervently that it will never come to Barracania. By what right do you have the effrontery to condescend to us? At heart, all you Europeans think us barbarians, or, as you say amongst yourselves, we are "just down from the trees."

Far into the night I discussed this matter with my father, and he is as disgusted as I. He agrees with me that any company whose senior staff think as you do is no place for any Barracanian proud of his culture and race. So much for all the company claptrap and specious propaganda about regionalization and Barracania for the Barracanians.

I feel ashamed and betrayed. Please accept this letter as my resignation, which I wish to become effective immediately.

cc: Production Manager

Managing Director

QUESTIONS:

1. What, in your opinion, did Baker hope to accomplish as a result of his conversation with Rennalls? Did he succeed? Why or why not?
2. Did nonverbal communications play a part in this case? Be specific and give examples.
3. What could Baker and Rennalls have done to improve the situation described in this case?

14

Decision Making

After completing Chapter 14, you should be able to:

Learning Objectives

- **Contrast** programmed with nonprogrammed decisions.

- **Identify** the steps in the decision-making process.

- **Discuss** priority setting.

- **Describe** the conditions governing alternative-outcome relationships.

- **Explain** the role of behavioral influences on decision making.

- **Compare** individual and group decision making.

- **Identify** specific techniques for stimulating creativity.

The focus of this chapter is on decision making, which is defined as the process of choosing a particular action that deals with a problem or opportunity. The quality of the decisions that managers make is the yardstick of their effectiveness.[1] Sometimes just one or two exceptionally good or exceptionally poor decisions can have significant effects on a manager's career or an organization's success. Union Carbide management made several poor decisions in the aftermath of the cataclysmic accident involving the release of methyl isocyanate in Bhopal, India, in 1984. This tragic event took the lives of more than 2,000 people. The accident itself, as well as subsequent decisions made regarding the handling of the accident, had profound effects on Union Carbide. Worldwide indignation and censure contributed to a collapse in the value of the company's stock, a downgrading of its credit rating, a hostile takeover attempt (by GAF Corp.), and damage claims totaling *billions* of dollars.

www.unioncarbide.com

Because decision making is so very important and can have such significant effects, as illustrated in the Union Carbide example above, it has been suggested that management *is* decision making. It would be a mistake, however, to conclude that only *managers* make decisions. Increasingly, important decisions are being made in organizations by nonmanagers. Thus, while decision making is an important managerial process, it is fundamentally a *people* process. This chapter, therefore, describes and analyzes decision making in terms that reflect the ways in which people make decisions based on their understanding of individual, group, and organizational goals and objectives.

TYPES OF DECISIONS

Managers in organizations may be separated by background, lifestyle, and distance, but sooner or later they must all make decisions. Even when the decision process is highly participative in nature, with full involvement by subordinates, it is the manager who ultimately is responsible for the outcomes of a decision. In this section, our purpose is to present a classification system into which various kinds of decisions can be placed, regardless of whether the manager makes the decision unilaterally or in consultation with, or delegation to, subordinates.

Researchers and experts in the field of decision making have developed several ways of classifying different types of decisions. For the most part, these classification systems are similar, differing mainly in terminology. We use the widely adopted distinction suggested by Herbert Simon.[2] Simon distinguishes between two types of decisions:

1. *Programmed decisions.* If a particular situation occurs often, a routine procedure usually will be worked out for solving it. Decisions are **programmed** to the extent that they are repetitive and routine and a definite procedure has been developed for handling them. For example, Land's End has a specific procedure that must be followed when a customer has a complaint about an order. Each step is tailored to respond as quickly as possible to the customer's complaints.[3]

www.landsend.com

---

[1]Ralph Sanders, *The Executive Decision Making Process: Identifying Problems and Assessing Outcomes* (Westport, CT: Quorum, 1999).

[2]Herbert A. Simon, *The New Science of Management Decision* (New York: Harper & Row 1960), pp. 5–6.

[3]See *www.landsend.com.*

EXHIBIT 14.1	**Types of Decisions**	
	Programmed Decisions	**Nonprogrammed Decisions**
Type of problem	Frequent, repetitive, routine, much certainty regarding cause-and-effect relationships	Novel, unstructured, much uncertainty regarding cause-and-effect relationships
Procedure	Dependence on policies, rules, and definite procedures	Necessity for creativity, intuition, tolerance for ambiguity, creative problem solving
Examples	*Business firm:* Periodic reorders of inventory	*Business firm:* Diversification into new products and markets
	University: Necessary grade-point average for good academic standing	*University:* Construction of new classroom facilities
	Health care: Procedure for admitting patients	*Health care:* Purchase of experimental equipment
	Government: Merit system for promotion of state employees	*Government:* Reorganization of state government agencies

www.digitalthink.com

2. *Nonprogrammed decisions.* Decisions are nonprogrammed when they are novel and unstructured. There is no established procedure for handling the problem, either because it has not arisen in exactly the same manner before or because it is complex or extremely important. Such decisions deserve special treatment. Individuals taking online courses in such e-learning companies as Digital Think, Skill Soft, Net G, and HighTech Campus occasionally are faced with problems registering, completing a competency test, or downloading a hard copy of a document noted in a Web-enabled course.[4] The technical help-desk in each of these firms must respond to these "exceptions." An exception is a situation, event, or problem that is nonroutine. The help desk employee must make nonprogrammed decisions to solve the problem. Each competitive company in the e-learning industry must handle as efficiently as possible nonprogrammed (exception)-type decision situations.

While the two classifications are broad, they point out the importance of differentiating between programmed and nonprogrammed decisions. The management of most organizations faces great numbers of programmed decisions in their daily operations. Such decisions should be treated without expending unnecessary organizational resources on them. On the other hand, the nonprogrammed decision must be properly identified as such, since it is this type of decision that forms the basis for allocating billions of dollars worth of resources in our economy every year. Unfortunately, it is the human process involving this type of decision that we know the least about.[5] Exhibit 14.1 presents a breakdown of the different types of decisions, with examples of each type, in different kinds of organizations. The exhibit illustrates that programmed and nonprogrammed decisions require different kinds of procedures and apply to distinctly different types of problems.

---

[4]The e-learning industry has become very competitive with firms attempting to solve customer problems immediately. Failure to solve such problems can result in lost clients, poor word-of-mouth publicity, and decreased revenues. An excellent report on the e-learning industry is found in Marc J. Rosenberg, *e-learning* (New York: McGraw-Hill, 2001).

[5]Sanders, *Decision Making Process.*

Expert Systems: A Form of Intellectual Cloning?

Computers have been tools for making decisions for several decades. Almost all routine, repetitive decisions that deal with quantitative data and have a definite decision procedure are programmed. Highly unstructured decisions, however, are rarely programmed. Until recently that is. In the last several years, the success of some expert systems has caught the attention of business executives. Expert systems are software systems designed to mimic the way human experts make decisions. In one sense, building expert systems is a form of intellectual cloning. The system designer builds into the system a knowledge base and an inference system. The knowledge base is derived from the expert's knowledge and experience in the field. There are two types of knowledge: (1) the facts of domain (widely shared knowledge, com-

monly agreed-upon practitioners) and (2) heuristic knowledge (the knowledge of good practice and good judgment in a field). Heuristic knowledge is what a human expert acquires over years of work.

Expert systems enable organizations to work faster and on a larger scale. The insurance and credit card industries are examples of sectors where expert systems are beginning to win over corporate converts because of the ability to deal efficiently with unstructured problems. Recent successes have also been reported for such applications as developing business plans, creating job descriptions, planning and tracking goals and progress toward goals, and even in improving the federal bureaucracy and making it more responsive.

Sources: "What's New for Management," *Fortune*, Winter 1997, p. 110; "Save the Bureaucrats," *Public Personnel Management*, Spring 1997, pp. 7–14; Sara Humphrey, "Tools Help Objectify Decision Making: Managers Can Quantify Risks, Rewards with Step-by-Step Analyses," *PC Week*, March 9, 1992, pp. 113–15.

Traditionally, programmed decisions have been handled through rules, standard operating procedures, and the structure of the organization that develops specific procedures for handling them. Operations researchers—through the development of mathematical models—have facilitated the handling of these types of decisions.

On the other hand, nonprogrammed decisions usually have been handled by general problem-solving processes, judgment, intuition, and creativity. Unfortunately, the advances that modern management techniques have made in improving nonprogrammed decision making have not been nearly as great as the advances they have made in improving programmed decision making.[6] Some important progress, however, has been made as Organizational Encounter 14.1 indicates.

Ideally, the main concern of top management should be nonprogrammed decisions, while first-level management should be concerned with programmed decisions. Middle managers in most organizations concentrate mostly on programmed decisions, although in some cases they will participate in nonprogrammed decisions. In other words, the nature, frequency, and degree of certainty surrounding a problem should dictate at what level of management the decision should be made.

Obviously, problems arise in those organizations where top management expends much time and effort on programmed decisions.[7] One unfortunate result of this practice is a neglect of long-range planning, which is subordinated to other activities, whether the organization is successful or is having problems. If the organization is successful, this justifies continuing the policies and practices that have achieved success. If the organization experiences difficulty, its current problems have first priority and occupy the time of top management. In either case, long-range planning ends up being neglected.

---

[6]John P. Kotter, *What Leaders Really Do*, (Boston: Oxford University Press, 1999).

[7]Sanders, *Decision Making Process*.

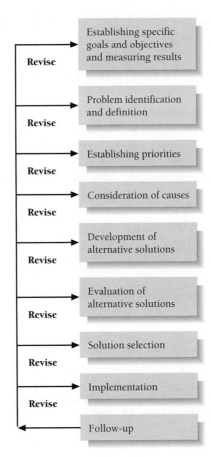

EXHIBIT 14.2
The Rational Decision-Making Process

Revise → Establishing specific goals and objectives and measuring results

Revise → Problem identification and definition

Revise → Establishing priorities

Revise → Consideration of causes

Revise → Development of alternative solutions

Revise → Evaluation of alternative solutions

Revise → Solution selection

Revise → Implementation

Follow-up

Finally, the neglect of long-range planning usually results in an overemphasis on short-run control. This results in a lack of delegation of authority to lower levels of management, which often has adverse effects on motivation and satisfaction.

A RATIONAL DECISION-MAKING PROCESS

Decisions should be thought of as a means rather than ends. They are the *organizational mechanisms* through which an attempt is made to achieve a desired state. They are, in effect, an *organizational response* to a problem. Every decision is the outcome of a dynamic process that is influenced by a multitude of forces. A rational decision-making process is diagrammed in Exhibit 14.2. The reader should not, however, interpret this outline to mean that decision making is a fixed procedure. It is a sequential process rather than a series of steps. This sequence diagram enables us to examine each element in the normal progression that leads to a decision.

Examination of Exhibit 14.2 reveals that it is more applicable to nonprogrammed decisions than to programmed decisions. Problems that occur infrequently, with a great deal of uncertainty surrounding the outcome, require that the manager utilize the entire process. For problems that occur frequently, however, this is not necessary. If a policy is established to handle such problems, it will not be necessary to develop and evaluate alternatives each time a similar problem arises.

Establishing Specific Goals and Objectives and Measuring Results

wwww.sony.com

Goals and objectives are needed in each area where performance influences the effectiveness of the organization. If goals and objectives are adequately established, they will dictate what results must be achieved and the measures that indicate whether or not they have been achieved. An outstanding example of effectively establishing goals and objectives and measuring results is the well-known Japanese firm Sony. One reason Sony is so successful is the fact that it closely tracks its progress toward established objectives and responds quickly when such progress is lagging. Sony's specific goals and objectives, coupled with its constant scanning of the environment to detect changes in consumer preferences and competitors' product mix, allow it to make sound decisions rapidly.

Problem Identification and Definition

A necessary condition for a decision is a problem—if problems did not exist, there would be no need for decisions. Problems typically result from a determination that a discrepancy exists between a desired state and current reality.[8] This underscores the importance of establishing goals and objectives. How critical a problem is for the organization is measured by the gap between the levels of performance specified in the organization's goals and objectives and the levels of performance attained. Thus, a gap of 20 percent between a sales volume objective and the volume of sales actually achieved signifies that some problem exists.

It is easy to understand that a problem exists when a gap occurs between desired results and actual results. However, certain factors often lead to difficulties in identifying exactly what the problem is.[9] These factors are:

1. *Perceptual problems.* As noted in Chapter 3, individual feelings may act in such a way as to protect or defend us from unpleasant perceptions. Negative information may be selectively perceived in such a way as to distort its true meaning or it may be totally ignored. For example, a college dean may fail to identify increasing class sizes as a problem while at the same time being sensitive to problems faced by the president of the university in raising funds for the school.

2. *Defining problems in terms of solutions.* This is really a form of jumping to conclusions. For example, a sales manager may say, "The decrease in profits is due to our poor product quality." The sales manager's definition of the problem suggests a particular solution—the improvement of product quality in the production department. Certainly, other solutions may be possible. Perhaps the sales force has been inadequately selected or trained. Perhaps competitors have a superior product.

3. *Identifying symptoms as problems.* "Our problem is a 32 percent decline in orders." While it is certainly true that orders have declined, the decline in or-

---

[8]David A. Cowan, "Developing a Classification Structure of Organizational Problems: An Empirical Investigation," *Academy of Management Journal,* June 1990, pp. 366–90.

[9]See G. P. Huber, *Managerial Decision Making* (Glenview, IL: Scott, Foresman, 1980).

ders is really a symptom of the real problem. When the manager identifies the real problem, the cause of the decline in orders will be found.

Problems usually are of three types: opportunity, crisis, or routine.[10] Crisis and routine problems present themselves and must be attended to by the managers. Opportunities, on the other hand, usually must be found. They await discovery, and they often go unnoticed and eventually are lost by an inattentive manager. This is because, by their very nature, most crises and routine problems demand immediate attention. Thus, a manager may spend more time in handling problems than in pursuing important new opportunities. Many well-managed organizations try to draw attention away from crises and routine problems and toward longer-range issues through planning activities and goal-setting programs.

Establishing Priorities

All problems are not created equal. Deciding whether to launch a new product in response to a competitor's move is probably a more significant decision than whether the employee lounge should be repainted. The process of decision making and solution implementation requires resources. Unless the resources the organization has at its disposal are unlimited, it is necessary to establish priorities-for dealing with problems. This, in turn, means being able to make a determination of the significance level of the problem. Determining problem significance involves consideration of three issues: urgency, impact, and growth tendency.

Urgency relates to time. How critical is the time pressure? Putting out a fire in the office is probably more urgent than fixing a stalled elevator. On the other hand, the elevator is likely to be more urgent than repairing a broken copier. The potential for stopgap measures also impacts urgency. For example, if there are people in the stalled elevator who can be released before the elevator is repaired, that reduces the urgency of making repairs. *Impact* describes the seriousness of the problem's effects. Effects may be on people, sales, equipment, profitability, public image, or any number of other organizational resources. Whether problem effects are short-term or long-term and whether the problem is likely to create other problems are also questions related to impact. *Growth tendency* addresses future considerations. Even though a problem may currently be of low urgency and have little impact, if allowed to go unattended it may grow. The decision to cut back on routine preventive maintenance of plant equipment as a cost-cutting measure may not create a significant problem immediately. Over time, however, major difficulties may arise.

The more significant the problem, as determined by its urgency, impact, and growth tendency, the more important it is that it be addressed. A critical part of effective decision making is determining problem significance.

Consideration of Causes

While not impossible, it is ordinarily difficult and ill-advised to determine a solution to a problem when the problem cause is unknown. The practice of bloodletting and the use of leeches are examples of solutions that formerly were applied to a variety of medical problems. If the causes of the medical conditions had

[10]Ian Palmer and Cynthia Hardy, *Thinking about Management* (Thousand Oaks, CA: Sage 2000).

been known, other solutions would have been implemented. If an organization wishes to address the problem of declining sales, how can it decide on an appropriate solution if it does not know the reason for the decline? If sales are falling because the product is no longer price competitive, possible solutions will be quite different than if it is due to poor service after the sale. Proper identification of causes helps the decision maker to avoid solving the wrong problem.[11]

Frequently, the search for problem causes leads to a better definition of the real problem. Causes can be turned into new—and better—problem statements. For example, a large metropolitan bank recently began to experience an increase in the number of customers who closed out their accounts. Defining the problem as "loss of accounts," the bank determined the cause was increased customer dissatisfaction with service. This cause then became the basis for a restatement of the original problem. In an effort to determine the cause of the restated problem, the bank contacted several former customers and learned they felt the tellers handling their transactions had gone from being friendly and pleasant to grumpy and irritable. Thus, this cause became the even better-defined problem: unfriendly tellers. The problem-to-cause-to-problem sequence was completed when it was determined that a poorly explained change in dress policy requiring all tellers to wear standard blazers was the *real* problem. It was easily addressed, and a special program for former customers who returned to the bank resulted in recouping virtually all the lost accounts.

Development of Alternative Solutions

Before a decision is made, feasible alternatives should be developed (actually these are potential solutions to the problem), and the potential consequences of each alternative should be considered. This is really a search process in which the relevant internal and external environments of the organization are investigated to provide information that can be developed into possible alternatives.[12] Obviously, this search is conducted within certain time and cost constraints, since only so much effort can be devoted to developing alternatives.

For example, a sales manager may identify an inadequately trained sales force as the cause of declining sales. The sales manager then would identify possible alternatives for solving the problem, such as (1) a sales training program conducted at the home office by management, (2) a sales training program conducted by a professional training organization at a site away from the home office, or (3) more intense on-the-job training.

Evaluation of Alternative Solutions

Once alternatives have been developed, they must be evaluated and compared. In every decision situation, the objective is to select the alternative that will produce the most favorable outcomes and the least unfavorable outcomes. This again points to the necessity of objectives and goals since, in selecting from among alternatives, the decision maker should be guided by the previously established

---

[11]J. M. Dukerich and M. L. Nichols, "Causal Information Search in Managerial Decision Making," *Organizational Behavior and Human Decision Processes,* October 1991, pp. 106–22.

[12]David B. Jamison, "The Importance of Boundary Spanning Roles in Strategic Decision Making," *Journal of Management Studies,* April 1984, pp. 131–52.

goals and objectives. The alternative-outcome relationship is based on three possible conditions:

1. *Certainty.* The decision maker has complete knowledge of the probability of the outcome of each alternative.
2. *Uncertainty.* The decision maker has absolutely no knowledge of the probability of the outcome of each alternative.
3. *Risk.* The decision maker has some probable estimate of the outcomes of each alternative.

Wouldn't it be wonderful if on a particular day early in the morning you knew for certain what the New York Stock Exchange was going to do that day? Knowing exactly what the future will be would lead to decisions about stock investments that would always optimize the results. Of course, certainty in most decision making at work, home, and in the stock market is not possible. There are more or less degrees of certainty.

The degree of certainty in decision making is expressed as a risk. When a decision maker lacks certainty about an outcome from a specific action (e.g., investment in a stock, receiving a promotion based on annual performance), there is a degree of risk. A probability expresses the degree of risk. For example, Amazon.com has not generated a profit since it opened its doors in 1994. Jeff Bezos, Amazon's CEO, expresses in specific terms that the firm will show a profit by 2002. There are some experts who are not as certain as Bezos. Some say that Amazon has a 50 percent or .5 probability of showing a profit by the end of 2002. That is, there is a risk or uncertainty factor associated with Amazon's belief of turning the profit corner.

Uncertain situations exist when managers have no or such little information that they are not able to even assign a probability to various decisions and their possible outcomes. By gathering information or studying a situation, the degree of uncertainty facing a decision maker can sometimes be reduced.

In a certainty situation, the decision maker has complete data, information, and confidence in the results of a decision he or she makes. In work organizations, having complete certainty is elusive. In most work situations, decision makers lack complete certainty but have some information and data to make decisions. This is the risk environment that is so common at work and in life. If a manager provides three subordinates with 5 percent merit raises, two subordinates with 2 percent merit raises, and three subordinates with no raises, there will be different employee responses. Predicting with certainty exactly how the eight employees will respond is impossible. The manager is operating with probabilities or risk regarding employee responses to the merit-based compensation decision.

James Papada, CEO and director of Technitrol, a producer of electronic components, leads his company in a manner that attempts to reduce uncertainty.[13] He believes that having no information or "compass" to make decisions is not acceptable. Papada wants his people to gather information, study markets and competitors, and make decisions that may involve risk but are not completely blind or uncertain. Technitrol, with 24,000 employees in 16 countries, understands that perfect certainty in decision making is not possible. However, as Papada illustrates by example, making decisions in a vacuum with

wwww.amazon.com

www.technitrol.com

---

[13]Christopher L. Tyner, "Technitrol's James Papada," *Investor's Business Daily*, September 7, 2000, p. A4.

no knowledge is unacceptable. Risk is a part of business; ignorance is a way to lose competitive advantages in the market.

In evaluating alternative solutions, two cautions should be kept in mind. First, it is critical that this phase of the decision-making process be kept separate and distinct from the previous step, identifying solutions. This is particularly true in a group decision-making context. When alternatives are evaluated as they are proposed, this may restrict the number of alternative solutions identified. If evaluations are positive, there may be a tendency to end the process prematurely by settling on the first positive solution. On the other hand, negative evaluations make it less likely for someone to risk venturing what may be an excellent solution for fear of being criticized or thought less of.

The second caution is to be wary of solutions that are evaluated as being "perfect." This is particularly true when the decision is being made under conditions of uncertainty. If a solution appears to have no drawbacks or if, in a group setting, there is unanimous agreement on a course of action, it may be useful to assign someone to take a devil's advocate position. The job of a devil's advocate is to be a thorough critic of the proposed solution. Research supports the benefits of devil's advocacy and the conflict a devil's advocate may cause, thus forcing a decision maker to reexamine assumptions and information.[14]

Solution Selection

The purpose of selecting a particular solution is to solve a problem in order to achieve a predetermined objective. This point is an extremely important one. It means that a decision is not an end in itself but only a means to an end. Although the decision maker chooses the alternative that is expected to result in the achievement of the objective, the selection of that alternative should not be an isolated act. If it is, the factors that led to and lead from the decision are likely to be excluded. Specifically, the steps following the decision should include implementation and follow-up. The critical point is that decision making is more than an act of choosing; it is a dynamic process.

Unfortunately for most managers, situations rarely exist in which one alternative achieves the desired objective without having some positive or negative impact on another objective. Situations often exist where two objectives cannot be optimized simultaneously. If one objective is *optimized*, the other is *suboptimized*. In a business organization, for example, if production is optimized, employee morale may be suboptimized, or vice versa. Or a hospital superintendent optimizes a short-run objective such as maintenance costs at the expense of a long-run objective such as high-quality patient care. Thus, the multiplicity of organizational objectives complicates the real world of the decision maker.

A situation could also exist where attainment of an organizational objective would be at the expense of a societal objective. The reality of such situations is seen clearly in the rise of ecology groups, environmentalists, and the consumerist movement. Apparently, these groups question the priorities (organizational as against societal) of certain organizational decision makers. In any case, whether an organizational objective conflicts with another organizational objective or

[14]R. A. Cosier and C. R. Schwenk, "Agreement and Thinking Alike: Ingredients for Poor Decisions," *Academy of Management Executive*, February 1990, pp. 69–74.

Reading 14.1

Agreement and Thinking Alike: Ingredients for Poor Decisions

with a societal objective, the values of the decision maker will strongly influence the alternative chosen.

In managerial decision making, optimal solutions often are impossible. This is because the decision maker cannot possibly know all of the available alternatives, the consequences of each alternative, and the probability of occurrence of these consequences.[15] Thus, rather than being an *optimizer*, the decision maker is a *satisfier*, selecting the alternative that meets an acceptable (satisfactory) standard.

Implementation

Any decision is little more than an abstraction if it is not implemented, and it must be effectively implemented in order to achieve the objective for which it was made. It is entirely possible for a "good" decision to be hurt by poor implementation. In this sense, implementation may be more important than the actual choice of the alternative.

Since, in most situations, implementing decisions involves people, the test of the soundness of a decision is the behavior of the people involved relative to the decision. While a decision may be technically sound, it can be undermined easily by dissatisfied subordinates. Subordinates cannot be manipulated in the same manner as other resources. Thus, a manager's job is not only to choose good solutions but also to transform such solutions into behavior in the organization. This is done by effectively communicating with the appropriate individuals and groups.[16]

Follow-Up

Effective management involves periodic measurements of results. Actual results are compared with planned results (the objective), and if deviations exist, changes must be made. Here again, we see the importance of measurable objectives. If such objectives do not exist, then there is no way to judge performance. If actual results do not match planned results, changes must be made in the solution chosen, in its implementation, or in the original objective if it is deemed unattainable. If the original objective must be revised, then the entire decision-making process will be reactivated. The important point is that once a decision is implemented, a manager cannot assume that the outcome will meet the original objective. Some system of control and evaluation is necessary to make sure the actual results are consistent with the results planned for when the decision was made.

Sometimes the result or outcome of a decision is unexpected or is perceived differently by different people, and dealing with this possibility is an important part of the follow-up phase in the decision process.

Alternatives to Rational Decision Making

Decision makers do not follow to the letter the decision-making process presented in Exhibit 14.2. Time pressures, incomplete information, limited human resources, and many other factors may impact the decision-making process.

---

[15]Paul Shrivastava and I. I. Mitroff, "Enhancing Organizational Research Utilization: The Role of Decision Makers' Assumptions," *Academy of Management Review*, January 1984, pp. 18–26.

[16]E. F. Harrison, *The Managerial Decision-Making Process* (Boston: Houghton-Mifflin, 1999).

March and Simon offered a descriptive approach that is described as the administrative decision-making model.[17] In this model decision makers are depicted as operating with incomplete information, being impacted by their cognitive abilities and by psychological and sociological factors. Managers who are faced with limitations and restrictions often use what is referred to as the **bounded rationality** approach. In this approach the decision makers are assumed to have a limited or incomplete view of the problems or opportunities facing them. The number of solutions that can be implemented is limited by the capabilities of the decision maker and the resources that are available. Since the information, data, and knowledge are not perfect, which decision is best is unknown.

In the bounded rationality approach, the following assumptions are made:

- Managers (decision makers) rarely have all the information they need or want.
- Decision makers are not aware of all possible alternatives and are not able to predict consequences.
- Early alternatives and solutions are quickly adopted because of constraints and limitations.
- The organization's goals constrain decision making.
- Conflicting goals of different constituents (e.g. employees, suppliers, customers, and boards) can restrict decisions, forcing a compromise solution.

These bounded rationality-type assumptions point to making decisions that are constrained, limited, but good enough. This type of decision is referred to as a "satisfying decision," that is, making a decision that is acceptable and good enough, but if everything were perfect might not be the optimal decision. Decision makers are satisfiers because of the circumstances and the need to move forward. For example, few people find their ideal, perfect, or optimal job. People need to earn a living, and, after what each considers to be a thorough search, a person takes an acceptable or good-enough offer. There is some degree of satisfying in almost all decisions that people make.

Southwest Airlines is a company that offers a no frills, typically on-time and competitively priced airfare. If a traveler wants an optimal experience with a good meal, refreshments, comfortable seating, and quietness, then Southwest is not the way to fly. A traveler (decision maker) would be satisfied by electing to travel Southwest, but he or she would not be making an optimal choice.

Managers sometimes simply make decisions based on a "gut" feeling or intuition.[18] An intuitive decision maker uses experience, self-confidence, and self-motivation to process information, data, and the environment or address a problem or opportunity. Intuitive decision making involves an unconscious process that incorporates the decision maker's personality and experience in reaching a decision. Intuitive decision making occurs frequently because:

- High levels of uncertainty about a problem, the goals, and the decision criteria can exist.
- In some situations there is no history or past experience to draw upon.
- Time pressures are intense.
- An excessive number of alternatives can be difficult to thoroughly analyze.

---

[17]James G. March and Herbert A. Simon, *Organizations* (New York: Wiley, 1958).

[18]W. H. Igor, *Intuition in Organizations* (Newburg Park, CA: Sage, 1989).

These factors suggest that when uncertainty is high, time pressures are bearing down, and complexity exists, intuitive decision making is likely to be involved. The rational and administrative explanation of decision making are appealing because there is some logic and system associated with these processes.[19] However, in chaotic, rapidly changing, and pressure-packed situations, there is likely to be a lot of intuitive decision making taking place. Perhaps it is best to combine the more systematic and intuitive approaches when attempting to reach decisions.[20]

BEHAVIORAL INFLUENCES ON DECISION MAKING

A number of behavioral factors influence any decision-making process (e.g. rational, administrative, intuitive). Some of these factors influence only certain aspects of the process, while others influence the entire process. However, each may have an impact and, therefore, must be understood to fully appreciate decision making as a process in organizations. Four behavioral factors—values, propensity for risk, potential for dissonance, and escalation of commitment—are discussed in this section. Each of these factors has been shown to have significant impact on the decision-making process.

Values

Exercise 14.1

How Biased is Your Decision Making?

In the context of decision making, **values** can be thought of as the guidelines a person uses when confronted with a situation in which a choice must be made. Values are acquired early in life and are a basic (often taken for granted) part of an individual's thoughts. The influence of values on the decision-making process is profound:

> In *establishing objectives*, it is necessary to make value judgments regarding the selection of opportunities and the assignment of priorities.
>
> In *developing alternatives*, it is necessary to make value judgments about the various possibilities.
>
> In *choosing an alternative*, the values of the decision maker influence which alternative is chosen.
>
> In *implementing a decision*, value judgments are necessary in choosing the means for implementation.
>
> In the *evaluation and control* phase, value judgments cannot be avoided when corrective action is taken.

It is clear that values pervade the decision-making process. As one example, consider the issue of ethics in decision making. An ethical decision can be viewed as one that is legal and morally acceptable to society; an unethical decision is either illegal or morally unacceptable.[21] To a large extent, a decision maker's willingness to make ethical or unethical decisions will be influenced by his or her val-

---

[19]Orlando Behling and N. L. Ecker, "Making Sense out of Intuition," *Academy of Management Executive,* February 1991, pp. 46–47.

[20]S. Shapiro and M. T. Spence, "Managerial Intuition: A Conceptual and Operational Framework," *Business Horizons,* January–February 1997, pp. 63–68.

[21]T. M. Jones, "Ethical Decision Making by Individuals in Organizations: An Issue-Contingent Model," *Academy of Management Review,* April 1991, pp. 366–95.

Ethics and the Challenger Decision

You Be the Judge

Millions of Americans of all ages watched the live TV presentation of the launch of the space shuttle Challenger on January 28, 1986. Less than two minutes after lift-off, the Challenger exploded. All seven crew members perished. In hindsight, it became clear that the launch should have been canceled. The issue we are examining here is, was it as clear before the launch? Consider the following:

During the evening before the launch, a teleconference took place between representatives of Morton Thiokol (manufacturer of the booster rocket), the Marshall Space Flight Center (MSFC), and the Kennedy Space Center. Morton Thiokol engineers expressed concern about the integrity of the O-ring seals at temperatures below 53 degrees (temperatures at the launch site were below freezing). The Thiokol senior engineer concluded that the data supported a no-launch decision. The director of space engineering at the MSFC indicated that he was "appalled" by the Thiokol recommendation but would not launch over the contractor's objections. At that point, the MSFC chief of solid rockets gave his view, concluding that the data presented were inconclusive.

Based on NASA's rule that contractors had to prove it was safe to fly, the statement that the data were inconclusive should have stopped the launch. However, a Thiokol vice president who was also on the line requested an off-line caucus to re-evaluate the data. During the caucus, two engineers attempted to make themselves heard as management representatives began a discussion. Their attempts were met with cold stares as management representatives struggled to compile data that would support a launch decision. Returning to the teleconference, the Thiokol VP read a launch support rationale and recommended that it proceed.

NASA, for its part, accepted the recommendation without any discussion. It was consistent with their desires. Several delays had already taken place and they feared a loss of public and political interest. Besides, the president was giving his State of the Union address that evening and surely the launch would get a favorable mention.

What is your opinion on the ethics of the decision? Recall that the text defines an ethical decision as one that is both legally and morally acceptable to society.

Source: M. P. Miceli and J. P. Near, "Whistleblowing: Reaping the Benefits," *Academy of Management Executive,* August 1994, pp. 65–72; R. March, C. Stubbart, V. Traub, and M. Cavanaugh, "The NASA Space Shuttle Disaster: A Case Study," *Journal of Management Case Studies,* Winter 1987, pp. 300–18; and G. Whyte, "Decision Failures: Why They Occur and How to Prevent Them," *Academy of Management Executive,* August 1991, pp. 23–31.

ues. Well-publicized scandals involving Wall Street insider trading, the savings and loan industry, defense contractor overcharges, the Iran-Contra affair, and many others have heightened awareness of the critical role values play in decision making. You Be the Judge presents another powerful example.

Ethical scandals continue to gain the public's attention. There are ethical problems in health care, the legal profession, government, and business organizations. The scandals are global.[22] Why do some individual decision makers in every profession, occupation, and country resort to unethical choices? Philosophers and social scientists have studied this problem and found that no one set of explanations apply to all cases.

---

[22]R. T. DeGeorge, *Business Ethics* (Old Tappan, NJ: Prentice-Hall, 1999).

Some of the most cited explanations of why decision makers still make unethical choices include:

- They feel pressure to perform exceptionally well. This pressure to produce top-level results (financially) is continuous.
- They think since everyone else is doing it, so must they to remain competitive. This is the keeping-up-with-the-Jones explanation.
- The practice of being secretive and nonrevealing is considered important in some organizations. This results in the practice of stonewalling or willingly hiding or holding on to relevant data and information. Examples of hiding research and survey information include Dow Corning's silicone gel used in breast implant studies, Ford Pinto's rear gas tank defect problems (resulting in explosions and deaths), and B.F. Goodrich's rewarding employees who falsified and withheld data on the quality of aircraft brakes.
- They fail to take responsibility for problems.
- They focus on cost before safety when there is a choice.

Improving the record of making ethical decisions is difficult.[23] Values are difficult to change. Some of the efforts used to promote ethical decision making focus on training, preparation of a code of ethics, having top executives serve as proactive role models, and personally examining the situation or decision to be made. When examining the situation, the decision maker should consider doing what is legal, doing what is right, being fair, and answering the question, "Could the decision meet the 'sunshine' test," or "if it is published in the newspaper, would the reader consider the decision ethical?"

Ethical decision making starts with the values that guide an individual's decision making. There are no simple prescriptions, but there are right, fair, honest, and open ways of making decisions. Many decisions have an ethical dimension that requires thought, reflection, caution, and attention.[24] Considering the rights of others, adhering to strong values, and living up to high standards of behavior are the starting points for facing inevitable ethical dilemmas when making decisions.

Propensity for Risk

From personal experience, you undoubtedly are aware that decision makers vary greatly in their propensity for taking risks. This one specific aspect of personality strongly influences the decision-making process. A decision maker who has a low aversion to risk will establish different objectives, evaluate alternatives differently, and select different alternatives than will another decision maker in the same situation who has a high aversion to risk. The latter will attempt to make choices where the risk or uncertainty is low or where the certainty of the outcome is high. You will see later in the chapter that many people are bolder and more innovative and advocate greater risk taking in groups than as individuals. Apparently, such people are more willing to accept risk as members of a group.

[23]Linda K. Trevino, G. P. Weaver, D. G. Gibson, and B. L. Toffler, "Managing Ethics and Legal Compliance: What Works and What Hurts," *California Management Review,* Winter 1999, pp. 131–51.

[24]Dawn-Marie Driscoll and W. Michael Hoffman, *Ethics Matters: How to Implement Values-Driven Management* (Waltham, MA: Bentley College Press, 2000).

Risk propensity is also affected by whether potential outcomes are characterized in terms of losses or gains. This, in turn, depends on how the decision maker "frames" the decision. *Framing* refers to the decision maker's perception, in terms of gains or losses, of the decision's possible outcomes.[25] When the choice is perceived as being between losses, there is a greater propensity to take risks than when it is perceived as being between gains. For example, when a large number of individuals are confronted with the choice of losing $100 for certain or taking a gamble on a coin flip with an equal expected value (i.e., if it comes up heads you lose $200; if it comes up tails you lose nothing), most people will choose the gamble. On the other hand, when confronted with the choice between a certain gain of $100 or a coin flip with an equal expected value (heads you receive $200; tails you receive nothing), most people opt for the certain $100.

Potential for Dissonance

Much attention has been focused on the forces and influences affecting the decision maker before a decision is made and on the decision itself. But only recently has attention been given to what happens *after* a decision has been made. Specifically, behavioral scientists have focused attention on the occurrence of postdecision anxiety.

Such anxiety is related to what Festinger calls cognitive dissonance.[26] Festinger's **cognitive dissonance** theory states that there is often a lack of consistency or harmony among an individual's various cognitions (attitudes, beliefs, and so on) after a decision has been made. That is, there will be a conflict between what the decision maker knows and believes and what was done, and as a result the decision maker will have doubts and second thoughts about the choice that was made. In addition, there is a likelihood that the intensity of the anxiety will be greater when any of the following conditions exist:

1. The decision is an important one psychologically or financially.
2. There are a number of foregone alternatives.
3. The foregone alternatives have many favorable features.

Each of these conditions is present in many decisions in all types of organizations. You can expect, therefore, that postdecision dissonance will be present among many decision makers, especially those at higher levels in the organization.

When dissonance occurs, it can, of course, be reduced by admitting that a mistake has been made. Unfortunately, many individuals are reluctant to admit they have made a wrong decision and will be more likely to use one or more of the following methods to reduce their dissonance:

1. Seek information that supports the wisdom of their decision.
2. Selectively perceive (distort) information in a way that supports their decision.
3. Adopt a less favorable view of the foregone alternatives.
4. Minimize the importance of the negative aspects of the decision and exaggerate the importance of the positive aspects.

---

[25]Glen Whyte, "Decision Failures: Why They Occur and How to Prevent Them," *Academy of Management Executive,* August 1991, pp. 23–31.

[26]Leon Festinger, *A Theory of Cognitive Dissonance* (New York: Harper & Row, 1957), Chap. 1.

Case 14.1

An Ethical Dilemma At Bridgestone/Firestone and Ford Motors

While each of us may resort to some of this behavior in our personal decision making, it is easy to see how a great deal of it could be extremely harmful in terms of organizational effectiveness. The potential for dissonance is influenced heavily by one's personality, specifically one's self-confidence and ability to be persuaded. In fact, all of the behavioral influences are closely interrelated and are only isolated here for purposes of discussion.[27] For example, what kind of a risk taker you are and your potential for anxiety following a decision are very closely related, and both are strongly influenced by your personality, your perceptions, and your value system. Before managers can fully understand the dynamics of the decision-making process, they must appreciate the behavioral influences on themselves and other decision makers in the organization when they make decisions.

www.siebel.com

Siebel Systems understands dissonance well and has a policy and process of decision making that in order to maintain focus and avoid second-guessing, decisiveness must take precedence. Tom Siebel, CEO, has perpetuated a style and process of decision making that centers on what he calls "clean" and decisive decisions. Good or bad, popular or unpopular, once a decision is made, the entire strength of the firm is behind it, and decisions are implemented within 90 days. There's no second-guessing or doubts. At the 90-day mark, Siebel resets the agenda and may find that the decision was wrong, but that is accepted as part of decision making.[28]

By *clean,* Siebel decision makers mean fast, firm, and no second-guessing. The company has grown to 6,000 professionals in 30 countries with annual revenues of over $1.5 billion. Siebel believes that professionalism, no second-guessing, a strong work ethic, and luck are responsible for a greater than 100% compound annual growth rate (CAGR). Cognitive dissonance is resisted at Siebel, and the results have been phenomenal.

Escalation of Commitment

Gamblers who place larger and larger wagers in an effort to recoup earlier losses are displaying a decision-making behavior called *escalation of commitment.* Decision makers who are unclear of their goals, have a fear of failure, are feeling pressure, and work in a culture with low trust are likely to be candidates for escalation of decision making. **Escalation of commitment** refers to an increasing commitment to a previous decision when a "rational" decision maker would withdraw.[29] It typically results from a need to turn a losing or poor decision into a winning or good decision. Examples of escalation of commitment abound in daily life. President Lyndon Johnson's decision to continue increasing U.S. troop involvement in the Vietnam war is a frequently cited example. The savings and loan crisis of the 1980s grew out of decisions made by loan officers to make increasingly riskier loans in an escalating effort to recoup losses resulting from previous poor loan decisions. The decision made by Bureau of Alcohol, Tobacco, and Firearms agents to move forward with the raid on the heavily armed Branch Dividian compound outside Waco, Texas, appears to have been an example of escalation of commitment.

---

[27]Richard Harrison and James G. March, "Decision Making and Post-Decision Surprises," *Administrative Science Quarterly,* March 1984, pp. 26–42.

[28]Thomas M. Siebel, "Cyberhouse Rules," *Forbes ASAP,* November 27, 2000, pp. 97–98.

[29]Barry Staw and his associates have done much of the work in this area. See, for example, Barry M. Staw, "The Escalation of Commitment to a Course of Action," *Academy of Management Review,* October 1981, pp. 577–87.

A particularly interesting example occurred several years ago when Robert Campeau, head of Campeau Corporation, began a hostile takeover bid for Federated Department Stores, owner of Bloomingdales, among other retail chains. Macy's, led by Edward Finkelstein, also wanted Federated. The resulting bidding war became personal. Ego, rather than economic rationality, drove the bidding, with Campeau becoming committed to winning the deal at any cost. He indeed did win the bidding war, but the price led Campeau Corporation into bankruptcy as the price of Campeau stock fell from a high of $26 a share before the bidding to $1 a share a year after the takeover.

Escalation of commitment can result, as it did in Campeau's case, from becoming too ego-involved in a decision process. Because failure is threatening to an individual's self-esteem, people tend to ignore negative information. It can also be the result of peer pressure which makes it difficult for a decision maker to reverse a course of action he or she has publicly supported in the past. In either case, it involves loss of objectivity in the decision-making process.

An area in which escalation of commitment is noticeable is among venture capitalists pouring money into start-up Internet companies. From 1998 through the summer of 2000, over $65 billion has been provided to Internet companies. Jay Hoag, a partner of a Palo Alto venture capital firm Technology Crossover, has had successes and failures.[30] Petopia, a "pet portal," was one of Jay's projects. Round after round of financing was provided to Petopia. He admits that he should have backed off, but he feared losing an Internet winner. He stayed in with investments long after he should have backed out.

www.tcv.com

Petopia never achieved its milestones. Now he realizes that operating a pet store online presents obstacles not found in a brick and mortar store. For example, pet food, which accounts for more than 50 percent of all pet product sales, weighs a lot, so shipping it is expensive. Many pet products cost more to ship than customers are willing to pay for them. Hoag is an example of escalating his commitment because of ego, fear of failing, and pressures from other firms wanting to be part of a "get rich quick" deal.

It should be noted that each of the behavioral influences we have just discussed—values, propensity for risk, potential for dissonance, and escalation of commitment—are influenced by the culture to which the decision maker has been exposed as well as the cultural context in which the decision is being made. As organizational decision making transcends national boundaries, cultural influences—and differences—become increasingly significant. Many cultural differences affect decision making. Organizational Encounter 14.2 provides some examples.

GROUP DECISION MAKING

The first parts of this chapter focused on individuals making decisions. In most organizations, however, a great deal of decision making is achieved through committees, teams, task forces, and other kinds of groups.[31] This is because managers frequently face situations in which they must seek and combine judgments in

---

[30]Melanie Warner, "Fallen Idols," *Fortune*, October 30, 2000, pp. 108–21.

[31]H. W. Crott, K. Szilvas, and J. A. Zuber, "Group Decision, Choice Shift, and Polarization in Consulting, Political, and Local Political Scenarios: An Experimental Investigation and Theoretical Analysis," *Organizational Behavior and Human Decision Processes*, June 1991, pp. 22–41.

Making Decisions in Diverse Cultures

Organizational decision making in the United States is presumed to be based on thorough and objective analysis of relevant information. Whether this is true in actual practice is arguable, but it does represent what is supposed to happen "ideally." This is not the ideal in every society, however. In some countries, it is inappropriate for senior executives to consult subordinates before making a decision; in other countries it is equally inappropriate for them not to consult subordinates. In almost every aspect of decision making, different cultural norms dictate different ways of proceeding. A few examples:

1. In some cultures (United States, for example), problems are more likely to be seen as requiring solutions, whereas in others (Thailand, for example), problems are more likely to be seen as situations requiring acceptance.
2. Americans value following the chain of command during the decision-making process. Swedes, on the other hand, will willingly go around or over someone in the chain if doing so is helpful to the decision process. Such behavior would be viewed as inappropriate in American organizations and perfectly acceptable in Swedish ones.
3. Italians, who value tradition and history, will tend to adopt tried and proven solutions to current problems. Australians are more present oriented—and more aggressive—and are more likely to try unique and innovative alternative solutions.
4. Germans tend to process their decisions through committees, frequently composed primarily of technical experts. The French, who tend to be highly centralized, would not likely use committees.
5. In high power-distance cultures like India, decisions are made at the highest level of the organization. In a low power-distance culture like Sweden, on the other hand, the lowest-level employees expect to make their own decisions.

The differences between Japanese and American management practices are often subjects of debate and discussion. Decision making is a part of management practice, and many differences in the decision-making process exist between these two countries. For example, the Japanese are much more consensus oriented than are Americans. Japanese decision making is often described by the word *nemawaski*, which means "root-binding." Each employee has a sense of running the organization because nothing gets done until everyone agrees. Many—if not most—American managers would find this approach frustrating and agonizingly slow. Japanese are also likely to spend much more time on deciding if there is even a need for a decision and on what the decision is about than their American counterparts. Because of this, they tend to direct their attention to major decisions, in contrast to American managers who often focus (by Japanese thinking) on minutia.

These, and other, examples help illustrate the many cultural variations in decision making. They also explain why cross-cultural decision making can be so very difficult.

group meetings. This is especially true for nonprogrammed problems, which are novel and have much uncertainty regarding the outcome. In most organizations, it is unusual to find decisions being made on such problems by one individual on a regular basis.

The increased complexity of many nonprogrammed decisions requires specialized knowledge in numerous fields, usually not possessed by one person. This requirement, coupled with the reality that the decisions made eventually must be accepted and implemented by many units throughout the organization, has increased the use of the collective approach to the decision-making process. Compaq Computer Corporation, the highly successful Houston-based personal computer manufacturer, attributes much of its success to the fact that group decision making permeates the entire organization. Group decision making at Compaq is practiced from the executive suite to (and including) the assembly line. Many companies, including General Electric, Ameritech, and GTE, are training managers to work in groups to solve problems.[32] The increasing use of self-directed teams, noted elsewhere in the text, also means that more group-based decision making is taking place.

Individual versus Group Decision Making

Considerable debate has occurred over the relative effectiveness of individual versus group decision making. Groups usually take more time to reach a decision than individuals do. But bringing together individual specialists and experts has its benefits since the mutually reinforcing impact of their interaction results in better decisions. In fact, a great deal of research has shown that consensus decisions with five or more participants are superior to individual decision making, majority vote, and leader decisions. Unfortunately, open discussion has been found to be negatively influenced by such behavioral factors as the pressure to conform; the influence of a dominant personality type in the group; "status incongruity," as a result of which lower-status participants are inhibited by higher-status participants and "go along," even though they believe that their own ideas are superior; and the attempt of certain participants to influence others because these participants are perceived to be experts in the problem area.[33] Additionally, framing effects occur more frequently in groups.[34]

Certain decisions appear to be better made by groups, while others appear better suited to individual decision making. Nonprogrammed decisions appear to be better suited to group decision making. Usually calling for pooled talent, the decisions are so important that they are frequently made by top management and, to a somewhat lesser extent, by middle managers.

In terms of the decision-making process itself, the following points concerning group processes for nonprogrammed decisions can be made:

1. In *establishing goals and objectives,* groups probably are superior to individuals because of the greater amount of knowledge available to groups.

2. In *identifying causes and developing alternative solutions,* the individual efforts of group members are necessary to ensure a broad search in the various functional areas of the organization.

3. In *evaluating alternative solutions,* the collective judgment of the group, with its wider range of viewpoints, seems superior to that of the individual decision maker.

4. In *solution selection,* it has been shown that group interaction and the achievement of consensus usually results in the acceptance of more risk than would be accepted by an individual decision maker. In any event, the group decision is more likely to be accepted as a result of the participation of those affected by its consequences.

---

[32]"Bye-Bye Smarties?" *Fortune,* August 22, 1994, p. 18.

[33]Richard A. Guzzo and James A. Waters, "The Expression of Affect and the Performance of Decision-Making Groups," *Journal of Applied Psychology,* February 1982, pp. 67–74; D. Tjosvold and R. H. G. Field, "Effects of Social Context on Consensus and Majority Vote Decision Making," *Academy of Management Journal,* September 1983, pp. 500–06; and Frederick C. Miner, Jr., "Group versus Individual Decision Making: An Investigation of Performance Measures, Decision Strategies and Process Losses/Gains," *Organizational Behavior and Human Decision Processes,* Winter 1984, pp. 112–24.

[34]Glen Whyte, "Escalating Commitment in Individual and Group Decision Making: A Prospect Theory Approach," *Organizational Behavior and Human Decision Processes,* April 1993, pp. 430–55.

EXHIBIT 14.3
Probable Relationship between Quality of Group Decision and Method Utilized

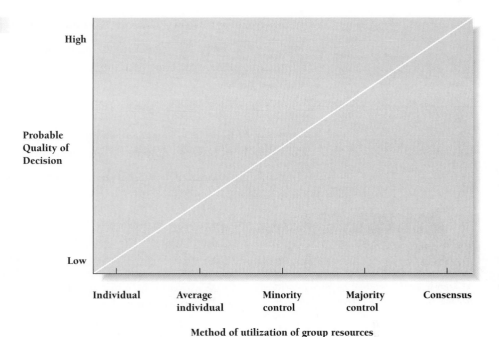

Method of utilization of group resources

5. *Implementation and follow-up* of a decision, whether or not made by a group, usually is accomplished by individual managers. Thus, since a group ordinarily is not responsible, the responsibility for implementation and follow-up necessarily rests with the individual manager.

Exhibit 14.3 summarizes the research on group decision making. It presents the relationship between the probable quality of a decision and the method utilized to reach the decision. It indicates that, as we move from "individual" to "consensus," the quality of the decision improves. Note also that each successive method involves a higher level of mutual influence by group members. Thus, for a complex problem requiring pooled knowledge, the quality of the decision is likely to be higher as the group moves toward achieving consensus.[35] The final section of the chapter examines ways to increase creativity in group decision making. Before progressing, however, examine the Management Pointer 14.1, which presents some techniques to increase your individual creativity.

Creativity in Group Decision Making

Since most decisions involve some degree of risk, there is a need for creativity to solve problems and seize opportunities. **Creativity** is a process by which an individual, group, or team produces novel and useful ideas to solve a problem or capture an opportunity. In organizations, moving away from logical, linear, or "in the box" thinking describes creativity. This is called *lateral thinking* or a process of generating novel ways to solve problems faced by an individual or group.

---

[35]S. Plous, *The Psychology of Judgement and Decision Making* (New York: McGraw-Hill, 1993).

Creative decision makers share some common characteristics such as:

- *Perseverance.* They stay longer attacking problems.
- *Risk-taking propensity.* They take moderate to high risks and stay away from extreme risks.
- *Openness.* They are open to new experiences and are willing to try new approaches.
- *Tolerance of ambiguity.* They can tolerate a lack of structure, some lack of clarity, and not having complete information, data, and answers.

www.ebay.com

These characteristics of creative individuals fit many of the popular stars of the general press, including Jack Welch (General Electric), Bill Gates (Microsoft), Carly Fiorina (Hewlett-Packard), and Herb Kelleher (Southwest Airlines). Their background and creativity characteristics are cited quite often. One less publicized, yet creative decision maker who personifies perseverance, risk taking, openness, and an ability to deal with ambiguity is Meg Whitman. She worked at Procter & Gamble, Barn & Co., and Disney searching for her ideal job.[36]

Meg Whitman joined FTD (flowers) as CEO and kept learning and making what colleagues call fast and no-nonsense decisions. She took an opportunity at eBay when it was somewhat of a maze of conflict, uncertainty, and risk. Whitman was open to ideas, withstood unrelenting criticisms for her decisions, and stuck to her plan. When the eBay system crashed and service was turned off, Whitman jumped in and corrected the problems. She persevered and creatively helped eBay achieve unheard-of success. She took risks, became wealthy, and serves as an example of an unrecognized (by most people) leader, serving as a role model and as a creative decision maker.[37]

Groups and teams have more creative potential than individuals such as Meg Whitman. This is especially true when the task is complex and novel and there is uncertainty. Groups also have creative potential because of possessing combined expertise, resources, and experience.

If groups are better suited to nonprogrammed decisions than individuals are, then an atmosphere fostering group creativity must be created. In this respect, group decision making may be similar to brainstorming in that discussion must be free-flowing and spontaneous. All group members must participate, and the evaluation of individual ideas must be suspended in the beginning to encourage participation. However, a decision must be reached, and this is where group decision making differs from brainstorming.

Management Pointer 14.1

INCREASING YOUR CREATIVITY

As knowledge/information-based organizations become the norm, it is becoming clear that creativity is a competence that these organizations need. The real value in organizations such as Microsoft, Hitachi, Compaq, and Kodak are not in their physical assets but in their intellectual assets—the ideas and insights in the minds of their employees. Such organizations cannot survive without creativity and are discovering that it is a skill that can be developed. Here are some tips for becoming more creative.

1. Get out of the office. A walk in the park or a trip to a toy store may be more productive than sitting at your desk with a pencil and pad.

2. Be childlike. Some believe this is the most important tip because creativity seems to be connected with age.

3. Be a maverick. The best ideas and decisions often come from those who don't care what others are thinking or how they are doing things.

4. Sit on the other side of the room. Break your routine, drive to work a different way.

5. Ask "What if . . .?" This question can stimulate thought for you and plenty of discussion in a group.

6. Listen. No one has a monopoly on good ideas. Ask others, and listen.

Techniques for Stimulating Creativity

It seems safe to say that, in many instances, group decision making is preferable to individual decision making. But we have all heard the statement, "A camel is

---

[36]Patricia Sellers, "These Women Rule," *Fortune,* October 25, 1999, pp. 94–134.

[37]Rochelle Sharpe, "As Leaders, Women Rule," *Business Week,* November 30, 2000, pp. 75–84.

a racehorse designed by a committee." Thus, while the necessity and the benefits of group decision making are recognized, numerous problems also are associated with it, some of which already have been noted. Practicing managers are in need of specific techniques that will enable them to increase the benefits from group decision making while reducing the problems associated with it.

We shall examine three techniques that, when properly utilized, have been found to be extremely useful in increasing the creative capability of a group in generating ideas, understanding problems, and reaching better decisions. Increasing the creative capability of a group is especially necessary when individuals from diverse sectors of the organization must pool their judgments and create a satisfactory course of action for the organization. The three techniques are known as brainstorming, the Delphi technique, and the nominal group technique.

Brainstorming   In many situations, groups are expected to produce creative or imaginative solutions to organizational problems. In such instances, *brainstorming* often has been found to enhance the creative output of the group. The technique of brainstorming includes a strict series of rules. The purpose of the rules is to promote the generation of ideas while, at the same time, avoiding the inhibitions of members that usually are caused by face-to-face groups. The basic rules are:

> No idea is too ridiculous. Group members are encouraged to state any extreme or outlandish idea.
>
> Each idea presented belongs to the group, not to the person stating it. In this way, it is hoped that group members will utilize and build on the ideas of others.
>
> No idea can be criticized. The purpose of the session is to generate, not evaluate, ideas.

Brainstorming is widely used in advertising where it apparently is effective. In some other situations it has been less successful because there is no evaluation or ranking of the ideas generated. Thus, the group never really concludes the problem-solving process.

The Delphi Technique   This technique involves the solicitation and comparison of anonymous judgments on the topic of interest through a set of sequential questionnaires that are interspersed with summarized information and feedback of opinions from earlier responses.[38]

The **Delphi process** retains the advantage of having several judges while removing the biasing effects that might occur during face-to-face interaction. The basic approach has been to collect anonymous judgments by mail questionnaires. For example, the members independently generate their ideas to answer the first questionnaire and return it. The staff members summarize the responses as the group consensus and feed this summary back along with a second questionnaire for reassessment. Based on this feedback, the respondents independently evaluate their earlier responses. The underlying belief is that the consensus estimate will result in a better decision after several rounds of anonymous group judgment. While it is possible to continue the procedure for several rounds, studies have shown essentially no significant change after the second round of estimation.

---

[38]Norman Dalkey, *The Delphi Method: An Experimental Study of Group Opinion* (Santa Monica, CA: Rand Corporation, 1969). This is a classic work on the Delphi methods.

The Nominal Group Technique (NGT)   NGT has gained increasing recognition in health, social service, education, industry, and government organizations.[39] The term **nominal group technique** was adopted by earlier researchers to refer to processes that bring people together but do not allow them to communicate verbally. Thus, the collection of people is a group "nominally," or in name only. You will see, however, that NGT in its present form combines both verbal and nonverbal stages.

Basically, NGT is a structured group meeting that proceeds as follows: A group of individuals (7 to 10) sit around a table but do not speak to one another. Rather, each person writes ideas on a pad of paper. After five minutes, a structured sharing of ideas takes place. Each person around the table presents one idea. A person designated as recorder writes the ideas on a flip chart in full view of the entire group. This continues until all of the participants indicate that they have no further ideas to share. There is still no discussion.

The output of this phase is a list of ideas (usually between 18 and 25). The next phase involves structured discussion in which each idea receives attention before a vote is taken. This is achieved by asking for clarification or stating the degree of support for each idea listed on the flip chart. The next stage involves independent voting in which each participant, in private, selects priorities by ranking or voting. The group decision is the mathematically pooled outcome of the individual votes. The NGT is illustrated in Exhibit 14.4.

Both the Delphi technique and NGT have had an excellent record of successes. Basic differences between them are:

1. Delphi participants typically are anonymous to one another, while NGT participants become acquainted.
2. NGT participants meet face-to-face around the table, while Delphi participants are physically distant and never meet face-to-face.
3. In the Delphi process, all communication between participants is by way of written questionnaires and feedback from the monitoring staff. In NGT, communication is direct between participants.[40]

Practical considerations, of course, often influence which technique is used. For example, such factors as the number of working hours available, costs, and the physical proximity of participants will influence which technique is selected.

Our discussion here has not been designed to make the reader an expert in the Delphi process or NGT. Our purpose throughout this section has been to indicate the frequency and importance of group decision making in every type of organization. The three techniques discussed are practical devices whose purpose is to improve the effectiveness of group decisions.

Decision making is a common responsibility shared by all executives, regardless of functional area or management level. Every day, managers are required to make decisions that shape the future of their organization as well as their own futures. The quality of these decisions is the yardstick of the managers' effectiveness. Some of these decisions may have a strong impact on the organization's success, while others will be important but less crucial. However, all of the decisions will have some effect (positive or negative, large or small) on the organization.

---

[39]See Andre L. Delbecq, Andrew H. Van de Ven, and David H. Gustafson, *Group Techniques for Program Running* (Glenview, IL: Scott, Foresman, 1975). The discussion here is based on this work.
[40]Ibid., p. 18.

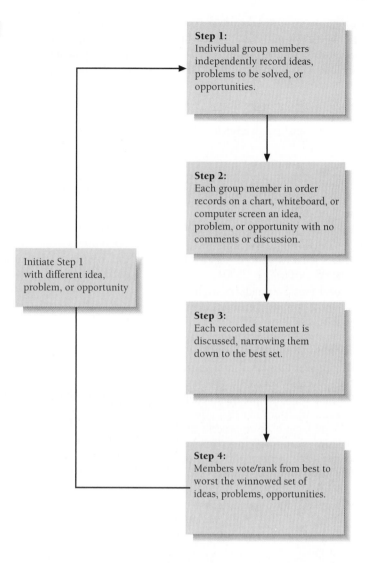

EXHIBIT 14.4
Four-Step Nominal Group Technique

Step 1:
Individual group members independently record ideas, problems to be solved, or opportunities.

Step 2:
Each group member in order records on a chart, whiteboard, or computer screen an idea, problem, or opportunity with no comments or discussion.

Step 3:
Each recorded statement is discussed, narrowing them down to the best set.

Step 4:
Members vote/rank from best to worst the winnowed set of ideas, problems, opportunities.

Initiate Step 1 with different idea, problem, or opportunity

Summary of Key Points

- Decisions may be classified as programmed or nonprogrammed, depending on the type of problem. Decisions are *programmed* to the extent that they are repetitive and routine and a definite procedure has been developed for handling the problem. Decisions are *nonprogrammed* when they are novel and unstructured and there is no established procedure for handling the problem.

- Because not all problems are of the same importance, it is necessary to prioritize them. How significant a problem is depends on at least three problem attributes: urgency, impact, and growth tendency. *Urgency* relates to time and how critical time pressures are in dealing with a problem. *Impact* describes the seriousness of the problem's effects. *Growth tendency* addresses the likelihood of future changes in problem urgency or impact.

- The relationship between alternatives and outcomes is based on three possible conditions. *Certainty* exists when the decision maker has complete knowledge of the probability of the outcome of each alternative. *Uncertainty* exists when absolutely no such knowledge is available. *Risk* is an intermediate condition, wherein some probable estimate of outcomes can be made.

- The decision-making process entails following a number of steps. Sequentially, these are: (1) establishing specific goals and objectives and measuring results, (2) problem identification and definition, (3) establishing priorities, (4) consideration of causes, (5) development of alternative solutions, (6) evaluation of alternative solutions, (7) solution selection, (8) implementation, and (9) follow-up.

- The decision-making process is influenced by behavioral factors. Different decision makers may behave differently at any step in the decision-making process. Behavioral factors include values, propensity for risk, potential for dissonance, and escalation of commitment.

- Research suggests that decisions made by groups are superior to those made by individuals. However, there are aspects of group decision making that tend to have negative effects. These include pressure to conform and the disproportionate influence exerted by a dominant group member.

- One of the advantages of group decision making is that it can facilitate the identification of creative and innovative solutions to problems. Three specific techniques for stimulating creativity in groups are brainstorming, the nominal group technique, and the Delphi process.

Review and Discussion Questions

1. How much risk can you tolerate in deciding how to be successful in your career?

2. Why is it important to establish priorities among different problems? Under what conditions might it be necessary to reevaluate priorities?

3. Increasingly today, decisions are made in a global context. Can you think of some techniques that might be employed to reduce the likelihood of difficulties when decision makers from different cultures are working together to solve a problem?

4. How do you cope with cognitive dissonance after making decisions? Are you successful? By what criteria?

5. Think of a reasonably important nonprogrammed decision you have made recently. Did you employ an approach similar to the decision-making process outlined in Exhibit 14.2? How good was your decision? Could it have been improved by using the decision-making process? Explain.

6. How important a role should ethics play in decision making? Should managers—and organizations—be evaluated on the extent to which they make ethical decisions?

7. What role does personality play in decision making? Can you think of an example from your own experience where the personality of a decision maker clearly influenced his or her decision?

8. Creativity requires nonconformity of thinking. Does that explain why so many organizational decisions are noncreative? Aside from the specific techniques discussed in the chapter, what can be done to stimulate creative decision making in an organization?

9. Bounded rationality appears to be a better explanation of how decision making actually occurs. What makes this better than a rational explanation of decision making?

10. "Decisions should be thought of as means rather than ends." Explain what this statement means and what effect it should have on decision making.

READING 14.1   Agreement and Thinking Alike: Ingredients for Poor Decisions

Richard A. Cosier, Indiana University
Charles R. Schwenk, Indiana University

EXECUTIVE OVERVIEW

People frequently believe that conflict is to be avoided in organizations. They think that meetings and decisions should reflect agreement and consensus. This article suggests that fostering disagreement in a structured setting may actually lead to better decisions. Two techniques for programming conflict into the decision-making process are suggested—the devil's advocate decision program (DADP) and the dialectic method (DM). In particular, evidence indicates that larger firms operating in uncertain environments benefit from encouraging structured conflict in decision making. This article challenges managers to consider either the devil's advocate or dialectic methods to program conflict into important organizational decisions.

Most of us believe that a major objective in organizations is to foster agreement over decisions. After all, agreement indicates cohesion and homogeneity among employees. People who are in agreement with each other are satisfied and secure.

There is growing evidence that suggests conflict and dissent are what organizations really need to succeed.[1] Corporate decisions should be made after thoughtful consideration of counterpoints and criticism. People with different viewpoints must be encouraged to provide thoughts on important decisions. Widespread agreement on a key issue is a red flag, not a condition of good health.

There is an old story at General Motors about Alfred Sloan. At a meeting with his key executives, Sloan proposed a controversial strategic decision. When asked for comments, each executive responded with supportive comments and praise. After announcing that they were all in apparent agreement, Sloan stated that they were not going to proceed with the decision. Either his executives didn't know enough to point out potential downsides of the decision, or they were agreeing to avoid upsetting the boss and disrupting the cohesion of the group. The decision was delayed until a debate could occur over the pros and cons.

Some contemporary managers, however, recognize the benefits of conflict. Gavin Rawl, chief executive officer at Exxon, follows a policy of "healthy disrespect," according to *Business Week*.

Even as he rose through the Exxon hierarchy, however, Rawl always had a healthy disrespect for bureaucracy. The company was obsessed with consensus. Proposals would wend their way through a maze of committees and task forces, through layers of staff. As Senior Vice President Charles R. Sitter says: "In a large organization, good ideas have lots of foster parents, and the bad decisions produce lots of orphans." Consensus, after all, is safer: The footprints are covered.[2]

Another example is the flamboyant Scott McNealy, Sun Microsystems' chief executive officer. McNealy encourages noisy, table-pounding meetings and debate among senior executives. Dissent and opinion is a natural part of the "controlled chaos."[3]

These managers, like others, have recognized the need to allow different viewpoints and critical thinking into organizational decisions. The type of conflict that is encouraged involves different interpretations of common issues or problems.[4] This "cognitive conflict" was noted as functional many years ago by psychologist Irving Janis. Janis, in his famous writings on groupthink, pointed out that striving for agreement and preventing critical thought frequently leads to poor decisions such as those made during the Bay of Pigs invasion and the defense of Pearl Harbor.

Cognitive conflict can arise in two ways: (1) it can reflect true disagreement among managers and surface through an open environment which encourages participation; or (2) it can be programmed into the decision-making processes and forced to surface, regardless of managers' true feelings. Although both methods may be effective, the second is decidedly less common. Given the potential benefits of programmed conflict in organizational decision making, companies would do well to im-

Source: Richard A. Cosier and Charles R. Schwenk, "Agreement and Thinking Alike: Ingredients for Poor Decisions," *Academy of Management Executive*, February 1990, pp. 69–74.

[1] Conflict has been frequently presented as a positive force in textbooks. See, for example, Peter P. Schoderbek, Richard A. Cosier, and John C. Aplin, *Management* (San Diego: Harcourt, Brace, Jovanovich, 1988), pp. 511–12.

[2] "The Rebel Shaking up Exxon," *Business Week*, July 18, 1988, p. 107.

[3] "Sun Microsystems Turns on the Afterburners," *Business Week*, July 18, 1988, p. 115.

[4] Tjosvold uses the term *controversy* to describe this type of conflict. He differentiates controversy from conflicts of interest which involve the actions of one person blocking the goal attainment of another person. See Dean Tjosvold, "Implications of Controversy Research for Management," *Journal of Management* 11 (1985), pp. 22–23.

plement it. While elements of both methods of conflict generation are reviewed, means for encouraging programmed conflict is a major focus in this article.

ALLOWING TRUE DISAGREEMENT

Allowing disagreement to surface in organizations is exemplified by Jack Welch at General Electric. *Business Week* observed:

> Welch, though, is convinced he can reach his aims. Like a man obsessed, he is driving G.E. through drastic fundamental change. Once formal, stable, gentlemanly, the new G.E. is tough, aggressive, iconoclastic. "It's a brawl," says Frank P. Doyle, senior vice president for corporate relations. "It's argumentative, confrontational." Working there can be a shock to newcomers. "There's a much higher decibel level here. I told Jack what passes for conversation here would be seen as a mugging by RCA people," Doyle says.[5]

The planning process involves scrutiny and criticism at G.E. Suggestions are expected and frequently offered and people are encouraged by Welch to speak their minds. This is consistent with organizational case studies that note the value of "forthright discussion" versus behind-the-scenes politicking in determining organizational strategy. In one case, the vice president for manufacturing and finance at a company showing strong performance stated:

> You don't need to get the others behind you before the meeting. If you can explain your view (at the meeting), people will change their opinions. Forefront (the fictitious name of the company) is not political at this point. But, you must give your reasons or your ideas don't count. (VP of manufacturing.)

> There is some open disagreement—it's not covered up. We don't gloss over the issues, we hit them straight on. (VP of finance.)[6]

Several studies on strategic decision making show that, in general, successful companies advocate open discussions, surfacing of conflict, and flexibility in adopting solutions. Other studies, however, suggest that strategy is facilitated by consensus. This contradiction raises an important issue. Consensus may be preferred for smaller, nondiversified, privately held firms competing in the same industry, while larger firms dealing with complex issues of diversification may benefit from the dissent raised in open discussions. Larger firms in uncertain environments need dissent while smaller firms in more simple and stable markets can rely on consensus. In addition, Dess concludes, "organizations competing within an industry experiencing high growth may benefit from a relatively high level of disagreement in assessing the relative importance of company objectives and competitive methods."[7]

Examples of the benefits of conflict in tactical problem-solving (short-term) situations are also common. Bausch and Lomb has established "tiger teams" composed of scientists from different disciplines. Team members are encouraged to bring up divergent ideas and offer different points of view. Xerox uses roundtable discussions composed of various functional experts to encourage innovation. Compaq expects disagreement during all stages of new product development. Stuart Gannes, writing in *Fortune*, explains, "But at Compaq, instead of just arguing over who is right, we tear down positions to reasons. And when you get to reasons you find facts and assumptions."[8] Apple Computer, Ford Motor Co., Johnson and Johnson, and United Parcel Service are other examples of companies that tolerate conflict and debate during decisions.

In general, successful leaders seem to encourage managers to speak their minds. While this allows conflict into decision making, it carries a potential high cost. Positions are frequently tied to people and competitive "zero-sum" situations in which perceived winners and losers are likely to develop. Clearly, "losers" are less likely in future discussions to give their opinions.

Also, unprogrammed conflict is likely to be emotional and involve personal feelings. Lingering dislikes and rivalries are possible after higher emotional interchanges. Coalitions form and long-term divisiveness ensues.

Corporate time and money may have to be diverted from problem solving to resolving emotional conflicts between managers.

What may, in fact, be needed is programmed conflict that raises different opinions *regardless of the personal feelings of the managers*. Although research exists supporting some options for programmed conflict, few, if any, examples exist in the corporate world.

PROGRAMMED CONFLICT

The Devil's Advocate

What can leaders do to experience the benefits associated with conflict in decision making, while minimizing the cost? Two options with potential are the devil's advocate

---

[5]"Jack Welch: How Good a Manager?" *Business Week,* December 14, 1987, p. 94.

[6]Kathleen M. Eisenhardt and L. J. Bourgeois III, "Politics of Strategic Decision Making in High-Velocity Environments," *Academy of Management Journal* 31 (1998), pp. 751–52.

[7]Gregory G. Dess, "Consensus on Strategy Formulation and Organizational Performance: Competitors in a Fragmented Industry," *Strategic Management Journal* 8 (1987), p. 274.

[8]Stuart Gannes, "America's Fastest-Growing Companies," *Fortune,* May 23, 1988, p. 29.

and dialectic methods for introducing programmed conflict into organizational decisions.

The usefulness of the devil's advocate technique was illustrated several years ago by psychologist Irving Janis when discussing famous fiascos. Janis attributes groupthink—the striving for agreement instead of the best decision in a group—to decisions such as were made during the Bay of Pigs and Pearl Harbor.[9] Watergate and Vietnam are also often cited as examples. Janis recommends that everyone in the group assume the role of a devil's advocate and question the assumptions underlying the popular choice. Alternatively, an individual or subgroup could be formally designated as the devil's advocate and present a critique of the proposed course of action. This avoids the tendency of agreement interfering with problem solving. Potential pitfalls are identified and considered before the decision is final.

While Janis' observations are generally well known and accepted, corporate implementation of devil's advocacy as a formal element in decision making is rare. This is despite recent research that supports the benefits of devil's advocacy.[10] The conflict generated by the devil's advocate may cause the decision maker to avoid false assumptions and closely analyze the information. The devil's advocate raises questions that force an in-depth review of the problem-solving situation.

A devil's advocate decision program (DADP) can take several forms. However, all options require that an individual or group be assigned the role of critic. It needs to be clear that the criticism must not be taken personally, but is part of the organizational decision process.

The devil's advocate is assigned to identify potential pitfalls and problems with a proposed course of action.

The issue could relate to strategic planning, new product development, or a formal presentation to the key decision makers by the devil's advocate raises potential concerns. Evidence needed to address the critique is gathered and the final decision is made and monitored. This DADP is summarized in Exhibit 14.5.

It is a good idea to rotate people assigned to devil's advocate roles. This avoids any one person or group being identified as the critic on all issues. The devil's advocate role may be advantageous for a person and the organization. Steve Huse, chairperson and CEO of Huse Food Group, states that the devil's advocate role is an opportunity for employees to demonstrate their presentation and debating skills. How well someone understands and researches issues is apparent when presenting a critique.[11] The organization avoids costly mistakes by hearing viewpoints that identify pitfalls instead of foster agreement.

Often, a devil's advocate is helpful in adopting expert advice from computer-based decision support systems. Behavioral scientists Cosier and Dalton suggest that computer-based decisions may be more useful if exposed to a critique than simply accepted by managers.[12]

The Dialectic

While the DADP lacks an "argument" between advocates of two conflicting positions, the dialectic method (DM) programs conflict into decisions, regardless of managers' personal feelings, by structuring a debate between conflicting views.

---

[9]See Irving L. Janis, *Victims of Groupthink* (Boston: Houghton-Mifflin, 1972).

[10]See, for example, Richard A. Cosier, "Methods for Improving the Strategic Decision: Dialectic versus the Devil's Advocate," *Strategic Management Journal* 16 (1982), pp. 176–84.

[11]Steve Huse, chairperson and CEO of Huse Food Group Inc., shared these observations in an interview with the senior author.

[12]A model is developed which recommends methods of presenting information based upon conditions of uncertainty and information availability in Richard A. Cosier and Dan R. Dalton, "Presenting Information Under Conditions of Uncertainty and Availability: Some Recommendations," *Behavioral Science* 33 (1988), 272–81.

EXHIBIT 14.5   A Devil's Advocate Decision Program

1. A proposed course of action is generated.

↓

2. A devil's advocate (individual or group) is assigned to criticize the proposal.

↓

3. The critique is presented to key decision makers.

↓

4. Any additional information relevant to the issues is gathered.

↓

5. The decision to adopt, modify, or discontinue the proposed course of action is taken.

↓

6. The decision is monitored.

The dialectic philosophy, which can be traced back to Plato and Aristotle, involves synthesizing the conflicting views of a thesis and an antithesis. More recently, it played a principal role in the writings of Hegel who described the emergence of new social orders after a struggle between opposing forces. While most of the world's modern legal systems reflect dialectic processes, Richard O. Mason was one of the first organization theorists to apply the dialectic to organizational decisions.[13] He suggested that the decision maker consider a structured debate reflecting a plan and a counterplan before making a strategic decision. Advocates of each point of view should present their assumptions in support of the argument.

The benefits of DM are in the presentation and debate of the assumptions underlying proposed courses of action. False or misleading assumptions become apparent and decisions based on these poor assumptions are avoided. The value of DM, shown in Exhibit 14.6, for promoting better understanding of problems and higher levels of confidence in decisions is supported by research.[14]

Critics of DM point to the potential for it to accentuate who won the debate rather than the best decision. Compromise, instead of optimal decisions, is likely. Managers will require extensive training in dialectic thinking and philosophy. Supporters of DADP argue that a critique focuses the decision maker on issues while the

dialectic focuses more on the process of structural debate. Nevertheless, Cosier and Dalton suggest that DM may be the best method to use under the worst decision-making condition—high uncertainty and low information availability. The dialectic may be a good way to define problems and generate needed information for making decisions under uncertainty. When information is available and causal relationships are known, computer-assisted or devil's advocate methods are preferred.

PROGRAMMED AND UNPROGRAMMED CONFLICT

It is not a major breakthrough in management advice to suggest that conflict can improve decisions, although it is useful to remind managers of the need to allow dissent. It is, however, uncommon for managers to formally program conflict into the decision-making process. Thus, regardless of personal feelings, programmed conflict requires managers to challenge, criticize, and generate alternative ideas. Compared to conflict that is allowed to naturally surface, programmed conflict may reduce negative emotional byproducts of conflict generation since dissent is no longer "personal." It also insures that a comprehensive decision framework is applied to important problems and issues.

Two options for implementing programmed conflict are based on the devil's advocate (DADP) and dialectic (DM) methods. We challenge managers to formally encourage controversy and dissent when making important choices under uncertain conditions. Encouraging "yes sayers" and complacency promotes poor decisions and lack of innovative thinking in organizations.

---

[13]Richard O. Mason, "A Dialectical Approach to Strategic Planning," *Management Science* 15 (1969), pp. B403–14.

[14]Ian I. Mitroff and J. R. Emshoff, "On Strategic Assumption-Making: A Dialectical Approach to Policy and Planning," *Academy of Management Review* 4 (1979), pp. 1–12.

EXHIBIT 14.6   The Dialectic Decision Method

1. A proposed course of action is generated.
    ↓
2. Assumptions underlying the proposal are identified.
    ↓
3. A conflicting counterproposal is generated based on different assumptions.
    ↓
4. Advocates of each position present and debate the merits of their proposals before key decision makers.
    ↓
5. The decision to adopt either position, or some other position, e.g., a compromise, is taken.
    ↓
6. The decision is monitored.

Exercises

EXERCISE 14.1   How Biased Is Your Decision Making?

Step 1: Answer each of the problems below.

1. A certain town is served by two hospitals. In the larger hospital, about 45 babies are born each day, and in the smaller hospital, about 15 babies are born each day. Although the overall proportion of boys is about 50 percent, the actual proportion at either hospital may be greater or less than 50 percent on any day. At the end of a year, which hospital will have the greater number of days on which more than 60 percent of the babies born were boys?
   a. The large hospital.
   b. The small hospital.
   c. Neither—the number of days will be about the same (within 5 percent of each other)

2. Linda is 31, single, outspoken, and very bright. She majored in philosophy in college. As a student, she was deeply concerned with discrimination and other social issues and participated in anti-nuclear demonstrations. Which statement is more likely:
   a. Linda is a bank teller.
   b. Linda is a bank teller and active in the feminist movement.

3. A cab was involved in a hit-and-run accident. Two cab companies serve the city: the Green, which operates 85 percent of the cabs, and the Blue, which operates the remaining 15 percent. A witness identifies the hit-and-run cab as Blue. When the court tests the reliability of the witness under circumstances similar to those on the night of the accident, he correctly identifies the color of a cab 80 percent of the time and misidentifies it the other 20 percent. What's the probability that the cab involved in the accident was Blue, as the witness stated?

4. Imagine that you face this pair of concurrent decisions. Examine these decisions, then indicate which choices you prefer:

Decision I

Choose between:
   a. A sure gain of $240
   b. A 25 percent chance of winning $1,000 and a 75 percent chance of winning nothing

Decision II

Choose between:
   c. A sure loss of $750
   d. A 75 percent chance of losing $1,000 and a 25 percent chance of losing nothing

Decision III

Choose between:
   e. A sure loss of $3,000
   f. An 80 percent chance of losing $4,000 and a 20 percent chance of losing nothing

5. a. You've decided to see a Broadway play and have bought a $40 ticket. As you enter the theater, you realize you've lost your ticket. You can't remember the seat number, so you can't prove to the management that you bought a ticket. Would you spend $40 for a new ticket?
   b. You've reserved a seat for a Broadway play for which the ticket price is $40. As you enter the theater to buy your ticket, you discover you've lost $40 from your pocket. Would you still buy the ticket? (Assume you have enough cash left to do so.)

6. Imagine you have operable lung cancer and must choose between two treatments—surgery and radiation therapy. Of 100 people having surgery, 10 die during the operation, 32 (including those original 10) are dead after one year, and 66 after five years. Of 100 people having radiation therapy, none dies during treatment, 23 are dead after one year, and 78 after five years. Which treatment would you prefer?

Step 2: Your instructor will give you the correct answer to each problem.

Step 3: Discussion. In small groups, with the entire class, or in written form, as directed by your instructor, answer the following questions:

Description:
1. How accurate were the decisions you reached?

Diagnosis:
2. What biases were evident in the decisions you reached?

Prescription:
3. How could you improve your decision making to make it more accurate?

Sources: From D. Kahnemann and A. Tversky, "Rational Choice and the Forming of Decisions," *Journal of Business* 59(4) (1986), pp. 5251–78; A. Tversky and D. Kahnemann, "The Framing of Decisions and the Psychology of Choice," *Science* 211 (1981), pp. 453–58; D. Kahnemann and A. Tversky, "Extension Needs Intuitive Reasoning," *Psychological Review* 90 (1983), pp. 293–315; and K. McKean, "Decisions, Decisions," *Discovery Magazine,* June 1985.

Exercises

EXERCISE 14.2   Group Decision Making

PURPOSE

1. Identify the pros and cons of group versus individual decision making.
2. Experience a group decision-making situation.
3. Practice diagnosing work group effectiveness.

INRODUCTION

Much of the work that takes place in organizations is done in groups. In fact, the more important a task, the more likely it is to be assigned to a group. There is a tendency to believe that groups make better decisions and are better at solving problems than individuals. However, the evidence on this subject is contradictory and seems to suggest that "it depends." Groups are more effective under some circumstances and individuals under others. There are assets and liabilities associated with both (Maier, 1967). Because so much important work is done in groups, it is necessary for group members to learn to minimize the liabilities and capitalize on the assets of the group problem solving.

INSTRUCTIONS

1. Read the directions and complete the Wilderness Survival Worksheet.
2. Form groups of five to seven people.
3. In groups, read the directions for and complete the Wilderness Survival Group Consensus Task.
4. Calculate your scores using the directions in the Wilderness Survival Scoring Sheet on pages 560–562.
5. Interpret your score.
6. Participate in a class discussion

PART I: WILDERNESS SURVIVAL WORKSHEET

Directions: Here are 12 questions concerning personal survival in a wilderness situation. Your first task is to *individually* select the best of the three alternatives given under each item. Try to imagine yourself in the situation depicted. Assume that you are alone and have a minimum of equipment, except where specified. The season is fall. The days are warm and dry, but the nights are cold.

After you have completed the task individually, you will again consider each question as a member of a small group. Both the individual and group solutions will later be compared with the "correct" answers provided by a group of naturalists who conduct classes in woodland survival.

Source: Wilderness Survival is reprinted from: J. William Pfeiffer and John E. Jones, eds., *1976 Annual Handbook for Group Facilitators* (San Diego, CA: University Associates, Inc., 1976). Used with permission. The Group Effectiveness Checklist is based on the ideas presented in I. L. Janis, "Groupthink," *Psychology Today,* November 1971; N. R. F. Maier, "Assets and Liabilities in Group Problem Solving: The Need for an Integrative Function," *Psychological Review* 74 (1967), pp. 239–49.

	Your Answer	Your Group's Answer	Expert Answer

1. You have strayed from your party in trackless timber. You have no special signaling equipment. The best way to attempt to contact your friends is to:
  a. Call for "help" loudly but in a low register.
  b. Yell or scream as loud as you can.
  c. Whistle loudly and shrilly.
	____	____	____

2. You are in "snake country." Your best action to avoid snakes is to:
  a. Make a lot of noise with your feet.
  b. Walk softly and quietly.
  c. Travel at night.
	____	____	____

3. You are hungry and lost in wild country. The best rule for determining which plants are safe to eat (those you do not recognize) is to:
  a. Try anything you see the birds eat.
  b. Eat anything except plants with bright red berries.
  c. Put a bit of the plant on your lower lip for five minutes; if it seems all right, try a little more.
	____	____	____

	Your Answer	Your Group's Answer	Expert Answer

4. The day becomes dry and hot. You have a full canteen of water (about one liter) with you. You should:
   a. Ration it—about a capful a day.
   b. Not drink until you stop for the night, then drink what you think you need.
   c. Drink as much as you think you need when you need it.

5. Your water is gone; you become very thirsty. You finally come to a dried-up watercourse. Your best chance of finding water is to:
   a. Dig anywhere in the stream bed.
   b. Dig up plant and tree roots near the bank.
   c. Dig in the stream bed at the outside of a bend.

6. You decide to walk out of the wild country by following a series of ravines where a water supply is available. Night is coming on. The best place to make camp is:
   a. Next to the water supply in the ravine.
   b. High on a ridge.
   c. Midway up the slope.

7. Your flashlight glows dimly as you are about to make your way back to your campsite after a brief foraging trip. Darkness comes quickly in the woods and the surroundings seem unfamiliar. You should:
   a. Head back at once, keeping the light on, hoping the light will glow enough for you to make out landmarks.
   b. Put the batteries under your armpits to warm them, and then replace them in the flashlight.
   c. Shine your light for a few seconds, try to get the scene in your mind, move out in the darkness, and repeat the process.

8. An early snow confines you to your small tent. You doze with your small stove going. There is danger if the flame is:
   a. Yellow.
   b. Blue.
   c. Red.

9. You must ford a river that has a strong current, large rocks, and some white water. After carefully selecting your crossing spot, you should:
   a. Leave your boots and pack on.
   b. Take your boots and pack off.
   c. Take off your pack, but leave your boots on.

10. In waist-deep water with a strong current, when crossing the stream, you should face:
   a. Upstream.
   b. Across the stream.
   c. Downstream.

11. You find yourself rimrocked; your only route is up. The way is mossy, slippery rock. You should try it:
   a. Barefoot.
   b. With boots on.
   c. In stocking feet.

12. Unarmed and unsuspecting, you surprise a large bear prowling around your campsite. As the bear rears up about 10 meters from you, you should:
   a. Run.
   b. Climb the nearest tree.
   c. Freeze, but be ready to back away slowly.

Individual Score

WILDERNESS SURVIVAL GROUP CONSENSUS TASK

Directions: You have just completed an individual solution to Wilderness Survival. Now your small group will decide on a group solution to the same dilemmas. A decision by consensus is difficult to attain, and not every decision may meet with everyone's unqualified approval. There should be, however, a general feeling of support from all members before a group decision is made. Do not change your individual answers, even if you change your mind in the group discussion.

Outcome	Group 1	Group 2	Group 3
Range of individual scores (low-high)			
Average of individual scores			
Group score			

Cases

CASE 14.1   An Ethical Dilemma At Bridgestone/Firestone and Ford Motors

An investigation indicates that over the last eight years, more than 100 people have died in accidents linked to Bridgestone/Firestone tires. The Bridgestone/Firestone crisis illustrates how secrecy and internal company policies may have played a role in some of these deaths. Lawyers, the families of victims, and Bridgestone/Firestone (BF) knew about defects in tires. However, the truth was kept silent by a series of secrecy agreements signed as part of Firestone's legal settlements.

Lawyers claim that for years Firestone's executives decided to seal documents that relate to safety issues. For example, one lawsuit shows that more than 1,400 tires made at a Bridgestone/Firestone plant in Wilson, North Carolina, were returned because of defects. This is eight years before the recall in 2000 because of belt separations or suspected belt separations.

BF recalled 6.5 million tires on August 9, 2000, as reports of accidents involving the failures mounted. Ford, BF, and the National Highway Traffic Safety Administration are investigating what can cause the tread to pull off the tire, sometimes as the vehicle is traveling at highway speeds.

SERIOUS PROBLEMS

It's no wonder that BF and Ford Motor Company appear to be circling the wagons these days. After acknowledging serious problems with Firestone tires on Ford vehicles, and in the wake of a massive tire recall with additional recalls possible, the companies are under assault from several different forces on many different fronts.

First, there is the legal assault on the two companies. The National Highway Traffic Safety Administration is reportedly investigating more than 750 complaints about Firestone tires alleging links between the tires and dozens of deaths and hundreds of injuries. Some of the families of these victims already have sued Bridgestone/Firestone and/or Ford for manufacturing and distributing allegedly defective products, and other lawsuits are sure to follow.

In fact, the publicity surrounding the tire recall is likely to increase dramatically the number of individual lawsuits brought against the companies by individuals who only now are realizing that there is a possible or likely connection between the tires and an accident they may have suffered on the road.

Now, although these lawsuits certainly aren't welcome at Ford and BF, it's fair to say that both companies probably are big enough to handle these particular lawsuits since, on a relative scale, they will be few in number. Big companies like Ford and BF routinely handle defective product claims and typically have some sort of insurance to help them pay both litigation costs and damage awards.

But the tire recall also looks like it will spawn class-action litigation against the two companies, and here is where the possible exposure to both Ford and BF is immense. Some of these potentially massive lawsuits reportedly are aimed at broadening the existing recall; others are reportedly alleging "emotional distress" on behalf of drivers worried about their vehicles crashing or even the resale value of their cars.

Source: Case prepared by authors from: Andrew Cohen, "Circling the Rubber Tired Wagon," CBS News, September 5, 2000; "Shakeup at Bridgestone/Firestone,"CBS News, October 2, 2000; and "CEO of Tire Maker Apologizes," September 7, 2000, *www.newsnet5.com.*

Not all of these lawsuits, of course, will make it to trial. The more creative the legal theory, the less chance there is that a judge will buy into it. But some of these cases likely will make it to trial and a few might even generate victories for large classes of plaintiffs.

Such victories, with punitive damages a possibility, could absolutely devastate either or both companies. Even a settlement in cases involving the strongest class-action plaintiffs could cost the companies' precious financial resources.

But it gets worse: Adding to the companies' legal headaches is the knowledge that they will have to spend millions and millions in legal fees just to fend off these challenges. And in addition to sustained court expenses, lawsuits bring the sort of corporate uncertainty that shareholders and market analysts simply hate—and that's also got to weigh heavily on the executives who run BF and Ford.

Then there is a congressional investigation. While the multilayered legal assault on the companies relates to their past performance, duties, and responsibilities, Congress could play a significant role in changing the way the companies are required to do business in the future. In the past, Congress has stepped in to help the automobile and tire industries when those industries faced certain regulatory action.

Then there is the regulatory front. Firestone or Ford faces potential fines for failing to recall the tires sooner, and they also face potential penalties for withholding documents. And while Joan Claybrook, a former administrator of NHTSA, astutely pointed out in the *New York Times* that those fines and penalties are a drop in the bucket compared to what the companies make, the real regulatory problem for Ford and Firestone may come down the road, in the form of more recalls and safety warnings by an agency angered by the actions and reactions of the companies.

These additional recalls and warnings obviously could and will affect sales of all Firestone tires and perhaps Ford vehicles as well, which means less profit for the two companies to work with as they fight the legal and political battles above.

Finally, there is the wild card in all of this, the possibility of criminal charges brought in Venezuela against the corporate officers or key decision makers of Ford and BF. Venezuelan prosecutors apparently are on the cusp of a criminal investigation designed to determine whether involuntary homicide and/or conspiracy charges could be sustained for producing faulty tires and then deceiving the government and failing to warn drivers there of the dangers of the tires.

KEY DECISION MAKERS

The top executive of the embattled U.S. division of Bridgestone Corp. will no longer manage its operations, the president of the Tokyo-based company said.

Masatoshi Ono, CEO and chairman of the U.S. operations and executive vice president of Bridgestone Corp., may remain with the company but his role has not been determined.

Bridgestone President Yoichiro Kaizaki told *Nikkei Business* magazine during an interview that he would discuss plans to restructure the U.S. subsidiary with "the person who will become the top management of Bridgestone/Firestone in the future."

The magazine quoted Kaizaki as saying: "To start with, we will renew Bridgestone/Firestone's top management and the company's organizational structure." The magazine also said that Kaizaki added: "We will let Mr. Ono go."

Bridgestone spokesman Ken Kitawaki insisted Monday that the company has not decided what will happen with Ono.

Ono, 63, was named BF CEO in 1993, replacing Kaizaki, who was promoted to Bridgestone Corp. president. In 1996, Ono also was named chairman of the Nashville-based U.S. subsidiary.

Rumors of Ono's demotion, firing, or resignation have circulated since August, when the company recalled 6.5 million ATX, ATX II, and Wilderness tires that have been linked to fatal crashes worldwide.

FORD CEO JAC NASSER

Ford CEO Jac Nasser said his company's vehicles are safe. "This is a tire issue, not a vehicle issue," he said, repeating what has become the company's standard defense.

"We have millions of Goodyear tires on 1995 through 1997 Explorers—the same specification tire operating under the same conditions—and they haven't experienced these problems," he said.

But NHTSA administrator Sue Bailey said many of the accidents were caused by a combination of flawed Firestone tires and characteristics of the Ford Explorer, which, like other sport utility vehicles, has a higher center of gravity and is more apt than a car to roll over.

It "clearly is a combination of situations that produced the outcome," she said.

Ralph Nader, consumer advocate and Green Party presidential candidate, said Ford and Firestone officials should be criminally prosecuted.

"It's a classic two-company cover-up in the most tragic ways for the families and individuals who lost their lives in these otherwise preventable collisions," he said in a Capitol hallway.

Helen Petrauskas, Ford's vice president of environmental and safety engineering, told the Senate hearing that Firestone had insisted the overseas tire problems identified by Ford were caused by road and repair problems and unfavorable driving conditions. Ford's own company testing found no defect trends in U.S. versions of the tires.

In the United States, there has been talk of legislation and lawsuits. In Venezuela, the Bridgestone/ Firestone and Ford executives who made decisions are facing a criminal investigation. The charge: involuntary homicide.

QUESTIONS:

1. Are executives who made decisions to continue producing (Bridgestone/Firestone) tires and using Fords responsible for engaging in unethical decision making? Explain.

2. How would you rate the ethical tone of legally sealing documents that revealed tire defects? Should the law be changed regarding sealing such documents?

3. What changes do Bridgestone/Firestone and Ford have to implement to eliminate the possibility of repeating the type of decisions that resulted in the tire defect scandal?

Video Case

IBM TURNAROUND, LOU GERSTNER, AND THE BODY SHOP

Lou Gerstner, head of IBM, and Anita Roddick, founder and head of the Body Shop, are two excellent examples of how today's business leaders can bring about both corporate and social change. Gerstner turned around a floundering IBM and over the course of three years increased the value of its stock fourfold. He acknowledged the invalid assumptions of the old IBM: "There's no question that we believed we could make everything and we could outcompete against everybody. That's not our view today." Gerstner had a vision for the future of IBM and realized he would have to lead the way. He emphasized the importance of problem solving instead of just building bigger computers, and he even changed the dress code from the traditional IBM "uniform" of dark suit and white shirt to more casual dress. Both of these changes fit in with Gerstner's vision of the future.

Anita Roddick started with an initial investment of $6,000 and a single cosmetics shop, and has since increased the number of Body Shops to over 1,300 stores in North and South America, Europe, Asia, Australia, and New Zealand. And, The Body Shop had net assets of over $96 million in 1996. Roddick had a vision that The Body Shop is "a movement by which we use our products as emissaries for social and political change." Roddick sees environmentalism as the most pressing issue of the next decade. She views The Body Shop as a role model for how business can lead the charge toward corporate and social responsibility. Toward that end,

Body Shop employees are expected to work on community projects on company time, customers are given information about recycling and animal and human rights, and The Body Shop is against animal testing and advocates the use of natural products that do not require testing. Company representatives teach third world workers new technologies to use the resources at their disposal to serve as suppliers to The Body Shop and are paid first world wages. Body Shop associates even gathered one million signatures protesting the burning of the Amazon rain forests and delivered them to the Brazilian embassy.

Anita Roddick and Lou Gerstner could both be described as true leaders. They are charismatic, and they innovate, inspire, and challenge the status quo. Both executives had strong visions for their businesses and transformed their companies by creating changes in their followers' goals and values.

DISCUSSION QUESTIONS:

1. In what ways was charisma exhibited by Roddick and Gerstner?
2. How did these executives transform their visions into real corporate change?
3. Should more business leaders view their corporations as instrumental in social and political change, as does Anita Roddick? Why or why not?

V

Part

Organizational Design, Change, and Innovation

Where there is an open mind, there will always be a frontier.
—Charles F. Kettering, *Quoted in Profile of America*

15
Chapter

Organizational Structure and Design

After completing Chapter 15, you should be able to:

Learning Objectives

- Identify the choices which must be made in designing an organization structure.

- Define what is meant by the term *division of labor*.

- Discuss the role of delegation of authority in design decisions.

- Describe several forms of departmentalization.

- Explain the importance of span of control.

- Define three important dimensions of structure.

- Compare mechanistic and organic organizational design.

- Identify the major advantages of matrix organization design.

- Discuss multinational organizational structure and design issues.

- Explain the meaning of the term *virtual organization*.

Organizational structure and design have always been important factors influencing the behavior of individuals and groups that comprise the organization; the new rules of operating in today's global business environment make structure and design considerations even more critical.[1] Today's managers are faced with an array of different structural possibilities.[2] Ultimately, it is through the design of the structure that management is able to establish expectations for what individuals and groups will do to achieve the organization's purposes. But before these purposes can be accomplished, somebody must do some work. Not only must people do some work, they must do the right work. And that brings us to organizational structure, because it is through structure that managers decide how the organization's purposes will be accomplished.[3]

Managers achieve coordinated effort through the design of a structure of task and authority relationships. Design, in this context, implies that managers make a conscious effort to predetermine the way employees do their work. Structure refers to relatively stable relationships and processes of the organization. Organizational structure is considered by many to be "the anatomy of the organization, providing a foundation within which the organization functions."[4] Thus, the structure of an organization, similar to the anatomy of a living organism, can be viewed as a framework. The idea of structure as a framework "focuses on the differentiation of positions, formulation of rules and procedures, and prescriptions of authority."[5] Therefore, the purpose of structure is to regulate, or at least reduce, uncertainty in the behavior of individual employees.

Organizations are purposive and goal-oriented, so it follows that the structure of organizations also is purposive and goal-oriented. Our concept of organizational structure takes into account the existence of purposes and goals, and our attitude is that management should think of structure in terms of its contribution to organizational effectiveness, even though the exact nature of the relationship between structure and effectiveness is inherently difficult to know. Structural decisions should also reflect company values and incorporate ethical and environmental considerations. Indeed, as illustrated in the You Be the Judge, many issues relating to values and ethics are at the core of some contemporary approaches to organizational design and structure.

DESIGNING AN ORGANIZATION STRUCTURE

Managers who set out to design an organization structure face difficult decisions. They must choose among a myriad of alternative frameworks of jobs, work projects, and departments. The process by which they make these choices is termed **organizational design,** and it means quite simply the decisions and actions that

---

[1]William McKinley and Andreas Georg Scherer, "Some Unanticipated Consequences of Organizational Restructuring," *Academy of Management Review,* October 2000, pp. 735–52.

[2]Wouter H. F. M. Contenraad, *The Corporate Paradox: Economic Realities of the Corporate Form of Organizations* (Boston: Klenver, 2000).

[3]John Hagel, III, and Marc Singer, "Unbundling the Corporation," *Harvard Business Review,* March–April, 1999, pp. 133–41.

[4]Dan R. Dalton, William D. Todor, Michael J. Spendolina, Gordon J. Fielding, and Lyman W. Porter, "Organization Structure and Performance: A Critical Review," *Academy of Management Review,* January 1980, p. 49.

[5]Stewart Ranson, Bob Hinings, and Royston Greenwood, "The Structuring of Organizational Structures," *Administrative Science Quarterly,* March 1980, p. 2.

Organizations Should Incorporate Ethics

You Be the Judge

All of us would acknowledge that organization designs should include considerations of work and technology. After all, the underlying purpose of organization structure is to regulate behavior to accomplish legitimate work. But who among us would argue that organization structure should include provisions for ensuring ethical actions on the part of all employees? That question is on the table for discussion in many organizations around the globe. One particular point of view advocates a radically new type of organization structure based on a philosophy of ethical management. Along with traditional management functions, the new design would incorporate six new functions of crisis management (preventing and responding to threats), issues management (assessing broad societal and industry trends), total quality management, environmentalism, globalism (ensuring that the organization's production, marketing, and administrative processes are tuned to the global political economy), and ethics (keeping tabs on the ethical and moral consequences of the organization's behavior, policies, decisions, and procedures).

The proposed new design integrates the six new functions. The resulting design encompasses four major divisions, or centers:

1. *A Knowledge/Learning Center.* The key issue of this division is: What do we need to know to produce and/or deliver world-class products/services?
2. *A Recovery/Development Center.* The key issues here are: How can we help our employees recover from whatever dysfunctions or problems they bring with them to the organization? Also, how can we help the organization as a whole recover from systemic dysfunctions and develop into a healthy system?
3. *A World Service/Spiritual Center.* The key issue of this center is: How can our organization use all of its resources to develop a healthier society and world?
4. *An Operations Center.* The key issue of the operations center is: How can we actually implement and operate a world-class manufacturing and/or service organization?

The advocates acknowledge that no organization currently embodies all features of their design. They correctly point out, however, that many organizations in both the public and private sector are experimenting with every one of the features of their idealized structure.

What opinion do you hold regarding the requirement that organizations should incorporate ethics in their organization designs? Whose ethics and values should they incorporate? Yours? Mine? The customers? You be the judge.

Sources: Ian I. Mitroff, "The Antediluvian Corporation," *Across the Board,* October 1994, pp. 59–60; Ian I. Mitroff, Richard O. Mason, and Christine M. Pearson, "Radical Surgery: What Will Tomorrow's Organizations Look Like?" *Academy of Management Executive,* May 1994, pp. 11–21; Ian I. Mitroff, Richard O. Mason, and Christine M. Pearson, *Framebreak: The Radical Redesign of American Business* (San Francisco: Jossey-Bass, 1994).

result in an organization structure.[6] This process may be explicit or implicit, it may be "one-shot" or developmental, it may be done by a single manager or by a team of managers.[7] However the actual decisions come about, the content of the decisions is always the same. The first decision focuses on individual jobs, the

---

[6]David A. Nadler and Michael L. Tushman, "The Organization of the Future: Principles of Design for the 21st Century," *Organizational Dynamics,* Summer 1999, pp. 45–60.

[7]B. B. Lichtenstein, "Self-Organized Transitions: A Pattern amidst the Chaos of Transformative Change," *Academy of Management Executive,* November 2000, pp. 128–41.

next two decisions focus on departments or groups of jobs, the fourth decision considers the issue of delegation of authority throughout the structure.

1. Managers decide how to divide the overall task into successively smaller jobs. Managers divide the total activities of the task into smaller sets of related activities. The effect of this decision is to define jobs in terms of specialized activities and responsibilities. Although jobs have many characteristics, the most important one is their degree of specialization.

2. Managers decide the bases by which to group the individual jobs. This decision is much like any other classification decision and it can result in groups containing jobs that are relatively homogeneous (alike) or heterogeneous (different).

3. Managers decide the appropriate size of the group reporting to each superior. As we have already noted, this decision involves determining whether spans of control are relatively narrow or wide.

4. Managers distribute authority among the jobs. Authority is the right to make decisions without approval by a higher manager and to exact obedience from designated other people. All jobs contain some degree of the right to make decisions within prescribed limits. But not all jobs contain the right to exact obedience from others. The latter aspect of authority distinguishes managerial jobs from nonmanagerial jobs. Managers can exact obedience; nonmanagers can't.

Thus, organization structures vary depending upon the choices that managers make. If we consider each of the four design decisions to be a continuum of possible choices, the alternative structures can be depicted as follows:

Division of labor:	**Specialization**
	High Low
Authority:	**Delegation**
	High Low
Departmentalization:	**Basis**
	Homogeneous Heterogeneous
Span of control:	**Number**
	Few Many

Generally speaking, organization structures tend toward one extreme or the other along each continuum. Structures tending to the left are characterized by a number of terms including *classical, formalistic, structured, bureaucratic, System 1,* and *mechanistic.* Structures tending to the right are termed *neoclassical, informalistic, unstructured, nonbureaucratic, System 4,* and *organic.*[8] Exactly where along the continuum an organization finds itself has implications for its performance as well as for individual and group behavior.[9]

---

[8]W. F. Joyce, *Megachange* (New York: Free Press, 1999).
[9]Ibid.

DIVISION OF LABOR

Exercise 15.1

Paper Plane Corporation

Division of labor concerns the extent to which jobs are specialized. Managers divide the total task of the organization into specific jobs having specified activities. The activities define what the person performing the job is to do. For example, activities of the job "accounting clerk" can be defined in terms of the methods and procedures required to process a certain quantity of transactions during a period of time. Other accounting clerks could use the same methods and procedures to process different types of transactions. One could be processing accounts receivable, while the others process accounts payable. Thus, jobs can be specialized both by method and by application of the method.

The economic advantages of dividing work into specialized jobs are the principal historical reasons for the creation of organizations.[10] As societies became more and more industrialized and urbanized, craft production gave way to mass production. Mass production depends upon the ability to obtain the economic benefits of specialized labor, and the most effective means for obtaining specialized labor is through organizations. Although managers are concerned with more than the economic implications of jobs, they seldom lose sight of specialization as the rationale for dividing work among jobs.[11]

Division of labor in organizations can occur in three different ways:[12]

1. Work can be divided into different *personal* specialties. Most people think of specialization in the sense of occupational and professional specialties. Thus, we think of accountants, software engineers, graphic designers, scientists, physicians, and the myriad of other specialties that exist in organizations and everyday life.

2. Work can be divided into different activities necessitated by the natural sequence of the work the organization does. For example, manufacturing plants often divide work into fabricating and assembly, and individuals will be assigned to do the work of one of these two activities. This particular manifestation of division of work is termed *horizontal specialization*.

3. Finally, work can be divided along the *vertical plane* of an organization. All organizations have a hierarchy of authority from the lowest-level manager to the highest-level manager. The CEO's work is different from the shift supervisor's.

Determining what each job in the organization should do is a key managerial decision. The important point to keep in mind for now is that jobs vary along a general dimension of specialization with some jobs being more highly specialized than others. Managers can change an organization's structure by changing the degree of specialization of jobs. For example, Procter & Gamble (P&G) CEO Edwin Artzt changed the degree of specialization of the company's sales reps. Artzt believes that sales reps interested in developing strong ties with customers lose their competitive instinct. He believes that team members devote too much

---

[10]Richard E. Kopelman, "Job Redesign and Productivity: A Review of the Literature," *National Productivity Review,* Summer 1985, p. 239.

[11]Donald J. Campbell, "Task Complexity: A Review and Analysis," *Academy of Management Review,* January 1988, pp. 40–52.

[12]Paul S. Adler, "Building Better Bureaucracies," *Academy of Management Executive,* November 1999, pp. 36–49.

energy to building relationships within the team and with the customers and too little attention to building volume and profit. He reversed P&G's team approach in favor of sales representatives who represent narrow sectors such as soap and food products. One organizational effect of Artzt's decision has been a move to create separate sales groups within each sector. In terms of specialization of labor, sales representatives now have more specialized jobs (they sell fewer different products) and the organization has more specialized units (the sales units in each of the sectors).[13]

The process of defining the activities and authority of jobs is analytical; that is, the total task of the organization is broken down into successively smaller ones. But then management must use some basis to combine the divided tasks into groups or departments containing some specified number of individuals or jobs. We will discuss these two decisions relating to departments in that order.

DELEGATION OF AUTHORITY

Managers decide how much authority should be delegated to each job and each jobholder. As we have noted, authority refers to individuals' right to make decisions without approval by higher management and to exact obedience from others. **Delegation of authority** refers specifically to making decisions, not to doing work. A sales manager can be delegated the right to hire salespeople (a decision) and the right to assign them to specific territories (obedience). Another sales manager may not have the right to hire but may have the right to assign territories. Thus, the degree of delegated authority can be relatively high or relatively low with respect to both aspects of authority. Any particular job involves a range of alternative configurations of authority delegation.[14] Managers must balance the relative gains and losses of alternatives.

Reasons to Decentralize Authority

Relatively high delegation of authority encourages the development of professional managers. No doubt Philip G. Barach (CEO of U.S. Shoe Corporation) has this point in mind when he describes his management style as organized anarchy because he tends to leave his day-to-day managers alone without any direction from his office (until things go wrong).[15] Organizations that decentralize (delegate) authority enable managers to make significant decisions, to gain skills, and to advance in the company. By virtue of their right to make decisions on a broad range of issues, managers develop expertise that enables them to cope with problems of higher management. Managers with broad decision-making power often make difficult decisions. Consequentially, they are trained for promotion into positions of even greater authority and responsibility. Upper management can readily compare managers on the basis of actual decision-making performance. Advancement of managers on the basis of demon-

---

[13]"No More Mr. Nice Guy at P&G—Not by a Long Shot," *Business Week*, February 3, 1992, pp. 54–55.

[14]Jeffrey A. Alexander, "Adaptive Change in Corporate Control Practices," *Academy of Management Journal*, March 1991, pp. 162–93.

[15]"Why U.S. Shoe Is Looking Down at the Heel," *Business Week*, July 4, 1988, p. 60.

strated performance can eliminate favoritism and minimize personality in the promotion process.

Second, high delegation of authority can lead to a competitive climate within the organization. Managers are motivated to contribute in this competitive atmosphere, since they're compared with their peers on various performance measures. A competitive environment in which managers compete on sales, cost reduction, and employee development targets can be a positive factor in overall organizational performance. Competitive environments can also produce destructive behavior if one manager's success occurs at the expense of another's. But regardless of whether it's positive or destructive, significant competition exists only when individuals have authority to do those things that enable them to win.

Finally, managers who have relatively high authority can exercise more autonomy and thus satisfy their desires to participate in problem solving. This autonomy can lead to managerial creativity and ingenuity, which contribute to the adaptiveness and development of the organization and managers. As we've seen in earlier chapters, opportunities to participate in setting goals can be positive motivators. But a necessary condition for goal setting is authority to make decisions. Many organizations, large and small, choose to follow the policy of decentralization of authority.

Decisions to decentralize often follow experiences with centralization. For example, in the early 1990s, Hewlett-Packard (HP) began to rethink decisions it had made in the 1980s. Those 1980s decisions had centralized operations at the expense of product manager's autonomy. The impetus for the decision to centralize was the increasing cost of duplication at the local level. For example, each HP unit once manufactured its own circuit boards for its own products, even though the circuit boards were interchangeable. This arrangement enabled local managers to have control and flexibility over volume and quality. But the cost of duplication became intolerable as competition forced down the prices of HP products. Circuit board production was consolidated in a few manufacturing sites under the direction of a single manager.

www.ibm.com

The downside of the decision was the creation of committees and procedures, a seemingly impenetrable maze of bureaucracy. The company reversed its earlier decision to centralize when it announced a major reorganization. John Young, HP's CEO, decided to go the way of many competitors, including IBM, by reducing the number of managerial levels in the organization structure and decentralizing decisions to managers of more or less independent operating units. Each unit has its own sales force concentrating on selling the unit's product. No doubt the reorganization will be worked out over a long time and with mixed results, but HP's way of the future seems to rest on decentralization rather than centralization.[16]

Decentralization of authority has its benefits, but these benefits aren't without costs. Organizations that are unable or unwilling to bear these costs will find reasons to centralize authority.

---

[16]Daniel S. Levine, "Justice Served," *Sales and Marketing Management,* May 1995, pp. 52–61, and "Hewlett-Packard Rethinks Itself," *Business Week,* April 1, 1991, pp. 76–79.

── Management Pointer 15.1 ──

**WHEN TO DELEGATE
AUTHORITY**

A manager can be guaranteed no simple answers to complex problems, but the following considerations can be taken into account when deciding how much authority to delegate to a particular job or employee:

1. How routine and straightforward are the job's or unit's required decisions? The authority for routine decisions can be centralized. For example, fast-food restaurants such as Kentucky Fried Chicken centralize the decision of food preparation so as to ensure consistent quality at all stores. However, the local store manager makes the decisions to hire and dismiss employees. This question points out the importance of the distinction between deciding and doing. The local store prepares the food, but the headquarters staff decides how to prepare it.

2. Are individuals competent to make the decision? Even if the decision is nonroutine (as in the case of hiring employees), if the local manager is not competent to recruit and select employees, then employment decisions must be centralized. This question implies that delegation of authority can differ among individuals depending upon each one's ability to make the decision.

3. Are individuals motivated to make the decision? Capable individuals aren't always motivated individuals. We discussed motivation and individual differences in earlier chapters. Decision making can be difficult and stressful, thus discouraging some individuals from accepting authority. It can also involve a level of commitment to the organization that an individual isn't willing to make. Motivation must accompany competency to create conducive conditions for decentralization.

4. Finally, to return to the points we made earlier, do the benefits of decentralization outweigh its costs? This question is perhaps the most difficult to answer because many benefits and costs are assessed in subjective terms. Nevertheless, managers should at least attempt to make a benefit-cost analysis.

Reasons to Centralize Authority

Managers must be trained to make the decisions that go with delegated authority. Formal training programs can be quite expensive, which can more than offset the benefits.

Second, many managers are accustomed to making decisions and resist delegating authority to their subordinates. Consequently, they may perform at lower levels of effectiveness because they believe that delegation of authority involves losing control.

Third, administrative costs are incurred because new or altered accounting and performance systems must be developed to provide top management with information about the effects of their subordinates' decisions. When lower levels of management have authority, top management must have some means of reviewing the use of that authority. Consequently, they typically create reporting systems that inform them of the outcomes of decisions made at lower levels in the organization.

The fourth and perhaps most pragmatic reason to centralize is that decentralization means duplication of functions. Each autonomous unit must be truly self-supporting to be independent. But that involves a potentially high cost of duplication. Some organizations find that the cost of decentralization outweighs the benefits.[17]

Decision Guidelines

Like most managerial issues, whether authority should be delegated in high or low degree cannot be resolved simply.[18] As usual, in managerial decision making, whether to centralize or decentralize authority can only be guided by general questions. Managers faced with the issue should answer the four questions raised in Management Pointer 15.1.

DEPARTMENTAL BASES

The rationale for grouping jobs rests on the necessity for coordinating them. The specialized jobs are separate, interrelated parts of the total task, whose accomplishment requires the accomplishment of each of the jobs. But the jobs must be performed in the specific manner and sequence intended by management when they were defined. As the number of specialized jobs in an organization increases, there comes a

---

[17]Jay Greene and Judith Nemes, "To Centralize or Not to Centralize: Centralization Paying Off at Not-for-Profits, For-Profits Cut Back at Corporate," *Modern Healthcare,* October 8, 1990, pp. 30–36.

[18]Richard S. Blackburn, "Dimensions of Structure: A Review and Reappraisal," *Academy of Management Review,* January 1982, pp. 59–66.

point when they can no longer be effectively coordinated by a single manager. Thus, to create manageable numbers of jobs, they are combined into smaller groups and a new job is defined—manager of the group.

The crucial managerial consideration when creating departments is determining the basis for grouping jobs. Of particular importance is the determination for the bases for departments that report to the top management position. In fact, numerous bases are used throughout the organization, but the basis used at the highest level determines critical dimensions of the organization. Some of the more widely used **departmentalization bases**[19] are described in the following sections.

Functional Departmentalization

Managers can combine jobs according to the functions of the organization. Every organization must undertake certain activities to do its work. These necessary activities are the organization's functions. The necessary functions of a manufacturing firm include production, marketing, finance, accounting, and personnel. These activities are necessary to create, produce, and sell a product. Necessary functions of a commercial bank include taking deposits, making loans, and investing the bank's funds. The functions of a hospital include surgery, psychiatry, housekeeping, pharmacy, nursing, and personnel.[20] Each of these functions can be a specific department, and jobs can be combined according to them. The functional basis is often found in relatively small organizations providing a narrow range of products and services. It is also widely used as the basis in divisions of large multiproduct organizations.

Manufacturing organizations are typically structured on a functional basis (Exhibit 15.1). The functions are engineering, manufacturing, reliability, distribution, finance, personnel, public relations, and purchasing. The functional basis has wide application in both service and manufacturing organizations. The specific configuration of functions that appear as separate departments varies from organization to organization.

The principal advantage of the basis is its efficiency. That is, it seems logical to have a department that consists of experts in a particular field such as production or accounting. By having departments of specialists, management creates efficient units. An accountant is generally more efficient when working with other accountants and other individuals who have similar backgrounds and interests. They can share expertise to get the work done. General Motors (GM) attracted considerable attention when it combined its traditional product divisions into two functional departments: production and sales. Now under the direction of a new chief operations officer (COO), GM has accelerated its consolidation of its auto divisions into one functionally organized entity.[21] The driving force behind

---

[19]Marianne Jelinek, "Organization Structure: The Basic Conformations," in *Organization by Design* (eds.), Marianne Jelinek, Joseph A. Litterer, and Raymond E. Miles (Plano, TX: Business Publications, 1981), pp. 293–302.

[20]Peggy Leatt and Rodney Schneck, "Criteria for Grouping Nursing Subunits in Hospitals," *Academy of Management Journal,* March 1984, pp. 150–64.

[21]James R. Treece and John Templeman, "Jack Smith Is Already on a Tear at GM," *Business Week,* May 11, 1992, p. 37.

EXHIBIT 15.1
**Functional
Departmentalization
Structure**

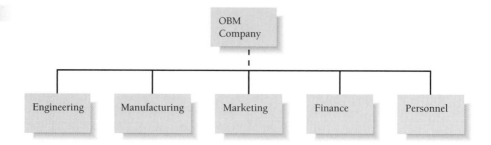

www.gm.com

GM's reorganization was a desire to reduce the cost of developing and marketing cars by realizing the efficiencies of function-based organization structure.[22]

A major disadvantage of this departmental basis is that, because specialists are working with and encouraging each other in their areas of expertise and interest, organizational goals may be sacrificed in favor of departmental goals. Accountants may see only their problems and not those of production or marketing or the total organization. In other words, the culture of, and identification with, the department are often stronger than identification with the organization and its culture.

Territorial Departmentalization

Another basis for departmentalizing is to establish groups according to geographic area. The logic is that all activities in a given region should be assigned to a manager. This individual would be in charge of all operations in that particular geographic area.

In large organizations, territorial arrangements are advantageous because physical separation of activities makes centralized coordination difficult. For example, it is extremely difficult for someone in New York to manage salespeople in Kansas City. It makes sense to assign the managerial job to someone in Kansas City.

Large multiunit retail stores are often organized along territorial lines. Specific retail outlets in a geographic area will comprise units, often termed *divisions*, which report to a regional manager who in turn may report to a corporate manager. For example, the manager of the Lexington, Kentucky, retail store of a national chain reports to the president, Midwest Division. The Midwest Division reports to the headquarters unit.

Territorial departmentalization provides a training ground for managerial personnel. The company is able to place managers in territories and then assess their progress in that geographic region. The experience that managers acquire in a territory away from headquarters provides valuable insights about how products and/or services are accepted in the field. Exhibit 15.2 depicts a territorial organization structure.

---

[22]Richard B. Chase and David A. Tansik, "The Customer Contact Model for Organization Design," *Management Science,* September 1983, pp. 1037–50.

EXHIBIT 15.2
Territorial
Departmentalization
Structure

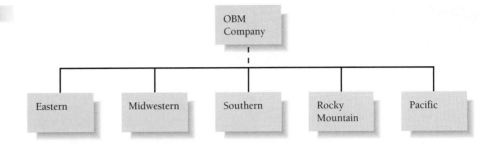

Product Departmentalization

Managers of many large diversified companies group jobs on the basis of product. All jobs associated with producing and selling a product or product line will be placed under the direction of one manager. Product becomes the preferred basis as a firm grows by increasing the number of products it markets. As a firm grows, it's difficult to coordinate the various functional departments and it becomes advantageous to establish product units. This form of organization allows personnel to develop total expertise in researching, manufacturing, and distributing a product line. Concentrating authority, responsibility, and accountability in a specific product department allows top management to coordinate actions.

The organization structure using products as the basis for departments has been a key development in modern capitalism. The term *divisional organization* refers to this form of organization structure. Most of the major and large firms of developed countries use it to some degree. The product-based divisions are often free-standing units that can design, produce, and market their own products, even in competition with other divisions of the same firm.[23] General Motors pioneered the divisional structure when it evolved into the five separate auto divisions: Chevrolet, Pontiac, Oldsmobile, Buick, and Cadillac. As we noted in our discussion of the functional form, General Motors has begun a process of moving away from the purely product-based, divisional form.

A product department organization is shown in Exhibit 15.3 with three product divisions (small household appliances, large household appliances, and commercial appliances) reporting to the OBM corporate headquarters. Within each of these units we find production and marketing personnel. Since managers of product divisions coordinate sales, manufacturing, and distribution of a product, they become the overseers of a profit center. In this manner, profit responsibility is implemented in product-based organizations. Managers are often asked to establish profit goals at the beginning of a time period and then to compare actual profit with planned profit.

Product-based organizations foster initiative and autonomy by providing division managers with the resources necessary to carry out their profit plans. But such organizations face the difficult issue of deciding how much redundancy is necessary. Divisional structures contain some degree of redundancy because each division wants its own research, engineering, marketing, production, and all

---

[23]Joseph T. Mahoney, "The Adoption of the Multidivisional Form of Organization: A Contingency Approach," *Journal of Management,* January 1992, pp. 49–72.

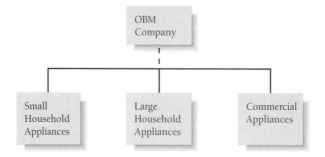

EXHIBIT 15.3
Product
Departmentalization
Structure

other functions necessary to do business. Thus, technical and professional personnel are found throughout the organization at the division levels. The cost of this arrangement can be exorbitant.

Customer Departmentalization

Customers and clients can be a basis for grouping jobs.[24] Examples of customer-oriented departments are the organization structures of educational institutions. Some institutions have regular (day and night) courses and extension divisions. In some instances, a professor will be affiliated solely with the regular division or extension division. In fact, titles of some faculty positions specifically mention the extension division.

Another form of customer departmentalization is the loan department in a commercial bank. Loan officers are often associated with industrial, commercial, or agricultural loans. The customer will be served by one of these three loan officers.

The importance of customer satisfaction has stimulated firms to search for creative ways to serve people better. Since the Bell System broke up, competition for customers has forced AT&T to organize into customer-based units that identify with the needs of specific customers. Prior to the breakup, the firm was organized around functions. The move toward customer-based departments at Bell Labs was accompanied by efforts to implement total quality management (TQM), a customer-focused management practice that is reinforced in the customer-based structure.[25]

Some department stores are departmentalized to some degree on a customer basis, as shown in Exhibit 15.4. They have groupings such as retail store customers, mail-order customers, institutional customers, and government customers. Organizations with customer-based departments are better able to satisfy customer-identified needs than organizations that base departments on noncustomer factors.[26]

---

[24]Alf H. Walls, III, *Rethinking Marketing* (Westport, CT: Quorum, 2001).

[25]Michael Maccoby, "Transforming R&D Services at Bell Labs," *Research-Technology Management,* January–February 1992, pp. 46–49.

[26]Jay R. Galbraith and Robert K. Kazanjian, "Organizing to Implement Strategies of Diversity and Globalization: The Role of Matrix Organizations," *Human Resource Management,* Spring 1986, pp. 37–54.

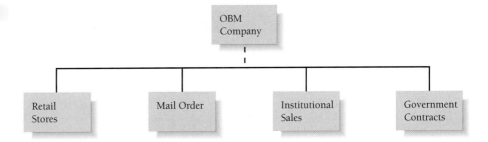

EXHIBIT 15.4
Customer
Departmentalization
Structure

OBM Company

Retail Stores | Mail Order | Institutional Sales | Government Contracts

SPAN OF CONTROL

The determination of appropriate bases for departmentalization establishes the kinds of jobs that will be grouped together. But that determination doesn't establish the number of jobs to be included in a specific group, the issue of **span of control.** Generally, the issue comes down to the decision of how many people a manager can oversee; that is, will the organization be more effective if the span of control is relatively wide or narrow? The question is basically concerned with determining the volume of interpersonal relationships that the department's manager is able to handle. Moreover, the span of control must be defined to include not only formally assigned subordinates, but also those who have access to the manager. Not only may a manager be placed in a position of being responsible for immediate subordinates, she may also be chairperson of several committees and task groups.[27]

The number of potential interpersonal relationships between a manager and subordinates increases geometrically as the number of subordinates increases arithmetically. This relationship holds because managers potentially contend with three types of interpersonal relationships: (1) direct single, (2) direct group, and (3) cross. Direct single relationships occur between the manager and each subordinate individually (that is, in a one-on-one setting). Direct group relationships occur between the manager and each possible permutation of subordinates. Finally, cross relationships occur when subordinates interact with one another.

The critical consideration in determining the manager's span of control is not the number of potential relationships. Rather it's the frequency and intensity of the actual relationships that are important. Not all relationships will occur, and those that do will vary in importance. If we shift our attention from potential to actual relationships as the bases for determining optimum span of control, at least three factors appear to be important.

Required Contact

In research and development as well as medical and production work, there's a need for frequent contact and a high degree of coordination between a superior and subordinates. Conferences and other forms of consultation often aid in attaining goals within a constrained time period. For example, the research and development team leader may have to consult frequently with team members so that a project is completed within a time period that will allow the organization

---

[27]V. Nilakant, "Dynamics of Middle Managerial Roles: A Study in Four Indian Organizations," *Journal of Managerial Psychology* (UK), 6, no. 1, 1991, pp. 17–24.

to place a product on the market. Thus, instead of relying upon memos and reports, it is in the best interest of the organization to have as many in-depth contacts with the team as possible. A large span of control would preclude contacting subordinates so frequently, which could impede the project. In general, the greater the inherent ambiguity in an individual's job, the greater the need for supervision to avoid conflict and stress.[28]

Degree of Specialization

The degree of specialized employees is a critical consideration in establishing the span of control at all levels of management. It is generally accepted that a manager at the lower organizational level can oversee more subordinates because work at the lower level is more specialized and less complicated than at higher levels of management. Management can combine highly specialized and similar jobs into relatively large departments because the employees may not need close supervision.

Ability to Communicate

Instructions, guidelines, and policies must be communicated verbally to subordinates in most work situations. The need to discuss job-related factors influences the span of control. The individual who can clearly and concisely communicate with subordinates is able to manage more people than one who can't.

The widespread practice of downsizing and "flattening" organizations of all kinds has direct implications for the span-of-control decision. Downsizing reduces the number of all employees, but relatively more managers (usually middle managers) than nonmanagers.[29] This increases the number of nonmanagers per manager; consequently, the average span of control of each manager increases. Whether the factors of required contact, degree of specialization, and ability to communicate have any bearing on the resultant spans of control can be debated. In fact, many middle managers whose spans of control have been widened believe that top management made the decision without regard to these factors. The Organizational Encounter describes experiences with downsizing in American firms.

DIMENSIONS OF STRUCTURE

The four design decisions (division of labor, delegation of authority, departmentalization, and span of control) result in a structure of organizations. Researchers and practitioners of management have attempted to develop their understanding of relationships between structures and performance, attitudes, effectiveness, and other variables thought to be important. This development of understanding has been hampered not only by the complexity of the relationships themselves, but also by the difficulty of defining and measuring the concept of organizational structure.

---

[28]Ronald J. Burke and Esther R. Greenglass, "Work Status Congruence, Work Outcomes and Psychological Well-Being," *Stress Medicine*, March 2000, pp. 91–99.

[29]Robin Bellis-Jones and Max Hand, "Improving Managerial Spans of Control," *Management Accounting* (UK), October 1989, pp. 20–21, and John S. McClenahen, "Managing More People in the '90s," *Industry Week*, March 20, 1989, pp. 30–38.

The Effects of Downsizing on the Spans of Control of Managers

Nearly every firm in the global economy either has downsized or has considered the implications of doing so. Some giants in the basic industries such as IBM, GM, Ford, Hewlett-Packard, Ford, and Chrysler as well as many of the 21 winners to date of the prestigious Baldrige Award have already reduced the number of middle managers and increased the spans of control of all managers. This decision is based on the idea that highly trained individuals throughout the organization, empowered with authority and competence, can manage themselves. The idea isn't new, but widespread application of the idea is new. Many firms, large and small, have reported their experiences with wider spans of control—some positive, others negative. Positive experiences stress the renewed commitment of employees who have the benefits of empowerment; negative experiences stress the additional pressures placed on managers to be responsible for the work performance of more employees.

One observer points out that for flattening to reach its full potential, managers and employees must exercise initiative to "add value" to the directives they receive. The idea of adding value implies that individuals take the directive and evaluate its full potential for adding to the organization's well-being and effectiveness. Another observer of flattening in the U.S. banking industry states that whether the practice works depends upon the willingness and ability of employees at the local level to provide quality service and high performance, even peak performance, of their assigned duties. But perhaps the most important factor bearing on the practice's success is the manager's ability to comprehend the new relationship between managers and nonmanagers: No longer can managers set themselves apart from those they manage; they must develop helping and coaching relationships with their subordinates.

Sources: Bradley L. Kirkman and Debra L. Shapiro, "The Impact of Cultural Values on Employees to Teams," *Academy of Management Review*, July 1997, pp. 730–37; Kim S. Cameron, "Strategies for Successful Downsizing," *Human Resource Management*, Summer 1994, pp. 189–211; John A. Byrne, "The Pain of Downsizing," *Business Week*, May 9, 1994, pp. 62–69; Anat Bird, "Organizational Flattening within the U.S. Banking Industry," *Bankers Magazine*, July–August 1991, pp. 67–70.

Although universal agreement on a common set of dimensions that measure differences in structure is neither possible nor desirable, some suggestions can be made. At present, three dimensions are often used in research and practice to describe structure: formalization, centralization, and complexity.[30]

Formalization

The dimension of **formalization** refers to the extent to which expectations regarding the means and ends of work are specified, written, and enforced. An organization structure described as highly formalized would be one with rules and procedures to prescribe what each individual should be doing.[31] Such organizations have written standard operating procedures, specified directives, and explicit policy. In terms of the four design decisions, formalization is the result of high specialization of labor, high delegation of authority, the use of functional departments, and wide spans of control.[32]

1. High specialization of labor (as in the auto industry) is amenable to the development of written work rules and procedures. Jobs are so specialized as to

[30]James P. Walsh and Robert D. Dewar, "Formalization and the Organizational Life-Cycle," *Journal of Management Studies*, March 1991, pp. 103–41.

[31]Robert W. Hetherington, "The Effects of Formalization on Departments of a Multi-Hospital System," *Journal of Management Studies*, March 1991, pp. 103–41.

[32]Poeter H. Grinyear and Masoud Yasai-Ardekani, "Dimensions of Organizational Structure: A Critical Replication," *Academy of Management Journal*, September 1980, pp. 405–21, discusses formalization in relation to centralization.

leave little to the discretion of the jobholder.

2. High delegation of authority creates the need for checks on its use. Consequently, the organization writes guidelines for decision making and insists upon reports describing the use of authority.

3. Functional departments are made up of jobs with great similarities. This basis brings together jobs that make up an occupation such as accountants, engineers, and machinists. Because of the similarity of the jobs and the rather straightforward nature of the department's activities, management can develop written documents to govern those activities.

4. Wide spans of control discourage one-on-one supervision. There are simply too many subordinates for managers to keep up with on a one-to-one basis. Consequently, managers require written reports to inform them. Although formalization is defined in terms of written rules and procedures, we must understand how they're viewed by the employees. Some organizations have all the appearances of formalization, complete with thick manuals of rules, procedures, and policies, yet employees don't perceive them as affecting their behavior. Thus, where rules and procedures exist, they must be enforced if they're to affect behavior.[33]

Centralization

Centralization refers to the location of decision-making authority in the hierarchy of the organization. More specifically, the concept refers to delegation of authority among the jobs in the organization. Typically, researchers and practitioners think of centralization in terms of (1) decision making and (2) control. But despite the apparent simplicity of the concept, it can be difficult to apply.

The difficulty derives from three sources. First, people at the same level can have different decision-making authority. Second, not all decisions are of equal importance in organizations. For example, a typical management practice is to delegate authority to make routine operating decisions (i.e., decentralization), but to retain authority to make strategic decisions (i.e., centralization). Third, individuals may not perceive that they really have authority even though their job descriptions include it. Thus, objectively they have authority, but subjectively they don't.[34]

The relationships between centralization and the four design decisions are generally as follows:

1. The higher the specialization of labor, the greater the centralization. This relationship holds because highly specialized jobs do not require the discretion that authority provides.

2. The less authority that is delegated, the greater the centralization. By definition of the terms, *centralization* involves retaining authority in the top management jobs, rather than delegating it to lower levels in the organization.

3. The greater the use of functional departments, the greater the centralization. The use of functional departments requires that activities of the several inter-

---

[33]Eric J. Walton, "The Comparison of Measures of Organization Structure," *Academy of Management Review*, January 1981, pp. 155–60.

[34]Jeffrey D. Ford, "Institutional versus Questionnaire Measures of Organizational Structure," *Academy of Management Journal*, September 1979, pp. 601–610.

related departments be coordinated. Consequently, authority to coordinate them will be retained in top management.

4. The wider the spans of control, the greater the centralization. Wide spans of control are associated with relatively specialized jobs which, as we've seen, have little need for authority.

Complexity

Complexity is the direct outgrowth of dividing work and creating departments. Specifically, the concept refers to the number of distinctly different job titles, or occupational groupings, and the number of distinctly different units, or departments. The fundamental idea is that organizations with many different kinds of jobs and units create more complicated managerial and organizational problems than those with fewer jobs and departments.

Complexity, then, relates to differences among jobs and units. Therefore, it's not surprising that differentiation is often used synonymously with complexity. Moreover, it has become standard practice to use the term *horizontal differentiation* to refer to the number of different units at the same level;[35] *vertical differentiation* refers to the number of levels in the organization.[36] The relationships between complexity (horizontal and vertical differentiation) and the four design decisions are generally as follows:

1. The greater the specialization of labor, the greater the complexity. Specialization is the process of creating different jobs and thus more complexity. Specialization of labor contributes primarily to horizontal differentiation.

2. The greater the delegation of authority, the greater the complexity of the organization. Delegation of authority is typically associated with a lengthy chain of command (that is, with a relatively large number of managerial levels). Thus, delegation of authority contributes to vertical differentiation.

3. The greater the use of territorial, customer, and product bases, the greater the complexity. These bases involve creating self-sustaining units that operate much like freestanding organizations. Consequently, there must be considerable delegation of authority and, thus, considerable complexity.[37]

4. Narrow spans of control are associated with high complexity. This relationship holds because narrow spans are necessary when the jobs to be supervised are quite different one from another. A supervisor can manage more people in a simple organization than in a complex organization. The apparently simple matter of span of control can have profound effects on organizational and individual behavior. Hence, we should expect the controversy that surrounds it.

Relationships between dimensions of organizational structure and the four design decisions are summarized in Exhibit 15.5. It notes only the causes of high

---

[35]Brian C. Robertson, *There's No Place like Work* (Dallas: Spence, 2000).

[36]Richard L. Priem and Joseph Rosenstein, "Is Organization Theory Obvious to Practitioners? A Test of One Established Theory," *Organization Science,* September–October 2000, pp. 509–24.

[37]Phillip G. Clampitt, Robert J. DeKoch, and Thomas Cashman, "A Strategy for Communicating about Uncertainty," *Academy of Management Executive,* November 2000, pp. 41–57.

EXHIBIT 15.5	Organization Dimensions and Organizational Decisions
Dimensions	**Decisions**
High formalization	1. High specialization
	2. Delegated authority
	3. Functional departments
	4. Wide spans of control
High centralization	1. High specialization
	2. Centralized authority
	3. Functional departments
	4. Wide spans of control
High complexity	1. High specialization
	2. Delegated authority
	3. Territorial, customer, and product departments
	4. Narrow spans of control

formalization, centralization, and complexity. However, the relationships are symmetrical—the causes of low formalization, centralization, and complexity are the opposite of those in the exhibit.

ORGANIZATION DESIGN MODELS

The three models of organizational design described in this section are important ideas in management theory and practice. Because of their importance, they receive considerable theoretical and practical attention. Although many variations on these three models can be found in practice, we will focus on the basic elements of *mechanistic, organic,* and *matrix* organization designs.

The Mechanistic Model

A body of literature emerging during the early 20th century considered the problem of designing the structure of an organization as but one of a number of managerial tasks, including planning and controlling. These writers' objective was to define *principles* that could guide managers in performing their tasks. An early writer, Henri Fayol, proposed a number of principles that he had found useful in managing a large coal mining company in France.[38] Some of Fayol's principles dealt with the management function of organizing; four of these are relevant for understanding the mechanistic model.

The Principle of Specialization   Fayol stated that specialization is the best means for making use of individuals and groups of individuals. At the time of Fayol's writings, the limit of specialization (that is, the optimal point) had not been definitively determined. Scientific management popularized a number of methods for implementing specialization of labor. These methods, such as work

---

[38]Henri Fayol, *General and Industrial Management* J. A. Conbrough (trans.) (Geneva: L International Management Institute, 1929). The more widely circulated translation is that of Constance Storrs (London: Pitman, 1949).

standards and motion-and-time study, emphasized technical (not behavioral) dimensions of work.

The Principle of Unity of Direction   According to this principle, jobs should be grouped according to specialty. Engineers should be grouped with engineers, salespeople with salespeople, accountants with accountants. The departmentalization basis that most nearly implements this principle is the functional basis.

The Principle of Authority and Responsibility   Fayol believed that a manager should be delegated sufficient authority to carry out her assigned responsibilities. Because the assigned responsibilities of top managers are considerably more important to the future of the organization than those of lower management, applying the principle inevitably leads to centralized authority. Centralized authority is a logical outcome not only because of top managements' larger responsibilities but also because work at this level is more complex, the number of workers involved is greater, and the relationship between actions and results is remote.

The Scalar Chain Principle   The natural result of implementing the preceding three principles is a graded chain of managers from the ultimate authority to the lowest ranks. The scalar chain is the route for all vertical communications in an organization. Accordingly, all communications from the lowest level must pass through each superior in the chain of command. Correspondingly, communication from the top must pass through each subordinate until it reaches the appropriate level.

Fayol's writings became part of a literature that, although each contributor made unique contributions, had a common thrust. Writers such as Mooney and Reiley,[39] Follet,[40] and Urwick[41] all shared the common objective of defining the principles that should guide the design and management of organizations. A complete review of their individual contributions won't be attempted here. However, we'll review the ideas of one individual, Max Weber, who made important contributions to the mechanistic model. He described applications of the mechanistic model and coined the term *bureaucracy*.

Bureaucracy   Bureaucracy has various meanings. The traditional usage is the political science concept of government by bureaus but without participation by the governed. In laymen's terms, *bureaucracy* refers to the negative consequences of large organizations, such as excessive red tape, procedural delays, and general frustration.[42] But in Max Weber's writings, *bureaucracy* refers to a particular way to organize collective activities.[43] Weber's interest in bureaucracy reflected his

---

[39]James D. Mooney and Alklan C. Reiley, *Onward Industry* (New York: Harper & Row, 1939). Revised in James D. Mooney, *The Principles of Organization* (New York: Harper & Row, 1947).

[40]Henry C. Metcalf and Lyndall Urwick (eds.), *Dynamic Administration: The Collected Papers of Mary Parker Follett* (New York: Harper & Row, 1940).

[41]Lyndall Urwick, *The Elements of Administration* (New York: Harper & Row, 1944).

[42]Michael Crozier, *The Bureaucratic Phenomenon* (Chicago: University of Chicago Press, 1964), p. 3.

[43]Max Weber, *The Theory of Social and Economic Organization*, A. M. Henderson and Talcott Parsons (trans.) (New York: Oxford University Press, 1947).

concern for the ways society develops hierarchies of control so that one group can, in effect, dominate other groups.[44] Organizational design involves domination in the sense that authority involves the legitimate right to exact obedience from others. His search for the forms of domination that evolve in society led him to the study of bureaucratic structure.

According to Weber, the bureaucratic structure is "superior to any other form in precision, in stability, in the stringency of its discipline and its reliability. It thus makes possible a high degree of calculability of results for the heads of the organization and for those acting in relation to it."[45] The bureaucracy compares to other organizations "as does the machine with nonmechanical modes of production."[46] These words capture the essence of the mechanistic model of organizational design.

To achieve the maximum benefits of the bureaucratic design, Weber believed that an organization must have the following characteristics.

1. All tasks will be divided into highly specialized jobs. Through specialization, jobholders become expert in their jobs, and management can hold them responsible for the effective performance of their duties.

2. Each task is performed according to a system of abstract rules to ensure uniformity and coordination of different tasks. The rationale for this practice is that the manager can eliminate uncertainty in task performance due to individual differences.

3. Each member or office of the organization is accountable for job performance to one, and only one, manager. Managers hold their authority because of their expert knowledge and because it's delegated from the top of the hierarchy. An unbroken chain of command exists.

4. Each employee of the organization relates to other employees and clients in an impersonal, formal manner, maintaining a social distance with subordinates and clients. The purpose of this practice is to ensure that personalities and favoritism do not interfere with efficient accomplishment of the organization's objectives.

5. Employment in the bureaucratic organization is based on technical qualifications and is protected against arbitrary dismissal. Similarly, promotions are based on seniority and achievement. Employment in the organization is viewed as a lifelong career, and a high degree of loyalty is engendered.

These five characteristics of bureaucracy describe the kind of organizations Fayol believed to be most effective. Both Fayol and Weber described the same type of organization, one that functions in a machinelike manner to accomplish the organization's goals in a highly efficient manner. Thus, the term *mechanistic* aptly describes such organizations.

The mechanistic model achieves high levels of production and efficiency due to its structural characteristics:

1. It's highly complex because of its emphasis on specialization of labor.

---

[44]Richard M. Weiss, "Weber on Bureaucracy: Management Consultant or Political Theorists?" *Academy of Management Review,* April 1983, pp. 242–48.

[45]Weber, *The Theory of Social and Economic Organization,* p. 334.

[46]*From Max Weber: Essays in Sociology,* H. H. Gerth and C. W. Mills (trans.) (New York: Oxford University Press, 1946), p. 214.

2. It's highly centralized because of its emphasis on authority and accountability.

3. It's highly formalized because of its emphasis on function as the basis for departments.

These organizational characteristics and practices underlie a widely used organizational model. One of the more successful practitioners of the mechanistic model has been United Parcel Services (UPS).[47] This profitable delivery firm competes directly with the U.S. Post Office in the delivery of small packages. Even though the post office is subsidized and pays no taxes, UPS has been able to compete successfully by stressing efficiency of operations. It apparently achieves great efficiencies through a combination of automation and organization design. Specialization and formalization are highly visible characteristics of UPS structure. UPS uses clearly defined jobs and an explicit chain of command. The tasks range from truck washers and maintenance personnel to top management and are arranged in a hierarchy of authority consisting of eight managerial levels. The high degree of specialization enables management to use many forms of written reports such as daily worksheets that record each employee's work quotas and performance. Company policies and practices are in written form and routinely consulted in hiring and promotion decisions. Apparently, UPS has found the mechanistic form of organization to be well suited for its purposes.

www.ups.com

www.usps.gov

UPS has more than 1,000 industrial engineers on its payroll. Their job is to design jobs and to set the standards that specify the way UPS employees do their jobs. For example, engineers instruct drivers to walk to the customer's door at the rate of three feet per second and to knock on the door. Company management believes that the standards aren't just a way to obtain efficiency and production, but also provide the employee with important feedback on how he's doing the job. All in all, the company's efficiency bears testimony to its use of the mechanistic model.

The Organic Model

The **organic model** of organizational design stands in sharp contrast to the mechanistic model due to their different organizational characteristics and practices. The most distinct differences between the two models are a consequence of the different effectiveness criteria each seeks to maximize. While the mechanistic model seeks to maximize efficiency and production, the organic model seeks to maximize satisfaction, flexibility, and development.

The organic organization is flexible to changing environmental demands because its design encourages greater utilization of the human potential. Managers are encouraged to adopt practices that tap the full range of human motivations through job design that stresses personal growth and responsibility. Decision making, control, and goal-setting processes are decentralized and shared at all levels of the organization. Communications flow throughout the organization, not simply down the chain of command. These practices are intended to implement a basic assumption of the organic model which states that an organization

---

[47]Kent C. Nelson, "Efficiency Wasn't Enough, So We Learned How to Dance," *Computerworld*, March 23, 1992, p. 33, and Richard B. Chase and Nicholas J. Aquilano, *Operations Management* (Homewood, IL: Richard D. Irwin, 1992), p. 533.

will be effective to the extent that its structure is "such as to ensure a maximum probability that in all interactions and in all relationships with the organization, each member, in the light of his background, values, desires, and expectations, will view the experience as supportive and one which builds and maintains a sense of personal worth and importance."[48]

An organizational design that provides individuals with this sense of personal worth and motivation and that facilitates satisfaction, flexibility, and development would have the following characteristics:

1. It's relatively simple because of its de-emphasis of specialization and its emphasis on increasing job range.
2. It's relatively decentralized because of its emphasis on delegation of authority and increasing job depth.
3. It's relatively informal because of its emphasis on product and customer as bases for departments.

A leading spokesperson and developer of ideas supporting applications of the organic model is Rensis Likert. His studies at the University of Michigan have led him to argue that organic organizations (Likert uses the term *System-4*) differ markedly from mechanistic organizations (Likert uses the term *System-1*) along a number of structural dimensions.[49]

The literature is filled with reports of efforts to implement organic designs in actual organizations.[50] Likert himself reports many of these studies.[51] One organization has received considerable attention for its efforts to implement organic principles. Aid Association for Lutherans (AAL) operates a huge insurance business. It has transformed its organization from a mechanistic to an organic structure in an effort to take advantage of benefits of the **self-directed team** concept. Prior to reorganization, AAL was organized mechanistically according to the traditional functions of the insurance industry, and employees were highly trained to deal with processing, underwriting, valuations, and premium services functions. Specialization resulted in considerable efficiency dealing with customers requiring the attention of one of the functions. But when multiple functions were involved, the organization became bogged down.

AAL's management explored potential benefits of establishing teams of employees that could handle all details of any customer transaction, whether health, life, or casualty insurance. The teams consist of individuals who once were responsible for functions; now they're responsible for customers and take initiative that once required management prodding. As a result of teams' assumption of responsibility for their own management, three levels of management have been eliminated from the organization. The organization is now simpler and more decentralized than before, and therefore more organic and less mechanistic.

AAL also implemented a form of employee compensation termed "pay for knowledge" to encourage employees to adopt the new work system. It provides individuals with pay increases for obtaining additional knowledge that enables

---

[48]Rensis Likert, *New Patterns of Management* (New York: McGraw-Hill, 1961), and Rensis Likert, *The Human Organization* (New York: McGraw-Hill, 1967).

[49]Likert, *New Patterns of Management and the Human Organization.* New York: McGraw-Hill, 1961.

[50]Joanne B. Ciulla, *The Working Life* (New York: Times Books, 2000).

[51]Likert, *New Patterns of Management and the Human Organization.* (New York: McGraw-Hill, 1961).

them to improve their job performance. In the context of AAL's organic organization, employees needed to learn not only new technical knowledge, but also new interpersonal knowledge because working with other individuals in teams is critical to the success of the new organizational design.[52]

Both the mechanistic and the organic models have their advantages and disadvantages. Either or both can be optimal depending upon circumstances. The matrix organization design model has special appeal because it can exploit the advantages of mechanistic and organic models and minimize their disadvantages.

The Matrix Model

An organization design, termed **matrix organization**, attempts to maximize the strengths and minimize the weaknesses of both the functional and product bases. In practical terms, the matrix design combines functional and product departmental bases.[53] Companies such as American Cyanamid, Avco, Carborundum, Caterpillar Tractor, Hughes Aircraft, ITT, Monsanto Chemical, National Cash Register, Prudential Insurance, TWR, and Texas Instruments are only a few of the users of matrix organization. Public sector users include public health and social service agencies.[54] Although the exact meaning of matrix organization varies in practice, it's typically seen as a balanced compromise between functional and product organization, between departmentalization by function and by product.[55]

Matrix organizations achieve the desired balance by superimposing, or overlaying, a horizontal structure of authority, influence, and communication on the vertical structure. In the arrangement shown in Exhibit 15.6, personnel assigned in each cell belong not only to the functional department, but also to a particular product or project. For example, manufacturing, marketing, engineering, and finance specialists are assigned to work on one or more projects or products A, B, C, D, and E. As a consequence, personnel report to two managers: one in their functional department and one in the project or product unit. The existence of a *dual authority system* is a distinguishing characteristic of matrix organization. The potential conflict between allegiance to one's functional manager and one's project manager must be recognized and dealt with in matrix organizations.[56]

Matrix structures are found in organizations that (1) require responses to rapid change in two or more environments, such as technology and markets, (2) face uncertainties that generate high information processing requirements, and (3) must deal with financial and human resources constraints.[57] Managers confronting these

---

[52]Donald J. McNerney, "Compensation Case Study: Rewarding Team Performance and Individual Skillbuilding," *HR Focus*, January 1995, pp. 1, 4; Dennis H. Pillsbury, "Team Concept Makes Vorpage 1 #1 for AAL," *Life & Health Insurance Sales*, October 1993, pp. 10–11; and Fred Luthans, "A Conversation with Charles Dull," *Organizational Dynamics*, Summer 1993, pp. 57–70.

[53]D. Lei, John W. Slocum, Jr., and R. A. Pitts, "Designing Organizations for Competitive Advantage: The Power of Unlearning and Learning," *Organizational Dynamics*, Winter 1999, pp. 24–38.

[54]Ibid.

[55]Paul R. Lawrence, Harvey F. Kolondny, and Stanley M. Davis, "The Human Side of the Matrix," *Organizational Dynamics*, September 1977, p. 47; George J. Chambers, "The Individual in a Matrix Organization," *Project Management Journal*, December 1989, pp. 37–42, 50.

[56]Paul B. de Laat, "Matrix Management of Projects and Power Struggles: A Case Study of an R&D Laboratory," *Human Relations*, September 1994, pp. 1089–1119.

[57]Lei, Slocum, and Pitts, "Designing Organizations."

EXHIBIT 15.6	Matrix Organizations			
	Functions			
Project, Products	**Manufacturing**	**Marketing**	**Engineering**	**Finance**
Project or product A				
Project or product B				
Project or product C				
Project or product D				
Project or product E				

circumstances must obtain certain advantages that are most likely to be realized with matrix organization.[58]

Matrix organization facilitates the utilization of highly specialized staff and equipment. Each project or product unit can share the specialized resource with other units, rather than duplicating it to provide independent coverage for each. This is a particular advantage when projects don't require the specialist's full-time efforts. For example, a project may require only half a computer scientist's time. Rather than having several underutilized computer scientists assigned to each project, the organization can keep fewer of them fully utilized by shifting them from project to project. Such flexibility speeds response to competitive conditions, technological breakthroughs, and other environmental changes. An important UK car manufacturer, the Rover Group, has found the matrix structure to be useful, as noted in International Encounter 15.1.

Advantages of Matrix Organization   A number of advantages can be associated with the matrix design. Some of the more important ones are as follows:

Efficient Use of Resources: Matrix organization facilitates the utilization of highly specialized staff and equipment. Each project or product unit can share the specialized resource with other units rather than duplicating it to provide independent coverage for each. This advantage is particularly so when projects require less than the full-time efforts of the specialist.

Flexibility in Conditions of Change and Uncertainty: Timely response to change requires information and communication channels that efficiently get the information to the right people at the right time.[59] Matrix structures encourage constant interaction among project unit and functional department members. Information is channeled vertically and horizontally as people exchange techni-

---

[58]Christopher A. Bartlett and Sumantra Ghosal, "Organizing for Worldwide Effectiveness: The Transactional Solution," *California Management Review,* Fall 1988, pp. 54–74; James K. McCollum and J. Daniel Sherman, "The Effects of Matrix Organization Size and Number of Project Assignments on Performance," *IEEE Transactions on Engineering Management,* February 1991, pp. 75–78.

[59]Christopher K. Best, "Organizing for New Development," *Journal of Business Strategy,* July–August 1988, pp. 34–39.

Rover Group Uses Matrix Organization to Great Advantage

The Rover Group (UK) has been developing innovative management practices that incorporate teamwork, total quality management (TQM), and corporate reorganization. Among its most successful achievements is the development of the K series engine, Rover's first volume car engine in 30 years. The K series engine development effort began in 1986. To spur along the process, Rover used a project management approach. This management approach combines the time and talents of individuals from throughout the organization from all functional departments. The company selected members for the K series project team on the basis of their ability and willingness to adapt to constant change. The 18 members of the team were trained to work with other people from different functions and with different educational and technical expertise. Although team members were a part of the K series project, they continued to report to the managers of their home functional departments.

As the cross-functional project approach proved successful, management created project groups to deal with quality problems and to launch the Land Rover Discovery four-wheel-drive vehicle. Each project group contains functional experts with demonstrated technical and interpersonal skills. Rover has found that these project groups integrate from the beginning all the concerns of the functional groups that must eventually bring the car to the market, from product design to production to marketing to sales. In traditional auto manufacturing plants, functional departments work in isolation and only after they've received information and specifications from the preceding department in the developmental process.

Thus, Rover's initial positive experience with project management has led it to integrate the practice throughout the organization. Nearly every employee has an assignment in a functional department and one or more product or project groups.

Sources: Alan Pilkington, "Learning from Joint Ventures: The Rover-Honda Relationship," *Business History*, January 1996, pp. 90–115; Alan Pilkington, *Transforming Rover: Renewal Against the Odds*, London: Bristol Academic Press, 1995; Frank Muller, "A New Engine of Change in Industrial Relations," *Personnel Management* (UK), July 1991, pp. 30–33; Ralph Bertodo, "Implementing a Strategic Vision, *Long Range Planning*, October 1990, pp. 22–30; and Ralph Bertodo, "Evolution of an Engineering Organization," *International Journal of Technology Management* 3, no. 6 (1988), pp. 693–710.

cal knowledge, resulting in quicker response to competitive conditions, technological breakthroughs, and other environmental conditions.

Technical Excellence: Technical specialists interact with other specialists while assigned to a project. These interactions encourage cross-fertilization of ideas, such as when a computer scientist must discuss the pros and cons of electronic data processing with a financial accounting expert. Each specialist must be able to listen, understand, and respond to the views of the other. At the same time, specialists maintain ongoing contact with members of their own discipline because they are also members of a functional department.

Freeing Top Management for Long-Range Planning: One stimulus for the development of matrix organizations is that top management is able to be less involved with day-to-day operations. (Environmental changes tend to create problems in cross-functional and product departments that cannot be easily solved by lower-level managers.) For example, when competitive conditions create the need to develop new products at faster than previous rates, the existing procedures become bogged down. Top management is then called upon to settle conflicts among the functional managers. Matrix organization makes it possible for top management to delegate ongoing decision making, thus providing more time for long-range planning.

Improving Motivation and Commitment: Project and product groups are composed of individuals with specialized knowledge to whom management assigns, on the basis of their expertise, responsibility for specific aspects of the work. Consequently, decision making within the group tends to be more participative and democratic than in more hierarchical settings. This opportunity to participate in key decisions fosters high levels of motivation and commitment, particularly for individuals with acknowledged professional orientations.

Providing Opportunities for Personal Development: Members of matrix organizations are provided considerable opportunity to develop their skills and knowledge. Placed in groups consisting of individuals representing diverse parts of the organization, they come to appreciate the different points of view expressed and become more aware of the total organization. Moreover, the experience broadens each specialist's knowledge not only of the organization but of other scientific and technical disciplines—engineers develop knowledge of financial issues; accountants learn about marketing.

Different Forms of Matrix Organization   Matrix organization forms can be depicted as existing in the middle of a continuum with mechanistic organizations at one extreme and with organic organizations at the other. Organizations can move from mechanistic to matrix forms or from organic to matrix forms. Ordinarily, the process of moving to matrix organization is evolutionary. That is, as the present structure proves incapable of dealing with rapid technological and market changes, management attempts to cope by establishing procedures and positions which are outside the normal routine.

This evolutionary process consists of the following steps:

Task Force: When a competitor develops a new product that quickly captures the market, a rapid response is necessary. Yet in a mechanistic organization, new product development is often too time consuming because of the necessity to coordinate the various units that must be involved. A convenient approach is to create a task force of individuals from each functional department and charge it with the responsibility to expedite the process. The task force achieves its objective, then dissolves, and members return to their primary assignment.

Teams: If the product or technological breakthrough generates a family of products that move through successive stages of new and improved products, the temporary task force concept is ineffective. A typical next step is to create permanent teams consisting of representatives from each functional department. The teams meet regularly to resolve interdepartmental issues and to achieve coordination. When not involved with issues associated with new product development, the team members work on their regular assignments.

Product Managers: If the technological breakthrough persists so that new product development becomes a way of life, top management will create the roles of product managers. In a sense, product managers chair the teams, but they now are permanent positions. They have no formal authority over the team members but must rely on their expertise and interpersonal skill to influence them. Companies such as General Foods, Du Pont, and IBM make considerable use of the product management concept.

www.dupont.com

www.kraftfoods.com

Product Management Departments: The final step in the evolution to matrix organization is the creation of product management departments with subproduct managers for each product line. In some instances, the subproduct managers are selected from specific functional departments and would continue to report directly to their functional managers. Considerable diversity in the application of matrix organization exists, yet the essential feature is the creation of overlapping authority and the existence of dual authority.

Exactly where along the continuum an organization stops in the evolution depends on factors in the situation. Specifically and primarily important are the rates of change in technological and product developments. The resultant uncertainty and information required vary.

A fully developed matrix organization has product management departments along with the usual functional departments. Such organizations have product managers reporting to top management and with subproduct managers for each family cereal product line.

MULTINATIONAL STRUCTURE AND DESIGN

As we have seen previously, four design decisions regarding division of labor, delegation of authority, departmentalization, and span of control shape the design of organizational structures. These decisions, in turn, are affected by a variety of factors. Foremost among them are the social, political, cultural, legal, and economic environments in which the organization is operating. Because of their very nature, multinational corporations frequently exist in very divergent environments. A multinational corporation may be categorized as consisting of a group of geographically dispersed organizations with different national subsidiaries.[60]

One approach to setting up a foreign subsidiary is that of replication. That is, the same organization structure and operating policies and procedures that exist in the existing domestic organization are used. For example, when establishing its foreign subsidiaries, Procter & Gamble created an "exact replica of the United States Procter & Gamble organization" because they believed that using "exactly the same policies and procedures which have given our company success in the United States will be equally successful overseas."[61] The potential difficulty with such a practice is that it may result in the reliance upon organizational designs and management practices that are simply unsuitable for the environment of the host country. This may explain why there is a tendency for foreign subsidiary organizational structures to evolve over time as the company becomes more internationalized.[62]

---

[60]S. Ghoshal and C. A. Bartlett, "The Multinational Corporation as an Interorganizational Network," *Academy of Management Review,* October 1990, pp. 603–25.

[61]C. A. Bartlett and S. Ghoshal, *Managing across Borders: The Transnational Solution* (Boston: Harvard Business School Press, 1989), p. 38.

[62]D. A. Ricks, B. Toyne, and Z. Martinez, "Recent Developments in International Management Research," *Journal of Management,* June 1990, pp. 219–53.

For multinational corporations, there are a number of factors that may have important implications for structure and design decisions, as well as general operating policies. We will briefly examine four of these.[63]

1. National boundaries are an important force in defining organizational environments. This is similar to the point we made at the beginning of this discussion. For many elements of structure, crossing national boundaries creates a necessity for carefully assessing the nature and extent of environmental differences.

2. National boundaries are of varying importance for different elements of organizational structure and process. Not all effects are equal. Some aspects of an organization may be significantly affected by distinct aspects of the environment of the host country. Other aspects may be affected by global or regional factors that are independent of a particular nation. Still other aspects may be relatively environment free.

3. Subsidiaries of multinational corporations can act as conduits that introduce changes into the host country's environment. In some cases, this may mean the direct replication of elements of a particular structure heretofore not used in the host country. More often, however, it relates to operating procedures that emanate from the subsidiary organization. An example would be Marriott Corporation's introduction of their five-day workweek into Hong Kong, a setting in which a six-day workweek is the norm.[64]

www.marriott.com

4. Subsidiaries of multinational corporations can act as conduits through which features of the host country's environment are introduced throughout the organization. This is the reverse of the previous point. It strongly suggests that beneficial changes can—and do—flow both ways. Organizations should be structured to facilitate both directions of change.

Of course, while there can be important cross-country differences that dictate making adaptations in structure, policy, and management practices, there can also be a great deal of similarity even between widely divergent countries. One of the challenges to organizational researchers is to provide data to help better understand the degree of similarity and difference across national boundaries that have implications for organizational operations.

Corporations that cross national boundaries must decide how to include foreign activity in the organization. How should international activities be coordinated? In fact, foreign activities are but extensions of the domestic businesses, and how they're coordinated to achieve strategic outcomes involves issues not much different from those of local activities.[65] Japanese corporations' outstanding success in international markets has initiated great interest in the ways firms can and should organize if they're to compete with the Japanese. At

---

[63]The following discussion is based upon P. M. Rosenzweig and J. V. Singh, "Organizational Environments and the Multinational Enterprise," *Academy of Management Review,* April 1991, pp. 430–61.

[64]Ibid, p. 354.

[65]Mohammed M. Habib and Bart Victor, "Strategy, Structure, and Performance of U.S. Manufacturing and Service MNCs: A Comparative Analysis," *Strategic Management Journal,* November 1991, pp. 589–606.

the heart of the discussion is which departmental basis is appropriate under which circumstances.[66]

The most prevalent departmental basis is *territory*. This arrangement has national and regional managers reporting to a headquarters in the same national or regional area. Territorial-based organizations for MNCs have the same characteristics as those for domestic organizations. Each national or regional office has all the resources necessary to produce and market the product or service. This organizational form is suitable for organizations with limited product lines such as ITT and Charles Pfizer Corporation.

MNCs having a diversified product line will find certain advantages in the *product-based* organization structure. This structure assigns worldwide responsibility for a product or product line to a single corporate office, and all foreign and domestic units associated with that product report to the corporate product office. Eastman Kodak uses the product-based structure to assign responsibility for worldwide research and development, manufacturing, marketing, and distribution of its products. The basic product unit, termed a line of business (LOB), makes its own decisions and succeeds or fails accordingly. Eastman Kodak believes this structure enables managers to respond more quickly to market conditions.[67]

MNCs with very restrictive product lines such as firms in the mining industry will use the *function* approach. According to this structure, a corporate office for each business function such as production, marketing, and finance has authority over those functions wherever they take place throughout the world. Thus, production personnel in Europe and South America as well as North America will report to corporate officials in charge of production.[68] Although MNCs share certain common managerial and organizational problems, how they deal with them will reflect their own national culture as well as the local, host country culture.

We can summarize our discussion of how MNCs organize by describing how many Japanese firms go about it. Typically they concentrate on a relatively narrow set of business activities, unlike their typical Western counterparts that enter several lines of business. One effect of this difference is that Japanese employees perform relatively fewer specialized jobs with relatively more homogeneous skills and experiences due to the fewer business specialties to be performed. The typical Japanese manufacturing job has less range than the typical Western manufacturing job. The authority associated with each job is relatively less in Japanese firms, although the Japanese practice of participative management enables individual workers to have a say in matters that immediately affect their own jobs. Middle managers in Japanese firms are expected to initiate opportunities for workers to be involved, and they are evaluated on this criterion as well as on economic and performance criteria.

Departments in Japanese firms are more often based on function and process than on product, customer, or location. The preference for the internal-oriented bases reflects again Japanese firms' preference to do business in fewer industries such that more complex divisional firms aren't as likely to develop. There are, of course, many diversified organizations in Japan, but these firms typically follow

www.itt.com

www.pfizer.com

---

[66]David J. Lemak and Jeffrey A. Bracker, "A Strategic Contingency Model of Multinational Corporate Structure," *Strategic Management Journal*, September–October 1988, pp. 521–26.

[67]Wilber J. Prezzano, "Kodak Sharpens Its Focus on Quality," *Management Review*, May 1989, pp. 39–41.

[68]Christopher A. Bartlett, "How Multinational Organizations Evolve," *Journal of Business Strategy*, Winter 1982, pp. 20–32.

holding company patterns of organization. The Japanese have developed the practice of creating close ties with supplier organizations and thus have avoided the necessity of vertical integration as is the case of many Western business organizations.

The differences between organization structures in Japan and in the West can be accounted for by differences in business practices. These business practices are no doubt due to national and cultural developments in how business is done, not in how organizations are structured.[69]

VIRTUAL ORGANIZATIONS

One of the fastest developing practices in business throughout the world involves firms in cooperative relationships with their suppliers, distributors, and even competitors. These networks of relationships enable organizations to achieve both efficiency and flexibility to exploit advantages of the mechanistic and organic organization designs. These "virtual organizations" have become so pervasive that some experts refer to them as the models for 21st-century organizations.[70] Cooperative relationships enable the principal organization to rely upon the smaller, closer-to-the-market partner to sense impending changes in the environment and to respond at the local level, thus relieving the parent organization of that necessity.

A **virtual organization** (e.g., meetings, teams, offices, firms, and alliances) is a collection of geographically distributed, functionally and/or culturally diverse aggregations of individuals that is linked by electronic forms of communication.[71] The virtual organization by necessity has to rely on somewhat blurred boundaries to forge relationships that are often governed by contract. The virtual unit is assembled and disassembled according to needs.

An example of a virtual organization is Barclay's global bank. The organization is a global network created by electronically linking extant networks of small, regional banks. Customers of the regional banks feel like they are a part of a large entity, Barclays, because they are provided with worldwide services. The feeling of being a part of a worldwide entity exists, as customers remain members of their local community banks as well.[72]

Exhibit 15.7 captures the main characteristics of virtual organizations. The characteristics are applicable to a movie production firm in which personnel are aggregated to complete a film, to an e-learning company preparing training courseware (that subject matter experts prepare) for delivery online to clients, to a manufacturing firm in which subcontractors both domestically and globally based provide raw materials, manufacturing processes, distribution and storage facilities, and research, and to development consortia, in which intellectual properties flow through the companies in a specific geographic region.

---

[69]J. Stewart Black and Hal B. Gregersen, "The Right Way to Manage Expats," *Harvard Business Review,* March–April 1999, pp. 52–64.

[70]Mangu K. Ahuja and Kathleen M. Carley, "Network Structure in Virtual Organizations," *Organization Science,* November–December 1999, pp. 741–57.

[71]Geraldine De Sanctis and Peter Monge, "Communication Processes for Virtual Organizations," *Organizational Science,* November–December 1999, pp. 693–703.

[72]P. R. Monge and Janet R. Fulk, "Communication Technology for Global Network Organizations," in Geraldine De Sanctis and Janet Fulk (eds.), *Shaping Organization Form: Communication, Connection, and Community* (Newburg Park, CA: Sage, 1999), pp. 81-110.

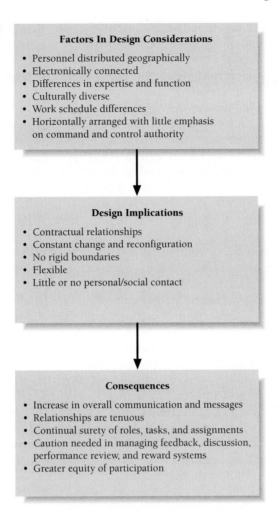

EXHIBIT 15.7
Characteristics of
Virtual Organization
and Some
Consequences

Factors In Design Considerations

- Personnel distributed geographically
- Electronically connected
- Differences in expertise and function
- Culturally diverse
- Work schedule differences
- Horizontally arranged with little emphasis on command and control authority

Design Implications

- Contractual relationships
- Constant change and reconfiguration
- No rigid boundaries
- Flexible
- Little or no personal/social contact

Consequences

- Increase in overall communication and messages
- Relationships are tenuous
- Continual surety of roles, tasks, and assignments
- Caution needed in managing feedback, discussion, performance review, and reward systems
- Greater equity of participation

Exhibit 15.7 summarizes some of the factors, implications, and possible consequences of virtual organizations. These attributes can be applied to any type of virtual team, unit, organization, or consortia. Proponents of the virtual-style organization propose that the benefits of this type of arrangement are faster response time, autonomy, greater flexibility, and more efficient use of technical, behavioral, and professional expertise. The critics argue that virtual organizations mean increased conflict, decreased loyalty, a lack of any coherence in plans and strategies, information overload, and no social interaction fulfillment.

The Realities of Virtual Organizations

An organization is typically virtual to some degree.[73] At one extreme, a firm is virtual to the extent that each step in the process of providing a product or service is outside the firm's boundaries. Some publishing firms typically perform

---

[73]Robert Kraut, Charles Steinfield, Alice P. Chin, Brian Butler, and Anne Hoag, "Coordination and Virtualization: The Role of Electronic Networks and Personal Relationships," *Organization Sciences*, November–December, 1999, pp. 722–40.

manuscript selection and marketing in-house, while writing, editing, printing, and distribution are done outside the firm and in many instances through virtual connectiveness.

The other extreme finds the fully integrated, mechanistic-type organization performing all aspects of management, production, sales, finance, and distribution. But even most of this type of traditional firm are making contractual and logistical arrangements to have some activities performed externally.

Transaction-cost theorists have studied why certain activities are kept within the firm while others are contracted or performed outside. The decisions are based on minimizing the combined cost of production and governance. If only production costs are considered, it is argued that these costs can be reduced as more production activities are performed externally. However, the costs of governance are often higher when firms purchase goods and services in the open market rather than in-house.

The virtual organization is distinctively different than the mechanistic, organic, or matrix forms that have hierarchy, layers of management, and face-to-face control. The line and staff arrangement in these organizational design approaches is in-house. Virtual organizations are not always the best or most appropriate arrangement. The work, expertise, and goals of the firm must be reviewed carefully. The requirements of personal contact, regular hours, in-person negotiations, and employee needs must be determined. When there is a reasonable fit among the work, expertise, goals, and requirements, then a virtual organization should be considered as an option.

Work in e-commerce, consulting, marketing, and job searching seems best suited for virtual organizations. These jobs are service-oriented, require extensive communication, are dynamics, and are knowledge-based. There is also the issue of whether an organization has the managerial competence suited to lead, coordinate, facilitate, and provide constructive feedback to virtual organization workers. These and similar issues should be carefully evaluated before taking a plunge into virtual organization discussions, plans, or implementation.

The viability of a virtual organization as the proper approach design is centered on two major issues.[74] First, is the conclusion that the virtual arrangement results in economic gains of acquiring goals and services from specialized firms, which are able to provide these factors efficiently? Second, is the assumption that computers and telecommunications networks reduce the costs of coordination, allowing organizations to achieve these economic benefits without incurring the higher transaction costs associated with buying from an external supplier?

The exact form of the appropriate virtual organization varies. Some organizations develop relationships only with key suppliers. Other organizations develop relationships with marketers and distributors. In the extreme case, the parent organization functions much like a broker and deals independently with product designers, producers, suppliers, and markets. The critical managerial and organizational decisions involve which of the functions to buy, which to produce, and how to manage and coordinate the relationships with their partners. Managers in these organizations have less environmental uncertainty to deal with because they have, in a sense, subcontracted that responsibility to their counterparts in

---

[74]Kraut, et al.

the network. Such organization structures are, in a sense, boundaryless organizations.[75]

Virtual organizations have come a long way since they originated in Japan where firms create alliances with other firms. These alliances take the form of cooperative agreements, consortia, and equity ownerships to establish networks of businesses. In Japan, this form of doing business is termed *keiretsu* and involves a very large financial institution, a very large industrial conglomerate, and smaller firms in a network of relationships that enable the large firm to produce the product and the smaller firms to supply components, do research and design, and perhaps distribute and market. The participating bank provides the financial requirements to support the network of cooperative relationships. This form of interorganizational network has enabled Japanese industry to grow without supply bottlenecks and damage to competition from domestic firms.

Boundaryless Organizations

www.motorola.com

www.oticon.com

www.cocacola.com

The command and control, top-down, mechanistic organization design is orderly, specific, and relies on defined roles for employees, managers, and nonmanagers. Companies such as Motorola, Oticon A/S, and Coca-Cola are continuously attempting to minimize and, in some cases, eliminate vertical and horizontal structures, tightly defined work roles, and top-down control. They are working to achieve what is referred to as a "*boundaryless organization.*" The assumption these and other firms are making is that rigid structure and too much specificity creates barriers within a firm and between a firm and its external suppliers and customers.

The minimization of layers results in a flatter hierarchy. There is still a hierarchy but there is less distance, less separation between top-level managers and other employees. There is also in the boundaryless organization an emphasis on participative decision making, multiple-hierarchy teams (executives, managers, operating employees), team building, and coordination. At Oticon A/S, a Danish hearing-aid manufacturer, hierarchy has been purposefully minimized. There is also a project-team emphasis used to oversee, coordinate, and plan all work. The functional departmental unit has been eliminated. Oticon A/S has concluded that functional departments create too many barriers to interaction, team building, and morale. Oticon A/S has decided to use project teams to tear down the barriers. Other firms, such as Xerox, use multidisciplinary teams that work on a single project from start to finish instead of using departmental units.

www.xerox.com

In order for Oticon A/S and Xerox to be effective with a more pronounced boundaryless design, there must be a high level of trust between employees. Trust in these arrangements exists when individuals make a good faith effort to behave in accordance with expectations, are honest in all interactions, and do not take advantage of others even when the opportunity is available.[76] There is also the

---

[75]Abbe Mowshowitz, "Virtual Organization: A Vision of Management in the Information Age," *Information Society,* October–December 1994, pp. 267–88; Heather Ogilvie, "At the Core, It's the Virtual Organization," *Journal of Business Strategy,* September/October 1994, p. 29; and "Learning from Japan," *Business Week,* January 27, 1992, pp. 52–55, 58–59.

[76]Larry L. Cummings and P. Bromiley, "The Organizational Trust Inventory (OTI): Development and Validation," in R. M. Kramer and T. R. Tyler (eds.), *Trust in Organizations: Frontiers of Theory and Research* (Thousand Oaks, CA: Sage Publications, 1996), pp. 302–30.

need for individuals to possess good skills and competencies so that work can be performed without constant managerial monitoring and feedback.

The effective boundaryless organization breaks down barriers with external constituents and distance. Strategic alliances and telecommunicating are examples of how to break down barriers. The Japanese *keiretsu* relationship is an example of a vertical alliance between large corporations and their suppliers. Typically, the large business takes a minority ownership (e.g., 10%) in a supplier. The two organizations become bonded in a strategic partnership for their mutual gain. There is little room for communication, decision making, and strategic choice barriers in alliances. The leveraging of resources, achievement of goals, and reduction of risks are some of the reasons why Coca-Cola and Apple Computer have adopted alliances to reduce unnecessary structural barriers with external constituents.

Telecommunicating (also called *teleworking*) is reducing barriers. The software engineer in Austin, Texas, and the engineering salesperson in Tacoma, Washington, are examples of millions of individuals who are doing their work outside of brick and mortar buildings. They represent a part of the virtual workforce. They are workers in boundaryless organizations that are connected via technology.

Conceptually the boundaryless organization involves the breaking down of structure, hierarchy, specific roles, and distance. The virtual organization already discussed is one variation or type of boundaryless organization.

Summary of Key Points

- Four key managerial decisions determine organization structures. These decisions are concerned with dividing the work, delegating authority, departmentalizing jobs into groups, and determining spans of control.

- The term *division of labor* concerns the extent to which jobs are specialized. Dividing the overall task of the organization into smaller related tasks provides the technical and economic advantages found in specialization of labor.

- Delegating authority enables an individual to make decisions and extract obedience without approval by higher management. Like other organization issues, delegated authority is a relative, not absolute, concept. All individuals in an organization have some authority. The question is whether they have enough to do their jobs.

- There are several forms, or bases, of departmentalization. *Functional* groups jobs by the function performed, i.e., marketing, production, accounting. *Territorial* groups on the basis of geographical location. *Product* groups on the basis of the department's output. *Customer* groups on the basis of the users of the good or service provided.

- Span of control relates to the decision regarding how many people a manager can oversee. It is an important

variable because managerial effectiveness can be compromised if spans of control are too large. Additionally, span of control affects the number of levels in an organization; the wider the span, the fewer the levels.

- Three important dimensions of structure are formalization, centralization, and complexity. *Formalization* refers to the extent to which policies, rules, and procedures exist in written form; *centralization* refers to the extent to which authority is retained in the jobs of top management; and *complexity* refers to the extent to which the jobs in the organization are relatively specialized.

- Two important organizational design models are termed *mechanistic* and *organic*. Mechanistic design is characterized by highly specialized jobs, homogeneous departments, narrow spans of control, and relatively centralized authority. Organic designs, on the other hand, include relatively despecialized jobs, heterogeneous departments, wide spans of control, and decentralized authority.

- A third organizational design, matrix design, offers a number of potential advantages. These include efficient use of resources, flexibility in conditions of change and uncertainty, technical excellence, freeing top management for long-range planning, improving motivation and commitment, and providing good opportunities for personal development.

- It is important to be particularly attentive to structure and design considerations in multinational organizations. Differences in the social, political, cultural, legal, and economic environments of countries hosting subsidiaries of domestic organizations can dictate the need for different answers to design questions.

- Virtual organizations have become important ways of getting work done. Often termed "empty organizations," they serve as focal points for getting all the functions accomplished but without having to directly manage them.

- Boundaryless organizations in which the hierarchy and chain of command are minimized and rigidly structured departments are eliminated are being implemented to reduce barriers between people and constituencies.

Review and Discussion Questions

1. Why would a virtual organization design be popular in the movie industry?

2. "The more authority that is delegated to nonmanagers, the less authority managers have." Is this necessarily a true statement? Explain.

3. What barriers are reduced or eliminated by adopting a boundaryless organization?

4. What are some of the factors which may have important implications for structure and design decisions in multinational corporations?

5. Characterize the following organizations on the basis of their degree of formalization, centralization, and complexity: the university you are attending, the federal government, and a local branch of a national fast-food franchise.

6. Can you think of a particular company or type of industry that tends toward a mechanistic design? What advantages and disadvantages could you see if that organization or industry adopted a more organic form?

7. What is the difference between organizational structure and design?

8. What cues might a manager have that suggest a problem with the design of an organization? Is changing an existing organization a different task from designing a brand new structure? Explain.

9. Changes in organizational size affect structure. In what ways might growth (increasing size) affect an organization's structure? In what ways might decreasing size affect structure?

10. What are some of the potential advantages of a matrix design?

READING 15.1   The New Enterprise Architecture

The ubiquitous Tom Peters predicts the imminent "disappearance of the organization as we know it." Is this a prescription for his brand of "liberation management" or a descent into chaos? One fact is certain: never before have so many enterprise leaders questioned the fundamental principles of traditional organization structures as during this turbulent period of the value decade. The pressure to become more customer-driven, and to manage horizontally with greater attention to core business processes, is creating the need to rethink the way we configure enterprises. New forms of "organizational architectures" are emerging that are fundamentally different from the "command-and-control" structures of the past. The third competency of the high-performing enterprise is to design an enterprise architecture that is consistent with the demands of becoming a superior value-delivering business.

An example of an enterprise that can cope with rapid change and that shows tremendous flexibility is Ross Perot's former company, Electronic Data Systems (EDS). EDS's goal is to "help define and exploit fast-changing markets." EDS is unique in that it is quite possibly the world's biggest and best professional service firm. What's different about EDS is an organizational structure that looks nothing like the typical corporate hierarchy that most people in the business world are used to. EDS considers itself to be in the "knowledge extraction, integration, and application business." It operates almost entirely on the basis of "projects." In other words, the company's 72,000 employees, in 28 countries, are organized primarily around the completion of client projects rather than into business functions.

In 1984, when the company became a wholly owned subsidiary of General Motors, it registered a profit of $71 million on $950 million in revenue. By 1991, the numbers were up to $548 million in profit derived from $7.1 billion in revenue. The rapid growth of the company is a reflection of the tremendous growth of information technology around the world. EDS "offers information systems consulting, total information systems development, information systems integration, and total information systems management for clients."

The company is divided into 38 strategic business units (SBUs), each responsible for its own profit; these are subdivided into 32 vertical industry units dealing with such sectors as finance, manufacturing, transportation, and communications. There are also six horizontal SBUs that deal with specific, across-the-board client information systems capabilities.

For each client project, EDS assigns 8 to 12 employees who work together for a time span that ranges between 9 and 18 months. Some members of the group work with the customer on a full-time basis. "Though the project's product/result is buttoned down, the formal structure of the project team is murky. . . . Who reports to whom is not critical. Getting the job done is."

However, there are usually three discernible "ranks" within project groups: (1) the individual performer, (2) the subproject team leader, and (3) the project manager. Individual performers will often become subproject leaders when their skills match certain requirements. Then they will return to performer status on subsequent projects. An individual performer will qualify for project manager status after displaying project management skills in his or her work. All of these designations are extremely informal in nature to everyone but the customer. "The ball, when it comes to on-time, on-budget results, is clearly in that leader's court, formal designation or not," says Barry Sullivan, EDS's marketing head:

> EDS is "loose and flexible," says one EDS executive—but damned disciplined. Accountability is unmistakable. If you're assigned a job, you're expected to get it done, even if nothing is written down, even if your "authority" doesn't come close to matching your "responsibility."

EDS demonstrates many of the characteristics of the new organizational structures of the future: customer-focused, team-based work units; temporary work assignments; high levels of employee autonomy based on demonstrated skill competencies; and a clear accountability to "get the job done." The traditional command-and-control model for organizational structure is giving way to a looser, flexible, and more freewheeling style. The "adaptive" organization in the value decade:

> will bust through bureaucracy to serve customers better and make the company more competitive. Instead of looking to the boss for direction and oversight, tomorrow's employee will be trained to look closely at the work process and to devise ways to improve upon it. . . .

Source: William A. Band, *Touchstones* (New York: John Wiley, 1994), pp. 59–76.

Raymond Miles, management professor at the University of California, Berkeley, likens the adaptive organization to ". . . a network where managers work much as switchboard operators do, coordinating the activities of employees, suppliers, customers, and joint-venture partners."

Apple Computer takes this idea to extraordinary lengths through its "Spider" system. This network of personal computers, with a videoconferencing system and a database of Apple employee records, provides project team managers with a record of every employee's skills, location, and position, plus color photographs. When a manager wishes to form a team to get something done, he or she is able to access Spider to identify and select employees from around the world.

What will the enterprise of the future look like? Former Harvard economist and now Secretary of Labor Robert Reich believes that, in the future, ". . . every big company will be a confederation of small ones. All small organizations will be constantly in the process of linking up with big ones." Welcome to the world of "no boundaries," "shamrocks," and "clusters."

"Boundaryless"

The requirements of the value decade place a premium on enterprise innovation and change. Your task is to design a more flexible organization, to break down the internal boundaries that make the enterprise rigid and unresponsive. However, as traditional organizational boundaries crumble, a new set of "psychological boundaries" must be successfully managed. These new dimensions can be identified as "authority," "task," "political," and "identity" boundaries. Each is rooted in one of four dimensions common to all work experiences, and each poses a new set of managerial challenges in the new work environment.

1. *The authority boundary: "Who's in charge of what?"* Even in the most "boundaryless" company, some people lead and others follow; some provide direction and others are responsible for execution. When managers and employees take up these roles and act as superiors and subordinates, they meet each other at the authority boundary and will want to know: "Who's in charge of what?" Traditionally structured organizations don't find this question difficult to answer, but more flexible organizations do. For example, the individual with the formal authority is not necessarily the one with the most up-to-date information about a business problem or customer need. In addition, to be an effective follower means that subordinates have to challenge their superiors, to push for the best solutions to business problems. When leaders and subordinates fail to communicate at the authority bound-

ary, they can't work together to achieve common goals.

2. *The task boundary: "Who does what?"* Work in complex organizations requires a highly specialized division of labor. Yet, the more specialized the work becomes, the harder it is to give people a sense of a common goal. This contradiction between specialized tasks and the need for shared purpose helps explain why teams have become such a popular form of work organization in recent years. Teams provide a mechanism for bringing people with different but complementary skills together and tying them to a single goal. If teams are to succeed, however, decisions have to be made to address "Who does what?" People at the task boundary divide up the work they share and then coordinate their separate efforts so that the resulting product or service has integrity. Again, in a traditional organization, "Who does what?" was an easy question to answer. In a more flexible environment, the old standby, "It's not my job," doesn't work anymore. To work effectively in teams, workers must take an interest not only in their own jobs but also in their coworkers'.

3. *The political boundary: "What's in it for us?"* Just because an organization does away with traditional boundaries, it doesn't mean that it's suddenly "one big, happy family." There will always be politics, because each group within the enterprise has different interests. This is normal and healthy because it ensures that all aspects of the enterprise are being "looked out for." For example, R&D has an interest in long-term research; manufacturing, in the producibility of a product; marketing, in customer acceptance; and so on. A director of a research lab who tries to protect his or her scientists from intrusions from marketing is engaged in a necessary political agenda. The only time the political boundary doesn't work is when negotiating and bargaining fail and people can't reach a mutually beneficial solution. This is the difference between a win/lose and a win/win situation.

4. *The identity boundary: "Who are we?"* When traditional functional or departmental boundaries are abandoned, a more common identity for all employees in the enterprise can be fostered. Having fewer boundaries helps to break down the "us against them" thinking that leads to conflicts within the organization. However, when the identity boundary is strong, "team spirit" strengthens. Groups within the enterprise need to feel that "they are the best" without devaluing the potential contribution of other teams. When this seemingly paradoxical balance is achieved, people feel loyal to their own groups and also maintain a healthy respect for others. In other words, healthy pride prevails.

Shared Authority

A more fluid, boundaryless organization will create more blurred roles for workers, and will require new types of skills of the senior executives of the enterprise. Authority will have to be exercised in new ways.

> Authority in the corporation without boundaries is not about control but about containment—containment of the conflicts and anxieties that disrupt productive work. . . . In the corporation without boundaries . . . creating the right kind of relationships at the right time is the key to productivity, innovation, and effectiveness.

Here's an example of how one human resources executive exercised authority and leadership in the collaborative style that is becoming more common in the flexible organizations emerging in the 1990s. This vice president of a high-tech components manufacturer was faced with managing a massive downsizing and reorganization as a result of a shift in his company's strategic plan. He also had to figure out how his own department could best serve the company's new strategy while laying off 20 people—40 percent of the staff in the department.

He decided to ask his subordinates to help him design a new and smaller human resources department. By asking them to help plan the cutback, he felt the layoffs might feel less arbitrary and impersonal. Meanwhile, those who did leave could do so in dignity.

He divided eight people into two teams. He asked both teams to come up with a wide range of possible configurations for the new human resources department and to recruit some of their own subordinates as team members. The teams considered issues such as reporting relationships, spans of control, organizational structure, and new combinations of functions. At the same time, the new departments had to operate with 40 percent fewer people, while taking on additional responsibilities called for under the company's strategic plan. By asking each team to design several alternatives, he was able to avoid potentially explosive turf wars among team members, who, in essence, were designing themselves out of a job. The teams were encouraged to think through all options without becoming wedded to one solution.

The VP gave the teams less than a month to come up with their plans. This was done to create a sense of urgency and to establish a momentum to break free from the inertia of day-to-day activities. He also offered to meet with each participant privately, to discuss his or her own future in confidence. This allowed each team member to openly vent frustrations and connect personally to the VP. Every participant was given the opportunity to discuss how he or she might fit into the new organizational structure or even how the VP might help with the search for a new job.

Nine proposals were presented, and, although discussions were stormy, each team collaborator was committed to the task at hand—even if it meant supporting a plan that eliminated his or her job. In the end, the VP sketched out a new organization that drew on elements from all nine plans.

The downsizing and implementation went smoothly for everyone involved. Each team member felt that all viewpoints had been heard and a fair and effective solution had been reached. The vice president never wavered from the goal of establishing a smaller department. However, he created a way in which conflicts could surface and be dealt with in a productive manner. He managed the "psychological boundaries" of the group effectively.

Shamrocks and Portfolio People

Besides enterprises "without boundaries," what other forms might an enterprise take in the value decade? Management observer Charles Handy proposes an unusual metaphor to illustrate his predicted organizational structure: the "shamrock," an enterprise that resembles a four-leaf clover.

The first leaf contains core workers—qualified professionals, technicians, and managers; people essential to the firm. The second leaf contains contract workers. Nonessential work is contracted out to people who specialize in one particular task and who did it well at low cost. The third leaf features the flexible work force, the part-time and temporary workers used as the organization expands and contracts its services to match customer requirements.

External customers form the fourth leaf. The customer is not viewed as separate from the organization, but as an integral part of the overall "shamrock."

The shamrock framework envisions relatively temporary links connecting everyone involved except the "professional core." As a consequence, Handy strongly believes that the worker of the future will have to be adaptive and flexible. The new worker won't have just a job, but a "work portfolio" made up of many different types of work. *Wage (salary)/fee work* will be done where money is paid for time expended or upon the completion of a particular job. *Homework* will include such things as cooking and cleaning. *Gift work* will be done for charity, for neighbors, or for the community. *Study work* will include the learning or training necessary to keep other work skills up-to-date and relevant.

Portfolio people will see themselves as "minibusinesses," continually contracting their skills where there is the greatest demand, then moving on when the assignment is finished.

Vineyards

D. Quinn Mills suggests, in his provocative book, *Rebirth of the Corporation*, the preferred architecture of the future will be "the cluster organization." He defines this concept as "a group of people so arranged as if growing on a common vine, like grapes." In business, the common vine is the vision; the employees are in groups arranged by the vision; and the vine and clusters together produce the wine of business success.

> Clusters succeed because they make it possible for a firm to hire the best people, develop an ongoing commitment to quality, be quickly responsive to shifts in the marketplace, and provide a process for rapid revitalization when performance declines.

In Mills's vision, people will be drawn from different disciplines to work together on a semipermanent basis. The six types of clusters are:

1. *A core team.* Comprised of top management; has the central leadership role and is akin to European management committee.
2. *Business units.* Clusters with customers external to the firm; they conduct their own business, deal directly with customers, and may be profit centers. Their flexibility, responsiveness, and autonomy allow a complex company to move at the same pace as far smaller firms.
3. *Staff units.* Clusters with customers internal to the firm, such as accounting, personnel, and legal. These units may price services to internal customers, and may evolve into business units with external customers.
4. *Project teams.* Assembled for a specific project. They lack the ongoing business orientation of the business unit, but projects may last a long time, and teams may appear semipermanent.
5. *Alliance teams.* Today's version of the joint venture. Teams involving participants from different corporations are becoming common in marketing, sales, and product development fields.
6. *Change teams.* Created for the purpose of reviewing and modifying broad aspects of firms' activities, their objectives are limited to achieving a specific end-result.

Even More Variations

Boundaryless enterprises, shamrock-shaped organizations, and companies that resemble clusters of grapes are only a few of the new forms of enterprise structures that are emerging. What other types of architecture might you consider for your company? The choice is wide, but the common denominator is a focus on flexibility and responsiveness.

- *Autonomous work teams.* These self-managed units are responsible for an entire piece of work or a complete segment of a work process. They provide their own supervision, cross-train and trade work tasks, and are empowered to take responsibility for the work process and results. They are used extensively in factories and will become more prevalent in knowledge-intensive work.
- *"Spinouts."* Rather than lose innovators who supply more opportunities than there is time to take advantage of, companies will "stake" entrepreneurs in the creation of new organizations in which they will retain equity. Spinouts may evolve into joint ventures, become fully independent companies, or continue to be associated with the parent, but will usually not end up fully integrated. In the future, there will be many "satellite" operations of this nature, with various degrees of coupling to the core business.
- *Networks.* Companies will evolve into a combination of wholly owned operations, alliances, joint ventures, spinouts, and acquired subsidiaries. These networks will be linked together through shared values, people, technology, financial resources, and operating styles.

TEAMS OF SPECIALISTS

The important components of the "new enterprise" architecture are small task-oriented collections of people who carry out essential enterprise activities, using team-based structures as the "linchpin" for delivering value to a clearly defined customer group. Noted management writer Peter Drucker models the new organization after a soccer team or a doubles tennis team; team members have designated positions on the field of play, but they also have the mobility to move into another area if that will produce the optimum result. Drucker writes:

> Because the modern organization consists of knowledge specialists, it has to be an organization of equals, of colleagues and associates. No knowledge ranks higher than another; each is judged by its contribution to the common task rather than by any inherent superiority or inferiority. Therefore the modern organization cannot be an organization of boss and subordinate. It must be organized as a team.

A highly skilled, more knowledgeable workforce brings new pressures on an enterprise. Unless the environment in the organization fosters innovation, creativity, and flexibility, the "knowledge worker," who has transportable skills, can easily leave and find an organization better suited to his or her needs. Team-based organizations work well in satisfying the needs of knowledge workers and improving business process efficiency.

As discussed in *Touchstone Two*, Hallmark is a good example of how team-based organizational structures work to better harness the talents of specialized technicians and creative workers. Approximately 700 writers, artists, and designers are responsible for creating the 40,000 new cards and other items Hallmark produces each year. The company recently reexamined its organizational structure because, although it was happy with the cards being produced, it took too long to turn an initial idea into a salable item. The long gestation period was caused by the sequence of sketches, approvals, cost estimates, and proofs that had to be completed as the product ideas moved from one department to another.

Hallmark staff members are now assigned to separate "holiday and occasions" teams. A Valentine's Day team, for example, consists of artists, writers, designers, lithographers, merchandisers, and accountants. At the head office in Kansas City, team members have been relocated for a closer physical proximity that allows them to work more intimately as a unit. A single card can now move through the production stages faster. This new way of organizing the work at Hallmark has cut cycle times in half, saved money, and made the company more responsive to its customers' changing tastes.

Hired Help

As employees within the enterprise become more specialized, a trend to hire outside subcontractors is emerging. Leading organizations are investing heavily in the training and development of their core staff—in building core competencies. They then "buy in" the expertise and services of outside specialists who can perform noncore tasks more effectively than in-house staff. This approach improves organizational flexibility and drives down costs. But new skills are required to smoothly mesh the efforts of outsiders with full-time employees.

Xerox Canada's former Director of Communications, Monica Burg, made subcontracting an integral part of her department. She restructured Xerox's marketing department and explored nontraditional partnerships with advertising agencies and other suppliers, such as printers, graphics companies, and individual copywriters. In what she termed "best of breed, best of price," Burg handpicked a cross-section of experts and put them together in a Xerox "partnership." The result: competitors became collaborators. Burg even went to the extent of making an agreement with her advertising agency of record (Young & Rubicam) to have a few of the agency's employees work out of Xerox's offices and cross-train with Xerox staff. Xerox benefited from the expertise of dozens of companies instead of going to only one agency for every service. Burg therefore eliminated the problem of mediocre services at high prices. "For the same budget that gave us one commercial last year, I did six commercials, a corporate video, and a national print campaign."

Subcontractors can be involved at all levels of the enterprise, including research and development. Apple Computer has maintained the lion's share of its "thinking function" at home, but utilizes software writers by the thousands, and hires independent contractors to help with its research and development.

It's important to treat your subcontractors as your own people. Train, share values, share information, and invite them to participate in your enterprise, just as Xerox Canada has. But there's a catch. Although outsiders must be given access to virtually all information, if "insiderization" becomes extreme, you lose the element of a fresh approach—the main purpose behind subcontracting in the first place. Innovation is imperative. Keep your enterprise "scouring the world for subs" who unexpectedly leapfrog your current partners' offerings.

Finally, don't "sub your soul." Determine what's special or unique about your organization, and make sure it doesn't get subcontracted out.

Self-Management

For core tasks that must be retained within your enterprise, how should the teams of employee specialists be governed? "Self-management" seems to be the answer for many innovative companies in the value decade. Self-management is not a new idea. For example, there are Procter & Gamble factories that have been worker-run since 1968, unbeknownst to competitors and even to some people at corporate headquarters!

Thomas A. Stewart predicts, in *The Search for the Organization of Tomorrow,* that the organization of the 21st century will be created through the convergence of three streams of reasoning:

1. A new emphasis on managing business processes rather than functional departments like purchasing and manufacturing;
2. The evolution of information technology to the point where knowledge, accountability, and results can be distributed rapidly throughout the organization; and
3. "The high-involvement workplace" where self-managing teams and empowered employees are the rule.

A classic example of self-managed work teams that has received wide attention is Johnsonville Foods. Johnsonville, a family-owned sausage-making company, was growing rapidly in 1988, but CEO Ralph Stayer still thought something was wrong. He looked around and found that none of his employees was having any fun; they were simply carrying out his orders. This discovery led Stayer to launch a program where self-managed work teams have become the rule.

To better prepare them for self-management, Johnsonville workers were encouraged to broaden their skills in any way they wished, with the company picking up the tab. Workers could take drama courses, painting, or karate, or upgrade their personal computer skills. The choice didn't matter, so long as each worker felt enriched as an individual.

Johnsonville workers are among the one percent or less in the United States who are encouraged, with company financial support, to study anything—job-related or not.

One Johnsonville "member" says:

> Look, anything you learn means you're using your head more. You're engaged. And if you're engaged, then the chances are you'll make a better sausage.

Self-management continues to be the backbone of Johnsonville Foods. As for the company's self-managed team formula, the following ingredients are included in Johnsonville's "recipe":

- Each team recruits, hires, evaluates, and fires its own people;
- Team workers regularly acquire new skills as the company sees fit, and train one another as necessary;
- Teams formulate, track, and adjust their own budgets;
- Teams make capital investment proposals as needed after completing support analyses, visits to equipment vendors, and so on;
- Teams handle quality control, inspection, subsequent troubleshooting, and problem solving;
- Teams are constantly improving every process and product;
- Teams develop and monitor quantitative standards for productivity and quality;
- Teams suggest and develop prototypes of possible new products, packaging, and other components;
- Teams in the plant routinely work with their counterparts from sales, marketing, and product development; and
- Teams participate in "corporate-level" strategic projects.

Johnsonville revenue has grown from around $7 million in 1981 to about $130 million in 1991. Stayer believes great results come about because "people want to be great." This CEO wants all of his employees to develop to their full potential, "to be the instrument of their own destiny. It is unconscionable for people not to have the chance to use their full talents."

Focus on Process

Organizing people around processes, as opposed to functions, permits greater self-management and allows companies to dismantle unneeded supervisory structures. This kind of structure also improves communication and eliminates the "crabgrass" that often grows between departments, "Purchasing buys parts cheap, but manufacturing needs them strong. Shipping moves goods in bulk, but sales promised them fast." Organizing around processes helps ensure that the overall goals of the enterprise are reached with greater ease.

Says Xerox's Richard Palermo, Vice President for Quality and Transition:

> If a problem has been bothering your company and your customer for years and won't yield, that problem is the result of a cross-functional dispute, where nobody has total control of the whole process; people who work in different functions hate each other.

Here are ten ideas for promoting a more horizontal structure:

1. Organize primarily around processes, not tasks;
2. Flatten the hierarchy by minimizing subdivision of processes;
3. Give senior leaders charge of processes and performances;
4. Link performance objectives and evaluation of all activities to customer satisfaction;
5. Make teams, not individuals, the focus of organizational performance and design;
6. Combine managerial and nonmanagerial activities as often as possible;
7. Emphasize that each employee should develop several competencies;
8. Inform and train people on a just-in-time, need-to-perform basis;
9. Maximize supplier and customer contact with everyone in the organization; and
10. Reward individual skill development and team performance instead of individual performance alone.

HIGH-PERFORMANCE WORK SYSTEMS

The work systems of superb value-delivering enterprises are designed for high performance. David A. Nadler, Marc S. Gerstein, and Robert B. Shaw define high-performance work systems (HPWS) as:

> An organizational architecture that brings together work, people, technology, and information in a manner that optimizes the congruence or "fit" among them in order to produce high performance in terms of effective response to customer requirements and other environmental demands and opportunities.

This sounds like a sensible idea, but what is the most superior configuration? There are two conflicting schools of thought about the "best" enterprise structure. Some observers promote the "melting pot" solution, which gives employee teams the freedom to organize themselves as they see fit; structure and hierarchy are secondary, if not irrelevant, to this view. Another group argues that somewhere "out there" is a perfect solution to your organizational problem. The solution can take any shape—hierarchical, matrix, parallel, team-based, or fashioned after a symphony orchestra. Whatever your own bias toward organizational design, keep these HPWS design principles in mind:

- Perfect structure is in the eye of the beholder.
- Complex problems sometimes demand complex solutions.
- In a turbulent world, structures must be flexible enough to allow "fleet-of-foot" responses to strategic opportunities and competitive challenges.
- Determining what does and doesn't work largely depends on the competency and attitude of leaders.
- Continuous assessment and improvement should be a way of life.
- The two key tests of an effective structure are: (1) the customer's needs are being met; and (2) the structure stimulates learning at all levels of the organization.
- There is a strong correlation between market responsiveness and flat structure.

The Zoological Society of San Diego illustrates the HPWS principles in action. Its management practices are as unique as the species it houses. With 1,200 year-round employees, $75 million in revenues, and 5 million visitors annually, the San Diego Zoo directly competes with amusement park heavyweights such as Disneyland. In addition to maintaining high technical standards, the zoo also champions environmentally sound business practices.

In 1988, the zoo remodeled its displays according to "bioclimatic zones." This was a radical change from its former method of display, which grouped types of animals together according to their species, such as primates and pachyderms. As a result of the new display philosophy, the zoo had to change its internal management structure as well. The old zoo was managed through 50 departments—animal keeping, horticulture, maintenance, food service, fund-raising, and so on; a traditional functional management structure was used. For example, if a groundsman, responsible for keeping paths clear of trash, was rushed or tired, he would sweep garbage under a bush, suddenly transforming his trash into the "gardener's problem."

After the zoo's redesign, the departments became invisible. Each bioclimatic section is run by a team of mammal and bird specialists, horticulturists, and maintenance and construction workers. The team tracks its own budget on a separate personal computer that is not hooked up to the zoo's mainframe. Team members are jointly responsible for their displays, and it's difficult to tell who is from which department. When, for example, the path in front of one of the buildings needed fixing one autumn, both the construction person and horticulturist did it. As team members learned one another's skills, teams have been gradually trimmed in size from 11 to 7. It became appar-

ent, when some staff left the zoo, that it was not necessary to replace them.

Because the teams are self-managed, zoo executives, who were once burdened with petty managerial tasks, have much more free time to focus on increasing attendance. In 1991, although the Gulf War and the recession had depressed California tourism overall, the San Diego Zoo enjoyed a 20 percent increase in attendance. Management attributes this success to the employees' new sense of ownership and their effort to improve the zoo attractions for visitors.

"High-Performing TV"

Other interesting examples of high-performing design principles can be seen in the television industry.

> When the Cable News Network (CNN) went on the air on June 1, 1980, it had secured access to only 1.7 million cable subscribers, far short of the 7.5 million "minimum" founder Ted Turner needed to cover 50 percent of operating costs. By 1992, the number had grown to almost 60 million in the U.S. alone.

Turner's dream was to revolutionize televised news programming by "delivering news on demand." Traditionally, newspapers and established TV networks delivered the news according to *their* schedules. Morning newspapers are delivered at about the same time each day regardless of when a major story breaks. Televised newscasts appear on air at exactly the same time each day and night, regardless of the events being covered. Only news announcements that have profound national or international consequences are aired immediately. Otherwise, it is rare for the major television networks to preempt regularly scheduled programming.

From the start, CNN was run contrary to established TV network practices. CNN's first president, Reese Schonfeld, advised everyone to "avoid slickness at all costs." Decisions that would take the major networks and newspapers hours to make were routinely handled by CNN executives in minutes. Furthermore, committees aren't part of the CNN decision-making process.

This formula continues. At CNN, the news is the "star," not the anchorpersons. Unlike the major networks, which require an entire team of people for a remote news report, CNN operates leaner and meaner. CNN "video journalists" (VJs) will often write, direct, and report a story solo. A VJ may even be responsible for sound; the only other CNN team member may be the camera person. VJs may be required to be on air "live" for many hours on end when a major story breaks in their area. (This was the case for Bernard Shaw, who reported live from Baghdad during the Gulf War.)

Atlanta, Georgia, is the hub for all the network's activities, and CNN's key decision makers are found there. The staff at this highest level has been organized in an extremely flat structure, and each member of the core group is very familiar with the others. However, the structure of remote video journalists and assignment desks pushes the responsibility for the live stories away from the "core."

> CNN is a superb example of radical centralization and radical decentralization—at once. Everyone at CNN is encouraged to take the initiative for split-second decisions. People on or close to the firing line have extraordinary autonomy, yet they must buy into the vision and understand how their piece fits into the larger puzzle.

Turner's vision has become a reality and a money maker. By 1984, he had lost $77 million in launching CNN. In 1985, the organization was in the black for the first time, recording profits of $13 million on $123 million in revenue. In 1991, CNN generated $479 million in revenue and $167 million in profit.

Fashion Television

Another high-performance success story is found in the design of CITY TV, a television station in Toronto. The unique aspect of CITY TV is that the station operates with no studios. Cameras are not "hard-wired" to studios and control rooms. A network of 32 exposed "hydrants" connects audio, video, intercom, and lights, and 90 miles of cable. Literally, any corner of the station can be on-air within minutes. All programming is casually broadcast from the desks and workspaces of CITY TV staff. CITY TV successfully creates live, interactive programming using workspaces, offices, or the station's lobby, roof, or parking lot as a living "set."

CITY TV's unorthodox and flexible organizational design has spawned several thriving "niche television magazines," the most successful of which is *Fashion Television* (FT). Although produced and edited locally in Toronto, the show uses the latest technology to combine and use "on-location" footage from all over the world. *Fashion Television* reports on sophisticated haute couture trends as well as on pop culture and other art forms. The flexible style of the show gives viewers the feeling they are "on the inside" with the latest fashion trends.

AN ARCHITECTURE THAT IS RIGHT FOR YOU

Where does all this leave your enterprise? Your task is to find the right framework—one that is responsive to the turbulence of the value decade. Four organizational components must be in fine working order if your organization is to achieve long-term success: (1) the work—the basic tasks to be done by the organization and its parts; (2) the people—the characteristics of individuals in the organization; (3) the formal organization—the various structures, processes, and methods created to get individuals to perform tasks; and (4) the informal organization—

the emerging arrangements regarding structures, processes, and relationships. Here are some design tips for creating a high-performing enterprise:

1. *Customer-focused design.* The design should start from outside the organization, beginning with customers and their requirements and then moving back to the work and organizational processes. The core purpose is to enable sets of people working together to deliver products and services that meet customer requirements in a changing environment.

   Xerox, formerly a traditional company—with separate vertical functions such as R&D, marketing, and sales—recently adopted a new, horizontal structure.

   > The new design creates nine businesses aimed at markets such as small businesses and individuals, office document systems, and engineering systems. Each business will have an income statement and a balance sheet, and an identical set of competitors.

   "Each business will be run by teams with a strong emphasis on the customer. Says Paul Allaire, Xerox CEO, "We've given everyone in the company a direct line of sight to the customer."

2. *Empowered and autonomous units.* Organizational units should be designed around whole pieces of work—complete products, services, or processes. The goal is to maximize interdependence within the unit and minimize interdependence among units, and the aim is to create loosely coupled units that have the ability to manage their relationships with each other. Teams, rather than individuals, are the basic organizational building blocks.

3. *Clear direction and goals.* Great latitude should be given in how work is done, but there is a great need for clarity about the requirements of the output. A clear mission, defined output requirements, and agreed-on performance measures provide the necessary guidance.

4. *Control of variance at the source.* Work processes and units should be designed so that variances (errors) are detected at the source, not outside the unit; information and tools required for early detection must be built in.

5. *Sociotechnical integration.* Social and technical systems should be inexorably linked. The design's purpose is to achieve effective integration between the two.

6. *Accessible information flow.* Members of autonomous units need to have access to information about the market, their output, and the performance of their work processes. The flow of information must allow members to create, receive, and transmit information as needed.

7. *Enriched and shared jobs.* The strength of a group effort is fortified if people are cross-trained in a variety of skills. Broader jobs increase individual autonomy, learning, and internal motivation. The unit's ability to reconfigure is enhanced, as is people's ability to participate in the design and management of the entire work process. Learning becomes an important driver for individuals.

8. *Empowering human resources practices.* There should be practices consistent with autonomous, "empowered" work units, such as locally controlled staff selection, skill-based pay, peer feedback, team bonuses, and minimization of rank and hierarchy.

Ralph Heath, president of Ovation Marketing, Inc., of La Crosse, Wisconsin, discovered that the path to "empowerment" isn't always easy. In the past, purchase requisitions and travel budgets had to be approved by both middle management and himself. This was time-consuming, for Heath in particular. Heath made a decision: employees were told to approve their own expenses.

Two weeks later, however, Health was still being swamped with purchases and expenses submitted to him for approval. Heath realized that his employees weren't comfortable with this responsibility and didn't trust that he was willing to let them operate without constant approvals. So, he called a meeting and explained again that requisitions were now an individual responsibility. He then set fire to his stack of purchase orders to prove how serious he was!

Not only hasn't he received any more purchase orders or expenses for approval, but six months later, Ovation's travel expenses were down 70 percent; entertainment expenses dropped 39 percent; car mileage dropped 46 percent; and office supply expenses dropped 18 percent. Ovation's profits went up 16 percent in 1991, compared to profits a year earlier. The "empowerment" of employees has paid off.

9. *Empowering management structure, process, and culture.* Ensure that the larger "host" system is supportive of the empowered autonomous unit. There will be different approaches in each unit to planning and budgeting, modes of decision making, management styles, types of information systems, and management processes. These differences should be acknowledged and accepted.

10. *Capacity to reconfigure.* The enterprise should be designed to anticipate and respond to changes quickly. Work units need the ability to act on their learning, either through continuous improvement or through large leaps of design.

Organizations in the future will clearly be flatter. The high-performing enterprise will be comprised of small units, linked together into networks. The team will be the basic building block of the firm, and the most-prized enterprise skill will be effective collaboration. Above all, the high involvement of all members of the workforce will be critical to success in the value decade.

Exercises

EXERCISE 15.1   Paper Plane Corporation

OBJECTIVES

1. To illustrate how division of labor can be efficiently structured.
2. To illustrate how a competitive atmosphere can be created among groups.

STARTING THE EXERCISE

Unlimited groups of six participants each are used in this exercise. These groups may be directed simultaneously in the same room. Approximately a full class period is needed to complete the exercise. Each person should have

Source: Louis Potheni in Fred Luthans, *Organizational Behavior* (New York: McGraw-Hill, 1985). p. 555.

assembly instructions and a summary sheet, which are shown on the following pages, and ample stacks of paper (8½ by 11 inches). The physical setting should be a room large enough so that the individual groups of six can work without interference from the other groups. A working space should be provided for each group.

- The participants are doing an exercise in production methodology.
- Each group must work independently of the other groups.
- Each group will choose a manager and an inspector, and the remaining participants will be employees.
- The objective is to make paper airplanes in the most profitable manner possible.

- The facilitator will give the signal to start. This is a 10-minute, timed event utilizing competition among the groups.
- After the first round, everyone should report their production and profits to the entire group. They also should note the effect, if any, of the manager in terms of the performance of the group.
- This same procedure is followed for as many rounds as there is time.

PAPER PLANE CORPORATION: DATA SHEET

Your group is the complete workforce for Paper Plane Corporation. Established in 1943, Paper Plane has led the market in paper plane production. Presently under new management, the company is contracting to make aircraft for the U.S. Air Force. You must establish an efficient production plant to produce these aircraft. You must make your contract with the Air Force under the following conditions:

1. The Air Force will pay $20,000 per airplane.
2. The aircraft must pass a strict inspection made by the facilitator.
3. A penalty of $25,000 per airplane will be subtracted for failure to meet the production requirements.
4. Labor and other overhead will be computed at $300,000.
5. Cost of materials will be $3,000 per bid plane. If you bid for 10 but only make 8, you must pay the cost of materials for those you failed to make or which did not pass inspection.

Summary Sheet

Round 1:

Bid: _____ Aircraft @ $20,000.00 per aircraft = _____
Results: _____ Aircraft @ $20,000.00 per aircraft = _____
Less: $300,000.00 overhead; _____ ×$3,000 cost of raw materials; _____ ×$25,000 penalty
Profit: _____

Round 2:

Bid: _____ Aircraft @ $20,000.00 per aircraft = _____
Results: _____ Aircraft @ $20,000.00 per aircraft = _____
Less: $300,000.00 overhead; _____ ×$3,000 cost of raw materials; _____ ×$25,000 penalty
Profit: _____

Round 3:

Bid: _____ Aircraft @ $20,000.00 per aircraft = _____
Results: _____ Aircraft @ $20,000.00 per aircraft = _____
Less: $300,000.00 overhead; _____ ×$3,000 cost of raw materials; _____ ×$25,000 penalty
Profit: _____

STEP 1: Take a sheet of paper and fold it in half, then open it back up.

STEP 2: Fold upper corners to the middle.

STEP 3: Fold the corners to the middle again.

STEP 4: Fold in half.

STEP 5: Fold both wings down.

STEP 6: Fold tail fins up.

Completed aircraft

Cases

CASE 15.1   Provident National Bank Trust Division

The December 31, 1986, issue of *Trust Division Newsletter*, the monthly newsletter for employees of Provident National Bank Trust Division, contained the following message from Tom Stewart, executive vice president and Trust Division manager:

> As 1986 draws to a close, I would like to thank all of you for the Trust Division's most outstanding year. Our results in 1986 and our future are, in a very important sense, dependent upon those who have preceded us. This year we will celebrate the holiday season without the leadership of Dick Boylan, Ted Mygatt, John Karnick and others who had so much influence over Provident's Trust Division. Their wisdom and guidance will be sorely missed. However, with such a talented and dedicated group of employees, I am confident that, with continued effort, teamwork, and a focus on results, we will achieve even more in 1987 as we continue to execute our strategic plan.

With that message, Tom Stewart captured the spirit and significance of a year that marked the end of one era and the beginning of a new one in the life of the Trust Division. Every one of the 400 Trust Division employees will remember 1986 as the year of leadership change, reorganization, and the strategic plan. The Trust Division's record of accomplishments impressed the financial services industry as innovative and groundbreaking. As Tom Stewart noted in his message, the strategic plan was a key to augmenting that record.

As 1986 came to a close, the Trust Division Fact Sheet noted that it was then the fifth largest trust department in the country in terms of assets managed by the holding company, PNC Financial Corporation. The division managed more than $30 billion in assets and generated revenues in excess of $70 million, establishing it as the largest trust operation in Philadelphia. It was the first to advise a mutual fund, one of the first to automatically sweep cash balances in trust accounts and package the service into a cash management account, one of the few banks to sell its investment research nationally and internationally, and the only one to deliver it electronically. Through the offices of direct and indirect subsidiaries, it manages the assets of mutual funds, acts as transfer agent

for mutual funds, provides clearing and subcustodial services for money market funds, and manages the assets of employee benefit plans. PNC Financial Corporation's report to the stockholders for the first nine months of 1986 noted that trust income was 21 percent higher than during the same period of 1985. This record of growth, innovation, and profitability was accomplished through the leadership of J. Richard Boylan, who headed the division from 1973 until his death on March 30, 1986.

THE BOYLAN STRATEGY

J. Richard "Dick" Boylan joined Provident in 1954, after a four-year stint with a securities firm. His first assignment at Provident was in the Investment Advisory Department, from which he moved rapidly through the ranks: assistant trust department officer (1956), assistant vice president (1963), senior vice president (1968), and vice chairman of the bank (1981). Throughout his career, Dick Boylan attracted attention by redefining what was thought possible in the trust business: where others saw obstacles, he saw possibilities. He was inventive and creative, capable of inspiring incredible loyalty and effort from those around him. However much of his success was due to personal traits, he was also a skilled strategist who had a plan for the development of the Trust Division.

Provident's trust strategy evolved from top management's decision to develop Provident's investment capabilities. When the bank looked at its trust business in the early 1960s, it found itself in fourth place in the Philadelphia market in terms of trust assets. Market surveys indicated that consumers did not differentiate among trust companies in terms of investment ability. The choice of a trust company was based on relationships and price. Provident decided that its best course of action was to spend heavily on people to improve its investment capabilities. By causing consumers to become more conscious of the investment performance of different banks, Provident hoped to differentiate its product in the regional market.

In 1972, Dick Boylan learned that he had cancer. He shared this information only with his immediate family and continued his unrelenting pace at Provident. By 1984, the issue of executive succession had become critical due to the recurrence of Boylan's illness. In that year, Thomas S. Stewart was named deputy division manager of Provident's Trust Division. From this position, Tom Stewart was expected to prepare for eventual succession to division manager.

Source: Adapted from "Provident National Bank Trust Division (A)" and "Provident National Bank Trust Division (B)," copyright © James L. Gibson and Bank Marketing Association. This case study is intended to provide a focus for discussion and to illustrate neither correct nor incorrect management policies, strategies, and tactics.

THE STEWART STRATEGY

Tom Stewart's career at Provident began in 1964, when he joined Provident National Bank as a management trainee. In 1965, he took a position in the Trust Division as personal trust portfolio manager, which he held until 1971. He managed employee benefit and endowment portfolios from 1971 to 1975, at which time he was named manager of the Personal Trust Investment Department. He managed this department until 1978, when he was elevated to manager of the Personal Services Group. Three years later, in 1981, Stewart was named director of economic and investment research, where he remained until his appointment as deputy division manager. In the course of Stewart's career, he has been associated with the two principal components of the Trust Division—investment and personal trust—as well as with numerous task groups to convert ideas into products and services. Thus, it came as no surprise to anyone when Tom Stewart was elected executive vice president and named manager of the Trust Division effective July 1, 1986.

Stewart expressed his philosophy of what the trust business could become in articles published in the journal *Estates and Trusts*. He argues that trust departments should be leading the banking industry's efforts to implement relationship banking. Trust departments, he believes, have always been relationship oriented, by the very nature of their traditional activities. But despite being the resident practitioners of relationship banking, trust personnel must, according to Stewart, make fundamental changes if they are to compete in the financial services market.

The first required change is to develop customer- and market-driven attitudes to displace product-driven attitudes. Too many trust departments express the attitude: "Here is our investment style, take it or leave it." That attitude must be replaced with one that begins with consultation with the customer to determine the customer's financial requirements as well as the customer's beliefs about money and wealth. This initial consultation provides the groundwork for continuing consultation as the customer moves through the financial life cycle. At each stage of the cycle, the consultative relationship will identify financial needs appropriate to that point in the cycle and plans for the next stage.

The consultative relationship with customers takes on greater significance in the contemporary financial market because the traditional trust customers, large wealthy families with established trusts for future generations, no longer exist in large numbers. To survive, trust departments must continue to serve families and individuals with established wealth, but they must begin to focus on those who are in the wealth accumulation phase of their financial life cycles.

Provident's Trust Division managers and employees generally understand Tom Stewart's ideas. They expected that when he assumed the job of division manager he would begin to implement the changes necessary to make his ideas the guiding principles of Provident's Trust Division.

INITIATING THE STRATEGIC AND ORGANIZATIONAL CHANGES

When 1985 rolled around, Tom Stewart had been in his new job for less than a year. It was already generally understood that he would be the next division manager. Despite his experience in the two most important line units in the division, Tom recognized that he had to tap the ideas of the entire management cadre to maintain the momentum of the Boylan years. During the first six months of 1985, he conducted a series of one-on-one meetings with all the group and major department managers. Exhibit 15.8 shows the organization chart at that time. These meetings stimulated discussions about where the division was headed in the coming years and what was to be expected of each group and department. These discussions were held against the backdrop of excellent performance in all areas of trust activities.

On August 20, 1985, Stewart reviewed the division's six-month performance for all officers of the Trust Division. According to Stewart, revenues for the first six months of 1985 were up 13 percent, while expenses were down slightly by .2 percent. Assets managed by the division were $25.9 billion, compared to $23.7 billion at the end of 1984. Moreover, all but one of the common trust funds exceeded the Dow Jones Industrial Average. Generally, all the performance news was good news. Little surprise then that the advice that Stewart got from some quarters was "don't fix what isn't broken."

Forces for Change

The impetus for considering long-run, strategic issues was reinforced by the actions of senior officers of PNC Financial Corporation, who had undertaken a comprehensive review of the holding company's strategic plan. In a September 20, 1985, memo to the 11 group managers of the division, Stewart stated:

> The growing complexity of the financial services environment requires that we pay more attention to the strategic issues which define the character of our business. We must ask the key strategic questions: What are the nature and direction of the organization? What is its basic purpose? And we must develop answers to these questions. Only then, after we know where we're headed, can we determine how to get there. Our meeting next Wednesday is designed to deal with strategic issues. It is not intended to result in a series of action plans. I am hopeful that a statement of mission can be developed and that we will leave the meeting with a better sense of direction. Then we can begin to determine our key objectives and what will be required in terms of resources and effort to achieve those goals.

EXHIBIT 15.8   **Provident National Bank Trust Division: Organization Chart**

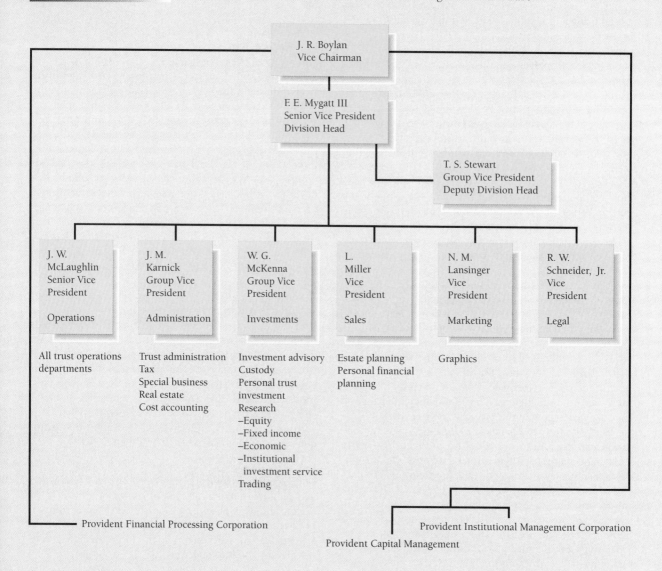

The *Trust Division Newsletter* reported the meeting of the group managers. The item noted that Tom Stewart had led a full day's discussion of the mission and direction of the division. It also reported that Tom Whitford would serve as coordinator of the planning process. Whitford had joined the Trust Division on September 3, 1985, as vice president in a position of planning and product development. Tom had been with Provident's Community Banking Division for two years, in product management and related activities. Prior to joining Provident, he had worked for Booz Allen & Hamilton as a planning consultant. With these announcements, the strategic planning process was initiated.

The first meeting of the strategic planning group resulted in several important conclusions. One of the most important conclusions was that the Trust Division's future driving force will be market needs. The market needs driving force focuses attention on taking advantage of market opportunities by providing product and services to meet current and emerging customer needs. The planning group believed that this driving force differed significantly from the existing products-offered driving force, although not so different from the driving force of some of the division's nontraditional trust businesses.

The transition from product-driven to market-driven strategy would be most important in the personal trust business, due to increasingly complex and competitive financial services and significant changes in customer needs. In particular, the redirection of the driving force would require greater efforts on market research to determine customer needs and then on developing, delivering, and servicing products to meet those needs.

Tom Stewart indicated to the planning group that the next several months would be spent in determining the current and future implications of market needs as a driving force on market scope, product scope, organizational structure, system and productions requirements, sales/distribution, and resource requirements/allocations. To determine these implications, Stewart directed the group to focus on what the financial services industry will be like in the 1990s. Defining and clarifying a vision for the 1990s will enable Provident Trust to develop a clear mission statement that will be more than an extrapolation of current product and service demand. Through the application of creativity and innovation, Stewart believed that the Trust Division could develop its own strategic direction that would be specific enough to guide current activities, yet flexible enough to permit adjustment to changing market needs.

Tom Whitford would meet with each member of the planning group to discuss his/her "vision for the 90s." Since the planning group consisted of group managers and major department managers, the focus of these discussions would be the contributions of existing organizational units to the achievement of the eight objectives. After these one-on-one meetings, Whitford would consolidate the information in a working draft, after which the planning group would reconvene to review the document and the preliminary tactics. A target date for the completion of these initial planning tasks was November 21, 1985.

The November 21 meeting introduced some themes that were to carry through the remainder of the planning process. The group reaffirmed the importance and implications of the market-needs driving force. It also acknowledged the importance of management development and human resources planning as necessary ingredients of strategic change. Details and issues began to surface regarding the division's market and product scope, environmental analysis, and key strategic issues. Tom Stewart reported that a consulting firm had been engaged to assist the division as it moved forward with its strategic planning.

Activities of the Consultants

Two consultants from a Boston-based firm spent several days in December 1985 and January 1986 interviewing key management personnel in the division, including members of the strategic planning group. The consultants, who had been retained after considerable discussion with Tom Stewart and Tom Whitford, proposed a process that emphasized the importance of shared values and wide participation in the process. With these two points in mind, the consultants proposed the following activities and timetable for obtaining a strategic plan by April 30, 1986.

The Strategic Planning Team

The first activity, to be completed in January 1986, was the appointment of a strategic planning team. The team would include key managers or representatives from the functional groups of the division. The team would be the forum in which the elements of the strategic plan would be deliberated during the next four months. The team that Tom Stewart headed contained the membership of the original planning group that had been meeting since September plus two other individuals representing key departments in the division—trust administration and investment research. The strategic planning team consisted of 14 individuals, including Tom Stewart. Tom Whitford continued in the role of internal coordinator.

The Task Forces

The second major activity was the appointment of task forces to develop general strategies around a limited number of key strategic issues. Discussions among the consultants and the planning team narrowed the key issues to seven:

1. The emerging affluent market.
2. The wealth accumulator market.
3. The wealth maintainer market.
4. The institutional market.
5. Human resources.
6. Technology.
7. Competition.

These seven issues reflected the general concerns that had been the focus of much discussions in the preceding months.

The first four issues referred to market segments that have distinctly different demographic profiles, sources of wealth, attitudes toward investments, and attitudes toward credit. Consequently, they have different needs for financial services and are appropriate bases for product differentiation. These four segments emerged from discussions within the strategic planning team on the issue of which markets Provident should target for strategic resource allocation during the next four to five years. If Provident was to be a market-driven organization, then it must identify which markets would drive it.

The emerging affluence market is 20- to 45-year-old, married college graduates with household incomes of $50,000 to $75,000 from employment sources. They are in the white-collar, fast-track professions but would like to start their own businesses. They are looking for means to build their asset base but are not all that sophisticated in making investment decisions.

The wealth accumulator market is individuals aged 45 to 65, with household incomes of more than $75,000. Their accumulated wealth derives from business, investment, and inheritance sources. They are members of professional occupations such as physicians, corporate executives, attorneys, and entertainers but also entrepreneurs.

The wealth maintainer market members are aged 55 and older, with liquid assets in excess of $75,000 and income from inheritance and employment-related income and benefit plans. They tend to have the same educational, career, and demographic characteristics as wealth accumulators, except their sources of income are relatively secure.

The institutional market segment consists of bank trust units, regional brokers, insurance companies, pension funds, investment advisory institutions, international banks and brokers, investment counselors, and mutual fund managers. This particular market segment had been the focus of much of Provident's innovative products under Boylan's leadership.

The human resources and technology task forces reflected the strategic planning team's understanding of the importance of assessing strategic issues for human and technological resources. They were charged with responsibility for identifying the contributions of people and technology to the achievement of market-driven strategic objectives.

Finally, the task force on competition was to add to the existing information and assumptions regarding the strategic direction of the financial services industry. Although separate entities, the three task forces were expected to initiate and to respond to interactions with the four market segment task forces.

Diagnosing Issues and Assessing Opportunities
Each of the task forces contained 10 to 15 members, including at least one member from the strategic planning team. The seven task forces met throughout the months of January and February 1986 with the expectation that each would prepare and present its report at a mid-March meeting. These reports were presented March 18 and 19. Each of the market segment reports contained detailed description and analysis of (1) the segment's characteristics, (2) its product and service needs, (3) Provident's current ability to serve the segment, and (4) key competitors. With this information as background, the reports identified strategic issues associated with the segment, strategies for targeting and serving the segment, and specific product and delivery proposals.

The human resources and technology reports emphasized the importance of developing these resources to be compatible with whatever strategic thrusts the division

adopted. The competition task force made this report; since its findings were incorporated in the market segment reports, it was disbanded after the March meeting.

Inappropriate Organizational Structure
The March meeting was pivotal because a number of issues crystallized during the discussion of the reports. One issue that attracted considerable discussion was that the current organizational structure does not always correspond to the needs of the market segments it is attempting to address. As one participant stated: "To be truly market driven, the organizational structure should be molded to fit the marketing strategy, and not the reverse. This implies the possibility of organizational changes that, in some cases, might be fairly major." Another participant echoed the same idea when discussing the division's markets and marketing: "Market segments, unfortunately, do not always correspond with the organizational structure. The organizational structure must eventually be altered to correspond to the needs of markets and market segments."

Inappropriate Organizational Culture
Along similar lines, the idea of appropriate attitude of managers in market-driven organizations began to take form, as noted by one individual: "Provident trust managers must practice thinking first of markets and customers, and second of products and services. Put another way, products and services can only be thought of within the context of market and customer needs. This is the essence of being market driven and is the basis of the inside → out approach to strategy formulation."

The theme of being market driven carried through the human resources task force report, which recommended that Provident's culture become more heavily influenced by incentives, targets, performance, and MBO-type systems. The key values in the culture should be risk-taking, cross-selling, accountability, technological literacy, and a marketing and customer focus. As stated by the chairperson of the task force: "Provident Bank must be prepared for major change within the Trust Division over the next five years—change involving people, organizational structure, systems and procedures, and culture. Since change is always a difficult, painful, and disruptive process, Provident's management must be prepared to orchestrate such change in the most positive and constructive manner possible." The human resources task force played an important and instrumental role by articulating the importance of "people issues" in the development and implementation of strategy.

Anticipating Implementation Issues
Implementation plans were important, not only from a planning and accountability perspective but also from an organizational perspective because the intensive nature of

EXHIBIT 15.9   **Provident National Bank Trust Division, Reorganized**

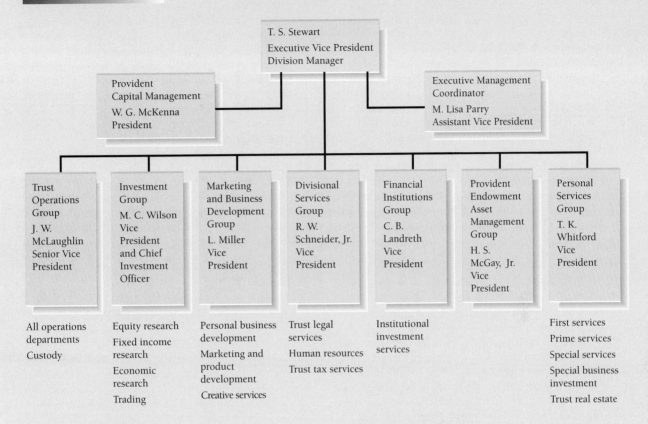

necessary intergroup communication and coordination became apparent. For example, the implementation plan for the wealth maintainer market segment identified individuals from the marketing, sales, trust administration, trust investment, institutional investment services, and operations departments who would be responsible for completing specific tasks related to the strategic plan.

It also became clear that effective implementation of the market-driven strategy would involve extensive and intensive interdivisional cooperation and coordination. Some of the activities could not be completed by the Trust Division alone; Provident's Commercial and Retail Divisions were key actors in many activities. For example, serving the emerging and accumulator market segments will require that some products developed in the Trust Division be distributed in retail, commercial, and private banking departments.

ANNOUNCING THE CHANGE

The Trust Division strategic plan was formally unveiled on May 15, 1986. Ted Mygatt, Robert Chappel, and Tom Stewart presented the plan to some 200 officers of the Trust Division and guests from the PNC affiliates as well

as other bank divisions. That presentation was followed by a June 18 letter from Stewart to all employees of the Trust Division, announcing the reorganization of the division. The reorganized division is depicted in Exhibit 15.9.

The new organizational structure derives directly from the strategic plan and is designed to enable the division to serve customers more effectively and efficiently. In the June 18 letter to the employees, Stewart stated that the changes in the organizational structure are intended "to facilitate communications—with our customers and among ourselves—and to enable us to execute our strategic plan." Top management had earlier decided to transfer Provident Financial Processing Corporation and Provident Institutional Management Corporation to the bank's Operations/Mutual Funds Division.

The June 18 letter explained the groups in the new organization as follows:

Trust Operations Group In addition to the operations departments now in the Operations Group, we are adding the Custody Department. Our custodial services activities have grown quite rapidly during the last few years, especially our involvement with investment counseling organizations. By becoming an integral part of the Operations Group, our Custody Department can develop new, more efficient ways to provide custodial services to institutions and individuals.

Investment Group Skip Wilson will continue to have overall responsibility for the Economic and Investment Research Group; in addition, he will become our chief investment officer. Rapid changes in the nature of the securities markets make it essential that investment research and securities trading activities be effectively coordinated. As a result, the Trading Department will become part of the Investment Group.

Marketing and Business Development Group By combining our marketing, product development, personal financial planning, and personal sales efforts into one group, our new business development activities will become more focused and more effective. We are merging the Personal Financial Planning Department into the Estate Planning Department, and the new entity will be known as the Personal Business Development Department. Nan Lansinger will manage the Marketing and Product Development Department, and the Graphics Department will continue to report to Nan.

Divisional Services Group This newly formed group will combine three departments that provide important services to the entire Trust Division. In addition to the Trust Legal Department, the Trust Tax Department will also report to Bob Schneider. We are forming a Trust Human Resources Department, which will support the division in its training and development, recruiting, and salary administration activities and which will act as a primary coordination point for our communications with the bank's Personnel Division.

Financial Institutions Group The Institutional Investment Service becomes the foundation for this new group, which will sell a variety of investment and other services to financial organizations in this country and abroad.

Endowment Asset Management Group In order to concentrate our efforts on serving the charitable market locally and nationally, we are creating a special group to address these customers. With an excellent base of Philadelphia area customers, this group will be staffed by several members of the Investment Advisory Department.

Personal Services Group (PSG) The most significant changes that will occur involve the transition from being organized functionally in our account management activities to being organized according to our customer segments. Replacing the Trust & Estate Administration, Personal Trust Investment, and Investment Advisory Departments, three new departments, Special Services, Prime Services, and First Services are being formed. Each department will consist of portfolio managers and trust administrators whose efforts will be directed to serving their customers as effectively as possible. Persons in the Trust & Estate Administration, Personal Trust Investment, and Investment Advisory Departments will, for the most part, be assigned to one of the new departments.

Existing account assignments will not be altered immediately. Over time, however, I anticipate that some changes in account assignments will occur as we work increasingly to segment our customer base and to provide high-quality but differentiated levels of service. New accounts will be assigned to the appropriate department beginning July 1.

To the extent possible, personnel in each department will have offices and work spaces that are located together. This will require a substantial number of physical moves, which will occur in the months ahead.

Recognizing the need to retain a mechanism through which the investment managers and trust administrators can communicate effectively about their functional specialties, Bob Warth and the managers of the investment management units will oversee portfolio management issues, while Lou Sozio and the trust administration unit managers will be responsible for trust administration matters.

By combining the Special Business and Real Estate Investment Departments into PSG, we expect to improve operating efficiencies in both departments. In addition, this group will develop more effective ways to serve business owners through close coordination with our commercial division.

Provident Capital Management Bill McKenna has been named as president of Provident Capital Management. PCM will continue to operate as an independent subsidiary providing investment and administrative services to the employee benefit market.

Executive Management Coordinator The purpose of this newly created position is to assist the division manager in a wide range of activities.

Stewart and the strategic planning team recognized that the most significant changes were to occur in the Personal Services Group. They anticipated that portfolio size would be the basis for assigning accounts to each of the three new departments. Initially, they thought that portfolios in excess of $2 million would be assigned to Special Services; portfolios greater than $500,000 but less than $2 million would be assigned to Prime Services; and portfolios greater than $100,000 but less than $500,000 would be assigned to First Services. The departmental managers would work together to settle important issues related to levels of service to be delivered in each of the three departments. The team also anticipated that important issues would arise related to interfaces among these three departments and Trust Division groups and bank divisions.

MAKING THE CHANGES WORK IN THE PERSONAL SERVICES GROUP

The strategic and reorganization plans had implications for every group in the Trust Division. The individuals and departments that focus on the financial needs of individuals played crucial roles. The Personal Services Group was formed from personnel previously assigned to the Administration and Investments Groups. Trust administrators had been in the Administration Group; trust portfolio managers had been in the Investments Group. The strategic planning process had identified the need to bring together in one organizational group all the tasks whether administrative or investment, associated with delivering personal trust services. The decision to relocate individuals in the new organizational unit and to establish processes, procedures, and performance expectations for the new unit set in motion a series of required implementation steps. The outcomes of these steps could be the critical factors in the strategic plan's success.

Tom Stewart appointed Tom Whitford as manager of the Personal Services Group. Stewart believed that the key to implementing the strategic plan in the Personal Services Group was the integration of "marketing thinking" into the account management area. Accordingly, he clearly communicated his expectation that while Whitford would be responsible for the account management and support services, Ludlow Miller, vice president for marketing and business development, would be responsible for sales and marketing in the Personal Services Group. Stewart expected that Whitford and Miller would work in tandem to develop the Personal Services Group's capability to achieve its mission and objectives.

The team of Tom Whitford, Ludlow Miller, and the three personal trust department managers undertook the difficult process of implementing the strategic plan and reorganization. They expressed considerable concern that the effects of the reorganization would not fall too heavily on employees and clients. As they viewed their tasks, four changes with severe implications for both groups were readily apparent:

1. Personnel had to be reassigned to each of the three new departments and be integrated in their new jobs and units.
2. Existing accounts had to be reassigned to the appropriate department and, within the department, to the appropriate individual(s).
3. Levels and types of service to be delivered in each of the three departments had to be determined.
4. Performance expectations for personnel assigned to each of the three departments had to be devised and made known to individuals.

Reassignment and Integration of Personnel

The reassigned employees numbered approximately 75. They were split more or less evenly between the administration and investment groups prior to reorganization. Previously, they had been located on different floors and were physically separated by functional responsibility. The reorganization plan called for individual administrators and portfolio managers to be assigned to one of the three departments.

Prior to reorganization, individuals were assigned responsibility for accounts largely on the basis of experience and maturity as administrators and portfolio managers. Consequently, the assignment of significant accounts to an individual was an important indicator of the individual's performance. The task that confronted Whitford and the three department managers was to deal with the attitude that assignment to the Special Services Department would be far more desirable than assignment to either of the other two departments. There also existed considerable uncertainty and anxiety that is quite normal and to be expected whenever an organization undertakes major change that dislocates key personnel.

One idea considered was the creation of an intern program. The program would enable members of the First Services Department to serve on a rotating basis as interns to administrators or portfolio managers in the other two departments. The interns would serve for three to six months and devote 20 percent of their time as backups to experienced senior trust officers. The program would enable interns to receive additional experience and exposure in dealing with large-client relationships and other administrative and portfolio matters. For example, the interns would assist with the preparation of account/relationship plans, development of investment programs, and other projects. The underlying purpose would be to enhance the depth and breadth of experiences of First Services personnel while maintaining their primary responsibility to their own accounts and departmental activities.

In addition to the difficulty posed by the perceived higher status of the Special Services Department, Whitford and his colleagues had to consider the compatibility of individuals who would work in tandem inside each market segment department. Prior to reorganization, each trust administrator would be assigned to accounts with any number of investment officers. Thus, an administrator would have to develop working relationships with as many as 20 different individuals. Teamwork was quite difficult under these circumstances. The reorganization plan recognized that the existing assignment procedure was cumbersome.

The initial plan was to assign an administrator and an investment manager to each account to work as a team. Thus, each account would be serviced by two individuals working together. Not all accounts would be assigned to two individuals, because the strategic plan anticipated that levels of service would have to take into account the size of the portfolio. Thus, many accounts in the First Services Department would be assigned only to an administrator, since the funds would be invested in the Trust Division's common trust funds (CTFs).

The 75 individuals assigned to the Personal Services Group were spread rather evenly throughout the three departments, with the Prime Services Department being somewhat larger. Robert Warth, an experienced investment manager continued as manager of the Special Services Department, Lou Sozio, an experienced trust administration manager, continued as manager of the Prime Services Department, and Karen Minyard, an experienced trust administrator, continued as manager of the First Services Department.

Reassignment of Accounts

The reassignment of accounts was no less troublesome than the reassignment of personnel. The reassignment of accounts to appropriate departments was to be based on size of account, as well as other factors that differentiated trust accounts. For example, some accounts required sensitivity to family relationships, while others were generally stand-alone accounts. Some accounts were highly complex in terms of portfolio composition, tax implications, longevity of the trust, and continuing trusts for successive generations, while others were simple agreements to invest portfolios in CTFs. Some accounts had significant implications for other banking and trust business, while others were relatively simple revocable accounts. Taken together, all these factors form three rather discrete clusters of accounts with different needs for service.

As long as the reassignment of accounts coincided with the reassignment of personnel, no major problems were encountered. But when an individual who administered accounts large enough to be assigned to the Special Services Department was assigned to one of the other two departments, he or she would have to give up the large account. And that created the problem, because the reassignment disrupted the close personal and professional relationship that develops between trust administrators, portfolio managers, and the family or individual whose assets are entrusted to them. Not only did administrators and portfolio managers object to being removed from the relationship but the client may, and sometimes did, object to the reassignment.

The close personal relationship between trust administrators, portfolio managers, and clients is a core professional value. Thus, administrators and portfolio managers were reluctant to relinquish their accounts, and many made persuasive arguments for retaining them even when doing so violated the spirit of the reorganization.

Whitford noted that it was important to maintain the appropriate balance between the reorganization objectives and the customer service objectives.

The account reassignment process involved developing a notification procedure for informing the client of the new status of the account. The procedure involved letters and phone calls from both the previous and new administrators and portfolio managers. The process also involved developing ways to transfer the accounts so as to maintain continuity of the trust agreements, relationships, and investment philosophies. Although the process would appear to be a rather straightforward transfer of information from one individual to another, it was complicated by the diversity of trust agreements and relationships that typified the unique requirements of trust clients and beneficiaries.

Determination of Service Levels

The strategic decision to create three departments in the Personal Services Group reflected the assumption that each department would meet the needs of a particular market segment through differentiated service levels. The existing personnel had sufficient experience to make first approximations of each segment's needs and to deliver those services profitably. These first approximations became topics of considerable discussion among Whitford, Miller, and the three market segment managers. As noted above, the accounts assigned to the three departments differed along several dimensions, notably but not exclusively the size of investable assets. The other important dimensions also had implications for service provided and fees to be charged.

The implementation team recognized that existing clients would have service expectations based on their historical relationships with Provident. These expectations would have to be honored regardless of profitability, or lack thereof. New business in the departments, however, would have to meet certain criteria related to the appropriate service level. In a general sense, the service levels would differ along the familiar high-tech/high-touch dimension. The First Services Department's service would emphasize the delivery of high-tech service wherever appropriate. The Special Services Department would deliver high-touch service. The Prime Services Department would provide a balance of tech and touch. However, these distinctions were to be general guidelines only and were in no way to reflect quality of service to be delivered in the three units.

The initial discussions focused on the components of service traditionally provided in trust departments. These components include the form and content of contacts and meetings with customers, responses to customer inquiries and questions, distribution of account and check schedules, payment of customers' bills, coordination of customers' needs with other units and divisions of Provident, appropriate investment vehicles, distribution of written materials, and nature of administration services. As the discussion of the optimum service levels developed, it was to be informed by market research, which would identify with greater specificity the characteristics and service needs of the three market segments.

Performance Standards

From the beginning of the strategic planning process, planners recognized that the plan and reorganization required the development of performance standards for personnel throughout the division. The strategic redirection and reorganization required new work behaviors, which required new standards to define appropriate levels of performance. The strategic planning task force advocated management by objectives as the approach offering the best chance of reducing ambiguity in these standards. Each group and department manager had to lead the way in the development of these standards.

The three PSG market segment managers had to develop performance standards for themselves and for their immediate subordinates. The standards were to be consistent with the service level definitions and strategic initiatives of the PSG. After the performance standards were defined for the managers of the units, the process would

move on to define standards for the investment and administrative personnel in each unit. The standards were to reflect the different missions of the three departments.

How to Do It All

As Miller, Whitford, and the PSG department managers reviewed the many tasks before them, they were impressed with what they had accomplished to date. But they also realized that easy tasks tend to be done first. In particular, they were concerned with the interrelationships among each of the tasks. They expressed a need to develop a fairly detailed plan for implementing the tasks. The plan would have to take into account the specific requirements of each task as well as the interrelationships among the other tasks and groups within the division.

QUESTIONS:

1. Evaluate the firm's organization design in terms of the important contingency factors which are relevant in this instance.
2. What changes would you recommend be made in the present organization design?
3. What do you believe will be the most important sources of resistance to changing the organization structure?

16
Chapter

Managing Organizational Change and Innovation

After completing Chapter 16, you should be able to:

Learning Objectives

- Define what is meant by *organizational change management*.

- Identify the major steps in undertaking organizational change effort.

- Describe the two major types of change forces.

- Discuss the role of problem diagnosis in the organizational change management.

- Identify a number of change methods and the relative depth of intervention each represents.

- Recognize the impediments and conditions that may limit change management effectiveness.

- Discuss the ethical implications of change management.

- Understand how adopting innovation is a natural outcome in organizations that effectively manage change.

Reading 16.1

Why Transformation Efforts
Fail

As managers contemplate the futures of their organizations in the 21st century, they can't escape the inevitability of change. *Change* is certainly among the most frequently used words on the business pages of every newspaper in the world. Not only have entire countries and empires gone through dramatic and wrenching changes, but also so have companies such as IBM, Amazon.com, Intel, and Oracle. The USSR no longer exists, but neither does Pan American Airlines. So it makes a great deal of sense for this text, that is devoted to the preparation of future managers, to address the issues associated with managing change.

Well-known business writers state that contemporary business organizations confront changing circumstances that put bygone eras of change to shame by comparison. The combination of global competition, computer-assisted manufacturing methods, and instant communications has implications more far reaching than anything since the beginning of the Industrial Revolution.[1] Popular literature including best-sellers warns managers that their organizations' futures depend upon their ability to master change.[2] Other authors state that change is a pervasive, persistent, and permanent condition for all organizations.

Effective managers must view managing change as an integral responsibility rather than as a peripheral one.[3] In addition to managing change, contemporary and future managers will have to develop approaches for adopting and implementing innovation. Innovative products, processes, and practices have become the rule rather than the exception, and managing change and innovation have become interwoven as the significant management responsibility of the 21st century.

But we must accept the reality that not all organizations will successfully make the appropriate changes or adopt the effective innovations. Some researchers believe that organizations with the best chance for success are relatively small and compete in industries in which research and development expenditures have traditionally been relatively high and barriers to entry are relatively low. Such firms in these industries have experienced change to survive and they are likely to be the survivors in the first quarter of the 21st century.[4]

This chapter explores issues associated with managing change and innovation through the application of specific actions intended to rely on reeducation and learning among individuals, groups, and organizations. Reeducation and learning comes about when managers perform analyses and take actions that when taken together maximize the probability that successful change will occur.

ALTERNATIVE CHANGE MANAGEMENT APPROACHES

Managers can undertake organizational change in various ways. In many instances the change process occurs at the expense of short-term losses in exchange for long-term benefits.[5] One extensive review of the literature identified several

---

[1]William A. Pasmore and Richard W. Woodman (eds.), *Research in Organizational Change and Development* (Stamford, CT: JAI Press, 1999).

[2]David A. Gavin, *Learning in Action* (Boston, MA: Harvard Business School Press, 2000).

[3]Danny Miller, "What Happens after Success: The Perils of Excellence," *Journal of Management Studies,* May 1994, pp. 325–58.

[4]Yury Boshyk, *Business Driven Action Learning: Global Best Practices* (New York: St. Martin's Press, 2000).

[5]Viktor Jakupec and John Gavick (eds.), *Flexible Learning, Human Resource and Organizational Development: Putting Theory to Work* (New York: Routledge, 2000).

approaches that managers can use to manage planned change.[6] Although the terms applied to the different approaches vary from author to author and from proponent to proponent, the underlying theme is the same. Regardless of the terms used, the approaches range from the application of power, in any of its forms, to bring about change to the application of reason. Midway between these two extremes is the approach that relies upon reeducation.

Managing Change through Power

The *application of power* to bring about change implies the use of coercion. Managers have access to power and can use their power to coerce nonmanagers to change in the direction they desire. Managers can implement power through their control over reward and sanctions. They can determine the conditions of employment including promotion and advancement. Consequently, through their access to these bases of power, managers can bring to bear considerable influence in an organization.

The application of power often manifests autocratic leadership, and contemporary organizations do not generally encourage managers to engage in such leadership behavior. In times past, autocratic management has been a factor in the rise of labor unions as counterweights to the arbitrary use of managerial power. Except in crises situations when the very existence of the organization is at stake, power is not a favored approach for bringing about change.

Managing Change through Reason

The *application of reason* to bring about change is based on the dissemination of information prior to the intended change. The underlying assumption is that reason alone will prevail and that the participants and parties to the change will all make the rational choice. The reason-based approach appeals to the sensibilities of those who take a utopian view of organizational worlds. But the reality of organizations requires that we recognize the existence of individual motives and needs, group norms and sanctions, and the fact that organizations exist as social as well as work units—all of which means that reason alone won't be sufficient to bring about change.

Managing Change through Reeducation

The middle ground approach relies upon *reeducation* to improve the functioning of the organization. Reeducation implies a particular set of activities that recognizes that neither power nor reason can bring about desirable change. This set of activities has been the subject of much research and application and is generally understood to be the essence of organizational development.[7]

The term *organizational development* implies a normative, reeducation strategy intended to affect systems of beliefs, values, and attitudes within the organization

---

[6]Louise Lovelandy, "Change Strategies and the Use of OD Consultants to Facilitate Change: Part I," *Leadership and Organizational Development Journal 5*, no. 2 (1984), pp. 3–5.

[7]Susan A. Mohrman, Allan M. Mohrman, Jr., and Gerald E. Ledford, Jr., "Interventions That Change Organizations," in Allan M. Mohrman, Jr., Susan A. Mohrman, Gerald E. Ledford, Jr., Thomas G. Cummings, Edward E. Lawler III, and Associates (eds.), *Large Scale Organizational Change* (San Francisco: Jossey-Bass, 1989), p. 146.

so that it can adapt better to the accelerated rate of change in technology, in our industrial environment, and in society in general. It also includes formal organizational restructuring, which is frequently initiated, facilitated, and reinforced by the normative and behavioral changes.[8]

The fact that organizational development is a process that brings about change in a social system raises the issue of the *change agent* (the individual or group who becomes the catalyst for change). Are change agents necessary for organizational improvement to take place? Once we recognize that organizational change involves substantial changes in how individuals think, believe, and act, we can appreciate the necessity of someone to play the role of change agent. But who should play the role? Existing managers? New managers? Or individuals hired specifically for that purpose? Depending upon the situation, any of these can be called upon to orchestrate the organizational change process.[9]

Managers who implement change programs are committed to making fundamental changes in organizational behavior. At the heart of the process are learning principles that enable individuals to unlearn old behaviors and learn new ones. The classic relearning sequence of unfreezing, moving, and refreezing is implemented in the systematic approach to change.[10]

LEARNING PRINCIPLES IN CHANGE MANAGEMENT

To better understand how changes are brought about in individuals, we must appropriate principles of learning. Managers can design a theoretically sound change approach and not achieve any of the anticipated results because they overlooked the importance of providing motivation, reinforcement, and feedback to employees. These principles of learning serve to unfreeze old learning, instill new learning, and refreeze that new learning.

Unfreezing old learning requires people who want to learn new ways to think and act. Unfreezing deals directly with resistance to change.[11] Individuals may not accept that they need more skill in a particular job or more understanding of the problems of other units of the firm. Some people recognize this need and are receptive to experiences that will aid them in developing new skills or new empathies. Others reject the need or play it down, because learning is to them an admission that they aren't completely competent in their jobs. These kinds of people face the prospect of change with different expectations and motivations. Determining the expectations and motivations of people isn't easy. It is, however, a task that managers must undertake to manage change: It is management's responsibility to show employees why they should want to change.

Movement to new learning requires training, demonstration, and empowerment. Training nonmanagerial employees hasn't been a high priority among American corporations, but recently lost market shares to foreign competitors that invest greater resources in training have encouraged American firms to make

---

[8]Elizabeth Wolfe Morrison and Frances J. Milliken, "Organizational Silence: A Barrier to Change and Development in a Pluralistic World," *Academy of Management Review,* October 2000, pp. 706–25.

[9]Ibid.

[10]Kurt Lewin, "Group Decisions and Social Change," in ed. Eleanor E. Maccobby, Theodore M. Newcomb, and Eugene L. Hartley (eds.), *Readings in Social Psychology* (New York: Holt, Rinehart & Winston, 1958).

[11]E. B. Dent and S. G. Goldberg, "Resistance to Change: A Limiting Perspective," *Journal of Applied Behavioral Science,* March 1999, pp. 45–47.

training a regular part of their employees' assignments. Through training and demonstration of the appropriateness of that training, employees can be empowered to take on behaviors they previously had only vaguely imagined possible. The new behaviors must be carefully and sensitively taught.

Refreezing the learned behavior occurs through the application of reinforcement and feedback. These two principles suggest that when people receive positive rewards, information, or feelings for doing something, they'll more likely do the same thing in a similar situation. The other side of the coin involves the impact of punishment for a particular response. Punishment will decrease the probability of doing the same thing at another time. The principle, then, implies that it would be easier to achieve successful change through the use of positive rewards. Reinforcement can also occur when the knowledge or skill acquired in a training program is imparted through a refresher course.

Management must guard against the possibility that what a person has learned at a training site is lost when that person is transferred to the actual work site. If things have gone well, only a minimum amount will be lost in this necessary transfer. A possible strategy for keeping the loss to a minimum is to make the training situation similar to the actual workplace environment. Another strategy is to reward the newly learned behavior. If the colleagues and superiors of newly trained people approve new ideas or new skills, these people will be encouraged to continue to behave in the new way.

If colleagues and superiors behave negatively, the newly trained people will be discouraged from persisting with attempts to use what they've learned. This is one reason why it has been suggested that superiors be trained before subordinates. The superior, if trained and motivated, can serve as a reinforcer and feedback source for the subordinate who has left the training confines and is now back on the job.

CHANGE AGENTS: FORMS OF INTERVENTION

Because managers tend to seek answers in traditional solutions, the intervention of an outsider is necessary. The intervener, or **change agent,** brings a different perspective to the situation and challenges the status quo. The success of any change program rests heavily on the quality and workability of the relationship between the change agent and the key decision makers within the organization. Thus, the form of intervention used is a crucial consideration.[12]

To intervene is to enter into an ongoing organization, or relationship among persons or departments, for the purpose of helping it improve its effectiveness. A number of forms of intervention are used in organizations.

External Change Agents

External change agents are temporary employees of the organization, since they're engaged only for the duration of the change process. They originate in a variety of organizational types including universities, consulting firms, and training agencies. Many large organizations have individuals located at central offices who take temporary assignments with line units that are contemplating

[12]N. A. M. Worren, K. Ruddle, and K. Moore, "From Organizational Development to Change Management," *Journal of Applied Behavioral Science,* September 1999, pp. 273–86.

organizational change. At the conclusion of the change program, the change agent returns to headquarters.

The usual external change agent is a university professor or private consultant who has training and experience in the behavioral sciences. Such an individual will be contacted by the organization and be engaged after agreement is reached on the conditions of the relationship. Ordinarily, the change agent will have graduate degrees in specialties that focus on individual and group behavior in organizational settings. With this kind of training, the external change agent has the perspective to facilitate the change process.

Internal Change Agents

The **internal change agent** is an individual working for the organization who knows something about its problems.[13] The usual internal change agent is a recently appointed manager of an organization that has a record of poor performance; often, the individual takes the job with the expectation that major change is necessary. How successful internal change agents undertake their roles has been extensively studied in recent years.

Raymond Smith's experience as an internal change agent clearly illustrates what such individual efforts can bring about.[14] When Mr. Smith became CEO of Bell Atlantic, he confronted the imperative of changing a slow-to-act bureaucracy into a fast-response entrepreneurial entity. The driving force behind the change was the deregulation of the communications industry. Rather than rely on outside consultants for transforming the organization, Smith took on the role of champion of change himself with full understanding of all the demands that the role would place on him. He immediately began fact gathering and consensus building via discussions with managers and nonmanagers throughout the organization. His intent was to demonstrate by word and deed that Bell Atlantic had to change in fundamental ways if it was to survive in the competitive, deregulated environment.

Signs of progress include breaking down barriers between departments, sharing resources, and developing attitudes that encourage teamwork and idea sharing. He attributes much of this success to creating a sense of empowerment among Bell employees. They believe if they act for the good of the company and succeed, they and the company prosper. But if failure is the outcome, failure is shared by all. He has reoriented the company to be consistent with the new environmental demands—competition.

External-Internal Change Agents

Some organizations use a combination *external-internal* change team to intervene and develop programs. This approach attempts to use the resources and knowledge base of both external and internal change agents. It involves designating an individual or small group within the organization to serve with the external change agent as spearheads of the change effort. The internal group often comes

[13]C. Johnson, "Moving at the Speed of Dell," *HR Magazine,* April 1999, p. 52.

[14]Rosabeth Moss Kanter, "Championing Change: An Interview with Bell Atlantic's CEO Raymond Smith," *Harvard Business Review,* January–February 1991, pp. 119–30.

from the personnel unit, but it can also be a group of top managers. As a general rule, an external change agent will actively solicit the visible support of top management as a way to emphasize the importance of the change effort.[15]

Each of the three forms of intervention has advantages and disadvantages. The external change agent is often viewed as an outsider. When this belief is held by employees inside the company, there's need to establish rapport between the change agent and decision makers. The change agent's views on the problems faced by the organization are often different from the decision maker's views, which leads to problems in establishing rapport. Differences in viewpoints often result in mistrust of the external change agent by the policymakers or a segment of the policymakers. Offsetting these disadvantages is the external change agent's ability to refocus the organization's relationship with the changing environmental demands. The external agent has a comparative advantage over the internal change agent when significant strategic changes must be evaluated.[16]

The internal change agent is often viewed as being more closely associated with one unit or group of individuals than with any other. This perceived favoritism leads to resistance to change by those who aren't included in the internal change agent's circle of close friends and its personnel, and this knowledge can be valuable in preparing for and implementing change. The internal change agent can often serve as the champion for change because of enlightened understanding of the organization's capability and personal persistence.[17]

The third type of intervention, the combination external-internal team, is the rarest, but it seems to have an excellent chance for success. In this type of intervention, the outsider's objectivity and professional knowledge are blended with the insider's knowledge of the organization and its human resources. This blending of knowledge often results in increased trust and confidence among the parties involved. The combination external-internal team's ability to communicate and develop a more positive rapport can reduce resistance to any forthcoming change.

Resistance to Change

Even in situations in which change can be considered the best choice in a work situation, there is fear, anxiety, and resistance. The more significant the change in structure, task, technology, and human assets, the more intense the fear, anxiety, and resistance. A large portion of whatever fear, anxiety, or resistance occurs is triggered by changes in routine, patterns, and habits. Researchers, however, have been more specific in categorizing resistance to change that results from individuals and organizational factors.[18]

---

[15]Warner W. Burke and W. Trahant, *Business Climate Shifts: Profiles of Change Makers* (Boston: Butterworth/Heinemann, 2000).

[16]Ari Ginsberg and Eric Abrahamson, "Champions of Change and Strategic Shifts: The Role of Internal and External Change Advocates," *Journal of Management Studies,* March 1991, pp. 173–90.

[17]Jane M. Howell and Christopher A. Higgins, "Champions of Change: Identifying, Understanding, and Supporting Champions of Technological Innovations," *Organizational Dynamics,* Summer 1990, pp. 40–55.

[18]Dent and Goldberg, "Resistance to Change."

Individual Resistance

Individuals resist change because they fear what will happen to them. A number of individual impediments have been uncovered through research conducted in organizational settings. Included as reasons for resistance are the following:

- The threat of loss of position, power, and authority.
- Economic insecurity regarding retaining a job or level of compensation.
- The possible alteration of social friendships and interactivity. Redesign, shifts in work processes, and movement of people are considered to be threats to friendships, patterns of social-on-the-job interactions, and routines.
- The natural human fear of the unknown brought about by change. The inability to predict with certainty how the new organizational design, manager, or compensation system is going to work creates a natural resistance.
- Failure to recognize or be informed about the need for change.
- Cognitive dissonance created because one is confronted with new people, processes, systems, technology, or expectations. The dissonance or discomfort created by what is new or different is another typical social psychological human process.[19]

Each of these and other individually oriented points of resistance can be addressed through increased communication, information, and data. Face-to-face meetings, newsletters, e-mails, reports, speeches, conferences, and other methods of communication can lead to a better understanding and trust about changes. Other methods for dealing with individual resistance include having people participate in the entire change process, using change champions from within the group to serve as facilitators, and engaging in negotiations about the type and pace of changes. These approaches require management skill in leading the change approach.

Unfortunately, some managers use coercion, threats, and manipulation to implement changes. The drawbacks to these hands-on, top-down approaches include resentment, withdrawal, slowing down, anger, covert sabotage, and unethical behaviors.[20] These methods provide little long-term benefits that justify their implementation.

www.monsanto.com

Trust, faith, and confidence in any change program are extremely important. Robert Shapiro, CEO of Monsanto, captures the essence of trust as follows:

> You can't get to good morale by lying. . . . You can't get innovation that way. You find an enormous amount of time and effort is dealing with the trust of others. Look at all the inefficiencies of lack of trust. It tells you that an honest organization is going to be much more efficient. It just makes good business sense.[21]

---

[19]Denise M. Rousseau and S. A. Tijoriwala, "What's a Good Reason to Change? Motivated Reasoning and Social Accounts in Promoting Organizational Change," *Journal of Applied Psychology,* August 1999, pp. 514–28.

[20]A. S. Judson, *Changing Behavior in Organizations: Minimizing Resistance to Change* (Cambridge, MA: Basil Blackwell, Inc., 1991), p. 48.

[21]D. Jones, "Driving Change—Too Fast?" *USA Today,* August 11, 1999, p. 6B.

Organizational Resistance

A range of forces within an organization poses barriers to the implementation of changes in structure, tasks, technology, and behavior. These organizational barriers to change include:

- The professional and functional orientation of a department, unit, or team. Engineers perceive changes from an engineering background and experience. Likewise, its member's education, training, and learning shape sales' and marketing teams' perceptions. The organizational unit also creates its own norms and standards of behavior. Changes may alter relationships that impact these norms and standards.

- Structural inertia creates a natural barrier. Organizations are structured to promote stability. The structural arrangement is created in a way that resists changes or forces that generate instability. This same type of structure at the organization level also exists at the group and team level. Strong norms are resistant to change because of group members' comfort with a certain flow and pattern.

- If change is considered a threat to the power balance in an organization, it will be resisted. The fear of losing position, status, and resource power or leverage creates a strong backlash. Change in how products are sold in mall stores, online, and through catalogues created resistance in Sears stores, units, and subunits based on the perception of power and its distribution in the firm. The online unit wanted more resources allocated to it while the store managers resisted the untested venture into online e-tailing.

- A failure at previous change creates an aura and folklore about the dangers associated with change. Entire units have experienced unsuccessful changes, such as Coke's experiment with changing the taste and flavor of Coca-Cola. Future attempts to alter anything associated with changing Coke's formula will likely be met with skepticism, doubt, and caution. The same type of failure-driven resistance existed at Ford Motor Company for at least a full decade after the monumental financial losses associated with the introduction of the Edsel automobile. Ford was reluctant to introduce major style changes and new products for at least 10 years after the 1957 Edsel failure.

Strategies for Overcoming Resistance to Change

The range of individual and organizational resistance factors involves fear, anxiety, team behavior, politics, and uncertainty. In analyzing change and resistance there are a number of key considerations.[22] First, individuals and organizations must have a reason to change. That is, there must be some motivation behind the change.

Second, the more involved people are at all levels of the hierarchy in the planning, implementation, and monitoring of the change, the higher the likelihood of success.

Third, communication is ongoing and not a one-time factor in successful change programs. There is always the need for even more communication in major change programs. Communication can educate and prepare the employees in a way that reduces fear, anxiety, and resistance.

---

[22]Rousseau and Tijoriwala, "What's a Good Reason to Change?"

Finally, the creation of a learning organization or one that has the capacity, resilience, and flexibility to change is ideal. In learning organizations, such as Cisco Systems, Wal-Mart, Baxter Laboratories, and Krispy Kreme, employees share ideas, make recommendations, and participate voluntarily in change from the outset.

Learning organizations have the following characteristics.[23]

- Open discussions and accessibility to information and data
- Clear vision expressed at all levels
- Strong emphasis on interdependence, worth, and importance of each person and unit
- Clear goals and concepts of performance expectations
- Commitment to learning, improving, and personal growth
- Concern for measurable results whenever possible
- A curiosity to try new methods, experiment, and accept failure

Any organization in any industry can become a learning system that can thrive on change. Setting aside old ways of thinking and minimizing the resistance to change can become a habit, especially in organizations who want to fit the learning model.

A MODEL FOR MANAGING ORGANIZATIONAL CHANGE

The process of managing change through reeducation approaches can be approached logically. The several steps of this logical process are suggested in Exhibit 16.1. The model consists of specific steps generally acknowledged to be essential to successful change management.[24] A manager considers each of them, either explicitly or implicitly, when undertaking a change program. Prospects of initiating successful change can be enhanced when managers actively support the effort and demonstrate that support by implementing systematic procedures that give substance to the process.[25]

The model indicates that forces for change continually act on the organization; this assumption reflects the dynamic character of the modern world. At the same time, it's the manager's responsibility to sort out the information that reflects the magnitude of change forces.[26] The information is the basis for recognizing when change is needed; it's equally desirable to recognize when change isn't needed. But once managers recognize that something is malfunctioning, they must diagnose the problem and identify relevant alternative techniques.

Finally, the manager must implement the change and monitor the change process and change results. The model includes feedback to the implementation

---

[23]Peter Senge, *The Dance of Change: The Challenges to Sustaining Momentum in Learning Organizations* (New York: Doubleday, 1999).

[24]Donald L. Kirkpatrick, *How to Manage Change Effectively* (San Francisco: Jossey-Bass, 1985), pp. 101–06.

[25]John P. Kotter, "Leading Change: The Eight Steps to Transformation," In J. A. Conger, G. M. Spreitzer, and E. E. Lawler, III. (eds.), *The Leader's Change Handbook* (San Francisco, CA: Jossey-Bass, 1999), pp. 87–99.

[26]Ralph H. Kilmann, "Toward a Complete Program for Corporate Transformation," in Ralph H. Kilmann, Teresa Joyce Covin, and Associates (eds.), *Corporate Transformation* (San Francisco: Jossey-Bass, 1989), pp. 302–29.

EXHIBIT 16.1   A Model for the Management of Organizational Development

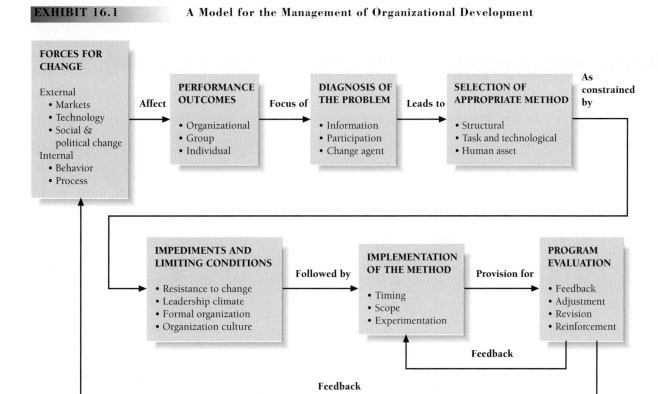

step and to the forces-for-change step. These feedback loops suggest that the change process itself must be monitored and evaluated. The mode of implementation may be faulty and may lead to poor results, but responsive action could correct the situation. Moreover, the feedback loop to the initial step recognizes that no change is final. A new situation is created within which problems and issues will emerge; a new setting is created that will itself become subject to change. The model suggests no final solution; rather, it emphasizes that the modern manager operates in a dynamic setting wherein the only certainty is change itself.

FORCES FOR CHANGE

The forces for change can be classified conveniently into two groups: *external forces* and *internal forces*. External forces are beyond management's control. Internal forces operate inside the firm and are generally within the control of management.

External Forces

Organizations seldom undertake significant change without a strong shock from their environment. The external environment includes many economic, technological, and social/political forces that can trigger the change process. Those who study and practice organizational change agree that these environmental triggers

AT&T Responds to Changes in the Competitive Environment

Since 1983, when the firm was broken up by events following deregulation, AT&T has been undergoing changes that have altered nearly every aspect of its organization and strategy. These changes reflect AT&T's responses to the necessity to compete in markets that reward fast adoption of new technology and adaptation to fickle customer demand. AT&T's organization structure at the time of deregulation proved incapable of bringing about appropriate behavior. According to Chairman Robert E. Allen, who took over in 1988, AT&T had a top-heavy bureaucracy that created unnecessary blocks to creativity and initiative. He began efforts to flatten the organization and bring top managers closer to the customer. Lower-level managers have more authority to respond to customer issues.

The change hasn't been without costs as reflected in the employee layoffs and early retirements since 1984. But to stay the course is essential, according to Allen. To combat the effects of these traumatic changes, AT&T has implemented policies giving managers and employees personal stakes in the businesses they run. Their salaries and advancement opportunities are tied to customer satisfaction. Allen claims to have no grand design for what AT&T will look like, but he insists that it must continue its efforts to create smaller, customer-oriented units.

Sources: "Bob Allen Is Turning AT&T into a Live Wire," *Business Week*, November 6, 1989, pp. 140–41, 144, 148, 152; Barry F. Dambach and Braden R. Allenby, "Implementing Design for Environment at AT&T," *Total Quality Environmental Management*, Spring 1995, pp. 51–62; and Benjamin Schneider, Arthur P. Brief, and Richard A. Guzzo, "Creating a Climate and Culture for Sustainable Organizational Change," *Organizational Dynamics*, Spring 1996, pp. 6–19.

are necessary but not sufficient to initiate change. Change also involves managers who are aware of the change and who take action.

The manager of a business has historically been concerned with reacting to **economic forces**. Competitors introduce new products, increase their advertising, reduce their prices, or increase their customer service. In each case, a response is required unless the manager is content to permit the erosion of her profit and market share. At the same time, changes occur in customer tastes and incomes. The firm's products may no longer have customer appeal; customers may be able to purchase less expensive, higher-quality forms of the same products. The Organizational Encounter describes the actions of AT&T in response to changes in economic forces.

The second source of environmental change forces is **technology**. The knowledge explosion has introduced new technology for nearly every business function. Computers have made possible high-speed data processing and the solutions to complex production problems. New machines and new processes have revolutionized how many products are manufactured and distributed. Computer technology and automation have affected not only the technical conditions of work, but the social conditions as well.[27] New occupations have been created, and others have been eliminated. Slowness to adopt new technology that reduces cost and improves quality will show up in the financial statements sooner or later.[28] Technological advance is a permanent fixture in the business world. As a force for change, it will continue to demand attention.

[27]Robert H. Hayes and Ramchandran Jaikumar, "Manufacturing's Crisis: New Technologies, Obsolete Organizations," *Harvard Business Review*, September–October 1988, pp. 77–85.

[28]Michael S. Morton, "The 1990s Research Program: Implications for Management and the Emerging Organization," *Decision Support Systems*, November 1994, pp. 251–56.

The third source of environmental change forces is **social** and **political change**. Business managers must be tuned in to the great movements over which they have no control but which, in time, influence their firm's fate. Sophisticated mass communications and international markets create great potential for business, but they're also great threats to managers who can't understand what's going on.[29] Finally, the relationship between government and business becomes much closer as regulations are imposed and relaxed.

Comprehending implications of external forces requires *organizational learning* processes.[30] These processes, now being studied in many organizations, involve the capacity to absorb new information, process that information in the light of previous experience, and act on the information in new and potentially risky ways. But only through such learning experiences will organizations be prepared for the 21st century.

Internal Forces

Internal forces for change, which occur within the organization, can usually be traced to *process* and *behavioral* problems. The process problems include breakdowns in decision making and communications. Decisions aren't being made, are made too late, or are of poor quality. Communications are short-circuited, redundant, or simply inadequate. Tasks aren't undertaken or aren't completed because the person responsible did not get the word. Because of inadequate or nonexistent communications, a customer order isn't filled, a grievance isn't processed, or an invoice isn't filed and the supplier isn't paid. Interpersonal and interdepartmental conflicts reflect breakdowns in organizational processes.

Low levels of morale and high levels of absenteeism and turnover are symptoms of behavioral problems that must be diagnosed. A wildcat strike or a walkout may be the most tangible sign of a problem, yet such tactics are usually employed because they arouse management to action. A certain level of employee discontent exists in most organizations—it's dangerous to ignore employee complaints and suggestions. But the process of change includes the *recognition* phase—the point where management must decide to act or not to act.

In many organizations, the need for change goes unrecognized until some major catastrophe occurs. The employees strike or seek the recognition of a union before the management finally recognizes the need for action. Whether it takes a whisper or a shout, the need for change must be recognized by some means; and once that need has been recognized, the exact nature of the problem must be diagnosed. If the problem isn't properly understood, the impact of change on people can be extremely negative.

DIAGNOSIS OF A PROBLEM

Change agents facilitate the diagnostic phase by gathering, interpreting, and presenting data. Although the accuracy of data is extremely important, how the data

---

[29]Huibert de Man, *Organizational Change in Its Context: A Theoretical and Empirical Study of the Linkages between Organizational Change Projects and Their Administrative, Strategic, and Institutional Environment* (Delft, The Netherlands: Eburon, 1988).

[30]Peter M. Senge, "The Leader's New Work: Building Learning Organizations," *Sloan Management Review,* Fall 1990, pp. 13–23; Peter M. Senge, *The Fifth Discipline: The Art and Practice of the Learning Organization* (New York: Doubleday, 1990); and Calhoun W. Wick and Lu Stanton Leon, "From Ideas to Action: Creating a Learning Organization," *Human Resource Management,* Summer 1995, pp. 299–311.

are interpreted and presented is equally important. Interpretation and presentation are generally accomplished in one of two ways. First, the data are discussed with a group of top managers, who are asked to make their own diagnosis of the information; or, second, change agents may present their own diagnoses without making explicit their frameworks for analyzing the data. A difficulty with the first approach is that top management tends to see each problem separately. Each manager views his problem as being the most important and fails to recognize other problem areas. The second approach has inherent problems of communication. External change agents often have difficulty with the second approach because they become immersed in theory and various conceptual frameworks that are less realistic than the managers would like.

Appropriate action is necessarily preceded by diagnosis of the problem's symptoms. Experience and judgment are critical to this phase unless the problem is readily apparent to all observers. Ordinarily, however, managers can disagree on the nature of the problem. There's no formula for accurate diagnosis, but the following questions point the manager in the right direction:

1. What is the problem as distinct from the symptoms of the problem?
2. What must be changed to resolve the problem?
3. What outcomes (objectives) are expected from the change, and how will those outcomes be measured?

The answers to these questions can come from information ordinarily found in the organization's information system. Or it may be necessary to generate ad hoc information through the creation of committees or task forces. Meetings between managers and employees provide a variety of viewpoints that can be sifted through by a smaller group. Interviewing key personnel is an important problem-finding method. Another diagnostic approach that obtains broader-based information is the attitude survey.

The survey is a useful diagnostic approach if the potential focus of change is the total organization. If smaller units or entities are the focus of change, the survey technique may not be a reliable source of information. For example, if the focus of change is a relatively small work group, diagnosis of the problem is better accomplished through individual interviews followed by group discussion of the interview data. In this approach, the group becomes actively involved in sharing and interpreting perception of problems. However, the attitude survey can pose difficulties for organizations with relatively low levels of trust in management's sincerity to use the information in constructive ways.

Identification of individual employees' problems comes about through interviews and personnel department information. Consistently low performance evaluations indicate such problems, but it's often necessary to go into greater detail. Identifying individuals' problems is far more difficult than identifying organizational problems. Thus, the diagnostic process must stress the use of precise and reliable information.

To summarize, the data collection process can tap information in several ways. Five different approaches are useful for assorted purposes.[31]

1. Questionnaire data can be collected from large numbers of people.
2. Direct observations can be taken of actual workplace behavior.

---

[31]Noel M. Tichy, *Managing Strategic Change* (New York: John Wiley and Sons, 1983), pp. 162–64.

3. Selected individuals in key positions can be interviewed.

4. Workshops can be arranged with groups to explore different perceptions of problems.

5. Documents and records of the organization can be examined for archival and current information.

SELECTION OF APPROPRIATE METHODS

Organization Development at
J. P. Hunt

Managers have a variety of change and development methods to select from, depending on the objectives they hope to accomplish. One way of viewing objectives is from the perspective of the depth of the intended change.

Depth of intended change refers to the scope and intensity of the change efforts. A useful distinction here is between the formal and informal aspects of organizations. Formal organizational components are observable, rational, and oriented toward structural factors. The informal components are not observable to all people; they are affective and oriented to process and behavioral factors. Generally speaking, as one moves from formal aspects of the organization to informal aspects, the scope and intensity increase. As scope and intensity increase, so does the depth of the change.

The choice of a particular development method depends on the nature of the problem that management has diagnosed and the depth of the intended change. Examining several specific development methods is the focus of the rest of this section. For purposes of our discussion, we have grouped these methods into three categories: structural, task and technological, and human asset. The classification of methods that we use in no way implies a distinct division among the approaches. On the contrary, the interrelationships among them must be acknowledged and anticipated. As an illustration of this, we close this section with a look at approaches that are "multifaceted" and cut across our three categories.

Structural Approaches

Structural approaches to organizational change refer to managerial actions that attempt to improve effectiveness by introducing change through formal policies and procedures. Actual structural reorganization is the most direct example of this approach. Mergers and acquisitions, as well as the recent interest in downsizing, may set the stage for a variety of structural reorganizations. Generally, restructuring tends to focus on creating flatter, more organic organizations.

Not all structural approaches necessarily involve making actual changes in the organizational structure, however. Introduction of a zero-based budgeting system, for example, may represent a significant change in both policy and procedure, without altering the existing structure. Many organizations are revising their reward systems, placing emphasis on pay for performance. In such systems, pay is determined by achieved levels of either individual or team performance. Reward systems such as these also represent a structural approach to organizational change.

One method representing a structural approach to organizational change that has demonstrated effectiveness is management by objectives (MBO). Another structural approach is referred to as *reengineering*.

Management by Objectives   Management by objectives (MBO) is a process consisting of a series of interdependent and interrelated steps designed to facilitate planning and control, decision making, and other important management functions. It is also a philosophy of management which reflects a proactive rather than reactive approach to managing.[32] Successful use of MBO depends on the ability of participants to define their objectives in terms of their contributions to the total organization and to be able to accomplish them.

The original work of Drucker[33] and subsequent writings by others provide the basis for three guidelines for implementing MBO:

1. Superiors and subordinates meet and discuss objectives that contribute to overall goals.
2. Superiors and subordinates jointly establish attainable objectives for the subordinates.
3. Superior and subordinates meet at a predetermined later date to evaluate the subordinates' progress toward the objectives.

The exact procedures employed in implementing MBO vary from organization to organization and from unit to unit.[34] However, the basic elements of objective setting, participation of subordinates in objective setting, and feedback and evaluation usually are parts of any MBO program. The intended consequences of MBO include improved contribution to the organization, improved attitudes and satisfaction of participants, and greater role clarity. MBO is highly developed and widely used in business, health care, and governmental organizations.

www.hp.com

Reengineering   Companies such as Mutual Benefit Life, Hewlett-Packard, and Ford, through initiative to change work flow, processes, and design, helped create what eventually became known as *reengineering.* The objective of reengineering is to create processes, systems, and structure that meets customer needs efficiently and in an economically sound manner. Instead of this objective catching the attention of managers, the notion of downsizing introducing computerized systems to replace employees and eliminating layers of management dominated discussions, analysis, and critiques of reengineering.

James Champy and Michael Hammer popularized reengineering in their book *Reinventing the Organization.*[35] They advocate an approach to structure and process that begins with a clear, blank sheet of paper. This fresh start enables managers to design an entirely new (reengineered) organization to meet the needs of customers. The new approach must be implemented with careful training, education, and documentation to prevent the old structures and processes from reappearing out of habit and inertia. Reengineering consists of a process that evolves from unfreezing, reinventing the new structures and processes, and freezing them.

---

[32]Original statements of MBO may be found in Peter Drucker, *The Practice of Management* (New York: Harper & Row, 1954); George Odiorne, *Management by Objectives* (New York: Pitman Publishing, 1965); and W. J. Reddin, *Effective Management by Objectives* (New York: McGraw-Hill, 1970).

[33]See Ronald G. Greenwood, "Management by Objectives: As Developed by Peter Drucker, Assisted by Harold Smiddy," *Academy of Management Review,* April 1981, pp. 225–30.

[34]Jan P. Muczyk and Bernard Reimann, "MBO as a Complement to Effective Leadership," *Academy of Management Executive,* May 1989, pp. 131–38.

[35]M. Hammer and J. Champy, *Reengineering the Corporation* (New York: Harper Collins, 1993).

Reengineering consists of three strategies: streamlining, integrating, and transforming. Streamlining breaks the core process into segments to eliminate waste, delays, and slow response time. An example of streamlining is to discover the most efficient way to repropose on-site, instructor-led training so that it can be delivered on the Internet through online, asynchronous courseware.

Integrating is the unification of systems, processes, or work-related activities across functional lines, combining the course preparation, instruction, and graphical design and hosting activities in producing online courses to fit the diverse needs of online trainees.

Transforming involves benchmarking to locate "best in class" organizations. An example of transforming is to forget how the firm currently prepares and delivers online training courses. What do trainees want, when and where? Is it possible to learn and pace the training skill, competency, or knowledge in such a way that each person literally controls and structures his or her own course?

www.tacobell.com

Taco Bell is a documented example of reengineering. The firm started its reengineering work by asking customers what they wanted when visiting a Mexican American fast-food restaurant. Instead of finding that customers wanted what other successful fast-food restaurants provided, Taco Bell found simplicity was the resounding response. Customers wanted from Taco Bell fast service, hot food, good tasting food, and cleanliness. Fancy surroundings, expensive internal designs and furniture, and soothing music were not mentioned.

Taco Bell reinvented itself, the restaurant design, the price structure, and the treatment of customers. Small lot cooking was replaced with a central kitchen which controlled food quality very carefully. The central kitchen dispersed the food to restaurants, which were 30 percent kitchen and 70 percent customer service area instead of the reverse design.

Taco Bell streamlined, integrated, and transformed its typical restaurant design, pricing, food preparation, and customer service. The results have been the preparation of good Mexican American food, served hot, and sold at a reasonable price in a clean environment.

Critics of reengineering point to the fear and anxiety raised by this structural change approach.[36] Reengineering has not lived up to the excessive hype and expectations established by a legion of management consultants and academic gurus. Despite the hype, some organizations continue today to use reengineering concepts such as streamlining, integration, and transformation. When these activities are used with caution, with concern for people, and with gaining and sustaining a fair competitive advantage, reengineering practices can be effective, well received, and cost efficient. On the other hand, when *reengineering* is the code word for downsizing, eliminating management layers, and having computers replace people, there is likely to be resistance, anxiety, and fear permeating throughout an organization.

Task and Technological Approaches

Task and technological approaches to organizational change both focus directly on the work itself that is performed in the organization. A task focus emphasizes job design changes, a topic discussed in detail in Chapter 6. Job enlargement, which increases range (the number of tasks performed), and job enrichment,

---

[36]Thomas H. Davenport, "The Fad That Forgot People," *Fast Company,* November 1995, pp. 70–75.

which increases depth (the amount of discretion and responsibility the jobholder has), are primary examples of task approaches. Some of the newer systems of work scheduling may also be classified as task approaches. Recall, for example, our discussion of flexible work schedules in Chapter 6. By allowing individuals to choose when they perform their assigned tasks, management is hoping to increase satisfaction, productivity, and performance while decreasing absenteeism and turnover.

Technological approaches emphasize changes in the flow of work. This could include, for example, new physical plant layouts, changes in office design, and improved work methods and techniques. Many technological changes are related to advances in equipment design and capability. For example, computer-aided-design (CAD) technology has transformed the job (and productivity) of draftspersons; laser-guided production equipment has dramatically increased the accuracy of many manufacturing processes; the desktop computer has altered literally millions of jobs; and, on a growing number of factory floors, robots are outnumbering people. Organizational researchers are just now beginning to examine some of the longer-term effects of technological change on individuals.[37]

An important aspect of task and technological approaches to organizational change is training. When jobs are redesigned, when work flow is changed, or when the use of new equipment must be mastered, training programs are an integral tool in providing the necessary new skills and knowledge. In fact, the most widely used methods for developing employee productivity are training programs.[38] A distinction can be made between on-the-job training and off-the-job training. On-the-job training generally focuses on teaching specific skills and techniques needed to master a job. It has as an advantage the fact that the employees are actually producing while undergoing training. Corning Inc., the well-known glass manufacturing company, is an example of an organization that is extensively involved in on-the-job training. As employees master each job requirement, they receive credits that become part of their performance evaluations. Training at Corning, however, is not restricted to specific job skills. The company has developed an interactive set of workbooks to train employees in company culture, values, and organization.[39]

www.corning.com

Frequently, organizations have provided training that supplements on-the-job efforts. Some of the advantages of off-the-job training are:

1. It lets executives get away from the pressures of the job and work in a climate in which "party-line" thinking is discouraged and self-analysis is stimulated.

2. It presents a challenge to executives that, in general, enhances their motivation to develop themselves.

3. It provides resource people and resource material—faculty members, fellow executives, and literature—that contribute suggestions and ideas for the executives to "try on for size" as they attempt to change, develop, and grow.

---

[37]See, for example, Marlene E. Burkhardt, "Social Interaction Effects Following a Technological Change: A Longitudinal Investigation," *Academy of Management Journal*, August 1994, pp. 869–98.

[38]D. Roth, 10 Companies That Get It: Southwest Airlines," *Fortune*, November 8, 1999, p. 115.

[39]Jeanne C. Meister, "Training Workers in the Three C's," *Nations Business*, September 1994, pp. 51–53.

The theme of the advantages cited above is that trainees are more stimulated to learn by being away from job pressures. This is certainly debatable since it is questionable whether much of what is learned can be transferred back to the job. Attending a case-problem-solving program in San Diego is quite different from facing irate customers in Cleveland. Nonetheless, despite the difficulty of transferring knowledge from the classroom-type environment to the office, plant, or hospital, off-the-job training programs are still very popular and widely utilized.

Human Asset Approaches

Directly or indirectly, all organizational change efforts involve the human assets of the organization. MBO programs, for example, are designed to help individuals set realistic performance goals and objectives, and a variety of job training programs are aimed at increasing skills and knowledge needed to perform tasks. Thus, both the structural approaches and the task and technological approaches typically involve changes related to achieving fairly specific and narrow outcomes. What we are calling human asset approaches, however, is a category of change methods designed to result in a far less specific and much broader outcome of helping individuals learn and grow professionally, and perhaps personally.

A necessary prerequisite to effective, lasting organizational change is individual change. Structural, task, and technological transformations will ultimately fail if the individuals involved are not receptive to change. Human asset approaches help prepare people for ongoing change and learning.

The "learning organization" philosophy stresses the importance of this. According to Peter Senge, a leading advocate, learning organizations value continuing individual and collective learning.[40] To increase effectiveness, Senge argues, organizational members must put aside their old ways of thinking, learn to be open with others, understand how their company really works, develop plans everyone can agree on, and then work together to achieve those plans.[41] Human asset approaches assist in achieving one or more of those objectives. The Organizational Encounter suggests a number of ways organizations have used to develop human resources through intensive developmental programs.

We will discuss two of the more widely known approaches: team building and the managerial grid. Additionally, we will introduce three recent approaches: ethics training, mentoring programs, and introspection development.

Team Building

In recent years, U.S. organizations have shown renewed interest in effectively using work groups, or teams.[42] Anyone who has ever operated a business or organized any kind of project requiring the efforts of several people knows the difficulties involved in getting everyone to pull in the right direction, in the right way, and at the right time. One approach to minimizing these difficulties is that of team building.

---

[40]Peter Senge, *The Fifth Discipline* (New York: Doubleday Publishing Company, 1990).

[41]Brian Dumaine, "Mr. Learning Organization," *Fortune,* October 17, 1994, pp. 147–57.

[42]G. L. Stewart, Charles C. Manz, and H. P. Sims, Jr., *Team Work and Group Dynamics* (New York: Wiley, 1999).

American Organizations Change to Deal with Diversity

American organizations have recognized that the composition of their workforce is beginning to reflect the composition of American society. Diversity of culture, religion, national origin, race, and gender now characterizes the employment rolls of all but the most isolated organization. In recognition of this fact of organizational life, organizations have turned to organizational change interventions to help employees learn to deal effectively with their fellow employees as well as a diverse population of suppliers and customers. For example, the Monsanto Company has devised a well-publicized organizational change effort that prepares its employees to cope successfully with differences between employees. The program alerts new and veteran employees to become aware of subtle forms of discrimination when dealing with other people and to develop skills to help employees confront differences and, at the same time, get on with doing business.

McDonald's Corporation undertook a determined effort in 1981 to recruit and hire mentally and physically challenged individuals. The program aims to find useful employment for individuals who might otherwise be unable to contribute their talents. McDonald's found during the course of its program that it was necessary to help other store employees understand what it means to be a disabled restaurant employee.

New York City has long been recognized for its diverse population. Recently, the New York City Police Department implemented sensitivity training to help police officers relate to the ever-increasing diversity of the city's population, the police department's constituency. Sensitivity training coincided with the department's new initiative to focus police efforts at community levels throughout the city.

www. mcdonald' com

Sources: R. Roosevelt Thomas, Jr., "Redefining Diversity," *HR Focus*, April 1996, pp. 6–8; Shari Caudron, "Monsanto Responds to Diversity," *Personnel Journal*, November 1990, pp. 72–80; Jennifer J. Laabs, "The Golden Arches Provide Golden Opportunities," *Personnel Journal*, July 1991, pp. 52–57; and Alan M. Webber, "Crime and Management: An Interview with New York City Police Commissioner, Lee P. Brown," *Harvard Business Review*, May–June 1991, pp. 110–26.

The purpose of team building is to enable work groups to get their work done more effectively, to improve their performance. The work groups may be existing or relatively new command and task groups. The specific aims of the intervention include setting goals and priorities, analyzing the ways the group does its work, examining the group's norms and processes for communicating and decision making, and examining the interpersonal relationships within the group. As each of these aims is undertaken, the group is placed in the position of having to recognize explicitly the contributions, positive and negative, of each group member.

The process by which these aims are achieved begins with diagnostic meetings. Often lasting an entire day, the meetings enable each group member to share with other members his or her perceptions of problems. Subsequently, a plan of action must be agreed on. The action plan should call on each of the group members, individually or as part of a subgroup, to undertake a specific action to alleviate one or more of the problems.

Team building is also effective when new groups are being formed because problems often exist when new organizational units, project teams, or task forces are created. Typically, such groups have certain characteristics that must be overcome if the groups are to perform effectively. For example:

1. Confusion exists as to roles and relationships.
2. Members have a fairly clear understanding of short-term goals.
3. Group members have technical competence that puts them on the team.
4. Members often pay more attention to the tasks of the team than to the relationships among the team members.

To combat these tendencies, the new group could schedule team building meetings during the first few weeks of its life.

Although the reports of team building indicate mixed results, the evidence suggests that group processes improve through team-building efforts.[43] This record of success accounts for the increasing use of team building as an organizational development, (OD) method.

Ethics Training

While many organizations have codes of ethics, with few exceptions ethics training, particularly organizationwide efforts, is a relatively recent development. While the content and methodology of ethics programs vary widely, most may be categorized as focusing on one or both of two general objectives: (1) developing employee awareness of business ethics and (2) focusing on specific ethical issues with which the employee may come in contact. By helping to develop employee awareness of ethical issues in decision making, for example, organizations hope to:[44]

Enable recognition of ethical components of a decision

Legitimize ethics as part of the decision-making process

Avoid variability in decision making caused by lack of norms or awareness of rules

Avoid confusion as to who is responsible for misdeeds

Provide decision-making frameworks for analyzing ethical choices

The second objective, that of focusing on relevant ethical issues with which employees may be faced, may include dealing with conflict-of-interest situations, white-collar crime, or discharging one's job responsibilities within the context of local, state, and federal requirements. This latter category could encompass such diverse activities as employee safety, EEO issues, product marketing claims, environmental protection, and sexual harassment.

Formal ethics training, particularly programs involving most or all levels within the organization, is too recent a phenomenon to draw conclusions regarding its effectiveness. It is clear, however, that however effective it may be, ethics training is not a cure-all. The accompanying You Be the Judge invites you to express an opinion regarding an ethical issue involving a major corporation.

Mentorship Programs

Formal mentorship programs represent an even more recent and less frequently used organizational change technique than ethics training. A mentor is a knowledgeable individual who is committed to providing support to other, usually junior, organizational members.[45] Mentoring programs help individuals develop by providing specific job instruction, disseminating organizational cultural norms and values, dispelling organizational myths, and generally transferring knowledge

---

[43]J. Lipman-Blumen and Harold J. Leavitt, " 'Hot Groups with Attitude': A New Organizational State of Mind," *Organizational Dynamics,* Spring 1999, pp. 63–73.

[44]Susan J. Harrington, "What Corporate America Is Teaching about Ethics," *Academy of Management Executive,* February 1991, p. 23.

[45]Belle Rose Ragins and Terri A. Scandura, "Gender Differences in Expected Outcomes of Mentoring Relationships," *Academy of Management Journal,* August 1994, pp. 957–71.

Ethics Training Doesn't Always Guarantee Positive Results

You Be the Judge

www.jnj.com

Johnson & Johnson has been a leading company in efforts to provide guidelines and training in ethical behavior. Any business source will include this company as one of the forerunners in ethical training. However, as managers of the company found out, ethical training does not always eliminate ethical problems.

What happened went something like this: A 3M employee obtained samples of a new 3M casting tape to be used by physicians to set broken bones. Hoping to enhance himself financially, he mailed these samples to four 3M competitors, including Johnson & Johnson. According to 3M, while none of the companies reported receiving the material, only Johnson & Johnson analyzed the samples and used 3M's proprietary technology in their own competing product. As a result, again according to 3M, Johnson & Johnson undermined 3M's efforts to win a larger share of the $200 million domestic market for such products.

In the inevitable litigation that followed, a U.S. District Court master ordered Johnson & Johnson to pay 3M more than $116 million for misappropriating trade secrets. Potentially more costly, Johnson & Johnson may have to remove some of its casting tapes from the market. According to court records, the sample was originally sent to the president of Johnson & Johnson's orthopedics company. Since he was away, the sample went to the company's product manager, who then sent it to the lab for analysis. The resulting lab report was sent to several orthopedic officials who failed to instruct company chemists not to use the findings in their own work.

Johnson & Johnson denies any wrongdoing. Ultimate resolution of the issue may take years. Whatever the final outcome, could the problem been avoided altogether? What should the official at Johnson & Johnson have done when he received the 3M information? Some experts say the official should have immediately notified 3M and the FBI. Others say the official should have simply acted as he did. Who is correct? You be the judge.

Sources: John A. Byrne, "Businesses Are Signing Up for Ethics 101," *Business Week*, February 15, 1988, pp. 56–57; Judy Nixon, Carolyn Wiley, and Judy West, "Beyond Survival: Ethics for the Industrial Manager," *Industrial Management*, May/June 1991, pp. 15–18; and Barbara Etorre, "James Burke: The Fine Art of Leadership," *Management Review*, October 1996, pp. 13–16.

gained through years of being part of the organization. Mentoring relationships, of course, are not new; mentors and "mentees" have existed as long as have formal organizations. Formalizing such relationships, however, is a very new and largely unexplored concept.

A number of positive benefits to the organization have been identified as outcomes of mentoring programs.[46] These include (1) early identification of talent that might otherwise go unnoticed, (2) sensing by mentors of employee attitudes and morale, and (3) transmission of informal organizational expectations (corporate culture). Organizational benefits of mentoring can accrue at all levels of the company, up to and including the individual(s) being groomed for the presidency.

There are some caveats to keep in mind, however. Formalized mentor-mentee relationships should always be voluntary, for both parties. Companies should not assume that every long-term employee who has the interest would make a good

---

[46]James A. Wilson and Nancy S. Flman, "Organizational Benefits of Mentoring," *Academy of Management Executive*, June 1986, pp. 305–28.

mentor. In this regard, some individuals should be discouraged from assuming this role, and it is a good idea for all prospective mentors to receive some training or coaching on effective mentoring relationships. Finally, organizations must understand that not everything passed from mentors to mentees will be factually correct or organizationally desirable. The potential payoffs, however, both in terms of individual and organizational change, make such programs worth considering.

Introspection Development

Dealing with constant change, both planned and unplanned, is a significant facet in a growing number of work situations. Companies are learning that taking time for reflection can be an invaluable activity for many organizational members. Major companies, such as Aetna, PepsiCo, and AT&T, are incorporating various forms of introspection training into their management change programs. AT&T, for example, devotes approximately 20 percent of its annual executive training budget to courses that encourage development of introspection. Introspection involves a close examination of one's own thoughts and feelings. Some companies, like AT&T, support specific training courses. Others, like Patagonia, the outdoor sportswear company, allow employees to take periodic sabbaticals to renew and recharge themselves. Regardless of the approach, successful introspection has a number of goals:[47]

www.aetna.com

www.pepsi.com

www.att.com

1. *Developing objectivity.* Successful reflection requires objectively seeking and processing information about oneself.
2. *Learning.* Learning must result from introspection, not just once, but continually. The objective is to create a process that filters experiences through reflection to produce better decisions.
3. *Improving self-confidence.* Reflection is designed to help individuals become comfortable with their weaknesses as well as their strengths.
4. *Increased sense of personal responsibility* and a willingness to look internally rather than projecting blame for negative outcomes externally.
5. Successful introspection should create an *increased tolerance for ambiguity and paradox,* attributes that are becoming virtual requirements for mastering today's organizational environments.
6. *Action taking.* Introspection does not mean we have to change, but it should enable us to more easily change when it is appropriate to do so.
7. *Achieving a balance in life.* Helping to sort out priorities in the conflict between work demands and one's nonwork life is an important payoff of successful introspection.
8. Introspection should open an individual's access to *creativity and intuition,* thus fostering innovation and higher-quality nonprogrammed decision making.
9. The ultimate goal is *egolessness,* or the ability to transcend selfish concerns. This translates into decision making centered on what is best for the unit, not what is most ego enhancing.

Introspection programs that allow time for examining one's self need to be scientifically studied. Instead of relying on common sense that self-examination

---

[47]Stratford Sherman, "Leaders Learn to Heed the Voice Within," *Fortune,* August 22, 1994, pp. 92–100.

sounds good, there is a long overdue need to rigorously study these types of programs. While their adherents are strong believers, well-designed evaluation studies are lacking, and until more results are available, this type of change will only be occasionally attempted.

Multifaceted Approaches

Not all organizational change interventions fit neatly into one of the three categories of approaches we have just examined. Sometimes techniques from different categories may be used together in a multifaceted approach to development. As an example, a silver-mining company combined team building (a human asset approach) and MBO (a structural approach).[48] The program was aimed at improving productivity and safety in the mine.

Other OD interventions may be considered multifaceted because the technique used is itself so broad-based that it cuts across two or even all three categories. Currently, the most popular such program is *total quality management*, or *TQM*. TQM is both a philosophy and system of management that, using statistical process control and group problem-solving processes, places the greatest priority on attaining high standards for quality and continuous improvement. Organizations such as IBM, Xerox, Ford, Johnson & Johnson, and Motorola have adopted some form of total quality management. Motorola's program, for example, focuses on achieving "six-sigma quality." Six-sigma is a statistical measure that expresses how close a product comes to its quality goal. One-sigma means approximately 68 percent of products reached the quality objective; three-sigma means 99.7 percent have reached the goal; six-sigma is 99.999997 percent perfect, or only 3.4 defects per one million parts.

There are many different versions of TQM. In actual operation, one company's TQM program may appear quite different from another company's. In spite of large operational differences, the major components of most TQM programs are similar. One researcher describes key TQM components in the following manner.[49]

Goal: The goal of TQM is to establish quality as a dominant organizational priority, vital for long-term effectiveness.

Definition of quality: Quality is satisfying the customer. All quality improvements must begin with an understanding of customer needs and perceptions.

Nature of the environment: TQM changes the boundaries between the organization and its environment. Entities formerly considered part of the environment (suppliers, customers) are now considered part of organizational processes.

Role of management: Management's role is to create a system that can produce quality results; managers and the system are responsible for poor quality.

Role of employees: Employees are empowered to make decisions and take necessary steps to improve quality within the system designed by management. Additional training provides needed skills for this broader role.

---

[48]Paul F. Buller and Cecil H. Bell, "Effects of Team Building and Goal Setting on Productivity: A Field Experiment," *Academy of Management Journal,* June 1986, pp. 305–28.

[49]Barbara A. Spencer, "Models of Organization and Total Quality Management," *Academy of Management Review,* July 1994, pp. 446–71.

Structural rationality: The organization is restructured as a set of horizontal processes that start with suppliers and end with customers. Teams are organized around processes to facilitate task accomplishment.

Philosophy toward change: Change, continuous improvement, and learning are necessary. Ideally, all organizational members are motivated toward constant improvement.

TQM represents one of the most comprehensive and far-reaching approaches to improving effectiveness. There are very few current or near-future organizational members who have not been or will not be affected in some way by TQM.

IMPEDIMENTS AND LIMITING CONDITIONS

The selection of any change method should be based on diagnosis of the problem, but the choice is tempered by certain conditions that exist at the time. Scholars identify three sources of influence on the outcome of management change programs that can be generalized to cover the entire range of interventions: leadership climate, formal organization, and organizational culture.

Leadership Climate

The nature of the work environment that results from the leadership style and administrative practices of managers is termed the **leadership climate**. It can greatly affect a program. Any program that lacks management's support and commitment has only a slim chance of success.[50] We can also understand that the style of leadership may itself be the subject of change. For example, total quality management (TQM) attempts to move managers toward a certain style—open, supportive, and group-centered. But we must recognize that participants may be unable to adopt such styles if the styles aren't compatible with their own manager's style.[51]

Formal Organization

The **formal organization** includes the philosophy and policies of top management, as well as legal precedent, organizational structure, and the systems of control. Of course, each of these sources of impact may itself be the focus of a change effort. The important point is that a change in one must be compatible with all of the others.[52] It may be possible to design organizations that not only facilitate change, but actually welcome change.[53]

Organizational Culture

Organizational culture refers to the pattern of beliefs resulting from group norms, values, and informal activities.[54] The impact of traditional behavior that's sanctioned

---

[50]Noel M. Tichy, "GE's Crotonville: A Staging Ground for Corporate Revolution," *Academy of Management Executive*, May 1989, pp. 99–106.

[51]Gary G. Whitney, "Vectors for TQM Change," *Journal for Quality and Participation*, October–November 1992, pp. 40–44.

[52]Kotter, *The Reader's Change Handbook*.

[53]Russell L. Ackoff, "The Circular Organization: An Update," *Academy of Management Executive*, February 1989, pp. 11–16.

[54]Mary F. Sully de Luque and Stephen M. Sommer, "The Impact of Culture on Feedback-Seeking Behavior: An Integrated Model and Propositions," *Academy of Management Review*, October 2000, pp. 829–49.

by groups norms, but not formally acknowledged, was first documented in the Hawthorne studies. A proposed change in work methods or the installation of an automated device can run counter to the expectations and attitudes of the work group, and, if such is the case, the selected method must be one that anticipates and manages the resulting resistance.[55]

Implementing a method that doesn't consider the constraints imposed by prevailing conditions within the present organization may, of course, amplify the problem that triggered the process. If management undertakes change in this way, the potential for subsequent problems is greater than would ordinarily be expected. Taken together, the prevailing conditions constitute the climate for change, and they can be positive or negative.

IMPLEMENTING THE METHOD

The implementation of the method has two dimensions: timing and scope. *Timing* refers to the selection of the appropriate time at which to initiate the intervention. *Scope* refers to the selection of the appropriate scale. Timing depends on a number of factors, particularly the organization's operating cycle and the groundwork preceding the program. Certainly, if a program is of considerable magnitude, it's desirable that it not compete with day-to-day operations; thus, the change might well be implemented during a slack period. On the other hand, if the program is critical to the organization's survival, then immediate implementation is in order. The scope of the program depends on the strategy. The program may be implemented throughout the organization. Or it may be phased into the organization level by level or department by department. The optimum strategy uses a phased approach, which limits the scope but provides feedback for each subsequent implementation.

The intervention that's finally selected is usually not implemented on a grand scale. Rather, it's implemented on a small scale in various units throughout the organization. For example, an MBO program can be implemented in one unit or at one level at a time. The objective is to experiment with the intervention (that is, to test the validity of the diagnosed solution). As management learns from each successive implementation, the total program is strengthened. Not even the most detailed planning can anticipate all the consequences of implementing a particular intervention. Thus, it's necessary to experiment and search for new information that can bear on the program.

As the experimental attempts provide positive signals that the program is proceeding as planned, there's reinforcement effect. Personnel will be encouraged to accept the change required of them and to enlarge their own efforts' scope. Acceptance of the change is facilitated by its positive results.

EVALUATING PROGRAM EFFECTIVENESS

Bringing about effective change represents an expenditure of organizational resources in exchange for some desired result. The resources take the form of money and time that have alternative uses. The result is in the form of increased

---

[55]Ivan Perlaki, "Organizational Development in Eastern Europe: Learning to Build Culture-Specific OD Theories," *Journal of Applied Behavioral Science,* September 1994, pp. 297–312.

organizational effectiveness: production, efficiency, and satisfaction in the short run; adaptiveness and flexibility in the intermediate run; survival in the long run. Accordingly, some provision must be made to evaluate the program in terms of expenditures and results. In addition to providing information to evaluate a specific organizational change effort, evaluation provides a literature that can be accessed by others who are deciding whether to undertake OD. Reviews of the relative efficacy of interventions appear regularly.[56] The evaluation phase has two problems to overcome: obtaining data that measure the desired results and determining the expected trend of improvement over time.

The acquisition of information that measures the sought-after result is the easier problem to solve, although it certainly doesn't lend itself to naive solutions. As we've come to understand, the stimulus for change is the deterioration of effectiveness criteria that management has traced to structural and behavioral causes. The criteria may be any number of effectiveness indicators, including profit, sales volume, absenteeism, turnover, scrappage, or costs. The major source of feedback for those variables is the organization's information system. But if the change includes the expectation that employee satisfaction must be improved, the usual sources of information are limited, if not invalid. It's quite possible for a change to induce increased production at the expense of declining employee satisfaction. Thus, if the manager relies on the naive assumption that production and satisfaction are directly related, the change may be incorrectly judged successful when cost and profit improve.[57]

To avoid the danger of overreliance on production data, the manager can generate ad hoc information that measures employee satisfaction. The benchmark for evaluation would be available if an attitude survey was used in the diagnosis phase. The definition of *acceptable improvement* is difficult when evaluating attitudinal data, since the matter of how much more positive employees' attitudes should be is quite different from the matter of how much more productive should they be. Nevertheless, for a complete analysis of results, attitudinal measurements must be combined with production and other effectiveness measurements.

In a practical sense, a program's effectiveness can't be evaluated if objectives haven't been established before it's implemented. A program undertaken to make the organization "a better place to work" or to develop the "full potential of the employees" can't be evaluated. If, on the other hand, measurable criteria that are valid indicators of "better places to work" and "full employee potential" are collected during the diagnostic phase and subsequently tracked as the program is undertaken, bases for evaluation exist. A considerable body of literature describes methods of evaluation, and managers of change programs should consult it for guidance in program evaluation.

---

[56]Reviews include John M. Nicholas, "The Comparative Impact of Organization Developments on Hard Criteria Measures," *Academy of Management Review,* October 1982, pp. 531–43; Anthony P. Raia and Newton Margulies, "Organizational Development: Issues, Trends, and Prospects," in Robert Tanenbaum, Newton Margulies, Fred Massarik, and Associates (eds.), *Human Systems Development* (San Francisco: Jossey-Bass, 1985), pp. 246–72; and George A. Neuman, Jack E. Edwards, and Nambury S. Raju, "Organizational Development Interventions: A Meta-Analysis of Their Effects on Satisfaction and Other Attitudes," *Personnel Psychology,* Autumn 1989, pp. 461–89.

[57]Bernard A. Rausch, "Dupont Transforms a Division's Culture," *Management Review,* March 1989, pp. 37–42.

Generally, an evaluation model would follow the six steps of evaluative research:

1. Determining the objectives of the program
2. Describing the activities undertaken to achieve the objectives
3. Measuring the effects of the program
4. Establishing baseline points against which changes can be compared
5. Controlling extraneous factors, preferably through use of a control group
6. Detecting unanticipated consequences

Application of these six steps isn't always possible. For example, managers don't always specify objectives in precise terms, and control groups may be difficult to establish. Nevertheless, the difficulties of evaluation shouldn't discourage attempts to evaluate.

HOW EFFECTIVE ARE CHANGE INTERVENTIONS?

The critical test of alternative change interventions is whether they help to improve organizational effectiveness. This can only be determined through research. There's a rather long history of such research. The current practice appears to have shifted the focus from interventions directed at informal components to those directed at formal components. In particular, structural interventions have been the most widely used method as reported in the literature.[58] The increasing use of structure and job targets reflects the increasing importance of production and efficiency criteria of organizational effectiveness, the specific targets of such interventions. The priority of these criteria reflects the importance of external competitive pressures that emphasize quantity, quality, and cost improvements. Structural interventions target these variables for change, whereas human asset interventions target somewhat more nebulous but nonetheless important variables such as attitudes, problem-solving skills, motivation, openness, and trust. It's also possible that interventions that attempt to change individual and group behavior have waned in popularity because it's difficult to evaluate them through rigorous evaluative research designs.[59]

Research reviews of the record-of-change efforts conclude that multi-method approaches have better success than single-method ones. Nicholas, for example, compared effects of sensitivity training, team building, job enrichment, and job redesign and concluded that no one method is successful in all instances (an expected conclusion, given what we said previously).[60] But he also found that significant changes occur when several methods combine. One such combination includes three discrete steps involving all levels of the organization. The three steps are (1) all employees participate in goal setting, de-

---

[58]Donald F. Van Eynde and Julie A. Bledsoe, "The Changing Practice of Organization Development," *Leadership and Organization Development Journal* (UK) 11, no. 2 (1999), pp. 25–30.

[59]Mark Wilson and George Engelhard, *Objective Measurement: Theory into Practice* (Stamford, CT: Ablex, 2000).

[60]John B. Nicholas, "The Comparative Impact of Organization Development Interventions on Hard Criteria Measures," *Academy of Management Review,* October 1982, pp. 531–42.

Management Pointer 16.1

STEPS TO TAKE WHEN MANAGING CHANGE

A manager confronted with the need to plan and implement change would be well advised to consider the following points:

1. Management and all those involved must have high and visible commitment to the effort.

2. People who are involved need to have advance information that enables them to know what is to happen and why they are to do what they are to do.

3. The effort (especially the evaluation and reward systems) must be connected to other parts of the organization.

4. The effort needs to be directed by line managers and assisted by a change agent if necessary.

5. The effort must be based on good diagnosis and must be consistent with the conditions in the organization.

6. Management must remain committed to the effort throughout all its steps, from diagnosis through implementation and evaluation.

7. Evaluation is essential and must consist of more than asking people how they felt about the effort.

8. People must see clearly the relationship between the effort and the organization's mission and goals.

9. The change agent, if used, must be clearly competent.

cision making, and job redesign, (2) employee collaboration is developed through team building, and (3) the organizational structure is reorganized to accommodate the new levels of participation and collaboration. Application of these three steps can go a long way toward meeting some arguments against specific methods. The overriding managerial concern is transfer of learning to the work environment.[61] Only under these circumstances can methods be considered effective.

SOME GUIDELINES FOR MANAGING CHANGE

What then can managers do when they recognize the need to change their organization? Although no absolute guarantees can ensure success in every instance, the accumulated experience of people involved with organizational change offers some guidelines. This chapter closes with Management Pointer 16.1, which identifies the important points that a manager should consider when contemplating a major organizational change.

Organizational change is a significant undertaking that managers should go about it in a systematic way. The model for managing change offers a systematic process for bringing about organizational effectiveness.

[61]Mark Mendenhall and Gary Oddou, "The Integrative Approach to OD: McGregor Revisitied," *Group and Organizational Studies*, September 1983, pp. 291–302.

Summary of Key Points

- The need to consider organizational change arises from changes in the inter- and extraorganizational environment. Changes in input, output, technological, and scientific subenvironments may indicate the need to consider the feasibility of a long-term, systematically managed program for changing the structure, process, and behavior of the organization. Even in the absence of environmental changes, organizational processes and behavior may become dysfunctional for achieving organizational effectiveness.

- The diagnosis of present and potential problems involves the collection of information that reflects the level of organizational effectiveness. Data that measure the current state of production, efficiency, satisfaction, adaptiveness, and flexibility must be gathered and analyzed. The purpose of diagnosis is to trace the causes of the problem. In addition to serv-

ing as the bases for problem identification, the diagnostic data also establish the basis for subsequent evaluation.

- To diagnose the problem, managers can consider these analytical questions:

  1. What is the problem as distinct from its symptoms?

  2. What must be changed to resolve the problem?

  3. What outcomes are expected, and how will these outcomes be measured?

  The managerial response to these questions should be stated in terms of criteria that reflect organizational effectiveness. Measurable outcomes such as production, efficiency, satisfaction, adaptiveness, and flexibility must be linked to skill, structural, task and technological, and human resource changes necessitated by problem identification.

- Through diagnosis, management associates the problem with structural, task and technological, and human asset causes and selects the appropriate intervention. If employee participation is inappropriate because the necessary preconditions don't exist, management must unilaterally define the problem and select the appropriate method. Whatever the sources of the problem the intervention must include provision for learning principles.

- The last step of the process is the evaluation procedure. The ideal situation would be to structure the procedure in the manner of an experimental design. That is, the end results should be operationally defined, and measurements should be taken, before and after, both in the organization undergoing change and in a second organization (the control group). If the scope of the program is limited to a subunit, a second subunit could serve as a control group. An evaluation not only enables management to account for its use of resources but also provides feedback. Based on this feedback, corrections can be made in the implementation phase.

Review and Discussion Questions

1. Identify the existing forces for change acting on your college. Compare these forces to those acting on a firm where you work or have worked. What are the important differences among these forces? Which are more powerful: the environmental or internal forces? Which organization seems more responsive to these forces for change?

2. Explain the concept *organization intervention* and why any particular management or organizational change can be considered an intervention.

3. Might some managers attempt to implement a particular intervention, such as TQM, without first diagnosing whether the intervention would be appropriate for their organization's problems? What would explain this behavior?

4. Explain why OD programs to bring about significant change often must use more than one form of intervention.

5. Evaluate the ethical issues associated with downsizing an organization by reducing its labor force to increase the organization's long-run chance of survival. What other ethical issues can you identify in the practice of organizational change as you understand it thus far?

6. Describe the relationships among the steps of the change model depicted in this chapter and the process of unfreezing-movement-refreezing. Which steps of the model are related to which elements of the relearning process?

7. How would you go about designing a training program that would cause managers in a small firm to recognize the need to change the way they manage if their industry has become more competitive in recent years?

8. What would be the characteristics of an organization or situation for which the use of reason would be an effective approach for managing change? Are such organizations and situations relatively rare?

9. Explain the difficulties that you would encounter in attempting to obtain diagnostic information from members of two groups who believe that they're competing for scarce resources.

10. Explain why an OD program should be evaluated and why such an evaluation is so difficult to do.

READING 16.1   Why Transformation Efforts Fail

by John P. Kotter

Over the past decade, I have watched more than 100 companies try to remake themselves into significantly better competitors. They have included large organizations (Ford) and small ones (Landmark Communications), companies based in the United States (General Motors) and elsewhere (British Airways), corporations that were on their knees (Eastern Airlines) and companies that were earning good money (Bristol-Myers Squibb). These efforts have gone under many banners: total quality management, reengineering, right sizing, restructuring, cultural change, and turnaround. But, in almost every case, the basic goal has been the same: to make fundamental changes in how business is conducted in order to help cope with a new, more challenging market environment.

A few of these corporate change efforts have been very successful. A few have been utter failures. Most fall somewhere in between, with a distinct tilt toward the lower end of the scale. The lessons that can be drawn are interesting and will probably be relevant to even more organizations in the increasingly competitive business environment of the coming decade.

The most general lesson to be learned from the more successful cases is that the change process goes through a series of phases that, in total, usually require a considerable length of time. (See Exhibit 16.2.) Skipping steps creates only the illusion of speed and never produces a satisfying result. A second very general lesson is that critical mistakes in any of the phases can have a devastating impact, slowing momentum and negating hard-won gains. Perhaps because we have relatively little experience in renewing organizations, even very capable people often make at least one big error.

ERROR #1: NOT ESTABLISHING A GREAT ENOUGH SENSE OF URGENCY

Most successful change efforts begin when some individuals or some groups start to look hard at a company's competitive situation, market position, technological trends, and financial performance. They focus on the potential revenue drop when an important patent expires, the five-year trend in declining margins in a core business, or an emerging market that everyone seems to be ignoring. They then find ways to communicate this information broadly and dramatically, especially with respect

Source: John P. Kotter. "Leading Change: Why Transformation Efforts Fail," *Harvard Business Review,* March–April 1995, pp. 59–67.

to crises, potential crises, or great opportunities that are very timely. This first step is essential because just getting a transformation program started requires the aggressive cooperation of many individuals. Without motivation, people won't help and the effort goes nowhere.

Compared with other steps in the change process, phase one can sound easy. It is not. Well over 50 percent of the companies I have watched fail in this first phase. What are the reasons for that failure? Sometimes executives underestimate how hard it can be to drive people out of their comfort zones. Sometimes they grossly overestimate how successful they have already been in increasing urgency. Sometimes they lack patience: "Enough with the preliminaries; let's get on with it." In many cases, executives become paralyzed by the downside possibilities. They worry that employees with seniority will become defensive, that morale will drop, that events will spin out of control, that short-term business results will be jeopardized, that the stock will sink, and that they will be blamed for creating a crisis.

A paralyzed senior management often comes from having too many managers and not enough leaders. Management's mandate is to minimize risk and to keep the current system operating. Change, by definition, requires creating a new system, which in turn always demands leadership. Phase one in a renewal process typically goes nowhere until enough real leaders are promoted or hired into senior-level jobs.

Transformations often begin, and begin well, when an organization has a new head who is a good leader and who sees the need for a major change. If the renewal target is the entire company, the CEO is key. If change is needed in a division, the division general manager is key. When these individuals are not new leaders, great leaders, or change champions, phase one can be a huge challenge.

Bad business results are both a blessing and a curse in the first phase. On the positive side, losing money does catch people's attention. But it also gives less maneuvering room. With good business results, the opposite is true: convincing people of the need for change is much harder, but you have more resources to help make changes.

But whether the starting point is good performance or bad, in the more successful cases I have witnessed, an individual or a group always facilitates a frank discussion of potentially unpleasant facts: about new competition, shrinking margins, decreasing market share, flat earnings, a lack of revenue growth, or other relevant indices of a declining

EXHIBIT 16.2   Eight Steps to Transforming Your Organization

1. Establishing a Sense of Urgency

    Examining market and competitive realities

    Identifying and discussing crises, potential crises, or major opportunities

2. Forming a Powerful Guiding Coalition

    Assembling a group with enough power to lead the change effort

    Encouraging the group to work together as a team

3. Creating a Vision

    Creating a vision to help direct the change effort

    Developing strategies for achieving that vision

4. Communicating the Vision

    Using every vehicle possible to communicate the new vision and strategies

    Teaching new behaviors by the example of the guiding coalition

5. Empowering Others to Act on the Vision

    Getting rid of obstacles to change

    Changing systems or structures that seriously undermine the vision

    Encouraging risk taking and nontraditional ideas, activities, and actions

6. Planning for and Creating Short-Term Wins

    Planning for visible performance improvements

    Creating those improvements

    Recognizing and rewarding employees involved in the improvements

7. Consolidating Improvements and Producing Still More Change

    Using increased credibility to change systems, structures, and policies that don't fit the vision

    Hiring, promoting, and developing employees who can implement the vision

    Reinvigorating the process with new projects, themes, and change agents

8. Institutionalizing New Approaches

    Articulating the connections between the new behaviors and corporate success

    Developing the means to ensure leadership development and succession

---

competitive position. Because there seems to be an almost universal human tendency to shoot the bearer of bad news, especially if the head of the organization is not a change champion, executives in these companies often rely on outsiders to bring unwanted information. Wall Street analysts, customers, and consultants can all be helpful in this regard. The purpose of all this activity, in the words of one former CEO of a large European company, is "to make the status quo seem more dangerous than launching into the unknown."

In a few of the most successful cases, a group has manufactured a crisis. One CEO deliberately engineered the largest accounting loss in the company's history, creating huge pressures from Wall Street in the process. One division president commissioned first-ever customer-satisfaction surveys, knowing full well that the results would be terrible. He then made these findings public. On the surface, such moves can look unduly risky. But there is also risk in playing it too safe: when the urgency rate is not pumped up enough, the transformation process cannot succeed and the long-term future of the organization is put in jeopardy.

When is the urgency rate high enough? From what I have seen, the answer is when about 75 percent of a company's management is honestly convinced that business-as-usual is totally unacceptable. Anything less can produce very serious problems later on in the process.

ERROR #2: NOT CREATING A POWERFUL ENOUGH GUIDING COALITION

Major renewal programs often start with just one or two people. In cases of successful transformation efforts, the leadership coalition grows and grows over time. But whenever some minimum mass is not achieved early in the effort, nothing much worthwhile happens.

It is often said that major change is impossible unless the head of the organization is an active supporter. What I am talking about goes far beyond that. In successful transformations, the chairman or president or division general manager, plus another 5 or 15 or 50 people, come together and develop a shared commitment to excellent performance through renewal. In my experience, this group never includes all of the company's most senior executives because some people just won't buy in, at least not at first. But in the most successful cases, the coalition is always pretty powerful in terms of titles, information and expertise, reputations and relationships.

In both small and large organizations, a successful guiding team may consist of only three to five people during the first year of a renewal effort. But in big companies, the coalition needs to grow to the 20 to 50 range before much progress can be made in phase three and beyond. Senior managers always form the core of the group. But sometimes you find board members, a representative from a key customer, or even a powerful union leader.

Because the guiding coalition includes members who are not part of senior management, it tends to operate outside of the normal hierarchy by definition. This can be awkward, but it is clearly necessary. If the existing hierarchy were working well, there would be no need for a major transformation. But since the current system is not working, reform generally demands activity outside of formal boundaries, expectations, and protocol.

A high sense of urgency within the managerial ranks helps enormously in putting a guiding coalition together. But more is usually required. Someone needs to get these people together, help them develop a shared assessment of their company's problems and opportunities, and create a minimum level of trust and communication. Off-site retreats, for two or three days, are one popular vehicle for accomplishing this task. I have seen many groups of 5 to 35 executives attend a series of these retreats over a period of months.

Companies that fail in phase two usually underestimate the difficulties of producing change and thus the importance of a powerful guiding coalition. Sometimes they have no history of teamwork at the top and therefore undervalue the importance of this type of coalition. Sometimes they expect the team to be led by a staff executive from human resources, quality, or strategic planning instead of a key line manager. No matter how capable or dedicated the staff head, groups without strong line leadership never achieve the power that is required.

Efforts that don't have a powerful enough guiding coalition can make apparent progress for a while. But, sooner or later, the opposition gathers itself together and stops the change.

ERROR #3: LACKING A VISION

In every successful transformation effort that I have seen, the guiding coalition develops a picture of the future that is relatively easy to communicate and appeals to customers, stockholders, and employees. A vision always goes beyond the numbers that are typically found in five-year plans. A vision says something that helps clarify the direction in which an organization needs to move. Sometimes the first draft comes mostly from a single individual. It is usually a bit blurry, at least initially. But after the coalition works at it for 3 or 5 or even 12 months, something much better emerges through their tough analytical thinking and a little dreaming. Eventually, a strategy for achieving that vision is also developed.

In one midsize European company, the first pass at a vision contained two-thirds of the basic ideas that were in the final product. The concept of global reach was in the initial version from the beginning. So was the idea of becoming preeminent in certain businesses. But one central idea in the final version—getting out of low value-added activities—came only after a series of discussions over a period of several months.

Without a sensible vision, a transformation effort can easily dissolve into a list of confusing and incompatible projects that can take the organization in the wrong direction or nowhere at all. Without a sound vision, the reengineering project in the accounting department, the new 360-degree performance appraisal from the human resources department, and the plant's quality program, the cultural change project in the sales force will not add up in a meaningful way.

In failed transformations, you often find plenty of plans and directives and programs, but no vision. In one case, a company gave out four-inch-thick notebooks describing its change effort. In mind-numbing detail, the books spelled out procedures, goals, methods, and deadlines. But nowhere was there a clear and compelling statement of where all this was leading. Not surprisingly, most of the employees with whom I talked were either confused or alienated. The big, thick books did not rally them together or inspire change. In fact, they probably had just the opposite effect.

In a few of the less successful cases that I have seen, management had a sense of direction, but it was too complicated or blurry to be useful. Recently, I asked an executive in a midsize company to describe his vision and received in return a barely comprehensible 30-minute lecture. Buried in his answer were the basic elements of a sound vision. But they were buried—deeply.

A useful rule of thumb: if you can't communicate the vision to someone in five minutes or less and get a reaction that signifies both understanding and interest, you are not yet done with this phase of the transformation process.

ERROR #4: UNDERCOMMUNICATING THE VISION BY A FACTOR OF TEN

I've seen three patterns with respect to communication, all very common. In the first, a group actually does develop a pretty good transformation vision and then proceeds to communicate it by holding a single meeting or sending out a single communication. Having used about .0001 percent of the yearly intracompany communication, the group is startled that few people seem to understand the new approach. In the second pattern, the head of the organization spends a considerable amount of time making speeches to employee groups, but most people still don't get it (not surprising, since vision captures only .0005 percent of the total yearly communication). In the third pattern, much more effort goes into newsletters and speeches, but some very visible senior executives still behave in ways that are antithetical to the vision. The net result is that cynicism among the troops goes up, while belief in the communication goes down.

Transformation is impossible unless hundreds or thousands of people are willing to help, often to the point of making short-term sacrifices. Employees will not make sacrifices, even if they are unhappy with the status quo, unless they believe that useful change is possible. Without credible communication, and a lot of it, the hearts and minds of the troops are never captured.

This fourth phase is particularly challenging if the short-term sacrifices include job losses. Gaining understanding and support is tough when downsizing is a part of the vision. For this reason, successful visions usually include new growth possibilities and the commitment to treat fairly anyone who is laid off.

Executives who communicate well incorporate messages into their hour-by-hour activities. In a routine discussion about a business problem, they talk about how proposed solutions fit (or don't fit) into the bigger picture. In a regular performance appraisal, they talk about how the employee's behavior helps or undermines the vision. In a review of a division's quarterly performance, they talk not only about the numbers but also about how the division's executives are contributing to the transformation. In a routine Q&A with employees at a company facility, they tie their answers back to renewal goals.

In more successful transformation efforts, executives use all existing communication channels to broadcast the vision. They turn boring and unread company newsletters into lively articles about the vision. They take ritualistic and tedious quarterly management meetings and turn them into exciting discussions of the transformation. They throw out much of the company's generic management education and replace it with courses that focus on business problems and the new vision. The guiding principle is simple: use every possible channel, especially those that are being wasted on nonessential information.

Perhaps even more important, most of the executives I have known in successful cases of major change learn to "walk the talk." They consciously attempt to become a living symbol of the new corporate culture. This is often not easy. A 60-year-old plant manager who has spent precious little time over 40 years thinking about customers will not suddenly behave in a customer-oriented way. But I have witnessed just such a person change, and change a great deal. In that case, a high level of urgency helped. The fact that the man was a part of the guiding coalition and the vision-creation team also helped. So did all the communication, which kept reminding him of the desired behavior, and all the feedback from his peers and subordinates, which helped him see when he was not engaging in that behavior.

Communication comes in both words and deeds, and the latter are often the most powerful form. Nothing undermines change more than behavior by important individuals that is inconsistent with their words.

ERROR #5: NOT REMOVING OBSTACLES TO THE NEW VISION

Successful transformations begin to involve large numbers of people as the process progresses. Employees are emboldened to try new approaches, to develop new ideas, and to provide leadership. The only constraint is that the actions fit within the broad parameters of the overall vision. The more people involved, the better the outcome.

To some degree, a guiding coalition empowers others to take action simply by successfully communicating the new direction. But communication is never sufficient by itself. Renewal also requires the removal of obstacles. Too often, an employee understands the new vision and wants to help make it happen. But an elephant is in the person's head, and the challenge is to convince the individual that no external obstacle exists. But in most cases, the blockers are very real.

Sometimes the obstacle is the organizational structure: narrow job categories can seriously undermine efforts to increase productivity or make it very difficult even to think about customers. Sometimes compensation or performance-appraisal systems make people choose between the new vision and their own self-interest. Perhaps worst of all are bosses who refuse to change and who make demands that are inconsistent with the overall effort.

One company began its transformation process with much publicity and actually made good progress through the fourth phase. Then the change effort ground to a halt because the officer in charge of the company's largest division was allowed to undermine most of the new initiatives. He paid lip service to the process but did not change his behavior or encourage his managers to change. He did not reward the unconventional ideas called for in the vision. He allowed human resource systems to remain intact even when they were clearly inconsistent with the new ideals. I think the officer's motives were complex. To some degree, he did not believe the company needed major change. To some degree, he felt personally threatened by all the change. To some degree, he was afraid that he could not produce both change and the expected operating profit. But despite the fact that they backed the renewal effort, the other officers did virtually nothing to stop the one blocker. Again, the reasons were complex. The company had no history of confronting problems like this. Some people were afraid of the officer. The CEO was concerned that he might lose a talented executive. The net result was disastrous. Lower-level managers concluded that senior management had lied to them about their commitment to renewal, cynicism grew, and the whole effort collapsed.

In the first half of a transformation, no organization has the momentum, power, or time to get rid of all obstacles. But the big ones must be confronted and removed. If the blocker is a person, it is important that he or she be treated fairly and in a way that is consistent with the new vision. But action is essential, both to empower others and to maintain the credibility of the change effort as a whole.

ERROR #6: NOT SYSTEMATICALLY PLANNING AND CREATING SHORT-TERM WINS

Real transformation takes time, and a renewal effort risks losing momentum if there are no short-term goals to meet and celebrate. Most people won't go on the long march unless they see compelling evidence within 12 to 24 months that the journey is producing expected results. Without short-term wins, too many people give up or actively join the ranks of those people who have been resisting change.

One to two years into a successful transformation effort, you find quality beginning to go up on certain indices or the decline in net income stopping. You find some successful new product introductions or an upward shift in market share. You find an impressive productivity improvement or a statistically higher customer-satisfaction rating. But whatever the case, the win is unambiguous. The result is not just a judgment call that can be discounted by those opposing change.

Creating short-term wins is different from hoping for short-term wins. The latter is passive, the former active. In a successful transformation, managers actively look for ways to obtain clear performance improvements, establish goals in the yearly planning system, achieve the objectives, and reward the people involved with recognition, promotions, and even money. For example, the guiding coalition at a U.S. manufacturing company produced a highly visible and successful new product introduction about 20 months after the start of its renewal effort. The new product was selected about six months into the effort

because it met multiple criteria: it could be designed and launched in a relatively short period; it could be handled by a small team of people who were devoted to the new vision; it had upside potential; and the new product-development team could operate outside the established departmental structure without practical problems. Little was left to chance, and the win boosted the credibility of the renewal process.

Managers often complain about being forced to produce short-term wins, but I've found that pressure can be a useful element in a change effort. When it becomes clear to people that major change will take a long time, urgency levels can drop. Commitments to produce short-term wins help keep the urgency level up and force detailed analytical thinking that can clarify or revise visions.

ERROR #7: DECLARING VICTORY TOO SOON

After a few years of hard work, managers may be tempted to declare victory with the first clear performance improvement. While celebrating a win is fine, declaring the war won can be catastrophic. Until changes sink deeply into a company's culture, a process that can take five to ten years, new approaches are fragile and subject to regression.

In the recent past, I have watched a dozen change efforts operate under the reengineering theme. In all but two cases, victory was declared and the expensive consultants were paid and thanked when the first major project was completed after two to three years. Within two more years, the useful changes that had been introduced slowly disappeared. In two of the ten cases, it's hard to find any trace of the reengineering work today.

Over the past 20 years, I've seen the same sort of thing happen to huge quality projects, organizational development efforts, and more. Typically, the problems start early in the process: the urgency level is not intense enough, the guiding coalition is not powerful enough, and the vision is not clear enough. But it is the premature victory celebration that kills momentum. And then the powerful forces associated with tradition take over.

Ironically, it is often a combination of change initiators and change resistors that creates the premature victory celebration. In their enthusiasm over a clear sign of progress, the initiators go overboard. They are then joined by resistors, who are quick to spot any opportunity to stop change. After the celebration is over, the resistors point to the victory as a sign that the war has been won and the troops should be sent home. Weary troops allow themselves to be convinced that they won. Once home, the foot soldiers are reluctant to climb back on the ships. Soon thereafter, change comes to a halt, and tradition creeps back in.

Instead of declaring victory, leaders of successful efforts use the credibility afforded by short-term wins to tackle even bigger problems. They go after systems and structures that are not consistent with the transformation vision and have not been confronted before. They pay great attention to who is promoted, who is hired, and how people are developed. They include new reengineering projects that are even bigger in scope than the initial ones. They understand that renewal efforts take not months but years. In fact, in one of the most successful transformations that I have ever seen, we quantified the amount of change that occurred each year over a seven-year period. On a scale of one (low) to ten (high), year one received a two, year two a four, year three a three, year four a seven, year five an eight, year six a four, and year seven a two. The peak came in year five, fully 36 months after the first set of visible wins.

ERROR #8: NOT ANCHORING CHANGES IN THE CORPORATION'S CULTURE

In the final analysis, change sticks when it becomes "the way we do things around here," when it seeps into the blood-stream of the corporate body. Until new behaviors are rooted in social norms and shared values, they are subject to degradation as soon as the pressure for change is removed.

Two factors are particularly important in institutionalizing change in corporate culture. The first is a conscious attempt to show people how the new approaches, behaviors, and attitudes have helped improve performance. When people are left on their own to make the connections, they sometimes create very inaccurate links. For example, because results improved while charismatic Harry was boss, the troops link his mostly idiosyncratic style with those results instead of seeing how their own improved customer service and productivity were instru-

mental. Helping people see the right connections requires communication. Indeed, one company was relentless, and it paid off enormously. Time was spent at every major management meeting to discuss why performance was increasing. The company newspaper ran article after article showing how changes had boosted earnings.

The second factor is taking sufficient time to make sure that the next generation of top management really does personify the new approach. If the requirements for promotion don't change, renewal rarely lasts. One bad succession decision at the top of an organization can undermine a decade of hard work. Poor succession decisions are possible when boards of directors are not an integral part of the renewal effort. In at least three instances I have seen, the champion for change was the retiring executive, and although his successor was not a resistor, he was not a change champion. Because the boards did not understand the transformations in any detail, they could not see that their choices were not good fits. The retiring executive in one case tried unsuccessfully to talk his board into a less seasoned candidate who better personified the transformation. In the other two cases, the CEOs did not resist the boards' choices, because they felt the transformation could not be undone by their successors. They were wrong. Within two years, signs of renewal began to disappear at both companies.

There are still more mistakes that people make, but these eight are the big ones. I realize that in a short article everything is made to sound a bit too simplistic. In reality, even successful change efforts are messy and full of surprises. But just as a relatively simple vision is needed to guide people through a major change, so a vision of the change process can reduce the error rate. And fewer errors can spell the difference between success and failure.

Exercises

EXERCISE 16.1   Organization Development at J. P. Hunt

OBJECTIVE

To experience an OD technique—in this case the use of survey feedback—to diagnose strengths and weaknesses and develop an action plan.

STARTING THE EXERCISE

Set up four to eight members for the one-hour exercise. The groups should be separated from each other and

asked to converse only with members of their own group. Each person should read the following:

J. P. Hunt department stores is a large retail merchandising outlet located in Boston. The company sells an entire range of retail goods (e.g., appliances, fashions, furniture, and so on) and has a large downtown store plus six branch stores in various suburban areas.

Similar to most retail stores in the area, employee turnover is high (i.e., 40 to 45 percent annually). In the credit and accounts receivable department, located in the downtown store, turnover is particularly high at both the supervisor and subordinate levels, approaching 75 percent annually. The department employs approximately 150 people, 70 percent of whom are female.

Due to rising hiring and training costs brought on by the high turnover, top department management began a turnover analysis and reduction program. As a first step, a local management consulting firm was contracted to conduct a survey of department employees. Using primarily questionnaires, the consulting firm collected survey data from over 95 percent of the department's employees. The results are shown in Exhibit 16.3, by organizational level, along with industry norms developed by the consulting firm in comparative retail organizations.

THE PROCEDURE

1. Individually each group member should analyze the data in the exhibit and attempt to identify and diagnose department strengths and problem areas.
2. As a group, the members should repeat step 1 above. In addition, suggestions for resolving the problems and an action plan for feedback to the department should be developed.

EXHIBIT 16.3   Survey Results for J. P. Hunt Department Store: Credit and Accounts Receivable Department

Variable	Survey Results[*]			Industry Norms[*]		
	Managers	**Supervisors**	**Nonsupervisors**	**Managers**	**Supervisors**	**Nonsupervisors**
Satisfaction and rewards						
Pay	3.30	1.73	2.48	3.31	2.97	2.89
Supervision	3.70	2.42	3.05	3.64	3.58	3.21
Promotion	3.40	2.28	2.76	3.38	3.25	3.23
Coworkers	3.92	3.90	3.72	3.95	3.76	3.43
Work	3.98	2.81	3.15	3.93	3.68	3.52
Performance-to-intrinsic rewards	4.07	3.15	3.20	4.15	3.85	3.81
Performance-to-extrinsic rewards	3.67	2.71	2.70	3.87	3.81	3.76
Supervisory behavior						
Initiating structure	3.42	3.97	3.90	3.40	3.51	3.48
Consideration	3.63	3.09	3.18	3.77	3.72	3.68
Positive rewards	3.99	2.93	3.02	4.24	3.95	3.91
Punitive rewards	3.01	3.61	3.50	2.81	2.91	3.08
Job characteristics						
Autonomy	4.13	4.22	3.80	4.20	4.00	3.87
Feedback	3.88	3.81	3.68	3.87	3.70	3.70
Variety	3.67	3.35	3.22	3.62	3.21	2.62
Challenge	4.13	4.03	3.03	4.10	3.64	3.58
Organizational practices						
Role ambiguity	2.70	2.91	3.34	2.60	2.40	2.20
Role conflict	2.87	3.69	2.94	2.83	3.12	3.02
Job pressure	3.14	4.04	3.23	2.66	2.68	2.72
Performance evaluation process	3.77	3.35	3.19	3.92	3.70	3.62
Worker cooperation	3.67	3.94	3.87	3.65	3.62	3.35
Workflow planning	3.88	2.62	2.95	4.20	3.80	3.76

[*]The values are scored from 1, very low, to 5, very high.

Cases

CASE 16.1   Implementing Total Quality Management at Thiokol Corporation

BACKGROUND

The Huntsville Division of Thiokol Corporation consists of approximately 700 employees and has been located in northern Alabama since 1949. It now occupies 256 buildings totaling over 1 million square feet of sheltered research, engineering, and production space. Products are primarily small to mid-size rocket motor propulsion systems for tactical and space applications, including Patriot, Maverick, HELLFIRE, Sidewinder, TOW, MK 70, Castor, and other rockets. The Huntsville Division is part of the Thiokol Corporation, a Utah-based $1 billion-plus company with eight operating divisions and 11,500 employees.

GETTING STARTED

Thiokol/Huntsville Division (THD) formally embarked on implementation of a total quality management process. The working definition of total quality that was developed for application throughout the business unit is as follows: *Doing the right things right, the first and every time, in a mode of continuous improvement, focused on customer satisfaction.* As part of an off-site executive total quality workshop, this definition was used as a basis for developing the following vision statement, which would provide direction for other business decisions and practices: *To be a recognized leader in our industry, working with pride, integrity and teamwork to provide products and services of unmatched quality and value to our customers.*

Part of the executive team's challenge was to "walk the talk" and show employees that our total quality/continuous improvement (TQ/CI) process was not just another program. We had had a lot of them, including "value management" and "zero defects" in the 1960s, "quality thinking" and "error-cause removal" in the 70s, and "quality circles" and "productivity teams" in the 80s.

One of the formal ways to ensure that our TQ/CI process was indeed not just another program was to establish measures of success. To define success, however, it became obvious quite early that the executive staff should have input from the employee population. An attitude and opinion survey was generated using Tom Peters's Excellence Audit Kit, which is based on his book, *Thriving on Chaos.*

Source: M. P. Charness, Director of TQM, Thiokol Corporation, Huntsville Division, Huntsville, Alabama. (Case presented at the 1992 ASQC Quality Congress, Nashville, Tennessee.) Reproduced here by permission of Michael P. Charness.

The audit was developed using input from a team of 10 employees, representing a diagonal cross section of the population, and was then administered to all 1,000 employees in small groups on company time. The survey contained approximately 50 business practices/philosophy areas, asking the following questions for each one: How much are we like this? and How important is it to be like this? A numerical rating scale was used, and we were able to use the data to determine the areas that were deemed very important but where we were not doing as well as we needed. Additionally, a section of the survey included traditional human-resource "climate" questions about how employees feel about their own jobs. An extract from that portion of the survey and the results are shown in Exhibit 16.4.

On a rating scale of 1 to 5, we considered 4 to be acceptable. We were encouraged that although a lot of areas were identified as needing improvement, basically employees felt that THD was "a good place to work." Data from the various parts of the survey were summarized and shared with employees through company newsletters and during interactive TQ/CI workshops.

Additionally, initial action plans were provided for the areas needing improvement. In this way, we were able to prioritize and publicize the first improvement targets within the business unit. Publicizing also put our management commitment to the test since we were putting in writing a major part of what we intended to do, and how we intended to do it. If we didn't "walk the talk" and follow through, the "new way" would have no credibility.

ADDING STRUCTURE

A Total Quality/Continuous Improvement Executive Steering Council was established and chaired by the vice president/division manager and included all of his direct reports. This group meets regularly to discuss issues related to the improvement process in a forum separate from other routine business issues. The steering committee provides prioritization, guidance, monitoring, sponsorship, and leadership for the improvement teams and other elements of the process.

To ensure that the TQ/CI process is consistent with business direction, the five-year strategic business plan was modified to add a section for total quality. In this plan, which is updated annually, the TQ/CI strategy is laid out, objectives and time frame established, and goals set. Long- and short-range improvement project plans are included from all functional organizations. The TQ/CI

EXHIBIT 16.4
Some of the Employee Survey Results

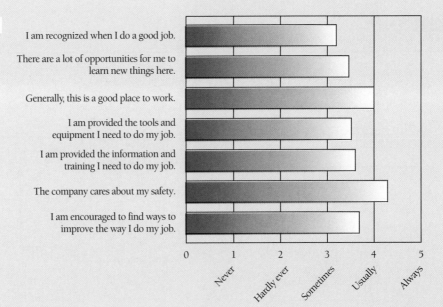

TRAINING

Early on, it was decided that the traditional approach to training for total quality would not produce the desired results in THD's culture and structure. A training plan was established for TQ/CI and was later expanded and integrated with THD's overall training plan. Within the first seven months after the initial attitude survey, all employees participated in a TQ/CI workshop. This workshop, representing Phase I of the TQ/CI training program, was normally eight hours, conducted in groups of 15 to 25 from a natural work group, and broken into two half-day sessions. Eight hours is generally considered "light weight" for training that is supposed to effect a major cultural change, but it was supplemented in a unique way that will be discussed shortly.

The workshops were conducted top-down with most supervisors going through them twice: once with their peers and their boss, and then again with their subordinates. Two complementary sets of the basic materials were developed so that the viewgraphs, videos, and exercises had enough diversity to keep the supervisors interested. Further, the supervisors kicked off the session for their subordinates, providing a constancy of purpose and support down through the organization.

Each eight-hour workshop was tailored to the work group in attendance, so that groups consisting of primarily supervisors were provided leadership/people-skills training to reinforce the change from a traditional, authoritarian style, to one of encouraging employee involvement without threat. Each eight-hour workshop covered the essentials of the TQ philosophy—effective organizations, visioning, human resource implications of TQ/CI, prescription for excellence (employee survey results), and implementation at the Huntsville Division. Statistical process control (SPC), alone on which many companies spend days of training, was only briefly touched on, giving an overview of the common SPC terms and charting methods so that the employee would be familiar with them when at some future point they were needed in her work environment.

One of the unique aspects of THD's TQ/CI training program is "just-in-time" training. Not just-in-time (JIT) in the sense of inventory management, but rather training that is provided *just in time* for when it will be applied. When an employee is selected or volunteers to participate in a process improvement team (discussed later), the team receives additional training as Phase II. Team participants are trained in the tools to implement the fundamentals of total quality on the process they are working on. This tailored training includes issues of customer focus, problem solving/process analysis (including more detailed SPC than in Phase I), measurement/feedback, team building, effective meetings, and goal setting.

As teams review their systems and processes, special courses/modules are provided to fill the needs for specific skills that have to be developed, such as Design of Experiments or Quality Function Deployment. This just-in-time training has not only proven to be cost-effective, but also to have the maximum possible impact on the employees' retention of the learned skills for application back in the normal workplace (when employees are not working on a specific process improvement team).

Executive Steering Council monitors activities of the plan and directs and manages changes as appropriate.

EXHIBIT 16.5
Process Improvement Structure

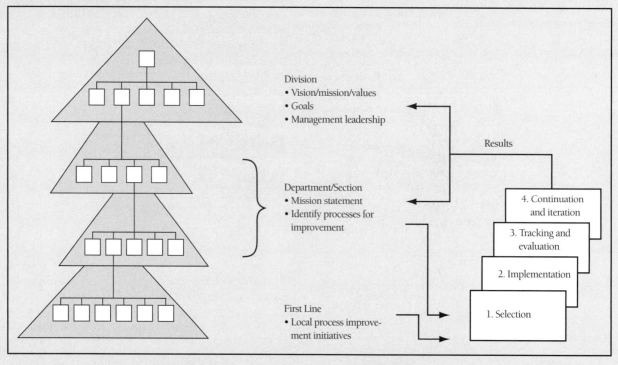

Division
- Vision/mission/values
- Goals
- Management leadership

Results

Department/Section
- Mission statement
- Identify processes for improvement

First Line
- Local process improvement initiatives

4. Continuation and iteration

3. Tracking and evaluation

2. Implementation

1. Selection

PROCESS IMPLEMENTATION TEAMS

Implementation of TQ/CI at THD is through two types of teams: departmental teams and critical process improvement teams. Departmental teams are designed around existing organizational structure and are based on the concept that every person is a member of the team made up of the department/group in which he works. This is in contrast to early implementation of quality circles in which participation was optional. Managers are members of departmental teams at two levels: the department team they manage and the team consisting of their peer group reporting to the next level manager. Mission statements are developed and improvement opportunities identified at all levels, as presented in Exhibit 16.5. Department teams are tasked with determining their supplier-customer relationships, defining customer expectations, mapping and reviewing departmental processes, establishing improvement opportunities, providing both internal and external feedback and measurement to monitor for continuous improvement, and reporting status to cognizant management.

When employees and management identify processes that are multiorganizational in nature and high in impact, a critical process improvement team is formed of a group of individuals whose background and experience allow them to evaluate specific processes for restructure and im-

provement opportunities. As multifunctional groups similar to ad hoc task forces, these teams are brought together as needed by the steering council and are given special training to aid them in their responsibility to map out selected major processes, identify root causes of problems and waste, select solutions, and, most important oversee the effective implementation of those changes.

MEASURES OF PROGRESS

To assess the effectiveness of the total quality process, a variety of measures are used at both local and macro levels. Thiokol believes that "what gets measured, gets improved." At the macro level, it was found to be very difficult to design a single, overall productivity measure for the business unit, so instead, several measures are used that are easy to collect and that link tangibly to day-to-day activities. Measures are posted on special performance boards throughout the business unit, and each manager is required to work with her people to establish improvement measures for their key activities and to keep progress charts visible in the work area. These measures are usually associated with specific process improvement projects, and serve to stimulate new ideas and often friendly competition between organizations that have similar goals.

Measurement is also key to the process analysis that is done by the process improvement teams. As they map out

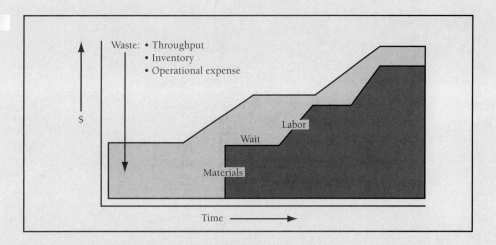

EXHIBIT 16.6
Improved Process

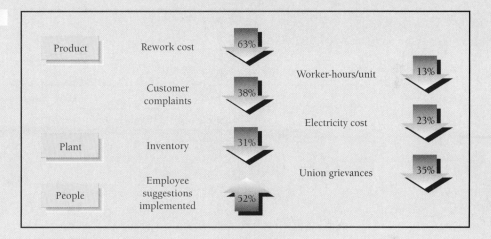

EXHIBIT 16.7
**Measures of Success—
Other Areas of Impact**

their existing process, they assess the amount of time and cost associated with each step in the traditional approach. While Thiokol/Huntsville uses this method extensively, some small, local processes are not treated to the full mapping; those processes may simply have a time/cost profile established as a baseline and then be reprofiled after the improvement project has been completed. The simple model used for this profile was established by the Westinghouse Corporate Quality/Productivity Center and is shown in Exhibit 16.6. It has also been an excellent tool to "roll up" a number of subprocesses to determine overall improvement. Any area under the curve is considered to be a waste of throughput, materials, inventory, and time and thus costs extra. While not easily quantified in hard dollars, the removal of any area under the curve is removal of waste and is considered worthy.

Examples of macro measures used by THD are shown in Exhibit 16.7 and indicate the level of success of the overall TQ/CI process. In a comparison of the most recent two fiscal years, all key areas show double-digit improve-

ment. The 63 percent improvement in scrap, rework, and repair costs follows a 34 percent improvement the year before, indicating that the improvement curve need not flatten out after the first year of the improvement process, but rather can accelerate. The same is true of most of the other indicators shown in Exhibit 16.7, proving that a company need not wait the traditionally espoused five years to have substantive results in the improvement process.

While it may be true that it does traditionally take about five years to change a company culture—the way people think—in the near term, management can strongly influence and even dictate if necessary, the way people *act,* and that is where the immediate improvement comes from. As success breeds success, the desired culture change is reinforced and follows naturally.

PROCESS IMPROVEMENT EXAMPLES

The outstanding results shown in the previous section are, in effect, a roll-up of processes being improved at all levels across the business unit. The previously mentioned

EXHIBIT 16.8
Targeted Processes—
Examples

Cross-Functional

Concurrent engineering	Purchase requisition flow
Environmental management	Information resource management
Supplier selection	Design-to-cost/producibility
Supplier quality and delivery	Proposal preparation/approval
Nonconforming material flow	Contract materials transfers
ECP/VECP flow	Performance recognition/
	suggestion awards

Departmental

Chlorinated solvent	Shop inventory
Maintenance materials flow	Mixer cycle time
Purchase order format/flow	Operating supplies
Components manufacturing	Work order scheduling

EXHIBIT 16.9   1990 Manufacturing Improvement Projects

Project	Program	Partial Listing Implementation Cost	Savings
Insulation wiping sequence	Castor	None	18.6 worker-hours per motor
Move chemlock control panel	Castor	3 hours	6 worker-hours per motor
Use of disposable tubing	Castor	$35 per motor	3.8 worker-hours per motor
Modified pot liner sleeve	Mk70	1 hour plastic shop	1.5 worker-hours per motor
Case unpacking location	Mk36	None	16 worker-hours per mix
Insulation cutting and installation	Mk36	None	32 worker-hours per mix
Rebalance inspection coverage	HELLFIRE	None	46 worker-hours per mix

Employee Attitude Survey, along with opportunity targets developed in the TQ/CI workshops, formed the basis for the initial process-improvement team activities. Examples of departmental and cross-functional processes addressed are shown in Exhibit 16.8. Many of the processes are specific to our industry, but the listing provides the reader with a feel for the type and range of processes being attacked.

An initial concern of management was that teams would recommend grandiose changes to processes that required investment in time and capital well in excess of near-term return. As it turned out, team-generated improvements of processes usually result in low- or no-cost

solutions to problems through streamlining and restructure. Some typical improvements in manufacturing and nonmanufacturing areas are shown in Exhibits 16.9 and 16.10.

EXTERNAL CUSTOMER/SUPPLIER INVOLVEMENT

To be successful, any process improvement effort must include a focus on external elements of the product and service chain—namely, external customers and suppliers. THD involves both customers and suppliers in our "concurrent engineering" of new products. Suppliers are brought in during the preliminary design phase to ensure

---

EXHIBIT 16.10   Process Improvement Examples

Nonmanufacturing

Deficiency Reporting/Dispositioning

• Average processing cost of 8 worker-hours reduced to one-half worker-hour on low-cost items (20 percent of all DRs).

Procedure Review/Approval Process

• Average cycle time of 66 days reduced to 14 days.

Contract Materials Transfers

• 4,000 CMTs per year reduced by 50 percent.

• 1,800 worker-hours per year savings.

---

producibility of the final requirements. Likewise, frequent communication with external customers ensures that integration and performance requirements will meet their expectations.

To optimize the communication and day-to-day management of supplier issues, THD is aggressively pursuing a reduction of our active supplier base by at least 10 percent per year in each of the next five years. It may sound a bit clichè, but "only the best will survive." This pressure is also being applied by our customers toward us in their striving for excellence and cost-effectiveness. To this end, a cost-based supplier rating and certification system was developed that allows buying decisions to be made based on historical true cost of doing business with a supplier, rather than awarding a contract primarily based on bid price. "Certified" suppliers are given an additional cost advantage of up to 10 percent when evaluating competitive bids, recognizing that there are additional cost benefits of developing long-term business relationships with proven performers.

MANAGEMENT ACTION AREAS FOR CHANGE

Where do we go from here? Any business enterprise that has been so successful in achieving improvement goals must be careful not to rest on its laurels. It has become evident that a number of areas need continued diligence to improve. Although significant results have been achieved at the bottom line in a short time, certain support systems need to be changed from the traditional approaches to ensure continued improvement.

THD has identified the following areas as targets for significant improvement over the next two years or so:

• Integration across functional boundaries.
• Compensation/reward system.
• Recruitment/selection.
• Individual job structure.
• Training/skill development.
• Organization structure.
• Evaluation and recognition.

Experience at the Huntsville Division of Thiokol Corporation has shown that it is not necessary to wait five years or more to achieve substantial bottom-line results from TQM. Through a commitment to integrating continuous improvement into all aspects of the business on an ongoing basis, these results come from implementation of a well-thought-out, comprehensive plan with top-management support and involvement. In the beginning, near-term results are achieved by dictating behavior and allowing the internalized "culture change" to follow in the longer term.

QUESTIONS:

1. What are the factors for success in the Thiokol case? What did the firm do that led to improvements in performance?
2. What strategy for change did the company use? Did the strategy for change have anything to do with the program's success?
3. Can the increases in performance be sustained if the culture does not change? Explain your answer.

Video Case

BIG APPLE BAGEL AND ST. LOUIS BREAD COMPANY: THE RESPONSIVE ORGANIZATION

In the past, a corporation was structured much like the military, with a formal chain of command and division of labor. Over time, many companies came to realize that the bureaucratic structure of the traditional corporation can often cause breakdowns in communication and lower efficiency.

Manufacturers of products in relatively unchanging environments often take a mechanistic approach to production. In such environments, employees strictly adhere to their job descriptions. However, companies that depend on their ability to continuously introduce new innovations usually take a more organic approach, giving employees more room to make decisions and communicate outside the chain of command. Some companies may choose to radically modify or reengineer their structure.

Big Apple Bagels and St. Louis Bread Company are two rapidly growing businesses that share a similar market. However, each organization is structured quite differently. Whatever the structure, for an organization to be successful, it must be responsive to its customers. This operating principle runs a lot deeper than just making sure the right kind of cheese gets put on a turkey sandwich.

Many companies are finding that changing the way in which they are organized improves their responsiveness. For example, they may choose to simplify their structure and reduce the layers of management, thus reducing the layers in the chain of command. Another option is to widen the spans of control. The traditional organization has a tall structure and a narrow span of control. This means managers have few subordinates who report directly to them. A company with a flat organizational structure has a wide span of control with fewer reporting levels.

Many companies are empowering their employees and allowing them to make decisions on their own rather than insisting that they report to various levels of management. When Paul Stolzer opened the first Big Apple Bagel store in 1985, he had no idea that in the short span of seven years his small store would grow into a franchise that boasts 75 stores with more opening all the time. Stolzer said, "The stores have changed quite extensively over the years. We are actually a fourth or fifth generation store right now. Initially the stores were set up as strictly bagel bakeries with a predominant product being bagels and cream cheese. We've progressed to a more aggressive stature, adding a few more dimensions to our operation in that we have dine-in facilities, a more extensive sandwich menu, and a very, very strong coffee program. We're still progressing. That's one thing that never ends."

One thing that hasn't changed is Big Apple Bagels' open-door policy. From top management to line workers, communication channels are wide open. Jim Lentz, director of training for the company, said, "At Big Apple Bagels we have an open door policy between the franchisee and the franchisor, and between the ultimate consumer and the franchisor in that we encourage people to come up with suggestions, new products, new ideas. We're never further than a phone call or a stop away. We're continually in the franchisees' stores to make sure that their operation meets our specifications."

In 1987, Ken Rosenthal opened his first St. Louis Bread Company store in Kirkwood, Missouri, with used baking equipment. Today, St. Louis Bread company operates over 50 stores in the St. Louis area, with stores opening in other midwestern markets as well. The growth happened quickly, forcing the company to change its organizational structure. Originally, it was a small store with 17 employees. When it became a large chain, employing over 1,000 people, a more traditional organizational structure was needed.

When a company is growing, it may need to use some of the concepts of reengineering. Reengineering entails the radical redesign of business processes to achieve major gains in cost, service, or time. For example, by mid-1992, St. Louis Bread was growing at a frantic pace. The partners decided it was time to slow down and take a breath. They began to realize that the opportunistic approach wouldn't work anymore.

They had reached a point where the controls and information systems they had in place were inadequate for a larger operation. New equipment was purchased to automate processes on the line. Thirty-thousand-dollar point-of-purchase cash registers were installed to track everything from sales per hour to sales per stock-keeping unit to sales by stores.

Doron Berger said, "The organization at St. Louis Bread Company is probably not atypical of many organizations. While we have a hierarchical structure in terms of someone is ultimately accountable for the results of the business, we do fight vigorously to maintain a flat organization. In other words, there aren't a lot of layers between the president, CEO, and the people who are on the front lines. I think we have succeeded because of the effort we have put into that."

In November of 1983, Au Bon Pain, the dominant bakery/café chain in the country, acquired St. Louis Bread Company. Au Bon Pain's stores were all in urban areas. St. Louis Bread would enable them to tap into the suburban market. David Hutkin said, "Our organizational structure has not changed dramatically. It really hasn't changed since the acquisition. We've continued to run the company very independent of the parent company, and we're still building stores and expanding the concept. As far as the organization, basically we're still doing the same things as we were doing before."

A company like Big Apple Bagels is considered to be a boundaryless organization. In such an organization, the corporate structure is more horizontal than vertical. Boundaryless businesses are typically organized around core customer-oriented processes, such as communication, customer contact, and managing quality. In order to enjoy the benefits a horizontal organization offers, four boundaries must be overcome:

- Authority
- Task
- Political
- Identity

Even a relatively boundaryless company has an authority boundary. Some people lead, others follow. To overcome problems that may arise, managers must learn how to lead and still remain open to criticism. Their "subordinates" need to be trained and encouraged not only to follow but also to challenge their superiors if there is an issue worth considering. As one Big Apple executive said, "I think there are some natural boundaries that occur between a franchisor and a franchisee, or an employee and an employer. What we try to do at Big Apple Bagels is to eliminate those boundaries by keeping the phone line open at all times as well as the fact that a lot of us have been franchisees as well as now being a franchisor so we know what it's like to sit on both sides of the table and to be able to talk to the franchisee from the standpoint of we were there at one time as well and we have that empathy for their position."

The task boundary arises out of the "it's not my job" mentality. A task boundary can be overcome by clearly defining who does what when employees from different departments divide up work.

The political boundary derives from the differences in political agendas that often separate employees and can cause conflict. This is closely related to identity boundary. The identity boundary emerges due to an employee tendency to identify with those individuals or groups with whom they have shared experiences, or with whom they share fundamental values.

To overcome the identity boundary, employees and management need to be trained to gain an understanding of the business as a whole and avoid the "us versus them" mentality. A good way to do this is by forming cross-functional teams, in which tasks are shared and cross training simply happens as a result of employee interaction.

The new boundaryless organization relies on self-managed work teams. It reduces internal boundaries that separate functions and create hierarchical levels. A horizontal corporation is structured around core, customer-oriented processes.

Lines of communication are very open, allowing line-level employees to communicate their questions and concerns directly to those at the management and executive level. Not all organizations are structured the same way. There are factors to consider such as organizational size, culture, and production volume. These factors may indicate that under some circumstances, a tall organizational structure may be more appropriate than a flat structure. Companies in the future may change or alter the way they operate, but customer satisfaction, quality, and efficiency will always be the primary goals.

DISCUSSION QUESTIONS

1. If companies today are working so hard to break down boundaries, why is it that there are boundaries in the first place?
2. What are some new technologies that will help managers keep lines of communication open to employees? To customers?
3. The video mentions that St. Louis Bread Company had to use a more traditional organizational structure when it grew rapidly. Why do you think that was necessary? What do you think the company gains by adopting such a structure? What does it lose?

Video Case

FALLEN APPLE

Started by Steve Jobs and Stephen Wozniak in a garage in 1976, Apple Computer was a corporate Cinderella story. From the early days, Apple grew to a net worth of $9 billion, with a 9 percent market share and 20 million users. But, Apple's success did not last forever. As Apple progressed through the organizational life cycle, it found itself to be in trouble. Apple must sell computers to a substantial piece of the 70 million U.S. homes without PCs in order to remain profitable and independent. Apple has experienced shortages of key parts, unfilled orders, executive turmoil, and users defecting to computers with other operating systems.

What is the cause of Apple's decline? Other companies in the industry soon learned how to make inexpensive, powerful computers with an operating system incompatible with Apple's. One business analyst attributes the decline to arrogance—Apple's leaders thought they had the best product and that the best product was going to win. Apple's executives failed to adopt a proper strategy to deal with the dynamic environment.

Recently, Apple has attempted to respond to its decline by developing a more powerful computer and cutting prices to match those of competitors. This strategy has cut into profits—so much so that over a three-month period profits dropped from $115 million to $60 million. Apple has also begun to license cheaper versions of computers that can use other companies' software. The case of Apple illustrates how organizations can move from inception to maturity and hover on the edge of decline. A few key strategic decisions made by Apple executives almost brought an American success story to the brink of disaster. Time will tell whether the appropriate strategic decisions can turn Apple around.

DISCUSSION QUESTIONS

1. Did Apple's size, technology, and/or strategy contribute to its decline? How?
2. How did the attitudes of Apple's top management contribute to its decline?
3. What should Apple executives have done to respond to the changing environment?

Glossary

A

adaptiveness   A criterion of effectiveness that refers to the ability of the organization to respond to change that is induced by either internal or external stimuli. An equivalent term is *flexibility*, although adaptiveness connotes an intermediate time frame, whereas flexibility ordinarily is used in a short-run sense.

attitudes   Mental states of readiness for need arousal.

attraction-selection-attrition framework   The concept that attraction to an organization, selection by it, and attrition from it results in particular kinds of people being in the organization. These people, in turn, determine organizational behavior.

authority   Authority resides in the relationship between positions and in the role expectations of the position occupants. Thus, an influence attempt based on authority generally is not resisted because, when joining an organization, individuals become aware that the exercise of authority is required of supervisors and that compliance is required of subordinates. The recognition of authority is necessary for organizational effectiveness and is a cost of organizational membership.

B

banking time off   A reward practice of allowing employees to build up time-off credits for such things as good performance or attendance. The employees then receive the time off in addition to the regular vacation time granted by the organization because of seniority.

baseline   The period of time before a change is introduced.

behavior   Anything a person does, such as talking, walking, thinking, or daydreaming.

behavior modification   An approach to motivation that uses the principles of operant conditioning.

big five personality model   A model of personality that suggests human personality is comprised of five central dimensions: extroversion, emotional stability, agreeableness, conscientiousness, and openness to experience.

boundaryless organization   A firm in which chains of command are eliminated, spans of control are unlimited, and rigid departments are replaced with empowered teams.

boundary-spanning role   The role of an individual who must relate to two different systems, usually an organization and some part of its environment.

brainstorming   The generation of ideas in a group through noncritical discussion.

broadbanding   A pay system that reduces the actual number of pay grades to a relatively few broadly based pay grades. Places an emphases on titles, grades, and job descriptions.

burnout   A psychological process brought about by unrelieved work stress, resulting in emotional exhaustion, depersonalization, and feelings of decreased accomplishment.

C

cafeteria fringe benefits   The employee is allowed to develop and allocate a personally attractive fringe-benefit package. The employee is informed of what the total fringe benefits allowed will be and then distributes the benefits according to his or her preferences.

centralization   A dimension of organizational structure that refers to the extent to which authority to make decisions is retained in top management.

change agent   A person who acts as the initiator for change activities. Can be internal members of the firm or external consultants.

charismatic leader   The charismatic leader is one who creates an atmosphere of motivation based on an emotional commitment and identity to his or her vision, philosophy, and style on the part of followers.

classical design theory   A body of literature that evolved from scientific management, classical organization, and bureaucratic theory. The theory emphasizes the design of a preplanned structure for doing work. It minimizes the importance of the social system.

classical organization theory   A body of literature that developed from the writings of managers who proposed principles of organization. These principles were intended to serve as guidelines for other managers.

coaching   To tutor, guide, direct, prepare, train, instruct, teach, or mentor someone.

coercive power   Influence over others based on fear. A subordinate perceives that failure to comply with the wishes of a superior would lead to punishment or some other negative outcomes.

cognition   This is basically what individuals know about themselves and their environment. Cognition implies a conscious process of acquiring knowledge.

cognitive dissonance   A mental state of anxiety that occurs when there is a conflict among an individual's various cognitions (for example, attitudes and beliefs) after a decision has been made.

command group   A group of subordinates who report to one particular manager constitutes the command group. The command group is specified by the formal organization chart.

commitment   A sense of identification, involvement, and loyalty expressed by an employee toward the company.

communication   The transmission of information and understanding through the use of common symbols.

complexity   A dimension of organizational structure that refers to the number of different jobs and/or units within an organization.

compliance   Being in agreement with specific legal, organizational, or official requirements.

compressed workweek   An alternative work arrangement in which the standard five-day, 40-hour workweek is compressed. The most popular form is four 10-hour days.

confrontation conflict resolution   A strategy that focuses on the conflict and attempts to resolve it through such procedures as the rotation of key group personnel, the establishment of superordinate goals, improving communications, and similar approaches.

conscious goals   The main goals that a person is striving toward and is aware of when directing behavior.

consideration   Acts of the leader that show supportive concern for the followers in a group.

content approaches to motivation   Theories that focus on the factors within a person that energize, direct, sustain, and stop behavior.

contingency approach to management   This approach to management is based on the belief that there is no one best way to manage in every situation but that managers must find different ways that fit different situations.

contingency design theory   An approach to designing organizations where the effective structure depends on factors in the situation.

continuous reinforcement   A schedule that is designed to reinforce behavior every time the behavior exhibited is correct.

counterpower   Leaders exert power on subordinates, and subordinates exert power on leaders. Power is a two-way flow.

cultural diversity   The vast array of differences created by cultural phenomena such as history, economic conditions, personality characteristics, language, norms, and mores.

D

decentralization   Basically, this entails pushing the decision-making point to the lowest managerial level possible. It involves the delegation of decision-making authority.

decision   A means to achieve some result or to solve some problem. The outcome of a process that is influenced by many forces.

decision acceptance   An important criterion in the Vroom-Jago model that refers to the degree of subordinate commitment to the decision.

decision quality   An important criterion in the Vroom-Jago model that refers to the objective aspects of a decision that influence subordinates' performance aside from any direct impact on motivation.

decoding   The mental procedure that the receiver of a message goes through to decipher the message.

defensive behavior   When an employee is blocked in attempts to satisfy needs to achieve goals, one or more defense mechanisms may be evoked. These defense mechanisms include withdrawal, aggression, substitution, compensation, repression, and rationalization.

delegated strategies   Strategies for introducing organizational change that allow active participation by subordinates.

delegation of authority   The process by which authority is distributed downward in an organization.

Delphi technique   A technique used to improve group decision making that involves the solicitation and comparison of anonymous judgments on the topic of interest through a set of sequential questionnaires interspersed with summarized information and feedback of opinions from earlier responses.

departmentalization   The manner in which an organization is structurally divided. Some of the more publicized divisions are by function, territory, product, customer, and project.

development   A criterion of effectiveness that refers to the organization's ability to increase its responsiveness to current and future environmental demands. Equivalent or similar terms include *institutionalization, stability,* and *integration.*

devil's advocacy   A form of programmed conflict in which someone or some group is assigned the role of critic whose job it is to uncover all possible problems with a particular proposal.

diagonal communication   Communication that cuts across functions and levels in an organization.

discipline   The use of some form of sanction or punishment when employees deviate from the rules.

downward communication   Communication that flows from individuals in higher levels of the organization's hierarchy to those in lower levels.

dysfunctional conflict   A confrontation or interaction between groups that harms the organization or hinders the achievement of organizational goals.

dysfunctional intergroup conflict Any confrontation or interaction between groups that hinders the achievement of organizational goals.

E

economic forces Forces in the environment that can influence what occurs within a firm, such as security markets, interest rates, foreign currency fluctuations, and competitors' pricing strategies.

effectiveness In the context of organizational behavior, *effectiveness* refers to the optimal relationship among five components: production, efficiency, satisfaction, adaptiveness, and development.

efficiency A short-run criterion of effectiveness that refers to the organization's ability to produce outputs with minimum use of inputs. The measures of efficiency are always in ratio terms, such as benefit/cost, cost/output, and cost/time.

emotional intelligence (EQ) The ability of people to understand and manage their personal feelings and emotions, as well as their emotions toward other individuals, events, and objects.

employee assistance program An employee benefit program designed to deal with a wide range of stress-related problems, including behavioral and emotional difficulties, substance abuse, and family and marital discord.

employee stock ownership plans (ESOPs) An employee reward program in which organizations make contributions of company stock (or cash to purchase stock) to employees. Stock allocation is typically, but not always, based on seniority.

empowerment Encouraging and/or assisting individuals and groups to make decisions that affect their work environments.

encoding The conversion of an idea into an understandable message by a communicator.

environmental certainty A concept in the Lawrence and Lorsch research that refers to three characteristics of a subenvironment that determine the subunit's requisite differentiation. The three characteristics are the rate of change, the certainty of information, and the time span of feedback or results.

environmental diversity A concept in the Lawrence and Lorsch research that refers to the differences among the three subenvironments in terms of certainty.

environmental forces Forces for change beyond the control of the manager. These forces include marketplace actions, technological changes, and social and political changes.

equity theory of motivation A theory that examines discrepancies within a person after the person has compared his or her input/output ratio to that of a reference person.

ERG theory A need hierarchy theory of motivation comprised of three sets of needs: existence (E), relatedness (R), and growth (G).

escalation of commitment An impediment to effective decision making, it refers to an increasing commitment to a previous decision when a rational decision maker would withdraw. It typically results from a need to turn a losing or poor decision into a winning or good decision.

eustress A term made popular by Dr. Hans Selye to describe good or positive stress.

expectancy The perceived likelihood that a particular act will be followed by a particular outcome.

expectancy theory of motivation In this theory, the employee is viewed as faced with a set of first-level outcomes. The employee will select an outcome based on how this choice is related to second-level outcomes. The preferences of the individual are based on the strength (valence) of desire to achieve a second-level state and the perception of the relationship between first- and second-level outcomes.

experiment To be considered an experiment, an investigation must contain two elements—manipulation of some variable (independent variable) and observation of the results (dependent variable).

expert power Capacity to influence related to some expertise, special skill, or knowledge. Expert power is a function of the judgment of the less-powerful person that the other person has ability or knowledge that exceeds his own.

external change agent A person from outside an organization who initiates change.

extinction The decline in the response rate because of nonreinforcement.

extrinsic rewards Rewards external to the job, such as pay, promotion, or fringe benefits.

F

facultative learning Learning that is made easier by practice.

felt conflict The second stage of conflict which includes emotional involvement. It is "felt" in the form of anxiety, tension, and/or hostility. See also **perceived conflict** and **manifest conflict**.

field experiment In this type of experiment, the investigator attempts to manipulate and control variables in the natural setting rather than in a laboratory.

fixed-interval reinforcement A situation in which a reinforcer is applied only after a certain period of time has elapsed since the last reinforcer was applied.

flextime An arrangement that provides employees greater individual control over work scheduling. In a flextime schedule employees can determine, within some limits, when they will go to work. In most flextime plans, employees may vary their schedule day-to-day, provided they work a specific number of hours a week.

formal group   A group formed by management to accomplish the goals of the organization.

formal organization   The recognized and sanctioned structure, policies, and rules of a unit or institution.

formalization   A dimension of organizational structure that refers to the extent to which rules, procedures, and other guides to action are written and enforced.

friendship group   An informal group that is established in the workplace because of some common characteristic of its members and that may extend the interaction of its members to include activities outside the workplace.

functional conflict   A confrontation between groups that enhances and benefits the organization's performance.

functional job analysis   A method of job analysis that focuses attention on the worker's specific job activities, methods, machines, and output. The method is used widely to analyze and classify jobs.

fundamental attribution error   A tendency to underestimate the importance of external factors and overestimate the importance of internal factors when making attributions about the behavior of others.

G

gainsharing   A reward system in which employees share in the financial benefits the organization accrues from improved operating efficiencies and effectiveness. Gainsharing can take many different forms including cash awards for suggestions and bonus plans.

general adaptation syndrome   (GAS) A description of the three phases of the defense reaction that a person establishes when stressed. These phases are called *alarm, resistance,* and *exhaustion.*

globalism   The interdependency of transportation, distribution, communication, and economic networks across international borders.

goal   A specific target that an individual is trying to achieve; a goal is the target (object) of an action.

goal approach to effectiveness   A perspective on effectiveness that emphasizes the central role of goal achievement as the criterion for assessing effectiveness.

goal commitment   The amount of effort that is actually used to achieve a goal.

goal difficulty   The degree of proficiency or the level of goal performance that is being sought.

goal intensity   The process of setting a goal or of determining how to reach it.

goal orientation   A concept that refers to the focus of attention and decision making among the members of a subunit.

goal participation   The amount of a person's involvement in setting task and personal development goals.

goal setting   The process of establishing goals. In many cases, goal setting involves a superior and subordinate working together to set the subordinate's goals for a specified period of time.

goal specificity   The degree of quantitative precision of the goal.

Graicunas's model   The proposition that an arithmetic increase in the number of subordinates results in a geometric increase in the number of potential relationships under the jurisdiction of the superior. Graicunas set this up in a mathematical model: $C = N \left(\frac{2N}{2} + N + 1 \right)$

grapevine   An informal communication network that exists in organizations and short-circuits the formal channels.

grid training   A leadership development method proposed by Blake and Mouton that emphasizes the balance between production orientation and person orientation.

group   Two or more individuals interacting with each other in order to accomplish a common goal.

group cohesiveness   The strength of the members' desires to remain in the group and the strength of their commitment to the group.

group norms   Standards shared by the members of a group.

groupthink   The deterioration of the mental efficiency, reality testing, and moral judgment of the individual members of a group in the interest of group solidarity.

H

hardiness   A personality trait that appears to buffer an individual's response to stress. The hardy person assumes that he or she is in control, is highly committed to lively activities, and treats change as a challenge.

Hawthorne studies   A series of studies undertaken at the Chicago Hawthorne Plant of Western Electric from 1924 to 1933. The studies made major contributions to the knowledge of the importance of the social system of an organization. They provided the impetus for the human relations approach to organizations.

health promotion program   See **wellness program**.

history   A source of error in experimental results. It consists of events other than the experimental treatment that occur between pre- and post-measurement.

horizontal communication   Communication that flows across functions in an organization.

horizontal differentiation   The number of different units existing at the same level in an organization. The greater the horizontal differentiation, the more complex is the organization.

I

impression management   A political strategy which refers to actions individuals take to control the impressions that others form of them. It represents a deliberate attempt to leave a desirable impression on others. The desired impression may or may not be an accurate one.

incentive plan criteria   To be effective in motivating employees, incentives should (1) be related to specific behavioral patterns (for example, better performance), (2) be received immediately after the behavior is displayed, and (3) reward the employee for consistently displaying the desired behavior.

influence   A transaction in which a person or a group acts in such a way as to change the behavior of another person or group. Influence is the demonstrated use of power.

informal group   Formed by individuals and developed around common interests and friendships rather than around a deliberate design.

information flow requirements   The amount of information that must be processed by an organization, group, or individual to perform effectively.

initiating structure   Leadership acts that imply the structuring of job tasks and responsibilities for followers.

instrumentality   The relationship between first-and second-level outcomes.

instrumentation   A source of error in experimental results. The error changes in the measure of participants' performance that are the result of changes in the measurement instruments or the conditions under which the measuring is done (for example, wear on machinery, fatigue on the part of observers).

interaction   Any interpersonal contract in which one individual acts and one or more other individuals respond to the action.

interaction effects   The confounding of results that arises when any of the sources of errors in experimental results interact with the experimental treatment. For example, results may be confounded when the types of individuals withdrawing from any experiment (mortality) may differ for the experimental group and the control group.

interest group   A group that forms because of some special topic of interest. Generally, when the interest declines or a goal has been achieved, the group disbands.

intergroup conflict   Conflict between groups; can be functional or dysfunctional.

internal change agent   A person, manager, or nonmanager, working for an organization, who initiates change.

internal forces   Forces for change that occur within the organization and that usually can be traced to *process* and to *behavioral* causes.

interpersonal communication   Communication that flows from individual to individual in face-to-face and group settings.

interpersonal orientation   A concept that refers to whether a person is more concerned with achieving good social relations as opposed to achieving a task.

interpersonal rewards   Extrinsic rewards such as receiving recognition or being able to interact socially on the job.

interpersonal style   The way in which an individual prefers to relate to others.

interrole conflict   A type of conflict that results from facing multiple roles. It occurs because individuals simultaneously perform many roles, some of which have conflicting expectations.

intervention   The process by which either outsiders or insiders assume the role of a change agent in the OD program.

intrapersonal conflict   The conflict that a person faces internally, as when an individual experiences personal frustration, anxiety, and stress.

intrarole conflict   A type of conflict that occurs when different individuals define a role according to different sets of expectations, making it impossible for the person occupying the role to satisfy all of the expectations. This type of conflict is more likely to occur when a given role has a complex role set.

intrinsic rewards   Rewards that are part of the job itself. The responsibility, challenge, and feedback characteristics of the job are intrinsic rewards.

J

job analysis   The description of how one job differs from another in terms of the demands, activities, and skills required.

job content   The factors that define the general nature of a job.

job context   The physical environment and other working conditions, along with other factors considered to be intrinsic to a job.

job definition   The first subproblem of the organizing decision. It involves the determination of task requirements of each job in the organization.

job depth   The amount of control that an individual has to alter or influence the job and the surrounding environment.

job description   A summary statement of what an employee actually does on the job.

job descriptive index   A popular and widely used 72-item scale that measures five job satisfaction dimensions.

job design   The process by which managers decide individual job tasks and authority.

job enlargement   An administrative action that involves increasing the range of a job. Supposedly, this action results in better performance and a more satisfied workforce.

job enrichment   An approach developed by Herzberg that seeks to improve task efficiency and human satisfaction by means of building into people's jobs greater scope for personal achievement and recognition, more challenging and responsible work, and more opportunity for individual advancement and growth.

job evaluation   The assignment of dollar values to a job.

job range   The number of operations that a job occupant performs to complete a task.

job relationships   The interpersonal relationships that are required of or made possible by a job.

job requirements   Factors such as education, experience, degrees, licenses, and other personal characteristics required to perform a job.

job rotation   A form of training that involves moving an employee from one work station to another. In addition to achieving the training objective, this procedure also is designed to reduce boredom.

job satisfaction   An attitude that workers have about their jobs. It results from their perception of the jobs.

job sharing   A form of alternative work arrangements in which two or more individuals share the same job. One job holder might work in the mornings, while a second job holder works in the afternoon. Job sharing increases employee discretion.

job specification   A product of a job analysis. A job specification identifies the minimum acceptable qualifications that a job holder must have to perform the job at an acceptable level. It may include specifications for educational level, knowledges, skills, aptitudes, and previous experience.

L

laboratory experiment   The key characteristic of laboratory experiments is that the environment in which the subject works is created by the researcher. The laboratory setting permits the researcher to control closely the experimental conditions.

leader-member relations   A factor in the Fiedler contingency model that refers to the degree of confidence, trust, and respect that the leader obtains from the followers.

leadership   Using influence in an organizational setting or situation, producing effects that are meaningful and have a direct impact on accomplishing challenging goals.

leadership climate   The nature of the work environment in an organization that results from the leadership style and administrative practices of managers.

learning   The process by which a relatively enduring change in behavior occurs as a result of practice.

learning transfer   An important learning principle that emphasizes the carryover of learning into the workplace.

legitimate power   Capacity to influence derived from the position of a manager in the organizational hierarchy. Subordinates believe that they "ought" to comply.

life-change events   Major life changes that create stress for an individual. The work of Holmes and Rahe indicates that an excessive number of life-change events in one period of time can produce major health problems in a subsequent period.

linking-pin function   An element of System 4 organization that views the major role of managers to be that of representative of the group they manage to higher-level groups in the organization.

locus of control   A personality characteristic that describes as *internalizers* people who see the control of their lives as coming from inside themselves. People who believe their lives are controlled by external factors are *externalizers*.

M

management by objectives (MBO)   A process under which superiors and subordinates jointly set goals for a specified time period and then meet again to evaluate the subordinates' performance in terms of those previously established goals.

manifest conflict   The final stage in conflict. At the manifest conflict stage, the conflicting parties are actively engaging in conflict behavior. Manifest conflict is usually very apparent to noninvolved parties. See also **perceived conflict** and **felt conflict.**

matrix organizational design   An organizational design that superimposes a product- or project-based design on an existing function-based design.

maturation   A source of error in experimental studies. The error results from changes in the subject group with the passage of time that are not associated with the experimental treatment.

mechanistic model of organizational design   The type of organizational design that emphasizes the importance of production and efficiency. It is highly formalized, centralized, and complex.

mission   The ultimate, primary purpose of an organization. An organization's mission is what society expects from the organization in exchange for its continuing survival.

modeling A method of administering rewards that relies on observational learning. An employee learns the behaviors that are desirable by observing how others are rewarded. It is assumed that behaviors will be imitated if the observer views a distinct link between performance and rewards.

modified or compressed workweek A shortened workweek. The form of the modified workweek that involves working four days a week, 10 hours each day, is called a 4/40. The 3/36 and 4/32 schedules also are being used.

mortality A source of error in experimental studies. This type of error occurs when participants drop out of the experiment before it is completed, resulting in the experimental and control groups not being comparable.

motion study The process of analyzing a task to determine the preferred motions to be used in its completion.

motivator-hygiene theory The Herzberg approach that identifies conditions of the job that operate primarily to dissatisfy employees when they are not present (hygiene factors—salary, job security, work conditions, and so on). There also are job conditions that lead to high levels of motivation and job satisfaction. However, the absence of these conditions does not prove highly dissatisfying. The conditions include achievements, growth, and advancement opportunities.

multiple roles The notion that most individuals play many roles simultaneously because they occupy many different positions in a variety of institutions and organizations.

N

need for power A person's desire to have an impact on others. The impact can occur by such behaviors as action, the giving of help or advice, or concern for reputation.

need hierarchy model Maslow assumed that the needs of a person depend on what he or she already has. This in a sense means that a satisfied need is not a motivator. Human needs are organized in a hierarchy of importance. The five need classifications are: physiological, safety, belongingness, esteem, and self-actualization.

needs The deficiencies that an individual experiences at a particular point in time.

noise Interference in the flow of a message from a sender to a receiver.

nominal group technique (NGT) A technique to improve group decision making that brings people together in a very structured meeting that does not allow for much verbal communication. The group decision is the mathematically pooled outcome of individual votes.

nonprogrammed decisions Decisions required for unique and complex management problems.

nonverbal communication Messages sent with body posture, facial expressions, and head and eye movements.

norms The standards of behavior shared by members of a group.

O

operant Behaviors amenable to control by altering the consequences (rewards and punishments) that follow them.

optimal balance The most desirable relationship among the criteria of effectiveness. Optimal, rather than maximum, balance must be achieved in any case of more than one criterion.

organic model of organization The organizational design that emphasizes the importance of adaptability and development. It is relatively informal, decentralized, and simple.

organizational behavior The study of human behavior, attitudes, and performance within an organizational setting; drawing on theory, methods, and principles from such disciplines as psychology, sociology, and cultural anthropology to learn about *individual* perceptions, values, learning capacities, and actions while working in *groups* and within the total *organization;* analyzing the external environment's effect on the organization and its human resources, missions, objectives, and strategies.

organizational behavior modification An operant approach to organizational behavior. This term is used interchangeably with the term *behavior modification.*

organizational climate A set of properties of the work environment, perceived directly or indirectly by the employees, that is assumed to be a major force in influencing employee behavior.

organizational culture The pervasive system of values, beliefs, and norms that exists in any organization. The organizational culture can encourage or discourage effectiveness, depending on the nature of the values, beliefs, and norms.

organizational development The process of preparing for and managing change in organizational settings.

organizational politics The activities used to acquire, develop, and use power and other resources to obtain one's preferred outcome when there is uncertainty or disagreement about choices.

organizational processes The activities that breathe life into the organizational structure. Among the common organizational processes are communication, decision making, socialization, and career development.

organizational structure The formal pattern of how people and jobs are grouped in an organization. The organizational structure often is illustrated by an organization chart.

organizations Institutions that enable society to pursue goals that could not be achieved by individuals acting alone.

P

participative management   A concept of managing that encourages employees' participation in decision making and on matters that affect their jobs.

path-goal leadership model   A theory that suggests it is necessary for a leader to influence the followers' perception of work goals, self-development goals, and paths to goal attainment. The foundation for the model is the expectancy motivation theory.

perceived conflict   The first stage of the conflict process. Perceived conflict exists when there is a cognitive awareness on the part of at least one party that events have occurred or that conditions exist favorable to creating overt conflict. See also **felt conflict** and **manifest conflict**.

perception   The process by which an individual gives meaning to the environment. It involves organizing and interpreting various stimuli into a psychological experience.

performance   The desired results of behavior.

person-role conflict   A type of conflict that occurs when the requirements of a position violate the basic values, attitudes, and needs of the individual occupying the position.

personal-behavioral leadership theories   A group of leadership theories that are based primarily on the personal and behavioral characteristics of leaders. The theories focus on *what* leaders do and/or *how* they behave in carrying out the leadership function.

personality   A stable set of characteristics and tendencies that determine commonalities and differences in the behavior of people.

personality test   A test used to measure the emotional, motivational, interpersonal, and attitude characteristics that make up a person's personality.

pooled interdependence   Interdependence that requires no interaction between groups because each group, in effect, performs separately.

position analysis questionnaire   A method of job analysis that takes into account the human, task, and technological factors of jobs and job classes.

position power   A factor in the Fiedler contingency model that refers to the power inherent in the leadership position.

power   The ability to get things done in the way one wants them to be done.

power illusion   The notion that a person with little power actually has significant power. The Miligram experiments indicated that the participants were obedient to commands given by an individual who seemed to have power (wore a white coat, was addressed as "doctor," and acted quite stern).

process   In systems theory, the process element consists of technical and administrative activities that are brought to bear on inputs in order to transform them into outputs.

process approaches to motivation   Theories that provide a description and analysis of the process by which behavior is energized, directed, sustained, and stopped.

production   A criterion of effectiveness that refers to the organization's ability to provide the outputs the environment demands of it.

programmed decisions   Situations in which specific procedures have been developed for repetitive and routine problems.

progressive discipline   Managerial use of a sequence of penalties for rule violations, each penalty being more severe than the previous one.

psychological contract   An unwritten agreement between an employee and the organization which specifies what each expects to give to and receive from the other.

punishment   Presenting an uncomfortable consequence for a particular behavior response or removing a desirable reinforcer because of a particular behavior response. Managers can punish by application or punish by removal.

Q

qualitative overload   A situation in which a person feels that he or she lacks the ability or skill to do a job or that the performance standards have been set too high.

quality of work life (QWL)   Management philosophy and practice that enhances employee dignity, introduces cultural change, and provides opportunities for growth and development.

quantitative overload   A situation in which a person feels that he or she has too many things to do or insufficient time to complete a job.

quality circle   A small group of employees who meet on a regular basis, usually on company time, to recommend improvements and solve quality-related problems. Frequently a part of **total quality management** efforts.

R

reciprocal causation of leadership   The argument that follower behavior has an impact on leader behavior and that leader behavior influences follower behavior.

reciprocal interdependence   Interdependence that requires the output of each group in an organization to serve as input to other groups in the organization.

referent power   Power based on a subordinate's identification with a superior. The more powerful individual is admired because of certain traits, and the subordinate is influenced because of this admiration.

reward power   An influence over others based on hope of reward; the opposite of coercive power. A subordinate perceives that compliance with the wishes of a superior will lead to positive rewards, either monetary or psychological.

role   An organized set of behaviors.

role ambiguity   A person's lack of understanding about the rights, privileges, and obligations of a job.

role conflict   Arises when a person receives incompatible messages regarding appropriate role behavior.

role set   Those individuals who have expectations for the behavior of an individual in a particular role. The more expectations, the more complex is the role set.

S

satisfaction   A criterion of effectiveness that refers to the organization's ability to gratify the needs of its participants. Similar terms include *morale* and *voluntarism*.

scalar chain   The graded chain of authority created through the delegation process.

scientific management   A body of literature that emerged during the period 1890–1930 and that reports the ideas and theories of engineers concerned with such problems as job definition, incentive systems, and selection and training.

scope   The scale on which an organizational change is implemented (for example, throughout the entire organization, level by level, or department by department).

selection   A source of error in experimental studies. The error occurs when participants are assigned to experimental and control groups on any basis other than random assignment. Any other selection method will cause systematic biases that will result in differences between groups that are unrelated to the effects of the experimental treatment.

self-managed team (SMT)   A relatively small group of individuals who are empowered to perform certain activities based on procedures established and decisions made within the group, with minimum or no outside direction. They may take many forms including task forces, project teams, quality circles, and new venture teams.

self-serving bias   A frequent attribution error which is reflected in the tendency people have to take credit for successful work and deny responsibility for poor work.

sensitivity training   A form of educational experience that stresses the process and emotional aspects of training.

sequential interdependence   Interdependence that requires one group to complete its task before another group can complete its task.

shared approach   An OD strategy that involves managers and employees in the determination of the OD program.

shared strategies   Strategies for introducing organizational changes that focus on the sharing of decision-making authority among managers and subordinates.

situational theory of leadership   An approach to leadership advocating that leaders understand their own behavior, the behavior of their subordinates, and the situation before utilizing a particular leadership style. This approach requires diagnostic skills in human behavior on the part of the leader.

social support   The comfort, assistance, or information an individual receives through formal or informal contacts with individuals or groups.

socialization processes   The activities by which an individual comes to appreciate the values, abilities, expected behaviors, and social knowledge essential for assuming an organizational role and for participating as an organization member.

span of control   The number of subordinates reporting to a superior. The span is a factor that affects the shape and height of an organizational structure.

status   In an organizational setting, status relates to positions in the formal or informal structure. Status is designated in the formal organization, whereas in informal groups it is determined by the group.

status consensus   The agreement of group members about the relative status of members of the group.

strategic contingency   An event or activity that is extremely important for accomplishing organizational goals. Among the strategic contingencies of subunits are dependency, scarcity of resources, coping with uncertainty, centrality, and substitutability.

stress   An adaptive response, moderated by individual differences, that is a consequence of any action, situation, or event and that places special demands on a person.

stressor   An external event or situation that is potentially harmful to a person.

structure   The established patterns of interacting in an organization and of coordinating the technology and human assets of the organization.

structure (in group context)   Used in the context of groups, the term *structure* refers to the standards of conduct that are applied by the group, the communication system, and the reward and sanction mechanisms of the group.

substitutability   The ability of various work units to perform the activities of other work units.

superordinate goals   Goals that cannot be achieved without the cooperation of the conflicting groups.

survey   A survey usually attempts to measure one or more characteristics in many people, usually at one point in time. Basically, surveys are used to investigate current problems and events.

system 4 organization   The universalistic theory of organization design proposed by Likert. The theory is defined in terms of overlapping groups, linking-pin management, and the principle of supportiveness.

systems theory   An approach to the analysis of organizational behavior that emphasizes the necessity for maintaining the basic elements of input-process-output and for adapting to the larger environment that sustains the organization.

T

task group   A group of individuals who are working as a unit to complete a project or job task.

task structure   A factor in the Fiedler contingency model that refers to how structured a job is with regard to requirements, problem-solving alternatives, and feedback on how correctly the job has been accomplished.

team   A formal group comprised of people interacting very closely together with a shared commitment to accomplish agreed-upon objectives.

technology   An important concept that can have many definitions in specific instances but that generally refers to actions, physical and mental, that an individual performs upon some object, person, or problem in order to change it in some way.

telecommuting   An alternative work arrangement in which an employee works at home while being linked to the office via a computer and/or fax machine.

testing   A source of error in experimental studies. The error occurs when changes in the performance of the subject arise because previous measurement of his performance made him aware that he was part of an experiment.

time orientation   A concept that refers to the time horizon of decisions. Employees may have relatively short- or long-term orientations, depending on the nature of their tasks.

time study   The process of determining the appropriate elapsed time for the completion of a task.

timing   The point in time that has been selected to initiate an organizational change method.

tolerance of ambiguity   The tendency to perceive ambiguous situations or events as desirable. On the other hand, intolerance of ambiguity is the tendency to perceive ambiguous situations or events as sources of threat.

total quality management (TQM)   A philosophy and system of management which, using statistical process control and group problem-solving processes, places the greatest priority on attaining high standards for quality and continuous improvement.

trait theory of leadership   An attempt to identify specific characteristics (physical, mental, personality) associated with leadership success. The theory relies on research that relates various traits to certain success criteria.

Type A behavior pattern   Associated with research conducted on coronary heart disease. The Type A person is an aggressive driver who is ambitious, competitive, task-oriented, and always on the move. Rosenman and Friedman, two medical researchers, suggest that Type As have more heart attacks than do Type Bs.

Type A managers   Managers who are aloof and cold toward others and are often autocratic leaders. Consequently, they are ineffective interpersonal communicators.

Type B behavior pattern   The Type B person is relaxed, patient, steady, and even-tempered. The opposite of the Type A person.

Type B managers   Managers who seek good relationships with subordinates but are unable to express their feelings. Consequently, they usually are ineffective interpersonal communicators.

Type C managers   Managers who are more interested in their own opinions than in those of others. Consequently, they usually are ineffective interpersonal communicators.

Type D managers   Managers who feel free to express their feelings to others and to have others express their feelings. Such managers are the most effective interpersonal communicators.

U

unilateral strategies   Strategies for introducing organizational change that do not allow for participation by subordinates.

universal design theory   A point of view that states there is "one best way" to design an organization.

upward communication   Upward communication flows from individuals at lower levels of the organizational structure to those at higher levels. Among the most common upward communication flows are suggestion boxes, group meetings, and appeal or grievance procedures.

V

valence   The strength of a person's preference for a particular outcome.

values   The guidelines and beliefs that a person uses when confronted with a situation in which a choice must be made.

vertical differentiation   The number of authority levels in an organization. The more authority levels an organization has, the more complex is the organization.

virtual organizations   A collection of geographically distributed, functionally and/or culturally diverse aggregations of individuals that are linked by electronic forms of communication.

Vroom-Jago model   A leadership model that specifies which leadership decision-making procedures will be most effective in each of several different situations. Two of the proposed leadership styles are autocratic (AI and AII); two are consultative (CI and CII); and one is oriented toward joint decisions (decisions made by the leader and the group, GII).

W

wellness program   An employee program focusing on the individual's overall physical and mental health. Wellness programs may include a variety of activities designed to identify and assist in preventing or correcting specific health problems, health hazards, or negative health habits.

work module   An important characteristic of job redesign strategies. It involves the creation of whole tasks so that the individual senses the completion of an entire job.

Name Index

Company Index

Subject Index

A

Absenteeism, reward program's effect on, 205
Accommodating approach, 360–361
Adjourning stage, 318–319
Administrative decision-making model, 540
Anticipatory socialization, 75–76
Arbitration, 369–370
ASA. *See* Attraction-selection-attrition framework
Assumptions, testing, 138–139
Asymmetrical power relationships, 388
Attraction-selection-attrition framework, 108
Attribution theory of leadership
    attributional leadership model, 461–462
    attributions, leader's, 461
    perception of responsibility, 461
    research support, 463

B

Big Five Personality Model, 126–127
    agreeableness, 126–127
    conscientiousness, 127
    emotional stability, 126
    experience, openness to, 127
    extroversion, 126
Biofeedback, 293
Boundaryless organization, 601–603
Bounded rationality approach, 540
Brainstorming, 551
Broadbanding, 208–209
Bureaucratic structure, 587–588
Burnout, 278–279

C

Change agents
    external change agents, 629
    external-internal change agents, 630–631
    internal change agents, 630
Change management
    alternative approaches, 626
        power, managing change through, 627
        reason, managing change through, 627
        reeducation, managing change through, 627–628
    application, 626
    case studies, 662–670
    change agents
        external change agents, 629
        external-internal change agents, 630–631
        internal change agents, 630
    development exercise, organization, 660–661

diagnosis of problem, 637–638
effectiveness, evaluation program, 650–652
ethics training, 645
failure reading, transformation
    anchoring change to corporate culture, 660
    guiding coalition, not creating, 656–657
    obstacles, not removing, 658–659
    short-term goals, not setting, 659
    undercommunicating, 658
    urgency, failure to establish sense of, 655–656
    victory to soon, declaring, 659–660
    vision, lacking a, 657
forces
    economic forces, 636
    external forces, 635–636
    internal, 637
    political change, 637
    social change, 637
guidelines, 653
human asset approaches, 643
implementation, 650
introspection development, 647–648
limitations
    formal organization, 649
    leadership climate, 649
    organizational culture, 649–650
mentorship programs, 645–646
model application, 634
multifaceted approaches, 648–649
principles, learning, 628–629
research studies, 652–653
resistance to change
    encountering, 631
    individual resistance, 632
    organizational resistance, 633
    overcoming, 633–634
selection, method
    importance, 639
    management by objectives, 639–640
    reeinginnering, 639–641
    structural approaches, 639
task approaches, 641–642
team building, 643–644
technological approaches, 641–642
total quality management (TQM), 648–649
total quality management exercise, 662–668
Change, rapidity of change, 6
Charisma, influence of, 391
Charismatic leadership
    components, behavioral, 466
    crisis-based leadership, 467–468

definition, 464
impact, 464
visionary leadership, 467–468
Chronic stress, 267
Coalition tactics, 405
Coercive power, 390
Cognitive component, 119
Cognitive dissonance, 120
Cognitive outcomes, 277
Cognitive techniques, 291–292
Command group, 315
Communication
    active listening reading demonstration, 517–523
    application, 492
    barriers
        communication overload, 509
        filtering, 508
        frame of reference, 506
        in-group language, 508
        selective listening, 506–507
        source credibility, 507
        status differences, 508
        time pressures, 509
        value judgments, 507
    case studies, 525–528
    determination of communication style exercise, 524–525
    diagonal communication, 499
    downward communication, 498
    e-mail, 501–502
    effectiveness, impact on, 492
    electronic meeting software (EMS), 502
    elements
        communicator, 494
        decoding-recieving, 495
        encoding, 494
        feedback, 495
        medium, 495
        message, 494–495
        noise, 496
    external communication program, 499
    horizontal communication, 499
    improvement methods, 510
        empathy, 511–512
        ethical communication, promoting, 513–515
        feedback, 511
        following up, 511
        grapevine, utilization of the, 513
        regulating information flow, 511
        repetition, 512
        simplifying language, 512–513
        timing, effective, 512
        trust, encouraging mutual, 512
    information richness, 500
    information technology, 500–501

READINGS, EXERCISES, AND CASES IN *ORGANIZATIONAL BEHAVIOR AND MANAGEMENT*
SIXTH EDITION